THE OCHBERG ORPHANS

AND THE HORRORS FROM WHENCE THEY CAME

THE RESCUE IN 1921 OF 181 JEWISH ORPHANS BY ISAAC OCHBERG,
THE REPRESENTATIVE OF THE SOUTH AFRICAN JEWISH COMMUNITY,
FROM THE HORRORS OF THE 'PALE OF SETTLEMENT'

This is Volume 3 of a sequel following
100 Years of Arc Memories – published in 2006 and
More Arc Memories - published in 2008
(*More Arc Memories* contains a section of 17 chapters on the Ochberg Orphans)

The Ochberg Orphans were placed in the care of
The South African Jewish Orphanage (now Arcadia Jewish Children's home) and
The Cape Jewish Orphanage (now Oranjia Jewish Child and Youth Centre)
The full proceeds from the sale of these books go to Arcadia and Oranjia which still
care for children in Johannesburg and Cape Town and need our support.

Book compiled by
David Solly Sandler

National Library of Australia Cataloguing-in-Publication entry

Title: The Ochberg Orphans and the horrors from whence they came.
The rescue in 1921 of 181 Jewish orphans by Isaac Ochberg, the representative of the South African Jewish community, from the horrors of the 'Pale of Settlement'
/ compiled by David Solly Sandler.

ISBN: 9780987106308 (hbk.)

Series: ARC (Arcadian) memories; v.3.

Notes: Includes index.

Subjects:
    Ochberg, Isaac
    Ochberg Orphans
    Arcadia (The South African Jewish Orphanage, Johannesburg)
    Oranjia (The Cape Jewish Orphanage, Cape Town)
    Pale of settlement--History
    Orphanages--South Africa--Biography

Other Authors/Contributors: Sandler, David Solly.

Dewey Number: 362.732089924

This edition first published April 2011

Cover designed by Sarah Natasha Myra Sandler

Every effort has been made to incorporate correct information, dates, statistics and photos. The publisher regrets any errors and omissions, and invites readers to contribute their up-to-date or additional relevant information to David Solly Sander, E-mail: <sedsand@iinet.net.au>

ISBN 978-0-9871063-0-8

The past is never wholly dead; it continues ceaselessly to whisper its secrets to newborn ages, telling their offspring of their unremembered ancestors, bringing to life long-forgotten memories. (Israel Abrahams "The Birth of a Nation")

Part one of this book tells the story of a forgotten part of Jewish History; a period completely overshadowed by the Holocaust; the horrors of war and pogroms and starvation and disease suffered by Jews in the 'Pale of Settlement' from 1914 to 1922. It details the horrors and the help given to these desperate people by Jewish communities established in the USA, Canada, Palestine and South Africa.

The book then focuses on, and follows up on the lives of the 181 Jewish Orphans rescued from the 'Pale of Settlement' in 1921 by Isaac Ochberg, the representative of the South African Jewish community. Half of these Ochberg Orphans, on arrival in South Africa, were placed in the care of the Cape Jewish Orphanage (later known as Oranjia) while the rest were sent to Johannesburg and placed in the care of the South African Jewish Orphanage (later known as Arcadia).

While the firsthand accounts of the Ochberg Orphans are included in part one of the book, the secondhand accounts, as recorded by their descendants, are in part two and part three of the book. Part two, *Cape Town, South Africa,* contains the history of Oranjia and the life stories of the Ochberg Orphans in its care and similarly part three, *Johannesburg, South Africa* contains the history of Arcadia and the life stories of the Ochberg Orphans in its care

I regard this book as a third volume on Arcadia (the Arc). The first volume published in 2006 *100 Years of Arc Memories* celebrated the centenary of Arcadia and contained the Arc memories of over 120 of its children. The second volume *More Arc Memories* published in 2008 contains the memories of over 100 further children including a section of 17 chapters on Ochberg's Orphans and it was almost complete when I started to receive, via the Jewish grapevine, the life stories of the Ochberg Orphans and I realised that we needed a third volume to properly record their history.

In total we have made contact with the families of over 140 Ochberg Orphans and this book contains the life stories of 130 of the 181 Ochberg Orphans. No doubt more will come to light in the fullness of time.

The book has three aims:
- To record the forgotten history, the horrors suffered by Jews in the 'Pale of Settlement' from 1914 to 1922 and the help given to them by their brethren, the Jewish Communities worldwide.
- To provide a legacy for the descendants of each of the Ochberg Orphans; a book which gives the history of the Ochberg Orphans and preserves the life stories of their Ochberg Orphan relative.
- To raise funds for Arcadia and Oranjia, the two Jewish Orphanages in South Africa, in whose care the Ochberg Orphans were placed. Both of these institutions still exist and still take care of Jewish children in need and all the proceeds from the sale of this book and the two previous volumes on Arcadia will be donated to them.

I feel honoured to be the compiler of this volume and the catalyst for its creation and regard these three volumes of life stories collected, as the property of the Jewish Community.

I thank all the many people who have helped me collect the life stories, and those who have opened their hearts and shared their, or their parents' stories. I dedicate the book to the deceased Ochberg Orphans, deceased Arcadians and to the generosity of the South African Jewish community which has always taken care of its own. In these difficult times in South Africa, I appeal to all ex South Africans to support their needy community left behind.

I end with the blessing that Doctor Lichtigfeld (Arcadia's Superintendent from 1952-1971) often bestowed on the congregation at Arcadia.

May the Lord bless you and keep you and make his face shine on you and give you peace and happiness and may there be peace in Israel soon.

THE STORY OF THE BOOKS

I spent most of my childhood, 1954-1969, in Arcadia from age three until 17, when I finished school. At the age of 28 in 1981 I left Johannesburg and I have lived in Perth, Western Australia, ever since.

In 1999 after a visit to the UK, Israel and South Africa, where I caught up with many of my Arc contemporaries, I 'published and distributed' a photocopied 16 page scrap photo album with all the photos entrusted to me by fellow Arcs during my visit. This scrap photo album was well received and very soon I started to receive letters from contemporary Old Arcs detailing their *Arc Memories*. This was the start of a very large project which seemed to grow and grow and very soon Old Arcs of all generations were sending in their *Arc Memories*.

The approach of the centenary of Arcadia prompted the first book, *100 Years of Arc Memories*, which was published in May 2006 to celebrate the centenary and completed a journey of over six years and a labour of love - though some call it a '*meshugas*'. Over those years, I was privileged to meet with, and get to know many fellow Arc brothers and sisters spanning many generations across the world. I am indebted to them all, for without their memories there would have been no book.

Over the next two years, 2007 and 2008, I continued to collect more Arc Memories and at the end of 2008 *More Arc Memories* was published. It was a great experience to meet more Old Arcs and their children, and the children of committee members.

Both *Arc Memory Books* contain memories recorded by Old Arcs long deceased including those of David Kotzen and Dr Solly Farber, two very close Arc 'brothers', who passed away in 2002. They encouraged me when alive, and have helped me compile these books with the very rich trail of Arc memories, from the *Arcadian* and other publications, they left behind.

It was only towards the completion of *More Arc Memories* that I started to receive, via the Jewish grapevine, the life stories of the Ochberg Orphans and I realized that we needed a third volume to properly record their history. I concluded the section of 17 chapters on The Ochberg Orphans (in *More Arc Memories*) as follows.

> "The Ochberg Orphans Memories, like Arc Memories, are a special part of South African Jewish History that needs to be preserved in a book. Though this second volume on Arcadia contains this section on the Ochberg Orphans, they really warrant their own book. Time and space did not permit me to properly complete this onerous and long overdue task of collecting the details of the "Ochberg Orphan" in this volume.

> I undertake to continue to collect their memories "through the eyes of their children" and PG when I have collected enough of their Memories will put them in a book and PG it will be a fitting memorial to the Ochberg Orphans as PG the Arc Books will be. I therefore invite the children of Ochberg Orphans to contact me, David Solly Sandler, on sedsand@iinet.net.au with their parent's details and story."

And so now, after a further two years of collecting memories, I am happy to present this third volume, The Ochberg Orphans.

The *Arc Memory Volumes* are still on sale in Australia, Canada, Israel, New Zealand, South Africa, the UK and the USA. They were funded by the generosity of Old Arcs. I hope to fund the printing and distribution of this book in a similar way. This means that the full proceeds of book sales go to Arcadia and Oranjia. By February 2011, almost R500,000 had been raised. With the books available in seven countries, you can pay for your order locally and have books delivered to you or to your family and friends in the country of your choice. Please visit our website www.arcadia.ca.com.au (or contact me on sedsand@iinet.net.au) and help us reach our target to raise R1,000,000 for Arcadia.

I hope you enjoy the read.

Best wishes and good health to you all, and may we soon see peace in Israel.

Shalom

David Solly Sandler

THE OCHBERG ORPHANS

Table of Contents

Chapter		Page

PART 1
THE 'PALE OF SETTLEMENT'
1914-1922

SECTION 1
THE HORRORS

This section tells not only of the wars and pogroms suffered by the Jewish Communities at the hands of the advancing and retreating armies, but also of the starvation and diseases suffered by Jew and Gentile alike.

While the war and pogroms resulted in the death of Jews in the tens of thousands, starvation and diseases took a very much higher toll on the population in general.

Chapter 1 – EUROPE, WWI AND LIFE IN THE 'PALE OF SETTLEMENT' 1914-1920

EUROPE, WWI AND LIFE IN THE 'PALE OF SETTLEMENT' 1914-1920

On New Year's Day 1914 Europe was at peace; there had not been a major conflict for 44 years.

France was smouldering because of the 1871 defeat and the German annexation of the provinces of Lorraine and Alsace. The war party in France wanted "revanche'. Germany knew that a war with France was inevitable and she was building her army as well as her navy.

With all this tension the nations were forming alliances. France and Russia had signed one and Germany knew now that a war with France would mean fighting on two fronts so she made an alliance with the Dual Monarchy, Austria/Hungary. Britain had the 'Entente Cordiale' with France since 1904. Russia had an alliance with Serbia.

Europe was actually a tinderbox – despite being at peace – and all that was needed was a spark for the whole place to blow up. That came on 26 June 1914, when Archduke Francis Ferdinand, the nephew of the Austrian Emperor, Francis Joseph, on a state visit to Bosnia was assassinated at Sarajevo in Bosnia. The assassination came to be called 'The shot that went around the world'.

Five days later Austria declared war on Serbia. Within a week the whole of Europe was ablaze. Serbia asked Russia for help and the Czar ordered a general mobilisation. Britain and Germany tried to avoid a war.

On 1 August Germany officially declared war on Russia because of the mobilisation of the Czar's soldiers and two days later on France. Britain was now in the war together with France against Germany. On August 4th, Britain officially declared war.

Meanwhile on the eastern front, Russia, in response to French urging, attacked on 14 August 1914 and two huge battles took place - at Tannenberg in East Prussia and at the Masaurian Lakes - which ended in a massive defeat for the Russians followed by a retreat. Paul Hindenberg and Erich Ludendorff were the victorious German generals.

The Germans advanced into Russian Poland and entered the area known as the 'Pale of Settlement'. These were the lands which the Czarist regimes had allowed Jews to settle in and it was estimated that there were four million Jews living there at this time. The 'Pale' stretched from Latvia in the north to the Ukraine and Galicia in the south. Regardless in which province the Jews lived, they were not welcomed and neither were the Latvians, Lithuanians, Poles, Ukrainians or Russians - they were all Jews. Those Jews, who were under Russian rule had been discriminated against, subjected to restrictions and regularly attacked in pogroms. On the other hand those Jews living in Austrian Galicia were relatively free from restrictions. In fact many of them served in the Austrian forces and also there were many Jews serving in the German armies.

As the German army advanced into 'The Pale' they were actually welcomed by the Jews. The war had caused a great deal of confusion for the Jews, for although they were ostensibly subjects of the Czar, he was more of an enemy to them than were the Germans. The Jews and the Germans spoke a similar language and the reports were that the Jews were well treated by the German soldiers. In fact the Jews had very little interest in the war other than to survive it. Between 1915 and 1917 battles waged across the areas where the Jews lived and many, many Jews died. No one knows the numbers.

In March 1917 the Russian Revolution took place under Gen Kerensky and the Russian army remained in the war. Eight months later in November, the Bolshevik Revolution led by Lenin and Trotsky took place and Russia withdrew from the war.

By the Treaty of Brest-Litovsk between Germany and Russia concluded in March 1918, Russia gave up most of the lands which had been in 'the Pale'. Russian Poland, Latvia, Lithuania, Estonia and Ukraine became independent. (By the Treaty of Versailles after the war ended Ukraine was returned to Russia and an independent Poland was established.)

Around the world the Jews looked on in horror at what was happening in Eastern Europe. Many had come from those areas where the fighting was fiercest. Some had only come very recently and had left behind parents, wives, brothers, sisters, families and friends. Many *Jews around the world* were in a state of shock and trauma. A few received messages from Europe detailing the death and destruction that had taken place.

The war had been followed by widespread pogroms and then, in 1920, by the 'flu epidemic which killed as many people again as had died in the war *and pogroms*. There were *hundreds of thousands of orphaned children*, hungry, sick and dying. The Jews asked themselves whether there was not something that could be done. Could they not help the survivors? Or at least rescue the children?

Jews around the world rallied to save their brethren in need and help arrived from many Jewish Organisations around the world.

This background history has been extracted and adapted from an article written by Lionel Slier in September 2004 and titled "The Ochberg Orphans"

Chapter 2 – POGROMS

THE POGROMS
Extracted from the Zionism and Israel - Encyclopedic Dictionary

The Bolshevik ("October") revolution of 1917 was followed by a civil war and a war with Poland. A large number of Jews, between 50,000 and 100,000 or even 200,000, died in riots and massacres. In the long history of European anti-Semitism, these were probably the largest-scale massacre of Jews to date. Because of the chaos prevailing in that period, and because of the interests of various sides in covering up the violence, the post-revolutionary pogroms are the least discussed and researched, and data about them are scarce.

Neglected Pogroms

The neglect of this period cannot be entirely accidental. The Proskurov pogrom, in which about 2,000 Jews were murdered on 15 February 1919, was a horrendous event. Eventually, about 10,000 Jews were murdered in that district. The events are barely remembered by Jews, and certainly not by anyone else whose ancestors were not from that unfortunate town. Yet at the time, the New York Times wrote:

The first of a new series of events which leave the scope of ordinary pogroms and assume the character of slaughter occurred in a city which will forever be written in letters of blood on the pages of Jewish history. (Jews Slain in Ukraine, New York Times, 19 September 1919, based on an article that had appeared in the Yiddish paper, *Der Tog* - the Day).

These pogroms were indeed a new and "improved" twentieth century version, which foreshadowed the mass murders of the Holocaust. Armies, rather than disorganized bands, often conducted the massacres, sometimes using machine guns. One might think that these events were simply overshadowed by the Holocaust, but, for example, the pogroms of Kishinev are quite well documented, though they killed far fewer people.

History of the Civil War Pogroms

Most of this violence was not the "natural consequence" of war, but rather the result of pogroms, aimed specifically at Jews. It is difficult to get more accurate numbers, or to know how many were murdered because they were Jews, how many died of starvation and disease and how many died fighting in the various armies.

The area of the greatest concentration of pogroms corresponded roughly to the Tsarist Jewish pale of settlement. It included Ukraine, Galicia, Belarus ("White Russia" on map), Moldavia, Eastern Poland, Eastern Romania, and Western Russia. The borders shifted around with the confused fighting.

Most of the pogroms and deaths occurred in the Ukraine, for several reasons. The first was that the Ukraine had the largest concentration of Jews in Russia. The second is that the Ukraine

Map showing the approximate area in which Pogroms took place in 1918-1921

was the scene of the bitterest and most prolonged fighting. In addition to the "White" (Volunteer) counter-revolutionary forces of General Anton Ivanovich Denikin, that operated in Greater Russia, and the Soviet Red Army, there were the Ukrainian nationalists of Petlura, and the Polish forces. Several wars occurred in the Ukraine and vicinity between Polish, Ukrainian, "White" Russians and Soviet troops. Western Russia had been the scene of fighting with the German and Austrian forces, and it held major concentrations of demobilized, hungry, armed and unruly troops. We cannot ignore, as well, the long history of Ukrainian anti-Semitism, going back to the time of Bogdan Khmelnytsky (Chmielnitsky).

The reasons or excuses for the pogroms were diverse. Everyone hated the Jews for religious reasons. The Poles accused them of being anti-Polish. The Ukrainians hated the Jews first because they were merchants and exploiters (bourgeois) and then because they were communists.

Russian human catastrophes of the twentieth Century tend to have a mind-boggling scale. There was chaos during this period, and afterwards the authorities destroyed or hid whatever documentation existed, though some of it is coming to light following the fall of the USSR.

REGISTER OF OCHBERG ORPHANS AT ORANJIA

If we examine the register of Ochberg Orphans kept at Oranjia and look at the causes of the deaths of their parents we find that many pages in the register mention that the families had suffered or endured pogroms or many pogroms and died in the pogroms or of starvation and typhus

3

THE UKRAINE TERROR AND THE JEWISH PERIL
Published in 1921 by THE FEDERATION OF UKRAINIAN JEWS, IN AID OF THE POGROM SUFFERERS IN THE UKRAINE. (Registered under the War Charities Act.)
26a, Soho Square, London, W. I.

PREFACE

This Pamphlet requires no preface. It contains a statement of facts, collected from trustworthy sources, as to the Terror in the Ukraine, since the conclusion of war, and the peril to the Jewish population in that country.

It is quite likely that some of the facts and figures cited in the following documents are below or above reality. A moments imagination will show the grave difficulty of eliciting the exact truth from witnesses who have fled from scenes in which they took part as victims.

Thus, when "Jewish representatives, recently arrived from the Ukraine, unanimously declare that the number of Jews massacred far exceeds a hundred thousand," we do not claim plenary accuracy. But this sentence is accurate: "The Committee of Jewish Delegations has in its possession reports on these massacres committed in more than 400 places."

Statistics are given below of the Terror, place by place. A very simple effort of computation will justify the aggregate estimate. Further in the report will be found some details of the Terror. These details do not encourage a minimisation of its effects. The conclusion should be read in the eloquent terms of the French Appeal in which men as eminent and humane as MM Anatole France, Henri Barbusse, Georges Duhamel, Charles Seignobos and Albert Thomas, "appeal to all peoples of the world against the unheard-of crimes of which a single people is the victim."

The burning words from the altar of French justice sear the conscience of mankind: "the Jews," we read, "who for centuries have been settled in Eastern Europe, have become the innocent and pitiful victims of struggles; national, political, and social. Millions of men, women, and children are suffering indescribable misery, and are handed over defenceless to death and dishonour.

Who is to defend them?

The Federation of Ukrainian Jews in London which is responsible for publishing these documents, is doing all it can to collect what is necessary to relieve their distress. This elementary duty is incumbent in the first instance on fellow-Jews, who are united with the victims by a religious bond, and whose constant tradition it is to express that bond in terms of charity. If this were all, the Federation might have refrained from making public the details of the Terror, and from adding to the evidence of unrest, which is accumulated from every country of Europe.

But the question of relief is not all, as the signatories to the French Appeal recognise. Relief is urgent and essential, not merely for the sake of the victims, pitiable though their plight is, but for the sake of Europe at large. The extent of the problem is too vast, to be left to the charity of co-religionists. Starving children are always the potential parents of discontented and anti-social men and women.

But the demoralised urchins from the Ukraine, with their childish memory of seeing a father shot or a mother violated by savage soldiery, present a problem beyond the reach of ordinary methods of relief. Such children seem bound to grow up with a grievance against society, unless a remedy is found for their moral as well as their physical wants. The latter may be supplied by a tremendous effort of charity among their own brethren; the former clearly depends upon the public opinion of civilized peoples. It is, first, then, to public opinion that these facts and figures are addressed.

One further reflection suggests itself. The Federation of Ukrainian Jews has no political axe to grind, and is neither Zionist nor anti-Zionist. Its functions begin and end (though, unfortunately, the end is not in sight) with the needs of the Jews in the Ukraine. "The rival ambitions of peoples, governments and parties, and all the folly of civil war, satiate themselves today upon the unhappy Jewish minority with criminal cruelty" : these are the words of the French Appeal and they lift the problem out of politics. But, however much detached from politics the attitude of the Federation may be it cannot but see in the facts, which it brings to the bar of public opinion, a meaning beyond the facts themselves.

It is freely asserted that Soviet Russia is under a Jewish domination, in which Jews alone are above the law, and that one of the chief objects of their misrule is to abolish the sanction of religion as the mainstay of the moral life. From this assertion it follows, that to destroy the Jews is to destroy destructive Bolshevism. Thus stated, the proposition moves in a vicious circle of destruction, out of which no sound principle is forthcoming. But the facts disclosed in the following pages seem to strike at the root of the argument.

Not even a nightmare could conjure up the vision of a Jewish domination, which would tolerate the Terror in the Ukraine, raging since 1918, and directed precisely at Jews. The unhappy victims of that Terror, so far from having lost their religious sense, find in the teachings of Judaism their sole, remaining comfort in life. They have seen their homes sacked and pillaged; their few worldly possessions have disappeared; their relatives, distant or very near, have been killed in their sight by a violent death; they include 150,000 orphan children, who will never find their parents' graves, and who are crying for food, clothes, and bedding, in a land where such commodities are unobtainable ; they have passed through a purgatory of suffering, so unimaginable and irrational, when measured by their limited experience, as often to drive them crazy — and yet they cling to the consolation of religion, and welcome the ministrations of their Rabbis.

We other Jews, watching with anguish the trials of our brethren in South-eastern Europe, and welcoming chiefly for their sake the prospect of a national home in Palestine, deplore the fallacies of half-knowledge, which confound the victims of revolution with the revolutionaries themselves, and even identify Zionism with Bolshevism. The Federation of Ukrainian Jews in London, which has no politics, and which is neither Zionist nor anti-Zionist, is not-concerned with the fight against anti-Semitism, though it seeks to alleviate persecution of the Jews. But, so far as the facts herein disclosed admit a general conclusion, apart from their particular conclusion to the urgency of swift relief, they do seem to show that a great wrong is still being organised against the Jewish population in the unhappy country which was Russia. Of Russia, in 1896, Lecky, the historian, wrote (Democracy and Liberty, I., 465):

"The Russian persecution stands in some degree apart from the other forms of the anti-Semite movement, both on account of its unparalleled magnitude and ferocity, and also because it is the direct act of a Government, deliberately, systematically, remorselessly seeking to reduce to utter misery about four-and-a-half million of its own subjects. . . .

Nowhere, indeed, in modern Europe have such pictures of human suffering and human cruelty been witnessed as in that gloomy Northern Empire. . . . Some of the most disgraceful apologies for the savage persecutions in Russia have come from writers who profess to be champions of nationalities, ardent supporters of liberty and progress."

Twenty-five years and a bloody revolution have neither tamed the Russian, nor changed the key of some of his apologists.

We would not conclude on a note, however mildly, controversial. This Pamphlet is published and distributed in the cause of humanity and charity. The conclusions which we have suggested may be disputed, or may not be accepted in all quarters. The facts which we narrate are indisputable, and their victims cry for assistance. We do not believe that the world has grown so callous as to turn down the appeal of the little destitute children who have survived the Terror in the Ukraine.

THE UKRAINE TERROR AND THE JEWISH PERIL
MEMORANDUM ON THE MASSACRES OF JEWS IN THE UKRAINE
Committee of Jewish Delegations, Paris, 10, Place Edouard VII. Geneva, 16 December 1920.

The Committee of Jewish Delegations, representing either by direct election or by written authority the Jewish populations of 22 countries, appeals to the League of Nations to obtain justice for the most terrible crimes that history has ever witnessed.

In Eastern Europe, in the Ukraine, a people numbering millions of souls has been massacred; intervention to put an end to these massacres demands the urgent attention of the human race and of the League of Nations, its spokesman.

The Committee deems that action in this direction is possible; it is a duty incumbent on civilized peoples.

If the League of Nations makes its voice heard, the first step will have been taken towards putting an end to these massacres. Categoric declarations made by the Governments who will co-operate in this matter will exercise a restraining influence on these acts of destruction.

Since December, 1918, there has been an uninterrupted series of pogroms in the Ukraine. Since the beginning of September, 1919, a report of the Red Cross Society at Kieff records that more than 30,000 Jews have been murdered. Since that date the number of murders has increased alarmingly. Jewish representatives, recently arrived from the Ukraine, unanimously declare that the number of Jews massacred far exceeds a hundred thousand. The Committee of Jewish Delegations has in its possession reports on these massacres committed in more than 400 places.

Many of the pogroms were specially serious on account of their long duration. The pogroms at Ovroutch lasted from 31 December, 1918, to 16 January 1919. Those at Vassilkof lasted from 7 to 15 April 1919; those at Zlatopol from 2 to 8 May; those at Tcherkassy from 16 to 21 May; those at Derajna from 7 to 17 of June; those at Rovno from 14 to 29 of May; those at Lytine from 14 to 28 May; and those at Balta lasted 9 days.

In other places massacres have been several times repeated ; Radomyal, Tcherniakof, Kornip, Volodarka, Elisabetgrad and several other towns were the scenes of massacres of 4, 5 and even 10 days' duration.

Hundreds and thousands of Jews have been wounded, ill treated, savagely beaten.

Up to the present more than a million Jews have been robbed and many of them have had literally their last shirt taken from them. The most refined tortures have been devised. Old men and children have been cut to pieces. Thousands of women and young girls have been outraged, and among these even little girls and old women. The victims have been terribly mutilated; the right arm and left leg have been cut off, or vice versa, the left arm and right leg; one eye has been torn out and the nose cut off. The houses in which the Jews took refuge were burnt, and all perished in the flames. The number of cases in which these unhappy victims were doomed to die a slow death of indescribable torture cannot be counted. Burning was the usual practice.

Besides physical torture, they were subjected to mental torture of a kind for which there is no parallel in history. Jews were compelled to dance and to sing in the presence of their torturers, to mock their own people and to praise their executioners; they had to dig their own graves and to commit shameful acts for the amusement of their murderers. These wretched people were forced to look on at the dishonouring of their daughters and of their wives, and children were compelled to hang their fathers.

The moral condition of the Jewish population of the Ukraine is near insanity; the terrible sufferings which all the population of this country is enduring through famine and epidemics, cannot be compared to the hell in which the Ukrainian Jews have been plunged for a year and a half. History has nothing to compare with it. The imagination of the greatest poet could not describe these scenes of horror. Dante's Inferno pales besides the realities of everyday life in the Ukraine.

Apart from the Jewish circles, the protests which have been made up to the present in many countries against this state of things have been merely the individual protests raised by eminent persons. And, however highly placed those persons were, they found that they were hopeless in the face of these crimes. It is a matter of urgent importance that the civilized peoples should make themselves heard. To keep silence is to become the accomplice of these murderers.

The vicissitudes of civil war in Russia have not in any way modified the duty of the League of Nations. Should the Ukraine fall temporarily under the sway of the Soviets, it must be realised that in the case of new upheavals these pogroms will break out with fresh violence. The blood of these victims is not yet dry, and we see at hand the moment when the crimes of the last two years will be surpassed by new acts of violence.

Firm intervention is urgently called for if three million human beings are to avoid complete annihilation.

Is an intervention of this kind possible? Will it succeed?

It is our opinion that, if at any moment during the course of this criminal butchery at which the world has passively looked on the public opinion of the civilised world and the Governments had expressed strongly its firm determination to put a stop to this state of things, the massacres would, in spite of all, have ceased. During the most disordered days, when it seems that no regular authority any longer exists, nevertheless there are some amongst the leaders of these savage bands who would listen to the cries of horror and indignation coming from the West, and would give way before a determined and authoritative protest.

The Committee thinks that the same will be true in the future. The extermination of the Jewish people will become impossible from the moment when order is restored and the League of Nations makes its voice heard. The principal murderers and the guilty ones are at the present moment in full liberty and go entirely unpunished, since most, if not all of them, have gone to countries within the sphere of influence of the League of Nations.

We demand that an exemplary punishment should be visited upon them, convinced as we are that this will give a determined and undeniable proof of the formal will of the people of the West to put an end to these massacres.

At the bar of the civilised world, at the bar of the League of Nations, which is the largest representative international body which has ever been brought into existence, we denounce as murderers the following persons: Hetman Strouk, who at the head of his men, massacred a thousand Jews, in 41 places in the neighbourhood of Tchernobel;
Colonel Hetman Tioutiounik

Hetman Sokolowsky whose troops massacred 3,000 Jews in 70 places in the neighbourhood of Radomysl-Jitomir:
Hetman Simossenko, who was responsible for the butchery at Proskourof ; and others besides.

We like to hope that the conscience of humanity will refuse to allow these murderers to remain in complete liberty to command their regiments and indirectly to ask for the protection of the civilized world. We ask the League of Nations, which represents the continuity of the brotherhood of man, to make a stern example of the culprits. It is a defiance, direct or indirect, to the principle of the League of Nations and to the most elementary principles of human justice to maintain amicable relations with men still red with the blood of their innocent victims, with men who have surpassed an hundred-fold, the horrors of the Spanish Inquisition.

We ask plainly for the punishment of these murderers. We hope that the whole of humanity will support our claim with all its might.

The President: N Sokolow
The Secretary General: L Motzkin

REPORT OF POGROMS IN THE UKRAINE
By the Kiev Pogrom Relief Committee of the Russian Red Cross

The wave of Jewish pogroms, unparalleled in history, which has covered the fields and towns of the Ukraine with rivers of Jewish blood, began on 31 December 1918. The pogroms had their origin in the civil war which broke out after the downfall of the German Empire and of the regime of the Hetman which was intimately connected with and dependent upon that Empire.

The civil war began with a victorious revolt of the newly-formed Directorate against General Skoropadski, followed by a no less victorious and violent movement of the Bolshevists against the Directorate. The troops of Petlura, driven westwards towards the frontiers of Galicia, began to break up into small gangs of freebooters and rebels, who remained in the localities occupied by the Communists, and who thus formed a very dangerous "internal front." This front became especially extensive when the detachments of Grigoriev, Tintiunik, Zeliony, Struck, Sokolowsky, and of many other chiefs who had at first joined the Bolshevists, separated themselves from the latter and started campaigns of their own.

During the first two years of the Revolution, commencing from 27 February 1917, there were practically no Jewish pogroms. There were, of course, excesses committed by demoralised detachments of troops, more especially during the demobilisation. These excesses were, if not exclusively, yet mostly, directed against Jews, but they were merely sporadic in character and never assumed a large scale. The assailants practically always limited themselves to acts of robbery and to the damage of property.

During the German occupation no pogroms took place in the Ukraine.

Equally the months of November and December, 1918, when the Directorate victoriously fought the Hetman, passed without these horrors. Pogroms only commenced when the Directorate suffered defeat at the hands of the Communists who rose against them. The more decisive these defeats were, the more often the beaten Petlura troops had to carry out evacuations of territories which they had occupied, the more cruelly the defeated and irritated troops began to revenge their setbacks and hardships on the peaceful Jewish population, and the more often they began to treat the Jews as Communists. The battle-cries, "Murder Jews and Communists!" and the "Jews are Communists!" soon sounded throughout the Ukraine, provoking sanguinary pogroms.

The first massacre broke out in the town of Ovrutsh and its environs. The defenceless Jewish population were at the mercy of a Petlura Ataman, and murder and robbery lasted from 31 December to 16 January. At the same period the Shitomir pogrom took place (7 to 10 January) and others of the towns of Berdichev, Tchernichov, and a good number of villages round Ovrutsh. The wave of pogroms in January was almost exclusively confined to the eastern portion of the province of Volhynia, where the Petlurists were severely pressed by the Bolshevists.

The February pogroms were more widely spread. By that time Kiev was already occupied by the Communists (from 2 February).

The Petlurists were then hurriedly evacuating the provinces of Kherson, Poltava, and Kiev. Pogroms took place in Elisavetgrad (4 and 5 February), in Novo-Mirgorod, Piriatin, and many other places of the province of Poltava. On many railway stations soldiers threw Jews out of the carriage windows and shot at them. In Lubny a pogrom was only prevented because a detachment — about a hundred men strong — came to the rescue of the threatened victims in time. This detachment lost 14 men killed, but the population was saved. The Jews of Krementshug, in order to escape a pogrom, were compelled to pay a ransom of one million five hundred thousand roubles.

During this period pogroms took place in the following towns of the Kiev province : In Vasilkov, 7 to 8 February; in Rossava, 11 to 15 February; most of the victims being murdered by the Soviet troops. Pogroms also occurred at this time in Stiepantzy, 14 February; Radomysl, 18 to 20 February; Skvir, at the beginning and at the end of February; and in Mtshna and Brovary.

The most terrible pogroms, however, took place far in the rear of the armies, in Proskurov (15 February) and in Felchtine (16 February). These pogroms were provoked by an attempt of the Bolshevists to raise a rebellion in Proskurov.

The March pogroms began when the Petlurists cut the front near Sarny in the direction of Korosten, and when they again came to within a hundred kilometers of Kiev. At that time pogroms took place in Korosten; in Ushomir (31 March), in Beloshitz (7 to 12 March), in Samgorodok. (13 March), in Tsherniakhov (11 March), in Shitomir, for the second time, on 23 March, in Yanushpol (25 to 29 March), in Radomysl (12 to 13 March, and again 23 to 31 March).

In Radomysl the pogroms assumed a chronic character, and were continuous because at that place and at that time the gangs of Sokolowsky had already started their bloody work. On 13 March a new pogrom was carried out by the red troops in Korosten. This pogrom was ended by a new advance of Petlura. In addition there were Petlura pogroms in Kalinovka, Kublitsh, Ziatkovzy, and other towns of the province of Podolia.

The pogroms in April 1919 were less numerous and not of a general character. The outstanding event of this month was the activity of Struck in the district of Tshernobyl. On 7 April his gang was raging in Tshernobyl itself. At the beginning of May, Gornostaipol and Ivankov were ransacked, and during the whole month the murderous gangs of Struck were plundering and slaughtering Jews in the surrounding villages, more especially in those situated on the shores of the Dnieper, where no steamer was allowed to pass without the Jews being taken off and drowned. Up to 27 August a total of 41 settlements in this locality had suffered. In addition to the above, Sokolowsky's activities continued in this district, and Korolevka was ransacked on 22 April, Malin, Rakitnoe and Kornin on 10 April. At this time another settlement — Emiltshenko — was ruined by a detachment of Petlurists, who were retreating from Gliebsk towards Novogradvolynsk.

The gangs of Zeliony worked near Kiev itself, carrying on their ferocious activities in Vasilkov, which was subjected to a pogrom lasting from 7 to 15 April, in Rshishtshev, 9 April, and in the village of Seplisetskoe, Olshanka, and others. It should be pointed out that in Vasilkov the pogrom was perpetrated by the Sixth Soviet Regiment. There were gangs of freebooters also in the region of Tarashtshansk, and the pogrom in Boguslav, which belongs to this region, lasted from 4 April to 25 April. In the Province of Podolia a large number of settlements were destroyed, among them Balta and Bratzlav.

The pogroms which took place in May were very numerous, and nearly all carried out by Grigoriev and his detachments. For most of them the Ataman himself and his assistants Uvarov and Netshaiev were responsible. Three quarters of all the pogroms took place in the south-eastern part of the province of Kiev, in the districts of Tsherkask and Tshigirin. Many pogroms were organised in the neighbouring districts of the provinces of Kherson and Poltava. Those pogroms for which Grigoriev was not responsible were organized by the local peasants, who were under the influence of the "Universals," which were then being issued by the contending Governments.

Chronologically the pogroms can be arranged as follows: Zlatopol, 2 to 8 May, 1919. Elisavetgradka, 15 to 17 May. Znamenieva, 3 May. Adjanka and Busk, 18 May. Lebedin, 5 May. Novy Boog, 19 May. Gorodishtshe, 11 to 12 May. Tshebkassy, 16 to 21 May. Orlovetz, 12 May. Raigorod, 20 May. Rotmistrovka, 13 to 14 May. Savdino Znamenski, 20 May. Belozorie, 14 to I9 May. Alexandrovka, 15 to 18 May. Matusovo, 13 to 14 May. Stepanovka, 18 May. Smiela, 13 to 14 May. Semionovka, 18 to 19 May. Grosulov, 20 May.

During the same period pogroms took place in Fumdukleevka, Medviedevka, stations Bobrinskaja Zvetkovo, Moshna, Globin, Kassel, Tomashov, Verstshak, Vessioly Koot, Vessioly Podol and others. At the station Ivanovka the men of Grigoriev murdered 62 Jews from Kodyma who were fleeing to Odessa to escape the pogroms. Many murders were also committed at other stations.

Directly attributable to Gregoriev's "Universals" are the pogrom in the Uman district, which geographically lies far away from the region in which his troops were acting. The most sanguinary pogroms were those in Uman, 13 May; in Doobovo, 13 to 14 May; Talnoje, 13 May, and in Christionovka, Lodishenko, Biezovok, Mankovka, Ivanka, Booki and others.

Thus the whole month of May was signalized by Grigoriev's activities, which in cruelty surpassed everything that had been committed by other gangs, and on the Petlura front in the provinces of Volhynia and Podolia. There were pogroms in Voronovitz on 9 May, in Rovno on 14 and 29, in Kremenetz on 12 May, in Litin on 14 and 28 May, in Kodyma and other places the dates of which are not yet established. The pogroms in Trostianetz on 10 May, and in Graisin on 12 May, may be classed among the most cruel ever perpetrated. In Kodyma, on 8 May, a pogrom was organised by one of Grigoriev's detachments, in which the peasants from the neighbouring villages co-operated

In connection with Grigoriev's revolt must be mentioned the pogrom in Zolotonosha, province of Poltava, on 12 May, committed by the Bogunsky Soviet Regiment. Obuchoff was ransacked on 17 May by the Sixth Soviet Regiment, and Pogrebishtshe on 18 May by the Eighth Soviet Regiment.

In June the provinces that suffered most were Podolia, Kiev and Volhynia. In the provinces of Kherson and Poltava only sporadic outbreaks took place. In Kiev the remainders of the Grigoriev groups continued devastating the localities through which they were passing, and on 15 June they ransacked Stavishtshe; on 16 June, Tarasttsha; on 20 June, Volodarka Ryshanovka; on 22 June, Skvir; and on 27 June, Alexandria, for the second time. Within Sokolowsky's sphere of activity the following towns suffered a second visitation: Brusilov on 13 June, Khodorkov on 15 June, Korosten on 20 June, Tcherniachov on 20 and 24 June. The towns of Kornin and Radomysl as well as that of Dubov suffered a second time. Ataman Zeliony ransacked Obuchov on 25 June, Rshishtshev and Kagarlyk on 3 June. In the province of Podolia murders and robberies were committed in the towns of Derashna, 7 to 17 June, Khmelynin, Golosovka, Maidan, Stryshanka, Staraia, Siniava and others. In the province of Poltava, Semenovka was the only place that suffered a pogrom during the month of June.

In July 1919 the pogroms assumed a more grave character, as they were mainly taking place in the same three provinces. The Kiev pogroms exceeded all others in cruelty. In this province 27 pogroms took place during the month, 12 being registered in Volhynia and 14 in Podolia.

In the Kiev province only dispersed gangs were operating, while in Volhynia and Podolia, they were joined by the Regular Petlura Troops. On 3 July Vorshtshagovka experienced a pogrom. On 2, 5 and 11 July pogroms took place in Volodarka, Dekov, Novo-Fastov respectively, but these names by no means exhaust the number of places which have undergone a

similar fate. Priluki was "pogromed" on 4 July, Sachnovka on 8 July, Turubov on 9 July, and Kalinovka on 14 July.

Sokolowsky was now repeating his exploits of the preceding months, and he again ransacked Roshevo on 3 July, Makarovo on 6 July, Brusilov on 5 July, Kornin on 9 July, Yannogorodka on 15 July, and Khavno on 13 July. Zeliony, too, was very active, and pogroms were organized in Radishchev on 1 to 13 July, Tagantsha on 8 July, Kosin on 17 July, and Pereyaslav on 15 to 19 July. At the very end of the month, on 29 July, Uman suffered a sanguinary pogrom, and on 31 July the stations of Potoski and others were ransacked.

In the province of Volhynia the following pogroms took place during the month of July 1919: Kodry, 6 and l0. Khamovka, 9 and 11. Kamenny Brod, Kotelny, Sarushnetzy and Dombrovitzy on 10. Xavrov, on 20. Slovetshna, 16 to 19; there were numerous victims from the neighbouring villages of Davidka, Bobrin and others.

In the province of Podolia the following pogroms took place during the month: Shmerinka, on 3 July. Brailov, Pikov, Voronovitzy, Obodin, all on 10. Yanov, on 11 to 15. Tulchin, on 14. Litine, on 18. The following places were pogromed on 15 to 20: Novo Constantinov, Teplin, Gaisin and Petchora.

During the month of August 1919 the number of pogroms decreased, but, in view of the fact that the front line moved nearer to Kiev, information on pogroms in the provinces of Podolia and Volhynia became scarce. On 7 August, Pereyaslavl suffered a second pogrom, at the hands of Lopatkin's gang. In Vinnitza a pogrom took place on 3 August, in Golovatchovsk on 4 August.

During the second half of August pogroms took place in the following towns: Tatiev, 24 August. Belaya-Tserkov, 25 August. Pliskov, 24 August. Boyarka, 3 September. Rushov, 24 August. Vasilkov, 3 September. Pogrebishtshe, 18 to 21 August. Germanovka, 28 August.

Shooting took place in Kiev itself on 31 August. Pogroms also took place in: Smela, Tsherkassy, Gorodishtshe, Orlovetz, Korsun, Fastov, Ustihovka, Ignatovka, Njeshin, Gostomla, Stepantzy, Takashtscha, Belotzerkovka, Priluky, and Ekaterinoslav.

By 9 September the number of places where pogroms were perpetrated amounted to 372, the actual number of pogroms being no less than 700. In several places pogroms occurred lasting many days, until the whole Jewish population was annihilated and their property destroyed.

According to Governments and districts the pogroms can be distributed as follows:

Province of Kiev. District of Tshernobyl (Struck) 43, Tripolie (Zeliony) 9, Tsherkassko-Tshigirinsky (Gregoriev) 23, Berditchev 5, Tarashtshansk 20, Uman 12, Skvir and Pogrebishtshe 30, Kiev 16 and Radomysl-Shitomir (Sokolowsky) 52. Total 210

Province of Volhynia. District of Ovrutch 26, Shitomir 20 and Rovno 10. Total 56.

Province of Podolia. District of Gaisin 29, Balta 8, Vinitza 16, Proskurov 8 and Kamenetz-Podolsk 1. Total 62

In the Province of Kherson. Poltava 23, Tshernigov 15 and Ekaterinoslav 6. Total 44

In all, 372 places which suffered from pogroms were registered. Comparing the dates on which pogroms took place we note that the most terrible months in this respect were those of the summer, namely May, June and July, 1919.

As to the part played by various gangs of pogrom makers in the sufferings inflicted on the Jewish population in the Ukraine the following statistics are available: Petlura's Regular Troops and Detachments. 120 places 15,000 killed, Gangs of Sokolowsky. 70 places 3,000 killed, Gangs of Zeliony. 15 places 2,000 killed, Gangs of Struck. 41 places 1,000 killed, The Gangs of Sokolow and others, 38 places 2,000 killed, Gangs of Grigoriev. 40 places 6,000 killed, Gangs of Yashtshenko, Golub and the others. 16 places 1,000 killed and The Soviet Troops, 13 places 500 killed Total 30,500 killed

To the above data new names must be added of towns which were ransacked and destroyed by the detachments of the Volunteer Army quite recently, at the end of August and September. They are as follows: Pogrebishtsche (400 killed), Bela Tserkov (300 killed), Boguslav, Smela, Tscherkassy, Gorodischtsche, Korsun, Fastov (over 1,000 killed), Ustinovka, Germanovka, Vasilkov, Makarov, Rakitnoie, Boyarka, Ignatovka, Neshin, Ekaterinoslav, Gostomyl, Stepantsy, Tarashtsha, Shabennoie, Belotserkovka, Priluki, Grebionka, Motovilovka, Borsna.

The entire number of registered victims who were killed in all these pogroms amounts to 40,000. The number of unregistered sufferers have also been very considerable, as there was no possibility of taking note of those who lived in the villages whose Jewish populations were completely destroyed. The number does not include the many who were done to death at points which have not yet been registered, because they are inaccessible. Such points are in the western parts of the Provinces of Volhynia and Podolia, and the southern parts of the Province of Kherson.

Not included in the above were those who died during their wanderings from one town to another in search of an asylum, those who were thrown out of trains and shot, those who were drowned in the rivers, and those who were murdered in forests and other lonely and sequestered places. In the above totals we have not included those who died from wounds, from infection, and from starvation and exposure.

It can be assumed that no less than 70,000 victims perished. Until quite recently the outstanding feature of Jewish pogroms in Russia was plundering and damaging Jewish goods, rape and other forms of violence, murder taking place comparatively seldom. Also refined cruelties were a rare phenomenon in Russian pogroms. The recent epidemic of pogroms, however, excels all other periods in its refined cruelty, in the merciless thoroughness of the acts of violence, and in the naked bloodthirstiness of the barbarous criminals.

The explanation of the tragic difference may, perhaps, be found in the fact that whereas the old pogroms were committed with the connivance of the Government, the newest pogroms were actually organised and directed by those who held administrative power in places where the Jewish population was, for days, weeks and even months, at their mercy, without the slightest prospects of relief from anyone.

It must further be added that never before has contempt for human life and other people's property been so openly expressed and so widespread as during the last years of the external war and during the whole period of the civil war with its White and Red terrors, forcible contributions, requisitions, searches, raids, round-ups, hostages, and so forth.

The following is a description of the average pogrom:
"The gangs break into the township, spreads all over the streets, separate groups break into the Jewish houses, killing without distinction of age and sex everybody they meet, with the exception of women, who are bestially violated before they are murdered, and men are forced to give up all there is in the house before being killed.

"Everything that can be removed is taken away, the rest is destroyed, the nails, doors, and windows are broken in search of money. On one group departing another comes, then a third, until absolutely nothing is left that could possibly be taken away. All clothing and linen is taken, not only from those who escape death, but also from the corpses of the dead.

A new administration is established in the place, and a deputation of the Jews miraculously preserved go to them or to the Christians who are supposed to be friendly to Jews, and request protection. As a rule the new authorities, consent to grant the protection on the condition that a certain contribution is paid by the Jews. With great difficulty a contribution is paid and then a new claim arrives from the authorities for contributions in kind, and it is the duty of the Jews to obtain a certain number of boots and a certain quantity of meat for the soldiers.

In the meantime small groups continue terrorising the Jews, exact money, murder and violate. Then the town is occupied by the Soviet troops who often continue the robbery of their predecessors. But soon all the gangs return, as the front fluctuates and the place continually changes hands. Thus, for instance, Boguslav was taken five times during one week. Every change of Government or administration brings about new pogroms, and the end of it is that the terrorised population, ruined and exhausted, naked and bare-footed, without a single coin in their pocket, flee heedless of the climatic condition and risking the dangers of the journey to the nearest town in the vain hope of getting protection there."

This is a typical picture of a pogrom, though, of course, there are variations in details, in the character of the murders committed, and the number of victims. Sometimes it happens that the contribution is exacted before the pogrom can break out. In such a case the Jews sometimes escape death, but are certain to lose all their property. Sometimes the raging gangs, or even the regular troops, organise a slaughter in the literal meaning of this word without a, single life being spared, regardless of sex and age. Details vary also in this respect, and in Belomitza (Province of Volhynia) all fathers of families were killed. In Trostianetz only males were killed regardless of age (370 people). In Volodarka, on 9 to the 11 July, seventy-three old men, women and children were slaughtered; all the rest took flight.

The bandits everywhere displayed great ingenuity and refinement in the method of killing. Shooting was most frequent, but before being; shot the victims were driven from one place to another until brought to a cemetery or a forest. But sometimes the bandits were short of cartridges and cold steel was used. In Proskurov, on 15 February, only bayonets and swords were used, and it took Samosenko's men four hours to slaughter in this way 1,600 Jews. In Dubovo the Jews were brought to a cellar and two bandits, by dealing blows on their heads, had to throw them either dead or wounded into this cellar. In Obodin (district of Bratzlav) only bayonets were used, because one cartridge cost 50 roubles. In Gorshtshik a group of rebels decided to kill the Jews by bayonets only, because shooting might create a panic among other rebels who were destroying a railway not far away.

In Tschernobyl district the usual way of killing Jews was by drowning. Jews were driven to the river and forced into the water, where they had to stay until drowned: rifles were used only when some of them succeeded in swimming to the other shore. Steamers on the Dnieper were stopped, Jews singled out from the crowds of passengers and thrown into the water. In the provinces of Poltava and Kherson, Jews were thrown out of trains running at full speed. In Elisavetgrad (1,526 killed) hand grenades were thrown into the cellars where Jews were hiding. In Rotmistrovka there were cases where badly wounded people were hanged or burnt in their houses.

In Klevan (district of Rovno) the soldiers of the Red Army invented a new method of torturing Jews by tearing their beards with a specially-adapted wire. In Ziadkovtzy (province of Podolia) during the second pogrom 15 Jews were thrown into a well alive.

The following is-the list of places with the largest number of victims: Proskurov, 15 February 1,650, Trostianetz, 10 May 370, Elisavetgrad. May 1,536, Novograd-Volynsk, 350, Fastov, 23 to 27 September 1,000, Shitomir, 23 to 26 March 317, Tscherkassy, 16 to 20 May 700, Yasov, 300, Feltin, 16 February 485, Teophipol, 26 June 300, Tulchin, 14 July 519, Belaia-Tscherkov, 25 August 300, Uman, 13 May 400, Krivoie-Osebo 280, Pogrebitshts, 13 August 400, Kamenny Brod, July 250, Gaissin, 13 May 350, Bratzlav 269, Fundukleevka 206, Litin, 14 May 110, Kamenetz-Podolsk 200, Vasilkov, 7 to 15 April 110,Golovatshevsk, 4 August 200, Ladyshenka, 14 May 100, Uman, 29 July 150, Novomirkov, 7 May 105, Priluky, 4 July 150 and Meshigorje 104.

All the wounds inflicted on the Jews were severe, and nearly always resulted in death. Very often the bandits were not satisfied with merely wounding but came back, until those whom they had left alive, though severely wounded, were killed. This is the reason why the proportion of killed to wounded is larger here than in real war. Violations of women in June and July increased in number tremendously, and on many occasions gangs of bandits broke into houses mainly for that purpose, though, of course, no house was left without being ransacked.

The bare recital of the numbers of the victims in no way shows the misery and affliction of the Jewish population, and the position of those who survived seems to exceed any imaginable depth of horrors. There are hundreds of thousands who have looked into the eyes of death and who have lived through all the horror of expecting death at any moment. These people, deprived of every possible means of subsistence, physically and morally ruined are faced with the problem of finding an asylum, of saving themselves and their children from starvation, from exposure during the coming winter, from infectious diseases and demoralisation.

We quote below a report of our commission on the Jews in Ladyshenka where an ordinary, simple pogrom took place with only 83 victims, and without the usual bestial accompaniments of other pogroms:

"On 9 July a peasant brought to the Jewish hospital in Uman the last two Jews from Ladyshenka (before the war Ladyshenka counted a Jewish population of 1,600). These were two young Jewish girls, frightfully beaten and bruised, one with her nose cut off and the other with her arms broken. They are both in Kiev now and both suffer from venereal disease.

"More than 1,000 Jews from Ladyshenka are now in Golovatshevsk. They are all naked, all bruised, and all, whether well or ill, live in the Synagogues, in the stables or the streets. Nobody knows what their lips, always firmly pressed together, could tell us and how these people live their day. Funerals take place very often in Golovatshevsk, and special collections are often made to provide the garments of the dead."

Pictures of other places are even more depressing and sadder. Sometimes the places of refuge where those who escaped death from the pogroms, expecting to find protection, become areas of new pogroms, with new hundreds of victims and the mass of misery is driven again in all directions.

It is impossible to calculate all the damage caused to the Jewish population of the Ukraine. If counted at the present values it would amount to billions. The vast majority of townships, and even many towns, are entirely cleared of Jewish property. In some of the places like Boguslav (5 April), Volodarka (11 July), Kutosovo (26 July), Voshtshagovka (9 June), Snamenka (3 May), Beloshitza (11 July), the Jewish houses were converted into heaps of smoking rubbish. But where there were no fires the Jewish houses look like ruins; windows are smashed, frames are torn out, and everything inside broken or carried away.

SOME STATISTICS OF WOMEN VIOLATED

(Extract from Documents of the Committee of Jewish Delegations.)

Tcherkassy 156, Kostolewitoh all the Women, Filchtine 200, Jgnatowka 250, Jitomir 200, Jampol all the Women, Belais-Tserkow 50, Talnoie 208, Stepantzy 150, Fastow 270, Rjichtchew 200, Kief 60, Khorodowo 60, Bakitnoe 100, Vassilkof 36, Horodichtche 40, Tripollie 170, Dymer 42, Pereiasslav 300, Krementchoug 350 and Borispol 18.

SOME STATISTICS ABOUT THE MASSACRES

(The following statistics (of people murdered)are based partly upon the report of the Russian Red Cross in Kieff, issued in September, 1919, and partly on the investigations subsequent to that date carried out by Jewish Commissions of enquiry.)

Ovroutch 120, Balta 190, Proskourow 1,754, Krivoie-Czero 250, Berschady 300, Kaniefk 506, Elisabetgrad 2,100, Bratzlaw 269, Tityewo 200, Zolotonocha 206, Tcherkassv 783, Foundouklewka 500i, Pogertbistche 400, Stepantzy 270, Filchtine 615, Kamenetz-Podolsk 200, Radomisi, 16 Pogroms 953, Golovanievsk 200, Toultchine 519, Rjichtchew 426, Ouman 550, Khodorowo 315, Teplik 400, Prylouki 150, Haissine 410, Vassilkoff 427, Petchera 1,100, Tripollie 300 Families, Trostianetz 378, Ladyjenka 100, Kamenka (Kief) 210, Zlatopol 289, Novograd-Volynsky 350, Novomirgorod 169, Matussowo 212, Pereiaslaw 400, Jitomir 412, Mejigorie 194 Drowned Janow 300, Borispol 780, Belaia-Tserkow 300, Nowo-Poltawka 120, Rotmistrowka 500, Kieff 550 and Kamenny-Brod 250.

SOME TYPICAL POGROMS IN THE UKRAINE

(Extracts from Documents of the Committee of Jewish Delegations.)

Pogrom of Ovroutch

At the head of the troops of Petlura was the hetman Kozyr-Syrko. The haidamahs started the pogrom by violating ten young girls. When a Jewish deputation came to the hetman to beg for mercy, Syrko answered, "Why have old men come? Send men here from 15 to 40 years of age." A terrible panic took possession of the town. During the night Syrko began to outrage and to humiliate the Jews whom he had forced to come to him.

While he lay stretched on his couch, the Jews, a clown's cap on their heads, were forced to dance and to sing Jewish songs.

On 16 January, when a delegation composed of the President and 22 members of the Jewish Community, came to see the hetman, the haidamahs with blows of the knout forced the representatives of the community to sing the Jewish song "Maiofis" and then murdered them with bayonets.

The Pogrom at Proskourov

The following atrocities were committed by order of the helman Simossenko, one of the commanders of the troops of Petlura, who authorized his "lads" to amuse themselves, for a few days. The massacres were perpetrated by the Cossacks who carried on their work coldly and methodically, going from house to house and from district to district. They hacked their victims before killing them, putting them to all kinds of torture. The murders were committed usually with the naked sword or bayonet. Some bodies bore on them thirty six wounds and cuts, others were cut in pieces, and in some cases the head was severed from the body.

Children were violated and murdered before the eyes of their parents, who were then themselves murdered.

By order of the same hetman the first-aid quarters were removed, so that the wounded had no means for taking refuge, even though the number of them was enormous.

The Jews were not allowed to bury the bodies of those who had been massacred by the Cossacks. These troops piled the bodies in hollows and then filled them up in order that the place of burial should not be recognised. By the order of Simossenko, who was the commander of a brigade, the massacres started at one o'clock in the afternoon, with cries of "Long Live Holy Ukraine" and "Death to the Jews" and finished towards six o'clock, when "the lads fatigued with their work," returned to the barracks to the sound of music only to start their dreaded work the next day.

The Pogrom of Filchtine (near Proskurov)

This pogrom commenced on 17 February and was carried out by detachments coming from Proskourow. By order of the commandant of the troops of Simossenko, the Cossacks billotted for the night in Jewish houses, seized all the exits from the town and commenced a general massacre of the Jews. Those who tried to escape were shot, women and children were hoisted on bayonets, bombs were thrown and garrets and cellars, where the panic stricken populace attempted to hide themselves, were burned. The whole place was destroyed by fire. Of the whole population, only 25 families remained alive. There was nobody to look after the wounded and bury the dead. Six hundred were killed and many wounded and mutilated.

The Pogrom of Balta

The detachments of Petlura drove the whole Jewish population from the town, which was then given up to looting. Ninety Jews were killed. Old women were violated. The loot was carried off in military trains. The pillaging lasted a whole week. They dragged from the trains Jews arriving from Balta, covered them with blows, and carried off all their goods. The pogroms were renewed on several occasions, causing each time numerous victims.

The Pogroms in Kornine

On the night of 20 February 1919, the troops of Petlura arrived in this city during their retreat and levied a contribution of

200,000 roubles. Drunken soldiers broke into the houses, attacked the population, carried off all goods of value on wagons and gave up all the rest to the populace. On 27 February a new detachment arrived which repeated the pogrom. Among those killed was the Rabbi whose body was cut open by the Cossacks.

Peasants who wished to shelter the Jews were threatened with death. When the Jewish population hid themselves in the surrounding forests, soldiers on horseback organised a beat and forced the fugitives to return to the town, and perpetrated unmentionable atrocities upon them.

The Pogrom of Bogouslaw

This town changed hands about 20 times in one week. The shooting and the pillage commenced again with every new occupation. Initially the unhappy population, having escaped so many horrors, and seized with terror, fled from these terrible places, without money and without clothes, in utter destitution.

The Pogrom of Ladyjenka

In July, 1919, a peasant brought to the Jewish hospital of Ouman, the two last survivors of the Jewish population of this city, where before the pogrom there were 1,500 Jewish souls. There were two young girls, both frightfully beaten, wounded and bitten. One had her nose cut, the other had her arms broken. They are at this moment in Kieff. Apart from their wounds they suffer from venereal diseases for which they are being treated (Report of the Red Cross).

The Pogrom of Krementschoug.

All the horrors which took place in the above-mentioned towns are nothing in comparison with what took place at Krementschoug, where the work of destruction commenced with the entry of the volunteer troops into the town. The cries of grief and lamentation arose on all sides. All the Jewish houses were sacked and pillaged.

350 women were registered as violated, neither children of twelve years nor old women of sixty being spared. After being violated the little girls were thrown into the water closets.

The Pogroms of Fabtov.

A terrible pogrom organised by detachments of Denikin broke out in this town at the end of September, 1919.

The pogrom took place during the occupation of the town, and afterwards, the bodies of those killed were left lying for several days in the streets. Thousands of people, gravely wounded, died without anyone being able to bring them any help. The dogs and pigs gnawed at the bodies killed and wounded.

A great number of women and girls were violated. It was with truly bestial fury that the soldiers threw themselves on young girls and violated them before the very eyes of their helpless parents.

Particularly revolting scenes took place in the court of the Synagogue where the Jews had sought refuge. The whole court was strewn with bodies of old men, women and children and violated girls. Many people went mad.

Many Jews sought shelter in the Church, but the soldiers surrounded it and killed the 60 Jews in it, and then burned all the Jewish houses in the town. More than two hundred houses were thus given up to the flames.

THE FRENCH APPEAL TO HUMANITY

In the name of human conscience, in the name of the moral responsibility, which every man bears towards his fellow men: the undersigned appeal to all people of the world and more especially to the French people.

A cry of terror and of poignant grief reaches us from Eastern Europe, from the Ukraine, from Poland, from Lithuania, and from Galicia: a whole people cries out despairingly for help.

The Jews who, for centuries, have been settled in Eastern Europe, have become the innocent and pitiful victims of struggles, national, political and the rival ambitions of peoples, governments and parties, and all the folly of civil war satiate themselves to-day upon the unhappy Jewish minority with criminal cruelty.

The pogroms of Tsarism, even the massacres of Kishinev have been surpassed by these recent atrocities.

In Bessarabia, occupied by the Rumanian troops, the military authorities tolerated wicked outrages against the Jews. In Eastern Galicia a wave of pogroms followed the Polish invasion, and at Lemberg the terror was at its height. The horrors of Pinsk, Lida and Vilna, added a page of tears and blood to the tragic annals of Jewish history.

In more than a hundred towns of the Ukraine, frightful pogroms have taken place and tens of thousands of victims have perished. The most terrible days of the Inquisition have returned, for the massacres have been accompanied by the most cruel tortures and the most terrible moral and physical torments. At Proskenow, thousands of Jews were massacred. At Filchtine, Jitomir, Balta, Ouman, Habidievka, Bobry (a Jewish agricultural colony), Litine, Kamenenetz-Podolsk, Kitaigorod, Trostinetz, etc., the number of victims is enormous. In the Ukraine the pogroms are still being carried on and threaten the Jews with complete extinction.

Millions of men, women and children, are suffering indescribable misery, and are handed over defenceless to death and dishonour. What the war has spared of the modest possession of the Jews is now systematically pillaged and destroyed.

In the very midst of civilised Europe, at the dawn of the new era for which the world awaits its charter of liberty and justice, the existence of a whole population is threatened. Such crimes dishonour not only the people that commit them, but outrage human reason and conscience.

The undersigned appeal to all peoples of the world against the unheard of crimes of which a single people is the victim.

Everywhere Committees for the defence of the Jews of Eastern Europe must be organised, and these Committees must unite for prompt and vigorous action against the oppressors.

Public opinion must be stirred up by the protest of the masses and by the great organ of the press which is at last fully and correctly informed.

Let the voices of the peoples' representatives in all the parliaments of the world be raised against these heinous iniquities. The duty is incumbent upon free peoples and responsible governments, to put an end to this monstrous violation of the rights of man.

We ask for the speedy organisation of Committees of defence against persecution. Committees invested with every authority which belongs to their high mission. Millions of oppressed Jews have no other safeguard than the consciousness of the moral solidarity of the civilised world, and they have put their supreme hope in the sacred right of all men to life and liberty.

Signed
Anatole France, Paul Appell, Membre de l'Institut, A Aulard, Professor a la Faculte des lettres de Paris, Henri Barbusse, Charles Bernard, Depute, Emile Combes, Senateur, ancien President du Conseil, Michel Corday, L Dispan De Fleuran, Professeur agrege au Lycee Lakanal, Georges Duhamel, Elie Faure, Charles Gide, Professeur a la Faculty de Droit de Paris, Ferdinand Herold, Vice-President de la Ligue des Droits de l'Homme, Gustave Herve, L Lapicque, Professeur a la Faculte, F Larnaude, Doyen de la Faculty de Droit de Paris, Ernest Lavisse, de Academie Fransaise, Directeur de l'Ecole Normale Superieure, Victor Marqueritte, Madame Menard-Dorian, Pierre Mille, Wilfred Monod, Pasteur, De Monzie, Depute, ancien Ministre, Moutet, Depute du Rhdne, A Prenant, Professeur a la Faculte de Medecine, Membre de 1' Academic de Medecine, Henri Roger, Doyen de la Faculte de Medecine, Gabriel Seailles, Professeur a l'Uni- Ch Seignobos, Professeur a la Faculte des Lettres de Paris. Albert Thomas, Depute, ancient, et Ministre. Abbe Violet.

Signed in the UK.
President The Very Rev Dr J H Hertz, Chief Rabbi.
Vice Presidents Sir Stuart M Samuel, Bart. Herbert Bentwich.
Patrons Haham, Dr. M Gasteb, Sir Robert Waxey Cohen, KBE, Nahum Sokolow, Solomon J Solomon, RA, Israel Zangwill, Dr S Bbodbtsky, Sir Adolph Tuck, Bt Nathan Daski, Prof A Buchler, B S Straus and Dr R N Salaman.
Chairman Dr D Jochelman,
Vice Chairmen Dr M. Pines, Morris Myer.

Treasurers Joseph Prag, JP M Shalit
Secretary S Goldenberg
Executive Committee Ekan Adler, J Kipernick, Rev Michael Adler, B Kogan, M Bagrit, M Liebeman, B Bernstein, J Landau, J Caplan, J Machower, Dr S Daiches, Laurie Magnus, Rev L Geffen, Rabbi I I Mattuck, M Grossman, Dr M Schwarzman, L Hut, L Schen, M Kaufman, A Tarlo, I Kalmenson and Dr I J Trivus. **Secretary** A. M. Kamer.

The following messages of sympathy were received at a Public Meeting held in London by the Federation of Ukrainian Jews in April 1921.

From Lord Parmoor
There is much misery in many European districts, and I wish that we in England could do more to help in the work of relief and restoration. I know that the Jews in some districts have suffered in a special manner, and I cordially would support your endeavour to awaken public opinion.

From Lord Weardale
I am sorry it will be impossible for me to be present at your mass meeting on Sunday next. I should have been interested in hearing the reports from representatives upon their visit to the pogrom areas of the Ukraine. I fear, however, that they can hardly be anything but most distressing, for passions have been running riot in all those districts, and although newspaper reports are not always reliable, there can be no doubt that cruel sufferings have been inflicted upon the Jewish inhabitants of those regions. The war seems to have greatly deadened the public conscience, or perhaps the existence of widespread disorders in so many parts of the world has rendered it painfully callous. We see what is now going on close to our own shores in Ireland, and, alas, we have no Gladstone among us who would rouse the public to condemn these terrible proceedings, both in Ireland and elsewhere. I rejoice to learn you are taking action at Mile End, and I trust that a powerful appeal will proceed from your meeting, calling upon all civilised Governments to intervene to save the unfortunate Jews of Eastern Europe from the appalling attacks upon them.

From Col Josiah C Wedgwood, MP:
The martyrdom of the Ukrainian Jews, culminating in the massacres of the last two years, must rouse the deepest indignation of all right-minded people in the world. By reason of our protectorate over Palestine, the British Government should exercise some restraining influence over these Polish, Russian, and Rumanian butchers. At least let the half-savage Governments know that our sympathies are with the Jews and not with the half-breed Dagos who persecute our friends.

Published in 1921 by THE FEDERATION OF UKRAINIAN JEWS, IN AID OF THE POGROM SUFFERERS IN THE UKRAINE. (Registered under the War Charities Act.) 26a, Soho Square, London, W. I.

Chapter 4 ~ THE PETLURA POGROMS

SIMON PETLURA

Symon Petlura is regarded as a hero by Ukrainians. For a short time in 1918 he gave them their independence. He was head of the Ukraine Army and State while his soldiers murdered many Jews. As you will read, there is some doubt whether he knew fully what was going on.

Extract from
THE HOLOCAUST - THE JEWISH TRAGEDY
by Martin Gilbert

Even as the First World War ended on the western front, more than 50 Jews were killed by local Ukrainians in the eastern Polish city of Lvov. In the then independent Ukrainian town of Proskurov, 1700 Jews were murdered on 15 February 1919 by followers of the Ukrainian nationalist leader, Simon Petlura, and by the end of the year, Petlura's gangs had killed at least 60,000 Jews.

These Jews were victims of local hatreds reminiscent of Tsarist days, but on a scale unheard of in the previous century. In the city of Vilna, the 'Jerusalem of Lithuania', 80 Jews were murdered during April 1919; in Galicia, 500 perished. 'Terrible news is reaching us from Poland,' the Zionist leader Chaim Weizmann wrote to a friend on 29 November 1918. 'The newly liberated Poles there are trying to get rid of the Jews by the old and familiar method which they learnt from the Russians. Heartrending cries are reaching us. We are doing all we can, but we are so weak!'

EVIDENCE OF MILE. HAIA GREENBERG,
a witness in the Petlura Trial
see more details below

The most notable witness called, was Mile. Haia Greenberg, 29, a curly bobbed-haired nurse. In a soft, low voice, she told of the carnage and raping ordered by Simon Petlura and of the blood-bathed home of her grandparents. Murmured she:

"I shall never forget the reddened snowsleds, filled with the hacked bodies, going to the cemetery to desposit their sad burden, in a common pit. They brought the wounded to the hospital— armless and legless men, mutilated babies and young women whose screams became faint as their wounds overcame them."

Then breaking down and sobbing convulsively she screamed: "Oh, no, no! I cannot go on! They are before my eyes!"

"Petlura was responsible. Even Ukrainian officers said so. His soldiers killed our people, shouting his name. One regiment had a band and it played while knives fell on the heads of innocent babies. Petlura could have stopped it, but he wouldn't listen to our pleas."

REGISTER DETAILS OF OCHBERG ORPHANS AT THE CAPE JEWISH ORPHANAGE - ORANJIA
courtesy Veronica Belling, Jewish Studies Library, University of Cape Town

The family details of Roza Gurwitz as recorded on page 93 of the register at The Cape Jewish Orphanage - Oranjia.

1 Name and surname: Roza Gurwitz
2 Father: Yitzhak 3 Mother: 4 Age: 10 years
5 From where: Felshtin   6 Who died: Both parents
7 General Comments: The father died from   The mother was murdered by Petlurists in 1918 in Proskuro. The child was left alone without any relations or help.

The family details of Nahman Gruntshtein as recorded on page 99 of the register at The Cape Jewish Orphanage - Oranjia.

1 Name and surname: Nahman Gruntshtein
2 Father: 3 Mother: 4 Age: 9 years
5 From where: Berditchev   6 Who died: Both parents
7 General Comments: The father was murdered by the Petlurists. The mother died from   The child was found with the granny in terrible conditions..

The family details of Hersh Stillerman as recorded on page 113 of the register at The Cape Jewish Orphanage - Oranjia.

1 Name and surname: Hersh Stillerman
2 Father: Shmuel 3 Mother: 4 Age: 12 years
5 From where: Lemberg   6 Who died: Both parents
7 General Comments: Both parents and a sister were murdered by the Petlurists in Felshtein (Proskurov's circle). The child was in   and a Petlurist chopped off his left hand. The child suffered greatly and was left alone.

Many other pages in the register simply mention that the families had suffered or endured pogroms or many pogroms without naming the pogrom.

SIMON PETLURA (Symon Petliura)
Extracts from Wikipedia, the free encyclopedia

Much has been written about Symon Petliura and below are some extracts. He was well educated and worked as a teacher and turned to publishing and writing.

Petliura was born on May 10, 1879, in Poltava, Ukraine, the son of Vasyl Petliura and Olha Marchenko, urban dwellers of Cossack extraction. Cossack, as opposed to peasant heritage, allowed certain privileges regarding land ownership, taxes and access to education in the Russian Empire, of which most of Ukraine was then part.

As the editor of numerous journals and newspapers, Petliura published over 15 000 critical articles, reviews, stories and poems under an estimated 120 nom-de-plumes. His prolific work in both the Russian and Ukrainian languages helped shape the mindset of the Ukrainian population in the years leading up to the Revolution in both Eastern and Western Ukraine. His prolific correspondence was of great benefit when the Revolution broke out in 1917, as he had contacts throughout Ukraine.

Symon Petliura's portait on a Ukrainian stamp

Rise to Power

Petliura attended the first All-Ukrainian Army Congress held in Kiev in May 1917 as a delegate, where he was elected head of the Ukrainian General Army Committee on 18 May. With the proclamation of the Ukrainian Central Council on 28 June, 1917, Petliura became the First Secretary for military matters.

Petliura became a member of the Directorate of Ukraine as the Chief of Military Forces and later became the leader of the Directorate of Ukraine in February 1919. In his capacity as head of the Army and State, he continued to fight both Bolshevik and White forces in Ukraine for the next ten months.

1919

With the outbreak of hostilities between Ukraine and Soviet Russia in January 1919, Petliura ultimately became the leading figure in the Directorate. During the course of the year, he continued to defend the fledgling republic against incursions by the Bolsheviks, Anton Denikin's White Russians, and the Romanians. By autumn of 1919, most of Denikin's White Russian forces were defeated — in the meantime, however, the Bolsheviks had grown to become the dominant force in Ukraine.

Petliura withdrew to Poland 5 December 1919, which had previously recognized him as the head of the legal government of Ukraine. In April 1920, as head of the Ukrainian People's Republic, he signed an alliance in Warsaw with the Polish government, agreeing to a border on the River Zbruch and recognizing Poland's right to Galicia in exchange for military aid in overthrowing the Bolshevik regime. Polish forces, reinforced

by Petliura's remaining troops (some two divisions), attacked Kiev on 7 May 1920 in what became a turning point of the 1919–21 Polish-Bolshevik war. Following initial successes, Piłsudski's and Petliura's forces were pushed back to the Vistula River and the Polish capital, Warsaw. The Polish Army managed to defeat the Bolshevik Russians, but were unable to secure independence for Ukraine. Petliura directed the affairs of the Ukrainian government-in-exile from Tarnów and when the Soviet Union requested Petliura's extradition from Poland, the Poles engineered his "disappearance," secretly moving him from Tarnów to Warsaw.

After the Revolution

Bolshevik Russia persistently demanded that Petliura be handed over. Protected by several Polish friends and colleagues, with the establishment of the Soviet Union in 30 December 1922, Petliura, in late 1923 left Poland for Budapest, then Vienna, Geneva and finally settled in Paris in early 1924. Here he established and edited the Ukrainian language newspaper *Tryzub* (Trident).

Promoting a Ukrainian cultural identity

During his time as leader of the Directorate, Petliura was active in supporting Ukrainian culture both in Ukraine and abroad.

Petlura introduced the awarding of the title "People's Artist of Ukraine" to artists who had made significant contributions to Ukrainian culture. A similar title award was continued after a significant break under the Soviet regime. Among those who had received this award was blind kobzar Ivan Kuchuhura Kucherenko.

He also saw the value in gaining international support and recognition of Ukrainian arts through cultural exchanges. Most notably, Petliura actively supported the work of cultural leaders such as the choreographer Vasyl Avramenko, conductor Oleksander Koshetz and bandurist Vasyl Yemetz,

Paris

In Paris, Petliura directed the activities of the government of the Ukrainian National Republic in exile. He launched the weekly Tryzub, and continued to edit and write numerous articles under various pen names with an emphasis on questions dealing with national oppression in Ukraine. These articles were written with a literary flair. The question of national awareness was often of significance in his literary work.

Petliura's articles had a significant impact on the shaping of Ukrainian national awareness in the early 20th century. He published articles and brochures under a variety of noms de plume, including V Marchenko, V Salevsky, I Rokytsky, and O Riastr.

Role in pogroms

Anti-Jewish pogroms accompanied the Revolution of 1917 and the ensuing Russian Civil War. The Ukrainian state promised Jews full equality and autonomy, and Arnold Margolin, a Jewish minister in Petliura's government, declared in May 1919 that the Ukrainian government had given Jews more rights than they enjoyed in any other European government. However, Petliura lost control over most of his armed forces, who then engaged in killing Jews. During Petliura's term as Head of State (1919-20), pogroms continued to be perpetrated on Ukrainian ethnic territory, and the number of Jews killed during the period is estimated to be 35,000 to 50,000.

The debate about Petliura's role in the pogroms has been a topic of dispute since Petliura's assassination and Schwartzbard's trial. In 1969, the Journal of Jewish Studies published two opposing views by scholars Taras Hunczak and Zosa Szjakowski, which are still frequently cited.

Some historians claim that Petliura, as the head of the government, did not do enough to stop the pogroms, and suggest that by this lack of activity knowingly encouraged them as a means to strengthen his base of support among his soldiers, commanders and the peasant population at large, appealing to antisemitic sentiments. They also suggest that many of the atrocities were committed by the forces directly under the command of the Directorate and loyal to Petliura. According to a Jewish former member of the Ukrainian government's cabinet, Solomon Goldelman, Petliura was afraid to punish officers or soldiers engaged in crimes against Jews for fear of losing their support. Nevertheless, Goldelman consistently defended Petliura and his record. Petliura is said to

have once said, "it is a pity that pogroms take place, but they uphold the discipline of the army.

It is time to realize that the world Jewish population—their children, their women—was enslaved and deprived of its national freedom, just like we were.

Historians have pointed out that Petliura himself never demonstrated any personal antisemitism, and it is documented that he actively sought to halt anti-Jewish violence on numerous occasions, introducing capital punishment for the crime of pogroming. Taras Hunczak of Rutgers University writes that "to convict Petliura for the tragedy that befell Ukrainian Jewry is to condemn an innocent man and to distort the record of Ukrainian-Jewish relations".

Because the USSR saw Petliura and Ukrainian nationalism as a threat, it was in its interest to tarnish his reputation. A propaganda campaign to this end included accusations of anti-Jewish crimes. Hunczak insists that "Petliura's own personal convictions render such responsibility highly unlikely, and all the documentary evidence indicates that he consistently made efforts to stem pogrom activity by UNR troops.

In 1921 Ze'ev Jabotinsky, the father of Revisionist Zionism, signed an agreement with Maxim Slavinsky, Petlura's representative in Prague, regarding the formation of a Jewish gendarmerie which was to accompany Petliura's putative invasion of Ukraine, and would protect the Jewish population from pogroms. This agreement did not materialize, and Jabotinsky was heavily criticized by most Zionist groups. Nevertheless he stood by the agreement and was proud of it.

Assassination

On 25 May 1926, while walking on rue Racine, not far from boulevard Saint-Michel, Petliura was approached by Sholom Schwartzbard. Schwartzbard asked him in Ukrainian, "Are you Mr. Petliura?" Petliura did not answer, only raised his walking cane. Then as Schwartzbard claimed in court he pulled out a gun and shot him five times Some state that there were two more after he was lying on the ground. That is how Schwartzbard described the incident:

"When I saw him fall I knew he had received five bullets. Then I emptied my revolver. The crowd had scattered. A policeman came up quietly and said: 'Is that enough?' I answered: 'Yes.' He said: 'Then give me your revolver.' I gave him the revolver, saying: 'I have killed a great assassin.' "When the policeman told me Petlura was dead I could not hide my Joy. I leaped forward and threw my arms about his neck."

Schwartzbard was claiming that he was walking around Paris with Petliura's photo in one pocket and his handgun in another, peering in the faces of the Paris residents just to find his victim.

Schwartzbard was a Ukrainian-born Jewish anarchist. He participated in the Jewish self defense of Balta, for which the Russian Tsarist government sentenced him to three months in prison for "provoking" the Balta pogrom and was twice convicted for taking part in anarchist "expropriation" (burglary) and bank robbery in Austro-Hungary. He later joined the French Foreign Legion (1914 - 1917) and was wounded in the Battle of the Somme. It is reported that Schwartzbard told famous fellow anarchist leader Nestor Makhno in Paris that he was terminally ill and expected to die, and that he would take Petliura with him; Makhno forbade Schwartzbard to do so.

The French Secret service had been keeping an eye out on Schwartzbard from the time he had surfaced in the French capital and had noted his meetings with known Bolsheviks. During the trial the German special services also informed their French counterparts that Schwartzbard had assassinated Petlura on the orders of *Galip*, an emissary of the Union of Ukrainian Citizens. He had received orders from the head of the Soviet Ukrainian government, Christian Rakovsky, an ethnic Bulgarian and a revolutionary leader from Romania. The act was consolidated by Mikhail Volodin, who arrived in France 8 August 1925 and who had been in close contact with Schwartzbard.

Schwartzbard's parents were among 15 members of his family murdered in the pogroms in Odessa. The core defense at the Schwartzbard trial was — as presented by the noted jurist Henri Torres — that he was avenging the deaths of more than 50,000 Jewish victims of the pogroms, whereas the prosecution (both criminal and civil) tried to show that:
(i) Petliura was not responsible for the pogroms and
(ii) Schwartzbard was a Soviet agent.

Both sides brought on many witnesses, including several historians. A notable witness for the defense was Haia Greenberg (aged 29), a local nurse who survived the Proskurov pogroms and testified about the carnage. She never said that Petliura personally participated in the event, but rather some other soldiers who said that they were directed by Petliura. Several former Ukrainian officers testified for the prosecution.

After a trial lasting eight days the jury acquitted Schwarzbard.

Petliura is buried alongside his wife and daughter in the Cimetière du Montparnasse in Paris, France.

"Home at last", painting by Moshe Maimon

STANISŁAW BUŁAK-BAŁACHOWICZ

As stated in the article (following later), from Wikipedia, the free encyclopedia

"For his resistance against Bolshevik forces that killed local Belarusian peasantry, members of Belarusian minority in Poland regard Stanisław Bułak-Bałachowicz as their national hero."

"In early years he had the reputation of people's defender, because he often was an arbitrator in disputes between farmers and the landlord. From these times he has got a nickname "Daddy" (Bat'ka). His other characteristic nickname became part of his surname—"Bulak"—which means in Belarusian language a man who is driven by the wind. "

This article on Stanisław Bułak-Bałachowicz (three pages below) makes no mention of the pogroms reported below.

**The two articles below come from the book
THE TOWNS AS THEY WERE IN THEIR TIME AND PLACE**

AN EXEMPLARY AND GLORIOUS COMMUNITY
Written by Baruch Melamed
Translated by Selwyn Rose

Israelite community in the town of Kamien-Koszyrski, in the district of Polesia, Poland - my eyes shed tears over your destruction, my heart aches over what the Czar and the enemy did to you, my poor pen is inadequate to tell of your life; I will try to put into a few words your memorial.

I first knew you with the end of the First World War.

The first to injure you and suck your blood, were the soldiers of Kaiser Wilhelm. After them came others in their place – all sorts of gangs and armies, that widened and deepened your suffering, until there came as robbers the gangs of the murderer Bulak-Balakhovich, who outdid by far in their destruction all who had come before them.

More than a hundred victims, pure martyrs from among your children were killed and incinerated that same Rosh Hashanah 5681 (1881/2), lost to unconstrained robbery and murder at the hands of those blood-thirsty wild men, and you – wretched, pillaged, long-suffering then, after everything, the events that beset you during those six years of war.

> The gangs of Hetman Bulak-Balachovitz raided the community in the 1920 pogrom and burnt 20 Torah Scrolls out of a total of 30 belonging to the community. (*Encyclopedia Judaica*)

CHILDHOOD IN THE SHADOW OF POGROMS
Written by Bracha Gazit (Gisis)
Translated by Selwyn Rose

I was born on the eve of World War One and my first steps were taken in an unsettled world, shaken and stormy. To our great sorrow and humiliation, most of the blows, the suffering and the torment fell on us the Jews. Throughout all the generations up until the present day, we have drunk copiously of the cup of bitterness to the very last drop. Our little town, *Kamen-Kashirskiy*, well-versed in suffering, that had passed all the most difficult and bitter of tests during decades of disturbances and pogroms, of burnings and assassinations, had withstood them all, thanks to the awareness and will to live and to survive in spite of all. She nurtured within her a type of Jew, loyal and proud until she was subdued in the Second World War, such as other magnificent Jewish towns and communities, by the black forces of Nazism.

I remember my town, its streets and lanes and especially its people, for we were so close to each other – like one big family. However, I will dwell here on the things that happened to me one week, during the pogroms that were visited upon us in those days, as they are unforgettably etched into my memory – and will remain so to my dying day.

I was a little girl then, about six years old and the days were days of riots against the Jews under the leadership of Batko Balachovich. They fell upon us and attacked us, robbed, burned, raped and murdered, young and old. Between Rosh Hashanah and Yom Kippur about 150 families lost dear ones – husbands, mothers and children. The number of widows and orphans who remained from that slaughter laid a shadow on the town that stayed a long time, and the wounds never healed. On one such autumn morning, we were awakened to the sound of loud knocking on the door. When my father opened the door, he saw before him three armed rioters who pointed their rifles at him, demanding money. My father stood before them and explained that there was no money, nor anything else of value, because others had been already and taken what there was. They didn't believe him, of course, and began searching. Two of them guarded father while the third started grubbing around all over, turning the house upside down and slashing the pillows and chairs with his sword. Our belongings and household goods were strewn all over the floor and feathers filled the house like a snowstorm. Enraged at not finding anything of value they started hitting my father with their rifle butts, cursing and abusing him and finally leaving us alone.

When my father recovered a bit he and my mother began to discuss what to do. My mother was for running and hiding but my father coolly and in a calm and considered fashion, explained that there was nowhere to run, since the hooligans were everywhere; there were already dead and wounded and we had nothing with which to defend ourselves, no weapon – nothing. Only with the help of heaven would we be saved.

My mother could not stay at home in that situation and dressing my little brother and me we went out. My father stayed at home. When we arrived at my grandfather's house – later our house – and went in, we were shocked. The house was in a far worse state than ours. Fear and confusion was everywhere. The doors and windows were smashed, the contents of the cupboards and bedding strewn over the floor. The air was full of a sea of flying feathers covering, as they settled, the torn books littering the floor. My grandfather, wrapped in his prayer shawl, was down on his knees trying to gather together the pages of the holy books from the confusion on the floor.

At the side of the room lay a dead person face down. Apparently shot in the back, he had fallen forwards onto his face. At this horrible sight my brother and I just wanted to get out, to leave our grandfather's house, so we grabbed our mother's hand and dragged her outside. From each and every house, every courtyard, frightened and worried faces looked out at us, sad eyed with the helplessness that was the lot of every Jew during the dreadful riots.

We walked in the direction of our lane and entered the homes of our neighbours. In every house we saw the same picture of destruction and fright, timidity and fear. But it was mainly fear that showed in the eyes of everyone, young and old alike.

However, a different sight met our eyes when we entered the home of Pesl Fugatch, who had a very sick, bed-ridden sister. The rioters, it seems, found nothing of value and left it untouched. Compared to the other houses we had seen it was a veritable Garden of Eden. I asked our mother to let me stay there with Pesl, and I would come home alone later. In this way, I separated from my mother and brother, and remained in that house with the woman and her sick sister. But we were not left in peace for long. That same day, in the afternoon, the rioters came and with shouts and blows, forced us from the house and drove us in the direction of Eli the tailor's house where they had gathered hundreds of other Jews, men women and children. When the house had been absolutely jammed full of people, with no possibility of forcing one more soul through the doors, they closed and locked the doors with a lock and bolted it, placing armed guards outside to make sure no one escaped. Their intention became clear very quickly: they demanded from us an exorbitant sum of money and threatened they would kill us one by one if we didn't give it to them, or burn us all together by setting the house on fire. The people cried and begged for their lives, throwing everything of value they had on them, like cash, watches or rings but nothing seemed to satisfy them and they demanded more and more – threatening the whole time to kill us.

Three long days and nights laden with the fear of death the people spent, without a morsel of food to eat. The overcrowding was so, that some people were even unable to stand any longer because of weakness and lay on the floors, one on top of the other. Adults prayed, children cried and screamed and the entire sight was shocking. I stuck close to the only "guardian" I had and tortured myself with the thought that all this had come upon me because I had left my mother and brother. The woman under whose care I was, pleaded with their leader to let me leave the house, for what benefit would they get by killing me as well. She explained that I was not her daughter and that it was my last request to see my mother before I died.

To this day I have no idea what it was that influenced him more – the pleas of the desperate woman, or the helpless face of a little girl. Whatever it was he let me go and even said he would take me himself to my mother. Perhaps he thought he would get some ransom or other benefit from my mother? In any event, he took me by the hand and walked me home and my joy knew no bounds at the thought of seeing my loved ones again. I ran with all my strength while he, the tall man in the Cossack's hat and long sword swinging at his thigh, ran alongside grasping my hand until I got to my grandfather's house and stood stock still. I didn't know whether to enter his house first or our own. And my appalling shock when I saw, in the barn separating our two houses, a man's body hanging....................

It was my father, hanging there on a length of wire, snorting his last breaths...... I don't think I shouted, because there was no strength left in me to shout, I only freed myself from the hand that held me and clung to my father's legs, silently whispering, "Daddy…" The man, who stood next to me, laid his rifle at my father's feet and lowered my father to the ground.

My father, for a change, clasped me to him and asked me where I had just come from and where had I been all the time. With legs that could barely hold us, we entered my grandfather's house. The house was full of people – alive and dead. On the floor the bodies of the murdered were strewn about and on the bed lay a wounded man with a severe head injury. My aunt was trying to staunch the bleeding with bread. In the meantime another group of hooligans entered, looking for some youngsters to torment and vent their anger on. And again they took my father and two others: Shimon the builder and his only son. They led them to our barn, stood them in a row and told them to count to three and walk forwards.

They shot Shimon's son in the back and he fell forward on his face like a felled tree in the forest. He was such a good-looking boy, sturdy and tall. His heartbroken father knelt down to pick him up but the murderers started kicking him and told him to start running if he wanted to live – and left them. My father and Shimon dragged the dead body into the house and laid it together with the other dead. My father went into our house that had been broken into and was now deserted, removed a board from the ceiling and climbed up to the attic where about 60 people had been hiding for a number of days, most of them youngsters. The ladder, which gave access to the attic, had been removed entirely from its fixture; thus they thought that they could save themselves, and their hiding place not be discovered. Through a small aperture in the eaves, they could see everything that occurred outside in the street.

One day, when a few of the hooligans were still running around like poisoned rats, seeking adventure, especially youngsters whom they could bully, three of them climbed up to the attic of our house, the entrance to which was blocked with bales of hay.

When my father sensed they were near, he quickly told those hiding there and one after the other they jumped from the roof to the mud-covered ground at the front of the house. The last to jump was my father, who blocked the entry of the hooligans to the attic with his body. Exactly at that time, the leader of the gangs gave the order to cease the killing and rioting and warned that anyone disobeying his order would be killed. They didn't stop their 'devil's dance' immediately however. They still went wild here and there, setting fire to houses, robbing and raping. I don't remember when it all stopped because as soon as I saw the faces of the people who had jumped from the roof, all covered and filthy in mud and blood, I started to run from that place. I arrived at the house of Itcha Berenholtz, where there were also many Jews concentrated, among them my mother.

I fell into her arms and fainted, since I was completely at the point of exhaustion and for a few days I was unconscious, fluttering between life and death.

ALTER BOBROV in an interview in 1971
"Balachouwitz a notorious Ukrainian fanatic descended on the city with his gangs and the pogroms raged for nearly a week.' When order was restored, supplies began to arrive first from the Juedischer Hilfsverein u Berlin, and then from the Joint Distribution Committee,

REGISTER DETAILS OF OCHBERG ORPHANS AT THE CAPE JEWISH ORPHANAGE - ORANJIA
courtesy Veronica Belling, Jewish Studies Library, University of Cape Town

---

The family details of Yontil Ellman as recorded on page 1 of the register at The Cape Jewish Orphanage - Oranjia.

1 Name and surname: Yontil Ellman
2 Father: Babil 3 Mother: Chanah 4 Age: 10 years
5 From where: Dematzewa 6 Who died: Both parents
7 General Comments: The father died of general weakness. Mother was killed by the Belachowitz in 1920.
The children were left alone without means to live.

The family details of Rosa Heft as recorded on page 11 of the register at The Cape Jewish Orphanage - Oranjia.

1 Name and surname: Rosa Heft
2 Father: Lazar 3 Mother: Beile 4 Age: 9 years
5 From where: Dematzewa 6 Who died: Both parents
7 General Comments: The father was killed by the Belachowitz in 1920. The mother died from confinement.
The children were left alone without means for development.

The family details of Saul Zvengel as recorded on page 31 of the register at The Cape Jewish Orphanage - Oranjia.

1 Name and surname: Saul Zvengel
2 Father: Hershel 3 Mother: Henye Golda 4 Age: 8 years
5 From where: Wlodawa 6 Who died: Both parents
7 General Comments: The father was killed by the Belachowitz. The mother died of typhoid.
The child left with no relatives to look after him

The family details of Sarah Margolin as recorded on page 63 of the register at The Cape Jewish Orphanage - Oranjia.

1 Name and surname: Sarah Margolin
2 Father: Abraham 3 Mother: Frume 4 Age: 9 years
5 From where: Pinsk 6 Who died: Both parents
7 General Comments:
The father died of typhoid fever in 1917
The mother died of typhoid fever in 1918
The older brother killed by the Belachowitz in Pinsk 1920
The child left with no relatives whatever

The family details of Simon Migdalawitz recorded on page 65 of the register at The Cape Jewish Orphanage - Oranjia.

1 Name and surname: Simon Migdalawitz
2 Father: Shmuel 3 Mother: Chana 4 Age: 8 years
5 From where: Pinsk 6 Who died: Both parents
7 General Comments:
The parents have suffered through the Poles and the Belachowitz and after being starves for a considerable time have both died of typhoid fever.

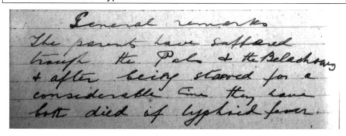

Translation of questionnaire of the Joint Distribution Committee Rovno for Moshe Lipshitz:

Region: Vladeve; City: Vladeve Province: Siedlicz; Date 5/II
Name and surname: Moshe Lipshitz
With whom is the child living: With the mother; Address 449 Vladeve Vishker Date of birth: 1914
Name of father: Avraham Yitzhak; Occupation: Land worker; Last address: Vishke in Vladeve
Name of mother: Sheindel; [Living with] family: Shneiderman
Which of the parents died: Father; Cause of death: He was murdered by the Baluchovitzes When: September 1920
Does he have any property: Everything was destroyed
How many children: 6; Boys 3; Girls 3.
Name and condition of the children over 14 years: Freyde, 17 years old, was raped by the Baluchovitz's; Perel 12 years old; Beile 9 years old; Pesakh 4 years old was adopted.
Has the child attended school: Yes; Which one: a kheyder.
Receiving a subsidy: Yes

Translation of questionnaire for the Pinska Family.

Names: Moshe 12, Zlata 9, Faivel 8, Feigel 5 (full orphans
Surname: Pinsky Father Aharon; Mother Yenta
Place of birth: Pinsk Father's occupation: carpenter.
Other comments:
Father died of hunger and the struggle to survive.
The mother died from the Balachovitches, she contracted syphilis from being raped by them.
The children had no where to go.

STANISŁAW BUŁAK-BAŁACHOWICZ
Extracts from Wikipedia, the free encyclopedia

Below are extracts about Stanisław Bułak-Bałachowicz who was well educated; a political essayist and writer of two books, and a skilled and highly decorated field commander.

Early life

Stanisław Bułak-Bałachowicz was born 10 February 1883 in Meyszty, a small village near Vilna (Vilnius, Lithuania, then Russian Empire), in a family of local landlord's cook and maid.

After the birth of Stanisław, his father left the landlord's kitchen and together with his brother acquired a small estate in Stakavievo near Vilna. Stanislaw had two brothers and six sisters.

He had been attending for four years agricultural faculty in Belmonty, was working as accountant and in 1904 started working as a manager of Duke Plater farms in Horodziec and Łużki.

In early years he had the reputation of people's defender, because he often was an arbitrator in disputes between farmers and the landlord. From these times he has earned a nickname "Daddy" (Bat'ka). His other characteristic nickname became part of his surname—"Bulak"—which means in Belarusian language a man who is driven by the wind.

Stanisław Bułak-Bałachowicz
President of the Belarusian Provisional Government
12 November 1920 – 28 November 1920

World War I

After the outbreak of the Great War and Duke Nikolai Nikolayevich Romanov's address to the Polish people, Bułak-Bałachowicz joined the Russian Imperial army. As a person of noble roots, he was drafted as an ensign to the 2nd Leyb-Courland Infantry Regiment. However, unlike many of his colleagues which were awarded the basic NCO grades for their noble ancestry only, Bułak-Bałachowicz proved himself as a skilled field commander and was quickly promoted. By December 1914, only four months after he entered the army, he was given command over a group of Cossack volunteers, of whom he formed a cavalry squadron. Together with the 2nd Cavalry Division he fought on the western front, most notably in the area of Sochaczew near Warsaw.

During the German summer offensive of 1915 Warsaw was taken by the Central Powers and Bułak-Bałachowicz's unit was forced to retreat towards Latvia.

On November 1915, Bułak-Bałachowicz was assigned to the special partisan regiment in Northern front headquarters as a squadron commander. His regiment under the command of colonel Punin L. was acting in the Riga area. For their audacious actions partisans were nicknamed "deathknights".

His unit was formed of four cavalry platoons: one of Cossack light cavalry, one of hussars, one of uhlans and one of dragoons. Thanks to the versatile and flexible structure of his

unit, Bułak-Bałachowicz managed to continue the fight behind the enemy lines until 1918.

For the German campaign Bułak-Bałachowicz was decorated with six orders and three soldier's Georgiev medals (2nd. 3rd, and 4th degree).

Stanisław Bułak-Bałachowicz also fought in the Russian Civil War the Polish-Bolshevik War.

Transferred to Brześć Litewski, the Bułak-Bałachowicz's unit was reformed into a *Bułak-Bałachowicz Operational Group*, sometimes incorrectly referred to as *Belarusian-Lithuanian Division*. It was composed mostly of Belarusian volunteers, as well as veterans of the Green Army and former Red Army soldiers, and received the status of an allied army. Because of the composition of his troops, Stanisław Bułak-Bałachowicz is sometimes referred to as a Belarusian.

On 23 July 1920 during the Bolshevik offensive towards central Poland, general Bałachowicz's group started an organised retreat as a rear guard of the Polish 3rd Army. During that operation, Bułak-Bałachowicz abandoned the withdrawing Polish troops and stayed with his forces for several days behind the enemy lines only to break through to the Polish forces shortly afterwards. During the Battle of Warsaw overnight of 14 August Bałachowicz's forces were ordered to start a counter-attack towards the town of Włodawa, one of the centres of concentration of the advancing Russian forces. On 17 September the area was secured and the Bułak-Bałachowicz's forces defended it successfully until 7 September against numerically superior enemy forces. Stanisław Bułak-Bałachowicz organised an active defence and managed to disrupt the concentration of all enemy attacks before they could be started. For instance on 30 August and 2 September his forces, supported by the Polish 7th Infantry Division, managed to attack the Soviet 58th Rifle Division from the rear, before it could attack the town of Włodawa.

On 15 September the unit was yet again advancing in pursuit of the withdrawing Red Army. That day the unit captured Kamień Koszyrski, where it took more than 1000 prisoners of war and the war materiel depot of an entire division. During the Battle of the Niemen River Bałachowicz's unit prevented the enemy from forming a defensive line in Polesie. Overnight on 21 September his unit outflanked and then destroyed completely the Bolshevist 88th Rifle Regiment near the town of Lubieszów. Perhaps the most notable victory of the Bułak-Bałachowicz's Group took place on 26 September, when its forces once again broke through enemy lines and captured Pinsk. The city was the most important rail road junction in the area and was planned as the last stand of the Bolshevik forces still fighting to the west of that city. After it was lost, the Red Army central front collapsed and the withdrawal turned into a panic retreat.

Failed uprising in Belarus

In October Stanisław Bułak-Bałachowicz was stationed with his forces in Pinsk, where they received supplies and a large amount of former Red Army soldiers who were taken prisoner of war after the Battle of Warsaw and volunteered for the service in anti-Bolshevik units. The unit was to re-enter combat in November, but on 12 October a cease fire was signed. On the insistence of both the Entente and Bolshevik Russia, the allied units were to leave Poland before 2 November. General Bułak-Bałachowicz was given the choice of either being interned in Poland with his units and then sent home or to continue the fight against the Reds on his own. He chose the latter option, just like most other White Russian and Ukrainian units fighting on the Polish side in the Polish-Bolshevik War.

On 10 November, 1920 Bułak-Bałachowicz entered Mozyr. There, two days later, he proclaimed the independence of Belarus and started forming a new Belarusian National Army. On 16 November 1920 he also created the Belarusian provisional government. However, the planned uprising gained little support in the Belarusian nation tired by six years of constant war and the Red Army finally gained an upper hand. On 18 November 1920 Bałachowicz abandoned Mozyr and started a withdrawal towards the Polish frontier. The Belarusian troops, hardened by the years spent behind the enemy lines, fought their way to Poland and managed to inflict heavy casualties on the advancing Russians while suffering negligible losses, but were too weak to turn the tide of war.

He was also a political essayist and writer of two books on the possibilities of a future war with Germany: "Wojna będzie czy

*A postal stamp of the Belarusian Democratic Republic,
issued on behalf of the Bułak-Bałachowicz Army*

nie będzie" (*Will there be war or will there be not*; 1931) and "Precz z Hitlerem czy niech żyje Hitler" (*Down with Hitler or long live Hitler?*, 1933). Between 1936 and 1939 he briefly served as an adviser to Franco's nationalists in the Spanish Civil War.

World War II

During the Polish Defensive War of 1939, Stanisław Bułak-Bałachowicz volunteered for the Polish army. He created a Volunteer Group that fought in the defence of Warsaw.

After the capitulation of Warsaw, general Bułak-Bałachowicz (formally retired) evaded being captured by the Germans and returned to civilian life. At the same time he was the main organiser of Konfederacja Wojskowa (*Military Confederation*), one of the first underground resistance groups in German and Soviet-occupied Poland. In early 1940 the Gestapo found out his whereabouts. He was surrounded with a group of young conspirators in a house in Warsaw's borough of Saska Kępa and arrested by the Germans. He managed to kill one of them with a knife hidden in his walking stick and was subsequently shot to death by the remaining Gestapo agents. Neither the exact date of his death nor the place of his burial are known.

For his resistance against Bolshevik forces that killed local Belarusian peasantry, members of Belarusian minority in Poland regard him as their national hero. Historians have often seen him to be an adventurer.

From Wikipedia, the free encyclopedia

Chapter 6 – THE DENIKIN POGROMS

ANTON DENIKIN

Anton Denikin was general of the Russian White Army that fought against the Soviets.

'The press of the Denikin regime regularly incited violence against Jews and his generals incited people to "arm themselves" in order to extirpate "the evil force which lives in the hearts of Jew-communists." ' (1)

REGISTER DETAILS OF OCHBERG ORPHANS AT THE CAPE JEWISH ORPHANAGE - ORANJIA
courtesy Veronica Belling, Jewish Studies Library, University of Cape Town

---

The family details of Abi Ellstein recorded on page 57 of the register at The Cape Jewish Orphanage - Oranjia.

1 Name and surname: Abi Ellstein
2 Father: Matoth   3 Mother: Rishke Yentil   4 Age: 11 years
5 From where: Pinsk   6 Who died: Both parents
7 General Comments:
Father killed by the Denikins in 1919
The mother died of hunger in 1920 after living in very difficult circumstances.
The children were left without support.
Father's yorzeit 27 Shevat
Mother's yorzeit 27 Tamus

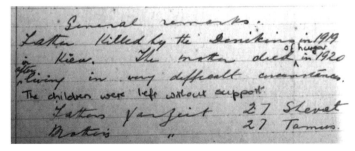

According to Nahum Gergel's 1951 study of the pogroms in Ukraine (quoted in Aleksandr Solzhenitsyn's book "Two Hundred Years Together"), out of an estimated 887 mass pogroms, about 40% were perpetrated by the Ukrainian forces led by Symon Petliura, 25% by the Ukrainian Green Army and various Ukrainian nationalist gangs *(Stanisław Bułak-Bałachowicz)*, 17% by the White Army (mainly by the forces under Denikin's command) and 8.5% by the Red Army.

Extract from Wikipedia, the free encyclopedia

"The retreat of the White Army intensified anti-Jewish violence in the areas not yet under Red Army communist control, as non-communist Russian and Ukrainian farmers, workers, middle-class businessmen, nobility and even some clergy effectively identified most or all Jews with "Judeo-Bolshevism", with communist violence, and with Lenin and Trotsky themselves.

Anton Ivanovich Denikin

Denikin resisted demands by human rights and Jewish organizations, and by British Secretary of State for War Winston Churchill, to issue specific orders against pogroms. In September, 1919, Churchill urged Denikin, both through the British military mission to South Russia, and in direct correspondence "to do everything in [his] power to prevent a massacre of the Jews in the liberated districts [and to issue] a proclamation against anti-Semitism." In October, 1919, with Denikin's order purging Jews from the volunteer forces (order #21,322), the campaign of pogroms against the Jewish population of Ukraine and Russia intensified.

When Denikin at last issued official orders against anti-Jewish pogroms, these orders were effectively ignored not only by the local population, but also by virtually all soldiers and no officers responsible for the former anti-semitic atrocities were brought to justice."

ANTON DENIKIN
From Wikipedia, the free encyclopedia

Childhood

Denikin was born in Szpetal Dolnyj village, now a part of the Polish city Włocławek (then part of the Russian empire). His father, Ivan Efimovich Denikin, had been born a serf in the province of Saratov. Sent as a recruit to do 25 years of military service, Ivan Denikin became an officer on the 22nd year of his army service, in 1856. He retired from the army in 1869 with the rank of a major. In 1869 Ivan Denikin married a poor Polish seamstress, Elżbieta Wrzesińska - his second wife. Anton Denikin, the couple's only child, learned to speak two languages (Russian and Polish) at the same time. His father's commitment to Russian patriotism and the Orthodox religion was crucial for Anton Denikin's decision to become a soldier.

The Denikins lived very close to poverty, the retired major's small pension being their only source of income. After his father's death in 1885, Denikin's family financial situation got even worse. Anton Denikin began tutoring younger schoolmates so that the family could earn an additional income. In 1890 Denikin began a course at the Kiev Junker School, a military college from which he graduated in 1892. Twenty-year-old Denikin joined an artillery brigade, in which he served for three years.

In 1895 he was first accepted into General Staff Academy. Denikin first saw active service during the 1905 Russo-Japanese War. In 1905 he was promoted to the rank of colonel. In 1910 he was appointed commander of the 17th infantry regiment. A few weeks before the outbreak of the First World War, Denikin reached the rank of major-general.

World War I

By the outbreak of World War I in August 1914 Denikin was a Chief of Staff of the Kiev military district with the rank of Major-General. He was initially appointed Quartermaster of General Brusilov's 8th Army. Not one for staff service, Denikin petitioned for an appointment to a fighting front. He was transferred to the 4th Rifle brigade. His brigade was transformed into a division in 1915. It was with this brigade Denikin would accomplish his greatest feats as a General.

In 1916 he was appointed to command the VIII Corps and lead troops in Romania during the last successful Russian campaign of the war, the Brusilov Offensive. Following the February Revolution and the overthrow of the Czar he became Chief of Staff to Mikhail Alekseev, then Aleksei Brusilov, and finally Lavr Georgevich Kornilov. Denikin supported the attempted coup of his commander, the Kornilov Affair, in September 1917 and was arrested and imprisoned with him. After this Alekseev would be reappointed commander-in-Chief.

Civil War

Following the October Revolution both Denikin and Kornilov escaped to Novocherkassk in southern Russia and, with other Tsarist officers, formed the Volunteer Army, initially commanded by Alekseev. Kornilov was killed in April 1918 near Ekaterinodar and the Volunteer Army came under Denikin's command.

In the face of a Communist counter-offensive he withdrew his forces back towards the Don area in what was known as the Ice March. Denikin led one final assault of the southern White forces in their final push to capture Moscow in the summer of 1919. For a time, it appeared that the White Army would succeed in its drive; Leon Trotsky, as commander of Red Army forces hastily concluded an agreement with Nestor Makhno's anarchist *Revolutionary Insurrectionary Army of Ukraine* or 'Black Army' for mutual support. Makhno duly turned his Black Army east and led his troops against Denikin's extended lines of supply, forcing him to retreat. Denikin's army was decisively defeated at Orel in October 1919, some 400 km south of Moscow. The White forces in southern Russia would be in constant retreat thereafter, eventually reaching the Crimea in March 1920.

In the occupied territories, Denikin's regime carried out mass executions and plunder. The press of the Denikin regime regularly incited violence against Jews. For example, a proclamation by one of Denikin's generals incited people to "arm themselves" in order to extirpate "the evil force which lives in the hearts of Jew-communists." In the small town of Fastov alone, Denikin's Volunteer Army murdered over 1500 Jews, mostly elderly, women, and children. An estimated 100,000 Jews were killed in pogroms perpetrated by Denikin's forces and other anti-soviet armies.

Facing increasingly sharp criticism and emotionally exhausted, Denikin resigned in April, 1920 in favor of General Baron Pyotr Wrangel. Denikin left the Crimea by ship to Constantinople and then to London. He spent a few months in England, then moved to Belgium, and later to Hungary.

Exile

From 1926 Denikin lived in France.

Denikin was a talented writer, and before World War I had written several pieces in which he analytically criticized the shortcomings of his beloved Russian Army. His voluminous writings after the Russian Civil War (written while living in exile) are remarkable for their analytical tone and candor, and are a "must read" to anyone interested in the Russian Civil War. Since he enjoyed writing and most of his income was derived from it, Denikin started to consider himself a writer

With the fall of France in 1940, Denikin left Paris in order to avoid imprisonment by the Germans. Although he was eventually captured, he declined all attempts to co-opt him for use in Nazi anti-Soviet propaganda. The Germans did not press the matter and Denikin was allowed to remain in rural exile.

From 1945 until his death in 1947, Denikin lived in the United States, in New York City. On 8 August, 1947 at the age of 74, Denikin died while vacationing near Ann Arbor, Michigan.

General Denikin was buried with military honors in Detroit. His remains were later transferred to St. Vladimir's Cemetery in Jackson, New Jersey.

(1) From Wikipedia, the free encyclopedia

MAN-MADE FAMINE IN SOVIET UKRAINE 1921-1923
Written by Dr Roman Serbyn

Much has been written in recent years about the man-made famine that ravaged Ukraine in 1932-1933 and caused the deaths of 7 million to 10 million people. This is in stark contrast to the largely ignored famine of 1921-1923 - the first of three famines that Ukraine's population has suffered under the Soviet Communist regime, and a famine that, contrary to popular belief, was not caused by drought and crop failures, but by the policies of the Soviet state.

What follows on the next few pages of The Ukrainian Weekly is a pull-out section about the 1921-1923 famine, featuring an article prepared and illustrations collected by Dr Roman Serbyn, professor of Russian and East European history at the University of Quebec in Montreal.

Grain requisition and export - not drought and poor harvest - were the real causes of the first great famine in Soviet Ukraine which occurred in 1921-1923. This is borne out by Western and Soviet documents alike.

The famine was concentrated in the rich grain-growing provinces of southern Ukraine, an area inhabited by about a third of the republic's 26 million citizens. It affected both the rural and the urban population. Most of the victims were Ukrainians; national minorities like Germans, Jews and Russians also suffered. Between the fall of 1921 and the spring of 1923, 1.5 million to 2 million people died of starvation and accompanying epidemics.

Saving this population would have required no more than half a million tons of grain or equivalent foodstuffs per year. During the two years of the famine, the Bolshevik government took from Ukrainian peasants many times that amount. Most of the confiscated grain was shipped abroad: the first year to Russia, and the second to Russia and the West. Ukraine was also obliged to send additional "voluntary" famine relief to the Volga, and to feed some 2 million people who came from Russia as refugees, soldiers and administrators.

At the time of the famine, many witnesses recorded the tragedy, and some of them even hinted at its criminal nature. But the passage of time dulled the memory of succeeding generations, and subsequent publications dealing with Ukraine and the Soviet Union said little of substance about this particular disaster. More surprisingly, the Ukrainian community itself has preserved but a vague memory of these events. Today most Ukrainians would be hard-pressed to explain why the famine had broken out, why it lasted so long and what was done to overcome it.

Famine and Epidemics

The High Commissariat of Dr Fridtj of Nansen was a Geneva-based international organization devoted to famine and refugee relief work. In his capacity as Dr. Nansen's representative,

Captain Vidkun Quisling toured Ukraine in early 1922, and filed some of the best informed and most detailed reports on the famine. On 25 February after inspecting the province of Zaporizhzhia, Quisling wired:

"The situation is terrible. Local official statistics show that of the province's 1,288,000 inhabitants, 900,000 are without food. This number will certainly grow by 200,000 before the end of April. Sixty percent of the famished are children. Public resources are exhausted and public institutions can provide only 10,000 rations daily."

Two days later he reported: "the situation in the province of Katerynoslav is just as bad...At this time it is estimated that 520,000 persons are without food, including 200,000 children. By the end of May there will be 730,000."

In mid-March, Quisling found that "in the province of Mykolayiv, about 700,000 persons, or half of the population, is without food. It is estimated that by the end of March the number will rise to 800,000, and by the end of April to 1 million... 40 to 50 percent of the starving children die...The situation is particularly bad in the city of Kherson and the surrounding district, where many villages have died out and remain desolate." By the fall of the same year, the city of Kherson was reduced to one-quarter of its normal population.

Quisling's most complete report, titled "Famine Situation in Ukraine," was written in March and published by the High Commissariat in April 1922. It gives a detailed account of the famine conditions in the five provinces completely overcome by starvation: Odessa, Mykolayiv, Katerynoslav, Zaporizhzhia and Donetske; it also describes the affected districts of three other provinces; Kremenchuk, Poltava and Kharkiv. A dozen photographs of famine victims and a map of the famine regions accompany the document. The report faults the Soviet government for not recognizing the famine in time and criticizes the regime for doing so little about it afterwards. It concludes that unless help comes quickly, the number of the starving will reach 7 million by the summer.

Weakened by malnutrition, the population of southern Ukraine easily fell prey to contagious diseases. In October of 1921, Volga refugees brought typhus and cholera to Ukraine, and in the next month the whole country was swept by epidemics. The epidemics continued, on and off, throughout the whole period of the famine. Although no complete statistics are available on deaths from diseases, we know that epidemic cases were recorded by the hundreds of thousands and that their mortality rate was very high.

The prime victims of the famine and the epidemics were children. They also were the main targets for kidnappings and cannibalism. A million children had been orphaned by wars and the famine, and they had to fend for themselves as best they could since neither the state nor state-controlled charitable organisations could care for them in any significant way. These children known as "bezprytulni," continued to pose serious social problems during the 1920s. Hordes of these children succumbed to starvation and disease; others resorted to petty crime. Still others became wanderers. They flocked to railway stations and rode freight cars in search of food and shelter.

Ukrainian railway stations became the main gathering centers for people fleeing the famine. Refugees lived for weeks in dilapidated wagons, waiting for a chance to board a train that would take them away. Penniless, they fought for space on wagon rooftops. In the winter, many train riders died of cold and exposure. Suzanne Ferriere, assistant secretary general of the International Save the Children Fund, visiting Poltava in 1922, was told that in that city 400 frozen children were removed from the train on two particularly cold days.

Mortality was so high during the famine that the corpses could not be buried fast enough. For days and weeks they lay in morgues and cemeteries, or simply where they fell. Many cadavers were devoured by hungry animals, and there were cases of starving people being reduced to anthropophagy.

Uniqueness of Ukrainian Famine

Simultaneously with Ukraine, the Russian Soviet Federated Socialist Republic (RSFSR) experienced a major famine along the Volga valley, in the northern Caucasus and the Crimea

It was the Volga disaster that attracted particular attention and became well-publicized. It later provided the focal point for the study of what is described by history books as "the Russian famine of 1921-1922."

In 1921, and again in 1922, southern Ukraine was subjected to a terrible drought. Harvests fell to between 10 and 25 percent of the normal crop yield, and in some cases the crop failure was complete. In spite of this, Ukraine as a whole had enough food to feed every one of its inhabitants. The crops in the northern part of the country generally were good, and there were still some reserves from previous years. To overcome the crisis in Ukraine it would have been sufficient to prevent grain from leaving the country and to organize food distribution in the south. Had the Soviet government- of Ukraine taken these steps - simple measures which any national government worthy of the name would not hesitate to take - there would have been no famine at all.

While famine ravaged the southern provinces of Ukraine, the Kharkiv government did virtually nothing to alleviate it. Instead it was very actively involved in organising famine relief for Russia.

Throughout the whole period, the starving areas of Ukraine were taxed, and forced to provide 'voluntary" aid for Russia. This amounted to criminal behavior on the part of the Bolshevik authorities and astounded foreign observers.

"Up to the time the American Relief Administration (ARA) began its activities (January 1922)," wrote H H Fisher, a former ARA worker, "neither the central government at Moscow nor the Ukrainian at Kharkiv had made any serious move to relieve the famine in the south [i e Ukraine]. In fact, the only relief

activity which went on in Ukraine, from the summer of 1921 to the spring of 1922, was the collection, for shipment to the distant Volga, of foodstuffs, for lack of which people along the Black Sea were dying."

"...not before the 11th of January of this year," wrote Quisling in the March 1922 report quoted above, "could the gubernia of Donets stop their obligatory relief work for the Volga district and begin to take care with all their forces of their own famine problem, at a time when already more than every tenth person in the Donets was without bread. In the beginning of March of this year, you could still see, in the famine stricken gubernia of Mykolayiv, placards with: 'Working masses of Mykolayiv, to the rescue of the starving Volga district!' The gubernia of Mykolayiv itself had at the same time 700,000 starving people, about half the population."

It was only in the beginning of 1922 that the Kharkiv government made a half-hearted effort to organize famine relief for the starving Ukrainian population. Meagre financial aid was allocated to the Sovietized Ukrainian Red Cross and the recently formed Pomhol (Famine Relief Committee). These organizations could not help even 10 percent of the starving Ukrainian population, as their main duty continued to be famine relief for Russia. Starving Ukrainians had to look for help elsewhere than to "their own" government. This aid eventually came from the West.

Foreign Relief

In July of 1921, anguished cries pierced the air, begging the West to "save starving Russia." Tikhon, patriarch of the Russian Orthodox Church, wrote to the pope and the heads of other Churches; the prominent Russian writer Maxim Gorky addressed Western intellectuals; George Chicherin, as commissar for external affairs, sent a message to the heads of states; and Lenin appealed to the proletariat of the world. This campaign received an immediate response. States, Churches and charitable organizations offered to supply food, medicine and clothing.

The most significant aid, by virtue of its size and quality, was that provided by the American Relief Administration, headed by Herbert Hoover, secretary of commerce in the Harding administration. At the height of its activities, in the summer of 1922, ARA fed 10 million people in the RSFSR and another 2 million in Ukraine. It also provided medical supplies and clothing.

The Soviet authorities begged the West to send aid to Russia, but interfered with its delivery to Ukraine, at least at first. Although as early as August 1921, the West knew from Soviet sources about the catastrophic conditions in Ukraine, Soviet representatives either denied that there was starvation in the country or played down its importance. Moscow insisted that all aid go to the Volga and assured the West that Ukraine could take care of itself and even help Russia. Not being eager to assume more financial burdens, the West found it convenient to ignore the Ukrainian disaster, even if it meant letting the country starve.

The situation improved at the end of the year when the American Jewish community decided to send massive help to starving brethren in the Soviet republics. The American Jewish Joint Distribution Committee put pressure on the ARA to organize distribution centers in Ukraine for the food parcels sent by American Jews to their friends and relatives living there. The "Joint" (as it was commonly known) also wanted the ARA to investigate the famine situation in Ukraine, since it was getting alarming news from Ukrainian Jewry. The ARA succeeded in persuading the Soviets to allow a delegation to visit Ukraine in December of 1921. The result was the Hutchinson-Golder report and a separate agreement signed by the ARA and Soviet Ukraine, which led to the extension of American aid to Ukraine.

Help came to Ukraine in two forms; food and clothing parcels and soup kitchens.

Since the fall of 1921, food parcels could be bought by private individuals and organizations in the West and sent through relief organizations to designated parties in the Soviet republics. Most of these parcels, costing $10 each and capable of feeding one person for one month, were bought in the United States and distributed by the ARA in Ukraine.

A small number of parcels were bought by Ukrainians. ARA records show that on 5 July 1922, the Rev. Basil Kusiw of Bloomfield, N J, paid $200 on behalf of the Ukrainian Relief Committee for food parcels to be distributed equally among five Kiev institutions: the (Shevchenko?) Scientific Society, the Ukrainian Academy of Sciences, the National Ukrainian Theatre, the Medical Academy and the Ukrainian Institute of Popular Education. Three weeks later, the Ukrainian Relief Committee of Newark, N J, bought $500 worth of food for

general distribution by the Ukrainian Red Cross in Kiev. But the Ukrainian American aid channeled through the ARA was insignificant when compared with the millions of dollars spent by the American Jewish community for Ukrainian Jewry.

Of much more significance for the Ukrainian population were the soup kitchens. These mass feeding stations began to be organized in May of 1922. By the summer of that year, the ARA was feeding about 1 million children and another million adults. Dining halls were also set up by various religious organizations, agencies of the Red Cross, and the international network of the Save the Children Fund. Representatives of the American and Canadian Mennonite communities were particularly active among the German Mennonite colonies set up on the former lands of the Zaporozhian Sich.

While the responsibility for organizing the American famine relief in Ukraine fell to the ARA, the actual costs of the soup kitchens were underwritten by the Joint. By the time the ARA decided to intervene in the Ukrainian famine, its own resources had been committed to the Volga relief. At this point the Joint offered to help finance famine relief in the Ukraine, on condition that the kitchens be set up in predominantly Jewish districts and that they carry Yiddish signs acknowledging the support of the Jewish organizations that sponsored them. The ARA was delighted by Joint's offer and only insisted that the kitchens be made accessible to all, regardless of religious or ethnic background. This was agreed upon and a wide network of soup kitchens was set up in Ukraine, frequented mostly by Jews but benefiting hundreds of thousands of non-Jews as well. Later on, Hoover even suggested that the Joint take over and run the operations in Ukraine by itself, but after some hesitation, the Joint declined the proposition.

Soup Kitchen a common sight – courtesy Brian Fine's Website

Chapter 8 – HORROR UPON HORROR - NEWS CUTTINGS

In the 20th century the great suffering of the Jewish People in Eastern Europe from after WWI and into the early 1920s is only overshadowed by the Holocaust. The suffering cannot be imagined and following are newscuttings and appeals of that period.

These news cuttings are from The Hebrew Standard (an Australian Jewish Newspaper) and are dated 1921 and 1922 and were kindly sent in by Brian Fine, the son of Zeidel Feinschmidt.

Friday, July 28 1922   THE HEBREW STANDARD   *Page 5*

HORROR UPON HORROR!!

THE UKRAINE GEHENNA

Help! Help! Help!

If there are any of our readers who have not been touched by the various articles that have from time to time appeared in our columns describing the almost indescribable hardships and cruelties that our unfortunate brethren in Eastern Europe have suffered during the last few years, surely the illustrations that appear in this issue must at least move them. So heartrending, so gruesome were the pictures received of which the pictures reproduced are but a sample, that one could but recoil in horror that such happenings were possible in this so-called civilised age.

The cry of distress has reached all quarters of the globe, and the response has exceeded by far that of any other appeal that has been made to our people. Although every section of Jewry in every country of the world has given, and given, in most cases, as it has never given before, the amount of suffering, misery and starvation is so great that the funds spent so far have but touched the fringe of relief, and unless more and still more is obtained, but little can be done to save the hundreds of thousands of our brethren.

The Sydney Committee of the Relief Fund are working hard that the response to the appeal in this city may not be behind that of others, but there is still too much apathy in this matter, and there are still too many in this city who do not realise that they must do more and still more, for their starving brethren.

MOVING CORPSES

The reports of the delegates of the Ukrainian Red Cross, who visited districts stricken by the famine, contain the following particulars:--

The streets of Yekaterinoslav are always filled with the constant crying of children and grown-ups begging for food in a heart-rending manner. The children, with earth coloured faces and exhausted to the highest degree, look like moving corpses. It is difficult to believe that they really are living children.

Here you can hear the hunger howl. A peasant lies down weeping or howling. Unconsciousness soon seizes him and he passes away.

From morning until night, unfortunate people are moving to and fro in the futile hope that they may find help, until they fall dead.

When a horse falls down a whole crowd, desperate and hungry, rush, armed with knives, cutting off pieces of the corpse and swallowing them sometimes raw. Not only the corpses of horses and dogs are eaten, but also the skins.

All these children died of starvation. Their so-feebled groaning, their plaintive demands did not reach out ears! The Ukraine is so far off. They died with this desperate word on their lips: "Bread!" We transmit to you this last cry. Do your duty please!

HUNGER MADNESS INCREASING

Things are not going on any better in the villages. Cases of hunger-madness are rapidly increasing. A mad woman badly cut the dead body of her father. Another ate her own child. (Report of the medical officer delegated to the government of Yekatarinoslav, February 27 1922).

In three southern districts of the government of Zaporoshye 190,000 people are starving. A quarter of them are lying down, without being able to move because of weakness. The population seems to be condemned to death. All dogs and cats have been devoured long ago. The provisions of dried weeds have reached their end. Anything is taken for nourishment. Skins of the animals are cut to pieces, boiled into a glutinous mess and then consumed.

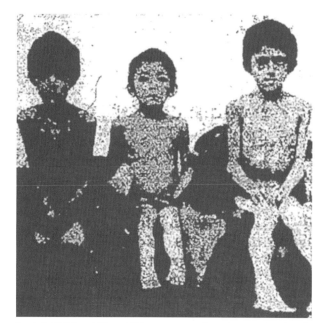

Jewish Children! The children you see here have not eaten for many a day. That is why their bodies are so thin and their legs swollen. They have no parents to whom to ask for bread. So please ask your parents not to let your poor little comrades die with hunger!

ATE THEIR CHILDREN

In the village of Blagiweschchenka, a family ate their own children, a boy of nine and a girl of seven years of age. (Proof of this has just come into our hands.)

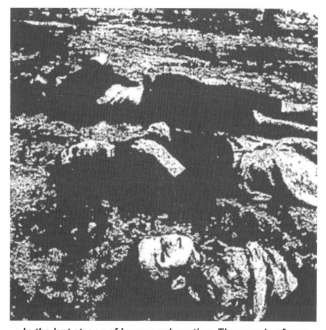

In the last stages of hunger exhaustion. Thousands of our brethren are suffering similar pangs! Help them!

In another family the hungry father killed his wife and both children by strangling them. Ten per cent of the working cattle still remain but the animals are exhausted from hunger and disease. In some districts no single horse is to be seen. In autumn ten times less has been sown than in any previous year. - Report of the medical department of Zaporoshye, 21 February 1922.

The physician of the Ukrainian Red Cross, delegated to this province, reports: In Zaporoshye 700,000 people are starving. These persons have not even linseed cake at all, but only miserably nourishing substitutes. In consequence there is a spread of all sorts of diseases. About 100,000 people, mostly children are already broken down and remain lying. At least 50,000 pounds of grain per month are needed to keep them alive. Besides this, attention must be paid to the way in which nourishment will be given. The people must be nourished and attended by a doctor at the same time. Careless feeding may lead to death. The weakened digestive tube is no more able to act regularly. Besides the gravest intestinal complaints, the cases of acute anaemia and general exhaustion are rapidly increasing. (25 February 1922.)

These ones have finished with their suffering. They are no more hungry. But what of the others? Those who desire death to escape the terrible tortures of hunger. And so little is wanted to save them! Are you doing your share?

Dr Bogen, who has recently visited Kiev, Jitomir, Berditchev, Vinnitza, Proskurov, reports:

"There were thousands of persons all huddled in a large dark hall, lying on the bare floor. There was a man with a terribly sick child, trying to get back to Riason, but he had no money. There was a group of women. They were sitting on their ragged belongings. They had no place to go; they had arrived in Kiev looking for food. The people were sick, miserable, dilapidated, broken humanity. At the feeding station were men, women and children all waiting in vain for food. The concentration shelters for refugees were a nightmare of horror. All human beings, men, women and children of various classes, huddled together in as small a space as possible. An expression in their faces and eyes of utter despair."

They must Not Die!

—These hundreds of thousands of starving and homeless Jews— in the pogrom areas of Ukraine

An Appeal to the Heart of Every Jew

The Martyrdom of Jews in the Ukraine is the greatest tragedy in the history of our people. The orgy of massacre, pillage and violation is breaking the spirit of three millions of our brethren in faith. Hundreds of communities have been wiped out, thousands of Jewish homes have been ravaged.

ONE HUNDRED AND FIFTY THOUSAND ORPHANS are left to-day as the result of this holocaust of butchery, and Jews in the devastated areas are in so terrible a condition that words cannot adequately depict their misery.

Jews in the British Dominions! Your brothers and sisters are dying by thousands, accused of no crime; brought to no trial, and guilty of no fault but that of being Jews. Help those who are left behind.

Jewish Mothers! You who are happy in the possession of homes and children in this land of safety, give thought to the children in these broken homes. Famine and disease are stalking throughout the land. HELP must be quickly forthcoming.

"**THEY MUST NOT DIE.**"

These hundreds of thousands of starving Jews in the pogrom areas of the Ukraine.

This appeal is made to every Jew and Jewess throughout the land. Give, and give liberally, even at great sacrifice. The spirit of Judaism is Charity, and no more sacred occasion has ever demanded its expression.

Send GENEROUS Donations at Once to the

Federation of Ukrainian Jews

IN AID OF THE POGROM VICTIMS IN THE UKRAINE.

(Registered under the War Charities Act).

26a Soho Square, London, W.I.

Telephone: Gerrard 6245.   Telegrams: "Ukrarelief, London.

Hon. President:
The Very Rev. The Chief Rabbi, Dr. J. H. HERTZ.

Hon. Vice-Presidents:
Sir ███ SAMUEL, Bart., and HERBERT BENTWICH, Esq.

Chairman: Dr. D. JOCHELMAN.   Vice-Chairman: Dr. M. PINES.

Joint Hon. Treasurers:
JOSEPH PRAG, J.P., and M. SHALIT, Esq.

Hon. Sec.: S. GOLDENBERG, Esq.   Organising Sec.: A. M. KAIZER, Esq.

News cuttings from the UK press sent in by Aubrey Berman,
the grandson of Charlotte Berman (Zlata Samurina).

31

Chapter 9 – HOW THE PARENTS OF THE OCHBERG ORPHANS DIED

The register of the Ochberg Orphans admitted to the Cape Jewish Orphanage contains the background details of the children in its care.

This register is written in Yiddish and contains the following information for each child

1. Name and surname
2. Father
3. Mother
4. Age
5. Birth place
6. Who of parents died
7. How parents died

Page 57 of the register - an example

Details as to how the parents died give us an insight into the the the conditions and suffering of those times. We have 79 children entered in the register from 51 families.

An analysis of the causes of the death of the parents reveals the following

Hunger, starvation and diseases		63
Made up of		
Hunger and typhus	20	
Hunger and starvation	20	
Hunger and cold	3	
Typhus and typhoid	8	
Influenza	4	
Other illnesses	8	
Pogroms		**15**
Balachowicz	5	
Petlurists	5	
Denikins	1	
Bolshevics	4	
Other causes of death		**19**
Russians	2	
War	13	
Unknown	4	
Surviving parents		**5**
Total		**102**

Eleven parents were also described as having suffered and endured pogroms – see example below.

We can see that over 60% of the parents were overcome by hunger and diseases while say 15% perished in pogroms.

We must bear in mind that this is a very small sample of a very larger picture. We will never know how many people, both adults and children were killed in pogroms or from hunger and starvation and the diseases that accompanied it.

PART 1
THE 'PALE OF SETTLEMENT'
1914~1922

SECTION 2
HELP GIVEN BY JEWISH
COMMUNITIES

This section tells of the help given on a mass scale by the American Jewish Joint Distribution Committee to relieve the hunger and starvation suffered not only by Jews but also by Gentiles, without discrimination.

While the American Jewish Joint Distribution Committee saved hundreds of thousands from certain starvation with their mass feeding programs Jewish communities from Canada, Palestine and South Africa rescued groups of approximately 200 Jewish Orphans each by transporting them to their respective countries and caring for them.

Chapter 10 – THE AMERICAN JEWISH JOINT DISTRIBUTION COMMITTEE

This chapter has been compiled from information and photos kindly supplied by Solly Kaplinski, Misha Mitsel and Lisa Margolin of the JDC

Since 1914, the American Jewish Joint Distribution Committee (JDC) has acted on behalf of North America's Jewish communities and others to fulfil the principle that "Kol Yisrael Arevim Zeh L'Zeh"—all Jews are responsible for one another. JDC is dedicated to serving the needs of Jews throughout the world, particularly where their lives as Jews are threatened or made more difficult.

From 1919 to 1921, JDC raised $33.4 million toward relief programs for well over a million impoverished and starving Jews in Europe as well as reconstructive aid to rebuild community institutions. It promoted economic development in Palestine, cared for war orphans and at-risk children there and in Eastern Europe, established Agro-Joint in the Soviet Union, and helped European Jews regain their economic footing.

In the Ukraine the JDC worked together with the American Relief Administration (ARA) where the Chief of Operations was Col. Wm. R Grove. While funds raised by the JDC were collected by Jews from Jews and for Jews in the Ukraine (and in other of JDC's operations) help was given on a non-sectarian basis.

EXTRACTS FROM COL GROVE'S REPORT TO HERBERT HOOVER ON FEEDING PROGRAMS IN THE UKRAINE

"An arrangement was made in New York on 9 March 1922, for a joint operation by the American Relief Administration (ARA) and the Jewish Joint Distribution Committee (JDC) to provide sufficient food for a maximum of 800,000 children and 400,000 adults - the maximum to be reached by 15 July. The adult program was carried out with the corn and corn grits from the Congressional Appropriation, but about 80% of the child-feeding was financed by the Joint Distribution Committee and the remaining 20%, as well as the medical program, were borne by the ARA, the administration of the whole to be strictly non-sectarian.

"It was also decided to include the larger cities outside of the famine area in the distribution of food as the refugees and patients in hospitals and other institutions in those cities were in many cases in a deplorable condition.

The first regular meeting to discuss affairs connected with the child-feeding program in the Ukraine was held in Kharkov early in April 1922 and attended by representatives of the Ukrainian Red Cross, the Ukrainian Co-operative Union, the Ukrainian Central Relief committee, the Nansen Organisation and Mr George P Harrington of the American Relief Administration. At this meeting, figures showing the population, the number of the starving, and the number to be fed by the government, were discussed.

"We have been unable to secure any reasonably accurate figures as to the percentage of starving people. This is not surprising when we consider the important facts involved. There is a difference between hunger and starvation, but the line is hard to fix. A family starving today gets a food package and is well fed for a month. Some districts estimate too high while others have such poor statistics that their estimates have proven lower than their actual wants. This is true of some of the extreme southern districts. In some of the non-famine districts it was found in March that there were many starving people, as certain sections in the southern parts of these districts had poor crops, and the people had no money to buy food.

"In some cities, such as Kherson, the people were dying in March at a rate which would have wiped the city out in one and one-half years.

"The best evidence we have as to starvation figures is that there were in the Ukraine on 31 July no known cases approaching starvation. It is evident, therefore, that the 1,923,435 persons being fed by the ARA on that date cover the real needy and those figures might be used as a maximum of starving people for the Ukraine. In fact, we were feeding hundreds of thousands who were at that time ready to go on the undernourished rather than the starvation list, but if the ARA food had not arrived these and many others would have starved, for the food we imported not only enabled these to survive, but released the food they would have consumed, thus making it possible for others to live.

Figures at that time given by the central government of the Ukraine were as follows:

ESTIMATE OF STARVING CHILDREN AND ADULTS, AND NUMBER THE GOVERNMENT PROPOSED TO FEED FROM ITS OWN RESOURCES (These figures are in 1,000s)										
Districts	Population	Starving			Government Intended to Feed			Remaining		
		Child	Adult	Total	Child	Adult	Total	Child	Adult	Total
Odessa	1 951	225	150	375				225	150	375
Nikolaiev	1 422	220	300	520	12	9	21	208	291	499
Zaporojsh	1 128	384	509	893	34	26	60	350	483	833
Ekaterinoslav	1 779	319	447	766	22	16	38	297	431	728
Donetz	3 112	402	279	681	28	20	48	374	259	633
Total	**9 392**	**1550**	**1685**	**3235**	**96**	**71**	**167**	**1454**	**1614**	**3068**

Organisation

"It was originally planned to feed a maximum of 100,000 children in the Ukraine, but when the joint ARA-JDC movement was inaugurated, and it was decided to increase the number, it became necessary to divide the Ukraine into further sub-divisions than those already used for food remittance work, so that each of the five famine districts was made a separate unit for child and adult feeding purposes, and as rapidly as they became available the personnel to start work was assigned. The personnel was increased until a total of 39, including the nine medical relief men, was reached.

Supervision and Control of the Feeding

"The feeding in the Ukraine has been under the supervision of the various sub-district supervisors and has varied with the available facilities and the temperament and ability variously constituted, but always with a view to continuing ARA control of the food until consumed. In the cities the Pelidist system of physical examination for children has been used and in many cities physical examination of adults has also been made to determine the most needy. In the rural districts, as a rule no examinations have been practicable or necessary as the most needy cases there can be reached without the danger of playing favorites. Control has been maintained by the use of a large number of Russian inspectors whose work was in turn checked by the ARA representatives as far as practicable. The general instructions given from the start were that no technicalities were to interfere with getting the hungry person and the food together at the earliest possible moment. Refinements were to be made at a later date, but the organisation of the work required the attention of the personnel to such an extent that the time for many of the refinements never came.

Effects of Child-Feeding

"The effects in a real starvation area of a ration such as the ARA has given in Russia are tremendous. In the city of Odessa, where prior to receipt of ARA food the situation was as bad as could well be imagined, the improvement within 30 days was very marked. In one kitchen visited on May 22nd, out of a total of 1,100 children there were about 100 cases of the typical starvation class; five weeks later in going through that same kitchen not one child was found that would be called anything but undernourished. Another very noticeable effect of the ARA feeding was the lively and cheerful attitude of the children after having been fed a month, as compared with their quiet demeanor before. In April Odessa was a desolate city with noiseless children; in July the streets were filled with lively youngsters playing and shouting and crying 'Arah' whenever an ARA automobile would pass. It is from the children that we get the spontaneous recognition of relief work, as they know nothing of politics and no amount of propaganda can convince them that their best friend is not the one that feeds them.

Rations

"The ration for adults in the Ukraine was one Russian pound (9/10 English pound) of corn grits per day per person. It was issued dry, no kitchens being operated for adults except special kitchens for students in Odessa and Ekaterinoslav. The ration was 780 calories for each child and the menu was varied daily, the following being a sample for a week:

Sunday - Maize gruel, cocoa, bread
Monday - Maize grits, bread
Tuesday - Dumplings, cocoa
Wednesday - Maize grits, bread
Thursday - Maize pudding, cocoa , bread
Friday - Bread, pudding, bread
Saturday - Maize gruel, bread

The maize gruel is made up of sugar, milk, corn grits and a small portion of salt. The maize grits consist of corn grits, fats and salt. The dumplings are made up of sugar, flour, fats and salt. The components of the maize pudding are sugar, milk, corn grits and a little salt. Sugar, flour and fats are the commodities used in the preparation of bread pudding. The child ration was given in kitchens to those between three and fifteen years, inclusive. Nursing and expectant mothers were also fed.

Conclusion

"It is not believed that any deaths from starvation occurred in the Ukraine after 15 July. If so, they were isolated cases where the starving were not brought to the attention of any of our personnel. We had difficulty in some of the cities, even after we were feeding the full number of known starving people, to get at all of the cases.

Occasionally a family would be found where the attention of the children had not been directed to an ARA kitchen. This seems impossible with so many kitchens operating in every city of the famine district, but it is nevertheless true and shows to what extent demoralisation exists. For instance, a family was recently found in Odessa where there were three children not eating at ARA kitchens and yet in a deplorable state. The father was dead, the mother lying sick, and none of the people in the house had taken the trouble to send these children to an ARA kitchen. The mother, when asked why they did not give them any attention, stated that the children were so dirty that she felt the neighbours were afraid to have anything to do with them for fear of getting disease from them. This is, of course, an isolated case.

"There is a very general feeling of appreciation of our work among the masses, this feeling being tempered only by the dread of the ARA's withdrawal and the attendant fear of the coming winter, when both fuel and food are predicted so short that the population of the cities fear great suffering, if not actual death, from these causes.

"It can be fairly said that the work of the ARA in the Ukraine in 1922 has left on the mass of people a very fine impression. It has been repeatedly told us by natives that they do not understand how a country 5,000 miles away could take such an interest in people not of their own blood, as to send so much food to them without cost. For some time they had a lingering suspicion that at the bottom of each sack of flour they would find an advertisement of somebody's superior seed wheat or propaganda of some character; but as the weeks went by and

People wait for a meal at a soup kitchen in Odessa. Ukraine. c.1923   Photos courtesy of American Jewish Joint Distribution Committee

Trade school, students working at the cabinet making workshop. Pinsk, Poland. c. 1923

the children were restored to health and no demon appeared, they began to appreciate the fact that we were here only to help. The result is that among the masses, and especially among the villagers there is a great appreciation of the general work of the ARA.

"Since it became widely known that the Joint Distribution Committee financed the Ukrainian program on a non-sectarian basis, much favorable comment has also been received as to this humanitarian contribution, but it is too early to say what effect, if any, it will have on the relations heretofore existing between the Jews and Russians in certain sections of the Ukraine. Like all similar movements, however, it must have a permanently beneficial effect in the minds of the large majority of people who are capable of appreciating such magnanimous action. A contributing influence in improving this relationship was the very able manner in which Dr Boris D Bogen conducted his work in the Ukraine for the Joint Distribution Committee. The nature of the operation required close contact with the district of Ukraine and the various sub-district supervisors, as well as the government representatives and a large number of Russian people. The broad-minded viewpoint of Dr Bogen left a fine impression on all with whom he came in contact"

Dr Boris Bogen. Russia, 1924

EXTRACTS FROM DR BOGEN'S LETTERS

Kiev, 13 April 1922

"In the early morning Col Grove and myself spent a little time at the railroad station where the refugees were concentrated. There were thousands of them all huddled in a large dark hall lying on the bare floor, moaning, picking vermin and suffering. There was a man with a terribly sickly child telling us how for months he was trying to get back to Riasan, but he had no money and the child was ill. There was a group of women - they were sitting on their ragged belongings, they had no place to go, they arrived in Kiev looking for food. There was a boy of about 14 years of age moaning and pitifully begging for a piece of bread. At the time of our visit the refugees were moved from one room to another so as to clean up the place and take away the sick and the dead and there in the corner a woman was arguing in a frenzy with a soldier not to touch the sick or perhaps dead man lying near her. Oh! This was a horrible scene. The air was foul, the people were covered with vermin, sick, miserable, dilapidated humanity.

"We followed up this investigation by visiting the home of refugee children, a kind of a hospital conducted by the government for the children of the famine district. At that particular time there were about 150 children there, all sick, some with typhus, dysentery and other diseases. The doctor in charge is Miss Brylowski. She pleaded for the sake of the poor children. They were all hungry she said. They receive nothing but bread and occasional supplies of other commodities.

"It was pitiful to see how the children huddled under the blankets. They have nothing else on their bodies. They are in bad need of clothing and linen. The place was clean but exceedingly cold.

"We visited also the refugee feeding stations, a horrible place. Here were men, women and children all waiting in vain for food and occupying their time in picking off the vermin. The lady in charge explained to us that they have tried to build a disinfecting plant and in fact she showed us the place where they had already begun the construction but the amounts required for this undertaking were so large that it had to be given up.

"We then visited the concentration shelter for refugees where they are taken care of for fourteen consecutive days. This was a nightmare of horror. The stories we heard there were enough to drive a person insane. There were all human beings, men, women and children of various classes huddled together in as small a place as possible (for the entire building could not be heated for lack of fuel) hungry, ragged, eaten up by vermin, without any hope and with an expression in their faces and eyes of utter despair.

"We went over the entire refugee situation with a lady physician, a representative of the government. She explained to us that the situation is becoming more and more serious for Kiev is one of the centers to which the refugees are attracted, that the city is already saturated with all that it can absorb, that the government was compelled to establish restriction points so as not to admit any more refugees, that the death rate is appalling and that epidemics are continually raging throughout the entire district. In this case the death was attributed to dysentery but on investigation it was diagnosed as a mild case of cholera undoubtedly due to starvation.

"There is no question in my mind that this situation is the most acute case of mass suffering due to neglect and want that I ever witnessed. It represents only a sample of the situation to be found in the other cities where refugees are concentrated. This condition cannot be permitted to continue without at least every possible effort made to meet the situation.

"I am telling you as I feel just coming from the field where I mingled with and talked to the people. Their faces haunt me, their voices ring in my ear and my heart bleeds because I know that among the thousands here there are many who are just as good as you and I.

"In this connection I want to tell you of the visit we made to a special hospital for children, the head of which is Dr Balaban. This was formerly a hospital modern in every respect. At the present time the entire equipment is dilapidated. There are about 400 children in this hospital. It was a blessing to see the good use that they made of the ARA blankets and shawls, the only things that keep them warm. Dr Balaban showed to us two examples of child starvation; one an actual skeleton and the other swollen with hunger. She explained to us that very few survive, especially in the winter. The department of infants was especially appalling. They had no milk in the place and the food that they get is not fit for children. They employ a large number of wet nurses but the latter cannot feed the children because they are not sufficiently nourished. The food they receive is absolutely insufficient and besides, imagine children suffering from dysentery, typhus, scarlatina and diptheria fed on black bread and a limited amount of lard.

Prosburov, 17 April 1922

Then we were taken to an infant home with 45 beds. This is an international institution for children of all nationalities. This institution was in the most horrible condition that I ever saw - dirty, very badly equipped, the children emaciated and in general it produced a most appalling impression.

"Next to that we visited the hospital with 200 patients, one of the worst institutions of this kind that I ever saw - no bedding, no blankets, dirty, unhygienic, no bathing or disinfecting facilities (while they have the equipment they have not the wood).

"This was only a prelude to an institution that they showed us in connection with the work for the refugee children. Imagine 194 little men and women huddled in rags on the floor without clothes to cover their bodies; they cannot leave the house for lack of clothes. They cannot move for lack of room; all of them looking emaciated and undernourished, some of them like skeletons. This was a horrible sight to behold. We were especially impressed with the terrible restraint that could be felt in the conduct of these children. They showed a kind of a fear in their eyes, they were almost motionless. I am especially picturing eight or ten children grouped in a corner on the floor throwing at us the most pitiful look. Upon further inquiry we found that these children came from the famine district; that because of lack of clothing, they cannot leave the rooms and as there are only two or three rooms designated for them they have no place to move around.

"I spoke to the matron and she informed me that the reason the children are in this shape is because they are suffering from long hunger and that even the feeding that they receive now is not sufficient and that it does not do them much good when they cannot move about.

"These children have no beds to speak of or blankets or any other thing on which to lie down and are practically speaking leading an animal existence. We were so strongly impressed with the critical situation that I was tempted at once to make arrangements to provide some clothing for the children but upon inquiry we found that it would be exceedingly difficult and very expensive.

"After discussing the matter with Col Grove we decided that we should send a telegram asking for an emergency appropriation of at least $50,000 worth of clothing and linen for children. This is a very insignificant sum but it will at least give us a chance to satisfy here and there some of the children who will perish on account of neglect and want. I hope that this request will be granted without delay."

Odessa, 21 April 1922
Ódessa is the most dismal town that we have so far visited. As soon as we arrived we could notice that the town is in desperate condition. There were very few people on the streets and in their walk and look we could see that they are disheartened and distressed.

"Everywhere I heard horrible stories of the raving disease and starvation death. The population of Odessa is about 500,000 of whom 60% are Jewish. The mortality rate per day is estimated as 500; about 110 bodies are daily picked up on the streets. In going through the various districts we saw a number of bodies which were not as yet picked up for burial. The recent order is that these bodies must be removed immediately but unfortunately the number are so great that even with this rule in effect it is difficult to keep up with the number. In the outskirts of the city some of the bodies have been devoured by stray dogs.

"We visited yesterday the City Hospital, an institution with a capacity of 2,000. There are only 300 patients there. The administration cannot accept any more because of a lack of food. In going through the wards we saw little children and men and women; all of them pleaded and prayed for bread. They did not get any allowance for the past four days. Many of the children were in the last stages of starvation. This was the most trying experience that I ever had. Col Grove and I decided that we cannot wait until the organisation is completed and we sent $50 worth of foodstuffs to this institution; this was done by buying an 'Internal Sale' with money that I had. I have written a letter to the Superintendent that this was a gift of the Joint Distribution Committee. Naturally, this is a very small proposition; the children in the other institutions are in the same deplorable state. Col Grove is trying very hard to start the feeding immediately.

People share a meal at a communal soup kitchen. Kharkov, Ukraine. c.1923. JDC was the largest single donor to ARA food programs in the Soviet Union during a widespread, prolonged famine. In the Ukraine alone, their contributions helped nearly two million Jews survive.

THE MIRACLE OF EKATERINASLAV
By Benjamin Pepper

When I expressed my willingness to go to the Ukraine, Mr Rosenberg begged me to keep a diary. I did so for the first ten days in Ekaterinaslav, but our hours of work were such that I could not keep it up and I therefore must write this account from memory. I left London on 7 April 1922 as an ARA man appointed by Colonel Grove, with Mr Benjamin Blattner, JDC accountant, Mr Frank L Price, a publicity man of the ARA, and two Englishmen employed as accountants by the ARA. I travelled via Ostend to Berlin and then to Riga where we obtained the necessary Russian visas permitting entrance into Russia. From Riga we went by train to Moscow (then a three day trip for what now takes a day and a half). Moscow had a drab, rundown appearance, but the only indications of famine were the many beggars on the street. On the day of my arrival, I received my inoculations against typhoid, paratyphoid and cholera and left the following day for the Ukraine. My first stop was at Charkov where I waited for Col Grove and Dr Bogen to arrive and assign me to my work. There I got my initiation into the horror of famine.

On my arrival in Charkov, it became necessary to pass through the main waiting room of the railroad station which is a room about one half the size of the main floor of the Grand Central Station. The floor of this room was literally covered with people, old and young - men, women, children, infants - all starving and a number already dead. At least 30 dead bodies were being removed daily from this station. To get out of the station I had to pick my way over these bodies of human beings lying there dying of starvation. Charkov was not in the famine area, it was a railroad center and these people were refugees from the famine districts who had gathered at all the various railroad centers throughout the Ukraine in such numbers that the Government had no place to put them, no means of feeding them nor any possibility of coping with the situation in any way and these gathering points were centers of pestilence and death.

After several days in Charkov, Col Grove and Dr Bogen arrived from their trip of inspection through the Ukraine. I received my instructions from them and departed for Ekaterinaslav, arriving there on the 28th of April. Ekaterinaslav, about 300 miles south of Charkov, is a city of 175,000 inhabitants, 76% of them Jews. At the railroad station I was met by the ARA district supervisor, Mr Thomas Barringer, who took me through the city to the ARA headquarters. The impression I gathered was that of a dead city. The street along which we rode was the famous Ekaterinenskai Prospect - a broad avenue wider than Fifth Avenue, four miles long in a straight line, with a once beautiful alley of acacias down the centre. But where there once was grass there was now bare dirt and where many a tree had formerly stood there was now a stump. Many of the buildings on either side were in ruins for there had been much fighting there during the war and revolution. Other buildings were boarded up and through the gaping broken windows, one saw empty wrecks of what had been stores and shops.

The ARA headquarters were located near the edge of the city on the Novo Dworanskai. Practically every building on this street excepting the one assigned to us had been damaged, although many a family still found shelter in these roofless, ruined, windowless homes. The building we had was a three storey, solid, cement and brick building about 50 by 50 feet and here the ARA had several months previously opened offices for the distribution of the $10 food package which it sold in America. The main floor and basement of this building were used for the clerical work and distribution warehouse of the food package work, the second floor was used for sleeping quarters and on the third floor we now prepared to organise the non-sectarian child feeding division.

My very first day at Ekaterinaslav had one most important meeting. I wish I could do justice to Dr Boris Chanis. Dr Chanis is a leader among the Jews and indeed among all the people in Ekaterinaslav, possessing the respect and admiration as well as the trust and confidence of all people with whom he came into contact. He is a man of about 35 years of age, ill of an incurable disease, frequently suffering intense pain, and yet devoting his time and his life unstintingly to the cause of helping his fellowmen. With us he devoted all his time to relief work and took barely enough pay to sustain life himself. His unselfishness and self-sacrifice combined with his keen mind and unflagging energy were a guide and an inspiration to us in our work. Upon meeting him I realised that he was a man who could and would be of immense service to us in our work and I immediately arranged with him to go on a trip of inspection the following day to some of the Jewish children's homes in the city of Ekaterinaslav, and on this next day I received my first picture of what the famine meant in the children's homes.

The home we first visited containing 50 children was quite near the ARA headquarters, a small two storey cement and brick house considerably dismantled, windows broken and lacking the ordinary facilities of sanitation. It was a dreary looking place without even the simplest equipment. There was not a single knife or fork for the children though that was unimportant, as they had nothing to eat with knives or forks, the diet at that time consisting almost entirely of a very watery soup and some indigestible black bread. Most of the children were in rags and some were actually stark naked. They were little tots, none older than 14 and most of them between seven and ten - all Jewish children. Due to the fact that they had already received some food from the JDC food packages, they had not had any deaths within the preceding month, though before that they had suffered severely from starvation. But the food packages had not gone a very long way in maintaining more than existence. The children were emaciated, some of them unbelievably thin and gaunt with skin drawn tight over the jaws and cheek bones and with deep sunken eyes, so that their faces looked like skeleton heads. They had a frown on their faces with deep vertical creases between their eyebrows which I later learned was the typical frown of starvation. Their skin was a sort of mottled brown which I later learned was also a sign of starvation. There were a few who had been through even more extreme stages of starvation, for their stomachs were bloated and swollen and one or two were even swollen about the joints of the legs and feet. These youngsters slept three and even four together in tiny cribs without mattresses at all or with mattresses made of coarse sacking stuffed with stiff straw. The two women in charge of this children's home were deeply ashamed for the condition of the house which it was obvious they could do nothing to prevent.

When I first came to Ekaterinaslav, one could find on the streets every day persons who crept wearily into some corner never to rise again. Beggars met one at every turn. I remember particularly one Jewish family, a mother with three weeping children lying on the sidewalk at one of the more busy corners. Another case that I shall never forget I saw at one of our kitchens in company with Dr Chanis. It was a woman with a tiny infant in her arms. The child seemed to me to be not more than six months old but what attracted our attention was its sunken, wrinkled face which was that of a man of 75. That child was four years old! In all the terrible time of revolution, banditry, bloodshed and famine, the mother had kept this child alive, but no more than that. She had had so little nourishment to give it that she had been unable to do more than maintain the spark of life, but the child, unable to grow, at the end of four years was still an infant in arms.

The first few days were spent at the ARA office getting acquainted with the problems and working out the details of the child feeding work with Mr Barringer, the ARA supervisor. The program which we were to carry out involved the feeding of 200,000 children and 150,000 adults in the district of Ekaterinaslav, a territory about 300 miles long and 150 miles wide. This district contained in addition to Ekaterinaslav itself, the smaller cities of Alexandria, Krivoi, Rog, Nikopol, Sinelnico, Povlograd etc. Fortunately for us, the railroad system in our district was very well laid out for our purposes, so that we were able to depend almost entirely upon the railroads for getting food to the various distributing points which we established throughout the district. From these distributing points the food was conveyed to the little villages and towns scattered over the district by the farmers of the villages who came with their little wagons and small cossack ponies or ox carts in long trains from all directions.

We had warehouses in all the cities that I mentioned above and Russian representatives appointed to supervise the management of the warehouse and the organisation of kitchens and distribution of food in the area surrounding each one of these points. This organisation, of course, was entirely Russian. For the whole Ekaterinaslav district we had only three Americans in the child feeding work and one additional American for the food package work - four Americans in all. I am not going into detail about our organisation, but am trying to give only a broad idea of the work in one district. By the 15th of May we were actually feeding 12,000 children, by the 30th of May 40,000 and at the height of the work on 1 August, we were feeding 210,000 children and 150,000 adults.

The child feeding and adult feeding work was entirely non-sectarian and conducted according to the principle of greatest need, which principle the ARA and JDC men worked out and carried through in entire accord. The child feeding was done entirely through kitchens or through giving food to institutions. In the entire Ekaterinaslav district there were 311 kitchens, in the city of Ekaterinaslav there were 22 kitchens. The houses for these kitchens were provided by the local governments and were also equipped by them with large kettles, pails and tin dishes. The children who came to the kitchens received one meal a day of about 670 calories food value. The food consisted of gruel of oatmeal grits, cocoa with evaporated milk, sugar, some fats and a quarter pound of white bread daily. I remember well the opening of the first kitchen at Ekaterinaslav on the Potiomkinskaia during the first week in May. This kitchen accommodated about 400 children. The preceding week the local committee of representative citizens living in this area had been busy selecting the children who should be fed and when the work was done word had gone forth that the kitchen was to be opened. From early morning the fortunate children with little mugs in their hands began gathering about the door while hundreds of others who had not been selected for feeding stood about hoping that something would happen so that they might also be admitted. It is impossible for anyone who has not seen it to picture these long lines and rows of thin, tragic faces and forms with their look of expectation as they waited there for the doors to open. One of the curious features of our feeding was that hungry as the children were, for a long time it was impossible to get them to drink the cocoa. They had never seen it in their lives, they did not know what it was and they were quite afraid of it. But after they had once acquired the taste they could not get enough of it. The feeding in the institutions was conducted in the same way as in kitchens directly under our control with regard to the menu and amount of calories per meal. We printed circulars showing the rations for each day and the ration per child allowed so that the only difference between the feeding in institutions and kitchens was that in one case we directly controlled the work, while in the other case we merely exercised a supervisory function. Wherever possible we used existing institutions.

The difficulties we had to contend with were of various sorts. On 30 June we were feeding 90,000 children which was up to schedule. Then suddenly the food ceased coming in and we were unable to expand our program as required. Daily messages to Odessa brought no response and Mr Barringer and I were frantic. In the first week in July Col Grove happened to come through Ekaterinaslav on a tour of inspection, we informed him that our program of expansion had stopped and we were in actual immediate danger of having to close our kitchens due to the fact that our food reserves were being exhausted. Col Gove was astonished. He said that he himself had signed the order for additional shipments and that he would investigate this matter instantly on his arrival in Odessa. There, as I later learned, he discovered that some clerk through whose hands our order had passed had decided that our warehouse space in Ekaterinalsav, which he had never seen, was not sufficient to accommodate the supplies ordered and that he had better hold up this requisition. He had therefore filed it away. It was through such occurrences that each day contained its drama. The food started to come in immediately after Col Grove reached Odessa and you may imagine the sigh of relief and delight which Mr Barringer and I heaved when the telephone call came from the railroad station that the trains had come in. Within 36 hours, 75 carloads arrived and the day was saved.

I ought to touch on one more matter and that is the adult feeding, particularly in the country districts rather than in the city. There originally had been no intention of feeding adults in the Ukraine, but investigation showed that the feeding of children was not sufficient to meet the problem of famine in this area and that unless something was done to save the adults, tremendous numbers of them would die and that furthermore the peasants in the villages had become so weakened from lack of food that it was highly probable that a large part of the harvest would be lost due to the fact that they were unable to harvest the crop. Therefore, upon very short notice, we organised our adult feeding work. This was done through the same agencies as our child feeding, but the food was not distributed cooked each day, but a two weeks' supply of uncooked corn grits was given out at once to each adult entitled to help. The object of this was to enable the peasant to remain at work in the field without the necessity of interruption, a long tramp to some kitchen and back each day. The importance of this adult feeding cannot be measured. I have had representatives of a number of villages come to me after the harvest and tell me with tears in their eyes that our food came at the time of most extreme need as though in answer to their prayers and that without it they and their village would have

been unable to save the harvest upon which depended not only their lives, but the lives of all the city workers.

The recuperative power of a human being is marvelous. One would have supposed that to save these haggard, skeleton-like children that I saw when I first arrived in Ekaterinsalav would have required years of careful feeding, yet it took no more than two months. The change which took place in Ekaterinaslav in that brief time was unbelievable. Where once the streets had been filled with beggars, without any other act than the opening of the ARA kitchens, these beggars disappeared from the streets as though some great hand had swept them away. Where one saw previously thin, pale little children with no strength in their limbs, with no laughter in their eyes, two months later these creatures were gone and in their place were merry, rosy-cheeked, happy youngsters. It is this unbelievable transformation particularly among the children due to no other factor than our feeding which I shall always look back upon as something akin to a miracle.

Awaiting the opening of a JDC Soup Kitchen Ekaterinoslav Ukraine, 1921.
Courtesy of American Jewish Joint Distribution Committee

JOINT DISTRIBUTION COMMITTEE

PARIS-FRANCE

Isaac O c h b e r g,
President of
THE CAPE JEWISH ORPHANAGE,
P.O. Box 2730,
CAPE TOWN. (South Africa).

Paris Address:
Executive Committee
of the Jewish World Relief,
Conference,
10 Place Edouard VII,
P A R I S .

Paris, May 20th, 1921

Dr. B. D. Bogen,
J.D.C., Paris.

Dear Sir,

I have to thank you sincerely for the kind interview you granted me yesterday afternoon and particularly for your promising to assist me in every way in my undertaking with regard to selecting and transporting a number of Jewish Pogrom orphans from Eastern Europe to South Africa.

For your information I take the liberty of giving you a few details in connection with my visit here:

Some time ago, when it became known of the great distress a large number of Jewish orphans were living through in the progrom area, it was resolved, on many large public meetings in various towns in South Africa, to bring a number of these children to be brought up in South Africa. In fact I may say that it is almost a unanimous opinion and desire of South African Jewry to support those unfortunate orphans by bringing them up in South Africa.

I have the honour to be President of one of our largest Jewish institutions of South Africa called "THE CAPE JEWISH ORPHANAGE" and we have on our books about 1600 regular subscribers. This institution unanimously consented to take charge of about 100 children and for this purpose we are now building a special wing adjoining our building in which we intend to accommodate the pogrom orphans that will come to South Africa.

An appeal has been made by us which has received a very liberal response from the Jews of South Africa as well as from the Gentiles.

We have approached our Government and they have spontaneously agreed to admit, without any restriction, such pogrom and war orphans that we may bring and for your information I attach you a copy of a communication, dated 14th August 1920, addressed to me by the Secretary for the Interior on behalf of the Union Government from which you will see that the above permission has been granted. I also attach a copy of the letter given to me by the High Commissioner of S.Africa in London and I might state that the principal Cabinet Ministers of the Union Government are very strongly in favour and are willing to support us in every way possible in the above object.

I am here at the unanimous desire of the South African Jewry to select and transport about 200 children from the pogrom and war orphans to South Africa and for this purpose I am anxious to secure the assistance from you which I feel sure will be of immense value to me and I take the opportunity of thanking you, Sir, in advance on behalf of the Jewish Communities in South Africa, as well as for myself, for the assistance you may render me.

On the advice of Dr.Leo Motzkin, President of the Executive Committee of the Jewish World Relief Conference, I am leaving tonight for Vienna to attend a conference that is to be held on the 24th instant, where, no doubt, many important opinions on this subject will be heard. From there I intend next week to proceed to Rovno in which neighbourhood I understand a large number of pogrom orphans are available. I am also informed that you have a branch of your organisation there.

If you require from me any further references, I shall be very happy to let you have them as I have with me various documents from important bodies of South Africa. Further, should you desire our bankers, the National and "Standard" Banks of South Africa, Circus Place, London Wall, London, will give you such guarantees that you may desire in connection with such expenses that you make on our behalf.

In conclusion, I would feel very grateful to you if you will kindly let me have a letter from you today which will enable me to present to any of your organisations with the object of securing their assistance in connection with my selecting etc. of the orphans that I require.

Thanking you once more, I remain, dear Sir,
                    Yours very faithfully,

            (Sgd) Isaac Ochberg,

                        President of the Cape Jewish Orphanage

REPLY FROM JOINT DISTRIBUTION COMMITTEE TO ISAAC OCHBERG

JOINT DISTRIBUTION COMMITTEE
Paris – France C.40.49

25 May 1921

Mr Isaac Ochberg
c/o Executive Committee of the Jewish World Relief
10, Place Edouard – VII
PARIS

Dear Sir

This will acknowledge receipt of your letter of the 20th May from the contents of which we were most interested to note that the Jews of South Africa are desirous of caring for one hundred orphan children of Poland.

We would much appreciate it if you would submit to us the authentic documents in your hands and also inform us of the exact sums your Committee has at its disposal to cover the transportation etc of these one hundred children.

On receipt of this data the Council will submit this proposition to our New York office, and in the meantime we shall be only too glad to place at your disposal all the facilities of our organisation and to co-operate with you in every way. It must, however, be clearly understood that the JDC, while giving every co-operation possible, assumes no responsibility whatever in connection with the task you desire to accomplish.

We are, dear Sir,
Yours faithfully

EUROPEAN EXECUTIVE COUNCIL
Per ME BAYNTON
Secretary

LETTER FROM SOUTH AFRICAN DEPARTMENT OF THE INTERIOR TO ISAAC OCHBERG

Departement Van Binnenlandse Zaken
Department of the Interior

Cape Town

14th August 1920

Sir

With reference to your interview with me recently and your communication of the 13th instant, I am directed to advise you that the Minister of the Interior has approved of your request to be permitted to bring into the Union of South Africa certain children from Russia, who are orphans as the result of the recent war. I understood from you when you interviewed me that you proposed to go over yourself and arrange all matters connected with the admission of these children to South Africa, and on receipt of definite information as to when you propose to leave London, I will communicate with the High Commissioner for the Union in London asking him to render you every assistance in your mission.

I am leaving for Pretoria on Tuesday morning and any communication you wish to address to me further on the subject should be directed to the Secretary for the Interior, Union Building, Pretoria.

I have the honour to be, Sir
Your obedient servant
(Sgd) R D SHOW
Secretary for the Interior

The President
The Cape Jewish Orphanage
P O Box 2730
CAPE TOWN

A BRIEF HISTORY OF THE AMERICAN JEWISH JOINT DISTRIBUTION COMMITTEE

It all began with a telegram. In 1914, US Ambassador to Turkey Henry Morgenthau, S. sent a cable to Jacob H Schiff, a well-known Jewish philanthropist, asking for $50,000 to feed starving Jews in Palestine caught in the throes of World War I. Within a month, the money was raised, and through the collaboration of three American Jewish relief organizations determined to aid Jews in Europe and Palestine, the American Jewish Joint Distribution Committee (JDC) was born. Since then, JDC has been fulfilling its mission on behalf of North America's Jewish communities and others, providing rescue, relief, and renewal of Jewish life, and carrying out its partnership with Israel.

JDC has been a Lifeline to Jewish Communities Worldwide for Nearly a Century

During World War I, JDC channelled funds to Jews in the warring countries who were suffering from hunger and malnutrition and had lost homes and livelihoods.

• From 1919 to 1921, JDC raised $33.4 million toward relief programs for well over a million impoverished and starving Jews in Europe as well as reconstructive aid to rebuild community institutions. It promoted economic development in Palestine, cared for war orphans and at-risk children there and in Eastern Europe, established Agro-Joint in the Soviet Union, and helped European Jews regain their economic footing.

American Jewish Distribution Committee: Original Medical Commission upon arrival to Paris. January 1921 consisting of eighteen men: thirteen physicians, two public health men, one dentist, one pharmacist, one secretary. Dr. Morry Plotz, Mr. Schmidt, Dr. J. Alcazar, Dr. MM. Anshin, Dr. Z.A. Bonoff, Mr. M. J. Cahan, Dr. R. Friedman, Dr. J.J. Golub, Dr. R. Kohn, Dr. J. Michlin, Dr. Newman, Mr. A. Horwin, Dr. S. Fox, Dr. H. Apfel, Dr. Z. Sagal, Dr. L. Silver, Dr. S. Wendkos, Mr. S. Flessig.
The first JDC medical unit of 18 physicians and sanitation personnel arrived in Poland January 1921. This unit, working with Polish-Jewish medical aid organizations, helped revive, transform and finance almost 500 medical and sanitation institutions, including public baths, dispensaries, hospitals, sanitaria. X-ray stations, nurses training schools, milk centers and well-baby stations. Thousands owed their recovery from war injuries and disease to these installations.

• Before and during World War II, JDC helped hundreds of thousands of Jews escape Nazi-occupied Europe and, wherever possible, provided a source of sustenance to those unable to leave.

• Between 1945 and 1951, JDC spent over $300 million in Europe, the newborn State of Israel, and other countries of refuge to salvage and rebuild Jewish lives ravaged by the Holocaust. In 1946 and 1947, JDC's relief efforts were helping 700,000 Jews a month—one out of every two living in Europe west of the Soviet Union.

• Responding to the unhealthy conditions faced by the Jews of North Africa and the Middle East, JDC helped combat malnutrition and infant and child mortality for tens of thousands of children through feeding and health programs. JDC supported relief, medical care, and cultural, religious, and vocational programs to help fight poverty and add to the dignity of Jewish life.

• In the largest mass migration in modern Jewish history, some 440,000 Jews reached the newborn State of Israel by the end of 1950; fewer than half were able-bodied. JDC devoted two decades to directly helping elderly and disabled new immigrants, then redefined its role to help Israel develop innovative social services to meet the needs of its most vulnerable citizens.

• JDC organized and financed Operation Magic Carpet—the largest human airlift in history—which flew some 48,000 Yemenite Jews from Aden to Israel between 1948 and 1950. It continues to help remnant Jewish communities in North Africa and Asia maintain Jewish schools and other vital institutions and care for their disproportionate number of elderly and impoverished.

• Fifty years after being expelled, JDC returned to the Soviet Union in the late 1980s to help Jews there rediscover their Judaism and re-establish Jewish community life. Two years after the 1991 collapse of the Soviet regime, JDC inaugurated the first in what has become a network of *Hesed* welfare centres that provide food, medications, and other vital forms of care to impoverished elderly Jews.

• Following years of assistance to Jews in Ethiopia, in May 1991 JDC played a central role in Operation Solomon, which airlifted more than 14,000 Ethiopian Jews to Israel over the course of 36 hours. It has subsequently worked with numerous partners to help Ethiopian-Israelis become part of mainstream Israeli life.

• Following six decades of furnishing Jewish community development assistance in Latin America, JDC's role shifted to providing basic food, medical, and housing relief to Jews plunged into poverty by Argentina's 2001 economic crisis. Partnering with local Jewish agencies, JDC established a network of social service centers that served a peak caseload of more than 36,000 "new poor."

• Responding to renewed terrorist attack, the Israel Emergency Campaign-funded "Keep the Children Safe" initiative sent hundreds of thousands of children to summer camps and after-school programs in 2002 and 2003. With IEC help, JDC provided emergency assistance to Israelis who faced war in the north in 2006, and it supports those facing recurrent rocket attacks in Sderot and the Gaza border region.

• Backed by over $19 million in contributions, JDC's International Development Program (JDC-IDP) organized relief and development projects in India, Indonesia, Sri Lanka, and Thailand following the December 2004 Indian Ocean tsunami. Later humanitarian responses include JDC-IDP's efforts following the May 2008 cyclone in Myanmar and the devastating January 2010 earthquake in Haiti.

• JDC's *TEVET* (Fighting Poverty Through Employment) partnership with the Israeli government is breaking the cycle of dependency among chronically unemployed population groups by helping them overcome social and cultural obstacles to employment and enhance their marketable skills.

• *Ashalim*, JDC's three-way partnership with UJA-Federation of New York and the Israeli government, has developed more than 300 programs for children and youth at risk in Israel. Meanwhile, the International Fellowship of Christians and Jews (IFCJ)-JDC Partnership for Children in the Former Soviet Union has expanded support for impoverished Jewish children in that region and is working to integrate them into Jewish community life.

THE MISSION OF THE AMERICAN JEWISH JOINT DISTRIBUTION COMMITTEE

Rescue whenever and wherever a Jewish community is threatened. In the early 1990s, JDC helped sustain and rescue 15,000 Ethiopian Jews. Today, JDC maintains global networks and contingency plans in the event of a crisis.

Relief for Jewish communities in distress. JDC has been providing food, clothing, and medicine to hundreds of thousands of impoverished elderly Holocaust survivors and children in need in the former Soviet Union and the world.

Renewal and discovery of Jewish heritage and Jewish community life. Since the fall of communist regimes in Europe, JDC has been helping Jewish communities rediscover their heritage and rebuild a vibrant Jewish communal life.

Partnership with Israel as it addresses the social service needs of its most vulnerable communities: children at risk, struggling immigrant populations, the elderly, and the disabled.

International Development Program (IDP): Non-sectarian aid in response to natural and man made disasters and long-term development assistance to non-Jews to fulfill the Jewish tenet of *tikkun olam*, the moral responsibility to repair the world and alleviate suffering wherever it exists. Often referred to as "the Joint," JDC has worked in over 85 countries over the course of its history and has played a role at virtually every major juncture of Jewish history since its founding.

For more information, please contact JDC at 212-885-0838 or via email at press@jdcny.org.
Web Site: www.JDC.org

In what was called the largest human airlift in history, JDC organises and finances Operation Magic Carpet, which flew some 48,000 Yemenite Jews from Aden to Israel. All photos are courtesy of American Jewish Joint Distribution Committee

46

JDC IN THE UKRAINE TODAY
Courtesy JDC and Ninio Reeva

Ukraine once served as a vibrant and vital center for Jewish culture. Beginning in the eighth century, it was an important refuge for Jews fleeing persecution. Centuries of pogroms and the depredations of World War II, with more than one million Ukrainian Jews murdered at the hands of the Nazis, devastated this once thriving community. Yet, despite the restrictions of the Soviet era, Ukrainian Jewish culture managed to survive.

Today, Ukraine is home to eleven Jewish communities. With almost 350,000 Jews in Ukraine, the community, its culture, and its heritage are growing stronger. In fact, while *aliyah*, or immigration to Israel, is still important, there is a growing trend of Ukrainian-born Israeli citizens to return to the Ukraine.

Following its declaration of independence in 1991, Ukraine suffered a major economic slowdown, losing more than 60% of its GDP by 1999 and suffering some of the worst hyper-inflation in Europe. The economy subsequently rebounded and Ukraine enjoyed consistent growth until the recent global financial crisis, but issues like aging infrastructure, poor transportation, and the country's dependence on Russia for energy supplies continue to hamper efforts to improve daily living. The elderly in the Jewish community have been particularly hard hit as the rising costs of daily necessities have put them at risk.

With many Ukrainian Jews cut off from Jewish traditions and culture for decades, there is a need to provide them with frameworks for learning more about their Jewish heritage.

JDC has a long history of work in Ukraine. In the 1920s and 1930s, JDC through Agro-Joint trained and resettled Jewish artisans and traders on newly established Jewish farm settlements in Ukraine. Today, JDC works to provide basic daily needs for at-risk elderly Jews and for young families that have children with special needs or disabilities through a network of Hesedim. Over the past two decades, JDC's Hesed welfare centers have given thousands of impoverished elderly Jews the opportunity to live the last years of their life in dignity and comfort – instead of the isolation and poverty that would normally await them. The Hesed provides services such as hot meals, medical assistance, a *moked* repair service, and sends homecare workers to assist the frailest and home bound clients.

Providing basic daily needs for at-risk elderly Jews

Young Jews explore and celebrate their identity

The Hesed welfare centers' unique approach even drew recognition from the Russian Academy of Languages, which adopted Hesed as a Russian word meaning "the provision of services with special compassion."

JDC also fosters community programs that are renewing Jewish culture. These efforts include:

- Thirty eight organizations providing welfare services
- Seven Hillel centers, where young Jews can explore and celebrate their identity
- The building and renovation of The Odessa Grand Jewish Community Home, which houses a *Hesed*, two local JCCs, and other Jewish organisations
- The opening of the renovated Beit Graham Jewish Home in Krivoy Rog, which now houses *Hesed* programs for children and the elderly in addition to JCC programming
- Opening of a new Wohl Jewish Center in Kharkov

Hundreds of thousands of Jews in Ukraine have benefited from almost a century of JDC's work and commitment. Currently, tens of thousands are served by JDC's Jewish Community Centers and Hillel centers, benefiting from services that provide:

- Three million, two hundred thousand hours of home care for more than 10,700 homebound elderly Jews
- Nutritional assistance for more than 6,000 children at risk
- Food cards for more than 48,000 clients, enabling them to purchase their food in local supermarkets
- Social and cultural interaction as well as basic needs for more than 5,800 seniors through day centers
- Annual medical consultations for more than 3,800 clients and medicines for nearly 36,000

Perhaps the most promising evidence of JDC's impact is the emerging Jewish leadership in Ukraine that, in locations like Zaporozhye, is raising its own funds to ensure the long-term sustainability and community ownership of the programs JDC has fostered

For more information visit the JDC website: www.jdc.org
Contact Information: Solly Kaplinski <sollyk@jdc.org.il>
Executive Director Overseas Joint Ventures

Chapter 11 – THE RESCUE OF UKRAINIAN ORPHANS BY THE CANADIAN JEWISH COMMUNITY IN 1921.

At the same time that Isaac Ochberg, the President of the Cape Jewish Orphanage and the representative of the South African Jewish Community was gathering the orphans to be brought out to South Africa there was a very similar scheme being carried out by the Canadian Jewish Community.

While the ship carrying the South African children arrived in Cape Town on 19 September 1921 the children arrived in Canada about three weeks earlier.

THE RESCUE OF UKRAINIAN ORPHANS
Courtesy Janice Rosen, Archives Director, Canadian Jewish Congress Charities Committee National Archives. Extracted from the books "THE JEW IN CANADA" compiled and edited by Arthur Daniel Hart and "LILLIAN AND ARCHIE FREIMAN Biographies" by Bernard Figler.

It was in the summer of 1920 that the pitiable condition of the Jewish child population of Ukrainia first came to the attention of Canadian Jewry in a direct and authoritative way. Professor Elie Heifetz of Ukrainia came to America in July of that year with a description of suffering and tragedy that would have seemed unbelievable had it not been fully substantiated.

There were more than 137,000 Jewish children in the Ukraine orphaned by the war, he reported, children of tender age practically living wild and semi-barbarous lives, without homes or means of obtaining regular sustenance beyond their own puny resources, which were mainly the garbage lots of Ukrainian towns and villages. When this course failed to provide for them they tried to assuage the pangs of hunger by eating such edible wild roots and herbs as were left in a territory that had been sadly ravaged by war and post-war excesses. It was felt that aid for these orphans was an imperative duty of the Jews of the American continent who had known nothing of such terrible privation.

While seeking relief supplies for Ukrainia through the People's Relief Committee of New York, Professor Heifetz had conceived a plan to rehabilitate many of the orphans by their emigration to America where they would be placed in foster homes. The United States laws, however, were not favourable to such immigration. He then turned to Canada in the hope that his scheme might be successfully carried out here.

A meeting was convened for this purpose in Montreal on 11 July 1920 presided by Lyon Cohen, president of the Canadian Jewish Congress. A Committee was appointed to examine the proposed plan. It became evident at the outset that the task was a huge one, requiring the active interest and support of all Canadian Jewry. It involved a campaign for a large sum of money for relief of the children in Europe; obtaining permission of the Canadian Government to admit a number of the children; finding reliable foster homes for their adoption; dispatching competent persons to Europe to select the children; preparing them for the trip and accompanying them to Canada.

Some of the Orphans – 1921

A national committee would have to be set up, headed by a prominent personality. Everyone agreed that the ideal person as leader of this undertaking was Lillian Freiman.

Four days later she was visited by a committee consisting of Professor Heifetz, Harry Hershman, representing the People's Relief Committee and Mrs Anna Selick of Toronto. The Committee placed before her all the facts in their possession regarding the Ukrainian orphans.

If there was anything calculated to stir her fullest sympathy it was a story of children in distress, particularly orphans. She promptly pledged herself to the pressing cause. She wasted no time getting matters started and arranged a conference with F C Blair, secretary of the Department of Immigration and Colonisation, attended by herself, Professor Heifetz and Hershman.

She explained to Mr Blair the urgent problem and asked permission, for the admission of 1,000 orphans from Ukrainia, to be adopted into Canadian Jewish homes. The department felt that the immigration of 1,000 children might be too big a problem to handle and therefore consented to the entry of only 200, as an initial experiment. Further numbers might be approved if the admission of the first 200 was made in a manner satisfactory to the Department of Immigration.

It was stipulated that the children must be in good health; not over 12 years of age; complete arrangements for their reception and adoption had to be made in advance of their arrival; a proper organisation had to be formed to execute the project. These conditions were immediately agreed to by Mrs Freiman and her colleagues.

On 8 August Louis Zucker, president of the Peoples' Relief Committee, and Professor Heifetz met with Mrs Freiman in Ottawa and went into further plans for the work and decided to appeal on Rosh Hashana for Canadian Jewry's support. The following day a conference was held in Montreal, attended by delegates representing more than 100 organisations. They formally named Mrs Freiman as Dominion President of the Ukrainian Orphans Committee, and Professor Heifetz, director. The following committee was appointed to direct the appeal in Montreal: Lyon Cohen, Rabbi H Cohen, Leon Meltzer, S D Cohen, Louis Zucker, Lionel Coviensky and Harry Barsky.

Mrs Freiman issued a stirring message to Rabbis and presidents of Synagogues throughout the Dominion, asking them to address their congregations on Rosh Hashana on the plight of the Jewish orphans in Ukrainia. Meetings were held with leaders of communities. Professor Heifetz addressed gatherings in Winnipeg and a conference in Saskatoon of delegates from western cities. A J Freiman spoke at two large meetings in Montreal, one of them in Prince Arthur Hall, at which great enthusiasm was aroused for the undertaking.

It was necessary to take steps to win the interest and support of Jews in all parts of the country. It was decided to convene a Dominion-wide conference. On 1 October 1920, telegrams, bearing the signatures of Lillian Freiman and Professor Heifetz, were sent to leaders of communities from coast to coast, inviting them to a conference in Chateau Laurier, Ottawa, 6 to 8 October. The telegrams read in part:

"Jewish hearts all over Canada have been deeply stirred by authentic accounts of suffering of these Jewish orphans and everywhere great enthusiasm prevails for our plans to rescue and bring some here for adoption in homes where they will be given the love and care they now so pitiably lack. May we not have your co-operation in this noble undertaking?"

This was one of the most momentous gatherings of its kind ever held by Canadian Jewry. Mrs Freiman presided. Delegates were present from many parts of the country. Present also were S W Jacobs K C, MP; Solomon Lowenstein and Charles Zunser, representing the orphans branch of the Jewish Joint Distribution Committee of America and Reuben Brainin, noted Hebrew author and journalist.

Harold Fisher, mayor of Ottawa, welcomed the delegates and F C Blair, Secretary of the Department of Immigration, explained the Department's attitude and promised all possible co-operation and assistance.

The Conference adopted the official name of the Jewish War Orphans Committee of Canada; elected Lillian Freiman, National President, and her husband Chairman of the Executive Committee, and an Executive which included Lyon Cohen, D S Freidman, Dr C J Gross, Lionel Coviensky, H Wolofsky, L Zucker, H Hershman, Nathan Sloves and representatives of a large number of communities. The Conference decided also to conduct a campaign for funds on 26-28 December 1920.

On Lillian Freiman's invitation, Mrs Arthur Meighen, wife of the Prime Minister of Canada, accepted the office of Honorary President of the Committee. Lady Davis, Lady Borden and Mrs Mark Workman became Honorary Vice-Presidents.

Her Excellency the Duchess of Devonshire, wife of the Governor General, was apprised by Mrs Freiman of the proposed undertaking and replied: "Under your leadership the scheme will be carefully worked out and will prove a very successful one" and desired to be kept informed of the progress of the Committee for the adoption of the first 200 orphans.

An executive office was opened in Ottawa with Sam Berger as secretary. Under the personal supervision of Mrs Freiman an extensive publicity campaign was planned and quantities of literature dealing with the orphans' situation in Ukrainia were sent out.

The Executive decided that it was of the utmost importance that a prominent person tour the country to explain the urgency of the undertaking, organise local committees and receive applications for adoption of orphans. They urged Lillian Freiman to undertake such a tour herself.

Early in November 1920, she set out, accompanied by Miss Ida Seigler of Montreal, editor of the Canadian Jewish Chronicle, to visit the leading cities from Halifax to Vancouver. They did not spare themselves. Mrs Freiman delivered scores of addresses, met delegations in every community, and assisted in the organisation of numerous local committees.

Many applications for adoption were received. These were turned over to the local committees for investigation so that the orphans would be assigned only to homes offering the right sort of care and assurance for their future. Many individuals and organisations also undertook to contribute annually $200 per child for the maintenance of orphans in their respective European countries.

Groups of women everywhere began to sew garments for the little ones. The hearts of mothers were filled with pity at the thought of thousands of boys and girls, like their own, wandering the streets of Ukrainian towns and villages, footsore, ragged and hungry. Enthusiasm was the greater as it became known that no other country had attempted the actual bringing of orphans from Ukrainia. Hadassah Chapters, B'nai B'rith Lodges, local councils of Jewish women, Synagogue Ladies Auxiliaries, were all co-operating in the work.

On her return from the four-week trip she said: "Canada's Jews are ready to open their homes to these children from Eastern Europe. We have received over 1,500 applications for adoption of children. The idea of financial adoption on the same plan as that carried out on behalf of the French and Belgian orphans is meeting with enthusiastic response. The little colony of Edenbridge, with 22 Jewish families has applied for adoption of 22 children."

Nor did she content herself with routine checking of the applications but personally investigated, as far as geographically possible, the prospective homes for the children, for she was worried lest any child 'of hers' may chalila be placed in the wrong home and not receive the proper care and upbringing.

The campaign that followed in December raised nearly $100,000, in addition to donations of large quantities of children's clothing, which were shipped abroad. Boys and girls were also urged to make sacrifices from their penny banks for the purchase of clothing and shoes for their less fortunate brothers and sisters in Ukrainia.

Non-Jews as well supported the cause, for through the very generous publicity given by the general press the sad plight of helpless children touched Christian hearts too. Thus, in Yarmouth, Nova Scotia, the mayor J M Walker, was treasurer and another prominent Christian, K Kilty, was an active member of the campaign committee.

SELECTION OF THE ORPHANS

In the meantime, the National Committee for War Orphans decided to send a delegation, or unit, to Europe to select the children, ascertain that they were in good physical health and otherwise comply with the requirements of the Canadian Immigration authorities, and to bring them to Canada.

There was unexpected delay in dispatching the unit to Ukrainia. It was hoped that its members would sail in November 1920, but Professor Heifetz, who was to head the unit, being a subject of Soviet Russia, could not obtain the documents indispensable to pass unhindered through different European countries. It was found necessary therefore to appoint a new director in the person of Gregory Sanders of Montreal. He was to be accompanied by Harry Hershman of Montreal, as assistant director, Dr Joseph Leavitt, Montreal, as medical director and William Farrar, Hamilton, director of transportation.

William Farrar, a non-Jew, and former alderman of Hamilton, was a popular figure with the Hamilton Jewish Community. For many years he had taken an active interest in Jewish affairs and even attended synagogue services frequently, especially on the High Holy Days. Mr Farrar was also an enthusiastic Zionist and attended the Eleventh Zionist convention held in Toronto 23-26 December 1910. At this Convention president Clarence I de Sola submitted a resolution to create a Land Fund to Purchase land in Palestine. When the resolution was

Harry Hershman with some of the Orphans

adopted de Sola and Treasurer A A Levin led with the firstcontributions and were immediately followed by Alderman Farrar!

When the committee learned that Mr Farrar would like nothing better than to serve as a member of the unit his appointment was unanimously approved for he was a prominent business man and organiser, with special knowledge of transportation problems. [It was characteristic of Mr Farrar that he later reimbursed the committee all the money spent on his transportation and maintenance while with the unit.]

In December Mr and Mrs Freiman and Mr Sanders went to New York where they were assured the facilities of the Joint Distribution Committee in Europe, including personnel, records, offices, warehouses, automobiles, etc.

Some contributors expressed the wish that relief be also extended to orphans in the part of Ukrainia under Soviet rule. The delegation had learned, however, in New York, that it would not be practical to enter Soviet territory. It was therefore determined to concentrate the work of the committee in Polish Ukrainia where the situation was perhaps more acute. As a matter of fact, however, many of the orphans that were rescued came from towns and villages in Soviet Ukrainia from which they had fled in terror following pogroms against the Jewish inhabitants.

On 2 February 1921, a conference was held in Montreal confirming the necessary change in plans, and arrangements were rushed for the departure of the unit to Europe. Unfortunately they suffered another setback when the wife of Gregory Sanders became seriously ill and he was obliged to resign as director and was replaced by Mr Hershman. The Department of External Affairs in Canada facilitated the task of the committee by issuing special documents, in English and French, requesting the co-operation of governments abroad. As all three members of the unit were British subjects the necessary passports and visas were speedily procured.

The entire Canadian Jewish community followed with quickened interest the departure of the unit on 5 February 1921 on the White Star liner 'Cedric'. Applications for adoption continued to flow to the Dominion headquarters at Ottawa where G Garrow-Greene, private secretary to Mr and Mrs Freiman, was the new executive Secretary. The applications, after careful scrutiny, were classified according to sexes and ages of the children desired, to facilitate the work of selection by the unit in Europe. Care was taken to distribute the children among as many communities as possible.

Upon arrival in Europe the unit met with Jewish leaders in Paris, Vienna and Warsaw. Considerable time was spent preparing in advance for the movement of the children to be selected, following conferences with the Polish Ministry of Foreign Affairs in regard to passports and with the Polish Ministry of Transportation to assure an adequate supply of railroad cars.

Although they had been prepared for very tragic conditions, the members of the unit were shocked to discover the indescribable plight of the war and pogrom sufferers in the small cities and villages of Polish Ukrainia. Writing from Warsaw, on 17 March 1921, Mr Farrar said "The Jews in Ukrainia have been in Hell. Young girls come here with the most heartrending stories. I am made sad from morning until night."

After completing the preliminary work in Warsaw, the unit proceeded on its way, reaching Rovno, which had been selected as the base for activity, on 3 April. It was the glorious hopeful season of spring, but alas, such a spring in Poland. How the thoughts of each member of the unit must have turned toward Canada, where the springs come year after year under happy circumstances. Spring meant nothing of what it had in Canada, to these Canadians in Poland. True, here and there, the trees were green with budding foliage, and the ground had splotches of grass, but there was so much of desolation that the signs of spring became insignificant. Trees everywhere gaunt and charred, met their gaze, trees that seemed to speak of war and pillage, and upheaval; and most indelibly impressive of all, was a population which faced the picture of utter hopelessness and misery. Women clutching their skirts, their eyes darting hither and thither were filled with the fear that experience had taught them to have. And the children! What horrible mute stories the faces of the little ones told. They did not need to speak. Children of perhaps four or five with features of aged persons, eyes sunken, cheeks nothing but skin and bone, bodies almost mere skeletons. Surely, thought these missionaries of humanitarianism, this was the saddest spot on earth.

There was no lack of children for the unit to examine. Thousands had been registered by the representatives of the Joint Distribution Committee, and the fortunate ones accommodated in the three homes that had been established in Rovno. But there were also many others living in sheds and in the open, for space in the homes was limited. Did they want to go to Canada? The excitement, and the anxiety to be chosen which prevailed amongst the children of Rovno, stirred pangs of pity in the hearts of each member of the unit, for sad though it was to decide that way, very few, if any of the children first

examined were fit to pass the physical and mental tests. With the valuable co-operation of the agents of the Joint distribution Committee, the unit set to work. The memory of the week that followed their arrival in Rovno will probably never be erased from their minds. Over 1,000 children were examined by Dr Leavitt and he found only 46 whom he thought might be of the standard required. The pale thin faces of the little ones, the eyes which mirrored years of intense suffering, almost unnerved the doctor. Over 8,000 children had to be examined eventually before the number brought to Canada was selected. Three children who came before the doctor were all that remained of a happy family of 15 members. All the others had been killed or had died of diseases brought on by wounds and hunger. One of the three was a cripple, and so the Jewish community of Rovno refused to allow the other two to be taken, as it was felt that they would likely be the sole means of support of the crippled child in later years. In a letter which he wrote to Mr Freiman from Rovno on 7 April, Mr Hershman said, "We examined children from the Felstin district, and out of 80, found only 15 to comply with our regulations. Most of the others are in a very poor physical state, some of them maimed and crippled from the effects of pogroms they were in." In this letter, Mr Hershman expressed the belief that it would take from two to three months longer to pick out the required number of children. And then, in a later letter, he wrote:

"Children born in the Ukraine from three to six years ago, could not survive, especially if they had become orphans at the ages of one or two years. Those who survived are the fortunate ones whose parents were spared, and only superhuman sacrifices on the part of the parents saved them."

By 21 April, Hershman cabled that the unit had already selected 60 children, between the ages of four and 12. As people in Canada were becoming impatient for the arrival of the children, the Ottawa headquarters cabled on 25 April to send the first party of children as soon as possible.

The unit in the meantime was meeting with tremendous difficulties. First, there were no suitable houses in Rovno where to place the children after they had been selected. There had been delay in the arrival of the cases of clothing, and the greatest difficulty of all was the absolute lack of official records relating to the birth of the children. This, of course, was vitally essential.

The parents of the children were dead; official records had been destroyed in the pogroms. Hershman had to make dozens of visits here and there, interviewing old residents who had known the parents of the orphans. In this way a sufficient record was built up and, when completed, the documents of origin were certified by the local rabbinate. One can appreciate the quandary of the unit in this respect as, for example, 55 of the children chosen were from the district of Novgorod, Wolinsk, which had been burned and pogromed no fewer than 15 times and records of vital statistics had been completely destroyed.

With the shortage of railroad cars following the war, the unit encountered further difficulty when different governments refused to allow their equipment to pass beyond their respective frontiers. During all this time the people of Canada were chafing a little at the protracted delay in the consummation of the undertaking, it being naturally hard for them to understand why it was taking so long to collect the children.

On 20 May 1921, Freiman cabled Hershman instructing him that, as conditions in Canada necessitated quick conclusion of the project, the number of children to be brought to Canada should be reduced to 150, instead of the original 200. One of the reasons that forced the committee to this decision was that most of the children found eligible for emigration were older than desired by adoptive families. Hershman had reported that there were few children under six years of age who had survived, whilst 70 per cent of the applications for adoption were for children under six.

As news arrived from the unit, and was conveyed by bulletins to all the local committees most of the applicants consented to accept children older than originally stipulated. A further cable was sent to Hershman instructing the unit to endeavour to finish its work by 15 June. At last the first party of orphans was ready for departure. They left Rovno on 14 June, in the words of Hershman "to the greatest joy of the children and the grief of the population."

There were 51 boys and girls in the first party. In two days they reached Vienna where they were comfortably housed. Here Farrar taught them some of the simple words of the English language and described to them in an interesting manner Canada, Canadians and Canadian customs, all of which, needless to say, increased the eagerness of the children to come here.

It was decided to gather all the children in Antwerp until the date of sailing. Finally, after the lapse of another month, the rest of the children had been selected, all obstacles surmounted and passports and visas secured. A cable was dispatched to Ottawa to purchase steamship transportation. All the children reached Antwerp on 6 August, just three days before the date of sailing of the *SS Scandinavian*.

SHE LEAVES FOR EUROPE

When word was received in Canada of the readiness of the children for the sea voyage Mrs Freiman prepared to leave for Europe in order to take charge of the orphans and accompany them to Canada. Before embarking she said: "I hope to be able to minimise the terrors of the voyage for the little ones and prepare them for the new and strange life they may expect to come to in their new Canadian homes."

She was accompanied by her cousin, Mrs Asher Pierce, of Montreal, who was a member of the Executive committee. Mrs Pierce was deeply interested in Child Welfare, being actively connected with the Children's Memorial Hospital and was also a board member of a number of communal organisations. Both were travelling at their own expense and both had applied for the adoption of orphans. They sailed for Southampton on 17 July.

Mrs Freiman's coming to Antwerp had a two-fold purpose: firstly, to become acquainted with the children before they were placed with their adoptive parents and secondly, to supervise carefully and unhurriedly their distribution to the various homes, and make certain, as far as possible, that each child will be assigned to the proper home.

The children were all well clothed and in good appearance, especially when compared with other European children. But when "mama" Freiman examined them with her motherly eye, she was not happy with the way they were dressed as "they lacked individuality". And she decided that they must have different clothes. She explained:

"It is true, as they say, that a diamond sparkles even when in the mire, but how much more beautiful is it when placed in a proper setting?"

She left at once for Paris where she purchased new and appropriate clothes for each according to age and physical build.

She examined each child and said: "This little girl has dark hair and dark complexion and needs this kind of dress and coat; this one has blond hair and rosy complexion" and so on for each one. This is the "mama" motif in the title "Mama Freiman" given her.

Hershman later told the moving story.

"I can still see vividly the unforgettable scenes, scenes of joy and tears, an ocean of tears, that followed Mrs Freiman's first meeting with her children. The great joy that shone from her smiling face and the flow of tears that stemmed from her eyes in pain over the fate of the 150 destitute and friendless orphans who now surrounded her and looked up to her as to a guardian angel, their Mama Freiman, and tears of joy that she had lived to see the fruit of her untiring work.

"Friday evening following her arrival, the children were seated at long tables, at the hotel where they were staying, with many leading persons of the Antwerp Jewish community. Mrs Freiman had brought with her the 'Loving Cup' presented to her by the Orphans Committee at the Conference held in Ottawa. At that time she had taken an oath not to make use of this gift until she had seen the children. And here she had lived to this great moment to see around her these children. Tonight she will for the first time use this cup and she honoured me by asking me to chant the Kiddush.

"The Loving Cup is a massive silver cup, with two handles. It is now filled with wine, provided by the Antwerp Jews, and is quite heavy and I have a 'job' to hold it high while pronouncing the Kiddush. But still more difficult than holding the cup is my struggle with the 'ivre', but thanks to the festive atmosphere, or perhaps by the grace of my forefathers, I successfully pronounced the entire Kiddush and handed the cup to Mrs Freiman.

"She then carried the cup to each child to taste from the Kiddush, and from her eyes flowed a stream of tears that nearly fell into the cup, but through the tears we could see her great nachas that she derived from this experience."

"PLEASE DON'T LEAVE ME BEHIND!"

In Antwerp, before the children were to be examined medically, Mrs Freiman washed and combed them and wept all the time like a child.

Suddenly another obstacle arose, with an outbreak of a skin infection, preventing several children from sailing with the group. The Jewish community of Antwerp undertook to accommodate and care for the stricken children till they were well enough for a subsequent journey across the Atlantic.

The turn to be medically examined came for a sweet-faced little girl whose golden curls and fair skin made her look like a typical 'Anglo-Saxon. Through a blow of some sort one of her nails had turned black. The examiners, who were unreasonably severe, refused to allow her to go on board unless the nail was removed on the spot.

As the ship was ready to sail at any moment this meant that there would be no time to administer an anaesthetic. Mrs Freiman was afraid to allow the child to undergo such torture and both she and Hershman were greatly agitated at the thought of leaving her behind.

The little girl, perceiving their agitation and seeing that something was amiss, begged them to tell her what it was. No one had the heart to tell her. Finally, Mrs Freiman told her, in her Yiddish, and the child, throwing her arms around her, cried out:

"Let them cut off my whole hand, but please don't leave me behind."

She went through the operation like a brick and as soon as it was over she rushed out to her friends and boasted, "It hardly hurt me at all," while the long-repressed tears ran down her cheeks.

The Polish Ukrainian Orphans brought out to Canada – Harry Hershman is the man with the beard holding a child

THEY SAIL

They now feverishly prepared for the ocean voyage; the racket with each one's packing, the big 'garden party' in the beautiful garden of Antwerp's Jewish leader, Mr Unterman, the parting with the children who must remain for a second boat, and finally they are aboard the *SS Scandinavian* with the first group of 108 children, in the ages of 2½ to 12. It is 19 August 1921 and they are on their way to Canada!

One can imagine the hearts of the little ones beating more rapidly as their thoughts centred on the land of promise to which they were bound at last.

Each child had an outfit of clothing and shoes, and fastened to each little jacket and blouse was a tag on which the identity of the child was inscribed. The steamship officials had made special preparations to ensure a comfortable and pleasant voyage, including a kitchen for kosher food. During the voyage Mrs Freiman and Mrs Pierce worked with the members of the unit in classifying the children for adoption so as to avoid delay in the assignment of the children on arrival at Quebec, the port of debarkation. Four special nurses had been engaged in Europe to accompany the children and attend to their wants.

CHILDREN DISAPPEAR

The trip is smooth, no storms, no fog. The children are well and happy and "mama" Freiman with them. But "mama" Freiman also has much "trouble", because it is difficult to keep them together. The older ones are constantly disappearing, led by their eagerness to examine the big ship, while the younger vanish in thin air. The reason for this is that many of them are so charming "Chainevdig" that the passengers of first and second class "kidnap" them and amuse themselves with them and shower them with attention and presents. The little ones were having a taste of the human kindness which awaited them in Canada.

One of the most popular children on the boat was a five-year old little girl, Yochele, a lovely child, with big fascinating dark eyes and exceptional brightness. Yochele also sang very beautifully Yiddish folk-songs. Time and time again she "disappeared" into the captain's or purser's cabin where a number of passengers are gathered and feed her with sweets and coax her to sing again and again. Far from shy, Yochele obliges with "Kukuriku Hundele" and other songs.

On the last day of the voyage they were sailing up the St Lawrence. Early morning Mrs Freiman was already on deck, around her a number of the older children who shower her with questions; "What place is this we are passing now? When will we arrive in Ottawa? And where is Montreal? And will Mr Freiman be at the ship when we arrive? They wanted so much to meet Mr Freiman!

Mrs Freiman struggles to speak to the children in Yiddish in reply to their questions, but her Yiddish is rather imperfect and the children have fun hearing her speak and smile secretly. One would suspect that the children deliberately ask her all

these questions just to hear her speak Yiddish. They delight not only with what she tells them but with her entire attitude towards them. Because she does not reply to a question just to dispose of it but embraces the questioner and with the gentlest motherly love gives her reply, no matter how childish the question.

ARRIVED!

The *Scandinavian* approached Quebec in the evening of Friday, 20 August. What excitement prevailed! The children spent the last few hours on the boat scurrying around, packing their little valises, their "baggage" consisting of many little keepsakes, toys, dolls and playthings given them by sympathetic Jewish persons of Vienna, Dresden, and Cologne where the children had passed through. And every few minutes they rushed to the side of the boat to gaze in wonderment at the twinkling lights on the shore.

Before landing in Quebec they were examined again and each child, terrified that he or she might be refused admission, begged: "Please, doctor, dear man, let me pass, do not keep me back."

A little boy whose eyes showed great terror was detained as not normal but was quickly released when Mrs Freiman threw herself at the doctor like a tigress and said that she will fight to her last breath for the child, who was well and healthy but was terrified of anyone in uniform. Whilst the youngster was kept a few hours under observation the rest of the children became frightened and did not want to go anywhere without their little pal. His little sister broke into such sobbing that they had to take her to her little brother, and she remained with him till he was released.

Once they were all assembled the children asked if they had to be examined again before landing and when they were told that there will be no more examinations they began to jump and sing and weep and kiss each other and hugged Mrs Freiman and Hershman.

THEY LAND!

It was Saturday morning. A steady rain was coming down. On the dock was gathered the entire Quebec Jewish community and members of the committee who had come from several cities. From Ottawa came A J Freiman and from Montreal, Horace R Cohen, Asher Pierce, Mrs H Wolofsky and D S Friedman.

The children were lined up on deck in neat rows, with the younger ones in the front. At a signal from Mrs Freiman they began to sing the "Hatikvah" and there was not a dry eye in the crowd assembled on the dock. They followed with "O Canada" and sang the national anthem with such fervor, like a prayer to God, to bless the land that gave them a home and freed them from fear and death.

A Quebec newspaper described this scene:

"Over a hundred little Jewish orphans from Ukrainia, bereft of parents, relatives and homes by the cruel fortunes of war and by the barbarous pogroms on defenceless people, which are one fruit of the still seething political conditions of Central Europe, landed from the ocean liner, *SS Scandinavian*, when she docked here Saturday morning. When they trod the soil of Old Quebec and saw the comforting Union Jack, flying in the breeze from the citadel, they sang "God Save the King."

The gangplank was lowered and the first to board the ship was A J Freiman. After embracing his wife he greeted the members of the Commission.

Then Lillian Freiman went over to the children and returned, leading by the hand a little girl of 11, with blue eyes and black hair.

"Archie", she said smilingly to her husband, "this is our new daughter."

Freiman bent down and kissed the child and asked her in Yiddish "What is your name, my dear?"

"Gitel" she timidly replied.

The community had arranged a reception and repast for the children in the community hall, some distance from the dock. On account of the Sabbath, however, the children refused to drive from the immigration quarters to the hall. They formed into a procession, each child carrying a tiny Union Jack, with knapsack on the back, and marched in the rain through the principal streets of the city.

Louis Lazarovitz, president of the community, presided at the reception. Mrs Lazarovitz greeted the children and their guardians in Yiddish, and Miss Rachel Smiley read an address of welcome to Mrs Freiman, in English. Speeches were also delivered by Mrs Freiman, A J Freiman, Farrar, D S Freidman and Hershman.

Mrs Freiman was too overcome by her recent experiences and by the constant watch she had kept over her little charges to be able to say very much. "I only wish", she said, "that every Jewish woman in this country had had the privilege we've had of being thrown into contact with these wonderful children. If they had, then I am sure there wouldn't be a Jewish home in Canada that wouldn't be clamouring for a little orphan. They will make splendid Canadian citizens, and above all, they will be loyal Jews. Those of us who have been so fortunate as to be allowed to adopt these children have been given a great privilege as well as a great responsibility. God grant that we may bring to the task the understanding, the sympathy, the helpfulness and the mother love that these little ones so sorely need."

As some of the speakers made reference to the great Jewish tragedy that had occurred in Europe, adults and children began to weep. It seemed for a moment as if it was Yom Kippur. A representative of the "Keneder Adler" then reminded the children that this Sabbath being "Shabbos Nachamu" – the Sabbath following Tisha B'Av – it was not a time for weeping but to comfort each other and to forget the past. The world was before them. Many of them will become the future Jewish leaders in Canada. They were the future Lillian Freimans and the Hershmans.

THE PARTING

That evening the children were embarked on their final destinations, Saint John, Montreal, Ottawa, Toronto, Winnipeg, care being taken to keep brothers and sisters together for adoption in the same communities.

A member of the committee related: "Those who did not witness how the children parted from each other and from Mrs Freiman and Hershman do not know the meaning of a shudder, have no concept of catastrophe."

The terrible experiences of the children had bound them together as one family and when the moment of parting came one saw the most tragic scene one can imagine. They fell on each other's neck and sobbed and sobbed. There were loving embraces, murmured endearments and promises to write.

When the moment came to part from Mrs Freiman and Hershman many adults had to leave the hall, so moving was the scene.

Each child fell on her neck and sobbed and begged her: "Darling mother, where are you sending me?" Will you come to see me?" Not once but ten times they turned back from the door and ran back to her and Hershman to bid them again farewell. Mrs Freiman's eyes were swollen, her face drawn from the worry and strain. Like a statue she stood there, hugging each child and sobbing quietly, and it seemed that in this weeping one heard a curse against those who brought such a terrible tragedy upon Jewish life.

Gently the children were separated and taken to the railway station where they were made comfortable in their berths. They were escorted to their various destinations: by Mrs Freiman, to Montreal and Ottawa; by Hershman to Toronto; by Myer Budovitch, to Saint John; and by Miss Hattie Silverman to Winnipeg.

On their arrival in Montreal a large crowd awaited them at the station. The children noticed that several persons held copies of the *Jewish Daily Eagle* which carried photographs of Mrs Freiman and Hershman. They began to plead that each be given a copy of the newspaper. A bundle of papers was soon brought and distributed among them.

One little girl sat quietly on a bench staring at the photographs and suddenly broke into heartrending sobbing and began hysterically to kiss the photographs. Many adults were moved to tears and Mrs Freiman embraced the child, and herself began to weep and could not calm herself for many minutes.

The parting farewells were repeated as Mrs Freiman had to leave for Ottawa a half hour before the children destined for Toronto and she had to bid each one goodbye. One little boy held onto her neck and refused to let go. He kept crying "I will not leave you, you are my mother, the best mother in the world and Mr Hershman is my dear father. I cannot live without you both …"

Returning to Ottawa, the Freimans also brought with them two young girls, one of them adopted by Lillian Freiman's parents.

FURTHER ARRIVALS

Less than two weeks later, though still fatigued from her ordeal, Mrs Freiman went to Rimouski where she boarded a ship bringing another 24 children who had been obliged to remain over in Antwerp. On this journey too she was accompanied by Hershman.

The ship arrived in Quebec on 3 September and was met by Mr Freiman, Mrs Asher Pierce and many others. Sixteen more children arrived on 24 September, one on 6 December and one on 24 January 1922.

The children became quickly accustomed to Canadian life and many of them showed intelligence and musical talent. A few months after her return Lillian Freiman boasted that her adopted daughter, Gladys, "speaks excellent English and has become a thorough Canadian, knowing more about the Queen's birthday than many of her Ontario-born associates."

Though Canada had received these few Jewish orphans of the Ukraine, thousands of orphans remaining in Europe were maintained by the charity of world Jewry. In Canada appeals were held from time to time to raise funds for this purpose. When a campaign on a larger scale was planned in 1925 it was but natural for people to turn to Lillian Freiman and H Hershman, whose names represented the highest concern for these orphans, to assume the leadership.

A campaign for $50,000 was launched under her chairmanship. Dr Leo Motzkin, Dr Oscar Cohn and Rabbi Dr Eisenstadt came to Canada as delegates of the World Relief Organisation to describe the plight of thousands of Jewish orphans in Ukraine.

In August 1925 the 'Conference Universelle Juive de Secours' of Paris nominated her one of three world representatives on the honorary committee of the first general congress for the children, which was convoked that month by the Save the Children Fund, International Union, in Geneva, Switzerland. The Congress discussed the problem of orphans and widows left by the war, measures for the increase and tightening of safeguards for uprooted women and children, as well as questions of charity.

The Conference elected her one of the Honorary Vice-Presidents of the Organisation. The award came in appreciation for her work on behalf of the Ukrainian orphans.

MICHAEL G PIERCE - ONE OF THE CHILDREN

The writer was curious to know if Mrs Asher Pierce, who had accompanied Mrs Freiman, had also adopted a child. He asked this question of her son, Sidney D Pierce, Deputy High Commissioner of Canada in London, England, and former Canadian Ambassador to Mexico.

"Yes," wrote Mr Pierce, "my mother did adopt a son, my brother Michael."

'Michel-Moshe' was a blond, blue-eyed boy of ten when he came to Canada.

"I was brought up by my grandmother", Michael told the writer, "after both my parents passed away. I do not know why I was so lucky to be chosen to be brought to Canada. My grandmother was reluctant to let me go. When, at the last minute, she finally consented, I had to run to catch up with the other children, who were already departing from our village.

"On board ship Mrs Freiman and Mrs Pierce were always together. Dr Leavitt was busy running around treating the children who were seasick. I was not seasick. I believe I knew on the boat that Mrs Pierce was adopting me. I remember that Mr Pierce was at the boat when we arrived in Quebec and that we motored to Montreal. Sidney took to me at once and always took care of me, like a brother. Often, when I came home late, he waited up for me and scolded me.

"I recall that my parents' name was 'Glatter' and to this day I write my name 'Michael G Pierce'.

"Asher and Ella [Vineberg] Pierce were wonderful parents to me, but I have lost them both, in one year. Mr Pierce passed away on 18 May 1936 and Mrs Pierce on 31 December 1936."

Michael served six years in the Canadian Army, in the Second World War, spending three years overseas.

***Note** There is only one known case where siblings went to South Africa and Canada.*
Rivka Kailer was one of the Ochberg Orphans while her sister Zippe (Celia) was part of the group that went to Canada. See chapter 67.

TELEPHONE: GERRARD 6245
TELEGRAMS: UKRARELIEF, LONDON.

FEDERATION OF UKRAINIAN JEWS,

IN AID OF THE POGROM SUFFERERS IN THE UKRAINE,

(REGISTERED UNDER THE WAR CHARITIES ACT, 1916.)

Central Offices :

26A, SOHO SQUARE, W.1.

Clothing Department :

33, BROAD STREET, W.1

SECRETARY :
A. M. KAIZER, Esq.

HON. PRESIDENT :
THE VERY REV.
DR. J. H. HERTZ,
CHIEF RABBI.

HON. VICE PRESIDENTS :
SIR STUART SAMUEL.
HERBERT BENTWICH, Esq.

CHAIRMAN :
DR. D. JOCHELMAN.

VICE CHAIRMEN :
DR. M. PINES.
MORRIS MYER, Esq.

JOINT HON. TREASURERS :
JOSEPH PRAG, Esq.
M. SCHALIT, Esq.

HON. SECRETARY :
S. GOLDENBERG, Esq.

EXECUTIVE COMMITTEE :

ELKAN ADLER, Esq.
REV. MICHAEL ADLER.
M. BAGRIT, Esq.
B. BERNSTEIN, Esq.
J. CAPLAN, Esq.
DR. S. DAICHES.
HAHAM DR. M. GASTER.
REV. L. GEFFEN.
M. GROSSMAN Esq.
L. HUT, Esq.
M. KAUFMAN, Esq.
I. KALMENSON, Esq.
J. KIPERNICK, Esq.
B. KOGAN, Esq.
M. LIEBERMAN, Esq.
J. LANDAU, Esq.
J. MACHOWER, Esq.
LAURIE MAGNUS, Esq.
RABBI I. I. MATTUCK.

London, 24th February 1921. 19

Isaac Ochberg, Esq.,
Cape Jewish Orphanage.

Dear Sir,

    With reference to our wire, sent you today, saying "await our letter", I now beg to give you a detailed reply to all the points mentioned in your previous letters. Our reply has been delayed as we have been waiting for the arrival of our delegate Mr Saltzman, who left tr REVAL. on the 8th inst., and whom we are expecting any day. We wished to hear all he had to say on the general situation in the Ukraine, and to consult him on the orphans question.

    We learn from his last report that the Moscow Relief Committee has formed a special Commission to deal with the care of the orphans, and according to the statistics, it appears that there are 500,000 orphans who are in want of immediate succour.

    The opinion expressed by our representative Mr Saltzman is that the plan for bringing the children out of the Ukraine to America Canada and Africa is both impracticable and undesirable, because, even under the best circumstances, we should be able to transport barely 5000 children. Even for this number the expense would be so great that we could, for the same money, support more than 50,000 children on the spot.

    The Soviet Government has put houses at the disposal of the Children's Commission to be used as homes for the homeless children, as well as provisions. It is, However, unable to supply any equipment. Mr Saltzman points out that a scheme could be brought into operation whereby every Jewish sympathiser would give, or subscribe for, the following articles, necessary for every child in the Homes :-

Dr. M. SCHWARZMAN.
L. SCHEN, Esq.
A. TARLO, Esq.
Dr. L. TRIVUS.

1 bed with mattress.	Outer garments.
1 pillow.	1 spoon.
3 pillowcases.	1 fork.
1 blanket.	1 knife.
2 sets of underwear.	2 plates.
3 pairs of stockings.	1 bowl.

Drugs for use in the Homes are, of course, a necessity. The actual organisation of these Homes would be primarily carried out by the above-mentioned Commission.

The same opinion is held by Dr. Boris Bogen, the European Director of the Joint Distribution Committee, who has just returned from a visit to those areas of the Ukraine occupied by the Poles, and with whom we have had a special interview on the subject of orphans.

He says that for ever a year the Joint Distribution Committee has been considering the problem of the orphans, and has come to the conclusion that it will cost considerably less to maintain the orphans on the spot than to take them out of the Ukraine and settle them elsewhere. According to Dr. Bogen, 5 orphans could be kept in the Ukraine for the same sum that it would take to get 1 orphan out. The Joint Distribution Committee has, therefore, opened several orphanages which are being managed by the local Jewish communities in Polish Ukraine. It has also evolved an Adoption Scheme, whereby any person in America can adopt an orphan by investing $100. at fixed periods for the maintenance of that child in the Ukraine. We are awaiting full and detaild particulars of this scheme from the Joint Distribution Committee, on receipt of which we shall investigate the matter thoroughly, and let you know the result. At the same time we shall also consider what activities we can undertake in that line.

Quite a different opinion is held on the other hand, by Canadian Jewry, who have formed a Jewish War Orphans Committee, with a special European unit who are already on their way to the Ukraine to bring to Canada as many orphans as they can. For this they have already obtained the permission of their Government. This Commission is comprised of Messrs. William Farrar - Master of Transportation, Dr. J. Leavit - Medical Director, H. Herschman - Assistant Director. These gentlemen, when in London, were interviewed by us on this subject. We learn from them that preference for the first batch will be given to those orphans who have lost both parents. The Commission think that they will have no difficulty in emigrating the orphans as, according to the Joint Distribution Committee, there already are 20,000 registered orphans in

Polish Ukraine.

From what we can gather from our representative, and from the Joint Distribution Committee, it would appear that this gigantic task of bringing the orphans out of the Ukraine, would require to be undertaken by a large and thoroughly organised body, which, if such can be formed, might make it worth while; otherwise, it would be far better to erect and equip suitable orphanages in the Ukraine, where the orphans could be cared for. Should your Committee, however, wish to follow the example of the Canadian War Orphans Relief Committee, before proceeding to Europe you should first be in possession of guarantees from a great number of prospective foster parents (1) as to their willingness to adopt an orphan or more (2) as to their financial ability to maintain and educate the orphans. When you have been well assured of these facts, you could send a special Commission, including a medical officer, to the Polish Ukraine to work in conjunction with the Canadian War Orphans Committee. We ourselves are not doing anything in the matter, pending full particulars from the Joint Distribution Committee and the arrival of Mr Sultzman, on whose report and advice we will be able to base our decisions. Should you decide to form a Committee for the transportation of orphans we shall give you all the help in our power.

I beg to enclose a Questionnaire Form used by the Canadian War Orphans Committee. You may, perhaps, find this of use.

Awaiting the favour of your early reply,

Yours faithfully,

Secretary.

59

Chapter 13 – Ukrainian Orphans Rescued and Transported to Palestine

ITZHAK BELSON, MY FATHER
Information obtained from Nili Rokach, the daughter of Itzhak Belson, living in Kedumim Israel.

In 1922 Israel Belkind, a Lover of Zionism and a visionary and builder who wanted to redeem the land of Israel, brought a group of about 60 children aged 10-18 from an orphanage in Rovno in the Ukraine via Vienna and Romania and Egypt to a children's village in Afulla, near Hadera.

This was in fact the second group of children that Israel had rescued from Eastern Europe, as in 1904 after the Kishnev Pogrom, he had also brought a group of children to Israel.

Itzhak, my father, was one of five children of Miri and Michael Belson. Miri died from TB around 1914 and Michael who had remarried was alive when the children came to Israel. It is assumed he perished in the Holocaust.

Sarah, the oldest sister was aged 19 and a seamstress, followed by Chayim, Itzhak, Chanoch and Miriam.

Israel Belkind, with great difficulty, collected the children from a children's house in Rovno and brought them to Israel.

The children attended the Tarbut school in Rovno which taught, using Hebrew as the medium. All the subjects including Mathematics and Nature Studies were taught in Hebrew.

Itzhak remembered the starvation in Rovno and collecting and eating the crumbs after they ate. The nearest main town was Livov with 20,000 who were mostly Jewish.

The children were taken via Vienna, where Itzhak remembered the zoo, to the port of Constanta in Romania, where they took a ship through the Dardanelles to Alexandria in Egypt and finally from there sailed to Jaffa. In Jaffa they came ashore in small boats and the children tasted their first green and black olives.

The children were first taken near Hadera, a swampy area with malaria. Later they were taken to a new children's village near Afulla run by the South African Zionist Federation. There was conflict between Belkind, who had no money, and the SAZF who provided the funding. Later the children ran away and joined Belkind in Svat where there was no water or food and there they brought water from Rosh Pinar. Itzhak remembers they were very, very poor but happy. They had a very interesting educational method established by the children.

The children were taken back to the children's village in Afulla where the SAZF taught religion and there was a religious way of life. The SAZF established the synagogue which still exists at the north side of Haemek Hospital. The village had about 100 children aged from 10 to 18 and there were six classes at school.

Itzhak remembers tricking the head of the store into giving the children food "for a very important visitor" and as it was a 1st of April prank they only received minor punishment.

Itzhak, when 25 and then later when 26, went to Rovno and married a cousin of 16. He stayed in touch with the children of the village and a teacher there was like an aunt to him and he and his children used to visit her.

ISRAEL BELKIND (1861-1929)
Extract from the Jewish Virtual Library

Israel Belkind

Israel Belkind was born in Byelorussia near Minsk. He received a Hebrew education from his father, who was a leader in the movement promoting Hebrew education in Russia. Belkind also attended a Russian gymnasium and intended to go on to university, but instead became involved in Zionist activities, which were intensified in the wake of the 1881 pogroms in southern Russia.

On the first of Shvat (January 21, 1882) Belkind invited a group of young Jews to his home and together they formed the first organised group promoting settlement in Eretz Yisrael. Originally called Davio, an acronym for the Hebrew words from Exodus, "Speak unto the children of Israel that they will go forward," Belkind changed the name to Bilu, an acronym for the words from Isaiah (2:5), "Beit Yaakov Lechu V'nelcha," "House of Jacob, come and we will go." He explained the significance of the change in name: "Rather than persuade others to go to Eretz Yisrael, we have decided to move there ourselves." Shunning diplomatic or political channels, the group's goal was a practical one: to settle in Eretz Yisrael.

Belkind was the head of the first group of Bilu pioneers, which reached Eretz Yisrael in July, 1882. He worked first in Mikveh Yisrael and Rishon LeTzion, and then moved to Gedera, the first official Bilu community. Belkind, however, did not succeed in adjusting to agricultural labor, and instead devoted himself to education. He taught first at a private school in Jaffa, and then moved to Jerusalem to teach at the Alliance Israelite Universelle. His goals as a teacher were to fuse Jewish values with practical labor. In 1903 Belkind founded an agricultural school in Shfeya, near Zikhron Yaakov, for youths orphaned in the Kishinev pogrom, but the school failed three years later for lack of money.

After 1906, Belkind wandered around Eretz Yisrael and countries abroad, never really finding a permanent home. He had published several textbooks while teaching, and continued his work as a writer. He contributed many articles to contemporary journals and wrote popular articles on history. He was an editor of "HaMeir," a monthly publication on settlement and the Yishuv, and in the United States during World War I, he published his memoirs, "The First Steps of the Jewish Settlement in Palestine" (1918). In 1928 he published a geographical work in Russian, "The Land of Israel Today." Belkind died in Berlin in 1929 where he had gone to seek medical treatment, and was later buried in Rishon LeTzion.

PHOTOS OF THE CHILDREN AT SHFEYA YOUTH VILLAGE FOUND IN TASHA ALTUSKA'S PHOTO ALBUM
Sent in by Sandra Rachman, Tasha's granddaughter from the UK

Tasha was an Ukranian War and Pogrom Orphan (one of the Ochberg Orphans) that was saved by the South African Jewish Community in 1921. Tasha (an older sister of three other Ochberg children) was a nurse on the journey to Cape Town who looked after the Ochberg children and accompanied them to Johannesburg and continued to look after them at Arcadia (SAJO). Tasha was more than just a carer to the other Ochberg Orphans (in the eyes of the children who had no family) but more like a relative, a mother figure to the little ones and an aunt or older sister to the older ones. I believe in Tasha's album we have photos sent to her by other Ochberg Children who would share their simchas and adventures with her with cards and photos as we would all share with family.

While we cannot identify any of the children in the photos we do know these photos are of children in a children's village (Meir Shfeya Youth Village in Palestine) where the rescued children lived.

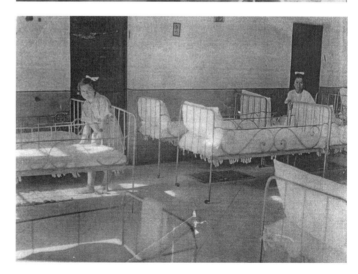

Girls from the Meir Shfeya Youth Village in Palestine working in the vegetable garden, washing clothes, working in the kitchen, and making beds.
NB The above photos were also found in the article following.

THE MEIR SHFEYA YOUTH VILLAGE
Extract from the internet

The Meir Shfeya colony was founded by Baron de Rothschild in 1890, near Zichron Yaacov. Its name is a combination of two words from a completely different origin: "Meir" is the name of the baron's father, while "Shfeya" is a distortion of the name of a village called Shveia which was located in the area.

The person responsible for the idea to establish a youth village near Meir Shfeya was Israel Belkind, one of the first members of the Bilu group, after bringing Jewish orphans rescued from the Kishinev pogroms to Israel.

Belkind named the place "Kiryat Sefer". The secretary of the children's village was Israel Shochat, one of the founders of the Hashomer defense organisation. After two years of dispute with the baron's emissaries at the colony, Belkind was prompted to move the children to Ben-Shemen.

By the way, in 1917, when the Turks expelled Tel Aviv's residents up north, the place temporarily housed the Herzliya Hebrew High School.

World War I left many orphaned children in Jerusalem. A girl's institution called "Aliza's care center" was established at the yard of the Diskin Orphanage on Neviim Street with the help of Hadassah, the Women's Zionist Organisation of America. In 1923, Aliza's care centre was moved to Shfeya, where it began developing.

Aliza's care centre was run in its first years in Shfeya by Chava (Hoz) Borodovsky. Chava was the sister of Dov Hoz, one of the founders of the Haganah organisation, and was the only passenger to survive a road accident in December 1940, which killed Dov, his business partner Yitzhak Ben-Yaacov, his wife Rivka Sharett and her sister Tirtza, and Chava's younger daughter Ora.

I found the photos for this article thanks to Ada (Borodovsky) Tamir, Chava's eldest daughter, and I thank her for letting me present them here.

Group photo at Aliza's care center:

Meir Shfeya Youth Village main building

A wedding at Shfeya

Girls at Aliza's care center

1923, the first British commissioner to the Land of Israel, Herbert Samuel, visits Shfeya.

KFAR YELADIM – THE CHILDREN'S COLONY

Nili Rokach, the daughter of Itzhak Belson, writes that her father, as part of a group of about 60 children, was rescued by Israel Belkind and taken to Kfar Yeladim in Palestine and that Kfar Yeladim was supported by the South African Zionist Organisation.

Extracts from THE SOUTH AFRICAN JEWISH WAR VICTIMS FUND confirm this.

The Jewish Relief Reconstruction and Orphans Fund.
Its first designation was *The Cape Russo-Jewish War Relief Fund*, then *The Relief Fund for Jewish War Victims of British and Allied Nations and Palestinian Jews*, and in 1920 it was changed to *The Cape Relief Fund for Jewish War and Pogrom Victims*.

Kfar Yeladim

To the Cape Fund belongs the credit for having formulated the scheme for the establishment of an Orphan Colony in Palestine, which eventually became what is now known as Kfar Yeladim.

The Children's Colony

Mr Belkind had brought to Palestine about 120 children from the Ukraine, and through various causes had found himself stranded with the children. Mr S Hillman, who was at this time on a visit to Palestine, investigated the position on behalf of the United Fund. Eventually the United South African Fund took over 86 of the Belkind children, and 44 children maintained by Durban, making a total of 130, obtained land from the Jewish National Fund in Balfouria erected buildings at an approximate cost of £12,000 and formed a children's colony at Givat Hamoreh.

The United Fund guaranteed the maintenance of the children for five years. Mr Richard Feldman of Johannesburg, while on a visit to Palestine, did yeoman service at the children's colony. The colony is now known as Kfar Yeladim, and on closing down of the Relief Fund was handed over to the South African Zionist Federation to be maintained as a children's colony in the name of South African Jewry.

Extract from RHODESIAN JEWRY AND ITS STORY PART 1V   written by Eric Rosenthal
At least one Bulawayo representative, Joseph Joseph, attended the inaugural meeting of the Actions Committee of the World Zionist Organisation in February 1920, while in 1923 Rhodesian Jewry undertook to be responsible for the immigration and maintenance of the 35 War orphans from the Ukraine, brought to Palestine through the efforts of Reconstruction Fund. Of these 25 were paid for by Matabeleland and Northern Rhodesia, while Mashonaland, more particularly Salisbury, undertook the responsibility for

another ten. These boys and girls were housed in a settlement called Kfar Yeladim, with which a connection was maintained for many years.

Boys looking after the cows – perhaps from Kfar Yeladim
Photos from Tasha Altuska's Album

We know of only one instance where the sibling of an Ochberg Orphan went to Palestine

In the life story of Nat Greenstein (Nachman Greenshtein) **(see chapter 64)** written by his grand daughter Lisa Greenstein we have an extract from a letter sent by Sam Gillad (Nat's brother) to Ben Greenstein (Nat's son) in June 1989 when Sam was 75.

Sam Gillad (Nat's brother) writes;
While Nat was an Ochberg Orphan. "I was attached to a group that was sent to Palestine. We were put in an orphanage that was supported by a group of kind Jews from Cape Town. It was a farming school. I grew up there to the age of 15."

These news cuttings are from The Hebrew Standard (an Australian Jewish Newspaper) and are dated 1921 and 1922 and were kindly sent in by Brian Fine, the son of Zeidel Feinschmidt.

ORPHANS FOR AUSTRALIA

Some time ago the Perth (Western Australia) Jewish Community unanimously decided to adopt 30 orphans from the pogrom areas and funds were raised for this purpose. The committee appointed to deal with the matter chose families of high standing as foster parents for the children. Negotiations have been proceeding for official permission for the entry of these children into Australia. The Federation has now been informed by the Migration and Settlement Office of the Government of Australia that official permission has been given. Steps are now being taken by the Federation to send a special representative to Eastern Europe to select these orphans and bring them to London. They will be the guests of the Federation before embarking for Fremantle.

2010 Follow up of Perth (Western Australia) connection
Written by David Sandler

I contacted Michelle Urban of the Jewish Historical and Geneological Society in Perth who referred me to two people:-
-Dr Oswald Tofler, who has done extensive studies on the Perth Jewish Community, analysing the intermarriage figures in Perth, has published his finding. He says he knows no one in Perth with this background and he believes nothing further eventuated.
-Phil Samuel, who has lived in Perth all his life, 70 years, knows no one having this history and suggested I send a letter to editor of the Maccabean, the Perth weekly Jewish Newspaper.

A letter to the editor and the 1921 news cutting were published in the Maccabean on 19 March 2010 and as at the time of printing this book not one response had been received.
One can only conclude that the attempt to bring out the children to Perth (Western Australian) was unsuccessful.

The following cable was received by the Rev J Danglow, President of the Melbourne Ukrainian Relief Fund, from Dr Jochelman, President of the London Fund:
"Gratefully acknowledge receipt of twenty-two hundred pounds; latest reports indicate position pogrom sufferers indescribable; over three million Ukrainian Jews destitute; six hundred thousand homeless children starving; one hundred thousand escaped refugees now scattered Eastern Europe; abject misery; money urgently needed; cable immediately all available funds - Jochelman, President Ukrainian Relief Fund."

We urge our readers who have not subscribed to this fund to send in their donations as early as possible, so that a further amount may be forwarded to London.

ORPHANS FOR SOUTH AFRICA
The Hebrew Standard

A party consisting of 250 little children from the Pogrom areas in the Ukraine will shortly arrive in London as guests of the Federation. These children are on their way to South Africa, and have been carefully selected from numerous Jewish villages by Mr Isaac Ochberg, President of the Jewish Orphanage, Cape Town. The difficulties in ultimately securing this number of children have been immense and in a report personally given by Mr Ochberg, at a meeting of the Executive Committee on Friday last, he related his experiences. It was necessary for him to travel from village to village, and take only those who were medically fit for sailing. It was heart-rending to have to refuse to take the many other orphans who were eager to be taken away from their unhappy surroundings. The cases met with were often of a very pathetic character. Amongst the party of orphans ultimately gathered there are children whose parents were buried alive, and others who are the sole remnants of what were once large Jewish families. When the task of getting this first group of children together was accomplished, Mr Ochberg was faced with the problem of housing them in Warsaw. In this work he was considerably assisted by the Warsaw Ukraine Committee, and now the children are temporarily housed comfortably and awaiting their transportation to Danzig. From the latter port they will journey to London, where they will stay a few days and then continue their journey to South Africa.

It was decided at the meeting of the Executive Committee abovementioned, that a special Reception Committee be appointed to take care of the orphans while in London. This committee consists of the following: - Mesdames J H Hertz, D Jochelman, N Wolf, Marcouse Rev Geffen, Messrs A Tarlo, S Goldenberg, and A M Kaizer with the power to co-opt. It was at the initiative of the Federation that South African Jewry became interested in assisting Jewish pogrom orphans. The Federation is therefore happy to receive these children and act as their host while in London.

It is hoped that this scheme of bringing over unfortunate war orphans to happier countries will be further developed and the Federation is interesting itself in securing the co-operation of Jewish communities in Australia and New Zealand.

University Students Help
The Hebrew Standard
A number of the University students have been collecting for the Ukraine Relief Fund, and to date have about £50 in hand. Among others whom they have approached was Mr G J Cohen, who has promised them the sum of £50, on condition that nine other contributions of a similar sum are received. Already two promises have been received. The sum of £500 thus obtained will mean the saving of the lives of 2,000 individuals. Others willing to contribute are asked to communicate with Mr S Goldberg, Medical School, Sydney University.

Chapter 15 – THE SOUTH AFRICAN "JEWISH WAR VICTIMS FUND"

Orphans in the Ukraine and Poland were helped in three ways through the generosity of the South African Jewish Community
-They were maintained and cared for in their towns of residence in the Ukraine and Poland,
-Some were transported to Palestine and maintained there; the group taken to Palestine by Israel Belkind to Kfar Yeladim (Children's village).
-Some were brought to South Africa and maintained there; Ochberg's Orphans who were placed in the care of the South African Jewish Orphanage (Arcadia) and the Cape Jewish Orphanage (Oranjia).

SOUTH AFRICAN JEWRY
Extract from THE JEWS IN SOUTH AFRICA Edited by Gustav Saron and Louis Hotz. Printed in 1955

"This may help to explain how South African Jewry has acquired the characteristics which distinguish it as a group. It has a world-wide reputation for liberality towards those of its co-religionists who are in need, and for staunch support of the Zionist movement. It is also recognised as a well-organised and relatively united community.

Being largely descendants of Lithuanian Jewry, South African Jews are a fairly homogeneous group, unlike those of the United States of America. They have inherited some of the qualities of the *Litvaks* - their warm-heartedness and generosity, their practical-mindedness, a strong feeling of Jewish solidarity, and a love of learning combined with a somewhat critical attitude to religious traditions, their religion being often more of the head than of the heart.

Enterprising and hard-working, they have been able to take advantage of the opportunities offered by a new and developing country."

THE JEWISH WAR VICTIMS' FUND
This article, kindly sent in by Ron Lapid, was first published in the The South African Jewish Year Book 1929 and it comes with a note "We are indebted to Mr A Cousin of Johannesburg for much of the information contained in this article."

The Relief Fund for Jewish War Victims of British and Allied Nations and Palestinian Jews, popularly known as the Jewish War Victims Fund, was established at Johannesburg on 27 January 1915, as a result of a meeting of representatives of Jewish organisations. Forty three Jewish institutions were represented at the meeting by 76 delegates. The resolution creating the organisation established the principle that the Fund should be administered and supervised by the South African Jewish Board of Deputies, and that the President, Treasurer and Secretary of the Board should fill these respective offices of the Fund. Mr Bernard Alexander, President of the Board, was the first Chairman and held the position for the following ten years.

The inaugural meeting was successful only after several ineffectual attempts had been made, and to the United Hebrew Polish Society of Johannesburg belongs the credit for its persistence in inducing the SA Jewish Board of Deputies to take the lead in this very necessary relief movement. Mr A Couzin, of

Johannesburg, was originally responsible in large measure for the activities of the United Hebrew Polish Society in respect of this scheme.

Almost simultaneously with the establishment of the Fund in Johannesburg, organisations with similar objects sprang into existence in Cape Town, Port Elizabeth, Kimberley, Bloemfontein, East London, Durban and Bulawayo.

Although there was no actual affiliation, there was close co-operation between the various organisations, and there was no overlapping of territory or activities.

At the outset the funds collected were allocated as follows: 65 per cent to Russia, Poland and Lithuania, 20 per cent to Palestine, 10 per cent to Alexandria for the relief of refugees there, and 5 per cent to Belgium.

Later, when the needs for Alexandria and Belgium became less urgent, this extra 15 per cent was added to the Russian, Polish and Lithuanian allocation. Branches of the parent organisation were established in every village and town, committees were formed, regular monthly collections instituted and functions and entertainments on a colossal scale were organised in augmentation of the Fund.

By 31 March 1916, twenty four thousand pounds had been collected and forwarded to responsible committees in the stricken areas.

By 30 May 1917, the Fund issued its first printed audited Revenue and Expenditure Accounts for the period 25 February 1915 to 31 March 1917.

The accounts make very interesting reading.

From the inception of the fund to 31 March 1916, the sum of £24,072 15s 1d was collected, and for the next succeeding 12 months the sum of £27,386 6s 6d was collected, making a grand total of £51,459 1s 7d. Of this amount £44,193 14s was sent to Russia and Poland, £5,313 to Palestine, £380 to Belgium and £90 to Alexandria.

The entire cost of collecting administering and despatching this large amount was £423 11s 9d, of which the major portion was spent in postage, printing and bank charges. Salaries amounted to the very modest sum of £355. This must surely be a record for economical and efficient management. The audited accounts are signed by B Alexander, President; I M Goodman, Hon Treasurer; P Cowen, General Secretary; and M Abrahams, Registered Public Accountant, Auditor.

In November 1920, it was announced that the Transvaal Fund had reached £129,843.

Owing to slackening off in the activities of many of the branches, on the initiation of the Doornfontein Branch, a Conference of War Victims Fund Branches was held in Johannesburg, and the connection of the Board of Deputies with the Fund ceased.

But the Conference resulted in a wonderful revival of activities. At the time of the Conference it was reported that 28,000 garments had been collected and shipped overseas for distribution in the war ravaged areas, and in the two years following the Conference an additional £76,604 was collected.

Cape Town

It is of interest at this point to record the progress of the sister fund in the City of Cape Town. The Cape Relief Fund for Jewish War and Pogrom Victims was established in December 1914. The territory over which the Fund had jurisdiction was the Cape Province, excluding Kimberley and district, Port Elizabeth and district, East London and district, and after the first two years, Paarl and district. These centres each had their own organisation and despatched their collections direct to the London Committee.

From December 1914, to 31 December 1920 the sum of £77,835 18s 5d was collected at a total cost of £1,220 3s 10d, truly a remarkable achievement, and a striking proof of self-sacrificing labours on the part of a comparatively small band of workers.

During these six years of the existence of the Fund, the following gentlemen held office: Chairman, Mr Morris Alexander; Vice-chairman, Rabbi M CH Mirvish, Hon Treasurers, Rev B Strod, Dr S E Kark, Mr A Brodie and Mr J Gitlin; Hon Secretaries, J Mirvish, I M Goodman, J Gesundheit and B Chideckel.

The following is a summary of the amount remitted to:

Russia	£39,000 0 0
Roumania	1,000 0 0
Poland and Eastern Europe	19,300 0 0
Palestine	12,150 4 0
Lithuania	2,000 0 0
Salonika	1,000 0 0
Hebrew Schools in the Palestinian Colonies	500 0 0
Russo-Jewish Prisoners of War	400 0 0
Relief of Persian Jews	300 0 0
Students at Basle	50 0 0
Vienna	300 0 0
	£76,000 4 0

In 1919 and 1920, 22,500 garments were collected and sent to Warsaw for distribution to the various stricken areas.

The Fund underwent several changes of name before it became finally merged into the *United South African Jewish Relief Reconstruction and Orphans Fund.* Its first designation was *The Cape Russo-Jewish War Relief Fund,* then *The Relief Fund for Jewish War Victims of British and Allied Nations and Palestinian Jews,* and in 1920 to *The Cape Relief Fund for Jewish War and Pogrom Victims.*

Kfar Yeladim

To the Cape Fund belongs the credit for having formulated the scheme for the establishment of an Orphan Colony in Palestine, which eventually became what is now known as Kfar Yeladim.

In addition to the organisations established in Johannesburg and Cape Town, active committees existed at Kimberley, Port Elizabeth, East London, Durban, Bloemfontein and Rhodesia.

Various attempts were made on the initiative of the Johannesburg Fund to bring the various organisations together, pool their resources, co-ordinate their activities, and generally unite for the good of the common objective. Following much correspondence with the various organisations occupied in similar work throughout South Africa, a Conference of all interested organisations was held in Bloemfontein in August 1922.

At this Conference, *The United South African Jewish Relief Reconstruction and Orphans Fund* came into existence, with headquarters at Johannesburg. All branches of the Transvaal movement and all centres in South Africa affiliated, with the exception of Port Elizabeth and Roodepoort.

Fate of War Orphans

For some time prior to the Bloemfontein Conference the question of the war orphans had agitated the minds of many of the workers, and several of the branches had forwarded resolutions and recommendations on the subject. While most of the workers felt that something should be done specifically for the war and pogrom orphans, there existed three distinct schools of thought on the subject:

(a)   That the orphans should be maintained and cared for at their present towns of residence.

(b)   That a number should be transported to Palestine and maintained there.

(c)   That a number should be brought to South Africa and maintained here.

Eventually all three schemes were in part adopted.

With regard to (a), South African Jewry maintained 2,250 orphans through the agency of the Central Relief Committee in Paris, at the following centres:

1.	Kherson	800 children	(by the United Fund)
2.	Odessa	500 "	(by the United Fund)
3.	Odessa	150 "	(by the Cape Jewish Orphanage)
4.	Tiraspol	300 "	(by the Cape Fund)
5.	Berezovka	100 "	(by Wynberg, CP)
6.	Lvovo	200 "	(by the Cape Fund)
7.	Lvovo	100 "	(by Krugersdorp)
8.	Otchakoff	100 "	(by Pretoria)

The children received food, clothing and medical attendance. In addition to this the United Fund equipped and maintained three hospitals under the control of OZE for a considerable period.

Chaluzim Assisted

The United Fund also remitted relief for the Chaluzim, to the Habin Bureau for Jewish War Sufferers in the Far East, to the Russian Jewish Students' Society in Switzerland, to Jewish sufferers in Japan from earthquake, to Jewish refugees in Romania, to the OZE to the ORT to refugees in Germany, and wherever else an appeal from suffering Jewry emanated.

In November 1922, an appeal was issued by the United Fund for clothing and within a short while 60,000 garments were collected and were carried rail free by the South African Railways and freight free by the Union Castle Steamship Co. The United Fund appointed Mr I Ochberg, of Cape Town as its delegate in the Ukraine, and right worthily did he carry out his mission in the field of relief work.

With regard to (b), after protracted negotiations with the Palestine Orphans' Committee of the American Joint Distribution Committee, and the Waad Leumi, of Palestine, it was ascertained that Russia would not permit the transportation of any more orphans beyond its borders.

The Children's Colony

It, however, transpired that a Mr Belkind had brought to Palestine about 120 children from the Ukraine, and through various causes had found himself stranded with the children. Mr S Hillman, who was at this time on a visit to Palestine, investigated the position on behalf of the United Fund. Eventually the United South African Fund took over 86 of the Belkind children, and 44 children maintained by Durban, making a total of 130, obtained land from the Jewish National Fund in Balfouria erected buildings at an approximate cost of £12,000 and formed a children's colony at Givat Hamoreh.

The United Fund guaranteed the maintenance of the children for five years. Mr Richard Feldman of Johannesburg, while on a visit to Palestine, did yeoman service at the children's colony.

The colony is now known as Kfar Yeladim, and on the closing down of the Relief Fund was handed over to the South African Zionist Federation to be maintained as a children's colony in the name of South African Jewry.

The Local Orphans

The third activity (c) remains to be dealt with.

In Cape Town and in Johannesburg there was a strong body of public opinion in favour of bringing out to South Africa war pogrom orphans principally with a view to their being adopted. The Cape Relief Fund fathered the movement at the Cape, but the scheme was eventually taken over by the Cape Jewish Orphanage. In the Transvaal the idea was taken up with much enthusiasm.

Mr I Ochberg, President of the Cape Jewish Orphanage proceeded to Europe and, at the request of the Committee of the Cape Jewish Orphanage and the Johannesburg Committee, brought with him from the Ukraine about 180 children. About half the number remained at the Cape Jewish Orphanage, and the other half were handed over to Johannesburg.

An arrangement was come to between the Relief Fund and the South African Jewish Orphanage in Johannesburg whereby the Relief Fund allotted £12,500 to the Orphanage to assist them in the purchase of their present building (*Villa Arcadia*). The Johannesburg children therefore became the charges of the Jewish Community of the Transvaal, just as the children at the Cape came under the care and protection of the Cape Jewish Community.

At the Cape an additional building was erected and the advent of the children for a time revived the activities of the United Fund in Johannesburg and brought largely increased funds to the Cape Jewish Orphanage.

Total Amount Collected

At the outbreak of the World War, the Jewish population of South Arica was about 55,000. In 1921 the official figures give 62,000. The Transvaal Fund up to the time of the amalgamation in 1922 collected £206,347 and the Cape about £100,000 making a total of £306,347. In the two years following amalgamation the United Fund collected £55,580 and the nett results of three fetes held in Johannesburg were £24,600. This brings the total up to £386,527. The total amounts collected by the Committees at Durban, Port Elizabeth, Bloemfontein, Kimberley, East London, Bulawayo and Salisbury in all probability exceed £100,000.

It can with all safety be stated that South Africa raised upwards of £500,000 for Jewish relief in the war and pogrom-stricken areas. Thus the relief funds subscribed by South African Jewry averaged over £9 per head of its Jewish population, a record which is hard to believe has been equalled by any other Jewish population in the world.

PART 1
THE 'PALE OF SETTLEMENT'
1914-1922

SECTION 3

ALTER BOBROW AND
THE THREE PINSK ORPHANAGES

This section tells of the three Pinsk Jewish Orphanages
established by Alter Bobrow and his companions in 1917

It was from these three orphanages and other similar established
orphanages that Isaac Ochberg selected children to go to South Africa

These orphanages were supported by
the American Jewish Joint Distribution Committee

Chapter 16 – ALTER BOBROW AND THE PINSK ORPHANS

PINSK ORPHANS 1917-1921
Written by Liebe Klug

In 1883 a son was born to Yachna Obrov and Leib Obrov in Pinsk. He was named Tzadk-Zander, but was never called by that name. The children born before him had died, either in childbirth or infancy. Instead he was known as Alter, the old one, in that way hoping that he would live to be an old man. In fact he died one week short of his 90th birthday. Members of the family and close friends, always called him 'Alter'. In later years he was known in the family as 'Alec', but only on official terms 'Alexander', the English transfer of Tzadek-Zander.

So Alter led the life of a Jewish child in Pinsk in the designated Pale of Settlement. He went to cheder, and to Shul, and when he was older to the Yeshiva. His father Leib, made a living by dealing in futures. Not futures on the stock market as we know it, but futures of the apple crop. Jews were not permitted to own land, so he did the next best thing. Every winter he visited the neighbouring peasant and did a deal with him. He would guess what the apple crop would yield, and offered him a price for the entire crop. In this way he would take a gamble on the possible worms that might enter the apples, a late frost that would kill off the blossom, a high wind that would shake the young immature apples from the trees, or any other misfortune that would ruin his 'futures'. If there was a late frost, Alter and his brother Itzik, would sleep in the orchard and burn smoke pots to keep the frost off the delicate blossoms.

Father Leib though, was also forward thinking in other ways. Alter was devoted to his Yeshiva learning, and it was clear that he was a good and committed scholar. Father Leib wanted his son to have a secular education, to go to Real Schule, a high school, and maybe get a profession at the University in Vilna. He was a far seeing man, and also wanted his son to be freed from the constraints of living in the Pale of Settlement, with its restrictions on movement, land ownership and occupations. A Jew who had a university degree, could get a passport that enabled him to travel and work anywhere.

Alter's father took him out of the Yeshiva and sent him to the Real Schule. Alter was heartbroken. To be enrolled in the Real Schule meant attending on Saturday, the Sabbath, and to Alter, Saturday was the holy day of prayer and contemplation in the synagogue. It was a real wrench for him to leave the Yeshiva, his teachers and his friends.

As a Jew there was a numerus clausus of 5% allowed to enter the university, so Jewish pupils had to achieve even higher grades than the general population. In the event Alter was accepted and studied to become an Analytical chemist. He never spoke about his student days, but was proud of his achievement. As an old man, sorting out papers, he showed me with pride his final degree marks. He achieved 5 for every subject. Every subject was marked out of 5, and that was the highest mark attainable Now as an Analytical Chemist with a new passport, he was allowed to move outside the Pale of Settlement, and took a job on a large sugar estate, where beet

Alexander (Alter) Bobrow –
"His surname was originally "Obrov" But I suppose that the pronunciation became Abrov. Later when papers for travel were issued, there was a mistake, and the name was written as "Bobrov". So to avoid confusion the papers were issued as Obrov-Bobrov! When my father reached Cape Town he dropped "Obrov". So his name became "Bobrow", as did his mother and family."

was grown. What seemed to stay in his mind, when he did talk about it, was the fact that he was allocated his own serf. As a socialist that was repugnant to him. The serf had to look after his every need, and what upset him was that the serf insisted on taking off his boots and cleaning them each night.

Alter went home regularly to his family and his friends in Pinsk. In 1917, the Great War raged, and Pinsk being a border town, received the brunt of the troop movements, back and forth. Germans, White Russian troops, Red Army Troops, devastating and laying waste towns, villages, farms. On this particular visit, he saw that amongst the rubble of what were streets of houses, were wandering young children, without food or shelter, or care. The orphans of the ravages of war. He belonged to a Zionist Socialist Group, and when they met together, suggested and persuaded them to give up their jobs and work together to rescue the children.

So it was. This small group went from street to street collecting the children. There was at first no coherent plan of what to do. However, the children were hungry, so they started a soup kitchen, no doubt helped with supplies from the Jews in the town. It fast became clear that the children had nowhere to go, no clothes, no roof over their heads. There was no going back. A disused Old Aged Home was taken over, and beds from a derelict hospital commandeered. The first Orphanage was formed. Within a few months there were three orphanages in the Pinsk area alone. All funded by the community, and staffed by voluntary workers.

Then there was the next step. What to do with the children during the day? Start a school of course. Not only the children of the orphanage went to the school, children of the town also joined. This is a story I heard from a cousin of Alter's, now living in Hamilton, Canada. She was an old lady then by the time I met her, and had been a much younger cousin. She remembers being very upset in the class, because when my father (who was teaching) asked a question of the class, and she put up her hand to give the answer, he never chose her. Eventually she complained to him. His answer was that she had a mother and a father, so she had no need to be noticed, and given a chance to speak. But for these children who had lost everything, to be noticed by the teacher had great importance.

The ongoing daily care was undertaken by the team of friends, who had collected the children and set up the functioning orphanage. The costs were probably met by the pockets of the Jews of Pinsk. A most important contributor and mainstay was the Jewish American Joint Distribution Committee. It was set up by Henry Morgenthau (later to be chief Secretary to the Treasury in the US) to provide help and rescue to Jews all over the world.

When crisis struck, as it did in the form of an epidemic of typhoid, the children were nursed by those self same rescuers. This story comes from one of the group, Rachel Bramson one of the group of friends, that emigrated to Israel, and who we met on one of our visits there.

There was a typhoid epidemic in the orphanage. We all worked together for weeks, nursing the children ourselves, and had had no time off for weeks. At that time I was engaged to be married, and as a result of the illness had not seen him for quite a long time. I asked your father - Alter, for permission to leave for a few hours. He was outraged and said to me. 'You ask to go out at a time like this!!! How can you!!' Of course I never left the building. He himself nursed the children for weeks, with not even time to go home to sleep. There were no extra beds, so he used to catnap on two chairs put together, and he was quite a tall man. Eventually, Alter caught typhoid and went home to be nursed by his mother. The children were quite upset by his absence. So, we devised a plan. We took them in groups to his mother's house, put a step ladder up against the wall, he was in an attic room, and one by one the children went up to give him a little wave, and he waved back. Having seen so much death, many of them saw their parents killed before their eyes, that to

have a surrogate father figure disappear must have disturbed them greatly.

Eventually Alter came back. The children were overjoyed. He took up his mandolin, and played. They formed a circle round him and danced, calling out 'Alter Alter Alter' as they skipped and hopped round him'.

Alter Bobrov gave an interview for the 50th Anniversary of the Cape Jewish Orphanage - Oranjia.

'So many children were found that soon we were obliged to set up three orphanages. At first Pinsk was isolated by the fighting, and we were thrown almost solely on our own resources. We had neither beds, bedding, nor clothes. I remember our using flour bags to make aprons and other garments for the boys and girls. At one time in the course of my duties, I had to walk through the streets in which shells were bursting. Balachou a notorious Ukrainian fanatic descended on the city with his gangs and the pogroms raged for nearly a week.'

When order was restored, supplies began to arrive first from the Juedischer Hilfsverein u Berlin, and then from the Joint Distribution Committee, including cocoa, condensed milk, cooking oil and milk. The entire area was in a state of furor. Rival armies were fighting for control, the Red Army against the Whites, as well as Allied contingents and unorganised guerilla bands. Law and order had broken down, transportation came to an end. The condition of Jews which had never been good, deteriorated even more. Famine, as well as diseases followed over most of the area. Pogroms were reported almost daily. The question arose - what to do to help the orphaned children?

By 1921 the Cape Jewish Orphanage was set up and functioning. The committee had heard of the plight of the Jewish Orphans in the Pale of Settlement and decided to help.

Contact was made with Dr Jochelman, President of the Federation of Ukrainian Jews in Britain offering help. The Prime Minister of South Africa, General J C Smuts and Mr Patrick Duncan, Minister of the Interior agreed to allow any children permission to land in South Africa. Isaac Ochberg proposed that the Cape Jewish orphanage be responsible for bringing the children out and taking care of them. A South African Relief Fund for Jewish War victims was already in operation and in less than a week £25 000 was pledged and a larger amount in due course was raised.

Isaac Ochberg offered to go to Europe to make the arrangements and to bring the children back to Cape town. He proceeded from town to town Minsk, Pinsk, Stanislav, Lodz, Lemberg, and Wlodowa.... The conditions in the area was dire, with pogroms an almost daily event. The children and their carers relied for their survival on the American Joint Jewish Committee.

The difficulty would be how to choose 200 children from amongst the several thousand being cared for in the orphanages. Only full orphans, that is those that had lost both parents were selected, and those who were healthy in mind and body. The selection was made in consultation with the Principal and Matron of each orphanage.

Alter Bobrov, was asked to accompany the children and stay for six months in Oranjia, as the orphanage in Cape town was named, with the children to help them to settle in. The children were issued with group passports with group photographs of 20-30 children.

I never heard of the journey directly from my father, but knew from bits and pieces that emerged from other people. They travelled first to Warsaw, where all the children from the different orphanages were collected, and then on to Danzig, where they boarded a boat to England. In London there was a shelter for any travelling Jews, who were immigrating to other countries. There the children waited until they embarked on the *Edinburgh Castle* in September 1921.

Many many years later, in Cape Town in 1968 where I was visiting for the funeral of my mother, I had a surprising graphic account of the journey to Danzig. It was high summer, and to cool off, it was customary to walk in the evening on a promenade by the sea, in a suburb of Cape Town called Sea Point. I was walking with my father. Due to the vagaries of immigration officials, his name was now Bobrow, Alexander. Still though called by his family, Alter, and the young members of the family, Uncle Alex. A man came up to us and said 'You don't remember me do you?' My father shook his head. 'I am one of the orphans who you saved in Pinsk, and brought to South Africa.' Then he went on: 'I well remember the journey from Pinsk. The train stopped at the little stations. The Jews had heard of the children from the orphanages and that they were being taken to South Africa. At each stop we were met with fruit and food and flowers. You Mr Bobrov, got down from the train with the children, and your mandolin. Together with those that greeted us, we sang and danced together with them, led by your mandolin.' He took my father's hand and shook it warmly, and went on his walk.

Over the years, I did hear a little of the journey on the *Edinburgh Castle*. My father had 60 of the children in his care. Twenty two from the orphanage in Pinsk that he and friends had started. Some had been severely traumatised by their experiences, having seen their parents killed before their eyes. Now having to cope with new circumstances and the unknown. There were many times when he brought children beset by nightmares, into his cabin and looked after them through the night.

The children were met by a warm and welcoming reception at Cape Town docks. For Alexander Bobrow, having once seen and lived in Cape Town there was no going back to Pinsk. Although he could not practice as an Analytical Chemist and could not afford to retake the South African examinations. When his contract with the orphanage expired, he lived in a little shack by the sea in a hamlet called Bakoven (it still exists) and grew his own fruit and vegetables. For a small sum he looked after a spastic child. He was always considerate to his parents and family in Pinsk and sent money regularly, which they saved. In 1934, they were able, with the money saved and his

intervention, join him in Cape Town. His father had unfortunately died in 1929.

There was another consequence of Alter's arrival in Cape Town. The policy in Oranjia, was not only to educate the orphan children, but also provide them with the means with which to earn a living when they were old enough to leave. To this end my mother Annie Gamsu (always called Channa, by close friends and members of the family) was employed to teach the girls dressmaking. One of her pupils was a beautiful 18 year old called Golda, with whom my mother became very friendly. She had been one of the orphans found and rescued by my father. Golda introduced my parents to each other, and five years later they were married. Golda was a bridesmaid, and the wedding photo is on the wall of my house.

Extract from "An Episode in the History of the Cape Jewish Orphanage" *Written by Jonathan Boiskin*

Ochberg had managed to secure helpers; a teacher named Alexander Bobrow, Boris Glasman and his wife, and a Miss Bettman.

Alexander Bobrow, one of Ochberg's helpers, was originally an Analytical Chemist in a sugar factory, but the war had turned him to social work in 1916, and he began to help the Jewish refugees in Pinsk. 'So many children were found,' Bobrow recorded, 'that we soon were obliged to set up three separate orphanages. At first Pinsk was isolated by the fighting and we were thrown almost solely on our own resources. We had neither beds, bedding, nor clothes. I remember using flour bags to make aprons and other garments for the boys and girls.'

Typhus broke out in one of these orphanages, and at one stage Bobrow, in the course of his duties, was compelled to walk through streets in which shells were exploding. Balachou, the notorious Ukrainian fanatic, descended on the city with his gangs and the pogroms they instigated raged for nearly a week. As order was restored, supplies began to arrive.

From the notes of Linda Press Wulf who interviewed Fanny Lockitch (Feyga Schrier)

In charge of *the Pinsk* orphanage was a giant of the Ochberg story, Mr Bobrow, who had been sent by Jewish organizations to Pinsk to help Jewish refugees in 1916, giving up his career as an Analytical Chemist in a sugar factory. He was put in charge of three orphanages in Pinsk, working with virtually no beds, bedding, food, clothes, or coal. At one point they made large aprons and other garments out of flour bags. A German Jewish welfare organization and then the Joint Distribution Committee were eventually able to send some supplies; cocoa, condensed milk, cooking oil.

When Mr. Ochberg finally gathered his 200 orphans, having spent three hazardous months travelling "through almost every village in the Polish Ukraine and Galicia, etc," Mr Bobrow accompanied him in taking care of the orphans on the way to South Africa, and he remained in South Africa for *many* years.

Written by Fanny Lockitch (Feyga Schrier)

Isaac Ochberg didn't know all the languages there. Although the First World War was over and the Russian Revolution was over, the fighting went on and the forests were infested with bandits and he went into the deep forests. He didn't know where he was going and believe me if we did not get together and notice all that and we said to daddy Ochberg, you are not going that way, and we begged the people that were helping him to engage somebody who knew the languages and we engaged a man. His name was Bobrov. He spoke seven different languages, seven languages spoken in Russia. He died in England at the age of 93 years.

He left from here to England afterwards. He used to play the ukelele, I'll never forget it, to us to sleep on the boat because a lot of the children use to get sea sick so that's how he used to get us to sleep.

LETTERS AND MESSAGES FROM ORPHANS AND COLLEAGUES LEFT BEHIND IN THE PINSK ORPHANAGES

Liebe Klug has exercise books, given to her father, from the three Pinsk Orphanages from which Ochberg Orphans were selected. These are exercise books with messages from the children and colleagues left behind.

These booklets are very special as many of the children would have perished in the Holocaust just 20 years later. Here are some of the letters.

PAGE 101

Be strong and of good courage
May they live!
Our brothers and our sisters who travel to Africa
Hoorah hoorah hoorah

In everlasting memory from the Hashamer Hastair Scouts
Pinsk – Orphanage Two
Rosensberg

PAGE 4

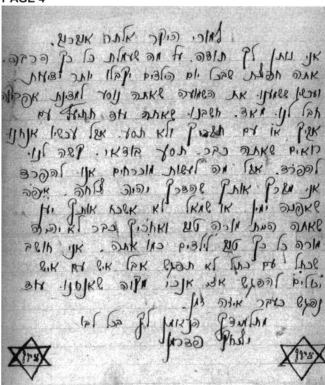

To my dear teacher Alter Abrov

I give my thanks to you for working so hard. You always wanted the children to acquire more and more knowledge every day and now we have heard that you are going to Africa. We are very sorry. We thought that you might still discuss things with your father and friends and would not go. But now we know for sure that you are going away.
It is difficult to say goodbye but what can we do – we have to say goodbye. I bless you and wish you a good trip.
Wherever I shall turn to the right or to the left, I will never forget you and will never find a teacher as good as you.
I think that one wall with another wall will never meet. But one person with another person has a chance to meet. So I hope that one day we shall meet.

Your faithfully [with all my heart]
Student Itzhak Federman

Letters translated by Rifka Gabbay

PAGE 24

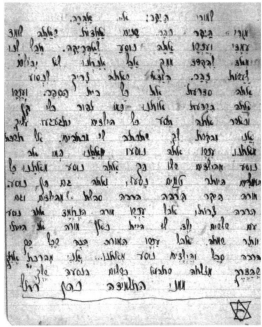

To my dear teacher A Abrov

Dear Teacher

You have taught us for many years and now you are going away to Africa. We are really sorry to say goodbye to you, but that is how it is. We can't change things. You have to leave. You, who have established the whole school, you are leaving us. We feel like a bird without a nest. All the children will miss you very much.

Please write to us and don't forget us. You are going away and we feel as if a father is leaving his children.

The good teachers have left and now you are also going.

Dear teacher you have suffered a lot from the children. You had a lot of trouble and now you are going together with 30 children. If you stayed here I would be much happier and now the teacher who suffered so much from the children is going away.

I wish you a good trip and a safe arrival at your destination.

From me, your student

Rachel Cohen

PAGE 26

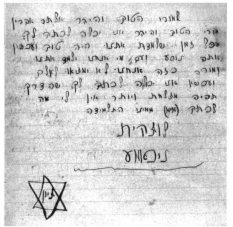

To my good and dear teacher Alter Abrov

My good dear teacher

I just wanted to tell you that as long as you taught us we had a good time and now you are going away.

Who will teach us? A teacher like you we will never find.

Now I want to write to you to wish you a good trip and there is nothing more I can say.

From your student

Nechama Lutzkit

PAGE 115

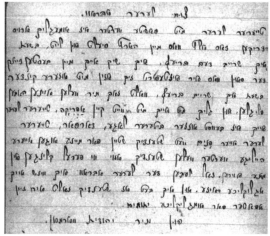

To the teacher Abrov

Dear Teacher, it is impossible to express in simple words the feeling I have in my heart while writing this letter.

I send you my greatest thanks and gratitude for taking an interest in our children.

As I am writing this letter I wish I had wings and could fly with you to far away Africa.

Dear teacher, you are aware of our bitter situation. Your face will always be in front of my eyes and your words will – like pearls – ring in my ears. May you live a long life. I wish you a good and blessed journey and I wish and hope that you will always be a father to unhappy orphans.

From me

Yehudith Wurman

PAGE 45

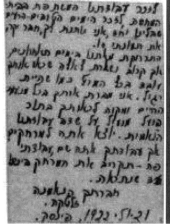

In memory of our common work in the house of shelter. In memory of our good days and bad days that we spent together, I give you, my dear friend, this photo of mine. In the last few days you seemed to be far away in your mind but you remained close to those who saw you working energetically and hard as you always used to.

I bless you with all the good things life has to offer and hope to see you continuing your useful nationalistic work. You are leaving to a far away land. But your work there and my work here will shorten the distance between us until we see each other again.

Your faithful friend
Zlatka
Pinsk 21st July 1922

PAGES 56 and 57

In memory
I just remember when I came from Poland I had nowhere to go. I didn't have a place to stay even for one night. Someone took me to the barracks and from there to Bagidel and there I wandered around for five months. They started building an orphanage and there was a teacher Abrov and he took me to that orphanage. He did not sleep day and night. He ran around to find a piece of bread to give me to eat. You were like a father to me and I did not feel lonely anymore. You were so dedicated and now you are leaving and I will be lonely again. I have a lot more to write but I can't express myself because my heart is very sad.

Be well, dear teacher Abrov
From me Gishe Gutshorbat

PAGES 67 - 69
Honourable teacher and best head master, when you were here with us we knew we had someone to care for us. But now when the time has come and you are saying goodbye to all our children you can imagine, dear headmaster, how horrible we feel in our heart. We feel even worse than before we first came to the orphanage.

We know well who established the orphanage. First G-d, then you together with Mr Goldsman. It is well known that no one was interested in the fate of the miserable suffering orphans. But G-d had pity on the poor lonely souls and sent two angles from heaven to help the unhappy orphans. It was a terrible time; no person wanted to go out into the street, the frost burnt like fire, the winds were howling and no one had pity on our orphans. Only two men had pity on us. They brought us back to life.

The streets were dangerous, bullets were flying over head and few people came to the orphanage, but the teachers Mr Abrov and Mr Goldsman were fearless, they ran around in an effort to bring something to put in the mouths' of the unhappy orphans in order to save them from hunger and keep their poor souls alive. We are deeply grateful for everything you have done for us. We wish you a good trip and everything you wish for yourself.

Before we were taken into the orphanage we're swimming in deep water with no shore in sight no one had pity on us only two men, Mr Abrov and Mr Holsman and saved us from death.

And now the day has come when we have to say goodbye you can quite well imagine how terrible we feel. If we had a problem we came for advice to our best friend but now that you depart we feel so terribly sad and so bitter.

We trust that when you arrive safely to your destination you will plead for us. We wish you a good trip and arrive safely, in good health.

Remember us
from me Ceril Supoznik
To our most faithful headmaster
Alten Abrov
5 July 1921

PAGE 85

I send this photo as a souvenir,
When you hold this photo you will know that you have a friend forever in a far away land – me Rosa Tsiz
I wish you a good trip and a safe arrival

From me – Rosa Tsiz

Letters translated by Rifka Gabbay

Chapter 17 – THE THREE PINSK ORPHANAGES

This chapter is copied from the website set up by Brian Fine www.ochbergorphans.com with his permission. Brian's father Jack Feinschmidt, was an Ochberg Orphan. I understand that most of the information in this chapter is from Liebe Klug, Alexander Bobrow's Daughter.

Alexander (Alter) Bobrow, a true hero of the Jewish People, established three orphanages in Pinsk and it was from these orphanages that Isaac Ochberg selected some of the children that he brought out to South Africa.

The Chief Rabbi of the British Empire declared:
" 1,000,000 human beings had been butchered and that for three years 3,000,000 persons in the Ukraine had been made 'to pass through the horrors of hell.' He said there were something like 600,000 homeless children, 150,000 orphans and 35,000 double orphans in the Ukraine who would die from cold, hunger or disease unless Jewish hearts remained human and came to the rescue."

PINSK 1917.

The year was 1917. The towns of the Pale of Settlement suffered from repeated incursions of White Russia Troops and Red Russia forces and was now occupied by the German army. Pinsk was cut off from the outside world.

Alexander Bobrow, known to friends as Alter was returning home to visit his family in Pinsk from the sugar estate where he was employed as an analytical Chemist.

As he travelled nearer to his home town he could see far and wide, how streets, homes and buildings had been razed to the ground. In the rubble he could see little figures moving, sitting or lying. Not trusting what he saw, he got down from the bus and walked through the devastation to his home.

ESTABLISHING THREE ORPHANAGES

Alter belonged to a Poale Zion Group and on his initiative, and at his insistence and with his example they all left their jobs to help.

Their big task was to walk from place to place and area to area, literally collecting children one by one from the wreckage which was their homes. Many had seen their parents, and in some cases, their entire families killed before their eyes.

Alexander Bobrow with a group of orphans

Once they were all assembled, it was obvious that without exception the children were starving. With the generous help of

the townspeople, a soup kitchen was started, to feed the children. Once regularly fed the next question was what to do with them? The answer was, to start a school.

The next question, where could the children sleep? Back in the rubble of their homes? No, of course not. The group commandeered a disused Old Aged Home and found beds in an empty hospital. The building was cleaned and disinfected. The first Pinsk Orphanage received their children

Within two years there were three orphanages in Pinsk alone. You see, the story of the Ochberg Orphans, is not complete. There is another story, an earlier story. Most of these stories came to me from either orphans or their saviours as I think of them. My father was Alter Bobrow, and he rarely talked of this remarkable endeavour. However many of the Poale Zion Group made Aliyah to Israel. One Rachel Bramsonrecca recalled the dedication of this group, and said that it was the spiritually strong leaders that were able to keep them all relational. They literally parented the children.

TYPHOID

They fed the children, clothed them, taught them and nursed them when an epidemic of Typhoid struck the area. Alter was there night and day. He never left the building and napped on two chairs put together. There were no free beds.

Eventually he succumbed to the illness and went home to be nursed by his mother.

The children were devastated and they panicked that he might die as did their parents. So a plan was devised. All the children, with a step ladder went to Alters family's home. His bedroom was in the attic. Then one by one every child climbed the ladders to peep in at the window where Alter lay in bed. To each one he waved. The children were reassured that Alter as they called him, was alive.

When Alter returned, the children were overjoyed and showed it by making a circle and dancing around him singing Alter,

Alter, Alter. And he, as was his way played the mandolin to them as they danced and sang together.

THE JOURNEY

Events then took an unexpanded turn and Alter was asked to accompany the children selected by Isaac Ochberg to go to South Africa.

In fact, the Orphanages Committee would only allow the children to leave if Alter accompanied them. Of course no one wanted him to leave; not his family, not the children or his colleagues. Notwithstanding their pleading he decided to go to Cape Town with the chosen children.

The children who were not chosen to go to South Africa with him, expressed their feelings in notes and drawings in three black school exercise books.

A MEETING ON THE SEA POINT PROMENADE
Written by Liebe Klug, Alexander Bobrow's Daughter

Many years ago, when I was on a visit to Cape Town following the death of my mother, my father and I were walking one evening on the Sea Point promenade.

A middle aged man came up to us and said. "You don't know me do you'?" My father said that he had no idea who he was.

I will quote you what this man said. "I was one of the orphans you saved, and I was one of the children chosen to go to Cape Town."

"I will never forget that journey. We were travelling by train to Danzig. The train stopped at stations on the way. At each station we were greeted by the Jews of the town with food and flowers. We the children got down from the train. Alter took his mandolin and together with the townspeople we all sang and danced together on the platform."

Whether this is the exact picture of the events we will never know. But what remains in this man's memory is that the journey was made a joyous one for the children.

POST CARD ALTER WROTE TO HIS PARENTS
THE NIGHT BEFORE HE LEFT PINSK.

My dearest parents,

Forgive me if I have caused you heart break. I am not responsible that my thoughts are not your thoughts.
Do not worry that I am going away. I am travelling. on a great and important mission. I hope that I will still have the possibility to repay you for all the good things that you have done for me.
Have no regrets over your son, who is devoted to you with his whole heart.

Alter

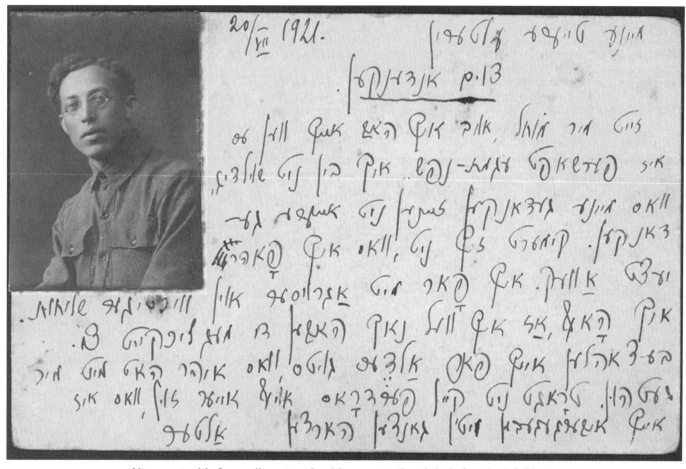

Alter wrote this farewell postcard to his parents the night before he left Pinsk,.

TWO OF THE LETTERS FROM THE EXERCISE BOOKS WRITTEN TO ALTER
BY THE CHILDREN WHO REMAINED BEHIND.

To Teacher Avrav –
Dearest teacher in memory
In the last days before your travel away you brought all the orphans together. You don't know what an impression you made on us.
God knows when we will see you again. When you are gone what will happen to us?
You have taken us out of the water and now we are back in the water.
Dear teacher you have been like a teacher and Father for two years that you were with us.
We have thrived like a plant and now we only hope that we will continue to thrive.
I wish you 'lucky' safe trip from me.
Shaska Dawidowsky
Year 1921

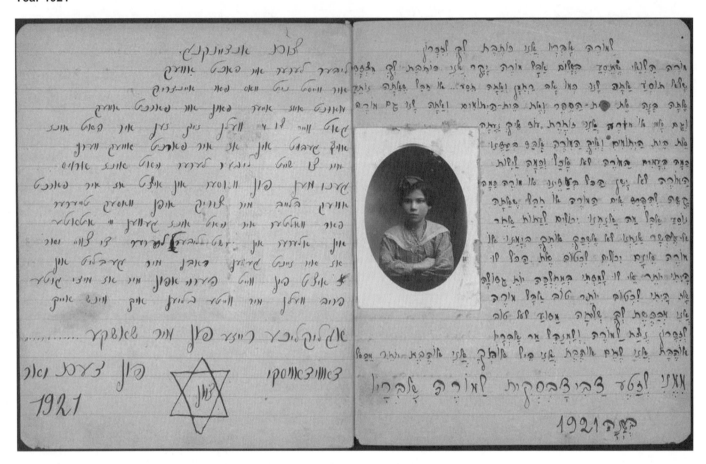

I'm writing in 'memory' (souvenir) to you.

Teacher I hope you travel in peace, but dear teacher I'm writing to say I'm sorry you are going.
You are like a Father but you have also built the school and the orphanage and you are also our teacher.
I know you have not slept or often not eaten for our sake.
How hard it was to separate from our teacher and 'benevolent' Father.
Sorry that you are leaving, but what can we do?
We will not forget you in all our days. I can't write as well as my learning is not enough. I'm sorry.
But dear teacher and Principal Mr Avrav whom I love more than ever.

From me Zeta Davidowsky
In the Year 1921

The letters were written in Yiddish and Hebrew and have been translated by octogenarian Old Arc Boys;
Eli Zagoria, an artist living in Perth and Michael Perry Kotzen an actor living in Sydney.

Photos of two of the three Pinsk Orphanages

PART 1
THE 'PALE OF SETTLEMENT'
1914-1922

SECTION 4
ISAAC OCHBERG AND THE OCHBERG ORPHANS

Many articles have been written about Isaac Ochberg,
the representative of the South African Jewish Community's
SA Jewish Relief, Reconstruction and Orphans Fund,
and the 181 Ukrainian War and Pogrom Orphans
rescued in 1921 and transported to South Africa.

While this volume contains several versions of this most heroic and
outstanding historical event in South African Jewish History,
there are two most authoritive articles, both titled
"The Ochberg Orphans" written by Johnathan Boiskin and
Lionel Slier respectively, and published in the preceding two
volumes; *100 years of Arc Memories* and *More Arc Memories*

Chapter 18 – INTRODUCTION TO THE POGROM ORPHANS 1921-1922

Written by Bertha I Epstein, the daughter of Isaac Ochberg, in THIS WAS A MAN, Cape Town, 1974

By 1920 when the whole of Eastern Europe was being involved in revolution and counter-revolution the Jews were helpless victims of pogroms and other atrocities.

When the stories infiltrated into South Africa my Father was torn with the agony of his luckless Jewish brethren and he yearned with every fibre of his being to find some means of helping them. He was fully determined that there must be something constructive he could do to alleviate the misery.

To this end he made up his mind that, come what may, he would somehow or other get to the Ukraine. Under prevailing conditions this was an extremely hazardous idea but, risky as it was, he planned very carefully against possible failure.

His first thought and concern was for the hundreds of destitute and abandoned parentless children who were known to be wandering in that area, even hiding in the forests and foraging in every conceivable place for anything they could find to eat.

He therefore approached the Union Government for permission to bring as many Jewish orphans as he could gather together in Eastern Europe to this country for settlement.

After many protracted consultations with the authorities, with the backing of many influential people of whom General Smuts was one, he was finally granted permission to bring 200 Jewish orphans to South Africa on the condition that the entire Jewish community made themselves responsible for the project and that at no time would these children become a burden to the state. This was a tremendous concession but it necessitated his travelling personally all over the country to every town and village no matter how remote to gain their support both morally and financially. It involved travelling by train, car, or any other available transport to any place where there were Jewish people. He made impassioned appeals from public platforms and in private, begging every Jew and Jewess to come forward with help whether in the form of money, clothing, food etc. But most important of all, he pleaded for offers of adoption of individual children into private homes where they would be able to receive loving care. Fund-raising efforts of every possible kind were organised by all sections of the Jewish community of South Africa, from Cape Town up to South West Africa.

My Father had himself photographed with the children at the Jewish Orphanage; it was made into a postcard and sent to every member of every congregation as a New Year greeting card. The message on it took the form of an appeal which read as follows:

"**With the compliments of the President and the Committee of the Cape Jewish Orphanage.**
May the divine Father of the orphans grant your heart's desire for the coming Holy festivals. May you lend a sympathetic ear to the appeal of the orphans in our midst, as well as to the heart-rending cry of the helpless little ones in the pogrom areas

With Compliments from the President and Committee of the Cape Jewish Orphanage.
May the Divine Father of the Orphans grant your heart's desires for the coming Holy Festivals and may you lend a sympathetic ear to the appeal of the Orphans in our midst as well as to the heartrending cry of the helpless little ones in the Pogrom Areas of Eastern Europe for whom we are making ourselves responsible, by donating liberally during the New Year and Day of Atonement for the upkeep of those who are parentless, homeless and helpless

of Eastern Europe. Make yourselves responsible for them by donating liberally during the New Year and the Day of Atonement for those who through no fault of their own are parentless, homeless and helpless."

He was prepared to bear much of the necessary expenses himself, whilst the Jewish Orphanages both in Cape Town and Johannesburg undertook to give the children shelter and attention when they arrived and for as long as it was needed, but he could not undertake this stupendous task without the whole-hearted support of the entire Jewish community.

The response in most cases was immediate and very encouraging, but not everyone was in accord with his ideas and he frequently had to fight hard to overcome opposition. Finally after many months of continuous travel around the country, he felt that he could embark on his proposed errand of mercy secure in the knowledge that he had the necessary support.

Isaac left Cape Town on March 18th, 1921 for London where further complicated arrangements had to be made for his sojourn in Russia, the transport of the children from Europe to South Africa and temporary shelter for them when they broke their journey in England.

His only hope of entering Russia without risking dire consequences was to travel under the aegis of the great Dr Nansen. This was the world-famous explorer who had become an humanitarian and was himself doing similar work as my Father. With his special 'Nansen Passport', issued only to people doing bona fide relief work, he left London on May 18th for Warsaw in Poland. The wording of this document reads:

Whereas an agreement in regard to relief in Russia was signed in Moscow on the 27th August, 1921 between Mr Georges Tchitcherin, peoples commissary for the foreign affairs of the Russian Socialist Federative Soviet Republic, and Doctor Nansen, High Commissioner for Russian relief, appointed by the Geneva Conference, and whereas under the terms of this agreement a committee should be formed consisting of a representative of Dr Nansen and a representative of the Soviet government and whereas Dr Fridtjof Nansen in virtue of the power conferred upon him has appointed John Gorvin to be his representative on the international Russian Relief Committee, now therefore Mr John Gorvin requests the Soviet Government to extend to Mr Isaac Ochberg, delegate du Comité Exécutif de la Conférence Universelle Juive de Secours, which is working under the Tchitcherin-Nansen agreement and in co-operation with the International Russian Relief Committee in Moscow, all the privileges and facilities granted by the Soviet Government and contained in the said agreement signed in Moscow on the 27th August 1921. All civil and military authorities in Russia are requested to give the said Mr Ochberg all help and protection. His person is inviolable and therefore the authorities of the Government Political Administration (G.P.U.) are asked to extend to him all possible protection and assistance. Mr Ochberg has the right of free movement in Russia.

It bears Isaac's photo and signature and is written both in English and Russian. It was absolutely in- valuable. He was at that time the first British Jew to be granted the right of free travel in Russia.

Photo and signature of Isaac Ochberg

During the whole of June and July he was moving from one devastated village to another, travelling by wagon or truck or any other means of transport which he could hire or commandeer. In this way he picked up the children wherever they were to be found, and in ones, two and threes, or more when possible, he took them to the special depôts where he had people waiting to take care of the children, whom he had specifically engaged for the purpose.

Most of the children were in a shocking state. They were starving, clad in rags and verminous. Many of them were ill from the trauma of the horrible experiences which they had had, and many were still in a state of shock from seeing their parents murdered before their eyes or having to watch their mothers and sisters being raped. Apart from all these horrors, typhus, cholera and smallpox were rampant, and my Father himself had to take every possible precaution to protect himself.

His life was in danger all the time, and if anything happened to him the whole project would have to be abandoned.

By August 1st he had gathered together as many as he could, and then came the tragic and heartbreaking task of having to select those who could be taken with him and those who had to be left behind. One thing he was meticulously careful about and that was never to separate or break up a family. If it was possible to bring brothers and sisters he did so; if not, rather than divide a family he had, most unhappily and reluctantly, to leave them.

Having performed his grim task, he left Warsaw with the 200 selected children and made his way with them to Danzig. There a ship which he had chartered was waiting to transport them to England. It was a small freighter called the 'Baltabor'.

He also took several older boys and girls, making them tutors and nurses as this was the only way they could legitimately be included.

On their arrival in London the children were clothed and fed by various Jewish institutions and taken care of whilst Isaac finalized arrangements with the Union Castle Company for their transport to South Africa.

On his arrival in London he had been extensively interviewed by the English press and here are some extracts:

Question:	What is the object of your visit to London?
Answer:	My object in coming to London was to see the High Commissioner of South Africa, also the Executive of the Federation of Ukrainian Jews with whom I have been in correspondence for some time.
Question:	What are the main proposals of your scheme?
Answer:	We shall invite every suitable Jewish family to adopt at least one child. (In South Africa) Those who cannot do so are asked to provide support for the children when they are kept in the Cape Jewish Orphanage or the Jewish Orphanage in Johannesburg.
Question:	Have you the support of the Union Government:
Answer:	I am happy to say that our Government has given us every possible help. Sir Thomas Watt, the Minister of the Interior has, on behalf of the Government, most readily given his permission to bring pogrom or war orphans to South Africa.
Question:	Is there any anti-Semitism in the Union?
Answer:	No, there is practically none. Jews play their rightful part in public life and readily support non-Jewish funds, such as the Governor-General's Fund (for war relief) or the University funds.

On September 2nd 1921 he set sail on the Edinburgh Castle together with his 200 wretched but more hopeful children. Everything had been most confusing for them so the voyage was a welcome chance for rest and recuperation. By now all the 200 children were calling him 'Daddy Ochberg' and most of them were reluctant to move away from him. They clustered around him like the proverbial lost sheep.

On September 19th the Edinburgh Castle with its strange load of human refuse sailed into Table Bay docks to be greeted by a tumultuous horde of hundreds of weeping, cheering people. The quay was lined with men and women anxiously waiting to welcome the waifs they had helped to rescue from oblivion.

How happy my Father must have been to see the welcome 'his' children were getting. In the difficult and troublesome days of the early twenties in those devastated areas it was at great personal risk that he had ventured into his self-imposed task of bringing succour to his oppressed people who might otherwise have been left to perish miserably, but for him it had brought its own reward.

To him Israel Zangwill's words 'Remember that in these wan creatures runs the blood that is your own', proved a veritable clarion call. Boldly and fearlessly he had set about the task that he conceived to be his bounden duty.

When the children disembarked they were immediately taken to 'Oranjia' (the Cape Jewish Orphanage) where the committee ladies had prepared the dormitories for their arrival. Everything was done to make them comfortable and as happy as was possible. Most of them, naturally, were confused and homesick; many of them were still ill, but they were medically attended to and nursed. The entire Jewish community rallied round and everyone was only too willing to lend a hand.

Soon the children adjusted themselves to their new living conditions and the allocation took place of those that were to go to Johannesburg to 'Arcadia', the Jewish Orphanage there, whilst those who had been offered adoption were given over to the people taking them into their homes. My Father had gone to endless trouble to investigate these homes beforehand so that he was as sure as it was possible to be that they would not be square pegs in round holes. Most of the adoptions proved very successful, and there were only a few isolated cases of misfits.

Over the years these children grew up to be worthy South African citizens and some of the boys gave their lives fighting with the Army in World War II.

It must have been a source of immense gratification to my Father to see them being loved and cared for and educated. To the end of his days they called him 'Daddy Ochberg', turned to him for advice and help, and when he died it was a great personal sorrow to them. Even now, greybeards and grandparents as most of them are, they say 'Kadish' for him and bless his memory. (The prayer for the departed.)

When he at last recovered from the stress and rigours of his experiences with the pogrom orphans, the hordes of homeless starving Jews whom he had seen wandering about hopelessly in Eastern Europe returned to haunt him. He felt he could not rest until he had tried to help them. To this end, he arranged a return visit to the Ukraine and went there again in 1922. This time he represented the French 'Conférence Universelle Juive de Secours' as well as the English 'Fund for the Relief of the Jewish victims of the war in Eastern Europe.'

He had attempted again to get permission from the Soviet Government to remove more Jewish orphans, but they were adamant in their refusal to allow any more Russian children to come under 'bourgeois' influence. I have a cutting from an Odessa newspaper, dated 28th December 1922, of which the translation reads as follows:

THE WORKER WILL NOT ALLOW THE BOURGEOISIE TO BRING UP HIS CHILDREN

The Government Committee has lately refused the director of the Children's Home in Cape Town, South Africa, burger Isaac Ochberg, who came to Odessa for the purpose of taking 50 children to the Cape Town Children's Home. The Government Committee has ratified this refusal, showing thereby that the worker will not allow the Bourgoisie to bring up his children.

Obviously there was little he could do to change this so instead he set about opening soup kitchens where the destitute could be fed and clothed with whatever was available.

It was middle of winter, bitterly cold, and there was widespread distress. Typhus was still raging, and once again he had to take excessive precautions to protect himself from contamination. Nevertheless he travelled undeterred through the ravaged and stricken areas distributing huge quantities of food, clothing and medical supplies. There is no doubt that he was instrumental in saving the lives of countless thousands, for without his timely assistance things would have been far worse and even more harassing for those unfortunate people.

Returning to London from his second mission in February, 1923, Isaac was acclaimed far and wide by his fellow Jews as well as many non-Jews for his humane work of alleviation of the distressing conditions in Eastern Europe. Receptions were held in his honour, presentations of illuminated addresses acknowledging his work were made, and many great and famous people paid him homage. One tribute the Ochberg family and its offspring will always treasure is signed by some of the most revered and illustrious Jewish names. Among them are the then Chief Rabbi of the British Commonwealth, the Rev J H Hertz, Lionel de Rothschild, OBE, the Right Honourable Lord Swaythling, Claude Montefiore, Otto Schiff, Charles de Sebag Montefiore and Sir Stewart Samuel. Not least among these tributes is a letter written by one of his own orphans, to 'Daddy Ochberg', laboriously done in English and with some remarkably erratic spelling!

He had the added satisfaction to be able to report to the committee of the Cape Jewish Orphanage, when he returned to Cape Town in May 1923, that under the auspices of the Jewish World Relief conference he had established a permanent food kitchen in Odessa able to feed and care for 150 children, which was to be maintained and supported by the Orphanage.

There must by now be many thousands of people who have benefitted by his generosity and thoughtfulness and have reason to bless his memory. If ever a human being has earned peace and repose in the after-life, he has.

I hope I will be forgiven if I say that Isaac was, in my opinion, the type of man born once in a generation. His magnificent service to the cause of humanity will long continue to be a fragrant memory to those who have benefitted by his munificence, and to those who will still continue to do so for many, many years. Generations have been influenced by his work, and many have followed his example.

For such as he are the salt of the earth, and there could be no higher praise than that.

Verily, as it is inscribed on his tombstone:

He was a good South African and a great Jew.

Isaac's tombstone in Cape Town

Isaac Ochberg

THE RESCUE OF THE UKRAINIAN POGROM ORPHANS

This chapter has been incorporated into a Hebrew booklet of published by Keren Kayemet Le'Israel (Jewish National Fund)

The rescue of 200 children, orphans of the Ukrainian pogroms, is, without a doubt, one of the most glorious chapters in the life of Isaac Ochberg.

But 'We will not allow the bourgeois Ochberg to take from here the children of the working class', shouted labour leaders at party meetings.

'The government refused to permit the bourgeois Ochberg, director of an institution for orphans in South Africa, to remove from here 50 children and take them to South Africa, so giving its sanction to the principle that the workers will not allow bourgeois to educate children of the working class', wrote a newspaper in Odessa on 22 December 1922.

'Children of the working class' are Jewish orphans, victims of fate, sick, starved, dressed in rags.

'An uncle of ours is looking for 'our' orphans and it is said that he wants to take them to his faraway land', thus went the rumour in the streets of Odessa and Kiev.
'Who is he that we should believe him?'

They even knew that his name was Isaac, son of Aaron, and that he was very rich. 'The damned Jews have all the luck; other Jews take care of them', so said the jealous Christian orphans.

That was in the early 1920s in Europe, war was over, but not so in the Ukraine and southern Russia where all continued to make war against all.

The fighting had been going on for seven years already, between Germans, Poles, 'Red' and 'White' Cossacks, the armies of Skoropedesky and Petliura, the gangs of Bentke-Machno and ordinary robbers. Cities and towns went from the control of one to another, each new 'ruler' incited violence against the Jews, and the number of Jewish orphans grew. Not only starving Jewish orphans wandered from place to place. Also millions of adults were slaughtered or died of hunger.

Some children were able to escape from the tentacles of death. The number of Jewish orphans was horrifying: 100,000, 200,000 or half a million - who could count them, estimate their number?

With the cunning of wolf cubs they knew how to evade the murderers. But hunger, cold and disease followed them wherever they went. Even among the masses of homeless they received the worst of treatment, were the last to be fed, the first to be beaten. The masses never forgot that they were the 'Zhids', Jews. Although the new socialist authorities were not particularly prejudiced against them, they had little food to give them. They thus remained without bread, without medicines, without clothing. 'To help, to rescue, before it is too late', went the call throughout Europe. The feeling of Jewish solidarity awoke.

Committees were established, people of good will were enlisted, money was raised, medical aid, blankets and clothing were collected. Then the question arose how and through whom should the aid be given. Who would ensure that it would reach those in greatest need?

The way to the Ukraine and the roads within it were fraught with peril, bands were still rampant and murderers lay in wait.
But fate was kind and a man was found - Isaac Ochberg ....
He had the idea to take from the 'bloody hell', as the Ukraine was then known, as many orphans as possible and bring them to a refuge, which at that time for the Jews was the United States, Canada or South Africa.

His idea was not easily accepted. It was bold. Even Jewish charitable institutions contended, 'How many will he succeed in transferring? Could not far many more be helped in other ways?'

'The Government of Russia is providing houses, but does not have the means of equipping and establishing institutions. This is what we should do with our funds!'

Ochberg did not relent: 'We can never truly help them as long as they stay in that house of death. What they need is a relaxed atmosphere, full of love and encouragement.'

Ochberg had already begun to work. 'The South African government was ready to accept 200 children. This was only a drop in the ocean. However, the real task of absorption would fall to the Jewish charitable institutions and they would have to cover the expenses.'

'Perhaps the Russian government will allow these 200 children to leave, provided that it is supplied with a detailed list of people prepared to receive the orphans and it must be proven that they are capable financially and characterwise to ensure a pleasant life and proper education for their wards.'

Even before he ventured into the Ukraine he travelled from one South African Jewish community to another, looking for families willing to adopt a child and arranging the official documents.

Ochberg, as was his way, was not content to leave the matter to drawnout correspondence nor did he delegate the responsibility to others, but did everything on his own, knocking on many doors, leaving no stone unturned. He was ready to bear any expense, but wanted to feel that the entire South African Jewish community was partner to his mission. So great was his belief in the justice of his cause and so great was his personal magnetism that even those who at first opposed him eventually became fervent supporters.

He regarded himself responsible toward the South African government that the children would in no way become a burden to the state.

When he embarked upon his long journey, he had with him not only money, clothing and medicines, but also promises from individual families that they would adopt the children.

His stopover was in London. There were complex and complicated arrangements for the transport of 200 children. On 18 May 1921 he left for the Ukraine, the unknown country. His most important 'personal effects' were his bold determination and hope for the success of his venture. He also had with him a special passport issued by the International Aid Committee of Dr Nansen. Ochberg was the first British Jew allowed to travel freely within Russia.

The summer of 1921 found him journeying by train, by horse and wagon, over highways and dirt roads, visiting city after city, community after community in which Jews had remained - always searching for the orphans. Thousands wanted to go; he had permission for only 200.

Isaac Ochberg had to decide who would go and who remained - 'that was the most difficult part of my journey' he said after he returned home. Alone, he had to make his decision, then assemble the children chosen at the various points of departure. On 1 August the ship *Baltbor* sailed and on it a very precious human cargo. To the 200 frightened, sick and hungry children, Ochberg was everything and everyone in their world. They simply called him 'Father Ochberg'.

Many of the present leaders of the Cape Town Jewish community today were on the ship *Edinburgh Castle* which brought them as 'Ochberg's Children'.

The picture of hungry children gave him no rest. He made a second trip to the Ukraine, but this time the Russian Government refused to allow him to take out a single child. The only thing he could do was to establish a kitchen for 150 children (the licence was limited to one year). 'At least I knew that 150 children were eating warm meals three times a day'.

He traversed areas where not only hunger was rampant but also typhoid, and distributed large quantities of food and drugs, clothing and money, without which thousands would have died the following winter.

For many years he was president of the Cape Jewish Orphanage and continued to look after his children who called him "Daddy Ochberg".

THE POEM OF THE ORPHAN
(ON HIS WAY TO SOUTH AFRICA)

Below is the English translation from Yiddish of a poem written by one of these children.

Merciful Father in Heaven
Who in His mercy toward children left orphans
Forced to leave their homes
Has sent father Ochberg to make us citizens of South Africa
God blessed us that we found ourselves among good people
Our worries ended when we received the letter.
Our group, hundreds of children, would not be separated, we would live as brothers!
A miracle will happen and when we grow up and stand on our feet
We will never forget the poor and needy.
Sins we have known
We will pray and ask blessings from heaven
We left behind us ruins when we started on our way
We took leave of our friends
And hoped that fate would allow
That we would live as Jews
To reach Zion is our dream.
Father Ochberg came to rescue us ....
And we will live as Jews
And to Zion come ......

So wrote an anonymous Jewish child from the Ukraine.

OCHBERG'S WORK FOR THE HEBREW UNIVERSITY

Isaac Ochberg's ties with the Hebrew University of Jerusalem and the assistance which he gave began already in the 1920s. One of his first contributions, made as soon as he had the financial resources to do so, was for £1,000 (pounds sterling). The year was 1928. Later, after the death of his daughter Ruth and his own recovery from a serious illness, he made a further grant of £10,000 for the endowment of a Chair of Agriculture in memory of his daughter.

Mrs Betha Epstein, the daughter of Isaac Ochberg, unveiling the memorial plaque at the University

In a speech given before the 'Dorshei Zion' organisation held to mark the founding of the Chair he said, 'Since the day the project of establishing the Hebrew University in Eretz Israel was proclaimed, the University was never far from my thoughts and I always wanted to sizably contribute towards its advancement.

The founding of an institution of science and learning in Eretz Israel is a great ideal. That day in our prayers, "From Zion will go forth Torah", is becoming a reality and the generations coming after us will look towards Eretz Israel as a centre of learning and science. I chose agriculture, since I am convinced that the establishment of a national homeland for the Jews in Eretz Israel will largely depend on the progress of farming. A Chair in Agriculture can be of benefit not only to the Jewish settlement but to the country as a whole.'

The Ruth Ochberg Chair in Agricultural Economics was one of the most important endowments of the Faculty of Agriculture in Rehovot at the time of its funding in 1937 and continues to be so today.

In connection with this contribution, one of Ochberg's friends tells a story. One day, when visiting Ochberg's office, he found him busy wording the text of a telegram, cutting out words so that it would be sent at the minimum rate. When asked what the telegram was about, Ochberg answered that he wanted to tell the Hebrew University of his contribution of £10,000. 'How ridiculous', said the friend, 'you give thousands of pounds and yet are making such a great effort to save a few pennies!' Isaac Ochberg laughed and remarked: 'Had I not made great efforts to save pennies all my life, I would not be able to make such a contribution today.'

Ochberg's concern with the Hebrew University continued to the last days of his life. In his will he left the University £10,000 'for the provision of scholarships'. He also bequeathed to the University part of his property valued at £130,000, the income of which was to be used by it. According to the terms of the will, the University was to establish a building for Botany on Mt Scopus to be named in his memory; however, the separation of Mt Scopus from Jerusalem after the War of Independence prevented realisation of the plan. Only 30 years after his death did Ochberg's dream come true. With the return of Mt Scopus, a wing of the library there will be named after the late Isaac Ochberg.

ISAAC OCHBERG –
THE MAN WHO WOULD NOT GIVE UP

Isaac Ochberg was born on 31 May 1878 in Uman in the Ukraine. It was a prosperous town and the Jewish community flourished. However, Jewish communal life in the Ukraine in the 19th century suffered from persecution and many Jews wanted to emigrate to where they could live in peace and educate their children without fear of pogroms.

At that time, every Jew who wanted to travel within Russia or leave its borders had to have special permission from the government. The 'Golden coast' of America and Africa beckoned to the persecuted.

Among those who left the land of their birth was Isaac's father, Aaron Ochberg. In 1893 he embarked for Cape Town. Aaron was an observant Jew, who was more interested in studying the Talmud than in business; however he managed to make enough money to enable his oldest son, Isaac, to join him.

At the age of 16, Isaac followed in his father's footsteps. After a long and wearying journey, he reached his destination in June 1985 and immediately became an apprentice to a watchmaker.

From his many friends he heard legends of the discovery of gold in the Transvaal region and decided to try his luck in Johannesburg. He worked as a waiter, but the climate of the city was damaging his health and in 1896 he returned to Cape Town. After 19 months of hard work he managed to save £200, a substantial sum in those days.

Isaac and his father bought a small hotel near the business district of Cape Town. At the same time he decided to try and obtain South African citizenship.

However, when he learned that his mother had fallen ill, he took the first boat back to Russia. He was 21 years old - tall, with intelligent blue eyes, light hair and a high forehead, a resolute young man knowing what he wanted.

When he returned to the town of his birth, he met a friend of his sister, a girl by the name of Paulina Borisovna Woldiner, a teacher of Russian in a school for orthodox children. A few months later they married and Isaac asked her father his permission to take his new bride to South Africa. The wedding took place in July 1900. Six weeks later Isaac was forced to leave for South Africa alone since the hotel had gone bankrupt.

At that point he could not afford to take even his young bride. In tears they parted and he promised that he would send her passage money as soon as possible.

After the hotel business failed, Isaac tried his hand at selling coffee. At night he would grind the beans and during the day he would go from house to house vending his wares. He chose the coffee trade because no one was prepared to loan him money to go into anything else. After nine months of hard work - day and night - he succeeded in saving enough money to send for his wife and rent a place to live in. He also put £25 in the bank, as a safeguard against any crisis that might compel his wife to return to her parents in Russia.

Before his wife came, he used to write her a letter every week, sometimes as long as 40 pages. Her boat was nine days late and Isaac was a bundle of nerves. Finally in June 1901 his wife arrived.
Those were the days of the Boer War; however, the young couple believed that they could establish their new home in South Africa and enjoy a pleasant life.

Soon their first child was born and at the same time Isaac had his first business success. This was 1902 and from that year onward, again and again, he proved his commercial talents; real estate, establishment of factories, agriculture, scrap metal trade etc. His beloved father was killed in 1905 in a train accident and Isaac became the sole support of the family (including his brother and four sisters who in the meantime had come to South Africa). However, his widespread business interests did not prevent him from taking an active part in the life of the Jewish community. Little time passed before he became well-known for his charitable work. His name was connected with every Jewish institution in the country and with many outside it. Throughout his life he helped people to whom fate had been cruel. He himself lived a modest life and also educated his children in that way.

In 1914, when he was already a rich man, Isaac, together with his wife and four children, travelled to England to expand his business interests. When the First World War broke out, he signed a contract with the British government to supply uniforms for the army. The following year the Ochberg family returned to South Africa, though not before he purchased a warship which had gone out of service.

He renovated the ship, brought it to South Africa, and rented it to the government to transport grain. To his great distress, the ship hit a sandbank off the South African coast.

Upon his return, he continued his real estate transactions. He loaned money to poor people to allow them to stand on their own feet. Today there are three flourishing suburbs near Cape Town which to a large measure owe their existence to the initiative of Isaac Ochberg.

Isaac was a Zionist since his youth and he never lost his belief in Zionism till his dying day. After his rescue mission of the The Ukrainian Pogrom Orphans, he devoted his time and energy to Israel. In 1926 he and his wife visited Israel. Jewish farming and the Hebrew University on Mt Scopus left deep impressions on him.

He summarised his thoughts in a press interview given in July of the same year:

'I believe that the Jewish problem will be finally solved in the Land of Israel, and only there. As a businessman I was very impressed with the industrial development of the country.'

After his return he tried to convince South Africans to spend their vacations in Israel. He described a visit to the country as an unforgettable experience. His devotion to Zionist affairs knew no boundary and in the course of time he became one of the pillars of the Zionist movement in South Africa. He was a fervent supporter of Herzl and after the publication of the Balfour Declaration named one of his offices in Cape Town *Balfour House.*

It is worthwhile quoting here one of the passages in his will concerned with agricultural settlement in Israel. 'The principal goal of the fund is to assist the settlement of poor Jews on the soil of the Land of Israel. I wish that preference be given to orphan children from Poland or Russia provided that they be suitable to become settlers on the land. The Jewish National Fund must purchase as soon as possible a tract of land suitable for agricultural settlement. A sum of £165,000 is allotted for this purpose.'

The enormity of the contribution becomes evident if one remembers that the year was 1937. The sum provided for the establishment of two settlements: Daliya and Gal'ed (Even Yitzhak Ochberg) in the Menashe Hills.

Daliya Memorial Pergoda

Isaac Ochberg, who did so much to help those in need, himself underwent great suffering in his personal life. His father was killed in a train accident, two of his children were victims of incurable maladies and his mother died of a malignant disease. In 1933 a further tragedy befell him. Ruth, the youngest of his daughters, died at the age of 17. At her grave the bereaved father called out, 'My God take me so that she can live.'

From the moment of her death, his health began to fail and he never recovered from the cruel blow of fate.

However, despite his personal tragedy, he did not abandon his Zionist work and continued to help in strengthening the Jewish settlement in Eretz Israel.

His health was poor. He went from doctor to doctor, from one European medical centre to the next - all to no avail. Later it was found that he had been suffering from cancer. In November 1937, during an ocean voyage, Isaac Ochberg died at the age of 59.

His body was brought to Cape Town for burial, and as provided in his will, he was laid to rest in a grave next to that of his daughter.

His funeral was one of the largest ever seen in Cape Town. Many of the children he had once saved came to pay their respects. He left most of his assets to the needy, mostly to public institutions, with the single largest sum going to the Jewish National Fund.

BENNIE PENZIK ADDS

The preceeding articles have been incorporated into a Hebrew booklet of 46 pages published by
Keren Kayemet Le'Israel (Jewish National Fund)
Division of Information   Jerusalem 1970

The Hebrew on the cover reads -
Flourishing Memorial in Ramat Menashe
To the Memory and Deeds of Isaac Ochberg

Aside from the recorded issues in this article, the publication has sections which deal with the mammoth task of clearing rocks from the area for the newly established kibbutzim Dalia and Even Itzhak in order to make the ground fertile.

"And the land is filled with stones. And in the first days of settlement there were only stones and thorns and masses of flowers, but the eyes searching the vistas saw only the stones. Endless, endless stones."

In the early days, the story is told of the area being out of bounds for Jews due to marauding Arab gangs and then goes on to deal with the improvement in relationships with the surrounding Arab communities once the land was redeemed by the JNF with the Ochberg bequest.

Chapter 20 – UKRAINIAN ADVENTURE

Jewish Affairs, August 1961
[With acknowledgements to
The Story of the Cape Jewish Orphanage.
Golden Jubilee 1910-1961 By Eric Rosenthal]

All activities of the Cape Jewish Orphanage since its foundation were to be overshadowed by a great enterprise commenced towards the end of 1920, that caught the imagination of South African Jewry as nothing else has done. This was the episode usually referred to as the 'Immigration of the Ukrainian Orphans'.

To understand its origin, there is a need to recall the circumstances existing in the former Russian empire after the crash of the Czarist regime in 1917. Rival armies were fighting for control - the 'Reds' on one side against the 'Whites', who hoped for the restoration of the Emperor, while in the middle were the Allied contingents as well as unorganised guerilla bands. With law and order rapidly melting away, transportation came to an end. Hundreds of thousands of demobilised soldiers roamed about, among equally vast armies of German ex-POWs trying to make their way home after the Soviets made peace with the Kaiser at Brest-Litovsk. Poor at the best of times, owing to the oppression to which they had been exposed for generations, the condition of the Jews in what had been Russia became even worse. Famine over vast areas was followed by epidemics of typhoid and other diseases. In this misery ancient antagonisms came to the surface. Polish and other peasants joined forces with reactionary officers and troops, to massacre whatever Jews came in their way. Pogroms were reported almost daily, of which the full details and numbers will never be known. In despairing letters, smuggled through the enemy lines, survivors asked their kinsmen in South Africa - and anywhere else in the world - for immediate help. A great surge of anger and pity swept the community. Why not try and bring some of the war victims to the Union - particularly the children? Overnight the idea took shape, spreading like wildfire from town to town. Before any organisation could step in, generous offers were made of financial and other help.

No one was more in sympathy with the plan than Isaac Ochberg, who immediately cabled to Dr Jochelman, President of the Federation of the Ukrainian Jews, in Britain, offering whatever help South Africa could give. Dr Jochelman replied, expressing his thanks, adding that his organisation was prepared to bring to London any children that could be saved, and then hand them over to a South African Committee.

Two further questions now arose - how could abandoned children be rescued, and would the Union Government create any difficulties in admitting them? Ochberg immediately contacted the Prime Minister, General J C Smuts, and Mr Patrick Duncan, the Minister of the Interior, who granted permission to land, without restriction, as many youngsters as could be saved.

A South African relief Fund for Jewish War Victims had already come into operation, when, at a special meeting called in his office on 19 August 1920, Ochberg proposed that the Cape Jewish Orphanage *take all the responsibilities of bringing the children out, and taking care of them*. In addition it should act as a clearing-house, whence they could be distributed among charitable people for adoption. 'I further suggest,' said Mr Ochberg, 'that a sum of £10,000 be raised by the Relief Fund and earmarked for this purpose'. This would suffice for the emigration of 200.

Less than a week later, at a record meeting in one of the Cape Town cinemas, crowds of Jews pledged themselves to give to the limit in helping to save the orphans. The original sum of £10,000 was forgotten and a target of £25,000 agreed upon, in its turn to be multiplied several times over.

Isaac Lewis, who only a few weeks before paid for another two plots adjoining the Orphanage, now offered to assist in financing the journey of the refugees. Hastening to Johannesburg, Ochberg gained not only the support there of the South African Jewish Orphanage, but of the community as a whole, the collecting campaign being extended into the country districts, where Archie Shacksnovis, a prominent advocate, carried the crowds with his eloquence. Assistance of many kinds, often unexpected, came from outside, as for instance the provision of free cinema slide advertising on the whole chain of the old African Theatre Trust.

As the details of the position in Europe leaked out, the tragedy of the situation became clearer. No fewer than 400,000 Jewish orphans were known to be destitute in Russia, so that whatever was done could only be a drop in the ocean.

By January 1921, when Bernard Alexander of Johannesburg persuaded the Union Government to give on a pound for a pound principle to the Pogrom Orphan Fund, it was felt that not 200 but 250 children could be brought to South Africa.

The next step was for someone to go to Europe and make arrangements on the spot. Without a moment's hesitation, Isaac Ochberg offered to undertake this responsible and by no means unhazardous task.

Hard at work in Eastern Europe, Ochberg, in a letter to the well-known Port Elizabeth communal leader, Adolph Schauder, outlined some of his adventures. Having thanked his friend for a note, only delivered to him after a delay of many months, 'owing to my movements in the Ukraine, where postal communications did not reach us', he expressed thanks for the cases of second-hand clothing just to hand.

'You will be glad to hear that I returned last night to London,' he continued, *'after living through a very trying time during the last three months on my mission in the Pogrom areas ... I have been through almost every village in the Polish Ukraine and*

Galicia, etc and I am now well acquainted with the places where there is at present extreme suffering. You can rest assured that I shall distribute the clothes your community have so kindly donated. I succeeded in collecting the necessary number of children, and I can safely say that the generosity displayed by South African Jewry in making it possible to remove them means nothing less than saving their lives. They would surely have died of starvation or disease, or have been lost to our nation for other reasons. I am here now [in London] with the object of arranging transport, and I hope to be able to advise telegraphically soon of my departure for South Africa with the children.'

The letter was written on a crudely-printed letterhead, reading:
"Jews War and Pogrom Orphan Transport – South African. Representative:
Isaac Ochberg, Esq. President Cape Jewish Orphanage, Cape Town, South Africa.
Temporary Shelter: Warsaw, Slika 28"

Ochberg proceeded from town to town, also visiting, amongst others, Minsk, Pinsk, Stanislav, Lodz, Lemberg and Wlodowa. (see interview of Fanny Lockitch)

In each case the Principal and the Matron were consulted before the final decision, care being taken to ensure that no child was taken away who did not wish to go.

Ochberg had managed to secure some helpers, including a teacher named Alexander Bobrow, Mr and Mrs Boris Glasman, and Miss Bettman, now Mrs Leah Marks, a well known Cape Town communal worker. Mr Bobrow is still living in Cape Town and able to give his first-hand testimony. Originally an analytical chemist in a sugar factory, the war had turned him to social work and in 1916 he was asked to join the 'Curatorium' formed to help the Jewish refugees at Pinsk. 'So many children were found,' said Mr Bobrow, 'that we were soon obliged to set up three orphanages. At first Pinsk was isolated by the fighting and we were thrown almost solely on our own resources. We had neither beds, bedding, nor clothes. I remember our using flour bags to make aprons and other garments for the boys and girls.'

Typhus broke out in an orphanage and at one stage Mr Bobrow, in the course of his duties, had to walk through streets in which the shells were bursting. Balachou, the notorious Ukrainian fanatic, descended on the city with his gangs and the pogroms raged for nearly a week. At one of the orphanages an old woman pacified the terror-stricken children by calling out: 'The Almighty will keep us and save us - Now you repeat it after me.'

As order was restored, supplies began to arrive, first from the Juedischer Hilfsverein in Berlin, and then from the Joint distribution Committee, including cocoa, condensed milk, cooking oil and clothes.

The Polish authorities were not very helpful and many children travelled to Warsaw by cattle-truck. Quaint old photographs show the youngsters lined up, their hands symmetrically folded in accordance with the taste of the cameraman. The passports themselves are probably unique. Though their covers carry the usual words in Polish and French, Paszport - Passeport, with the Polish Eagle, they were made out 'in quantity'. On the pages usually devoted to the prescribed form of thumbnail snapshot, with personal particulars, group photos appeared, some with as many as 30 or 40 small children sitting in rows. On the face of each one whose name was eliminated in the passport the Polish official had inked in a cross, through which the pathetic little countenances stared as though behind prison bars.

Many years later one of these documents was put into use afresh, as indicated in a letter from Mr Jan Majewski, Consul for Poland in the Union, who wrote to the President of the Cape Jewish Orphanage on 9 February 1942:

'I am returning herewith Collective Passport No 4074E issued by the Government Commission at Warsaw on the 16th of August, 1921, containing the names of 21 minor children, which you were good enough to hand to me in connection with the investigations to establish the citizenship of Mr Morris Gersznader ...'

'We set off for Africa,' said Mrs Lockitch, 'each with a tiny package of the clothing that had already been sent to us from overseas, and a few pitiful trifles like photographs or dolls. We travelled in slow overcrowded, dirty trains to Warsaw. In the middle of that city was a restaurant, belonging to a Jewish woman who became a legend to the children on account of her kindness. 'Panya' [Mrs] Engle, she was called. During the several months the Ochberg orphans stayed in schools near here Panya Engel, with a few friends, worked incessantly to ease their way. Just as it seemed as if most of the difficulties had been overcome, there was an outbreak of a serious eye disease - trachoma - which held up their departure for many weeks more. Fresh delays occurred when, as a result of his hardships, Ochberg himself was taken ill. Some of the senior boys and girls were selected to act as 'monitors' as in school, and then the great trek began.

'We said goodbye to Warsaw,' said Mrs Lockitch, 'and travelled by river boat down the Vistula to Danzig. There, on the Baltic, we boarded a steamer bound for London, and then other kind people took charge of us, and put us up in a hotel. As a sign of our appreciation, we were taught to sing 'God Save Our King' for the entertainment of our visitors, while we waited for the ship to take us to South Africa. A few of us were again taken ill, and spent the time in London in hospital, one lad by the name of Srulik Ellman, having to be left behind and only joining us in Cape Town a year later.'

But all the troubles were finally sorted out, and early in September 1921, with Mr and Mrs Maman as Principal and Matron, the party set off in the Edinburgh Castle. Ochberg too was on board, and all the passengers took the most friendly interest in the small emigrants.

'Never until my dying day,' said Mrs Lockitch, 'shall I forget our first sight of the lights of Cape Town, and then the tremendous reception when we came ashore on 21 September with half the city apparently waiting on the quay for us.'

So large was the group of children that the Cape Jewish Orphanage could no longer house them all, and a considerable number went to Johannesburg, where they were installed at Arcadia, the corresponding institution in that city. Special English-language classes were organised, in which Mr Cohen of Cape Town Central School took a leading part. Many youngsters presently entered Cape Town High School, where Mr AP Blair was principal. At a later date this school was taken over by the well-known historian and scholar, Dr Louis Herrman. A new extension to house the Ukrainians was officially named the Isaac Ochberg Wing.

The warmth of the friendship and the hospitality of South Africa showed itself in numberless invitations to Jewish homes, not a few of the children being directly adopted. Subsequent events more than justified the experiment of bringing the Ukrainian children, not a few of whom became persons of consequence in their new fatherland. The touching affection which they showed to Ochberg in particular, was never forgotten, and more impressive than any words, is the plain fact that one of the boys, who gave his life in World War II, left his property to the Cape Jewish Orphanage.

Later, schemes were put forward to bring further orphans from Eastern Europe to South Africa, but practical difficulties supervened and instead it was found advisable to arrange for their emigration from Eastern Europe to Palestine. This brought the supporters of the Cape Jewish Orphanage into contact with the Zionist organisation, and as a result of the visit from the distinguished leader, Dr Schmarya Levin, a special home for Pogrom and War victims was set up overseas. This however, falls outside the scope of the history of the Orphanage proper.

PANYA ENGEL

Panya Elgel looked after the children in Warsaw as Isaac Ochberg was gathering them from the various orphanages.

The photos below have three things in common; Panya Engel, the woman with the hat seated in the middle with hands on lap, a face blanked out and the children looking very sad.

Ursula Rembach, the daughter of Leah Altuska sent in this photo and caption."The children on the day they had their passport picture taken. Small boy third from left with white top is Chaim Altuska. The little girl on the extreme right is Leah. She is holding a small porcelain doll which she told me she placed on her mother's grave before she left.

Brian Fine comments
This picture must have been taken in Brest while the passport photos were taken in Warsaw. If this was taken on the day that Ursula's mother visited the grave of her mother then it must have been in Brest as Warsaw was a day's journey away (on a good day that is). Have a good look at the clothes the kids are wearing definitely winters. Warsaw pictures were taken outdoors in last stages of summer. The tall boy front row with coat and cap is my father Zeidel Feinschmidt.

Tania Jacobson comments
This photo was taken before the children left Brest Lltovsk and I am sure my father Isaac Bornstein is in the second row far left looking very sad.

Estell Hammar, daughter of Sima Samurina, sent in this photo commenting "Don't know who they are"

Chapter 21 – ITINERARY AND EXPENDITURE FOR THE PROJECT

ITINERARY FOR POGROM ORPHAN PROJECT 1921

18 March	4.00 pm	Left Cape Town for London
4 April		Arrived in London
4 June	8.00 am	Left Warsaw for Brest
4 June	6.00 pm	Arrived in Brest
5 June		I visited Dematchewo and Wlodowa with a motor car and returned the same day to Brest
6 June	10.00 am	Left Brest for Pinsk
7 June	6.00 am	Arrived in Pinsk
do	11.00 pm	Left Pinsk for Rovno
8 June	8.00 pm	Arrived in Rovno
13 June	12.00 am	Left Rovno for Livov to arrange about an orphanage
13 June	7.00 pm	Arrived in Livov
19 June	8.00 am	Left Livov for Warsaw to arrange another Orphanage
19 June	10.30 pm	Arrived in Warsaw. Made an Orphanage at Warsaw
26 June	3.00 pm	Left Warsaw for Brest
26 June	10.00 pm	Arrived in Brest. .
27 June		Visited Dematchewo and Wlodawa with a motor car to send away the first batch of children from Dematchewo through a Mr Friedman for Warsaw
28 June	4.00 am	Arrived again in Brest
28 June	10.00 pm	Left Brest for Pinsk
29 June	6.00 am	Arrived in Pinsk
30 June	11.00 pm	Left Pinsk for Rovno
1 July	8.00 pm	Arrived in Rovno
3 July	6.00 am	Left Rovno and met Mr Glassman and together we left for Sarna
3 July	11.00 pm	Arrived in Sarna
4 July	1.00 pm	Left Sarna for Rovno
4 July	6.00 pm	Arrived in Rovno
7 July	10.00 am	Left Rovno with Glassman for Wiswa
7 July	6.00 pm	Arrived in Wiswa
8 July	11.00 am	I left Wiswa for Kowel and Glassman left at 5 p.m. with a few children for Warsaw
8 July	2.00 pm	Arrived in Kowel
9 July	5.00 pm	Left Kowel for Sarna
10 July	1.00 am	Arrived in Sarna
10 July	5.00 pm	Left Sarna for Kowel
10 July	12.00 pm	Arrived in Kowel and met Glassman
11 July	4.00 am	Left Kowel for Kamin-Kashirsk with Dr Zachanowitz and Glassman
	10 a.m	Arrived in Kamin-Kashirsk
11 July	3.00 pm	Left Kamin-Kashirsk for Pniwna with a wagon with Dr Zachonowtiz. Mr Glassman with Mr Jaffe left with a wagon for Graceluscho, Klainluscho and Doravito and brought three children to Kamin-Kashirsk the following day.
11 July	7.00 pm	Arrived in Pniwna
11 July	8.00 pm	Left Pniwna for Doravock with a wagon
11 July	10.00 pm	Left Doravock for Pniwna with a wagon. Slept in Pniwna in an attic.
12 July	5.00 am	Left Pniwna on a wagon for Kamin-Kashirsk with orphans, on the road I met with a big storm.
12 July	5.00 pm	Arrived in Kamin-Kashirsk and met Glassman with other Orphans. In Kamin-Kashirsk I met some very nice people of the Committee
13 July	12.00 pm	Left Kamin-Kashirsk with Orphans for Kowel
13 July	3.00 pm	Arrived in Kowel
13 July	5.00 pm	Sent Orphans with a lady and gentleman to Warsaw
14 July	1.00 am	Left Kowel for Lubomil with Glassman
14 July	4.00 am	Arrived in Lubomil
14 July	8.00 am	Left Lubomil for Shask on a wagon
14 July	2.00 pm	Arrived in Shask
14 July	8.00 pm	Left Shask with Orphans
15 July	4.00 am	Arrived in Lubomil with wagon of Orphans. Left the Committee 60,000 mark for collecting the Orphans

THE TOWNS VISITED AS PER OCHBERG'S ITINERARY – This is not 100% accurate as no single map exits.
Names have been added and placed where they should be. Some towns no longer exist. Map courtesy Brian Fine

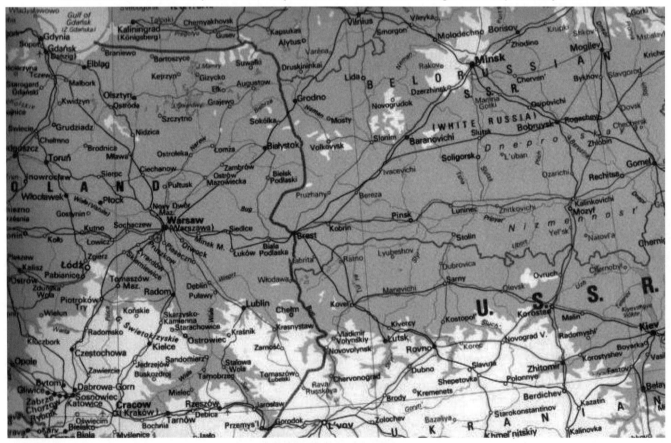

GENERAL MAP OF AREA

15 July	11.00 am	Left Lubomil with Orphans for Warsaw. Glassman left for Rovno.
16 July	6.00 am	Arrived in Warsaw
18 July	11.00 pm	Left Warsaw for Lubomil
19 July	3.00 pm	Arrived in Lubomil and met Glassman
19 July	11.00 pm	Left with the Orphans and Glassman for Kowel
20 July	3.00 am	Arrived in Kowel
20 July	11.30 p.m.	Left Kowel for Livov to get children. Glassman and the children left Kowel for Warsaw and then he left Warsaw to fetch the children from Rovno, Sarna Kostopol and brought them to Warsaw.
21 July	9.00 am	I arrived in Livov
23 July	12.00 am	Left Livov for Warsaw
24 July	8.00 am	Arrived in Warsaw
1 August	8.00 pm	Left Warsaw for London. Glassman left for Brest, Kowel and Rovno to get the children and brought them back to Warsaw

POGROM ORPHAN FUND
STATEMENT OF RECEIPTS AND PAYMENTS
BY MR ISAAC OCHBERG IN CONNECTION WITH BRINGING TO AFRICA
175 ORPHANS WITH STAFF, FROM RUSSIA

EXPENDITURE				RECEIPTS			
Expenses bringing children from Pogrom area to Warsaw, temporary home, Railway and Wagon Fares, Food, Clothing, during their stay at Warsaw etc. Less Sale of Bedsteads. 5,062,340 Polish Marks	963.	10.	0.	Cash from Orphan Fund Johannesburg Cash from Cape Jewish Orphanage Cash from friends of Orphans Cash from Rev Wilder Cash Interest on Deposit	5000. 3500. 321. 30. 93.	0. 0. 4. 0. 12.	0. 0. 0. 0. 0.
Expenses at Danzig	16.	0.	0.				
Steamship Fares from Danzig	638.	9.	0.				
Telegrams to Warsaw	4.	0.	0.				
Railway Fares from Southampton to London Children and Staff	35.	0.	0.				
Expenses at London	14.	0.	0.				
Cables & Wireless Messages to Cape Town and Johannesburg	27.	16.	0.				
Boots for children	42.	18.	1.				
Taking Film children	11.	6.	6.				
Expenses re Passports	11.	10.	0.				
Medicine	15.	10.	0.				
Caps	5.	3.	0.				
Steamship Fares per "Edinburgh Castle" London to Cape Town	2005.	18.	0.				
Expenses on children at Madeira	12.	10.	0				
Expenses on Board to Cape Town	29.	0.	0.				
Washing on Board to Cape Town	8.	0.	0.				
Bonus for (Staff)	60.	0.	0.				
Total Expenditure to Date	**3900.**	**9.**	**7.**				
Refund to Orphan Fund Johannesburg	2500.	0.	0.				
Refund to Cape Jewish Orphanage	1000.	0.	0.				
Additional Refund to Orphan Fund Johannesburg	600.	0.	0.				
Additional Refund to Cape Jewish Orphanage	600.	0.	0.				
Balance in hand to meet undischarged Liabilities	344.	6.	5.				
	£8944.	**16.**	**0**		**£8944**	**16.**	**0.**

I beg to report having audited the above statement of Receipts and Payments together with the corresponding vouchers and am satisfied the above Statement exhibits a true and correct account of
Mr Isaac Ochberg's transactions.

I am unaware on what basis the refunds to the Institutions concerned have been made.

I LEVY
Incorporated Accountant
CAPE TOWN   7.11.21

THE NUMBER OF OCHBERG ORPHANS RESCUED

While permission was given for 200 children to be brought out to South Africa, and this is the number used in many articles only 167 arrived initially in September 1921. While 89 remained in the Cape, 78 were taken by train to Johannesburg. To this 167 must be added the three 'nurses' older sisters who looked after the children and children who were initially held back because they were ill, and only arrived later.

Extract from AN EPISODE IN THE HISTORY OF THE CAPE JEWISH ORPHANAGE
Written by Jonathan Boiskin

Isaac Ochberg said that he had collected 233 orphans, brought them to Warsaw and placed them in the temporary shelter set up with the help of Regina Engel. Unfortunately, 37 of them ran away and others took ill, so that only 169 were taken to London, but two took ill just before sailing, so he arrived with 167. Seventy-eight of these children were taken by train to Johannesburg on their arrival in Cape Town.

Extract from ARCADIA GOLDEN JUBILEE SOUVENIR 1906-1956.
THE WAR ORPHANS FROM EASTERN EUROPE.

It was in 1921 that the late Mr Isaac Ochberg, the President of the Cape Jewish Orphanage, working in conjunction with the Jewish Relief, Reconstruction and Orphans Fund, brought out to this country 167 Jewish war orphans from Eastern Europe, 89 of whom were taken over by the Cape Orphanage and 78 by the Fund in Johannesburg. A number of these orphans were privately adopted, and the Fund remained with 67 orphan children on its hands.

THE CHILDREN THAT RAN AWAY

1.	Kawerberg	M.	13	Kowel
2.	do	E.	4	do
3.	do	M.	9	do
4.	Feldman	F.	6	Shazk
5.	do	G.	9	do
6.	Nejman	A.	13	Lubomel
7.	do	M.	11½	do
8.	Krejn	L.	12	do
9.	do	H.	10	do
10.	do	J.	8	do
11.	do	M.	7	do
12.	do	B.	5	do
13.	Wajsberg	L.	12	do
14.	Majer	R.	13	do
15.	Machluk	C.	10	do
16.	do	M.	11	do
17.	Saja	B.	13	do
18	Naiditch	R.	11	Pniwho
	do	I.	6	do
	do	G.	6	do
	Ginsburg	S.	9	Shazk
	Fridland	S.	5	do
	Pomeranez	B.	9	Brest
	do	S.	8	do
	Dekter	I.	7	Kamin-K

Names of Children who ran away from Orphanage in Warsaw

A MOTHER PLACES THREE CHILDREN IN THE CARE OF ISAAC OCHBERG TO TAKE TO SOUTH AFRICA.
See letter below translated courtesy Jack Goldfarb and Veronica Belling

12 July 1921
I, signing this letter residing in the village of Pniawna Gmina (district) Ugrinczynska Powiat (county) Pinskie, who is a caretaker of my under aged children Rosa 10 years, Iser 8 years and Dwora 6 years last name Noydutsh left after their father's death Leib Noydutsh without any material support, I testify that I intend to better their wellbeing. I freely gave up them for the director of African Mission Mr Ochbergezawi to be sheltered in Africa with citizens who are trustworthy.

Signature Chaya Noydutsh

Witnesses: Yehezkel Shulman
            Yekutiel Shulman

What happened to these children? They are not on the list of children who went to South Africa.

We find the three children on the list of children who ran away from the Orphanage in Warsaw – see 18, 19 and 20 on list above. They would have been with the group for only a few weeks

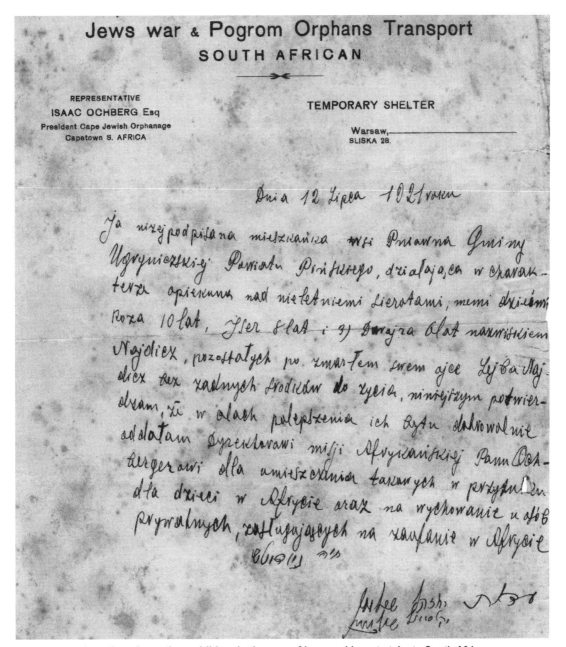

Jews war & Pogrom Orphans Transport
SOUTH AFRICAN

REPRESENTATIVE
ISAAC OCHBERG, Esq
President Cape Jewish Orphanage
Capetown S. AFRICA

TEMPORARY SHELTER

Warsaw,_____
SLISKA 28.

A mother places three children in the care of Isaac ochberg to take to South Africa

Dale Romanovsky in the story about his father MANNIE ROMANOVSKY (MENDEL FELDMAN) wrote

Isaac Ochberg took *Mendel* with another four or five children that were picked up from Wlodawa to the orphanage that he had established in Warsaw, where he was accumulating the children.

It was at this orphanage that my grandfather told us that it was his happiest time, due to the fact that he met his older brother and sister again, as they had been picked up in a village three or four villages further down. However, just before they were to leave to unknown lands, the kids got very nervous and approximately 25 of them escaped that night and in that 25 was

my grandfather's brother and sister, who he never saw again. My grandfather was then brought to South Africa and ultimately adopted by the Romanovsky's.

Selwyn (Ram) Romanovsky adds

My Dad's real parents were Feldman and we do not know their first names. He had three siblings all who perished; Fieval, an older brother, Chia, an older sister and a younger sister who's name we don't know. My Dad never heard from his Mom or family again.

We can conclude that F and C Feldman, no 4 and 5 on the list above, were Mendel's siblings Feival and Chia.

Chapter 23 – GROUP PASSPORT PHOTOS AND NAMES

The following passport photos and names accompanying the photos were kindly provided by the Jewish Museum in Cape Town and Lauren Snitcher.

I understand that the lists of names below accompanying the photos are generally in no particular order in relation to the

passport photo and that the number after the name is the age of the child but that it is not always accurate and sometimes less than the ages found on other documents.

Lastly children who are crossed out on the photo for various reasons did not finally come out to South Africa.

GROUP PASSPORT ONE

LIST OF NAMES ACCOMPANYING GROUP PASSPORT ONE

1. Ortman Regina	7 lat	13. Razer Ides	7 lat
2. Bethman Zhnla	5	14. Razer Perl	8
3. Bethman Salomon	7	15. x Rozenbaum Leon	7
4. Bethman Szendel	8	16. Rynzler Charnel	8
5. Broder Jano	5	17. x Wajdman Srejndel	7
6. Broder Bina	7	18. Rubin Chane	6
7. Lille Rose	8	19. Rubin Dawid	7
8. Drylina Jude	8	20. x Sztrosner Fejga	7
9. Gies Jetti	8	21. Frachtel Jaro	8
10. Zanni Tojba	8	22. Kull Chane	5
11. Nemel Beile	5	23. Srlanger Dery	9
12. Razer Nason	5	24. Zwyrn Osiasz	4

25. Zwyrn Berner	5 lat
26. Mordechan Gahe	8
27. Mordechowin Elel	6

GROUP PASSPORT TWO

LIST OF NAMES ACCOMPANYING GROUP PASSPORT TWO

1.	Lewin Sora	5.	14.	Weiman Chanon	9	27.	Gajer Mojze	4½
2.	Gaber Czarna	7.	15.	Koledner Jeze	5.	28.	Koledner Sora	10.
3.	Hajer Rywen		16.	Szajer Jacob	7.	29.	Laurat Fajba	8.
4.	Beniewicz Rywen	4.	17.	Rajer Chaim	7.	30.	Mejsterman Wolf	8.
5.	Margolin Soro	7.	18.	Belman Chana	10.	31.	Josel Anna	5.
6.	Gerenberman Jocke	5.	19.	Swarc Josif	9	32.	Gajer Sora	9
7.	Mejsterman Rywin	8.	20.	Garbuz Szmul	9			
8.	Samyrino zTato	9.	21.	Urzleja Aba	8			
9.	Karman Benjamin	5.	22.	Lewin Chaim	9.			
10.	Rozenblit Szamaj	6.	23.	Buchoers Szulem	4.			
11.	Lipajo Mojsze	5.	24.	Elman Ajzyk	7.			
12.	Mijdalowicz Nochros	5.	25.	Rajzman Chaim	9.			
13.	Pentix Chaja	7.	26.	Kaufman Szloma	5.			

GROUP PASSPORT THREE

LIST OF NAMES ACCOMPANYING GROUP PASSPORT THREE

1. Hilman Israel	
2. Koladner Iван	
3. Grinszleyn Israel	8.
4. Bauer Chaim	7.
5. Borgairskja Iван	8.
6. Surman Salomo	8
7. Fainszmid Zydel	9
8. Gruszenobel Moyses	8
9. Wolynec Israel	8.
10. Wolynec Irene	10.
11. Lydergendel Fryma	7.
12. Kowalcewwa Jacob	8
13. Gibreenker Srewe	3.
14. Bormaer Sare	8.

15. Berenwiez Chawa	7.
16. Orljanski Abram	8.
17. Piaxer Chawa	8.
18. Piaxer Chaja	7.
19. Pomeranc Becalel	6.
20. Pomeranc Salomo	7.
21. Strajer Fyga	8.
22. Strajer Jacob	7.
23. Altsuno Sam	9
24. Liberman Ryvca	9.
25. Grinszleyn Froim	8.
26. Hitman Chanon	9.
27. Pinler Moyze	8.
28. Szkjner Mirca	8.

29. Kudler Chaja	7 ½.
30. Kudler Chana	6
31. Kudler Bevl	5.
32. Kudler Berel	3.
33. Dragit Sovie	6.
34. Dragit Ester	5.

GROUP PASSPORT FOUR

LIST OF NAMES ACCOMPANYING GROUP PASSPORT FOUR

1. Szkjner Chanul	5 lat	5. Dexter Srul	6 lat	29. Hauenberg Meir	4 lat
2. Rajchman Abram	9.	16. Dexter Max Ber	5.	30. Ganzjol Jecol	5 lat
3. Rajchman Chaim	7.	17. Ginsberg Szymen	7.		
4. Szkjner Izaak	6.	18. Frydland Srmul Josl	8		
5. Gornicka Abram	10.	19. Machler Mendl	6.		
6. Elman Jankl	7.	20. Majer Ruwen	8		
7. Aluser Chaim	8.	21. Fajnberg Srl	9.		
8. Cwengel Saul	7.	22. Majer Majer	4.		
9. Ortreabaum Srmul	9.	23. Rojn Juden	6.		
10. Kaufman Salome	5.	24. Rojn Merz	9.		
11. Engelman Jacob	7.	25. Rein dejer	10.		
12. Borowa Srajs	9.	26. Ptasin Dawid	10.		
13. Salan Salome	7.	27. Hauenberg Majer	10.		
14. Fehrlejn Josef	9.	28. Hauenberg Max	8.		

LIST OF NAMES ACCOMPANYING GROUP PASSPORT FIVE

1. Neustlyn Solomon 5 lat	13. Miodotwier Syma 6 6l	25. Dinter Fajwel 6 la
2. Berger Abram 7.	14. Ruclocki Aron 7.	26. x Miodolowie Aborn 7.
3. Milerman Herez 10.	15. Ruclocu Fajwel 6.	27. x Helman Benjamn 6.
4. Abraberman Wolf 8	16. Gades Samel 9.	28. Dewehodni Isa 10.
5. x Berger Josef 9.	17. Lidewner Herez 10.	29. Dewehodni Szda 7.
6. x Benler Herz 7.	18. Elorba Abo 8	30. Herman Iser
7. Cyrulnix Izaak 10.	19. x Sem Abam 9	
8. Cyrulnix Jonas 8.	20. Elirlyn Sloma 8.	
9. Rebl Herman 8.	21. x Rucho Isachar 9	
10. Trespel Jazaw 5	22. Nahan Mordwah 10.	
11. Frimel Maks 9.	23. Nahan Sachew 7.	
12. Rejzender Rubin 9.	24. x Helman Aporx 7	

GROUP PASSPORT SIX

LIST OF NAMES ACCOMPANYING GROUP PASSPORT SIX

LIST OF NAMES ACCOMPANYING GROUP PASSPORT SEVEN

1. Elman Bluma	3l.	13. Lerman Dwojra	6l.	25. Joffe Frjdel	9l.
2. Lerman Nechama	3l.	14. Heft Rosa	7l.	26. Ganifas Gitel	12l.
3. Jahr Pepa	4l.	15. Mandelblatt Pesse	8l.	27. Zaika Mania	8l.
4. Petricwicz Regina	4l.	16. Haus Roza	7l.	28. Zaika Lizel	3l.
5. † Bexler Leja	9l.	17. Haus Nesia	8l.	29. Dragif Chasia	7l.
6. Elman Fejga	5l.	18. Goldman Sryfre	10l.	30. Dragif Dwojra	3l.
7. † Margolin Sore	7l.	19. Majxejer Franervu	8l.		
8. † Gesenkerman Josha	5l.	20. Blind Salxa	8l.		
9. Genefas Malxa	7l.	21. Majslerman Sorro	8l.		
10. Gabaj Gitla	6l.	22. Derlowicz Chana	8l.		
11. Nejszkejn Sala	5l.	23. Gesenkerman Srijne Roele	10l.		
12. Mussman Reizel	4l.	24. Samarina Ztala	4l.		

LIST OF NAMES ACCOMPANYING GROUP PASSPORT EIGHT

1. Krejn Pinezo	5lo	13 Auber Brajndel	7lat	25 Borowix Rachile	9.
2. Fellezix Fejga	4	14 x Guber Crarno	7.	26 x Tenenboum Sara	10
3. Lewin Pesra	4	15 Feldwau Chaja		27 x Helman Chasra	8.
4 x Lewin Sora	5.	16 Machter Chaja	S	28 Libssewe Perl	11.
5 Gerunluman Brjndle	9.	17 Fajler Siba	9.	29 Guber Chaja .	8.
6 x Samurino Sima	7.	18 Gajer Sora	9.	30 Srapiro Matra	6.
7 Gorniszhja Chanexc	6	19 Kosler Ryrere	8		
8 Pinsro Ztalo	6.	20 Pencx Chane	8.		
9 Kaufman Cytoro	5.	21 Pinsro Duojre	10.		
10 Joffe Cini	6.	22 Kawerberg Mirjam	10.		
11 Echtorkja Taubo	7.	23 x Holodnet Labe	10.		
12 Krejndel Rejrel	7.	24 Bernfeld Chaio	10.		

LIST OF NAMES ACCOMPANYING GROUP PASSPORT NINE

1. Helewan Tayba	8 lat	13 x Rozenblat Aronuj	6 lat
2. Helewan Chaim	7.	14 Nauman Troad	6.
3. Gabor Chaje	13.	15 Echrlyn Oscer	6.
4 Knukowiec Ztala	11.	16 Feldman Fajwel	5.
5 Gabaj Sino	9.	17 Elorlyn defil	5.
6 Alluxra Lejo	6.	Nxdytoraje Alejxe	5.
7 Vanifar deic	8.		
8 Forfil Roza	7.		
9 Bernfild Hexon	18		
10 x Nanman Benjamin	5		
Trolexya Lujbo	6.		
12 Rorinblt gdelgo	7.		

106

Chapter 24 – 1921 News Articles

1921 NEWS ARTICLES OF THE OCHBERG ORPHANS

These old newspaper cuttings were kindly sent to me Solly and Sylvia Jossel and then later by Jenny Segal and other people, but the photos were copies of copies and therefore of poor quality.

A very big thank you to Dov Penzik who took the trouble to obtain and send us these clearer copies.

ORPHANS FROM UKRAINIA
Islington Daily Gazette, London – 25.8.1921

A party of 137 orphan children from Ukrainia whom the Ukrainian Relief Federation have rescued from destitution arrived in London yesterday en route for South Africa. The Jewish population in South Africa has offered to support and train them, and half of the children are being sent to a home in Cape Town and half to Johannesburg.

100 POGROM ORPHANS EN ROUTE FOR THE CAPE
London, August 22
Rhodesia Herald, Salisbury – 26.8.1921

A telegram from Warsaw states that over one hundred Jewish children left on Saturday for Cape Town. All are orphans whose parents were victims of Bolshevist atrocities, in the Ukraine two years ago.

The representatives of the Cape Jewish Orphanage stated that it was a common thing to find small children aged two or three years, hiding in woods or fields, and living on grass and berries. Many were terrified at the approach of strangers and numbers were ignorant of their names.

Most of them had seen their parents killed.

The children are now well fed and clothed. They left via Danzig for London, where they will be entertained for a week previous to embarkation for Cape Town – (Reuters)

FOUNDLING'S FUTURE DESTITUTE THROUGH MASSACRE OF THEIR PARENTS
Sheffield Independent, Sheffield – 26.8.1921

A party of 137 orphan children from Ukraine, rescued from destitution, arrived in London yesterday en route for South Africa.

The children come from Jewish families massacred by bandits in Ukraine. They were mostly found lying ill and starving by the roadside or in the fields.

The Jewish population in South Africa has offered to support and train them. Half of the children will go to a home in Cape Town and half to Johannesburg.

Daily Graphic, London – 27.8.1921

RESCUED CHILD VICTIMS OF THE RUSSIAN TERROR

A batch of refugees with their beloved interpreter in the middle

Ready for a meal. The children have known actual starvation

The interpreter is a favourite with the youngsters

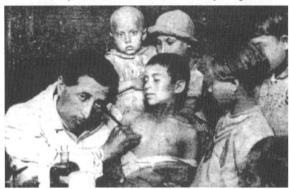

A skilled doctor made a careful examination of each arrival

Picked up by the Jewish relief agents in ruined Ukrainian towns or roaming in the woods on the verge of starvation a batch of 137 children have just reached London. They are now being sent to a good home in South Africa by the Federation of Ukrainian Jews.

CHILDREN VICTIMS MUTILATED BY BOLSHEVISTS
South Wales News – Cardiff – 26.8.1921

Orphaned victims of Bolshevism, 137 Russian children were given their first meal on English soil yesterday. They arrived from Warsaw in the morning.

Brought to England by the Emigration Committee of the Federation of Ukrainian Jews, they will stay in London for a few days, and will then be taken to South Africa where a home has been found for every one of them. As they appeared yesterday they were mostly sturdy children between 2 ½ and 12 years of age, the boys alert and intelligent, and the girls who are in a majority, unusually beautiful. But the face of nearly every one bore the marks of premature age stamped there by experiences horrible almost beyond belief.

They have all been for many weeks in hospital at Warsaw, where flesh has been put on the bare bones and smiles on

faces that before had shown nothing but sorrow. Most of them were found by the Jewish relief agents begging crusts in the streets of ruined Ukrainian towns. Not a few were actually living in the woods on berries, homeless wild, and so frightened of all grown-ups that they tried to flee from those who sought to save them. Many did not know their own names.

When questioned through an interpreter, they told piteous stories. One after another related that they had seen their mother and father killed before their eyes; some had seen brothers and sisters mutilated.

Harris Stileman, a sad-faced boy, ten years of age, with one hand cut off at the wrist, said that the bandits of Petloura (the semi-Bolshevist adventurer who made himself dictator of the Ukraine) had come to the house of his father, who was a prosperous peasant, and then, because his father would not join them, they killed him and the boy's mother, while their children watched. Then they put out his sister's eyes, and cut off the boy's hand before leaving the children to starve before a burning home. The sister is dead; the boy carries his mutilation to his grave.

As an advertisement of the horrors of Bolshevism the stories of these children can hardly be surpassed.

Safe in bed after many trials and grim adventures

RUSSIAN ORPHANS
100 LITTLE STRANGERS FOR CAPE TOWN
London, August 22
Bulawayo Chronicle, Bulawayo, SA – 27.8.1921

A telegram from Warsaw states that over a hundred Jewish children left on Saturday for Cape Town. All are orphans whose parents were victims of Bolshevist atrocities, in the Ukraine two years ago.

The representatives of the Cape Jewish Orphanage stated that it was a common thing to find small children aged two or three years, hiding in woods or fields, and living on grass and berries. Many were terrified at the approach of strangers and numbers were ignorant of their names and most had seen their parents killed.

The children are now well fed and clothed. They left via Danzig for London, where they will be entertained for a week previous to embarkation for Capetown – (Reuters)

UKRAINIAN ORPHANS
Daily Telegraph, Fleet Street, London EC4 – 27.8.1921

It is just fifteen years since the Jewish communities throughout the world were stirred to their depths by the pogroms in Russia which rendered thousands of Jewish families homeless and made hundreds of orphans helpless and hopeless. The relief which is never absent on such occasions was quickly forthcoming, and a fund was raised which realised £120,000. A commission was sent out, consisting of the late Mr Carl Stetlauer, representing the London Russo-Jewish Committee, the late M David Feinberg, representing the Alliance Israelite Universell, and Dr Paul Nathan of the Hilfsverein der Deutscher Jüden, to Russia. On their advice, the funds were distributed, and, incidentally some hundreds of the destitute orphans were absorbed in England, France, Germany and the United States. History is now repeating itself, for some hundreds of the stricken children in the Ukraine are about to find homes in South Africa, Canada, the United States, and England. It is a merciful project which redounds to the credit of the Jewish community, and which is in accord with its highest traditions of warm-hearted philanthropy.

The little ones are now in London and are the guests of the Federation of Ukrainian Jews. The whole 130 odd, now on their way to South Africa, were carefully selected from numerous Jewish villages by Mr Isaac Ochberg, president of the Jewish Orphanage in Cape Town. It was necessary for him to travel from village to village and take only those who were medically fit for sailing. The task was a heart-rending one. Among those ultimately chosen there were children whose parents were buried alive; others who are the sole remnants of what were once large, prosperous Jewish families. It is hoped that before long another 150 children will be sent to Canada, whilst the United States will doubtless, absorb a number in keeping with the importance and size of the Jewish community in America. Already it has adopted a scheme of financial responsibility for the maintenance of destitute children within the Ukraine, a system which is working admirably. French and English Jews are also alive to their responsibilities and can be relied upon to fulfil their duty towards those unfortunate children. It is hardly necessary to add that the 137 little transmigrants are receiving the warmest hospitality at their temporary home in Bow-road.

RUSSIAN CHILDREN
Nottingham Guardian – 27.8.1921

One hundred and thirty seven Russian children have reached England, where they will be fed and cared for until they can be sent to South Africa. They are of varying ages, but they are all reported to be sturdy and strong, and they are all orphans, whose fathers and mothers have been murdered by Bolsheviks. They were all found destitute and starving by rescue agents and some of them had been so terrorised by the horrors they had seen that they were frightened of the people who were trying to save them.

They will be cared for in South Africa by a Jewish organisation, and brought up as British citizens. They will, there is little doubt, be a source of wealth to South Africa in years to come, and it is a pity that more of the Russian children who are starving

cannot be settled in some part of the British Empire, where they would be valued. The stories the children are telling of the horrible brutalities they have witnessed throw a red light upon the working of the Bolshevik system, which must have been inspired by devils, if there are any, and from whom all trace of human kindness is absent. Fortunately, the political news from Russia, is better. The authors of the Bolshevik system have realised their failure and are making efforts to get back to something like the old conditions.

Leeds Mercury, Leeds – 30.8.1921

POLISH ORPHANS FOR SOUTH AFRICA
Some of a large party of Ukraine children in London
on their way to new homes in South Africa.
Many suffered terribly under the Red regime.

YOUNG ARRIVALS FROM RUSSIA *(Daily Sketch)*
Looking all the better for their voyage these little
Jews arrived in London from Russia yesterday.

The neatly-dressed youngsters coming ashore.
They were delighted at the change (Daily Sketch)

JEWISH ORPHANS FOR PALESTINE
The Star . Johannesburg – 27.8.1921

Durban, Saturday – The Durban committee of the Palestine Restoration fund has placed £1,100 at the disposal of Dr de Sola Pool, Director of Palestine Orphanages, for the purpose of transferring to Palestine about 50 Jewish orphans from the pogrom-stricken areas of the Ukraine and Poland. A further sum of £600 is about to be transmitted for the upkeep of these orphans for three months, six of these children being adopted by the Durban Jewish community which is undertaking their maintenance until they are self supporting. – (Reuter)

SUCCOUR FOR POLISH CHILDREN
South Wales News, Cardiff – 2.9.1921

South African Jews have banded themselves together to help the destitute and starving children of Poland, the Ukraine, and Galicia. Mr Isaac Ochberg, president of the Cape Jewish Orphanage in Cape Town, is now in London with 200 children who have been collected in Warsaw from the more distressed districts, and will leave with them for South Africa to-day. The children, who are all under nine years of age will be taken care of by the Jewish Orphanage and by the trustees of the Jewish War Victims' and Orphans' Fund in Johannesburg, and the intention is to distribute them among Jewish families and to bring them up as British citizens.

In the course of an interview with a Press representative, Mr Ochberg said that the children he had now in his charge formed the first contingent of those who would be taken to South Africa. "They are all", he remarked "victims of some pogrom or disturbance and when I found them they were roaming about the towns or in the forests, filthy, worse than naked, and starving. In most of the places there was no food, and disease was rampant, and in some of them I was glad to get even a crust of bread to eat. The Jewish community in South Africa have taken up the idea very favourably, and the Dominion Government have extended their sympathy and have given us every assistance possible, especially in the way of withdrawing the restrictions against the immigration of orphan children."

POLISH CHILDREN FOR SOUTH AFRICA
Scotsman, Edinburgh – 2.9.1921

South African Jews have banded themselves together to help the destitute and starving children of Poland, the Ukraine and Galicia. Mr Isaac Ochberg, president of the Cape Jewish Orphanage in Cape Town, is now in London with two hundred children who have been collected in Warsaw from the more distressed districts, and will leave with them for South Africa to-day. The children, who are all under nine years of age, will be taken care of by the Jewish Orphanage and by the trustees of the Jewish War Victims' and Orphans' Fund in Johannesburg and the intention is to distribute them among Jewish families and to bring them up as British citizens.

JEWISH ORPHANS FOR SOUTH AFRICA
South Africa, London – 2.9.1921

The problem of the war orphans of Eastern Europe presents many difficulties and it is hoped to lessen these by finding homes for the destitute children in various hospitable countries. So it comes about that some 140 Jewish orphans whose parents, it is stated, were massacred by bandits in the Ukraine, are on their way to South Africa. Their support is entirely in the hands of the Jewish organisation there – an extremely rich body, which has branches all over the sub-continent – presumably they will eventually develop into useful citizens. A representative of *South Africa* who made inquiries into the matter learned that the Union Government have not been involved in any expense. They were merely asked to give their permission for the children to enter the country subject to certain necessary regulations.

Daily Mail, London – 3.9.1921

OFF TO SOUTH AFRICA.

Orphaned victims of Bolshevist atrocities in the Ukraine, recently arrived from Warsaw, leaving Waterloo Station yesterday on their way to South Africa.

AID FOR POLISH CHILDREN
Daily Telegraph, Fleet Street, London, EC 4 – 2.9.1921

South African Jews have banded themselves together to help the destitute and starving children of Poland, the Ukraine, and Galicia. Mr Isaac Ochberg, president of the Cape Jewish Orphanage in Cape Town, is now in London with 200 children who have been collected in Warsaw from the more distressed districts, and will leave with them for South Africa to-morrow. The children, who are all under 9 years of age, will be taken care of by the Jewish Orphanage and by the trustees of the Jewish War Victims and Orphans Fund in Johannesburg, and the intention is to distribute them among Jewish families and to bring them up as British citizens.

Sheffield Independent – 3.9.1921

RUSSIAN REFUGEES – A party of children rescued from the famine stricken area of Russia and brought to London, left Waterloo yesterday for South Africa, where they will be adopted.

ORPHANS' FRESH START
JEWISH REFUGEES' NEW HOME IN SOUTH AFRICA
Observer, London – 4.9.1921

This week-end there has left London, for South Africa by the Union Castle liner Edinburgh Castle a party of some 160 Jewish orphan children from Russia who have been staying for eight or nine days at the Atlantic passengers' hostels in the East-end, and while awaiting the sailing of the boat have been receiving the hospitality of members of the Jewish race in London.

All the children are orphans, and, a sad history is associated with every one of them, as all have lost their parents in the Ukraine as the result of the troubles which have beset the unhappy land of their birth.

One day this week the children were taken in char-a-bancs for an outing as far as Ruislip and given a very happy time. The children as a body have shown remarkable intelligence and several of them in the few days they spent in London picked up and were able to pronounce quite a number of English words. This large family of orphans has been taken from Russia to be provided with a home in South Africa through the generosity of a wealthy Jewish gentleman, and it is understood that further steps in the same direction with regard to other children are contemplated by the same benefactor.

Reynolds Newspaper, London – 4.9.1921
LITTLE RUSSIANS OFF TO SOUTH AFRICA

A party of children numbering about 200, *rescued from the famine stricken area of Russia and brought to London, left Waterloo Station en route for South Africa, where they will be adopted. The children are with their nurses on the platform before departure.*

ORPHANS FROM RUSSIA
People, London – 4.9.1921

This week-end there has left London for South Africa by the Union Castle liner, the "Edinburgh Castle", some 160 Jewish orphan children from Russia, who have been staying for 8 or 9 days at the Atlantic Passengers' Hostels in the East End. This large family of orphans has been taken from Russia to be provided with a home in South Africa, through the generosity of a wealthy Jewish gentleman, and it is understood that further steps in the same direction with regard to other children are contemplated by the same benefactor.

SUCCOUR FOR POLISH CHILDREN
South Africa's Aid
Yorkshire Herald, York – 5.9.1921

South African Jews have banded themselves together to help the destitute and starving children of Poland, the Ukraine, and Galicia. Mr Isaac Ochberg, President of the Cape Jewish Orphanage in Cape Town, is now in London with two hundred children who have been collected in Warsaw from the more distressed districts and were to leave with them for South Africa last Friday.

The children, who are all under nine years of age, will be taken care of by the Jewish Orphanage and by the trustees of the Jewish War Victims' and Orphans' Fund in Johannesburg, and the intention is to distribute them among Jewish families and to bring them up as British citizens.

In the course of an interview with a representative of the press, Mr Ochberg said that the children he had now in his charge formed the first contingent of those who would be taken to South Africa. "They are all", he remarked, "victims of some pogrom or disturbance, and when I found them they were roaming about the towns or in the forest, filthy, worse than naked, and starving. I have been from village to village to pick them up. In most of the places there was no food and disease was rampant, and in some of them I was glad to get even a

crust of bread to eat. The Jewish community in South Africa have taken up the idea very favourably, and the Dominion Government have extended their sympathy, and have given us every assistance possible, especially in the way of withdrawing the restriction against the immigration of orphan children." Mr Ochberg spoke with gratitude of the help given by the British officials in the districts of the favourable terms given by the steamship companies for transporting the children. He deplored, however, that the Polish authorities had not been so ready to help in the matter, their attitude having, he remarked, generally been apathetic.

Nottingham Journal – 8.9.1921
POLISH ORPHANS

The Federation of Ukrainian Jews in London has sent a relief committee out to the Ukraine to bring some of the orphan children starving there. They are being cared for at a hostel at 193 Bow Road, where they will stay for a few days, after which they will be sent to South Africa, and a home found for everyone of them. Our picture shows the first party which arrived. In the centre can be seen Anco, their beloved interpreter and guardian.

JEWISH ORPHANS FOR SOUTH AFRICA
Liverpool Post & Mercury Liverpool – 5.9.1921

There has left London for South Africa by the Union-Castle liner Edinburgh Castle a party of some 160 Jewish orphan children from Russia who have been staying for eight or nine days at the Atlantic passengers' hostels in the East-end, and while awaiting the sailing of the boat have been receiving the hospitality of members of the Jewish race in London. All have lost their parents in the Ukraine as the result of the troubles which have beset the land.

This large family of orphans has been taken from Russia to be provided with a home in South Africa through the generosity of a wealthy Jewish gentleman, and it is understood that further steps in the same direction with regard to other children are contemplated by the same benefactor.

JEWISH WAR-ORPHANS
Christian, London – 22.9.1921

The first group of Jewish War-orphans has just sailed for South Africa, under the care of Mr Isaac Ochberg, of Cape Town who, after overcoming tremendous difficulties, brought the children out of the Ukraine. On their arrival in Africa, the children will be cared for at the Cape Jewish Orphanage, and from there they will be gradually dispersed among reliable Jewish families, who will adopt them and bring them up as their own. It is the intention of the South African Jewish community to continue with this work; and it is hoped that as time proceeds, others, to the extent of a few thousands, will find happy homes in this new country. The hospitality of the Federation of Ukrainian Jews was extended to the children during their short stay in London.

JEWISH ORPHAN CHILDREN FROM EASTERN EUROPE
Cape Town, September 20
South Africa, London – 23.9.1921

Two hundred Jewish orphan children collected from the pogrom areas of Eastern Europe who are to be taken into the care of the Jewish Orphanage at Cape Town and the trustees of the Jewish War Victims and Orphan Fund, have arrived here under the charge of Mr Ochberg, and have left for various destinations. – *Reuters*

THE ATTEMPT TO SAVE THE STARVING RUSSIANS
Sphere, London – 10.9.1921

Mr Nansen, the famous explorer, who is acting as the intermediary between the Moscow Government and the various fereign Governments, arrived in London last week-end in connection with the international scene for the relief of famine-stricken Russia. Here he is seen on arrival at Victoria with Lord Weardale of the "Save the Children Fund" (on left), Mrs Snowden and Miss E Jebb, the honourary secretary of the fund.

A group of Young Russian Refugees in London. This party of young Russian children has been brought over to England from Russia in an effort to save the child-life of that unhappy country. These children are being housed and fed at a hostel in Bow Road London

ORPHANS FROM THE UKRAINE
The Herald, Glasgow – 26.9.1921 and The Daily Telegraph Correspondent

Johannesburg. Thursday (delayed) – The Jewish community assembled in great force at the station today and gave 75 orphans from the Ukraine a rousing reception. The children will be housed in the Jewish Home for the Aged temporarily. Three big sunny rooms have been arranged as dormitories, with rows of camp beds and snowy pillows and sheets. These little orphans were warmly welcomed by the rest of the fraternity. Judging from their appearance the children should be an asset to the Jewish community in Johannesburg.

Photos courtesy
International Press Cutting Bureau
New Bridge Street, London EC4

Thank you to the many people who sent in these news cuttings and a very big thank you to Dov Penzik who went to a much trouble to obtain better copies for us.

THE UKRAINE TERROR – ORPHAN'S PATHETIC APPEAL
The Jewish Guardian dated ~August 1921

"Can you provide me with a rubber arm?" asked Harry Stillerman, one of the Jewish war orphans from the Ukraine who are now domiciled in Bow Road, en route for South Africa, when our special representative visited their shelter. His story is typical of the 137 boys and girls who have been brought to this country by Mr Isaac Ochberg, President of the Cape Town Jewish Orphanage, having been adopted by Jewish residents in South Africa. The tale of their journey, their selection and approval by the Immigration Authorities, is sufficient to prove that Mr Ochberg was untiring in his efforts to bring happiness and health to the bereft children. What is more, he will provide for them in South Africa a home where they will receive again a mother's love and a father's care from the benevolent Jewry of that country.

But, Harry Stillerman's story remains to be told. He is 12 years of age, slightly built. Very intelligent and sensitive. He recited his experiences unhaltingly yet wistfully. It appears that his family were the victims of the notoriously cruel sack of Filchtine, where probably the greatest pogrom in the whole history of the occurrences in Eastern Europe since 1916 took place. It was here he lost his arm as he called it: as a matter of fact the hand only is missing. In 1918 Petlura's army was operating in the neighbourhood. His father and mother were bayoneted before his eyes. He and his sister attempted to get away, but they were caught and subjected to a form of mental torture which surpasses the wit of the most prolific imaginative writers of the ages. He was given a candle and was told to burn his sister's eyes with the flame. Needless to say he refused. The punishment that was passed upon him for refusal was again the conception of a maniac. First he saw his sister put to death with the bayonet, and then, as though he had not suffered sufficiently mentally, he was made to suffer bodily also.

One of the soldiers took hold of his left hand and severed it from the arm with a sabre. He was rescued by some peasants and taken to a hospital near Proskurov and was kept there for about two months. Hence the pathetic plea, 'Can you give me a rubber arm?' There is little more to say of his history, though in that short period his sufferings must have been intense. He was rescued eventually by Mr Katz, who went out to the Ukraine about two years ago, and while there acted as a representative of the Federation of Ukrainian Jews, under whose auspices the orphans arrived in London. The lad was taken to Lemberg and was placed in an orphanage there, and from the large number who found refuge in the building Mr Ochberg chose a large number. There is a charming sequel to this story, for on Monday morning last young Harry found, much to his surprise, that a visitor to the Settlement at Bow Road was none other than an uncle who has been resident in this country for 15 years. Obviously the ties of family suggested to the old gentleman that he should adopt Harry. The lad, however, has made his own place in the little orphan community, and when asked by our special representative whether he would prefer to stay with his uncle or go to South Africa, replied, 'I want to go with the other children to South Africa,' and to South Africa Harry was due to go yesterday. Questioned as to his education said he could only speak Yiddish and had spent a great deal of time in the *Talmud Torah* until the pogrom occurred which sent him and about 86 others in search of refuge.

The whole of the party, under the auspices of the Federation of Ukrainian Jews, was taken to Ruislip by motor charabancs on Tuesday afternoon, and were regally entertained by the Federation. Feasted and entertained, they arrived home in a state of happiness and tired contentment that bore living testimony to the good and noble work of the Federation.

Ochberg leaving Danzig for London with children on board SS Baltara – August 1921

The children disembarking in London - en route to Cape Town

The Edinburgh Castle entering Cape Town harbour - 21 Sept 1921
News cuttings courtesy Lionel Slier

Chapter 25 – A SECOND VISIT TO THE UKRAINE

FROM CAPE TOWN TO THE UKRAINE
Jewish Relief News – England 1923

Bringing Happiness to the Hungry

Mr Isaac Ochberg was born in Uman, a town in the Ukraine. His father Aaron had gone to South Africa and there Isaac followed him at the early age of fourteen, making the trip alone. Several years later he got into business and very soon established himself. His successful business career has especially been interesting for his ventures in ship buying and it is on account of these that the Cape Argus described him as the plucky shipowner. Important purchases of properties have also given Mr Ochberg a high standing in the business world.

His Jewish Communal work has been of equal importance. He is a leading member of a number of institutions in Cape Town and his special interest has been making helpless children happy. For seven years he has been very active as President of the Cape Jewish Orphanage, and it was in this connection that he formulated a scheme for bringing over pogrom orphans from the Ukraine to South Africa. In 1921 he travelled to the part run over by the Balachovitch's bandits, and brought back with him 200 orphan boys and girls. Of these 100 were taken to the Cape Jewish Orphanage, whilst the others were taken over by the Johannesburg Relief Reconstruction and Orphans Fund of which Mr Bernard Alexander is President. It was Mr Ochberg's burning wish, however, to see how his fellow-Jews in the heart of the Ukraine were faring. After great difficulty he succeeded in getting permission to enter the country. He was placed in charge of a special delegation appointed by the World Relief Conference, which sent through him a shipment of 1,100 tons of food-stuffs, and medical stores, amounting to thousands of pounds. Clothing parcels were also sent through him by the Federation, while the War Victim Fund asked Mr Ochberg to distribute for them £1,000 amongst the Jews in Kovno and Wilno districts. After four months' stay in Russia and the Ukraine Mr Ochberg returned to London.

A group of 150 Orphans maintained in Odessa by the Cape Jewish Orphanage. Mr Ochberg is in the centre – courtesy Jewish Relief News

MR ISAAC OCHBERG RETURNS
The Cape Argus – Monday, 7 May 1923

Work of Cape Jewish Missioner in Russia's Devastated Areas

Mr Isaac Ochberg returned by this morning's mail-boat from his second mission to the Ukraine, where he distributed huge quantities of food and clothing, and in the name of the Cape Jewish Orphanage, opened a relief kitchen in Odessa.

In a conversation on board the Saxon with *The Argus*, Mr Ochberg stated that he fortunately arrived in the stricken area at the right time, as the unfortunate people were feeling the rigours of winter and, but for the timely assistance he was able to render, there would have been acute and widespread distress. Mr Ochberg held a mandate from Professor Nansen's Relief Committee, which protected him against being searched or arrested.

He is the first British Jew to be granted the right of free travel in Russia, and European Jewish organisations took full advantage of his visit to place at his disposal both funds and material, in order to make as great success as possible of his mission of relief.

The American Relief Organisation has done wonderful work, and have funded, according to Mr Ochberg, enormous quantities of food, including hundreds of cartons of wheat and flour.

Internal Conditions

Mr Ochberg was naturally very circumspect in his remarks about internal affairs in Russia, and did not enter into political or economic problems, but it is evident that internal Russia is "still in the shadows".

Mr Ochberg, who started from Warsaw and visited Khiev, the districts on the Baranowitch border, Odessa, Nikolaieff, Cracow and Moscow, formed the impression that there was a slight economic improvement. Business premises in the larger towns are re-opening and there is an approach to commercial activity. At the same time the agriculturists are making no attempt to product more than is required for their necessities, and until freedom in trade is restored there can be no definite improvement in the condition of the masses. In South Russia conditions are still extremely bad.

Jewish Defence Force Stops Pogrom

The kitchen at Odessa, which feeds 150 children every day, will be run for a year; at least the Cape Jewish community have undertaken full financial responsibility for that period, and it is hoped that arrangements can be made by the end of the year for bringing another 30 orphan children from the Ukraine to South Africa to make up the complement agreed to by the Government.

The Jewish Self-Defence Force, which was authorised by the Russian Government in those districts inwhich pogroms had become frequent, numbers about 10,000, and the fact that such a force is in existence had a beneficial effect in improving the living conditions of the Jew, removing the dark clouds which continually threatened to break.

Enthusiastic Welcome

Mr Ochberg had an enthusiastic welcome home this morning. He was looking remarkably well, and was delighted to return after his absence which had lasted just a year. In addition to a large number of friends who were at the boat side were the committee of the Jewish Orphanage led by Mr J Kadish president, and Mr L Raphaely, treasurer. There will be a special gathering tonight in the Gardens Synagogue in honour of Mr Ochberg.

The above photograph shows Mr Isaac Ochberg after his arrival by the Saxon this morning, leaving the ship with his wife and daughter, friends and members of the committee of the Cape Jewish Orphanage.

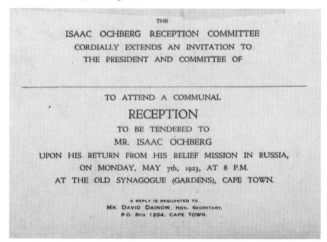

THE

ISAAC OCHBERG RECEPTION COMMITTEE
CORDIALLY EXTENDS AN INVITATION TO
THE PRESIDENT AND COMMITTEE OF

TO ATTEND A COMMUNAL

RECEPTION

TO BE TENDERED TO
MR. ISAAC OCHBERG
UPON HIS RETURN FROM HIS RELIEF MISSION IN RUSSIA,
ON MONDAY, MAY 7th, 1923, AT 8 P.M.
AT THE OLD SYNAGOGUE (GARDENS), CAPE TOWN.

A REPLY IS REQUESTED TO
MR. DAVID DAINOW, HON. SECRETARY,
P.O. Box 1204, CAPE TOWN.

Cynthia Zukas, the granddaughter of Isaac Ochberg, writes from Zambia.

First of all, I don't remember my grandfather at all, he was in Cape Town, we lived in Johannesburg and I was only five when he died.

What I do remember was that during my student days in Cape Town, I used to go with my Mother every year to celebrate second night Passover at the orphanage. Fanny Lokitch was still there, and I think cousins Phyllis and Dick as well. They were happy occasions, and when one of the kids found the matzo my Mum had arranged a big gift, sports equipment or a new gramophone etc. It was great to hear the children singing all the songs with gusto.

I'm trying to remember why Noreen and I cut ourselves off from the Ochberg praises. Partly, as I said, embarrassment at him being portrayed as a 'saint', and partly as students we didn't want our friends hearing that we had a very rich grandfather.

You probably know my parents divorced when I was about six or seven, and my Dad had a very different memory. Yes, he admired the philanthropy, but said Isaac was a hard and difficult man in business!

But since meeting Lauren, I have met a couple of other children of orphans, including Mr Sandak-Lewin and Mrs Levenkind (from Zim), and feel very proud of him.

I have just reread bits of my Mother's book on bequests. I had a friend at UCT doing architecture, Kenny Dixon and was surprised to hear he received a grant from Oranjia. Also, I remember the small dowry for girls getting married. I wonder if these small grants were given to Arcadia as well as Oranjia?

By 1971 my husband, Simon Zukas and I were both political exiles from South Africa and living in Zambia. When the organisers tried to get me special permission to attend the Jubilee they refused. I think it was petty and spiteful of them!

I enclose a photo of an illustrated plaque I inherited after our Mum died.

Maybe 30 years ago, we were in Israel to visit my mother-in-law and paid a visit to Kibbutz Dahlia, which was quite inspiring.

I am an artist and I run an Art Charity that gives grants and scholarships to talented Zambian artists. We have two sons, one here, one in UK, six grandchildren and one great granddaughter.

Extract from THE JEWS OF ZAMBIA by Sharon Rosen

When Zambia became an independent nation in 1964, the country's Jewish community, which numbered approximately 700 families supporting seven shuls, dwindled to 100 families supporting one shul in Lusaka. Most of the Jews immigrated to South Africa, England, Israel and the United States. Simon and Cynthia bucked the trend, returning to Zambia in 1965.

Simon Zukas provided advice and counsel to Dr. Kenneth Kaunda's new government. He later became the first white to

Photo of an illustrated plaque I inherited after our Mum died. The letter on the left is from "Fund for the relief of the Jewish Victims of the war in Eastern Europe" 1923 and the letter on the right is from "Conference Universalle Juive de Secours" 1923

serve in a Zambian cabinet (first as minister of agriculture and then as minister of public works) when Frederick Chiluba became president in the 1990s. Simon takes pride in the fact that he supported African justice and independence from the 1950s to the present.

Cynthia, an accomplished fine artist, also took part in Zambia's nation-building by serving on the board of the National Museum and the National Arts Trust. She chairs the Lechwe Trust, which provides grants and scholarships to Zambian artists, enabling them to create at home and study abroad.

Cynthia said she feels that living in Zambia gave her the opportunity to accomplish more than she could have in London. "I was determined to do what I could to help here," Cynthia said. "One can't give up just because of the poverty. You can't put money in one man's pocket to affect change. Simon and I tried to look at the bigger picture, he in politics and I in the art world."

Simon and Cynthia represent one of the seven Jewish families still living in Zambia.

FUND FOR THE RELIEF OF THE JEWISH VICTIMS OF THE WAR IN EASTERN EUROPE

28, Throgmorton St., London, E.C.2

March 21st. 1923

Isaac Ochberg Esq,
Constitutional Club,
Northumberland Avenue,
London. W.C.

Dear Mr. Ochberg,

We feel that we ought to place on record our great indebtedness to you for the help and advice that you have so kindly given us during your stay in London.

Your mission to the Ukraine undertaken by you at great personal sacrifice and expense was of the utmost benefit, not only to the sufferers in the stricken areas, but also to all Organisations working in Europe for their relief. The information and reports which you have brought back have been valuable because we had an opportunity of being guided by your personal experience.

The members of our Committee who had the pleasure of meeting you and of hearing your statement on the present conditions in the Ukraine, were impressed by your sincerity. They admired the courageous action which you have taken in braving the risks of a journey through the diseased and ruined districts in which you spent four months.

South Africa has raised large sums of money for the relief of our fellow Jews in Eastern Europe. It is, however, the sympathy and devotion, at the back of these collections, which have impressed us very much. We especially appreciate the fact that yours was the first visit within recent years to the Ukraine by Jewish representative from the British Empire.

118

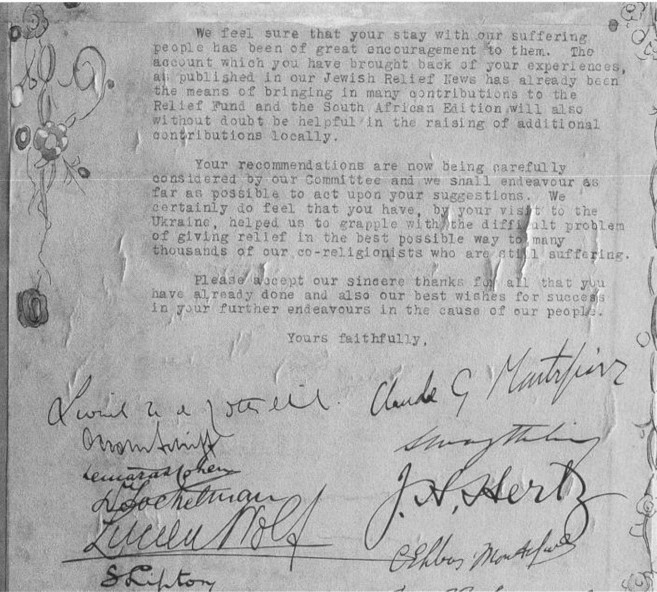

We feel sure that your stay with our suffering people has been of great encouragement to them. The account which you have brought back of your experiences, as published in our Jewish Relief News has already been the means of bringing in many contributions to the Relief Fund and the South African Edition will also without doubt be helpful in the raising of additional contributions locally.

Your recommendations are now being carefully considered by our Committee and we shall endeavour as far as possible to act upon your suggestions. We certainly do feel that you have, by your visit to the Ukraine, helped us to grapple with the difficult problem of giving relief in the best possible way to many thousands of our co-religionists who are still suffering.

Please accept our sincere thanks for all that you have already done and also our best wishes for success in your further endeavours in the cause of our people.

Yours faithfully,

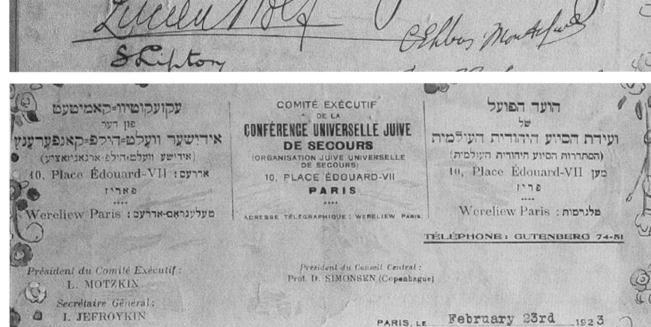

עקזעקוטיוו-קאמיטעט
פון דער
אידישער וועלט-הילף-קאנפערענץ
(אידישע וועלט-הילף-ארגאניזאציע)
10, Place Édouard-VII :ארדעם
פאריז
····
Wereliew Paris :טעלעגראם-אדרעם

COMITÉ EXÉCUTIF
DE LA
CONFÉRENCE UNIVERSELLE JUIVE
DE SECOURS
(ORGANISATION JUIVE UNIVERSELLE
DE SECOURS)
10, PLACE ÉDOUARD-VII
PARIS
····
ADRESSE TÉLÉGRAPHIQUE : WERELIEW PARIS

הועד הפועל
של
ועידת הסיוע היהודית העולמית
(ההתדרות הסיוע היהודית העולמית)
10, Place Édouard-VII מען
פריז
····
Wereliew Paris :מלגרמות

TÉLÉPHONE : GUTENBERG 74-51

Président du Comité Exécutif :
L. MOTZKIN

Secrétaire Général :
I. JEFROYKIN

Président du Conseil Central :
Prof. D. SIMONSEN (Copenhague)

PARIS, LE   February 23rd   1923

Mr. I. OCHBERG,
National Bank of South Africa
LONDON.

N° 15467

Dear Mr. Ochberg,

In presence of the marvelous and so important work you accomplished during your mission in the Ukraine where you so devotedly lent a helping hand to our sinistred brethren, we wish, on your return, to express to you our most hearty feelings of sympathy and gratitude.

You have not had a moment's hesitation to sacrifice months of your existence already filled with other duties. Neither did you fear to expose your health, nor spare your forces and your means. You undertook this journey which you considered as a holy pilgrimage.

Your efforts remained not fruitless. The observations you gathered, the effective work you did, the judicious advices bearing the stamp of your good sense which you offered to your collegues of the mission and to our Executive Committee, finally the practical conclusions and those of principle you brought back from your mission and which you so remarkably outline in your reports, all this served highly our relief work and will enlighten our way in future.

Reiterating our thanks, we beg to remain,

with our kindest regards,

Yours very sincerely

THE GENERAL SECRETARY

J. Jefrojkin

THE PRESIDENT

L. Motzkin

These tributes were kindly sent in by Cynthia Zukas, the granddaughter of Isaac Ochberg

CAPE TOWN ZIONIST FAMILY HONOURED
Daily News, Cape Town, 29 September 1970

The Hebrew University of Jerusalem has honoured the memory of a prominent Cape Town Zionist family, the late Mr and Mrs Isaac Ochberg, by establishing a new wing in their law faculty named after them.

The wing, built on the University's Mount Scopus campus, was officially opened last week by the daughter of Mr and Mrs Ochberg, Mrs Bertha Epstein. The board of governors and a number of South Africans and former South Africans, now resident in Israel, attended the opening ceremony.

When Mr Ochberg, died at the age of 59 in 1937, he left what was then the largest single bequest ever made to the community, a sum of over a quarter of a million Palestine pounds (over US$500,000 at that time) which was divided between the Jewish National Fund and the Hebrew University of Jerusalem.

Bequest

The University used the bequest to build the new wing housing the law faculty's library and two of its research institutes, that for Jewish law and for legislative research and comparative law.

Mrs Pauline Ochberg also established at the university the Ruth Ochberg chair in the faculty of agriculture, in memory of their daughter, and made available funds for student scholarships.

In a tribute at the opening ceremony to Mr Ochberg, Mr Justice Joseph Herbstein recalled that his former colleague had travelled to his native Ukraine in 1921 and again in 1922 first to bring 200 destitute Jewish children to South Africa where he persuaded the Jewish community to undertake full responsibility for their welfare, and again in what was virtually a one-man rescue mission, to set up soup kitchens to aid others who could not leave.

THIS WAS A MAN
Zionist Record 7 February 1975

CAPE TOWN- Bertha Epstein has published in a limited edition, a book on the life of her father, Isaac Ochberg, entitled *This Was a Man*.

In a warm, filial fashion, she traces the life of 'the type of man born once in a generation', from his birth in the Russian Ukraine to his deeply-lamented death.

This man of indomitable courage, far-sightedness and business acumen, made full use, she says, of every opportunity that came his way.

He was best known perhaps, to the Jews of South Africa as an ardent Zionist and philanthropist. Mrs Epstein recalls his bravery in getting his family from Russia, and the 200 orphans he brought from the Ukraine to *Oranjia*, the Jewish orphanage of Cape Town in 1921.

It seems almost impossible that a man should have accomplished so much in one lifetime. Mrs Epstein brings vividly to life his dynamic personality, his courage and his ever-present concern for his fellowmen.

His Will bears testimony to his love for South Africa, the land of his adoption, and for Israel.

DRAMATIC RESCUE OF CHILDREN RECALLED
The Argus, Thursday, 31 March 1977

After World War 1, when Jews were being massacred in pogroms in Poland and Russia, a Cape Town businessman set out alone to save as many of the children involved as possible.

He braved dangers and discomfort to find and bring out 200 orphans who he took from Danzig to London in a chartered ship.

Then he brought them to Cape Town.

His name was Isaac Ochberg and he was born in Russia but came to South Africa with his family as a child. He became president of the Cape Jewish Orphanage.

The story of his rescue operation is told in an exhibition of treasures from the archives of the Jewish Museum which is being held at the Old Synagogue in Government Avenue during the Cape Town Festival.

Passport

His passport, with visas and entry stamps for Poland and Russia, is among the exhibits together with an identifying armband worn by one of the 'Ochberg children' – Mr Jack Shrier, who now lives in Sea Point.

Mr Shrier was one of the 100 children who were taken in by the Cape Jewish Orphanage. The others went to an orphanage in Johannesburg. Many were later adopted, and some still live in Cape Town.

This fascinating exhibition also has touches of humour. There are photographs and cartoons of Mr Hyman Liberman, who was not only the first Jewish Mayor of Cape Town but is believed to have been the first Jewish Mayor in the whole of Southern Africa.

Cartoons

The cartoons include ones drawn during his period of office when the City Council acquired its first mayoral car. It shows the Mayor and city councillors driving along the 'road to ruin' in a car labelled *mad expenditure.*

Other cartoons show a trip up Table Mountain to inspect the reservoirs which the Mayor and councillors made on donkeys and mules.

And there is a light-hearted report of a City Council meeting told entirely in cartoons.

So although this exhibition – with photographs of momentous occasions in the life of the Jewish community in Cape Town, and beautiful illuminated addresses to former ministers – is of particular interest to the Jewish community, other people would also find it worth visiting.

It will be open from 10.00 am until 5.00 pm on Tuesdays, Wednesdays and Thursdays and on Sundays from 10.00 am until 1.00 pm throughout April, except for Passover and Easter. Passover this year is on the same weekend as Easter.

THE OCHBERG LEGEND
Published in the Cape Jewish Chronical
December 1986

In the third week of September 1921 the sleek Edinburgh Castle entered Cape Town Harbour after a two-and-a-half week voyage from England. The 200 children on board had travelled from much further than England in the preceding six months. They had come from the devastated villages and destitute ghettos of Eastern Europe where all of their parents had died. Isaac Ochberg, a cheerful red-haired man in his early forties appeared on deck, and the children immediately swarmed around him.

In the political and social upheaval following World War I, a destructive wave of programs, famine and epidemics engulfed much of Eastern European Jewry. Civil war raged in Poland, the Ukraine and Russia. Bolsheviks, monarchists and bands of guerrillas fought bloody battles. Murderous pogroms in Jewish towns were reported daily. Influenza and typhoid epidemics were responsible for innumerable deaths and it was estimated that about 400 000 Jewish children had been orphaned.

In Cape Town, an extraordinary meeting of the Jewish community listened as Isaac Ochberg, himself a Ukrainian immigrant, proposed a rescue effort for as many children as could be saved. It was hoped that £10 000 could be raised. But how many children without parents would the government allow in?
Prime Minister Jan Smuts and Interior Minister Patrick Duncan were approached, and permission was promptly granted for the entry of an unrestricted number, provided they were all in perfect health, reasonably intelligent, and would not become a burden on the state. The Cape Town Jewish Orphanage

agreed to assume responsibility for looking after them and trying to place them for adoption. A figure of 200 youngsters was decided upon if the money could be raised. Ochberg, who after years of struggle in Cape Town and Johannesburg was now a well-to-do businessman, offered to go to the Ukraine at his own expense to gather and bring back the children.

The money for what was officially called 'Immigration of the Ukrainian Orphans' was quickly raised. At an enthusiastic meeting in a Cape Town cinema in August 1920, hundreds of people pledged a total of £25 000. Funds and offers of help poured in from communities all over South Africa.

Seven months later, Isaac Ochberg sailed for Europe on what was certain to be a hazardous mission. Epidemics, gangs of bandits, and lack of transportation were but a few of the dangers awaiting him in the areas he was headed for.

He was armed only with a Nansen passport (a safe-conduct document issued by the International Russian Relief Committee established by Fridtjof Nansen, the Arctic explorer), for refugees and relief workers.

Ochberg began choosing children. Many of them had lived through hellish experiences, seeing their parents killed or their mothers and sisters raped and mutilated. Selection was an agonising responsibility for Ochberg, but he applied two criteria: only those children who had lost both parents and only those who wished to go.

The children were assembled in Warsaw for the journey to South Africa. Some travelled in slow dirty trains to Warsaw – clutching a precious doll or a dog-eared photograph. In Warsaw Madam Panya Engel cared for the children.

Sorely needed supplies began arriving: from Berlin and the United States: condensed milk, cocoa, cooking oil, 16 cases of clothes arrived from South Africa.

The children travelled under group passports, and when some of the children were held back or dropped out for various reasons, the authorities crossed out their sad little faces from the group photo. A small Baltic steamer ferried the children to London.

Ochberg enlisted a number of British volunteers to accompany the children to South Africa and on September 2, 1921, the Edinburgh Castle sailed from England with Isaac Ochberg and the 200 orphans on board. Each child carried a knapsack laden with an issue of clothing and a few meagre belongings. The Union Castle Line helped out with greatly reduced fares and a supply of kosher food.

On the voyage fellow passengers took a warm, friendly interest in the little immigrants, and at dawn on September 19, the ship eased into Cape Town harbour. Thousands of weeping, cheering people lined the quayside in an emotional greeting.

Chapter 28 – DAVID DAINOW – A HERO

AN UNIQUE MEETING IN CAPE TOWN
The South African Jewish Chronicle – 19 Dec 1952

A meeting of an unique character took place on a recent Tuesday evening in Cape Town. Those present were members of an Old Boys' and Girls' Union. They were not graduates of a college or a university or of any fashionable educational institution. Actually they had been residents for a number of years – (in the old days the word *inmates* would have been used) – of the Cape Jewish Orphanage in Oranjezicht. Now grown up – one *old girl* is a grandmother – they banded themselves together some years ago into a *Union* which helps to raise funds and to supply amenities to the present residents of this fine institution for unfortunate Jewish children.

Hearing that the previous Director and Secretary of the Orphanage, in the person of Mr David Dainow, was on a recuperative stay in Muizenberg, after a recent severe illness, a request was made to him to address the members of her group.

Mr Dainow readily consented, especially when he heard that some of the *graduates* of the institution, who would be present at his talk, had come over to South Africa with the group of two hundred children, which the late Mr Isaac Ochberg had brought to South Africa from the pogrom areas of the Ukraine some thirty one years ago.

'An historic event occurred at that time,' said Mr Dainow. 'The faraway community of Cape Town felt it was not enough to give money to funds for relieving Jewish victims of the first World War. It also wished to save lives.

'It was then that a great idea was born – the project for the bringing over of a large group of stricken war orphans to be adopted by South African Jewry.'

Mr Dainow added that the idea fired the imagination of the late Isaac Ochberg, who was then President of the Cape Jewish Orphanage. Busy man as he was, he decided to undertake the holy mission of redemption personally and to enter the dangerous areas of the Ukraine borders to rescue some of the children.

'At that time, I was a uniformed member of the staff of the Joint Distribution Committee in Warsaw,' went on Mr Dainow. 'One day my chief, the late Dr Boris Bogen, sent for me and told me that a gentleman had arrived from South Africa to take over a group of pogrom orphans. No other Jewish community in the world had undertaken such an activity and the gentleman concerned was having a hard time.

'I understood that Mr Ochberg had already journeyed into the interior of the Ukraine. He had chosen quite a number of children whose parents had been killed in the pogroms. Difficulties, however, arose with the temporary authorities of that wild country. Ochberg, with the children, had to flee into Poland as their lives were in danger.

'The children', went on Mr Dainow, 'were placed in temporary orphan homes in various parts of Poland, whilst Ochberg chose further orphans who had escaped from the Ukraine and who were roaming about uncared for in most unhappy conditions.

'So earnestly did Mr Ochberg devote himself to his task that he did not notice that a great prejudice had sprung up against a stranger who had come to take away human lives.'

'It was at this stage that I, who was the only British Jew on the 'Joint' Staff, was asked to help. As a representative of this great official distribution agency – which was so deeply respected by Polish Jewry – I managed to calm harassed and anxious Jewish communal leaders and to assure them that the stranger's purpose in taking the children was a noble one, and that a fine and generous Jewish community many thousands of miles away would adopt the orphans and be their new parents.'

'Finally, all local opposition was overcome and gradually the people began to understand the generous hand being held out to them. Until that happened, however, Ochberg went through a terrific crisis. This all must have had an effect on his health, which took its toll in later years.'

Mr Dainow went on to relate how when all the children had been finally gathered into Warsaw, Ochberg had to face tremendous difficulties from the disturbed Polish Administration at the time, to obtain all the necessary permits, documentation, passports, travel tickets, etc.

An accompanying staff of nurses and assistants had to be engaged to travel with the large party of children to South Africa. Ochberg interviewed hundreds of applicants before making the final choices. When all was ready, there was tremendous difficulty in chartering a special boat to take the children and staff to London. Ochberg worked like a Trojan and a boat was secured.

On their safe arrival in London, under the personal care of Isaac Ochberg, whom the children had now learnt to adore, they were taken to the Jews' temporary shelter and were well cared for by London Jewry.

It took weeks before all the arrangements could be made to place the children on a boat for their journey to South Africa. Mr Ochberg was, of course with them.

'The rest of the story is generally known,' added Mr Dainow. 'The children were loyally welcomed and cherished. Half their number were adopted by Johannesburg and Transvaal Jewry and many were adopted by private Jewish families. The rest of the children were brought up with every attention love and care in the orphanages of Cape Town and Johannesburg.

Mr Dainow came over in 1922 at Mr Ochberg's cabled request to help in placing the children in homes and institutions. A year later the work was ended and he then entered the service of the Zionist Federation.

Mr Dainow said finally: 'The work of Isaac Ochberg was a shining light in the story of philanthropic endeavour. The whole project was unique and proved a lasting credit to South African Jewry.

Mr Schneider, Chairman of Old Boys' and Girls' Union, expressed deep thanks to Mr Dainow for his illuminating and informative address. ***Article sent in by Lionel Slier***

PART 1
THE 'PALE OF SETTLEMENT'
1914~1922

SECTION 5
FIRST HAND ACCOUNTS OF THE OCHBERG ORPHANS

This section contains first hand accounts of the
Ochberg Orphans, most of whom have now passed away.

Most where interviewed by Rainmaker Films
for its documentary, some left written accounts of their lives
while others were interviewed by their children.

All secondhand accounts of Ochberg Orphans, compiled
by their descendants, will be found in Parts 2 and 3 of this book.

We start off this section with the first hand account of Feiga Mirel,
a mother of two Ochberg Orphans, Rose and Mannie Shamis.

Feiga Mirel Shamis tells her life story; her struggle to survive in the first two decades of the twentieth century in the Ukraine and Poland and to bring up her twelve children, including two, Rose and Mannie, who were later taken to South Africa by Isaac Ochberg.

Two copies of this book were written in long hand in Yiddish and sent by Feiga then living in Israel to Rose and Mannie living in South Africa. Mannie had the book translated into English by Mrs Luba Cesman in 1991 and in 1998, four years after Mannie's death, Nora Favish, his wife, had the book edited and published as a legacy for Rose and Mannie's children, grandchildren and great–grandchildren.

Judy Favish the daughter of Mannie has kindly shared the book with us

SHALOM SHALOM MY DEAR CHILDREN
Written by Feiga Mirel Shamis

Now dear children, I your mother will describe what I have done in this beautiful good world, with lots of *tsores,* ever since I was young. I was born Feiga Mirel Misler in a small *shtetl* called Verba in 1878 and my father died when he was still very young. We were five children when he died and my mother was pregnant. We all worked and helped, and the elder sister was

engaged but my father had not been able to take her to the *chupa.* He had organised a religious husband with *peyote* for my other sister.

I missed my father who had gone on business to Dubno where he took ill. We were called out on a Sunday when he died and the funeral was held there on the Monday. When we returned my mother was a widow with orphans.

Imagine our troubles when we lost the head of the home. What did we have left? We looked like wandering sheep, and they say a widow is very bitter even if she has a golden roof. But we knew that we could do nothing. It was God's will.

After my father's death I wanted to go to Rovno to study in high school but my mother prevented me from going.

'There is no father so there is no high school', she said. 'We have to look after the shop.'

'You have other children,' I told her, 'let them be in the shop.' But I was very capable and could look after the business better than the others, so she would not let me go. I wanted to study nursing and become a sister to help the doctors, but she would not let me. I promised to return the money that she would have to spend but it was 'no', and one has to listen to a mother sometimes.

Kalman Shamis 1876-1918 and Feiga Mirel (Misler) Shamis

As time passed she forced me to go into our business and she made a businesswoman out of me. I was able to go out and buy goods without getting lost, but thank God I had completed the Russian primary school early.

The *tsores* was growing like weeds. God dishes out the good and the bad and one has to accept it. My mother married off Rosa and she then had two more children, giving me another brother and sister.

My brother, who produced vodka at his home, did not live long. Peasants who wanted vodka came into his home and tied up his wife and children. A woman who heard their screams arrived and the peasants ran away but my brother died soon after that. His wife and children later went to live in Palestine.

My mother had an aunt in Kishinev who sent a cable to say that she was marrying off an orphan, as she herself was childless, and she invited my mother to come. Mother said she would not go and leave her children behind, and so I asked her to send me.

'The train will take you somewhere else,' she replied, 'and I will have to go and look for you.'

'I have a mouth,' I said, 'I can enquire at every station.'

'Do you have any money?'

'I'll find the money,' I told her, and I sent a cable to the aunt in Kishinev who sent me 50 roubles. So I told my dear mother that I had received the money and would go soon. Then I took leave of my sister in Vishneviets, a very nice and *frum* woman. After four days with her I went back to my mother's house for *Shabat* and left for Kishinev on the Sunday.

I planned not to return from Kishinev. I wanted to leave behind all the *tsores*. It was not bad in my mother's home, we had a nice house but I knew that I would have to study for something and I have been sorry until today that I did not study further.

I went from Verba to Dubno and from there to Zhdolbunof and Radziel from where I sent a telegram to my mother and another to my aunt and uncle asking them to meet me at the station. A porter took me to the carriage and said I would reach Kishinev in the morning. When I arrived there I saw a man and woman looking into the carriages and realised that they were my Aunt Zlata and Uncle Shlomo.

When they came nearer I said, 'Are you my aunt and uncle?'
The uncle replied, 'Are you the Polish girl?'
'Yes, I am,' I said. 'You guessed right, this is I.'
So we were all very happy and went to their home.

They lived like very rich people. Their hobby was to marry off poor girls. They took me on a tour of the city and they took me to the theatre and the cinema and they bought me a present. My aunt took me shopping for clothes and you can imagine how I felt when she said: 'You are ours, I will leave everything to you in my will.'

After the grand wedding of the orphan they were marrying off, my uncle engaged me as a cashier. My Aunt said I should learn to speak Ukrainian so that I could converse with the customers and a young woman came to teach me and I progressed very well. I would not go anywhere without my aunt and I did whatever they told me. I was very happy and they were happy with me.

My teacher used to come in the daytime to give me lessons so I was surprised when she arrived one evening. She told me in confidence that the Cossacks (or Russian peasants) were going to organise a *pogrom* and she advised me to go home. I told my aunt to go to her sister in Balta until the trouble was over but she wanted to be clever.

'I have worked hard for my possessions,' she said, 'and I don't want to give them to the Cossacks.'

'Let's call your neighbour,' I pleaded, 'and ask his advice because many Jews have already left for Balta.'

So the neighbour, who was also a very rich person, said: 'Your aunt does not want to go and we should not force her. Come with us, and we'll go even further than Balta. I already have two children; let me think that I have three.'

I thanked him very much and replied: 'I'll go home to my mother because I'm afraid that she will be worried.'

My aunt said she would not let me go, so I said: 'Dear aunt, come to us in Verba for four weeks. See how many people are leaving. But if you don't want to go, I must go.'

I decided to go home and the neighbours went to Balta for four weeks. If I had been clever I would have followed the neighbours and would have gone to high school with their son and then married their son and my life would have been wonderful. I would never have gone back to that forsaken place, Verba.

When the time came for the *pogrom* they strangled my uncle and stole everything. My aunt remained with her troubles and I suppose it is all from God.

Later I received letters from my friend's father in Kishinev and also from his son. They wanted to send me money so that I could go there but my mother would not allow it. I had come home and she was very pleased with me.

'I told you not to go,' she said, 'and one should listen to a mother.'
'I will listen to you the second time,' I replied.
'My child, you have become so clever suddenly.'

'Mother, when was I a fool? I was always clever and in a big city one becomes clever because one mixes with clever people.'

I did not even want to see the village of Verba, but one cannot take only the good things. It comes from God.

Time passed and my friend from Kishinev came to visit us. He was very educated and he wanted to take me to the big city with him. I was hoping to go there because I very much wanted to study nursing. But my mother would not allow it and after two weeks my friend went home. I could do nothing with my mother and I felt that she had robbed me of my life. Nowadays one does not consult a mother, a mother is not such an important person any more. Children do what they want to.

Time passed and then my mother said she had written to my sister in Vishneviets asking her to find a good looking, educated man as a match for me.

'If that's what you want I'll go back to Kishinev to my friend,' I said, and they are very rich people.'
My mother said, 'NO'.

Then my sister came on a visit and I told her what had happened.

'Why do you have to go to Kishinev?' she asked. 'There is a very nice young man in Vishneviets. He is educated and he is decent. If you want him he can come to you.'

'No, not to me,' I said. 'I will accompany you when you return home and you can invite him to visit you. Then, if I do not like him, nobody will know.' I said this because I agreed with Hershele Ostropoler who believed that if one has an opportunity one should use it, and also because my mother liked to marry her daughters off when they were still very young. So I went to my sister and she invited the young man who greeted me very warmly. Then he went away and I went home. He asked my sister if I could write and, if so, if I would write to him, and I said, 'not so soon' because I did not want to get too fond of him. I still preferred the one from Kishinev.

However he came to visit us. He was from a very rich family and he brought his uncle with him because he was afraid he would be cheated without his uncle. He was very attractive and well educated and he became attached to me like glue, but my heart did not permit me to love him.

My mother kept on asking me: 'Do you like him?'
'I prefer the one from Kishinev,' I said. 'He is from a big city and this one is from a *shteltl.'*

I forgot about him and worked very hard for the business, and went to collect money in the village, nothing was too much for me. Then I received a letter from my sister saying that the young man wanted to visit us again, this time accompanied by my sister as well as his uncle. But the *Mazel* was far from me. This is something one cannot take for oneself, one has to ask God for it, only He has the key for the *Mazel.*

My sister was now also very keen on the match. They were nice, religious people, the young man was very well educated and we understood each other. There was a match.

My dear children, I was not yet seventeen and your father was twenty years old, and he died at 42. When we became

engaged I had a pain in my heart. He spent two weeks with us and all the people envied me because he was a very nice lad. He bought me a gold chain and he admired me but I felt nothing. I knew that everything had gone and I did not want to speak to my mother.

My mother gave him a thousand roubles as a dowry, and a gold watch and the wedding was arranged for the Saturday after *Shavout,* after the winter. I wrote to him sometimes in Yiddish and sometimes in Russian and he liked my letters. When the time came, he came to us and we had the *chupa.* Like me he had no father, only two sisters and a mother, and my mother organised a very good wedding, even though there was no father.

We were not short of troubles but when there are troubles one gets used to them. I was lucky that your father was a knowledgeable man, dear children, and after the wedding he did not want me to struggle in a

shop. He wanted to be a businessman and I agreed on condition that he would earn well because a man must provide for his wife, and I helped him.

As happens with the Jews we had children quickly. After a few years my father's sister died and their house was transferred into my name because they loved me very much and they had no children. So we had a home of our own, and your father treated me very well. When we sat down to meals the atmosphere was wonderful and I was very happy. The main thing was that he was educated, and I never needed money, except after *Havdala.*

He became a civic leader in the little town and we had a nice office in my home with a picture of the Tsar hanging there. He used to issue travel documents and things like that and once a year people used to come from the ministry to check the books and see if everything was correct. If they were satisfied he was given a train ticket and a holiday, wherever he wanted to go to.

Some years passed and a few more children came. People have smaller families these days but your mother had 12 children. Your father sent two of them to America before he died and left me with children who are now spread all over this world.

Then war broke out. They were training soldiers in the forest near our *shtetl.* There were many soldiers and officers and much shooting. It was very unpleasant because the soldiers would loot. They wanted money and food and, if we did not have any, they took our cows and the harvest from the fields. Later we organised food in our kitchen and soldiers who passed through stopped to eat at our place.

They wanted to enlist your father and he said to me: 'Who knows if I will survive, I can't go.' So he advised the soldiers to go on to Dubno and return later and they took this advice because he had an office with a picture of the Tsar on the wall and they held him in high esteem. They left, and your father remained.

Later the fighting grew worse. They started shooting from both sides of the *shtetl*. Germans on the one side and Russians on the other, and we were caught in the middle. Most of the Jews fled but we could not leave because the Cossacks wanted our horses and they worried us until we felt like the wicked in the next world.

A Jewish soldier said to us: 'Run away, they will burn you.'
'Where to?' we asked.
'Anywhere, wherever you can go.'

So we kissed the *Mezuza* and left. We went from one *shtetl* to another, with each child carrying a bundle and walking all the way because there were no horses. We could not go by train in the war, and they had burned down the station. It was dark and I was pregnant and I felt terrible and, dear children, it started raining. We reached Dubno where we rested for a few days and then went on, with the police behind us.

Life was very bitter. We reached Ostro where your father took ill. Fortunately a Jewish blacksmith approached us and took us into his home and we stayed there for four weeks. They were very good people. Then God helped us, we heard that the Germans were retreating, and we decided to go back to our home because I was in the ninth month.

Our new friends in Ostro did not want me to go. They said I should give birth to my baby in their home. They offered me a special room and said they would provide a midwife and give me everything of the best. But I thought we might be able to get back to our own home, so I risked my life and we started off.

On the way we met a soldier with a wagon, so I gave him three roubles and he took us to Varkovitz. In this town a woman gave us a room that had not been swept in at least ten years, but I told your father that I would clean in up. Luckily we were there for only four days. Soldiers told us to leave and go to Aziran because there would soon be shooting and, as we left, the shooting started. The children were crying, and I cried with them.

A wagon came by and the owner was a Jew. I begged him to take us to Dubno, which he did, and I thanked him but he would not take any money. We were not short of troubles but I felt better when I saw Dubno where we stayed for two days before going on to Verba. A Gentile took us part of the way but your father took ill again and we carried on like real Gypsies. Everyone suffered. It was war.

We reached Verba, home at last. We spent that night with another family because we were afraid to go to our own home. When we went there the next day we found a hole dug in the middle of the room, and nothing else. The home was cleaned out like before *Pesach*. The Germans had looted everything and sent it away to their families in Germany.

I felt bad and I was due any day. There was no midwife in the *shtetl* so your father, dear children, went to the village and brought back a Gentile woman who had worked for me years before and had taken my children for walks in the forest. When she arrived I gave birth to a daughter, a war baby. My new daughter was called after my mother's mother but we could not name her in the *Shul*. You can imagine, my children, how bad it was, with not a drop of milk. But the old woman, Ditoska, had brought a loaf of bread and some potatoes and we boiled water for tea.

We stayed at home for a while but then soldiers and officers arrived and things were bad again. We were chased out of our *shtetl* to the village of Nosivits, four verst (about 4 km) away, with such a tiny baby. You can imagine how bitter I was. We did not even see Gentiles on the way and the soldiers told us to carry on to Stopets where we stayed with Gentiles for six days. Then they left and we went to the village of Komerivke with the police on our trail again. We walked all the way and it was raining, it was a terrible ordeal.

The children were wet right through and my heart broke for them, and of course we had the baby with us. Not even many Gentiles were there any more but we did come across some old peasants in the village and we started meeting soldiers again. It was bitter. The children wanted to eat but we could not stop because the soldiers wouldn't allow it and we couldn't find a wagon, so we carried on. You can imagine the wonderful 'tour' we had.

We passed through Danishkevits where we stayed in the home of a wonderful peasant family. We rested a bit there and they roasted potatoes for us and gave us tea in the morning before we carried on to Teruea. From there it was very far to Terye and a soldier took us on his wagon. We spent *Shabat* at the home of a peasant in Terye and on Sunday, although we barely had the strength to live, we went on like Gypsies through the village of Sapiniets and reached the city of Kremenents. We had passed through about twenty villages and had suffered a lot with the children. It is difficult to describe.

Conditions in Kremenets were good so we stopped in the centre of the city where a butcher approached us and I told him our troubles. He kindly directed us to his house and we went there. The children were tired and wet so we dried them and fed them and put them to bed. Then I cried and cried.

I cursed the day I was born, and from travelling like that your father had taken ill from sorrow. We spent a long time at the butcher's home; they were very nice, religious Jews.

One morning, while we were having breakfast, we heard shooting and the windows were broken. Kremenets is a city of hills and they fired over the hills, as if I hadn't had enough, and a shell landed in the garden. It destroyed the whole garden and left a deep hole. The house was full of old people and if the shell had gone any further they would all have been killed. Thank God everyone was still alive. This was 'real life' and we went back into the house in case it happened again. After all, it was a war.

I discovered that there was a Jewish militia in Kremenets and I went to them and told them all that had happened to us. I asked them if they could find a room for us because your father was ailing and could not manage to do anything. That was my life. Later that day they said they found a place with two rooms and a kitchen for 16 roubles a month. So I went and paid the 16 roubles for the month and we moved into our new abode. Your father's health failed again and I was very distressed at seeing him lying there so ill in that lovely little room.

When the month was up the landlord arrived on a Friday and I thought he had come to collect the 16 roubles for the next month.

But he said: 'I can get 30 roubles. You must move on Sunday.' He was holding a stone in his hand and he shouted: 'If you don't move out I'll hit your husband with this stone.'

I stood there and thought the man was mad. What kind of person speaks like that?

But he repeated the threat: 'On Sunday you must not be here.'

'Maybe you will not live until Sunday, Mr Spiegel,' I replied, 'I am not afraid of you and your stone and you will come to remember me. My husband is afraid, not me. I will take the stone to the police and go to see the President of the City and ask whether you are allowed to evict people in this manner during the war.'

Next morning your father felt better and went to the synagogue. I said to him: 'What would we have done if that man had killed you with the stone? I will not keep quiet about it.'

The landlord and landlady went into hiding but their two daughters remained at the house. I went off to see the President. It was a long way but I was determined and I arrived at his castle where there was a guard standing outside.

'You are not allowed in here,' he said.
'Last night someone was going to kill my husband,' I told him, 'if you won't let me in I will go home and telephone the President direct.'

'Wait here,' said the guard, 'I will ask him. Maybe he will come out.'

After five minutes the President came out in his shirtsleeves and told the guard to let me in. I told him in Russian what had happened and he said: 'All right, all right, I will come with you now.'

We took his carriage and we went right through town where all the Jews stood and looked at how the President was travelling with a Jewish woman. He was not a very good man, but he was good to me. One has to know how to speak to important people.

I had told him that my husband was a leader, that he had been a Mayor for eight years under Tsar Nicolas and that a picture of the Tsar had been on the wall in our office. I also told him that our landlady locked all the doors and refused to let my children use the toilet.

'We will teach them a lesson,' he said.

He came with me right up to the entrance to the yard, then he whistled and police arrived. All the people who lived in that street came to see what was happening. The landlords were not liked and the people were happy that I had been brave enough to report them.

The President said to the daughter: 'Where are your mother and father?'
Then I said: 'Mr President, they are hiding from you.'

He ordered the police to break down the doors that were locked and I invited him to look at my room which the daughter had told him was dirty. The room was clean and the President told the daughter that he could see from my appearance that my room would be clean.

'Your father will have to pay a large fine,' he told her, 'and when you have to run from Kremenets will you please take your house with you on your shoulders. Your father wanted to kill a civil servant who has worked for the Tsar for eight years. He will sit in jail for this.'

The President was there for an hour. He wrote down everything I told him and sent a letter to the government in Warsaw. He instructed the police to guard us at night and said that the two rooms and the furniture remained with us. I thanked him very much and I thanked the police and gave them some vodka.

Mr Spiegel sat in jail for three months. He should have been there much longer but he managed to buy himself out for a lot of money.

We stayed for a few months, then many soldiers and officers arrived and they liked our rooms so they said we should leave and go to Shomsk. So we travelled like Gypsies again from *shtetl* to *shtetl*, from village to village, from town to town and we travelled after dark because it was wartime.

We arrived at Shomsk late at night, there was mud and rain and the children were crying and I cried with them. I cursed the years I still had to live, I could not stand it and I did not want to live any more. We stood in the middle of the *shtetl* in flooded streets, wondering what to do when a man presented himself as Itche Meier. I asked him to take pity on the children who had suffered so much and he said he could give us a room. We stayed at his house for two weeks and our families came to like each other very much.

We then found a suite of two rooms and a kitchen, with a separate entrance, in a Polish woman's house. We moved in with nothing, no beds, no table, nothing, and we slept on the floor. Still, it was wartime and the children were safe and your father was feeling better and I was grateful for those things. But I just couldn't stop crying.

Your father met the rich man of the *shtetl* and told him that I wouldn't stop crying and the man, his name was Mr Kofke, said that he and his wife would visit us. They came in the evening and I said to them: 'Dear visitors, I would ask you to sit but I have no benches.' Then I started crying.

'If you promise not to cry I will send you all the furniture you need tomorrow,' said Mr Kofke, 'but you must not cry.'

They spent about an hour with us and, the next day, the furniture arrived. There was a table with stools, two beds, a sideboard, crockery and everything one needs, all on condition that I did not cry. I thanked them very much and our families began to visit each other and your father did business with them.

We lived like all the Shomsk Jews and I was happy. A year passed and then your father took ill again. He lay ill for some months and you can imagine how I felt. Doctors saw him often and God helped him and he recovered. I thought all was well, but then my dear children, I received a letter from my mother to say that your father must come to Verba immediately, it was a matter of life and death.

Some Jews from Verba had bought two wagonloads of sugar from an officer and had taken them to Shomsk at night. A soldier had seen them, and he had been given a bag of sugar to keep him quiet, but he still reported them and ten Jews were arrested. I knew from your father's books that people could be shot for doing that in wartime. You can imagine the *Tsores,* with your father lying ill and me not knowing what to do.

'I will go to Verba and see what is happening there,' I said to your father, 'and if it is very bad I will send a telegram for you to come.' Then I sent a telegram to your father's mother, for her to come immediately so that your father would not be left alone with the children. It was bad to leave him and I left with bitterness in my heart, but I had to go.

In Verba it was terrible. My mother was crying because both her brothers had been arrested and the women were saying that it was a big sacrifice for the Jews to have their men in jail, and there would be an outcry in the heavens. What can one do, dear children.

'I will do better for you than my husband could have done,' I told them. 'Give me a thousand roubles and I will go and see the Prosecutor in Dubno, and God will have to help me.' So I took the money and we left for Dubno at five on the following morning.

It was very difficult to reach the Prosecutor who had the right to shoot me. I could speak Russian very well and went into the first office where they stopped me. I was not afraid of them and gave the person at each desk five roubles so that I could go further, and God helped me. I came to a door where there was a waiter and he would not let me pass. But I had to have my way and I gave him a gold ten-rouble piece.

'If I write a letter to the Prosecutor will you knock on the door and give it to him?' I asked. 'I will write it immediately and pour my heart out to him.' The waiter said he would, so I gave him the letter and he took it in to the Prosecutor. I was then asked to come into the office where I felt faint and the Prosecutor's secretary gave me some water to drink.

'Why are you so frightened?' asked the Prosecutor.

'Mr Prosecutor, you will shoot me'

'After such a letter how can I shoot you? Your letter is very dear to me.'

I thanked him and began to feel more confident. Then I greeted him officially by handing him the money. He went into another room, obviously to count it, and came back looking sad. I got the shivers.

'Why are you so sad, Mr Prosecutor?' I asked him. 'I can tell you a nice story from a novel I have just read.' So we sat down and I told him the contents of the novel. He seemed happier, and did not return the money to me.

Then I asked him: 'Perhaps you would like a letter from Peter Swetnikoff? He is a very rich man who used to buy from my mother's business. When I was a young girl he would come and tease me by taking off his monocle and putting it over my eye. He managed to get my two brothers out of the army.'

'I know him well,' said the Prosecutor, 'and now please tell me, what is your request?'

We went into another room and I told him the horrible story about the ten Jews who had bought the two wagonloads of sugar from the officer and had been arrested.

'Please Mr Prosecutor, save their lives.'
'All right, all right,' he said, 'I can see that you are a good person. I never knew until now that a Jewish woman could write such a wonderful letter in Russian. How did you know I was a good man?'
'Because you allowed me to speak to you.'

Then he picked up a book and read, and laughed out loud. It is the money laughing, I thought. Thank God he had accepted my 'greeting'. I knew then it would be all right. He had kept me a long time and I was worried about the women of the arrested men who were out in the street waiting for a verdict. What could I do when I was in his hands? Still, one has to know how to speak to such a personality.

'Mr Prosecutor, is there anything else you want to tell me?'
'No.'

I wondered whether to ask him again, bearing in mind, my dear children, that he had the right to shoot me.

Then he said: 'Your writing and your speaking will do you good. I will come to your house tomorrow morning. Put a bag of sugar in your house where I can see it. I will then ask you what you are doing with that sugar and you will answer that it was left there by soldiers who were passing through and said they would collect in on their return.'

I thanked him and asked him to give me a letter in the meantime which would allow the arrested men to be released. I was afraid they might be sent to Rovno that same night and be executed immediately. In wartime they do that. So he gave me a letter which released the men from prison.

Then I said: 'Mr Prosecutor, I have another request.' 'Nothing is enough for us Jews.

'If it is possible I will do it for you, write to me about it.'
I did, I wrote to him about a terrible officer who treated Jews very badly and the man was later transferred to Rovno.

Then he said: 'I do not normally travel in wartime but to you I will travel.' I though, this is God's wonder.
'Are you still afraid that I will shoot you?'
'I have to try for our Jewish nation,' I replied very diplomatically. I took my leave of him and he kissed my hand.
'I am coming to see you tomorrow, Madam,' he said.

I asked him if his secretary could give me some more water to drink. I did this so that I could thank her, and I also gave her five roubles.

The meeting with him was such an experience that I cannot, dear children, describe it well enough. You can imagine what your mother went through while completing her mission during wartime when we were all in danger of being shot.

I came out of the building to find the wives of the condemned men crying and waiting anxiously for news. I forgot that I had left your ill father and the children on their own. All I could think about was the ten families I had saved.

'It is *Simchat Torah*,' I shouted. 'Dance all the way home, you will have your husbands.' I gave them the formal letter from the Prosecutor.

'Deliver it quickly,' I said, 'and your husbands will be released. They will be free.'

On the way home I bought a bottle of wine and some other delicacies and the next day I stood at the window waiting for my visitor to arrive. When I saw him I opened the door quickly and he came in carrying a big cross and a book. He kissed my hand again.

'Madam Shamis, I keep my promises. I said I would come and I did.'

I thanked him, knowing that he did not travel anywhere in wartime. He looked around.

'What is that bag of sugar doing there?' he asked, pointing.
'Mr Prosecutor, some soldiers who were passing through put it there and said they would come and take it away when they return. I have not seen them since.'
'Good, good,' he said and wrote something down in his notebook. He had two hours to spare before his train left for Dubno so I invited him to sit down and have something to eat. My two brothers and my brother-in-law were present and my sister-in-law arrived with a roast chicken and a bottle of Vishniak.

The Prosecutor asked me to come and visit him.
'Mr Prosecutor I have a sick husband at home. When he is well again we will certainly come and visit you.' I said.

Then he told my sister-in-law about the letter I had written him and how he would not even have let me into his office had it not been for that letter.

Turning to me, he asked yet again: 'Are you not still afraid that I will shoot you?'

'When I travelled to see you I was very nervous,' I said, 'but not any more.'

I have managed to do such a *Mitzva* through him, I thought, that I am not afraid of him now. Let him be afraid of me. He asked me to accompany him to the station and on the way I told him that my husband had been in charge of passports for eight years, in the service of Tsar Nicolas, and that a picture of the Tsar had been on the wall in our office. He was very impressed.

'I recognised right away that you were a very important woman,' he said.

I thanked him and we chatted and we became good friends. Then I pointed out to him that there was a railway truck full of sugar standing at the station.

'Go and buy it,' he said. 'Nothing will happen to you. Your wonderful letter will not allow anybody to do you harm. I will keep your letter all my life, and I will show it to my friend Mr Swetnikoff who used to do business at your mother's shop.' He bade me farewell and kissed my hand as his train left.

I went and bought the truckload of sugar and sent it to your father in Somsk. Some Jews complained about this and the police went to see the Rabbi. But I gave each policeman a bag of sugar.

I wish I had a truckload of sugar now, dear children. I would then have the opportunity to visit you and come back to Israel. In our *Shtetl* they wanted to give me 500 roubles but I would not accept it. I did not want to sell the *Mitzva*. I said goodbye to the people and went home to your father and my children, thank, God for that. I told your father about everything that had happened to me since I left home. He was very impressed.

The following day I went to Vishnieviets and sold the sugar to a winery at a profit but it gave me no pleasure because your father was lying ill again and I could think of nothing else. He remained ill in bed for another four months. There were trains going to Kiev with soldiers and I decided to take your father to hospital there. It was a very difficult journey.

We arrived in Kiev at 3 o'clock on a Monday and at 10 o'clock on the Thursday night your father died. I was at his bedside. He held my hand and talked to me, and until the last moment of his life he was concerned about how I would manage on my own with the children.

He said: 'My advice to you, dear mama,' 'is that you should not die.'

I cried.

'They are calling me and I must go,' he continued. 'and you know that. Firstly you must teach the children. They must be educated so that they will always be able to make a living. And they must not trouble you.

'Dear Kalman' I said, 'after you die I will look after the children and I will not attend celebrations and I will not get married again because you have treated me very well. For ten years I will honour your wishes, dear Kalman.'

I continued to talk to him but he could not answer me. He took my hand and kissed me softly so that the children and I would stay well. Then he fell asleep. So died a Russian civil servant and my pain was very deep. The war had done this to him. Ever since the Cossacks had first driven us from our home I knew he would not survive the war. And so it turned out to be.

Imagine, dear children, the sun had risen by the time I left the hospital but I could not see anything in front of me. All I could see was your father as I left him.

In Kiev they do not remove a body from the hospital without a death certificate. I went to the *Gabbe,* Mr Maisel, and I went to many places before I found the department that issues death certificates. And when I took the certificate to the hospital they sent me back to get another certificate and your father's passport.

I walked ten blocks and my feet were very painful. When they gave me the two certificates I put them in my pocket and forgot they were there.

It was already late on Friday and the hearse had not yet arrived, so I went out into the street and started to scream and cry. A Jew who was passing by asked me what the matter was.

'My husband died at ten o'clock last night and the hearse has not yet come.' I stammered.

'If we 'phone them they will come quickly,' he said.

We went into a shop and he 'phoned them and five minutes later the hearse arrived. I asked him to come with me into the hospital until the body had been taken away. But they would not release the body without the certificates and I had forgotten where I put them. Fortunately the Jew was there. He signed an undertaking to produce the certificates on the Sunday and they allowed the body to be taken away in the hearse.

On Sunday I found the certificates in my pocket. The Jew arrived and together we went to the cemetery to present the certificates. We could not find your father's body there. Then they told us they had organised a funeral on the Saturday night. Can you imagine what I felt, dear children?

'How could you organise the funeral of my husband without me?' I screamed at them. I did not mince my words and I wanted to tear up the burial place. But nothing could be done, it was too late.

The Jew took me back to the hospital where he asked the nurses to give me food and look after me. He even said that if I wanted to rest for a few weeks I could stay at his house and he gave me his address.

I thanked him. There are good people in the world. If it had not been for him they may have cremated your father after he died, or kept his bones for study and research.

In Kiev there were many friends from our *Shtetl* who had moved there before the war. I told them that I wanted to jump into the river. How could I go back to my eight children without their father? And such a father, I did not want to live without him. My friends would not let me travel and they looked after me for eight days. I began to realise that it would be bad enough for my children to be fatherless and it would only make things worse for them to be without a mother as well. So I did not throw myself into the river.

Now, dear children, I had to go home from Kiev by train. When I got onto the train some soldiers said Jews were not allowed and wanted to chase me out of the carriage. I would have been squashed between two trains.

A Russian soldier said to me, 'Mama, I have not eaten for two days. Give me 50 kopeks and I will look after you. If the soldiers push you out you may be killed.' I gave him a whole rouble. He helped me off the train and took me to another one with instructions on where to change trains for Kremenets. From there I went by wagon to my home and my children at Somsk. I had bought the *Mitzva* from the Russian soldier for a rouble, and he had saved my life.

When I returned, my children, you both had measles and scarlet fever and then you both caught colds and you got bronchitis. Can you imagine that, after all the 'real life' I had been having. I cursed the minute I was born. I cried with blood, not tears. I wanted to take poison but when I looked at my orphans my heart broke. Where will eight children be without a mother? I did my children no harm, I fed them and I brought them up well but they had no luck. Let them all be well. I asked God for the strength to carry on because I hope to see them all again during my lifetime.

I needed a doctor for my children. I was completely confused and did not know what to do. For four weeks I stayed in my room and cried. My mother-in-law was staying with me and some very nice people, refugees from Radzivil and their wives, came to visit. One of them suggested that we should be partners and open a business. I went out and bought eight pieces of linen and two hundred pairs of old trousers. We were to share the profits but it turned out that he gained the profits and I risked my life.

I went a few times and bought goods, dressed like a peasant because they did not search peasants. But carrying the goods gave me palpitations and I felt it was harmful to my health.

One day he said to me: 'When are you going again?'

'You go this time,' I replied. 'Do you think you have found a fool to work for you?'

That business ended then, but one cannot be idle and live on capital. I decided to make vodka and went looking for someone to make the sales. The children had recovered, thank God, but I still had to pay rent. I went to the *Schochet* of the *Shtetl* and told him: 'Avraham, I am going to produce vodka, and I am looking for a salesman.' He gave his approval so I started and I risked my life again. But to do nothing is worse.

I made vodka until two weeks before Passover and then I couldn't carry on anymore. It is hard to make a living and I got palpitations from the vodka. I used to work right through the winter nights making it and pouring it into bottles and then I would have to wash all the barrels and put them outside. Every minute I thought someone was coming. I felt worse than the wicked in the next world and finally my conscience would not let me make it anymore.

I bought two kilograms of *matzos* for the children for *Pesach* and a lot of potatoes, but there was no wood for a fire so I went with another woman to the forest to find some and we carried it a long way on our backs. Eight days before *Pesach* some Jews came to my home and said:

'Mrs Shamis, we hear you are making vodka, so you must give us twenty roubles per month.'
'If you find one drop of vodka in my place you can have a hundred roubles a month,' I said.

They searched and found nothing.
'You've missed the boat.' I told them, 'you should have come six months ago.'

One of the children took ill again and we needed things so I went to the *Schochet* again.

'Avraham, I want to buy empty bags and exchange them for salt or matches or sugar or whatever I can get. Will you look for buyers?'
'I am fearful about this,' he said.
'Put your fear to one side,' I told him, 'I have to go on with this.'

I went to see the biggest thief in the village, a peasant who knew how these things were done. I dressed in his wife's clothes and became a peasant again. That way it would be more difficult for people to recognise me as a Jewess and, as I have said before peasants were not searched very often.

God helped me and I managed to buy salt and matches and sugar with the empty bags. Sometimes my goods were confiscated but I did not lose heart. I struggled like the wicked in the next world but I managed to earn what we needed and, thank God, the children were well. My troubles grew like weeds but, I thought, a bitter leaf from God is better than a sweet one from a person, and I knew that God would help me again.

On the eve of Passover we saw people wearing red hats in the streets. They were bandits, so I took all our possessions from our room and hid them, leaving the room like *Tisha B'av* when one mourns the fall of the temple. They were terrible bandits who robbed and killed. We heard shots and screams. One couldn't go out into the streets, one was even afraid to go to the window. They were in the *shtetl* until after *Pesach*. We hid for the full eight days of Passover. You can imagine, dear children, the *Yomtov* we had.

The bandits left after killing some Jews and then new bandits arrived, at the same time as Poles who were looking for Communists to kill, and we were in the middle. We overheard them saying that they should kill all the Jewish children so that the Jews would die out. Every so often a new group would arrive and they robbed and killed. They attacked the Rabbi and hurt him so badly that he died four weeks later. We were hungry because we could not go out to get food but fortunately our rooms were in the house of a Polish woman who was sometimes able to go out and bring us potatoes.

When the police arrived it was just as bad because they were completely wild. They broke the doors and shattered the windows and killed anyone they suspected of being a Communist. When I said I wanted to complain to an officer they threatened to kill me. They shot and wounded a Communist who managed to stagger to my door and ask for water. I gave him some but he died. Then the Polish bandits wanted to cut up his body right near my door.

'Can't you do that somewhere else?' I begged them. 'I am frightened and my children are frightened.'

They moved off saying, 'The dogs should eat this Communists's body.'

After this group left things became quieter and we could go out and buy food. But there was starvation in the area, there was no bread and people were frightened of each other. Then there was shooting in the forest again and many peasants came into our *shtetl* from the village. The peasants said they would not allow the Poles to come in.

Two peasants came to the house and asked if they could sleep there. They looked like decent lads from a nice home so I gave them the children's room. I told them how I had suffered since my husband died and they said they had never harmed any Jews. Then my landlady arrived and said there were two bandits staying at her house who had that very day killed four Jews in our *shtetl.* You can imagine how I felt. When I told the peasant lads about it one of them said that I should leave the lamp in our room burning through the night and he would stay awake. If I needed help I should call him.

I hid the children under a large round table and covered them with a sheet. I did not sleep, I guarded the children as they lay there like chicks. At about 2 o'clock there was a knock on the outside door. First I went to see if the lad was awake, and he was. So, without being nervous, I opened the door. My heart nearly stopped as a bandit burst into the room and went straight for the children.

I grabbed him by his throat and shouted at him: 'How can you come here at night to kill my children?'

Then the lad came into the room and slapped the bandit so hard that he nearly lost his face.

'You are going to kill people at night, are you?' the lad screamed at him. Then he threw the bandit out through the door like a dog. If it had not been for the lad we would have been slaughtered. God had looked after us.

One day there were some shots in the forest and some bandits arrived with an officer who boasted that on the previous day they had killed forty Jews. But we have a good God. Members of the militia followed the officer and a companion to see where they went and what they were doing. They stopped near a Jew so the militia surrounded them. They tried to run away but they were caught. The officer refused to answer questions but his companion said they went around looting and had killed many Jews. The officer was shot dead on the spot and his companion took the militia to where they had hidden the silver and money they had looted. Everything was recovered.

Thank God the Jews in the *shtetl* stayed alive. But they had had a bad time. The Bolsheviks came and there was shooting again. One of them came into the house and said: 'You will see how I shoot and kill Jews.' I thought, if he is going to kill me what should I do?' I took one of my children in my arms and sat near the window. He fired a shot through the window to frighten me and the panes were shattered and I fainted from fright and fell over still holding the child. Fortunately my landlady heard the shot and brought the doctor immediately. I think the child and I would have fallen asleep for good if he had not come.

One Sunday a Bolshevik came to the house dressed as an officer. He looked a bad man and I thought I recognised him as the same person who had frightened me by shooting through the window.

'I will bring you a gift that will keep you awake all night,' he said.

'No,' I cried, 'I have young children.'
'And I will kill all the Jews in the *shtetl*,' he added.
It was terrible to hear such words from a bandit. I was speechless and I could not move, then I got the shivers.

He left and towards evening he returned with his 'gift', a soldier who had been wounded in the head and had gone mad. He put the madman in my bed. Every now and then, right through the night, the man would wake up and shout: 'Where is my money, where is my horse?' Then he would fall asleep again. I stayed up the whole night trying to console the children who were beside themselves.

In the morning I went to the authorities and asked them to take the man away. I said the children were very nervous and our lives were in danger. They said they would take him away on the following day and again that night I did not sleep. But God helped me, they did come and they took him away. He was a Jew from Odessa and they sent him back there, as a gift to his mother.

There had been shooting for ten days and much of the *shtetl* had been destroyed. Most of the people who survived were ill.

It was terrible. We sighed with relief when the group left. Then, on a Sunday, new people arrived wearing long grey coats with red stripes and white hats with red bands. One of them approached one of your brothers who was 16 years old.

'Go and tell your Polish landlord I want to speak to him,' he commanded your brother.
When the landlord arrived the man said: 'I want a horse.'
'He does not have a horse,' said your brother.
'If you open your mouth again I'll shoot you,' said the man.

The landlord pleaded with him not to touch your brother who then ran upstairs and hid under the roof. The man followed him and searched for him but could not find him. Can you imagine, dear children, what I went through? I had no way to protect my child because I had to hide in the wardrobe.

Towards evening I went upstairs and found him. He was ill with shock. We called the doctor but he died the following day, a Saturday at 11 o'clock. He was a lovely lad. The funeral took place on Monday night at 10 o'clock. You can imagine, dear children, how sad it was when such a wonderful person was taken from my family. I had lost two men, my husband and my son. What could I do?

In order to tell you everything that happened at that time, I would have to write for a year. There were many murders and people were being assaulted. We were afraid even to go to the window. The bandits tortured me and there was nowhere to run. Then the bandits were shot at by the Bolsheviks and finally the Red Army came. They handed out leaflets saying they would not harm anybody and they gave the Jews food and cigarettes. They also looted but they did not hurt anybody.

One of the officers came to my house and asked me if he could have a room for two weeks. I could see he was decent, and I didn't want to be evicted, so I gave him the children's room. He returned late that night and I made him tea.

'I am sorry, dear sir, that I have no sugar,' I said.
'I know many people and I will bring you sugar,' he offered.
I thanked him and added respectfully, 'I can live without sugar.'
'I will also install lights in your home for you,' he said.

I felt shivers. One must beware of people like this. He told me he was a senior officer and that he came from a very rich family in Moscow. There were two children, he and a sister, and his family owned forests and four houses.

'We have plenty of money but everything is very expensive.' He said.
'If there is plenty of money nothing is expensive,' I suggested.
'Where are you from?' he asked.
'I come from a small *shtetl* called Verba near Dubno.'
He went on asking questions.
'When you know everything you will grow old very soon,' I said.
I doubted whether he was telling the truth. People like this are a long way from home and sometimes their minds wander.
'If your father is so wealthy, with only two children and so many houses,' I asked him, 'why are you in this place following the bandits?'

'For talking like that I can shoot you.'
I was not afraid of him, one must be strong and not give in.
'When you are at home do you also threaten to shoot people,' I said, 'or do you go to church with your father?'

'I could shoot you, and your children, but I won't because I like you.'

My neighbour had come in with his two daughters and we talked, sometimes seriously and sometimes laughingly, until three in the morning.
'Give me your money,' I said, 'and I will show you that I can lead the army better than you.'
'I see you are very clever,' he answered, 'For that I will take you and your children to Moscow where you can stay with us and have plenty of money.'
'I don't want to go to Moscow, I don't want money, my children are my wealth.'
'But as a mother on her own with children you struggle. I can see your life is hard. I am begging you to come to Moscow with me, Mrs Shamis.'

'First you want to shoot me, then you want me to come with you. When I leave this place it will not be with you. The God who has helped me until now will help us further.'
'Where is your God, in heaven?' he asked. I have no God and I am rich on earth.'
'I have children so I am richer than you. You run around from place to place and you have nothing. God will improve my lot, not you.'
'Then I have no choice but to shoot you.' He drew an empty gun and made as if to shoot at the door.
'You are being unkind,' he continued, 'when I first saw you I noticed that you are a very pretty woman with a good figure and lovely dark eyes.' He went on telling me about my virtues and added that he had never done any harm to Jews.

'Thank you for that,' I said, 'but I have suffered very much and have had to hide my children from the bandits.'

'You need not suffer any more. Now you can have it very good, if you come with me.'

'If you arrive home with me and my children your father will chase us away. Go home to your big city where you can find a nice girl. I am old and I have many children.'
'You are younger than me,' he said.

'No, you are an important man and you have a rich father, you can easily find a beautiful girl in Moscow. You can help me and my family if you want to but you must get married to someone in Moscow. You can invite us to the wedding.'

'You make trouble for me,' he said, 'I lie awake at night thinking about your lovely dark eyes, and I become delirious and I clamp my teeth.'

My neighbour interrupted: 'Why do you pester Mrs Shamis like this?'

'Because I am as lonely as a dog. If she will come with me I will do whatever she asks, throw away all my possessions if she wants me to. I will listen to her.'

'If you listen to me,' I said, 'you will look at my neighbour's two lovely daughters and ask one of them to come with you.'
He laughed, 'I only want you.'

'My husband was a Commissar under Tsar Nicholas for eight years,' I said, 'and we had a picture of the Tsar on the wall. I have no need to become a Russian *grande dame*, but I will come with the children to visit you in Moscow.' Then we all went to bed.

Early next morning he wanted tea, and he said: 'Mrs Shamis I had a dream last night. In that dream I gave you a big box of money and you came with me to Moscow.'
'No, I didn't. And I don't want your money. I have said before that my children are my riches.'

When he left our home he gave me his address and asked me to write to him. 'If you don't write' he said, 'I will not come and shoot you – I will shoot myself.'

It was a stick from God that such a man had stayed with us. But we Jews hope that the stick will break one day and flow with the stream to the sea, and there will be the best Jewish life. If I had lost my pride, or my sense of humour, he would definitely have shot me.

One day soon after he had left, Gentiles wearing masks arrived and robbed every home and broke the locks on the shops and threw goods into the street. They demanded money, got drunk, smashed the telephones and murdered and assaulted people. We could do nothing because there were no police. It was real anarchy and the children and I spent the whole day hiding in the cellar of our Polish landlady's house. They departed towards evening and shot at doors and windows as they left. They simply took our souls from us.

The *Pintele Yid* is not good. One gets used to such things, one learns to live with the *tsores*.

A Chinese group then arrived. Nobody knew where they came from. The first thing they did was to take away the wood I used for making fires in the stove and then they took my table and benches outside and chopped them up for firewood. They said if I locked the door they would smash the windows and one of them said: 'You have so many children. We will take two of them when we leave and cook them when we have nothing to eat.'

I got a terrible fright and asked my neighbour to take the children and hide them. For several days I did not know where they were. My *Mazel* was under a black cloud, I had to be a mother and a father to my children. I did not sleep at home while the Chinese were there and before they left one of them held a knife to my throat and said, 'I will slaughter you.' Thank God I survived them.

The next people to arrive were French, about two hundred including soldiers, officers and members of a military band. They seemed very nice people and they appeared to be rich. A colonel spoke to me in English but I did not understand English so I took him to an interpreter and learned that the officers wanted my room. When I complained that the children would have nowhere to go it was agreed that they would come only for meals, four times a day. They brought many good things with them, I boiled eggs for them and baked bread for them and they liked it very much. Yente was a beautiful child and was taken by them to eat at the table.

The Colonel asked me through an interpreter who I was and where I came from. I told the interpreter to tell him my story and about the various groups of bandits, and how I had suffered with my children.
The Colonel was astounded. He said he would give me a letter of introduction to a rich Jew in France who would allow us to stay with him and would see to it that the children were educated. Then, when he returned to France himself, he would set us up in a home and I would be rich and things would be all right.

I thanked him and said I had previously received a similar offer from a Commissar in the Red Army who had also threatened to shoot me. I told him that I wanted to take my children to Warsaw and educate them there. He and the French soldiers then went to another village but they came back twice to visit and brought me flour so that I could bake for them and brought me a bag of potatoes. Then they said farewell and went back to France.

Thank God it was quiet for some time, but one must carry on. I had lost my whole world because of my children, I had lost my youth, but I was prepared to do anything for them, even break iron if I had to. So when I heard about a peasant who had second hand soldiers' clothes I went to find him even though he lived quite far away. On the way I met two strange soldiers.

'Where are you going?' they asked.
'I'm not sure myself.'
'Are you interested in buying old clothes or new clothes?'
'I will buy anything you bring me,' I said.

I did not continue on my journey to find the peasant and took one soldier back to my house to show him where they should bring goods at night. At about 2 o'clock that night they returned with two bags of clothes. I washed all night to get the dye stamps off the clothes and in the morning went around the houses to sell them. Thank God I made a good profit.

One night they brought me a white saddle and I was really afraid. I cut it up and sold the pieces of leather to the shoemakers. I kept on buying from them and risked my life in doing so. Before they left our *shtetl* for the last time they gave me a coat as a gift for the children. Then I went to a village far away where I found old hats and arranged with a peasant to come every two days, late at night, and bring me whatever he had. I sold them to the tradesmen who made hats and that is how I earned money.

The time came when I wanted to educate the children so we left Shomsk for Kremenets with the intention of going from there to Warsaw. In Kremenets I hired a room for two months because we were not sure when we would leave the place. We struggled there, sometimes I earned money and sometimes not, and there were always new bandits.

I had suffered enough from them in Shomsk, I had lost your father, dear children, and your brother. I kept on having palpitations and I suffered from headaches. Sometimes I felt that I couldn't take it any more. My dear child I suffered much more than I have written about, even friends did not give us a good deal. One night I slept in a little kitchen which was so cold that my headscarf froze. But I made sure my children were well, and thank God I overcame the problems.

I married off your sister Leika in Kremenets. Her husband was a clever man who came from a good family and they had a very nice house. But who knows what is happening now with that 'wicked man'?

I had thought that I would get rid of the bandits in Kremenets but still they worried us and threw stones through the windows. They were terrible people and I was afraid that I would lose all the money I still had. So I went ahead with the plan to go to Warsaw and sent one of the children ahead to start studying. Four of the children I would leave in Kremenets with some money and I had a letter of introduction to an editor in Warsaw called Polotski, a Jewish Commissar who was a very rich man with a sister in Kremenets.

In the meantime shooting from the mountains around Krements had started again. I saw some of the bandits involved, they had long hair and big eyes and rode on small horses. They had long, warm coats and carried shotguns on their shoulders and other guns and knives at their sides. They murdered people and blood was flowing. It was terrible, I could not allow the children to go out. Then police arrived and arrested the bandits and confiscated their arms.

When things had quietened down a little I went to the station to take the train to Warsaw. They did not want to sell me a ticket so I asked to speak to the man in charge. I told him that I had to go to Warsaw to find a home for my children and that I had left four children behind in Kremenets, and my tears flowed. He took pity on me and took me to the train himself. I never paid.

When I reached Warsaw I asked a Jew to direct me to the editor's office.

'If you give me 50 zlotys I will tell you where to go,' he said.
'No,' I said, 'Rather you give me 50 zlotys and I'll take you right through Warsaw.' I managed to find the office on my own.

I was shown in to Mr Polotski and gave him the letter of introduction. And I told him about the lot of the Jews in the area I came from. He told me that I should have gone to the police. Then I asked where the office was for refugees who want to emigrate to America. He gave me a letter and sent a man with me to the Centre for Refugees where it was agreed that I would work as a matron. I remained there and was able to send money to the children for *Pesach*.

I worked hard to make the thirty families at the Centre feel that it was really *Pesach* and a Mr Peroaz and his wife, who were very rich people and had donated money for the purpose, came to see if everything was being done properly. They were very satisfied and invited me to their home for *Pesach* but I declined because my children were not there.

After *Pesach* they sent for me and said that refugees would soon be sent to Mexico. So I borrowed 300 zlotys from them and went to Kremenets to fetch the children. When I arrived the children cried with joy and so did I, and I felt so guilty about having left them that I couldn't sleep that night. The children had grown and I thanked God that they were well.

I went back to Warsaw with the children and we stayed at the Centre. When Mrs Peroaz went on leave for four weeks I ran the Centre better than she had. I wrote down who arrived and who left and doctors came every day and I kept everything clean and they liked my daughter Yente very much because she is such a pretty child. However, I thought it would be better for the children to be in the orphanage, so I took them there.

There were 60 Jewish children at the orphanage which was very clean and well run by a Professor and Mrs Engel. Two of the girls were married off there. A Professor Shor performed the ceremonies (*Chupa* and *Kidushin)* and bought clothes and spent 20 dollars of his own money on each bride. I always knew your sister Vanka would marry a doctor, and so she did. There were many doctors present, a band was playing and it was a very nice wedding.

I was asked to remain working at the Centre until all the refugees had left but my first concern was to provide for my children. What would people say, I thought, if I leave my own children and go on camps with other children? My children would be lost without their mother. I protected them from the bandits and I won't desert them now. I knew that God would not forsake me because I am a widow.

My daughter Tzilla who is now at Givat Chaim in Israel worked at the children's hospital in Warsaw and in the evenings she went to meetings of the *Chalutzim* (pioneers) to be trained like *Hachshara.* She wanted to get a certificate to go on *Aliyah* to Palestine. It was not easy but I managed to earn some money and eventually she received the certificate and left for Palestine. Vanka went to work at the hospital as a sister but who knows how she is getting on with that 'wicked man'.

I remained with two children, you, dear Rosa, and you, dear Manes. I worked at a Jewish Centre for the Jewish congregation and during the holidays I went on children's camps. I was recommended by Professor Shor and took you, Rosa, and Reysele and Manes with me on the summer camp when I worked as a matron and they were very satisfied with me. We spent two months in Zakopany and when we returned there was a letter from Tzilla saying she was very happy in Givat Chaim. She said she would arrange for me to go to Palestine.

Then came a man from South Africa, a Mr Isaac Ochberg. He wanted to take about two hundred children who had been orphaned by the First World War to South Africa where they could be looked after and begin a new life. He also wanted us to go and I was convinced that I would accompany the children.

However, Mrs Engel then told me that children only, and no parents, would be going to South Africa.

I approached Mr Ochberg and asked him to return my two children. I told him I would look after them and educate them even if I had to carry stones in order to do it. But he said he had already obtained visas for them and refused. I was deeply distressed.

You can imagine, dear Children, how Mrs Engel broke my heart when she said I could not go. You can imagine what a mother feels when she has to part with small children. You, dear Manes, were only eight years old and you dear Rosa, were ten. I read in the newspapers that there was no food for them on the train taking them to the boat on which they would go to London. We heard there had been a storm in which the boat nearly sank. The children were already dressed in lifebelts but God helped them and the boat was saved. They stayed in London for a while and then left, again by boat, for South Africa.

After six months I received a letter from Mr Ochberg saying that my two children were missing. I was so upset that I cried right through the nights. I sent Mr Ochberg an airmail letter in which I told him to return my children or arrange for me to come to South Africa and find them myself. After a while he sent me another letter saying that the children were no longer missing. I sent a second airmail letter and this time he replied saying the children were well and had settled down. I did not believe him, but what could I do? If the sea had not separated us I would have gone to join them.

I had written ten letters to the children before I received one from them. They said I should not cry and sent photographs. You can imagine how I felt when I saw those pictures of my children. I looked at those photos at night and cried. Such little children who need their mother, I regretted having sent them away. It's a shame when a mother exchanges her children for paper and I never received any 'paper' anyway. When I asked them in Warsaw whether I could go on a boat to South Africa they said: 'We are taking men only, no women.'

I was rewarded twenty years later when manes came to see me. He told me he was coming from South Africa on a visit, he did not tell me that he was in the South African Army and had been sent to Egypt, from where he came to visit me in Palestine. He did not want me to know he was a soldier because he thought I would worry. But I had the feeling all along that he was in the army, his mother is not a fool. I took consolation from the fact that he was only one of many soldiers, it was the Second World War.

One thing that worried me when the children were still young in South Africa was that they sent me money. Where did they get the money from? I wrote a letter to the teachers at their orphanage and asked them where the children had managed to get money. They wrote to tell me that the children had come first in their classes at school and had been given prize money which they sent on to me.

Then I read in the newspaper that there had been a terrible earthquake in Africa. I fainted and was unconscious for an hour before the doctor revived me. I sent a letter to the orphanage and the children replied saying that the earthquake had been in another part of Africa, far away from them. I thanked God for that.

Sometimes I did not have the will to live. I thought of suicide but, fortunately people looked after me. And I decided to write to you about my life because I want you to know how I suffered. I hoped, dear children that you would all be happy and that one day I would see you again.

Tzilla wrote from Givat Chaim saying that she wanted me to come to Palestine. She had been there for three years and had finally managed to obtain a certificate for me to enter the country. I had no husband to support me so I needed money to support myself, and I also needed money for travelling. I worked at a school camp where I looked after 300 children and then at another camp in Zakopany where I had an unpleasant experience.

A doctor arrived there and said he had heard that the place was dirty. I took him round and showed him all the floors and he saw that everything was clean. I suspected that he was trying to frighten me and that he wanted a bribe. I did not give him one but I gave him a good lunch with plenty of wine and sent him on his way. When I left there I had enough money for the tickets to Palestine and I was proud that I had earned it through my own labour.

I went to Lvov, took out a passport and paid for it. On a Tuesday I took the train which connected with the boat which left on Wednesday. We all wanted to reach the destination as soon as possible. Many people were sick on the boat but I felt well. I met a young woman from Lvov who was going to visit her parents and had a child of four with her. She befriended me and invited me to share her cabin. Her name was Esther Steinberg and her husband worked in Haifa. She invited me to visit them in Haifa and one day I will do that. Every minute of the time I thought about the fact that I was going to be with my daughter in Palestine. I was very happy.

At 3 o'clock on a Sunday afternoon we disembarked at Haifa and stood in a long queue to be inoculated against smallpox. It grew late and Esther Steinberg invited me to sleep at her house but I declined because I had arranged to stay with my sister-in-law who has three children and lives in Meshek Yagur. I travelled there that night and on the following day your sister Tzilla came and took me to her home in Givat Chaim.

They had a meeting at Givat Chaim and a Mr Zimmerman and a Mrs Sima Liberman told me that I could not be accepted there. I was stunned, and your sister Tzilla wanted to commit suicide.

'Bad luck follows me wherever I go,' I told her. 'I have suffered so much in Europe, finally I manage to get to Palestine, I stand here with no money left and no home, and I get this kind of welcome.'

I thought they wouldn't send me back to Poland because I no longer had a home there. But they found a middle way. 'You can stay,' Mr Zimmerman said, 'but only for four months, as a visitor.'

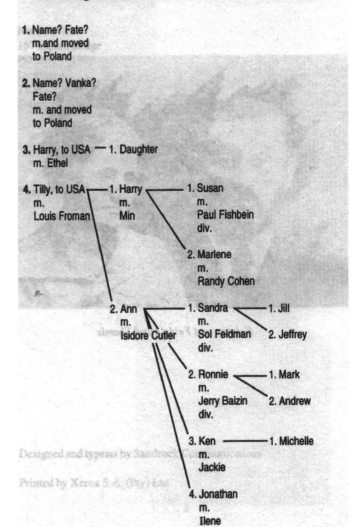

The Descendants of Kalman Shamis b.1876 d.1918 and Feiga Mirel Misler b. 1878 d. Israel 1950

1. Name? Fate?
m. and moved to Poland

2. Name? Vanka? Fate?
m. and moved to Poland

3. Harry, to USA — 1. Daughter
m. Ethel

4. Tilly, to USA
m. Louis Froman
  — 1. Harry
     m. Min
       — 1. Susan
          m. Paul Fishbein div.
       — 2. Marlene
          m. Randy Cohen
  — 2. Ann
     m. Isidore Cutler
       — 1. Sandra
          m. Sol Feldman div.
            — 1. Jill
            — 2. Jeffrey
       — 2. Ronnie
          m. Jerry Baizin div.
            — 1. Mark
            — 2. Andrew
       — 3. Ken
          m. Jackie
            — 1. Michelle
       — 4. Jonathan
          m. Ilene

5. Leika
m. Hirsch Freedman
Died in Holocaust

6. Ichiel
Died in Holocaust

7. Jacov ———— Four children
m. Bracha
Died in Holocaust

8. Tzilla
m. Chaim Ben-Zvi in Palestine d. Israel 1998
  — 1. Batsheva ——— Two children
     m. in Israel
  — 2. Zwia ——— Five children
     m. in Israel

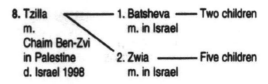

138

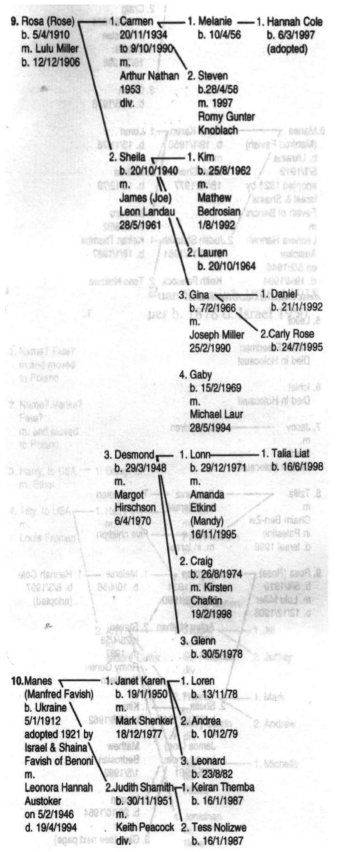

9. Rosa (Rose)
b. 5/4/1910
m. Lulu Miller
b. 12/12/1906

— **1. Carmen**
20/11/1934
to 9/10/1990
m.
Arthur Nathan
1953
div.

— **1. Melanie**
b. 10/4/56

— **1. Hannah Cole**
b. 6/3/1997
(adopted)

2. Steven
b.28/4/58
m. 1997
Romy Gunter
Knoblach

2. Sheila
b. 20/10/1940
m.
James (Joe)
Leon Landau
28/5/1961

— **1. Kim**
b. 25/8/1962
m.
Mathew
Bedrosian
1/8/1992

2. Lauren
b. 20/10/1964

3. Gina
b. 7/2/1966
m.
Joseph Miller
25/2/1990

— **1. Daniel**
b. 21/1/1992

2. Carly Rose
b. 24/7/1995

4. Gaby
b. 15/2/1969
m.
Michael Laur
28/5/1994

3. Desmond
b. 29/3/1948
m.
Margot
Hirschson
6/4/1970

— **1. Lonn**
b. 29/12/1971
m.
Amanda
Etkind
(Mandy)
16/11/1995

— **1. Talia Liat**
b. 16/6/1998

2. Craig
b. 26/8/1974
m. Kirsten
Chafkin
19/2/1998

3. Glenn
b. 30/5/1978

10. Manes
(Manfred Favish)
b. Ukraine
5/1/1912
adopted 1921 by
Israel & Shaina
Favish of Benoni
m.
Leonora Hannah
Austoker
on 5/2/1946
d. 19/4/1994

— **1. Janet Karen**
b. 19/1/1950
m.
Mark Shenker
18/12/1977

— **1. Loren**
b. 13/11/78

2. Andrea
b. 10/12/79

3. Leonard
b. 23/8/82

2. Judith Shamith
b. 30/11/1951
m.
Keith Peacock
div.

— **1. Keiran Themba**
b. 16/1/1987

2. Tess Nolizwe
b. 16/1/1987

11. Janica (Yenta)
d. in Holocaust

12. Moishele
d. in infancy

Note: *These details are incomplete because not all the information is available.*

'Then give me the money to go to America where I have a daughter,' I said, 'or send me to South Africa where I have a son and a daughter.'

What would happen after four months? I did not know, I was very unsettled. I started working, mending and altering linen from six in the morning until four in the afternoon. There was no room for me where Tzilla stayed and I would have had no place to sleep if a member of the community called Sarah had not given me shelter for four months. I am still grateful to her.

Then a case arose where they had to go and look for a member's mother in Russia. So all the members in this community where decisions are taken collectively said: 'But this mother (meaning me) is already here, why can't she stay?' That is how I managed to remain there. I want to thank all the boys and girls who voted for me and wish them success in whatever they do.

The Redemption should come soon. We should be redeemed from the hand of the 'Wicked Man'. He is the only stick and the stick will be broken. Let him drown in the sea and the Jews will swim to Redemption. We Jews should be proud and not lose hope, everything will be all right and it is not long to wait.

Now my dear children, you deserve to hear about the good years I had. Your mother was 17 when she married your father who was 20 and they lived together for twenty two years. I had twelve children and your father sent two of them to America. When he died at 42 your father left me with eight children. Two of them died at home and I married off Leika and Vanka. I remained with four, Yente, Tzilla, Rosa and Manes. They all swam over the sea to different lands. Yente was left in the hands of a 'wicked man', God knows if she is still alive, Rosa and Manes went to South Africa and I am here in Israel with Tzilla.

I ask God to allow me to see my children again while I am still alive. I would like to be with you, even four weeks would be enough to chat with you.

I finish my writing, dear children, with a big SHALOM.

Thus writes the mother of Rose Miller and Manfred Favish.

THE VERBA AREA

Map by courtesy of the Johannesburg Reference Library

Chapter 30 – CHAYA BERNFELD (CLAIRE KLEIN)

MEMORIES OF CLAIRE KLEIN (CHAYA BERNFELD)

These memories are extracted and adapted from the original transcript of an interview of Claire Klein.

Events have been arranged into a chronological order and headings included to help the narrative flow.

MY EARLY MEMORIES

I was born in Warsaw *on 14 July 1911*. My birth name was Bernfeld. I was *Chaya* Bernfeld. When I was on the boat to South Africa there were a few ladies who said my English name must be Claire so I stuck to Claire.

Life was ok. I had food and what more do you want when you are a child? I remember my parents. I remember my father. He was killed in the army. I remember my mother, but I don't know the name. In fact we were sick. We were both taken to hospital at the same time with typhoid fever or some fever and she died and I recovered. You know that a child has got much more stamina.

Chaya's mother, Feiga Bernfeld

THE REGISTER AT ORANAJIA

The record below shows that Chaya Bernfeld aged 12 (and her brother Hersh, who was then aged 11) were from Warsaw. Their father Yash "was killed in the war by the Germans. The mother Feiga died of hunger and typhus leaving much suffering." "The children remained alone without support"

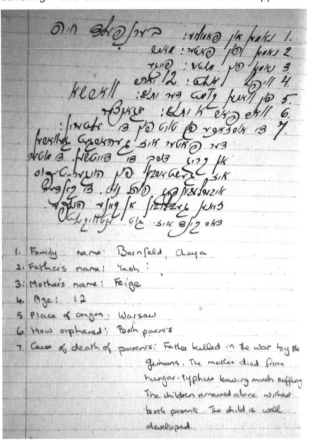

Family details of Chaya Bernfeld as recorded in the register at Oranjia – The Cape Jewish Orphanage.

Group Passport 8 – Chaya is in the middle of the back row 5th from the right

Chaya Bernfeld from Group passport photo 8.
"I recognise my mother as the girl in the back row, with a bow in her hair, no. 65 in that photo. It is interesting that I have a picture of myself as a child with exactly the same style of bow in my hair."

We were quite happy; my mother, my father and the kids. We didn't worry about anybody else. I was at school. I remember when I was very young, probably about three or four, we had a maid and she used to be a Roman Catholic. Every morning she used to take me and my brother to the Roman Catholic Church; that I do remember. There were buses. We had buses there and it was very cheap. I suppose for about three or four cents we had a ride on the bus.

At one time I was cold and hungry when my mother died and my sister didn't have much money. I don't know where she got the money from. She might have sold my mother's jewellery because my mother had very nice jewellery. You see, my father had a factory and he used to manufacture panama hats in winter for summer. He used to work with little things to tie it up to keep your ears warm in winter. And they used to work in summer for winter and winter for summer. That I do remember.

When my father died, I don't know what happened to the factory. But when he used to go to Panama to buy the straw he always used to bring some jewellery for my mother so when she died there was a lot of jewellery there.

My sister gave me a ring with a red stone because it was my birth stone and that's all I had and then when I was at the orphanage one of the kids borrowed it and I never saw it again.

I had a sister and a brother and Harry and then when Ochberg came he said would I like to go to South Africa and so I said yes and my sister was already engaged to a chap who was in Buenos Aires and he sent her a ticket to come over. And that's what happened. She went to Buenos Aires. Her fiancée sent her a ticket. My other brother remained there. I think he was killed in the Holocaust. We never heard.

First I went to stay with my sister in her flat and then I went to this particular school and Anje was there as well, and she said come and stay with me. My aunty won't mind. She didn't have a mother. She had an aunt and a granny I think and so I went to stay with them. She married an Avon I think. He had something to do with the Hebrew School and she settled in Israel.

I was only a kid *during the war,* about five and we were not supposed to go out at night but I used to go out at night. I could have been shot, but I went out…By the police because we were not allowed out.' Till 6 o' clock everybody was allowed to play and walk. After that nobody was allowed out except the police. I remember going to school, a Polish government school.

MEETING ISAAC OCHBERG IN WARSAW

The Jewish people in Johannesburg and Cape Town decided to make a collection and send over Mr Ochberg, who was a millionaire living in Cape town and he was supposed to bring back 200 children as young as possible, because they wanted young children for adoption. But he could only get so many young ones and not so very young either.

It was June and the schools broke up for about three months I think and somebody recommended this particular boarding school to collect the children and bring them there. He needed accommodation for 200 children and it was a big boarding school. So as he collected *the children* he put them there. And so he brought a few children and an adult and left them there, and he went to collect some more children, brought another adult and that's how it went on.

Now I was staying with a friend whose aunty was in charge of all the cleaning and when I met Ochberg he couldn't speak a word of Polish and I was born in Poland and could speak perfect Polish. He decided to come to this school and then he brought one girl. I had to look after her. Then he wanted to do certain things in Warsaw and he didn't know the language so I helped him. I helped him out. Somebody said, "She speaks Polish very well. Why don't you ask her to help you?" and that's how I helped him. He wanted to go to certain places in Warsaw and I knew my way very well and I used to take him there by horse and cart. There were no cars. I used to ride with him and he was very nice to me and I was 11 years old.

He asked whether I would like to come to Cape Town, to South Africa. I said yes why not. So he asked have you got somebody younger than you and I said yes I've got a brother who's a few years younger than me and Anje, who was the girl, my best friend whose aunty was in charge of the school and so he said she could come as well.

Isaac Ochberg used to go to all the little *dorps* to collect the children. I don't know, he probably went to, say, the little places like, what should I say, like Constantia, I mean it wasn't as nice as that. He probably spoke to the head, maybe of the Jewish school, or the Hebrew school. Probably there must have been

Hebrew synagogues and I suppose that's how he collected the orphans. All I know is every time he came back he had about 10 children or 12 children. In the *shtetls* often there was a pogrom where they killed the Jews.

And so, eventually he collected 200 children from Russia, Latvia, Lithuania and I think there was one girl, from Hungary, but otherwise it was Russians, Lithuanians and Latvians .There were no children from Warsaw because he was supposed to bring back the orphans from outside.

He gathered the 200 children and a few grown-ups. I think there were about six grown-ups if I'm not mistaken. Dr Solly Mark's mother, was one of the grown ups looking after children and there were a few others.

They said they need children *in South Africa*; that people want to adopt certain children and that the Jewish community has collected all the money and we wanted to come with and that's what happened.

Ochberg was a millionaire. He couldn't sign his name. He would put a cross instead of his name and he owned a lot of property in Adderley Street and he had a daughter. She married a Robinson and I think he had a daughter who was not quite right and she was at a special school in England in London and he did that for nothing. He didn't get any money, he didn't need it.

LONDON

We were in London for about eight days and I remember I liked London. Some of the Jewish people were very nice. They brought us fruit. Otherwise nothing happened. We were waiting there for a ship. And when the Edinburgh Castle arrived we all got onto the ship and by the time we got to Cape Town I was speaking a perfect English because the sailors were teaching the children. You know sailors are very fond of kids and so I spoke a very nice English.

It was wonderful. I was very happy to travel. I always loved to travel and it was good. I didn't know what South Africa was like but I was quite content to leave Warsaw.

ARRIVING IN CAPE TOWN

We arrived in Cape Town. Then they separated the children with 100 for Cape Town and 100 for Johannesburg. And I was left in Cape Town with my brother and Anje and we decided we would rather be in Cape Town.

There were very few adopted I can tell you that. People were not keen to adopt .There weren't any two year olds and three year olds. I think there were one or two adopted children. I remember one very wealthy family who didn't have any kids so they adopted a boy and then she fell pregnant and she didn't want the boy, so the boy had to come back to the orphanage. It wasn't very successful. There were very few adoptions.

I decided to stay in Cape Town because I was very fond of the sea. They didn't mind. They didn't ask anybody where they wanted to stay. My brother, Harry, was going to Johannesburg but I said "no he stays here with me, that is my brother" so we both landed in Cape Town.

I went to school. I went up to standard 9 because I wanted to start work and be independent. Although the principal wanted me to stay on and do matric but I didn't. I planned to work and to go to commercial college and I took shorthand typing, business methods. I was smart. I did the course in about eight months instead of a year. My brother, Harry was still in the orphanage.

When we went to the orphanage in Cape Town, they got a man from England and he was a very good man. He ran the orphanage very well. When we were in the orphanage we used to go to shul on Saturday mornings and the principal of the orphanage, Isaac Ochberg, he used to entertain us after shul and always give us little presents; little baby boxes of crayons. Every Saturday he used to give us something.

AFTER LEAVING ORANJIA

Harry, *my brother*, did very well. He started off with a firm, a very big firm of fish people but he didn't like it because his clothes always stank of fish.

I got a job with the Karasol who was the secretary of several organisations; the orphanage, the old aged home, maybe one or two others and I got a job there.

We only met Thelma Friedman and Arthur after leaving Oranjia. We were very good friends. We were very friendly. We used to go for tea every Sunday afternoon. We used to go for a drive to Muizenberg. We had another friend, Thelma and we used to go there for a Saturday afternoon. We had tea and it was very nice.

I couldn't speak a word of Yiddish. Polish was my language and that's what I spoke. The only time I ever learnt Yiddish was from my mother in law when she came up for Pam's birth. She stayed with me and she wouldn't go back to Cape Town. We were in Port Elizabeth at the time.

One of her daughters stayed in Cape Town. My father in law used to deal in cattle so he wouldn't come to Cape Town but he used to come for weekends sometimes but my mother in law lived in Cape Town and that's where I met my husband.

I wouldn't be here today if it wasn't for Mr Ochberg. He was a very good man. He did a lot for the children. He put himself out.

Definitely it was fate *that I go to South Africa* because otherwise I would have remained in Warsaw and I might have landed up in the holocaust. Who knows? My sister was in Buenos Aires, South America. She might have sent for me and I didn't mind going anywhere.

Chapter 31 ~ SOLLY BETTMAN

MEMORIES OF SOLLY BETTMAN

These memories are extracted and adapted from the original transcript of an interview of Solly Bettman.

Events have been arranged into a chronological order and headings included to help the narrative flow.

MY EARLY MEMORIES

My name is Solly Bettman, Solomon Bettman. I was born in 1915 in Chodrov. I have four sisters and my father was Hirsch.

My late father was taken away to the Polish army and my late mother, she was very upset about it and she was waiting, waiting for him to come back. When he came back in 1918 he had a sickness, you know, that everybody died from. He had the doctor and he had "bankes" then he passed away a month later. I went to the funeral of my late father. I was three years old and they buried him there and there is no stone or anything like that.

My late mother died a month later because she didn't want to live without her husband. Then I was taken down to the orphanage in Stanislav. In the orphanage the war was on down there and there was quite a lot of children down there. They had to take me to hospital. I had a big operation. I was there six months and during that time the Cossacks were there with their big lances and they used to kill the people and I used to run about. I had to run away from the orphanage because the Cossacks used to come to the orphanage and then we used to come back.

I remember in Chodrov we stayed in a little house and there was a kitchen and upstairs, on top of the kitchen there was a "badem", what they call in Jewish a "badem" and there we used to sleep on top because it was warm. And otherwise on Saturday we didn't cook on Saturday, we only cooked on Friday for Saturday so we could sleep on Friday night and Saturday on top of the stove. It was a very difficult time because my late father was already taken to the army, to the Polish army. They came to fetch him. They searched all the houses and they would have got him anyway.

I can't remember exactly what my father did but he used to go away. He used to be a "smouse" you know. He used to go away for four or five days and come back but I was too small to remember all this. We stayed in a very small village and we had no other way of knowing anything and Friday nights we used to go to a little shul down there and otherwise I can't remember very much.

Well we were very poor. We had very little clothing but we had enough food to eat. My late mother and my eldest sister, Leah, she used to work and we used to get a little bit of food in the house but we were very very poor. We had other relations, an uncle down there, they used to help us. I can't remember anything else.

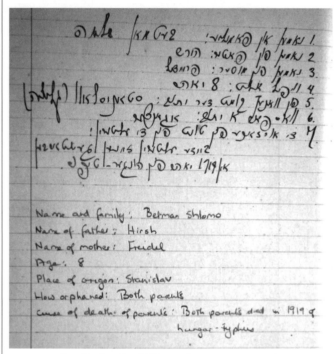

Family details of Shlomo Bettman as recorded in the register at Oranjia – The Cape Jewish Orphanage.

I went to the market once with another child and we were looking for food and there was a woman standing there with bread, selling bread and she had a long dress on and there was a coal under it, you know, the fire and a little boy there, my friend, took and pulled her dress at the back and I stole a loaf of bread because we were hungry. We had nothing to eat and we ran away. Of course they didn't catch us. Then we went back to the hostel down there.

When I was in the orphanage I remember looking for food because the Cossacks used to come to the orphanage and then we used to look for food down there and we used to find the potato peels, and we used to eat them. At that time it was very nice but food was very scarce.

Every few days another group arrived; the Germans arrived and the Poles arrived and the Cossacks arrived and nobody knew where they were. Food was very very scarce and children were running all over the place because a lot of them lost their parents. But I was one of the lucky ones because I stayed in the orphanage down there. But of course we had to, when the Cossacks came down there, we had to run away because they used to kill them, but what we saw was very very tragic, but you know too at my age to remember all these stories, it takes a little bit of time and to actually tell the proper story I will need very much more time than what I have got now.

We didn't know what we were because we were youngsters mostly three years and four years and five years old and we didn't know what religion we had. In the part of Poland where the family stayed, we didn't know anything about Jewishness because we didn't have anybody to advise us or tell us. It is something that if you would read about it maybe but at my age when I was brought out to this country by Mr Ochberg my late sisters and myself, we were in a dream or in a different dream altogether because what we lived through in Poland and what we had here was something different altogether. All the bad things actually vanished when we arrived here. The thoughts were not in comparison to South Africa. But when we arrived here and they gave us a meal, they gave us bread and they gave us jam and we didn't understand that we had arrived sort of from nowhere. But there were 200 children who arrived here and a lot of them can tell, they were older than I am and they could tell very much more stories how they lived. You can actually get books from the Jewish library or whatever. Maybe you can read it because I myself only know certain things. I could, if I stay long enough and if I talk long enough I may remember much more.

The only thing I remember about the Cossacks is that the children used to walk in the streets looking for food and we used to see these Cossacks in bunches and they used to have these long spears and sometimes they used to take these spears and kill the people, because to them it was like a sport. They weren't a long time down there they were a week or two weeks and then they went somewhere else; where I don't know and then the Germans arrived and then they arrived back. It was a changing, a different world altogether. We don't know what happened to a lot of these children that were running about without parents because they killed the parents and Mr Isaac Ochberg went to many many many cities and villages and picked up 200 children and 100 remained in Cape Town and 100 went to Johannesburg.

All I remember from my late father was that they made a minyan at shul. They picked him up and they took him to the Jewish cemetery and they carried him. There was no box, "targigim", and they buried him and there is no stone at the moment because there is nobody to put a stone there and none to this day. Maybe I will go down there and put down a stone….and that was the end of my late father's funeral.

When I came back from the funeral we packed up. We stayed in a very little poor house and we put everything in a cart and we walked and the Jewish Community put me in the orphanage and one of my sisters, my sister, Leah, I don't know where she went to, but the two others went somewhere else. They were working and eventually Mr Ochberg found all of us and put us together. That's how we arrived in South Africa.

You ask me what happened. I mean I'm 86 years old and I was three years old then so tell me how can I remember.

MEETING ISAAC OCHBERG

You know when Isaac Ochberg came to the orphanage and he picked me, I didn't even know that my sisters were with me. I didn't know; they picked me up; they said I must go to such and such a place. They took me to such and such a place. They took us on a train. There was nothing on the train. It was a goods train. No food, no nothing. How can you remember all this? It is very very difficult. Very few people can remember from 83 years ago. But as I say, sometimes it comes back when you sit down by yourself, sometimes it comes back, but otherwise you can't remember everything.

Well they fetched me and they found my four sisters. They took my sister, Leah, the eldest one, she was 16. They weren't allowed to take children of 16 years old but she came here as a teacher and Channah was also older. She came as a nurse, servant and Salka was a youngster and I was a youngster and Perly was a youngster. Perly was my youngest sister and all my sisters are gone now and I am the only one who is left and it's very very sad. They all passed away now. We came from Stanislav to Warsaw. We went in a train. The train was one of these Nazi types of trains. There was no food, there was no nothing and they put us in a train and how long we travelled I don't remember, a few days I know. We stopped, we started and we stopped and we started until we arrived in Warsaw and when we arrived in Warsaw they took us all into one big big hall and they had beds and that's where we slept and that's where they gave us bread, they only gave us bread to eat. They had nothing else because the late Isaac Ochberg was a very good man and he was all over Poland while we were there, he was looking for other children.

Eventually Mr Isaac Ochberg arrived and he picked on me and my four sisters. My four sisters were not with me all the time. My eldest one, Leah, is passed away now, and then I had another one by the name of Channah and then I had another one by the name of Salka and one named Perly. And I was the second youngest.

And then we were taken by Mr Ochberg. They collected all the 200 children and my four sisters and myself were amongst the 200. We went to Lemberg and we stayed down there until Mr Ochberg made arrangements to take a boat. We arrived in the port of Danzig and from Danzig we all went on a ship. It was the first time on board ship, it was very very slow in going and from the ship we went to London.

From London we stayed seven days, and it was a different life altogether in London because it was peace down there and they took us to Hyde Park for a ride on a horse and I was very lucky, I fell off the horse and they brought us back home. Then they got a boat for all the children and we went from the boat and we came to South Africa from London.

So when we were on the boat they gave us bananas and it was the first time I saw bananas, but I didn't eat it because I didn't know what it was and I didn't like it.

LIFE IN SOUTH AFRICA

We arrived in South Africa and we went to the Cape Jewish Orphanage. We had a big welcome and half the children went to Johannesburg and half remained in Cape Town.

I was in the orphanage till I was 13 years old. I had barmitzvah there in the Gardens Shul when the Reverend Bender was the Rabbi and after a while I went to work for a Mr Reitz in George and I worked there for 12 months. And I got a big pay, three pounds a month. An old pound. And I left there and I came to Cape Town.

I've got three lovely children. I've got eight grandchildren all lovely people and I'm all right. I don't have to come to them thank goodness, but I had a very very hard life. I had to earn my own living and I had to make my own way of life. There was nobody that could help me. I was no professional. Of course I went to school here. I only finished standard five and there was no alternative but to work and to open a business.

I got married and I got a beautiful wife. She had cancer but she passed away. She was very good. She helped me and we did very well and now today I am retired. I've been retired since 1966. Since 1966 I retired and brought up the children. The children are all right. They are well looked after. They all earn good wages and got houses and cars. They have got things that we didn't have. And we are very happy about it. That's all that I can say.

The regret is that my parents died very young, when I was very young. I had no parents. I was so small when my parents died, I didn't know about them. But it's better to have parents and know and learn and talk to them and live to a ripe old age. When you're small it's very difficult but I had good people looking after me. For my first job I went to Reitz in George. I was working for a year. I was just over 13 and then when I worked for I Marks and company and then I came back to Graaf Reinet and from Graaf Reinet I went to Port Elizabeth and I met my wife, my late wife, a beautiful girl and we married and we worked very hard together and we did very well and we retired from Port Elizabeth and we came to Cape Town and I am still retired.

My children can work. My sons go to work. But my one son doesn't work. And the other one is an accountant and my daughter is married very nicely so I am very happy at home. That's all I can tell you.

I was very lucky. 20 years ago I had an agency to keep me going. Well, I saw many people, business people, and I went around and I play bowls. I still play bowls. I enjoy my children and I enjoy my life. How long I don't know. Nobody knows. That's all I can tell you what I'm feeling now. But hopefully I will see my children again. My son is here from Sydney, Australia. My other son is also in Australia. He comes here often about once a year. This one comes four times a year. My daughter stays here in Cape Town. She is married very nicely. She is very happy and that's all I can tell you and then I am happy. I live in Esplanade, a flat called Esplanade. I stay in Sea Point.

Group Passport 1

"You asked whether we could identify my mother, Bettman Sheindel, listed as number 4 on PASSPORT NO 1) list, in the above photo. We think she is the girl third from the right in back row". Aubrey Sheiham

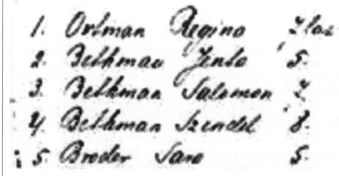

The first five children listed on Group Passport 1

Chapter 32 – TOIBA ECHSTEIN (TILLIE RABINOWITZ)

TILLY'S ORIGINAL TESTIMONY
Arnold Rabinowitz, the son of Toiba (Echstein) Rabinowitz, writes

Here are excerpts from Tilly's somewhat disjointed memoirs. Cyril my brother has 20 pages, I have three double sided pages and David another brother also has some pages

This is the first eight pages of about 20 that Cyril has and is in the process of transcribing. I think Tilly must have written it in about 1990 when she was staying with us in our house in Spain. I know she was working on something but didn't want us to see what. It's a pretty graphic story of the time and gives some fascinating detail about her life, her family and her parents.

I think Tilly decided to write some of her memoirs in the third person because she felt she could more accurately portray emotions and events that way. I think she felt that she was constrained by being Toiba (AKA Tova, Tilly and Tabi) and that this way was freer for her.

"She huddled close to her nine year old sister as her five brothers also wept, on learning of the death of their mother, the centre of their universe. The mother was almost a stranger most of her time being occupied caring for her brood. Her death was caused by the birth of the eighth child who mercifully died.

How vividly that scene is recalled by Tabi seventy years later, when she surveyed her eldest son's Spanish holiday home. Her mother died in a windowless room as are the living rooms in this house reputed to be 300 years old. But wait – these bedrooms had windows. Tabi is so certain about the dark death room – with their grim father – always grim and unapproachable - and the grandmother – so broken and of no help or consolation. Tabele always controlled her emotions There wasn't anyone to be demonstrative to – everyone was so shattered – showing emotion wasn't encouraged. Events moved so fast. The mother wasn't there – but her mean spirited sisters were. Tabi can't recall once being hugged by either parent grandparent, sister, brother or aunts. Although physically comfortably housed, fed and clad it was an undemonstrative family - kisses and hugs were entirely absent.

Meanwhile the war raged unabated – taken in its stride by the family who lived in this sprawling house surrounded by large grounds containing a cow and horse and the tomatoes her Father loved. Although all pork products were avoided, when the Father was in hospital, the mother told the children, he was forced to eat chazer (pork products).

There wasn't a mother's protection when the robbers burst into the house and herded all – even little Tabi against a wall, the robbers at their back with levelled guns and demanding money in their harsh Polish language. Sure a massacre would have resulted if someone hadn't arrived at the house of mourning disturbing the would be murderers and robbers. The only ones who would have survived would have been the three youngest

boys; Osher Joseph and Mordechai. They weren't standing facing the wall as they were sleeping

Incidents like standing and quaking were soon forgotten when racing across the fields falling frantically to the ground to avoid the war planes flying over Brest Litovsk to the battle field not too far distant.

After the planes disappeared Tabi and her brothers and sister all older than her; Samuel, Beryl and Sirke inadvertently encountered a Polish landowner and Aristocrat. All Poles were aristocrats; so the children had been told, specially the neighbour who was riding a bicycle. Because the children obstructed his crossing he cursed them and the children knelt crying, "Proske pani – proskepani forgive us we beg your pardon."

Arriving home breathless and hungry, some food was always there prepared either by their servant (much loved Polish peasant, the children's favourite adult) or the grandmother who had quite a brood to care for; the sour looking aunts and their brother Label.

Was it only a few months ago that the shoemaker had called to measure the children's feet for the new shoes periodically required? Now Tabi's shoes were too small and new ones had to be bought, the oldest aunt undertaking the task of finding new shoes for seven growing children.

Aunty Raizel was as different to her two younger sisters as could be imagined. She had just become engaged, was in love happy and always smiling.

Four months after the mother died Father left home with his business partners to purchase cattle and horses for their trading. Their clientele came from all walks of life. The gentry needed the best riding horses for their stables and breeding bulls and cows for the supply of milk.

Tabi's family was rich even after the war. They lived in a large house fronted by a barber shop. The barber was also the dentist and his main function in that field being extracting damaged teeth which caused much pain both before the extraction, during the struggle between patient and dentist, and many days after. Altogether a very undignified exercise dreaded by all.

The daily servant was an added luxury, the farm hands mostly young peasants, who cleaned the outdoor latrines, the horse, and cow stables, milked the cow, groomed the horse, all for food and a pittance of a few kopeks a week.

When Tabi's father left on his business trip the maid cooked and cared for the children. The grandmother often visited and of course the unpopular aunts came to amuse their young nieces and the younger of the five nephews; the two older nephews were almost the same age as the aunts, quite a normal situation in Europe with Mothers and daughters giving birth simultaneously. Sometimes the Uncles or Aunts were younger than the nieces and nephews.

Doing some end of year clearing I finally found the pages that Tilly wrote for me about her earliest days in Russia. I found it quite difficult to transcribe as it was so emotional and affecting. It has many details that I did not know and I am sorry I haven't read it more closely until now. It's often like that with things that are so close to the heart.

Tilly's handwriting is very clear and it was not difficult to transcribe. I have done the transcribing absolutely accurately and not corrected any spelling mistakes.I did not have to: there were none! Not a single one. There are some missing capitals and similar errors but I have kept the writing as it is and not corrected these either. She must have gone to a school with excellent teaching and have been an excellent pupil. The pages were written when she was about 82 and dated 16 June 1993.

This is my transcription of the three double sided pages that I found.

"Reviving all these memories isn't doing me any good but before my courage fails me I feel I owe it to my children to record.

After my mother died, my next recollection after the attempted hold-up, is being herded into a courtroom to view my slain Father's body-- He was wearing a bloodie white coat, and the murderers were all lined up.

Another memory - soon after my father died, there was an end to hostilities and the town was overrun with soldiers. Our home was near the station. Soldiers were climbing in and out our windows and through the house as a short cut - I don't know who was chasing who, but I can remember the sight. I remember that during winter time we had double windows. In between the windows there were wads of cotton wool.

When I came from school one day I was told that our cow had died and I sat down and cried. I wasn't even fond of the cow. I think my sister was crying too.

Did I tell you that I had one sister and five brothers?
I should not have been selected to leave Poland - too young, confused and obviously stupid. There I go - crying for self pity.

All the children selected were sent to a camp (house) in Warsaw. We embarked in Danzig. I remember that we all loved the lady who was in charge while we were in Warsaw.

The boat was terrible. Confined to the hold of the vessel, I was sea-sick all the time. There was a doctor who was always busy with the ladies.

Gosh! The sight of the first black man I ever encountered, a giant with huge arms!

Soon after we arrived from Cape Town, the people who had asked to adopt kids came to inspect. In Cape Town we were separated - some remained there and I and Jack were sent to Johannesburg. Oscar had measles so he remained in Cape Town in the Orphanage. There wasn't an orphanage in Johannesburg so we were accommodated in the Jewish aged home - there weren't too many old people there. I don't remember any.

I was told at some later stage that the children were listed or graded. Those who came from good backgrounds were placed at the top of the list. Oscar, Jack and I there at the top of the list, so my adopted cousin Esther Abrahams (later Esther Hurwitz) told me! I didn't know the meaning of that until much later.

Jack had been promised to Mr and Mrs Cohen, leading Johannesburg citizens and socialites. I was to be adopted by Mr and Mrs Cumes a very wealthy family. Jack left first. Mrs Cumes used to visit me every day and sit and sew dolls clothes for me.

I don't know who cared for us or educated us. When I arrived in South Africa I entered standard three without knowing an English word.

One day Esther Pincus and Millie Miller came to the home. I'd never seen them before. I was told to go with them and was taken out by a back gate I hadn't noticed until that day. I never saw Mrs Cumes again. I don't know why the original plan was changed.

I came to Esther's house and met Saul and two little girls for the first time. I know it was night because I was put to bed in the room with the little girls. I think I was bathed. I don't remember.

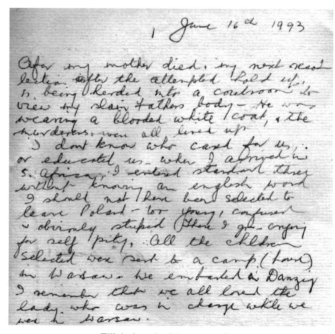

Tilly's handwritten memoires

I was taken to my new home and met Mrs Abrahams - she was 50, old to me and her two sons and two daughters. I remember Rosy was over 21, Becky about 26, Doddy 24 and Isaac about 30. I realise now it was a very poor house. My bedroom only had a bed, nothing else. They were such old people. Mrs Abrahams and her daughters shared one room. Isaac and Doddy shared another.

Rosy started sewing clothes for me. Esther took me to a dressmaker to have a dress made.

Oh, it was all so strange but I wasn't afraid. But this memory makes me feel cold now. No one ever kissed me or showed any affection.

I now realise some time at first I slept in the same room as Mrs Abrahams and Becky. She looked like a witch (Becky) and slapped me quite often saying I was cheeky. Mrs Abrahams used to shout at her and Becky used to shout at the servant and chase him with a broom.

Doddy was very handsome and so were Isaac and Esther and Rosy. Doddy used to work for his brother-in-law Saul Pincus until he had a nervous breakdown.

In my first year with the Abrahams family Esther and her three little girls went on holiday to Umkomaas with another family. The husbands stayed home. During the holiday the eldest child Miriam developed meningitis and died within days. Remember this was about 1923/4. It was my first experience of other people's grief. I just wandered around.

Soon after this incident Esther left her little girls with us who were looked after by their Nurse, an elderly spinster whom we called Miss Locker; that was her name.

One day this Miss Locker tripped and as I saw her coming down the steps hands first I burst out laughing. As soon as Miss Locker straightened she came after me and slapped me so hard just for laughing. I never knew what was the right thing to do. I was criticised about my manners, my eating habits, my freckles etc. I became so sensitive. No one ever told me how to do anything, just mockery and often laughter.

At the time the Cohens were having trouble with Jack who was rebelling about everything; over separation, maybe, and I aged nine was called in to counsel him.

When I think of it now, I never said no to anything. I was eating breakfast and was offered a bad egg but I was eating it until Isaac smelled the stink and told me not to eat it.

Sometimes when I came home from school the house was locked and the neighbour spied me so lost she called me into her house until someone came home.

Tragedy started afflicting the Abrahams. After Miriam's death Mrs Abraham's eldest brother, who had fathered eight children, and was grown up when I met them, committed suicide because of financial troubles. Two of his daughters were killed in a motor accident before my arrival.

When Doddy started hitting his head against doors or walls, he was taken to see various doctors or they came to the house and the family was thrown into a panic.

By that time I had finished school in Standard Six and was sent to business college. I was never consulted about what I wanted. I was 14 and I'd never been out of Johannesburg in that time.

At school I excelled in sport and was good at arithmetic and writing essays. All the pocket money I collected and sent home. In those days two (shillings) and six (pence) was a lot. I never owned a toy or a doll or a book of my own.

If I didn't finish my food Isaac would threaten (that) he would take away my samples, my only possessions. He used to get them for me when he worked in a pharmacy. He worked for a Mr Khan, a bachelor who gave me two tiny books. I still have them - or did. You must have seen them, both Omar Kyams. Isaac wasn't a qualified pharmacist".

Arnold Continues
Of the characters that Tilly describes in the Abrahams household:

I remember Becky and Doddy very well. Becky certainly looked like a witch and she scared the life out of me each time we met. She was hatchet faced, small but jerkily active and with long black hair streaked with grey and white. Doddy was amiably childlike and always wanted to play games, specially his own version of boxing, when we met. I must have been around ten or so last time we met. They lived in a decrepit house somewhere in Yeoville, in a lower ground floor flat that I was always scared to enter.

Rosy Abrahams married Nochem (Naom) Brozin and went to live in Middleburg, a good half of which I am sure he owned eventually. They had six children, one who died in early adulthood. Some live in South Africa and some in Israel. One of them, Max, is/was a very driven, successful businessman. He and one of his sons are responsible for Nando's, that South African competition for Kentucky Fried Chicken.

Isaac Abrahams, who had the same dark, almost kohl surrounded eyes as Doddy, married Ethel Rabinowitz, my father's sister. They had four children, the eldest of whom was named Miriam. She still lives in Johannesburg. One of the children, Samuel, a year younger than me, lives in Sydney.

Esther married Saul Pincus. They had three daughters, one of whom, Zelda, died in London about six years ago. She and my uncle Max, my father's younger brother who died in Toronto about four years ago, were childhood sweethearts. We were able to bring them together, both in their 80's, at a restaurant in Highgate, London, about eight years ago. It was a very touching meeting.

That is where the six pages end and it is all that I have.

Here's another fascinating instalment of Tilly's story, much the same as before but with some additional and very emotional detail. It was transcribed by David and is all he has.

Tilly's piece is, again, written in the third person. I think she decided to do this in order to enhance her work. I think she always felt disenfranchised and powerless and very much the luckless, powerless orphan refugee. Writing in the third person was, I think, her way of making her story universal but it's interesting how quickly she lapses into first person narrative when her emotions are raised. It is interesting too how she has "re-yiddishised" (my neologism!) many of the names in this later version: Echstein/Hochstein, Toiba/Tovah and so on.

Toiba's Story from David's transcription

"How many crimes are committed in the guise of charity, kindness, unselfishness or saintliness?

Tovah Hochstein was ruminating about the circumstances of her adoption which had occurred five years ago when Tovah was nine years old.

She was orphaned together with her five brothers and sister when her mother died while giving birth to her eighth child and her father was killed four months later. To Tovah these occurrences were being taken as merited. Her three brothers were younger than Tovah who never felt sorry for herself.

At this time an organization was formed in South Africa. It's main object to seek out 200 orphans in Poland and Russia soon after the 1914-18 world war. The delegation that arrived in Warsaw was headed by Mr Hochberg *(sic, I am sure she must have meant Ochberg)*, a wealthy bachelor from Cape Town. He had organized a dedicated committee to assist him in his humane task. The committee consisted of people living as far apart as from Johannesburg to Cape Town, a distance of 1,000 miles. When he arrived in Warsaw, he and his committee began the heartbreaking task of selecting the lucky boys and girls. Tova Hochstein and two of her younger brothers were chosen and together with personnel such as doctors and house-mothers and nurses were brought by boat to Cape Town.

By this time the people who had applied to adopt children had been chosen.

When Tovah and her brothers landed in Cape Town one brother, Osher, had developed measles and stayed in Cape Town. Joshe and Tovah went on to Johannesburg. A big fuss was made when Tovah and the other children met the prospective parents.

Joshe's name was changed to Jack and he had been promised to Mr and Mrs Cohen, a prominent and wealthy family who already had three children.

Tovah had been adopted by Mr and Mrs Cumes.
For the next few months Mrs Cumes came to the orphanage daily to sit with Tovah and make dolls' clothes while Jack or Joshe had gone to the Cohen house.

One day two ladies arrived at the depot where the orphans were being temporarily housed, collected Tovah in the clothes she was wearing and she was taken to Mrs Pincus' house. The other lady was Mrs Miller, aunt to Mr Pincus, Mrs Abrahams's sister.

Mr and Mrs Pincus had three daughters. Mrs Pincus was very beautiful and Mrs Abrahams' daughter. (I'm repeating myself and getting emotional and need some oxygen. Better!)

The next day Tovah was taken to Mrs Abrahams who had adopted her and saw her new home for the first time. Mrs Abrahams was 50 years old, a widow, and had two sons and three daughters being supported by her three working children. Although Tovah had never been to school, she didn't remember one, she was placed in the same class of the other children of the same age. By the end of the one year Tovah was coming top of class and promoted with the other classmates. She had learnt English for one year yet her essays were top in the class all the time.

After four years in school Tovah went to a business college to learn shorthand typing. She was employed in Mr Pincus' shop till her marriage four years later to Dannie, who was handicapped and had worked only for his father in the hide and skin business.

Tovah was absolutely ignorant about life as she didn't have a friend. When she returned from school to an empty house as Mrs Abrahams was visiting, she would sometimes be invited by a neighbour to play with the baby. She didn't own a toy. Rosy the youngest daughter used to make her clothes.

Mrs Abrahams never showed Tovah about any aspects of social life. Tovah always stayed home with "Ma", as Mrs Abrahams was called, on any evening. Tovah didn't feel deprived as she accepted the indifference of the adults and was raised in the tradition that children should be seen but not heard.

When Doddy suffered a nervous breakdown and "Ma" was adised to take him to London to consult doctors Tovah who was in business college stayed with relatives. When the house was rented out, Rosy went to live with Esther (Mrs Pincus) and Isaac shared accommodation.

Tovah wonders if her life would have been different living with the Cumes, Mrs Cumes a young mother of two children. Tovah feels despite her obvious kindness, deprived her of life for return of an impoverished home and never giving her any love, she basked in the glory of taking an innocent child, taking everything from that child.
("Damn her," was scratched out in the original).

Unfortunately the family paid a terrible price.
Becky, the middle daughter, was slightly handicapped after falling from a horse, always behaved like a witch.

Tovah endured two or more mothers, embarrassed the more the family from their so-called generosity as she was paraded as the poor orphan they opened their poor home, their empty home.

The handsome Doddy never recovered from his mental collapse.

Soon after Esther Pincus and her aunt stole Tovah away, from the very embarrassed Cumes, her older daughter died from meningitis, one of the first cases on the Natal coast.

Tovah was continually homeless, deprived and frustrated. Being a gifted student she had ambitions to study. When Tovah heard that pleading poverty, her Hebrew education, was accepted free, she couldn't attend any more classes. Tovah always felt like the adopted charity case.

Tovah harbours no grudge against the offspring descendants who have been paying a bitter price for Milly Iller, Ma Abrahams and Esther's folly, but that's another story. Maybe they would have suffered without the sins of the older generation. She wonders why so many afflictions should have befallen the descendants even to the fourth and fifth generation.

During these events Tovah was ten years old – obviously the most innocent and ignorant child imaginable. The six year old brother Joshe knew what was what. As he rebelled at being separated from his brother and sister to the extent that the Cohens sent for Tovah to quieten him down as the Cohens were totally at a loss of how to handle their problem and again that's another story.

Obviously Tovah had an air of being wise and very mature for her age. Huh!! Maybe she was cunning. When a classmate heard that Tovah came from Russia he promptly asked if she knew Napoleon too. Her reply was "of course". As Tovah grew older she regarded herself as the orphan and not entitled to any solicitude that she noted other children accepted as a right.

Tovah was very sensitive and cried easily. She never fought. Becky the middle sister of the Abrahams family limped as the result of an accident

I was brought to Esther's house from the aged home and spent the night in the little girl's room and the next day was taken to my new home. I was told Mrs Abrahams was my new mother. She was 50. Issac, Becky, Doddy and Rosy lived in the house. I came there with the dress and underwear I was wearing. That was all my possessions. That night I slept in a room that had a bed. I don't remember any other furniture, or when I received more clothes. I do remember I was just a frozen ten year old. Jack who was four years my junior had more sense. I think he started rebelling from the moment he reached the Cohen's house, and objected to everything- to being separated from Osher and me. The Cohens asked me to come to their house to pacify him. I remember being told that we were at the top of the list for the most desirable children, being educated and coming from a fine family. Fat lot that meant!

Doddy was working for Saul Pincus. Becky who limped helped in the house. Rosy, 21, was working in a solicitor's office. Isaac was working as a pharmacist's assistant for Mr Kahn. When Doddy started ailing I was going to business college.

He was taken from doctor to doctor and finally a decision was made. South Africa didn't have highly qualified neurologists or psychiatrists, so it was decided that Becky, Ma and Doddy would sail to England to seek a cure.

One evening, I maybe was 12 or 13, I was playing with Ma's long braids and tangled them up so much most of her hair had to be cut off and I was ashamed.

At sports I was the fastest runner. All school work was so easy for me. I came first in my school career, all four years of it. That's all the schooling I had! Rosy left school after standard six and so did I.

Rosy was 13 years my senior – always cosseted and loved. She was very good natured. She was already working when I came to the Abrahams house. Actually, I was stolen from Mrs Cumes, who came to claim me a day after I left the home. Who knows what kind of life I may have had brought up in comfortable surroundings, by young people.

I was always Mrs Abrahams' companion when the rest of the family went out. I was such a tomboy that when I got my first period I was afraid and ashamed to tell anyone. Eventually Becky found out and gave me some rags to plug the leak, but did not tell me it would happen every month. I thought it was only happening to me. Oh, I was ignorant and stupid.

Tilly (Toiba Echstein) and Arnold Rabonowitz – 1985

Chapter 33 – SHEWA GELERNTER (HILDA MODLIN)

MEMORIES OF HILDA MODLIN (SHEWA GELERNTER)

These memories are extracted and adapted from the original transcript of an interview of Hilda Modlin.

Events have been arranged into a chronological order and headings included to help the flow of the narrative

MY EARLY MEMORIES

The name that I was born with was Sheva Gelerenter. My adopted name was Hilda Seligson and my name now is Mrs Hilda Modlin.

I remember always being hungry and I used to walk a lot, always looking down on the ground. I thought maybe I'd pick up something to eat but I never did. I was always hungry. I also remember being cold. I remember being poor. I remember being hungry. Maybe there wasn't enough food at that time because there was a pogrom going on and there wasn't enough food at the orphanage. I was brought up in an orphanage.

I don't know myself how old I was. I was told that I was five. I had a brother as well but I don't remember him. He was older than I was by three years. He didn't come to South Africa. My mother didn't send him because she thought that when he grew older he could support her.

I suppose my mother never had enough food at home because my father was already dead. He died before I was born. I had letters from my brother afterwards to say that he, my brother, was a locksmith and I think that was the only letter I had from him. Well, the letter was actually from my mother to say that he was working and he was a locksmith, and that's all I remember about him.

My father was killed actually by a train. You know, he was deaf from the First World War. He had to cross over a railway line and he didn't hear the train coming on and the train killed him. That's what I was told. I don't know more than that.

I remember my own mother, very, very vaguely. I seem to remember a lady with a doek on her head, a scarf sort of tied under her chin. I don't remember what she looked like.

I don't remember coming here, or the boat trip. Well, I must have come by boat. But I don't remember that part of it. I also don't remember going with Mr Isaac Ochberg together with a lot of other children.

I was adopted from the Cape Jewish Orphanage. I don't know how long I was in the orphanage before I was adopted and I was taken from there. I was always very, very shy. I couldn't speak English, not one word, and it took me quite a time, you know, to learn. I had Christian friends and they spoke in English and I couldn't, didn't know what they were talking about, and I used to just make signs with my hands, you know, I didn't understand anything.

One or two years later I started going to school and I could say a few English words from there, and little by little I learnt, and

then I started learning elocution and they had to teach me how to pronounce words properly,because I used to speak half English, half Yiddish.

I remember people saying that, you know, I came with a lot of other children but I didn't know any of them. I was always very shy. I never spoke to anybody. I always sort of kept to myself.

Well, after my adopted mother died in 1937, a lady from the orphanage committee came to see me and she brought me a letter. The letter was from my mother, my own mother, and to say that I've got a brother as well and she told me all the details, and I suppose she used to keep in touch with the orphanage committee, and that's how I knew. Then afterwards I started getting letters from her, from my mother, and the letters came until the war broke out, you know the Hitler war, and the letters came until Germany invaded Russia because Brest-litovsk was on the border of Russia, and when Germany invaded Russia she took all the border places away, and then the letters stopped. I never heard any more.

I didn't feel anything. Because you know my adopted mother was very good to me and I never thought of any other mother, so I didn't feel anything and that's all. I was then 20.

I remember I saw Mr Ochberg once. He was in Malmesbury. You know, every family, they came out once for a whole day to Malmesbury and every Jewish family had to take one or two children in, you know, spend the day with them and that's where I met him. Mr Ochberg.

I always thought maybe I dreamed it. I wasn't sure what I thought. I thought maybe it was just a dream, you know. I thought there is enough to eat now. Maybe I just dreamt it. Well, I've got to learn to accept it, that it wasn't a dream, it was real, it did really happen. I just didn't dream it, it happened.

I never gave a thought to how it happened or why did it happen. You know, a young child doesn't think of these things.

I might have been dead now. As a matter of fact I'm sure I would have been. I wouldn't have been sitting here today. I wouldn't have lived to this age that I am now. If it wasn't for Isaac Ochberg I wouldn't be here at all. I would have died the same way that so many millions of other people died. It is just due to the one man, Mr Isaac Ochberg that I'm sitting here and able to tell you all this.

You know sometimes I don't sleep at night and I start thinking of the past and I think did it really happen or did I dream it? From what age does a child really start remembering? I don't know.

Well, I thought maybe it was just a dream that I had, you know, but it was a nightmare. That's all I remember and now that I come to think of it, it was traumatic.

May it never happen again, never ever!

Chapter 34 – FREIDL JOFFE (FREDA LARSEN)

CHILDHOOD MEMORIES OF FREIDL JOFFE (later known as FREDA LARSEN)

These memories were recorded by Freda's son, Peter Larsen, in 1987 when Freda was about 77. The recording was transcribed virtually verbatim. Events were rearranged into a chronological order and headings and words in italics were included to help the flow of the narrative.

MORRIS MY FATHER

My father's name was Morris (Moshe). I remember him quite well. He was a handsome tall man, about six foot tall. He had curly black hair like me and my son Peter. He was a bookkeeper. My mother had light hair like my sister Sylvia.

It was 1905 – before I was born. My father was then a family man living in Latvia at the time and he was in trouble because he didn't go fight the Japanese with the Russian Army. He sort of absented himself and was a deserter in a way.

He thought to himself, now what do I want to go fight wars with the Japanese. They called it a "Japonska milkhome" (*Japanese War*) I don't think he deserted deliberately from what I heard as a little child, but when he went there to report the commander was already gone and instead of going to the head office, and saying I've come a bit late and can I join with the next complement, he did not. *Perhaps* they *would say* come back in about six months, they are not sending anymore at the moment. *So he did not go fight* with the Russians rather against the Japanese, they would have killed him in any case. Anyway *that's* what he thought. My mother pointed that out afterwards.

At that time my sister Sarah was only six months old and I wasn't on the scene at all. We're talking about 1905 and not about 1914 when the war started. Anyway Sarah was six months old. So my mother told us afterwards that my father thought: well there's a six-month-old baby; he's a young man who had just got married and has a young child and he has got to fight against the Japanese. Some of them were so against fighting for anybody, even for the Russians, they used to cut off their toes and work it so they got dysentery so they did not need to go. They mutilated themselves not to go to that war. He would have got out of going *into the army* too. Now, my poor father was also in trouble *as he was regarded as a deserter.*

Because *his family* were well to do, they helped us, our aunty and so on living in Brooklyn America. This was his sister actually, and they wanted to get us over to America; to take him and my mother and us over to America. After the war they found out where we were and they used to send us parcels of food.

The Russians *were* still in command and he was hiding from the Russians *because he had deserted* and therefore could not apply to get a passport. He wrote to his sister and said its no use you going to a lot of rigmarole to obtain passports and he

would like to come, but could not because he could not travel around because he was a deserter. They'd shoot him on the turn!

He dare not declare himself! If I was a person who is hiding from somebody, I can't go travelling around –they'd soon discover me. He could not go to America because he was a deserter from 1905.

So to avoid contact with the Russian Military our family moved to Pinsk.

THE 1914 WAR.

I remember the war in 1914. We would go to the soldiers with a little bucket and they would fill it up with soup. Then a big truck would come along with potatoes and we had a *stick with a* nail on one of them and *we would try* hook a potato. I used to go into the barracks and ask for food.

What happened was the war broke out in 1914. My father wasn't dead yet in 1914. So they used to come and collect *men*, a whole bunch of them. He hid under the bed once. And what do you think they did? The Germans, the enemy was there. They picked him up, collect them all and they must go and dig graves. He stands there, remember he is not a soldier, he is not in the army, he was a romantic man I believe he came from a very highly educated family. He came from a different society.

The whole position was this; Germans come along then he must go and dig the graves. They don't know you see. They can't get hold of him because he is not a Russian and he is not anything; they don't know about what happened to him that he was in danger with the Russians for deserting *at the time of* the Japanese war, but not with the Germans – they don't worry about that. So he digs and he digs and he digs about half a day and then he thought he would leave it.

He comes along and sees the Germans are coming towards him. They recognised him and asked what are you doing here? They said, didn't we tell you that you must stay there dig graves? He said yes, but I thought I'll go home for a bit of food, I'm hungry. They said we'll give you some of our bread, but you come back straight away otherwise we'll shoot you!

At one stage the Germans said, we give you a time limit – bag of potatoes, bag of flour even, they said everything must put down to the depot - because you see they were hungry too! They are fighting a war – if they have no food then the soldiers are in trouble, isn't that so? It's a case of survival of the fittest, that's all it is.

FORCED LABOUR CAMP AND FATHER DIES

The thing was that after that he has got to go there or he has got to go here and his life was a misery. They come along and give a command that they are collecting *men*, they are going

153

from house to house to all the houses and the men must come along with them. They bring along the big truck they are going to collect *men* the whole lot they got to go somewhere to work in a labour camp. The Germans wanted them for labour for factories etc during the big war. *(Note1)*

They thought they were going to work somewhere. They didn't tell them that they are going to treat them so badly. They gave them the peelings of six potatoes to eat. Other people who were there told us. Somebody told us that if you were tired and pushing along wheelbarrows and if they fell down in the wheelbarrows - some of them are very sick already suffering from dysentery and all kinds of things - they threw them down on the side, it was a bit like a mountain. They were on the top and down below was the valley and they just throw them down. That's how they treated them.

They didn't throw my father down, but he became very ill and they didn't feed them properly. But he became very ill from the food, they didn't give him food or nothing so he became very ill, but the one man told us he died during Chanukah and that's why I have a sentimental feeling around Chanukah time.

My father wasn't actually killed by the Germans, but he died of diseases, but that man told us they died of dysentery and diphtheria.

My father played the violin beautifully. As sick as he was he played to all of them while they were dying - so the ones that came back told me. Of about 6,000 only six survived. They collected 6,000 men as labourers not just from Pinsk, from everywhere and I remember us waving to him when he was on the trucks that came to collect them and if anyone didn't want to go, they shot them on the turn!

He died of disease - they didn't treat them for any sickness that they had. You had to just live or die, one of the two. They had typhus, dysentery, diarrhoea. He died of dysentery. The man said it was dysentery. My father was ailing for quite a time there, but he said they allowed him to take the violin with and while they were all lying there groaning, and they were all dying he was going up and down in the ward or the barracks and played the violin for them. That man told us.

Anyway, six of them came from the big crowd that they collected from all towns – not only our town – six! But otherwise you must have been very lucky to survive, even six! Because if you fell down and you couldn't do your work, they chuck you down the ravine. They had no mercy whatsoever. That's the Germans.

Note 1 - Editors note
Although Peter says that Freda had a very good recall and a good feel for languages and she would have been aware of whether soldiers were German or Russian (Soviets) there is some doubt as to which of the two committed these attrocities during WWI.

"Following the collapse of Czarist Russia in 1917, Ukraine was able to bring about a short-lived period of independence (1917-20), but was reconquered and forced to endure a brutal Soviet rule that engineered two artificial famines (1921-22 and 1932-33) in which over 8 million died."...... Extract from the internet.

ANNIE BOROVIC AND RACHEL BOROVIC,

So some they killed. Annie Borovic with Rachel Borovic, they came from Brest-Litovsk and they used to shoot in the street and some of them got killed in the crossfire. If we say now I'm going to the market with my mother and there is some of them, they used to shoot out because they are from the enemy that shouldn't be there, then they start shooting and anybody that is going along would be shot with them. That happens quite a lot.

Anne Borovic's parents, the mother *had died* and father was killed in front of them. That's how they happened to come here *to South Africa* you see. Because they lost their parents altogether, but they were not from Pinsk.

THE STILLERMAN BOY

They killed some of them. The one that we adopted here, the blood was still on the wall where they killed them. So they cut off another boy's hand because they wanted him to take a candle to burn the sister's eyes out because he refused and put up a fight you see; well they killed the whole lot. They would have killed him as well. They cut off his arm. He was adopted by very wealthy people afterwards when he came out here, but they chucked him under the table they thought he was dead, but he wasn't! They all left, the others came to see who can they save, you know - and they saw this child was still alive.

THE DINNER

My mother and my sister weren't there at the time, but the Germans looked around in the houses to get all the girls, or men or whoever it is, and my father was already dead, so they couldn't get hold of him again, and they are coming along with the big things, a big heavy armament (rifles) – they come in there -tramp, tramp, tramp- , him and another one. I'm lying there underneath, I was very cold. I was by myself in bed. I hear them - tramp, tramp, tramp - so I put the blanket over my head. I could have been about eight or nine. So I'll tell you what happened then. I'm underneath there, so they thought well somebody's lying down there; they thought it could have been a big girl or somebody – just a little treat for them that day! They had a look at me and I started crying you see, but I was cute, I must have been very cute because they said, "What are you crying for?" I said, "I'm hungry". Now, that broke their heart - I suppose they left a few children at home somewhere. If I was older, if I was 17 they might not have played any games at all.

What happened was I am in bed. They asked what are you crying for, I'm hungry. They didn't say very much, they took off the things from their back – it must be that God was with me because they could have given me a hit on the head you know, or do anything, they could have done it if it wasn't that certain people are sent to people at a certain time, you understand, that's my idea. It's like angels you know that look after certain people - not all. So anyhow, why I'm so lucky I could write three or four books never mind putting it here, of the different things that have happened to save me.

They take the things off their back and there are lovely tins of condensed milk, and there was bully beef and there was sausages and there was bread. I suppose they felt they could get it somewhere else, you know. They took out all the food and they put it all onto the table. They thought well I don't know what's going on here, but at least that child will have something to eat. They thought well, she can't be alone in this place, there must be someone belonging to her who are not here at the moment.

They left and my mother arrived, looked around. She said *"Vos iz do gegangen?"* (What is going on in here?) Where did you get all these things? They were afraid to touch it, they thought they might have just put it there in the meantime they will come along and collect it just now.

So I said, well they put it down because I said I was hungry. They took it out of their little bags and put it all on the table. My mother made a nice dinner with the sausages and the bully beef and whatever else they had and the chunks of bread that she cut up. We had a plate full of food. Very seldom get a plate of food. And that's how we had to *survive. It was* survival of the fittest.

MEMORIES OF UKRAINE

Our house was quite a nice little cottage. We must have had some blankets – some of the natives perhaps they're struggling and suffering and they haven't got a blanket and they're cold. There was no electricity. We had lamps with wicks and so on. I think there were coal stoves, I remember my father going to make one in Poland. We were refugees there for three years. That's what saved us; by sending us to Poland when they were fighting in that Russia. Before they leave they would have killed the lot of us when they put the town on fire from four points, to burn it, from four directions.

We used to play with the children. A woman who was older used to collect a lot of us and we used to go to the forest, to go and pick blackberries.

We are very lucky because some of other children ran around without any shoes or anything in the snow. My mother used to take off her petticoat and make little shoes for some of them.

I'm lucky to be alive. I nearly fell down when I was stealing the potatoes. Those potatoes were almost in a line where they were, you understand, but if that started to roll down and I go down with them then they would not have been able to get me out you see. As soon as my mother noticed it, she asked me to come back, and not to take any potatoes. It was a depot, where they kept the food, and I took the chance, because we were hungry and I climbed in. We were stealing I suppose so. You could put a little child through the bars. It was about three or four o'clock in the afternoon. My mother was there with us and she had a bag. I was handing over the potatoes and I filled it up and it lasted us quite a time.

Then there was a shortage of salt, you couldn't get any. Don't forget this is a war. You either get this or you don't get that. We had a shortage here in South Africa of sugar at one time.

How do you think they tried to treat up a meal a little bit? You can't eat potatoes without a bit of salt. They used to go to the shop and get a tin or a bottle of sauce from the herring and they used to get a few herrings as well and they'd cut it up a little. It doesn't go off there because it's cold always there. There were no fridges and I remember my mother putting some in the potato. Not only for us.

MY MOTHER

My mother could speak German, she came from Latvia, which was mainly German speaking. She would have been able to speak to the soldiers in German. They used to always send her out to talk for them if they wanted to. My mother was a dear woman. She was a very sweet, charming person and she went next door when the woman was dying of typhus and nobody would go near her. They said no we are frightened, if you go there you will get the same thing. My mother said, it is quite OK, I'll go there, and I'll help her and she went in there and she washed her. Mind you, it was a very courageous thing to do. She washed her and she washed the floor and gave her plates of soup. Every time she cooked a bit of food for us she would bring some to her. Well, even a little bit of soup with a potato swimming around is also better than nothing. And all the others that you saw were running around naked, cold and hungry and some of their stomach was like that (swollen) from *kwashiorkor.*

My mother was a very good cook. We had very nice meals in the beginning. She cooked beautiful fish and would make bulkelach, jam tarts and the little pantry had five or six kinds of different kinds of jam. Yes you could manage reasonably at times but not when they came to take the town and put it on fire and things like that!

The schooling came later on, not at the beginning and they taught us Hebrew, and they taught us Jewish, they taught us even sums, some of them. And if we didn't get in, we used to look through the window and watch them learning you know. You see we had a desire for that. But then we started to get hungry and we started to get miserable and we wouldn't take much notice or attend to anything. The children are hungry.

My mother didn't make enough money. There was a time when there was no food for anybody. Everyone was suffering. There were general shortages after the war was declared. When the enemy was there they took away everything. After the war you can't rehabilitate. There's no husband. There's nothing! There's just a woman with three small children. My Mother used to sew and make a bit of money, but not as much as we needed. And then they came along and wanted to take the children.

Lots of other families they took the children, they were suffering from malnutrition, kwashiorkor. They killed the mother and father. The children ran around without any parents. So you know what we used to do? We used to go into the veldt and pick some radishes or something and some of them were just eating grass. It was very hard to survive, we used to run around bare feet, my mother used all her petticoats, she used to wear about four or five, and she would make them little shoes, she knew how to make it, not only for us but for all the other little kids in the neighbourhood.

They suffered more than we did, because we still had a mother. Some died of dysentery. We survived because she helped us as much as she could, but should she have died, and she was suffering from very severe dysentery, we would not have survived, because who is going to help us.

When the enemy came to Pinsk, if you've got dysentery, they used to pack you up in a big truck and take you away and they used to burn them alive some of them. They wanted to take my mother away because she had that and we had to put her under the mattress so nobody could see when they came to make an inspection. So you see what we had to put up with there.

When she was very ill, the neighbour said don't let her lie on top of the bed, put her underneath the mattress. Make up the bed like there is nobody there, because the soldiers came along, collected them all and burnt them alive, if they had anything like infection. They are looking after the soldiers, they are not looking after us. If they found you had typhus, you didn't stand a chance because that was a very serious matter, it could spread through the army personnel. It was a bit like plague you know. I had it, on the top of my head, and they chop off your hair but I survived it and then I was in hospital for something else and they could see the marks. I also had diphtheria.

We did have fruit. I remember going into some orchard. There was a lot of cherries, and I overate myself on those cherries. We were not short of fruit. They can't collect all the things from the trees. The Germans can have some of the flour, but they can't commandeer the fruit on the trees. That country grows fruit not like ours. Their apples are different, their pears are different. They are 100% in the things that were there. There was a thing called *yagdes*, (berries) or something, you don't get it here. Not only the blackberries, but there was something else, greenish like. I think we get something here, small ones, but green, beautiful, but we used to call them *yagdes*. They were very tasty, my mother used to make pots of jam out of them.

SARAH

Sarah, she was our oldest sister and she was a nice girl. She had to remain with my Mum. They had relatives in Latvia, and don't forget others are in America, and they wanted to bring them over from Pinsk.

Why was our family in Pinsk? We were Latvian people, not White Russians at all, but because *our father* did that (absented himself from the Russian army) they advised the family to come to Pinsk. All that revolved around it, you understand. Latvia was a different country, but Pinsk belonged to white Russia. My father was a fugitive. They could catch him at any time and murder him there on the turn! Now Pinsk was in another country, not Latvia where he had deserted, but in White Russia. It saved his life for a little while but not for very long!

My father and my mother are Latvians. At the time that he deserted he was a Latvian. Then he escaped to Pinsk but unfortunately it changed his life for a little while. It changed his life but not for very long *as he soon died.*

They wanted to send Sarah to Latvia where there was someone who might have married her without expecting a *nadan* (dowry). But they were all eventually killed (WWII) before they could get to Latvia. Even if she could have, it would have been no good because they were killing them in Riga too!

My father worked as a book keeper for private people. He was very clever. For all of them that couldn't write any language, he used to sit there, when their husbands were away at the front, and he used to write letters for them because they were illiterate. They were jealous and we thought they would report us. That's why when I see my sister Sylvia when she signs herself a little bit, there a few words in there, I kiss them, 'cause I think she was such a tiny little girl. She even wet herself there on the bench. They were sitting in school but she learnt to be able to write that. I am touched about that you know because she was only a little girl.

She was quite sensible, quite clever to be able to write, because the others, my father had to sit and write letters for all of them. You know what else happened? When I was in that home, in Arcadia, those children can't write. They want to write to their mothers and fathers and aunties and would say "Freda write a letter for us." I used to sit the whole time and write letters for them because I could. Well, I was older, there was a school, I learnt to write in the school.

I remember Sarah to a certain extent. I remember her coming to the train when we were going, when they were collecting us and she came there with my mother to say goodbye. That was another incident. They cried bitterly. I on the other hand, being small, I wanted them to now go so that I could get on with the train *journey*. You see, in other words I'm selfish in some ways and didn't begrudge them in other ways. But I thought because I am the one that's going then I want that train to "chook chook", it must go on!

WAITING FOR THE TRAIN

Nothing bothers me you know. I was different to what I am now. I was about ten. Nothing bothers me, I can tell you even when they were taking those refugees to Poland, they were all dying there of the cold and what do you think I did with my sister, I go in there by the officers that are sitting there doing all their work, but they also got fires, I sat myself down on the bench, everybody else is freezing, they are nearly dying, and I am sitting there.

And then *the officers* said, you better go back to the train, the train is going to go off. At the time, it was the time the train was going off you see. So I left and said *a dank,* (thank you) but I sit there in the warm, *while the others* were dying of cold. My sister she followed me after *I went in*, because the two of us are sitting on a bench. We very were young and waiting for the train.

They said, My G-d they could have chased you out, they could have done this, they could have done that, but somehow nobody chased me and then the whole lot wanted to come in.

THE SHOOTING OF THE RUSSIAN SOLDIER

There was a Russian soldier on a horse. He *was in* the town when *he* should go away. The Russians you know, they *had withdrawn* because the *German soldiers* were coming. He might have been staying with somebody and overslept himself. We are all standing there and they said that we must go and get into our houses, but you know me, you can see that I am different to what I am now, I was courageous I was everything.

Then he was going on that horse. Some people told him *vihodi!* (Come out) but he might have been drunk even. The *German soldiers* used the long guns (rifles) and they are training it on him and they killed him. We all saw it. The Germans shot the Russian.

He should have vacated. You know go away from here and the enemy is going to come, he shouldn't be here, he should be with the rest, but he overslept, drunk. They were all soldiers.

It was not only the Germans that we had to put up with but also the Austrians. Suddenly one morning we woke up and the Austrians were in charge.

ALONE ON THE TRAIN WITHOUT A TICKET

One little story I wanted to keep to myself, *it's* very sad and I have never forgotten it, because we were still in a bad way, we were starving and my sister was too young to do anything. My older sister, they were more afraid to do anything like that than the middle one. Now what do you think? They make up their minds that I must go to a place. I must go to Luliniez, or something like that, outside of Pinsk.

They couldn't afford to buy me a ticket as we haven't got the money for it. I must go. There's a lady they happened to know there. So they give the address and so on. In the meantime when the man came along to look for tickets they used to put me underneath the bench, but how I survived all this I don't know.

The story was that my mother wanted me to go there to see if I can't collect something or bring something back and so on. I begged her, I never forgot, I cried that I'm frightened to go on my own, I haven't got a ticket, if they catch me, and if I haven't got a ticket they'll murder me! They would have chucked me out of the train; I don't know what they would do! I spoke to the ladies that sat there about it, and they said it's no use going to the toilet there, because they check them. They said go underneath the seat. I went underneath the seat and when the ticket inspector went away I'd come up again. Well they helped me with some sandwiches and so on and so forth.

When we arrived at that lady's place, because I had an address, I showed somebody and they took me there.

Now I saved them a lot you know I saved them because my mother afterwards came to this lady's place with my sister. My sister was full of sores you know, big ones on her neck. I think it was from hunger or starvation or malnutrition you'd call it, terrible sores.

That lady said all right you can ask your mother to come along as well. You see, some have more and some have nothing. It all depends.

Anyway, the whole family arrived. They see me there and that woman takes me in and all the rest of it and she helped us. She says we can stay there. My Mother had arrived, she is there with Sylvia and Sarah and the lady helped us as much as she could. She was quite well off.

I'll never forget the one thing made me sad. Instead of going to the toilet, which they didn't have or was probably outside, I went to the front door, because it was snowing, it was cold and miserable, how I survived I'll never know and I used to open the door to go outside and pass water instead of waking them up to ask them where I must go. I mean you know when I lie down here I say my God you know the little native girls are better off, because we had a harder time than some of them have here. That I can tell you and it looks to me like it!

Then we stayed there. My mother used to sew for them, because if you have that skill in your hands, you've got something, that you can help, or you can do something. If she used to go to another home like in Pinsk to help with sheets or pillowcases or whatever they've got, they used to feed her as well.

We had a sewing machine and you know that when we were travelling we saw they put the machine on top of the trucks where the train is and we'd say "Oh there is our machine!" They'd pick it up wherever we went, or if we were refugees or so we took it with. It was a foot pedal sewing machine. She took it and so it helped her a lot. When she used to sew for them even if they didn't pay them they would give her the food and the children as well, say they can come along, you know.

If my father didn't die, if he could have lived, it would never have come to that. But then they wouldn't have taken us into the orphanage, so we wouldn't have come to South Africa.

SYLVIA NEARLY ADOPTED

So we were there, a little town near Pinsk not in Pinsk. At one point Sylvia was on the verge of being adopted by a very rich woman near Pinsk but my mother would not allow it.

A Jewish woman, she was a well to do person, she took us in. She had a nice home. Sylvia was after all the smallest, the youngest and that woman had no children. So she took her, if you don't mind, she takes her and keeps her in bed with her. You can do that with a small child, you know, when you have no children you make a fuss of them. So that woman takes her in bed and she is sleeping with her in the beautiful bed and we are refugees, we don't know where we are, we haven't got a meal to our name or anything or food or anything or clothing.

She gave her everything, dressed her up like a princess if you don't mind. I don't think she would remember it though. I was older, I remember it. They dressed her like a princess, me too, she dressed us both, but my mother was there staying with somebody else and she politely said to my mother, "Wouldn't you like your child to remain here." She said I would like to keep her and look after her, I've got no children.

So my mother, it was fated like that because she would have (eventually) died there. They killed them there. My mother had a bit of sense. That woman would have died, the whole lot would have died.

In the episode with that woman my mother had a bit of sense. A person is hard up and all that, but they got to have a bit of sense. My mother said, when we go, we all go together. Wherever I go, whatever will happen, I take both my children. My mother said at one time that she was tempted, like when she left Latvia, she was tempted to avoid being killed or starved, I mean if you're in the land of the living you've got a bit of hope, but if you hold onto a child and you've got nothing the child dies. It's very difficult.

PINSK ORPHANAGE AND ISAAC OCHBERG

"This is the beginning of my story of why I am here *in South Africa*;

Because of the terrible conditions my mother wanted to have us admitted into an orphanage, but they wouldn't take us. They said no they can't take us because we have a mother. I was about 12, and Sylvia was nine. They said listen, we can't take you in the orphanage because you have a mother. We are not allowed to take any children unless they have no mother and no father. In the end they took Sylvia, they consented to take Sylvia and took her to the Karlin orphanage, which is a different one to where I went afterwards.

Pinsker orphanage is a very nice place, but they didn't take us. It is a big place and everybody would say 'Take my child, take my child,' and so they had to be strict.

Things were bad, we were hungry, we were starving, we suffered badly, but they weren't going to accept children for that reason, they were only going to take you in if you have nobody.

So all right, how do you think did I overcome that hurdle? I didn't do it purposely but G-d had led me like that.

It was very cold, it was winter time and freezing, and we had no coal or anything like that, no fires. I don't like to even think about it, or to relive such sadness you know. So you know what I did, and I say it in our Lord's name, and I would not tell a fib. In those days my Mother somehow wasn't as you would be or I would be, and we were fighting for our very existence. My Mother was a funny person, she said we must lie down here and wait for Death to come and fetch us, for there was no food of any kind, you see, that's why previously I had to go and get a few potatoes. So you know what I did, and I never forgot it and now I want it to be recorded. So I don't tell my Mother anything, I go in. There was a school next door, a school, nobody was there, it was at night don't forget, middle of the night and

nobody was there, but there was a lovely big fire going, a beautiful fire in the fireplace.

I see this lovely fire there in the fireplace, so I sit myself down there and spend the night there. I spend the night there if you don't mind because it was nice and warm. What must I do? My mother is starving, and they are cold and they are miserable and they die of frostbite and everything else. It is difficult to explain to you what I did go through. So anyway, it is unbelievable, but if you haven't got the courage, you would never survive you see. They died of *kwashiorkor* or whatever they would have died from. So anyway, I didn't know anything about it, I was too young to realize it was a very dangerous thing to do for a young child to sit there all night. Anybody could have attacked me, but that didn't get into my head you see, I didn't know anything like that, but what they did was, and this is the real truth and may G-d punish me if I tell one lie.

After they found out what I had been doing t*he people running the orphanage* called me in afterwards and asked, "Why did you stay there in the school?" I said I'm cold and I'm hungry and I have nowhere to stay. I saw this fire here and I thought it will be nice and warm here. They questioned me you see, they didn't want to punish me or anything but they wanted to look into this matter. First the mother wanted them to take me into the orphanage. They wouldn't allow it. Now the child has got nowhere to stay. The mother is evidently neglecting them and now the child is all by herself in the school. They put a different construction on it you see. They thought well if that's the case, it's like a child has been neglected you know, street children. They said well in that case they called the Committee and they had a committee meeting and said, that the child is evidently not looked after by anybody. G-d made it like that because through that I am here; but step by step He works, His miracles to perform.

One of the committee ladies was pointing at me in the playground and I could see she was questioning my admission to the orphanage and they were talking, talking, talking, then she shut up! Evidently the others presented their idea about it you see.

So they said well in that case we must take them in. They left it at that. By then I was in the home (orphanage) and that home wasn't bad. It wasn't bad and when I had a sore throat, they attended to me. They took me in and arranged it that my sister must come from Karlin orphanage to come to the Pinska orphanage because I was there. Otherwise they might have taken me only and left her behind. They would not take our oldest sister Sarah into the orphanage as she was too old.

I liked it there and you know what I did? G-d is my judge. If they give us bread or they gave us anything, or they gave us food I used to keep mine, I didn't eat it. I ate some of it, but I kept it in my locker so that when I go visiting, I could give my mother the food and my sister. *Don't let me have to recall bad memories* like that which should be forgotten. You mustn't live in the past!

So anyhow, let me tell you what happened there. It is quite something to be able to go through and survive, because some of them didn't. Anyway, a lot of them died. I remember seeing their stomachs were standing like that. I remember seeing them like that as well. Anyway, so you know what happened, that part I never told you, but anyhow that's how we happen to be in South Africa.

So I'm staying in that orphanage. It's quite nice. There was a bit of food more, definitely, there was little bit of supper and I would hide that, that I never forget, so I would hide it so that I could take some to *my mother and sister*. Even when I went to wash a floor somewhere and they gave me half a loaf of bread, I wouldn't eat it; I gave it to my mother. Wash floors, mind you, like the picanins! You know that's something like on a par with the picanins who would also wash a floor.

I wasn't greedy, I wasn't selfish, I thought of them all the time. G-d knows it. I'm not making it up.

GENERAL ADMISSIONS FORM USED IN JEWISH ORPHANAGES IN POLAND

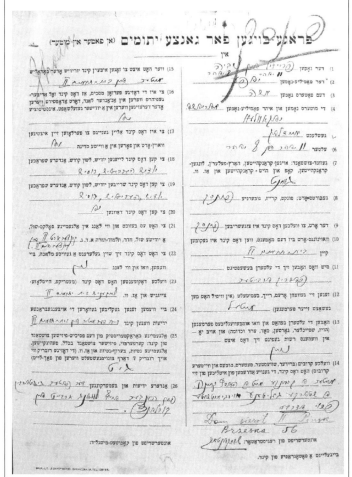

General admission form of Frejdel/Freidl and Sima/Cijwa Yafe/Yofe/Jaffe/Joffe – written in Yiddish

Veronica Belling has very kindly translated the general information form,

"This is a copy of a general admission form for Jewish Orphanages in Poland and the Ukraine. There is a place on the form to fill in the city, but generally it isn't filled in. There is another form that was issued by the Joint Distribution committee in the Rovno District in the Ukraine. Let me stress again that there is very little information in the forms. The form I translated for you for Joffe has more information than most that only have names and ages and not much else. I hope this makes it clear."

Questionnaire for Full Orphans: (without father or mother)…

1. Name **Frejdel and Sima/Cijwa**
2. Surname **Yiddish: Yafe/Yofe (English: Jaffe/Joffe)**
3. Father's name **Moshe**
4. Mother's name and maiden name **Mariasha….**
5. Sex **Female**
6. Age **11 and 8**
7. State of health. Eye disease, heart complaints, lung-complaints, head and skin diseases, etc. **Healthy**
8. Place of birth, place, circuit, district. **Pinsk**
9. Place where the child was assigned **Pinsk**
10. Address before the child was admitted to **Orphanage II**
11. What was the parents occupation. … **worker**
12. Were they poor, rich, average (estimate of their worth) **average**
13. Did the parents own immovable property (house, granary/barn, garden, sod, land, etc.) If yes, who is looking after it now. **None**
14. Relatives (brothers, sisters, uncles, aunts, and further relatives) Does the child have the exact address of any of them. **Mother has a cousin who has a heart ailment, suffers badly, worn out. Address: Dom Sieret II, Pinsk, Brsesna 56.**
15. Who has legal authority over the child: **Matron from Orphanage II**
16. Is this person agreeable that the child be taken away to another country, to be adopted or to be brought up in a Jewish environment, institution there. **Yes**
17. Is the child itself inclined to leave his present home and to travel to a faraway country
18. Can the child read Yiddish, Hebrew, other languages? **Yiddish, Hebrew, Russian**
19. Can the child write Yiddish, Hebrew, other languages? **Yiddish, Hebrew, Russian**
20. Can the child *daven*? **Yes**
21. Has the child attended a general folkshul, a Jewish school, *kheyder*, Talmud Torah, etc. and for how long: **Orphanage II**
22. Has the child learnt a specific trade, with whom, where, and how long **No**
23. What certificates does the child have (matric, school leaving certificate etc.) O**rphanage II**
24. From whom is the information about the child obtained **Matron of Orphanage II**
25. General psychological-physical condition of the child: build, general physical condition, abilities, general inclinations, vocational leanings etc. (this section as well as section 7 should be filled in by trades people. **Good**
26. Other information and comments. **Father… died of hunger…. long years of working in Kurland.**

So anyway, we stayed there for quite a little time, could be about a year or so, when all of a sudden, who should come out but Mr Ochberg. It was the Jewish welfare organisation said we would like to send that man (Ochberg) to collect some children for us. We called him Uncle Ochberg because we loved him such a lot. We have such wonderful memories of him. Now he became wealthy, but before he was a poor man. He bought up a lot of ships that were going down or something and he made a fortune that way. He became a wealthy man in other words.

Then the people made a big fuss of him. He comes from England or wherever he comes from. And he was made a fuss of, this Mr Ochberg.

So he arrives, and now what does he want to do? He wants to collect some orphans who have lost their parents, lost everything. They prepared him on account of me sleeping there in that school you know, that's what it was. That's how they got hold of me and another thing is that none of them wanted to go. Very few wanted to go. And some that he collected they suddenly take it into their heads they wanted to go back. They didn't all want to go to South Africa. They said it was a black country, you would become black and you become this and you become that. You know what it is. I am talking about 70 years ago!

I had a choice either to stay in Cape Town or go to Jo'burg. I had a chance to go to America because I had an aunt there. That's where I copped it you see and that's why I chose Jo'burg. Why I chose Jo'burg. G-d wanted me to come to Jo'burg, that's why. My Mother said it was the train ride (desire to travel) that made me decide to go to Jo'burg and being the older one my word counted and I decided for my younger sister, Sylvia was nine. I could have been almost 12, something like that. It would have been 1921.

Mr Ochberg arrives, he is collecting the children. He said that that child showed great tenacity, great courage in fighting for her survival. Let's see if we shouldn't send her in the office instead of someone else perhaps. They only had a limited amount of children going to South Africa. They didn't only take children from Pinsk, they took from other places too. There were a lot on the boat that came from other places.

The thing is, I come now to the office. They said, will you speak Hebrew to us if he asks you? And I'll tell you who knows about it, it is the Levy girls, Ethel Levy and the other Levy. There were four daughters. They said we remember how you used to speak Hebrew. But nobody would believe it unless those girls that I happened to know, you see. So he speaks to me. You see I'm rather good at languages. I can pick up a language with no trouble. I have got an aptitude for that language. I speak Hebrew, I tell you and his eyes grow big, I remember him looking. He was really over-awed. He says now, he asks me, am I by myself, I said no I got a sister.

My older sister Sarah could not come as it also depended on the age, one mustn't be too old, one mustn't be above 12. One mustn't be after 15 at all and the ones that were older had to help with the babies.

He said would you like to come to South Africa? I already had my mind made up. I used to pray about it that they should pick me to go to America because I had an aunt there and they did take some to America. But after the war in 1921 they knew there were some orphans who have been neglected with no parents at all. So I tell fibs to him I said, well I have got nobody. I dare not say that my mother will stop them and she wouldn't want me to go.

I said I had a sister and they called her in. She's got nice big blue eyes with blond locks. She took after her mother who was a fair woman and I took after my father with black hair. They say would you like to come, I said yes we would love to come. I thought what should I go languish in that place, because I like to travel around.

TRAVEL PERMITS ISSUED BY THE MAGISTRATE OF PINSK

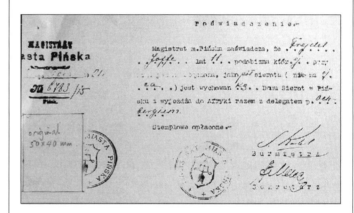

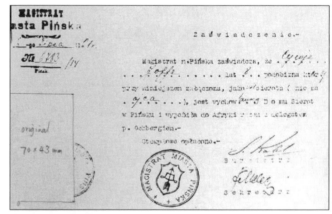

Travel Permits Freidel (Freda) and Cywje (Sylvia) Joffe

The documents in Polish are travel permits issued by the magistrate of Pinsk and the two photos with the writing and blue stamp are part of these documents.

Here is a translation of the travel document from a similar one done by Jack Goldfarb

The two similar affidavits grant permission for the two Joffe siblings to be placed in the care of Mr Ochberg for the journey to South Africa. The Affidavits were written in Polish. Pinsk was actually located in White Russia, an area ceded to Poland in 1918, but then returned to Russia later.

6783/15 & /14) Affidavits Issued by the Magistrate of the Town of Pinsk on July 6, 1921.
The Magistrate of Pinsk states that FREIDEL JOFFE (and CYWJE JOFFEE) , of eleven (and eight) years, whose photograph is attached, and is an orphan without parents, who resides in the Orphanage, is to depart for Africa with Caretaker OCHBERG.
Stamped and Sealed by two secretaries of the Magistrate of the Town of Pinsk.
Below are the passport pictures of the two sisters Freidel (Freda) and Cywje (Sylvia) Joffe which Peter Larsen photographed at the Kaplan Centre Archives in Cape Town. He also took the photos of their travel permits and a questionnaire.

Freidel (Freda) and Cywje (Sylvia) Joffe

They made a fuss of us there. They collected us up with a whole lot *of other children*. They brought us all to Warsaw where there was a place where they collected us to feed us up and see that nobody was sick and all that kind of thing before they go on the long journey. There they looked after us and we had nurses to bath us and also make sure there were no lice.

In the meantime, my mother, she was not with us, she was not in Warsaw. You can imagine. She had nothing, but she sold a couple of pillows so that she could get the money for the fare. *She came to Warsaw* to bring us home, but not with Sarah, she left Sarah behind She wanted to bring us home and if not to bring me home then Sylvia. Many wanted to take their children home and Ochberg nearly had to abandon the project and he had to collect children from many different orphanages.

My mother said I'm taking Sylvia home. She is the youngest. I was more or less self-sufficient; I ran around and brought them food but Sylvia was more or less helpless.

To cut a long story short, *there were* all kinds of *decisions we* had to go through and experiences. My mother was there. I said leave Sylvia to come with me. This is what *I said and* I'll never forget these words. I said leave Sylvia to come with me. I said I'll look after her like (I'd give) the eyes from my head –

Nokhkukn nokh geben mayn eygn van kop! You can imagine *the dilemma of my mother considering* how small Sylvia was. They put us in barracks and we were all sleeping there. My mother is sleeping, she was a bit tired, she wanted to sleep but Sylvia said she must look at her with one eye. My mother said I can look at you. I'll open one eye to look over you with one eye. A child loves her mother you know, a small child. So we went for a couple of nights

My mother stayed two or three days in Warsaw and then was going to catch a bus home. The buses come round, so she's on the bus. We're standing there, she's crying and we're crying. So she went out of the bus again. She left about two or three times the different buses to go on. She goes out of the bus to stand with us. Well there must be an end to it sometime. Either she takes us and tells the people we're not going, 'cause some of them didn't go, or she must go home.

Poor old thing. That will be a thing in my memory I suppose for the rest of my life.

And then we saw her getting into that bus and the bus pulled away.

I don't suppose she could ever get over it. Yes, everybody loves children you know.

ENGLAND

Understand that when we came to England, we spent *one* month in England. Women used to come and bath us, wash us and they promised money, to the ones that were helping themselves, and drinking big cans full of milk. Naturally, for six months they kept us there. They give us something if we are going to drink the milk and eat that thing, because we are all a lot of shadows never mind anything else from wherever they've taken us. But they said if they are eating, helping themselves, then they will give them a shilling or sixpence or something, – you know what a child is - like a reward.

I think I said to one lady, but that was in London, not here *in South Africa*, I said can we have as much bread as we want to? She said you can have as much as you want, you can eat, you can eat yourself full if you want to you see. We didn't think that we can eat as much as we like.

I was lucky in a way. I was going to be adopted in London by very wealthy people, very wealthy, and they saw us there as we walked along at the station. The others looked like woebegone waifs you see and I had this beautiful black hair hanging down and they thought that's a nice pleasant little girl you see and they went to them and they said no they are not allowed. They said you got to come to South Africa and take one and go back again, but we cannot leave them in between because we signed a contract with the Government in Pinsk that we have to deliver them in South Africa.

I might have died in England if those people would have adopted me. During the Second World War of course. They bombed them and I might have copped it. In South Africa I was a bit more protected.

CAPE TOWN

When we arrived in Cape Town, I am standing in the queue. So naturally Sylvia didn't have much to say and she is standing next to me. Johannesburg had an arrangement that they would take a certain lot. Some children remained in Cape Town. I could have picked, I had a choice, definitely. I had a choice. Some could stay in Cape Town, some could go to Johannesburg.

I was not such a fool, it did not pay me off in some way, but G-d wanted it like that I suppose. He works everything, you don't think so but He does.

Now, when I said I'll go to Johannesburg, they asked with your sister? I said yes. I chose to go to Johannesburg, because I wanted to travel. I always had this wanderlust and my mother would jokingly say, "Ikh muz aykh oys for!" (I must send you away!)

My mother wanted me to go to Cape Town. My sister had no say. She was too young to understand at that time. She was controlled by me particularly. They wouldn't separate us. The older one has got the say.

So now we're in the train. Now they all know that we are coming, like the royalty, they all know that we are going to different stations. And the people were collecting there. The people know *we are on the train*, they advertised all this. The children from the home are coming through. That group of children is coming through to Johannesburg. The blooming station was packed, like it was for the Queen. You want to see the boxes of chocolate that they brought, we didn't know that they would do that, but they chucked a whole lot of beautiful lovely big boxes of chocolate. Everything. Whatever they can do.

JOHANNESBURG

We arrived in Johannesburg now, now we are in Jo'burg. The train was very nice because they chucked everything in and some of us took them and we arrived in Johannesburg and we had all these things that we had collected up. The others wouldn't take it from us you see. So we arrived. There were lovely ladies, ladies from the benevolent society, I suppose well to do, wealthy with the diamonds and all the rest of it. They were bathing us, doesn't matter how big you were. That is now a mitzvah like. A blessing for them. I wouldn't mind if a lot of children came along that were saved from starvation and saved from being killed and all that. I would also have to come and give a hand. I'm sure you would give a hand if you knew something like that, wouldn't you? So anyway they bathed us and looked after us and they dressed us and everybody had their separate clothes, you know South Africa is not poor. Well South Africa was not in the war you know, you musn't forget that. If they had nothing in Pinsk, it's not to say that it means the same thing here.

In Johannesburg we were housed in an old age home until they acquired Arcadia. So you know me, I pal up with some man

Photo and inscription Sylvia and Freda Joffe from the photo album of their "nurse" Tasha Altuska

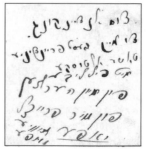

For remembrance

To my best friend
Tasha Altuska
With much love from my heart
from me
Freidl Joffe,
Livia Joffe

there in the old age home. He was walking around on crutches and was a proper cripple he was. I explained to him how my father died and about my mother and I told him I wanted to send *my mother* a pound. I only had some of the money and he said I will give the rest. In those days, 1921, that was a lot of money. He said I'll give the rest, give me what you got and I'll keep it and see if it can be sent away because it would be difficult for a child to organise it. He was a nice man and my mother received the pound and thanked us. Sarah bought herself a beautiful pair of shoes for 50 pence. They thought they were rich. A pound was a lot of money in those days.

Also I won some money picking out some actresses and I sent that to them. I wouldn't buy a thing for myself, you know, as she said what's going on there and because money was very precious there.

My mother Maria could sew and so could my eldest sister Sarah. But my sister Sylvia - we're growing up now - now she got to know George and his mother. And his *mother* was a nice old woman in a way. She used to give her some money for our mother. My mother was a dressmaker. She used to sew dresses and could make beautiful eiderdowns. She did that at home.

We spoke to Mr Shear *when we were at Arcadia* and asked him if we could *arrange for Sarah to come* out. Sarah was working already *in Poland but he said* that we cannot leave our mother behind. There must be the two of the family there and the two of you here. You know, my sister Sylvia and I here, and she (Sarah) must look after our mother *in Poland.*

Then comes along that stupid Arthur and he wants to marry me. I said no my mother won't allow it. He said your mother is 6000 miles away! What does she know! I forget you don't know him.

It was a very courageous thing for my mother to let us go 6000 miles away. When I last heard from them it was in 1939. You Peter were born in 1938. It must have been not straight away, that war, because I sent photos of your *Bris.* They even saw that. And then they wrote us the last time and said don't send money and don't send letters. They are reading our letters, we are getting into trouble. They only corresponded till 1939. You were about a year old Peter. They told us to leave it alone, because they were reading the letters. They are opening letters when there is a war. They cut them off. We don't know how long they survived, but we worked it out.

Your dear father took a great interest, and I love him for that, he used to pick up the papers and he used to have it on the bed, you were only a year old. He used to read it in the paper. No, he said, there was a concentration camp just outside Pinsk. We knew everything that was happening, because they wrote about it, but what can you do? My husband said, well they have gone already, so they hadn't survived very long. My Mother and Sarah must have lived a year or two before they collected them up. He said those concentration camps are right next to Pinsk. We knew about it, because they wrote about it in South Africa. I said to my husband at that time, can't they intervene. Can't somebody come along and tell them to stop. He said, no we've

declared war. We are the enemy now. You can't do anything when they have declared war.

Before the war we used to correspond. I wrote about Sylvia, I sent them photos of us and I used to get letters until the war broke out. The letters disappeared, unfortunately I didn't keep them. You know a person moves around, suitcases here, suitcases there and you never know what happens to things. I had a lovely photo of my mother and my sister and my sister is sitting on my mother's lap. She's only six months and there is another one of me when I was small and I'm standing there on a little bench. I was short like, and it was a lovely photo of us. I don't know what happened to it. You take it around here and there. There was no law and order in those days. In the course of time these photos and letters get lost.

Some correspondence was lost or discarded inadvertently Looking through various papers one was inclined to discard some but Arthur once stopped me when he recognised one as being a letter from my mother. My husband tried to make me aware of holding on to letters.

I don't think I have any now and I don't remember getting their later letters, my sister must have some. We stopped writing letters.

There was a beautiful dress a lady in Johannesburg gave me. I will never forget it. It was pink with lovely greens right round. It was out of this world. You know what happened? When they had concerts they used to come and ask me can I lend them that dress to the one who was acting or something like that because it was so beautiful. So I said yes I lend you that dress. Yes all right you can have it. It was an orphanage don't forget and they can't go and involve themselves in buying such an expensive dress because somebody's got to pay for it.

Mariasha and Sarah

While Freda and Sylvia went to South Africa with Isaac Ochberg, Mariasha their Mother and Sarah their older sister remained behind and are believed to have perished in the Holocaust

Chapter 35 – CHONAN MIGDALOWICZ (CHARLES MIGDAL)

MEMORIES OF CHARLES MIGDAL

These memories are extracted and adapted from the original transcript of an interview of Charles Migda.

Events have been arranged into a chronological order and headings included to help the narrative flow.

MY EARLY MEMORIES

My name is Charles Migdal. I was born in Pinsk in Poland in 1908 and it was quite a big community. There were 38 000 people; Yidden staying there.

I remember my father bought a hat for me. I must have been about five and a little boy got hold of my hat and threw it on the ground and as the mud was knee-deep I couldn't go to shul for Yontev.

We lived in a house and had a big garden and there we had 24 hours notice to get out and in 24 hours the garden was empty.

They took 36 children and they put them against the wall and they shot them, Jewish children and we had 24 hours notice to get out because there was a big fight between the Russians and the Bolscheviks.

And then the train came. If you wanted to stay; you can stay on your own responsibility. But the train came and we got onto the train. There were thousands on the trains, hanging on the doors, on the windows, and all over on top of the train and under the train. The train left.

Later we arrived at a certain place and I don't think there were any houses. The town was flat. There was a big hall with no windows and no doors. It was winter and the frost must have been anything between 20 to 25 degrees below zero. It must have been that. If you put a cup of boiling water down in a second it becomes a block of ice. We had no clothes, no shoes. We had to cover our feet with pieces of rag.

Anyway there my mother died, probably from exhaustion or from malnutrition or whatever.

And then we travelled to various places and then we came to another place in Russia where we saw how the people were bayoneting one another and corpses falling. We were in a house looking through the windows we could see that corpses are falling and soldiers chasing one another on horseback. Who it was I don't remember, but they were chasing one another. It made a very bad impression on my young mind but I couldn't see that. We looked through the window and I could see all that. There were other things actually but I really can't remember what happened to me in that short period of time.

The train left. We all had to get off the train. We were travelling to various places. There were no telegraph poles. There was

Charles Migdal

nothing. Just like the middle of the sea. A man came along; a policeman or a general, I don't know. The train stopped. He chased us all off the train and we all jumped into the snow and the frost was terrible, terrible. Then my father said to another man, there must be a village here or there and they left. My father had his luggage in a handkerchief tied to a walking stick on the back and they went to different areas. They came back about midday.

People came with horses and sleds from all areas and they took us to the various villages and we stayed there. Then we went two or three days without food and we were very very hungry. There we had to sleep on an oven. We weren't allowed to play in the house although it was my father's house, our house, but then my aunty was there and her daughters and she wouldn't allow us in the house. And my father had to force the door open and the snow is falling. The frost was bitterly cold and we had to be on the oven.

Cholent smelling too beautiful, delicious. So we came off from the oven and opened up the oven and we had a good time with the cholent and we had a marvelous time. In the morning my father went with that man to shul and they came from shul and they opened the oven to take the cholent out and there's no

164

cholent. We got a hiding for it but it was worth the hiding. We had a marvelous time after two or three days without food, can you imagine?

Then we left for other areas; where I don't know; to Deep Russia and when we came back to Pinsk hardly any houses were standing from a Yiddishe population of 36 000. My mother before we left she opened up the flooring and put in her suitcase with all her belongings in suitcases. When we came back there were hardly any houses standing. We didn't know where our house stood or what happened to the suitcases. That was the time Ochberg came and took us to South Africa, without clothes, no food.

A wagon came with half a loaf of bread and those who were lucky enough to catch the half a bread, were lucky. Those who didn't did without. In Kosovo, in the Russian Revolution now, reminds me exactly what happened to me. I was about six or five and there was a plank with two buckets of water. I had to go far away to a well to carry water. I had to go without food or clothing. We wrapped our feet in pieces of rags, and that was it. It was certainly not pleasant at all.

In winter we would take the bucket by hand and put water in it and take the water, put it in the buckets, quite a long distance to the house where we stayed.

And then after a while my father couldn't manage us so he put us in an orphanage in Pinsk. We must have been there about a year perhaps, something like that and we all had to darn our own socks. They could see that I darned the socks very well so they gave me the job to darn everybody's socks. There must have been about 250 children. They put me into a room there by myself to darn socks. The wages I got was Friday night an extra slice of bread. Each one had one slice of bread. Friday night my wages was an extra slice of bread.

My cheder was next to the hospital. I could see my father dying. I asked him how old I was. I was 8. I asked if I was a Cohen or a Levy at the age of 8. I had that in mind. He said just ordinary, you're not a Cohen or a Levy. Anyway he died.

MEETING ISAAC OCHBERG

Anyway, after that Ochberg came when I was there for about a year. We heard a man coming from South Africa to take children whose parents were killed in the war, pogroms or otherwise. He interviewed me and all the children, but he interviewed me especially, I don't know why. And he said to me how did my parents die. Well I didn't know what he actually meant by it, so I said well, they died a natural death. As I said a natural death so he wouldn't take us. So he took from our orphanage 36 children and he marched them to a certain destination. There were three orphanages, Jewish orphanages in Pinsk.

I was the eldest of three brothers, there were four actually, but I couldn't get hold of my elder brother. I would have also brought him out, but he was out of town I couldn't get hold of him. I saw children marched off to a certain destination so I said to the children, my brothers, I said "Come, let's go after them. They don't know who they took or didn't take. I said come, let's go after them." We marched after them. Then we came to Warsaw. Then from Warsaw I had to go to shul to say kaddish for my mother. They had a big shul there. There I think is where Kosevitsky davenned, Moishe Kosevitsky, he must have been at shul.

From there we took a boat to Danzig and then to London. I wasn't a bit afraid because I knew in my mind that they won't send little children back home to nowhere.

We toured London nicely. We saw the palace. We saw everything. It was very nice and each of us got two pennies a present and I had the pennies until I came to South Africa.

SOUTH AFRICA

So we came to South Africa from London. In Cape Town, all the children got off the boat and they called out their names and our names weren't there. So I was not a bit afraid because I knew in my mind that they won't send little children back to Russia, Poland these places. It must be the Jewish Zionist Federation or these people got hold of General Smuts, he was the Prime Minister at that time. He got hold of Jan Hofmeyr, he was the Minister of Interior that time. They would not let us off the boat. We had to be on the boat all the time. After about an hour we left, they took us off the boat and that's how I came to South Africa.

Then I was in the orphanage. They put us in an orphanage and half went to Johannesburg Orphanage. I remained in Cape Town Orphanage. Then Mr Ochberg came to me and he said Chonkele, he said I like you very much and I'd like to see a future for you. He said there's a lady in Durban and she's an old lady and she wants to take charge of an orphan. Would you like to go? She's a rich woman and I'd like to see you have a future for you and there may be a future for you there. So I thought to myself, what have I got in the orphanage. I have no future in the orphanage and the children as soon as they pass barmitzvah, they send them out anyway in the country amongst Dutch and Christians, so I went there.

The old lady was very kind. She had four very good properties and she had already adopted two children and then when I came to the old lady, the older one was already in his thirties and the other boy was already about 24. Her husband died some 16 years before and it was an intestate estate *and when she died everything was left to the son.*

Well, I was left in the street, I had nothing, I starved. It came Pesach and nobody invited me because they knew that that man who married the Rabbi's daughter, he would invite me naturally. Anyway they didn't invite me so I went to my room. It was the first and second Sederim and I had a glass of water, a good cry and I went to sleep. And I will never forget.

I had no holiday for 18 years. When I came to Cape Town I couldn't recognise my brothers. I had no other holidays. I was in the house for all those years.

Chapter 36 – SALOMON NEUSTEIN (SOLLY JOSSEL)

MEMORIES OF SOLLY JOSSEL (SALOMON NEUSTEIN)
These memories are extracted and adapted from the original transcript of an interview with Solly Jossel. Events have been arranged into a chronological order and headings included to help the narrative flow.

MY EARLY MEMORIES

My name was Salomon Neustein which was afterwards changed when I was adopted in South Africa to Shleime Josselowitz and then shortened to Solly Jossel. I was born in Drohobitch in Poland on 27 July in 1914. My family moved to Lemberg where eventually I was brought up.

Lemberg was a very big city and we knew nothing of pogroms in Lemberg. Lemberg was a city of Jewish study. Famous Rabbis of the world came to Lemberg. The only thing is that when the war started, the Poles were all busy with the war instead of attacking Jews. From Drohobitch we moved to Lemberg. Lemberg was in Poland.

My father was conscripted into the Polish army and he used to come home for weekends. One weekend he came home when my mother was six months pregnant with me. He was sitting at home and they heard some voices from outside about a woman being attacked so my mother said to my father "Will you go outside and see what's happening?" and he went outside and the Cossacks were attacking an elderly woman and he interfered and the Cossacks shot him and my mother went outside to see what was happening and he died in her arms. She was then six months pregnant.

After that of course I was born and she couldn't support me so she put me into an orphanage at the age of two as the orphanage would not accept children under the age of two. She used to come at weekends to take me out but she had to work so I used to play around in the market on a Saturday or on a Sunday. As a treat she used to buy me an apple. One Sunday I saw a very big apple for the price of a small apple so of course I bought the big apple, but it was a cooking apple and I couldn't eat it and unfortunately she had to buy me another one. I remember in the orphanage food was very short and my brother used to come in the school holidays or in the school terms and take me for a meal at the school where he was studying so that I should be able to get a decent meal.

It was during the war 1914 to 1918 and I remember the soldiers use to parade in the streets and we couldn't get through the streets because they were parading so we used to wait for them to stand at ease and we would go under their feet to get to school to get a meal. My brother use to come and see me. I had a family of two brothers and a sister and unfortunately my mother was very depressed and very poor so we stayed in one room, five of us were on a double bed, head to foot and that room was the bedroom, the bathroom, the kitchen and the toilet and unfortunately the only way we used to bath was in a tin bath. We put hot water in it and the family had a bath.

Salomon Neustein

I remember we lived in one room and unfortunately my mother had to bring up four children and my brother, I remember that my brother, whose name was Feivel. Feivel died of typhoid fever when he was about 17. I remember his funeral. I remember I was about six. When we lived in Poland, our main food was salt herrings and boiled potatoes and sour cream. That seemed to have all the vitamins, very nourishing. My mother of course couldn't support us and as I say at the age of two I landed up in the orphanage until the age of six.

In the orphanage there was nothing to eat. Food was very short and we used to sleep on the floor on the carpets. I used to lie on the lawn all day long, all by myself. I was always a loner. I never liked to play with other children. And that's how they found me in South Africa as well. I was always a loner.

THE MAN FROM AFRICA

A man arrived from Africa who said that he was going to take children to Africa on the condition that he wasn't going to split the family so the children who he was going to adopt or bring to South Africa had to be orphans, pure straightforward orphans. They weren't allowed to have mothers or fathers because he did not want to split the families.

I was just fortunate because the matron of the orphanage was very kind to me and she realised that I was a loner and my mother and my brother used to tell me that I would lie on the lawn all by myself looking at photographs and books and I think she had pity on me and she did not tell Mr Ochberg, the gentleman who arrived from Africa that I had a mother. There were 400 orphans in my orphanage and Mr Ochberg was only able to choose eight children per orphanage and I was just fortunate that I was one of the eight.

My mother of course agreed to me being taken away, because she had no future for any of us here and she felt that if one of her children had an opportunity to have a better life he should be taken away. At that time my mother was the only woman who saw us off at the station because she was the only mother the children had. All the others were orphans. At the station I was very excited because I was going for a holiday. I did not realise that I'd never see her again [he cries and is silent for a long time] and she was of course very upset at leaving me and she had no clothing for me so she took my brother, my eldest brother's [he cries again and is silent], she took my brother, my eldest brother's shorts and altered it for me so that I could have a pair of shorts and a shirt. That's how we went. All the other children had no clothing. That was the only clothing we had and that was how we were going to Africa. Of course we did not realise we were going to Africa. My mother gave me a note, a bank note and she gave me an envelope with a mailing address and her photograph. Of course she kissed me. [he cries again and is silent for a while]. Anyhow she kissed me goodbye and I was very excited while she was so sad. I did not know that I would never see her again. Of course she went home and I went on with my travels with the other children and the first station we came to I used that bank note to buy boiled eggs for as many children as I could and that was the rest of my food.

Anyhow we travelled through Europe and every now and then we stopped at the station. It was after the 1914-18 war and there were no passenger trains so they put us into a cattle truck. In the cattle trucks we had to stand up because there wasn't enough room for all the children to sit in so there were two cattle trucks, about 100 in each cattle truck and we had to stand all the way. We used to stop at a station for the engines to put in water and to fill up with coal. At the station we had an opportunity of having a drink of water because there was no food and he used to give us a plate of soup at night. Some children of about 15 years of age scared us and said they were feeding us at night because they were giving us worms and snakes to eat and of course we were scared as we were kids. I was then six, and we were scared to eat the food because they frightened us.

At one station I remember a man came to the station and said to me, I don't know why he picked on me, but he said to me let me take you to my room and I'll give you a meal. I was scared to go because I said the train will go away without me so he said "don't worry, come with me and I'll see that you're back in time". So I went with him in his room and he gave me a meal, something to eat because we were all starving. Right through Europe there was no food so whatever they could give us, whatever they could give, they fed us. Now the children were from the age of six months to 15 years. There was a little girl of about three who had a sister of six months and they asked her, tell me what is your sister's name? She said I don't know, so they called her Tsippora because she was little as a bird and

that was the name she remained with. Tsippora was found with her sister under a tree and the name Tsippora means a little bird in Hebrew.

I don't remember that I was in Warsaw. It was just a passing phase. I don't think we were there very long. I don't remember anything. I was too frightened. We were busy travelling. I was too frightened to remember any names. I was too small. I was only six years of age.

Also at certain places we had to board boats. These boats couldn't go into harbour, so they used to put us in big boxes and tow the boxes to the boats. Some of these older children said "oh they were putting us in the boxes because as soon as they were out in the sea, they'll drown us". And of course all of the 200 children cried as we were all scared thinking whatever they're telling us is true.

Anyhow, that was some of the experiences that I remember and then we arrived in London. London was the first place where we had a decent meal. As a matter of fact the photographers in London showed the children grabbing for bread because that was the first meal we really had. In London we were supposed to have boarded a ship, I think it was the Edinburgh Castle to go to South Africa.

First of all General Smuts wouldn't allow 180, and said 150 children and Ochberg begged him. So after persuasion he said, all right. I'll allow you 200 children. If one of them is ill, mentally or physically, I'm gonna send all the 200 back. So of course we were thoroughly examined to see if we were all fit. And this one boy in London got some eye disease and he waited for him to get better and he wasn't getting better quickly, so we decided to go, to leave him in London and the other, the balance of the 200 children would go to South Africa.

During our stay in London Mr Ochberg got ill and he landed up in hospital and the children were very scared that he may die. So the elder children were sleeping in the passages, they wouldn't leave the hospital. They were scared of what would happen to all of us if they lost him. Anyhow, fortunately he got better.

But I'll tell you before he left South Africa, Mr Ochberg appealed to the people, to the Jews of South Africa for funds. He was very well off. He was also kind to us orphans. When he arrived from Europe to South Africa, he was on his own. He was very fortunate. He got into the right crowd. He was very well off. But of course he couldn't afford to bring 200 children to South Africa so he appealed to people in South Africa for funds which they donated very generously and that's what helped him. Now he was exact with what he spent. Exactly every penny that he spent on this trip he paid out of his pocket but whatever he spent on the children he of course was reimbursed when he came to South Africa.

On the trip from London to South Africa, to Cape Town actually I was very friendly with a little girl called Regina. She was the same age as me but we were very friendly together and we spent the trip from London to Cape Town together.

SOUTH AFRICA

We arrived in Cape Town and the Cape Town orphanage couldn't afford to keep 200 children and they made plans with the Jewish Orphanage in Johannesburg to take 100 children. Now we didn't know how they were going to separate us so they asked of each, "Where would you like to go? Would you like to go to Cape Town or would you want to go to Johannesburg?" Of course, being babies, we didn't know, so some of us chose Johannesburg and the eldest children said "oh… you made a terrible mistake because it's so hot there and there are lions in the street." So I went back and I said look I want to change my mind. And they said no, you can't change your mind. Once you said Johannesburg, you've got to go to Johannesburg.

So we travelled to Johannesburg and when we came to Johannesburg they had no facilities for us, because there was only a small Jewish orphanage there so there was an old age home in Doornfontein, one of the suburbs of Johannesburg. They put us into that old age home and the old people slept in beds and the youngsters slept on the floor. They gave us mattresses and we slept on the floor. The first time there, the Jewish people of Johannesburg heard that the orphans had arrived and of course they all came to see us.

Through them there was a Mr and Mrs Josselowitz who also came to see us and I don't know what it was, but she sort of appealed to me. She sort of reminded me of my mother and I went up to her and said "mamma will you take me?" She couldn't understand me, I could only speak Polish and she Jewish and English. I don't know how we communicated with each other, but she said to me, it was 6 'o clock, "go and have your dinner, and when you have your dinner I'll take you home." She had no intention of adopting anybody, but I wouldn't let her go and so she said all right. I was scared to go into the dining room because I felt that she may go home. I wouldn't go anywhere so she said all right. I'll sit in the dining room with you. So she came into the dining room and I finished my supper and she took me home. They were very poor people. They had that little store in Doornfontein and a daughter of 27 who was qualified teacher. And of course they were elderly people, having a daughter of 27 and they had no facilities for me so I had to sleep in their bed until they managed to scrape enough money to buy a bed for me.

Anyhow when I slept in the bed I was very scared. I used to have terrible dreams. Darkness used to approach me and I was scared and I used to shout in my sleep. "Pappa", (in Jewish), I don't know how I learnt the Jewish, but I said "Pappa, I'm undressed, I'm uncovered". So my pappa said come into my bed. That became a habit because I was scared to sleep by myself. I don't know how, I had dark visions, the darkness flowing towards me used to wake me up.

The Josselowitz family used to spoil me very badly. If they did not give me my way, I used to get under the table and kick my legs from temper until they gave in. And then to hurt them I used to say "you're not nice to me, I'm going back to the orphanage" and of course that hurt them very much. I was a

naughty boy, but they were wonderful to me. And I tried to reciprocate as much as I could later on in years.

You see the thing is that when I was living in Poland I wasn't living with my mother. From the age of two I was living in the orphanage. I did not realise what a mother was. The only thing I knew was that she used to see me on Sunday, to take me out just to give me a change and she had no time for me either, because she had to bake bread and sell it on the market and when she took me out all the time I spent with her was in the market so I had sort of no mother. You see I had no feeling. The only mother I really had was a mother in South Africa.

Anyhow, as I was growing older I would sit in the backyard with the African servants who taught me English and then they sent me to a kindergarten school in Doornfontein and I sort of gradually learnt English and one day we were having a concert and I was in the concert. They found they had to sing and I had no voice for singing so they threw me out of the concert. I came crying home to my people. So my father went to the school and said to them [long silence – he's crying]. He said, in those days he used to call me Shlomo, that's Hebrew for Solomon and he said "Shlomo is an orphan. [crying] Try to be kind to him. Help him. Put him into the concert." [crying] I came crying home every night. So they said to me "All right, you're in the concert, but don't sing." [little giggle]. So they put me into the back row of the concert and then afterwards I was studying. They sent me to a Hebrew school to learn Hebrew and then I went to Jewish Government School in Doornfontein where I stayed until standard five. The teacher also knew I was an orphan. They were very nice to me I must say.

At the Jewish school there was a teacher by the name of Mr Lewis and he would send me out of school on Fridays to buy bargains for him. He used to lend me his bicycle and I would go from Doornfontein to town. There was a place in Harrison Street called New York Grocers and I used to go there and buy him Friday loaves and he pushed me through school. I was very fortunate. I think I flunked the standard five exams but he pushed me through so I could go to high school. My parents couldn't afford to send me to high school. So there was a commercial school, called Commercial High School which was a government school and I went there up to standard eight when they turned round to me and said "Look we can't afford to carry on with you anymore. You must go try and get a job." But just before then I was still a youngster.

It was during the war years. I hadn't heard from my family and after that I got news in 1935 from my mother. She got somebody who wrote in English to me. The last letter was in 1935 where she wrote to me and said "one day I hope that I will still meet you."

These people Josselowitz were very nice people, absolutely marvelous people, they were marvelous to me and when I started they said they couldn't afford to let me go to school. So they said that I must find myself a job.

I looked through the newspapers and I found a job as a dispatch clerk with a firm called F Malk Ltd in central

Johannesburg. I met with Mr Malk who was a very difficult taskmaster and I still wore glasses and he said to me why are you wearing glasses. He was scared he was going to employ somebody who was not going to give him his value. So I explained to him I had a stigmatism in one eye and that's the reason why I'm wearing glasses. Anyhow he employed me at five pounds a month which was then a very good salary and I decided that I've got to improve my position so I used to go at 5 'o clock, after work to night school. I took a Bachelor of Commerce degree and I took my Chartered Institute of Secretaries where I became a fellow of Chartered Institute of Secretaries.

The school teacher at that time was a Mr Coleman and it was business college, called The Johannesburg Business College in Jeppe Street and the children who attended the classes were so tired from working all day that we used to fall asleep at school and he was so sorry for us that he let us sleep. How we passed our exams, I don't know. He himself was a very poor bloke who was studying for law. Eventually he became a judge. He was Justice Coleman and when I went to school, Commercial High School, we also had a fellow by the name of J R Sutherland who was a master of economics. He wrote a book of economics and he would take us for economics at the night school. During the day Mr Malk as I say was a very difficult taskmaster and he made me deliver parcels on a bicycle.

At that time my sister, my adopted sister, Ethel, she married a man by the name of Solly Joffe who was a structural engineer and I would go on this bicycle, parcels on the front, parcels on the back, and deliver parcels. And one day he was driving behind me. He was scared I was going to have an accident and he followed me. I did not know that he followed me. I had to go to Jeppe, from Johannesburg to Jeppe which was about four or five miles on the bicycle.

At night we had to pass by Mr Malk and in case we stole something he made us empty out our pockets to see if the whites and the blacks weren't stealing anything. Anyhow I had this job as a dispatch clerk. I had to pack up parcels with two Africans and we were in the basement and the only way that I could study was while the Africans were packing goods. I used to sit there and study my books. I could see him coming down the steps because he used to watch to see if I was working so as soon as I saw a pair of legs, I used to take my books and hide it amongst the stock so he wouldn't see that I was studying.

So I got through the examination and I wanted to be a chartered accountant but in those days a chartered accountant had to do articles and had to work for six years as an articled clerk and you had to pay to become articled and of course my family couldn't afford it. I decided to take B.Comm as a chartered secretary which was the closest to a chartered accountant. My South African mother used to write regularly to my mother in Poland to tell her how I was getting on and they were such wonderful people in spite of the fact that they needed money.

My South African Mother sent my Mother in Poland the first five pounds that I earned at Malk in spite of the fact that they themselves were so badly in need of the money.

When I was 22 I was offered a better job because of my qualifications. It was a better job in Springs in a concession store as a bookkeeper so I said to my parents that I've been offered a better job. I was getting 15 pounds a month in those days, and this job was offered to me for 20 pounds a month which I thought was a fantastic job and I told my parents I was offered this job in Springs so my brother-in-law said if you're running from job to job, people will think that you're not a capable man. Stay with Malk for five years. It doesn't matter what you've been offered. Stay with him for five years and then you've got a reference that you've been there for five years. Every month that I worked for Malk, I was scared that I would get the sack because he was so difficult to work for. Every month he threatened us that "if you don't work I'll throw you out." He use to say, "Why are the shelves dirty?" so I said I didn't put any stock in. "So how can you sell from empty shelves? Put stock in." So when we put stock in, he asked "who told you to put stock in. I did not tell you to put stock in." He was very difficult. Anyhow, then one day a traveller came along, one of Mr Malk's travellers who didn't bring him any orders and he said to him "you know you're so hopeless that I can send little Jossel who's working in the basement, I'll send him traveling. He'll be better then you."

So he gave me a car and a driver to go travelling. In those days Vredendal was an Indian area so I went to Vrededorp and I said to these people if you don't give me any orders, I'll get the sack. So they all felt sorry for me and they gave me orders and then I went to Jeppe. I got a very big order for canvass shoes which in those days came from Japan and then I got a very big order for special price which was very much below the price Malk allowed me to sell and I came to Malk and I said well look I've got a very big order but this is the price so he called the traveller in and he said "you see how well Jossel did. Look at all the shoes he sold" so he sent out that order for shoes.

Then after five years I decided I would go for this job that had been offered for me in Springs that was still waiting. So I went. I was scared to go to Malk. I was scared to talk to him because he was so difficult. Now how am I going to go to him to give him notice? Eventually I decided I had to give him notice. I went to Malk and said Mr Malk I've been offered a better job in Springs and I'm sorry I've got to leave you. He said "why didn't you tell me? I would have increased your salary. I would've made you a traveller. Think of the opportunities you've lost. Why must you leave me? Don't leave me." I said I'm sorry but I have committed myself. Anyhow I left Malk and I got this job in Springs as a bookkeeper in the concessions store with these people who were cousins, in a firm called Blumberg & Lipman. I worked for them as a bookkeeper and I used to cash up and then the business grew and they had five concession stores. After getting all these concession stores I said to them, "look you've got such an outlet of goods why don't you open your own wholesale business?" So they said to me, "so who's going to open this for us?" So I said, "let me open a wholesale business and let me supply the stores with goods." So they said "all right." That was from the age 23.

When I was 27 I contracted an ulcer, a stomach of bleeding ulcers and I had to give up my position. I went to a doctor before I married Sylvia to inform her of my ulcerated stomach condition and to make sure that she still wanted to marry me. The doctor assured us that I had as much chance of living a long life as everyone else and that there was more danger when I left his rooms of getting knocked over by a car in the road.

When I was about 16, the Rabbi of the Reform Congregation of Johannesburg, Rabbi Weiler went to Poland and met my mother in Lemberg. She must have heard that there was a Rabbi from Johannesburg visiting Lemberg and she went to see him and when he came back here he got hold of me through the telephone book. He looked up all the Josselowitzs. My mother knew that my name was Josselowitz. He looked up all the Josselowitzs and he phoned me and he said come to see him at lunchtime and he was a Reform Rabbi so he did not keep the Jewish dietary laws and he was eating there and he gave me something to eat so he told me that he met my mother and that she sends of course all her love to me. I thought that was a very nice gesture of his. The thing is that the last letter I got from her was 1935 when she said she hoped still to see me.

During the time that I was living in Johannesburg I know my sister got married and my mother sent me a photograph of her husband and herself on the day of their marriage and I knew afterwards that she had two children, a son and a daughter and I didn't know what happened to my mother because after that letter in 1935 I haven't heard from her again because of the Germans marching into Poland. You see when the Germans marched into Poland, my brother, who happened to be in the Polish army was sent across to Russia the Polish Army went across to Russia and that saved his life. When he came back to Lemberg he couldn't find my mother and he used to go to the cemetery to look for Jewish people and there he found an elderly woman who befriended him and he became a gas fitter and a plumber and he was working for the Communist Government and he found me, I didn't find him. He wrote a letter to the South African Police in Johannesburg, Doornfontein and landed up in the Doornfontein Police Station and it was addressed to me. My brother in Poland knew he had a younger brother called Josselowitz but he didn't know where. He had no address because my mother was not available. She was killed. And the Police went across the road to a store, a dairy run by somebody called Hock and asked "do you know a family Josselowitz who has a connection with a family in Poland." So this woman rang up all the Josselowitzs and they all came to claim the letter. After Hitler everyone was looking for some relation and the police interviewed these Josselowitzs and they said no this letter does not refer to you. My mother and father were then living in Braamfontein. They had a shop in Braamfontein and this Hock family approached them and they said to me "go down to Doornfontein Police Station and see if the letter is for you." I must have been still very young because I went down with a bicycle hoop with a stick. I ran all the way from Braamfontein to Doornfontein Police Station and

the police asked me certain questions which pertained to the letter and they said this letter is for you. And the letter had the name and address of my brother so we wrote him a letter to tell him that he found me. And then afterwards when we got married, my wife Sylvia corresponded with him and used to send him goods. Money wasn't any good to him because the value of money was not as good as black market stuff. So we used to send him silk stockings and penicillin and other medicines which he could then sell on the black market and that's what kept him going. We then decided to try and bring him out here. The South African government wouldn't give him a visa to bring him out here. So when we went to Rhodesia, I asked the Rhodesian Government and the Rhodesian Government said to me as long as you get him out of behind the iron curtain, we will give you permission to bring him here. So I wrote to him and I said to him "get out of behind the iron curtain and we'll try and get you." So then he got out of the iron curtain. He went to Italy. When he was in Italy, the Israeli Government helped him to come to Israel. When he got to Israel, Sylvia and myself went to meet him and from there we brought him to South Africa but the Israeli Government said, "look we're not a transit depot, we don't bring people here to take them out. If we bring people here we want them to remain in Israel, not to be a transit depot." So I said well I'll pay you whatever it cost you. And they said, "all right, if you cover our expenses, we'll let him go." And then we took him out to Rhodesia and the Rhodesian Government allowed him to stay.

I was brought out to South Africa by a charitable institution and I always felt I should pay back all that was done for me. So the first thing I did when I turned 17 was I became the secretary of the Hebrew Congregation in Braamfontein. From there when people moved out of Braamfontein, it became a poor area and the Jewish people from Braamfontein moved to Parktown and Rosebank or to other areas. In those days, Yeoville was popular, Berea was popular, Braamfontein was a non-entity. And so the synagogue had no funds to support the Rabbi. So I used to arrange concerts in this place called The Orpheum and another place which doesn't exist today. So we had concerts and with that money I supported the synagogue. I always felt I'd like to repay what was done to me that other people should get benefit and that's how I got involved with all these very charitable institutions.

There was 500 000 orphans in Europe and that's why I always felt that I won a lottery because I was one of the 500 000 orphans that was brought out to South Africa. There were only eight of 400 selected from the orphanage and I was one of those eight. It shows you that this was my destiny and I feel that the Lord above brought me to South Africa to do good work and that's what I did. I spent all of my life doing charitable work, religious work, political work, communal work. I did it all in 35 years. Fortunately I had a wonderful wife who helped me. She used to work. I used to work up to 4 o' clock every day. From 4 o' clock up to 7 o' clock I did charitable work and Sylvia used to look after the business. We are now married 58 years and for 58 years we worked together.

I married my wife Sylvia in 1944 and together we had three children. The only holiday Sylvia ever had was about three months after each child was born. We worked together all our married lives and we still work together TG. She was a wonderful companion, a wonderful friend and a wonderful woman. She used to help me with all my charitable work and would take over our business completely from 4 pm till 7 pm whilst I spent that time doing all the charitable work, and still managed to do her own work at the same time besides doing mine.

I was the president of the Bulawayo Hebrew Congregation for eight years. I was the chairman of the Jewish Board of Deputies for two years. I was the chairman of the Zionist Organisation. I was life chairman of the SPCA. I was on the Jail Society and I visited jail twice a month to help people in jail and I used to communicate with their wives and husbands sometimes to help them to get on their feet. So I was connected with everything.

As a matter of fact my daughter was one day at school asked "what does your father do" and she said "you name it, my father's on it." I was in every single institution and as a matter of fact I was named in the The Jewry of South Africa. I've got an article of all the good work that I did. I started a movement in Rhodesia. I became the first President of Springs and I was the President of Johannesburg. I was also a free mason. Wherever I could be associated, I was associated and as a matter of fact I've even got a photographs of Professor Chris Barnard and myself when he came to Rhodesia. We invited him to do some charitable work and he came along with his first wife. And I've got a photograph of Ian Smith who I also worked with. I also worked with Nelson Mandela and Sylvia has always stood beside me.

JOSSEL, Solly. B.Com. F.C.I.S. F.S.A. F.I.S. F.F.C.S. F.F.C.B. A.E.I. Company Director. Born Poland, 27th August, 1914. Came to South Africa, 1920. Educated Jewish Government School, Commercial High School, Johannesburg. Correspondence College. Director of 17 Companies. Member of Bulawayo Hebrew Congregation, President for 10 years, 1964-1974. Central African Zionist Organisation (Southern Division), Chairman 1970-74. Executive Member Savyon Lodge (Old Aged Home) 1970-1974. Foundation President Hebrew Order of David of South Africa 1974. Lodge Askelon No. 39. Executive Member Central African Jewish Board of Deputies 1960-74. Vice-President Central African Zionist Organisation 1970-74. Trustee Bulawayo Chevra Kadisha. President H.O.D. Sir Herbert Samuel Lodge, Springs 1939-43. Councillor City of Bulawayo 1962-70. Treasurer Rhodesia Prisoners Aid Society 1958-1974. Vice-Chairman S.P.C.A. 1972-1974 and Treasurer. Married Sylvia Bonner, 13th August, 1944. Two sons, one daughter. Foundation Member Balfour Park Club, Johannesburg, member Parkview Sports Club, Bulawayo. Served in S.A. Forces in World War II from 1939-42. Recreations: Charitable, Religious and Communal Work. Add: 43 Pauling Road, Suburbs, Bulawayo. P.O. Box 1633, Bulawayo.

Extract from South African Jewry 1976-7

"Solly's 96th birthday - Left to Right - Adam and Jodi Fittinghoff (our granddaughter and husband), middle is Solly and Sylvia and then Kerryn and Adam Thal (our grandson and his wife). Back Row - Bernice (our daughter) and Barry (our son-in-law) (Jodi"s Parents) in the middle of them Tayne (our great-grandson) - Jodi's son." from Sylvia Jossel

MEMORIES OF MOLLY COHEN (MALKA SCHAPIRA)

These memories are extracted and adapted from the original transcript of an interview of Molly Cohen. Events have been arranged into a chronological order and headings included to help the flow of the narrative.

MY EARLY MEMORIES

Well, I'm Molly Cohen and I was born Shapiro but I heard that it wasn't exactly Shapiro. My name had a different spelling: Schapira, and so I don't know which is the correct one. I was born in 1913 in a little town near Poland, Sarny.

I don't remember my parents because I have no memory of them except a little incident here and there like when I used to come into the room and my father, I think it was my father, put me on his knee and played with me and gave me a swing up and down. That was my treat for the day. That I remember, but I don't remember exactly whether I had a mother and a father because I never experienced it through my life.

And what I did see wasn't very much to talk about. It was very sad at the time and I imagine that was the time that I had lost both my parents on the one day.

It was a very sad thing because I was a little child and I was put on to sort of a kist of linen with those brass hinges they had. It mesmerized me a bit, you know. Looking at those brass hinges and so I looked up and I saw a house or a room full of people crying, sobbing and I was wondering what was the matter when I noticed they had candles on the side of, must have been, my parents. They were both lying on the ground. I remember that the candles were on either side and I watched everybody crying so I started to cry and that's when they took me out of the room and that's all I remember of my parents. I hate to talk about it but that's why, people must know what happened in a small child's life.

I don't remember if my family were religious. But of course in that room that I was telling you about, it also had people with a tallis, but not the small one, the large tallesim that covered their heads when they were standing and praying and crying over the bodies. That's the only religious, sort of, item I can think about now. I wouldn't have been able to tell you then and there you know, what it was all about. But that's what happened you see. So I don't know whether my parents were perhaps part of the shul life or whatever. But that's the religious part I remember now that I know what it's about. I have seen it since in shuls here, you know, they have a certain time when they do have this kind of thing, with it all over the heads and they stand to the one side and pray. But that's what happened in that room now that I think, you know, there were candles and the sadness and when I looked up everybody was weeping and sobbing and praying at the same time.

Well, I don't remember pogroms, but I did hear about it you know. It was only those people that are hard and bad and they

Malka Schapira

attack a group or people that haven't got any defense. Those are the ones they just go for. And not understanding anything about the Jewish religion they make up stories like Jews killing Jesus or anything else, I don't know what else makes people kill and do the bad things they do. But that's why I say they start on the weak because they themselves are cowards. That's where they go and it's the same today, the same today. It didn't change.

I try to throw the death of my parents out of my mind altogether. It's very indelibly printed on my mind, you know. Thank G-d it's never spoilt my image of myself. I have kept myself as steady as I could. But I tell you, saying now at this age and in middle years that to lose your parents is a terrible punishment to anybody. I'm flushing, I feel all tense, you know, when I think of what can happen to innocent people that were out in the fields. To lose your mother and father is a terrible thing to happen. Thank goodness this community, this Jewish community was so loving and caring that they went to pick up the children and care for them. Most of us forgot the horrors and led a normal life as a young person and parties and this and that you know.

I lost so much that parents can give you. Their guidance and the love and care. It's all very nice you know, you have friends, but when you have the rock of your family and your parents behind you your life is far different. That's what I lost.

I was told that I had another two sisters who died from, typhus, they used to call it. There was no food. You know people scrounged around for a bit to eat. Thank God that they looked after me. I was too little to care for myself. I was told that I had the two sisters besides myself and another three brothers. Now, I found two brothers about ten years ago, perhaps a little longer, in Israel. The two brothers, one came from Poland and the other one I remember Mr Ochberg gave him money to get out of the city or whatever it is, to go away from all the trouble and he also happened to get through somehow to Israel, so that's where I met them. But I didn't meet the one brother because I didn't know that he was there while I was visiting. It's only after I went that I found that I had him, but he was already too old to visit. I wasn't so young myself and so I haven't really met him but I wrote to him and he corresponded, but I never saw him.

I've got two nephews and a niece there in Israel and that's from the one brother. The other one who I haven't met I think he's also had a daughter, married and so and so I mean, you know, from them I gleaned a little bit about my brothers, my sisters, you know, because I didn't know myself. I'm not speaking of knowing of them you know. So it's difficult, it's very difficult, you know, in a war situation and just to survive is a nightmare. But I'm surprised that no-one ever, sort of, could tell you a little more.

And the youngest brother, I heard but I haven't seen it, was picked up from the road, from the street and taken away. They used to do that. They used to put a gun into these young people's hands and use them as gun fodder. They just wanted to try out a place that was, you know, a lot of people or a lot of soldiers or whatever it is. They used to take these youngsters and give them a gun. They didn't even know how to use a gun and just put them into the front line. I never saw my family during that time. I'm talking now about a time much later. So this is what I heard.

My older brother did not come to South Africa because there was a certain age limit, you see. They were taking the younger children who couldn't care for themselves and he was already an older chap. You know, he was able to and was lucky to get something. But it was because of that.

The other bigger children that came along used to help with the little ones. So this was why my older brother got this money from Mr Ochberg and he saved himself and he went out of this town altogether.

After my parents died I suppose either my father's or my mother's family were just looking after me to keep me alive because there was no food, there was no shelter, there was nothing. You know how these things are. When you're small you accept everything. You just live through the day, you know. Sometimes it happens you can't do that for yourself. I don't remember but I must have been taken great care of because I was very young and they didn't want to lose us you know, they wanted to save us. But what can I say, what else can I tell you. I don't even know who was looking after me; their names or anything.

I wasn't in an orphanage initially, because I remember sometimes there were chickens there and the geese that I told you about and so it must have been a private place, a little out in the country farm somewhere. I didn't know anything about the war. I was born into a war so I don't know. I know a very tiny bit about the way I was or how I happened to survive. I can't tell you very much because I was too young to understand what exactly was happening.

People were frightened. Everybody was waiting to have this war to be over. I suppose there was nothing really to say except sitting around and waiting for the thing to go over. It's difficult for children because they don't know what's going on.

I was just kept alive and most probably we were hiding somewhere or running somewhere or doing so that you survived. The other children also felt like that, you know. There were other children from different parts of the world. My late husband came from Latvia. Now that's funny. I'm from one part, he's from another and we meet here. You know broken up homes, they break it up, just for the pleasure of it. And that's it, mainly on the Jewish community because we were always a minority wherever we were.

I remember there was a horse because it looked enormous to me when I looked up. This big beautiful animal I remember. But the ngaika and the tall hat I didn't really understand that until I was older. I heard people talk about these things. This is what I mean so that's why I said to you in the beginning I don't know what more to tell you other than what I have already told you, you see. But that's what war does. It never does any good to anybody. It's destructive, that's all it is. It destroys.

COMING TO SOUTH AFRICA

All I remember about coming to South Africa is a crowd of children that I was put in, and feeling a bit awkward, shy and afraid. It was all so frightening.

We stopped in England. I didn't know it was England but I mean we stopped there and they took us into a war orphans' home. People that got us through to come into the country, looked after us and we stayed there. I don't know what they exactly need to know before they let you live there, but of course I was out of that. I didn't know. We stayed there and then they took us onto the boat again.

Well, I used to play on board the ship with all the other children. But I don't remember anything special except that sometimes it wasn't so good because the boat was swinging, you know, and I didn't know why, but I wasn't feeling so nice. But, you know what a child is. They accept whatever is there and ask no questions. The nicest part of the travelling, you know, was being with the rest of the children.

I remember quarantine now that I understand what it was all about. One of the little ones, younger even that myself even, had something, measles or something that they didn't want to let it in, in case we made the rest of the people sick too, it was catchy. I remember having to stay over there on the boat not being allowed off. But that just made it a longer journey.

We were 200 of us on the boat and half of us remained in Cape Town and the other half went to Johannesburg. But I was lost until the orphanage here, when I made friends with the other youngsters.

I remember *Mr Ochberg* amongst the children and we were all trying to get near him and talk to him. In the end when we came here we eventually renamed him "daddy Ochberg". But otherwise we were just in a crowd.

I was just happy to be with the children and I didn't know where we were going or why we were going or anything like that. But of course later on when I did realise it, like I said before it was a wonderful Jewish Community here. That Ochberg knew to come and rescue us and they must have arranged all this. It was a wonderful thing to do, to send Ochberg from Africa and he went to pick up the children.

I don't know if I would have survived if I did not come to South Africa. It all depends whether the people from my family would have enough to keep me, to put me somewhere else or do something about me or just abandon me. I mean I don't know. I wasn't sure who was in my family and there were lots of Jewish children who were taken in by other homes, just maybe adopted or something like that. It did happen to some that were, roaming around and not having homes and not having anything. I don't know what the fate could be, most probably not too wonderful, but on the other hand it could have worked out. It depends on who took you or took notice of you. But I don't know.

You know when you are shocked enough it doesn't go away but I was very young so it helped because, you don't concentrate on it all, but it is indelibly printed. Never mind what you do, where you are, and this follows you, it just is there you know. Also a wonderful pleasant thing, it can also be indelibly imprinted on your mind but mainly it's something that you abhor.

Well, be honest, the trauma of not having parents didn't do all that for me, because I was much too young to absorb it that way. It was only when I was almost middle aged that I realised the terrible part of it. You know, with me, I thought that everybody's put into places and given food and looked after. I didn't know about why or wherefore about these things and only when you grow up you start thinking why haven't I got a mother and a father? You think, what a difference it makes to my life, what would they say about a kallahment, being ready for marriage you know. You want to talk, you want someone to be there and of course that's how you know you were different. But I say it again, thank goodness for this wonderful community who has given me life and living here and having my own family and from me, from this little girl.

I have two great grandchildren in New Zealand and another one in Cape Town and unfortunately I lost my oldest son about 12 years ago but I have a wonderful son here in Camps Bay and his wife, Nesta. They have been very good to me. We talk to each other about everything and that's where I am today, a great granny and a granny.

Yes and when you see their gain and you think, to multiply me a few times. What has been done so now we really have to say a big thank you to the people who thought about us.

No, no I can't say that alone without Ochberg. There were lots of people behind Ochberg. You know there was the Jewish Community, lots of talk about it and everything and arrangements that there were some marvelous people in the community. But he was a wonderful man because he undertook the journey and he took this journey, but then he wanted to go again and he went again but they didn't allow it anymore. So I mean it's not only Mr Ochberg. He's a wonderful chap because he knew the layout, it was where he was born but it was the Cape Town Jewry, the way that they treated us afterwards and they made us forget about everything, the horrors. To come and pamper us and look after us like we were being something wonderful. And so you see my family, I can't say that I was ever in prison, neither can my offspring so there you are.

I am an old lady now you see and looking back you appreciate a lot of things that you wouldn't have done as a youngster. You know about being a teenager and it gets you thinking and it gets you appreciating that I'm, thank G-d, still well, that I can think for myself and this little place I can run and be my own ballaboste as they say so thank G-d for that. I'm going to be 92 in November.

I'm talking to you a lot about what didn't happen to me, but what I heard during my life. This one said one thing and that one another thing. There were some older children than myself, you know, I was a very young round about eight. I'm sure, because we were all bunched together that they should have remembered something.

Molly Cohen

174

Chapter 38 – FEYGA SHRIER (FANNY LOCKITCH)

MEMORIES OF FANNY LOCKITCH (FEYGA SHRIER)

These memories are extracted and adapted from the original transcript of an interview of Fanny Lockitch. Events have been arranged into a chronological order and headings included to help the flow of the narrative.

MY EARLY MEMORIES

I was born in Brest-litovsk. It's a town that has a fortress and we were really in a suburb called Malarita. Malarita was a little village, part of Brest-litovsk, like any other one so it doesn't matter.

Brachah was my mother's name and she married a Zimmel Schrier, my father who was gassed in the war. At 33 he was gone. At 29 she was gone. She left five children.

I can tell you they were bitter years. I remember my mother was a doctor, she used to doctor people. And she made friends with a lot of Christians because she was doctoring them when they got sick.

What I do remember, we were in a house when my mother was still alive and I remember cherries, cherries were growing. We had five trees of cherries outside our place and we were able to stretch our hands from the window and pick the cherries and that's what we used to do before we went to bed.

We went to school, and we learnt Yiddish at school. We went to Jewish schools. But we had to learn Russian. No question about it. The first language had to be Russian. Everyone of us must talk Russian.

So we put our food in their oven for cholent on Saturday so that we would have a warm cholent and they used to allow us to do that.

My father was gassed, gassed in the army. That's the only time he had left and he went to visit my brother on a cold snowy day. He used to ha-ha-ha-(pant), he used to come from outside in the cold weather, he used to sit in front of the fire ha ha ha (pant) until he caught his breath. We thought he would be gone. Well this time he died on the way and he was buried in the snow. There's a plaque there still if you pass there may be today, *"Here lies Schrier Ziebel Schrier".*

My dad was only 33. They took them to the army so early. Oh I'll never forget when he used to come on a cold day when it was snowing. He would sit in front of that fire panting and trying to get the breath through. All of us used to start crying. We used to walk out of the room and we were finished. We couldn't watch it. Eventually he decided to go to Moscow and visit his brother. His brother was actually a mayor of Moscow. They hated the Jewish but gave them positions, I don't know how. My sister told us he died on the way.

My sister got married in Brest-litovsk. She met a fellow from Israel and then he took her to Israel and she promised to bring

us there. That's why she was so cross that I wanted my younger sister to come with us, and she stopped her. She would have been alive. She stopped her. But she herself went there and promised us she said when we get on she said then I'll bring you out. But she never brought her out in time. She died in the gas chambers during the Second World War. Yes. She would've been alive. She didn't mean it. She meant well. She said to me you've got Jack to look after you. I'll look after Mindele.

I got very big family in America, enormous, very big. They also, came from Russia, they were running to America and my sister, wrote to them and sent them letters and sent them photographs. She was a teacher. How they became teachers or doctors, I don't know because they were not allowed to. They only had to do everything with the doctor there. But they managed. They used to have school underneath the ground. My elder sister got married in Brest-litovsk and to an Israeli boy, a very nice man and together they went over and she lived in England.

My dad was in the army and my mother was going to get a little piece of bread and butter for the children and the bombs were flying all over her. But she couldn't help it. She had to get some food for the children or else we would have starved to death. The First World War, don't forget, was 1914 – 1918. It went on all the time. But the Russian Revolution was terrible. The Russian Revolution started at the same time and they were killing all the Jews. They made special wars. That was the Revolution. For the special wars they called up Jews because they wanted the Jews to be killed out and that was the Russian Revolution, to kill the Jews.

The Cossacks, they were cruel people. The Cossacks aaah, when they came along, they didn't care where they hit you or how they hit you. They had a free way. They could do what they liked. They could hit you, they could smash you, they could do what they liked. Nobody would report them. They were frightened. Everywhere, everywhere.

When the Cossacks appeared, everybody ran, not only the children, the grown ups as well. The Cossacks used to come so often you've got no idea. They roamed the streets. They did what they liked. You were not allowed to walk in the streets after 10.00pm but they were allowed.

And when bombs starting flying we were told we must move and we went into cattle trains to move. You can imagine that I moved with my family, my mother, my little brother to Vooranej, as far as Vooranej, Vooranej is Deep Russia in Brest. It is between Poland and Russia. So you can imagine the distance we went and we lost a little brother of five months. My older brother who came with me to South Africa to look after me, died in 1994. He got sick and he died and at that time he was quite oldish.

But by G-d, my mother went out at night and one day she got so sick, so ill and I, I stood with the little bit of food at her head and her eyes became big. It was not my mother. I cried and cried and cried and normally she used to stop us from crying and this time she says, "Look Fanny, it's all right, you can cry. You can cry one times, two times, you don't keep on crying, it's enough." And she died the next day. She was only 29 when she died.

I remember also she had a cousin, a nephew or a cousin, I can't remember who he was. After 10, you weren't' allowed to be in the street as there was a curfew and he wanted to come and see her because she was so sick and he went late at night and he was banging and banging at the window. The children didn't hear it. We were already starting to sleep. Banging, banging. My mother was so sick, she couldn't get out. And they ran after him. They stuck him with a knife and it made a hole on this bone there. And eventually she crawled out and opened up the door and it was him and she started cleaning up the wound. They wanted to kill him. They would have killed him because he broke the curfew.

They smashed him with a wire rod and he was bleeding. My mother was a doctor and she dressed his wounds. It was bleeding like anything. They don't care. They nearly murdered him. Luckily she was there and she dressed it. With wires, with wires they used to hit you. Raw wires, that's what he said, because it looked like a hole from a wire. Those pogrom areas and those days of the pogrom were terrible.

I come from a family of five children and I married into a family of five children. I had three sisters and two brothers and I married into a family of three sisters and two brothers and what became of them? I am the only one left out of our family. But my husband's family, how many are left I can't remember. But of course we went through the Russian Revolution. You were lucky if you came out alive.

I don't know how we grew up. Ever so often we got the baggage together and moved from one town to another because the moment they were bombing one town we had to get into a train, a cattle train, any train and move. And my mother lost her young baby of five months in the train as we were going on. He died in front of us.

There was no chance for any child to grow up. Where would you grow up with bombs? They wanted to kill all the Jews. Why? I don't know.

The people from the orphanage got to know about us. Our neighbours told them I think. Somebody told them and they came and fetched us. Yes, yes. The one thing about the Jews in Russia they kept their Jewishness. Maybe they wouldn't have been so persecuted if they didn't. You could pick them out as Jews. They wouldn't give up their Yiddishkeit. No. In the schools they had to talk Russian. They had to speak everything in Russian but when they came home, they spoke Yiddish. They wouldn't forget their Yiddish. And I think that's why they suffered.

Afterwards, when my parents were gone, I went to an orphanage, there was an orphanage there in Brest-litovsk. And I can remember very well bombs flying in the air. When the war started, when they used to start fighting and "boom boom" we used to hear and we used to rush under the beds. Month and months and months we slept under the beds because it was safer because the windows were shattered by the bombs that were flying around. For six months at the orphanage of the Brest children we slept under the beds. Yes, little children under beds heard noises. Is that a good thing?

DADDY OCHBERG

I am one of the survivors of 200 orphan children which our daddy Ochberg, brought in 1921. We called him daddy because to most of the children he was the only daddy they knew. He brought us here from the pogrom stricken areas of Europe; Russia, Poland, Lithuania and Latvia. He gathered them from all over. And how he managed to come through alive has been a mystery to me ever since.

When Isaac Ochberg arrived I already didn't have parents and was in an orphanage. And he came to our orphanage in Brest-litovsk and they called a few children. He took a fancy to me and he said would you like to come? And I said yes. I had a brother. Because I was younger than my brother and I wanted my brother to come so that he could look after me. My brother died in 1994 here.

So he took our names down and everything else and my eldest sister, she stayed with our uncle. Funny enough although they were anti-Semitic, this uncle was the mayor of Brest-litovsk. How he comes to be the mayor of the town I don't know.

Then they gathered us together to catch the ship. We had to go by water to London from Danzig. In Danzig we boarded a ship to take us to London. From London we went into the proper boat. After that they destroyed it. It was a battle ship that we came in, the Edinburgh Castle. After we arrived here that Edinburgh Castle was scrapped because it wasn't any good anymore.

My older sister did not come along and she says oh no. I wanted my younger sister to come with us as well. I wished she would have. She would have still been alive instead of dying in the concentration camp in the 2nd World War. She said well Jack is going to look after you and I want to look after Mindele. My older sister was with the uncle and she took my younger sister back and then a couple of years later we heard that she died; not a nice death but a cruel death. In the concentration camp you do not die a nice death. That was our upbringing.

My older sister wouldn't allow me to go and she dragged me back from the station but he came to fetch me and here I am. She took me back. I went back. I did not catch the boat and I came into my bedroom. My nose was bleeding for two weeks. I knew something drew me to South Africa then. I had to go. Something drew me. I was so sick, I didn't want to eat, I didn't want anything and what do you know?

I don't know why I wanted to go. I was crying for two weeks. Something drew me to South Africa. I don't know what it was. I never followed anybody but daddy Ochberg I followed. He wanted me to come and I wanted to go. I'm the only one that he came back for and he brought me and I went.

A miracle happened. Daddy Ochberg has never gone back to any town to fetch anyone. He took a liking to me. He came back to Brest-litovsk. Then he came into my room and he says well, are there any more children that want to come. I said yes, I want to go and he took me. If he didn't come again, I wouldn't have been here. Oh my brother was so pleased that I was with him and I was pleased that he was there to look after me. We were very devoted children to each other. I was in the orphanage already, my mother was gone. I told you how she died.

In the end my older sister said my brother must come. I'm too small and my brother must come to look after me and she will look after Mindele, a sister I had, younger than me which I wanted to come. If she had come with us she would have been alive. But what happened to her? She died in the concentration camp in the 2nd World War. She dragged her back to death.

Daddy Ochberg didn't know the language here. Although the First World War was over, the Russian Revolution was over, the fighting went on and the forests were infested with bandits and he went into the deep forests. He didn't know where he was going and believe me if we did not get together and notice all that and we said to daddy Ochberg, you are not going that way, and we begged the people that were helping him to engage somebody who knew the languages and we engaged a man. His name was Bobrov. He spoke seven different languages, seven languages spoken in Russia. He died in England at the age of 93 years.

He came from here to England afterwards. He used to play the ukelele, I'll never forget it, to us to get us to sleep on the boat because a lot of the children used to get sea sick so that's how he used to get us to sleep.

Ochberg met a nice lady in Warsaw. Panye Engel was her name. She had a big restaurant and every lunch time we, the 200 orphaned children, used to line up and walk with daddy Ochberg to her restaurant. She and daddy Ochberg were very great friends. She helped him such a lot, you got no idea. She wasn't Jewish, but she helped him. I doubt if he would have got out of Poland without her help. Every lunch hour, we had a beautiful lunch in her restaurant. We walked to the restaurant. She was very proud of it. Panye Engel. Before we left Warsaw she gave us each a little booklet with her photograph in it. You know, with love, she remembered us. They were all anti-Semitic, or supposed to be, and she had a heart of gold. She did what she was not supposed to do, but she did it and she showed Ochberg the way and where to go, how to go and who he must see, because she was a very cultured person. She knew the ins and outs of everything.

ARRIVING IN CAPE TOWN

When we arrived at the quayside it was early in the morning and we thought we were in Fairyland with all the lights on Table Mountain and everything else. And as the lights were getting brighter and getting later and later, the people there rushed towards the quayside. They wanted to see what monkeys Ochberg had brought.

Ooooo, there was a lot of opposition for Ochberg to go and fetch them, so he said "Bugger you. I'm going!" With his money, he laid out the money, he got the money to bring us out, and he said to the people, "Bugger you I'm not letting those 200 children die. They are going to come."

And they came. Ooooo, there was a lot of opposition, but once we were here, every Sunday they used to come to the orphanage and we used to serve them coffee. Every Sunday the playground used to be crowded. They used to come and visit the Russian children and we were beautiful. Everyone of them turned out a success. We didn't have any failures.

Oh he had people with him that he knew and they helped him. And when he came to the orphanage he had the matron and the principal and all the men, that were in the know, very intelligent, they helped him. He was doing a work of mercy, of course they helped him.

The thing is this, he had to ask permission from Smuts who was in power at that time. He had to ask permission, whether he could bring out children at all to this country and they decided whoever was, Smuts was in power then, he says I don't object, you can bring as many children as you want, but they mustn't be sick children, they mustn't be children who suffer from some disease. And they must have a clean history like any other child, then you can bring them. They had to be very careful.

And all of a sudden while we were travelling, a lot of the children that came from Pinsk got a head disease called parsh, you know. My G-d, and we were standing in line and we had to hide them behind. We used to be examined before we went off the boat and when we used to go into a train they used to examine us to see if we're alright as they're not taking in some sick children. Once we went into a train, you know, we were escaping from that town. When they came from Pinsk and on the train, the children got a disease on their heads. All of them caught it. It was very contagious and inspectors used to get onto the train to inspect whether the children that he's taking are in good health. We had good health and that they are perfect and my G-d they used to be, they started from the front and how these children used to jump everytime towards the back and they got through. And they were treated here and they were perfect. It was a miracle that those children didn't get more diseases, whatever, you know, as in war you get all sorts of diseases.

Smuts told him he could bring as many as he can. Unfortunately, he didn't have more money than 200 children and if he had more money he would have brought more children. He left a lot behind. He couldn't take 200 from one place. He gathered them from many towns; from Minsk, Pinsk, Smolensk, Warsaw, a lot of towns. And 200 children divide by 10, is only about 20 children from a place. Our orphanage at Brest-litovsk was considered quite big. Don't forget our orphanages were supported by America because the letters from the Jewish people were smuggled out and they got to know of the pogroms so they started sending clothes, and everything to help them. But none of them thought of bringing some children out. I wished they would have, but they helped.

Ochberg had to collect the money himself and to bring out 200 children costs a lot of money and he collected it and gave most of it from his own money.

We traveled by bus and by train. There were lots of buses in Russia and Poland. I can't even remember if Ochberg used a motorcar overseas, I don't think so. He had a motor car here. You know Ochberg used to come and visit the orphanage here. He worked very hard because he had to bring his family out. He came out first and then when there was enough money he brought his family out. But he worked hard. You've got no idea. I know.

When he first arrived in Cape Town Isaac Ochberg had a room with the Policansky's. He used to get up very early in the morning and put on a pot of water with potatoes in and meat and all vegetables and covered it with water and it was on a Bunsen burner and he knew exactly when to switch it off. One of the maids of the Policanskys, who were very rich people, used to switch it off five or six 'o clock. When he came it was all ready. And that was his supper and cheap. Every night he had a stew that he made himself. He was only happy. He didn't know the Policanskys and they took him in. He told them the story. And that I got from Mrs Policansky herself. She gave him a room and that's how he lived. He lived sparingly to collect the money to bring his family out and he did.

He had a lot of sadness in his life. Two of his children were slightly backward. He married a cousin, a beautiful woman. He had to leave them behind and they died in London. And the youngest child was brilliant and his oldest daughter who wrote that book, "This Was A Man", she was very educated. She went to University. She was highly respected and she represented her father in many, many places. Everything in "This was A Man" is absolutely true

I cannot understand how he got through without being killed. How he managed to get through that forest which was infested with bandits. And he got through it. I can't understand it. He took his life in his hands. He took such a chance, you've got no idea.

We felt better, even the children felt better when we engaged Mr Bobrov. I told you he spoke seven languages and we knew that that man would be able to carry him through. I don't think he would be able to get through without that man, Mr Bobrov, who died at the age of 93 in London.

A lot of food they gave us, we've never eaten before, for instance bananas. We never saw a banana in Brest-litovsk. We started eating it with the peel on and then people came along and told us no, no, no, that you must take off the skin and then we liked it and they kept on buying it. They import it. I've never seen a banana on a tree and you know Russia has got a climate for fruit. We used to have cherries on the trees. The fields used to be full of strawberries, blackberries, all the berries in the world, it grows there. But the bananas, who's ever seen a banana? Apples? Nice apples you could get there. Pears. Its all cold countries you see. You got all that. I never saw a tomato till I came here. A tomato, I didn't know what it was.

When we arrived here, we arrived early in the morning. The ship landed very early in the morning about, five or six in the morning and we were looking through the portholes. It was the most magnificent sight. All the lights on Table Mountain in rows. We thought it was Fairyland! And we shouted and we went on deck and they called us away, and they pushed us away and we came back. We couldn't sleep anymore. And early in the morning they brought us off from the boat and at Oranjia.

You should have seen the crowd who came to see us. They thought what monkeys did Ochberg bring? But I can tell you, he brought wonderful children. Each and every one made good and why? They wanted to do it for our daddy Ochberg. He died like that and he remained like that. He deserved it.

He was a man that loved children. When he used to come to visit us I want to tell you it would take him three hours to get up the stairs. One child would pull at his little finger, the other one would pull at the jacket, the other one would pull at his trousers. He just couldn't move. So much did the kids love him. And I can tell you, if he was alive today, daddy Ochberg would have seen we wouldn't have been short of anything.

He was an uneducated man when he came to this country. I don't know what happened. Whatever he touched, turned to gold. But he saw that his orphanage and his children were looked after. They were his children.

They called me Feygele but I became Lockitch in 1935 I got married. Well, they translated Feygele to Fanny. My name was Feygel. And my mother used to call me Feygele. They used to call me Flossy here. I was so fair, my hair was so fair it was always white and so they called me Flossy. I regret not to have to sing and I sang at many, many occasions. There was a teacher who wanted to teach me but there was a teacher who taught me elocution as well. So I grabbed it, I grabbed everything I could get hold of so she'll accept me to eisteddfod and what must I recite, Ulysses. Ulysses is one of the hardest recitations, also there's so much accent there. But I got through and I won a medal. Not a gold medal, but I won a silver one. I butchered the language, but (laughs), they couldn't get over it. Ochberg couldn't get over it you see and he thought I was the cleverest little girl he's ever met. I'll tell you another thing without thinking anything of me, I'm not trying to blow my own trumpet. When his daughter told him she was going to write a book about him, he says one thing you must do is ensure Feygele Schrier must get that book. I don't care if you don't give any of the others, but give one to Feygele Schrier. She sent me one. And she said it was my father's wish that I should give you my book but it was pinched from me, from here. Barry my son, borrowed it, he read it, he gave it back to me. I remember distinctly. But since then I have never found it. It was pinched.

Chapter 39 ~ LISA, MANYA AND ZIZZA ZAIKA

THE THREE ZAIKA SISTERS; LISA, MANYA AND ZIZZA
Written by Cissy (Zizza) Harris

My parents, Esther and Ephraim Zaika lived in Kostopol Ukraine. My father was the equivalent of a fitter and turner, he made the metal rims around cart wheels. My Mom did all the work at home. She was very sick from her first child and her body lacked calcium.

My father died from dysentery at age 44 as there were no hospitals in the area, the nearest being some 13 miles away.

My mother died in 1920 from cancer in the throat at age 39 and we remained living in the house. An American organisation came around looking to take orphans but Lisa, our oldest sister, would not let us go unless they took all of us.

A friend of Lisa, Sonia Goring, (1) persuaded her to take up the offer that the three sisters go with Isaac Ochberg to South Africa.

At that time, our family consisted of three girls; Lisa who was 20, Manya 10 and I was three and two brothers; Asriel who was 15 and was sent to an orphanage in Vienna and Jack our oldest brother.

As Lisa was already 20 years old, she had her own passport and Isaac Ochberg took her as a nurse to look after the children. Manya and I travelled on group passports.

Jack remained behind to sell the house and later went to Palestine. He lived in Tel Aviv and worked building the roads. He wrote to Lisa in South Africa begging her to bring him out to South Africa. Lisa saved 40 pounds over three years and also borrowed money from the father of a friend to pay his fare and he came out to join us in South Africa in around 1924.

Asriel lived in Vienna for about 10 years then we also brought him out to South Africa in around 1931.

While I don't remember anything from Eastern Europe, I do remember coming on the boat and recall a woman wanting to hit me as I was sick on her bed. My sister Lisa then carried me everywhere on the boat to protect me. I don't remember landing as I was only three. I do remember they gave us each an orange. It was the first time in my life I had seen an orange and I hung on to it and took it onto the train till we arrived in Johannesburg, a journey I hardly remember.

When we arrived in Johannesburg we lived in Beit Street in a double storey building. There was no Arcadia at the time but there were premises in Kensington.

Note 1: Sonia Goring was the mother of Gad Jacobi who became Minister of Labour in Israel. They remained in Kostopol and later immigrated to Israel.

Group Passport 7 – Zizza Zaike front row second from right

We arrived in early October 1921 and I was not long in the home and one of the first to be adopted. When my new parents came to adopt me they were looking for me and I was hiding under the table.

Extracts from the register kept by the South African Jewish Orphanage in JHB that cared for the three siblings. The age of the children is listed after the name and Sisel went to live with R Koselowitz who lived at the Royal Arcade.

My adoptive parents had no children of their own and were considering separation after 25 years of marriage. They were pressured by their family to adopt as in those days it was frowned upon to separate.

My adoptive father Harry arrived in South Africa from Radvilizik Lithuania and travelled on a cattle truck during the Boer War to Cape Town. His name was Koselowitz but when they applied for naturalisation they were unable to spell his name they gave him the surname Harris and he became Harry Harris.

My mother was Becky (Rebecca Hotz) oldest of 12 children. Her mother from Shavel Lithuania had sent her to a rich aunt in South Africa to find her a husband.

JACK ZEIKA

Jack, our oldest brother, came out from Palestine in about 1924 and he married Gerty Sacks from Durban. They lived in Holfontein in the Orange Free State and had a General Dealer Shop. They had no children and later had a shop in Geduld extension near Springs. Later they moved to Bulawayo Rhodesia and worked in a gift shop, Tivoli, owned by Gerty's sister. Gerty died and after her tombstone was laid Jack returned to Johannesburg and then later joined Lisa his oldest sister in Haifa. Jack passed away in 1984 aged 89.

LISA ZAIKA

Lisa was already 20 years old and Isaac Ochberg had taken her as a nurse to look after the children. When Lisa first arrived in Johannesburg she helped with the children in the Orphanage. She wanted to nurse but could not work at the General Hospital because she knew no English (or Afrikaans).

A Jewish lawyer, Alexander I think, arranged for her to go into the Klerksdorp hospital to become a nurse and she went to a training school there. It was a four year course and also taught English and Afrikaans and the exams were in English.

So in four years she leant the two languages English and Afrikaans and she just missed a first class pass because she did know one medical term. She was brilliant and at times knew more than the doctors.

After she left Klerksdorp she went to do a Midwifery course at the Queen Victoria hospital in Johannesburg. After she had trained at Queen Victoria as mid wife she worked as a private nurse for the Nursing Association and was sent out to work in the farming areas of Bethal and Zeerust or wherever they needed a nurse. She was as good as any doctor.

On one occasion she was sent to a farm where a man had a large open wound on his stomach which was full of maggots. The doctor had given up hope saying the man could not live long and she had to care for him.

She let the worms have their fill and cleaned and stitched closed the open wound and stuck on a clean dressing of cotton wool in gauze and solution which she changed regularly. The man recovered and was so grateful, however, the cheque never arrived in payment of her services.

She nursed on another farm and knew all the Jewish farmers in the area.

She later worked a year in Windhoek South West Africa. On Yom Kippur the doctor she was working with asked the local Rabbi to give her permission to eat so that he could help him as he had to perform several operations. She told the doctor, "You did not have to ask Rabbi. I'll work and won't eat!"

After her nursing assignments she always returned to Johannesburg.

In 1938, together with a few friends, Lisa decided to visit Israel and arrived in Israel with a visa that allowed her to stay for a month or two. She decided to stay on in Israel and because she did not have a visa, the British were looking for her. She had a friend in police who always warned her so when they came looking for her she was not to be found.

She married a Dr Saul Abend some time before the War of Independence. Saul had been locked up by the British and could not go back to his home in Poland (Galicia) as he had been away for more than five years

Isaac Ochberg and Lisa   *Lisa and Manya*

while he studied medicine at the University in Cadua, Italy. He could not return and never saw his parents again.

He arrived in Israel by boat during the time of the British blockade and the boat was beached near Ashkelon at midnight and all the passengers who swam and waded ashore were caught and arrested by British.

Saul was introduced by a friend to Lisa and they got married. He worked as a doctor in Sejera in the Lower Galilee with Lisa helping as his nurse.

Lisa

Lisa and Saul Abend

At the kibbutz stands a statue of three people, a farmer, soldier and another. He was the farmer.

At one stage Lisa worked for the Hadassa Hospital and they were very happy to have her. She spoke eight languages; Yiddish, Polish, German, Russian, Lithuanian, Latvian and English and Afrikaans. She could switch from one language to another without thinking. She also knew a little bit of Arabic but not so much Hebrew so they would not give her a pension.

On one occasion in Israel there was a patient with a rare disease which she recognized from South Africa and she saw the doctor was treating the patient incorrectly. She told the doctor so and the doctor said, "You know what to do. You nurse him!"

Eventually they settled in a home in Haifa in the German colony where he went into private practice. At that time there was something in the water affecting the children and he discovered the bug that was the cause. He wrote about it in a medical journal and won an award. Later he took a job at the Kupat Cholim (Medical Aid). They never had any children.

Lisa had the most wonderful sense of humour and could entertain a house full of people. Her husband was very shy and she would entertain all the guests. She could tell such stories!

ASRIEL ZAIKA

When my bother, Asriel Zaika, was 15 he was sent to an Orphanage in Vienna and there he learnt to be a dental mechanic. Around 1931 he came to SA on the last boat that carried Jews from Vienna. He lived with my parents and I in the city and went to work in Randfontein as a dental mechanic.

Later my two brothers had a shop in Malvern but it did not work. Jack then opened a business in Geduld Extention and Asriel opened a bicycle and watch repairing shop nearby.

Asriel lived with Jack and Gertie and met Doreen Pincus, a young widow, who had been married for a short while. Her husband had died and she had a young daughter.

Asriel married Doreen when the little girl was five years old and they had two children Ethne, named after Esther and Errol, named after Ephraim. They lived in Springs and later in Benoni then went to live in Israel when Ethne married. Asriel continued to repair watches and died aged 95 in 1995.

Ethne (Esther) went to finish her studies in Israel and got married to Eliyahu Cohen Arazi who is now a Rabbi. They have 12 children while a neighbour has 17 children!

Errol came to Israel to study in the Yeshiva after finishing school at Benoni High. While studying he met a girl from Switzerland, Elisheva Hausman. They married in Israel and had four children, one of whom died. They lived for some time in Switzerland. In the morning Errol teaches at a Yeshiva and in the afternoons he works on the computer at a hotel and has been there for years now.

On one occasion they were called out by a husband to help a woman in labour with a difficult birth in a nearby village on the Syrian border. The father-to-be had come with a donkey to transport Lisa and Saul to the village. There were sheep and goats in the room with the mother in labour and the first thing that Lisa did was chase the animals and everyone out. She successfully delivered the baby and, on the way back to the kibbutz, the grateful father asked Saul "Old man, how much did you have to pay for Lisa?"

Lisa nursed Paula, Ben Gurion's wife and his brother and one of the Bar Lev officers.

When the Israeli War of Independence broke out they fled to Haifa taking only a suitcase and were subsequently provided with a house by the custodian of enemy property.

During a visit to Kibbutz Negba, Saul met a cousin from Kostopol, Zalman Shochet, who was a founder of the kibbutz.

MANYA ZAIKA

Manya was in Arcadia for about six years but told me very little about her stay there. We used to visit her at Arcadia and take her to enjoy the zoo.

Frank Adler the son of Manya Zaika writes.
Herewith the little I can tell you about my mother's stay in Arcadia as told to me by her.

She said that when she arrived at Arcadia and saw the garden with its many fruit trees it seemed like the Garden of Eden. She remembered the unpleasantness of the weekly spoon of castor-oil she and the other children were given each week.

She started work when she was 14 working in the despatch section of the medical supplies firm Sieve Bros and Karnovsky.

She used to go to dance and ballet classes, one memorably run by a good woman called Madame Revodna. She later moved on to a number of boarding houses including one run by a Mrs Sachs from where she began to teach ballet herself. While there she met my father Nathan Adler who was articled to a firm of lawyers, Alexander Bros.

Until a few years ago my mother had a marvellous memory for Jewish life of '30s and '40s Johannesburg. Unfortunately after a fall and a time in hospital her memory and her mobility steadily reduced until today she has hardly any memory and almost no mobility.

Manya and Nathan Adler with Frank and Erika

ZIZZA ZAIKA

My new adoptive parents Harry and Becky (Rebecca Hotz) Harris had a tea-room bioscope, the Popular Bioscope, that showed a film and gave tea and a snack to its patrons. The family lived above the cinema between Pritchard Street and Kerk Street near the Royal Arcade. I first went to Fairview Junior School and then later to Troyeville middle school and finally to Jeppe High. We lived in Kensington in Merlin Street.

We were very comfortable for a while but then my uncle, who was my father's partner did something contrary to the agreement signed with Schlesinger Organisation and we lost the right to show the films. When we could not get pictures my Dad with my uncle ran the Popular Bioscope without films for a year or two quite successfully on the corner of Eloff and President Street. They ran a Vaudeville show with some very good artists some of whom went to the US.

After two years we moved to Fordsburg and my Dad operated this artists' theatre for a further six months. However, It was unsuccessful as he had no money to get good artists.

We rented a room for thee months in Mayfair trying to make this pay but then went back to the house in Kensington.

My father developed leg trouble and a Russian man who drew blood (steelen bunkes) helped heal him. He used a warm glass on the cut to draw out blood. Slowly he recovered and opened a little vegetable shop and later a grocery shop. I was nine at the time and helped in the shop.

We let the house and opened the grocery shop at the border of Jeppe Extension and Malvern, in Jules Street, the longest straight road in Johannesburg. We made a living and the three of us managed.

Cissy Harris (right) with Habonim friends on Edinburgh Castle. Port Elizabeth

Cissy Harris (right) with Habonim friends at camp

After finishing school I stayed at home working in the shop. Later I worked at an electrical firm in Pritchard Street that had not been in business for long.

I worked for Jewish Appeal for a while and went back to the electrical shop, Electo-import, Electrical Engineers and Building Construction, which did everything. I worked there from 1938 to 1979 and I did everything starting from being the office girl.

They fitted out big buildings with electricity, machines and lights. I drove the boss around and I would go and inspect the work etc when he was away. My niece and nephews, Asriel's children, came to me for their holidays and kept me busy and full of surprises!

The firm supplied diamond cutting factories, installing the cutting and sawing machines and fitting out the offices.

When the boss passed away, they were obliged to sell. The third partner had been bought out years before and the second partner could not run it. After that they did not need me and I went to work in the office for one of the diamond cutting firms. They would send me to the different shops where things were wrong and eventually they went in as there was a lot of monkey business from staff.

Then I worked for the Beth Din. My car was stolen at Wolmarans Street Shul, the Great Synagogue, and subsequently found in Botswana. Later my car was stolen from outside the Beth Din in Yeoville where I worked mornings and in the afternoon I worked for the Law Shop selling law books.

In 1991, following a desperate and terrible cry for help from my sister Lisa, and after living 70 years in South Africa, I went to live in Israel and, as I couldn't schlep everything, I had to leave a lot of letters and documents behind.

Lisa had lost her husband Saul and was in a home and a man was in charge of her money as she had dementia. He denied her basic things like a TV, telephone and fridge and she only had one dress that she washed each night. She needed me to help her and take care of her.

After going through a difficult and traumatic time I eventually took charge of her affairs and I made things easier for her by being there for her.

Lisa, who had spent many years looking after my brother Jack and who had so many friends, had a very sad, poor ending and it was a very sad funeral.

I have always lived on my own and I hate cooking and hate kitchen work.

In Johannesburg I rented a flat and had a car and I went to every show. Now in Israel I bought a flat and live here opposite the sea. I go on my own twice a week to a club and I'm always very busy.

I watch the children playing soccer and trees growing in a new park near me. On the weekend, the park is packed with people sitting on the lawn and having picnics.

You are very safe here; kids of ten walking around at ten at night, girls parade at midnight and if you see a crowd of blacks coming, you don't run away because they are Jewish Blacks wearing kippot!

We are all very thankful and grateful to Isaac Ochberg.
Thanks to him, if not for his actions, none of us would be alive today.

Cissy Harris with Bennie Penzik - Israel 2009

Nobody was interested in our story and I tried to encourage Lisa to write. In 1967 a journalist wrote about our story.

When I went in 2006 with the film company to Kostopol, Jon Blair, the producer, was wonderful and he took me to see a couple with the name Zaika. The man, Alexander Zaika, said he had a grandfather by the name Moshe from Zlavota but otherwise he knew nothing about his ancestors.

Chapter 40 - MANYA ZAIKA

MEMORIES OF MANYA ZAIKA (ADLER)

These memories are extracted and adapted from the original transcript of an interview of Manya Adler.

Events have been arranged into a chronological order and headings included to help the flow of the narrative.

MEMORIES OF KOSTOPOL

When my mother died she'd had six children. There was a baby after Cissie, Fagella Rochol, who only lived six weeks I think and the poor thing just didn't survive, I suppose my mother was too ill too have any more children.

Fagella Rochol was born at home with a midwife like Cissie and I remember it but it was a quieter birth. When Cissie was born I had a very bad reaction.

I was standing beside my mother and she was cooking and our stove was a strange sort with a ring on a white brick surface and that surface opened into an oven all white where my mother baked bread and cake, biscuits, anything for Saturday's lunch. The food went in on a Friday afternoon and it was closed up and Saturday you opened it up and you had a hot lunch. And so my mother put every meal, other meals were cooked on those surface white brick with a large ring on it and that's where my mother used to prepare the meals. It was a wood fire. Coal in Russia was at a premium, most of our heating was done by wood, blocks of wood. We used to store it in the underside of our house not laid up.

Before Cissie was born I was standing beside my mother and every now and then she'd say oh, and so I would ask what's the matter mother, aren't you well? No, and then I'd say "what is it momma," and she was stirring the soup, standing preparing the super, eventually she said to me, "you're going to, there's going to be a baby here", and it didn't, it meant nothing, a baby, where from?

Where does it come from? So my poor mother says you know it comes from the chimney. It was a chimney. It comes down the chimney so I looked at her very puzzled. Then during the night I heard my poor mother screaming and the midwife, such as they were in those days, was there and apparently she delivered the rest of the family. My poor mother was screaming and I and my poor father was walking up and down from the dining room to the lounge, walking up and down quite worried and my mother was in labour.

In the morning when I woke up there was *Cissy*, a red faced baby lying in a basket, next to my mother and I went up and saw an ugly red face. I was so disgusted I ran out of the house and on the outskirts of Kostopel. I wouldn't talk to a soul. Whoever wanted to stop me, talk to me, asked me why I was so hot, so upset, so fed up. I was in such a state. I hated everyone. I hated my family. I hated everyone I saw and everyone in Kostopel and I ran round a couple of times and eventually came home and I didn't want to have anything to do with anyone. It took a while and I suppose I quietened down and when I got to know this baby she was the most darling little thing you can imagine, and I adored her.

Cissy was only two when we came to South Africa, can you imagine? Cissy was two I was ten, I'm eight years Cissy's senior and I remember I would try and carry her, but I once dropped my neighbour's baby so I was very careful. They let me hold the little boy. The neighbour had a house full of children they were Jewish, they came from a place called Corrin and he was a musician, a fine looking man, always at home. He played the violin and they had a house full of children.

Asreil, my second brother, had his friend and I had a friend who was a couple of years my senior and we were friends with the neighbour's family. They must have been very poor musicians and the mother used to milk our cow for us and my father used to pay her. I suppose as musicians they'd play at weddings and so on, but they had a huge family.

When I was small my father used to make little rabbits out of his white handkerchief and make them jump and I used to laugh my head off. I was so amused at how my father could do this; make these things live and jump.

We had friends further down the road, other neighbours with whom we were friendly and they had a horse and cart. I think he had a fruit farm because often he used to have fruit on the wagon and she was a hefty looking woman who had a corset and she once showed me a corset. I said my mother hasn't got one of these. My mother didn't need a corset; she had a lovely slim figure and was tall and slim and the woman was squat.

Then I remember another occasion when Cissy was already walking. We had a big kist in which my mother used to keep her clean linen and so I opened up the top, lifted Cissy and put her in it and closed it and the poor child was terrified. I thought it was a big joke and she was so thrilled to get down when I lifted her out.

The first time I saw a living little thing was a mouse in a trap but I didn't know what a trap was for. I saw this little creature was very small and I was thrilled to the marrow. I hugged my father. I was so thrilled he took me to the neighbours' barn where they kept the horse to show me this little animal but what happened to it of course he never told me.

Those neighbours had two daughters, Mini was my age and Mini contracted scarlet fever, and my mother said to me don't ever go there until I tell you it's alright. She's sick and if you go there you'll get sick. My poor mother how she put up with me I don't know. I wasn't an obedient child and when my mother said take the cloth and dust the chairs I would run out and meet my friends. There were about 12 of them of all nationalities and we all played together and it was fun I loved that we had large grounds that led on to the cornfields through which I would go if I wanted to go to my granny and my aunt, my father's sister and uncle and cousins or if my mother wanted to send me to the choffert which I found I wasn't old enough to realise what a chauffeur did to the fell. We had a German girl who used to do the rough work in our house.

I used to see the poor chicken running around after it had its throat cut and I laughed and years later thought children should be told that things like that are painful. I just didn't know and I came back with the basket to carry the chicken.

The corn was much taller than I was and I used to pick blue cornflowers which were lovely and make things to put round our heads when we played as children. There was a well trodden path through the cornfields and Kostopol was in a hollow. We were higher up and on the other side of the field was Kostopol, the town as it was, down below and then we had a forest about two miles away. I used to get so worried as my father often used to stand at the window and look out into the dark and I used to stand beside him and we could hear the wolves howling and I used to be terrified. My father said they could never come to our house, you must never worry.

We had a glass factory in Kostopol I didn't know it but what I did know that is my shoes always went under my bed. I used to love running barefoot over the broken glass and in the afternoon when I was resting and my father would be at home he knew how to take the glass out of my foot and how to disinfect the *cuts*. The factory burnt down and I remember that large area full with broken glass.

I remember on one occasion quite a few of us were in fields of sweet peas and we thought it was great fun to pick the *peas* which had elastic in them and in the end we ran away. The peas were in pods and so we used to pick the pods but it was really difficult to run over these pods that catch your legs and so every now and then we'd look up. We thought it was fun to do it and our parents never knew we did it.

Suddenly somebody shouted, They're coming! They would have decapitated us if they'd caught us. The people, the Ukranian peasants and we started running. It wasn't easy to get out of this area running with the peas and we ran very fast and we got to the barn were I saw that mouse. They had barrels and what they had in those barrels I don't know: perhaps fruit, perhaps herring but they were standing upside down and we hid each other under the barrels and you could see through the opening in the barrel and through the doors. They'd come right through our area and were looking for us and they looked inside and I thought it's the end of me. If they catch me; if they turned up the barrels they would have, I'm sure, massacred us.

So I stayed there for hours and eventually when everything had quietened down and it was getting darker and we were sure of being able to get home we all climbed out and went home and I was walking towards our house and my father was standing at the window. My father never spoke much but I remember he didn't say a word, not a word but at night I had to sleep with my mother, for years, I suppose months I couldn't sleep I was so frightened that they'd come.

On the whole my father got on with everyone. I remember once I was crossing a bridge and there were gentile boys throwing stones. We were coming from the forest.

Liza came from boarding school and she knew which mushrooms you could pick and so I'd go with her into the forest and there were huge oaks with lots of leaves under the oaks and underneath you'd get mushrooms; they were the size of a round plate. So we used to pick lots of mushrooms and my mother knew how to make delicious mushroom. Peasants also used to come to our door and they'd make little containers from a birch tree, which is the Russian national tree, and they used to wear shoes and boots made from that bark. They used to make little containers filled with different kinds of blueberries, mulberries, strawberries and wild things. They were delicious and my mother used to buy lots of mushroom and dry them and in winter we used to have them the most delicious barley soup with mushroom. It was a marvellous, marvellous food.

I used to go very often to the butcher to buy liver or whatever my mother used to write down and bring it home from the butcher. My mother was a good cook, we loved her food.

I remember Jack, my oldest brother, had gone to the war. I heard that quite a few people had gone into the forest to hide to avoid the summons to the war but Jack had gone. My father must have suffered very much and my poor mother. We were on a main line from north to south as it were, from Sauna to Robner and soldiers used to come and my mother used to give them plates of soup and make them welcome. They'd sit round the table and she used to enquire whether they'd ever come across Jack, and of course they never did.

My mother used to make parcels and wrapped them with her linen and send it to the front wherever Jack happened to be. Jack saw Trotsky in Russia he heard him talk at Kronstadt, that was the name of the place, and when Jack came on leave he just couldn't face it. He had such a gentle nature Jack, that for him to shoot people was impossible, so one fine day Jack must have chopped his thumb as he was chopping wood so that he couldn't hold a revolver again. Jack used to chop up wood very often to heat our house and we had logs and a strange sort of opening into a wall where you had a double wall and inside you made a fire and in the evening we also used to make clever on the coals that were left after; it was a tenacious tasting food it was lovely.

So after that he was spared from the army. After we had gone in 1921 Jack still sent us money. I remember a friend of Jack's and Liza's coming to Warsaw when we were already in Warsaw and bringing us money and so Jack remained in our hearts for quite a time.

Asreil, after we left for South Africa, left for Austria Vienna. He was going to take up dentistry and Jack did dentistry for a while but Liza said that the gas or something didn't agree with him. Asreil apparently used to do dentist work in Vienna but when he came to South Africa he had to take new exams. We couldn't afford it so Asreil did at first dentures; he made dentures and sold those and in the end Jack opened a business in Freiheit and afterwards in Springs and he and Asreil had the place next to each other and he stayed at Jack's place but he was quiet you know.

Liza was in a boarding school called Isalobeil in the Ukraine which my father could only afford. She wanted to be a doctor but it would have taken years and he couldn't afford that. My father was an engineer, a mechanical engineer and he invented, Liza told me, an agricultural machine, which the owner for the firm that my father was working took, and never gave my father anything for it. I think his name was Zimmerman because Liza was close friends with his daughter Rosa.

Liza said it was my father's invention. He invented it and this man Zimmerman took it as if it belonged to him. My father was very good to keep Liza at this boarding school and Liza used to come home for the holidays and we had a very big map of Russia with the mountains and rivers and there seemed to be millions of them and Liza used to sit on the floor and study the rivers and mountains and I'm sure she knew each and every one. She had such a memory.

We had a cow and my mother used to make her own butter and we had cream always and milk. The cow's name was Manka, they named her after me, and was a lovely black and white cow and when Liza used to come home she used to go to our pantry and take off all the cream. She was very fat when she was young. She used to take all the cream from the jugs and enjoy herself.

We had lots of ground. When Liza saw our house in Johannesburg she said our garden was much bigger than this ground. We had every conceivable kind of vegetable in the garden and father got a piece of ground and grew tobacco there but what did he know about curing tobacco? Nothing, so they rolled their cigarettes. So my poor father must have had cancer because I remember when he got ill he had a big wound. It must have been in his lung and in Kostopol we had a hospital but I don't think it was a first class hospital. We had doctors and Felshaw was not quite a doctor but a woman who eventually became a doctor, and when I got scarlet fever she used to come see me. I used to think she was related to us. She was a close friend of ours and was always coming to see Liza and Jack who had close Russian friends who lived opposite us and he was, I think, a general. He had umpteen medals hanging all with the uniform and Liza and Jenya the Russian friend were similar ages. Liza sometimes used to go to church with her. She didn't bend you know, but she'd go and Jenya was always at our house and Pavloshka was Jack's friend and Jack played the concertina and my father used to be very hard on him. He didn't like him, he was handsome and young and used to go out and my father used to hit him when he came back. My mother used to suffer. She adored Jack. My father used to say you've got to stay at home and study, you have to study but he never did. My father adored his girls.

I didn't talk about making the buns and making things to sell to people before. I never mentioned it I know, Liza didn't like to talk about it. I remember once only in my life my mother not being kind to me, I mean she smacked me once. I said I'm going to tell my father and when my father came home, I said, I told you I'd tell and I told him, I said mother and why, why was I angry? I only remember her smacking me once. It's possible she may have smacked me before but I don't remember it and I was so hurt because she'd put away certain apples to make a strudel for the Saturday and the apples were missing. Who took them? I never told my mother lies, nor my father and I told my father, mother accused me of taking the apples and I told her I didn't take them. I was so hurt not about the smack about my mother disbelieving me. I was very upset.

He said shall I smack her, I said yes so he went behind her back and I looked and I said you didn't smack her. My mother and father had a wonderful relationship.

The last child must have been too much for her. She was called Fagella Rochol and only lived six weeks and it was sad.

Somebody once said to me that my father and my mother had a really good relationship; my father was a strong character my mother was gentle and she'd give in to him. They had one row I remember, once and I was so depressed over it but it passed and that's the only time I remember they had a quarrel. They were close, very close and so when my father died first, it was a terrible blow, a terrible shock.

My mother worked hard and baked special sweets and then even I used to go to the station when soldiers used to pass. I would sell them and Liza would go and sell buns that my mother used to make. She'd get up very early and bake and we had a room where she used to keep these things that we used to sell but it wasn't enough. My poor mother got ill and she went to Robsner to a hospital there and she had cancer at 38. I remember Jack calling me into the room every time that she looked bad and so I remember crying when my poor mother lay there naked. They allowed me to see her and it was winter and I wasn't permitted to go to the funeral. So that's what happened. So anyway, it was after my parents died that Liza met Ochberg.

Do you know when my mother fell ill Lisa shared her bed in case she'd wake up and no one would hear her so she slept in mother's bed. My mother had cancer of the throat and she must have died of hunger. Years later I discovered in South Africa that there had been famine in the Ukraine. There were times when we were short, just short periods when we were short.

I was no angel, I mostly didn't listen if my mother used to say, here's a cloth just wipe these chairs or wipe the table. We had a German girl Katja and we used to call her Cuts and she used to come and do the silver and copper things and whatever needed to be done. My mother used to embroider beautiful covers for the beds.

Liza says that she never knew what my mother and father said when they spoke to each other. When they didn't want us to understand she never understood and she didn't know which language it was. It wasn't Yiddish, not Russian not Polish not German because all these lived in our town and we used to converse with them. They had another language.

Children learned to understand each other's language easily and forget easily. Liza understood languages and said they never knew what language, maybe Esperanto. We never knew what it was that mother spoke with father.

Lisa and my granny, our father's mother, used to bake things for us and also my aunt. My mother had a wonderful sister who died.

Asreil and Liza told me that when my mother and sister died half the town closed up shops, closed up businesses and went to the funeral. If she knew someone who was in need she would immediately go and get things for her and bring them, and my mother too. In winter you couldn't see through the windows for the snow was so thick. So they'd open the door and if anybody would pass or looked as though they could do with a plate of hot soup my mother would call them in and give them a plate of hot nourishing soup and it was wonderful.

My granny, my father's mother, stayed with her daughter Rochol, my father's sister quite nearby, in town, in Kostopel down below. Schupa was my mother's sister and Schupa died fortunately. She didn't survive the terrible things that happened. I used to think why did my parents die so young but after the Holocaust I was thankful that they had died young, as to have gone though the Holocaust would be frightful.

Schupa's husband I remember always used to bring me money at Channeke; it's a custom, money at Channeke you bring money. I used to have a little bag round my neck and put the money in the little bag. And Christmas time when they'd come outside our window and sing Christmas carols we always used to throw Kopeks out.

Anyway Liza told me that my father was excommunicated from the synagogue because we had Russian books on our shelves. My father was a great reader; he was a scholar and he wanted Jack to be a scholar, he wanted all of us to be and he was so gentle with us girls, so kind. He was an important part of the synagogue, Liza told me all this I remember none of it. And so he had quite a following when he left from the synagogue. They bought a Torah and Liza said they walked though the streets, which shows you that Kostopol was still not anti-Semitic, they walked through the streets with the Torah and there was music to celebrate the occasion and they founded a new synagogue and they formed this new synagogue and that's how my father was quite an important man there apparently.

Jack used to play the accordion, Liza used to play the guitar and they had lots of friends visiting them, students you know.

My father was quite an important man in the synagogue, I of course don't remember this, but Liza told me. My father was religious but thank god he wasn't fanatically religious. He had books. He had a special friend called Perchas, I think Perchas Lebas was his name but I remember his first name. I remember his face, black hair he had and dark eyes. Only twice my father experienced anti-Semitism, otherwise nobody ever worried us. He didn't himself experience it but he saw it. My father had a little black beard and I think a moustache and it suited him. Hennola looked very much like him. Once he came home on a Saturday from synagogue and he said that as he was walking home, he saw some gentile men walking about with scissors trying to catch people who came from synagogue and cutting their beards. That was a terrible thing to do for him to see, he was quite shaken by it.

My father's name was Betrayan and my mum was Esther or Erika. Esther Lieber and Leiber was named I think after dad's mother's mother. And Hennola was named after dad's father his name was Harrison. He died young, he was only 63.

My mother was 38 when she died. She married very young and also dad's mother married young, 15 I think, 16 or 17 I think. At 21 she had three boys, dad's mother, but she was very youthful looking. She could easily have passed as his sister sometimes, she was tall, striking and she looked very young.

Now Rochol's husband was a striking man, wide forehead and tall and he travelled about a lot. What he did I don't know but I know he used to come back from Livrov, (Livrov is Lamberger), and bring beautiful shawls and all sorts of things. They were very well to do. They had this home in Kostopol which was lovely. My granny was a short little woman and always wore a silk white scarf. I never saw her work. She was twice married, and lost both her husbands.

ADOPTION AND THE CLOCHNY SKIRTS

I think my mother must have already died, and Liza was home and I used to be jealous of Liza. She had a good sense of dress and she had clochny skirts; not pleats, tight at the waist and the special Russian name a clochny. She used to look so lovely in it and I used to be so jealous of her. I had my own clothes but I liked hers.

We had these people who were related to us, but how, I never found out. I remember going to Robner and my father bought me a beautiful little handbag and a lovely coat and I looked so smart. Robner, like Kostopol, was a small town but it had lots of trains and different lines going through it. Robner was an important railway junction.

This family in Robner they had an only daughter who used to come and visit us. She was tall willowy, beautiful, very, very graceful and she always wore white large brimmed hats and her name was Fagella, Fagella Rochola I think. We thought it was the end of the war but apparently there was still snipers and she went out on their balcony and was shot. That was the end of her, and we couldn't believe it. She was such a lovely person, such a beauty and that was that. After some time her parents wanted to adopt me because I had no parents and was an orphan in some poverty.

They wanted a child. They had a large shop like Marks and Spencer's, a big business with lots of material and different types of things. I thought they wanted me to teach me to take an interest in their business and I didn't want that. I loved school. I remember going to school, just when we were able to. I can't remember whether the teacher's name was Mallumud or whether Mallumud in Hebrew means teacher so we used to call him Mallumud, Mr Mallumud. He was a tall fellow and he asked questions and I got out my seat and answered the question and he said Zaika knows it, Zaika

When Fagella was shot accidentally when she was on the balcony we were very shocked but I said I'm not going to be adopted. I'm not going to them and you know Liza and Jack said they won't take you into their business. You'll be educated as you wish to be. It is in your interest and your advantage. This is an opportunity they talked so much and I was such a donkey at that age and I said alright if Liza gives me that flared skirt, I'll go, and so Liza had no hesitation she took the flared skirt and said there you are, she had packed a little suitcase for me and Liza took me to the station.

Now the station was the one meeting place if you wanted to meet your friends, it was well lit up at night. In the late afternoon you could go there to see who was leaving who was coming back and it was a meeting place so I knew it quite well and so we went to the station and Liza and I sat there and waited and the train's supposed to come at half past nine. At half past nine no train, ten o'clock no train, so Liza said I'll go and ask the station master this is ridiculous the trains were always punctua. So she went to ask the station master, the station master says, no good the train has been de-railed and it's no use so Liza said, come and let's go back. She said it's fate that you shouldn't go and then we went back and I didn't mind I didn't say a word and I think Liza left the skirt with me I can't remember that. But I didn't go.

I can't remember whether her parents came and tried to persuade me again, that was that, so there was no more question of me going. Liza said it's fate.

FAMILY

Rochel, my mother's sister had a big family and I haven't seen a princess as beautiful as she looked. She used to wear a black muff with a black veil on her face, a smart hat and was very smart and walked beautifully. She had such a graceful figure and although her father had black hair, she was as fair as a lily.

I used to love my mother's sister and I used to sleep with my cousin's friends when I used to go there. They wouldn't let me go so I used to stay in their beds. I loved them and I think they had a third daughter who was in America. It used to take seven weeks for a letter to arrive from America. I remember Tchupa always telling my mother she got the letter from her daughter. I never knew her, but these two cousins I knew they must have perished in the war.

I don't know anything about where my mother's family came from, except that her brother Smolig lived in Selisht and my father's sister lived in Kostopol. They had a beautiful home where my granny was with them all that time.

She has a younger sister as well called Manya, she was lovely, but during the war I suppose, certainly after the war there was an illness called Sleeping Sickness and Manya got it and they didn't let us go and see her, but my father used to go whenever he could and my aunty Rochol's husband used to travel a lot. He used to go all over and used to bring back such beautiful things, shawls and lovely things, but so he may have been away when my father went, he used to sleep there to give his sister some company. They had lots of children: there was Aron and Celia.

My mother had a brother in Selisht otherwise I don't know any of her family. Her parents were no longer alive, and I never met my mother's parents. Zalman was on my mother's side I think as my mother used to take me there quite, quite frequently.

Only my grandmother, my father's mother was alive that's all. And Rochol who was his sister, and Aron and Mandelan who had meningitis when he was a little boy, they were Rochol's children. We used to go to Hottinger where they had a huge, estate. We could only go on Shabbat and my father used to carry me most of the way, I used to go in front and kick up the sand and make a mess in the middle of the road. It was lovely on either side so beautiful and if we went there not on a holy day we'd go by horse and cart.

If mother wanted to send a message to her brother, Smolig, she'd sent Asriel and he would take me along, I liked going there. This was in Selisht and my mother's brother had this land but the Ukrainians worked it for him and he used to teach Hebrew on a long table and when I could go there I used to sit at the table and see and listen to what was going on. He was a Hebrew teacher. Mary Magid's father was my cousin on Uncle Smolig's side, my mother's brother's side. And she's got a sister called Manya, her husband so these two sisters remained and Kalamust have been married to my cousin because Kala's father was Manya and Mary Magid's and her sister's father so Kala must have been his wife. So she survived.

My father's mother, my granny was twice married but I don't know anything about the background. My father came from a place called Slobuta and I've never been there but I used to hear all about Slobuta and it transpires that Chernobyl is near Slobuta because one of the descendants, he's a doctor in Moscow who had his parents in Slobuta had to get permission to get them out of Slobuta to come to Moscow.

And his bother is the one who is in Kelyachmona whom Sarah met in Russia, David Kuverschmidt. You know it seems to me that Kuverschmidt is related on both sides, but exactly how I can't remember.

I was three when the war broke out and the war must have occupied their lives. Do you know Ukrainians killed Uncle Smolig and it broke my heart to hear it.

The first world war we were driven out of our home twice and we stayed near Uncle Smolig he had a big family he stayed nearby and my father buried a lot of our furniture in the garden but a lot of it was missing when we came back.

Soshana and Java were sisters and I think they were Uncle Smolig's daughters. Smolig was my mother's brother.

Soshana and Jack and Soshana's husband and a whole crowd went fairly early in the twenties from Kostopol as Lutzig (pioneers) to Palestine.

Soshana came from Kostopol. Soshana was a young person when she came to Israel and her husband also came. Uri is Soshana's son, Uri and the daughter. They stayed on their small holding and they had chickens, and had a farm on a Moshav. She was a nice person and Uri became a bus driver did very well after that. Uri apparently was very courageous.

His wife had died and his wife's sister looked after the children. I remember seeing a lot of them. He had a son called Jasco who had something wrong with one leg. Uncle Smolig had a big family but I can't now remember them. Uri's sister was happily married and she suddenly became a little too promiscuous and the husband divorced her. I think she married somebody else again, but I think she regretted what she did. I remember her children as kids. We used to bring them presents.

We used to love going to Uncle Smolig, a friendly warm lovely family. They had big families and they were so nice.

Uncle Smolig was killed by the Ukrainians who worked his land. Ukrainians were very poor peasants and Hitler spread his poison everywhere and they killed him. Kala just escaped with her life apparently, Kala and Java.

My aunt Rochol was very stylish. She lived in a lovely house and with lovely clothes. They were very wealthy and they had a beautiful home in town and I remember when I used to go there had a special chair where the top used to come over your head. All sorts of lovely things were spread out there and I loved Mandalen he was so beautiful. It's extraordinary, my father was dark, with black hair and dark eyes and his full sister was as fair as a lily. The daughter Celia she was very fair and so was her sister Manya, really fair.

My granny lived until she was about 98 in spite of all the hardships they must have been through. I remember Liza who used to earn about £5 a month as a trainee nurse, used to send my granny some money. I remember we lived in a flat called Sunridge Court not far from the hospital. When dad was earning not a great deal, I would take £5 on occasions and save this for granny and one day when I said to Liza I can give you £5 now she said she won't need it any more. I was really heart broken. So she told me.

What my poor Aunty Rochol must have experienced and her children under Hitler. I used to wonder why it was that people should be punished that our parents should have died so young but when Hitler did that to the Jews, but thank G-d that our parents didn't live to have such an end.

Liza said 40 members of our family died. She didn't want to tell me at first. Rochol and the uncle and the children and the grandchildren, and my mother's sister had children, they must have been married. The sister was such a good woman, Liza said when she died the town closed their shops and went to her funeral, she was such a good person. Whenever she knew that anyone was in need she was the first to go and help.

Tchupa was my mother's sister, and she had Yenta and Vela two daughters whom I was very close to. We were friendly with all the neighbours, Jewish, non-Jewish and German. We all used to play together.

My friend Minya, where I first saw the little mouse in their barn where I hid under the barrel, developed scarlet fever and my mother said to me you are not to go and see her, she's very ill. Well when my mother said something to me I did just the opposite, I didn't listen to my mother, my poor mother and I went to see Minya.

I went to the forest and loved picking blueberries and mulberries with Liza. She'd take me to the forest and we'd also pick mushrooms. Liza knew which were the right mushrooms to eat so we came from the forest everything seemed to be a little bit not as it should be. I came home and I fell into bed, my

mother immediately sent for Tchupa and she came immediately, they were very close sisters. I had the scarlet fever. There was a woman, I don't know until today whether she was a relation or just a close friend of ours, she eventually was a doctor in Rochobot and she helped me.

GYPSIES

I remember something that Liza doesn't remember and I remember it as clearly as I'm sitting here. We lived barely two miles from the forest. I think a *bearst* is like a kilometre. Gypsies often used to come in and one thing they needed and that is salt and I remember being on our balcony and Liza sitting and we were talking and this gypsy I still remember the colour of the *duch* (headress) she was wearing, red with little sort of spots on it and she said in Russian or Ukrainian, "if you give me salt I'll tell you're your fortune."

And Liza had come from Slavil and was home now. What the occasion was I can't remember; whether it was her final. They tried very hard to talk me into leaving Kostopol and I wouldn't hear of it. I adored my granny I was so close to her. This gypsy read Liza's hand and she said you are going overseas and I remember Liza and I laughed. We thought it was the funniest joke out. We'd got to Robner. They would go to various places in the Ukraine perhaps beyond the Ukraine. We had relation in Bad Dichov and you know we'd go to places in Russia but to travel overseas was a big joke and we laughed uproariously. We gave her the salt and it came to pass that Ochberg came at that time.

MEETING OCHBERG

Lisa went to Kotz high school and became a teacher and so it was at a soiree she met a man from South Africa called Ochberg. He was sent to the Ukraine because in South Africa it was in the papers that lots of Jewish children had been orphaned in the war and they were in a bad way and the Jews got together and they sent this man. I suppose they gave him a certain sum of money to get started and so he could find the homeless Jewish children.

Anyway so this Ochberg told Liza who he was and what he's come for and he said to Liza, you're a teacher here would you consider coming to South Africa. So she said to him. I have two young sisters in our home.

We went to Warsaw first of all and in Southampton we were examined to see that we were able to go on the ship and Cissy was just recovering from measles but they passed her. How they passed her was a miracle, if she had been turned back we would have had to go back so we went to Madeira. Madeira that's where we stopped for a while the ship stopped for a while.

Liza was looking after me and Cissy and also helping with the other children. There were about 200 children, girls and boys half remained in Cape Town and half to Johannesburg.

There was one girl whose father went to Brazil and he sent for her. In South Africa she became a hairdresser. She was a beautiful girl, really intelligent and we were close friends. Charlotte Aronowitz was her name. She was a lovely person and she went to her father in Brazil. Also quite a few of the children went from South Africa to America. One of them had a sister in Poland who survived and came and took him and they went off to America. I remember another one and a third, quite a number of them, who had two relations in America.

ADOPTIONS IN SOUTH AFRICA

What was sad that we came to South Africa was that there were no laws there for adoption, people came and took children and there was one family who was very wealthy. They had a house that they lived in like a park. They had been married 15 years they had no children. They adopted two children a boy and a girl who were not related but because they were adopted and lived with these people and learned to call them papa and mamma they became close and when they adopted these children the woman became pregnant and when they had a child you won't believe it. It's unbelievable too unbelievable! They returned both children, and the agony on this poor girl I think she'd never been right since. Her name was Kruger and his name was Appel, a dark little lovely boy. It was tragic that it was those two.

Then there was another girl she had a sister and she was adopted and she came to visit us afterwards and she said she was learning French. I still remember her teaching us *le jardin* yes and a few French words and she was so proud she had taken their names and after a time apparently that family had children and they resented another girl and they sent her back. She went quite funny and it took years before she became more or less normal.

CISSY

I didn't want to be adopted myself but Cissy was sitting beside me and Mrs Harris's sister, a younger sister, Stella Hallman, she chose Cissy. The Harris's had no children, apparently they were married young. They had a cinema a bioscope where you paid sixpence to see a film and got a cold drink with it and in between there was a marvellous tap dancer and a singer.

The Harris's weren't a happy couple and Cissy once asked Liza why she let them adopt her. You know they didn't want African girls to look after them. Cissy had to do the shopping and Cissy had to do everything they wanted. Poor Cissy was deprived as she had elderly parents and they just used her. They both worked in a shop and apparently Mr Harris had a farm before and after they sold the farm they found diamonds on it.

Cissy and the Harris's had the shop in Kensington and the place where they lived was Orange Grove opposite the Infairlers and there was a family Segal. Now Mrs Segal was in Arcadia with me

JACK

After we left Jack sold the house and a whole group of young Halultzim went to Palestine as pioneers.

Jack got malaria because at that time Israel was full of malaria mosquitoes, and he eventually agreed to come to South Africa. Liza borrowed the money from friends in South Africa. She paid

them back later and brought Jack up and he was green. His complexion was green, he'd had malaria so badly. He didn't suffer though from malaria in later years. No, thank G-d god he recovered and he was happily married to Gerty and Gerty's sister Flori, as you know was at Grahamstown University with dad. Jack was very happily married with Gerty.

It was an accident that Jack met Gerty. He met her on the beach in Durban. She asked him some question and they discovered that he knew Gerty's sister and that's how Jack got to know Gerty. It was a miracle an absolute miracle, he was so happy with her.

THE SOUTH AFRICAN JEWISH ORPHANAGE

When we came to Johannesburg from Cape Town there was a South African orphanage in Johannesburg and we were asked to go to an old age home in Doorfontein. There was a Mr Wilson who could play the piano and he played the piano and taught us the Fox-trot and he used to dance with us so we used to take a partner and dance and it was fun.

The South African Jewry that was in Johannesburg decided to buy a mansion in Park Town. I can't tell you how many acres of ground it was. It was called *Villa Arcadia* and the SAJO retained the name Arcadia. It had an orchard and different levels of lawn. The gardens were laid out in terraces. The mansion stood, right up on a ridge in a sort of light forest up to Nathos Road which was at that time called the Ottobite Lane. Ottobite was quite a well known man in South Africa and he must have left a home there for the recuperation of anyone who needed it after they'd been to hospital so that was the Ottobite Home.

Sometimes we used to walk up through the forest or we used to sit in the forest when we had time. There was a tennis court and we were also given some chores, at the table, and different things that needed to be done, so that the time we had was not really a great deal and we had to do homework.

We had a matron In Arcadia and we used to call her mother the moustache as she had a moustache growing. Her mother was there for quite a time and when she was too old and she lived in such a tumbled down place, a shack somewhere in Doorfontein. They must have been quite poor.

And there was a late middle aged committee man, a bachelor Mr Isaacson. He used to come and was a friendly old man in his late middle age. She we used to call her the blue lips as she used to have fainting fits from time to time but she was strict as a sergeant major and she always had blue lips, so we called her blue lips. Eventually this committee man married this Mavis Myers. She had a terrible thing about her that we disliked; she was cruel in a sense. She could have been so nice but she had a sadistic streak.

For instance if Cissy's parents invited us to go to their cinema, Mavis Isaacson would wait until the last day before when we could go shopping and hoping to go to the cinema she'd find fault with something and she'd say it's cancelled you're not going and it was such a blow because we had so little really as a diversion.

Arcadia was beautiful to look at; it had a long drive, a magnificent orchard and the boys used to from time to time and the girls too, go in the orchard and they had such a variety of fruit and we'd take the fruity. They would say, don't go to the orchard but you know children can't be told don't go and take something in between meals so we used to go from time to time, singly or we'd go with somebody else and disappear. There the gardener sometimes used to say oh such and such had been but mostly he was nice.

We had several matrons after Miss Myers married Isaacson. They bought the Warmbaths Hotel and she had experience and so people who suffered with arthritis used to go to Warmbaths. I used to see them and a couple of times we stayed at that Warmbaths Hotel. She was quite a different person there, as she wanted people to come there.

MR AND MRS SHEAR

Mrs Shear had been a teacher in London with Uzangua and she used to be quite proud to boast that she'd taught in London under Ibra Uzangua. He was man who had written quite a lot about Jewish life here and she used to ask us questions and finally she and her husband, both of whom had come from Lichtenberg. He I think was a tailor there she was a teacher, a really plain looking woman. They had two daughters, one was called Naomi and the other was Ruth. Ruth went to college to become a teacher like the mother.

She promised me that I would learn the piano and Liza urged me to press it and I asked her and she made me prefect and gave me extra responsibilities to do but I thought it is well worth it waiting for the time she'd let me learn the piano. People used to come and teach gratis. She didn't do it and one day I plucked up courage and said, when am I going to start learning the piano. I used to be so envious when I used to hear them play the scales or whatever they'd learnt. I wanted so much to play. Oh she said, that's for the older girls. I could have cried I was so angry. She didn't let me learn music I was so heartbroken.

Anyway Arcadia was a palatial place with a tennis court and some of us used to play when we had the time. Arcadia was a rambling place but gradually slowly it began to close in, you felt you were getting tighter and tighter.

Pearl Potash and I became quite close friends. She was a very nice girl. Now she knew that her mother said she would come to fetch her when she turned 16 and sure enough I happened to come into the office to ask about something and I saw the likeliness immediately. She came with a little suitcase of clothes, dresses. We had to wear the school uniform and a sort of a uniform at home with the same colour dresses. She came back from school and the mother turned up and this girl locked herself in and she said I'm not going. The mother waited, waited and waited and she left the clothing but she never saw her. Eventually she married a Rhodesian man.

SCHOOL

I was one of those who was privileged to go to high school because I was good with Hebrew and in Hebrew I used to get books because it came easily to me, I used to get books as prizes.

They looked at our reports and they wanted to send me to Cape Town to train as a nurse first of all. I could have gone to university but I didn't want to be a nurse.

In Arcadia the first person who came to teach ballet was a woman called Pearl Adler. her father was a gold mining magnate, very well to do. She had an assistant called Lillian Browse who was lovely. She liked me and I loved her and she used to point me out.

And then there was a Hollander who used to come every Sunday morning and teach gym, with wooden clubs. We learnt exercises with these clubs which was excellent.

Mr Lilly was a lovely man he used to teach at school, we went one evening to an exhibition of his work it was beautiful.

I'd left school and the teacher sent a note asking me please to come back because I was good at it but I'd made up my mind when I was fourteen, I'm not staying there any longer. It had become so unbearable at my age and Liza was the one who kept my spirits up. I had my appendix out. Nothing wrong with my appendix but because I was bored to death there, bored stiff. If you wanted your tonsils out they took it out.

AFTER LEAVING ARCADIA

I got a room with Mrs Pickford and started working at Transvaal Drug where I met Izzy and we were close. He lived at Mrs Sach's at that time. I went from Mrs Pickford where I had been for a short while to Mrs Fine and from there I went to Mrs Sach.

I met Izzy when I was fifteen and we got engaged. He was a very youthful looking, he was a year older than I was but he didn't look it. He went overseas and after two years of waiting I met dad.

I met dad (Nathan) through a friend of Lisa who often used to arrange soirees. I think when I was seventeen and I hadn't seen Izzy for two years.

LIZA

You know at one time Liza became the theatre sister in Windhoek. I think she looked for somebody there. She was heart broken and dad was wonderful you know and he said, you need a change and he bought her a ticket G-d bless him, he was such a beautiful person. She went to Naples. I don't know why she went to Naples and from there she caught a boat to Palestine.

Liza's lovely. She was delightful, so content also so comfortable but also so gracious in the way she walked around and it was lovely the way she spoke to people and she had such a brilliant sense of humour and it was lovely to see her and to hear her.

I must say she was someone quite exceptional. The children used to love her, she was so good and she did so much. She knew so much and was a big personality. I can't remember her having a nasty side. I couldn't see that at all. She wasn't revengeful or mean not at all but a generous person.

PART 2
CAPE TOWN, SOUTH AFRICA

SECTION 6
THE HISTORY OF THE CAPE JEWISH ORPHANAGE - ORANJIA

The Cape Jewish Orphanage was established in 1912 and was later known as Oranjia

Isaac Ochberg was the President of the Cape Jewish Orphanage and half the Orphans he rescued from the Ukraine were placed in its care.

This institution, currently called Oranjia Jewish Child and Youth Centre still exists and still takes care of children.

You can read about the Cape Jewish Orphanage in some of the individual life stories of the Ochberg Orphans and there were a few descendants of Ochberg Orphans who were also placed in its care

Chapter 41 – CAPE JEWISH ORPHANAGE: BES YESOYMIM (1911-1939)

Written by Veronica Belling (1)

The commandment to care for the widow and the orphan, the most vulnerable members of society, is one of the most basic precepts of Judaism. Although the oldest Jewish organisation in South Africa, Cape Town's Tikvath Israel congregation, was founded in 1841, a Jewish orphanage in that city was only established in 1912, eight years after that of the South African Jewish Orphanage in Johannesburg. Prior to its establishment, abandoned and destitute children were sent to Norwood, the Jewish Orphanage in London. After the establishment of the orphanage in Johannesburg, the general feeling was that one Jewish Orphanage in South Africa was sufficient, and six Cape Town orphans were sent there. The proposed establishment of an orphanage for Cape Town was first raised and discussed at the Cape Town Jewish Philanthropic Society in 1907.

The idea of founding this body was first conceived by Mrs Natalie Friedlander, a prominent charity worker in the Cape Town Jewish community. At the end of 1909, in response to a rumor that there were Jewish children living in a state of great neglect in the Western Boland, Mrs. Friedlander, accompanied by Miss Henrietta Hill (at the time a high school student), discovered three Jewish children – two boys and a girl, aged eight or nine – who had been living with a Colored family in Piquetberg since their parent's death. The children were found at the back of a hotel washing bottles and glasses from the Bar! Another little boy was subsequently found on a farm in Namaqualand. These children were brought to Cape Town and homes found for them, but the question was what would happen to future cases. An Orphan Aid society was established by the Cape Town Hebrew Congregation, but this was clearly not enough.

Mrs Friedlander inspired her friend Joseph Kadish, a Cape Town jeweler well known for his public-spiritedness, to convene a meeting. This took place on 15 July 1911. Participants were Kadish himself, his brother, I Kadish, J Isaac Wittenberg, one of South Africa's earliest clothing manufacturers, Louis Gradner, a printer and future mayor of Cape Town, Meyer Lintern, a hairdresser in Long Street; Simon Frank from Gordon Street, J Isenstein, William Street shopkeeper in District Six, and the Reverends B Strod and Weinberg. As the Very Reverend Dr Adler, Chief Rabbi of the United Congregations of the British Empire, had passed away only a few days before, it was proposed to name the institution "The Doctor Adler Jewish Memorial Orphanage." This name is written across the first page of the minute book, but is never heard of again.

(1) Biog: Veronica Belling has been the librarian at the Jewish Studies Library, part of U.C.T. Libraries and the Kaplan Centre for Jewish Studies and Research, for the last 28 years. She is the author of *Bibliography of South African Jewry* (1997), *Yiddish Theatre in South Africa* (2008), and the translator of Leibl Feldman's *The Jews of Johannesburg* (2007) and *Yakov Azriel Davidson: His Writings in the Yiddish Newspaper, Der Afrikaner, 1911-1913* (2009).

Within a month, the committee had expanded to include Advocate Morris Alexander, Parliamentarian and Jewish community leader, the Policansky brothers, well known tobacco merchants, popular theatre impresario, Harry Stodel, the medical doctor, S E Kark (who offered his services free), Messrs R Barnett, M Davies, R Weinberg, M Papert, and Isaac Ochberg. The latter was to play a pivotal role in the history of the Orphanage. The committee was joined by the charities: the Hebrew Dividing and Benefit Society, the Grand Order of Israel, the Wynberg Synagogue, the Roeland Street Synagogue, the Helping Hand Society, the Bnoth Zion Association and the Jewish Girls Circle. A system was devised whereby all Hebrew congregations, charities and societies of various kinds that took out annual subscriptions to the orphanage would also be members of the committee.

While the original committee was predominantly a male affair, by October a Ladies committee consisting of fifteen women, chaired by Natalie Friedlander with Mrs A H Stodel, wife of Harry Stodel, as vice chairlady, was appointed. In the meantime the new institution was officially named the 'Cape Jewish Orphanage, *Bes Yesoymin.*'

There were four basic preconditions for the orphanage's establishment, viz. money, a building, a matron to care for the orphans, and the orphans themselves. All were achieved in the short space of six months. Money was the most pressing requirement. The Jewish community of Cape Town and surrounding districts already had a well-established tradition of fundraising and a communal network comprising a numerous Hebrew congregations and charities. One hundred subscription lists were initially drawn up. The first lists were sent to Simonstown, Diep River, Hopefield and Port Elizabeth, indicative of the policy of the orphanage of catering for the whole of the Cape Province. Within a fortnight the first contribution of £8 17s 6d was received.*(2)* Yet notwithstanding institutional support and that of the wealthier patrons, it was noted at a meeting in May 1912 that the majority of the subscribers came from the poorer section of the community, proving how necessary this institution was to Cape Jewry at large. Anyone donating £50 or more was eligible to endow a bed that would bear a plaque bearing the donor's name. The beds, however, could only be endowed in the name of living people; the names of those deceased persons would be inscribed on a Memorial Board at the entrance.

The task of finding a suitable house was not easy. Committee President Joseph Kadish offered a house that he owned in Mill Street, but it did not have any grounds and with the shop attached could only accommodate between 12 and 14 children. A house in Hatfield Street belonging to the Cape Town Hebrew Congregation that could accommodate fifty orphans was initially favoured, but it was considered to be too central and the congregation was not agreeable. A certain Louis Elias, a member of the Grand Order of Israel, offered a plot 80' by 100' in Upper Mill Street. This offer, which was bound to the condition that the ground only be used for an orphanage, was finally abandoned. *(3)*

194

As no other houses were available, it was decided to use Kadish's Mill Street house from 11 December 1911. Renovations were immediately set in motion and the house was soon equipped by generous donations of linoleum, furniture, beds linen, toys, and books. The Orphanage was opened in February 1912 by Colonel David Harris. Colonel Harris, while being deeply sensitive to the compliment paid to him, "regretted that such an institution was not kept by the state" and that, as it was sectarian, it would only be supported by the Jewish community. Still he "hoped that they would receive outside support, as the Jew had always proved himself to be a reliever of human suffering." *(2)*

By June 1913, the house in Mill Street was running out of space. It was proposed that plans should be put forward for the erection of a building that could accommodate fifty orphans. Two plots were considered: the first was in Upper Mill Street that could be leased from the Cape Town Municipality at a nominal fee, and the second was in Montrose Avenue in Oranjezicht, that was far more expensive but could be bought outright. Reservations were expressed about the possible penetration of Coloreds into Upper Mill Street, as well as the possibility of the area becoming more industrial. It was decided that the Oranjezicht plot would be the better asset, and it was duly purchased. South Africa Governor General Lord Buxton laid the foundation stone of the new building. *(2)*

With the flu epidemic of 1918, an extension to the building was envisaged. The following year, it was reported that there was space for another three more boys and six more girls. In January 1920, a scheme was outlined to build on two extra wings that would each be able to accommodate thirty six children. In February 1921, just before the arrival of the Ukrainian orphans, it was reported that there were 51 children from 19 different families in the home.

Even before advertisements were put in the paper for applicants, the committee made sure to ascertain whether there were any Jewish orphans who were being kept at any of the Christian orphan asylums in the city, such as the St John's Home, Nazareth House or the All Saints Home. One Jewish girl was located at St Michaels Home. Rumours surfaced from time to time about Jewish children who were being kept by Malay or Colored families, but these did not always prove to be accurate.

A set of criteria for admission was devised. First and foremost, the child had to be halachically Jewish. Secondly, the child had to be an orphan. Before the arrival of the Ukraine orphans, there were relatively few cases of full orphans, with only one of the parents having passed away in most cases. Priority was given to a child who had lost both parents; next came the child with no father; and third in line was a child with no mother. The criterion that the child had to be an orphan was adhered to very strictly in the early years and a child whose parents were both alive was almost automatically rejected. This principle was upheld steadfastly until September 1920, when, because of the case of a young child from Port Elizabeth whose parents were alive but who were unable to care for her, it was first set aside, with the following proviso:

To make explicit the rule with regard to the admission of children to this orphanage, which shall include not only orphans

in the ordinary accepted meaning of that term, but also such distressed children whose parents are in such circumstances that they may be considered dead.

The threat of children becoming Christian was also an incentive for this principle to be waived. Four children in Kimberley, whose father had deserted their mother and who were being supported by the community in a Christian Home, were also admitted. On occasion, the reason for refusing to admit the children of separated parents was that this would be an inducement for them to remain separated. Another determining factor was a means test. If a parent had the means to support the child, it was unlikely to be accepted. In all cases, parents were required to contribute towards the child's upkeep according to their means. Grandparents and aunts and uncles were also exhorted to contribute.

It is interesting that there were no applications for the admission of children from unwed Jewish mothers during this period. However a newborn male baby, found abandoned in a basket at the Home in April 1933, could have been the exception to this rule. This anonymous child was unanimously declared to be Jewish, circumcised and given the name of 'Abraham', the first Jew in the Bible. ('Theodor Herzl', the first name suggested, was ultimately rejected). The baby was then put up for adoption by a Jewish couple.

It was initially resolved that no more than two children from a single family should be admitted. This criterion was put to the test in the case of the very first application received in December 1911, when only two of the four applicants were admitted, but was subsequently abandoned. The home also initially refused to accept children who were under five years of age, but this criterion too fell away. It was not until 1928, however, that the first set of infants were admitted - aged three and a half, two and a half, and six months - and a Nursery Department established. Besides a minimum age, a maximum age was also determined, fourteen years for boys and fifteen for girls. This could be extended if the boy or girl had not yet passed Standard Seven. In January 1925, the maximum age was increased to sixteen.

Admissions were on the whole restricted to the Cape Province. Children from elsewhere, such as the Orange Free State or Durban were refused, although children from Bulawayo and from Elizabethville in the Belgian Congo were accepted. On the other hand, three children from Beira in Mozambique were advised to apply to the SA Jewish Orphanage in Johannesburg. Children who were physically disabled or retarded were also excluded and their families were referred to the community charities. Very early on, it was laid down that the home was for poor and destitute orphans who were physically healthy.

The circumstances of the applications reflect the exigencies of the time. A particularly poignant case was that of a woman who had arrived from Russia only seven months before to join her husband, who was acting as a *shoykhet* in Sutherland, Western Cape. When he suddenly passed away, she was forced to apply to the Orphanage to admit her two sons aged six and seven. In another instance, a ten year old boy whose mother had died in Vilna was placed in the orphanage by his father, who was working as an ice cream vendor and could not look after him. Similarly another six year old, who had been deserted by his mother in Russia, was admitted because his father was working as a bus conductor.

The Ukrainian pogrom orphans

The number of orphans at the home was doubled with the arrival of the Ukrainian pogrom orphans. The first mention of them appears in the minutes of 8 August 1920, when Isaac Ochberg, by then President of the Orphanage, reported that due to the war and pogroms, there were about 300 000 Jewish orphans in the Ukraine and stated that it was imperative that some of these be brought out to South Africa. By the time that he approached the Committee, Ochberg had already made contact with Dr Jochelson of the Federation of Ukrainian Jews, who was willing to bring the orphans to London, and had obtained the permission of the Minister of the Interior, Patrick Duncan, to bring them into the country. Ochberg initially envisaged bringing some 50-100 orphans at a time. He saw the Orphanage as acting as a clearing house, putting the children up for adoption and keeping the remainder at the Orphanage. Looking back, it was an amazingly romantic and heroic scheme and one that reflects the character of its originator. Isaac Ochberg, himself an immigrant from the Ukraine, had become a very wealthy man in South Africa. He was totally committed and involved with the Orphanage, on one occasion describing it as being his "whole life".

It was suggested that £10 000 should be raised by the Cape Relief Fund and that a public appeal should be published in the press to adopt the orphans. The SA Jewish Orphanage was also approached to co-operate. The Committee sent out appeals for funds as well as to ascertain how many orphans would be adopted, so as to determine how many children to bring in the first batch. The public was asked to subscribe £25 000 towards the scheme and it was decided that Ochberg himself should travel to the Ukraine to fetch the children. By January 1921, fundraising tours to the country districts had raised over £15000. The Johannesburg Committee had in the meanwhile succeeded in convincing General Smuts to agree to contribute towards the fund on a pound for pound basis. Immediately on Ochberg's return in September, the campaign to raise £25 000 was set in motion.

Ochberg originally collected 233 orphans and brought them to the Temporary Shelter in Warsaw, but 37 ran away while others took ill so that it was impossible to take them to London. He finally departed for South Africa with 167 on the *Edinburgh Castle*, on which special accommodation for the orphans had been arranged. Various welcoming receptions were arranged in Cape Town including a Memorial and Thanksgiving Service in the synagogue. It had been agreed that the children be divided equally between Johannesburg and Cape Town, with seventy ultimately being sent to the former while the balance was accommodated at the Cape Jewish Orphanage. Ochberg also brought along a Mr and Mrs Maman to act as the new principal and matron respectively, a Mrs Zalkow to be an assistant doctor and a Miss Bettman to teach Hebrew. Fortunately, the incumbent matron had recently married and volunteered to retire.

At the 8th SA Zionist Conference in January 1922, it was proposed to bring out more orphans and to take some of them to Palestine. Although Ochberg had originally envisaged bringing 500 to 1000 orphans, in May 1922 a resolution to bring in more orphans from Eastern Europe was opposed in the light of the upheavals on the Rand and the resultant wave of antisemitism throughout the country. Instead, it was decided to establish a temporary home for a maximum of 100 Jewish pogrom war orphans in Eastern Europe, to be maintained by funds provided by the Cape Jewish Orphanage, until such time as would be suitable to bring them out to South Africa. A sum of not less than £3000 would be donated to the Orphans Fund in Europe.

Through the arrival of the Russian orphans in 1922, numbers at the Orphanage peaked at 100. At the institution's May 1922 AGM, it was reported that 44 of these were South Africans (21 boys and 23 girls) and 53 were Russians (20 boys and 33 girls). The question of the adoptions became urgent. Preference was to be given to couples who had no children and next to couples who had girls and wanted a boy, and vice versa. It was determined not to split families if possible. By November 1921, twelve of the orphans had been adopted, with the number rising to 21 by the following month. By 1931, numbers in the Home had dropped to 64. In the next two years, they increased slightly to 73 and 77, rising to 83 in September 1936 (39 boys and 44 girls).

The employment of a suitable matron proved to be the biggest problem in the very early years. Advertisements were inserted in the local papers as well as in London. While it was never specified, the matron had to be of the Jewish faith, hence the applications of several Christian ladies who responded were not entertained. She further had to be educated and able to maintain the home in a kosher manner.

Between January 1912 and April 1913, three different matrons served the home. Standards were strictly Victorian, and the first matron was dismissed after three months, having been found with a man in her room at 9.45 p.m. *(4)* The second stayed only for six months, leaving of her own accord to join her husband. The third, a Miss R. Davids, was a volunteer and a member of the committee, who stood in between matrons and proved to be extremely popular with the children. Finally, in January 1913, Miss Lily Berliner, who came highly recommended from London, was engaged. Except for a period from October 1914 to November 1915, she served the Orphanage continuously until June 1918. Generally, her service was considered exemplary other than a complaint of excessive punishment when she was accused of plastering the children's mouths! Her response was that this form of punishment was common in Europe, but if the Committee objected she would not do it again.

The administration of the Orphanage was completely changed with the arrival of the pogrom orphans and the employment of the Mamams, who had accompanied them from Warsaw. The Matron was replaced by a Principal, Mr. Maman, who would also supervise the Hebrew education and teach the boys for their barmitzvahs while his wife took charge of the domestic side of things. However, the couple did not prove that popular and when their contract expired at the end of 1926, it was not renewed. In March 1927, a Mr. and Mrs Beresinski were employed in their place. Mr. Beresinski had been the principal of a large orphanage in Israel, where his wife had been the Matron. He was also a competent Hebrew teacher and could replace the current incumbent, Mrs. Gordon.

The Beresinskis remained for eight years until 1935, when they resigned to return to Palestine. In October of that year, they were replaced by a young British couple, Mr. and Mrs. Hickman. They lasted for five months before being summarily dismissed in April 1936. It would seem that they were too rigid in applying the rules of the home, on one occasion leaving a widowed mother of six who arrived unexpectedly to visit her children, out in the grounds and in the corridor in a howling southeaster. Moreover Mr. Hickman was not a competent Hebrew teacher, a very important function that the former principal had carried out. *(5)* In May 1936, the Beresinskis re-applied for their former positions and were accepted unanimously.

Conditions at the Home

First and foremost, the Orphanage aimed to ensure that the children were brought up as observant Jews, and Jewish law was strictly enforced at all times. At the outset, a member of the community was engaged to make the Friday night *Kiddush*, and the Matron was instructed to take the children to the synagogue on Saturday mornings. A regular *minyan* was held at the home and it was laid down that "No boys other than those who are not necessary to make a *minyan* should be allowed to join any synagogue choir." The children were to attend Reverend Bender's Sabbath afternoon services at Gardens Synagogue. Passover *Seders* were conducted at the home; the Cape Town Jewish Philanthropic society donated such necessities as *matzos* and wine, and donations were received to buy the children new clothes. On the High Holidays, services were generally conducted at the Home. Barmitzvahs were celebrated in the local synagogues, followed by a tea at the Orphanage. In September 1936, a Consecration Service for girls was introduced. The children were not allowed to attend amusements on Shabbat and Festivals (a performance of the Yiddish operetta, *Shulamis*, by Goldfaden, at the Opera House in May 1925 was refused because it was scheduled for a '*yontef*'). On the very rare occasion when the children were invited out on a picnic, they were not permitted to go unless the food was kosher. Offers of domestic employment for orphan girls in homes that did not observe *kashrut* were not entertained.

To prevent parental interference, in January 1914 the Orphanage applied to the courts for power of guardianship over the children. Holidays presented a problem, with parents applying to take the children out for those occasions, and which was generally refused to avoid favoritism. On the other hand, Morris Alexander's offer to take two orphans to his home in Muizenberg on weekends was greatly appreciated. For very specific occasions, such as a child's birthday or a relative's barmitzvah, the parent was sometimes allowed to take his/her child out. Considerable problems were experienced with parents coming to visit their children at all times, and in October 1914 it was declared that visiting hours would be displayed on a plaque on the door and would also appear on all stationery.

Life was Spartan for the children. Clothes were made from blue serge, but an offer of second hand boots was refused on the grounds that the children were only to wear new clothes. A crisis occurred when one of the girls was allowed to spend a month with a family in Ceres. Apparently, on her return she refused to dress the same or have her meals in common with the other children. However, within a month she seems to have relented. In September 1925, it was resolved by fourteen votes to eight that no scrubbing was to be done by the children! In June 1929, for the first time provision was made for the children to acquire dressing gowns and slippers. It was also resolved at that time that either the Matron or the Principal were to be present at all meal times, and that once a month a lady investigator should arrive unannounced to a meal and to inspect the kitchen. *(6)*

Entertainments and treats were few and far between. In June 1912, the children were taken to a matinee at the Tivoli, but it is not until December 1914 that we hear of another such outing. In that year, the children were taken to the circus, the Sea Point Pavilion and Hout Bay. Annual outings to Stellenbosch were organised by the Stellenbosch Young Israel society, and once a year the children were invited to a picnic at the Balmoral Hotel in Muizenberg.

Entertainments and lectures were also held on occasion at the Orphanage on Saturday nights. However, these could not have been too well patronized as the children were specifically exhorted to attend them. In 1925, it was decided to hold a holiday camp, either at Hout Bay or Kommetjie. Muizenberg was very specifically excluded. Later, extremely successful holiday camps were organized at the Strand during the Christmas break. In 1937, the camp moved to Muizenberg.

Education

The first children were sent to the Hope Mill School at the top of Government Avenue. By 1911 Hope Mill, the original Hebrew Public School, had become a government school, and the School Board agreed to provide the children with free education. Three years later, however, the children were transferred to the West End Public School as it was closer to the Orphanage. In the earliest years, the children's education generally ended at Std 6, the end of elementary school in those days. The writer found only one case before 1915, where a young girl was considered worthy of being transferred to Good Hope Seminary to study beyond Std 7. Discussion was initiated in September 1915 over having the older girls attend Higher Grade Schools. In June 1922 a teacher of dressmaking was engaged for the girls. In later years extra-murals were even provided for the children: in 1933 15 children (13 girls and 2 boys) were taking piano lessons, while elocution, physical culture, Scouts, and Girl Guides were also provided.

The children's Jewish and Hebrew education was regarded as crucial. In the words of the famous Yiddish playwright and traveler Peretz Hirschbein, who visited the home together with his wife in May 1921, the importance of this could not be over emphasized. In the beginning, Hebrew classes were provided by volunteer teachers until, in response to complaints by Rabbi Mirvish as to the poor standard of the children's Hebrew, it was decided that those over nine years old should be sent to the Talmud Torah. Two in-house Hebrew teachers were employed for the younger children, and Mark Cohen, principal of the Hope Mill School, was engaged to teach the senior boys. In January 1939, it was recorded that the children were studying Hebrew for five and a quarter hours a week. Older children who joined late with little or no Hebrew education studied longer hours. Although it was claimed that children in private homes attended Hebrew lessons 8-10 hours a week, the Orphanage children, also attended *shul* twice a day. In July 1939, it was suggested that due to the disparity of knowledge of the seventy children learning Hebrew, a third teacher should be employed.

The first hurdle for the pogrom orphans was to learn English. As recorded in the minutes, they were initially sent to Normal College for this purpose. However, this did not prove to be sufficient and a special English teacher was employed at the Home. The senior girls, who were working in the morning, studied English in the evening, and an English teacher was also hired for the adults. Extra teachers were employed to teach Hebrew. Unfortunately, between 1922 and 1925 there is a gap in the minute books, so it is not known exactly how the Russian orphans settled down in their very first years in South Africa.

The boys were sent to the Hope Lodge School and the girls to the Central Girls School, where there was provision for thirty percent of the pupils to be educated free of charge. Over the years, a running battle developed between Rosa van Gelderen, the Jewish principal of the Central Girls' School and a progressive educationalist, and the Principal, Mr Beresinski. In October 1932, when it was decided to transfer the girls to the Tamboerskloof school, it was only through the intervention of Reverend Bender and Morris Alexander that a compromise was reached, and they were allowed to stay on. The last straw came in July 1933, *(7)* when it was finally decided to transfer the children to the Tamboerskloof School at the beginning of 1934. *(8)*

After-Care Committee

The future prospects of the orphans presented the biggest problem. Their lack of academic prowess made this extremely difficult. Very few managed to pass the Junior Certificate. A list of eleven senior boys aged between fourteen and seventeen, compiled in 1929, reveals that three had passed Standard 5, four Standard 6, one Standard 7 and two JC. Of four girls, three (15, 16 and 17), had passed Std 6, and one (16) had passed JC. In only two cases - in 1926 and 1927 - were two children allowed to stay on at the Orphanage so that they could obtain a matric. Both were girls. In the 1930s, the situation improved slightly. More girls went to Underwood and did Shorthand and Typing, but only one completed her matric. In 1938 it was recorded that no child should leave the home without a JC at least. Between 1912 and 1939, only one boy was sent to university. He did the four year teaching course, T1, as he was considered not "mentally or physically fit to stand behind a counter".

Not long before the arrival of the Ukrainian orphans, in December 1919, Ochberg established an After-Care Committee to oversee the orphans from the time they left the Home until they were able to earn a living. This Committee was to act as guardians of the children until the age of 21. It succeeded the Education and Vocational committee, established in August 1916 and which had secured apprenticeships for boys with jewellers, electricians, dentists and farmers; and for girls with dressmakers, milliners and hairdressers. Ochberg recognized this as the most crucial time, when the Orphanage needed to provide supervision, maintenance, and education. According to the rules, the children had to leave the Orphanage at age fourteen for boys and fifteen for girls, when on average they had only passed Standard Six, did not have a trade, and were at their most vulnerable. In January 1925, the age of leaving the Orphanage was increased to sixteen.

Two senior girls were on different occasions appointed as assistant to the Matron at a nominal salary. One of them subsequently joined the permanent staff. Other options that were entertained were to send the orphans to Palestine. However the children were not keen. It was proposed to establish a Technical and Industrial School, or to create a farm settlement where the children could learn some type of trade or work on the land. This idea later merged with that of the Chalutz training scheme of the Zionist Youth movements, that aimed to send young people to Palestine, as it was believed that "to train poor lads as farmers for this country was creating more Poor Whites." Once the children were working, they were boarded out. It was generally felt that on apprenticeship to a trade or a business, the employer, was obliged to provide the children with a home. In December 1926, a hostel was established for the girls with Miss Berliner, the former Orphanage Matron, as the Hostel Matron.

In 1930, a special memorandum was drawn up regarding the unsatisfactory methods of finding work for the boys and especially for the girls. It was reported that the girls tended to be employed in bazaars where the work was heavy and often irksome, the pay small, the general influence bad and the prospect of eventual independence virtually nil. The boys were 'pitch-forked' into whatever could be found, with little consideration of suitability, future prospects or influence on their characters. Once a billet and a home had been found, no more interest was paid to the children, provided that they held their jobs. It was resolved to adopt a method that had been in vogue for many years in London: that each member of the Sub-Committee choose an individual child for whom he would act as guardian, helping him/her to find a suitable job and receive follow up reports from his employer. However, nothing was done as in December this resolution was reiterated. For girls, the best prospects often lay in marriage. A bequest to the home by A S Nathan provided a Fund to supply the girls with dowries of £20 each. By 1930, at least five of the girls were married. Most of the pogrom orphan girls as well as the local girls married.

When Isaac Ochberg passed away in December 1937, he left a bequest to the Orphanage of £1000 and a Fund for Higher Education of £10 000. Although it was initially hoped that this bequest could assist one of the Orphanage boys to become a

Isaac Ochberg and the Children at the Cape Jewish Orphanage (later called Oranjia) – 1922

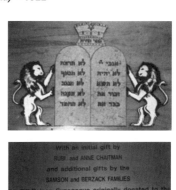

The Entrance to Oranjia   **The entrance to Oranjia and the Oranjia Shul relocated at the Sea Point Shul**

The Oranjia Shul relocated at the Sea Point Shul - Photos sent in by Peter Larsen

candidate for the Rabbinate, it was more realistically decided that it should be used for the purchase of High School and Hebrew books, to pay for extra tuition, and towards the board and lodging for children who were continuing their education.

Conclusion

Isaac Ochberg was responsible for one of the most successful undertakings of South African Jewry: the rescue of the children from the Ukraine. This venture showed the community at its best. It was never replicated. Various schemes to rescue children from Nazi Germany and from Nazi Occupied Europe were entertained, but none of them came to fruition. In July 1936, the admission of fifty German Jewish children of no older than ten years was contemplated. In June 1938, a proposal to bring 25 children, between the ages of six and ten, from Austria, was dismissed by the SA Jewish Board of Deputies "owing to likely legal and public reaction." In May 1940, the possibility of saving fifty orphan Dutch Jewish children, between the ages of two and twelve, was entertained, but never materialized.

Besides rescuing the Ukrainian orphans, the Cape Jewish Orphanage played an indispensable role in the years between 1912 and 1939, helping destitute immigrant families and ensuring that their children remained Jewish. The lack of educational attainment of the children is attributable to the standards at that time and to the children's disadvantaged backgrounds. In the case of the Ukrainian orphans, they also had to overcome earlier traumas, learn a new language and adapt to a foreign land. The Orphanage might not always have been the warmest place, akin to a real family, but what was never lacking was a sense of responsibility and identification with the children, as being among their own, as *eygene*, as members of the Jewish community, who would under no circumstances be abandoned even after they had left the Home. To quote from the Minutes: "our children were not treated as orphans but were happy in their home." All in all the children were, "no worse and no better than the average child in decent homes."

The war years proved to be a watershed for the Orphanage, as it was for the community. The immigrants began to prosper, becoming more established in their new homes. The Orphanage became less and less of a home for orphaned children than a place of refuge for children from broken families. In due course, it became better known as the Oranjia Jewish children's home than as the Cape Jewish Orphanage. Today, its official title is the Oranjia Jewish Child and Youth Centre.

NOTES

Most of the information above has been extracted from the Minutes of Oranjia, Cape Jewish Orphanage, BC 918, Manuscripts and Archives, U.C.T. Libraries.

(2) Eric Rosenthal, The Story of the Cape Jewish Orphanage: Commemorating the Fiftieth Anniversary of Oranjia, Cape Town: Oranjia, Cape Jewish Orphanage, 1961.

(3) It seems as if Elias regretted his initial offer as he progressively increased his stipulations, and finally under the apparent influence of a Johannesburg committee member, even seems to have questioned the need for an orphanage in Cape Town. Minutes, 3 January 1912.

(4) She was also accused of sending the children out on messages, and not reporting a robbery that had been committed at the orphanage to the committee. When asked to resign she had put her case in the hands of solicitors. Minutes, 27 March 1912.

(5) When in April 1936, three boys who were due to celebrate their barmitzvahs were found to be so unprepared that their barmitzvahs had to be postponed, it was unanimously decided to dismiss the Hickmans. Minutes, 27 April 1936.

(6) A grocery investigation later that year revealed that only 14lbs of meat a day was being consumed for 72 people, that was considered to be grossly insufficient, 14 November, 1929.

(7) Despite the girls' poor reports, Van Gelderen, who did not believe in homework, absolutely refused to abide by the request to provide the girls with extra arithmetic homework. Minutes, 25 July 1933.

(8) Rosa Van Gelderen's educational experiments were very progressive and worked extremely well with the children from more advantaged backgrounds, however, they were not always suited to children from deprived backgrounds such as those at the Orphanage. The Orphanage After-School program devoted considerable time to supervised homework, which she refused to support, but which might have been advantageous to the children. Minutes, 28 June, 30 August, 27 September 1932.

Chapter 42 – THE RABINOWITZ SISTERS AND THE CAPE JEWISH ORPHANAGE (1918-1926)

THE RABINOWITZ SISTERS
AND THE CAPE JEWISH ORPHANAGE
Written by Ron Lapid, Ra'anana, Israel June 2009

The grandfather that I never knew, Benjamin Rabinowitz, died at the age of 40 in the small town of Calvinia in the Cape Province in October 1918. He was one of the estimated 20-40 million victims across the world that died in the horrific flu epidemic at the end of the First World War. In South Africa alone, 130,000 people died, the majority in the Cape.

Benjamin had arrived in South Africa from Poneveyz, Lithuania about 1898. A few years later (we have never discovered exactly when), he married Bessie Neimark who had come from Vilnius, Lithuania.

Benjamin and Bessie Rabinowitz 1908

Nancy a few months old 1914

Fanny, Nancy and Tilly 1922

Between time spent eking out a living in Johannesburg, Queenstown, Cape Town and then Calvinia, the couple had five daughters. When Benjamin died, Bessie was about 35. The eldest daughter, Yettie was nearly 12, Rachel ten, Fanny eight, Tilly six and Nancy four.

Bessie's plan of survival was to join her younger brother Abe Neimark, a barber in Johannesburg, with Yettie and Rachel, and put the three youngest girls into the Jewish Orphanage in Cape Town. And so that is where they spent the next eight years!

At the end of 1926, Bessie requested to get the three daughters back, and the subject was raised and approved by the Board of the Orphanage. See the letter below which Isaac Ochberg wrote, updating Bessie of the decision, but imploring her to leave Fanny at the Orphanage for another year so that she could complete her Matric.

The letter is very emotional, and reflects most positively on the wonderful person that Isaac Ochberg so obviously was.

1920 Group photo of the children at the Cape Jewish Orphanage (over two pages)

This photo was sent in by Ron Lapid who writes,
"A group photo that was sent as a postcard to the family. It is date marked 10th September 1920.
The girl in front who has been circled is my mother Nancy. The girl second from the left in the middle row is Fanny, and Tilly is on the right hand side of the same row."
Isaac Ochberg sits in the middle holding a little girl

Message on the bottom of the card

With Compliments from the President and Committee of the Cape Jewish Orphanage.
May the Divine Father of the Orphans grant your Heart's desires for the coming Holy Festivals and may you lend a sympathetic ear to the appeal of the Orphans in our midst as well as the heartrending cry of the helpless little ones in the Pogrom Areas of Eastern Europe for whom we are making ourselves responsible, by donating liberally during the New Year and Day of Atonement for the upkeep of those who are parentless, homeless and helpless.

1920 Group photo of the children at the Cape Jewish Orphanage (over two pages)

The reverse side of the group photo
It is date marked 10th September 1920 and the stamp says "Paid 1/2 penny".

LETTER WRITTEN BY ISAAC OCHBERG TO BESSIE RABINOWITZ

ESTABLISHED 1895

ISAAC OCHBERG

P O BOX 1305
TELEGRAMS: OCHBERGCO
CABLES: OCHBERG
TELEPHONE: CENTRAL 72

CODES:
A B C 5TH EDITION.
BENTLEY'S PHRASE.
WATKINS. PRIVATE.

COMMISSIONER OF OATHS

OCHBERGS BUILDINGS
ADDERLEY STREET
CAPE TOWN

7th December,1926.

Mrs. B. Rabinowitz,
16 Nind Street,
DOORNFONTEIN.
Johannesburg.

Dear Mrs. Rabinowitz,

At the last Committee Meeting of the Cape Jewish Orphanage, your application for taking your children away came forward and it was decided to send them to you and also to pay their fares. In a way I was glad because of the fact that the children will be happy with you and no doubt you will be happy with them.

I congratulate you on these three children of yours as they are children that any mother can be very proud of. I probably love them more than any other children in the Home, though I have naturally never shown it to them, as one does not want to establish any jealousy amongst children. Fanny is an exceptionally brilliant child, also Tilly is a very nice child indeed and as far as Nancy is concerned, I think she is the sweetest child one can come across. I am sure I will miss them very much when they are gone.

My object however, of writing you today is with regards to Fanny. I may frankly tell you that I strongly suggested to the Meeting that we should urge upon you to leave Fanny at the Orphanage for another year so that she can take her matric for certain, on which I was opposed by some members. I forced the matter to a vote and only lost my proposal by one vote. I feel absolutely worried to think that there may be a possibility of Fanny not continuing with her education. The Almighty has gifted her with a wonderful brain, which possibly one out of thousands have. She has been our brightest child in the Orphanage, as far as education goes, for years and now that it has been decided that the child should be returned to you, you will forgive me if I take the liberty to urge upon you in the very strongest words one can that you should let Fanny continue with her education until at least she takes her matric in the hopes that she may then get a Bursary and continue her education further.

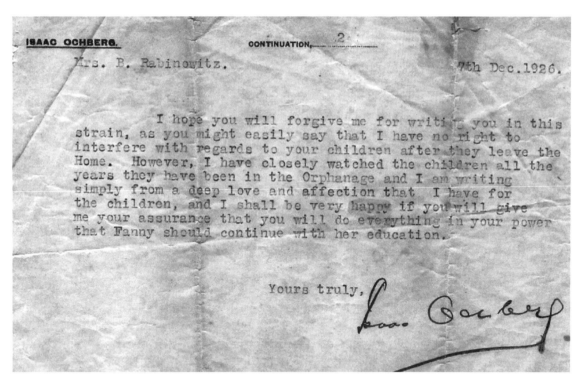

ISAAC OCHBERG.   CONTINUATION,........2........

Mrs. B. Rabinowitz.   7th Dec.1926.

I hope you will forgive me for writing you in this
strain, as you might easily say that I have no right to
interfere with regards to your children after they leave the
Home. However, I have closely watched the children all the
years they have been in the Orphanage and I am writing
simply from a deep love and affection that I have for
the children, and I shall be very happy if you will give
me your assurance that you will do everything in your power
that Fanny should continue with her education.

Yours truly,

"This afternoon I was at Kibbutz Tzora, where I was formerly a member, and was chatting to Zvi Herr. We were looking at the Arcadia MORE ARC MEMORIES book and he mentioned Isaac Ochberg.
I told him that I had a letter that Isaac wrote in 1926, and Zvi told me that he was sure you would be interested to see it. So here it is!
The Nancy Rabinowitz mentioned there was my mother, and Fanny and Tilly were my aunts. My mother lived to nearly 92 and passed away only three years ago." Written by Ron Lapid   7 June 2009

Ron continues:
Fanny, Tilly and Nancy all moved to Johannesburg to join their mother and Uncle Abe.

FANNY

The dire economic situation in the family did not allow Bessie the luxury of letting Fanny carry on at school, and Fanny went straight out to work to help support the family. She never did her Matric. She resented this to her very last day, and it was she who kept the letter written by Isaac Ochberg.

Fanny worked in the book keeping department at the SA Zionist Federation for several decades.

She developed into an outstanding sports woman. In 1948 she became the South African Table Tennis Champion. She also played tennis and was an avid adventure hiker.

She remained single till the age of 48, when she married Barry Martin.

On retiring in the mid seventies, they moved to Israel and lived in Ra'anana. Fanny carried on working till well into her eighties and played tennis almost till then. She died in 1999, aged 89.

Fanny, Max holding Ron and Nancy

205

TILLY

Tilly Rabinowitz Nurse – North Africa WW2

Tilly married Bill Koen-Cohen and they had two children - Ivor who lives in Atlanta, Georgia, and Reina who passed away in Cape Town in 2007. Reina and I were both named after our aunt Rachel who passed away in her twenties. Tilly passed away in Johannesburg in 1984 after a long illness very bravely endured.

Ivor and Tilly holding Reina

NANCY

Nancy and Max Lipschitz wedding 15 June 1941

In June 1941 Nancy married Max Lipschitz and they became my parents and of my younger brother Arthur. I was born 'Ray Lipschitz' and shortly after moving to Israel in 1966. I took out the Hebrew name 'Ron Lapid' ('Lapid' means "torch" like the Olympic Torch.)

Max was born in Johannesburg in 1908. Both his parents, Leon Lipschitz and Gruna Reuvid, grew up in Shavel in Lithuania. They immigrated independently to South Africa around 1900, and married in Johannesburg in 1907. Max spent 50 years of his working life at Sive Bros & Karnovsky (later to become South African Druggists Ltd.). As many of his generation, he was a keen sportsman. This included running. One of his more unusual feats was to take part in a "Gold Run". On behalf of a would-be investor he raced with four pegs and a hammer in his hands from a starting point to an area where he staked out a plot that the investor would buy. He got paid for the running, but unfortunately had no part in any gold which may have lain under the area he staked out.

Like her sister Fanny, Nancy also worked for many years at the Zionist Fed in Johannesburg. Even after retiring from there and moving to Israel in 1977, she carried on working as a book keeper till the age of 85. We used to think that she was embarrassed to stop working while her older sister Fanny was still on the job! Nancy passed away in 2005 well into her ninety second year. She remained in pretty good health almost till her death. In fact she was still playing bridge till a couple of months before the end.

My brother Arthur and I both live in Ra'anana. I moved to Israel in 1966 with my young wife Riwa Durbach. Unbeknown to her, she had several cousins who spent many years in Arcadia. We were six years on Kibbutz Tzora and then moved to Ra'anana. We have four married children and nine grandchildren all living within a 30 minute drive of us. We do count our blessings!

Arthur came on Aliyah in 1978. He has three daughters and four grandchildren.

Arthur, Nancy and Ron 2004

I never heard the sisters talk of their experiences in the Orphanage, and now regret that I did not have the foresight to directly ask them about it. I do not even know if they visited their mother during these eight years. What is for sure is that all three developed into survivors, into determined women who would doggedly carry on no matter what obstacles were placed in front of them. None of them ever took material comforts for granted and appreciated what ever they had. I am sure that all these traits were sharpened and strengthened by their eight years of childhood spent in the Orphanage.

Nancy surrounded by some of her offspring 2004

EULOGY OF NANCY LIPSCHITZ
29/03/1914 - 27/10/2005.
By Ron Lapid

When I think of you Mom, I don't think of the very last, very short but very difficult period.

I think of the photo of the baby born in Calvinia before the outbreak of the First World War - a baby who over nearly a century watched the world change in almost every aspect.

I think of the four year old losing her father and then spending several years in the Cape Town orphanage. That is probably where you honed your survivor instincts and your appreciation of the little things of life.

I think of the photograph of you water skiing when that was not a common activity for women.
I think of the photo of you balancing precariously on an overhanging rock above a ravine.
I think of you getting your driver's licence when roads were not tarred.
All this was before my personal memory.

Then I think of you in your longstanding marriage with your beloved husband and our father Max.
I think of you, my mother, as the only female travelling salesman I ever knew,
I think of you playing tennis for many years and only giving it up when bowls became and remained a passion in your life for decades.

I think of you always busy and intense to the end with everything you did.
I think of your 25 years at the Zionist Fed in Johannesburg, and then your aliyah at age 63.
But even in Israel at retirement age you never slowed down.
You carried on driving a car into your eighties and only stopped because the car gave in before you.
You carried on working till the age of 85, and only retired because the business got sold.
And always - bowls, and bridge, bridge and bowls.

Your little family expanded rapidly from two sons to two sons and two daughters in law and 13 grandchildren with their spouses and 10 great grandchildren- almost a tribe, with you as the matriarch.

When Kipling wrote asking perhaps doubting that it could be done "If you can fill the unforgiving minute with sixty seconds worth of distance run." he obviously did not know you.

Because Mom, your life was even fuller than that- you lived every minute of every hour, of every week, of every month, of nearly 92 years.

But now the race is over and the distance has been run.

May you rest in peace.

Ron Lapid.

THE CAPE JEWISH ORPHANAGE
REPORT AND BALANCE SHEET
For the period ending 30 April 1920

Office Bearers (1919-1920)
President: Isaac Ochberg, Esq
Vice President: J Kadish, Esq
Hon Treasurer: J B Shacksnovis, Esq
Chairlady: Mrs H Stodel
Vice Chairlady: Mrs A Leve
Hon Treasurer (Clothing Guild): Mrs Henry Harris

COMMITTEE:

Mr O Basson	Mr H Harris
Mr C Baker	Mr H Kadish
Mr A Benson	Mr M Lentin
Mr A Friedlander	Mr I Mauerberger
Mr J Frank	Mr L Raphaely
Mr S Goldstein	Mr S Sachs
Mr E Goldsmith	Mr D Shargey
Mr L Gradner	Mr R Weingerg

LADIES' GENERAL AND HOUSE COMMITTEE

Mrs I Barnett	Mrs A Silbert
Miss L Blumeneau	Mrs L Schrire
Mrs N Friedlander	Mrs J B Shacksnovis
Mrs B Hill	Mrs W Stern
Mrs B Jacobs	Mrs T Velenski
Mrs M Lentin	Mrs R Weinberg
Mrs I Ochberg	

TRUSTEES:

Mr Adv M Alexander, KC, MLA	R Herman Esq

DELEGATES:

Mr W Satusky: Woodstock & Salt River Hebrew Cong.
Mr N Emdin: Muizenberg & Kalk Bay Hebrew Cong.
Mr M Wisnekowitz: Paarl Hebrew Congregation
Mr S Marcus: Stellenbosh Hebrew Congregation
Mr L Goldberg: Worcester Hebrew Congregation
Mr L Rosenzweig: Robertson Hebrew Congregation

HON OFFICERS:

Ise Levy Esq	*Hon Auditor*
Messrs C & A Friedlander	*Hon Solicitors*
Dr S E Kark	*Hon Medical Adviser*
S Sachs Esq	*Hon Chemist*
S Koonin Esq	*Hon Dentist*
Messrs Winer & Baigel	*Hon Hairdressers*

STAFF:

Mr Mrs D Levin	*Matron*
Miss R Cohen	*Assistant Matron*
Miss R Tieger	*Secretary*
Mr Sandrusier	*Authorised Collector*

REPORT OF THE CAPE JEWISH ORPHANAGE

Ladies and Gentlemen

After the full and comprehensive report submitted by your Executive to the general body of members on the 28th December, 1920, your General Committee decided, in order to save expense, to publish for submission a short report only, together with the necessary financial statement up to the end of April, 1920 at the forthcoming General Meeting. As to the general working of the Home, we have to report that all members of the staff fulfilled their duties to the entire satisfaction of the Management. The health of the children has been everything that can be desired; the educational progress of the children has been favourably commented upon by all who have had the pleasure of noticing the splendid progress they have made both in secular and religious instruction and we can say with confidence that the good name already established by the Cape Jewish Orphanage has been very much enhanced, not only in the Province of the Cape but throughout the whole of South Africa. It is therefore with feelings of pride and pleasure that we have to report these pleasant facts in the hope that all members, donors and sympathisers will experience satisfaction in the thought that they have been the means of the Holy work being carried out successfully and that they will also in the future endeavour by every possible means to strengthen and support our Institution which may be termed the premier charity of the Cape Province.

The number of children in the Home at present is 52.

The Board of Management here wish to place on record their heartiest thanks to all the Honorary Officers for the valuable services they are rendering to the Home.

The most important and outstanding matter we have pleasure to record, is the decision of your Committee and the General Body of Members to bring from the Pogrom Areas in Eastern Europe a number of orphaned children and provide accommodation for some of them in our Home and for others to obtain a Home for them with some private members of the Community. After the appalling trials experienced by the Jewish population in common with their non-Jewish fellow countrymen during the World War, in which they bore more than their part of sacrifice and sorrow and of hopes for a happier future, however an even more terrible storm burst upon them in the shape of a new war – a war of extermination exclusively against them – a war of Pogroms. During the past two years the most thickly populated centres of Jewish life in Eastern Europe have been swept by an endless succession of these terrible pogroms, and as a result, official reports state that many Jewish Communities in the Pogrom Areas have been entirely wiped out.

Most terrible disasters and cruelties were inflicted, and the agonies and sufferings of our Nation in the terrible Pogrom areas are not paralleled in the two thousand years history of our people. The inhuman hordes, with no other thought but to kill, dishonour and exterminate the Jewish Communities, have destroyed Jewish homes and maltreated and murdered their peaceable and innocent inmates with a fury and beastiality which defy description. Everywhere men and women, the old and the young, the aged, infirm and the helpless were outraged, burnt and buried alive; every Jewish house either a ruin or a wailing place. One of the results of these terrible happenings has been that over 400 000 children are left parentless, homeless, naked and hungry, wandering in the woods, and forests and streets of Eastern Europe. Never in the history of the Jewish Nation has the Pogrom Monster inflicted such terrible atrocities. What torrents of blood and rivers of tears has he made to flow! How many victims has he deprived of life? It is with this spectacle before us that we, as an Institution for Jewish orphans, decided on the holy task of saving at least a few of the many thousands of Jewish children from what may be rightly described as a 'Hell on Earth'. What greater charity is there than to save human life, and more particularly so when the saving of such human life means the saving of innocent, helpless, hungry and starving children? Your President and Treasurer decided to bring home to the Jews of South Africa the duty they owe to their Nation, by making a strenuous effort to gather together £50 000 to assist in carrying out the noble work of saving some of the Jewish orphans in the Pogrom Areas of Eastern Europe. A tour was arranged and the following itinerary was duly completed:- Bloemfontein, Bredasdorp, Brandfort, Caledon, Claremont, East London, Hermanus, Kroonstad, Maitland, Malmesbury, Muizenberg, Oudtshoorn, Observatory, Paarl, Port Elizabeth, Simonstown, Stellenbosh, The Strand, Woodstock and Wynberg. As a result of this tour a magnificent sum was promised.

One thing your President and Treasurer can say, that they found the Jewish hearts most responsive to the appeal for this particular charity and wherever they addressed meetings they were received with true national enthusiasm and the response which followed was one which you would rightly expect from the 'Rachmonim bnei Rachmonim'. The only regret that has to be recorded is that owing to certain circumstances the tour undertaken by your President and Treasurer could not be completed, and as a consequence many important centres which should have been visited were omitted; but there is every hope that in the near future these places too will receive a visit, and we trust that the appeals there will be as successful as in the other centres. So much has been completed. Now as to the future – we earnestly appeal to every Jewish man and woman in South Africa who has not yet been approached for a contribution towards the Fund to save poor innocent Jewish Orphans to answer the heart-rending cry of these little ones in Eastern Europe. If each and every Jew would approach the subject from a personal point of view, and look upon this matter as if their own little children were homeless and helpless amidst a band of ruffians and human beasts and then ask themselves the question what would be their duty towards these helpless little ones. Once we are able to realise the terrible agonies of these hungry and naked children roaming about in thousands without a glimmer of hope in their innocent little lives we shall then out of sheer gratitude to God who has preserved us for our children, decide that not only must we give in the ordinary way, but we must make the great sacrifice which the Father of Orphans demands from us. In this way, and in this way only

can we justify our Judaism and display the true Maccabean spirit which has been the means of keeping our Nation alive during the last two thousand years of massacres, persecutions, and hopeless and helpless wanderings. Realising this, we again and again earnestly appeal to the Jewish hearts of South Africa and feel confident that a liberal response will be made to the heartrending cry of these poor orphans, and that unstinted support will be given to the Management of the Orphanage to carry out in full the noble task they have set themselves. Yes, even today a cry of panic and distress reaches us from large tracts of the Ukraine and other Pogrom areas, and it is our bounden duty to answer that cry in a practical manner. We specially appeal to all our Jewish men and women in South Africa to do all in their power to make the adoption scheme a complete success by taking one or more children into their private homes or elsewhere. In this way, and in this way only, will it be possible to save thousands of these poor little orphans. The Management will be pleased to receive applications for adoption as soon as possible, so as to give our President an indication as to the number of orphans that will be absorbed under the adoption scheme.

As a preliminary we have already started to build a suitable Home to accommodate the poor orphans on their arrival in Cape Town. Our many subscribers, donors and sympathisers will be gratified to learn that your President Mr Isaac Ochberg offered to the General Committee to go to Europe at his own expense to bring the first batch of these children; your Committee accepted your President's offer, and he has already booked to leave early in March for Europe. We wish him Godspeed on his mission of mercy, and may the Almighty bless and protect him and bring him and the orphans safely back to us. Further you will realise the enormous task of transporting about 100 orphans from Eastern Europe to South Africa over continents and oceans. All this needs *money* and the Jews of South Africa will appreciate that during the next 12 months or two years they must strain their hearts and nerves and sinews and make every endeavour to rescue as many of these orphans as possible and to make necessary provision for them, so that they will receive the care and protection they so richly deserve.

Finally, we feel it our duty to make special reference to extracts from correspondence that has passed between your President and Dr Jochelman, President of the Federation of Ukrainian Jews, London, in connection with the Pogrom orphan scheme.

The thanks of the Jewish Community are due to the Government of the Union of South Africa for their response in giving us permission to bring as many Pogrom orphans as we may desire to this country. We feel certain that this concession given by the Government to the Jews will rebound to the credit of the Government of South Africa for in after years they will find that these poor homeless and helpless little boys and girls will rank among the best citizens in South Africa.

The 'Cape Times and 'Argus' deserve our best thanks for granting us advertising space free of charge in their valuable papers, and we feel that the Management of these papers have, by their liberal response to the cause of the orphans, accomplished a very good and noble work. In mentioning the above papers we must not fail to thank the 'Zionist Record' for the assistance given us by way of free advertisements in connection with the Pogrom Orphan Appeal.

In the preparation of the advertising notices your Committee received valuable assistance from Messrs C J Sibbet, Wm Redford, H F Grapes and C Sims, and to these gentlemen we tender our sincerest thanks for the valuable honorary work they rendered to the cause. Likewise are our thanks due to the African Theatres Trust for displaying slides on their screens in their places of amusements free of charge.

As the work of our Home is rapidly increasing from day to day the Committee trusts that many willing helpers in the Community will come forward and assist in the noble task of ministering to the wants of those who are entitled to our care, affection and protection.

FOR THE BOARD OF MANAGEMENT
ISAAC OCHBERG (President)
J KADISH (Vice President)
J B SHACKSNOVIS (Hon Treasurer)

Extract of letter from Mr Isaac Ochberg, Cape Town to Dr D Jochelman, London

Dr D Jochelman
26a Soho Square
London W 1

Dear Sir

From the 'Jewish Chronicle" I notice 4d that you are Chairman of a Committee formed to collect funds in aid of War and Pogrom sufferers in the Ukraine, and I therefore take the liberty of addressing you.

It is stated that in many towns in the Ukraine there are hundreds of Jewish children left orphans, whose parents have been murdered during the Pogroms. I do not think that the assistance of money alone can give the help required for these unfortunate children, as I presume they have practically no one to look after them.

South Africa has been living through some fairly prosperous times during the last few years and the feelings here amongst the Jewish Community are very sympathetic towards the unfortunate members of our nation who have recently suffered from Pogroms etc in the Ukraine and elsewhere, and I feel that, if necessary, the sympathy of our Jewish people out here could be enlisted to support a scheme which would enable us to bring to this country a number of Jewish orphans, say between 200-300, who would receive here proper support and education, etc that would be necessary to bring them up to be good Jews and citizens, and I should be glad to hear from you on the subject so that I could put the matter more fully before the leading members of our Community.

Yours truly

(Signed) ISAAC OCHBERG

Extract of letter from Mr A M KAIZER, Secretary of the Federation of the Ukrainian Jews to Mr Isaac Ochberg

Isaac Ochberg, Esq   30 June 1920
Cape Town

Dear Sir

Dr D Jochelman has handed me your letter of the 11th inst addressed to him, receipt of which I beg to acknowledge.

The proposition made by you regarding the Jewish orphans of the Pogrom sufferers is received by my Committee with great satisfaction, and Dr Jochelman himself thinks that this is just the kind of work most needed at the present time.

He considers it would be a great thing in itself to take 200-300 Jewish children from the Ukraine to South Africa, but that the main point is that such a proposition, if carried out, will give an impulse to relief work amongst the larger Jewish communities on the other side of the Atlantic, possibly resulting in their bringing over thousands of Jewish orphans. The plan indicated by you will receive the full support of my Committee.

Yours faithfully

(Signed) A M KAIZER

Extract of letter from S Goldenberg Esq, Hon Sec Federation of Ukrainian Jews, to Mr Isaac Ochberg

Isaac Ochberg Ewq   27 November 1920
President Cape Jewish Orphanage

It will certainly be a splendid piece of constructive work if finally South African Jewry will have brought out, two thousand children and be responsible for their upbringing.

We note the various conditions you make with reference to the age and health and sexes of the children, who are to go to South Africa, and of course these instructions will be carefully studied when the time arrives for their consideration.

(Signed) S GOLDENBERG

Hon Secretary

Chapter 44 – THE BERESINSKIS - MATRON AND PRINCIPAL

CHLAVNE AND DORA BERESINSKI, PRINCIPAL AND MATRON OF THE CAPE JEWISH ORPHANAGE
Written by Itiel Bereson

My parents, Chlavne and Dora Beresinski, were appointed to the position of Principal and Matron of the Cape Jewish Orphanage – later called Oranjia in 1926.

Previously my father was House Master in a boarding establishment run by Dr Moliver in Jerusalem. He was recruited overseas in Palestine by Mr Polly Ansky who interviewed my parents to come look after a Jewish Orphanage in Cape Town.

My parents left the orphanage in 1935 and returned in 1936 where they again took charge of the Cape Town Jewish Orphanage until the end of 1944.

In 1936 there was a plan to bring out children from Europe but it fell though. At that time my father was a good friend of Dr Apt who was connected with Arcadia. My father was great friends with the Mayor of Cape Town Louis Gradner. They lived in Oranjiasig and his son, Weineich Gradner who later also became the Mayor of Cape Town. The secretary of Oranjia was a Mr Kloot who had been a principal of a school.

Early in the war the Orphanage housed British evacuees from both Catholic and Protestant denominations and was frequently visited particularly by the Catholic and Anglican Archbishops. Needless to say, the Jewish element was managed as usual. It was funny to see them saying their prayers before meals when we recited ours.

I remember going on outings with the children at Oranjia to Paarl and Stellenbosch in the cars of committee members and we were driven by their chaufeurs.

In 1945 my parents left the Orphanage to become the first Principal and Matron of Herber House in Johannesburg. This was a boarding school establishment, mainly for Jewish children who came from remote areas. My Father arranged supervision on the same lines as he did at Oranjia.

Dora and Chlavne Beresinski, Matron and Principal of Oranjia

The students were educated in different day schools where my Father taught Hebrew to Matriculation level at Athlone and Jeppe High schools. At the end of 1945 my Father, together with Rabbi Zlotnik (Avida), established the first Hebrew teachers' seminary at Yalta Court in Yeoville which became a feeding area for Talmud Torahs over a wide area. After the war my parents and I left South Africa to join family in Australia.

The Jewish Historical Society in Cape Town should be the repository of memorabilia and archival material from Oranjia which today no longer exists. I know there are many photos and one particular large one which contained superb photos of the Executive and committee and my parents in 1932. The archival material should be found in the old Cape Town Synagogue adjacent to the beautiful Garden Synagogue where all the boys had their Barmitzvahs.

Photos on next two page
Cape Jewish Orphanage President and Committee 1932
Illuminated address to Beresinskis in 1935 after nine years service

Children of Oranjia welcoming my parents back in 1936
Dora on right and Chlavne is fourth from right wearing a hat

CAPE JEWISH ORPHANAGE
CAPE TOWN

ד' ישמר־צאתך וכואך מעתה ועד־עולם
יברכך ד' סציון וראה במוב ירושלים כל ימי חייך

TO Mr & Mrs CH. BERESINSKI

Dear Mr & Mrs Beresinski,

The Executive and Committee of the Cape Jewish Orphanage are glad to have this opportunity of giving formal expression to the high opinion they entertain of your character and attainments and, of the services you have rendered during the past nine years to this Institution and its children; and through them, to the entire Jewish Community.

As Principal and Matron respectively of the Cape Jewish Orphanage, you have always given of your best and have successfully helped to mould the lives & characters of a considerable number of orphan children, who, but for your guidance, instruction and example, might have become derelicts on the sea of life: you have so directed and trained them that they have developed into sound Jews and Jewesses and loyal South African citizens.

As the Father and Mother of the large number of children who have had the inestimable advantage of years of association with you, you have always extended to your charges much of that warmth of love and devotion that they have missed in their young lives through the unfortunate early demise of their natural guardians.

As the Hebrew Teacher for some years; of our senior boys and girls, you, Mr Beresinski have trained them with marked success in the sacred tenets of our Faith, and have developed in them a sound knowledge in, and a warm love for our History, our Ritual and our Language.

As the Mother in Israel of our Home you, Mrs Beresinski have attended faithfully and ably to all those sacred and housewifely Jewish practices so estimable and desirable in the conduct of a Jewish Home.

The Committee of the Cape Jewish Orphanage regret exceedingly that they are to lose your services, services which you have rendered so ably, with credit to yourselves, benefit to those young people placed in your care, and loyalty to the Committee and the Community.

The Committee are happy, nevertheless to know that you are leaving these shores in the possession of full strength and vigour, and are starting on a new life full of excellent prospects in our Ancient Home-Eretz Yisroel.

They trust that the experiences you have gained in the active pursuit of your onerous Orphanage duties will stand you in good stead in your new and wider sphere, and that you will carry with you many happy memories of your beneficent work in Capetown and of your association with South African Jewry.

The Committee bid you both and your young son Eitel 'God Speed' and while they regret the severance of your connection with Orphanage work and with themselves, which has been honourable to yourselves, satisfactory to your Committees, and beneficial to the children, this regret is tempered by the knowledge that you are starting out on your new career with high hopes of future success.

All connected with the Cape Jewish Orphanage trust that these hopes will be fully realized, and join in assuring you that your work in Capetown has been good; and that you carry with you to Eretz Yisroel their esteem, regard and sincere good wishes.

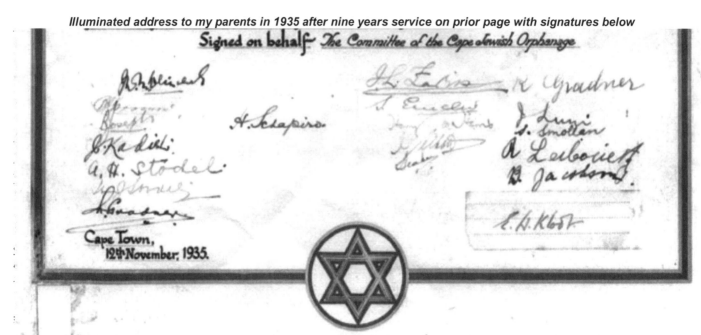

MEMORIES OF ISAAC OCHBERG, MY GODFATHER.
Written by Itiel Bereson

I was born in South Africa in 1927 and am the Godson of Isaac Ochberg who brought out the children from Eastern Europe in 1921. My parents were Chlavne and Dora Beresinski.

Isaac was a good friend of my father who was the principal of the Cape Jewish Orphanage. My father arrived in South Africa in 1926 and he was principal while my mother was matron. My parents had close contact with Isaac Ochberg and they looked after the children at Oranjia from 1926 to 1944 with breaks and sabbaticals when they went on visits to Palestine and Europe.

Although my memories of Isaac Ochberg are scant I remember him as a warm, kindly, loving man. I remember sitting on his knee and him cuddling me and using his many tikkies (threepences) to buy chocolate at the corner shop.

He was called Daddy Ochberg by everyone. I was told by others that he used to like me as a son. Even today I remember his smile, his face, his cuddles and feel close to him. He used to visit the children, my parents and the orphanage and was on the committee. He would have meals with my parents.

I was ten years old in 1937 when Isaac Ochberg died. I remember his death. It resounded with mourning and tributes which researchers may be able to find in the secular and Jewish newspapers particularly the Cape Jewish Chronicle.

We have been in Australia since 1948 and in 1957, 20 years after Isaac Ochberg's death, I received a letter informing me that he had left me a small bequest after his wife died.

In Australia I've been the principal of two high schools in Melbourne; Essendon High and Resevoire High. I believe I am the first Jewish principal of a non Jewish High school. I've written 16 books on subjects of Australian history and modern European History.

Itiel Bereson – 1970s

THE BUILDING AT ORANJIA

The building at Oranjia is a beautiful structure placed on the slopes of Table Mountain overlooking the city and sea. A short time after World War II started the building was modernised. The beautiful facade was kept. The building from its inception was set in beautiful surrounds on the slopes of Table Mountain in full view of Cape Town City and the Bay.

Besides Oranjia itself there were separate buildings; a hospital for infectious ailments, a beautiful synagogue which also serviced the local community, an enormous hall for indoor sports and meetings, a separate board room for committee meetings, a library largely unused containing many valuable first editions and other books bequeathed, a separate school area of about five classrooms for the teaching of Hebrew after school and also used for purposes of homework where there was supervision by their own school teachers at Cape Town High.

There are many lists of the children in Yiddish and English and handwritten and typed. Following are two lists

Cape Town

#	Surname	First name	Age	Place of birth
1	Elman	Jentel	6	Domatchevo
2	Soudax	Symcha	13	Wlodava
3	Cwengel	Saul	8	"
4	Kaufman	Solomon	7	"
5	Kasur	Chaim	11	"
6	"	Isaac	8	"
7	Shtern	Solomon	9	"
8	Kaverberg	Meer	13	Kovel
9	Migdalowitch	Symon	9	Pinsk
10	"	Chonon	10	"
11	Stilerman	Hersh	12	Loon
12	Bettman	Solomon	8	Stanislav
13	Jagolcovsky	Jacob	12	Brest
14	Orliansky	Abram	12	"
15	Gershenabek	Moisha	12	"
16	Perechodnik	Iser	12	Pinsk
17	"	Shepsel	9	"
18	Ruchozey	Aron	9	"
19	"	Fayvel	8	"
20	Gornshtein	Abram	11	"
21	~~Bornshtein~~ Solomon/Isaac		12	Brest
22	Bernfeld	Hersh	12	Warsaw
23	Feldman	Mendel	8	Shepz
24	Shteiner	Chaysel	7	Pinsk
25	"	Isaac	8	"
26	Engelman	Jacob	9	Wlodava
27	Lifshitz	Perel	11	"
28	Tenenbaum	Chaia	16	"
29	"	Sara	11	"
30	Fremd	Max	10	Livov
31	Mankes	Debora	7	"
32	Roht	Herman	10	"
33	Neishtein	Solomon	10	"
34	Rexler	Leya	6	"
35	Treppel	Jacob	8	"
36	Lila	Rosa	9	Stanislav
37	Rubin	Chana	6	"
38	"	David	7	"
39	Kingler	Chaykel	8	"
40	Rosenbaum	Leon	7	"
41	Shtainger	Pepy	9	"
42	Dreiling	Juda	8	"
43	Rosenblit	Ghalia	8	Sarny
44	Mussman	Isaac	9	"
45	"	Reisel	7	"
46	Fayfer	Lila	11	Kovel
47	"	Bluma	10	"
48	Ganffas	Gittel	12	"
49	"	Leya	11	"
50	"	Malka	10	"

Children remaining in Cape Town showing age and place of birth - pages one and two of three

No.	Name		Age	Country
	Boys			
1.	Elman	Yentel	5	Domatchewo
2.	Bondak	Eymcha	13	Wlodawa
3.	Cwengel	Saul	8	do
4.	Kaufman	Solomon	7	do
5.	Rasuv	Chaym	11	do
6.	do	Isaac	8	do
7.	Shtern	Solomon	9	do
8.	Kanerberg	Mees	13	Pynsk
9.	Migdalowitch	Hyman	9	Pynsk
10.	do	Chonon	10	do
11.	Stilerman	Hersh	12	do
12.	Betman	Solomon	8	Stamslawor
13.	Yagolkowsky	Yakow	12	Brysr
14.	Orltansky	Abram	12	do
15.	Gershenabel	Moisha	12	do
16.	Perrchoaduik	Yssr	12	Pynsk (Pynsk
17.	do	Shepsel	9	do
18.	Ruchocky	Aron	9	do
19.	do	Faiwel	8	do
20.	Gerynshtein	Abram	11	do
21.	Ochstein	Solomon	9	do
22.	Bornshtein	Isaac	12	Brysk
23.	Bernfeld	Hersh	9	Warshaw
	Girls			
1.	Elman	Bluma	5	Domatchewo
2.	do	Feyga	9	do
3.	Heft	Fosha	9	do
4.	Mandelblat	Pesha	11	do
5.	Lehrman	Nechama	5	do
6.	do	Dwoira	8	Wlodama
7.	Kaufman	Cypora	9	do
8.	Ginsburg	Mintcha	8	do
9.	Rasur	Yenta	10	do
10.	Gabay	Chaia	14	Kowel
11.	do	Pesha	11	do
12.	do	Gitel	9	do
13.	Kolodnew	Liba	12	do
14.	do	Yenta	8	do
15.	Miler	Braindel	8	do
16.	Pianka	Chama	13	Brest
17.	Barmatch	Sara	12	do
18.	Berkowitch	Chama	12	do
19.	Samyvina	Zlata	12	Pynsk
20.	do	Zoina	10	do
21.	Gefsunterman	Sheana Rochel	12	do
22.	do	Braindel	10	do
23.	Margolin	Sara	10	do
24.	Neishtein	Sala	7	Lemberg
25.	Harnis	Nesha	11	do
26.	do	Rosha	9	do
27.	Shtrasner	Feyga	6	Stamslawow
28.	Waidman	Sheindel	7	
29.	Wachtel	Sara	9	do
30.	Bertman	Laya	19	do
31.	do	Chama	13	do
32.	do	Yenta	8	do
33.	do	Sheindel	8	do
34.	do	Solomon	8	do
35.	Shapiro	Malka	9	Sarny
36.	Knubowie	zlata	12	Pynsk

CONTINUED:

No.	Name			
37	Gorynshtein	Chana	9	Pynsk
38	Gebengolc	Rochel	15	Shack
39	Bernfeld	Chaja	10	Warsav
40	Derlowitch	Chana	10	do
41	Kahan	Golda	17	Pynsk

51	Koloduer Liba	12	Kowel
52	Miler Braindel	8	"
53	Pianka Chava	13	Brest
54	Barmatch Sara	12	"
55	Berkovitch Chava	12	"
56	Samurina Sima	10	Pinsk
57	Gebunterman Sheina Rochel	12	"
58	" Braindel	10	"
59	Neishtein Sala	7	Loor
60	Hans Neshe	11	"
61	" Rose	9	"
62	Shtrasner Feyga	6	Stanislav
63	Waidman Sheindel	7	"
64	Wachtel Sara	9	"
65	Bettman Leya	19	"
66	" Sheindel	9	"
67	Shapiro Malke	9	Sarny
68	Knubovey Zlata	12	Pinsk
69	Gornshtein Chana	9	"
70	Gebengolz Rachel	10	Shaja
71	Bernfeld Chaia	10	Warshar
72	Berkovitch Chane	10	"
73	Kagan Golde	17	Pinsk
74	Markofer Franziska	9	Loor

Children remaining in Cape Town showing age
and place of birth - page three of three

Cape Town Contingent of Pogrom War Orphans arrived by the
"Edinburgh Castle" on 19 September 1921

THE YOUNG LADIES IN THE "LADIES SECTION"
Written by Jenny (Flink) Segall

Here are group photos of Ochberg Orphans as young ladies. They all grew up in Oranjia, and then remained in what they called the "Ladies section" and although I can identify some of the girls, most I cannot, so it will be interesting to see if people around the world can identify others in the photos. Incidentally, every single girl in the orphanage had to learn 'trades'.

They had to do dressmaking, millinery, etc. My mom became a well known dressmaker both in Cape Town, and ultimately in Johannesburg, but inevitably landed up just sewing for her and me! My Aunt, Nellie Frankal (nee Hans) did millinery, and worked for hat firms in Cape Town for many years.

Chava (Eva) Berkowitz was an Ochberg child who attached herself to my mom and aunt from the time they were little ones at the Orphanage until their deaths. She never married and was a Yiddish actress on stage in Johannesburg.

Other friends are the Pinsky's (Zlote Dembo) and her brother and sisters and Clara and Sally. Clara was married to Isaac Steiman and her daughters are Issa Werb and Judy Levin.

This crowd was brought up and lived all their lives at Oranjia, and the girls continued to live there in a Ladies Section even when they went to work. Socials were held there, and my Dad, went to a social that Oranjia held every Saturday night for the ladies (girls) of the orphanage, and my Dad met my Mom there.

Seated in front: Unknown and Zlata (Charlotte) Samurina
Middle row: Chava Pianka, unknown, Rywka Kailer and Chava Berkowitz and
Top row: Yetta Bornstein, unknown, Sima (Thelma) Samurina and Chaya Gaby

Ochberg girls on Muizenberg Beach - "My mom Rosie Flink (nee Hans) sitting in striped dress" Jenny (Flink) Segall
"My mom Pesha Mandelblatt wearing a striped dress standing on right" David Kapelus

SATURDAY NIGHT DANCES
Written by Celia Isaacman, the daughter of Regina Artman.

There was a hostel for girls who left the Orphanage in Forest Road in Oranjezicht and my mother stayed there and had some very happy times. There would be dances on Saturday nights and the girls could drop the names of young men they would like to invite into a box and those in charge of the hostel would invite the guys to come without mentioning who was actually the person asking them. In this way the hostel became a place where the young Jewish men could have a fun evening out and meet the girls.

A Saturday Night Dance in Cape Town –
Many girls met their husbands at these socials

"Typical Social (party) in Cape Town where my mom, Rosie Heft (front centre) met my dad, Julius Hoffman." Lazar Hoffman

"This is a photo of my Parent's wedding; Salka Bettman to Joseph Sheiham." Aubrey Sheiham – see chapter 53

"My mother, Sarah Wachtel, was a bridesmaid to Salka" Rhona Wolpert – see chapter 83

Chava Berkowitz in spotted dress and other Ochberg girls

A group photo of the Ochberg Girls at Muizenberg beach. "The second one is my mom Rosie. The fifth one is late Yetta (married name Bornstein) they lived in Cape Town when she married an Ochberg boy 'Borny'. Her children live in Cape Town. Her two daughters are Tania (Bornstein) Jacobson, and another daughter Rita Shorkend who is in the aged home in Cape Town now, not well. The sixth girl is late Eva Berkowitz and one of the girls in the photo is also my Aunty Nellie, but I just can't identify her." Jenny (Flink) Segall

Chapter 47 – ORANJIA TODAY

This article has kindly been sent in by Belinda Slavin, the Programme Director of Oranjia Jewish Child and Youth Centre.

Part of the proceeds on sale of this book will go to Oranjia.

HISTORY

The Oranjia Jewish Child and Youth Centre was established in 1911 as an orphanage. With the passage of time and with advances in medical science the number of Jewish orphans decreased. However, a new need arose; children who were in need of care and who had at least one biological parent alive. And it is this type of child who Oranjia currently cares for. Indeed, not a single child at Oranjia today is an orphan and each has at least one biological parent alive. All the children at Oranjia have been removed from their families by Order of Court in terms of the Children's Act.

In the 1980s with increased research and understanding in the field of childcare, it became abundantly clear that that institutional settings epitomized by large impersonal buildings were counter-indicated for the objectives that had been set, namely to provide an alternative specialised, professional context to remediate the consequences of removal to the children placed in our care. It has always been Oranjia's objective to construct a context within which such children can continue to grow and develop physically, psychologically, spiritually and emotionally.

In 1986, Oranjia laid the foundations for a shift into a new model of childcare, away from custodial principles. A group home was opened. The success of this group house living experience lead to the old institution closing and two more group homes being opened in January 1992.

From 1996 the number of residential admissions decreased resulting in the closure of first our Gorge Road Unit and then our Gardenia Avenue Unit. Currently in 2011, we are only operating one residential unit at Frank Ave.

RESIDENTIAL CARE

Residential care is a very specialised form of intervention that happens when a family is in dire need of help, change and support and the necessary support structures in the community are not in place or not specific to their needs. To remove children from their families and place them in a residential environment, albeit a caring, therapeutic milieu, stays traumatic and requires a lot of understanding and skill from all the professionals involved; to act in the best interest of both children and their families. The ultimate aim of residential care is to help families to function optimally in their own communities therefore re-uniting children and their families after successful and intensive intervention where possible.

To change set behaviour patterns and learn new skills takes a long time and requires hard work. Children and families in our care have to face these challenges every day and often against overwhelming odds. Our job is to be there 24 hours a day, every day, every step of the way encouraging, teaching, supporting and applauding.

In the new paradigm, emphasis is placed on "prevention" and community based support structures to prevent the use of more drastic measures like residential care as far as possible. This is good and definitely the way to go in the future. Children's homes should become resource centres for the communities they serve.

But there will always be those families that will benefit most from residential care, and we owe it to them to have those facilities in place, and staff them with people who are true professionals in their field and who will provide these families with the best possible care they can offer.

Oranjia currently in 2011 has one residential home which can accommodate 10 children. In 2009 our home underwent a massive renovation in order to provide a facility that would serve the community's needs for the next 20 years.

Oranjia is managed by a group of committed volunteers who oversee the overall managing of the home and ensure by their fundraising efforts that there are sufficient finances to enable the on-going running of the home. The professional staff is accountable to the management committee.

ORANJIA'S VISION AND MISSION

Oranjia aims to provide child and youth centred services as well as residential group care to children of the Jewish Community who have been found in need of care in terms of the Children's Act.

The philosophy of care is based on the core principle that children and youth at risk need opportunities for competency, development and personal growth.

Children and youth with emotional trauma and distress present with interpersonal and social difficulties.

Our emphasis is on the development of the whole child and youth in a context that actively promotes personal growth and development by building trusting and safe relationships between professional staff and residents.

These meaningful relationships are characterized by concern for physical and emotional needs, trust, understanding and awareness of the child and youth as an individual in a social and communal context.

SERVICES OFFERED

Residential Services and Group Care

- Group home offering 24 hour residential care for children and youth of the Jewish community, operated by a team of trained and skilled youth care practioners.
- A structured but flexible therapeutic milieu and routine to meet individual and group needs.
- Management of children and youth with emotional and behavioural difficulties.
- Provision of physical, emotional, social and spiritual care.
- Clinical assessment of children, youth and families.
- Treatment programmes for children, youth and families.

The programme provides services to meet all needs in a Jewish environment for children and youth aged from two to eighteen, after which a transition can be made to an aftercare programme.

Residential Aftercare

This service is offered to residents of Oranjia who have reached the age of 18 but are unable to return to their families and are not ready for independent community living. These residents are allowed to remain at Oranjia while they are assisted to further their education, find employment and acquire the life skills necessary to make the transition into independent living.

Aftercare and Daycare

When children and youth of school going age are ready to leave the residential programme, they and their families need support in making the transition. Oranjia will continue to offer them practical and emotional support for a considerable amount of time, the period of time being determined by the needs of each individual case. This can include the child or youth coming to Oranjia on a daycare basis. This service is crucial in assisting the transition from residential care back to family living in order to prevent re-admissions.

Social Work and Counseling Services

- Individual and group work with children and youth in residence and in aftercare.
- Family work including practical, social and emotional support and crisis intervention with families.
- Parent support
- Case management and assessments and liaison with other professional.
- Recruitment of host families for residents.

DAYCARE

In 2006, Oranjia started a Daycare programme aimed at children and youth that had never been in residential care, but had been identified as children "at risk." This preventative programme was identified as a need in the community and is in line with South African Child and Youth Care Practice. Children came to Oranjia after school, returning to their parents in the evening. Currently at the moment we are not running this programme as our residential unit is full. When residential numbers decrease more children could be admitted onto the daycare programme.

We are proud of the fact that of the over 70 children who have been in Oranjia's care since the move to the Group Homes in 1992, very few have become dependent on community resources and welfare. The majority have developed into self-sufficient adults who are making valuable contributions to society. This is not only gratifying in terms of the personal achievements of our past Oranjia children but also in terms of the significant financial implications for the community, i.e. not becoming welfare dependent adults.

ORANJIA'S CENTENARY

In February 2011 Oranjia turned one hundred years old.

In order to celebrate our centenary and this auspicious occasion we are planning to hold a Gala Dinner later this year and to launch a centenary book.

We appeal to all past residents of Oranjia who would be willing to write a short paragraph or be interviewed for the book to make contact. See contact details below.

All proceeds from the Gala Dinner and the sale of the book will be used towards the running costs of Oranjia.

If you would like to make a donation, see our bank details below.

FUNDING

Oranjia relies on the generosity of members of our community for funding. A large part of our funding comes from our allocation from the United Jewish Appeal in the Western Cape, donation and bequests as well as fundraising efforts such as our Friends of Oranjia draw and our annual Golf Day.

We are indeed most grateful for all donations. Our banking details are below:

Oranjia Jewish Child and Youth Care Centre
Bank: ABSA
Branch: Heerengracht
Branch Code: 506009
Account No: 4053384318
Swift Code: absa zajj

Please help us to identify your contribution by advising us by email or fax of any direct deposits made. Fax: 021 – 461 0693, or email Admin Director Jean Mausenbaum <mausenbaum@oranjia.com> Telephone: 021-465 5009

Or mail your contribution to: P.O Box 1204, Cape Town 8000.

PART 2
CAPE TOWN - SOUTH AFRICA

SECTION 7
OCHBERG ORPHANS WITH CHILDREN IN THE CAPE JEWISH ORPHANAGE ORANJIA

In this section you can read about the Cape Jewish Orphanage through the individual life stories of the Ochberg Orphans where their descendants were also in the care of the Cape Jewish Orphanage (Oranjia).

INTRODUCING ISAAC OCHBERG AND THE OCHBERG ORPHANS

Written by Charlotte Cohen[1]

Isaac Ochberg, the eldest son of Aaron and Sarah Ochberg, was born in Uman, a small town in the Ukraine in 1879. His father came to South Africa in 1893. Isaac followed in 1895, aged 15, making the trip alone. Several years later, he established himself as one of Cape Town's leading entrepreneurs – as a timber merchant and in part owing to his ventures in buying ships. Important purchases of property also gave him a high standing in the business community.

In her book *This was a Man* (Cape Town, 1974), Ochberg's daughter Bertha Epstein writes of her father: "He never refused to support a worthy cause. His creed was that since he had been enabled to achieve success in his own enterprises, he had a moral duty to help those less fortunate".

In the aftermath of World War I, as pogroms ravaged Eastern Europe, famine and war raged throughout Russia, and the Spanish Influenza epidemic burned through South Africa decimating Cape Town's population, Ochberg became the President of the Cape Jewish Orphanage. At a special meeting on 19 August 1920, he proposed that the Orphanage take all the responsibilities of bringing pogrom orphans out and caring for them; and that it act as a "clearing–house", from where the children could be distributed for adoption. In less than a week, at record meetings in Cape Town cinemas, crowds of Jews pledged themselves to the limit to help save the orphans.

As details of the position in Europe leaked out, the tragedy of the situation became clearer. No fewer than 400,000 Jewish orphans were known to be destitute in Russia. Whatever was done could only be a drop in the ocean.

By January 1921, Bernard Alexander of Johannesburg persuaded the Union Government to give, on a pound for pound principle, to the Pogrom Orphan Fund. It was felt that, with this, 250 children could be brought to South Africa. Someone had to go to Europe and make immediate, 'on-the-spot' arrangements. Without hesitation, Isaac Ochberg offered to undertake this responsible and by no means unhazardous task.[2]

Almost the worst problem confronting Ochberg was how to choose from the vast number of destitute children. Finally, he decided to choose eight children from each institution, to make up the total of 200 for which he had sufficient funds. Since the Union Government had laid down that any children coming in must be of good health, this demanded careful selection. Only full orphans (those who had lost both parents) were accepted.[3] Ochberg left London for Warsaw on 18 May 1921. After five weeks in the areas of Galicia and the Ukraine, he reported the experience as "appalling, the position desperate, the people terribly persecuted and ill-treated".

One of Ochberg's chief difficulties was to find a place in Poland where he could assemble a large number of children before he could begin to book their passages. Once this was done, he began his arduous journey, moving from one devastated village to another, travelling by any means of transport he could hire, to collect little children.

Nearly all the orphans had lost both parents, and were in a wretched state. Ochberg found children roaming around towns and forests in a filthy, naked, verminous and starving condition. Many of them were traumatized; physically ill from the privations they had endured, still in a state of shock from witnessing the murder of their parents or from seeing their mothers or sisters raped.

By 1 August, Ochberg had gathered as many as he could from Minsk, Pinsk, Vladivostok, Stanislavov, Brest-Litovsk and Warsaw. Then came the heartbreaking task of having to select those who could be taken with him – and those who would be left behind. If it were possible to bring brothers and sisters together, he did so.

Ochberg and the orphans then traveled by riverboat down the Vistula to Danzig. There they boarded a steamer bound for London.

Ochberg had actually placed 233 orphans in the temporary shelter set up in Warsaw. Unfortunately, 37 of them ran away and others took ill, so that only 169 were actually taken to London. As two children became ill just before sailing, he arrived with 167 orphans. English Jews provided for them during their week's stay before they left for South Africa. On 2 September 1921, with Mr. and Mrs. Maman as Principal and Matron, Mr Ochberg and his party of small immigrants set off from London in the *Edinburgh Castle* bound for Cape Town.

The *Cape Times* recorded their arrival in Cape Town as follows: As the children disembarked and proceeded to take their places in the motorcars, they were besieged with people pressing fruit, sweets and cakes on them. Everyone was struck with their happy, healthy condition, and except for a case or two of measles on the trip, they had a clean bill of health.

On their arrival, seventy-eight of the children were taken by train to Johannesburg.

In 1922, Isaac Ochberg went again to Russia as chairman of a delegation under the auspices of the Conference Universale Juive de Secours. He traveled through the starving areas of Russia, distributing great quantities of food, clothes and medication. By so doing, he saved many thousands of lives. In 1971, at the commemoration of the arrival of her father's Ochberg's Pogrom Children in South Africa, the words of Bertha Epstein say all that can or need be said:

Honour has been paid where honour was due, with love and affection, in the living presence of my father's greatest humanitarian achievement. This has been a Golden Jubilee to remember: the reunion of Isaac Ochberg and his beloved Pogrom Orphan children. God bless them all.[4]

'The Highest Form Of Wisdom Is Kindness' (Talmud)

---

[1] The author thanks the Jacob Gitlin Library for its assistance received in locating and providing sources of reference, including: *South African Jewish Yearbook 1929 – 5689-5690*; Rosenthal, E, *The Story of the Cape Jewish Orphanage*, Cape Town, 1961 (Golden Jubilee commemorative publication); Boiskin, J, 'The Ochberg Orphans', *Jewish Affairs*, Winter 1994.
[2] Rosenthal, E, *The Story of the Cape Jewish Orphanage*, Cape Town, 1961, p13
[3] Ibid., p15

[4] Epstein, B, *This was a Man*, Cape Town, 1974, p93

Chapter 48 – MALKA SCHAPIRA (MOLLY COHEN)

CONNECTIONS AND RECOLLECTIONS:
REMEMBRANCES OF AN OCHBERG ORPHAN
Written by Charlotte Cohen

Molly Cohen (Schapiro/ Schapera), my ex mother-in-law, is the last surviving Ochberg Orphan in Cape Town. Born 18 November 1913, she is a charming person, in good health, clear-thinking and lucid. She lives at Sea Point Place. I am still in contact with her on a regular basis.

I interviewed her in 2007 and in many ways, our coffee date could have been a poetic picture-postcard. We sat in a coffee bar in Sea Point. It was Autumn, but with the sun shining and just a slight nip in the air, it was a still lovely day. We sipped our coffee and nibbled a croissant.

Questions were posed, probed and prompted. And her memories from the early 1900s filtered through. Scenes from the past began to percolate - descriptions, emotions, recollections of people and places were brought back to life.

She recounted what she remembered, lucidly and clearly, recalling events and memories of the time when she was brought over to South Africa by the late Isaac Ochberg.

On the table lay a program from a function to mark the Golden Jubilee Pogrom Orphan reunion of the arrival of the 'Ochberg Orphans' in 1921.

As the families of the survivors were included in that 50th anniversary reunion in 1971, I also attended the function. I was married to Molly's son. My grandson is her great-grandson. She is still beautiful – well groomed, tidy, soft-spoken and ladylike. Contained, clear in her thinking and perspicacity, she is interested in all that goes on around her. Molly Cohen is the last surviving "Ochberg Orphan" in Cape Town.

THE INTERVIEW

Q: What was your maiden name, date and place of birth? What are your earliest memories of being in Europe during the war?

A: I was born in the Ukraine on 18 November 1913, some months prior to the First World War. My maiden name was Schapera (changed to Shapiro when I came to South Africa in 1921 at the age of seven). I do not remember my parents at all, but heard later that I had three brothers and two sisters. My memories of Europe are scant. I remember being shunted around, living with different families, being pushed from pillar to post. That was the way of life. I knew nothing else. One older brother was with me at the last place where I lived. Then I remember being put on a ship with a lot of children. It took us longer than expected to reach South Africa, as we stopped at a port because one of the children had mumps.

Malka Schapira, is the little girl front row, 5th from the right
Group passport number 8

Q: What do you remember of Isaac Ochberg.?

A: "Daddy Ochberg" - That's what we called him. That's what he was to us. Isaac Ochberg was always 'there'. When letters came for the children written in Yiddish, he would translate them into English, and then read them to us.

Isaac Ochberg was also Ukrainian. He came to live in South Africa. He was an attractive man with good business acumen. I think he had dealings with the timber industry and also bought and repaired second-hand parts of ships. He was a man of exceptional kindness and great courage. He went into the war zone to find and save the children of families he knew. The children were not only from the Ukraine. He fetched children from other areas as well. He made arrangements to bring out about 200 children. Approximately half went to Johannesburg, and the rest remained in Cape Town. He later went back on a second trip to fetch more children, but they would not let them out. We were the lucky ones. Once we arrived here, we were called "The Ochberg Orphans".

As there was an age restriction on the children who could be brought from Europe, my brother could not come with us on the boat. I think he asked Isaac Ochberg to assist him financially to leave the Ukraine, which he did. My brother then made his way to Egypt and then Palestine. After he settled there, he married a girl who came from Poland. I visited him in the early 1950s. I later discovered I had another older brother who had also managed to get to Palestine.

NOTES

Charlotte Cohen is an award-winning short story writer and poetess, whose work has appeared in a wide variety of South African publications since 1973.
Charlotte's interview and an article on Isaac Ochberg were published in 2007 'Jewish Affairs', a prestigious quarterly magazine produced by the South African Jewish Board of Deputies, edited by David Saks in Johannesburg. The interview was published in the Temple Israel Rosh Hashona Annual in 2006.

Q: How would you describe your childhood, growing up in South Africa?

A: We arrived in Cape Town in 1921. We stayed at the Orphanage, which had been established in 1911 (today, it is known as the Oranjia Jewish Child and Youth Centre) The matron and principal were married and lived at the Home. They were very good to the children.

One of the 'minders' married a Mr Marks – a well-known man in business circles. They were active in communal affairs. We attended a government school in Buitenkant Street. The principal was a Mrs Rosa Van Gelderen. We were taught in English – one half hour a week was set aside for an Afrikaans lesson, given by a Miss Goldblatt. We attended *cheder* after school.

The shul was on the premises of the Home. Saturday afternoons and weekends, we would congregate at the playground and play or watch hockey and soccer. I watched.

On Sundays, it seemed as if the whole Jewish community came to visit us, to talk to us and ask questions. Many country people also came to the Home to visit. Often a prospective parent would come to choose an orphan for adoption.

There was a group of us who did not want to be adopted. I was very happy at the Home and had many friends. I did not want to be separated from them. I also did not want to change my name, as I still had contact with my brother. Occasional letters came from him, written in Yiddish.

The community was loving and caring, totally committed and involved with the children and the running of the Home. It was never short of funds and *we* were never short of anything. If a child showed talent and wished to extend his or her capabilities or study further, they were totally and wholeheartedly assisted and given every encouragement. The community was involved with every aspect of our lives. They continued supporting and visiting the Orphanage for years.

We were extremely fortunate. We had the best of a sheltered, cared-for upbringing. We played, attended school and were given a religious background. We were surrounded by friends and by a devoted community, and never felt unloved.

Q: As you grew older, how did your life change?

A: It was when I reached my early teens that I was hit by the reality that I was alone, that there was no one close for me to lean on, no family to support me. The feelings of loneliness I experienced *then*, were the lowlight of my life.

I left school after passing J C (Junior Certificate, Standard. Eight). After working for a while as an assistant at the CTC Bazaars, I was later employed as a clerk at Zuckermans Wholesalers. When I was 17, the boss's son asked me out on my first date. A house had been opened up next to the Orphanage, into which they moved the older girls. A lady was appointed to take charge of us. Approval and permission to go out on dates was given by her.

Having parties was our form of socialising – and there were lots of parties. We would each bring something to eat, meet at the station and catch a train and walk to wherever the party was being held. There we would put on the gramophone and dance. Mountain climbing was also a great recreation and I met my husband-to-be on a climb when I was eighteen. I married a year later. Mr and Mrs Louis Gradner, who were the mayor and mayoress of Cape Town and also on the Oranjia committee, were *Unterfuhrers* at my wedding.

Q: What was the most important lesson you learned?

A: That when all is said and done, ultimately, you only have yourself to rely on - and it was a lesson I learned very much later in my life!

Q: Looking back at your life, do you think there was a 'higher plan', or that providence prescribed or pre-empted your life?

A: One has to wonder. Hundreds of thousands of children perished in Europe. Isaac Ochberg went back a second time to rescue more children but was unable to bring them out. We were the ones who were taken to safety by a man inspired to do so. We were the ones who were given a chance to lead a decent, meaningful and happy life with love, care and support – and to give life to future generations. I have been able to live a full life – seeing grandchildren and great-grandchildren.

I must believe in my own experience and what I see before me now. But, at the same time, there is so much more *beyond* what I can see. I realise there is so much I *don't* understand, so much I *don't* know. There is so much to think about, so much to wonder about…

Q: How would you sum up your life?

A: (Molly thought a while and answered in Yiddish)
Men lernt zach a ganzen leben un shtarbn a nar ("You live and learn your whole life and die knowing how little you know!"

Q: How did those early years as an 'Ochberg Orphan' affect your life?

A: They were happy years. The one thing that remains in my mind is the exceptional generosity of spirit and kindness we experienced. We were adopted by the whole Cape Town community. There were always people visiting the Home. They were a *part* of the home - and we were part of the community. We were taken into *their* homes - and more importantly, into their hearts.

More than anything, the care, concern and outstanding kindness extended to us by the Jewish people of Cape Town is something I have always carried with me. It is something that has sustained me, for which I have been appreciative, grateful and valued all my life.

ADDITIONAL FAMILY HISTORY
Recorded in 2009 from Molly

I have no memory of my parents, but I remember I never had a permanent place to live and I was moved from one place to another to keep me alive. I heard my parents were murdered on one day, but I heard this only later. They kept these things from the children

Joseph, my brother was about 15 when we left Poland. He was too old to go with us to South Africa and he looked after me and took me to the orphanage to be taken away. He asked Isaac Ochberg to help him to leave to go to Israel. He used to write to Isaac Ochberg enquiring about me and Isaac Ochberg read his letters and translated them for me. I don't have these letters.

Joseph was married to a Polish girl in Israel. They had two sons and one daughter and I saw him later in Israel in 1950. So I have a niece and two nephews still living in Israel.

Moshe is about 75 and had a wife called Ziva who died a few years ago, Avinoam has three children and I think the daughter is named Chaia and she has two daughters in America.

Shaika was my oldest brother and at least five years older than Joseph. I only found this out later and he was in Poland and later went to Israel.

I heard we had a younger brother than Joseph, but I don't know what happened to him. It was war time and a very hard time. Also I believe I had two sisters but they perished from typhoid.

I remember Betty, Gittel and Peggy at the Cape Jewish Orphanage but I can't remember their second names. I also remember a Tziporah. We girls who were too old to be in the orphanage stayed in a house nearby that was owned by the Jewish Community and we were still under the care of the Cape Jewish Orphanage. I stayed there for only three years and I worked at the OK Bazaars behind the counter.

I married Isaac Cohen in 1934 when I was 20. His name was previously (Kuzzon or Kagon) and he came from Vilna. After we married we had a little place in Woodstock. I don't know what work he had with his mother and father. I never saw him at work.

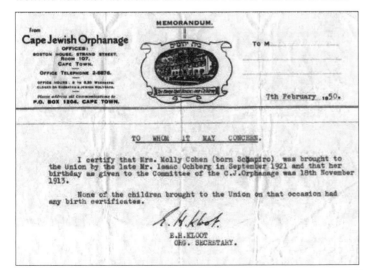

Wedding of Isaac Cohen and Molley Schapiro - 1934

*Molly back right with husband Isaac
In the middle are Isaac's parents with baby Hymie*

227

Molly with Hymie - 1936

Arthur and Hymie with their Grandparents

I lost my husband very early and he was 38 when he died of a heart attack. I was left with two little boys, Hymie and Arthur and we had a little shop and as I could not manage, I put my children into the orphanage and they were there a little while and went to SACS School in Cape Town.

Arthur and Isaac with cousin Harold

Arthur and Hymie with their Grandmother

My younger son, Arthur, is a Chartered Accountant and he lives in Cape Town. He has three children. I have four great grandchildren; two live in New Zealand and two in Cape Town. I now live at Sea Point Place an old aged home

I lost my older son, Hymie when he was 57. He was married and I had two grandchildren from him, Rodney and Steven. Tragically, Rodney passed away in 2006 at the age of 45.

Jon Blair took pictures of me in my son's house and he said he would show me the pictures. Now I'm telling you all my secrets. Sorry I could not tell you more. It's not something you can make up.

228

Arthur and Nesta Cohen continue

Molly's eldest brother Shaika had just one daughter who married and had two children, but Molly never got to meet him, and there was virtually no contact between them except one letter written from Israel where he finally came to live. This letter was written in Yiddish, and was received in about 1970 - up to that time Molly was not aware that he had survived, was alive, or that he was living in Israel.

Joseph/Yosef (another brother of Molly) had three children;
   -Chaia, who was married to Zvi Sarig (deceased), and they had three daughters, two of which live in Canada and one in Israel, named Orit.
   -Moshe (eldest son of Joseph) married Ziva, no children.
   -Avinoam (the youngest of Joseph's three children), married Liora, and have three children - a son and two daughters.

Molly with her grandson Rodney

Molly's eldest son Hymie, married Charlotte, had two sons, Rodney, who passed away three years ago and Steven, who has a son Aidan.

Hymie and Charlotte's wedding.
Molly third from left with Arthur behind her

Molly with her grandsons Rodney and Steven

Arthur, Molly's younger son, is married to Nesta and they have three sons. Saul (eldest) and his wife (Beverley) daughter (Hannah), and son (Ethan) live in Napier, New Zealand. Michael (middle son) is unmarried and lives in Israel. Alon (youngest) is married to Iva and they have a daughter, Lois (just five months old) living in Cape Town.

Hymie and Charlotte and Rodney

Arthur is a Chartered Accountant, trying to retire! Nesta, together with her colleague, run "Giftime" at Astra Centre (the Jewish Sheltered Employment Centre,) a similar operation to the Selwyn Segal Gift Shop.

THE CAPE JEWISH ORPHANAGE, ORANJIA.
Written by Arthur Cohen

Arthur, the son of Molly Cohen, and his late brother Hymie were in the care of the Cape Jewish Orphanage from late 1945 until 1949 and he lives in Cape Town.

The Cape Jewish Orphanage, later called "Oranjia", was located in an entire block fronting onto Montrose Avenue, overlooking the city area and harbour of Cape Town, and tucked into the slopes of Table Mountain. Being a steep-graded plot, the building was divided into two sections, joined by a fairly wide ramp.

The higher back section contained a large hall that was used both by residents and Jewish children in the neighbourhood for indoor activities such as Habonim meetings, gym, table tennis, etc. It also contained a shul (which was well attended on Shabbat and festivals), and a basic medical section. In later years a section of the area was used as a pre-school/nursery school for the general Jewish community.

The front section comprised, of an entrance hall which lead off to the principals living apartment, right to the general office, and centre to the communal lounge. The lounge adjoined the dining room (also used for doing school homework) and kitchen, and had stairs to the upper level landing which had boys (left) and girls (right) dormitories (each sleeps about 10 and grouped by ages of the children) communal bathrooms and in the middle was the exit/entrance to/from the ramp connecting with the back section. The outside surrounds were very extensive. In the front was a tiered section of ground, on which we were encouraged to individually stake out a small patch as a vegetable garden, split by a substantial number of stairs from the gate to the front door.

Hymie and Arthur

Hymie and Arthur

On the east and left of the buildings were top (gravel) and bottom (grassed) playing fields which was also used as a soccer ground when the Jewish community neighbours come to play with us. At the end of the bottom field was a section of trees, and on the retaining wall running between the top and bottom fields, was a narrow ledge with a few boulders on it.

Boys will be boys so it was not too long before we decided to construct a makeshift cable slide consisting of a tube with a rope through it, and tied at either end to a raised object, a fence pole on top field and tree branch on bottom field, and strung high enough to allow for the length of our body to be clear of the rocks protruding from the connecting ledge that we would pass over. Being its chief designer I was given the privilege of the first ride.

By now I'm sure you have guessed I ended up needing to use the services of the medical section and suffered a scar that I shall carry to my grave. Needless to say my approximately nine year old brain did not figure out that the weight of the hanging body will cause the rope to stretch and sag enough to collide with the waiting rocks which my desperate attempt to avoid was in vein. Thankfully it did not indispose me for too long, as I was soon, walking to and from Herzlia school, situated then in it's original location in Hope Street and opposite the Zionist Hall, so as to save the bus fare so I could buy a treat at the corner shop, now converted and developed into a popular deli cum coffee shop, the corner Montrose and Orange diagonally opposite the Sank home in which Barney and Abe, who both have championed and still do the cause of Oranjia for many decades, lived.

Another quite hair-raising activity was to take the staff delivery bike, one of us on the saddle and another perched on the handlebar basket, and go careening down Molteno Road which formed the west border of the campus block. Fortunately nothing but an occasional scrape of elbows and knees was the order of the day from this ongoing lark. My lifelong friend Michael Padowich, who was one of our neighbours and an eager participant herein, and I were recently recalling doing this.

Saturday afternoon and Sunday morning was a time when those that had families would be taken out for a while. Those not visited would sometimes be taken for a drive by a caring member of the community. Long after having left Oranjia, I recall one day hitch-hiking on De Waal Drive in the hope of a lift to Muizenberg, a popular seaside suburb. Whom should drive by but Joe Schneider (one such angel) in his big brown Hudson which I instantly recognised from the frequent visits he made to Oranjia during my stay there. Obviously I got excited at the prospect of a lift, and waved so as to draw Joe's attention, and he duly pulled over. I was chest fallen to see that the car was crowded with passengers and luggage, said thank you for stopping and wanted to have him move off. He would have none of it, and insisted in squeezing me in. To him I was like family because I had lived in Oranjia. Caring and concern for the wellbeing of the residents often did not cease when a resident moved out of the home e g a fund specifically for study bursaries was available for those old boys or girls in need and wishing to get a university degree.

Notwithstanding the fellowship spirit and feeling of belonging, the principal was very austere and was generally feared rather than liked. One got a grounding in Hebrew (as it was a school subject), went to shul, and observed the festivals, so secular and traditional education was enjoyed by all. The relationship with the staff (other than the principal) was relaxed and natural, and completely free of racial tension in the case of black employees. The atmosphere in the home, and the attitude of the residents to each other, was as siblings and friends. There was no suggestion that the young be obliged to do the bidding of their seniors (as usually applies in boarding school and university hostels). Also absent (or possibly undetected by my youth and naive view) was any sexual relations in spite of the close proximity and constant contact of boys and girls living in the home.

Those of us that experienced the campus days of the original home, must in the main have fond memories thereof. The ready association of the old boys and girls - in service or donations - is evidence thereof.

In memory of Isaac Ochberg and his worthy associates, and on behalf of Molly, I wish you great success with the progress and distribution of your book on the twin histories of Johannesburg's Arcadia and Cape Town's Oranjia.

Arthur, Molly, Moshe, son of Yosef, and Hymie ~1990

Arthur, Nesta, Saidee, Saul, Abe and Molly – 1990
Saul's Graduation (Saidee and Abe are Nesta's parents)

Steven Hymie and Rodney – 1984 Betty's Bay

Arthur, Molly holding great grand daughter Lois and Alon
Four Generations May 2009

Chapter 49 – SHEWA GELERNTER (1916-2003)

HILDA MODLIN (LIPSHITZ) - SHEWA GELERNTER
Written by Fay Lipshitz

My late Mother, Shewa Gelernter was born in Brest-Litovsk (Poland at that time) in 1916. Her parents were Gittel and Yitzhak. She had an older brother Haim. Her mother and brother were alive at the time Isaac Ochberg collected her.

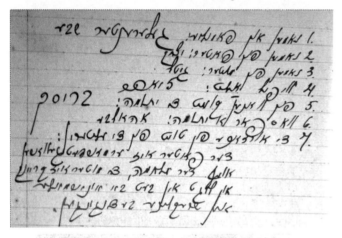

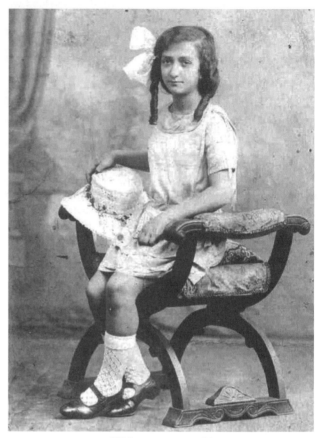

Hilda as a young girl

Details of Sheva Gelerenter as recorded in register at Oranjia
1 Name and surname: Sheva Gelerenter
2 Father: Yitzhak 3 Mother: Gitl 4 Age: 4 years
5 Place of origin Brisk
6 Who died: One parent
7 General Comments: Father was murdered in the War.
The mother is sick and lies in bed in abnormal and horrific
conditions

She didn't know what the circumstances were under which she came to be separated from her mother and brother and brought to South Africa; whether she was "given up" or had become separated from them. She was one of the youngest of the children he brought over. She continued to get letters in Yiddish from Gittel and Haim until 1938.

In South Africa my mother was adopted by Mr and Mrs Seligson, who gave her a loving home and called her Hilda, and she thus became Hilda Seligson. In 1937 she married my father, Barney Lipshitz and during the next few years I and then my brother were born. My brother was given the name Haim (Hymie) after her poor doomed brother. My parents divorced after a few years, and in 1955 my mother remarried, to Joe Modlin.

My dear mother died in Highlands House, Cape Town, in February 2003 at the age of 86. In the room opposite to hers at Highlands House was Mr Migdal, who had travelled with her to South Africa with Isaac Ochberg.

Hilda aged about six with the Seligson Family

FAMILY LEFT BEHIND AND LETTERS SENT

Hilda's mother Gittel and her older brother Haim were alive at the time Isaac Ochberg collected her. Later, during the Holocaust, they probably shared the fate of the rest of the Jews of Brest Litovsk and were drowned in the River Bug.

Gittel Gelernter, the mother left behind

Haim Gelernter, the brother left behind

Hilda was unaware of the Gelerenter family while she was growing up with the Seligsons and was only told by two members of the Orphanage Committee when she was about 16 years old and her adoptive mother had passed away. She then made contact with her family in Poland

These letters were written by Gittel to her "machatonim" Hilda's husband's parents, who would translate her letters for my mother, who couldn't read Yiddish. It was written after Hilda's marriage in 1937. The letters are not very informative, as you'll see, and was written, to judge by the orthography, by a simple soul. There is not much information to be gained, unfortunately, as to their lives, which were shortly to end so tragically.

Letter 1:

To our dear beloved machatonim,

Write and tell us how is the machatenester's health, how is she feeling now? We were very upset. May G-d send her a speedy recovery. Do not be afraid, it is not a dangerous illness. She must be careful what she eats, and not eat spicy food, and if her legs are swollen, she should wrap them in silk bandages, and G-d will send you good health, because you are taking care of my daughter. You must be a healthy mother for your beloved children all the while you still must bring them to the chuppa, together with your husband.

Be healthy, and may you make a speedy recovery.
 I am sorry about your illness.
From your machatenester,

Gittell Gelernter.

Letter 2:

My dear mechutan,

How is your health? How is your business going? How are the beloved children and grandchildren? I thank you, dear mechutan, that you read our letters to my daughter. She writes that you read our letters to her, and I am very happy about that. And may G-d help our machateneste to have good health. We beg you to write soon, as we are worried because our mechatenet is not well, and so we would like an early reply. The mechutenet whom you don't know wishes you good health.
Gittel Gelernter.

My son, who doesn't know you, sends you greetings and also wishes you good health. We bless your children and grandchildren. Please let us have an immediate reply.

On the address please write Haim Gelernter. He has two names, Haim Leiser, but on letters he uses just Haim, because it happened once that the postman did not know the address.

So please write just Haim Gelernter. Please send our letters to this address (address written below in Polish).

Hilda and Barney at their engagement

In 1937 Hilda married my father, Barney Lipshitz, whose parents had immigrated from Plinyan (Plungian) in Lithuania in the early years of the last century. Unfortunately the marriage was not a success, and several years later, after I and my brother were born, they divorced. After some further years, my mother remarried, to Joe Modlin, a good man but poor like herself.

Hilda on her wedding day – 1937

The writer Flaubert's phrase, "A Simple Heart" precisely describes my mother. She was always poor, and without much in the way of education, resources or support, and all her adult life she worked at the Kosher counter at the OK Bazaars. She lived simply and frugally, without envy or bitterness, was kind, compassionate and a humble soul.

After her arrival in Cape Town in 1921, she remained there all her life, except for some visits to Israel after I moved here. She died in Highlands House in Cape Town on 8 February 2003. If there is a Gan Eden, I believe she must be there, if anyone is.

MY STAY IN ORANJIA
Written by Hyman Meyer Lipshitz

After my parents were divorced, I was put in Oranjia at the age of four where I grew up, 1950 to 1962, together with my sister Fay.

Hilda holding Fay   *Hilda with Fay and Hymie in pram*

I am Hyman Meyer Lipshitz, 64 years son of Hilda Modlin (Gelernter). I am named after Hilda's brother (Chaim Meyer) who remained behind in Poland and was murdered by the Germans before I was born.

We were therefore second generation "Orphans" .I do recall the Arc kids coming down to Muizenberg during December holidays in the early 1960s and living in tents near to where our holiday camp was.

Hyman (Hymie) and Fay

Hyman (Hymie) and Fay

Hyman (Hymie) and Fay

My stay at Oranjia was a wonderful one. I always had friends to play with, we had a soccer field, tennis court and a section for the smaller kids with swings. We had a second home in Muizenberg which we moved to in year end holidays and that was when the fun time started.

Habonim Group at Oranjia – Hymie back row second from left

My mother Hilda used to see us every Sunday. When I was small she would walk the two kilometers up to the Home to save bus fare to fetch us for the day. When we were older we went on our own to visit her on Sunday.

When I was about 13 Hilda remarried to Joe Modlin who also had a daughter in Oranjia and that is how they met.

I have many wonderfull memories and a few bad ones of my stay in Oranjia 1950-1962 (12 years) but on the whole would not wish for anything better. When I come across an ex "Orphan" in later years it is like meeting a lost brother or sister and the feeling is much stronger than meeting an old classmate.

Hymie, Hilda and Joe Modlin - Muizenberg

While at Oranjia, I do recall celebrating Ochbergs birthday annually but by that stage he had already passed away. His daughter, I forget her name, used to celebrate the event with us and give us sweets. In the dining room of Oranjia there was a huge picture of Ochberg hanging on the wall whose eyes used to follow one around the hall.

I attended the reunion party in 1972 together with my mother and wife to celebrate the 50th year of the arrival of the children in Cape Town. We were all seated according to the area of origin. We saw a movie of the ship landing in Cape Town and the children arriving .That movie still exists today.

Group picture Oranjia 1957
Hymie bottom left next to Milton Kahn and his brother Neil

Group Photo Oranjia – 1953 – names on next page

The children starting from the back row and left to right: Gerry Gamaroff, Louis ?, Claire Moss, Fanny Wistow, Maureen Levy, Alma Mausenbaum, John de Combes, Rosalie Kuyk, Esther Simanowitz, Doreen Modlin, Woolfie Simanowitz, Eric Mausenbaum, Michael de Combes, Bennie Gamaroff, Hymie Mausenbaum, Rosalind Pichanik, Peter Mayer, Anna Kaplan, Fay Lipshitz, Sunya Kaplan, Yvonne Meyer, Henry Meyer, David De Combes, Myra Meyer, Estelle Joselowitz, Ray Katzeff, Beryl Levy, Enid Joselowitz, Hymie Lipshitz, Denbigh Kuyk, Sylvia Meyer, Yvonne Mayer, Sandra Dunstan, Edith Gellert, Charlie Meyer, Josephine Gotthilf, Rachel Gamaroff, Felix de Combes.
On the left are Mr and Mrs Harris, from England, the "Matron and Principal" and we called them "Matron" and "Sir"
Hymie 2nd row 1st left Fay 4th row 2nd left

No 2- Group photo Oranjia ~ 1956

I'll give you names of kids I recognise more or less in "rows" as they appear: from bottom up and left to right
Hymie Lipshitz, Myra Meyer, Benny Gamaroff, Milton Kahn, Edith Gellert, Sandra Dunstan,Hymie Mausenbaum, Felix de Combes, Josephone Gotthilf, Rachel Gamaroff, David and John de Combes, Anna Kaplan, Ray Katzeff, Beryl Levy, Esther Simanowitz, Enid Joselowitz, Doreen Modlin, Sunya Kaplan, Eric Mausenbaum, Woolfie Simanowitz, Fay Lipshitz, Peter Mayer.
Recognizable Adults in pic (left to right): Sylvia Gottlieb (an Orphanage Committee member, and at least till a couple of years ago was still alive and working at Highlands House), "Auntie Mollie" (Mollie Nochomowitz - she lived on the premises and was a motherly figure for us all), Julius Simenhoff, Mr Harris (the Principal), Fannie Lockitch (active on the Orphanage committee until her death a few years ago- also an Ochberg orphan), Dave Lockitch (committee) and Mrs Haussman (wife of "Photo Haussman" the photographer.

No 3- Oranjia group photo 1958

Top row: Estelle Joselowitz, Beryl Levy, John and Michael de Combes, Henry Meyer, Fay Lipshitz, Emanuel (Brand?) Enid Joselowitz.
2nd row: Walter Kahn?, Myra Meyer, Charlie Meyer, Trevor Bouwer ?, Bennie Gamaroff, Ray Katzeff, Sandra Dunstan, Yvonne Mayer, ?, ?, Lenny Kahn?.   3rd row. I can pick out Hymie Lipshitz, Rachel Gamaroff, Anna Kaplan, Hymie Mausembaum, Felix de Combes,Milton Kahn, David de Combes, Malka Bouwer, and Neil Kahn 4th row down: Sandra Dunstan, Maureen Levy, Esther Simanowitz, ?, Matron and Principal Mr and Mrs Wagman, Nurse ?, Sunya Kaplan, Ray Katzeff
Bottom row: can't identify the little ones but the Wagmans' two daughters are there - Judith and ? and David Bouwer Marcell de combes Graham Bouwer

Group photos sent in by Hymie Lipshitz and captions are from Fay Lipshitz

No 3 - Group photo Oranjia ~ 1958 - names on prior page

No 4 - Group photo Oranjia at Muizenberg holiday home ~ 1954 - names on next page

No 4 - Oranjia group photo at Muizenberg holiday home

I can't make out most of the kids - but these are the adults I recognize, from back forwards: Mrs Ray Gradner (matriarch of the Committee), Auntie Mollie, Jack Stodel, and, near the front right, Mrs Getz (sitting between Enid Joselowitz and Ray Katzeff), Mrs Getz was a seminal figure in my life - wife of Harry Getz, well-known sportsman at the time (swimmer?) She, Rhoda Getz, ran the library at the orphanage, and through her I started my lifelong love affair with books. Her daughter, Lyndall Gordon, is today a well-known literary scholar in Oxford (T.S. Eliot) and wrote a book about her circle of friends in Cape Town and Good Hope School. Once a year Mrs Getz gave "library prizes" to the kids. I always got the prize for having read the most books - but everyone got a prize, such as "a prize for having a lovely smile", etc. She was the most important figure in my life in those years.
The man with the guitar is I think Cyril Stodel, brother of Jack. Both were committee members.
We went to Muizenberg every year during the summer holidays and I guess I liked it.

Film evening at Oranjia Hilda 2nd row right, Hymie back eating and Joe Modlin right centre

MY ORANJIA EXPERIENCE
Written by Fay Lipshitz

The Oranjia experience was a difficult one for me. I hated feeling different from the other "normal" Jewish girls from comfortable homes in Oranjezicht, and growing up in an institution led to me feeling worthless and lonely. Unfortunately for very many years thereafter I was angry with my poor mother, and never had an intimate relationship with her.

It was only in her last years, when I was already in Israel, that I came to understand and accept her reasons for putting Hymie and me in Oranjia (my father was out of the picture and my mother was left with no support, financial or social, and had to work hard all her life in the OK Bazaars.

Children at Oranjia – Fay seated on right

Both Hymie and I were at Oranjia from age five to 16. He had a much healthier response to the experience, and even has good memories. Of course now that she's gone I feel so sorry that I was not more compassionate and kind.

Fay and Hilda – 1966

Fay and David Lidsky

Fay and Hymie in Israel

I have been living in Jerusalem since 1973. I am married to David Lidsky and we have a son Daniel. I sometimes think it would have gladdened Gittel's heart to know that her granddaughter was living in the land of Israel.

Hymie Continues

When Joe Modlin passed away in 1983, Fay and I bought a flat in Sea Point for Hilda where she stayed until she went to Highlands House in 1999. She passed away on 8 February 2002 aged 86.

When in Highlands House, she had a room opposite Mr Migdal who was also an Ochberg Orphan

I (Hymie) married Charlene Miller in 1971 (it is already 39 years how time flies). We have two daughters, Sharon born 1975 and Deborah born 1978. They both have married men from Johannesburg. Sharon married Anton Lopis and they have a daughter Jenna born 2008. Deborah married Paul Grusd and they have no children as yet.

Fay, Daniel and David Lidsky

Sharon, Charlene, Hymie, Deborah and Hilda
Sharon's batmitzvah 1987

Sharon, Charlene holding granchild Jenna, Hymie and Deborah and in front are Anton and Paul

My Granny was a real, gentle soul and I remember on a Saturday afternoon she would visit us, or we would visit her. We used to drink tea and she would always have a chocolate for my sister and myself. She taught me how to crochet and we would play cards together. Those were the days.

Hilda with grandchildren Sharon, Debbie and Daniel

MY GRANNY
Sharon Lopis daughter of Hymie Lipshitz writes

This is an incredible journey to look back at our ancestory and I'm so impressed with the photos of my late granny Hilda Modlin!

Fay and Hilda 1999. Note the height difference due to bad nutrition in Poland in early years of Hilda's life

Hilda

53 Years later – Milton Kahn, his brother Neil holding original plaque rescued from the scrap yard when Oranjia was demolished, and Hymie

PART 2
CAPE TOWN, SOUTH AFRICA

SECTION 8
LIFE STORIES OF OCHBERG ORPHANS PLACED IN THE CARE OF THE CAPE JEWISH ORPHANAGE ~ ORANJIA

In this section you can read the individual life stories of the Ochberg Orphans who where placed in the care of the Cape Jewish Orphanage ~ Oranjia

Chapter 50 – MALKA AND FREDA ALTSEFRUM

MALKA (MOLLY) AND FREDA

In 1921 Malka and Freda were young ladies of 26 and 22 years old and were 'attendants' to the children and this explains why they were not on the list of children that are in Ochberg Orphan group passport photos.

Lauren Snitcher writes about the Altzefrum family.
"I have found Freda and Malka's names on the ship's manifest. They were indeed part of the Ochberg orphan group and they are listed as attendants. That is all the information I have on them other than their ages where Freda is listed as 22 and Malka as 26.

Molly (Malka) and Freda Altsefrum

THE ALTSEFRUM FAMILY
Written by Aron the son of Molly

My father's name was Jack Suntup, he married my mother Molly in 1924. Her adopted name was Molly Wilder but her birth name was Malka Alzufrum. She was adopted by her uncle Chazen Wilder who was the Rabbi at the Cape Town Synagogue. My mother told me that she lived in a village in Galicia in Russia on the border of Austria and Poland. The King at the time was Franz Josef.

My mother's father's name was Sholem Alzufrum, she had a brother Yankel who died of influenza and also had three sisters; Sarah-Bella, Esther-Chaya and Freda. Sarah and Esther were sent to Bergen Belsen and she never heard from them again. Her mother and father were both murdered by the Cossacks in pogroms in front of them. My mother and Freda escaped and hid on a hop farm which their father owned. The workers on the farm who loved the family dug a hole, covered it with a roof and hid them there for a long time bringing them food and water.

Molly and Freda were eventually sent by ship to Cape Town, organised by Isaac Ochberg. Because Molly was one of the more senior girls, she was asked to look after all the younger children. When Molly arrived in Cape Town she lived with her uncle Chazen Wilder until she left to take up a position as the Matron of the Cape Town orphanage.

Molly and Freda's parents and grandparents were all Rabbonim going back hundreds of years. We were raised in a very religiously observant home but unfortunately my mother gave this up after she lost her sisters and other extended family in the Holocaust.

THE ALTSEFRUM FAMILY
Related by Sadie and Rachelle, the daughters of Freda.

The Altsefrum family lived in a small town in or near Libov in Poland and when the Bolsheviks came into the town they killed the Mother, Father and their Brothers and Sisters. The two sisters hid under the house and they chopped off our mother's hair.

Our Mother, Freda Altsefrum and her sister Molly (Malka) were part of the group of Ochberg Orphans who were brought out to Cape Town South Africa in 1921. They did not go up to Johannesburg but were placed in the care of Oranjia, the Jewish Orphanage in Cape Town.

Isaac Ochberg took the sisters and the rest of the children via Danzig to England. The sisters had an Uncle Rev Wilder living in Cape Town, however, they stayed in the Orphanage. Freda lived in the Cape Orphanage and became a matron there.

(Our Aunt Molly told Hilda, her daughter, two stories about how our parents died; "Died in the flu" and "murdered by the Bolshviks" I don't know what is correct.)

MOLLY'S FAMILY
Related by Aron the son of Molly

Molly moved up to Johannesburg and met my father Jack Suntup. They married in 1924 and had three children; Hilda, Solly and Aron (myself). My Dad passed away when I was 16 years old and my Mom died 20 years later. Solly also passed away about five years ago and Hilda is living in a retirement village in Cape Town.

My wife and I together with my three children, Lyn, Gary and Robyn migrated to Australia in 1990 and have been living in Sydney ever since. Thank G-d we now have six lovely grandchildren ranging in age from two to 18.

FREDA'S FAMILY

Freda's married name was Segal and she had three children; Sadie (now Lurie) born in 1927, Rachel (now Meyers) was born in 1931 and Charlie Segal born in 1940. Freda was not well and in 1940 when Charlie was born the two older girls were placed in the care of Arcadia.

Charlie was placed in the care of Arcadia in 1942 and left in 1957. There is an article on him in the Arcadia Centenary Book "100 Years of Arc Memories". He was a most talented trumpet player but sadly he was troubled and took his own life in 1957.

SADIE (SEGAL) LURIE

Sadie (Segal) Lurie (daughter of Freda) was born 18 June 1927 and writes;

My sister Rachelle born in 1931, my younger brother Charlie (Tsatske) born in 1940 and I were put in the care of Arcadia in about 1942 because our mother could not look after us. She had Alzheimer's at an early age.

I remember many many fellow Arcs including Willie, Celia and Sheila Aizakowitz. I was in the Arc for a few years and then worked as a switchboard operator and typist.

SADIE'S ARC MEMORIES

It is with pleasant Memories I recall the few years of my childhood spent at Arcadia.

There didn't seem to be a problem with my having the fact that I came there after having lived with an aunt in Norwood and was also placed in a convent and being placed in a convent takes some adjusting. This shoving around didn't affect me much despite hardships as I have a shiny, happy disposition. I loved the spirit of the place.

I loved the hustle and bustle of it all, lots of happy kids making noises of all different volumes. Here we were coming from all different walks of life for different reasons but mostly due to dire straights we were placed in Arcadia. Under such strange circumstances this for me was a new adventure.

In the bus which took us to school every morning Senior Boys would occupy the one side of the seating and us girls the other. Each morning I couldn't wait to run downstairs to find a seat that was just opposite this very good looking fellow called Donald Goldman so that I would be able to get a glimpse of him. My heart would go pitter patter when I saw him hoping he would notice me. Well thank goodness the great day arrived. He noticed me and we started a beautiful relationship. We used to walk down the driveway whenever possible. What beautiful surrounds there was to enjoy and admire. I was the envy of many a young lass. Our friendship lasted for many years. He loved his soccer. I used to go and watch him play. We used to

have a secret place just under the trees below the stairs overlooking Oxford Road and discuss our lives and what we would do after we left the Arc.

Well I went my way and became a Hairdresser and eventually owned the Business. He went his way. We did see each other from time to time at Arc functions but unfortunately with the passing of time and other issues this was not to be. Just thought I would give you some part of my stay at Arcadia. Of course there is lots more. Many beautiful and wonderful memories, from time to time us old Arcs get together but with the passing of time there are not many of us around. Lots have left the country and so forth.

Recently we had an event in the Sandton Shull Hall. It was great. Unfortunately we only enjoyed the pleasure of a couple of oldies.

My late brother *Charlie* was quite a guy. I didn't realise how popular and talented he was and the photos in the book of him look excellent.

Sadie married Gerald Lurie and had two children, David and Charmaine.

Sadie's Family: Gerald Lurie with David and Charmaine

A young Sadie with the Girls Hostel in Harrow Road behind her   *An older Sadie*

Granddaughter Shereen, son David and daughter Charmaine

Sadie

RACHELLE MEYERS (RAE SEGAL)

Sadie's sister, Rachelle Meyers (Rae Segal) born 11 July 1931 who now lives in Kinross South Africa writes.

I went to Athlone school and was in the Arc from age nine to age 16 and then had to leave and look after myself in the strange world. At age 16 I started working and supported myself. I stayed in the Josselyn Hotel. I met my Husband, Sammy Meyers, when I was 28. We were married 15 years and I have now been on my own for 30 years.

Rachel Segal married Sammy Meyers in 1962

Josef Vider, Samuel and Vider 1987

My Father came from Covno Geberna (in Russia) and my daughter Lana married Josef Vider, whose parents were in the concentration camps.

Rachel married Sammy Meyers in 1962 and they had one daughter Lana Vider (nee Meyers) who is married to Josef Vider and had one child Samuel.

245

CHARLIE (TSATSKE) SEGAL

Freda (nee Altsefrum) Segal's son Charlie was born in 1940. He was placed in the care of Arcadia in 1942 and left in 1957. Charlie was a most talented trumpet player but sadly he was troubled and passed away tragically at a young age.

There is a wonderful story about Charlie written by the late Solly Farber in the Arcadia Centenary Book "100 Years of Arc Memories"

Extract from the 1959 *Arcadian* – Au Revoir

"Tsatske was a very popular boy which is proved by the fact that he won 'the most popular boy award' twice. He was regarded as one of the finest sportsmen ever to be produced by the Arc, until he gave sport up in favour of his trumpet and school work. Tsatske did exceedingly well in both these things, passing matric with a University pass and receiving colours for the orchestra and military band. Tsatske was prefect and chief Chazen at the Arc in his last year."

Solly Faber remembered

"Charlie was as lean as a beanpole and had a head of tightly curled blond hair. As a small chap he was extremely cute and was nicknamed *Tsatske*, which in Yiddish is a plaything, a toy, a bauble. For Charlie this was a very suitable name. Our friendship was based on a mutual passion for music and specifically for the harmonica or the mouth organ as it is referred to by Philistines who don't know better. We had a harmonica band at the Home. Charlie played melody in the band and I played countermelody."

Charlie playing trumpet and the harmonica

David Sandler Remembers

I remember Tsatske Segal as tall with curly blonde hair, and always smiling. I remember him wearing a jacket and playing a shining silver trumpet. He played very well with crisp very clear and loud notes. The two songs "Oh my Papa" and "Danny Boy" spring to mind. Also as I remember it, he spoke very fast and swallowed his words.

Charlie Segal blowing the Shofar

Ronny Schreeuwer Remembers

That's about what I remember of Charlie as well. I used to sit and listen to him play on the steps behind the middle dormitory and was always fascinated by the beautiful sound that came out of that trumpet. I never knew that his nickname was Tsatske.

Solly Farber - Charlie's other favourite tune was "Cherry pink and apple-blossom white"

David Sandler - After many many enquiries I found someone who knew the tune "Cherry pink and apple-blossom white". It is very familiar and I recall Tzatske playing it and how he used to really hold onto the 4th note.

MY THREE YEARS OUTSIDE ARCADIA
Written by Charlie Segal

It seems like an eternity since I left Arcadia. I feel that the first three years of an Ex-Arcadian in the outside world is one of the most important periods in his life.

While we are at Arcadia, we are bound together like one inseparable family. Should a problem arise, we need only to turn to one or more of our companions for help. Once out in the open world, we very often are confronted with problems we must solve alone.

I therefore think that it is most important for us to set ourselves a goal in life and take full responsibility for the outcome, come what may. By instilling in us this sense of duty, not only to ourselves, but to our family, friends and business associates, we are bound to succeed in life where every opportunity for success exists.

It requires our sincere and undaunted initiative to achieve it.

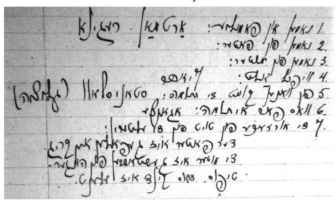

Family details of Regina Artman as recorded on page 143 of the register kept by the Cape Jewish Orphanage (Oranjia).
1 Name and surname: Regina Artman   2 Father: Unknown
3 Mother: Unknown   4 Age: 7 years   5 Place of origin: Stanislav
6 How orphaned: Both parents
7 General Comments: The father fell in the War.
The mother died of hunger and typhus.
The child is alone.

REGINA ARTMAN
Written by her daughter Celia Isaacman

My mother was born in 1914 in Stanislav, in what was once Poland but which was during her early childhood there, invaded by Germany and later by Russia. She had memories of the German occupation when the soldiers handed out white chocolate to the children in the streets, but terror when the Russians came when she and her family were hidden away in a haystack. Her father fought in the First World War with the Polish army and returned home ill and there being no hospital facilities for Jews, he died shortly after, leaving his wife with two little girls, my mother Regina and her younger sister Frieda.

Her mother struggled to support her little girls by herself for some time but found this an uphill battle so when she heard of a man coming from South Africa to rescue orphaned children and take them to a better country, she decided to try to get her children accepted by him. As they were not strictly speaking orphans, she took the drastic step of abandoning them so it would appear that they were orphans. She took them to a nearby village and told them to sit and wait for her on the steps of a building. At this time my mother was about six and her little sister must have been about two or three. Regina was given strict instructions that she must look after her sister and never let her out of her sight. My mother took this instruction very seriously. The two of them sat all day waiting for their mother to come back for them, but she never came.

Frieda the younger sister left behind. Stanislava 1933
Inscription on the back reads "In remembrance. From your sister Frieda. Please send me your photograph.

An older lady noticed that they had been sitting there all day and came up and spoke to them and ended up taking them home with her and then tried to find out where their mother was. When she failed to find her, she decided she might keep the girls herself as her children had grown up and gone, however, when her own children heard this they were horrified and told her to take them to the Jewish orphanage, which she subsequently did.

The orphanage was very overcrowded and my mother remembered that the beds were pushed right up against each other to make room for all the children. The matron took a liking to my mother who had beautiful red-gold hair which fell naturally into ringlets, and when Isaac Ochberg came to select a few children from the orphanage to take back to South Africa, she suggested to him that he take Regina as one of those children. My mother was woken up when it was still dark, dressed and taken with the few chosen children to go on the big adventure. She did as she was told and only when they set off, did she realise that her sister was not to come with her. She was devastated by this and was inconsolable. Maybe her sister was considered to be too young. She cried all the way to

Regina in her school uniform.
On the back was an inscription "To Daddy Ochberg, with love from one of your children, Regina"

London as she felt she had disobeyed her mother's instructions and let her little sister down.

When she told me this, I always believed that she must have been exaggerating as how could anyone cry all the way from Poland to London? However one day many, many years later when my mother made contact with Solly Jossel she asked him if he remembered her and he wrote back that the only Regina that he remembered was a little girl who cried all the way from Warsaw to London!

When she reached London it was found that she had measles, and she was separated from the other children and taken to the Great Ormond Steet Hospital to recover. As she did not speak any English, they found a Jewish lady who could visit her. This lady was very kind and gave her a little present of a chocolate shoe. My mother loved chocolate, but could not bring herself to eat this beautiful high healed shoe and so took it with her on board the ship when she eventually went to Cape Town to join the other children. She was too young to travel on her own, being either six or seven and so they found a young man who had been studying the violin in London and who was now preparing to sail back to Cape Town who agreed to keep an eye on her. They became good friends and he visited her once she had settled in the Orphanage and he decided to try to adopt her. This was refused as he was unmarried.

My mother's memories of Oranjia, the Orphanage in Cape Town, are a bit mixed. She remembered how there was a Principal who was there in her early years who was quite cruel and who would come into the room early in the morning and wake them up with a blast on his whistle. Anyone who did not immediately jump out of bed was hit with his cane. As she slept in the bed nearest the door she was usually the first to taste his punishment, but she soon developed good hearing and as soon as she heard footsteps nearing the room, she would jump out of bed to avoid his cane. There was a Ladies Committee that must have suspected that something was wrong as they would come to the children in the playground and question them about what happened in the Orphanage, but no one dared to say anything against him. They did however give him the nickname of Loki, the devil.

Regina's mother and sister Freda – 1931

She also had very good memories of her days there. On Sundays visitors would come to see the children but my mother was rather shy and retiring and was sure no one would come to see her and so hid in the toilet and would stay there with a book, reading. Isaac Ochberg, who of course knew all the children, would ask where she was and would always send someone to fetch her. He tried to make all the children feel special and wanted. When later he made a second trip to Europe to try to rescue some more children, my mother begged him to find her sister and bring her back with him. He was not able to do this and unfortunately it seems that she and her mother perished in the Holocaust.

In later years she attended Cape Town High School and when she finished Standard 8 (Year 10) she left school so that she could earn some money to try to get her sister and mother out of Poland. There was a hostel for girls who left the Orphanage in Forest Road in Oranjezicht and she stayed there and had some very happy times. There would be dances on Saturday nights and the girls could drop the names of young men they would like to invite into a box and those in charge of the hostel would invite the guys to come without mentioning who was actually the person asking them. In this way the hostel became a place where the young Jewish men could have a fun evening and meet the girls. She got a job at Fig Brothers, a firm in Sir Lowry Road and to try to save money would walk there and back every day. By this time she started to get letters from Poland from her sister, her mother and other members of her family begging her for money as they were restricted more and more in their ability to earn money to live. She would send whatever she could back to try to help them, but her salary was meagre and she was still only in her teens so it was never what she would have liked to give. When World War II began, the correspondence with her family in Poland dried up and even though she tried to trace Frieda after the war, she never managed to find her or to positively establish her final fate.

Regina the mountaineer – 25 February 1934

Muizenberg Beach - 8 March 1931
Regina second row second from left

Rosha (Rosy) Heft is the girl with the dark hair and the girl with the lighter hair (in fact a reddish colour) is Regina Artman.
"My Mom was one of Rosy's friends in the Orphanage and later they both enjoyed mountaineering together on weekends."

Regina with friends

249

Regina looking over the world

REMEMBERING REGINA ARTMAN
Written by Sam Chait, the son of Daniel Chait, the long serving groundsman of Arcadia.

We the family knew Regina as Jean and our family history with Jean really begins after she had already been brought out to South Africa and settled in the Oranjia Cape Town Jewish Orphanage.

My wife Judy's family, farmed in the Willowmore District in the Eastern Cape. This was a huge farm, the main produce being citrus (oranges), seeds, sheep and goats and of course ostriches.

Judy's parents, David and Ada Gellman were sponsors and supporters of Oranjia. On many occasions children at the orphanage were invited to come and spend holidays at the farm.

Amongst the children who went were Jean and Norman Migdale, who were both Ochberg orphans. After many visits by Jean a strong bond developed between her and the Gellman family. So much so, that Jean was officially adopted and became part of the family.

Regina Weintroub (Nee Artman) taken in the garden while on holiday at the Gellman Farm, Zandvlakte, Distict Willowmore, Cape Province

In her later years Jean married Hymie Weintroub. She bore two sons and a daughter. Her husband Hymie passed away many years ago. The older son Edgar, lives in Israel where he has been for many years. Celia, the daughter resides in Perth. Michael, the younger son also lived in Perth, but unfortunately passed away a few years ago.

Celia Isaacman continues

When my mother left Oranjia and worked just outside the City, she tried to save as much money as she could to send back to Poland. One of the things she did was to walk wherever possible and to economise on clothes and food. As a result of this she became ill and it was suspected that she had Tuberculosis. A doctor suggested that she move to a drier climate, but this was of course impossible for her, knowing no-one outside Cape Town. Help came from an unlikely source.

Regina was enjoying the freedom of her teenage years and of the experience of meeting new people when she fell in love with Norman Migdale. They must have been in their late teens or maybe only 20 and it must have been quite a love affair because there is a whole photo album with pictures of the two of them which my Mother kept all her life.

Norman Migdale and Regina Clifton Beach - 9 December 1934　　　　*Norman Migdale*

Norman was, I believe, what was called a commercial traveller who went around from village to village and to isolated farms in the districts to sell them goods. One of these farms was owned by a Jewish family called Gellman and over time Norman became quite friendly with them. When mother was diagnosed with possible TB, Norman told them her story and about her illness and they immediately invited Regina to come and stay with them. As Mrs Gellman said, they would feed her up on good wholesome farm produce and make her well again. It was quite an offer, especially as her condition could have been contagious and as they had never even met Regina.

My mother travelled to the Little Karoo to a small place called Willowmore, to a large and very isolated farm in the district called Zandvlakte where the Gellman family welcomed her and made her feel at home. She stayed with them for some months during which time her health improved considerably and she felt loved and welcomed by the whole family. The youngest

Gellman child was Judy, who much later married Sam Chait, whose father's story is also in the Arcadia Books as his father was the groundsman there.

At this stage she was very little maybe three or four and she became a great favourite of my mother. When it came time for my mother to leave and go back to Cape Town, Rifka and David Gellman told Regina or Jeankele as Mrs Gellman affectionately called her, that she was now one of their family and that she should refer to them as Mom and Dad. My mother who all her life had wanted to belong somewhere, was overwhelmed and felt that these were the kindest people in the world, especially as they had six children of their own. The relationship was a lasting one and while I was growing up, I together with my older brother had several holidays on the farm visiting our 'grandparents'. They always remembered our birthdays and it was due to their kindness that all three of us attended University and all ended up with degrees. They were truly an amazing family.

Jean on her wedding day

In this way my Mother's life was once more saved and we always felt that she had a guardian angel looking after her.

It was some time later that my mother met my father, Hymie Weintroub. He was from London and had also been brought up in a Jewish orphanage, a large one called Norwood where he and most of his brothers and a sister had been sent after their mother had died soon after giving birth to her sixth child. Hymie was only three at the time, but he soon learned that he did not wish to live in London and as soon as he was old enough to leave Norwood, at the tender age of 14, he took his barmitzvah money and bought a ticket to sail to South Africa to join his older married sister, Lily. Thus he came to Cape Town and later met and fell in love with my mother and they were married in 1938 in July with a number of the Oranjia Committee Ladies there at the Shul to wish them well.

They lived in a small flat in Sea Point and in time had three children, Edgar, Celia and Michael. Edgar went to Israel shortly after he got his degree and once he had turned 21, to join his Habonim friends and first lived on Kibbutz Yizrael and later moved to Jerusalem where he lived with his wife and two sons, Ohud and Lior. I qualified as a High School teacher after first obtaining my BA degree and later married Avroy Isaacman and together some years later we emigrated to Australia. We had two children, Lindsay our daughter and our son Gavin. My brother Michael qualified as a Social Worker and two years after we left Cape Town, he and my Mother came to live in Perth. He met and married an Australia girl, Erica Rappeport, and they had Andrew, now an accountant, and Nicki who is currently studying at Curtin.

That in a very brief form is the history of our family. As I look at it, it is quite a sobering thought that had it not been for Isaac Ochhberg, my mother would have perished as we believe her sister and mother did in the Holocaust, and none of us would have been here. What an amazing man and how could he have imagined the consequences of his actions and the number of descendants of those orphans and how well they did for themselves despite the traumatic experiences they all had in their home countries before coming to South Africa.

Jean surrounded by her family

Chapter 52 – CHAVA BERKOWITZ

Father was killed in 1914 War.
The mother died of hunger + need in 1916
when
in pogroms. The child suffered a
lot and is alone

Family details of Chava Berkowitz as recorded on page 125 of the register kept by the Cape Jewish Orphanage (Oranjia).
1 Name and surname: Chava Berkowitz 2 Father: Avraham
3 Mother: Chaya 4 Age: 12 years 5 Place of origin: Brest
6 How orphaned: Both parents
7 General Comments: Father was killed in 1914 War.
The mother died of hunger and need in 1916 when in pogroms.
The child suffered greatly and is alone.

Eva (Chava) Berkowitz

EVA (CHAVA) BERKOWITZ
Written by and photos from Jenny (Flink) Segall
News cuttings and programmes from Veronica Belling

Eva's parents were shot and her brother Zalman was perhaps five years old when he died. Eva took her brother Zalman into the forests. She hid him in a dustbin when she went to look for food, and one day she came back and found the Russians had shot him. She never got over that.

Eva and was on the boat with my Mom and Aunt (Ruza and Neta Hans) when they were brought out to Cape Town in 1921 by Isaac Ochberg. The three remained life long friends and 'family' and she was an 'aunt' to me. So she was one of the Ochberg children as well, attaching herself to my mom and aunt from the time they were little ones at the Orphanage until their deaths.

She had very bad sinus and was operated on her face and had awful scars. In those days the scars could not be fixed. She was a wonderful person. I saw her almost every day of my life and she was part of our family.

Eva never married. She had a sad life, and became one of the great Yiddish Actresses of the stage in Johannesburg from her 20s to her 50s. She was associated with the Yiddish Folk School in Johannesburg for many years.

When she died my husband and I put up her stone, and put on it in memory of her late parents, who were shot, and her late brother Zalman.

Eva (Chava) Berkowitz

Eva was a wonderful Yiddish actress, who played on stage with the best actors that came to South Africa to act. She played the piano well and also taught it. She led a full life. I do have a photo of the stone we put up for her.

Eva (Chava) Berkowitz

All I can tell you is that she was a wonderful friend and family to us and needs to be remembered as well.

Eva (Chava) Berkowitz

"MOTKE FROM SLABODKE"

Amusing Yiddish Play at Standard

Full houses at the Standard Theatre, Johannesburg, during the week have appreciatively received the sparkling Yiddish musical comedy "Motke from Slabodke" presented by Madame Sarah Sylvia's company of players, featuring Miriam Kressyn and Hymie Jacobson, of the Second Avenue Theatre, New York.

"Motke from Slabodke" tells the story of a 'Greener' from the "old country" who comes to America with his fiancee, Hanele, and looks up his old friend Rachmiel, who used to go to school with him. Rachmiel has become a renowned opera singer. He and his family warmly welcome the arrivals from Slabodke, and Rachmiel is particularly interested in Hanele, who has a most pleasing voice which he undertakes to train and thus make the young lady an opera star. He takes her to Italy for two years, where, incidentally they fall in love with each other, so that when they return, Motke's dreams are unhappily shattered. Nevertheless, the play ends on a happy note, with Motke marrying another member of the cast.

The play gives wide scope for the sparkling talent of Hymie Jacobson in several delightful comedy situations and shows Miriam Kressyn to advantage as an actress of ability and the possessor of a most pleasing soprano voice. The humour was good and avoided the vulgar, and the audience showed their appreciation in warm applause.

The supporting cast was responsible for some good work particularly Mr M Angorin as Itzick, one-time melamed to Motke and Rachmiel, who gave a most satisfactory character interpretation; and Miss Eva Berkowitz, who was excellent as his wife, Hashe Riva. As the mother of Rachmiel, Esther Metz made a dignified widow, and Max Rosenthal took the singer's part becomingly. Inka Behrmann was funny as Fritz von Shnobel, and Eva Shapiro was suitably cast as Francis L Galvin, was inclined to overdo the 'bouch' aspect of his part as Rachmiel's rich uncle Haim Ber, while Vera Kanevski was competent as Slatke, the servant who finally marries Motke.

Madame Sarah Sylvia and African Consolidated Theatres, Ltd are to be congratulated on treating local Yiddish-speaking audiences to this fine theatre fare.

Eva (Chava) Berkowitz

DAS GROSS GEVINS (THE GREAT WINDFALL)
by Shalom Aleichem 1950 Produced by Meier Tzelniker.

סידני מאַרקס

איז אַן אויסגעפּרובירטער שוישפּילער און האָט אַלעמאָל
גלענצנד אויסגעפירט זיינע ראָלן. טעאַטער־גייער וועלן
אים געדענקען פון אַ סך פריערדיקע אויפפירונגען. סידני
איז אַן איבערגעגעבענער מיטגליד פון „יאַט" און ווען אַ
ייִדיש טעאַטער וועט דאָ אויפגעבויט ווערן, וועט סידני
זיכער פאַרנעמען אַ זייער חשובן פּלאַץ. סידני שפּילט
די ראָל פון „מאָטל".

מאָריס קאַץ

געהערט צו דער אַלטער גוואַרדיע — אַ פעאיקער אַרטיסט
— איז אויף דער בינע שוין פון יאָרן. האָט ליב טעאַטער
און שפּילט זיינע ראָלן מיט פאַרשטאַנד. מאָריס קאַץ שפּילט
די ראָל פון „אשר פיין".

Hava Berkowits

ח. ו. ה. בערקאָוויטש

A talented artist - has performed many tim...

אַ פעאיקע אַרטיסטין — איז אויפגעטראָמן אַ סך מאָל
אויף דער בינע מיט גרוים דערפאָלג. חוה פיין —
„פרוי פיין". *with great success. She plays "Mrs. Fine"*

שלמה רובין

אַליין רעזשיסירט עטלעכע פיעסן און אויך געשפּילט מיט
דערפאָלג — האָט זייער ליב טעאַטער און איז בכלל אַ
טעאַטער־מענטש. שלמה רובין שפּילט „קאַלטון".

יאַנקל טאָביאַס

אָנגעהייבן זיין אַרטיסטישע קאַריערע אַלס סופלאָר, שפּע־
טער אַרוים פון סופלאָר־בודקע אויף דער בינע און גע־
שפּילט זיינע ראָלן מיט ערנסטקייט און פאַרשטאַנד. יאַנקל
שפּילט די ראָל פון „סאָלאָמאָן פיין".

מאַשע אייצלער

אין נאָמען פון אַלע אַרטיסטן פון „יאַט" און אויך פון דער
קולטור פעדעראַציע באַדויערן מיר זייער, וואָם מאַשע איצ־
לער נעמט ניט אַנטייל אין אונדזער הײנטיקער אויפפירונג
צוליב איר אָפּװעזנהײט. מאַשע איז אוועקגעפאָרן קיין אַמע־
ריקע מיט איר זונעלע פּערסי. מיר ווינטשן אַז איר
רייזע זאָל זיך דערפאָלגרייך, זיי זאָלן ביידע קומען געזונט
און מאַשע זאָל אַנטייל נעמען אין די ווײטערדיקע אויפ־
פירונגען פון „יאַט".

THE CAST:

Shimele Soroker	Meier Tzelniker
Ettee-Mene	Nechame Yaches
Beilke	Ira Glaser
Motel	Sidney Marks
Kopel	Israel Zygielbaum
Osher Fine	Morris Katz
Mrs. Fine	Chave Berkowitz
Solomon	Yankel Tobias
Soloweitchik	Benny Ozinsky
Himmelfarb	Moishe Miller
Mendl	Fred Bachmeier
Rivtche	Feigele Kramer
Kaltun	Shloime Rubin
Vigdartchik	
Rubintchik	
Pessel	Bertha Englender
Butcher	Meilach Pasklinsky

Jews, Jewesses, etc.

Music arranged by H. Ichiltchi
Conducted by Shura Kryzhovsky
Stage Manager Israel Glaser
Prompter Toni Englender

משה מילער

אַן אַלטער און איבערגעגעבענער מיטגליד פון אונדזער
היגער אַרטיסטן־משפחה, אַ פאַרשטענדיקער שוישפּילער
און פירט דורך זיינע ראָלן זייער צופרידנשטעלנד. משה
שפּילט — „הער הימעלפאַרב".

פייגעלע קאַפעלאָוויטש־קראמער

אַ טאַלענטירטע שוישפּילערין — באַזיצט זיך צו טעאַטער
זייער ערנסט, פאַרשטייט שטענדיק איר ראָל און שפּילט
מיט באַגײםטערונג. פייגעלע איז אַן איבערגעגעבענער מיט־
גליד פון „יאַט" און שפּילט אין „דאָם גרױסע געווינס" די
ראָל פון „ריווטשע" — די דינסט.

Chava Berkowitz; a talented artist has performed many times with great success. She plays "Mrs Fine

255

SHAIKE LETZ

A Musical Comedy in 3 Acts by L. Katsowitz
Produced by Jacob Mansdorf

CAST

1.	Avrokom Tsodick — The Parnes	B. OZINSKY
2.	Sifreh — His Wife (Mirele's Stepmother)	NIUSIA GOLD
3.	Mirele (His Daughter)	IRA GLAZER
4.	Shaike Letz	JACOB MANSDORF
5.	Maitse — Innkeeper	JULIUS LAZARUS
6.	Chena — His Wife	CH. BERKOWITZ
7.	Chiam Lipe — Their Son	N. GREENBERG
8.	Rov	M. POSLINSKY
9.	Zalmen Wulf (Gabeh)	A. GLAZER
10.	Meishe Chatze (Gabeh)	R. KATZ
11.	Azriel (Ex-soldier)	K. LURIE
12.	Sender Badchen	H. BAILEY BERMAN
13.	Yidel Mitn Fiddel	S. MARKS
14.	Yekel Bas	G. POTBURY
15.	Tsemach Faifel	I. GURWITZ
16.	Orke der Reidiker	M. KATZ
17.	Yachne Dvose	N. JACHES

Music by H. Kan Kohn
Decorations designed by M. Rubinger
Constructed by Nachomson and painted by Miss Watkin
Costumes made and designed by M. Kelmowitz-Mansdorf
Stage under the direction of I. Glazer, I. Teperson, A. Sament, T. Richter and A. Morris
Orchestra under the direction of Harry Epstein
Dances directed by Henna Seinik

Action — White Russia.   Time — Middle of the 19th Century.

Eva in black dress with pearls

256

Shaike Letz

This comedy which is being performed tonight, takes place in the middle of the last century somewhere in White Russia. In those days Jesters and Tricksters were common in Jewish communities. Such a one was "SHAIKE LETZ".

The Jews then lived in Ghettos. In every Ghetto there was a "PARNES" or "Head of the community", who not only controlled all religious and social affairs but also acted as liason between the Jews and the Czarist Government. He had to collect Taxes and provide the State with Jewish boys as recruits for Military service for a period of 25 years. The word "LOVE" was taboo and Jewish Girls were compelled to do the behests of their parents and marry according to the choice of their parents.

During that period however, the age of enlightment begun, and Jewish girls read books secretly and a resistance against artificial matchmaking commenced.

The first act takes place in MAITSE'S Inn. The gang of Klezmer (Minstrels) is discussing the pranks played by Shaike Letz. The Parnes is planning fresh gains and is prepared to betrothe his daughter "Mirele" to the Inn-keeper's son, the half-wit CHAIM LIPPE, for financial gain. Mirele however is in love with Shaike. As soon as the proposed match becomes known to Shaike he begins to devise ways and means to marry Mirele. He persuades the Klezmer to disguise as "PURIM SHPILER" and attend the Purim Feast of the Parnes.

The second act takes place in the home of the Parnes. The Purim Feast is in progress when the disguised Actors appear. They perform the play, in the course of which Shaike, who plays the part of a Jester orders the Hall to be decorated. Suddenly a Canopy (Chupe) appears, and in the confusion which follows Shaike places a ring on Mirele's finger and utters the words "Harei-Aht" . . . Mireles Stepmother, who is also in love with Shaike causes a disturbance by snatching the ring from Mirele's finger and placing it on her own finger claiming that Shaike had married her. Mirele is dragged away and Shaike with his fellow Klezmer remains crestfallen.

The Third Act takes place in the Court-room of the Parnes. Shaike Letz is brought in for trial. Zalmen Woolf proposes to send him for 25 years compulsory military service. Meanwhile Azriel, sent by Shaike, arrives in the disguise of a messenger and brings the news that Shaike has inherited a fortune from a deceased Uncle. The Parnes who is greedy for gain immediately gives his consent to the marriage. Shaike thereupon summons his fellow Klezmer to celebrate their great triumph.

PROGRAMME

"SOULS FOR SALE"
Melodrama in 3 Acts and 4 Scenes by W. Segal

Shloime Sharf	J. Dembo
Peshe	S. Portnoy
Ben Zion	L. Galvin
Note	B. Karlin
Gitel	E. Berkowitz
Fishel Rudnik	H. Hirsch
Viole	J. Kopeowitz
Luba	Sarah Sylvia
Mishka	I. Reiss
Dan	B. Ozinsky
Angela	Alice Sylvia
Ivan Ivanovitz	H. Hirsch
Michail	B. Ozinsky
Shames	S. Marks
Boy	L. Yevelov
Kol Nidrei and Choir	I. Fine

The action of the Play takes place in America   Produced by Sarah Sylvia

THE STAR,
FEBRUARY 3, 1939.

JEWISH OPERA SUCCESS

Joel Myerson's International Yiddish Opera Company at the Standard Theatre presented the third and last piece of their season last night, selecting William Segal's melodrama, "Children's Gratitude."

As there was no hesitation in criticising adversely the second play, so there is every readiness in commending the choice of their final presentation, which was in great contrast to "Kol Nidrei," and the manner in which it was acted. It is to be regretted for the players' own sakes that "Children's Gratitude" and dramas of a similar type were not given preference.

Here was a homely story, with its tears and smiles, its hopes and despairs, its joys and disappointments, a story that is seen every day in all spheres of life.

Without exception the cast are to be congratulated on as good an all-round performance as has been seen for a long time in a play of this type. Each player had his or her part that suited splendidly and they combined in a manner that brought out the moral of the story in a striking manner.

William Segal is a master of this class of melodrama and he had the good sense to finish on a tragic note instead of the usual happy ending.

As previously mentioned, both players and roles were admirably suited and all did fine work. Madame Vera Kanevska, in the part of the mother who sacrifices much for the sake of ungrateful children, was in her element in that type of characterisation we have commented upon as being her forte. It gave her fine scope to display her dramatic talents and the result gave great satisfaction, with commendation for herself.

Mr. Joel Myerson was better suited by the straight part of Dr. Seligson and Mr. L. Galvin was an impressive Bennie. Miss F. Karpelowitz looked and did well as the unsympathetic Tootzie, while the Refoel and Zlate Feige was a nice study of an aged musician and his wife by Mr. Silpert and Miss M. Leven. Miss I. Shapiro was a lovable Sylvie and confirmed the good opinion held of her.

The Shepsl of Mr. M. Angorn and the Saltshe of Miss I. Berkowitz, are left to the last because they deserve a paragraph to themselves for their "comic stuff." Mr. Angorn surprised with his really clever work as a character comedian and it is only fair to say that his part could not have been bettered. Miss Berkowitz's Saltshe was the third distinct type of part she has had in the three productions and her success was amply merited in all. Her ability in broad character parts was a welcome surprise also.

"Children's Gratitude" should enjoy and is entitled to full houses for the remaining nights of the season.

Yiddish Folkschool & Nursery School in Johannesburg In Collaboration With African Cons. Theatres, Ltd.

ייִדישע פֿאָלקסשול און קינדערגאַרטן אין יאָהאַנעסבורג צוזאַמען מיט „אַפֿריקען קאָנסאָלידײטעד טעאַטערס"

Programme

of

The Gold Diggers

Comedy in Three Acts and Five Scenes

by

Sholem Aleichem

Staged in commemoration of the 30th anniversary of the death of the Great Jewish Humorist, at the Standard Theatre, Johannesburg, from 4th to 9th November, 1946. Evenings at 8.15 p.m.

Matinee: Saturday, 9th November, at 2.30 p.m.

שלום־עליכם
1916—1946

פּראָגראַם

פֿון

„די גאָלדגרעבער"

קאָמעדיע אין דריי אקטן און פֿינף בילדער

פֿון

שלום־עליכם

אויפֿגעפֿירט אין יאָהאַנעסבורג, צום 30־טן יאָרצייט פֿונעם גרויסן ייִדישן הומאָריסט, אין „סטענדערד"־טעאַטער פֿון יאָהאַנאַג, דעם 4־טן, ביז שבת, דעם 9־טן נאָוועמבער, 1946 — איינשליסלעך; שבת, דעם 9־טן נאָוועמבער, אויך א נאָכמיטאָג־פֿאָרשטעלונג

אָהײב פֿון די אָװנט־פֿאָרשטעלונגען 8.15 אַװנט מאַטינע 2.30 ביי טאָג

THE CHARACTERS AND THEIR IMPERSONATORS :

LAIVE MOZGOVOYER (the man of brains) — I. ZYGIELBAUM
BAS-SHEVA (his wife) — — — — MRS. YACHATZ
ESTHER (their daughter) — — — — MISS KAZUREK
BENNY BEN (Bas-Sheva's nephew, a visitor from
America — — — — INKA BERMAN
EPHRAIM LAKEERDE (a Lithuanian sceptic) — B. KARLIN
MENDL BORD (a yes-man) — — — S. RUBIN
NISSL DERBAREMDIKER (a yes-man) — INKA BERMAN
YIDDL TORBE (a money lender) — — I. SANDLER
ITZIK (his little son) — — — — J. BOCHER
First Woman Stall-holder — — — MRS. KATZ
Second Woman Stall-holder — — MISS E. BERKOVITZ
Third Woman Stall-holder — — — MRS. S. RUBIN
HOLOVESHKA (Czarist policeman) — M. KATZ
VLOTZLAVSKY(a Yiddish-speaking Pole) — H. HERSH
AVREMELE MELAMED — — — — M. PASKLINSKY
ELKE THE WIDOW (a chatterbox) — MISS EVA BERKOWITZ
THE VILLAGE RABBI — — — — H. BERMAN
ZELDE THE COOK — — — — MRS. S. RUBIN

The plot represents a small Jewish town in Poland in the 'eighties.

FIRST ACT — At the Market Place.

SECOND ACT — At Moʐgovoyer's.

THIRD ACT — At the Old Cemetery.

Dream scene at the end.

★

Producer—F. ZYGIELBAUM.
Music arranged by SOLLY ARONOWSKY.
Decorations by RENE SHAPSHAK.
Stage Manager—BERNARD BEHRMANN.

Members of the Orchestra: D. Golante, Sarah Gordon, M. Pertz, Th. Boskin, B. Brazg and L. Riskovitsh.

חוה בערקאָוויטש

א פֿיאיקע אַרטיסטין — אין אויפֿגעטראָמען א סך מאָל אויף דער בינע מים גרוים דערפֿאָלג. „פֿרוי פֿײַג..."

Chava Berkowitz - A Review
A talented artist who has performed many times with great success.

Chapter 53 ~ CHAYA AND HERSH BERNFELD

CLAIRE KLEIN – CHAYA BERNFELD
Written by Pam (Klein) Jacobs

My Mother never spoke much about her childhood. When pressed, she told us that she was an orphan who lived in Warsaw, Poland.

Her father was killed in war, and her mother died some time thereafter, but she never said exactly what had caused her death. I found out recently that her mother had died of hunger and typhus.

Her father had a factory in Warsaw making Panama hats. He used to travel overseas every year to buy materials for the hats. On his way back from one of his trips, he was caught up in a war and was killed.

My mother said she was the third of four children. She had an elder brother, David, who she said was studying medicine at university. Her older sister, Genia, was engaged, and left with her fiancé to live in Buenos Aires. That left my mother and her youngest brother, Harry.

She remembers visiting her grandmother in Poland, and eating apples in a loft.

When she became an orphan, my mother (and I think, Harry) lived with an aunt of her good friend, Anya. This woman was the caretaker of a school in Warsaw, and I understood that they lived in a flat in the school grounds.

When Mr Ochberg went to Poland, my mother said that as she spoke Polish well, she travelled with him as his translator. I imagine that this travel was in and around Warsaw.

Before he left to return to South Africa, Mr Ochberg asked my mother whether she would like to go to South Africa to an orphanage there. She replied that she would like to go, but only if her brother, Harry, could go too.

My mother told me that although her birth date was shown as 1911, she was born a few years earlier. Apparently, when she left for South Africa, they made out that she was younger than she actually was, because, as I understood it, they felt that younger children were more acceptable.

My mother and Harry ended up at Oranjia Jewish Orphanage in Cape Town. She seemed to have been happy there. She went to school nearby, but left before matriculating. However, she was very bright academically and told the story that during maths classes, she very often got the correct answer before the teacher did.

After she left school, she took a job working in a furniture shop. Her employer was Jewish and treated her well.

Claire and Harry - young adults

Harry and Claire at Oranjia

Claire on her wedding day - Cape Town 1938   and Claire in town

My mother met my father, Joseph Max Klein, in Cape Town. His family had a farm, I think in Malmesbury, outside Cape Town, but later came to live in Cape Town. My father had one brother, Dr Willie Klein, a dermatologist in Port Elizabeth, and three sisters, Minnie Elliot, Leah Velk and Sarah Snitcher. My mother and father married in January 1938, and went overseas by ship for their honeymoon, to Europe.

Claire and Joseph Max Klein on their honeymoon

On their return to South Africa, they settled in Port Elizabeth, and lived in a block of flats, Harrodene, in 4th Avenue, Summerstrand, for a short while, until I was born. I am an only child. They then moved to a house up the road, 6-4th Avenue, Summerstrand, where I was brought up.

My father owned a shoe factory for many years. My mother used to help with the bookkeeping.

After the death of my father (at 62 year of age), my mother came to live with me and my husband, Marcus Jacobs, in Port Elizabeth.

We loved having her with us. She was a fantastic cook, and baked wonderful cakes, scones, crumpets etc. She was very capable in everything she turned her hand to. She was always helpful and never intrusive. She loved the grandchildren and they adored her.

She went on several overseas trips to Europe and Israel, with her sisters-in-law and with Marcus's mother. She also went to South America, to Buenos Aires to meet her late sister's family. It always amazed me that the sisters never tried to trace each other. By the time my mother made the trip to Buenos Aires,

she managed to trace her sister's family, but by then her sister had passed away.

She was an excellent bowls player and won a trophy at Wedgewood Country Club, Port Elizabeth. She was also an excellent bridge player.

Her mind was razor sharp right until the end.

When my husband and I, and our family immigrated to Australia, my mother came with us. She was 80 years at the time, and it could not have been easy for her. However, she made friends easily and played bridge once a week until well into her eighties.

Claire, granddaughter Michele, grandson Sydney and daughter Pam Jacobs at Michele's graduation as a doctor at Wits. in 1989

Claire on right next to granddaughter Dr Michele Jacobs, at her wedding in Cape Town in 1991 to Dr Mark Herman who stands next to his grandmother.

My mother remarked that she had three lives - the first in Poland, where she was born; the second in South Africa, and the third in Australia.

She passed away in 2005, just before her 94th birthday, leaving a great void in our lives.

Granddaughter Jennifer Jacobs with Claire

HARRY (HERSH) BERNFELD
Written by Pam (Klein) Jacobs

When Harry left Oranjia, he went to Rhodesia where he was employed by Mr Harry Margolis. I believe Mr Margolis owned a General Store in the town of Inyazura, and he may have been involved in farming as well.

When WW2 broke out, Harry joined the army and fought in the war until 1945. To the best of my recollection, he was stationed in North Africa, Malta and Italy (Montecatini).

I remember that my mother used to send him parcels. He would send her letters with cryptic messages to try and let her know where he was. One of these, which my mother recounted to me, contained an anecdote about a dog – a poodle – from which my mother deduced that Harry was in Malta.

On his return to Rhodesia, after the war, Harry bought a tobacco farm at Mrewa, near Salisbury. Later he also owned a cattle ranch, and a townhouse in Salisbury.

Before my mother married, she would visit Harry every year. He would send her a train ticket to Rhodesia, and would see to it that she had an enjoyable stay, taking her to places of interest such as the Victoria Falls.

While I was growing up, my mother and I visited Harry every second year in Rhodesia. We travelled there by train, and he would meet us in Salisbury.

He also liked us to spend a few days in Salisbury, at Meikles Hotel, as he felt we might be bored if we spent all our time on the farm. The farmhouse was large and comfortable, and a short stroll away was an orchard with many fruit trees and a dairy.

Harry would entertain friends for dinner while we were there, and we were often invited to the neighbouring farms and to his farm manager for meals.

He always looked after us very well, and took us on trips to Bulawayo, Inyazura, Leopard Rock, and the Matopos.

Harry did not marry until later in life. He met Ray, who was tall, dark-haired and slim. They fell in love, married and had about 20 happy years together before she passed away. They had no children.

Harry was kind, gentle, well-mannered, softly spoken and generous. He was a true gentleman, always courteous and never had a bad word to say about anyone.

A few years after Ray's death, he found friendship and companionship with a lovely lady, Franzie, who was a widow. They travelled overseas together, played bridge, went out to dinner etc. They remained friends until Harry passed away, while visiting us in Cape Town. He was in his early seventies.

Harry was very much loved by my family, but especially by me. He was my favourite uncle.

Harry carrying rifle with a friend

Chapter 54 – THE BETTMAN FAMILY
LEAH, CHANA, SHEINDEL, SOLOMON AND YENTA BETTMAN

The Memories of Solomon (Solly) Bettman are recorded in the firsthand accounts in Part One of this book.

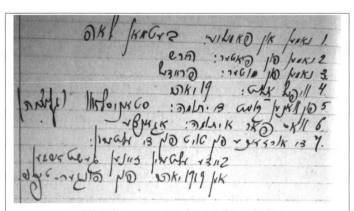

Both parents died in 1919 of hunger-typhus

The Bettman family details as recorded on pages 147, 149, 151, 153 and 155 of the register kept by the Cape Jewish Orphanage (Oranjia).
1 Names and surname: Leya (Lea), Chana (Hana), Sheindel, Shlomo and Yenta Perel Bettman
2 Father: Joseph
3 Mother: Freidl
4 Ages: 19, 13, 9, 8 and 6 years
5 Place of origin: Stanislav
6 How orphaned: Both parents
7 General Comments:
Both parents died in 1919 of hunger and typhus.

Group Passport One includes three Bettman children; number 2 Yentl Bettman aged 5, number 3 Solomon Bettman aged 7 and number 4 Sheindel Bettmanaged 8
"We think my mother, Bettman Sheindel, is the girl third from the right in back row." Aubrey Sheiham
While Chana Bettman is listed no 18 on Group Passport Two as aged 10, Leya is not shown on any Group Passport.

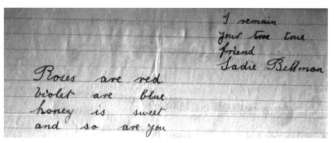

Letter written by Sadie Bettman to Isaac Ochberg

SHEINDEL BETTMAN
Aubrey Sheiham writes

As you may know, people like my mother and her siblings did not speak much about their lives. As four of the five Bettman children were very young when they came to South Africa their recollections are patchy. My mother never spoke about her early experiences. She talked about some of her friends in the Orphanage, but that was all she told us about. So there is nothing I can pass on to you.

I have compiled a detailed list of the families and offsprings of the Bettmans and have checked it with their children.

THE BETTMAN FAMILY - LEYA, CHANA, SHEINDEL, SOLOMON AND YENTA (PEREL) BETTMAN

The parents of the Bettman orphans, Joseph Hirsch and Freidel Rosenberg, lived in Chodorov, Poland. Both died in 1918 of hunger and typhus. The five orphaned children, Leya 19, Chana (Hana) 13, Sheindel 9, Shlomo 8 and Yenta (Perel) 6 were in an orphanage in Stanislav. They were brought out to South Africa by Ochberg in 1921. All the five Bettman orphans are now deceased and their family details are listed below.

Leah (Leya) Bettman married Peisel (Philip) Marks in Cape Town 1922. They had five children; three daughters and two sons.

Freda Marks married Charles Davis (deceased 1993) and settled in Johannesburg. Freda now lives in Cape Town and has four daughters:
Denny (Denise Ilona) married to Geoffrey David Belchetz. They live in Toronto and have two sons:
Lance (partner Tanya Snowe) 3 children-Tanya, Ethan, Luke, Gregory m. Ali) 3 children - Peyton, Leo, Ella.
Marilyn Ruth married/divorced Lenny Shulman and they had four daughters and live in Johannesburg; *Nicola* married Neal Manashe (UK) and had three children; Racquel, Jesse, Rafael, *Jacqui* married Sean Meyersfield and had two sons: Jamie,

Benjamin, *Candice* (London) and *Megan* (Johannesburg).
Helen married Raun Melmed, Phoenix, Arizona and had four daughters, Sarit (NY), Anamay (NY), Kara (Phoenix) and Lisa (Boston).
Vanessa married/divorced Neville Jossel, London. They had two daughters and a son; Victoria who married Micky Nurtman, Sarah (UK), Jonathan (Las Vegas).

Jossy (Joseph Hirsch) Marks married Judith Pogrund (deceased 2010) and lives in Cape Town and had three children. *Shuli* married Paddy Veitch and had two daughters: Julia and Tamaryn. *Debbie* married Rafael Weiner and had two sons: Benjamin and Robert. *Stanley Marks* lives in Davis, California.

Solly (Israel Nathan) Marks married Inge Chaimowitz (nee Ruschin). They live in Cape Town and had two children. *Sean Bettman Marks*, (deceased 2003) who had a son, Justin Marks. *Karen* married Lance Tollman and had two daughters: Sam and Candy. Inge has two sons from previous marriage, Gary who married Donna Cook from Hamilton Ontario and Stephen Chaimowitz who has a son Daniel.

Ida Marks married Alec Surovsky (deceased 2008).They had two daughters and two sons and lives in Cape Town.
  Michelle married Jerry Cheslow (New Jersey). They had three children Adam Baff, Daniella and Lara.
  Bryan Surovsky married Yael Tombak, lives in Jerusalem and they had five children: Elisheva, Elazar, Rafael, Ayelet, Ahuva.
  Rebecca married Danny Bryer, lives in Cape Town and they had two children: Gregg and Megan.
  Bernard married Marlo Besnoy, lives in La Jolla, California and they had three children: Jacob, Cayla and Sean.

Shooshy Marks married Harry Buchinsky. They had a daughter and a son and live in Cape Town.
  Lauren married Russel Glaun, lives in Boca Raton, Florida and have four children: Gabriel, Amy, Samuel and Ruth.
  Roy married Lynn Kamenir, lives in Cleveland, Ohio and they have three children: Danielle, David and Rachel.

Chana (Hana) Bettman married Hymie Schneider in 1933. Hymie had three sons in Oranjia at the time and his wife had died. They had three children

Rosie Schneider married Avi Hechter. Settled in Kibbutz Tzorah and have four daughters; Ora, Rutie, Gili and Rachel.
  Ora married David Yaalon, lives on Kibbutz Tzorah has four children.
  Rutie married Shimshon Chen, lives on Kibbutz Kalya and has four children.
  Gili married Zeev Rozner, lives on Kibbutz Tzorah and has three children.
  Rachel married Yaacov Israel, lives in Modiin, Israel and has three children.

Freda Schneider married and divorced Harold Sher, lives in Vancouver and has three children
  Dalya Klein married Rael Klein, lives in Vancouver and has two children
  Brian Sher who lives in Vancouver

Avron Sher who married Elisa Shrock and lives in Sydney Australia with two children.

Harry Schneider married Shirley, lives in Cape Town and has two children:
  Lianne married Andre Trantz lives in Israel with two children Eitan and Emma and *Gavin* married to Romy Stern, lives in Cape Town with a child.

Sheindel Salka (Jane) Bettman married Joseph Sheiham in 1932 and lived in Graaff Reinet. They had three children; Agnes, Aubrey and Hilda.

Agnes Sheiham (deceased) married Issy Goldman and had four children, Yaron, Yigal, Elana and Jonathan.
  Yaron married to Sandra Baum from Lichtenstein, lives in Charlotte, NC and has four children, Noah nearly 14, Mia 11, Benjamin 8 and Sarina 6.
  Yigal married to Maria Manuela Branco born in Mozambique. They have five children: two step-daughters; Marcela 24 and Carla 22, two step-sons 22 Barry 29 and Pierre 24, and Daniel 10.
  Elana married Michael Moore and lives in Cape Town with two children: Casey 16 and Ryan 12.
  Jonathan married Renee, lives in Toronto with two children, Danielle and Joshua.

Aubrey Sheiham married Helena Cronin. London.

Hilda Sheiham (deceased) married Ken Prissman and had three children, Geoff, Karen and Anthony.
  Geoffrey Mark married Tal Kissos and had two children: Sarah and Isaac.
  Karen Prissman lives in Johannesburg.
  Anthony Prissman, born 6/07/1971, married Leanne Slotar and lives in Johannesburg with three children: Adena Hila 13; Joshua nearly 11 and Hannah Mika 9.

Solly (Solomon) Bettman was born in Chodorov, Poland on 21 August 1911. Solly Bettman married Freda Gutstein. Freda`s parents were Devorah and Jacob Gutstein. They had three children:

Harold Joseph Bettman married Shirley Rothenberg. They live in Sydney, Australia and have two sons
  Kevin is married to Kellye Joseph and they have twin boys Josh and Zak and a daughter Tami.
  Shaun lives in Sydney.

Erica Ann Bettman was married to Cyril Benn and had three children with him: Adrienne, Simone and Gerard.
She divorced Cyril after 11 years of marriage and married Lewis Chesler who had two sons, Martin and Russell.
  Adrienne Jody is married to Jonas Weil from Sweden, lives in Israel and has three children: Alice Emily and Adam.
  Simone lives in Melbourne Australia with her partner Anthony Condon and they have two girls: Aimee and Hannah.
  Gerard Warrick lives in Glasgow, Scotland.

Philip Aubrey Bettman was married and divorced to Cathy Street. They have three children. Philip Bettman is now married to Caren Elstein on 17 February 2011 and lives in Sydney.

Neale Jeremy is married to Sally Paris and lives in Sydney.
Andrew Grant is married to Lisa Manuel and lives in Sydney.
Jenni-Lee is married to Steve Sault. They live in Canberra with Lana and Joe.

Pearl (Yenta Perel) Bettman came to the Cape Jewish Orphanage at age three. She was adopted immediately after arrival by Freda and Solomon Friedman. She married Samuel Isaac Trapida in May 1937. They have three daughters.

Ray Cynthia Trapida married Frank Belcher.

Joyce Trapida married Abraham Jowel Swersky and they have two children:
  Alison Janet Swersky married Paul Benson and they had two children Charlie and Abraham Benson
  Adam Jeremy Swersky.

Shirley Laura Trapida married Errol Shak and they have three children: Ian, Hilary and Hilton.   **22 February 2011**

PEARL (YENTA) BETTMAN
Joyce Swersky (Trapida) writes:

I have no good feelings about the stories my mother told me about her young life. She indeed was brought out by Ochberg. Her name was not Yente. She was known as Pearl. She was three years old on her arrival at the Cape Jewish Orphanage.

There were four sisters, Leah, Chana, Salka and my mom, Pearl, and one brother, Solly.

I don't think my mother spent long at the orphanage. She was small, cute and pretty and the orphanage was cash-strapped so when people of any age or type came looking for children to adopt, the orphanage co-operated happily.

Her adoptive name was Friedman. She was adopted by Freda and Solly Friedman from George. She later became Pearl Trapida after marrying Samuel Isaac Trapida. She never spoke of the orphanage, only of her subsequent very unhappy life.

I'm afraid that was the start of a very unhappy life for my mom and writing any more than this could only open a very sensitive familial can of worms.

"This is a photo of my Parents' wedding; Salka Bettman to Joseph Sheiham.
My Mother's sister is next to my father, and my father had a bow tie on that indicates it was their wedding.
It may have been the party after wedding because my mother was not in." Aubrey Sheiham

FEAR OF BEING SOLD INTO SLAVERY

Today an honorary life president of three Cape institutions, including the Women's Mizrachi, Mrs Leah Marks (Bettman) was a 17 year old orphaned schoolteacher when she met Mr Ochberg in Poland for the first time.

Mrs Leah Marks

'I was terrified at the time as I thought he was coming to kidnap the young girls at the school and sell them into slavery - which was a common thing during the Revolution,' Mrs Marks said at her home in Fresnaye today.

'I was very young when the Russians came to take my father away from our home in Lemberg. The only thing I can remember about it was my mother throwing a parcel to him - and then he was gone.

'A month after we heard my father was dead, my mother died. She was only 35 but I think the experience was too much for her.'

Mrs Marks said that she then fortunately managed to get a bursary to study.

'My three sisters and a brother were sent to various orphanages in Russia. After completing my studies I returned to Lemberg to teach - and it was there that I met Mr Ochberg.'

Between helping Mr Ochberg, Mrs Marks undertook a hazardous journey to Kalush Hospital where her sister, Chana, was suffering from a contagious disease.

They would not let me take her with me so I stole through a window, found her and carried her piggy-back to the station two miles away.

'Fortunately the train was delayed for four hours and we eventually managed to join up with the rest of the group gathered in Warsaw.

'Life was very cruel then and we never knew if there would be a tomorrow,' she added.

Mrs Marks said the orphans were in a terrible state when Mr Ochberg found them.

From Warsaw, they travelled to Danzig in cattle-trucks. Food was scarce and to keep their spirits up the orphans sang innumerable songs.

The arrival in Cape Town was overwhelming', according to Mrs Marks, and on Cape Town harbour she met her present husband, Phillip Marks.

'Since then I have continually devoted my life to charitable work because I feel the need to help those who cannot help themselves. Even today I also remain grateful to Mr Ochberg who saved us from the horror of the pogroms and the fire we would have faced later during the Nazi regime.'

Today Mrs Marks has only one regret - and that is that through illness - she has a broken leg - she might not be able to attend the golden jubilee celebration.

Daddy Ochberg with some of the "Young Ladies" Ochberg Girls. Cape Point 11 January 1931

"In the picture of the "Young Ladies" Ochberg girls the one on the right with glasses and a necklace is I am sure my mother Chana (Bettman) Schneider." Freda (Schneider) Sher from Vancouver Canada

Chapter 55 – CHANA DERLOWITZ

ANDJA AVIN (CHANA DERLOWITZ)
Written by Yvette Shiloh

Chana or Andja Derlowitz was one of the 200 children that were saved from the ruins of World War I ravaged Eastern Europe by the South African philanthropist, Isaac Ochberg. It took many years for me to grasp the miracle of his deed. There were many thousands of orphaned Jewish children all over Eastern Europe begging to be saved from the indescribable catastrophe of this war and its aftermath. Only a tiny drop in that sea of unfortunate children was saved and Andja was among the lucky ones.

The South African Jewish Community funded Mr Ochberg's mission, as he sought to alleviate the terrible plight of the Jews of Europe. The guidelines for the mission required that a child be orphaned of both parents. The task was huge, as every child Mr Ochberg and his team encountered was worthy of consideration. During their travels from city to city and village to village, the team came upon many, many children whose situation was heart-wrenching.

A miracle occurred and fate stepped in. Andja, was orphaned by her mother only. Her father had disappeared and she was brought up by her maternal grandmother, Devorah. Devorah, together with a daughter, Lonya, ran an orphanage for Jewish children in Warsaw and when Mr Ochberg arrived, he was persuaded by Devorah and Lonya to take Andja too.

Chana (Andja) Derlowitz as a very young child

The voyage to Cape Town was in all probability arduous, and it could not have been easy for a young child to be abruptly yanked from all she knew and loved. Andja was about 10 years old at this time and she must have felt totally abandoned. She never saw her grandmother or her aunt again, and she missed and longed for her beloved cousin, Yaakov, Lonya's son. Years later she learned that they had immigrated to Argentina but, unfortunately, never sought any contact with her. Later she discovered that her father, Solomon, had also immigrated to Argentina, where he remarried and had a second family. The orphanage, with the help of The Jewish Agency, eventually succeeded in contacting Solomon. Andja even sent him a photograph of herself. He responded by sending her a photograph of himself sitting at a desk on which stood the framed picture of Andja. This photograph of Andja on my "grandfather's" desk baffled and confused me for years. I did not know that the man was my mother's father or that she had sent him the picture.

Her childhood years passed and she realized that the orphanage had provided her the best home possible under the circumstances. She appreciated her life at the orphanage; nevertheless she must have longed for her family. Andja spoke very little of this period. I do recall that as a schoolgirl, I visited the Cape Town Jewish Orphanage in Orangezicht and

Little Andja, her mother, Sylvia and her grandmother, Devorah.

Andja (back row second from right) with a group of Ochberg Orphan friends

was overwhelmed with emotion. The outside of the orphanage was set in vast, luxuriant, rich gardens with playing fields and tennis courts, but the interior seemed so sparse and bare to me. I couldn't imagine my mother growing up in that place and did not feel that it had any connection to either my mother or to me. My mother referred fondly to a Polish caregiver, who came to South Africa with the children, and to whom she spoke Polish, thus ensuring that Andja never forgot her mother tongue. Andja had an older friend, Claire, who, I concluded, was my mother's confidante. Claire moved to Port Elizabeth as an adult, and she occasionally corresponded with my mother over the years.

The wedding photo of Andja and Isaac Avin

As a young teenager Andja left the orphanage and moved to a hostel run by "Granny Belina". When I was a child, our family visited Granny Belina at her retirement home. She lived in a studio flat in one of the suburbs of Cape Town, perhaps Rondebosh or Newlands. I was always so excited with anticipation when one of these visits approached, but the visits were often trying and unsatisfying. Granny Belina had no patience for young children and I have a memory of her being pleased when the visit was over. Years later, we visited Granny Belina in Fish Hoek, to where she had moved, and this was the last time we saw her.

Andja as a young lady

Andja turned out to be a very pretty young lady; her most prized attribute was her long, wavy auburn hair. She began to work and her first job was as a textile saleslady at Ackerman's Department Store in Cape Town. She referred to her department as the "Manchester Department". After a few years at Ackerman's, she went on her first real holiday. She bought a train ticket to Johannesburg and on the ride there, or possibly on the return ride, she met my father, Isaac Avin. Isaac was the most handsome, charming young man possible. She fell in love instantly, or so I like to believe. Not long after that, they married in the Old Synagogue on Hope Street in Cape Town. Mr.

Ochberg gave her away and I believe she was the last bride for whom he had the pleasure of performing this honour.

Married life wasn't always easy for Andja. Although Isaac was a wonderful, kind, helpful husband, he never became rich, as did many European-born Jews who came to South Africa. He came from Dvinsk in Latvia, following his older brother, Zalman. Zalman was a Hebrew teacher and later the principal of Herzlia, the Jewish school in Cape Town. Isaac's second brother, Jack, also immigrated to South Africa, leaving behind their sister, Eda and youngest brother, Michale, who later immigrated to Israel. These were Andja's only 'relatives', her own family having abandoned her.

Andja's only other 'family' was our revered 'Aunty Pauline' who lived in Washington, D C, far away in America. How she arrived there, I never knew, but I did know that she was married to Uncle Jack and that they had no children. For years and years, Andja dreamed of joining this aunt. It was almost an obsession. Aunty Pauline possibly encouraged this dream by writing regularly and by sending Andja and her children gifts over the years. The gifts were mainly beautiful clothes, and as Uncle Jack was a goldsmith, we children always made sure to check the pockets and cuffs of the garments to see whether some locket or gold-chain was tucked inside. Her dream of Pauline's adopting her never materialized. I believe that there was some age limitation for a child's potential adoption and immigration to the US, and I think that this is possibly the reason that Andja misstated her age in official documents. To immigrate she had to be younger than she was, and I think she may have had legal assistance in this matter. Aunty Pauline eventually visited Andja in Israel shortly before Aunty Pauline died in Washington. Their meeting was laden with accusations and misunderstandings and all the illusion that "Aunty Pauline" had represented evaporated.

Isaac and Andja had a number of grocery stores over the years, where they worked very hard together. At different times they

Andja and Michael, the oldest son

had a shop in Southfield, Ottery, Tamboerskloof, Klapmuts and finally in Sea Point.

In 1960 when Andja was over 40 years of age with a family of five children, Isaac decided that it was time to fulfil his dream of moving the family to Israel.

On a windy March day, Issac, Andja and their four daughters boarded the Edinburgh Castle bound for Southampton. My brother Michael had already left for Israel.

I was very excited and the only thing that ruined my pleasure was the sight of Betty crying on the quay. Betty had worked for us for nearly 15 years and we were her 'family'. Over the years she had borne her own children, three or more babies that she had taken to her aunt in Mossel Bay and abandoned. In later life, I often wondered what Andja felt when we left, but like many things, Andja did not share her thoughts and feelings with me or it seemed, with anybody.

On 10 April 1960, the family arrived at the port of Haifa. I don't think Andja was enthusiastic about the move at all, but in all probability she thought that she had no choice in the matter. She could not have imagined just how difficult this move would

Isaac and Andja

Andja with Faye and baby Debbie

prove to be. Initially the family settled on Kibbutz Kfar Blum in the Upper Galilee, but very soon Andja made her utter dismay known. There was no way that she could conform to the kibbutz mentality or accommodate herself to the circumstances. She worked mainly in the kibbutz laundry. Her year on the kibbutz was probably the most miserable year of her adult life. Isaac could not ignore Andja's plight and made plans to leave the kibbutz. With the help of a cousin he got a job as a buyer for the Sugat sugar plant in Kiryat Gat. They left the kibbutz in October, 1961 and settled in Kiryat Gat in the south of Israel. I remained on the kibbutz for another two years, during which time I occasionally visited my parents in Kiryat Gat.

The highlight of this period was when she inherited a large sum of money from her Aunt Pauline. With this money, she bought a house in Kiryat Gat and moved from their Sochnut apartment. I like to believe that she found contentment in this house. She had a magnificent garden with a granadilla archway from the garden gate to the front door which when in season bore the most beautiful purple fruit. There were also flower beds abundant with roses, sweet peas and carnations. The garden could be seen from the street and gave her much pride. Andja did not, however, like to cut flowers for indoor arrangements, saying that flowers should be in the garden and not in vases. By this time she had a number of grandchildren who regularly came to visit, but I think that it was her great love of gardening that gave her the most pleasure. A marvellous hammock hung under the big tree in the front garden and there was always a contest among the grandchildren as to who would get there first. A very big and diverse orchard took up the entire back yard. There were fruit trees of all sorts as well as large containers of potted plants.

There was also a large patio with tables and chairs and on various holidays, Andja with Isaac's help, would entertain the children and grandchildren with fancy holiday meals. These meals were something special. We were served gefilte fish and 'kichel' with chopped herring and brisket and all sorts of foods that I hadn't eaten since my South African childhood. The most enjoyable were Andja's tagelah. These she cooked in a large pot with 'real' syrup. She was also proud to recall that she had learned to prepare these dishes from Betty, who had worked for another Jewish family before she came to us.

It is my mother Andja whom I have to thank for my love of beautiful things. She was always occupied with some handiwork. She knitted for the whole family throughout our childhood and each garment was a work of art. She crocheted, embroidered, weaved and worked in many different media, the results of which were always beautiful objects, including lampshades, handbags and tablecloths. She passed her creative spirit, her love of beautiful things and her love of gardening to her children. My sister, Debbie, is an acknowledged painter and I too have always painted.

Andja died in May of 1984 of a heart condition. She had not been feeling well and walked to the local clinic. Her walk proved to be too much for her. When she returned home, she lay down and decided to wait until the next morning to tell Isaac of her discomfort, so as not to upset him. An ambulance took her to the hospital in Ashkelon. She lived for another few days,

during which time I visited her. It did not occur to me that she was going to die as she was only 68 years old (her age as we believed) and it was a shock when she died. Isaac was beside himself with grief, repeating that he had not said 'goodbye' to her. He was bed-ridden and could not go to the hospital in Ashkelon to visit her. He lived for another year and a half and never recovered from having lost his beloved Andja.

MY MOTHER ANDJA (CHANA) DERLOWITZ
Written by Debbie Eshel

I do not know exactly how old my mother, Andja, was when I was born. Until a few years ago I believed that she had arrived in South Africa at the age of four, lived in the orphanage until she was 16 and married my father when she was 18. I was not aware that there were discrepancies between these chronological events and her actual age. I knew that I was born when she was 37 years old, the fifth child in the family and this was my truth. From my perspective the exact facts are irrelevant.

My mother shared her memories with me by often repeating her sad childhood stories, thus endeavouring to come to terms with her difficult past. Apparently I wasn't always attentive or empathic although some of these stores were heart wrenching. I remember one particular story she recounted about a parcel of girl's clothing, possibly from America, that had arrived at the orphanage. This should have been a joyful day, full of expectations and excitement, but many times such days ended in disappointment. The garments were not to my mother's liking, perhaps not her size or not fashionable. My mother's innate wish as a teenager, to don an outfit that was hers alone, dress up and be unique, was thwarted. Such disappointments manifested themselves in her behaviour in later years. We immigrated to Israel in 1960 and settled on Kibbutz Kfar Blum. I was seven years old, and for the occasion my mother bought me two beautiful dresses. The kibbutz demanded that she give these dresses to the communal clothing store for the kibbutz children. My mother's childhood experience at the orphanage led her to strongly resist handing over the dresses. She refused to allow *her* daughter to share her dresses with the other girls. I was mortified by the situation. Today it pains me, that at the time I was unable to understand her, treated her angrily, and in defiance handed the dresses over to the kibbutz.

My mother showed us, her children, pictures of her aunt and children who had immigrated to Argentina. I viewed these pictures with detachment and failed to appreciate my mother's pining for family and for contact and the yearnings which were always her lot in life. These pictures were all that remained of a childhood marred by separation and disconnect.

My mother was unable to verbally express emotions and pain. There was no one to teach her this skill and I learned to express my feelings only as an adult. I learned from her that there could be payback if I were to reveal my feelings; that I could be vulnerable if I were to divulge my thoughts or cry in public. I assume that this is the way she grew up, struggling to find her place. When my mother was young there was nobody to raise her spirits, value her abilities or talents, pay attention to her pain or help her procure her place in the world. Perhaps this explains her great love of little babies. My mother adored babies; her countenance would soften and a smile would brighten her face. She was ready to embrace any baby and completely surrender to its innocence and softness. Her grandchildren, when they were babies, melted her heart and allowed her to express all the love that had built up. Love was something that she did not always know how to bestow. Her many grandchildren were a comfort to her. My heart fills too, when I ponder my mother's life and that of my father and realize that their lives continue to flow through me and my children. I'm sorry that my two sons knew her for only a few short years, and that my daughter was born after my mother died.

For better or worse, it is because of her that I am who I am today. I grew and matured and learned to regard my mother with compassion and empathy. Blessed be her memory.

ANDJA DERLOWITZ
Remembered by Sylvia Latter

My twin Yvette Shiloh, and my youngest sister, Debbie Eshel, wrote about our mother's childhood and life in the Cape Town Jewish Orphanage. They related that she and my father eventually settled in the town of Kiryat Gat, Israel and they told of her subsequent life there. My family and I lived a stone's throw from my parents' home. My children were very close to them and loved both of them very much. As my sisters affirmed, she had a special way with small children and they responded in kind. They loved playing in "saba and sabta's" beautiful garden.

I worked as a nurse in Kiryat Gat for many years. My mother had a good friend whose daughter worked with me at the local clinic. A number of years after my mother's death, my colleague told me that my mother had told her friend that she was extremely proud of me. It saddens me to think that my mother was unable to tell me that in person. I realise, today, that her traumatic early childhood experiences inhibited her ability to verbally express her approval of me directly to me.

Andja might not have been able to articulate her emotions, yet it was obvious to me that she had a very happy marriage and that my parents loved each other very much. I remember an occasion when she and I were looking at a photograph taken on her wedding day on the steps of the Old Gardens Shul in Cape Town. She said to me that if it were not for Isaac Ochberg, the man who "gave her away" at her wedding, she would not have been alive and nor would we. She did not explain herself then and it is only recently that the full implication of her statement has dawned on me I am grateful and appreciative that Mr Ochberg, a remarkable man, had initiative, courage, and the determination to go into the war-torn regions of Poland and the Ukraine to save Jewish children from certain misery and death.

DESCENDANTS OF ANDJA

Andja and Isaac produced five children. The first is my brother Michael, who today lives on Moshav Talmey Yafe in the south

of Israel, has four children and nine grandchildren. Next they had twin daughters: my twin sister Sylvia, a retired nurse who has three children and five grandchildren and lives in London, and me, Yvette. I am retired from the Technion in Haifa and have two sons and four granddaughters. My sister, Faye, is the fourth child and she lives in Reno, Nevada with her husband. They have one daughter. Lastly there is my sister, Debbie, who lives in Nir Hen in the south of Israel. She has three children and one granddaughter.

Andja's five children – Ashkelon 2006
Standing are Yvette Shiloh and Michael Avin and seated are
Debbie Eshel; Sylvia Latter and Faye Schwimmer.

Many of Andja's descendants – Ashkelon 2006 -
5 children, 14 grandchildren and 19 great grand
children and growing!

Chapter 56 – YANKEL, FEIGA, BLUME AND ISRAEL ELLMAN

The registers show that Yankel (Yontil) Ellman aged 10 and his younger siblings Fanny aged nine and Blume aged five were from Domatchewo.

Their father Bebil died of "general weekness" and their mother Chanah killed in 1920 by the Belachowzis. The children were left without the means to live."

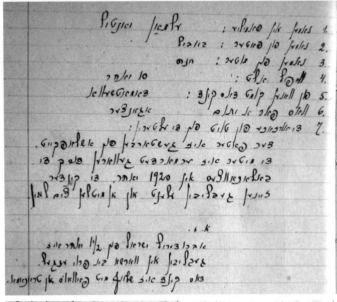

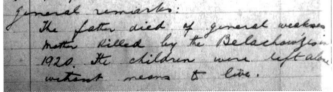

Family details of Yankel (Yontil) Ellman as recorded in the register kept by the Cape Jewish Orphanage Gloria was surprised to see that her father's father is named other than "David Eliezer", which she had always believed to be her grandfather's name.

JOE (YANKEL) ELLMAN
Written by Gloria (Ellman) Ben Shmuel

My father was born on 12 May 1909 in Brest Litovsk but grew up in Domatchewo, Poland, on the Russian border. His mother, Chaya, died in childbirth and his father, David Eliezer, married his wife's younger sister, Chana. They had three children, Feige (Fanny), Bluma and Israel (Issy).

Before Issy was born his father died a "natural" death from hunger or disease. When Issy was a few months old the Cossacks came to Domatchewo and in the resulting pogrom the mother was killed, and the children were left alone. My father, being the oldest, had to take care of his siblings, and would go out at night and dig up frozen potatoes from the fields for them to subsist on.

Blume Rosie Joe and Fanny

My father also had a first cousin, Rosha Heft whom he took responsibility for.

On arriving in Poland, one of the first places Mr Ochberg visited was Domatchewo. The children were temporarily taken to an orphanage in Warsaw while he went in search of more children. Issy was a sickly baby, and consequently when the children left with Mr Ochberg on their journey to England and then South Africa, he had to be left behind. The lady in charge of the orphanage in Warsaw took a great interest in Issy and wanted to adopt him. She wrote to my father in Cape Town asking his permission but he wanted her to send Issy to him in Cape Town to be together with the family. (At a later stage he was also sent to South Africa).

My grandfather, David Eliezer, had two brothers, Avraham and Shimon and their families who had been living in England for many years. My father knew that he had family in England and when the ship docked, reporters were on the scene and asked whether any of the children had relatives in England. My father said that he had uncles and cousins, and this was published. Two of his cousins came to meet the children and were prepared to take one child each. But when they saw there were four children, who didn't want to be separated, there was no alternative but for them to continue their journey.

Fanny and Issy Ellman, Rosie Hoffman and Blume Ellman

In South Africa, the children all grew up in Oranjia, however, my Dad, to my knowledge, never spoke about Oranjia.

After he left the orphanage, my father learnt to be a cabinet maker. Eventually he opened a concession store in the country, Brackenfell. My parents met through an uncle, my maternal grandmother's brother. They got married in November 1942. My father used to say that he didn't have a mother-in-law, since she was more like a mother to him. They had three children, Gloria (myself), David Eliezer and Charles (Chone).

My mother Gerty Lifshitz, was born in Cape Town on 7 of April 1915. She had a younger sister. My grandfather, Rav Uri, was a sickly person who passed away at the age of 47. My grandmother. Rahel Zlatta, worked day and night, sewing and knitting and selling her work in order to make ends meet. After my parents' marriage they lived in Boston Estate, Bellville. We moved to Tamboers Kloof for a short period, and then to Oranjezicht.

My father was always ready to help people whenever he could. At home he did all the fixing, electrical and otherwise. In Oranjezicht we had a house with a slate roof which constantly needed repair. Whenever the black South-Easter wind blew, he had a job on the roof, replacing missing or broken slates. He loved outdoor life, mountain climbing, camping and walking.

I left for Israel on 1 March 1967 by boat via England, so that I could meet "Ellmans". It was wonderful to meet David Ellman, my father's first cousin and his two sons, and other cousins as well. Growing up in South Africa, we only had my father's cousin Rosie Hoffman (nee Heft) and so meeting further cousins on my father's side was the highlight of my trip.

Shortly after my arrival in Israeal I heard that my father was very ill with heart disease. I returned to Cape Town, and on 17 August, 1968. He passed away at the age of 59. I found a job and stayed in Cape Town to be with my mother and brothers until 1975, when I returned to Israel. My mother visited Israel a couple of times. She passed away in Cape Town in 1989 at the age of 74.

On the list of Ochberg orphans my father's name appears as Yankel (Yaakov). It seems that after some time in South Africa he became known as Joe. We have no idea how and when this happened.

My father's sister, Fanny (Feige) died of tuberculosis in 1940 at the age of 27. She is buried in Maitland Cemetery very near to the graves of Isaac Ochberg and his beloved daughter Ruth.

A younger and older Fanny (Feiga)

Blume, her sister died in 1973 in her early 50s, leaving no children.

Issy was sent up north during WWII and was stationed in Egypt. He persuaded his superiors that, being so close to Palestine, he had to go there. He was very impressed with the country.

Postcard from Issy in WWII to Blume

On his return he married Fay Segal, and they had three children; Rochelle, Annette (Chana, named after our grandmother and Allan. Each had only one child. Only Annette's daughter, Blume, is married. She lives in England and has five children.

My brother Charles has one daughter, Tao. My brother David Eliezer has one daughter, Amy, and two sons, Aaron and Jonathan, who is married and lives in Israel. I have one daughter, Rachel Sarah, who is married and has three children. I am married to Michael ben Shmuel, from France, and we live in Jerusalem.

THE ELLMAN FAMILY
Written by Lazar Hoffman, the son of Rosha Heft.

Mom was aged nine and the only one of her family who came out to South Africa with Isaac Ochberg in 1921. She did, however, come out with her cousins the four Ellman siblings; Joe (Jankel), Blume, Feyga and Issy (Jentl).

Blume and Rosie Heft

Feyga died at a very young age of consumption

Issy was also in the Army and had a car breakdown service in Cape Town called Gardens Garage which he ran from home. He worked very hard and married Fanny Segal, the sister of Louis and Izzy Segal and they had three children; Alan, a younger daughter Annette, who took her own life and an older daughter, Rochelle.

Joe did not join the Army and was a storeman and married Gertie Lifshitz. They had three children; David a bookkeeper living in Cape Town, Gloria who lives in Israel and Charles, a Naturalist who lives in the Cape.

Blume worked for the in laws of Izzy Ellman, Louis and Izzy Segal, Clothing Importers, as a bookkeeper. Blume married Ruby Kaye (Kangisher) but later they were divorced and she was left with nothing. She had no children.

Issie Ellman   *Issy and Joe Ellman*

Joe and Gerty Ellman

Fanny Lockitch in an interview commented
"A baby of one year, Issie Elman, was sick and we had to leave him behind, but Ochberg promised him that he would come back and get him and he did."

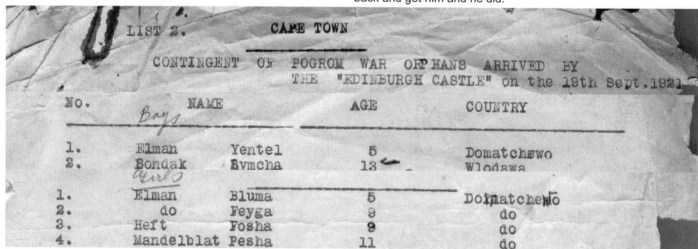

NO.	NAME		AGE	COUNTRY
	Boys			
1.	Elman	Yentel	5	Domatchewo
2.	Bondak	Svmcha	13	Wlodawa
	Girls			
1.	Elman	Bluma	5	Domatchewo
2.	do	Feyga	9	do
3.	Heft	Fosha	9	do
4.	Mandelblat	Pesha	11	do

Extract from list of children arriving 19 September 1921 by the "Edinburgh Castle"
Note: Issie Elman is not listed.

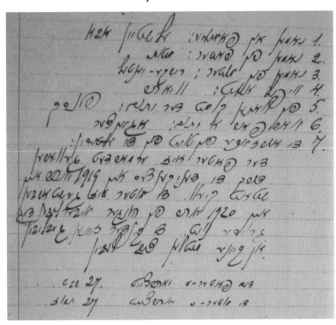

Family details of Abo Elshtein as recorded in register at Oranjia
1 Name and surname: Abo Elshtein 2 Father: Matoth
3 Mother Rifka Yentel 4 Age: 11 years 5 place of origin: Pinsk
6 Who died: Both parents   7 General Comments:
Father killed by the Deniking in 1919 in Kiev.
The mother died of hunger in 1920 after living in very difficult
circumstances. The children were left without any support.
Father's Yortzeit 27 Shevat Mother's Yortzeit 27 Tamus

Shlema Elstein – Photo from Pinsk Travel Document

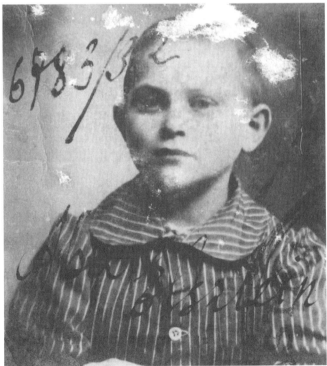

Abo Elstein – Photo from Pinsk Travel Document

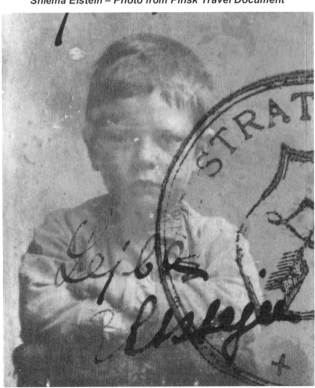

Leibl Elstein – Photo from Pinsk Travel Document

ABO AND SHLEMA ELSHTEIN
Written by Berenice Berger (Rubel)
Photos and captions by Maureen Katzeff

I am nearly 70 years of age and only now beginning to understand my father, Shlomo Elshtein and who and why, he was who he was.

There were three brothers Abo, Shlomo and Laibel. All three were adopted very soon after their arrival in the Cape by a Mr. and Mrs Rubel (Bessie and Faivel (Phillip) Rubel)

The three Elshtein boys at the Cape Jewish Orphanage.
My father Shleima (Solly) is the middle boy.
Abo is the oldest and Leibl the youngest.
This is the only photo that we have of my dad's youth

My father Solly Rubel (Shlema Elshtein), never ever talked about his childhood or life in Cape Town and his brothers. And there were also two adopted sisters, who I believe were both born in Cape Town.

The oldest brother Alf Rubel (Abo Elshtein) moved to Rhodesia and lived in Bulawayo and we never ever met him. My late mother did occasionally correspond with him. He only married very late in life to a woman Selma who we did not know. In fact I never knew my uncle, but I remember I received a cheque from him when I got married. Selma had a son from a previous marriage and as far as I know he lived in London. Consequently there are no descendants of Alf Rubel.

We did from time to time visit the Cape Town families; Louis Rubel and family and the sister Leah Kaplan who never had any children. The other sister Annie came to live in Johannesburg and was around often until she married out of the faith and my father no longer welcomed her to our house.

I think from what I can glean that both Bessie and Philip Rubel must have died when the boys were in their late teens, at which stage Alf left for Bulawayo and my father for Johannesburg. Solly married Jayne Singer some time in the late 1930s. I was born in 1941 and my sister Maureen in 1945.

קול ששון וקול שמחה קול חתן וקול כלה

Mrs. C. Singer
Mr. & Mrs. S. Baum
and
Mr. & Mrs. B. Sinder
request the pleasure of your company at the marriage of

Jayne Singer
to
Solly Rubel

at the Yeoville Synagogue,
On Sunday, 6th March, 1938 at 7 p.m.

Reception 8 p.m.
Ginsberg's Hall.
Gordon Terrace.

Bride's Residence:
38 Sharp Street,
Bellevue.

My parents wedding invitation. As my dad had no family the unterfires for my dad was family of my mother. We as children went under the surname of Rubel. It is only of late that we discovered my fathers surname was in fact Elshtein. The Rubels fostered the three boys.

My father was always a devoted husband and father. He loved entertaining and was full of naughty boy pranks. My mother contracted cancer at the age of 30 and my father looked after her in every which way until she died 17 years later. He never believed she would not survive and when she was at home with a day and night sister and on oxygen he arrived at my apartment distraught because the doctor had said the end was near.

He was a lost soul after her death in 1964 which is the day my eldest daughter, Kim turned six months. Our doctor said she pushed herself to live to see her first grandchild.

In 1968 my father married Sarah Garsh (nee Klein) from Kimberely in the Cape.

My late parents at Berenice's wedding on the 29/01/1961.

*Shleima Elshtein a few years before he passed away.
He was 65 years of age when he passed away and
was buried at Westpark cemetery Johannesburg,
where he lived from his early twenties*

My sister never had any children. I had three, Kim, Joanne and Brad. Kim Smyatsky has two daughters Leila l6 and Kiah12 and lives in Cape Town. Joanne Kirshenbaum has Nikita 13, Jason nine and Shira three and lives in Dallas and Brad lives in Tel Aviv and has two boys, Lev five and Max three. These are the only grandchildren and great grandchildren of the three Elshtein brothers.

MEMORIES OF LOUIS RUBEL'S (LIEBL ELSHTEIN)
As told to and related by his children Beth Miller and Dennis Rubel

My father was born in Pinsk the youngest of four children.

At a very early age he remembered marauding soldiers coming to their home and taking their father away (they could have been Bolsheviks or the Red Army).

A little later he recalls that soldiers again forced their way into their home and his mother told the children to hide in their bed which was over the fire place to protect them. He being an inquisitive two or three year old, and the youngest of the family, peeped through the curtains surrounding the bed and his blue eyes were seen by the soldier in the fire light, and he was forcibly removed from his hiding place, and a boyonette was struck through his tongue.

His mother struggled on but finally died of starvation or illness, I am not sure which.

The oldest child a daughter, Dora, took her three younger siblings, all boys, and they hid in the forest surrounding Pinsk.

They would forage for food in the bins in the town at night.

They luckily were found by Isaac Ochberg and taken into safe custody.

Unfortunately Dora, who was older than 16, was left behind and the last communication my father had from her was a picture taken at her wedding in 1938 in Brussels, Belgium when she married Maurice Kittenkorn. We have never been able to trace her after the Holocaust.

My father's memories were of the journey to London where they stayed in an Orphanage and the journey by boat to Cape Town.

He arrived in Cape Town at the age of four and his first sight was of dark people milling around on the quay and the hot weather and told himself that he must stay out of the sun otherwise he would become dark skinned. This never changed and he would never be out in the sun unless he could help it.

On arrival at the orphanage he was ill and was taken to Somerset Hospital were he spent some months recuperating.

In the interim there was a couple Phillip and Bessie Rubel who lived in Maitland and had previously adopted two girls (not related) and decided that they would adopt the two Elshtein boys.

Every Sunday they would visit my father at the Somerset Hospital and when it was time for him to be discharged they decided that they could not split up the family and adopted him as well.

About a year later Bessie thought that the boys seemed to have settled down well and it was time to question the oldest son, Alf, and ask him about his parents and where they had come from.

She discovered that they had adopted her own sisters' children.

My father recalled that she ran down the road carrying him shouting and crying, telling all her friends and neighbours the unbelievable news.

Unfortunately Phillip died when my Dad was 12 and Bessie died when he was about 18; but nothing can take away the unbelievable love and care they gave these three boys, who otherwise would probably not have have such a wonderful family life.

Grave stone of Louis Rubel (Leible Elshtein)

Beth, daughter of Louis

Wedding Rosalyn Pauline Wade to Louis Rubel (Leible Elshtein)

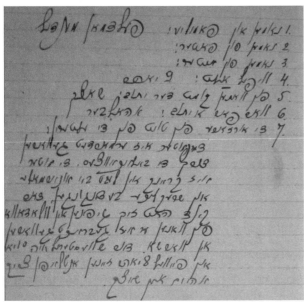

Mannie at ~10 years old in South Africa

Family details of Mendl Feldman as recorded in register at Oranjia
1 Name and surname: Mendl Feldman 2 Father: --- 3 Mother ---
4 Age: 9 years 5 Place of origin Shatzkh 6 Who died: One parent
General Comments: Father murdered by Bolsheviks.
The mother is sick and lives in terrible conditions. The child found
itself in Wladawa from where he was taken to Warsaw. The little
sister Chaye and Faivel, 8 years old ran away.

MANNIE (MENDEL FELDMAN) ROMANOVSKY
Written by Dale Romanovsky

My Grandfather, Mannie Feldman, was born in a small town in approximately 1914, in the western Ukraine. The town was called Shask. This was a small village with approximately 500 Jews. It was a desperately poor village with my great grandfather being the local shoemaker.

The Russians went off to fight in the First World War and it did not go well for them as there were perhaps a million to two million Russian foot soldiers killed in this war, due to the inefficiencies of the generals. On the return of these poor war veterans there was tremendous unrest in the Russian territory. The communists obviously took advantage of this unrest and commenced the Russian Revolution. Supposedly, many of the revolutionists were Jewish. The Czar, in an attempt to quell this revolution, sent out the Cossacks across his land with a primary intention of killing Jews, to curtail this revolution.

It was a Friday, and it always seems to be on our Sabbath that the Cossacks appeared in the village of Shask. Their intent, which was to kill all the male Jewish adults of this village, was very clear. My great grandfather went to hide in the attic of the local Synagogue from the Cossacks. After approximately two days of mass killings, the Cossacks had completed their dastardly deed and they moved on. My great grandmother then called upon my grandfather, who was approximately six at this time, and told him to take some food to his Grandfather in the attic of the synagogue. My grandfather then set off down the road with the food but unbeknownst to him or his mother, not all the Cossacks had moved on and he was soon spotted with the food and they followed him, finding his father. They brought his father down out of the attic and shot him right in front of him. My grandfather had great difficulty in dealing with this, because as a six year old, he felt he had betrayed his father.

My grandfather remained in the village about six weeks to two months, but it was very difficult to determine how long as to a six year old, time had no real relevance. During this time his mother approached the family and from what we could establish the family consisted of an older brother of twelve years old, a sister of ten my grandfather of six and a younger sister of nine months. My great grandmother told them that the Cossacks were returning to kill the rest of the Jews. Whether this was factual or mass hysteria, we could not establish, but nevertheless she told them that they should follow the mass of humanity and get to safety. She stated that she would not go with them as she didn't want to undertake such a difficult journey with a nine month old child. What also has to be understood, it was the middle of winter and a very, very cold one. We did track the temperatures and it was a very severe and cold winter during that year. It should be further understood that these children were not wealthy and were not traveling in Gore-Tex shoes or Gore-Tex jackets. We traced that my grandfather walked from Shask to a placed called Wlodawa, which would be the equivalent of walking from Toronto, Ontario to Lindsay, Ontario (approximately 130 km).

My grandfather had holes in his shoes and his older brother and sister made the first wrong decision in that they filled his shoes with paper to prevent him getting frostbite. However the paper soon got wet and my grandfather started suffering from frostbite. After about two days, the older brother and sister realized that my grandfather was going to kill them. What I mean by this is that he kept on saying to them how tired he was and that they would have to carry him and that he was hungry and he needed more food and they soon realized if they were ever going to get to their destination, wherever their destination was - they would have to abandon my grandfather. Therefore at six years old, they abandoned my grandfather on the side of the road. After a period of time my grandfather was overcome with hyperthermia and collapsed in a snow bank. The next thing my grandfather remembers was waking up in a Ukrainian farmer's hut. A farmer had come across him in the snow bank and brought him to his hut or cottage and revived him. After approximately two days my grandfather was again on the road. He then proceeded for a period of time, which was impossible for us to establish, but was probably another three to six months, and he walked to Wlodawa, stealing and begging, finally arriving in the town of Wlodawa, which was situated on the border of the Ukraine and Poland, and there he became a street child.

This is where the true hero of the story, Isaac Ochberg discovered him. Isaac Ochberg had heard of the plight of these children and was committed to saving them. We actually discovered the records of Ochberg, who kept fairly good records, and it was on an afternoon that he appeared by wagon in Wlodawa. He went to the local grocer, as it should be realized that not all the children were picked up from orphanages. Many were simply picked up off the street. In this regard he went to the local grocery store owner and asked if there were any children stealing his groceries. The grocer said yes and often they were sometimes behind the store. Ochberg then went behind the store and by chance found my grandfather there and started speaking to my grandfather in Yiddish, to which he replied and Ochberg then obviously realized that he was one of the Jewish orphans. We actually have the notes that he took when he interviewed my grandfather at that time. It should be noted that my grandfather had probably lived on the street at this time for six months to a year and was certainly not going with any adult. Ochberg persevered and from what we are told where he actually tied my grandfather up and put him on the back of the wagon. He took him with another four or five children that were picked up from Wlodawa to the orphanage that he had established in Warsaw, where he was accumulating the children.

It was at this orphanage that my grandfather told us that it was his happiest time, due to the fact that he met his older brother and sister again, as they had been picked up in a village three or four villages further down. However, just before they were to leave to unknown lands, the kids got very nervous and approximately twenty-five of them escaped that night and in that twenty-five was my grandfather's brother and sister, who he never saw again. My grandfather was then brought to South Africa and ultimately adopted by the Romanovskys.

My father and sister have done a tremendous amount of research on my grandfather. They went to the University of Cape Town and found a tremendous amount of information. The thing I found the most incredible about their research was a letter they found from the Romanovskys to the Orphanage requesting to adopt my grandfather.

Selwyn (Ram) Romanovsky adds

My Dad's real parents were Feldman and we do not know their first names. He had three siblings all who perished; Fieval, an older brother, Chia, an older sister and a younger sister whose name we don't know. My Dad never heard from his Mom or family again.

In South Africa he was adopted by Solomon Romanovsky and his wife, who had no children and were well into their fifties. They were very poor and wanted a child to look after them in their old age and died a few years after adopting my Dad.

My Dad went to Wynberg Boys' High School till grade eight and then went to work in a furniture store that he ultimately purchased from the owners he had worked for. He met and later married Fanny Krawchuk who had recently arrived from Grodno Poland in 1937.

My Dad's life in South Africa was very uneventful running furniture stores and he was able to provide a comfortable life for his family. He would never talk about his prior life and it was only my daughter's persistent looking and getting in touch with Lauren Snitcher that directed us to the Kaplan library where we found his details and confronted him with it and the stories came out when he was in his late eighties. We then encouraged him to have a video made of his life which was incorporated into the movie you have hopefully seen. I heard that Rainmaker were in South Africa trying to find out about Ochberg, at that time my Dad had passed away and I gave them whatever we had: tapes videos etc and made a financial contribution . The rest as they say is history.

One has to try and understand the trauma the children went through. They were simply picked up by Ochberg and sent to a different planet, that being South Africa. There was no counseling or help and they wanted to have nothing to do with their past and shut it in the deepest part of their memory and then tried to live a normal life. Was this possible? Of course not but it was not something my Dad was willing to share.

I remember before he passed away and we spoke to him he was embarrassed that when he lived as a street child in Poland he defecated in his pants. That was something that I think haunted him his whole life. The trauma that he went through was all related to that action. Maybe it was easier for him to deal with that one trauma than the other things that we can only imagine.

Mannie ~2000

He wanted to give us so much and was determined to give us what he never had and I remember he was determined to give us each R1,000,000; why that figure I do not know. The greatest tragedy was he died a penniless man and the fact that his kids had to support him in his old age was for him a greater tragedy than his youth. Can you imagine? He wanted to give his family all the love and comfort he never had and when he could not do that financially it was too much for him.

I know you want the day to day stuff but that was very ordinary as that is what he wanted for his family. Ordinary, safe and loving and that is how we want to leave it. We want his life in South Africa to be remembered as ordinary, safe and loving. I hope you understand that.

I would love to see the book as we got very involved in the movie and I ended up being one of the excutive directors; more as a tribute to Ochberg as I was very aware if he did not go rescue those kids I would not be here today and neither would be my kids. As my Dad always said, "A truly great and remarkable man!"

FAMILY DETAILS

My father (Mannie) and mother (Fanny) had four boys; Phillip, Gerald, Selwyn (Ram) and Leon.
-Phillip married but later divorced.
-Gerald married Jillian (I don't know her last name). Gerald and Jillian had two girls, Nicole and Justine.
-Selwyn married Elaine Cohen. They had three kids. Adam, Dale and Lindy. Adam married Amanda Kirkham in 2005 and Dale recently married Jennifer Devon this past summer.
-Leon has never married.

Therefore what was it like living with a man who as a child suffered so much? As it would have been like living with any father you loved so much. He could never discipline us as he always craved for his lost youth and he was determined that his kids would have only love. I remember thinking, boy it would be great to be punished and having a stern Dad not knowing why he let us do anything and supported whatever we did. I was never told "No you cannot" by my Dad.

Mannie and Fanny's Wedding ~1942

Mannie and family~1960

Mannie Playing Bowls

Mannie and Fanny and grand children 1985

Mannie and Fannie at son's graduation ~1973

Mannie and grandson ~1980

Mannie and grand children 1993

Mannie with son Gerald and granddaughter 1995

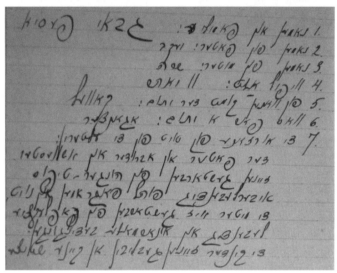

Group passport number nine
"We think my mother, Pesah Gaby, is in the top row fourth from right. She looks like me when I was a little boy."

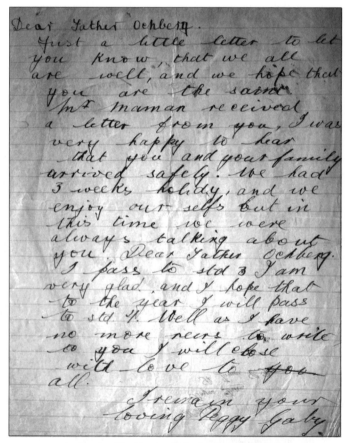

Family details of Pesye Gabai as recorded in register at Oranjia
1 Name and surname: Pesye Gabai 2 Father: Yakov
3 Mother: Sarah 4 Age: 11 years 5 Place of origin Kowal
6 Who died: Both parents
7 General Comments: Father died of hunger–typhus.
The mother died of 'Poplecsie'. A brother and a sister also died of
hunger-typhus after suffering many pogroms and suffering.
The children remained without any support.

PEGGY GREENBERG (PESAH GABY)
Written by Neil Greenberg

My late mother and two aunts were all part of the Ochberg Orphan group. They were the Gaby sisters, Pesah (Peggy Greenberg) my mother, Gittel (Shnaps) and Chana (Clara Penzik).

While growing up in Cape Town we all knew about the Ochberg Orphans especially since my late father, Harry Greenberg, was involved with the Cape Jewish Orphanage his whole life. However nobody ever mentioned it or talked about this chapter of history though I do remember seeing a film that was shown of the orphans disembarking from the ship in Cape Town. They were all bald as their heads had been shaved because of the problem with lice but other than that nothing much was said.

When my wife and I were in Cape Town in 1969, on honeymoon from Israel, many of my parents' friends were introduced to us and only then was it revealed that they had also been Ochberg Orphans. In my early twenties I went out with a young lady, who will remain nameless, and my parents were all excited because she was the daughter of another of the orphans. It was not until very much later after the advent of the Internet that I really started getting interested in knowing more about these few hundred extremely lucky children and the man who saved them.

Letter sent by Peggy Gaby to Isaac Ochberg

In 1998 my wife and I were in Cape Town for a family wedding and we paid a visit to the Jewish Museum where while perusing the exhibits we saw one entitled Polish Immigrant Passports. One of them just happened to be opened and I saw the name Penzik. Dave Penzik was my Uncle who had married Chana (Clara) Gaby and had gone off to live in Pretoria. I got very excited and the curator very kindly let me go through all the Polish Passports where I came upon the picture of my mother and her two sisters in one of the group pictures and had myself a good cry in the museum.

Peggy Gaby – 1921 Oranjia

My daughter who was with us and has a masters degree in Anthropology visited the archives at UCT and managed to track down the reports made by the Joint Distribution on the Gaby family. The father had died of "overwork" and the mother of "Apoplexy".

My greatest regret today was that we never sat down with her or my aunts or any of her friends and spoke to them or recorded their memories. I would have loved to have heard Fanny Lockitch (a great friend of the family) describe her life in her wonderfull gravelly voice.

I do believe that my Uncle Maurice also married one of the girls but we have lost touch with that side of the family in the "Great South African Jewish Diaspora". Hopefully we will be able to track them down. My cousin Benny Penzik who lives now in Israel is very active and we are in constant touch.

I have two children and two grandchildren all thanks to Isaac Ochberg.

Ivan Greenberg continues

I know nothing of my mother's other deceased siblings except that I was named after one of her brothers. I was told that the rest of the family had perished from typhoid and perhaps Bennie Penzik or Gerald Shnaps may have more information.

I managed to find some photos of my mother, Peggy Gaby and her sisters, Clara and Gittel.

Peggy Gaby about 14 years old

Personally, I have another strong connection to Oranjia other than through my parents. In 1958 I married Sarah Potashnik, the only daughter of Major Jacob and Pnina Potashnik who at one time were Principal and Matron of Oranjia. Major Potashnik was the Senior Jewish Chaplain in the South African army during the Second World War.

I actually met my wife for the first time at a Seder in 1947 at Oranjia. Sadly she passed away in 1985. We had three children, Lisa Kusevitsky (UK) Adrienne Behrmann (USA) and Peter Greenberg (Cape Town). I have five grandchildren. I married Jacquie Burman in 1988 and we are still going strong. (No children together).

The wedding of Peggy (Pesha) Gaby and Harry Greenberg 7 February 1933 at the Gardens Shul CapeTown. The small bridesmaid is Gittel Shnaps and Clara and David Penzik are recognizable among the family. Isaac Ochberg is in the crowd. Maurice Greenberg and Becky Greenberg (Rywka Kailer)) are also on the steps of the Shul at the back.

283

Peggy and Harry Greenberg

Ivan and Neil
1946

Peggy and Ivan – Adderley Street Cape Town 1940

*Back: David Penzik, Yonah Harpaz and Rita Penzik, bride and
groom and Bennie Penzik.
Front: Gittel Shnaps, Clara Penzik, Peggy and Harry Greenberg.
Sam Shnaps is kneeling in the front. I suspect this might be one of
the few photos showing all the Gaby sisters and their spouses.*

Chapter 60 ~ GITTEL GABY

GITTEL (GABY) SHNAPS
As remembered by her son, Gerald Shnaps

My mother, Gittel (born Gabai aka Gaby) was born in Kowal. She had told me that she was one of about six siblings and was nine years old when she arrived in Cape Town with her beloved "Daddy Ochberg", whom she regarded as her father and saviour as did her friends with whom she had a close relationship all her life. She travelled with her two older sisters Clara (Chaya) and Peggy (Pesye). Her only possession was a dress which had been made from sack cloth.

Peggy, Clara and Gittel Gaby.

Spring Buttress Stepover Table Mountain   **Gittel**

My mother was a very quiet little lady and during her lifetime she never mentioned a word of what had happened in Ukraine, other than that she had other siblings who had died. She was too young to remember what had happened, or possibly too traumatised to ever speak about it.

She told me that when they were chosen to accompany Ochberg, the policy was not to split up siblings. Her sister Clara was too old to be adopted, so she accompanied the orphans as an assistant or nurse aide. She did not ever tell me about the trip from Ukraine to England and never mentioned ever having been there.

She remembered growing up at Oranjia and how a family, Jochelson always wanted to adopt her, but she declined because she insisted that her two sisters be adopted as well.

When she was about 16 years old she attended Normal College (now Cape Town High School) and when she left school, she worked as a shop assistant at Ackermans in Plein Street, Cape Town.

Clara Penzik and Gittel Shnaps

Gittel Gaby and Samuel Shnaps getting married

At some later stage she met my father Samuel Shnaps, whose parents were both on the Oranjia committee at the time the Ochberg orphans arrived at Cape Town. My mother was married in the Great Synagogue Cape Town, Gardens Shul on 6 February 1938. They had two sons Gerald born on 17 December 1940 and Hillel was born 3 August 1944

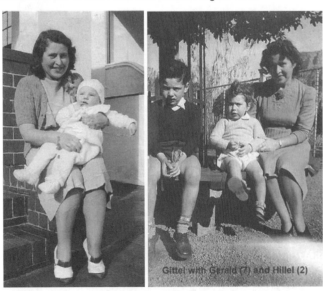

Gittel with Gerald (7) and Hillel (2)

Gittel and Gerald

During their younger years, my parents spent their recreation time hiking and mountaineering on Table Mountain and other nearby mountains in large groups. This was at a time when few of them had their own motor vehicles and they used public transport to reach their destinations.

My mother was a wonderful lady and an extremely proud grandmother.

I married my wife, Brenda (nee Gersh) and we have two children. Our daughter Beverly is married to Marc Morris. They have two sons, Sam and Adam and live in New York. Our son Mark is married to Peggy (nee Rabb) They have a son Eli and a daughter Maya who live in Cape Town.

My brother Hillel married Peta (nee Isenberg). They have two daughters, Michal and Merav and a son Iddo who live in Israel.

*The Gaby sisters at Clara and Dave Penzik's
40th wedding anniversary*
Gittel   Clara   Peggy

Beverly, Gittel's grand-daughter writes
Whenever I asked questions about her childhood, she'd offer me something to eat, mostly biscuits!!! She would always say I was the most beautiful, luckiest girl in the world!
The only thing I recall her saying about her childhood is that she would play with her siblings... I also remember the first time she showed me photos of herself as a kid, we both laughed - I think coz her hair was dark?"

Chapter 61 – CHAYA GABBE (1907-1987)

Clara Gabbe and her two sisters Peggy (Greenberg) and Gittel (Shnaps) were three of Ochberg Orphans who were in the care of the Cape Jewish Orphanage (Later called Oranjia).

Clara married David Penzik who together with his three siblings; Mina (Minnie), Chana (Hannah) and Chaya (Helen) were also Ochberg Orphans who were in the care of The South African Jewish Orphanage (later called Arcadia).

David Penzik (born 1908) married Clara Gabbe (born 1907) on 15 February 1931 at a ceremony held in the grounds of Arcadia and they had three children, Ruth, Bennie and Rita (Harpaz).

You can read more about the Penzik siblings; Mina (Minnie Davidow), David, Chana and Chaya (Helen Green (Meyerowitz), in MORE ARC MEMORIES and in Part Three of this book.

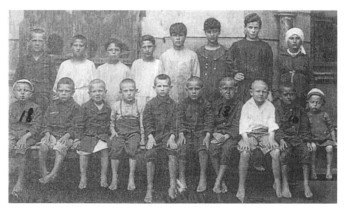

Group Passport no 9 - Chaya Gabbe is no 3 on the list

Beloved and Faithful Father Ochberg

I begin writing quickly in connection with our health, thank God I bring you good tidings. Beloved father, I can write to you now that we are completely healthy and everything is absolutely fine, the only thing is that you are not here. We only hope to God that in time we will be with you. Beloved father I can write to you that we are content and learning hard. Most of those who are not going to school are studying, etc. Mr Maman teaches us English and that is how we pass the time. And besides that I have no news. I end off fully knowing and hoping that my letter will find you in the best of health. From me your faithful and forever remembering, Chaya Gaby. I greet you from the bottom of my heart, I send greetings to your wife from the bottom of my heart, and I send greetings to your children from the bottom of my heart. End.

From me Chaya Gabbe

MY MOTHER CHAYA (GABBE) PENZIK
Written by Rita Harpaz (nee Penzik)

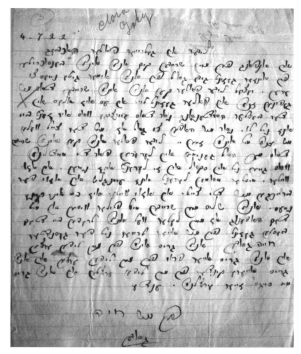

Letter written to Isaac Ochberg by Chaya Gabbe with translation by Veronica Belling

Chaya Gabbe in the middle with friends – mid 1920s

Chaya Gabbe - 1932

It was in Johannesburg that Mom and Dad reunited and married at Arcadia in February 1931.

Mom told me that when they rented a small house after they were married, they let out the one room for board and lodging to help to cover expenses. She said that she would buy a tickey or sixpence soup meat and soup-greens. She would prepare the soup, then serve the vegetables from the soup and use the meat to mince and make meatballs! These chores in addition to being pregnant and running a home.

My parents' early years of marriage were filled with the usual hardships of young couples but tragedy struck in April 1936 when their firstborn child, Ruth, aged 4, died as a result of an appendectomy. Mom was always of a nervous disposition and we had no doubt that the devastating loss had a massive impact on them both. Neither could speak of Ruthie, as she was known by all who knew and loved her, and we sought to spare them further agony by questioning. All I have is a lock of Ruthie's hair, her bracelet and a recollection by my late Aunt Helen who said that she was mature beyond her few years and was always saying to Mom "Don't worry, Mommy!" where it applied.

Dad told me that he had started to write the story of their lives but he was constantly consumed with distress after the first few pages.

I can honestly conclude this brief tribute by saying that the forty-six years with which I was blessed to spend with Mom and fifty with Dad were marked by constant love and affection and a harmony that has been my challenge to emulate.

Dave and Clara Penzik on their Golden Wedding Anniversary in 1981. Rita and Bennie are standing behind them.
"As you can see I inherited all the looks." Bennie

A close friend once described my Mom in the following words "She was the epitome of a lady, softly spoken, gentle, loving, kind and just the sweetest thing. Not an evil bone in her whole body!" This appraisal was echoed some years earlier by none other than the late and revered Isaac Ochberg (of blessed memory) who wrote to my Dad "I am sure that you have found out by now that she has a golden character and is really a sweet little woman and I am sure she will make you very happy."

Mom was 'little' and under five foot in stature and it was years before we appreciated that she was indeed the "power behind the throne" in the manner in which she made many astute observations while partnering Dad in investment decisions, particularly property, areas which we erroneously thought were beyond her domain.

She had a keenly developed sense of business, beginning with her entry in the field of dressmaking, leaving Cape Town in the twenties to start her new venture in Johannesburg with her good friend, Pearl Potash, the lady who subsequently boarded with us in Pretoria, elegant in army uniform and working in the military.

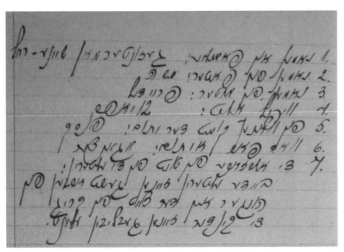

Details of the Gesunterman family as recorded in the register at Oranjia. 1 Names and surname: Sheine Rochel, Braindel and Jocheved Gesunterman 2 Father: Moshe 3 Mother Freidel
4 Ages: 12, 10 and 8 years 5 From where: Pinsk
6 Who died: Both parents
7.General Comments:
The parents died of starvation during the War

Jochevet Gesunterman
Photo on Pinsk travel document

PINSK TRAVEL DOCUMENTS

The children that came from Pinsk had in fact two travel documents; the group passport with the group photo and list and there was an individual affidavit issued by the Pinsk Magistrate with an individual photo which stated;

"NUMBER XX
Affidavit Issued by the Magistrate of the Town of Pinsk on July 6, 1921.
The Magistrate of Pinsk states that XXXXXXXXXXX, of XXXX years, whose photograph is attached, and is an orphan without parents, who resides in the Orphanage, is to depart for Africa with Caretaker OCHBERG.

Stamped and Sealed by two secretaries of the Magistrate of the Town of Pinsk."

The affidavits grant permission for the child to be placed in the care of Mr Ochberg for the journey to South Africa.

The Affidavits were written in Polish. Pinsk was actually located in White Russia, an area ceded to Poland in 1918, but then returned to Russia later.

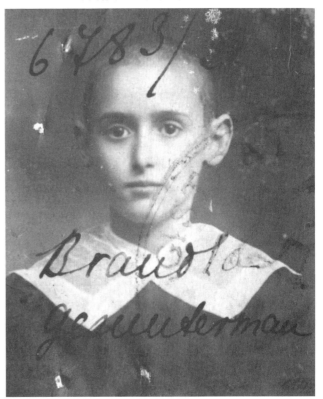

Braindel Gesunterman
Photo on Pinsk travel document

SHEINA-ROCHEL GESUNTERMAN-JANE ODDES
Written by Blume Sakinofsky

My mother never spoke to me about her childhood in Pinsk or about the time she and her sisters spent in the orphanage nor about the trip they took to South Africa via London with Isaac Ochberg. I can only surmise that the hardship and trauma she suffered was so great that she repressed all those memories.

She did tell me once though that she remembered hiding in the forest with her sisters and when they returned to the village they thought it was snowing until they discovered that what they saw was white feathers flying about in the wind after the *perenes* (duvets) had been sliced by the sabres of the Cossacks. My sister Maud agrees that our mother spoke very little about Russia and that once, when they returned home after hiding in the forest, they saw feathers tinged with blood that she thought was snow flying about in the sky. My mother also told me that at least on one night my grandmother gave my mother and her siblings salt water to drink instead of their supper before they went to bed, and saying to them, "Tomorrow will be a better day". It seems to me that their circumstances at that time must have been abysmal without prospects of improvement.

My mother told Maud about begging the authorities at the orphanage in Pinsk to allow her sisters to go to South Africa along with her. They had been very ill and there seemed to be a real possibility that they would be left behind because good health was a pre-requisite for selection to accompany Ochberg. Her sisters were isolated in the orphanage sickbay and she remembered climbing up the wall to peep through the window and see them. She told Maud that she had promised her mother to take care of them. My other surviving siblings, Blanche, Eli and Hymie (our eldest sister Freda died some years ago) confirmed that she never spoke to them of her childhood and of her life in the shtetl.

I remember my mother as a very beautiful woman, proud matriarch of six children. She was devoted to her family and instilled in us all the good values that included a sense of duty to the family, a charitable heart, and gratitude for all the good things in life. She also taught us to deal with adversity with a sense of acceptance and to do the best that one could under the circumstances with what one had. She was a devout woman who would say in the face of difficulties, "It is God's will". She remained close to her sisters throughout her life and saw them as often as she could in spite of the considerable geographical distance that separated her from them. I continue to marvel that she was such a wonderful human being in spite of the loss of her birth parents at such an early age and in spite of all the deprivation and traumas that she and her sisters had to endure.

Isaac Ochberg saved the lives not only of Jane, Bessie and Jessie Gesunterman but he is directly responsible for the existence of Jane and George Oddes' six children, 18 grandchildren and 23 great- grandchildren. May he always be remembered for his great heart and foresight.

Among the photographs is one that was taken in a vintage car showing the three Gesunterman girls rescued by Isaac Ochberg. From left to right Jessie, who later married Issy Sher

Sjeine-Rochel Gesunterman
Photo on Pinsk travel document

Jane as a young girl

Jessie, Bessie and Jane Gesunterman

who became president of the Great Synagogue, Gardens, Cape Town, Bessie who later married Morris Morris, and Jane who married my father George Oddes, with whom she had grown up after being taken into the Oddes home as a daughter but never formally adopted. George was a schoolboy at Sacs in Cape Town when his parents asked him to pick out one of the Ochberg little girls as a "sister". Apparently he looked over the kids who were put forward by the orphanage people and asked to see any others that were not included. Of course

Jane had not been included because, presumably, they were looking for a family that might adopt the three sisters and keep them together. As soon as he set eyes on her he said without hesitating, "that's the one". When they grew up they fell in love and it turned out to be a wonderfully harmonious union for many years until his death from cancer in 1961.

George and Jane Oddes around the time of their wedding

The only picture I have of them as a young couple is this wedding picture. They were married by the Reverend Klein in a small dorp called Williston in the Karoo. There was no local photographer. They honeymooned, however, in Cape Town and had a photographer take the picture there post hoc in their wedding clothes. The picture is undated but it must have been 1927 or 1928.

Jessie, Ouma Jane and baby Freda her eldest child

Freda's wedding 1951. On the steps of Jessie's flat in Oranjezicht. In front is Freda Oddes, becoming Friedman, second row Blanche and Maud Oddes, third row Blume Oddes and Phena Morris - they were all bridesmaids. .
Behind are Ouma Jane and mother-in-law, Esther Friedman.

Blume on her wedding day with her mother Janie

Jane and her children at Julie's wedding - 1980
Maud Nowosenetz , Blanche Phillips, Hymie Oddes,
Jane, Freda Friedman, Eli Oddes, and Blume Sakinofsky.

Julie the daughter of Maud and Sid Nowosenetz married Howard Phillips, a professor of history at the University of Cape Town and she herself is a lawyer and they have two very bright children, Laura and Jeremy.

By a freak of coincidence Blanche married the father of Howard Phillips who ended up marrying her niece Julie, the daughter of Maud and Sid.

(Blume Sakinofsky lives in Toronto. Her husband, Saki, is an emeritus professor of psychiatry, Professor Dr Isaac Sakinofsky).

Jane at her 80th birthday celebration at Jaffa in Pretoria.
Jane is surrounded by her children and grandchildren.

Lesley Friedman, Jane's grand daughter, writes

My grandmother had six children, four girls and two boys, all as beautiful as Blume, Lauren's grandmother, Bessie Gesunterman, had one gorgeous daughter, Phena, who in turn had four very handsome children, two girls and two boys. The third Gesunterman girl, Jessie, died very young and had no children.

We are planning to compile our full family tree, showing that as a result of Isaac Ochberg's fantastic achievement, there are at

least 50 successful Gesunterman descendents spread around the world - what a guy! Like most South Africans, everyone is scattered around the world.

We think Phena might be named after the river Pina which runs through Pinsk, where the Gesunterman girls came from. We also think they were in Alexander Bobrow's (Liebe Klug's dad) orphanage there.

My Ouma also sent her sons to Sacs in Cape Town, but they boarded at Herzlia, where Liebe's father was the housemaster and she must have felt they would be safe with him, like she and her sisters were safe with him. But I just suspect this, I have no proof – my Ouma Jane said nothing to me about her life, except to give her permission for us to make the film Ochberg's Orphans. However, she did ask us to try to find the oldest Gesunterman sister, who had left the younger girls in the orphanage and was never seen again. Her name was Freyde Gesunterman, and I have not been able to find any trace of her. My mother, Freda, my grandmother's oldest daughter, was clearly named after her.

To back up where Blume has written that my grandfather chose the woman he went on to adore and spend his life with, I quote from the file copies of two letters sent by the president of Oranjia, Isaac Ochberg, which can be found at the Kaplan Library.

The first, dated 11 November 1921, is headed 'Re Adoption' and is addressed to my grandfather. It reads

Dear Mr Oddes
With reference to our conversation I should like you to see the following children of which I might be able to give you one, namely: Pesha Mandelblatt, Brandle Miller, Liba Kolodner, Sima Samurina also the little kiddie Regina Hartman who only arrived from Europe this week.
Please let me know when you can come over to see these children and I will try to be with you.
Yours faithfully,

IO/DC   President

The second letter, dated 24 November 1921, is written to my great grandparents, Mr and Mrs Oddes, Williston and reads.

Dear Sir and Madam
Your son and Mrs Klein have spent some considerable time with me at the Home and they have finally picked on your behalf a beautiful child by the name of Shana Rochel Gezunterman as your adopted daughter. Your son has signed the contract as he stated that he had authority from you by wire and letters, but it is essential we should have your signature. I am therefore enclosing herewith contract and you will kindly sign same and have your signature witnessed and return the contract to me.
Extending to you, your son and the new member of your family the best of wishes and good luck.
I am, yours truly,
IO/DC   President

Our family history might have been very different if my grandfather had not fallen in love!

BRAINDEL GESUNTERMAN-BESSIE MORRIS
Written by Lauren Snitcher

This is the story of my maternal grandmother, Bessie Morris, born Braindel Gezunterman in Pinsk in what is now Belorus.

As a very little girl of about five or six years old, I would always ask my Ouma, with whom I had an exceptionally close and loving bond, "Ouma, tell me about when you were a little girl? Tell me about your life?" Her stock answer to me was always, "Laurentjie, I never was a child. I was too poor to have a childhood." Now, to my child's mind, I imagined that my Ouma just arrived on this planet at the age I knew her in her White Bowls outfit with her long skinny legs and always ate fried fish, soup and toast. But something inside me was not satisfied and I yearned to know more and so I kept on hakking her for many years until she eventually, exasperated, told me I was like "Malherbe se hond!" which in my family meant to go on and on with the same topic like a broken record player and probably in an attempt to get me to stop asking her questions, she eventually told me that her mother's name was Frieda, her father's name was Moshe and that he had a long red beard and that they had a cow at the bottom of their garden and that they lived in a little shtetl called Pinsk. I accepted this information but on some deeper level I knew that was not the full story and so, I kept asking away until as a teenager, my ouma eventually told me that she was one of the 176 orphans that Isaac Ochberg brought out to South Africa in 1921. It was then I knew my questions had been answered. And it was then I knew why I had not been satisfied with the story I had been given. Because I now understood that my ouma's past was inextricably linked with my future and had Isaac Ochberg not brought her and her two sisters as well as the other orphans to South Africa, they would have been murdered by the Nazis two decades later and I and over 3 000 descendants of the original Ochberg Orphans would not be here.

It was this tenuously fine line between life and death that ignited a fire and a passion in my soul which culminated in a need to tell the story and so began many years of dedicated research to fill in the gaps.

My ouma tells the story of how her parents would take them into the nearby forests and show them what berries, fruit, leaves, bark and plants they could eat to

Sheine-Rochel—I think is back row either extreme left or what I think is more probable—4th left – Passport 7

My ouma Braindel Gezunterman is middle row extreme left with the collared dress and the arms folded - Passport 8

sustain themselves when the Cossacks rode into their *shtetl* and they would have to flee into the forest for safety. This was something they did throughout the year. During the summer they would look for shade under the trees and in winter they would burrow into the snow to keep safe from the roaming starving wolves. They could stay in the forest from a few hours to a few days depending on how long the marauding bands of Cossacks would be kept busy plundering the village and killing the villagers.

My grandmother's sister, Janie Oddes (b Sheine-Rochel Gezunterman) relates the following image. She said that on returning from hiding in the forest during a particularly cruel and vicious pogrom, the three sisters came out of hiding and looked down onto their village and saw the most beautiful sight—there was pink snow falling all around, transforming their shtetl into a surrealistic, pink, wonderland. It was only on closer inspection that they realized what in fact they were seeing. It was the blood soaked feathers of the *perinehs* that the Jews had been sleeping or cowering under when the Cossacks attacked them and slashing through their bed coverings had massacred so many of them. Till the day she died, my aunt never wore red and white mixed together.

That same aunt tells the story how both her parents were sick with what was probably the Spanish flu and that at seven years of age she was in charge of giving them their medication. She was not able to tell the time yet and so the Doctor showed her that when the hands of the clock are in the various positions, that would be the time when she would have to giver her parents their medicine. She tells of how all three sisters would sleep in the bed with their parents for warmth and also because that was probably the only bed in the house and how they woke up one morning to find that both her parents had passed away during the night, leaving the three sisters orphaned and alone.

It needs to be remembered what the backdrop at this time in that area of the world was. There were about half a million Jewish orphans in Eastern Europe at that time; orphaned because of the First World War, the Russian Revolution of 1917, the famine of 1921-1923, the Spanish Flu Epidemic of 1918, general poverty and of course the notorious Pogroms carried out by the cruel Cossacks as well as general Anti Semitic massacres.

It was onto this scene that Isaac Ochberg arrived as hero, rescuer and saviour of our ancestors.

My Ouma tells me that she had an older step sister, also called Frieda who was not able to look after them. She never spoke disparagingly of her, but I picked up in her narrative, a sense that Frieda didn't or couldn't take on the burden of caring for her step sisters. It was then that my ouma and her two sisters were placed in an orphanage in Pinsk. There were three Jewish orphanages in Pinsk at that time according to the memoirs of Charles Migdal, another Ochberg Orphan.

In 2001 I went to Pinsk and with the help of a genealogist, found the original Yiddish names of my Ouma and her two sisters and was able to trace the orphanage they stayed in. The building does not exist any more but we went to the actual location and looked at the view and the trees that surely 80 years earlier my ouma, too had seen.

When Ochberg arrived in Pinsk, my Ouma was in hospital with typhus, which was rampant amongst the populace at that time. My aunt heard that there was a man from Africa who was looking for children to take back to South Africa. The process whereby Ochberg chose his precious human cargo was that he would visit the orphanages and speak with the matrons/carers. He wanted children between the ages of 5-15 who were full orphans in that they had lost both their parents, were healthy emotionally and physically and as far as possible he wanted to keep siblings together. So at only 10 years of age my aunt made her way into the hospital and managed to find her sister, my ouma and together they shimmied down the drainpipe and all three sisters were selected by Ochberg and made it to safety. Till the day she died, my Ouma and her sister spoke and saw each other regularly and were extremely close.

When they arrived in South Africa, my Ouma and her sisters stayed at Oranjia, the Jewish orphanage in Cape Town.

Shortly after their arrival, my aunt Sheine-Rochel (Janie) was chosen to be the "adopted" daughter of the Oddes family of Williston. Their son, George, was at school at Sacs and he was sent by his parents to choose an orphan girl. The idea was probably, that this little girl would help to run the home. What in fact did transpire was that she and George fell in love and eventually married each other. Her story has been told by her daughter, Blume.

But for the two sisters left behind in Oranjia, their security in the form of their older sister had been, once again, taken away from them and this after only having been in South Africa for three months.

I quote from a letter written by the President of Oranjia dated 2 December 1921. "As you are probably aware, Shana has two younger sisters at the orphanage, and you could not do a greater Mitzvah than to find homes in your town for the other two sisters. It seems to be extremely hard for this family to part and her two little sisters have had many cries since Shana left and I beg and appeal to you to complete this great Mitzvah by finding homes in your town for the other two sisters so that the three children of this family could be near one another so that they could see each other if only occasionally. Whoever will adopt them will never regret doing so as these children will never give a day's trouble. I say without exaggeration that they are the finest set of children I have had amongst the party of orphans I brought from the Ukraine."

The reply was as follows "with reference to your remark that I should try to get homes for Shana's other two sisters here - personally I think this would not be the correct thing. Three adopted daughters - all sisters - in the same village and different houses would only cause dissatisfaction among these children and they would never be able to grow up as the daughters of their adopted parents, as being sisters and having different parents would only make them more uncomfortable when they reach an age of discretion. In a city it would be a different matter."

My Ouma and her younger sister, Jessie (Yochevet) went on to live at the orphanage during their schooling. Bessie eventually became a hairdresser and married Julius Morris who owned the Caltex garage at the site of the present Claremont Pick N Pay in Cape Town. They had one daughter, Phena Morris who then married my dad, Norman Snitcher.

An interesting point to note is that the River Pina runs through Pinsk. Whether that had any influence in my Ouma calling my mom Phena, we will never know.

Unlike today, none of these traumatized children ever received any counseling or therapy and it is a testament to the orphanage and the Jewish community and perhaps to their innate strength of character that they all grew up to become stable, solid contributing members of society.

Brandle (Bessie) Gesunterman

Julius Morris and Bessie on their wedding day

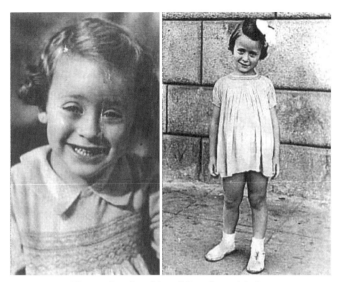

Phena, the daughter of Bessie and Julius

Bessie and Julius on their daughter's, Phena's, wedding day

Two Gesunterman sisters, Brandle (Bessie) and Janie (right) walking in Cape Town

Bessie and Julius in later years

Bessie Gesunterman married Julius Morris and they had one daughter Phena who in turn had four children, two girls (one being Laruren Snitcher) and two boys.

Lauren Snitcher, Phena's daughter and Bessie's granddaughter, lives in Cape Town, South Africa.

Since 1996 Lauren has been involved in setting up and maintaining a database on the Ochberg Orphans and was one of the driving forces behind the creation of a documentary film about the Ochberg rescue mission that was short listed for an Oscar in 2008.

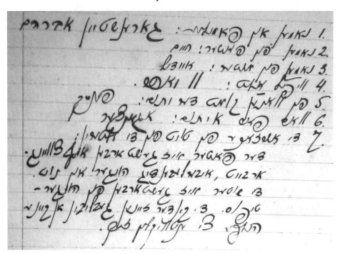

The Gorensteyn Family Details as recorded on pages 71 and 73 of the register kept by the Cape Jewish Orphanage (Oranjia).
1 Names and surname: Abraham and Chana Gorensteyn
2 Father: Chaim   3 Mother: Eidel   4
Ages: 11 and 9 years   5 Place of origin: Pinsk
6 How orphaned: Both parents
7 General Comments: The father died when he was taken to government work.
The mother died of typhoid having lived through hunger and need.

Chana Gorensteyn
Photo on Pinsk travel document

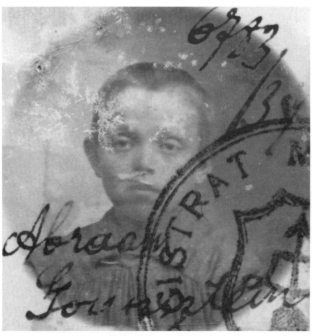

Abraham Gorensteyn
Photo on Pinsk travel document

AVRAM GORENSTEYN *(1910-1998)*
Written by Charles Levitt - August 2009 Sydney, Australia

Avram (Abe) was born 14 November 1910 in Pinska, Eastern Poland (Belarus). His grandfather, Matisyohu Gorensteyn lived in Orli, 20 miles from Pinsk, and was a Rabbi and Hebrew teacher.

Abe's father was Chaim Gorensteyn, and was the manager of a factory in Pinsk. Chaim was married to Aidel.

Aidel died of typhus in ~1917, and Chaim passed away from cancer of the stomach in ~1920. This left Avram and his younger sister Chana (Connie) as young orphans, destitute, starving and I cannot even begin to imagine how lonely and scared the two young children must have been to find themselves in the precarious predicament that they were in. Abe and Connie spoke Hebrew, Yiddish and some Russian.

Thanks to Isaac Ochberg's endeavours, Avram and Connie won the ultimate jackpot and were saved from certain death if not from the anti Semitism in Eastern Europe at the time, then later from Nazism.

up as/a good Jew and Jewess. For that purpose they shall shall be instructed in a traditional history, religious rites, and all other ceremonies ordinarily or ~~properly~~ *properly* taught to a child in a Jewish home; and the home of the Party of the other Part shall be regulated by Jewish ideas and customs. The children shall be instructed in Hebrew and otherwise all necessary steps shall be taken for the confirmation (Bar Mitzvah) and **otherwise** for the children.

8. It shall not be competent for the Party of the Other Part at any time to alter the name of the children adopted under this Indenture, but it shall **be permissible** for them to add the name of the adopting father as one of the christian names, so that the children to be adopted may be known as

Connie Gorenstein ~ Levitt

Abraham Gorenstein ~ Levitt

THUS DONE and signed at CAPE TOWN aforesaid on the day and in the month and year first aforewritten in the presence of the subscribing witnesses.

AS WITNESSES:

1. *Justinian M. Cohen*

2. *Howard Damon*

p.p. *I. Ochberg*

B. Braun

S.B. Levitt

Page 4 of the adoption papers of Abraham and Connie

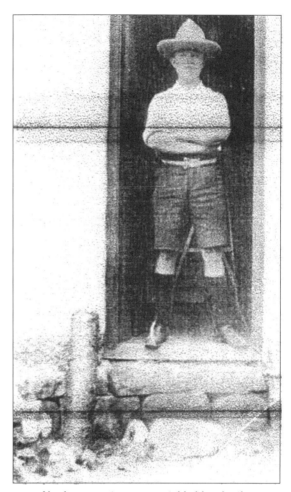

Abraham as a teenager outside his adoptive Parents' shop in Dealesville OFS

They arrived in South Africa on 23 September 1921, not being able to speak a word of the local languages, but to the credit of both, they learnt both English and Afrikaans and spoke both languages without a foreign accent.

After living in the Jewish Orphanage in Cape Town, they were adopted by Samuel Barnard Levitt and his wife Lottie Kümmel, who had no children of their own.

Abe was a highly intelligent person, and after schooling in the Free State and Johannesburg, studied medicine at the University of the Witwatersrand, graduating as a doctor in 1944.

Abe married Sylvia Krawitz in July 1948, at the Wolmarans Street Synagogue, and they lived in Barkly West in the Northern Cape, where Abe practised as a much loved and respected General Practitioner.

Abe Levitt and staff outside his adoptive parents shop in Dealesville OFS

Wedding photo July 1948 - Sylvia and Abe with Samuel Barnard Levitt and his second wife Taube

Sylvia and Abe – Durban 1948

Sylvia and Abe – Durban 1948

Sylvia, Abraham with Sharon, Charles and Allan Muizenburg – December 1955

Abe and Sylvia had three surviving children; Charles born 9 June 1949, Allan born 8 October 1950 and Sharon born 14 April 1953. The family moved to Johannesburg in 1958, and lived in Emmarentia. Charles matriculated at Greenside High School, Allan and Sharon at King David, Victory Park.

Charles and Allan qualified as doctors and Sharon obtained a BA degree at the University of the Witwatersrand.

Abe was a general practitioner of the old school, loved by family, friends and patients alike.

Sylvia passed away in 1970, and did not live to see her grand children. Abe married Fanny Rudolph in December 1972, and they shared a loving relationship for 27 years. Abe loved all his grand children; Sascha and Zoë; Charles's children, Brigitte and Andrea, Allan's daughters and Syndi, Lara and Tarryn, Sharon's daughters. Abe passed away 19 February 1998.

Sylvia passed away in 1970, and did not live to see her grand children. Abe married Fanny Rudolph in December 1972, and they shared a loving relationship for 27 years. Abe loved all his grand children; Sascha and Zoë; Charles's children, Brigitte and Andrea, Allan's daughters and Syndi, Lara and Tarryn, Sharon's daughters. Abe passed away 19 February 1998.

As a family, Charles, Allan and Sharon were unaware of his experiences as an Ochbherg Orphan during Abe's lifetime. No-one ever had a bad word to say about Abe. He must however have been emotionally scarred by his experiences as a young child. However he was a stoic person, and never complained, nor harped about the past.

Abe was very proud of his three children, and loved and was loved by all his grand children, who affectionately referred to him as Zeida or Zeids.

Avram and Sylvia, and later Fanny are forever in my thoughts, and out of the ashes of horrendous adversity, and a grateful thanks to Isaac Ochbherg, Samuel and Lottie, we as descendants are here to tell Abe's story.

ABRAM AND CHANA GORENSTEIN
Written by Sharon Abro

Group Passport Four
"Abe/Avraham is the little boy in the top row, 3rd from the right."

I refer to the article placed in the Jewish Report 07-14 May 2010 seeking descendents of Ochberg orphans. It appears that my father may be the "Abram Gerynsthein" listed in the article. We only know that his name was Gorenstein and we do know that he was one of the Ochberg orphans.

My brothers and I were told by our parents that my dad (Abraham – Abe) and his sister Chana (Constance - Connie) Gorenstein lived in Pinsk on the border of Russia and that they lost their parents in a typhoid epidemic. We are not quite sure whether was true or not. Apparently there were uncles and aunts Gorenstein who immigrated to the USA. My cousins have tried to find out if there was any connection in the USA but they were unsuccessful.

Having spent some time at the Cape Town Jewish Orphanage, my dad and aunt were adopted by Barney and Lottie Levitt and were renamed Abe and Connie Levitt. From the documents held by Lauren Snitcher in Cape Town, the only reference to Mr and Mrs Levitt, was that they were considering adopting a child. There is no official record that they had completed the adoption process. We believe that my dad would not agree to be adopted by them, unless his sister was part of the package. His life may well have been completely different, with my aunt having been brought up in the orphanage and losing contact with her!

Barney and Lottie lived in Uitenhage in the Eastern Cape and then moved to a farm near Boshoff in the Free State. My dad learnt the Afrikaans language, thereafter English and he grew up as a farmer at that time. My brother Allan tells me that when my father went for his driver's licence, the official said "Little Levitt (and he was little, barely over 5 foot 1 inches) you have got your licence, I saw you driving your father's tractor"! My father actually passed his Matric in Afrikaans, however his English was impeccable without any accent, neither Yiddish nor Afrikaans.

Lottie passed away in ~1936 and thereafter my grandfather married Taube Goldberg, who had a son Ralph from her first marriage.

My father started studying medicine at Wits University in 1932. He had to break his studies to help "Oupa", as we called our grandfather, on the farm because of the Depression and World War Two. He resumed his studies and qualified in 1946. He set up practice in Barkly West, a small Diamond Mining "dorp" (village) near Kimberley and on the Vaal River, in partnership with Shim Klein with whom he had studied medicine. My dad and Shim sustained a lifelong friendship.

My grandparents moved from Boshoff to Johannesburg. They lived in Kensington and owned a petrol station in Malvern. When my grandfather retired, they moved to Muizenberg and lived in a little house called "Wherry House" in Wherry Road next door to the Muizenberg Shul Hall, known as the Weizman Hall.

My aunt Connie married Adie Treiser and they had three children Ruth, Essie and David. Ruth stayed in South Africa (she has passed away) and Essie and David moved to Melbourne.

In 1948, my father met my mother Sylvia Krawitz, from Johannesburg. She had a B-Comm degree (most unusual for a woman in those days) and worked as a Bookkeeper for Suzmans (I think that is the forerunner of Capital Tobacco). They married in July 1948 and settled in Barkly West for a few years, where they had three children, Charles Hayman, Allan Maurice and me Sharon Miriam. Our mom was a full-time mother, did all my dad's accounts and was very involved in the Women Zionist League and the Jewish Women's Benevolent, both in Kimberly and later in Johannesburg.

I remember very little of Barkly West, only that it was very dusty and we lived near the river. My brothers attended the school in Barkly West. Charles moved to Kimberley Boys Primary as a weekly boarder for about one year. My late Aunty Lulu Liebesman (my mother's sister) told us a story, that on a visit to Johannesburg, Charles spoke to her in a broad Afrikaans accent. "I comes to Jo'burg and I comes in a trein"!

As my parents decided that we children needed to grow up in a Jewish environment, in 1958 we moved to Johannesburg. We lived in Emmarentia near the Dam and my father joined a General Practitioner medical practice in partnership with Sidney Sash. They had two sets of rooms, in Church Street, Mayfair and in Jan Smuts Avenue, Parktown. Most of my Dad's patients lived in Mayfair and surrounds and many were Afrikaans speaking. His patients loved him, not only was he their doctor, he was their friend, marriage councillor and brawl breaker etc etc!

Our father was the most amazing person and doctor. He was very small (always reminded me of Mickey Rooney), but a heart of gold for his family, friends and patients. It was nothing for him to get up in the middle of the night to visit sick patients. I also remembered he had a small room at home at the bottom of the house where he attended to patients. It always seemed to happen in the middle of dinner!

My older brother attended Greenside Primary School and then Greenside High. Allan and I both attended Greenside Primary and then we went to the very fledgling King David School in Victory Park. (Charles could not go, as he was older than the oldest class). My brothers both studied medicine and qualified at Wits University.

My mother died when I was 17 in 1970 and my father married a wonderful woman Fanny Rudolph in 1973, who was with him for the rest of his life.

Charles married Michelle Hillhaus (they are divorced). They moved to Adelaide where he specialised in Radiology and then moved to Sydney, where he lives today and works in a Radiology practice (funnily enough for a South African Doctor, Dr Van der Westhuizen). Charles has a son Sasha and a daughter Zoe. Sasha is married to Christine, they live in London and have a baby boy Alexander. Sasha works for Deutsche Bank. Zoe works in a hotel in California.

My brother Allan married Lorraine Seligman from Pretoria in 1974. Allan specialised in Paediatrics, but decided to remain as a General Practitioner and set up practice in Wendywood. They lived in Gallo Manor and had two daughters Brigitte and Andrea. Lorraine passed away at the age of 33. A couple of years later Allan married Wendy Millstein, however they divorced after 10 years. Brigitte and Andrea live in Cape Town. Brigitte is a personal trainer at Virgin Active and Andrea works at the Grand Westin Hotel on the Cape Town Foreshore. Allan worked for about five years as a doctor at the Sandringham Jewish Old Aged Home, but now is in private practice in Northcliff.

As for me, I married Ivor Davkin in 1972, am divorced from him and remarried Mel Abro. I live in Sandown and my husband and I are business brokers. I have three daughters. Syndi married Jared Kahn, lives in Cape Town, has one son Finn aged three and is expecting another boy in September. Syndi is an artist and also freelances as a graphic designer. Lara married Brett Duveen, lives in Savoy, has a daughter Noa aged three and a son Adi aged one. Lara is a Chartered Accountant and works for Ernst and Young. My youngest daughter Taryn lives in Douglasdale and is also a freelance graphic designer.

Over the years my father and my aunty Connie sustained a loving brother and sister relationship and their lives were intertwined. My father was the family doctor for my aunt and uncle, her second husband, her children and grandchildren for many years.

My dad practiced medicine into his eighties. He was half blind and still visited patients with his trusted medical sister, who used to drive him around. We were petrified that he would make a mistake one day! Eventually he was forced to give up medicine and from that day on, he deteriorated at a rapid pace and was in a wheelchair for the last couple of years of his life. One evening my children and I spoke to him and asked if he remembered anything about his birth parents, but it was very vague, he just said his mother was very tall. I cannot believe that as both my dad and his sister Connie were very short! My dad died in February 1999 and his wife Fanny passed away about one and a half years later.

My father was open about being a orphan, but we only learnt much later that he was an "Ochberg Orphan". My Aunty Connie blanked it out of her mind until just a few years before she passed away. Unfortunately Dad did not tell us the actual events up to the time of leaving Europe.

Dad was supposed to have been eleven when they arrived in South Africa on the boat, but we think he was older than that as we believe had his Barmitzvah in Russia. We also believe that as he and his sister Connie were so small as adults, the authorities at the Orphanage in Russia could have distorted their ages, in order for them to qualify to join the other orphans.

I have never written about our family before and looking back at this, it is so wonderful that my father and his sister were given the chance to live their lives and contribute, not only to their families and friends but to their communities as well. From my dad, there are three children, seven grandchildren and four and a half great-grandchildren and many more to come, please G-d! My aunty Connie has many more descendents. This would not have happened had there not been an Isaac Ochberg. My dad and his sister, had they survived after the First World War in the Orphanage in Europe would have more than likely have perished in the Holocaust.

Zeida's seven grandchildren ~1984.
Sasha at back Lara, Brigitte and Syndi,
Andrea and Zoe and Tarryn in front

CHANA AND AVRAHAM GORNSZTEJN
Written by Essie Nestadt

Group Passport Eight - "We think Chana is the little girl sitting in the front row on the very left."

Connie (Chana Gorenstejn) – ten years old

Connie ~1937

My mother and her brother were born Chana and Avraham Gornsztejn.

They came from a little village near Pinsk in the Ukraine (somewhere I read it was actually in Belarus) so I'm not sure.

They came to the Cape Town Orphanage with the group of Ochberg orphans on 23 September 1921.

They were then both adopted together by Free State farmers Barnett and Lotte Levitt who had no children of their own. They lived in Dielswil/Boshoff area where Barnett bred mules for the mines.

My mom went to Greenhill Primary School in Bloemfontein where she boarded, and then onto Unisi High School - also in Bloemfontein, where she also boarded.

After finishing school she studied music and the piano. She finished her course and passed the University of South Africa Music Piano Forte Final Division.

Her brother Abe, worked on the farm for 10 years and then went to the University of Witwatersrand to study medicine. He became a successful Doctor.

The Levitt family moved to Malvern East Johannesburg where Barnett Levitt bought a small shoe factory. Later he sold it and bought a Garage and Filling Station.

Our father Aron Treiser had come to South Africa to settle, from Germany in 1936. He also bought himself a Garage/Filling Station which happened to be near the Levitt's Garage.

He met my mother Connie, asked her to teach him English and the rest is history. They were married in 1937. They had three children. Ruth (deceased), Esther and David, (both in Melbourne) and we are the Ochberg orphan descendants.

Aron died in 1969 and Connie married Salvotore Alhadeff in 1975. They had a good 25 years together then he passed away. Connie's last years were spent back in Cape Town (where her daughter Ruth lived) at Highlands House Jewish Old Aged Home. She passed away aged 87 in 2002.

My mother was the sweetest, friendliest lady, who never knew what a "farible" was.

My husband, Ernie always said she was the best mother- in - law because she never ever interfered with us and never ever told us what to do. She worked side by side with our dad in the business, never spending too much time in the kitchen. She loved playing the piano and sang many Yiddish songs. She adored her brother Abe, who was adopted with her by the same Levitt family.

Even in her later years when she was living in The Jewish Old Aged Home in Cape Town and her health was failing, she always had a smile and never ever complained.

Addi (Aron) Treiser and Connie
1937 wedding at Wolmarans Shul

Addi (Aron) Treiser and Connie
Holiday in Durban - 1939

Aron, Connie, Ruth, David and Esther
The family on holiday   Durban 1946

Ruth, David, Connie, Essie and Jodi,
daughter of Ernie and Essie

Ruth, Michael and wife Maetie, Illana
Essie, Connie and Ruth's youngest Beverley

Connie with Essie and Ruth and
grandchildren

NAT GREENSTEIN (NACHMAN GREENSHTEIN), MY GRANDFATHER
Written by Lisa Greenstein

My name is Lisa Greenstein. I am one of the grandchildren of the man we knew as Nat Greenstein. This is not really Nat's story, because Nat never really told his story. This is my story of the grandfather I grew up with, and the man I have learned about since.

MY MYSTERIOUS GRANDFATHER

Growing up, my brother and I knew nearly nothing about my grandfather's childhood. But it is easy to imagine the missing details. Because the man we know inspires imagining. He is a playful, magical impresario, a man who can talk himself into or out of anything, who can hold a child enraptured on his knee for hours. He can whistle old-time songs and play the harmonica and make up unrepeatable limericks. He tells stories that will delight you or terrify you or leave you laughing in wild disbelief, begging for more, wondering whether he is telling the truth or some fantastical fiction.

Grandpa Nat convinces us that swallowing watermelon pips will make vines grow out of our ears. He teaches us how to make delicate origami boxes out of bits of chocolate wrappers. We litter the lounge table with our attempts. He stands with us on the balcony of his brother-in-law's 23rd floor flat in Mutual Place and cheers us on as we send paper planes swooping down towards the pool at the Sea Point pavilion across the Beach Road. Someone downstairs complains. Nat chuckles.

If he isn't enchanting the children with stories, my grandfather likes little better than to shock friends and family. Once, at an Italian restaurant, he warns my brother and me that if we don't stop squabbling we'll end up face-first in our spaghetti. A few minutes later, my brother, dripping forehead to chin in bolognese sauce, discovers that Nat is not a man of vain promises. His rudeness charms us. We are too young to notice that his lack of social grace eventually gradually embarrasses and isolates my grandmother until she seldom invites visitors, for fear that he would go too far and insult or offend them badly.

In rare moments, we notice a dark exchange of looks between the adults, a hushed conversation, a flurry of worried telephone calls. But we are too small to understand, and this is a shadow that no one wants to see, or perhaps a shadow that no one really knows how to explain.

We are told that Nat's grandmother let go of his hand at a harbour "in Russia" when he was four years old, and that he was sent over to South Africa as an orphan. But we know nearly nothing about his childhood. He never speaks about it, and he certainly never mentions the hardships in Russia that led to that journey.

So we imagine. We imagine a child abandoned by his grandmother and mother. We cannot imagine the pain, so we imagine a tough survivor, a dreamer, a joker, because we

Group Passport Six Nachman Greenshtein is no 14 on the list of children on the passport
Melwyn writes, "I am almost sure that my Dad is in the back row on the far right. He was about eight years old when he came out."

Lisa writes "Poring over the group passport photographs of the Ochberg orphans, I make out the name 'Grynstyn, Nachman, 8'. And there, in the dark, grainy photograph, I recognise the dark stare, the eyebrows straight and hard-set as though chiselled in two straight strikes."

cannot imagine our grandfather as anyone else. We imagine a hopeful Oliver Twist, a quick-witted Fagan, a wild ruffian child with nothing but his own wits and dreams and stories and talents to keep him one step ahead of trouble.

Grandpa Nat occasionally mentions his escapades at the Jewish Orphanage in Cape Town, Oranjia. He tells me that there were some cows kept at the orphanage for milking. He liked the sound that the cows made when they chewed crunchy straw, so he stole the other children's straw hats and fed them to the cows so that he could listen to the sound. We imagine the stolen hats, the oblivious cow, the crunching, the secret pleasure of the ragged child.

Later we will learn that he was a troubled man, and we will remember some strange, uncomfortable moments - sharp words at a table, a glowering figure in his chair. But we see few traces of the demons that plague our grandfather, and we do not think to ask. On rare occasions, his face darkens, and he warns us: One day you will forget your Grandpa Nat. We shift uneasily around these moments, and quickly the shadows are obscured by joking and laughter. Relieved, we let ourselves be enchanted once again by the magic that he weaves together to keep his demons out of sight for just another moment. His eyes sparkle as he invents rude poems, stories, games and songs to entertain us.

My father tells us how they would go down to the Green Point common to fly kites, and my grandfather's homemade kites, fashioned from brown paper and string, would fly higher and longer than all the other kids' expensive store bought kites. My uncle tells us how Nat could make anything out of leather, out of cloth.

One time, Grandpa Nat builds me a little birdcage with a breeding box at the back. I peep with wonder into the little box when, a few weeks later, a tiny egg appears, and the budgies fuss and chatter over it. I lay awake at night listening to the sounds of the newly hatched, tiny pink chicks. This is what my grandfather brings: wonder, possibility, new life. There is nearly nothing that can't be made or fixed. And if it really can't be fixed, there is no sorrow too great to be soothed by a song or a story.

I do not hear the name Isaac Ochberg until much, much later, more than 20 years after my grandfather takes his own life, in June 1989.

A DESPERATE CHILDHOOD REVEALED

Poring over the group passport photographs of the Ochberg orphans, I make out the name 'Grynstyn, Nachman, 8'. And there, in the dark, grainy photograph, I recognise the dark stare, the eyebrows straight and hard-set as though chiselled in two straight strikes. I discover that my grandfather's name was Nachman, not Nathan. He was 8, not 4, years old when he came to South Africa, and he came from a town called Berdichev in the Ukraine. I discover that the entire Jewish population of Berdichev was gassed in a concentration camp two decades later.

I find a letter from my grandfather's brother, Sam Gillad, written in 1989. The letter reveals some of the mysterious, harrowing details from my grandfather's past. The history is painful, but in no way unique. The details that echo those I've subsequently read in accounts by others of my grandfather's generation, who lived through famine and terror in Eastern Europe.

Nat's father, Moshe, a skilled leather craftsman, owned a leather factory in Berdichev, Ukraine. One night, a family friend warned them that the Russian authorities had been informed that Moshe had deserted the army in the Russo-Japanese war in 1905. If they stayed in Berdichev, Moshe would be sent to Siberia. That night, Moshe and his wife packed what they could. They gave all their jewellery and money to border smugglers to get them across the river to Austria.

Tombstone of Moses Greenstein
"Nat's father, Moshe, a skilled leather craftsman, owned a leather factory in Berdichev, Ukraine."

Eddie and Pearl Greenstein, Nat's siblings
"The second girl, Pearl, left too and married a man in Lwow. The fifth sibling, Ephraim, made his way back to Russia and disappeared for good.

Nat was a baby at this time, with five older siblings; Gila, Lazer, Mordechai, Pearl and Ephraim. Soon afterwards, a seventh child, Sam, was born, and World War I began. Moshe got them to Vienna, where he found work in a factory making artificial limbs for war invalids. They starved all through the war, and eventually made their way back to what had become Poland. Nat's parents made felt slippers at night, and Moshe would trek to the villages and peddle the slippers in exchange for potatoes and other food.

An eighth child, Luba, was born in 1919. Shortly afterwards, Moshe died in a typhus epidemic, leaving his wife destitute with eight children. Sam's account continues with this summary of Nachman's childhood family:

"The older children in order [from youngest]: Sister Gila got married to a young Jewish baker and moved to Lwow, a big city. The second: brother Lazer and brother Mordechai went away. The second girl, Pearl, left too and married a man in Lwow. The fifth, Ephraim, made his way back to Russia and disappeared for good.

"Mother was left with your dad, Nachman, me and baby Gila. She finally went to Lwow and found a small cellar in a building, where she did the cleaning as rent. The two [older] daughters did not help her much. She finally found a baker who let her deliver rolls and other small bakery things to kiosks all around town. She would get up at 4 in the morning, summer and winter, and deliver all the rolls. We were starving.

"At that time my mother's mother, an old and disturbed woman, joined her from Russia, and made her life very difficult. About that time, my grandma found out that Jewish war orphans were being gathered to be sent to find new life in other lands. Your dad was attached to a group that was sent to Cape Town, by help of Jews there. I was attached to a group that was sent to Palestine. We were put in an orphanage that was supported by a group of kind Jews from Cape Town. It was a farming school. I grew up there to the age of 15."
(extract from a letter sent by Sam Gillad to Ben Greenstein in June 1989. Sam was 75.)

Ochberg's records state that both of Nachman's parents were murdered, and that he was found with his grandmother 'in terrible conditions'. I can only guess that the grandmother lied about both parents' having been murdered in order that the child might have a chance to leave Eastern Europe.

A TURBULENT FAMILY HISTORY

According to family legend, a wealthy and prominent man arrived at the orphanage to adopt an orphan. He noticed that one of the children had run off and hidden in a tree in the orphanage's huge gardens. When he asked to see that child, the orphanage staff warned him off Greenstein, the *wilde chaya* of the place. Not put off, the man insisted on taking my grandfather home with him. Here the legends diverge. Some sources say that he returned Nat to the orphanage after a week. According to my uncle Ben, my grandfather ran away and was not seen again until *"he rocked up as a young man in Johannesburg totally broke and no friends apart from a jeweller called Dave Lockitch whom he may have met at the Kimberley Big Hole diamond diggings.*

"I'm afraid we may never know what he did during the time between running away as a child and his appearance in Jo'burg as a stone-broke young man.. He certainly never told me. As far as I know, he conned Lil's mother into thinking he was loaded until the point of no return. He was highly skilled as a leather worker as was his father and could make his own suitcases. He was also a dab hand at the sewing machine and somewhere along the line learned how to make neckties. He could create a spider's web of promises about the millions he was going to make..."

Nat as a young man

Lil as a young lady

Nat and Ben

Ben and Melvyn

A MIXED BLESSING

It's June 1989, midwinter in Cape Town. I am 14 years old. I have been left at a friend's house, even though it is a school night, and already dark. I know something is going on with my grandparents, though no one has said anything aloud. My grandmother has moved in with her sister, Freda, and my grandfather has taken to drinking a lot of whiskey. The hushed phone calls have become more frequent. But tonight it feels like someone has died. My mother eventually arrives, takes me into the friend's mother's bedroom and sits me on the bed. It's Nat. How, I ask, although I don't need to ask. So they explain the details. They never really sink in properly, of course. Like the rest of the story, there is much we fill in ourselves.

It was a strange, mixed blessing that Mr Ochberg bestowed on Nachman Greenstein, for the journey to South Africa that no doubt saved his life was also, in some ways, the unmaking of him. He took his own life by gassing himself in his car. When they found him, the engine was not running; he had, apparently, turned it off. After Nat's death, my grandmother no longer answered to the name of Lil: she insisted that we call her by her birth name, Rachel Leah.

Nat and Sam his brother

Nat meets my grandmother, Rachel Leah Mallach, and somehow persuades her to marry him. He has no family network, no fortune, no education. In my imagination, he is the cowboy with crazy charisma and irresistible eyes, sweeping through town to claim the woman all the other men are vying for. She's tall and arrestingly elegant. She has a younger sister, Freda, and since their mother died young, she has already spent half her life keeping a family together. He calls her Lil.

In later years Lil will tell us she should have listened to her family's warnings. She will tell me - without any trace of self-pity - about the hardships that her marriage brought. She will never use the word 'regret'. I have never heard anyone from the Greenstein family use the word 'regret'.

So they are married, and they have two sons: my uncle Ben, and my father, Melvyn. Nat can't keep a business going, or stay settled in one place for very long, and the family is constantly on the move.

Nat and Lil

THE FAMILY LEFT BEHIND

Following are the remaining contents of the letter (not covered in the narrative above) that was received from Sam Gillad, Nat's brother, that tells us about the family left behind.

June 7, 1989
Dear Ben, Lorraine, Adam and Saul

I was very grieved about my brother's passing. I wish we were closer, but fate drove us apart as children. I hope he found peace.

I feel it is my duty to tell you about the past of our family.

Your dad was attached to a group that was sent to Cape Town, by help of Jews there. I was attached to a group that was sent to Palestine. We were put in an orphanage that was supported by a group of kind Jews from Cape Town. It was a farming school. I grew up there to the age of 15." (Note 1)

After coming to Palestine, I constantly kept in touch with my mother and with Nachman, your dad. He seemed to hold an unforgiving grudge against his mother that sent him away. He never realised how lucky he was. If he stayed in Poland he would have had no future.

After I grew up, I became a policeman at age 16 ½ and served two years, then I resigned and went to work in the building trade and did well. I was about 20 when I decided to help my mother and sister Luba to come to Palestine. I sent them papers and money and they came; first my sister, who had emotional problems that her sisters in Lwow did not tell me about. I was crushed of what to do. Then my older brother, Mordechai, who lived in Jerusalem, came to Haifa, where I lived and worked, and I took her to him. She was about 16 and very wild. He tried to marry her off to a young Jewish butcher. She ran away and found English missionary women. They converted her to Christianity and married her off, to a high-ranking British police officer. She was very pretty and they had three children.

Then my mother came and I had to look after her. The economy deteriorated and I could not find work in Haifa so I went to Jerusalem, where I found work in the British broadcasting service as a technician. I took mother to Jerusalem and supported her with one third of my salary every month. She had a small room of her own. My older brother, who drove a taxi cab, did not help at all. At that time, the clouds of WWII were gathering. There was very bad inflation and I struggled to make ends meet.

I was getting nine pounds a month. I asked your dad in a letter if he could help his mother a little with one pound a month. He still hated her and did not write to us any more.

It saddened me very much about him. I don't mind now to mention it to you. He refused to help. It was 1942. The war was

raging, many young men and women in the Jewish community volunteered to serve in the British armed forces. I volunteered to serve in the RAF as a radio technician, where I was to the end of the war in mid 1946. All that time my sister used to come occasionally to visit her poor mother but never helped her a little (family trait). In 1947, the Arabs attacked the state of Israel, which was founded then. I joined the Israeli army, where I served to 1951.

I then decided to go to America to study industrial electronics. I arranged for my mother to be admitted to an old age home in Tel Aviv, where she lived out her life to age 82, died of cancer.

In 1951, at age 37, I came to Los Angeles and was accepted in the Los Angeles City College to study vocational electronic. I had no high school diploma. I never went to high school as I had to support my mother, and it was hard for me.

I had to take all the prerequisites for college. I struggled through and in 1955 I got an Associate of Arts degree. I did exceptional work at a part-time job, which I had to do to keep alive. At the end of school they asked me to stay on as a specialist and got me a permanent resident status from the immigration department and I remained here. I eventually got work in the television industry here. I met and married a girl from England that lived here. We had a sad marriage of about five years, then she left me and returned to her unhealthy brother in London and we broke up. I have been working here ever since, remained alone, where I am today.

At 75 I feel very much alone. I manage financially and try to promote some good inventions. I invented a real breakthrough in a possible source of energy with a magnet motor, that could work continuously without any fuel input. I also developed a theoretically possible flywheel motor that would do the same. I also have good ideas for 3D motion pictures (which I actually built) and lately I found a superior way to see 3D TV, which I may try to peddle to Japan, that has 3D TV now.

Sam Gillad
1323 N. Bronson Ave
Los Angeles, California 90028

THE NEXT GENERATION
Written by Lisa Greenstein

I am one of Nat's four grandchildren, and I see traces of him in each of us. His resourcefulness, his music, his flashes of genius, his flashes of anger. My uncle Ben married Lorraine (nee Saitowitz), and they moved to the United Kingdom in the 1970s. Ben is a scientist, a published author, and has exhibited his paintings and drawings in London. They have two sons, Adam and Saul. Adam made his way through school with several scholarships for his brilliant skill as a violinist. Today he is a prominent physician in Manchester, also widely published, and is married with two daughters, Ursula and Romy. Saul is an entrepreneur and runs an antique jewellery business in London.

My father, Melvyn, launched his own business ventures in the schoolyard, where he used to sell his school sandwiches (on my grandmother's famous homemade bread) for extra pocket

---

Note 1 Probably the group rescued and transported to Palestine by Israel Belkind, that lived in Gan Yeladim and was supported by the South African Zionist Federation. See Part One of this book.

money. As a young man, he was employed in the delicatessen industry, working for Patlansky Brothers (Patley's), where he developed a knowledge and appreciation for fine cheeses and meats. However, he soon moved towards his own business and travelled as a rep selling watches, clocks and jewellery to little towns and villages all over South Africa and Namibia (then Southwest Africa).

He met my mother, Anita (nee Immerman) in Cape Town in the early 1970s. Perhaps because of his turbulent upbringing, my father was determined that his family should be secure, settled and well provided for. In 1972 he bought a jewellery shop on Voortrekker Road in Parow. The shop, called Wolf Brothers, had been established in 1902 by two brothers, Angel and Isador Wolf.

My father steadily built the business, which today comprises six branches - four in Cape Town and two in Johannesburg. Wolf Brothers has become a household name in Cape Town.

I was born in 1974, and my brother Robert, was born in 1977. I went and studied theatre, literature and journalism at Rhodes University, and work today as a writer and editor, with more than 35 books in print internationally. I also perform regularly with a theatre group, Theatre Sports. Robert studied Business Science at the University of Cape Town, and after several successful years working as a business systems consultant, joined my father in Wolf Brothers, opening and running the Johannesburg branches of the business.

Robert is married to Hayley (nee Roach), and they have a son, Aiden Noah Greenstein, born in 2009. I have a son, Kolya Nathaniel Greenstein, born in 2008, named after my grandfather, Nat.

When I think back now, I can still hear him whistling and singing, always the same tune, both merry and achingly sad:

Show me the way to go home
I'm tired and I want to go to bed
I had a little drink about an hour ago
And it went straight to my head
Wherever I may roam
On land or sea or foam
You will always hear me singing this song
Show me the way to go home.

My Dad, Melvyn (centre), surrounded by my mom, Anita (back left), my brother Robert (front left) and I'm (Lisa) at the back on the right. The little boy is my son, Kolya Nathaniel Greenstein.

Melvyn Maurice Greenstein writes

We went to the screening of the Ochberg's Orphans movie and I was very moved.

I am married for 39 years to Anita and have two children Robert and Lisa. I have one brother who is married with two talented and brilliant sons living in London.

Unfortunately my father was very badly affected from his childhood and was always very unstable in his jobs etc. My mother was a very beautiful and astute business woman who worked every day of her life. Her marriage was always difficult although my father adored her. My father was terrible to my older brother who was an incredibly talented man who could play any instrument by ear and he could play any sport well. He had read all the classics.

Fortunately my brother and I have learned the lessons and have very stable lives and are blessed with stunning intelligent children.

Neil Greenberg writes

I have re-established contact with several of my friends from the sixties back in Cape Town who had an Ochberg parent and I was not aware of the fact at the time.

When we lived in Doverhurst we had neighbours a few floors down by the name of Greenstein. I was very friendly with the two sons Benny and Melvyn. Mr Greenstein manufactured neckties. I very vaguely remember Dad remarking to me one time that Mr Greenstein was an Ochberg orphan .

Wouldn't it be fantastic if these were the same Greensteins from nearly fifty years ago.

Anita, Melvyn, my son Kolya, me (Lisa) and Aiden, Robert's son

RUZA AND NETA HANS
Written by Jenny (Flink) Segall

My late mom Ruza (Rosie) Flink (nee Hans) standing and seated is my late aunt Neta (Nellie) Frankal (nee Hans).

My late Mom Ruza and her sister Neta were Ochberg orphans. They were about eight or nine years old when Ochberg brought them to Cape Town.

Mr Ochberg was the "Father" of the children and a great man who did this magnificent job of finding these orphans in the forests and bringing them to Cape Town and some to Johannesburg.

My mom was Rosie Flink (nee Hans). Her Polish name was Ruza. My aunt was Nellie Frankal (nee Hans). Her Polish name was Neta. This is the story of my mom and aunt.

Their parents were shot, and when the children found their bodies in the streets they ran for shelter to the woods. My mom and her sister had a brother, Hirschel, about eight months old. They hid in the forest for, what to them, seemed forever.

When Ochberg found them they were ill and he put them into some house somewhere to gain strength. When selecting who he could take, he took my mom and aunt, but the brother Hirschel (Hersz) had been stung by a wasp and it was risky for

Ruza and Neta Hans

the baby to go on board, so he left him in an orphanage in Poland.

He grew up there, and in later years they sent letters to Ochberg to ask if he could be sent to Cape Town, but they could not take him. Anyway, Hitler took care of him and they never saw each other again.

The town they came from was called Rawaruska, and I was sent a map identifying where this is, and it seems it was on the Ukraine/Poland border.

Ruza and Neta Hans (Rosie and Nellie)

ROSIE AND AIZER FLINK

My Dad, Aizer Flink, came by boat from Lithuania via London, to Cape Town. After he met my Mom he went out with her twice, always accompanied by someone. Then he left by train for Johannesburg, and within a few months he sent for her and they married. However I have no photos of that. They married in the Lions Shul in Doornfontein, and lived in Sivewright Avenue for many years. They then moved to Ascot Road in Bertrams and we lived there for 52 years.

My mom and dad's pole holders were great friends of his, from 'der heim' and one of them married an Ochberg girl. Her name was Tilly and I remember she had a sister, but I cannot remember their last name Tilly's married name was Feinstein and they never had children.

Benny Penzik's parents and my mom and aunt were all on the boat together and remained friends all their lives, and so Benny and his sister and myself all grew up together even though they lived in Pretoria and us in Johannesburg. (the parents married years before I am speaking of).

Rosie (Nee Hans) and Aizer Flink

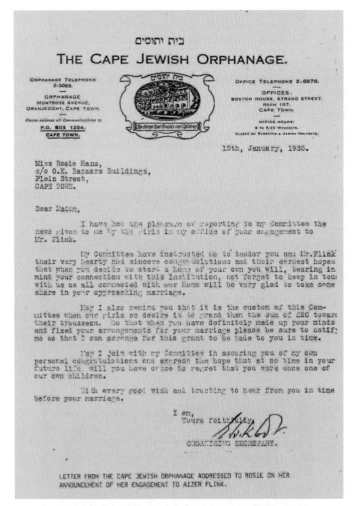

Letter from the Cape Jewish Orphanage to Rosie on her announcement of her engagement to Aizer Flink

MY HUSBAND CHAIM AND I

Chaim and myself at my 70th party at work in 2008.

My maiden name was Flink and I married Chaim Segall. My husband Chaim and I used to run the Bikkur Cholim Camp for 14 odd years, and of course the Arcadians used to come to our camp every year. You name the names and they were with us. I remember Eli Osrin and Solly Farber, just to name two.

Ellie Osrin was the best man at our wedding. We remained life long friends with Eli and also with Solly Farber and with many others from the Arc including Jerry and Mona Levy.
We also served on the committee of Arcadia with Bella Lubner and crowd, through our work with Bikkur Cholim.

My hubby Chaim was the Administrative Director of the IUA/UCF and National Youth Director of the Board of Deputies for 42 years and we were always connected with many organisations in Johannesburg.

Three Ochberg Girls; Nellie Frankal (Neta Hans), Eva (Chava) Berkowitz and Rosie Flink (Roza Hans)

NELLIE FRANKAL (NETA HANS)
Written by Cecil Frankal

Whilst staying at Oranjia, my mother Nellie, attended school at Good Hope Seminary and then Cape Town Girls' high school, together with her sister Ruza. Her first job, as far as I can recall, was making ladies hats in the millinery department of one of the most exclusive department stores in Cape Town, Garlicks. In fact, this was the only job that she had, as far as I can recall.

On Friday nights the youth gathered at Rosecourt in the Gardens area, where they used to hold socials, dances, parties and just get-togethers. My father lived across the road from Rosecourt, in Mill Street, where he was the only son, along with two sisters, of Meyer and Rebecca Frankal. My grandparents owned a CNA shop, coupled with a ladies hairdressing salon, and my two aunts were the hairdressers. On these Friday nights, my father would join in the fun at Rosecourt, where he played the piano for the dancers.

It was there that he met my mother, and the courtship began. I can sort of pinpoint the date by a leaf of a silver leaf tree, placed in one of our old photo albums, and it is inscribed "Kirstenbosch-1925", alongside a photo of the two of them.

I never stopped to think about it, but that means she was 15 when they were dating, and 23 when she married my father in September of 1933. His parents were against the marriage for a few reasons; firstly because she was an orphan from an unknown country, with poor English skills, and socially not good enough for my aunts. Also, my father was needed in the family

business, and he was about to be lost to the family from an everyday point of view. They moved to fashionable Muizenberg, and my brother was born in 1934. I followed in 1939. During their courtship days, their friends were nearly all from Oranjia, and I can still recall many of the women, but only by their married names-Gittel (Shnaps), Yetta (Bornstein), Fanny (Lockitch), Rose (Kapelus), and more.

After moving to Muizenberg, they befriended local couples, and started to play rummy, or just visit, neighbours or people with no connection to the past. But I do recall our annual trip to Oranjia for the Pesach seder, to which we all went with the Lockitch family.

My childhood in Muizenberg was brought to life every year at Pesach time, when my parents and I would make the hour-long trip to Cape Town, in order to attend the seder at Oranjia. This was the highlight of my life, to see how happy the children were and I really envied them!

The tables were often arranged according to the villages from which the parents came, and we always sat at Rawa Ruska, somewhere in Poland. My parents' closest friend, Fanny Lockitch, was a tireless worker for Oranjia, and we always accompanied her each year.

The father of another friend of mine, John Weinreich, was the president of Oranjia when I was growing up, maybe in the 30s, 40s or 50s. I clearly remember seeing his photo in the halls of Oranjia, along with many wonderful group photos of the children over the years.

311

My mom was active in the local Jewish affairs, and also attended shul regularly. In 1962, Muizenberg had passed its prime, and we moved to Sea Point, mainly to facilitate my lectures at UCT in the city.

Shortly afterwards my dad passed away, aged 56, and my mom lived on her own from then on, as my brother and I both married. She lived to the age of 81, succumbing to cancer, and it was only then that I realised how little I knew of her family.

She had a South American connection in Argentina, and exchanged letters in Yiddish with a family called Hecker and Sausner. I have seen wedding photos of men in military uniform, brides and cousins, all labelled in the photos, but she never spoke of them, and I was never able to make further contact. It was her reticence to talk of the past that has robbed us of the possible continuity of what little family we had.

Today there is only my cousin, Jenny Segall in Houston, and I.

SEEING THE MOVIE

I had attended a wonderful talk given by Lauren. When I arrived at the hall to register, I was made to feel very welcome, being the only man amongst all the women on a Wednesday morning. One lady came up to me and introduced herself to me as Noreen, and promptly sat down to enjoy her tea and scone with me. She was Isaac Ochberg's granddaughter! Two minutes later, her daughter came up and again introduced herself as Tessa, both from London. What an honour it was to meet them both.

When it was time for the lecture, it was very eloquently introduced by Tessa, who spoke easily, and then Lauren took to the podium. She is a gifted speaker, referred to no notes at all, and spoke at length about her passion for her great-great-grandfather, and told us that all she ever wanted to do since her early childhood was to find out as much as possible about him, which she did so well.

The movie that was assembled was incredible, and I am amazed that they were both able to find such footage after so many years.

Oranjia will always be part of my life - I am only so sorry that my mother's reticence to talk about her past has left many unanswered questions, particularly what her maiden name was. Hans? Ganz? Harris? Who knows? I had a long chat with Veronica Belling, who was convinced that it was Ganz or Gans, because there is very little use for the "h" sound in the language, but of course there is no final proof either way.

Jenny Segall, my cousin, and I are the only survivors of this generation, but luckily she had far more photographic material than I did.

NELLIE FRANKAL (NETA HANS)
Written by Jenny Segal

Nellie (nee Hans) and husband Sidney Frankal

It was thought that Nelie was the older child of the two children Rosie and Nellie (Ruza and Neta), as she was taller than my mom, so the orphanage just gave them both birth dates.

Nellie was a milliner and worked on other jobs as well, she married Sydney Frankal in Cape Town and they had two sons Raymond and Cecil Frankal.

Raymond passed away from cancer a few years ago, and he has a wife Isabel Frankal and three children (one in Melbourne and two in Cape Town) I don't have too much information on the Raymond's wife and children.

My cousin Cecil is a widower with three daughters, he still lives in Cape Town, he is an accountant, and we are in touch on a daily basis. He has one married daughter, one to be married in December 2009 and one single daughter.

Nellie was a humorous person and loved to play cards and poker. She was always on the go, had lots of friends, and most of them were the ladies of the orphanage that she grew up with. She was a popular woman and loved by all who knew her.

HIRSCHEL HANS
Written by Jenny (Flink) Segall

Hirschel Hans in Poland

The following letter written in 1932 translates as follows;

In the name of the Orphans Caretaking Association in Lvov, I am notifying you that Hersz has turned out to be a worthy boy.

He behaves well and lives with the family Shapiro where he is an apprentice. He has gained affection from the family and they treat him well. We hope he will turn out to be a good tradesman.

Hersz is healthy and would very much like to be with you. May I enquire if this is possible? We would like to be helpful in this regard. Please notify of how things are going with you and what your business is. From the address we assume you are not in an orphanage.

With hearty greetings to both of you.

The letter above was written in 1932 and it seems that the war interrupted the possible negotiations to bring Hirschel to South Africa. We believe Hirschel must have perished in the Holocaust.

Hirschel on the left
The last photograph we received from him

ROSIE HOFFMAN (ROSHA HEFT)
As related by her son Lazar Hoffman

My mother's mother died during childbirth and we don't know what became of the child. Her father went out on horseback one day and never came back. There were two older sisters who were 'too old' to be brought out by Isaac Ochberg so my Mom was the only one of her family to be saved. The older sister sent postcards with photos to my Mom but their names are hard to make out and we don't know their names. My Mom's birthday was 8 May, the same day chosen for a lot of children, as many did not really know their dates of birth.

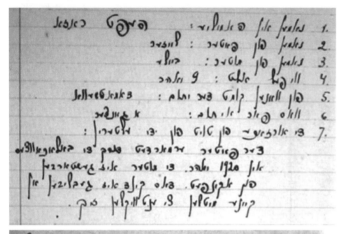

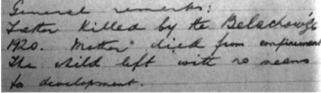

The family details of Rosha Heft as recorded on page 11 of the register at Oranjia. 1 Name and surname: Rosha Heft
2 Father: Lazar   3 Mother: Beile   4 Age: 9 years
5 From where: Dametzewa 6 Who died: Both parents
7 General Comments: Father killed by the Belacowitz in 1920.
Mother died from confinement.
The child left with no means to development.

PASSPORT 7 Rosha Heft is number 14 (back row 2nd from right) on the list while Feiga Elman is number 6.

Postcard photo of older sister and her children above with their messages below

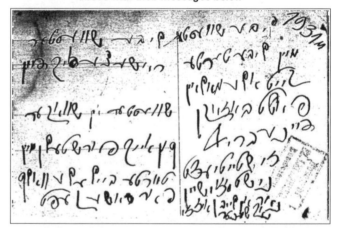

1931   Dear Sister
My dear daughter always goes and looks in the post for a letter from you – she still is not standing and is a pretty little girl.
Dear Sister Rosie
From your sister and brother-in-law. I am introducing my daughter, Beila Kocha, to Rosie Heft.

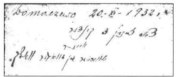

20 November 1932
These are our children, sister, from your sister and brother in law.   Wolf

My Mom was in the group that was placed in the care of the Cape Jewish Orphanage on their arrival in South Africa and they would have all gone to school and lived there until finishing school.

1928 Daily Timetable at Oranjia

-The children get up in the morning at 6.20, then they wash and make their beds which takes till 7 o'clock. Mr Beresinski is in attendance with the Boys and Mrs Beresinski with the Girls. From 7.00 to 7.25 they have prayers, and breakfast from 7.30 to 8 o'clock.

-Examination of the children, as regards clothes or cleanliness from 8.00 to 8.15. At 8.15 they leave for school taking with them a fairly liberal supply of sandwiches, such as fruit or eggs etc.

-The children arrive from school at three different times - some at 2.00, some at 3.00 and some at 4 o'clock. Then on their arrival they receive a light meal consisting of eggs bread and butter and pudding, also coffee or milk. After that they play for a little while and then do their homework. Some do their Hebrew lessons at home and some go to the Talmud Torah. Mr Simonhof assists till 6.30.

-From 6.30 till 7 o'clock they have prayers and conversation and supper at 7 o'clock, that is the usual. Dinner consisting of soup, meat, vegetables fruit and desert, ie pudding or jelly etc.

-The smaller children have their supper at 6 o'clock and at 7.00 they go to bed. The bigger children have their supper at 7 o'clock and go to bed at 8.15 up to 9 o'clock.

-Very often they have socials amongst themselves which takes up to about 10 o'clock. On Saturdays they have sometimes concerts and sometimes debates.

All the girls and boys of Oranjia used to go mountain climbing every Sunday and the start of the mountain climb was only five minutes walk from Oranjia which was perched high up on the mountain slope. They used to take pots and pans and cook and have picnics on the mountain. One day they even bumped into Jan Smuts.

After a certain age the girls were moved into a hostel. At Oranjia they were all encouraged to do a trade and Rosie became a seamstress with Foschini. Once she left Oranjia she did not have much contact with the other children except for the Ellman Family, her cousins, and a friend Brenda (Brina) Margolin who had a daughter Sara who worked in the Kaplan Library.

Above and top of next page - Rosie mountain climbing and on the beach with friends from Oranjia and cooking and rowing

Rosie and Julius   *Julius and Rosie*   *Julius in uniform*   *Rosie and Bella*

My Mom was standing at the entrance of Oranjia one hot day. A young man was walking up the hill to visit a friend. My mother offered him some water and this began their friendship and he, Julius, was to become her future husband. My Dad was Julius (Yehuda) Hoffman, the son of Rev Israel Hoffman, and was born in Pretoria. They were married 4 of September 1937 at the Roeland Street Shul by Reverend Bender. My older sister Bella was born in 1938 was named after my mother's late mother.When the war broke out things were tough and there were not many jobs around and my Dad joined up and went 'up North' for about six years. During this period my Mom had to bring up Bella by herself. My Dad was in Alexandria Egypt and was an instructor and had rank and was awarded some medals. After the war, in 1948, I (Lazar) was born and was named after my mother's late dad Lazar. We lived in Prince Street near Oranjia.

My mother was a housewife, a good Jewish cook and a gentle, caring and loving mother. She made me sandwiches and walked me to Primary School each day. She did knitting and all alterations. My Dad was an accountant at the railways and was on the committee of Oranjia.

As a child we went to Oranjia often. We went there as a family for Pesach Seders and I went there with my Dad for committee meetings and for Habonim on Sundays. Sometimes we took a boy, who was at a loose end, out on Sundays. Sheila Rosman who I married used to help a child at Oranjia with their homework whilst she was at University.

I remember on many an occasion going to the OK Bazaars Kosher counter where Hilda (Lipschitz) Modlin served. My Mom knew her well and would buy from her and have a bit of a chat.

Rosie, Lazar, Bella and Julius   *Bella and Lazar*   *Julius and Rosie*

Julius Hoffman

Lazar married Sheila Rosman of Uppington and became a Pharmacist. He owned a pharmacy for many years in Adelaide Australia, worked a short time in the USA and then settled in Perth Australia working in his profession. They have two sons; Julian an accountant who lives in Melbourne and Rodney who studies in Perth and aspires to be an Events Manager.

Rosie and Lazar

Mom was aged nine and the only one of her family who came out to South Africa with Isaac Ochberg in 1921. She did, however, come out with her cousins the four Ellman siblings; Joe (Benjamin), Blume, Feyga and Izzy (Jentl). She was always very close to them and after leaving Oranjia she remained in touch with them.

Bella married Charlie Wulf, the son of Devorah (Lehrman) Wulf, an Ochberg Orphan. She was a Comptometer Operator who worked for Stuttafords and Groote Schuur Hospital. Charlie died several years ago. Bella lived in the Cape all her life. They had no children and Bella now lives in Rondebosch.

317

Chapter 67 – RIVKA, ZIPPE AND MOSHE KAILER/KOHLER

BECKY GREENBERG (RYWKA KAILER/KOHLER)
Written by Basil Greenberg

I believe my Mother was born in 1909. She always used December 24 as her birthday but was not sure if that was correct. I believe that she was probably older than most of the other Ochberg Orphans when she arrived in South Africa.

My mom never spoke of the "old country" and rarely of her time in the Orphanage.

She and my dad married in June 1929 and my sister, Marion, was born in June 1932. I was born in December 1935.

For many years we remained connected to the Orphanage through my Dad and his brother, Harry, Ivan Greenberg's father, who served on the committee of the Orphanage. As a result, all of our families attended Pesach Seders at the Orphanage for many years.

When I was about 11 years old, we were living in a large flat in Sea Point and for a few years my Grandfather, Peter, lived with us too. Later he moved to live with Harry and his family where he remained until his death. Shortly after he moved, my mother started producing a variety of household soft goods for soft goods wholesalers from a room in the flat that she converted to a "factory".

The CMT (Cut, make and Trim) operation was common in those days and as for as long as I can remember my mother had excellent sewing skills. The "factory" became very busy and eventually my mother employed two coloured ladies as machinists to help her churn out the product. I remember that one of them was called Edith who remained an employee for many years.

Eventually, because of complaints from neighbours, the landlord insisted that she "close" the factory or we would be given notice to vacate.

She then moved to commercial premises in Sea Point where the business expanded considerably. I believe that at one time the staff exceeded 20 or more. My father who worked as a salesman in Sacks & Futeran for many years, resigned soon after the move and joined my mother in the factory which they called Vermont Manufacturing Co.

However, business became very much more competitive and they were both forced to work very hard for longer and longer hours. In about 1953/4 they closed their business and purchased a General Dealer store in Saldanha Bay. In 1960 my Dad was diagnosed with lung cancer and passed away in August that same year. My mother was then in her early fifties but she was unable to run that sort of enterprise on her own so I continued to run the business with her until 1967 which was about when I met my ex-wife.

The family details of Rivka Koiler as recorded on page 89 of the register at Oranjia. 1 Name and surname: Rivka Koiler 2 Father: Baruch 3 Mother: Miriam 4 Age: 9 years 5 From where: Kowal 6 How orphaned: Both parents 7 General Comments: Father fell in battle in 1915. Mother died from hunger-typhus. The child remained alone with no support.

*Group Passport no 8
Rywka Koyler is no 19 on list and aged 8*

No.	Name	Age	Place of birth
146.	Lewin Sara	5	Pinsk
147.	Guber Tcharna	7	Pniwno
148.	Kailer Rywka	8	Kowel
149.	Kolodner Liba	10	"
150.	Margolin Sara	8	Pinsk

*Extract from list of 163 names of Ochberg Orphans
Rywka Kailer is no 148 on list and aged 8*

Mom and I closed the business and both moved to Cape Town. When I married in 1968, mom was on her own and remained so for some years. I immigrated to Canada with my family in 1977. My late sister, who lived a very short distance from her, then bore the responsibility of watching over her. Later my mom moved into the Jewish Old Aged Home where she died in 1995.

I contacted my cousin in Montreal who has researched some of our family history. She says that as far as she is aware our family name was Kohler but sometimes Koyler was used.

Ivan Greenberg, whose uncle Maurice Greenberg was married to Rywka writes

My Mother was Peggy Gaby ex Oranjia, sister to Gittel (Shnaps) and Clara Gaby (Penzik).

However, I have a mystery to solve regarding my Aunt, Becky Kohler who was married to my Father's brother. Morris Greenberg. I know that Becky was an Ochberg orphan and was in Oranjia with my mother. I know that she came from Pinsk but I can find no reference to her in any documents which I have seen. Her son, Basil Greenberg, my first cousin, lives in Hamilton, Ontario, Canada. Basil and I have recently re-connected after many years of not corresponding.

Both my father, Harry Greenberg and his brother Morris were very active at Oranjia, both having married Oranjia Orphans, in fact I am pretty certain Morris was elected a Life President of Oranjia at one time. I also know that Becky had a brother who landed up in Halifax, Nova Scotia as she visited him on more than one occasion. I did some research for information on Becky at the Kaplan Centre UCT but could find no reference to her.

SOLVING THE BECKY KOHLER MYSTERY

Email from David Sandler
Ivan I read your email with much interest.
You say that Becky was an Ochberg Orphan but the Kaplan Centre UCT could find no reference of her.
The key to solving this mystery is in finding her correct name at the time of her coming to SA...
Becky is an English name! What was her original name? Also what was her original surname before Kohler? Was Kohler her adoptive name?
I see there is a Rywka Kailer. This fits, doesn't it?

Email from Ivan Greenberg
In the words of the immortal George Bernard Shaw in Pygmalion, "By George, I think you've got it"
Rywka definitely is Rebecca and Kailer could easily have been transposed to Kohler in South Africa. I wrote to her son, Basil Greenberg and perhaps he will confirm.

Ivan Greenberg writes to Basil.
The photo below definitely has your Mom and mine included. If the girl smack in the centre is not your Mom then it must be her twin. My Mom is on the right with the white beret and Gittel

Isaac Ochberg surrounded by Ochberg Children

Shnaps is at the top holding her head in her hands. I'm very glad that your Mom was finally identified and could be included in the history of Oranjia.

It is quite fascinating to read all about people who were known to us when we were children and now realise that most of them were regarded as relatives or best friends of our parents. Women such as Polly Kapelus, Yetta Bornstein, Molly Cohen were all in and out of our homes, either visiting or playing cards. I remember our fathers going to Orphanage meetings every month and years later having constant contact with Fanny Lockitch and the rest of the committee. I also remember someone not mentioned so far in the Oranjia correspondence, someone who in the 50's and 60's was regarded as the "Doyen" of Oranjia, that was the late Rae Gradner, wife of a former Mayor of Cape Town, who was noted for the fact that when the girls became ready for them, she was the person who always bought their first brassieres! Do you remember her? I hope you don't mind me also sharing this message with the group

Ivan writes "The Oranjia Social. I think my mother, Peshe Gaby is in the back row extreme right.
Rywka Kailer is in the middle row, second from right."

ZIPPA KOYLER

Documents and photos and extracts from Zippa's File courtesy Janice Rosen, Archives Director, Canadian Jewish Congress Charities Committee National Archives.

While Rivka was sent to South Africa with the Ochberg Orphans her younger sister Zippa (Celia) was sent to Canada as part of a group of 150 Polish and Ukrainian Orphans sent to Canada.

See chapter 11 of this book and the news article below telling the story of the rescue of these orphans by the Canadian Jewish Community.

JEWISH WAR ORPHANS ARRIVE IN CANADA
The Jewish Guardian of 9 September 1921

"An indescribably touching and, at the same time, picturesque scene was witnessed at Quebec last Friday on the arrival of the SS Scandinavian from Antwerp, carrying the Jewish orphan children rescued from Ukrania through the efforts of the Canadian Jewish War Orphans' Committee. The orphans arrived in charge of the Committee that was sent out to select them, as well as Mrs A J Freiman of Ottawa, who was responsible for the formation of the organisation, and Mrs A Pierce of Montreal. These two ladies had crossed over to Antwerp to meet and assist in caring for the children on the sea voyage.

At Antwerp the children were examined by the Canadian and United States immigration physicians when it was found that 40 of them were suffering from the effects of severe mosquito bites and had to be left behind for medical treatment.

Permission was given by the Canadian Government to the Committee to bring out 200, but only 150 of the best mentally and physically were selected. Even these had to be nursed, strengthened and fed for six months before they were in a condition to bring out to this country. On their way from Ukrania they had to pass through half a dozen small republics and in each of them had to have the general passport and visas.

After all the other passengers had left the Scandinavian, the war orphans, boys and girls, were marshalled on the deck of the steamer, and, carrying miniature Union Jacks aloft, walked down the gangway to the Louise Docks where they were met by a delegation from a number of the cities to which the orphans were distributed. They were next conducted to the immigration buildings for inspection, which was short, as the children, whose ages range from four to thirteen years, were perfectly healthy. After the inspection they were free to mingle with the large crowd that had gathered to meet them. Here was witnessed a beautiful sight of true human charity as the children were overwhelmed with affectionate attention by the members of the Reception Committee. The children are not only pretty but intelligent in appearance: some of them could speak four languages and had learned to say 'God Save the King' 'For he's a jolly good fellow'. They were absolutely clean and well dressed in clothing given them by the Jewish War Orphans' Committee, and while the girls carried small valises, the boys carried knapsacks on their backs containing a change of clothing, all of which was made in Canada, and went over for them.

At 11 o'clock, Saturday morning, the children went to Synagogue, where service was held by Rabbi Eliasoph, and were afterwards conducted to the Merger Building Hall where they were entertained to a regular banquet, provided by the Quebec Jewish community, who looked after them the whole day.

The next two days the Committee were busy separating the children and sending each to their future home: 55 went to Toronto, 16 to the Maritime Provinces, 12 to Winnipeg, 5 to Ottawa, and 2 remained in Quebec. The children had been so long together that it was sad when they had to part. An enthusiastic welcome, however, awaited them in the various cities in which their new homes are located.

Mrs A Pierce has adopted one of the boys and Mrs A.J. Freiman one of the girls. Mrs Freiman states that on her arrival in England more than 100 postcards from the children awaited her, inscribed with the English words: 'Welcome to Europe'. When she arrived in Antwerp one of the little girls stepped out from the others and asked her if she had received the postcards. Mrs Freiman said she had, and the little girl replied she wanted also to give a personal welcome and embraced her. Mrs Freiman decided this was to be her own child and adopted her. Her name is Leppa Gittle, she has bright eyes and red cheeks and is ten years old.

On arrival in Ottawa, Mrs Freiman, and the orphans accompanying her, were given a rousing welcome. The concourse on the station was so great that travellers could scarcely pass and the crowd broke into cheers and handclapping as Mrs Freiman came through the gate with her wards following close behind.

Apart from the five Jewish war orphans, there were two non-Jewish children brought from Poland with the party by direction of the Canadian Government. The little boys and girls were at first rather overawed by the warm welcome given them from all sides, but they were soon taken charge of by their foster parents and driven to their new homes.

The ocean voyage was uneventful, said Mrs Freiman: it meant, of course, a great deal of attendance upon the little ones on the part of those in charge, as all the children suffered more or less from sea sickness. However they soon became prime favourites with all on board from the Captain down. Mrs Freiman herself took motherly care and the children soon became very attached to her and she to them. She said it made her heart heavy to have to part with them, as after the weeks of intimate association she felt as though they were her own children. Twenty more children, who did not accompany the party on the 'Scandinavian' under the wing of Mrs Freiman were expected to arrive at Montreal shortly. They sailed on the SS 'Corsican' on Tuesday, August 23rd. Most of them will be placed in foster homes in Montreal and Ottawa.

An attempt will be made to approach the Canadian Government for permission to bring out to Canada another party of Jewish war orphans, and a meeting was held at the Chateau Frontenac, Quebec, on Saturday evening, August 20th, to promote this object."

NOTES ON ZIPPE KOYLER'S (CELIA JACOBSON'S) FILE

Family details

-The father was an employee in trade. In 1915 he was mobilised and in battle under fire he was killed by a bullet.

-It was a very bad time for the family. The mother worked for stangers. She became sick in 1918 from dysentery and died.

-Amongst the seven surviving orphans the oldest three had low wages and this was the source of their living

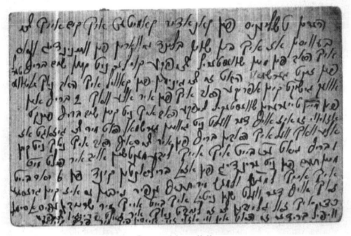

Letter from older siblings
Translated by Morris Zimmerman – New York

June 25
To Jewish War Orphans Committee of Canadian

I come to let you know that I am virtually blind from crying because I have not received any mail from my niece Tsippy since Hirshman has taken her from Kavill. I have another niece Rivka that I sent to Africa, and I get two letters every week from her. From my dear niece Tsipporah I have not received any mail, just as though she doesn't exist. Hirshman had promised me that every week I would receive mail from her. Instead, I have not yet received one letter. G-d I appeal to you dear people that you sympathize with my pain from not hearing from such a brilliant six year old child. I appeal to you to please answer me. Is she still alive? I beg you to write me a note so that I can believe that she still lives. You should let Tsiporah how many brothers she has and how they care about her.

Peretz (Pearl) Koyler

Marm Rapp writes

The older siblings wanted a better life for these two little ones. Little did they know what was in store for them all. Unfortunately, they all perished and these two little siblings survived, as did Morris, my father and he went through the Holocaust.

Zippa (Celia) as a young girl

I also had the post card translated by a very close friend of mine and I found it heart wrenching.

The letter below is covered in dots and the explanation is that each dot represents a tear that her brother has shed for his little sister since she left home. It shows that they really cared for these children and as my ever optomistic mother explained, they felt that they were given a chance

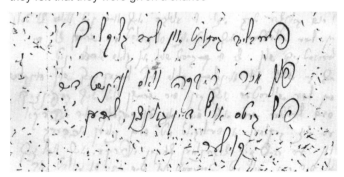

Jewish War Orphans Committee of Canada
EXECUTIVE HEADQUARTERS
OTTAWA, ONT.
♦♦♦

Montreal...............192

Mr......B. Jacobson......

......659 Main St   St John N.B.......

Dear Sir:—

On our records of adopted orphans your name appears as the party who has adopted the orphan

......Zippe Koiler......

Whereas, the committee is now preparing the necessary documents for your child, we would ask you kindly to fill in the following questions and return to the undersigned as soon as possible.

(1) Name of the child.. *Celia Jacobson*
(Please give full name the child has adopted)

(2) Is the child attending school?.. *Yes! Public school*
(Please inscribe whether English or Jewish or both)

(3) Sign your full name in order to make sure that we have your correct name

...... *Barnet Jacobson* ......

(4) Inscribe the name of your wife. *Esther Jacobson*

(5) Your address *659 Main St*

(6) Remarks. For remarks please use the reverse side of this sheet.

Please return as soon as possible to H. Hershman, 555 St. Lawrence Boulevard, Montreal.

Sincerely yours,

N. Hershman

Further notes on file

-Celia Jacobson attends Public school for English. Next year we will send her to Jewish School as she is too small for both.

-Mr Jacobson is a successful merchant of St John conducting a shoe business on the Main Street. The child is attending the English and Jewish School. Foster parents are very attached to the child, and the child behaves so as if she would have been their natural born child. The Jacobsons have a boy of 14 years and Zippe is the only girl in the house.
This is an A1 home.
Visited on 7 of February 1923

QUESTIONAIRES ON CHILD

MY MOTHER'S SIBLINGS
Written by Basil Greenberg

My mom was not a sole child and she had an older brother, after who I am named, who I believe was married when she left home. She also had a younger brother Morris, and sister Celia both of whom ended up here in Canada. Celia, younger than mom but older than Morris, was adopted by a Canadian family who were a well to do family in Halifax Nova Scotia where Celia lived for the rest of her life. Celia married twice but never bore any children. She did, however, adopt two girls Sandy and Cheryl. Sandy is married and lives with her family in Toronto. Cheryl married several times and now lives in the USA. I do not have much contact with her but I believe she has a daughter. Her son died tragically in an accident a few years ago.

Celia, mom's sister, was a great favourite of mine who, because I lived in Edmonton, did not see nearly as much as I would have liked. She died about 20 years ago very suddenly after a short and acute illness.

Morris, the younger of the children, and the father of my two cousins Analee and Marim (who is the Montreal cousin) remained in Europe throughout the war and ended up with his wife and the two very young girls in a refugee camp in Europe after the war. It was Morris who was completely instrumental in faciliting my immigration to Canada.

After the war, Mom and Celia, through their joint efforts traced Morris and his family to the refugee camp and Celia and her family arranged to have them immigrate to Canada, probably in the very early 1950s. Morris, on his arrival was set up in a tiny business in Halifax by Celia and her family and because of his very hard work and intelligence, eventually became a very comfortable man. Morris died a few years after our arrival in Canada, succumbing to long term illnesses that might have been attributable to severe malnutrition endured during the war. His wife, Ina, aged 93 survives still in relatively good health and still lives in the same home that she moved into on her arrival in Halifax!

In 1952 my mom (on her own) set sail for Europe and from there to Canada to meet with her brother and sister for the first time in about 30 years. In subsequent years she visited Canada several times and her siblings visited her once in South Africa.

I am in ongoing contact with my cousins (Marim and Analee) who are both younger than me.

MOSHE (MORRIS) KOHLER
Written by Marm Rapp

My dad Morris was the middle brother of the two girls, *Rivka and Tziporah*, that were sent away *to South Africa and Canada.*.

Rivka born 1910, Morris born 1913, and Tziporah born 1915 were all born in Poland. They had four older siblings, all married with children; Eli, Peretz, Hannah, and Leah.
Their father Boruch was married and divorced. He had one offspring in that first marriage. He was a son and he went to

America before my father was even born. He went under the name of Keller.

When my family came to Canada, my father tried to locate him. After much effort he finally found the widow, Mae living in Brooklyn New York. The half brother had died by that time but there was a daughter Roslyn Gitlin, her husband and three children.

The parents had died and the little children survived by going from one house to another. Conditions were very bad and when the opportunity arose to send the girls away, the eldest brother felt he was giving them a chance for a better life.Moshe was not eligible for transport as he wore glasses and was considered a handicapped child. Only perfect children were eligible.

My father Moshe (Morris) survived and married my mother in December 1939, and they lived in a little town in Manevietche.

The Germans had invaded their town and on July 23, 1941 Chaike, my mother, being pregnant with me had to leave home with her husband and they both ran to Russia.

Moshe was conscripted into the Russian army and Chaike managed to survive and after the war they found each other and were reunited. They went back home and no one of my fathers family had survived. In my mothers family, two sisters survived and also some cousins as they ran to the woods and joined the partisans.

The family was then placed in a displaced persons camp until it was decided where we should go. My father remembered that he had a sister in Canada, wrote to the Canadian government and they located her in Halifax. They found each other and Celia, (Tziporah) sponsored us for immigration to Canada.

Morris and Chaya (Ina) Kohler and their children Maria (Marim) and Annalee arrived at Pier 21in Halifax, Novia Scotia on October 15, 1948 aboard the General MB Stewart

In 1952 Celia and Morris sent for Becky to come visit her siblings in Canada in 1952. It was the first time in 26 years that they were reunited and since they were separated as children in 1921.

I have a beautiful photo taken of the three siblings when they were reunited in Canada 1952. Celia and Morris sent for Becky to come to Canada for a visit. It was the first time that they had seen each

Morris Marim and Ina
Morris is displaying Russian medals that he received. "Those medals were sent to Ina's uncle in Brooklyn and he threw them in the garbage. What a shame, they would be a treasure to have today" Marim.

Morris Celia and Becky 1952
The three siblings reunited in Canada

Celia died in January 1986, Morris died 6 August 1980 of Alzheimers.

My mother Ina cannot remember too much of the family in Poland so I am sharing with you whatever it is that I remember.

CELEBRATING INA'S 90th BIRTHDAY
Written by Marm Rapp

Dear family and friends,

Shabbat Shalom and welcome one and all. Brachim habayim.

We are gathered here this morning to celebrate a life. To celebrate a special day in the life of Ina Kohler, a very special birthday. The birthday of a woman who has a warm spot in the heart of each one of us here.

But before I begin, I want to tell you a beautiful story, a fairy tale in a way, but a fairy tale that is true.

The year is 1920 and the place is Ottawa and the person is Mrs. Lillian Freeman. Someone comes to Mrs Freeman and says- Mrs Freeman did you know that there are 137,000 starving Jewish orphans in Europe? She mobilised a committee across Canada, raised money and brought to Canada 147 young boys and girls who were taken into Jewish homes.

Our Aunt, our father's sister, was one of those orphans. She came to Canada as Tzipke Kojler and then became known as Celia Jacobson. She was given a home, brought up as their own child by Barney and Esther Jacobson, grand-parents of Joel Jacobson and I'm sure that there are a number of people in this room who remember her very fondly.

The committee was very selective in their choices and I remember Dad telling us that he was not eligible for transport because he wore glasses and therefore considered a handicapped child.

Twenty-five years pass, my parents meet, marry, survive the holocaust and find themselves after the war in a displaced persons camp, with two small children. They had gone back to Poland, their home, and found that practically all their families had been exterminated.

Mom, having always had Zionist leanings, wanted to go to Palestine. The time is 1945-46 and there is great excitement about the formation of the state Israel. Dad remembered that he had a sister in Canada and said that is where they must go. They must go to his sister Tzipke.

He started a correspondence with the Canadian Government and they located her in Halifax, married to Myer Zwerling.

So brother and sister connected once again on 15 October, 1948, and our small family made its way to Halifax, entered Pier 21, and together started a new life in Canada.

My parents bought a small grocery store, worked very hard to support their family. They worked very hard, but at least they were free and could make a good home for themselves and their children. I remember that first year, there was an oratorial contest and I spoke. My topic was "Now I am a Canadian". I believe that I received an honourable mention for that!

The Jewish community in Halifax took an interest in our family and various members would come out to visit the little shop and give encouraging words.

Shortly thereafter, my parents brought the Spatz family to Halifax. As many here may recall, Mom and Riva had a model relationship. Carol Anne Silverman called them nuns- they never went out alone. They were true soul mates, sharing all their joys and adversities. At this point I must thank and commend Jim and Marcy for sharing the love and joys of their lives with Mom and including her in their family life. Thanks Jim and Marcy.

The Children were educated, the family grew, and Anne's family grew up here and were an integral part of the community and I believe the community takes great pride in their achievements. I settled in Montreal, the home of my husband and his family, and built our wonderful family life there.

My parents established themselves in Halifax and also became important members of the Jewish Community.

A number of years before Dad died, he had the idea to sell Israeli bonds to non- Jewish corporations, and he was successful in establishing that milestone. The company that bought the first Israeli bond was Farmers Dairy.

In 1980 my dad died. It was a difficult time for all of us. Mom carried on in her usual optimistic fashion and truly endeared herself to all around her. She is 90 years old this year and to know her is to love her. She is kind and generous to a fault. She never forgets a birthday or a special occasion. Always there to render comfort and support and her wise counsel is always greatly appreciated. She always takes a special interest in her grandchildren and great grandchildren and is in touch with them on a daily basis. All of them are here today in great respect and love to her.

But all of these qualities are nurtured in her by a loving and nurturing community as well. So in paying tribute to her, we also wish to thank the Jewish Community of Halifax for acting in a symbiotic relationship with her- for loving her, caring for her and looking out for her, just as she does for each and every one of you. Mom does not want to leave Halifax. She loves her life here and she loves all of you.

Recently, Anne and I were talking about the possibility of Mom moving to Toronto and Mom answered that she would rather stay here with help in her home. So I think that says it all.

So let's raise our glasses and drink to a great lady. We all love you Mom, and wish you continued, good health.

Chapter 68 – BENJAMIN KARMAN (1912–1974)

The records below show that Benjamin Karman aged seven was from Sarne. His father Yeshaya and his mother Ita "died of hunger- typhus, surviving many pogroms and the child was left alone without any help".

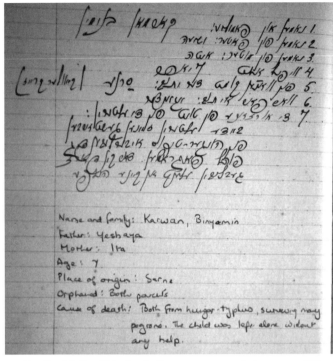

Family details of Benjamin Karman as recorded on page 115 of the register at Oranjia – The Cape Jewish Orphanage.

**Group Passport no 9
Benjamin Karman is no 10 on list and aged 5
Benjamin is in the front row 4th from the left**

Comment from Benjamin's children

"Unfortunately, it is also very difficult for us to make a positive identification of him from the photo you sent and we're wondering how in fact you were able to identify him. We've never seen that photo before."

Benjamin as a child.

BENJAMIN (KARMAN) RADOMSKY
Written by Bernice Hirsch (Haifa)

According to our late father's naturalisation certificate, he was born in Brest, Poland to Ita and Yehoshua Karman, the youngest of four children. His parents and siblings were wiped out during the Pogroms in the early 1920s. He was among the orphans brought out to South Africa by Isaac Ochberg, aged nine. Unfortunately, we do not have too much information about our late father z"l as he was very reluctant to talk about his childhood. The only time that he really mentioned the circumstances of his arrival in Cape Town, was, when in 1972, the Cape Town orphanage arranged a reunion of all the Ochberg Orphans and their families.

David vividly recalls that event and remembers specifically the showing of a cine movie of the orphans boarding the mail ship in Southampton, England. David's current work frequently takes him to the Isle of Wight, and when travelling there on the car ferry from Southampton, it evokes the memory of our father travelling from the same port.

Benjamin was adopted by Fanny and Joseph (Joe) Radomsky, of Grahamstown, their only child, where he grew up and was schooled. He left school at an early age to help Joe in his general dealer's business.

Bennie with Fanny and Joe Radomsky

Our parents, Bennie, as he was known to his family and friends, and Rae, as she was known to her family and friends, (Rachel nee Baskir) met on a blind date, arranged by a mutual friend and in 1942 they were married in East London. They moved back to Grahamstown where they lived for about four years before returning to live in East London. Benjamin went into the family business with our maternal grandfather and uncles. He later became involved in communal affairs and served on the Chevra Chadisha for 15 years.

We were fortunate to have known Fanny and Joe and have lovely memories of spending holidays with them in Grahamstown.

Bennie also became a travelling salesman, selling costume jewellery and during school holidays I sometimes accompanied him on his travels.

Bennie and Rae's wedding 27 December 1942

Fanny made enquiries through the various Jewish organisations and discovered that Bennie had a nephew, Marcel, living in Paris. He was the son of the eldest sister, so he and my father were about the same age. They kept up a correspondence with our father writing in English and Marcel writing in French. They managed to find someone to translate their letters. In 1960 our father brought Marcel out to East London to meet all the family. The common language between them was Yiddish. It was a most heart-warming and wonderful experience. After Benjamin passed away, the family kept up a sporadic correspondence which after some years stopped and we never heard from Marcel again.

I was born in Grahamstown and four years later Michael was born in East London and some eight years later our younger brother David was born in East London.

Our family moved to Cape Town in 1962, where our father went into business. Over all the years our mother Rachel worked as a bookkeeper. They had a wonderful marriage which lasted 33 years, until the untimely passing of our father in July 1974, and our mother remained a widow until she passed away in 2005.

Bennie was always one for the down and out and underprivileged and would never pass a beggar in the street without giving them something. He was a very strong-willed person, was never afraid to confront anyone and tell them what

Michael and Bernice standing with Bennie, Rae, and Marcel (Bennie's nephew) seated.

Bennie

he thought. He was an understanding father, although very strict at times and only wanted the best for his children.

We grew up in a very traditional home, always celebrating and enjoying Shabbat and the Chagim. Our Dad always felt good when he went to Shul, feeling uplifted after attending Shul services. He always had a keen eye for Ladies Fashions, which Michael and David seem to have inherited. Bennie was always known as a thorough gentleman by all who came into contact with him.

I married in 1964 and divorced in 1990. My two children Hilton and Faye were very young when their grandfather passed away. In 1978 we made aliyah, where my children grew up and were schooled. Today they are married with children of their own. They are fully aware of their grandfather's story and the grandchildren have written of their family roots at school including Benjamin's story.

Michael married Laura in 1977 and they have two daughters, Debbi and Lindi.

David married Naomi in 1987 and they have three sons, Binyamin, Avner, Yehoshua and a daughter, Shifra. Their eldest son is named Binyamin after our late father and Yehoshua is named after Benjamin's biological father, the name given on the naturalisation certificate.

Our father had a striking resemblance to Yitzhak Shamir, the 7th Prime Minister of Israel in 1983, so much so that when a charity collector from Gateshead, England, UK once entered David's home, he asked him if he was related to the then Prime Minister!

Sadly Benjamin z"l passed away in 1974 at 62 years of age. Had he been alive today, he would have been the proud father of his three children, grandfather of his eight grandchildren, great grandfather of 12 with another PG on its way.

Rae

Chapter 69 – LIEBA, YENTA AND ISAAC KOLODNER

Pages 75, 77 and 79 of the register kept by the Cape Jewish Orphanage (Oranjia) show that Liebe Kolodner aged 12 and her younger siblings Yenta aged eight and Isaac aged four were from Kowel.

Both parents had died.

Their father Levi "fell as a soldier in a battle in 1915" and her mother Henya Mirel "died of typhoid fever and having experienced hunger and hardship.

The children were left without the means to live."

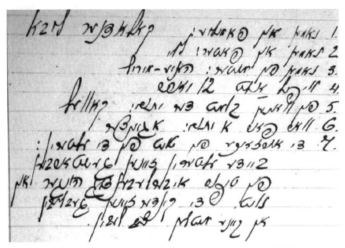

Family details of Liba Kolodner as recorded in Yiddish in the register kept by the Cape Jewish Orphanage

LIEBE SINGER (KOLODNER), (1909-1974).
Written by Aviva Singer

Here is the story of my grandmother, Liebe Singer (née Kolodner), who, along with her younger siblings Isaac and Hetty, came out with the Ochberg orphans. I have struggled to put together anything coherent because it was a taboo topic and my father, Leon Singer, who's now past 70, finds it distressing.

I am Aviva Singer, granddaughter of Liebe Kolodner Singer (1909-1974). The best person to tell you Liebe's life story would be my father Leon Singer, but he finds it very difficult to talk about these things, as Liebe did in her lifetime. She was an intensely private person.

There's not much of a narrative, because we only know fragments. As pointed out in earlier correspondence, Liebe is sitting in that group picture holding her younger brother Isaac. She was born in Kovel, Ukraine in 1909, making her around 12

PASSPORT 6: Yente Kolodner (later Hetty Nick) is second from left in the front row.

PASSPORT 2: Liebe is sitting in the the second row, second from right - bare-headed with scarf around her neck - holding Isaac on her lap. I also recognise her life-long friend Sarah Glaser (nee Wachtel) as the girl in the back row fifth from left.

in 1921. The shipping manifest on the Edinburgh Castle lists her as being seven (probably for immigration or fare purposes), while the passport lists her as being 10.

Her siblings were Itzik Kolodner (later Isaac Aronowitz 1918-85?) and Yente Kolodner (later Hetty Aronowitz and then Nick c.1914-1990). We had thought Hetty to have been four in 1921, and the group passport lists her as such, but at her death in 1990, she was recorded to have been 76, which would have made her seven at the time.

My father believes the Kolodner parents were teachers. Apparently Liebe did not speak a good Yiddish (my grandfather Solomon Singer re-taught her), and in South Africa, where the vast majority are of course Litvaks, some people affectionately called her "di Peilisher" (the Polish woman). Secular education in Kovel would have been conducted in Polish, so that bears out that she came from an educated home. The only time she was ever heard speaking that language though, was on her deathbed, when my mother told me she was counting in Polish. When Liebe had a minor stroke a couple of years earlier, she was also heard to speak Russian.

Liebe's father was Levi Kolodner and her mother Henya Mirel Kolodner (possibly nee Singal). The parents were reported to have died of typhoid, according to Lauren Snitcher, although we had hitherto believed them to have been pogrom victims.

Liebe in her early teens

Lazarus and Rebecca Aronowitz with Liebe, Hetty and Isaac

The story of how Isaac Ochberg's workers found the Kolodner children is unknown. My father says Liebe fled into the forest with Isaac and Hetty, but she never spoke further of this and the other two were too young to remember. The only possession she brought with her from Kovel, according to my father, was a torn machzor (prayer book). I asked when he gleaned any information, and he says he asked her when he was very young and didn't realise the hurt it caused her. As he got older, he knew never to broach the subject.

Liebe's siblings, Isaac and Hetty, were adopted by a couple from King Williamstown, Lazarus and Rebecca Aronowitz. My father says Liebe refused to be adopted, insisting: "I already had parents." However, she did visit Hetty and Isaac after their adoption and the Aronowitzes were very kind to her.

She stayed at Oranjia until age 16, and was then placed in a residence with other Ochberg girls. They trained to be dressmakers and Liebe worked for what my father describes as "a high-class fashion shop", Réjane, in Cape Town until her marriage to Solomon Singer in Cape Town in 1929. We know that she made life-long friends in the orphanage, such as Sarah Glaser and Peggy Greenberg. Liebe lived with us when I was a child and she died just before my ninth birthday and I remember Sarah Glaser being a regular visitor.

Liebe's husband Solomon Singer was 15 years her senior. He had come to South Africa from Riteve in 1913 to escape conscription to the Czar's army. He was at times an hotelier and cattle dealer, and made and lost money, so it was a hard life for Liebe. They settled in Saldanha Bay, where Singer relatives had a butchery and farm.

Liebe Kolodnerwith Oranjia friends. She must be around 16 because she still has the long ringlets. She's holding the hand of Chaia Gabay (Clara Penzik).

In 1930 or 1931, Solomon and Liebe's first daughter, Hannah, was born, but she tragically died of diphtheria aged five. They then moved to Cape Town and at the end of 1936, my father, Leon, was born. Having moved back to Saldanha, another little girl, Jean was born about two years later, but she too died aged five, despite a desperate dash to Cape Town for medical treatment. The existence of these two girls was a family secret until after Liebe's death in 1974. Liebe lived with us and was very close to my mother, her daughter-in-law, but neither she nor my father mentioned it, so it was a great shock for my mother to discover this when sorting through Liebe's possessions after her death.

Liebe ran the general store in Saldanha Bay until after her husband's sudden death in 1952. My father says she worked herself to the bone. Not only did she suffer the deaths of her children, but she had to work full time, do the household chores expected of a woman in those days and cook and care for members of my grandfather's family at various times. As an aside, my grandfather's younger brother, the late Harry Singer, served in North Africa with an Ochberg orphan, Isaac Rosier, who was killed in action. My father says it was Harry who buried him.

After being widowed, Liebe decided to sell up and move to Cape Town. She took a flat in Sea Point with my father, who was then a student at UCT. Shortly thereafter, at age 47, she suffered a massive heart attack and my father was told she had only days or at best weeks to live. In those years, there was no ICU or open-heart surgery, but somehow she confounded the doctors and survived another 18 years. However, from that time she remained very weak and at times was a semi-invalid. My parents married in Cape Town in 1961 even though my mother was from Johannesburg because Liebe was too ill to travel. However, the birth of my sister in 1963, her first grandchild, must have been a tonic and I remember my mother telling me

that "Granny's hair grew back." She lived to see all four of her grandchildren, which one hopes was of comfort to her.

Despite being young when she died, I remember her as "Granny", the head of our household. I sensed that her word was final although my mother says she never interfered or questioned how we were parented. However, we knew she was sick and had to be treated with great care. From about the time I went to primary school I knew Granny had been an orphan from "Russia" and I remember seeing the name "Liebe Kolodner" on an old photo and studiously copying it down. I knew it was a big secret and not to be talked about. I used to lie in her bed with her every afternoon when I came home from school. She had a radio next to the bed, which used to softly play the serials of which she was fond, a bottle of Eau de Cologne, a flagon of water, an old dictionary and a notebook in which she used to write words where she was unsure of the spelling and keep tally of minor spending.

Regular visitors included her sister Hetty, who moved to Cape Town from East London after being widowed,

Liebe on right next to Sarah Wachtel (Glaser)

and Hetty's younger daughter. Hetty and Liebe were very different characters; Liebe was very austere and reserved compared to Hetty, who seemed more light hearted. Their brother Isaac was an architect in Mafeking and I only remember seeing him a handful of times. He seemed quiet and pleasant. Isaac's oldest daughter, my cousin Avril, remembers "Aunty Liebe" visiting their home in the 1950s. They were fond of her and assumed she was a relative. Only after Liebe's death did Isaac reveal his true origins in a letter to his adult children. This naturally came as a shock. Isaac had obviously not felt able to reveal anything during Liebe's lifetime, perhaps out of respect for her feelings.

As previously mentioned, she never spoke of her origins, and the only clues we had were the few things she'd mentioned to my Dad when he was young and some sepia photographs kept in a chocolate box. Apparently around 1960 a relative called Usher Singal wrote to Liebe from Brazil, but she tore up the letter. He continued to write to Isaac in Yiddish (I have not seen these letters).

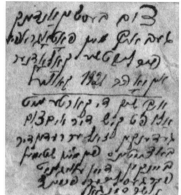

The little portrait and card is from her relative Usher Singal, who later went to Sao Paolo, Brazil. This is a card from their hometown, Kowel, written in 1921.

"For best memory, I give you my photograph for [can't make out first name] Kolodner in the year 1921.
Very difficult to make out what is written under the line.
I am sending the card with…. In memory…"

Avril has made contact with his daughters in Sao Paolo, but there is a language barrier and at the moment, I am none the wiser. In Liebe's possessions there was a tiny headshot of a young Usher Singal in army uniform, a New Year's card from him and photographs of children with a strong family resemblance.

The other clue is a portrait of a very well dressed young man, possibly taken in the late 20s or early 30s. He addresses the card in Yiddish "to my dear sister…" and begs her to send a photograph of herself or at least an answer. It is signed, "Your brother, Yaakov Kolodner." So Liebe had at least one surviving older brother, but she seemingly refused any communication with him and never spoke of him either. We can only guess at why. Perhaps she felt these male relatives had abandoned them. Avril has recently told me that there were eight Kolodner siblings in all. Why the younger ones were separated from them we don't know. My father thinks they may have already been living outside Kovel.

Liebe, Solomon and little Leon with Isaac

What can we make of Liebe's life? She was a reserved person, I don't remember her laughing or going out much although she was given to pithy observations, but I do remember that we loved her and that she was a person to be respected. People said of her that she "was a lady" in the very best sense of the word. For years after her death I would pore over her boxes, containing the few faded photos, postcards and trinkets, but I always think she left us, metaphorically, with boxes of sadness never spoken of or unpacked.

Liebe with her son Leon at his wedding -1961

THE FAMILY LEFT BEHIND
Avril Sibony writes

From letters received during the 1960s from a cousin, Usher Singal who had taken his family from Kowel to Brazil in 1934, we now have information that the parents, Levi and Henia Mirel Kolodner had eight children; Chaya Sura (Sarah), Malka, Moshe, Haim (Hirsh) Yankel (Yaacov), Liebe, Hetty (Yente) and Isaac (Yitzhak).

According to the Singal letters, the siblings and all of their children died during the holocaust. We have never been able to understand how the three children were separated from the main family group that all lived in Kowel.

Aviva Singer who sent in the photos and letters continues

Two of three older sisters and unknown cousins

Two of the three older Kolodner Sisters

Unknown niece and nephew

Three Levin Nephews

A photo of three Levin boys- the sons of one of her sisters

The inscription on back of portrait of the three Levin boys.

It says: *"Tsum bestn andaynk fur mayn lieber shvester Liebe fun mayne 3 zin Shmuele un Reuven mit Avrom Leven 1930 22/XI."*
Translated as: *"With best wishes to my dear sister Liebe from my three sons Shmuele and Reuven with Avrom Leven. 1930/22/11."*
Looking again, it could be that only the one boy is a Leven. What is clear is that this is a completely different handwriting from Yaakov Kolodner, so these are not his children. Therefore, the card must come from another sister or brother.

Yaakov Kolodner – a brother

Yaakov Kolodner – a brother

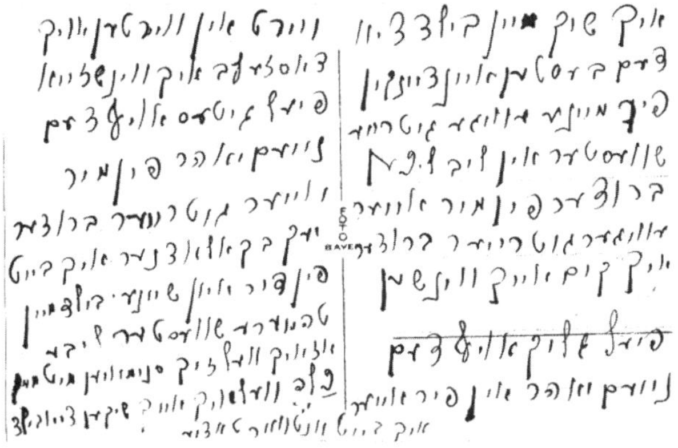

The back of the card from Yaakov Kolodner

"Ikh shikh mayn bild tsu dem bestn andeynkung fin mayne evige getraye shvester in lib libn bruder fin mir a yer eviger getraye bruder. Ich kum aych vintshn fil glik oyf dem nayen yohr..... dein getraye bruder Yaakov Kolodner. Ich beyt fun dir a sheyne bild, mein ??? shvester Liebe.. az ikh vil zikh ?? mit mayn khale vel ikh aykh shikhn ??? Ikh bayt antvort dir."

So basically, he says: "I'm sending my portrait as a keepsake for my ever faithful sister with love from your ever faithful brother. I want to wish you much happiness for the new year... your faithful brother Yaakov Kolodner. I beg you to send a lovely picture, my ???? sister, Liebe... with my wife, I want to send ???.
I beg you to send an answer".

Usher Singal – a cousin in South America

This card inscription in the ornate handwriting is the back of a New Year's card from Usher Singal, addressed to Liebe.

I can't make head or tail, except for his signature, but my mom has translated the following fragments:
Dear Liebele dir shikh herzlikhn dank dayn karte. Mayn choiv' iz (duty) iz ich tzu skikhn a Shana Tova.
I will write you a long letter. I wish you mazel.
"Ich bin aykh a fraynt mit ganse gevissen..."

So he's telling Liebe he's a friend to her, and she must have at that stage, when he was still in the Old Country, sent him a card, but later she shunned contact with him.

It seems as though Usher had a special relationship with these three as he kept trying to make contact

Other photos were taken in Kowel. The children and teens' pics are stamped with a photographic studio there. However, there is no writing on the back of these, so I assume that the women in the headshots are Kolodner sisters and their children.

Unknown Teenagers – cousins?

ISAAC ARONOWITZ (KOLODNER)
Written by Tobi Rosenberg

I am Tobi Rosenberg sister to Avril Sibony and younger daughter of the late Isaac Aronowitz Kolodner.

Until 1987 we didn't know that our father had been adopted. Our father felt that he did not want us to suffer in any way and his adoptive parents, Rebecca and Lazar Aronowitz, he loved more than a real son and maybe he was scared that it would affect our relationship with them. I was besotted by my grandparents and spent as much time with them as I could. Our father, Isaac, was artistic and became a successful accomplished Architect and both grandparents painted, hence we always said that his talent and ours was inherited from them! Little did we know the real truth.

Our beloved father, two to three years before he passed away, wrote us a letter telling us that he was adopted and that with the pogroms in Belarus his family I think two parents and five siblings suffered and only three survived; Isaac, Hettie and the eldest Lieba.

They were sent to the Cape Jewish Orphanage and at that time our grandparents had a baby who had died at three years and as my grandmother could not conceive more children, they were looking to adopt a girl child. My father was the exact age of the deceased child and they were happy to adopt him.

Hettie (Yenta) was also adopted but Lieba was almost my grandmothers age and did not want to be adopted by them. My father and his sister were taken to a small town King Williams Town to live and a few years later moved to East London where there were good schools and a big Jewish community. Evidently a neighbor would see him returning from school and refer to the adopted child and this upset him.

Isaac and Hettie

***Rebecca and Lazarus Aronowitz with
Isaac and Hettie***

Liebe stayed on in Cape Town and at the age of eighteen married Shlomo Singer. My grandparents kept close contact with her and visited her periodically. As a child I remember my parents made journeys to Cape Town to visit as well. The distance was great and the roads not good so these journeys were a great effort.

My father was an amazing man well read and very active in the UJA and a member of the Lodge and Rotary organizations. He was an ardent Zionist and donated a lot to Israel and the different causes.

Two years ago I saw the Documentary film made in Cape Town and spotted my father and his eldest sister in one of the pictures. I realized that there must be archives somewhere.

A short while later I was in Cape Town visiting my brother and we made enquiries and visited the Kaplan Institute. We search and searched and my brother was not enthusiastic at all but we persisted and slowly a whole wealth of information was discovered. It was winter and I was freezing but did not feel the cold. I can't begin to explain the emotions we felt. My husband, brother and I were overwhelmed by what we saw. We found the original register written by Isaac Ochberg, the minutes of the meetings planning the whole journey, the information about their journey to England and the arrival in South Africa. We found the correspondence of my grandfather with the orphanage and the adoption papers. It's amazing and a pity my father didn't make enquiries during his life time. I suppose he in his own way was a survivor and was not able to talk about his survival. Living in Israel we are never far away from the Holocaust and suddenly we also have our story.

Today Isaac Kolodner Aronowitz is survived by three children seven grandchildren and eight great grandchildren and some of them live in Israel fulfilling Isaac's dream. All this is thanks to Isaac Ochberg.

HETTY AND ISAAC KOLODNER
Written by Avril Sibony

We have never been able to understand how the three children Liebe Kolodner, aged about eight, Hetty (Yentel) Kolodner, aged about three years and Isaac Kolodner, aged about seven months, were separated from their family in Kowel in the Ukraine around 1917. During this time of the Russian Revolution and with pogroms raging in the area life was uncertain and families were torn apart.

From letters received during the 1960s from a cousin, Usher Singal who had taken his family from Kowel to Brazil in 1934, we now have information that the parents, Levi and Henia Mirel Kolodner had eight children; Chaya Sura (Sarah), Malka, Moshe, Haim (Hirsh) Yankel (Yaacov), Liebe, Hetty (Yente) and Isaac (Yitzhak).

According to the Singal letters, the siblings and all of their children died during the holocaust.

During the late 1950s Usher Singal had approached the Yiddish press in Johannesburg and asked for information about three children that had been taken to South Africa in 1921. A cousin on both my mother's (Robin/Rabinowitz) and my father's sides (Aronowitz/Leibowitz) of the family, Samuel Leibowitz, who read and contributed to the Yiddish press heard about this request, informed my parents and assisted them in making contact with the Singal family in Brazil. Today we have letters in Yiddish that Isaac received from Usher, but there seems to be very little information as to how the children were separated from their family.

Usher Singal and family, Sao Paolo, Brazil, late 1950s.

We were told that after a terrible pogrom, in which our father's parents and family were killed, three children, Liebe, Hetty and Isaac, like many others, managed to hide. When things quietened down they joined other children that had survived and began walking from village to village in the Ukraine until they were collected by Isaac Ochberg, put on a ship and taken via Southampton to Cape Town to the orphanage. According to a letter written to us by our father in 1979, they spent a while in

the UK until the necessary papers had been organized with the South African authorities and that they landed in Cape Town 21 September, 1921. He writes that at this point he was three, Hetty was seven and Liebe was eleven years old. Isaac and Hetty were adopted by Rebecca and Lazar Aronowitz and Liebe remained in Cape Town and married Solomon Singer in about 1927.

From what we know, in South Africa word had gotten out and there was great excitement amongst the Jewish Community, who went to Cape Town to see what could be done to help these children.

Rebecca and Lazar Aronowitz, from King William's Town were a young couple who had recently lost a baby in childbirth. According to information that I have from a cousin Dave Michelson, Rebecca had undergone a hysterectomy during the birth process and was unable, thereafter, to have children of her own. The couple went to Cape Town in order to adopt one of the children that had arrived. They had heard of the little boy (Isaac) who was about the age of the child that had been lost in childbirth would have been had he lived. On their arrival in Cape Town they realized that Isaac had two sisters, Liebe and Hetty.

Liebe refused to leave the orphanage, she was older than the other two and remembered her parents Levi and Henya Mirel Kolodner, who had died of Typhoid fever. We understand that Hetty refused to allow Rebecca and Lazar to separate her from her little brother.

My sister Tobi Rosenberg, now living in Israel, visited Cape Town a few years back and managed to find the original adoption contract between Lazar Aronowitz and Isaac Ochberg, made out in Cape Town at the Cape Jewish orphanage and dated 14 October 1921, for the adoption of Yentel and Itzik Kolodner, after which the children would be known as Itzik and Yentel Kolodner Aronowitz. Among the papers found by Tobi are letters to Isaac Ochberg, then the President of the Cape Jewish Orphanage, that Rev H Hirshowitz, Rebecca's father had also written to Issac Ochberg asking for a little girl aged between two and four and promising to assist with the upbringing of a child, should the young couple be allowed to adopt. Later Lazar writes in a letter dated 5 October, 1921, that they agree to adopt a girl of about five years of age and should the child have a brother or sister, they would be happy to adopt them together so as not to separate them from one another. At this point they were staying in the Strand with Rev Hirshowitz and his family so as to be closer to the orphanage when the adoption came through. By the 26 of October, 1921 Lazar writes to Isaac Ochberg, the President of the Cape Jewish Orphanage and thanks him for all he has done, advising him that they had arrived home safely in King William's Town, SA, and that the children had been given a very warm welcome on their arrival. On 23 November, 1921, Louis Wolk wrote to Isaac Ochberg telling of the successful adoption of the children and of how they are thriving, Ochberg writes back on the 29 November, 1921, that he is deeply touched by Mr. Wolk's letter and that Liebe, "aged about 12" is still at the orphanage and that he would be pleased if someone would like to adopt her as well, hoping that she could also live in King William's Town with her siblings.

Isaac and Hetty with Rebecca and Lazar, granny Ida and other members of the family on the veranda in Tamacha.

ISAAC AND ELLA ARONOWITZ

My parents, Ella and Isaac Aronowitz married in June 1944 and had three children, myself Avril, my sister Tobi and my brother Hirsh. We lived in East London, South Africa, so as to be near my father's parents and moved to Mafeking in 1961. Today I live in Beer Sheva, Israel and am still looking for my father's roots in the Ukraine.

Isaac and Ella Aronowitz on their wedding day with Ella's brother and sister, the best man Eli Robin and the maid of honor Ethel Robin, 18 June, 1944.

Hettie, Lazarus, Rebecca and Isaac

My father writes that during the early years they lived in Tamacha near King William's Town where Hetty started school. Later, in 1924, they moved to East London and he was educated at Selborne School for Boys from Sub A to Matric, and then Architecture at Witwatersrand University in Johannesburg where he met my mother, Ella Robin. He served as a surveyor with the Sappers during WWII and helped prepare the maps of South West Africa. He writes that Liebe kept up contact with the remaining family in Europe until "Hitler intervened" and that as far as they know the entire remaining family perished in the holocaust.

Isaac on his wedding day - 18 June, 1944.

Lazar holding Hirsh with Avril and Tobi ~ 1958.

Hetty and Jack Nick with Sheila and Mervyn in 1943

Mervyn, Sheila and Rosalie Nick, 15 January, 1951

Liebe, Aviva and Mara in 1971

Hetty and her daughters Rosalie and Sheila, plus Avril, Tobi and their mom Ella at Leon's wedding in 1961

HETTY (ARONOWITZ) AND JACK NICK

Hetty married Jack Nick and their children are Mervyn, Sheila and Rosalie.

Hetty, Rebecca, Mervyn, Lazar, Jack and Isaac in 1941

MY GRANNY HETTY (KOLODNER) NICK
Written by: Lindy Ress (nee Nick), the daughter of Mervyn Nick

My gran always came across to me as someone who was rather reserved and quiet. But she knew how to keep secrets. I only wish she hadn't felt the need to keep her life story as one. One of my special memories that came to mind when I thought about secrets was the time that I was playing at home as a child and somehow broke a picture that was hanging on the wall. I was petrified about the consequences but my gran, who must have been visiting at the time, came to the rescue, glued the picture back together and my parents were none the wiser.

The copies of letters and archive documents that I have seen as well as the stories already written by our cousins about my gran's siblings, has touched me deeply. Although I don't know much about her past, I can only imagine that she must have had a life of hardship. Now that I am a mother myself, I can appreciate even more how difficult it must have been to raise three children alone after being widowed at an early age.

My gran was a selfless person, and I can remember her as being a real lady. Maybe that's why her dog that she had when she lived with her daughter Rosalie and my cousins, who was called Lady, was so attached to her. So much so that she also went through a period of mourning after my gran passed away.

My gran was a worker. With her hair in curlers and a cigarette in her mouth she was always busy with something. Cooking, cleaning and fixing or playing her favourite card game 'patience'. She also always gave to others before herself, I am specifically thinking about all those apples that were peeled and cut up for us at the table.

I have a very special relationship with my cousin Janine with whom my gran lived, so I got to see my gran regularly during school holidays even though she moved home around South Africa quite a bit.

My father mentioned that when he asked his mom about her past she always said "I'll tell you later", which of course never happened. He remembers that his mom lived for her children and did everything for them. She sewed clothes for her two daughters and even made a gown for him.

She had a great deal of patience, especially for older people when others did not. She was also a stubborn lady who was incredibly independent and did not want favours from others.

My father recalls that some of the values which he feels that my gran tried to teach her children were to always save for a rainy day and to have patience for others.

He also remembers a phrase that she frequently used which he thinks she may have taken from one of her favourite radio programmes; "It's being cheerful that keeps me going"!

MY BEST GRANNY HETTY (KOLODNER) NICK
Written by Janine Yankovitch (nee Kalish), the daughter of Rosalie (Nick) Kalish

I am not sure where to begin......ever since I heard about the book that was to be written on the "Ochburg Orphans" I have been full of emotions. I have learnt so much more about my gran from correspondence sent from various family members regarding the book.

I knew that my gran arrived in South Africa by ship with her two siblings at a very young age. I never knew that there were other siblings left behind in the Ukraine (I always thought that she was from Poland) who were lost in the holocaust. I now live in Israel and once a year we mourn the six million Jews killed in the Holocaust with a Remembrance Day ("Yom Hazikaron") which from now on will have a whole new meaning to me.

My gran will always have a very special place in my heart. Ever since I was a baby, she lived with us and my father always used to joke that he had three children, me, my brother and my gran. I have never known another person like her; she gave so much to others, always putting them before herself, caring so much for others, and never putting herself first. She was always

there for us, my mom used to work and we were greeted daily after school by this tiny smiling lady, who only wanted to spoil us for the rest of the day.

My gran had a hard life, starting off as an orphan and thankfully being adopted by good people, she later went on to marry Jack Nick, who sadly passed away at a very young age leaving my gran, once again "alone" with three young children to take care of. She subsequently raised my Uncle Mervyn, Aunty Sheila and my mom Rosalie by herself, yet again giving herself totally to her children and leaving little for herself.

My mom tells us of how my gran used to sew them clothes when they were children, and I remember her talents with knitting. She taught me how to knit and embroider and always had to finish off what I started. She used to love playing "patience" the card game, and did she have patience for that game. I used to play rummy with her, and the two of us used to have competitions that went on for days.

She was a very quiet lady, not a lady of many words, and when asked how she was, she was always "fine", when asked if she was feeling ok, she would always answer "leave me alone", one never knew how she was really feeling. She was a tough lady and you would never hear her complain about anything. She let people get on with their lives, never interfering and asking questions or trying to change them, she was very accepting and if she did not agree with something, she kept it to herself.

I made aliyah in 1987 and she used to write me the most wonderful letters, telling me about her daily life and how much she missed me, I know it was hard for her when I left and it really hurt me.

I was with my gran when she passed away and I will never forget the peaceful look on her face, we don't even know if she suffered before she passed away, as she would never have told anyone if she did. I have a very special place in my heart for her and only wish she could have lived to be a great grandmother to my two boys. I constantly think of her and her memory will be with me forever.

Aviva writes "A photo of me, my son Taro Amichai (age 8) with his dad Tetsuya taken at Pesach. (Taro's second name is after Liebe's Hebrew name, Ahuva)"

Chapter 70 – DWORA LERMAN

DWORA WULF (LERMAN)
Written by Linda Press Wulf

What I heard from my husband, Stanley Wulf, is that his mother Dora (or Debbie) Wulf, formerly Dwora Lehrman, and his aunt, Nechama (later Naomi Stein/Naomi Miller), as small girls, were the only survivors of a pogrom in the village of Domachevo. His mother remembered a woman, perhaps their aunt, standing in front of her and her little sister as a Cossack charged on his horse. She shouted something like "Don't kill the children" and he shot and killed her, then reared up on his horse and, to the girls' disbelief, rode away without harming them further. She remembered lines of light or fire from his gun.

Dwora and Nechama Lerman in South Africa

Family details of Dwora Lerman as recorded on pages
7 and 9 in the register at Oranjia – The Cape Jewish Orphanage.

Some undetermined amount of time later, in 1921, when they were approximately eight and four years old, they were included by Isaac Ochberg in his group of orphans brought to safety in Cape Town.

Group Passport Photo Eight – taken in Warsaw 1921
Jules Miller comments "I'm 90% sure that my mom, Nechama, is in the front row 2nd from the right, and her sister Dwora is in the 2nd row, 3rd from the right."

In the 1990s, Dora Wulf's daughter, Freda Glaun, went to the UCT Archives, where the documents of the Oranjia orphanage are housed, and found her mother's and her aunt's adoption documents, which list their father's death as caused by "a swelling" and their mother's death as a result of "hunger-typhoid fever". The documents state, poignantly, "Lived through many pogroms and sorrows. The children left alone and could find no place for them."

"Stanley and other family members spelled the last name "Lehman" but in the orphanage records at one point it is spelled variously Lernman and Lerman, while Devorah is spelled variously Dwoyra and Dvora. In the Yiddish section of the handwritten adoption records, it is written as lamed ayin raish mem aleph nun for Nechama, but for Devorah, it is written - probably mistakenly - as lamed ayin raish noon ayin noon." There is no other information on this at all.

According to orphanage documents, Louis Stein, Ladies' Tailor of 19 Hope Street, Cape Town, with no children of his own, had written on 26 September 1921, five days after the orphans arrived, initially requesting a little boy of three temporarily housed in the "Home for the Aged". Mrs Stein was sent a letter re their successful application on 16 November. Two and a half months after the orphans arrived, the Steins adopted Nechama Lerman on 8 December, 1921.

The Kagan family applied some months later in a letter of 20 January 1922, from Joseph Kagan, Photographer, formerly of Muller's Buildings on Plein Street in Stellenbosch as well as 95 Caledon Street, Cape Town. By the time of the letter, the gracious script saying Muller's Buildings had been crossed out and only the Caledon Street address remained.

The letter said he had decided to adopt "the child Deborah Lerman" and asked Ochberg to bring the matter before the committee of the Cape Jewish Orphanage and let him know of the result as soon as possible. There is a private reference letter, concerning Mr Kagan, from another Cape Town photographer on 24 January and a personal reference letter from Mrs L Lehmime.

A letter of 21 February went back from the president to Mr Ochberg with concerns about Mr Kagan's contagious illness, but a 15 February doctor's certificate said Mr. Kagan had "made a very good recovery" from TB. There is an Adoption Contract, signed by Ochberg and Kagan, dated 20 February, concerning "Dwoyra Lerman".

Dora became Dora Wulf when she married Hymie (Hebrew name, Chaim) Wulf, the middle one of three brothers (Isaac and Berl) from Ponovez, Lithuania. Berl Wulf led the Upington shul for many years and Chaim himself had a beautiful baritone voice, assisting his brother at the High Holidays and also leading high holiday services in Rondebosch and in Brantford, Orange Free State.

Hymie and Dora developed a business in what was called "weeklies", beginning with Hymie carrying sacks of coffee and tea to the "Colored" areas of Cape Town and selling it by the cupful; then branching out into clothing when a woman asked them to bring a dress for her next time they came from "town" and promised to pay them back in instalments; and working up to the sale (still on the weekly instalment system) of clothes, tablecloths, and linen (Dora) and furniture (Hymie).

Their first two children, Charles (1934 - 2006) and Freda (born 1936) were given more food while their parents made do with little, and even Dora's late-born son Stanley remembers his mother weighing their plates in her hands to estimate that the children received about the same amount of food.

By the time this last child was born in 1952 (18 years after Charles and 16 years after Freda), the "weeklies" business had improved. Hymie had a storehouse for furniture in Woodstock and they owned the family house on Brunswick Road, as well as four other houses that were rented out, but Dora and Hymie worked hard until the end.

Hymie got colon cancer and died in January 1970 at the age of 62. That same year, Dora's younger sister Naomi, the wife of Harry Miller and the mother of three children called Blume, Jules, and Mary-Anne, died of breast cancer at the age of 53. Four years later, in December 1973, Dora, age 60, also died of breast cancer. Subsequently, Naomi's daughter Blume died of breast cancer in 1986.

Before they died, Dora and Hymie had the pleasure of visiting their grandchildren (Freda's sons by Dr Ivan Glaun of

Dora or Debbie Wulf (originally Dwora Lerman)

Thornton: Mark, Russell, Asher, and Braeme) and the satisfaction of seeing their son Charles happily married to Bella Hoffman.

There are several coincidences in this story: Dora was an Ochberg child; her son Charles married the daughter, Bella Hoffman, of an Ochberg orphan, Rosha or Fosha Heft (who became Shoshana Heft and then Shoshana Hoffman; and Dora's grandson Russell married Lauren Buchinsky, granddaughter of an Ochberg orphan, Leya Bettman (who became Leah Marks). Finally, Dora's last-born child won, by another coincidence, the three-year Isaac Ochberg Award at UCT medical school.

Stanley remembers his mother as hardworking, determined, and deeply scarred by her childhood experiences. She felt it was important to keep one's head down and not be noticed, in order to avoid danger.

His late older brother Charlie remembered his mother as being "a practical woman who didn't talk much about the past" or waste time lamenting. "She had backbone and courage as well as humility."

His older sister Freda adored and was intensely loyal to her mother. The relationship between Dora and Hymie became extremely strained halfway through their marriage, and their youngest child, Stanley, was raised in an atmosphere of silence between his parents. However, Judaism and Israel were strong shared values. Dora travelled to Israel with her older son Charlie in her 50s.

Harry Miller, widower of Dora's sister Naomi, remembered a story about Hymie discovering another member of Dora and Naomi's birth family, an older sister who emigrated to Israel, but there is no evidence or record confirming this.

THE OCHBERG ORPHAN STORY
Written by Linda Press Wulf

The following rough notes came from my general research (not specifically about Dwora) and from two interviews with Fanny Lockitch a couple of years apart. The quotations below are almost all from Fanny. She and her older brother Jack were chosen by Ochberg from an orphanage in Brest-Litovsk.

Fanny was no longer young at the time so some of the facts may not be exact but Fanny's memory was vivid and wonderfully valuable to me in writing my book.

Fanny said the Czar's conscription agents would wait for Jewish men outside the shul when services were over and "when they sent you back, you were already half dead," gassed by the Germans in the war. (I read that 650,000 Jews served in the Russian army during the war and one in six died.)

Fanny said her mother used to tell her, "Shh, don't talk," because there were paid informers or spies who were encouraged to report Jews to the government and then they were executed or imprisoned. And my husband says his mother Dwora had a fear of his standing out or being noticed, because if you did, there would be trouble from anti-semites.

In charge of the Pinsk orphanages was a giant of the Ochberg story, Mr Bobrow, who had been sent by Jewish organisations to Pinsk to help Jewish refugees in 1916, giving up his career as an analytical chemist in a sugar factory. He was put in charge of three orphanages in Pinsk, working with virtually no beds, bedding, food, clothes, or coal. At one point they made large aprons and other garments out of flour bags. A German Jewish welfare organisation and then the Joint Distribution Committee were eventually able to send some supplies; cocoa, condensed milk, cooking oil.

When Mr Ochberg finally gathered his two hundred orphans, having spent three hazardous months travelling "through almost every village in the Polish Ukraine and Galicia, etc," Mr Bobrow accompanied him in taking care of the orphans on the way to South Africa, and he remained in South Africa for years.

Fanny said, "One day we heard that a 'Man from Africa' was coming. He was going to take some of us away with him and give us a new home on the other side of the world.

We all liked the idea of going to a beautiful new country, but we also heard stories of robbers and wild animals, and that we might be eaten by lions. We will be thrown in the sea. We would be sold to the natives as slaves. We might be eaten by cannibals.

However, when Mr Ochberg appeared, with his reddish hair and cheery smile, we all took a great liking to him and soon called him 'Daddy.' He would spend hours talking to us, making jokes and generally cheering us up. He had a lovely, kind face and he loved children."

He decided to choose eight children from each institution to make up the total of 200. When Ochberg reached each orphanage, there was a selection process with the assistance of the matron or director, with the criteria being that the children were full orphans, of good physical and mental health, of reasonable intelligence, and giving their consent to being chosen.

"Some brothers and sisters were separated because selected children had to be 100% fit and well. There were some bigger children, 13-15 year olds to be in charge, but mostly younger. We didn't know the language or the area; there were bandits in the forests. "Don't you think I was brave to trust him?"

"We set off [from individual orphanages] for Africa each with a tiny package of the clothing that had already been sent to us from overseas, and a few pitiful trifles like photographs or dolls". Most of them travelled in slow, overcrowded, dirty trains to Warsaw "clutching a precious doll or a dog-eared photograph."

The Polish authorities were not very helpful and many children travelled to Warsaw by cattle-truck. There were dangerous moments before the orphans reached the gathering point in Warsaw, Fanny said some of the children had an eye disease called trachoma, and that there were inspectors checking the passengers of the trains who would force infected passengers to get off. "When the examiner started moving through the train to Warsaw, we learned to keep moving back to avoid him."

The "Temporary Shelter" for the "Jews War and Pogrom Orphan Transport - South African" was at Sliska Street 28, Warsaw. The children stayed in school for several months until all the children had gathered. Fanny called it a "battered schoolhouse, badly damaged by war, with broken windows".

Miss Lette, a Cape Town communal worker, and Boris Glasman and his wife arrived from Cape Town to help Mr Ochberg and Mr Bobrow

"Mr Bobrow spoke nine languages, and he used to sing and he played the ukelele. He taught us English, which was written phonetically in Yiddish for us. For years I thought that the British anthem contained the words "Rong to ray uber us" (Long to reign over us) and "God say the King."

There were delays while they waited in Warsaw, and then Ochberg himself became ill as a result of his hardships. "Two hundred children sat outside his room and prayed that Daddy Ochberg would get better."

In the group photos (21 children, for example) for collective passports, some heads were crossed out by officials with large black Xs when several of the children dropped out or had to be left out of the group "A baby of one year, Issie Elman, was sick and we had to leave him behind, but Ochberg promised him that he would come back and get him and he did."

The orphans went by river boat down the Vistula River (which goes through Warsaw) to Danzig (in Polish: Gdansk) on the Baltic Sea. Then a small Baltic steamer ferried them to England.

From the Orphanage book or newspapers of the time: [In England] Children came down the wide gangway in rows of two or three, helped by adults, all wearing neat hats. The first few stopped uncertainly at the bottom for photographs by the newspapers, squinting into the sun, the others backed up in a long broad line up the gangplank and along the side of the ship. As a sign of our appreciation, we were taught to sing "God Save Our King" for the entertainment of some of our visitors while we waited for the ship. A few of us were again taken ill and put in hospital. Fanny says, "We were in England for a couple of weeks and stayed in a big hostel paid for by Jews in England.

Finally, on 2 September 1921, the group began a two-and-a-half-week trip to South Africa on the "sleek" Edinburgh Castle with greatly reduced fares and a supply of kosher food provided by the Union Castle Line. "Each child carried a knapsack laden with an issue of clothing and a few meagre belongings." The ship had carried troops during the war and the children slept in bunks with some partitions. Some were seasick and bilious. Ochberg and a number of British volunteers accompanied them and "fellow passengers took a warm and friendly interest." Two

older girls with some knowledge of nursing picked up along the way helped the other children on the boat.

Also on the boat were; Shooshy Buchinsky's mother Leah, who served as an older Hebrew teacher. Her granddaughter Lauren married the grandson, Russel Glaun, of fellow passenger Devorah Lerman.

Another passenger was Shoshana Heft, aged 11 or 12 with no birth certificate, whose daughter Bella later married Devorah Lerman's son Charlie! Shoshana was one of a family of quite a few children and at least two older sisters were too old to come and later asked her to send them the money to get out, but she didn't have enough and they were killed in the Holocaust. She travelled on the boat with several cousins to whom she remained close in Cape Town; they were never adopted and she later told her daughter Bella she wasn't interested in being adopted; she left the orphanage when she was apprenticed to a dressmaking company at the age of 14 or 15.

Also there was one poor little boy, who had his hand hacked off by some ruffian and he became a successful man in Johannesburg,

At dawn on 19 September, the children had their first sight of the lights of Cape Town, the lights on the mountain. A huge crowd waiting at quayside, weeping and cheering, and Fanny said, "The whole town turned out to see what monkeys he had brought." Once at the orphanage, Fanny remembered, "They gave us hot baths; we were tired." The orphanage had a long driveway and there was a forest there.

"The Oranjia Orphanage in Cape Town took 100, but there was no more room and after a couple of nights with 100 children sleeping in each of two dorms, 100 children went to Arcadia Children's Home in Johannesburg."

When the huge crowd of orphans arrived, Fanny (quoting Mr Ochberg, I think) said they "stretched the walls." The small building had been built in 1916 for only fifty children, and two dormitories had been added in 1920 to hold 36 children each. In addition to the two hundred new orphans from Europe, there were 75 South African children already in the orphanage. At first all the European children were kept together; later they were mixed with the other children. "Isaac Ochberg built an additional wing at the back of Oranjia and we slept 12 children per room, but I was so happy to have so many friends. It was wonderful to be able to talk openly, not to have to look over one's shoulder to see who was following."

Not one of the children had parents, and they "swarmed around Ochberg" and showed touching affection to him for years afterward. "Ochberg used to get out of the car and the children would run to reach him. It would take ages for him to get up the few stairs because children would be holding onto a finger or a pinch of the cloth of his jacket, [so the crowd would go] slopping along, take an hour to creep up the stairs to get to the diningroom. He came to see us nearly every night. (Later she said: "he visited at least twice a week.")

Ochberg had employed a principal and matron in London, Mr and Mrs Maman. (At that time there was in the Cape Town orphanage only a house matron for the mere 75 children already there.) "He spoke perfect Yiddish but she had only broken Yiddish." Later Fanny said there was "a young couple (the same couple?) running the orphanage - he played rugby and tennis; she didn't play games but she was very nice."

"The principal of Cape Town High school, Mr Cohen, volunteered to help us and asked his staff to help us. We didn't have normal classes for several months but were taught simple English by walking around, mainly outside, while things were pointed at and named. Then we suddenly got books -- oy, it was painful. Cohen's son and daughter graduated as teachers and Cohen sent us to be in their regular classrooms because he knew they would be kind to us.

"We also went to a school on De Villiers Street, which was called "Miss Rosa's school" because Rosa Van Gelderin, a Jewish woman from Holland, was the principal there. (My friend Adrienne Folb in Cape Town, a freelance researcher of Jewish history, rented a house from Rosa years later, and remembers her as an extraordinary woman, a lesbian out of the closet before her time.)

"The only way for me to reach the top was to educate myself, to get possession of the English language. [My life was] working and studying. If I want to get anywhere, I have got to study and learn. I walked to Cape Town High and to De Villiers, a long way, coming home in the heat. We would all start off together and then some would lag behind.

"In the afternoons we would do homework and in the evenings we would talk or play games. Every Saturday night there was Debating Society. Judge Herbstein was the moderator, and other lawyers. Sometimes ballet dancers would come and dance for us and once the famous pianist Adelaide Newman came to give us a concert. On Sundays the playing fields and tennis courts were full.

"Some of the bigger boys, 15 years old, were sent to the country to stay with Jewish farmers and shopkeepers. They would get up at 5 am and worked very hard, but they saved money and eventually employed other people. For example, one of the boys sent to the country became the mayor of Durbanville, Mr Perch (used to be Perchodnik). Two girls were claimed by two aunts in South America.

"We had neat clothes, no longer ill-fitting garments, and there were many invitations to homes. [When we arrived in South Africa] they told us not to "be afraid of the black and colored people in South Africa, whom we saw of course as maids and cooks, but because of their broken English and our lack of English we couldn't communicate."

Fanny said by far the majority of the Ochberg children were not adopted out of the orphanage and she certainly was happy to stay there. "Adoptions began but not too many were adopted - maybe only ten. We were just told whether we would be adopted or not and we were meek and just accepted. We knew they came to rescue us, that they were kind to us."

"THE NIGHT OF THE BURNING"
A book written by Linda Press Wulf

Published by Bloomsbury in the UK in 2007 and 2008, and by Farrar Straus Giroux in the United States in 2006 (can be ordered through any bookstore)

The book is historical fiction, based on the meagre bones of fact that my husband was told about his late mother's childhood. That is, early in the twentieth century, young Dwora Lerman (later Dora or Debbie Wulf) and her even younger sister, Nechama (later Naomi Miller) were left alone after a pogrom in their village of Domachevo in Poland. Their aunt died shielding them from a Cossack. Some time later, in 1921, they were selected for rescue by an unusual visitor - a South African philanthropist called Isaac Ochberg.

When the sisters reached the safety of South Africa, they were placed in the Cape Town Jewish orphanage. In a new and perhaps avoidable tragedy, within a year they were adopted into two separate – and rather different — families, and their subsequent emotional relationship became very complicated.

Summary of Awards and Reviews

Awards
Selected for the New York Public Library's "100 Titles for Reading and Sharing, 2006"
Selected by the Forward's reviewer (USA) for "Best Children's Books of 2006"
Listed by the Financial Times (UK) as one of the (seven) teen books of 2008
A Sydney Taylor Book Award Honour Book
A Sydney Taylor Manuscript Award

Reviews
"Devorah's narration alternates between flashbacks to life in the sisters' Polish village of Domachevo and their later experiences as orphans, and both tales are equally touching and engrossing; her observations of the way black South Africans are accorded underclass status within their own country leads to provocative comparisons with her own sudden class reversal as a member of a relatively privileged white community." - *Bulletin of the Center for Children's Books*

"With bittersweet overtones, it reminds the reader of human savagery yet also shows the caring strength of one man and the power of sisterly ties." - selected and reviewed by Lesley Agnew, leading independent bookseller, for "Teenage Previews for March-June," *The Bookseller*, U.K.

"Linda Press Wulf displays great skill in her poignant handling of one of the darkest periods of 20th century history. The two sisters at the heart of her story are drawn with remarkable sympathy and understanding . [A] very impressive achievement, one which succeeds in conveying to young readers some notion of the depths of evil to which humanity can sink, but at the same time demonstrating to them the strengths of resilience, tolerance and love." -Robert Dunbar, Children's Book Reviewer, *The Irish Times*

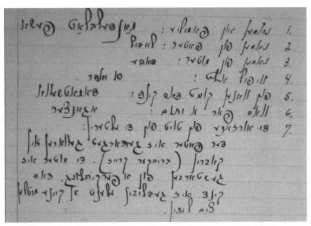

PASSPORT 7
Pesha Mandelblatt is third from left in the back row

The family details of Pesha Mandelblatt as recorded on page 13 of the register at Oranjia.   1 Name and surname: Pesha Mandelblatt 2 Father: Leibel 3 Mother: Dabe 4 Age: 10 years 5 From where: Dametzewa 6 Who died: Both parents 7 General Comments: Father killed in Kabryn in Poland. Mother died of influenza. The child left without means.

David Kapelus wrote after receiving the copy of the register
"I only wish I had this information sooner as we did not know my Mom's parents' names and were not able to record them on her tombstone."

POLLY KAPELUS (PESHA MANDELBLATT)
Written by David Kapelus

My mother was rescued from the orphanage in Damachevo which was and still is a small village or hamlet on the border of Poland and Belarus. The nearest major town in Belarus is Brest and in Poland, Wlodawa.

We never knew her parents' names until we received a copy of the register. Her father Leibel was killed in the civil war following the first WW and her mother Dobre died from influenza shortly thereafter. They were from Damachevo a hamlet in the Brest region (Belarus) close to the Polish border, the closest Polish town being Wlodawa. Sobibor the notorious death camp is close by and I have no doubt that this is where my mother would have ended her life had she not been brought to South Africa. She would have been murdered along with the other Damachevo Jews in 1941 .

Children at a temporary shelter in Warsaw.
My mother is wearing a white scarf and is to the right and behind Isaac Ochberg

Polly (Pesha) as a young girl at Oranja

My mother wearing a striped dress in Muizenberg

Calvinia district. My grandfather was born in Plungian (Yiddish Plumyan) Lithuania close to Memel and came to South Africa as an 18 year old in 1898. My father came to Cape Town after finishing high school and did a bookkeeping course. He originally worked for an aunt in the furniture business and later bought a partnership interest from Sam Spiro in a business called Spiro's furniture. His uncle and aunt's store was in

Morris Kapelus and Polly (Pesha) Mandelblatt
on their wedding day.

She told me she was about seven years old in 1921 although the exact date of her birth is unknown. She arrived and remained in Cape Town where she stayed at the orphanage. My mom did not say much about her stay at Oranjia good or bad. She worked before her marriage as a seamstress and did not work again after marrying at age 22-23.

She met my father, Morris Kapelus, at an Oranjia social. He was born in Ceres and grew up in Niewoudtville a hamlet in the

Observatory and Spiro's was in Salt River. My grandfather was Yehudah Leib (Louis in English) and my grandmother was Sarah Marcus.

My parents married in 1934, lived in Woodstock, Vredehoek and finally Sea Point and had three children Theresa, Arthur and David.

We used to go to second night Seder at the orphanage for many years. The Seder was conducted by Major Potashnik.

My mom was friendly with Gittel Shnaps and Peggy Greenberg (sisters) Yetta Bornstein and Thelma Freedman (surnames are married names). She also had a friend Freda Levit (an Ochberg orphan) who moved to Johannesburg.

My mother was a loving mother and grandmother and a good wife. She had no interests outside her home and family. I wish I could expand but there is nothing unusual in her life. She was very generous and was always giving her things away. She gave my wife some of her jewellery when we were still engaged. She cared nothing for material possessions even though she came from an impoverished background. In later life she used to visit a home for the Jewish mentally retarded in Cape Town and derived joy from the happiness the residents derived from her love and affection, This at a time when many people shunned the mentally challenged. This sums her up.

My father died in 1976 and had a large funeral as he was well known in the community and was secretary/treasurer of the Woodstock shul until his death. My mother died in 1990 by which time most of her contemporaries had also died.

Like many of her generation she was a housewife from the time she got married and essentially lived an uneventful life in SA. She had no surviving relatives that she was aware of after WWII and as well did not have any siblings at the time of her rescue.

My late sister Theresa (Cooksie) was born in 1935, my late brother Arthur was born in 1939 and I was born in 1945. My mother remained in South Africa I left in 1970 immediately after I married and lived in London for two years before immigrating to Canada.

Both my siblings are deceased. My sister had four children and was married to Keith Sher. Three of her children live in Australia and one in Johannesburg. I have three children (all girls) and two grandchildren and live in Canada.

Polly surrounded by her family
Standing: Keith Sher (son in law) Michelle Kapelus (grand daughter and David's daughter) Lee-Anne Sher
(grand daughter) Arthur Kapelus (son) Cooksie Sher (daughter) David Kapelus (son) Fay Farber (sister in law)
Seated: Helen Kapelus (daughter in law and David's wife) Ruth Kapelus (grand daughter and David's daughter)
Polly (Pesha) Kapelus and Gavin Sher (grand son)
Seated in front: Beverly Sher (grand daughter) Melanie Kapelus (grand daughter and daughter of David)
Missing: Lindy Sher (grand daughter)

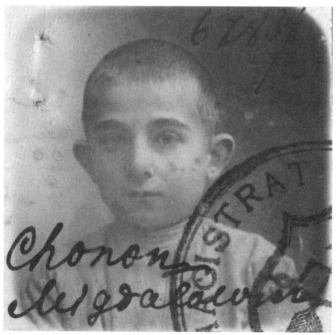

The Migdalowicz Family Details as recorded on pages 65, 67 and 69 of the register kept by the Cape Jewish Orphanage (Oranjia).
1 Names and surname: Chonan, Simon and Nachman Migdalowicz 2 Father: Shmuel 3 Mother: Chana
4 Ages: 9, 8 and 7 years 5 Place of origin: Pinsk
6 How orphaned: Both parents 7 General Comments:
The parents have suffered through the Poles and the Belachowitz and after being starved for a considerable time they have both died of typhoid fever.

Nachman Migdalowicz
Photo on Pinsk travel document

CHONON, NACHMAN AND SZYMON MIGDALOWICZ
Written by Cecil Migdal (Migdale Migdalowicz)

GROUP PASSPORT 5
No 13 on the list Szymon Migdalowicz aged 6
No 26 on the list Chonon Migdalowicz aged 7

Chonon Migdalowicz
Photo on Pinsk travel document

Chonon is on far right, middle row, and
Szymon could be 2nd on left, middle row, next to no.27

GROUP PASSPORT 2
No 12 on the passport list is Nachman Migdalowicz aged 5

Front row, no 5 from either side, could be Nachman

My Grandparents were Szmujka (Szmulka), and Heni Migdalowicz, (Shmuel and Chana),and they came from the area around Pinsk. They had four sons, Chonon, Nachman, Szymon and an older brother who's name is unknown. My Dad, Chonon, told me 50 years ago, but to my great sorrow, I don't remember.

Of the three brothers who came out to South Africa with Isaac Ochberg, my Dad was the eldest. The forth brother must have been older, as my Dad once told me that he didn't want to come to South Africa because he wanted to join the Russian Army.

Exactly where they were born, remains a mystery, as in one version (an interview with Lauren Snitcher when he was 91) he says he was born in Pinsk, but in an earlier interview he told us that our Grandmother died from typhus when the children were very young, and towards the end of the WW1, to escape the pogroms, our Grandfather took them on a trek to Pinsk.

My Dad said he was born in Pinsk, but the story he told me, was that they walked through forests for a few days, only moving at night, to hide from the White Russians or Cossacks, until they got to Pinsk. The children were under clothed, and had rags on their feet for shoes. I don't know for how long, but after some time, the children were put in an orphanage, as my Grandfather could not manage them.

I looked at a map of the area, and for sure the area was full of forests, so they must have come from a surrounding town. It could have been town called Lenin or Luninyets.

Enter Isaac Ochberg, and the three Migdalowicz boys where selected to go to South Africa. I think that my Dad told me that the fourth Brother didn't want to go to South Africa.

On the list of Ochberg Orphans there is a forth Migdalowicz boy, Hyman Migdalowicz who has 'missing' noted next to his name.

Lawrence Migdale, a nephew from the USA writes:
I think that Hyman was the oldest brother (who died before they got to Africa) but I am really not sure.

Cecil Migdal, a nephew from the Israel writes
Of the three brothers who came out to South Africa with Isaac Ochberg, my Dad was the eldest. The forth brother must have been older, as my Dad once told me that he didn't want to come to South Africa because he wanted to join the Russian Army.

The forth brother is a mystery as he did not come to South Africa with the rest. I know absolutely nothing about him. My father did tell me his name about 50 years ago, but I have forgotten. It's very interesting. My cousins, Seymour, Lawrence, and Leonie, don't know, as I asked them before. Sadly, it's mystery that will never get solved. I am still trying to find out where they were born, and maybe go from there, but am drawing blanks.

The orphans of Pinsk were originally given individual travel documents

The travel document of Nachum Migdalowick from the website www.ochbergorphans.com set up by Brian Fine

From Pinsk the children were taken to Danzig, where they boarded a ship called the Baltara for England, and arrived in August 1921.

The Baltara that brought the Ochberg Orphans from Danzig to England

In England they could have stayed in the Temporary Jews Shelter. In September 1921, they boarded the Edinburgh Castle, and arrived in Cape Town on 19 September 1921.

This is the ship which brought the Ochberg orphans to South Africa from England.

Norman and Charles at Cecil's wedding in Cape Town

It appears they never went to Arcadia and were not part of the Ochberg children that were transferred to Johannesburg. One brother went to Johannesburg, but only later in life, so as far as I'm aware, none went to Arcadia

For a while, our surname was Solomon, as a Family Solomon (who I met as a youngster) either adopted them, or took them under their wing. My Dad then became Charles Migdale. Due to a mix up on my birth certificate, I was registered as Migdal. Now the boys were known as Charles, Norman, and Simon.

My Dad was naturalized on 11 December 1936, and went into business in Caledon with Simon, and were famous, as the boys from the "Caledon Algemene Handelhuis". Simon never married, and died in Caledon in 1977.

My Dad married a Blanche Bessie Domp, and I came along. My Dad passed away in Cape Town in 2001 at the age of 92 or 93 of Blessed memory to all.

Lawrence and Seymour have an individual passport of Nachman and I have a passport photo of Chonon.

MY FATHER NORMAN MIGDALE
Written by Seymour Migdale from New Zealand

My father Norman (originally Nachman) never really spoke very much about his prior life in Poland and the trip over to South Africa and so I really have only a sketchy knowledge of his experiences in his early life but I would be very happy to share any memories that I do have.

Incidentally you will note that I spell the family name Migdale whereas Cecil spells it Migdal. This is because Cecil's father (Charles) originally Anglicised the name Migdalowicz to Migdal, whereas my father Nachman (later changed to Norman) anglicised it to Migdale.

I left South Africa in 1976 and lived in the USA until 1990 at which time I moved to New Zealand.

NORMAN MIGDALE (NACHMAN MIGDALOWICZ)
Written by his son Lawrence Migdale

Norman Migdale, was a self-made man. He relied on himself. He believed in working hard and he respected others who he saw were doing their utmost to get ahead. He lived for the business he built up over the years. *South African Shoulder Pads* was his life and his passion.

The business grew from one machine he installed in the family garage in Johannesburg to eventually employ about 150 workers in a large factory in the Industrial section of the city.

He knew every part of the business and was always checking to see that the products he sold were of the very highest quality.

Norman sold the business when it was clear that none of his children would follow in his footsteps. But retirement was a chore for him.

He loved his chevra. The other six Jewish guys who sat around the poker table with him were his best friends and confidants.

I remember when he was the youngest man at the table and then in later years, as one by one the older men passed away, how he kept each one's memory alive with terrific stories. You never knew if my Dad was kidding or telling the truth when he told a story.

He had a poker face when he wanted it.

The memory of him has been kept alive by all the interest and energy that so many of the Ochberg descendents have poured into the various projects.

Such a mitzvah. My Dad would be proud.

Nachum was always called Norman in the years I knew him. He married Jean Cohen and they had three children; Leonie, Seymour and Lawrence (me). Leonie has a daughter Arja

ARJA SALAFRANCA writes from South Africa

Here is my grandfather Norman Migdale's birth certificate. It is in Polish and is translated below.

Jack Goldfarb a freelance journalist from New York, writes;

This document issued in Poland and almost 100 years old is obviously time-worn and parts of it somewhat unreadable also because of the taping holding it together.

It is a Birth registration (Number 77) and testifies to the Circumcision of a Male Jewish Child.
The name of the Mohel: "Sztein" (Stein).
The date of the Circumcision appears to be April 7, 1913. (In the Hebrew month of Nisan).
Name of the Father:(illegible) **Migdalovch.**
Name of the Mother: (Genia?) (Illegible.) (Possible Maiden Name: "Abram") **Migdalovich.**
Name of the Child: **Nachman**
Certification of Copy with Seal. Issued: January 29, 1939.in Pinsk Region of Poland.
Although incomplete, I hope this information helps

MY GRANDFATHER: NORMAN MIGDALE
Written by Arja Salafranca

In the weeks after he died all the electrical appliances I salvaged from him went haywire and died too. It was spooky. My grandmother alone for the first time in almost fifty years, stayed with us for a weekend and other days and nights.

My grandmother was four years older than my grandfather: She was 30 when she married him in 1939 and he was 26. It must have seemed almost scandalous back then in a time of hats, impending war, white gloves, proprietary, girdles, and Caesarean scars that sliced a woman's stomach vertically in half. It wasn't something you advertised, or were proud of, either a four year age gap that went the wrong way, or the fact that you were thirty by the time you had finally found a man to marry.

What I know of my grandparents' early life has come in to me in snatches delivered by my mother Leonie: second-hand and third-hand tales, memory distorts, and broken telephone will always twist the truth further. I have a fragmentary picture, I've filled in the details by looking through the old black and white photographs, made up my own mind, and yet sometimes I accept that I'll always know and see something half done, a cake that never quite mixed right. It's unfortunate now, when I want to know the truth, that my grandparents are no longer around to tell me, or not, as the case may be.

My grandfather was born Nathan (Nachman) Migdalowitz, a name he changed in the 1930s. Migdalowitz became the more anglicised Migdale, and later on, Nathan became Norman, hard, gruff sounding, less Jewish? I seem to recall that he changed his name around the time of his marriage, from the softer-sounding Nathan to Norman, yet it wasn't a change that was ever officially recorded. My grandmother, in turn, became Jean, after having been born Janée. No one ever explained these changes to me – but then, perhaps I didn't ask.

I was 16 in 1988, the year my grandfather died of a heart complication, just two years after he had undergone a bypass operation that was meant to prolong his life for many years. We, my mother and I, had taken him to the hospital just a few days earlier

He was a child of his times, I understood years later. A man born into Eastern Europe on the cusp of World War 1 – he was born in 1913 I discovered from his actual birth certificates, not 1911 according to some obviously inaccurate ID books I found. There was no limit to the fudging and smudging out of dates within the Migdale family. When my mother told me about his background, I envisioned a cold northern European place. Four brothers scrabbling through dustbins looking for potato peels to eat, both parents dead. Father shot by pogrom invaders, the mother dead of starvation and exhaustion. My grandfather mentioned nothing of his early life, and I pieced his history together from my mother's words. The brothers, now orphans, being picked up by Ochberg, taken to South Africa and raised in luckier circumstances as orphans in a children's home in Cape Town. At fourteen my grandfather was kicked out, now old enough to earn his living. He found work in a tobacco factory. After that he lived in the country and was a quasi dentist of sorts, using pliers to pull out the rotten teeth of black labourers who couldn't afford dental care. These are the vague semi-organised facts. At some point he made his way to Johannesburg and worked at the CNA, a stationery shop, which is where he was working when he met my grandmother and married her. My mother remembers he earned 18 or 20 pounds a month at the time.

My grandparents married in 1939; she wore a sweet, short white waistcoat over her white dress, her hair garlanded with flowers, and they look happy, as happy as in a photo taken before the wedding or just after. Those wedding photos tell a story of hope, joy and pleasure. The orphan was finally starting a new life, his own family.

I learned that after the CNA my grandfather had started work in a shoulder-pad factory, his boss a man with a German sounding name. It was there that he got the idea of starting up his own factory. My mother remembers living in a house in Orange Grove, and the spare room was full of sewing machines. He was gradually buying machines in preparation. He opened up a factory in Fordsburg, made a huge success of his business and became comfortable. He was his own boss, at last, financially successful, with two children born in the 1940s. In 1951 the last child, Lawrence, followed.

My grandparents watched their own children finding happiness and other lives through moving countries.

I speculate here, but the orphan in him must have craved a family life and my grandmother obviously offered something here. She had a family originally from the Cape and was living in Johannesburg when they met. Her parents attended the

wedding; there was the sister, soon to live in Durban, a younger and an older brother. The older one immigrated to Australia; the younger remained a bachelor all his life.

And then he started his own family. My mother remembers him sitting down with them at night, telling them bedtime stories about the "happy man". The Happy Man lived underground, where he had a whole kingdom. He came up to earth to do good deeds, before going back into his world.

The factory in Fordsburg took off. The stress took its toll, the cholesterol-inducing Jewish food mixed with hereditary factors, and the inevitable heart attack.

Norman in his 20s some time in the 1930s

Walking in Johannesburg

Jean and Norman's engagement

Jean and Norman's wedding 1939

Jean and Norman's wedding 1939

It's 1976, and I am beginning to know my grandparents. At first my grandfather is a vague, almost forbidding presence still working, spending days at a goods store he owns. At eight he starts spending Friday nights there and I start spending nights at my grandmother. My mother complains that I returned quiet, subdued, unnaturally so. It soon stops. At this point my grandfather is still a far way, forbidding male figure. Although I am not close to my grandmother, she takes me to movies occasionally and I am more comfortable with her.

Yet, my grandparents were ever present. Sunday tea times when they came for cake, tea or coffee, the ritual handing over of the monthly cheque. My mother could not make all her expenses on her salary. Or, religious holidays, celebrated with food rather than prayer or ritual.

At times I try and detect a trace of Polish or Yiddish accent in his voice. But there's nothing there. I'm looking for the foreigner in him but his accent is neutral to my ears. At age eleven he tells me he doesn't like fiction, "it's just other people's made up stories. It's not real." This is disappointing to hear: I am a budding writer starting to receive praise at school for my first attempts at fiction, but it doesn't stop me.

Memories drift through: he gets lost going to the airport. At age 10 we pick up my grandmother from a recent trip to visit "my boys" and he gets lost. When, eight months later he takes us on the same journey, we are to visit the US, he gets lost again.

These could be endearing characteristics. He smokes, refusing to give it up, even though his wife rails against it. He sits on his corner chair in the lounge and smokes as we watch TV. My grandmother sits on the couch; my mother at the other end. As I grow older I migrate to a chair of my own, no longer sharing the couch.

And then it turns, and on the cusp of teenage hood I declare my lack of belief in the faith of my grandparents. I argue religion, and I argue politics. While, in time, we agree to disagree, there is still movement now within our relationship. Something changes, although I do not realise it at the time, and won't realise it till years later. We grow closer in a sense, although at age 13 and 14 I neither realise or accept it. When my grandfather has his bypass operation in 1986 and I don't visit him on one of the nights, he asks my mother where I am, asking after him. I make sure I see him the next time, his chest livid with stitches and yellow medicine, the operation that is meant to extend his life. He is just 73 that April 1986. Born on April 1st, he refuses to celebrate his birthday on April Fool's Day – sometimes his birthday moves to the second, sometimes the 3rd or fourth.

At fourteen, fifteen, he pinches my cheek affectionately when he comes to visit on Sundays. He comes sometimes in the mornings, without her, bringing her later for tea. I am learning to make doughnuts, and trying to make that elusive glazing, he eats, the only thing I have learned to cook.

Sometimes I still dream of him. He visits in dreams, as though, I sometimes, feel he's trying to tell me something, or, perhaps I have that wrong and I am trying to tell him something. Perhaps I'm also trying to reach out in some gesture of adult understanding.

I still don't know where you came from, I have no way of knowing or understanding what it means to be an orphan, to see your parents shot or die of starvation, to be raised with brothers but no family, and to try and create a family that was denied you as a young boy in Eastern Europe. I don't know your weaknesses, or your lack of understanding. You came from a time and a place in history, and you never pushed against what you knew or were told to believe. And I don't know you, or have any answers, except vague facts, crumbling with time, in which I attempt some sort of understanding and peace.

It was only when I started asserting myself and rejected your religion, that strangely, you started to take me seriously, to like me, in fact.

You have been dead for twenty-one years, and your voice is long gone from my memory. In a bizarre twist, when I summon up your sounds, all I hear is your familiar exclamation, you used it all the time to express your grief at life's lack of propriety, and the Yiddish words rolled off your tongue, as they never did before or at any other time, finally echoes of the past in your guttural rendering of "Gott in himmel"

Norman and Jean
taken in their flat in Johannesburg in the 1980's.

Norman Migdale (Nachman/Nathan Migdalowicz)

Chapter 73 – ZALKA NEISHTEIN (CELIA RAKOFF)

Zalka Neishtein later called Celia Rakoff
Written by Dr Vivian Rakoff

I realise that I know very little about my aunt Celia Rakoff, born Zalka Neishtein.

The family story as I remember it was that my grandparents, Barnett (Beryl) and Genesha Rakoff, visited the Cape Town Jewish Orphanage where the children had been housed and to see the children requiring adoption. Celia was among the last of the group 'unclaimed' by people willing to adopt them.

The story goes further that she hid behind a chair and as they were leaving she said in Yiddish "Nem mir" (take me) which they did, although they were by no means prosperous having five children and not much money.

She was a small plain child and I like to believe that she was treated with great affection which she reciprocated particularly towards my protective and loving Bobba.

Celia grew up deeply attached to my Bobba. She lived with my grandmother and some family members in the same house until my grandmother's death. She was overcome with grief and moved out of the family home to live alone in a flat on the Main Road in Sea Point. She never married.

Although we all knew she had been adopted, it was never mentioned and we were given to understand that it was a forbidden topic. In later years I heard that she had a brother living, I think, in Argentina who had tried to contact her before World War II. Her response was frantic agitation and refusal to have anything to do with him since it threatened her relationship with my grandmother.

When my Bobba died some zealous person tried to stop her from cutting her clothes because "she was not really a child". Celia was humiliated and angry and nevertheless she persisted, in tearing her garment in defiance of the busybody's prohibition.

She was lovingly reared and completed high school. After that, I know, she worked in a hairdressing salon "Maison Bruno" for a while, but the major part of her working life was spent at "Pinn' " a high end Jewish jewellery store in Cape Town.

She seemed to be very much part of the Pinn family and we were constantly told stories of the Pinn children who were, from her reports, infinitely more talented sophisticated than the Rakoff cousins. When she retired from the store after decades of service there was a dispute about her pension, and the matter was taken to the Cape Town Beth Din.

But dismal as the end was, she had a terrific time during her working years. She developed an "Aunt Mame" persona. She liked the rich customers, the touches of glamour and the perks that went along with the trade: Free stays at the Savoy Hotel in London, gift certificates to expensive London stores such as Fortnum and Mason's, ocean trips to South America. She was always full of stories about her interactions with important wealthy people, who I suspect responded to the waif-like neediness which first caused my grand-parents to 'take' her.

She died suddenly at age 70. I wasn't in Cape Town at the time but I am told that groups of people, none of whom knew one another, came to her funeral. It was as though her life was made up of a number of secret compartments. Indeed this was one of her characteristic modes: She would tell a story, of no apparent importance, with numerous demands that we keep it secret and "not to tell a soul".

Shortly before she died I was on a visit to Cape Town and the day before I left for England she met me downtown, and with a show of conspiracy, with many looks over her shoulder and fingers to the lips she gave me a cylindrical cardboard parcel which, when I unwrapped it, contained a Meissen china parrot on a branch with insects crawling over it. "It was a gift" she said "from a woman who collected parrots.

This odd object sits on top of a bookshelf where I can now see it. It is, I guess, as displaced, unrooted and idiosyncratic as Celia was.

I was deeply attached to her and she was a colourful and beloved member of the Rakoff family throughout my childhood and early adult years.

Chapter 74 – YSER AND SZEPSEL PERECHODNIK

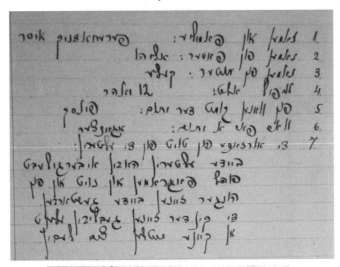

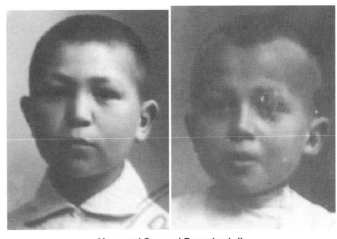

Yser and Szepsel Perechodnik
Photos from Pinsk travel document

Both parents have lived through many pograms & other difficulties have died of starvation.

The Perechodnik Family Details as recorded on pages 35 and 37 of the register kept by the Cape Jewish Orphanage (Oranjia).
1 Names and surname: Yser and Szepsel Perechodnik
2 Father: Eli 3 Mother: Keli
4 Ages: 12 and 9 years 5 Place of origin: Pinsk
6 How orphaned: Both parents 7 General Comments:
Both parents have lived through many pogroms and other difficulties. They have died from starvation..

GROUP PASSPORT FIVE
Yser Perechodnik is 28 on list and aged 10 while
Shepsel Perechodnik is 29 on list and aged seven.
Yser is back row on the right end while
Shepsel is most likely 2nd row 2nd from the right.

Pinsk travel document – Yser's above and Szepsel's below

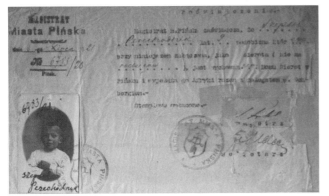

A THIRD UNKNOWN BROTHER
As recalled by Ivan Perch

I remember Uncle Oscar relaying to me that in the mid thirties, he and my dad, brought out from I don't know where, their brother who had not arrived with the Ochberg Orphans.

My father also mentioned to me over dinner in the Sea Point Hotel, that he couldn't understand why his brother was not happy in South Africa and that he and Oscar had paid for his return, I think to Poland.

To the best of my knowledge this third brother was never heard of again. I don't even know what his name was.

SAMSON (SAM) PERCH (SZEPSEL PERECHODNIK)
Written by Ivan Perch

My recollections of my father's early years are very vague, as I was born in April 1953 and at this stage my father was already 43. My late mother 14 years younger, was 29. Dad retired in 1969 at the age of 59. My mother passed away from Parasitic cancer of the brain at the very young age of 45. I was only 16 at this stage.

My father's age was a bit questionable, as his death, naturalisation and marriage certificates all state that he was born on the 6 March 1910. If this was the case he would have been 11 when he arrived from Poland in 1921. His passport stated that he was seven, the travel documents from Pinsk stated that he was nine. It is my opinion that he was about seven and he was most probably born in 1914.

My father left Pinsk (Under Polish Rule) on 6 of July 1921 (as per the Pinsk Travel Documents) and as per Visa C11329 in his group Passport left for South Africa via Danzig and the United Kingdom on 18 August 1921, and arrived in Cape Town abroad the Edinburgh Castle on 19 September 1921. He was brought up at Oranjia Orphanage and in ~1928 he had to leave without completing his studies to seek employment. He was a highly

Szepsel Perechodnik as a young boy

intelligent man and he many times made reference to the fact that if only he had the chance to study further, he would like to have studied law. Nevertheless this never stood in his way to become a successful business person and a highly respected person in the community.

To the best of my knowledge he travelled to the Transkei and worked in a trade store there. If I remember correctly this store could have been owned by the Stoch Family. He must have worked there for some years as he conversed in Xhosa fluently. On his return to Cape Town he started a General Dealer business with his brother Oscar (Yser/ Jser) in a small town on the West Coast of Cape Town called Riebeeck West. This business was called Perch Brothers and became a very successful outlet in this Town.

Szepsel Perechodnik with unknown man

Szepsel Perechodnik in the centre with unknown friends – 13/9/24

MY UNCLE OSCAR (YSER/JSER)

Unknown friend Samson Perch and Oscar Perch with dog

My Uncle Oscar remained a bachelor and remained in this business until he passed away in about 1970. I remember him coming to spend weekends with us at our home in Bellville and always enjoyed an outing with my Mother and the kids to Muizenberg. My mother always took great care of him and his welfare was always of great importance to her. She was one of the most charitable and kind women and the inscription on her tombstone really depicts her generosity and kindness

Oscar   *Oscar with his dog*

"Bella the daughter of Yaakov She did good through all her days and her good deeds will be praised in the gates ".

She many times would take me to Riebeeck West to visit my Uncle for the day. This always was a great outing for me in my youth, as uncle would treat us to the local country hotel for lunch and I would return laden with sweets and goodies from his store. The premises of my Uncle's store was originally owned by the Smuts family related to General Jan Smuts the first president of The Union of South Africa, who also hailed from Riebeeck West.

My uncle lived all the years in a small attached cottage to his business which was set in a wonderful garden with a small rivulet running through the plot. Oscar passed away not too long after my mother and due to immense stress and depression on my father's side, he sold this wonderful property, which today has been registered as a National Heritage building. I visit the now Boutique Guest House on many occasions en route to my farm on the Piketberg Mountains.

Sometimes with great joy, other times with great sadness, I recollect days gone by. Recently when I visited the property I sat in my car wondering what kind of a life Oscar must have had all alone in this small town, with no Jewish community to talk about.

Wedding of Samson and Bella Perch – 9 June 1946

He and my father were both very dignified and men of not too many words. One can only surmise that their youth had definitely left certain scars on their personalities. My father parted from the Perch Brothers business and before his marriage to my mother he bought some land in Kraaifontein, a very small town about 30 kilometres from Cape Town, and he had built a small building which was the start of Central Stores on the Old Paarl Road in Kraaifontein.

He married my mother Bella Bender on 9 June 1946 in the Gardens Synagogue and the marriage was solemnized by Rabbi M Abrahams. It was quite a coincidence that when I visited my cousin, Rabbi Karpol Bender and his wife Rena, nee Zambrowsky, in Israel in December 1986, we were invited to Rena's parents Rabbi and Mrs Zambrowsky for tea in Jerusalem and low and behold Rabbi Abrahams widow, was living in an apartment below Rena's parents. Rabbi Abrahams had married my parents and they had made Alliyah to Israel after his retirement from the Gardens Synagogue in 1968, and

My mother's grandparents on her father's side
Mr and Mrs Benderowitz

unfortunately he passed away in 1973. She was a Bender and Reverend Bender was one of the founder leaders at the Gardens Synagogue.

Rena the most interesting Rebbetzin I have met is a highly reputable artist with works in the Metropolitan Museum of Art and Yeshiva University Museum, both in New York City. Karpol spent many years in the States as the ambassador for the Bar Ilan university and returned to Israel to resume work for the University and lived across the road from the latter in Ramat Ilan. I am going off course, but just wanted to add a bit about my mother's rabbinical background.

After their marriage my father bought a house in the northern suburbs of Cape Town called Bellville. Bellville was 20 kilometres from Cape Town and about 14 kilometres to his business in Kraaifontein. The reason for choosing this suburb, is that it had the largest Jewish community in the Northern Suburbs, was close to his business and had better schools for his future family. He served on the Bellville Hebrew Congregation for many years and served two terms, as chairman of the community. Strangely the second term was the year of my Barmitzvah, which was on 7 May1966.

As stated before, he was a highly intelligent and furthermore well respected, quietly spoken gentleman with an outstanding reputation for being highly honourable both in his social and business interactions with people. Years after his death I met one of the Directors of Stellenbosch District Bank in Stellenbosch, and it was so warming to be told what respect the bank had for my father. My father as a Jewish man, once again was respected by one and all including the Afrikaans business sector, which in smaller towns in those days were very prone to be anti Jewish. The bank also had a branch in my father's complex in Kraaifontein and until his death he had a very large share holding in this Bank. Sam Perch, as he was fondly called, was a public speaker of note and many times at ceremonies in Bellville he was called upon by Community members to propose toasts at weddings, celebrations and Jewish functions in the town. He was very popular amongst the Jewish

My Mother and her parents, Jacob and Sarah,
outside their home in Bird Street Stellenbosch

Bella Bender aged 25

congregates in Bellville and I will always remember him as having a lot of passion for his fellow beings.

I clearly remember that there was a family in Bellville that was struggling financially and my father supplied them many times without being paid for groceries from his business. Likewise my late mother assisted people with no transport, served on many charity organisations including the B'noth Zion and Jewish Guild and was also chairlady on occasions for these organisations.

My father's business grew leaps and bounds in Kraaifontein and there were many additions, extensions and renovations to the first humble little building and it landed up as being the largest shopping/office complex on the Old Paarl Road, inclusive of a Shell Service Station as the final extension.

He became a prominent businessman in the area and served on the local Council for many years and served two terms as mayor of the town, quite an achievement for a Jewish man in a

totally Afrikaans speaking town. I refer back to my fondest memories of him, and they are definitely the wonderful respect that people of all kinds showed him and I have tried to base my life on these wonderful principles that he has passed down to me.

Dad never enjoyed joining mom and myself to a day at Muizenberg beach. He would always stay at home and recuperate from the week's hard work on these Sundays and public holidays. He would leave for his business at six in the morning and often return after six in the evening, including half days on Saturdays. I have found over the years that the beach and sand is not one of my favourite pasttimes. If a game of poker was available, he would be in his element. Many evenings were spent at our house and at the other homes of the school of players.

Mom on the other hand enjoyed her game of rummy and had a regular school going amongst the Jewish ladies in Bellville.

Samson Perch aged 33

These were wonderful times for me as they would bake and try and compete for wonderful eats at interval. When they gathered at our house guess who was in the kitchen waiting for the leftover goodies to appear from the dinning room.

They were both members of the Bellville Bowling Club and very much enjoyed this sport for recreational purposes. Mom was the better player of the two and I remember her receiving many trophies for championship events. She also served as chairlady of the club one or two occasions.

His last commercial venture was with his life long friends in the community of Bellville. They partnered and bought commercial land on one of the main roads in Bellville and erected a commercial complex called 26 Durban Road. He retained an office in the complex for the duration of his stay in Bellville.

He semi retired in 1968 after selling his businesses in Kraaifontein and retaining the complex as rental income for retirement.

Tragedy struck when my dear mother passed away at the tender age of 45 in hospital in 1969, after two brain operations.

My parents were a close and very dedicated couple and enjoyed a fulfilled and wonderful marriage. The shock of her death at this very young age was the result of this very powerful man's downward trend both physically and mentally, and after trying to get a housekeeper to look after the home in Bellville which eventually didn't work out, he decided to sell up the contents of the home, let same and he moved to a suite on the beach front in Sea Point in 1971.

Rev Zucker Mrs Zuker, Dad myself and Mum -
Ivan's Barmitzvah 7 May 1966

He was at times very depressed and I remember over dinner at the hotel one evening, I mentioned to him that he should start trying to put the past behind him and his answer to this was that the loss of his parents from starvation and living through pogroms in Poland was severe enough at that time, coupled with leaving as an orphan to a foreign country was a great enough loss for him, and he just couldn't at this stage of his life get over another loss of the passing away of my mother.

This was the one and only time that my father had ever discussed his past with me, as I know nothing more about his childhood or anything else from his past in Pinsk. This is very sad you know. I only started to understand what the Ochberg Orphans went through after ten years of lengthy research to put in an application for a Polish Passport, with the assistance of the Jewish Museum and the University Of Cape Town Jewish Archives.

I arrived at the Hotel to visit him and he was complaining of internal bleeding. I organised for him to see a specialist and he diagnosed that my father had a huge growth on the pituitary gland. I begged him to seek further medical advice abroad, but he refused as he was so mentally run down. They eventually did radiation on the area and unfortunately things didn't turn out well as they over radiated the area, and damaged part of his brain. He came back into the hotel and progressively started to lose his memory. He eventually had to go to Highlands House, because at this stage he was like a child and didn't even recognise me on my daily visits to The Jewish Old Aged Home.

He sadly passed away on 13 August 1974 at the age of 64, the year of my 21st birthday.

I remember words from a book of poems I read many years ago. "If I should die think only this of me that there was a part of life that was forever us". Ivan Kenneth Perch.

MY PARENTS' TOMBSTONES

Here is interred
My Beloved Wife, Our Beloved Mother
BELLA THE DAUGHTER OF YAAKOV
She did good through all her days
And her good deeds will be praised in the gates
She passed on in "with a good name"
19 Sivan 5730
May her soul be intertwined with the souls of the living

Here is interred
Our beloved father
R' SHIMSHON THE SON OF R' YISROEL
Who did good through all his days
With a love for others, and through acts of kindness
He passed on "with a good name"
25 Av 5734
May his soul be intertwined with the souls of the living

Chapter 75 – CHAWA PIANKA (1910-1983)

EVA SMULOWITZ (CHAWA PIANKA)
Written by Rae Sank

I am one of Eva Smulowitz's (Chawa Pianka) grand-daughters. I am writing this on behalf of her surviving children, Edith Friedlander (my mother) and Sonny Shmueli, (my uncle).

My Bobba was an amazing woman, but unfortunately, we only realised how amazing she was, years after her passing. She never spoke of her early life in Russia and very little of her time as an "Ochberg Orphan". It was a story we simply took for granted, that she had been one of the chosen two hundred. More than that we didn't question or show interest in her story. How very sad when I think of all the questions we should and could have asked.

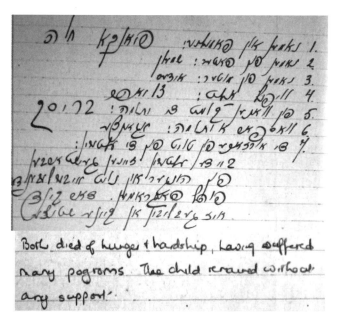

Chawa Pianka

The family details of Chawa Pianka as recorded on page 121 of the register at the Cape Jewish Orphanage (Oranjia).
1 Name and surname: Chawa Pianka
2 Father: Shimon   3 Mother: Ides   4 Age: 13 years
5 From where: Brest   6 How orphaned: Both parents
7 General Comments: Both died of hunger and hardship, having suffered many pogroms.
The child remained without any support.

GROUP PASSPORT THREE - Chawa Pianka (Eva Piankin) is sitting in the middle row, third from the left

Chawa Pianka, my maternal grandmother, was born in 1910 in Brest Litovsk, Russia. One afternoon, her little brother was standing in the doorway of their house, when the Cossacks swept through the town. They saw a small Jewish boy, leaned over their horses, and snatched him up for the Tsar's army. He was never seen or heard from again. Her parents died in either the 1918 Flu Pandemic or were killed in the chaos of war or pogroms.

When she was about 11 or 12 she met Isaac Ochberg and was one of the few children chosen to start a new life in South Africa. However, her older sister, Leah, fearful of the rumours of wild beasts and slavery, refused to sign the permission papers. Eva, who must have been very bright and determined, took the initiative herself and asked the matron of the orphanage to sign for her instead, which she did.

From the photos we've seen, she was a beautiful young girl. She had green-blue eyes, well marked eyebrows, high cheekbones and dark wavy hair. When they arrived in Cape Town harbour, the whole Jewish community came to greet them. Eva was sent to live in the Oranjezicht orphanage, Oranjia. She changed her name to Eva Piankin and stayed there for about five years. When she was 16 or 17 she was sent to Port Elizabeth to live with one of the prominent Jewish families there. It seems as if she and a nephew of the family fell

361

in love. However, the family didn't want to take responsibility for her and she was dispatched back to Cape Town, broken hearted.

Meanwhile, a young man, David Smulowitz, some 14 years older than she, journeyed from his home in Tsolo, Transkei, via East London and Port Elizabeth, to Cape Town, probably to find a wife. While there, he visited Oranjia. Someone asked where he was from and jovially, he replied :"Oh, I'm from lots of places.. Tsolo...East London... Port Elizabeth...."

"Port Elizabeth " she cried, "Why, we have someone here who was just in Port Elizabeth!" Eva was immediately called downstairs to 'meet a man from Port Elizabeth.' Thinking it was the boy she loved, she flew down the stairs, only to be greeted by a much older stranger. She was crushed with disappointment. However, David invited her out for lunch with his sister. Jumping at any chance for an outing, she accepted.

Although my grandfather was probably instantly smitten by this lovely young woman, the feelings were not returned as quickly. However, within a few weeks, Eva was persuaded to marry him by the chairlady of the Oranjia Committee and she decided to take her advice. She left the orphanage and went to stay with Baruch Chidekel, my grandfather's step brother, until her wedding day. My grandfather came from Bubne, Nevel, Vitebsk (the hometown of Marc Chagall). His father's name was Zalman, his mother, Hodes. He had three brothers, Samuel, Morris and David, a sister, Yetta and a half brother, Baruch Chideckel with the same mother. He and his brother Morris immigrated to South Africa in the 1900s as did other siblings.

She was 18 when she got married and was the first of the Ochberg orphans to do so. "Daddy Ochberg" gave her away.

SMULOWITZ – PIANKIN WEDDING
SA Jewish Chronicle – 6 April 1927 [pp 367-368]

Miss Eva Piankin, who was married at the Great Synagogue, *in Cape Town,* to Mr David Smulowitz, of Tsolo, was one of the group of orphans brought over from Russia, some six years ago, and it was on a recent visit to the Orphanage in Oranjezicht that Mr Smulowitz succumbed to the charms of his bride, and shortly afterwards his engagement was announced, culminating in "Tuesday's happy ceremony.

Although there were counter attractions, there was a fair attendance at the Mother Synagogue to witness the marriage ceremony which was conducted by the Rev A P Bender, assisted by Rev L Kirschner. The young bride made a pretty picture in her gown of white georgette with silver embroideries, and her veil of Brussels lace was arranged á la Russe over a headdress of orange blossoms. She was attended by Misses Sarah Barmash and Walt as bridesmaids, and two pretty little mites held the trailing veil.

The bride approached the *chupa* on the arm of Mr Isaac Ochberg, who, brought the Russian orphans to this country, and who has since taken a personal interest in her. Her future home will be in Tsolo, and there is no doubt that the training

she has received in the Home and the loving care and attention bestowed upon her since her arrival with her little fellows in this country will ever be remembered by her.

The hope expressed by the Rev Bender, in his address to the young couple, that she will uphold the traditions and ideals of Judaism and that she will maintain a true Jewish atmosphere in her household, will, I feel sure, be consummated.

In the Synagogue I noticed Mr H J Stodel, President of the Cape Town Hebrew Congregation; Mr L A G Neumann, Mr and Mrs Policansky, Mrs J Lurie, Mr and Mrs A Silbert, Mrs H Hamburg, Mrs R Myers, Matron of the Orphanage; Miss A Gamsu, Supervisor of the Dressmaking Department at the Home; Miss E Kupowitz, of the Orphanage Secretarial staff, and many of the children.

She returned with her new husband to the tiny hamlet of Tsolo, set in the beautiful but isolated hills of the Transkei, where my grandfather ran a general dealer store. Later it grew into a smallholding with cattle and fields of maize. She was horrified to find how tiny and lonely a place it was, however, being a woman of immense courage, strength and determination, she threw herself whole heartedly into the activities of the village. She taught herself to become an outstanding cook and baker using a wood stove as there was no electricity in those days in the Transkei. She learnt how to can and preserve fruit and made delicious bottled peaches and jams. She made wonderful homemade cheese and butter and baked her own bread. She became an accomplished bridge player and a competent tennis player competing in tournaments and even winning a trophy or two. She taught herself how to knit and was an expert at knitting socks for soldiers during WW11. In addition to the English she'd learned when she was brought to South Africa as a little girl, she added Afrikaans and Xhosa to her language skills.

Eva as a young lady and with her first born Edith

362

Most importantly, she had three children, Edith, Sonny and Rae, whom she adored. For years she had been agonising over her two older sisters, Leah and Clara, whom she left behind in Russia. She begged my Zaida to help her bring both of them over from Russia. It was not an easy task, but they persevered, and to her great joy, her sisters eventually made their way to South Africa. It must have been a very difficult and expensive thing to do, but he achieved it. He must have been a compassionate man, who obviously loved his wife very much.

When Sonny was only eight years old and my mother merely ten, (and later when my Aunty Rae was older, she joined them as well), my Zaida decided that it would be better for them to live in Cape Town, among the Jewish community, and get a Jewish education. I cannot imagine what it must have been like for my Bobba sending her children so far away from her so young. They would only come home again twice a year, for school holidays. The journey to Cape Town was three days by train and communication between my grandparents and their children was almost nonexistent, except for letters. My mother recalls that they made only one telephone call to Tsolo in all the years they lived in Cape Town! In our age of instant communication, cell phone, skype and the like, it is very difficult to comprehend.

Then, in 1960, tragedy struck the family. In March of that year, my vivacious and beautiful Aunty Rae died tragically young, leaving behind a little girl of two. Less than three months later, my Zaida died as well. He had been struggling with ill health, and the loss of his beloved daughter shattered him. He was a kind and generous husband and a loving if sometimes strict father. I wish I could have known him, but sadly he died the year I was born. My Bobba was left a widow at the youthful age of fifty.

She left Tsolo and moved permanently to Cape Town to live with us. For the next twenty three years, she tirelessly helped my mother in every way you can imagine. I remember her as a wonderful, loving, caring, hardworking, doting grandmother,

whom we called "Bo". Her bulkes, babke, bagels, taiglach, cakes, biscuits, brisket, roast chickens and everything she baked or cooked was outstanding and delicious. She played bridge with a group of friends each week but mainly just devoted herself to us her family: her daughter, son in law and grandchildren. She visited her son and family in Israel whenever she could but she never spoke of her early years in Russia or Oranjia.

My amazing, brave, unselfish, unforgettable Bobba, Eva Smulowitz died too young, in 1983, and is buried in the Old Cemetery in Pinelands, Cape Town. When she passed on, she left two children, eight grandchildren and a great grandchild -

and many more descendents since then.

We will always remember her with deep love, appreciation and admiration for what she achieved and of course the gift of life that she gave us all through her courage, intelligence, strength of character and foresight

Eva Smulowitz
(Chawa Pianka)
in her later years

EVA'S TWO OLDER SISTERS, LEAH AND CLARA

Not only did my Zaida arrange for his Eva's sisters to immigrate to SA, but when they arrived, he arranged for them to stay with family and friends. He also followed up and made sure they got married, which in itself was a wonderful mitzvah. He was living in the 'bundu', had very limited resources, financial or otherwise, but still managed to achieve an almost impossible task. He was definitely a true mensch.

Both the sisters eventually got married. Clara and her husband lived in Cape Town and had two children, but the circumstances of their lives are somewhat vague. I know my Bobba kept in touch with her sister over the years, but it was not a very close relationship for various reasons.

She was closer to Leah, who married a kind if simple man and lived in Butterworth, Transkei and Port Elizabeth, until moving to Cape Town a few years before she passed away. Sadly they weren't blessed with any children and my Aunty Leah died relatively young. Her husband, (Uncle) Nathan, then came to live with us for about 15 years or more, until his death.

Eva and family ~1961 - Kenneth Friedlander (son in law), holding Wulfie, Eva, with Rae on her lap, Edith (daughter), and Hessel

YETTA ROSIER (RAZU) AND ISAAC BORNSTEIN
Written by Tania (Bornstein) Jacobson

Both my parents were born in Brest Litovsk and came out with the Ochberg Orphans to South Africa in 1921.

YETTA CHAYIM AND ITZIK ROSIER

My mother spoke to me throughout my childhood of her experiences and the circumstances of her coming to Cape Town which I will try to relate to you.

The family was very poor and my grandfather was a teacher. They lived through a time when the Cossacks would come riding into the village and they would have to flee for their lives. My grandmother gave birth to her youngest child on the road out of town. There were five children and an adopted daughter. At the end of the 1914-1918 war conditions were very bad and a flu epidemic broke out. My mother told me how both parents landed in hospital and she would visit them every day. One day she came there to find both their beds were empty. They had died during the night.

The family could not do much for the children and suggested that the baby, Yossele, aged three, go into an orphanage. They promised to take care of him, but he unfortunately died. The oldest daughter, Elka, was taken to a nearby village to live with

Itzi, Yetta, and Chaim Rosia (Isaac, Yenta and Chaim Razu)

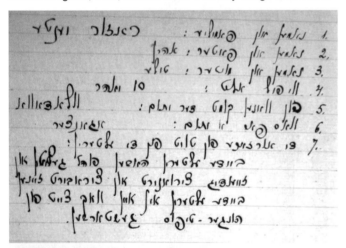

The Rosier family details as recorded on pages 17, 19 and 21 of the register at the Cape Jewish Orphanage (Oranjia).
1 Names and surname: Yetta, Hymie and Isaac Rosier
2 Father: Aaron   3 Mother: Tilly   4 Ages: 10, 9 and 8 years
5 From where: Wlodawa   6 How orphaned: Both parents
7 General Comments:
Both parents suffered a lot during the War.
They have both died within a week of hunger and typhoid fever.

an aunt with a view to finding a shiddach for her. She met someone and later went to settle in Palestine and finally got to America where she prospered.

Meanwhile the rest of the children, Yetta, Chaim and Itzik, were left to their own devices. Hearing about a man who wanted to take some children to Africa, my mother discussed this with her brothers. She at the time was ten and the others eight and six. They met with Isaac Ochberg who agreed to take them and so their journey began.

As we know, they travelled from Warsaw to Danzig and then to London where they were cared for before leaving for Cape Town. The children were all medically examined and my Uncle Chaim was found to have a strange black patch on the back of his head. He was kept behind for further investigation till it was found to be a mark from his pen which he wiped on the back of his head. I hate to think of the trauma it must have caused the children to be parted from him.

ISAAC BORNSTEIN

About my father Isaac Bornstein there is very little to tell. He was evidently brought up by his grandfather and not much is known about his parents except that his mother's surname was Pivacic. He said that the only relative he had was Leah Altuska but never spoke of her sisters.

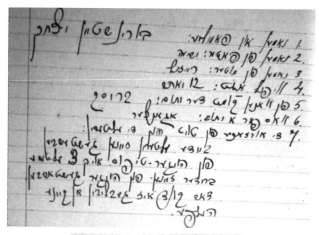

Family details of Yitzhak Bornstein as recorded on page 133 of the register at the Cape Jewish Orphanage (Oranjia).
1 Name and surname: Yitzhak Bornstein
2 Father: Yeshaya 3 Mother: Reizel 4 Age: 4 years
5 From where: Brest 6 How orphaned: Both parents
7 General Comments: Both parents died of hunger and typhus. Also the older brothers died of hunger.
The child remained without help.

Isaac Bornstein

AFTER ARRIVING IN SOUTH AFRICA

My father, mother and her two brothers remained in Cape Town where they lived at Oranjia. After their schooling most of the girls went out to work and they left the orphanage to live in a hostel in Oranjezicht run by a previous matron of the orphanage, a Miss Berliner. Mother worked in the millinery department of Ackermans, a department store in Cape Town.

Having met my father on the ship, they realized they were from the same town and became friendly. Meanwhile a close friendship existed between all the girls and they remained close for all their lives and became my family, all my "Aunties". We always referred to them as Aunty Peggy, Aunty Nellie, Auntie Polly etc. All the names were anglicised.

My parents met in the Orphanage and married when my mother was 20 and my dad 21. They married in 1930 and Mr and Mrs Max Policansky, gave her away. They were patrons of the orphanage and it was a beautiful wedding.

Isaac Bornstein and Yetta Rosia getting married
Cape Town August 1930.

In 1939 when war was declared and the Second World War started, my father and my mother's two brothers, enlisted and went off to fight. I was two years old and my mother was left to care for my sister Rita aged five and me.

Yetta and Isaac with daughters Rita and Tania

We are very close as we never had any family except the "aunties" from Oranjia. My sister's married name is Rita Shorkend.

Unfortunately my Uncle Itzik was killed up North which broke my mother's heart as he was such a very special and wonderful young man. I have letters which he wrote to us during the war and reflect his special qualities.

My Uncle Chaim came back to Cape Town, married and had two daughters, one now Dawn Goodman.

After the war my father came back and they lived in Muizenberg where they had a shop and then my father became a bookmaker and we lived well.

In 1950 my mother met her oldest sister in America after she had contacted the Red Cross to find them. I now keep in touch with her son in Los Angeles.

Isaac and Yetta Bornstein (Rosier)
on their 40th wedding anniversary

ELKA RAZU – AN OLDER SISTER LEFT BEHIND
Dawn Goodman writes

In the 1960s my Dad Chaim Rosier, got a phone call out of the blue, from the International Red Cross to ask whether he was related to a certain Elka Rozu who was living in Los Angeles and had been searching for her two brothers and a sister. The little ones had been separated from her when their parents had died of the flu epidemic raging through Eastern Europe around 1917, extreme poverty and starvation. That is what it says on my father's passport about his parents' death.

Elka was too old to be part of the Orphan group, and had a boyfriend anyway with whom she had decided to attempt to reach Palestine, which she and her future husband successfully did, going on to New York then LA as they became more affluent over the years.

Anyway, my father was quite shocked to learn that their elder sister was alive and trying to contact him and his sister and their younger brother Itzak, who came from Poland with them and sadly died in a battle in North Africa with the Germans as part of the South African Army Corp during World War Two.

In those days it took Elka two months to get to South Africa. She spent a few months here, and all I can remember of her visit was that every evening after work my father would go to Auntie Yetta's flat and the three of them would just weep and chat for hours- the weeping never stopped! Quite extraordinary!

The long lost sister Ella (Elka Razu) with her children
Alan and Ellen Rosen.~ 1952

Chapter 77 – ITZIK ROSIER (RAZU)

Letters sent in by Itzik's niece, Tania (Bornstein) Jacobson

LETTER FROM ITZIK TO HIS SISTER, YETTA BORNSTEIN (ROSIER/RAZU) - 7/11/1941

My darling sister,

Firstly let me assure you of my good health and cheerfulness. By now you are probably back in the good old Hansen Street home. I pray that you, Rita and Tania will have all the luck in the world and that only perfect health and happiness will follow you into Berelheim Villa (name of our house).

It will be a long time till I see Bornie again. We will have moved away from this unit but I had a chance of saying goodbye to him before we left. He was a little downhearted at my leaving but otherwise he is OK. But don't you be downhearted, dear sister. One of us or both of us will soon be back with you. Don't get upset when a batch of our fellows arrive in Cape Town and Bornie or I are not amongst them. There are still many married men up here with us and you must console yourself with the fact that we are here to do a job of work and we would like to see it finished. I am very confident that the whole business up here will soon be over and we shall be able to celebrate a permanent reunion. I promise that I will take good care of myself and with Captain Weinstein's blessings I will come back to you safe and sound. The greatest day in my life will be when I can gather you, Rita and little Tania in my arms again and kiss you all hullo.

Please write to me more often and I shall try to write to you with every mail.

G-d bless you all and with love to you, Rita, Tania, Chaim and Cecelia.

Your loving brother

Itzik

LETTER FROM CAPTAIN WEINSTEIN, JEWISH CHAPLAIN TO YETTA BORNSTEIN - 11/12/1941

My dear Mrs Bornstein,

A month or so ago it was my very pleasant task to pen glad and encouraging tidings to you. My heart was then overflowing with joy and pride at the achievements of one of my most precious congregants.

Today my heart is empty and pained. The pen is obstinate. Itzik, dear Itzik is no more with us. He was called to his mother and father.

Not a hundred yards from me and within a stone's throw of his pals with the ack-ack platoon, he received a direct hit from a bomb during an air-raid. His death was instantaneous. He suffered no pain.

My own brother's death could not have moved me or shocked me so much, for he was more than a brother and a friend.

If one has to consider a man religious when he is kind, unselfish, self sacrificing, with a strong sense of justice, a hater of wrong and a lover of good - then consider that Itzik was one of the most religious people I have been privileged to meet.

Itzik Rosier who fell in WWII

He was one of the most popular Jewish soldiers with the Dukes. Both officers and men loved him. As a Jew he was unique. His soul was Jewish and his love for Jewish matters was deep. Such I found him.

To his last moment he was joking - one of the finest characteristics he had. In his company one felt warm and relieved.

But such is war. Sacrifices are demanded if the fight for liberty has to be waged successfully. It is beyond us to know who the next victims may be.

In this hour of your very sad bereavement I extend my heartfelt sympathy. May God bestow his twofold blessings on you and your dear ones who have already suffered so much. May better days lie ahead and may the great day of Victory come soon - that day for which you have already given so much.

If there is anything I can do for you, please do not hesitate to let me know.

I wish you a long life of good health and happiness.

Let us think of our dear departed one as the pleasant symbol which he represented.

Captain Weinstein,
Jewish Chaplain, First South African Infantry Brigade.

HYMIE ROSIER (CHAIM ROZU)
Written by Dawn Goodman

When the 'Ochberg' children arrived in London and were being processed for their final journey to South Africa it was found that Chaim had a strange black mark on his hair which was puzzling. He was therefore not allowed by the medical authorities to travel with his group to Cape Town and that was another traumatic situation to experience after the long trip from home. The mark turned out to be from his rubbing a pencil on his hair while writing but it had to be checked out! He went on a later ship without his beloved siblings and eventually joined them in the Orphanage Oranjia in Cape Town where they grew up.

He spoke little to us, his family, about his life growing up except once to tell us that his father had been a Hebrew Teacher in a small poor village, and his memory and description of their home was of a small primitive place with the family bathing once a week in the bath centered in the kitchen area which was covered by a door that acted as a multi-purpose unit for preparation of food, ironing, homework for the children etc and all of them sleeping in this room which was warmed by the cooking oven.

My father grew up to become active in the early days of the liberation struggle in South Africa, being banned by the Apartheid government and when most of his friends exiled the country to continue the struggle out of our borders, decided to remain here giving up politics which was very dangerous in those days if one was an activist.

Therapists I have chatted with have explained to me that as an orphan being brought away from his home under the extremely harsh conditions he came from and went through as a child, Chaim would not have been able to bear another trauma of such huge magnitutude as exile from the place he had made his home and felt so secure and happy in. Unfortunately he did not live to see his dreams of a non racial democracy come to fruition.

My father left the Orphanage in his late teens and went, as did many other young Jewish men who were not well educated, to work in a country village of the Western Cape as shop assistant for some years. He learned to speak Afrikaans fluently which was the language in the countryside at that time, eventually returning to the City of Cape Town where he became interested in the politics of the Left joining the Congress of Democrats and the Communist party. He felt strongly about the oppression and discrimination of the masses of this country having seen first hand how the farm labourers, all coloured and black folk, were treated. Being very much affected by this, he decided to actively try to do something about this state of affairs.

He met my mother at one of the 'Party' meetings and they married at the Muizenberg synagogue. He went off to war and when he returned he opened a fresh fish shop in Parow, again a mainly Afrikaans speaking area. Here he worked very hard, getting up at 5.00 am every morning, starting the day with a

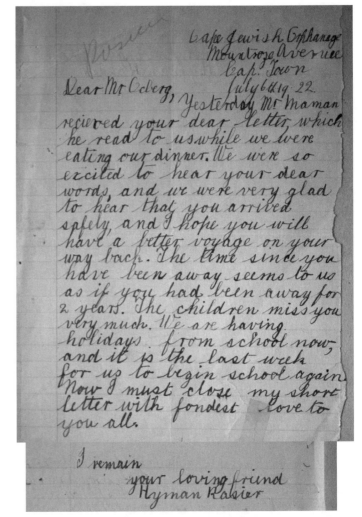

Letter from Chaim to Isaac Ochberg

visit to the local harbour to purchase fish, then driving quite a long distance to his business to return quite late in the evening, day in and day out for years until the shop he rented was sold. He then moved the business to the upmarket area of Sea Point eventually retiring to his little beach cottage at Clifton, which today is one of the most desirable places to live in this country, but then it was a simple low income area, mainly.

During our childhood years I remember well the terrible pressure of living with constant harassment by the Special Branch of the Apartheid Police force who were brutal in their activities and telephones were tapped. There was the fear of being arrested at any time which happened to my mother who was released from 'detention without trial' after months on medical grounds.

Chaim died suddenly of a heart attack in his mid '60s. He unfortunately did not live to see his dreams of a free South Africa realised.

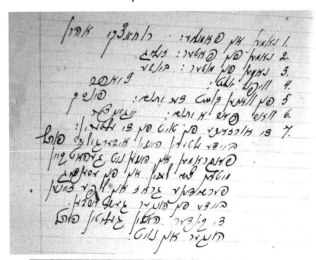

The Ruchocki family details as recorded on pages 43, 45 and 49 of the register at the Cape Jewish Orphanage (Oranjia).
1 Names and surname: Aron, Philip and Sholem Ruchocki
2 Father: Selig   3 Mother: Bashe   4 Ages: 9, 8 and 7 years
5 From where: Pinsk   6 How orphaned: Both parents
7 General Comments:
The parents had no means for livelihood and were eating grass and potatoe peel. The children were hunger stricken.

Pinsk Travel Document of Aron Ruchocki

Pinsk Travel Document of Faiwel Ruchocki

Parents Zelig Ruchocki born 10/4/1885 and Basha (Domoszicki) born 17/6/1889 who both died ~1920 photo taken in Pinsk

PINSK TRAVEL DOCUMENTS (AFFIDAVITS)

The children that came from Pinsk had in fact two travel documents. One was the group passport with a group photo and one was an individual affidavits given by the Pinsk Magistrate with an individual photo.

The affidavits grant permission for the child to be placed in the care of Mr Ochberg for the journey to South Africa. The Affidavits were written in Polish. Pinsk was actually located in White Russia, an area ceded to Poland in 1918, but then returned to Russia later.

The affidavits translate as follows.
NUMBER XXXXXXX **Affidavit Issued by the Magistrate of the Town of Pinsk on July 6, 1921.**
The Magistrate of Pinsk states that XXXXXXXXXXX, of XXXX years, whose photograph is attached, and is an orphan without parents, who resides in the Orphanage, is to depart for Africa with Caretaker OCHBERG.
Stamped and Sealed by two secretaries of the Magistrate of the Town of Pinsk.

AARON, FAIWEL AND SHOLEM RUCHOCKI
Written by Marjorie, Lynne, Robyn and Stan Ruch

Aaron (Archie) Ruchocki was born on 4 September 1909, Faiwel (Philip) Ruchocki was born on 5 January 1911 and Sholem (Solly) Ruchocki was born on 15 January 1913 in Pinsk, Poland.

They lived through many pogroms and life in Poland was hard. Philip's recollections from this difficult time included the extent of their hunger forcing them to eat whatever was available, including raw onions and potato peels.

After their parents Zelig and Basha died in 1920, Aron, Faiwel and Sholem went to an Orphanage in Pinsk. We are unsure if Zelig and Basha passed away from malnutrition or the epidemic that swept through Eastern Europe at the time

Philip's early years had been very traumatic and difficult for him and he chose not to speak about them, hence the lack of detailed information of this time in his life.

Philip recalled looking through the palings of the fence of the orphanage onto the street and watching the soldiers go by. He thought they couldn't see him because he was behind the fence. On asking Philip in his latter years how he felt about leaving Poland, his comment was, "I was so happy to get out of that place."

In 1921, Aron, Faiwel and Sholem were amongst the fortunate children selected by Isaac Ochberg to move to South Africa.

Archie, Philip and Solly arrived in Cape Town on 21 September 1921 on the Edinburgh Castle with approximately 200 other Ochberg Orphans. Archie, was 12, Philip was 10 and Solly was 8 according to known birth dates.

On their arrival they went to the Cape Jewish Orphanage, later called Oranjia in Oranjezicht, Cape Town.

The bottom left hand side of PASSPORT FIVE
I guess Faiwel is 2nd from left - 95% sure
and Aaron 4th from left - 90% sure

UNKNOWN RELATIVE

Jacob (Yakov) Ruchocki Pinsk

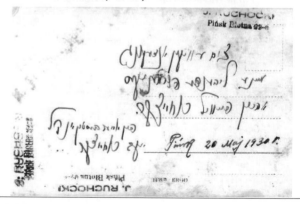

PASSPORT 5 no 14 on list is Aron and 15 is Faiwel
(Szulem (Sholem) is no 23 on passport 2)

Message on back of photo dated 20th May 1930 Pinsk
"In Eternal Memory. My beloved nephews
Aharon Faiwel Ruchocki.
From your uncle Yakov Ruchocki."

ARCHIE AARON RUCH (AARON RUCHCKI)
Written by Jerome Ruch

Aaron Ruchocki – photo from Pinsk Travel Document

Philip and Archie

From my earliest years, I never recalled anyone addressing my dad as Aaron. He was always known as Archie to everyone, although his full name was officially recorded as Archibald Aaron Ruch.

Like Philip and Solly, he also grew up in the Oranjia Orphanage. He always had a good sense of humour and had to work extremely hard for his entire working life in order to make ends meet and to make sure his family was looked after. His family always came first and everything he did, he did for the benefit of his family.

Archie stayed with the Kagan's (Nina and Grisha) at some point (probably when he left the orphanage and Philip left for George) before he got married and also worked for Grisha in his printing works which was situated on the corner of Roeland and Buitenkant Streets in those days. I think it was called Elite Printing Works. They were very fond of Archie and treated him as part of their family. When Grisha died and I was born, Nina Kagan became my godmother and used to call me "Grishinka" which I guess is "small Grisha" in Russian, but am not entirely sure as I don't speak any Russian. Both Nina and Grisha were of Russian descent.

Archie was naturalized on 30 June 1931 and he and Gwen were married on 14 November 1943 in the Gardens Synagogue, Cape Town. Gwendoline Pam was the daughter of Moses Benzion Pam, born 10 December 1875 and Cecilia Solomon, born 25 April 1883.

Archie and Gwen had three children; Monty born 28 October 1944, Barbara born 30 April 1948 and Jerome born 13 October 1953.

From an early age Archie loved walking on the Sea Point beachfront and made a point of swimming in the freezing water of Graaf's Pool, Sea Point as often as possible, no matter what the weather was like. He also trained as a life saver and had extremely strong and bulky calf muscles. He also loved animals and always had at least one dog and a cat living at home. Rinty, our Alsation, was like a forth child and even went to work on a daily basis with Archie.

Archie loved singing, had a great voice and sang in the Gardens, Sea Point and Schoonder Street Synagogue choirs at various stages of his life. He also composed a number of songs, including one, which was dedicated to Brenda. A number of these songs were sung at our wedding by a professional singer.

Archie, although an apprenticed compositor by trade, loved wholesale and retail trading and started a company called Archer Trading Company which sold paper and stationery products to the independent shops and cafes. After a period of time, he felt that our family should consider emigrating to Montreal as he did not feel totally at ease with the situation in South Africa. He then decided, in conjunction with my mom, to sell our house in Buxton Ave, Oranjezicht, as he did not have sufficient funds to pay for the air ticket to Montreal. The family then moved into a flat in Vredehoek while my dad flew off to Montreal to meet his family, Sam and Miriam Smith.

Sam (formerly Ruchocki) had been shipped out to Montreal at about the same time as Archie had been shipped out to Cape Town.

Archie lived with the Smith's for the duration of his stay in Montreal, but could not find sustainable employment and eventually returned to Cape Town, where he opened a similar business to the one he had before his trip. This business was

Gwen and Archie's wedding photo

called Archer Sales Corporation and he incorporated the logo "An Archer Product Always Hits The Mark" into the company letterhead, something which I still fondly remember.

A short while before our wedding, Archie was diagnosed with throat cancer and his condition deteriorated rapidly. However, being the special family type of person that he was, he insisted that we go away and enjoy our honeymoon and assured us he would still be around to see us on our return, even though he was already critically ill. He was true to his word. We saw him on our return, but very sadly, he passed away three days later on 30 June, 1976.

DESCENDANTS OF ARCHIE (AARON) RUCH

Monty and Barbara were both not well from an early age and needed lots of attention and special caring from their teens. Barbara passed away suddenly after having a very serious epileptic fit at the young age of 48. Monty lives in Johannesburg with his companion Gail. Jerome and his wife Brenda live in Camps Bay, Cape Town. They were married on 6 June, 1976 and have three children, Gillian, Mark and Hilton.

Barbara's batmitzvah: Front row: Archie Ruch, Jerome Ruch
Back row: Barbara Ruch, Gwen Ruch, Monty Ruch

Back: Jerome, Barbara, Monty and Philip
Front Brenda and Marjorie

Jerome Ruch, Barbara Ruch, Monty Ruch

Ruch Family Oct 2009 - Jerome and Brenda Ruch with their children Archie's grand children Hilton, Gillian and Mark

PHILIP'S STORY
Written by Marjorie, Lynne Robyn and Stan Ruch

Faiwel Ruchocki – photo from Pinsk Travel Document

Philip stayed at the orphanage for the next seven years during which time he attended the Central Boys School (Primary school) and Cape Town Boys High School. In 1924, while at Central Boys School he received a prize for being placed first in Standard 4.

In 1926 he won an essay prize for English. During this time Philip also sang in the Gardens Synagogue Choir and loved the tickets to a cinema café which they received in gratitude for their services, from the choirmaster.

It appears that all was not happy at Oranjia during this time and at the age of 17 (1928) Philip left Cape Town for George where a trustee from Oranjia (perhaps Boris Crasnow) had found him a job at Ress Brothers. He stayed with the Ress Family for about nine months and then went to Postmasburg in 1929 where he had a job with Voigt Brothers and Davidowitz, a shop and hotel. Philip helped run the shop.

Voigt Brothers and Davidowitz was owned by Kolly Davidowitz, brother of David Leopold Davidowitz, Isaac Ochberg's brother-in-law. David was called Mr Dee, D L Dee or 'Leffeld' which was the way it was pronounced with a Latvian/Russian accent. This was the beginning of a lifelong connection with the Davidowitz and later Friedberg families.

It seems that during this time, the Ochberg family were looking out for Philip and Solly as can be seen by Philip's employment opportunities and also a letter written by Solly to Philip in April 1929 where Solly wrote that *"Mr Ochberg told me that he would*

not let me return to the Orphanage on any account and so now I don't know where I'll be going to when I leave the hospital"

This excerpt is from a letter written by Solly to Philip while he (Solly) was ill in the New Somerset Hospital in Cape Town. From the letter it can be seen that Solly was also unhappy at Oranjia and that it was promised to him that he would not have to return there when he left the hospital. Unfortunately, Solly never recovered from his illness and passed away at the hospital on 26 April 1929 at the young age of 16. This was just five days after he wrote the letter to Philip. He was buried at Maitland Cemetery, Cape Town

Meanwhile, in 1931, Philip left Postmasburg together with Kolly Davidowitz and they went to Springfield. Here Kolly had a general dealership and a farm. Philip worked for Kolly in Springfield until 1934 when he and Kolly went to Douglas to work for Joe Friedberg at Friedberg Brothers, which was also a general dealership. Joe was Kolly's brother-in-law, brother to his wife Chassie. Philip developed a close relationship with Joe, his wife Anne and their four daughters.

Kolly's niece, Phyllis Friedlander, nee Davidowitz and daughter of Leopold, would often visit her uncle in Douglas during the winter holidays. She fondly recalls the time she spent there and has said "I thought Philip was such a good looking youth who I thought "taught" me to drive. That is he allowed me aged about six to sit on his lap in the car and turn the wheel of the car. I thought I was driving!"

Archie and Philip or Solly

On 19 July 1934, Philip became a naturalized South African. Philip stayed in Douglas at the Douglas Hotel from 1934 to April 1948. During this time he first worked as a bookkeeper at Friedberg Brothers, and later became a partner in the business, cementing his connection with the family. Unfortunately Joe passed away in the mid 1930s and in 1948 Friedberg Brothers was sold to Theron and Theron.

Philip joined the Herbert Unit of the NRVC (National Reserve Volunteer Corps) attached to the Dukes Regiment, in part time service from 14 October 1941 to 12 March 1946.

Philip was then invited to become a partner at Southern Timbers in Plumstead, Cape Town. The business was founded in 1923 and was run by Anne Friedberg's brother-in-law Solly Israel, her brother Joe Immerman and Solly's brother-in-law Chaim Aaron. Southern Timbers was a builders' merchant and hardware business situated on Main Road, Plumstead.

Through Isaac Ochberg and his brother-in-law, Leopold Davidowitz, Philip was closely connected to the extended Davidowitz, Friedberg, Israel family and this strong connection and closeness endured over the years.

Southern Timbers was an extended family business which grew from strength to strength. When there were no family members to continue the business and an offer was made by Checkers Supermarkets to purchase the land in 1983, the partners decided to wind things down and move on into retirement. The Checkers complex still stands on the site today.

Philip was a stickler for detail and accurate record keeping. He always conducted his business and all aspects of his life with the utmost integrity. Each night at home he would recheck and initial every invoice issued during the day. Once the business had been sold, Philip continued to sell off the remaining stock from a property they owned over the road from the original Southern Timbers. It was always a family joke that his method of stocktaking was by counting the screws and other small items, one at a time, lest he should make the smallest error. The last remnants of the Southern Timbers stock now fill a shoe box in Marjorie's garage in Lindfield, Sydney.

Archie and Gwen, Marjorie and Philip, the wedding couple and Reuben and Bess, Majories parents

Marjorie and Philip

Back in 1948, Philip lived in Cogill's Hotel, Wynberg. His interest in seeking out a Jewish social life, lead him to the Badminton Club, run at the Wynberg Shul. Here he not only enjoyed playing badminton, but it was at the Club in 1949 that he met the love of his life, Marjorie Ecker, who had migrated to Cape Town from England in 1947. They were married at the Gardens Synagogue, Cape Town on 17 August 1950, where the two witnesses were Leopold Davidowitz and Boris Crasnow, both of whom Philip had met when he first arrived in Cape Town in 1921.

Philip had met Leopold Davidowitz's daughter Phyllis many years earlier in Douglas and he and Marjorie and Phyllis and her late husband Dick continued that friendship after they were married and through their adult years. Marjorie and Phyllis still remain in contact today.

Philip and Marjorie always had a strong connection with the Cape Town Jewish Community. Philip served on the Committee of the Claremont Hebrew Congregation for about 30 years. He mostly was responsible for the maintenance of the building. Marjorie was heavily committed to the Ladies' Guild of the Shul where she served as Chairlady for a few years. She also was involved with the Union of Jewish Women from 1951-1992. They ran a traditional Jewish home and one of the highlights of the year was the annual Simchat Torah party held at their home following the shul Simchat Torah celebrations at the Claremont Hebrew Congregation. Each child happily received a chocolate bar and the numbers at the Ruch's annual party grew from year to year.

Another tradition which continued for about twenty years was that two months before Pesach, Marjorie and Philip would go to one of the Vineyards in Constantia and buy 160lbs of hermitage grapes to make wine. They pulled the grapes off the stalks, added the sugar, bunged up the barrel and left it to ferment for about six weeks. An important job in the wine making process was cleaning the barrel after bottling. This task was given to the gardener, Michael, who chose not to wash it out but to drink it out… He was found very incbriated one afternoon under the protea bush. Philip and Marjorie were well known for their delicious home made wine which they would use at the seder and throughout the year and also give as gifts to friends.

In 1969, they decided to take the family on a holiday to reconnect with Philip's roots in Douglas. The Douglas Hotel no longer existed so they stayed at the Frederick Hotel. Unbeknown to them, a wedding party had also checked in to the hotel during this time. It was the era when one put one's shoes outside the room, for them to be cleaned. When they woke up in the morning they found that the wedding guests had played a prank and taken all the Ruch family shoes home with them! Barefoot in Douglas.

Philip enjoyed his sport including golf and weekly tennis games. As a youth he was an excellent soccer player. He also loved his bridge and he and Marjorie played at least twice a week with two different card schools.

Philip was a quietly spoken and reserved man who was always willing to help others. He was considerate, respectful and charitable and was also involved with communal organisations.

Philip also took immense pride in his home and in providing the best he could for his family, always ensuring that the family's needs came first. He loved gardening and tinkering around the house. He maintained a magnificent garden with many manicured flower beds, a variety of fruit trees, as well as a thriving vegetable patch.

During their life in Cape Town, Philip and Marjorie, lived in seven different homes in the Kenilworth area, two of which were built by Philip. As their family grew, so their housing needs changed. Stanley was born 2 November 1951, Lynne 4 November 1953 and Robyn 10 March 1960. Once all the children had left home, they decided it was time to downsize to a flat. They purchased a flat in Dennekamp, a building which was built by Southern Timbers, with Philip overseeing the construction, in 1953. They had come full circle.

The Ruch offspring all migrated to Australia from South Africa. Stan married Kay Rickerby in 1993 in Sydney and they now live in Lennox Head, NSW. Lynne married David Michel in South Africa in 1982. They have four children, Jonathan, Beth, Daniel and Gideon. Robyn married Ian Satill in South Africa in 1984.

Philip and Marjorie with their children Stanley and Lynne and little Robyn in front

They have two children Brent and Lauren. The Michels and Satills live in Sydney, NSW.

Philip and Marjorie followed their children and migrated to Sydney Australia 30 August 1992. Here again they involved themselves in the community participating actively in the Seniors Club, regularly attending shul services and functions, hosting family Shabbat dinners and playing bridge with friends. Sadly, for about the last ten years of his life Philip suffered from Dementia/Alzheimers. He continued to stay at home where Marjorie lovingly cared for him until he passed away 11 August 2003, 13 Av 5763.

As the inscription on Philip's tombstone so aptly put it, "He lived his life with courage and integrity" and he is lovingly remembered by his family and friends.

EULOGY OF PHILIP RUCH - 12 August 2003
Delivered by Rabbi Freedman

My friends – we gather together today to bid farewell to a remarkable man, so dearly loved and cherished by his family and so warmly respected by his friends. As we accompany Philip Ruch on his last journey – our thoughts turn automatically towards his family – and we trust that the Almighty will comfort those closest to him – his dear wife, Marjorie, his son Stanley, daughters Lynne and Robyn, of course with David and Ian – together with his precious grandchildren – Jonathan, Beth, Daniel, Gideon, Brent and Lauren. To you all, may we wish you Long Life and Please G-d – much joy in the future to overtake the sadness of this hour. May you only hold wonderful memories of your husband, father and grandfather.

I was standing in shul this morning – and while reciting the Shemoneh Esreh – the Amidah – I was struck by a contradiction – our Rabbinic sources make it very clear that while reciting the Amidah we must not allow our voice to be heard by anyone else. Lo Yashmia Kolo – we should not allow our voices to be heard – rather we should confine our prayers to our own hearts and pronounce the words only with our lips, just loud enough to be able to hear the words with our own ears.

Yet, standing there in shul this morning, I was acutely aware of the words in the Amidah – Shema Koleinu Hashem Elokeinu – Hear our voice O Lord our God – how can Hashem hear our voice when it is stilled, how can He hear our sounds when they are not emitted. And yet of course – Baruch Ata Hashem, Shomea Tefillah – somehow Blessed is God – for He is able to hear through the silence and among the whispers and listen to our prayers. Just as in the story of Elijah – when he discovered that God Almighty was not in the loud and vocal – storms and earthquakes and fires – but within Kol Demamah Dakah – inside the still silent voice – in other words the inner being of man – within our soul and within our psyche.

And in having these thoughts as I stood in shul – I thought of Philip, who for so many years now has been like that Kol Demamah Dakah – that still, silent voice, and I realized profoundly that while we could not hear his voice in these latter years – His Maker, His Creator, His God had been listening to him all the time and taking note of his prayers, his concerns and his welfare.

Unquestionably, in answering those prayers, that were so quiet, so quiet that none of us could hear them – God answered his prayers and sent Philip an angel – an exceptional and remarkable partner. Marjorie – you are an example to each and every one of us – your family and your friends for the most incredible patience and loyalty, love and devotion that you have displayed. May each of us merit a partner as you have been for Philip. And your children learnt well from you and the love and care that I personally have seen from the family in recent years and of course most strikingly in recent days has been quite awe-inspiring and humbling. I have seen the true meaning of Kibud Av Va'em – respecting Parents and Ahavat Habriyot – the love for a fellow human being.

In a sad way this world of silence began for Philip in his childhood – Born in 1911 in Pinsk, he was only a young boy when his parents died and left him and his brothers as orphans. Those who would normally be attentive to his voice – his own parents were taken from him at a tender age. But once again God was listening to prayers that no-one else could hear. For in an act of true Chesed, Isaac Ochberg – a South African Jewish philanthropist went to the Ukraine in 1921 and literally rescued 200 Jewish orphans – including Philip and his two brothers Aron and Sholem. They came to South Africa on the Edinburgh Castle where he was placed in the Cape Town Jewish orphanage and eventually he attended Cape Town High School.

Again – the unheard voice of Philip – resulted in him not completing school – but going to live in the country – to Douglas. But once again, incredibly, – where no one else was listening - God heard his prayers – and he met the Friedberg family who were to become his adoptive family. Years later in 1947 he left Douglas and returned to Cape Town –where not only he was successful in business, running a company right up until 1983, but much more importantly he met Marjorie in 1949 and they married in August 1950.

It is a sad irony that the last full day of shiva, next Sunday – would have been your 53rd wedding anniversary.

From such humble beginnings – Philip achieved so much – he was successful in business and he enjoyed a Shem Tov – a fine reputation amongst his colleagues. He was fastidious when it came to honesty and his word was his bond.

He had a long and fruitful marriage – he raised outstanding children whom we here in Kehillat Masada can call our friends – and he saw the next generation step forward – he was at Jonathan's Bar Mitzvah and Brent's too, and also Beth's Bat Mitzvah. It should not be overlooked that he gave back to the Jewish community and that he and Marjorie were leaders in the Claremont Shul in Cape Town. While Marjorie was head of the Ladies Guild – Philip ran the Building Committee of the shul – and as we can see from those in our shul who are currently heavily involved in our building program – it involves hours upon hours of time and effort until success is realised. And Philip did all of this with dedication, distinction and success.

Finally on a personal note, I will miss Philip very much – he was in shul every Shabbat – Marjorie bringing him and then ensuring that his friends on the men's side were there to look after him during the service. And also at my monthly shiur for the senior members of the community – he would come and sit, often with a relaxed smile on his face – maybe (hopefully) he found my voice soothing – and he would absorb words of Torah in my home.

May God be ever watchful over his soul, May Philip himself now act as a *Melitz Yosher* – as an intermediary on behalf of his family and ת נ צ ב ה

May his soul be bound up in the bond of eternal life – Venomar Amen.

SOLLY (SHOLEM) RUCHOCKI

Solly the youngest of the brothers, born 15 January 1913, was placed in the care of The Cape Jewish Orphanage after arriving in South Africa. He attended the Cape Town Central Boys School and in December 1924 received a prize in Std IVB for Diligence. He passed away aged 16 in April 1929 (16 Nissan 1929) in the Somerset Hospital.

Sholem Ruchocki – photo from Pinsk Travel Document

SOLLY'S LETTER

The letter following was written by Solly from the New Somerset Hospital to his brother Philip in April 1929, shortly before he died.

Unfortunately, Solly never recovered from his illness and passed away at the hospital on 26 April 1929 at the young age of 16. This was just five days after he wrote the letter to Philip. He was buried at Maitland Cemetery, Cape Town

New Somerset Hospital
Cape Town 21-4-29

My dear Brother Philip

Thanks very much for your letter of the 15th inst and for handsome allowance of 10/- enclosed.

I gave this money to Aaron to put in my 2nd Post Office Book in which I will now have saved £3.10/-

You must be anxious about my health; but, dear Philip there is little to worry about now. The fever has now thank God passed

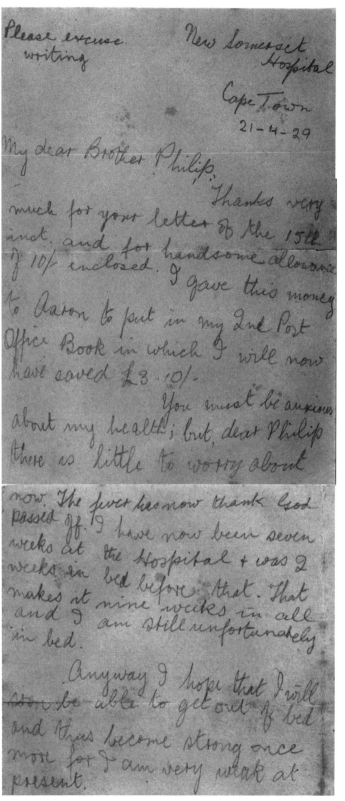

Solly's Letter

off. I have now been seven weeks at the hospital and was two weeks in bed before that. That makes it nine weeks in all and I am still unfortunately in bed.

Anyway I hope that I will soon be able to get out of bed and thus become strong once more for I am very weak at present.

I might inform you that this illness really started at Muizenberg through bad food and overwork with "Our Friend" a magazine we lately began to publish at Home.

Mr Ochberg told me that he would now let me return to the Orphanage on any account and so now I don't know where I'll be going to when I leave the Hospital. As I am still in bed I am not worrying about it.

You will most probably receive this letter on Pesach so I have the chance of wishing an enjoyable celebration of the Festival. I don't suppose you'll have a seder at Postmasburg so we will both be in the same boat for there is no seder.

I am sorry for not having written to you before but you can understand why. Now however, it is different. I get food from the Kosher kitchen and I hope to be getting better within a short time.

I now conclude with fondest love from

Solly

Solly's Letter

**IN LOVING MEMORY OF OUR DEAR
BROTHER SOLOMON RUCHOCKI WHO
PASSED AWAY ON 26 APRIL 1929
BORN 15 JANUARY 1913
MAY HIS DEAR SOUL REST IN PEACE**

The records below show that Zlata Samurina, aged 12, and her younger sister Sima Samurina, aged 10, came from Pinsk. They were the children of David and Esther who had both died from starvation and had witnessed many pogroms.

Isaac Ochberg rescued the children from an orphanage in Pinsk and took them to South Africa where they were placed in the care of The Cape Jewish Orphanage.

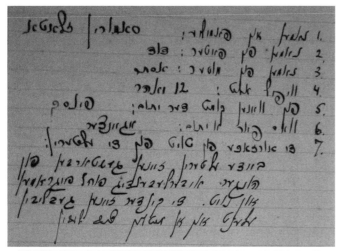

Photo of Zlata Samurina from Pinsk Travel Document

The Samurina family details as recorded on pages 39 and 41 of the register at the Cape Jewish Orphanage (Oranjia).

Pinsk Travel Document of Zlate Samurina
(This affidavit, written in Polish and issued by the Pinsk Magistrate with an individual photo, grants permission for the child to be placed in the care of Mr. Ochberg for the journey to South Africa.)

CHARLOTTE BERMAN (ZLATA SAMURINA)
Written by Aubrey Berman

My mother remembered having eight sisters and a brother who died in the forest from an acute attack of appendicitis. They were in hiding and could not reach a doctor. There was simply no medical supplies nor any medical assistance available.

My mother and her sister who were the youngest of the siblings were the fortunate ones as when Ochberg came to select orphans to escape a very good chance of death, he chose the youngest ones who would have less chance of survival if they had to fend for them selves in such a hostile environment. The older ones would have a better chance of survival in such harsh conditions.

When the ship docked in London my mother's sister Thelma said that someone wanted to adopt her in London but she would not be separated from her sister, so they did not force her to stay behind in London and leave her sister. All they had was each other and they wanted to remain close to each other. Life had been traumatic enough losing their entire family and they were not going to lose each other now after such a long ordeal.

Group Passport no 2
Zlata Samurina is no 8 on the list

Thelma and Charlotte (Sima and Zlata Samurina)

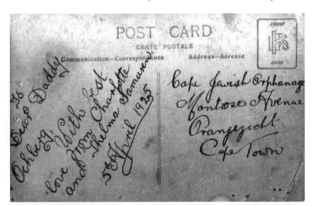

Message on the back of the photo of Thelma and Charlotte

My mother never spoke about her life before her arrival in South Africa and vaguely remembered being in a large ship that brought her to South Africa. She did at times talk about her life at the orphanage (Oranjia – The Cape Jewish Orphanage) where she lived and was educated.

At the age of 15 or 16 she was organised a job at a dress shop through the Orphanage as an assistant and later was taught to do certain alterations and taught how to become a seamstress. She later became more experienced and got a job as a seamstress at one of the leading fashion outlets in Adderley Street called Rejanes. At this stage she was being courted by my father and when she married him , her Unterferer was none other than "Daddy" Isaac Ochberg.

My Mother started sewing at home and doing alterations for private customers. She earned the same as when she worked for a boss but was still able to look after her children and do the housework while working to earn a living. When the customers started increasing she took on assistants who worked with her from the home as well until it outgrew the home and they rented a small shop to continue manufacturing on a larger basis. At this stage my father who had returned from military service after the end of the Second World War, joined her and went on the road looking for larger customers to take up the excess capacity. They were not financially highly successful but they earned a living and we were never short of anything that was necessary.

I attended the Oranjia 50th Anniversary celebrations with my Mother before they closed the Orphange and sold the property in favour of small family type units of families living together.

DESCENDANTS OF ZLATA SAMURINA

My mom had three children, all boys.

My eldest brother David was born in 1936 and passed away at the age of 63. He had three boys who are all married. Two of them, Lionel and Michael are still living in Cape Town, and one has two children and the other three children. The third son, Jonathan is living in Dallas, Texas and has one son and two daughters.

My older brother Solly, was born in 1939 and passed away aged 58. All his family are in Sydney Australia. He had two boys; the eldest Gary, had two girls and a boy while the other son, Anthony had two girls.

I have two boys currently living in San Diego and a girl living in Connecticut. My eldest son, Bradley is not married. My elder son Grant has two boys and a girl and my daughter Leigh has a boy and two girls.

OLDER SIBLINGS LEFT BEHIND

My mother always had a yearning to find out if any of her other siblings had survived and approached a tracing agency which they always referred to as HIAS, however I am not sure whether that was the correct name or not.

They traced a woman to a Kibbutz in Israel who was also an orphan from Russia from the same district with the same surname as theirs, but when questioned by the tracing agents, she would not cooperate with them and ran back to her room.

She could have been a sister but possibly out of fear was not interested in finding out if she had any living relatives.

They subsequently traced a women to New York that also fitted the possibility of being my mother's sister and when they discovered that she indeed was my mothers sister that she had not seen for 39 years, my parents went to America to meet her and all her family. I do not know how much older than my mother she was but she seemed much older from the photographs. Her married name was Sonia Falkowitz, nee Samurena, who had a daughter Esther who married an American named David Stein and lived in Long Island New York at the time.

Both my brothers made contact with them but I was very young at the time and did not have the opportunity of meeting them. Unfortunately both my parents and both my brothers have passed away and I have no one else left to ask as to their whereabouts other than them living somewhere in the States.

I immigrated to San Diego two years ago to be with my family when my wife passed away and have tried to trace them but have not had any success as I simply do not have enough information to track them down. It would be great meeting them and discussing the two families' histories which span over a century and would make an interesting story.

MY BOBBA CHARLOTTE
Written by Anthony Berman

My Bobba Charlotte often used to tell us that when they knew that the Kosacks were coming through the town they where made to hide in the woods, or sometimes under desks. She was never clear about it, and would change the subject if you asked further. She sometimes mentioned her sister that went to live in America, but without communication in those days she lost touch with memories. When I used to ask her why she ate the fish head, she said that it was because there were no bits to be left behind, we shouldn't waste any food.

She worked hard, loved us all a lot and always had a smile for all the grandchildren.

THELMA FRIEDMAN
Written by Dudley E Friedman

My mom was very bright and perceptive but she always had her background in her thoughts so we were never allowed to waste food and nothing was ever thrown away. She never spoke of her youth or always changed the subject. All in all I think her early life affected her and also influenced her greatly.

She was bright, shrewd, a good business person and very popular. She loved reading, sewing and knitting and even at the end when she was blind she would still be able to knit for charity I was always amazed how she could cast on and knit so fast and she even taught me.

She was also a difficult lady and could not tolerate fools and would say exactly what she felt sometimes sounding tactless, so you knew were you stood in my mom's opinion.

She tried to give us a happy and good childhood which I am very thankful for. She made many sacrifices I suppose like all good Jewish mothers and when she passed away I really did not expect to be so affected by my mother's death.

An older sister and other family left behind

Sima Samurina is the younger sister of Zlata whose life story is told in the previous chapter.

Sima Samurina's photo from her Pinsk Travel Document

Group Passport no 8
Sima is the 2nd girl in the middle row (arms folded and marked no 6)
sitting to the right of her friend Braindel Gesunterman

Cape Jewish Orphanage,
Montrose Avenue,
Oranjezicht,
Cape Town.

Dear Mr Ochberg,

I am just writing 4-7-22.
to you a few lines of English
because I do not know much
English, but I have written you
alot of Jewish. How are you
and your family keeping. All of
us at the orphanage are quite
well at present, Thank God.
Mr Maman told us that he receive
a letter from you and you
wrote that you arrived safely
(Please Turn Over.)

at London and I hope you will
arrive safely at Cape Town soon.
Now I must end my letter with
best love to you and all your
family from all of us here.
I remain,
Your loving friend,
Thelma Samurena.
My sister Charlotte Samurena
also sends her love to you.

Letter written by Thelma to Isaac Ochberg above and below

THELMA FRIEDMAN SIMA SAMURINA
Written by Estell (Friedman) Hammar

I remember a story my Mom told me.

Before Ochberg fetched the children my Mom told the story of when she and Bessie Morris (Braindel Gesunterman) where sick with dysentery and they were in hospital and had nothing to eat so her sister visited and gave them brown bread to eat which was forbidden to eat because of the dysentery. After eating the bread they recovered.

My mother said that Bessie and her were chosen to be part of the Ochberg orphans but said she would not go without her sister Charlotte.

My Mom never talked much about her youth. She used to say she loved the Friday nights at the Orphanage. Nellie Frankal and Zlote Dembo were her very good friends.

After leaving the Orphanage my mother lived in a boarding house in Oranjezicht and in the photo above I recognize my mother. She is the top row second from right and I think Charlotte is front row on the right. She was an apprentice hairdresser. She went on holiday to Durban by boat where she met my father, Arthur Friedman.

My parents were married on 15 October 1933. Charlotte who was already married to Nathan Berman at the time gave my mother away. My Mom married Arthur Friedman and they lived in Oranjezicht.

After their marriage they worked together in Woodstock. They had a Secondhand Furniture business called Southern Auctioneers. After five years of marriage they moved from

Arthur and Thelma

Oranjezicht to Muizenberg where I was born in 1943 and Dudley in 1936.

My Mom was very intelligent, funny and very open-minded and modern in her outlook on life. She worked all her life and loved playing bowls winning quite a few tournaments. In later years she volunteered at the Jewish Old age Home in Cape Town doing hairdressing.

When I was married I moved to Israel in 1973 and in 1977 my father died. Two years later my brother moved to London and in 1986 my mother immigrated to Israel.

Wedding of Thelma and Arthur Friedman – 1933

Estell, Dudley and Thelma in Israel - 1989

In Israel she stayed in a small flat on Moshav Regba where I lived and still live with my husband since 1973.

When my mother moved to Israel she met a member of the Moshav whose name is Mendel Glazer. His mother and her sister were in the orphanage in Johannesburg. His mother's sister's name was Zlata Dembo who was a good friend of Thelma - quite a coincidence.

While living on the Moshav in Israel she volunteered her help in our communal laundry. After a number of years her eyesight began failing her but she continued knitting baby clothes for her future great-grandchildren whom she never got to see and making knitted dolls. She was very independent to an extreme. My Mom passed away in 1998.

Our eldest son Steven

Thelma in her later years knitting

Robert and his wife Ayelet

THELMA'S DESCENDANTS

My married name is Estell Hammar. My husband's name is Leonard. We have three children Steven, Robert and Oren. Robert is married with two children; Tom and Aytan. Oren is married with one child Shai and Steven is still single.

Aytan and Tom – children of Robert and Ayelet

Estell and Leonard

Oren his wife Elinor and their daughter Shai

Chapter 82 – SIMON SANDAK-LEWIN

MY FATHER'S HOUSE
Written by Gloria Sandak-Lewin about her father,
Simon Sandak-Lewin

BACKGROUND

On 19 September 1921, Isaac Ochberg (1879-1938), a Ukrainian-born South African Jew, returned to Cape Town on the Edinburgh Castle with a group of about two hundred Jewish pogrom orphans whom he had found wandering, starving, traumatized and destitute, in post-World War I Eastern Europe.

At great personal risk, cost and effort, he had spent five months in Poland and the Ukraine, combing the countryside, determined to rescue as many Jewish children as possible, and personally searching for and selecting them wherever he could find them. My father was one of those children.

SYNOPSIS

The poem is in seven movements, each depicting an aspect of the children's hazardous journey from Eastern Europe to South Africa, and of their arrival here, and interweaving my father's personal story with the general historical background.

The movements are entitled:
I.   19 September 1921
II.   The Rape of Wlodawa
III.   The Arrival
IV.   The Pocket-Book
V.   The Adoption
VI.   Courtship and Marriage
VII.   The Meeting

MY FATHER'S HOUSE
I write your truth, your history

I. 19 SEPTEMBER 1921

1

A hard coming they had of it,
Just the worst time
For a journey, and such a long journey:
The ways cruel, and the weather sharp,
The iron heart of wartime.
And the children clamorous and tired,
Pale-cheeked, suffering from pallor,
And you one of them, ill,
Still rooting for berries and rats.
The shores of Danzig moved out from you,
The great ship shuddered and shook.
Wlodawa - forests of Wlodawa,
Minsk, Pinsk, River Bug,
And Lublin shadow of a town,

Great Warsaw, that war-walled city,
Where Pania Engel gave you warmth,
The queen of queens gave you light.
And the bunks hard and narrow,
And the children settle down to sleep.
Father Ochberg watches over you now,
The 'Man from Africa' kisses away your dreams.

2

Tate, tate, where are you?
I brought you a bowl of porridge,
I crept up to the prison wall,
I heard your voice behind bars.
But when I felt the lash of the Polish whip
I dropped the bowl, and ran into the nearby forest.
Did they feed you, *tate*, after that?
Did they give you the porridge that I dropped?

3

In the forests of Poland a blackbird flies from
                         tree to tree.
They are turning the hay now.
The rats are gnawing the berries
In the sun-lit forests of Poland,
The forests empty of children.

4

Only the best children they chose:
Those steady of eye
Those limber of wit
Those fired by the sun
Those striking for life:
You clamoured to survive:
They did not refuse you.

5

'We shall be sold into slavery!'
'The lions in the streets will eat us.'
'They will cast us into the sea.'
'We shall drown before we get there.'
And one small boy tried to shoot through a
                         porthole
To lose himself in the sea,
The angry vinegary sea.

6

'On their own feet they came', or by handcart,
Or carried on the shoulders of brothers and sisters,
Or in slow, overcrowded dirty trains,
Or huddled in cattle trucks trundling through Europe
(Having to relieve themselves there where they stood)
Towards Warsaw.   Then
By riverboat to Danzig
Where, on the Baltic, they boarded a London-bound
                         steamer.

'The Almighty keep us and save us,
The Almighty keep us and save us,
The Almighty will keep us and save us,
God Save the King!'

7

'"I am returning herewith Collective Passport No. 4074E, issued by the Government Commission at Warsaw on the 16th of August, 1921, containing the names of 21 minor children ..."'

They set off for Africa
('Africa' was on every child's lips)
You wore your apron with the others
(The chalky flour-bag apron that de-sexed you,
Issued alike to eager boys and girls).
Above the dirt-green multiple passport —
The multiple passport made out '"in quantity"' —
Rzeczpospolita Polska / République Polonaise —
The Polish eagle tongues his crownèd pride.
Row upon row of neat little girls and boys,
          arms solemnly folded,
(No smiling thumbnail sketch, with personal particulars)
Across a few, no.14, no.19, another numberless —
A typhus-ravaged face, its body couched in ticking,
Stares fixedly ahead, its fate unseeing —
A cross inked by some dutiful Polish official
Bars it forever from a land of freedom:
To die in the deathchambers, twenty years later.

8

The Poem of the Orphan on His Way to South Africa
(written by an anonymous Jewish child from the Ukraine)

Merciful Father in Heaven
Who in His mercy toward children left orphans
Forced to leave their homes
Has sent father Ochberg to make us citizens of South Africa
God blessed us that we found ourselves among good people
Our worries ended when we received the letter.
Our group, hundreds of children, would not be separated
[W]e would live as brothers!
A miracle will happen and when we grow up and stand
          on our feet
We will never forget the poor and needy. ...
We left behind us ruins when we started on our way
We took leave of our friends
And hoped that fate would allow
That we would live as Jews[.]
Father Ochberg came to rescue us [...]
We will live as Jews
And to Zion come ...

II. THE RAPE OF WLODAWA

1

'The earth was red and good for bricks
There was a watermill ... a steam-mill
There were twelve timber factories where we Jews worked
The timber went on barges down the Bug ...'

'I was born in Wlodawa in nineteen hundred and twelve.
I remember the red-brick houses, the peaked wooden roofs
I remember the River Bug — a big wooden bridge
On the other side of the bridge was a small town Wlodawka
It was a holiday town, I remember, there were forests of firtrees
I remember a hammock between the trees.
There were no Jews in Wlodawka.'

'I remember, in the town's centre, a large monument
          to the Czar ...
My mother used to repair fish nets.. she enjoyed that ...
We lived in Ulica Solna - the street of the Synagogue ...
The magistrate's court stood opposite our house ...
The statue was in the centre of the town.
Everyone raised his hat to the Czar's statue.'

Somewhere, in the distance, a roof burned ...

2

First there was you, Mojecki,
Author of nine blood-libels, of Jews as traitors to Poland,
Who believes that God rewards those who persecute Jews,
Who commends the measures of France, Spain and Germany:
You spread your thoughts with a fine poison-pen.

Then you, Miczyński, scurrilous lampoonist,
Who made Jews responsible   for
All   bad   things
In the kingdom of Poland, and of its people:
Desecrators of icons, profaners of Catholic festivals,
Implacable enemy of innocent Christians.

And you, Chmielnicki, 'Chmiel the Wicked',
You seventeenth-century Haman, you unripe Hitler,
Jew-butcher, responsible for this blood-sports holocaust:
100,000 killed, 300 communities:
Nemirov, Tulchin, Bar, Polonnaye, Lvov:
The twentieth day of Sivan was a bad day.

And not forgetting you, Petlyura, you murderous tyrant,
Atamàn, '*Batiushka*', ' "little father" ' of the Ukrainians,
' "Their apostle of liberty, their saviour" ',
Who personally ordered the terrible Proskurov pogrom
And met your fate in the streets of Paris with Schwarzbard.

3

Ashes of Sobibor, soil of Wlodawa
The cherries now
Bloom red in the *shul* where Jews have prayed for centuries
(They turned it into a grain-and-produce store)
Spiritual essences, essence of fire
Sweet *shtetl*
Where the great Yiddish writer Shalom Asch
Secretly came to barter books
To buy a rabbi's signature for his pains
But could not buy or have at any price:
Ashes of Sobibor, soil of Wlodawa

III. THE ARRIVAL

A flat bulbous shadowy outcrop of rock,
So flat we could eat off it,
Rising suddenly in a swathe of light;
With all the pinpoints of Cape Town shining right up to it
And all the people waiting at the quayside to greet us
And Witke, dear old Witke, waiting at the quayside,
Waiting with horse and cart, patiently waiting
To take us to our new homes, always waiting.
We were 'child guests', then, remember, no longer orphans
We 'foreigners' wore peaked caps, neat grey suits:
Our first words 'Thank you', 'please', 'bananas' ...
Africa...

IV. THE POCKET-BOOK

Somewhere in this giant plastic bag
I found your notebook
This little green notebook in which you jotted down
                          your history;
Your first careful words in an alien tongue.
These pages give the clue to you, the key
                    to your childhood.

You could not even write your name – (you tried out
                          spellings)
You tried your name three ways, three times
(Hastily you wrote as best you could).
These pages give the clue to you, the key
                    to your childhood.

'War' was your first word : 'the Russians fled'
'The Germans came' – you all fled – lost your parents –
'Yankiel taken as a soldier: mother died'.
You returned to Wlodawa – became a shepherd boy:
Your brother Itsca died.
In summer you dug potatoes, dragged water in winter
Slept on the floor at Motlan, one night in the
                      Bais Hamidrash.
War again. The Poles fled. The Bolsheviks came and fled.
You flee with your father to Malaritah, starving of hunger.
The Poles drive out the Bolsheviks – a pogrom:

Ballachofzas kills many Jews – cuts their beards and
                    flesh off
Kills many Jews   you escape   take some food
                    to your father
I took some food to my father   a soldier hit me
Sjambokked me till I bled   my father was swollen
They released him from prison   my father went to his
                    brother
He was swollen   he went to his brother
                  he stayed there a short while
He stayed there a while   he was swollen
                  he stayed with his brother

Your father died

                It was Shevat Shevat -
Your father's Yahrzeit is Rosh Chodesh Shevat 14.

Isaac Ochberg came. He took you away to Warsaw
 Your brother Nachman was then a shepherd in Briss.)
You boarded the ship for Cape Town nine weeks later
You stayed at the Cape Jewish Orphanage about one month
You were adopted in nineteen hundred and twenty-one.
These yellowed pages give the clue to you, the key
                    to your childhood.

V. THE ADOPTION

These silver candlesticks
These candlesticks testify
All that remains of those times,
All that remains behind.

A solid man
A solid heavy man, 'one of the old type of Yidden',
Moshe Lewin, housepainter, husband, grandpa,
Sucking peppermint drops as he puffs up the hill
Or sipping sweet-sour tea on the red polished stoep:
They have ghosted him into eternity
He lies now in an unknown nameless grave.

We used to beg him to take us to the 'bioscope':
'But it is *Shabbes*,' he pleaded, 'it is *Shabbes*.'
We plucked his sleeve to hurry faster, faster.
He wheezed down past Abrahamson's store,
              down Upper Mill Street.
The nicotine stains stuck fast in his soft white stubble.
They have ghosted him into eternity
He lies now in an unknown nameless grave.

'Hy het in sy ouderdom met meneer Mankowitz
               in sy huis saamgebly.'
'He was very lonely – he never asked for charity.'
'He was short of money – always short – that's why
              he went to Johannesburg.'
His wife, Hannah Hinde, an unknown form,
              an unknown entity:
Where did he come from, where, which was his shtetl?
Kovno, Legum, no, no one seems to know for certain:
Maitland, Pinelands, where, where was he buried?

And you, father, you who took the giant stride
From Warsaw to Cape Town
Shepherd — to schoolboy
War orphan — adopted son;
Who with earnest endeavour grappled with the
              English language —
'Describe a shooting accident and how you
              helped your friend'
(*Shoot, shoot* – 'Yankiel taken as a soldier')
'Do not write more than 25 lines in all'
('War again - the Poles fled - the Bolsheviks
              came and fled').
'Write down on your answer paper the opposite words: ...
"I must *engage* a cook ..." ("We were starving of hunger")
"The culprit *denied* his guilt ..."('They killed many people') '

Now comes the hard part, having to pay your end
              of the bargain,
Having to support and bear your elderly adoptive parents:
Now you are lost amidst figures digits and numbers
Now you are crushed beneath papers books and files.
They have ghosted him into eternity
He lies now in an unknown nameless grave.

VI. COURTSHIP AND MARRIAGE

The house implodes with bitter conflagrations
Frenzied shouts jostle darkly in the air
A brass Egyptian table stands there:
haunting sideways figures, sloping eyes
Glance sideways into eternity, dreaming of death.
Impressed in brass, these slender Egyptian women
Smile enigmatically at another world.
I love Mummy and Daddy:
A child's innocent graffito is shocked into punishment
Children whisper secrets in the yard
A door closes; pull down the windows; shut in the uproar:

Silence lies thick above my father's house.

VII. THE MEETING

Two brothers, twinned in a single bed,
Womb babies,
Whisper and cuddle like two young mischievous children,
Exchanging secret vows in the deep narrow bed,
And breaking silence far into the night.

And the years fall away, and they talk, and they
                            cover the years:
Write, brother, write, why do you never write?
I thirst, thirst for news of you
(They disappeared in Sobibor)

'Distant brother, cherished unknown sister:
 I want to acquaint you with my present position:
 Our house burnt down: I had to move with my family:
 In this new place I haven't a roof of my own.
 Give me some help; send me some assistance. ...
 Summer is coming; the work is very scarce. ...
 I hope that you will not refuse my urgent request.
 Your brother Nachman (1934).'
(They disappeared, disappeared in Sobibor)

'Dear Mrs Grosskopf, thank you for your letter,
 Thank you for telling me you saw my only brother
 In the Wetzlar Camp. ... It is twenty-nine years
                            since we met. ...
(No doubt he has told you the story of our lives. ...)
I've been trying to bring him and his family
                    to South Africa,
 So far without success. ...
 Thank you once again for all your care and trouble. ...
 Yours sincerely. ... (1948)'

Write, brother, write, why do you never write?
(They disappeared in Sobibor)

In an old string bag, tears streaming down your face,
You put our good discarded second-hand clothes
Packed neatly, snugly, folded lovingly,
Weeping as you did so, weighed it, inked on the address,
Stitched the coarse rank hessian at the top:
I helped you pack the parcels, fold the clothes.

Write, brother, write, why do you not write?
I thirst, thirst for news of you.

'Thank you, brother, thank you for the favour.
 I can let you know about the things you sent us.
 For my wife I kept the sweater with white embroidery,
                            the lady's handbag,
 Some of the things I sent to our Motlan. ...
 (You suffer with your eyes – you work too late, perhaps;
 And may God help that you should receive a healing. ...)'
(They disappeared in Sobibor:
Motti, Yankiel, the children, and the rest ...)

POSTSCRIPT

'Your father was always hungry'

'He was inclined to be *frum*'

'He was very small when I knew him,
                            very thin'

'He was always alone
    Lonely and alone'

Jeszcze Polska nie zginęła, kiedy my żyjemy!
Poland is not lost as long as we live!
Poland is not lost as long as we live!
Poland is not lost as long as we live!

I remember nothing
I remember only the image of an empty house
                            9 October, 1983.

Simon Sandak-Lewin

388

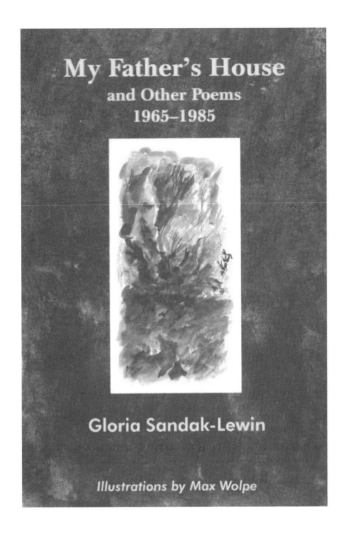

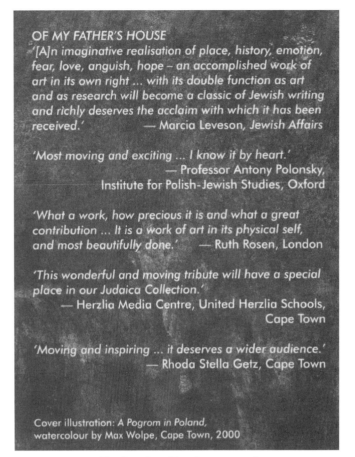

The front and back covers of
MY FATHER'S HOUSE and Other Poems 1965-1985
by Gloria Sandak-Lewin

SIMON SANDAK-LEWIN
(SIMCHA BEN HERZL SANDAK)
Written by Gloria Sandak-Lewin

My father was born Simon Sandak (Simcha ben Herzl Sandak) in 1910 and came from Wlodawa (Poland) on the River Bug. He was the son of Herzl and Golda (née Rossman) and had four older brothers, Mottel, Yankel, Itzchak and Nachman. Of the family only he and Nachman survived.

Herzl Sandak, his father, was imprisoned following a pogrom. He was severely beaten in prison and passed away three weeks after being released.

Golda died of heartbreak on hearing that one of her sons, Yankel, was being conscripted into the Russian Army.

The oldest brother, Mottel, about 20 years Simon's senior, and his family probably perished in Sobibor.

Yankel was conscripted into the Russian army for 25 years. He came on a brief visit when their mother Golda died and was never heard of again

Itzchak probably died of poverty and starvation.

Nachman, after much pain and travail, managed to make his way to Israel in 1949 after being in a Displaced Persons camp.

Simon was one of the Ochberg Orphans and unfortunately, contrary to the policy of Isaac Ochberg, who did not want to separate siblings, his brother Nachman was left behind or chose to remain behind in Poland.

My father was very ill at the time of the departure of the Orphans and had to persuade Isaac Ochberg to take him on board. Miraculously he recovered during the voyage and arrived in Cape Town on 19 September 1921.

He remained in the Oranjia Orphanage, Cape Town, for one month and was apparently so traumatized by his experiences in Eastern Europe that he was almost immediately adopted by very poor but kind-hearted Litvaks, Moshe and Anna Lewin, who had no children.

Although he was, from school reports, a very bright student, he had to leave school in standard 7, aged approximately 14, in order to support his elderly adoptive parents. He incorporated the surname of his adoptive parents into his name and became Simon Sandak-Lewin.

He became a registered Public Accountant and was Founder of the Faculty of Accountants of South Africa, as well as Founder of the South African Association of Certified Secretaries. He had a small accounting practice and an insurance brokerage, which in later years my brother Harold incorporated into his practice. He married Naomi Biall, daughter of Max Biall (Moshe – a Kohen) and Hilda Mary Biall (née Ritevsky) in about 1933.

Max (Moshe Biall), my maternal grandfather, came from Vilna and was apparently a talented violinist who played at weddings and on festive occasions before his violin was stolen. In South Africa he had various occupations: a smous, highly respected by the Afrikaans farmers with whom he traded, a photographer, and an hotelier running the very clean and antiseptic strictly kosher hotel, the Rose and Crown, in District Six.

Max was a Kohen, strictly halachic and very much involved in Shul Activities and became chairman of the Shul Committee planning the construction of the Schoonder Street Shul. (commonly known as the Round Shul).

I did not know my maternal grandmother from Lithuania, Hilda Mary Biall (Neé Ritevsky) as she passed away shortly after I was born; but by all accounts she was a refined, cultivated and genteel lady whom my father loved.

SANDAK - LEWIN, Simon (Sandy), F.S.A.A. (I.), B.Com., M.Com., F.A.I.A. (Lond.) F.F.C.S. (Eng.), F.I.A.C., F.A.C.S. (S.A.), M.C.I.A.(Lond.), Accountant and Auditor. Son of Herschel and Golda Sandak. Educated at Normal College and South African College Schools, Cape Town. Director of Companies, Commissioner of Oaths for the Magisterial area of the Cape. Was Senior Audit Clerk to a firm of Certified Accountants, London; in 1928 commenced practising as Public Accountant and Auditor. Vice-President of the British Society of Commerce; Registrar of the S.A. Association of Certified Secretaries; Founder, General Secretary and Treasurer of the Faculty of Accountants of South Africa; Founder of the S.A. Association of Certified Secretaries; representative in the Republic of S.A. for the Incorporated Association of Cost and Industrial Accountants (Lond.), Society of Commercial Accountants, British Society of Commerce and the Faculty of Secretaries; for many years served on the Council of the Institute of Accountants of S.A., Limited; for several years was Hon. Secretary of the Association of International Accountants (Lond.). Member of the Valkenburg Bowling Club; runner-up, Western Province Maccabi Association, final bowling tournament "Paddy" Purwitzky Cup, 1953. During World War II served with the South African Forces in 22nd Battalion C.D.C. Married, has one son and two daughters. Recreations: Bowls, swimming, walking, reading. Add.: 205 Costa Brava, Beach Road, Sea Point, Cape.

South African Jewry 1967-68

My father Simon Sandak-Lewin and my mother Naomi had three children: Harold, Gloria and Hilda.

Harold was a Chartered Accountant for 25 years and then went into the property business. He married Helga Fabian and had three children, Jonathan, Linda and Mark.

Gloria, after teaching at Herzlia High School and tutoring and lecturing part-time at the University of Cape Town, became a poet and writer. She married Robert Herzl Kaplan and had one son, Gad Simeon. They were divorced in 1985.

Gloria is the author of the long historical poem about Isaac Ochberg, *My Father's House* (1985, 1997) and the poetry collection *My Father's House and Other Poems* (2000), as well as a collection of short stories entitled *A Separate Life. Tales of a Woman Estranged*.

Hilda, my sister, became a very well-known opera singer with the Cape Performing Arts Council (CAPAB). She also specializes in a variety of folk music, including singing in Hebrew, Yiddish, Ladino, French, Russian, Turkish, Italian and Afrikaans and accompanying herself on the piano accordion. Hilda never married.

A younger Simon

Simon and Naomi

Naomi and Simon with their children: Gloria, Harold and Hilda

Afternoon tea at my parents' house in Three Anchor Bay, on the occasion of Harold Sandak-Lewin's 18th birthday.
Back: Harold Sandak-Lewin third from left Middle: Simon Sandak-Lewin on left; Naomi Sandak-Lewin second from right
Front row (L-R): Hilda and Gloria Sandak-Lewin, a maternal cousin Marion Kasimov and Helga Fabian, Harold's girlfriend

Wedding of Gloria Sandak-Lewin and Robert Herzl Kaplan
Isaac and Jesse Kaplan, Robert Herzl Kaplan, Gloria,
Naomi Sandak-Lewin (née Biall) and Simon Sandak-Lewin

Hilda Sandak-Lewin
as a young woman

Gad Simeon Kaplan
son of Gloria Sandak-Lewin

Harold and Helga Sandak-Lewin, with their son Jonathan,
graduating with a B.Social Science degree (UCT).
(He also has a B.Compt. (Honours) (UNISA).

Chapter 83 – FEYGA SCHRIER (FANNY LOCKITCH)

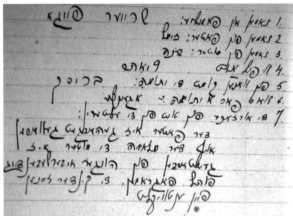

The Schrier family details as recorded on pages 127 and 129 of the register at the Cape Jewish Orphanage (Oranjia).
1 Names and surname: Yakov and Feiga Schrier
2 Father: Ziml 3 Mother: Brachah 4 Ages: 11 and 9 years
5 From where: Brisk 6 How orphaned: Both parents
7 General Comments: Father killed during the War.
The mother died of hunger, experiencing many pogroms.
The children are   and well developed.

GROUP PASSPORT THREE
Feiga Schrier is number 21 on the list
Feiga is in the front row third from the left
(Jacob Schrier is number 16 on Group Passport Two)

Soon after her arrival in South Africa Feyga was adopted by the Solomon Family of Palmer Road Muizenberg – see adoption papers below..

Fanny was the spokesperson for all the children and their informal leader and she gave many many years of service to Oranjia.

CAPE JEWISH ORPHANAGE ADOPTION CONTRACT *of Feygala Schrier by the Solomon Family*

THIS INDENTURE,

Made and entered into at Cape Town, in the Province of the Cape of Good Hope, in the Union of South Africa, on this the 25th day of the month of November in the Year One Thousand, Nine Hundred and Twenty-one (1921), between :—

ISAAC OCHBERG

in his capacity as President for the time being of the CAPE JEWISH ORPHANAGE,

(hereinafter styled and referred to as "THE said Orphanage") of the One part,

and *Samuel Solomon*

of Palmer Road

Muizenberg

(hereinafter styled and referred to as "the party of the other part.")

WHEREAS the said society has brought into this country from Central Europe certain male and female children said to be orphans, for the purpose either that such children shall be housed, maintained, supported and educated by the Jewish Community of South Africa, or, that such children shall be given out and placed with such person or persons who shall care to adopt any such children, as the said Society shall decide,

AND WHEREAS the said Society has assumed the guardianship of the said children,

AND WHEREAS the Party of the Other Part has applied to the said Society for the adoption of certain of the said children,

AND WHEREAS the said Society, after due and careful investigation, has come to the conclusion that the Party of the Other Part is a fit and proper person to adopt such child(ren)

Now therefore these presents Witnesseth :—

THAT the said Society does hereby give to and place with the Party of the Other Part certain child(ren) named *Feygala Schrier*
of the children hereinbefore referred to, under and subject to the following conditions :—

1. The Party of the Other Part does hereby adopt the said child(ren) and undertakes and binds himself take the said child(ren) into his home to treat the same as his own, and at his own expense hereafter to properly maintain, support and educate such child(ren).

2. Notwithstanding anything hereinbefore to the contrary contained, it is hereby distinctly understood and agreed that should at any time hereafter the said Society or any authorised Committee thereof, be of opinion that the said child is not being properly supported, maintained and educated or upon the breach of any term or condition of this Agreement on the part of the party of the other part, the said Society shall have the right immediately and without the necessity of any legal proceedings whatsoever, to take back the said child(ren) and in such event the Party of the Other Part does hereby authrise and empower the said Society, or its representative to enter upon the premises where the child(ren) may for the time being be, and to take and remove the said child(ren) therefrom.

3. The said Society shall have the right of ceding this Agreement so far as the Society is concerned, to the South African Jewish Board of Deputies or other organisation.

4. It shall be competent for any person duly authorised by the Society at any time or from time to time to see the child(ren) and ascertain that the child has been duly and properly maintained, clothed, fed and educated.

5. The Party of the Other Part shall not remove the child(ren) from the Union of South Africa except upon a notice in writing to and the written consent of the Society given not less than one month prior to the said contemplated departure. Anything to the contrary herein before contained notwithstanding, it shall be competent for the Society to with-hold its consent and to require the return of the children to its care and custody, in case of such contemplated departure of the Party of the Other Part. Any contemplated change of address of the Party of the Other Part within the Union shall be notified to the Society in writing from time to time.

6. The Party of the other part shall forthwith cause an Insurance on his life to be taken in a Society of standing in the sum of £   Sterling, in favour of the child(ren), and of the Society jointly, falling due on the   birthday of the said child(ren), and shall make payment of all premiums due thereunder and otherwise comply with and fulfil all the terms and conditions of the said policy. Should the Party of the other Part at any time fail to make payment of any premium, it shall be competent for the Society to do so and require payment forthwith. The obligation upon the Party of the Other Part in regard to the provisions of this last mentioned clause shall be and remain of full force and effect even in the event of the said child(ren) being taken from his custody by virtue of and under the conditions of this Contract.

7. It is a condition precedent to this Agreement that the Party of the Other Part shall take all requisite steps for the said child(ren) to receive all necessary instruction so that the said child(ren) may be brought up as a good Jew(s) or Jewess(es). For that purpose, it (they) shall be instructed in a traditional history, religious rites, and all other ceremonies ordinarily or properly taught to a child in a Jewish home; and the home of the Party of the other Part shall be regulated by Jewish Ideas and customs. The child(ren) shall be instructed in Hebrew and otherwise all necessary steps shall be taken for the confirmation (Bar Mitzvah) and otherwise for the child(ren).

8. It shall not be competent for the Party of the other part at any time to alter the name of the child(ren) adopted under this Indenture, but it shall be permissible for them to add the name of the adopting father as one of the christian names, so that the child(ren) to be adopted may be known as *Feygala Schrier Solomon*

THUS DONE and signed at Cape Town aforesaid on the day and in the month and year first aforewritten in the presence of the subscribing witnesses.

Solomon

As witnesses :

1.   *Jenny Solomon*

2.   *Rose Solomon*

FANNY LOCKITCH REMEMBERS

'I was born, Fayga Schrier in the town of Voronesz, which came into the news during the Second World War, but I hardly remember anything of that. My father, who was in the Russian Army died in a gas attack, while my mother passed away during the 1918 influenza epidemic.

Somebody put me into an orphanage in Brest-Litovsk, where the Germans and the Soviet had signed the 1917 Peace Treaty. I was only a little thing, but my brother Jack, two years older, now living in Salisbury in Rhodesia, was also there, and that made the placc a little more homely for me.

'Although the war was over, we were suffering from lack of coal, lack of clothes, from lack of food and from lack of care. To give an idea of conditions, I can remember how we had the Russians in the city at one moment, and a few days later the Poles. Looking out of the Orphanage windows, one could see some of the hand-to hand battles with bayonets, and the corpses lying in the street that led up to the fortress.'

Several hundred children in the orphanage, as well as those looking after them, depended for survival upon the famous Jewish-American organisation, the Joint Distribution Committee, which was again to do such wonderful work in the struggle against Hitlerism about 20 year later.

'One day, we heard that a 'Man from Africa' was coming. He was going to take some of us away with him and give us a new home on the other side of the world. Nearly all the orphans had lost both parents, many of them in pogroms, on the Ukrainian border. One poor little boy, who afterwards came to South Africa and is now a successful man in Johannesburg, had his hand hacked off by some ruffian.'

'Among us children the news aroused mixed feelings. We all liked the idea of going to a beautiful new country, but we also heard stories of robbers and wild animals, and that we might be eaten by lions. However, when Mr Ochberg appeared, with his reddish hair and cheery smile, we all took a great liking to him and soon called him 'Daddy'. He would spend hours talking to us, making jokes and generally cheering us up'.

Almost the worst problem confronting the visitor was how to make his choice from the vast number of destitute boys and girls. In the end he decided to choose eight children from each institution, to make up a total of 200 for which he had sufficient funds.

Since the Union Government had laid down that any children coming must be in good health, this demanded a very careful selection. Only full orphans, ie those who had lost both parents, were accepted, and then only if they were reasonably intelligent. Those suffering from mental defects were immediately eliminated, and in the words of one worker, 'the cream of each orphanage was picked.'

'How well I remember the scare stories that went around. 'We will be thrown into the sea', was one. Another said, 'We would be sold to the natives as slaves,' and a third, 'we might be eaten by cannibals'.

Fanny Lockitch 1961

SPOTLIGHT ON FANNY LOCKITCH
Written by Ernest Tivel
Cape Jewish Chronicle August 1995

Many factual articles and interviews, all steeped in praise, have been published over the years about our well-known Cape Town personality, Fanny Lockitch, whose life has been so closely bound up with Oranjia from the day she arrived in South Africa. Many accolades have been paid to her magnificent work in the Cape Town community. There are however special aspects of her life that are worth remembering.

Chance plays a major part in all our lives and it was chance that brought little Fanny to South Africa. In the 1920s civil war was raging in Russia and Jews were being massacred in their thousands day after day. Those who managed to survive died later in the concentration camps.

What chance did a mite like Fanny have to survive in such hopeless circumstances? No chance or very little. But a miracle was about to unfold. 'Daddy Ochberg' appeared on the scene and, after extraordinary efforts, he managed to rescue 200 Jewish children and bring them to South Africa. To make 'Ochberg's List' required certain qualities. You had to be in good health. You had a certain degree of intelligence and you had to have a pair of appealing eyes. Little orphan Fanny made the *List* and arrived in Cape Town in September 1921. She went to live in Oranjia with a number of other destitute Jewish orphans.

Even without parents, life for the orphans at Oranjia was neither sad nor deprived. In the words of Fanny Lockitch, 'It was a miracle that we were alive and we were pleased to be living in a warm, safe house with a bath and food. Here people were so kind and we were like a big family of brothers and sisters'.

Fanny left Oranjia in 1935 to marry Hymie Lockitch. However her relationship with the Home did not end there. Once she had brought up her family she returned to Oranjia as an honorary worker and her dedicated efforts there over some 55 years, particularly in regard to her extraordinary fund-raising abilities, were so much appreciated that she was made an Honorary Life Member and subsequently Honorary Life Chairlady.

Fanny has raised a small 'empire' of her own in Cape Town. She has three sons. The eldest bobby, married to Gillian is a Chemical Engineer and they have three children. The next son is Barry, a Chartered Accountant, married to Carole, with four children, and there is Brin, the youngest, married to Sharida, with two children. He is a Body Stress Release practitioner.

There is a total of fifteen in Fanny's empire. It is very likely that the family often looks back in grateful appreciation at that moment in time long ago when Fanny was chosen to join *Ochberg's List.*

INTERVIEW OF FANNY LOCKITCH
By Noreen Alexander

Noreen Alexander
Deliverance from persecution is not anything new to the Jewish people. In fact, it was one of the major factors that led to the founding of the Cape Jewish Orphanage which has a most interesting history dating back to 1921 as I learnt when I talked to Fanny Lockitch, who has been involved with the Orphanage for over forty years.

Fanny Lockitch
The Orphanage actually started in Cape Town far earlier, but we really start from 1910. Now you know that in 1910 the Union was formed and people were looking forward to a more prosperous time and, of course, the Jews started thinking about their destitute people, particularly the children, and it started really in a very strange way. In the village of Piketberg, three Jewish children, two boys and a girl, about the age of eight or nine, had been living in the care of a Coloured Family since their parents' death. They found them working at the back of an hotel – washing bottles and glasses for the bar! Later, on a farm in Namaqualand, they came upon another little boy, of about the same age, in a dreadful state of neglect. These children were immediately brought to Oranjia, and this is how the Orphanage started.

After that of course, they started accumulating children from all over and this led up to the big influx of the two hundred children from the pogrom stricken areas of Europe in 1921. This was our biggest, biggest helping hand that the Jewish community is very proud of.

Now you know at that time the bloodbath of Europe came to a close. The Csarist Russia Revolution was over and the now half forgotten Spanish influenza which carried away more victims than even the First World War had done, that also was over, yet the fighting went on! Civil War was raging in Poland and elsewhere and after the crash of the Czarist regime, rival armies were fighting for control and law and order was rapidly melting away. Poor at the best of times, owing to the oppression to which they had been exposed for generations the condition of the Jew in what had been Russia became even worse. Famine over the vast areas was followed by epidemics of typhoid and other diseases. In this misery ancient antagonism came to the surface. Polish and other peasants joined forces with the reactionary officers and troops to massacre whatever Jew came in their way. Pogroms were reported almost daily, of which the full details and numbers will never be known.

In despairing letters smuggled through the enemy lines, survivors asked their kinsmen anywhere in the world for immediate help. A great surge of pity and anger swept the Jewish communities. As details of the position leaked out, the tragedy of the situation in Europe became clearer. No fewer than 400 000 Jewish orphans were known to be destitute in Russia. South Africa then decided to bring some of the war victims to the Union, particularly the children. No-one was more in sympathy with the scheme than Daddy Ochberg, who is really synonymous with this whole project, even as grown-up people today, we refer to him by no other name than 'Daddy Ochberg', because to some of our children he is the only Daddy they could ever remember.

He immediately cabled to Dr Jochelman, President of the Federation of Ukranian Jews in Britain, offering whatever help South Africa could give. Dr Jochelman replied expressing his thanks and adding that the organisation was prepared to bring to London any children that could be saved and then hand them over to a South African Committee. A further question arose – would the Union Government create any difficulties in admitting the children? Daddy Ochberg contacted the Prime Minister, General Smuts, and Dr Patrick Duncan, the Minister of Interior, who granted permission to land without restriction, as many youngsters as could be saved, but of course, they had to be in perfect health. They had to have a degree of intelligence. Any little child that showed the slightest defect was immediately rejected, but of course he only had enough funds for two hundred children. In March 1921, Daddy Ochberg departed for this responsible and by no means unhazardous journey. He arrived there and believe me, what confronted him and how the man came through, I don't know, because he was so ill after a time that it was only our prayers that brought him back to life. He had to go through forests infested with bandits. He was strange in the country and of course, there was a Civil War raging in this country still. It wasn't settled. Anyhow, there were so many children that to make a choice was virtually impossible, until he decided that he would take eight children from each institution.

He took children from Minsk, Pinsk, Vladivostock, Stanislav, Brest-Litovsk, Warsaw, Lamberg, all over. Eventually he gathered the two hundred children. They didn't have any more funds. He would have saved more and I wish to God he would have, because the rest must have perished 20 years later under the Hitler regime – no doubt. He really snatched us from the jaws of death you can say, because, if we hadn't died then from famine and disease, we would have perished 20 years later in the gas chambers.

Anyhow, he managed to collect these children and we were all sent off to Warsaw. Warsaw was the headquarters of all the children that came from the various towns and there we met a very wonderful woman, who became a legend with us children, she was called Pania Engel – Pania means 'Madam' in Polish, and I remember we used to line up in a row and go to her every afternoon for a midday meal, and she gave Daddy Ochberg great assistance.

After that, he managed to get people to help. People from that country who knew the area, who knew where to look for the children and things became a little bit easier. But it wasn't all that easy. Disease broke out amongst the children, they got a very terrible eye disease called Trachoma and it delayed the actions, and Daddy Ochberg became very ill and that delayed things too, but anyway, after some time everything was ironed out and we were on our way.

The 'Great Trek' began!

We went down from Warsaw to Danzig. In Danzig we boarded a little steamer which brought us to England. In England we were taken over by other people, although Daddy Ochberg was the Chief of course. There I remember, we were taken into a huge hotel, and the first thing we had to do, was to sing 'God Save the King' as a mark of appreciation to our visitors, and of course, none of us knew any English, and we really massacred that song, but we sang it nevertheless. Also the first words we were taught were 'thank you very much', but we didn't say that – we had a girl called Barmuch, and we used to say 'dank you barmuch' and that helped us a lot. But, I must say when we finally got onto the boat to go to South Africa, everybody was really very kind to us. Daddy Ochberg was on the boat and he managed to get a Mr and Mrs Maman, who became the Principal and Matron of our Home, and with the two hundred children, he travelled, and I want to tell you that the children used to surround him – he was like God to us. If he could move one inch it was quite an achievement. We did not let him move once we got hold of him. I don't think there has ever been a man alive that had so much affection from so many children as that man had, because to us he was really our saviour.

Finally we arrived – well, that I'll never forget. In the early dawn when our boat, the Edinburgh Castle landed in Cape Town with all the lights shining right up to the Table Mountain, and all the people of Cape Town waiting at the quayside for us, the wonderful reception they gave us, it really made us feel at home because we came with very mixed feelings. There were so many stories told; we would be sold; we would be thrown into the sea, but really Daddy Ochberg made all the difference. Anyhow, when we came here we were soon absorbed into the Jewish community. We started learning English and I must say our children, nearly all of them, made good. We can look back with pride at what we have achieved. Amongst our past boys we have given to this country Doctors, Lawyers, Accountants, Architects, and many well respected leaders in Commerce and Industry. Our girls too have achieved high honours in the field of communal work. Hundreds of children have gone through the portals of Oranjia.

Noreen Alexander
What sort of children in fact do you take nowadays?

Fanny Lockitch
Well, we were children who were complete orphans who had an early foundation of love. But I must say today, it's mostly from broken homes. We are told, inaccurately, that nothing can replace parental love. It is true, nothing can replace parental love at its best, but there are many broken homes where children are neglected, overlooked and unwanted and these children find in Oranjia the love and understanding they have never known.

Noreen Alexander
Do you take children from all over South Africa?

Fanny Lockitch
Yes, we take children from all over South Africa. We take children from all walks of life, and our primary aim is to make them not only good Jews and Jewesses, but first class citizens of this country, because when they are old enough to leave us, we like them to go out with a proper feeling of confidence and a sense of responsibility which I have proved to you they have done.

We are really proud of what we are doing and as I say, a lot of thanks is due to the public, to the Committee too, because without them we could not achieve the high standards that we can so proudly show.

MY MOTHER FANNY LOCKITCH
Brin Lockitch who sent in most of the news cuttings writes

Fanny was determined, dominating, self-assured, confident, conceited, kind, rude, full of chutzpah, full of nonsense a lot of the time, sporty, humorous, a character of note and an incredible woman.

She very definitely left an indelible footprint.

MESSAGE FROM MRS FANNY LOCKITCH CHAIRLADY ORANJIA – 1961

In this, the fiftieth anniversary of Oranjia, those who work for the home are filled with a justifiable sense of pride.

Our children are drawn from all walks of life and our primary aim is to make them not only good Jews and Jewesses, but also first class citizens so that, when they reach the age when they must leave us, they will go out into the world with a proper feeling of confidence and a sense of responsibility. Among our past boys we have given to the country many Doctors, Lawyers, Architect and Accountants besides well-respected leaders in Commerce and Industry. Many of our girls, too, have achieved high honours in the field of communal work. Hundreds of children have passed through the portals of Oranjia and nearly all have made good – therein lies our best and only reward.

I want to thank my executive, my enthusiastic ladies' committee and the general committee as well as the public for the co-operation and support that they have always given me – without their assistance we could not possibly achieve the results that we can so proudly show. They all realise that the welfare of our children is the concern of the whole Jewish community and not only of the few who serve on our committee. I pray that all who have assisted us in our work may be blessed with good health and long life so that their children and their children's children may never know what it is to be bereaved at an early age.

By GILL TURNBULL
Staff Reporter

"When you're a small child alone in the world, the most important thing is to educate yourself — be the best there is. Then people will recognise you and you become somebody".

MEET Fanny Lockitch who with 200 other Jewish orphans, escaped the horror of the Polish ghettos and pogroms in 1921 and grew up in Oranjia Jewish Children's Home in sunny Cape Town.

Small in height, large in character, Mrs Lockitch has reason to celebrate 1986, the 75th anniversary of the home — the institution which was her home from 1921 when she was seven until she married in 1935.

One hundred of the 200 Lithuanian and Polish Jewish orphans permitted by the South African Government to settle here lived in Cape Town. The others went to the Arcadia Home in Johannesburg.

The orphans were rescued by a Cape Town businessman, Mr Isaac Ochberg, himself a Ukranian immigrant. At his own expense he brought the children out of pogrom-torn Europe.

Daddy Ochberg

This cheerful, red-haired man became Daddy Ochberg to the children who, as adults, are still known in the Jewish community as the "Ochberg orphans".

The children were rescued from certain death (tens of thousands of those who were left behind perished) and fear was no stranger to them.

Even so, they approached South Africa with some trepidation after hearing horror stories [ ]ions roaming the streets and [ ]ren being eaten by canni-

Fanny Lockitch

But Cape Town with its warm sunshine and the even warmer welcome from its Jewish community was a revelation, said Mrs Lockitch.

"We left a devastated Europe — dark and cold — where for months we slept under the beds. Bombs fell all around, the whole place was shaking, there were bayonetted bodies in the gutters so when we arrived in Cape Town at dawn and saw all the twinkling lights around Table Mountain it looked to us like fairyland."

Once her three sons had grown up she returned to work for Oranjia and to be honoured with the coveted Honorary Life Chairmanship for the fund raising effort which saved the home from closing down.

Ambition

Mrs Lockitch attributes her personal success and popularity in life to the early childhood ambition to be educated which drove her to win bursaries to pay for her own schooling.

It was not easy for a Russian-/Yiddish-speaking girl to master the intricacies of English but she persevered and also passed the highest taalbond examinations to become fluent in Afrikaans.

Later, as a young widow, she raised her children alone and put them all through university.

Even without parents, life for the orphans at Oranjia was neither sad nor deprived.

Mrs Lockitch: "It was a miracle we were alive and we were pleased to be living in a warm, safe house with a bath and food. Here people were so kind, and we were like a big family of brothers and sisters."

The home was started in 1910 to house local orphans who were discovered living in labourers' cottages on farms and washing glasses in country bars.

Haven

Later there were four episodes in which Oranjia acted as a haven for refugee children.

● After the London Blitz in 1940 a large number of non-Jewish children were rescued and cared for.

● In 1960 a large number of Jewish children were evacuated from the Congo during the revolution — Mrs Lockitch said there were so many "the walls had to be stretched".

● And in 1975, to meet the needs of a modern society in which women are obliged to work to support themselves and their children, a creche was established to help widowed and divorced working mothers in financial distress. Some children start there from as young as two years old.

The home is supported by the Jewish community and the emphasis has always been on education — as an investment for the future.

"When they have nothing it's the least you can give them."

Fanny Lockitch – a woman with a passion for children

Hilary Benjamin

An outstretched arm in a time of need from one of Cape Town's unsung heroes is what gave Sea Pointer, Fanny Lockitch (née Schrier), the basis for a love of children that was to become an overriding passion throughout her long life.

In failing health, Fanny died last week aged 94. Her family and community members paid tribute to the woman, who was an orphan and who spent her life helping others in the same position.

Fanny was an honorary life member and honorary life chairperson of the Cape Jewish Orphanage "Oranjia", in Oranjezicht.

The early years of Fanny's life reads like a rollercoaster. She was one of the "Ochberg children", so called after the Cape Town philanthropist and humanist Isaac Ochberg, who decided to risk his life to bring 200 Jewish orphans to South Africa from war-torn Eastern Europe – where they were threatened by famine, neglect and genocide.

In Fanny's case, she was one of a family of five who had lost first their mother in World War I and then their father, after he died following an illness contracted after being mustard-gassed.

Coming from the Russian/Polish border, from a town called Brestliovsk, just after the Tsarist revolution, at a time when the pogroms in the area were obliterating Jews, Fanny and a brother (only two of the five left Russia at that time) thought they had arrived in the promised land when they set foot in Cape Town.

She recalls in an interview for SAfm: "We left a devastated Europe – dark and cold – where for months we slept under the beds. Bombs fell all around, the whole place was shaking and there were bayonetted bodies in the gutters.

"So when we arrived in Cape Town at dawn and saw all the twinkling lights around Table Mountain, it looked to us like fairyland."

"Daddy Ochberg", as he came to be known by the children whose lives he saved, placed 100 of the children in the Oranjia orphanage and sent the rest to the Arcadia orphanage in Johannesburg.

He kept in touch with all of them, maintaining a benevolent and much-needed fatherly presence in their young lives.

Fanny was a Russian and Yiddish-speaking youngster of seven when she arrived in the Cape but she was a fast learner, later she attended Cape Town High School, and quickly managed to pick up both English and Afrikaans.

She won bursaries and schooled herself, later becoming a bookkeeper and working for, among other companies, United Motors, Lewis Stores, Empisal and Universal.

She married and had three boys, living at first in Muizenberg but settling in Sea Point later.

She was also an active member of the Clovelly Tennis Club and,

according to one of her sons, "at 5ft 2in, had a peculiar overhead smash that she was renowned for".

She was very community-minded and because of her background, had a keen sense of what children needed in their lives.

It was no surprise that the outlet for her charitable nature was the orphanage which had given her shelter and love as she was growing up.

She believed a good education was an absolute necessity and wanted to make sure that all the children at the orphanage had this opportunity.

While the children's home changed over the decades, eventually taking in children from problematic circumstances rather than just orphans, Fanny still believed its fundamental message was one of love and understanding. She used to hate to think any child should be made to feel separate – as she had most probably felt when orphaned at such a young age and in such dire circumstances.

Fanny took on huge amounts of committee work but was probably most famous for her orange (Oranjia) collection box drives. She would

drop off her fundraising boxes at shops and offices and then return to pick up the full ones.

Arriving and departing in her faithful orange Volksi Beetle, she became known and loved for her untiring fundraising work as well as for her annual cake sales.

The money from all of the boxes was counted personally by hand, cent by cent, and her family tell how she would pride herself on the fact that it was always correct – the bank used special weighing scales to calculate the amount.

Fanny worked for the orphanage for over 50 years and during that time, Oranjia served refugee and needy children in different ways. They homed non-Jewish children after the London Blitz in 1940, they cared for Jewish evacuees from the Congo during the revolution in 1960 and they later opened a creche to help young widowed and divorced working mothers in financial distress to care for their youngsters.

Fanny's enthusiasm and personal contribution towards this cause never waned and her family and friends remember her as a dynamic and selfless person.

Throughout her life she paid tribute to her own saviour, "Daddy Ochberg", who she always remembered and of whom she said: "He was like God to us – I don't think there has ever been a man alive that had so much affection from so many children as that man had, because to us, he really was our saviour."

Fanny leaves three sons, nine grandchildren and four great-grandchildren and her family has settled all over the world, from Cape Town to England to Canada.

■ Fanny Lockitch with two of her grandchildren, Michael and Tara Lockitch.

Obituary

'Aunty Fanny' fought for orphaned children

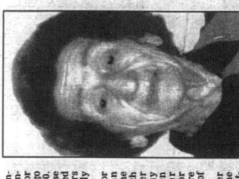

Granny figure: Fanny Lockitch was dedicated to helping others.

FANNY LOCKITCH, who arrived in South Africa as a World War 1 orphan more than 80 years ago and then dedicated her life to helping other orphans, has died. She was 94.

Born on April 22, 1911, Lockitch, née Shrier, and her brother Jack Shrier were among 200 orphans who arrived in Cape Town in 1921, when Lockitch was only 10.

The siblings, from the Russian/Polish border town of Brestiliovsk, were brought here by Isaac Ochberg who had obtained permission from the South African government to bring more than 200 healthy Jewish orphans from Europe.

They group became known as the "Ochberg children", named after the businessman, philanthropist, humanist and father figure who became known to them as "Daddy Ochberg".

On arrival, 100 of the orphans were placed at the Cape Jewish

FANNY LOCKITCH
Born: April 22 1911
Died: November 5 2005

Orphanage in Vredehoek, known today as the Oranjia Jewish Child and Youth Centre, while the remaining 100 were sent to Johannesburg's Arcadia Orphanage. Ochberg, however, managed to keep in touch with all of the children.

Lockitch only spoke Yiddish and Russian when she arrived in Cape Town but quickly learnt English and Afrikaans. She won bursaries and schooled herself, later becoming a bookkeeper for several companies in the city.

She married Hymie Lockitch and had three sons – Brim, Barry and the late Robert (Bobby) who died in Vancouver, Canada, five years ago.

Lockitch, who lived in Sea Point, never forgot her early

years in the orphanage and worked for it for more than 50 years, eventually holding the position as its honourary chairperson.

She was an active member of the Clovelly Tennis Club for many years and was also recognised for her involvement in community work.

She was most popular for her Oranjia collection box drives. Lockitch would leave fundraising boxes at various shops and later return in her orange Volkswagen Beetle to collect them.

She will also be remembered for her annual cake sales and was known to look after destitute and needy children – all done in honour of the man who had helped her, Isaac Ochberg.

"My mother said that when he (Ochberg) got the permission to fetch the orphans, he literally walked through the towns like the Pied Piper, collecting children," said Barry Lockitch.

Lockitch helped house non-Jewish children after the London Blitz in 1940 and cared for Jewish evacuees from the Congo during the revolution in 1960. She later opened a creche to ease the burden of young, widowed and divorced working mothers who were struggling financially to care for their children.

"She was known as a mother or a granny figure," said Jean Mosembaum, who works at the Oranjia Jewish Child and Youth Centre. "We used to call her 'Aunty Fanny', and even my children and all the children from the home called her *Mamla*, the Yiddish word for mother. She was a mother figure who fought for the children of the home."

Lockitch is survived by her two sons, Brim and Barry, nine grandchildren and four great-grand children.

– Natasha Prince

FANNY LOCKITCH (1911-2005) A Woman of Worth – Eishet Chaiyal
Cape Jewish Chronicle December 2005 / January 2006

Fanny Lockitch passed away on 5 November 2005. A true woman of worth, she gave a lifetime of devotion and service to the children of Oranjia.

Fanny and her brother arrived in Cape Town together with 200 Jewish orphans who had escaped the horrors of the Polish ghettos and pogroms in 1921, and grew up in the then known Cape Jewish Orphanage. These orphans had been rescued by Isaac Ochberg, a Cape Town businessman, who himself had immigrated from the Ukraine. Mr Ochberg brought these children out of pogrom-torn Europe at his own expense. They referred to him lovingly as "Daddy Ochberg".

Fanny attributed her personal success and popularity in life to her early childhood ambition to be educated. This drove her to win bursaries and pay for her own schooling. It was not easy for a Russian-Yiddish speaking girl to master the intricacies of English but she persevered and also passed the highest Taalbond Examinations to become fluent in Afrikaans.

As a young widow, she raised her three boys alone and put them through university, after which she returned to work for the Cape Jewish Orphanage and was honoured with the coveted Honorary Life Chairlady position for her fundraising efforts which saved the Home from closing down at the time.

Throughout the years during Fanny's term on the committee a number of highly significant events occurred. In 1940 a large number of non-Jewish children were brought to the Cape Jewish Orphanage, to escape the effects of the London Blitz while some twenty years later, in 1960, a large number of Jewish children were evacuated from the Congo during the revolution.

Further major moves occurred in 1975, when the Sarah Bloch Creche was established to meet the needs of women who were obliged to go out and work, and in 1992, which saw the sale of 25 Montrose Avenue and the move to the Group Homes.

During her years of devoted service to Oranjia Fanny built up a Box Collection scheme, spending five days a week going from door to door in the community to raise funds. Over the years she brought in over R1 million from boxes collected. Over and above this she held an annual cake sale in Sea Point, and had her special band of ladies who faithfully assisted her each year with her various fundraising activities. Fanny continued to work tirelessly until her retirement in 2002.

Fanny is survived by her remaining two beloved sons Barry and Brin, her daughters-in-law, grandchildren and great grandchildren. Her son Barry is currently a trustee of Oranjia, and a valued member of the Oranjia committee.

Aunty Fanny will most certainly leave a void in the lives of all those associated with Oranjia.

'A woman of worth who can find? For her price is far above rubies. Strength and majesty are her clothing; and she laugheth at the time to come. She openeth her mouth with wisdom; and the law of loving-kindness is on her tongue. Give her of the fruit of her hands; and let her works praise her in the gates." (Proverbs XX1 10-31)

Family details of Sara Wachtel as recorded on page 145 of the register kept by the Cape Jewish Orphanage (Oranjia).
1 Name and surname: Sara Wachtel 2 Father: Siyume
3 Mother: Mindel 4 Age: 9 years 5 Place of origin: Stanislav
6 How orphaned: Both parents
7 General Comments: Father fell in the war. Mother died from hunger and typhus. The child still had two brothers: the one in Stanislav and the second in Hungary.

Transit Visa to proceed to South Africa via Danzig and the UK

GROUP PASSPORT 1
Sara Wachtel is no 21 on the list of children
Sara is in the back row sixth from the left.

Sarah Wachtel (Glaser), left, and Lieber Kolodner at Oranjia
"My mother become a millinary apprentice and left school in standard eight so she would have been 16 or 17 when she left to go to work and found other lodgings."

SARA GLASER (WACHTEL)

Extracted from a family booklet "The Glasers of Piltene" written by Leon Glaser

On my mother's side I have been less successful in gathering family information. After making a good start at the Kaplan centre research library, the trail unfortunately seemed to end in the town of Bacau in Romania to which at least one of her brothers escaped. Even having actual street addresses and the verbal support of a number of Romanian officials the quest appeared fruitless and always ended abruptly. Little did I imagine what I was to discover once I was lucky enough to make the acquaintance of Dr Dan Jumara, a genealogist living in the town of Iasi, which is close to Bacau.

While my journey into the Glaser male line history was exciting and yielded its own emotions and rewards, the very start of the adventure into my mother, Sarah's, background was highly emotional from the moment I first made any progress. I need to repeat the incident concerning the events which occurred when I arrived one evening to visit my mother and found her tearfully destroying a whole box of family records and documents in the expressed belief that no one would ever be interested in them.

I am sure many families have a similar little box filled with history and I can only strongly advise and hope that the information be lovingly preserved. I saved what I could and tried to join the scraps together as in a jigsaw puzzle with what I then thought little success. She had often expressed her sense of loneliness because of the fact that she had no immediate family in the form of her brothers or cousins with whom to confide and interact.

One of the very few stories she told us of her childhood was her memory of sitting on the malamed's, (Hebrew teacher's) lap when he came to teach her brothers their barmitzvah portions. What was very intriguing was that she did on occasion talk of the "zigeuner" (gypsies) but I have no idea why and I can only surmise it was because they too were being persecuted and worse.

The years passed and after completing the first part of the story of my male line, my mind turned once again to my mother's story. All we knew was that she came to Cape Town as an "Ochberg " orphan. Her maiden name was Wachtel.

The story and the life of Isaac Ochberg and his amazing deeds in saving children are well known throughout the world. His story is summed up in the Cape Jewish Chronicle of December 1986, which was the 75th anniversary of the arrival of "his" orphans.

Sarah had two brothers, David and Wolf. Amongst the documents she destroyed that night were letters she had received from David. The last which I could save was probably written in 1934 and after that, silence. As they knew her address, we can only put the worst possible construction on the silence.

When David moved to Bacau he changed his surname from Wachtel to Rosenfeld, which was my mother's maiden name, and his first name to Heinrich which was the Romanian form of Chaim. Two reasons were given for these changes: firstly, that Wachtel was dangerously Jewish and secondly to avoid army conscription. It appears both these objectives were not

achieved as can be deduced from the letters where he says he is a soldier in a regiment and in fact landed up in the military in Romania. Times became steadily worse for him and his family to the point where he was demeaned and humiliated to the extent of having to beg for help to sustain his daughters.

Sarah was born in Budapest on 19 May 1910 (but there is a three year discrepancy about this date) and then as far as I can establish, the family moved to Stanislavov which was a town with a large Jewish population. After the loss of her father and mother, she was probably cared for by the Jewish orphanage which had been established by the local Jewish community. To talk of being "fortunate" in these circumstances stretches the imagination but in this case it is beyond doubt that being chosen as eligible to be sent to Cape Town as an "Ochberg" orphan was the difference between life and death.

Subsequently I visited the Kaplan Centre at the University of Cape Town where all the old records from the Oranjia Jewish Orphanage are kept. It did not take long to discover the actual entry, which shows her admission details to the orphanage in the register. This entry was an exciting find and was a fund of information. It confirmed that her father's name was "Sumner", a detail which had caused us some concern at the time of her passing, as we were told by all concerned that there was no such name. (My later visit to Yad Vashem confirmed the existence of such a name.) Much more than that; for the first time we discovered that her mother's name was Mindel. You must bear in mind that just to say her mother or her father is to talk about my grandparents of whom we previously knew nothing.

The causes of their deaths were also noted, with Sumner having died in a prisoner of war camp almost certainly in the Austria Hungary war against the Russians. In today's terms this would have meant he fought for the Germans against the Russians. Strange to think relatives on both sides of the family fought for the Germans against the then Russian oppressor.

Mindel died from hunger and typhus arising out of the unsanitary conditions caused in part by the movement of the country folk, whose all was destroyed by the Nazis, to the towns and villages in search of sustenance. The existing infrastructure could not cope with the influx of refugees. With the rape of the countryside, food was in desperately short supply. It is frightening to think this could happen while we sit in luxury only two generations later. When some of us are so quick to debunk the values and ethics and practices of our recent ancestors, it maybe behoves us to think of them and consider the values they stood and died for. While the dates and exact circumstances of their passing are unknown to me, a passage in letter No 6 seems to indicate that they died on the 23rd and 14th August in a year which is not clear but before 1921.

Now suddenly my maternal grandparents became real people with whom at this stage of my life I had "met" for the first time and whose suffering was now my suffering. My mother never spoke about her parents and whether this was subconscious or deliberate, I regret to say I never really questioned. The truth in retrospect is that in the nature of things she was probably too young to remember them and over the years consciously or subconsciously forgot about them.

I returned to the cardboard box and re-discovered the pieces of the jigsaw puzzle which I had managed to put together as well as a few other letters. They were written in German. After making a few enquiries I contacted a teacher at the local German school who was able to translate a major part of the letters as shown opposite. These few letters are dated from 1922 to 1935.

I thought long and hard about printing the letters here, and after reminding myself that this effort is for the benefit of my grandchildren, I came to the conclusion that it was appropriate to print them with due regard for their sensitivity and I do so here in translation. I trust they will serve as a memorial to the memory of those I never knew. When I read these letters for the first time from an Uncle *David* I never knew and learnt of his wife Taube and their children, my cousins Mindel and Laura, it was an unbelievably emotional experience for me. I spent the whole day as if I had just lost family. That Shabbat in shul I could do no more than think of them, close family I had never met and who almost certainly perished in the holocaust.

But herein lies a further mystery; as the letters were written in German so they were probably also answered in German. We never knew or guessed that my mother was literate in German and she never gave us the slightest hint of her ability. I can only assume it was too traumatic and brought back horrible memories. She was fluent in Yiddish and maybe used Yiddish in her letters.

Here follow the letters from David (Sarah's brother, Chaim Wachtel) and while there appears to be an error in the dates and sequence the intent and content is very clear.

Letter number one, dated 25 June 1922
Beloved Sister Sara,
I am able to tell you, that we are, thanks be to G-d, healthy. G-d grant that we may hear the same from you. Dear Sister I beseech you not to be angry that I have till now not written to you. You do not have to excuse me, as you know I am a soldier and my wife is not so well with the child which she (illegible) and I cannot burden her with expecting her to write. I am on holiday for thirty days and take this opportunity to write. I cannot write otherwise. I have not heard from Wolf. I beg you, if it is possible to protect my wife. I shall be grateful and pay you back, because life is very difficult. I cannot write to you from the regiment.   Greetings and kisses a thousand times.
Your brother, sister in law and child' Taube, Lora and David.

And on the reverse side; Please answer immediately,
Heinrich Rosenfeld, Florilor St, 12, Bacau, Romania

Letter number two, dated 22 January 1927
——— Sister,
I can write that your letter and photograph arrived.———
were very happy. Your brother is healthy.
Dear Sister I can write that my wife gave birth to a daughter on 24/11/1926 and she is named after my —— Lora,
Otherwise I must sign up———
I have no work now, many people have no work here, otherwise there is no news.
I have had no mail from Wolf.
Many greetings and a thousand kisses from your brother and daughter Lara and Taube.

Letter number three, dated 14 June 1931
Much beloved sister Sara and brother in law,
I am able to tell you that I received your wonderful letter and we were very happy to receive it and to hear you are married and that you are well. Dear sister Sara, I can tell you we are well, my wife and I and the children, thanks to G-d.
I am not earning any money as there is no work. You ask what I occupy myself with. I have a good trade, but there is no work. I work painting rooms and putting up wallpaper.
Dear Sister and Brother in Law, if all is well with you, I would like to come and work there, as here it is not possible to live. If possible you could send our children something, we would be very grateful. Otherwise nothing is new here.
Please write and tell us exactly what it is like there. I shall send you a photo of the children in the next letter.
We greet you and kiss you a thousand times.
Your brother and sister in law and the children
David Taube Lara and Mina,
Please reply immediately

Letter number four dated 17 February 1932
Beloved Sister Sarah,
I can tell you that I have received your loving letter which made me very happy. I believe you will also be happy to hear from us. Dearest Sarah I let you know that, thanks to G-d we are healthy and all well. May G-d grant we hear good news from you too.
Dear sister Sarah I do not understand what is wrong with you. You have not once written clearly what is going on with you. I beseech you to write everything exactly whether you are married to this young man with whom you have been photographed.
But in the previous letter he already refers to a brother in law. As your elder brother I would like to know everything. So you should write everything to me and a larger (photograph?). I have had no mail from our brother. I am also angry —— Wolf. Nothing new otherwise and we greet you and kiss you.
Your nephew? Lara and Mina brother and sister in law Taube.
Please answer immediately.
Mina was named after our blessed mother Mindel

Letter number five undated
Beloved Sister I can tell you that we received your loving letter which made us very happy. I can tell we are all healthy thanks to G-d. G-d willing we hope to hear the same from you, because all is not well with us.
Dear sister you wish from me a photo. Believe me of me——I would have sent you know that I am with the military. I can write to you——.———Wolf is in Russian____.____ is one year and five months old.———cannot write any more to you. I have not had mail from Wolf.
Your Sister in Law and brother and child
Taube ——-your nephew——.

Letter number six
This seems to be the end of a longer letter so date unknown.
——but all at once we gave your—— and you will now have the fourth letter—-I received your correct address. Dear sister I can tell you that I received——and in case I receive an answer to this letter I shall send you a photograph——.
I can tell you that——Wolf?—is in Stanislavov and it is very bad. No address—-.
Maybe it is possible for you to—-with support because—-

Dear sister, you ask—— our parents, G-d rest their souls. I can report that the year is (1922?) 23 August 1922 Tevet) and the year of mother is 14 or 15 August (14 or 15 Shvat)

What was most important to me was the information that at the end of hostilities those Jews who survived were allowed, on the giving up of their Romanian citizenship in terms of decree 487, to leave for Germany or Israel. As my cousins would now be 70, 77 and 80, it is not without the bounds of possibility that they could be alive. (This account was written in 2006.)

Many of the survivors who went to Israel, settled in Zichron Yaakov and Rosh Pina as pioneers. I have finally initiated a search in Israel, especially as I have learnt of a Mrs Branders who describes herself as a sister-in-law who had made attempts in 1957 to find Wachtels from Stanislavov and had indeed discovered a few whose names unfortunately are not the same names that I have discovered. It appears very likely that there were thus at least again two families Wachtel in Stanislavov and it is quite likely they could be related. The father's name of this family in the Yad Vashem document is given as Moishe, and he could well have been a brother of my mother's father, Sumner.

The fate of Wolf is unknown to me, with two possibilities both having the same end result. The last letter from David said he was in a Russian—— (indecipherable) which could only lead to one conclusion. Furthermore, the admission form to Oranjia confirms that one brother left Stanislavov and the other remained.

I then recalled that we went on a tour of Israel which included a visit to Yad Vashem. Nothing could persuade my mother to enter the monument/memorial and she was traumatically upset. I realise in retrospect that she knew far more than she had told us. Having visited the new Yad Vashem, a most fantastic memorial, I am once again trying to trace the family. In fact I tried a few Rosenfelds in the Haifa area phone book and although one was also Heinrich, we couldn't identify common family.

Writing of this incident has reminded me of another which I didn't question at the time. We had gone to a seder, which was led in the Polish manner and in the Polish "tunes" by Pinchas Gutter, who was himself a Warsaw Ghetto survivor. This resulted in my mother being unbelievably moved for days afterward. Again she never said anything but again in retrospect it seems highly feasible that she was taken back to her childhood days and remembered the seders and tunes from her parents' home. I don't know.

SARAH WACHTEL
Written by Rhona Wolpert

As an Ochberg Orphan, Sarah Wachtel, my mother, remained at Oranjia till she completed standard eight and was then apprenticed to a milliner, a job at which she excelled to the point of even making hats for herself well into her married life. I well remember the wooden blocks she had for making up these hats.

My mother never spoke much about her life in the orphanage in Poland, but always told me that when Isaac Ochberg came to

this orphanage, he tucked her under her chin, told her that she was a pretty little girl and asked if she would like to go with him. The tragedy is that she left two older brothers behind. She also used to tell me how Polish children would throw stones at the Jewish kids on the way to school. She arrived here not knowing a word of English, but could converse in Russian, Polish, Hebrew and Yiddish, which was faultless. We, as a family, knew many of the women with whom she came to Cape Town.

My parents, Sarah Wachtel and David Glaser married in 1933 and had three children, Leon, Herschel and myself. We all live in Cape Town. My mother was a most accomplished seamstress and knitted beautifully and never with a pattern. She was most reticent about telling us any stories about her youth. She and my father had a wonderfully happy marriage and in later years, they took to travelling the world. My father passed away in 1978 and my mother in 1988.

Wedding photo of Salka Bettman and Joe Sheiham

I was overwhelmed by the photo submitted by Aubrey Sheiham of the party at the wedding of his parents, Salka Bettman and Joe Sheiham. My mother was a bridesmaid to Salka and they remained life-long friends. She is in the photo in the centre directly behind Joe, the man with a bowtie and the woman on his left. I am unable to find my father in the photo. My younger brother Herschel immediately recognised our mother in that wedding party photo.

The most amazing story that goes with this is that when Salka and Joe's late daughter Hilda married Kenny Prissman in late 1964, Salka insisted that my parents bring me to the wedding! She said that there were all these Johannesburg boys coming down to Cape Town to be pole-holders and I was placed at the table with these rowdy young men!

Needless to say, I took one look at the tall young man opposite me, a fellow by the name of Sydney Wolpert and two years late we were married!

Two more men I recognise in the photo were part of our family's circle of friends, also forever. The young man sprawled on the floor on the left is Joe Talberg, and the man in the front row, third from the right was Kollie Kolevsohn. Joe was married to Bessie and Kollie's wife was Polly. They were all very great friends of my parents. My mother also remained very close to Liebe Kolodner Singer.

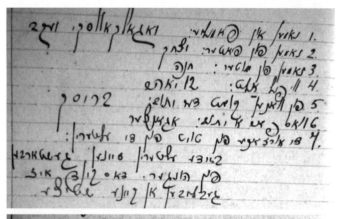

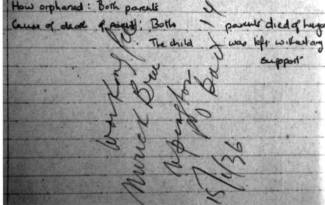

Family details of Yakov Yagalkowsky as recorded on page 135 of the register kept by the Cape Jewish Orphanage (Oranjia).
1 Name and surname: Yakov Yagalkowsky 2 Father: Yitzhak
3 Mother: Hana 4 Age: 12 years 5 Place of origin: Brest
6 How orphaned: Both parents
7 General Comments: Both parents died of hunger.
The child was left without any support.
Note dated 15/1/36: Working for Nurick Bros.PO Box 14 Upington.

JACK YALKOVSKY (YAKOV YAGALKOVSKY)
Written by Sally Sher from Israel.

I wonder whether Jack Yalkovsky's name has been recorded as an Ochberg Orphan. I dont know anything about his early life besides that he did live in the *Oranjia* Orphanage and had been brought to Upington by a childless couple Mr and Mrs Gotschalk.

From a young age he worked for my grandfather Abraham and his brother Morris Nurick in the shop on their farm Exteenskuil. He never married. He did not come into town and associate himself with anyone and to use my father's expression "he threw himself away." He was a real recluse. However he was loyal and worked well.

Morris was the elder. The firm was Nurick Bros. (Pty) Ltd. The address was P O Box14 Upington. Jack probably worked in the

farm shop for about 20 years. It would be interesting to know how he came to work for The Nuricks.

The farm Exteenskuil was about an hour by car from Upington. My family lived in Upington and went daily to the farm whereas Jack lived on the farm. He occasionally went to Upington to get stock for the shop that he ran on the farm. I found amongst our family tree Jack's surname spelt Yalkovsky.

My uncle Abe Rosman, now aged 90, who lives in Sea Point. together with my father ran the farm and produce section of the business. Abe said that Jack bought a piece of farming ground adjacent to Exteenskuil which he farmed until he was murdered. My grandfather bought the ground. Abe does not know what happened to the money and Jack's estate. While I have such a clear recollection that Mr and Mrs Gottschalk were instrumental in bringing Jack to Upington, Abe has no recollection of this.

Neither Abe nor I had ever seen a photograph of Jack. As far as descendants go Abe said that Jack had a coloured daughter. The girl's mother was a coloured woman living on the farm. I can't recall ever seeing the mother or daughter. I always heard about the relationship. Abe does not know what happened to her after he died. As I said previously he was a recluse.

Sadly one night in December 1956 two coloured men, an older one and a younger one, knocked on his door with the pretext that they needed petrol. The petrol pump was outside his house. They murdered him for the money in the safe.

Rhoda, Sally's sister writes

Although Jack was like a ghost in the background I was always intrigued by him and felt so sorry for him. I would have liked to hold his hand or kiss him. I definitely knew that originally he came to stay with the Gottschalks but they could not communicate with him, hence him going to live on the farm.

I remember going with my father to the farm and Jack had lunch with my father and Abe. He was clean and nicely dressed.

He used to come to Upington for Yom Kippur and I remember him sleeping over on the stoep. When my mother asked him if he slept well, he said he couldn't sleep there was too much traffic! My parents thought that was so funny. On the corner of our house was a stop street sign and maybe three cars at the most might have stopped there in the early evening!

I remember when he was murdered and the three murderers were apprehended near Kenhardt. They had used an axe to slice open his head and they were later hung! I remember hearing my father speak and arrange a tombstone to be put on his grave.

What I never ever heard was that he had a daughter and we suppose her mother was a coloured lady. I'm pleased he had some sort of normal life.

Chapter 86 – TEN MORE POGROM ORPHANS ARRIVING 1925

In 1925 ten Progom Orphans arrived in South Africa thanks to "the philanthropy of Cape Jewry, under the stewardship of Isaac Ochberg, the president of the Cape Jewish Orphanage, and with permission granted by the ex Governor General of the Cape of Good Hope and by J C Smuts."

Five of these children were siblings of the Slavin Family and came from Alexandrovsk in the Ukraine while the other five were the Solomon siblings from Pavlogrod Russia.

All ten children were adopted by Isaac and Lisa Solomon, shopkeepers in Wellington in the Cape, who had no children of their own. Lisa was the aunt of the Slavin children and Isaac the uncle of the Solomon children.

This chapter has been written by Barry Slavin

THE FIVE SLAVIN SIBLINGS; SOSA, LUBA, RACHEL, NAUM AND ABRAM

The Slavin family came from Alexandrovsk (Zaporozyhe) in the Ukraine. They belonged to a vanishing group of people who arrived on South African shores between 1880 and 1930. They were Eastern European Jews who suffered periodic pogroms and racial prejudice, were restricted in their educational horizons and prevented from reaching their true development potential. They were taught privately by parents and grandparents and by Rebbonim, how to read Hebrew and the Scriptures and to preserve their inherent Jewish traditions.

Around 1905 the Slavin family, Dov-Ber and Sheina and their three children Sosa, Luba and Freidel, left the Ukraine via Sevastopol for London where the youngest daughter Ray (Rochel) was born. The family could not integrate into an emigrant society and returned to Alexandrovsk in 1907. At about this time the Dov-Ber's brother emigrated to Canada.

The family had two more sons, Natie (Naum) born in 1909 and Abram in 1911. Freidel died in 1917, the father Boris (Dov-Ber) in 1919 and the mother Sheina in 1922. The two oldest children, Sonia (Sosa) and Lily (Luba) assumed guardianship of their younger siblings Rachel, Naum and Abram. Sonia was a nurse at the local hospital and was the only sibling who could read and write. Sheina's siblings, Jack, Israel and Maryassa, had already left the Ukraine for South Africa some years before.

The siblings suffered from abject poverty and starvation during the Revolution years, and scavenged like ferule creatures in order to survive. Sonia wrote to the United Kingdom Jewish Refugee Fund in 1923, endeavouring to trace another of her mother's sisters, Liza Gordin, who had left the Soviet Union for the United Kingdom in the early 1900's. The United Kingdom Jewish Refugee Fund responded to the letter received from Sonia and in turn forwarded her letter to Liza Gordin, now Solomon, who resided in Wellington, Cape Province, South Africa. Liza had married Isaac Solomon in London in 1906, and the two had immigrated to South Africa where they became shopkeepers in Wellington, and remained childless. Upon receipt of the correspondence from her niece Sonia from Alexandrovsk, Ukraine, Liza Solomon and her husband Isaac appealed to the philanthropy of Cape Jewry, under the steward-

Isaac and Lisa Solomon shopkeepers in Wellington

ship of Isaac Ochberg, the president of the Cape Jewish Orphanage, and with permission granted by the ex Governor General of the Cape of Good Hope and by J C Smuts (later to become Field Marshal and Prime Minister of South Africa), they were granted permission to enter South Africa on the strength of deputations made and undertakings given by Lisa and Isaac Solomon, and by Jack and Israel Gordin, to adopt the orphaned Slavin children. Isaac Solomon also secured refuge for orphaned children of his deceased siblings also left in the Soviet Union in similar circumstances. All of these ten children arrived in Wellington Cape in two separate groups, approximately six months apart. Isaac Solomon's siblings' orphaned children were Ray, Louise, Sima, Sara and Isaac.

The Slavin children departed Alexandrovsk in June 1925 travelling via Moscow, where they paid respects to Vladimir Lenin who had died in January 1925, and then proceeded via Riga, Latvia, where they were fed and clothed at the refugee station, bound for Southampton in the United Kingdom. They travelled steerage on the Union Castle Line's, *Walmer Castle*, bound for Cape Town, arriving on 25 August 1925.

Russia in Reality.

A Terrible Tale of Actual Experience.

ORPHANED CHILDREN NOW SAFE IN BRANDFORT.

Miss Ray Solomon, of Brandfort, has in her short life traversed many vicissitudes. She has climbed many steep hills and endured many fiery trials. The adopted daughter of Mr. and Mrs. Isaac Solomon, of Brandfort, she was, writes our Brandfort correspondent, one of a family of eleven born in Pavlogrod, Russia. Her father, a man in good circumstances, carried on the manufacture of buttons, and held the tender from the Russian Government for the supply of lead seals for the Russian postal administration.

During the revolution of 1919 all her father's worldly possessions, the result of 41 years of strenuous, energetic effort, were confiscated by the Bolsheviks. Her mother and father were tied hand and foot, the latter placed face to the wall, and with a pistol held to his neck his money demanded. After being subjected to considerable abuse and ill-treatment, they were thrown from their home on to the snow-clad earth. Within six days of this treatment her mother, father and two of the children died from hunger, shock and exposure.

The surviving members of the family, left destitute and penniless, passed through sordid privations, which beggars description, until eventually, at the instance of their uncle residing in America, they went to that country, there only to find on their arrival that the refugee quarter was so crowded that accommodation was unprocurable. They were then sent to Southampton to await the next batch of refugees, and were delayed seven months.

Arriving in America eventually, they were brought before the American Supreme Court at the instance of President Coolidge, on the appeal of Senator Perlman, and were again rejected and returned to Southampton.

In desperation, they then appealed to their uncle, Mr. I. Solomon, in South Africa, who provided their passage to this country and guaranteed the costs of their Southampton sojourn. They came to South Africa and were adopted by him.

Eight months later the widowed sister of Mrs. Solomon died in Alexandrosk, leaving a further five orphans penniless. These Mr. and Mrs. Solomon also adopted and brought them to South Africa. Five of these children are now earning their own livelihood in South Africa. Four Mr. Solomon is still educating, and Miss Ray's engagement has just been announced.

Mr. and Mrs. Solomon's devotion to human interests in the absence of any children of their own is one of the many admirable, practical humanitarian demonstrations by the Jewish community in South Africa to emancipate their relatives from terrible social conditions.

Isaac and Lisa Solomon of Bradford and their 10 adopted children from the Slavin and Solomon families

AFFIDAVIT.

I the undersigned, Isaac Solomon, presently residing at Wellington in the Province of the Cape, South Africa do hereby make oath and say:-

That I am a Naturalized British Subject who has resided in this country for the past 18 Years.

That I carry on the business of a General Dealer at Wellington aforesaid.

That I am a married man but we have no family

That my wifes sister Mrs.Sonia Slavin, born Gordon who resides in Aleksandrovsk, Ukrania, Ekaterinoslavska Russia is a poor widow and I have offered to take her daughter Luba Slavin, aged 18 Years and her son Nachum Slavin aged 15 Years into my home and to educate them and provide for them generally.

That the said Mrs. Slavin is not in a position to provide for the children mentioned and that I will do so if they are allowed to come out to this country.

That the Reverend Bender of Cape Town can further vouch for the accuracy of my statement.

Sworn to before me at Wellington C.P.this 11th,day of June 1924   J.Solomon.

Commissioner of Oaths.

In order to integrate the Solomon's ten new children, five from Liza's family and five from Isaac's family, education for the youngest and employment for the eldest of the orphaned children was prioritised, as well as English Language tuition.

Natie was sent off to Pondoland (now Transkei) to Mount Frere and Lusikisiki, to work for a Jewish Russian shopkeeper, where he spent two years as one of only two Europeans amongst the black rural populace. During this time Natie, who never had a single day's formal schooling, was able to teach himself to read and write and to understand financial matters, which facilitated his integration into this new foreign world. Apart from Russian, Xhosa was Natie's second language, and by the time he returned to Wellington approximately two years later in 1927, he had assumed the basic "Life Skills" of reading and writing and speaking passable English, all achieved by self study illuminated by candlelight in the back room of a primitive trading post. His main source of education was a copy of the renowned "Pears Encyclopedia", which he studied from cover to cover, its well worn pages filled with pencilled markings

copying the letters of the English alphabet. This document remains in the family as a cherished memento.

In 1927 the Solomons sold the General Dealership in Wellington, Cape, and purchased the Brandfort Hotel in the Orange Free State. Life was a struggle and the family supported one another by pooling common assets for the benefit of siblings and relatives.

NATIE SLAVIN

Natie relocated to the Transvaal in 1928 and found employment at an African Mine Concession Store at Croesus Mine on the Gold Reef. Here he worked together with several other Jewish emigrants who, in later life, were to become renowned businessmen in their own right. The Great Depression of 1929, the rise of National Socialism in Europe, and the knowledge that the old world left behind in Europe and Russia was being systematically destroyed by Anti-Semitism and Nazism, made for difficult and traumatic times. Natie befriended members of the Lithuanian Jewish community in Johannesburg, and through his association with them, developed a passable Yiddish. He lived in the centre of Johannesburg, in Pritchard Street, and as a young man took up bodybuilding and ballroom dancing, complete with Tuxedo and Tails.

In 1937 he was introduced via a friend, Jake Kaplan, to Rebecca (Betty) Matheson at the Shiva House for her late mother Rosie Matheson. Natie had now joined Charles Outfitters in Eloff Street Extension, and eventually purchased the business from a Mr Lapidus, the owner.

World War two broke out and, being stateless, Natie could not enlist in the armed services. During the war years there was a dire need for any form of shopping bags. Natie's sister Sonia, now a Russian translator at the General Post Office, secured some finance which was pooled, together with a loan secured by Natie's younger brother Abie, an employee at L Suzman & Co, tobacco wholesalers, thus facilitating the beginning of a home industry in the living room of his rented apartment in Gordon Road, Bertrams.

Together with the assistance of his fiancée Betty, Natie would draw the patterns and cut out the leather by hand and punch the holes around the outer edge of the leather, which Betty would then take to the local ladies in the area to thong together as bags. From these humble beginnings, Slavin Handbags grew to become the largest handbag manufacturer in South Africa and an element of a new Stock Exchange flotation in 1968.

Natie and Betty were married on 24 October 1946 in the Wolmarans Street Synagogue. They had a son Barry in 1947 and a daughter Sharon Roslyn in 1948. Business was thriving in the post world war years, and Natie actively participated in communal affairs and was a pioneering member of the Emarentia / Greenside Synagogue.

Natie had a wide range of business contacts and interest, but yet he remained a very private person. He loved South Africa and welcomed the toppling of the apartheid government. His legacy left South Africa a richer place as a result of his contribution and inspired his progeny to cherish and live out his memory.

Page left blank on purpose

PART 3
JOHANNESBURG, SOUTH AFRICA

SECTION 9
THE HISTORY OF THE SOUTH AFRICAN JEWISH ORPHANAGE - ARCADIA

The South African Jewish Orphanage was established in 1906

The Ukraine War and Progrom Orphans sent to Johannesburg
were initially in the care of the War and Progrom Orphans Fund.
In 1924 when the palatial estate of Rand lord Sir Lionel Phillips, Arcadia, was
acquired partly with proceeds from this fund, the children were placed in its care.
The South African Jewish Orphanage adopted the name Arcadia

.

Arcadia Jewish Children's Home, still exists in Johannesburg under the
Chevra Kadisha umbrella and still takes care of children in need.

You can read more about Arcadia and its children in
100 Years of Arc Memories and *More Arc Memories*
(Contact David Solly Sandler <sedsand@iinet.net.au> or visit website www.arcadia.ca.com.au)

Chapter 87 – THE HISTORY OF THE
SOUTH AFRICAN JEWISH ORPHANAGE (1899-1923)

This early history of the South African Jewish Orphanage is extracted from the Golden Jubilee Souvenir 1906-1956.

INTRODUCTION

As is mentioned on every letterhead and in every official publication of the Orphanage, the Institution was "founded by the Jewish Ladies' Communal League". It is therefore appropriate that the history of the South African Jewish Orphanage should begin with an account of the League, which, among its other activities, inaugurated and carried on the work of an Orphanage in the Community until 1921, when the South African Jewish Orphanage was established as a separate and independent Institution and took over all the Orphanage work and property and assets connected with that work from the League.

JEWISH LADIES' COMMUNAL LEAGUE

The League was brought into being on 30 November 1898, at a meeting held in the President Street Synagogue of the Witwatersrand Old Hebrew Congregation. Neither the Synagogue nor the Congregation now exist, the former having been demolished and the latter absorbed in the United Hebrew Congregation of the present day. Although the Minutes of that meeting call it "a Meeting of Ladies," a number of gentlemen were also present, and indeed the Chairman and Honorary Secretary of that meeting were men.

It was due to the initiative of Rabbi Dr J H Hertz (then the spiritual head of the first Jewish Congregation in Johannesburg and later Chief Rabbi of Great Britain) that this meeting was called, and when Mr S Goldreich, who presided, opened the meeting, he called on Dr Hertz to explain the object of the meeting. In doing so, the Rabbi mentioned that the purpose was to form a Society of Ladies to be a friend in need of the poor young, the fatherless orphan and the stranded stranger, to look after the Hebrew and Religious classes of the Congregation, and to try and foster a Judaic fervour amongst the Jewish Women of the town (for some hidden reason, the word "women" is in inverted commas). He then moved the following resolution, which was carried unanimously:-

"That the ladies here assembled resolve to organise at once a Jewish Ladies' Communal League, and that a Provisional Committee be elected to draft a Constitution and Bye-Laws."

The meeting then proceeded to elect Mr S. Goldreich as President, Mr E.M. Davis-Marks as Honorary Secretary, and a Committee of ten ladies, as follows: Mesdames George Albu, Naph. H. Cohen, D.L. Freeman, A. Goldstone, Leopold Graham, K. Klagsbrun, J Rosenthal, E. Rubenstein, M Seltzer and A Solomon.

The first General Meeting of the League was held on 25 June 1899, at which the first Committee of the League was elected,

as follows: President, Mr. S. Goldreich; Honorary Treasurer, Mr A. Goldstone; Honorary Secretary, Mr E.M. Davis-Marks; Mesdames E.M. Davis-Marks, M Levine, J. Kahn, E. Rubenstein, M. Seltzer, J. Jacobs, M. Levy, W. Woolf, D.M. Fogelman, S. Strauss, S. Sonnenfeld and Miss S. Green.

BOER WAR INTERREGNUM

Then came the Boer War. There is no record of any meeting being held during the war, and this is borne out by the fact that the second General Meeting of members was held on 26 November 1902.

FIRST MENTION OF AN ORPHANAGE

At the second Annual Meeting, the first mention is made of Jewish orphans in a proposal put forward at this meeting that endeavors should be made to start a Jewish Home for orphans, or, alternatively, to try and get them accepted by the Jewish Orphanage, in Norwood, England.

The first orphans' case considered by the League was that of two girls, at a meeting on 6 January 1903, when it was decided to call a meeting of the Committees of the Jewish Institutions to discuss the raising of the requisite amount of £600 so as to send these two orphans to England. This meeting of representatives of Jewish Institutions was held on 13 January 1903. The Chairman, Mr S Goldreich, explained the object of the meeting, which was to send Jewish orphans, who were in the Nazareth Home and in the Undenominational Home, to the Jewish Orphanage in London.

The representatives were all against this scheme, and suggested alternatives, such as getting the children adopted, placing them in private homes, etc., one speaker saying that this case of the two girl orphans would create a precedent, to which Dr Hertz replied that this was to be expected, and that the care of orphans was a sign of civilization which had until now been quite neglected.

Dr Hertz proposed that a Jewish Orphanage be started in Johannesburg, but this was not agreed to, and the proposition was withdrawn. Eventually, the meeting was adjourned after appointing a Sub-Committee to find private homes for the children. No better success was achieved at the adjourned meeting, the Institutions refusing assistance to send the children to London, or to establish an Orphanage in Johannesburg, whilst any attempts that may have been made to find private homes were evidently a failure.

At a League meeting on 3 February 1903, it was reported that Mr Max Langerman had offered to donate four stands in Kensington for an Orphanage.

FIRST ORPHANS' HOME ESTABLISHED AT 51 PRETORIA STREET, HILLBROW

At the General Meeting of the League on 26 May 1903, at which Mrs Max Langerman was elected President and Mrs Davis-Marks Honorary Secretary, the President proposed, and it was agreed, that authority be given to the Committee to rent a house in order to start an Orphanage, and the offer of M. Langerman of the four stands was accepted with thanks. A number of houses were inspected by members of the Committee, and eventually, on 13 July 1903 the offer of a house by Mr A D Alexander was accepted, at a rental of £35 a month, and arrangements were made to start an Orphanage without delay. The house was 51 Pretoria Street, Hillbrow, and was officially opened as an Orphanage on 18 August 1903, by Mr L J Reyersbach, the President of the Witwatersrand Old Hebrew Congregation.

The first Matron appointed was Miss Celina Lowenstock. Drs D Horwich and A Goodman were appointed Honorary Medical Officers and Dr Brinton the Honorary Ophthalmic Surgeon. These gentlemen offered their services, which were gratefully accepted.

GOLDEN JUBILEE YEAR DATE

At this stage it is appropriate to mention that there are those who maintain that the date abovementioned – August 18th, 1903 – marked the beginning of Orphanage activity in the South African Jewry, and that "Arcadia" is nothing more nor less than just the present-day development of that activity in our Community; therefore that date should be regarded as the real birthday of the Orphanage, and that consequently the Golden Jubilee should have been celebrated in 1953. But the 1931 Committee of the Orphanage, as officially recorded in its Minutes, decided that 1906 was the year of birth of the South African Jewish Orphanage, and consequently celebrated in 1931 its Silver Jubilee of twenty-five years' existence by holding a Silver Jubilee Ball at the City Hall. The reason for that decision was that the Committee held that it was in 1906 that the first home owned and erected by the South African Jewish Orphanage was established, whereas the previous homes were just ordinary dwelling houses rented by, but not belonging to the Orphanage, to accommodate for the time being the orphan children. That being the official decision, it was adhered to by the present Committee.

SOUTH AFRICAN JEWISH ORPHANAGE

A special meeting of the League, held on 20 July 1903, resolved that the home be named "The South African Jewish Orphanage," and that it be worked in connection with and under the control of the Jewish Ladies' Communal League. Thereafter, and until 1921, when the Orphanage was established as a separate and independent Institution, the Annual Reports were headed "The Jewish Ladies' Communal League and the South African Jewish Orphanage."

A week after the opening of the Home in Pretoria Street, the Committee arranged with the Mother Superior of the Nazareth Home and with the Undenominational Home to transfer the Jewish children in their Institutions to the Jewish Orphanage.

Although there were only eight children when the Pretoria Street House was opened, applications for new admissions soon began to increase in volume and urgency, so that the necessity for larger premises soon became apparent. At a special meeting of the Committee on 7 June 1904, it was resolved "that, in view of the numbers of applications and the limited accommodation available, that a building be erected upon the stands at Kensington so kindly donated by Mr Max Langerman, at a cost not exceeding £4,500, but that the building should not commence until £2,000 shall have been collected."

So many were the applications that several deserving cases had to be turned down on account of lack of accommodation. Incidentally, it can be mentioned here that even later, in the Kensington days, applications had to be refused because of lack of accommodation, and that only since 1923, when Arcadia became the Home of the Orphanage, the boast, mentioned in many of the Annual Reports since 1923, that no applications for admission have been refused because of want of accommodation, has been proudly made and justified.

ESSELEN STREET, HOSPITAL HILL

The number of Jewish children in need of home and shelter became so large that in July, 1904, the Orphanage rented a larger house, at 23 Esselen Street, Hospital Hill, and the Pretoria Street premises were vacated.

But the demand for accommodation kept on increasing, for the Jewish community was growing in size, as was also the number of orphan children. Not only were applications for admission from Johannesburg applicants increasing, but they came from all over the country. The Committee felt that the financial support from the country was very poor, and not at all commensurate with the size or economic position of Jewry outside Johannesburg. For instance, in December, 1904, an application from Cape Town for the admission of two boys was answered by the Committee regretting inability to accept any applications at the present time owing to the Home being full and that the meagre support from large towns other than Johannesburg has prevented a Home being erected.

The fourth Annual Report submitted to the General Meeting held on 19 March 1905, stated: "Your Committee have for a considerable period contemplated the erection of an Orphanage on the ground so kindly presented by Mr Max Langerman.

At last this long-cherished wish is about to be consummated. Your Committee are proud and happy to be in a position to report to you that within the next few days the foundation stone of the Jewish Orphanage for South Africa will be laid."

A few days after this meeting, on Thursday, 23 March 1905, the foundation stone of the Kensington Home was laid by Mrs Max Langerman. At this time there were twenty children in the Esselen Street Home. The Kensington Home provided accommodation for 32 children.

BENBOW STREET, KENSINGTON

The Kensington Home was ready for occupation in October, 1905, and on the 31st of that month the children were moved from Esselen Street to Kensington.

The Kensington Home was formally opened by Mrs Max Langerman on 6 May 1906, in the presence of a large and representative gathering. The opening ceremony was participated in by Rabbis Dr Hertz and Dr Landau, Revs, S Manne, W Woolf and D W Hirschowitz and the combined Choirs of the Witwatersrand Old and Johannesburg New Hebrew Congregation. Congratulatory speeches were delivered by the Mayor of Johannesburg (Councillor J W Quinn) and Mr L J Reyersbach.

The first indication of the setting up of the Orphanage as an independent Institution appeared in the year of 1906, when, at the Annual Meeting of the League in May of that year – the same month as when the Kensington Home was officially opened – the late Mr J H Isaacs (who was President of the Johannesburg Hebrew Congregation) asked the Committee to consider the idea of the separation of the Orphanage from the League, but this was strenuously opposed.

In 1907 the number of children in the Home had increased to 43; and already the lack of accommodation was being felt. The Annual Report complained of lack of support from the Communities outside Johannesburg, and mentioned that if more assistance from them was not forthcoming, the Committee would not be able to cope with the increasing demands of the Jewish population in South Africa.

Four extra stands adjoining the Kensington Home were purchased this year for £500 from the estate of the late Alfred Beit

A booklet containing the "Rules and Regulations for the South African Jewish Orphanage," which had been drawn up by the Committee, and was the subject of a number of meetings, was printed in 1907. This set out that the Orphanage was controlled by a Committee of three, one of whom was the Chairman, Treasurer or Honorary Secretary of the League, and the other two members of the League committee. This Committee met once a week, and reported to the League Committee once a month.

The first South African Jewish Orphanage in Kensington

The Official opening of the first South African Jewish Orphanage in Kensington – photo from Arlene Beare

Only genuine orphans were to be admitted, that is to say, children who had lost one or both parents, and no applications from parents or guardians were to be considered unless they were resident in South Africa for at least a year. This latter rule is still in force, but it is more honoured in the breach than the observance. Orphans must be between the ages of four and eleven at the time of admission. Boys must leave the Home at the age of fourteen, and girls at the age of fifteen.

Now, of course, it is different. Destitute children as well as orphans are eligible for admission, and the age of admission is from two years to twelve. In addition, applications for admission of children under two are also considered, and if granted, the child is placed in Cotlands Babies' Sanctuary, where the Orphanage pays for its keep until the age of two, when the child is taken into Arcadia.

In 1907 the continued financial depression caused a falling off in subscriptions and general revenue, which that year totalled only £1,268. That year the Johannesburg Municipality made a grant of £100 to the Orphanage, which annual grant still continues.

On 25 November 1908, the foundation stone of the private hospital (actually an Isolation Ward), erected in the grounds, was laid by the late Sir (then Mr) George Albu, to commemorate the tenth anniversary of the Jewish Ladies' Communal League.

By 1917 there were 58 children in the Orphanage, and the accommodation was very strained. Many were the schemes and discussions at the Committee and Annual Meetings for either enlarging the existing buildings or erecting new buildings.

The Orphanage veteran Honorary Life President, Mr I Heymann, joined the Committee in 1918, and in 1920 was elected as a Trustee in place of Mr Max Langerman, who had died the previous year, and the same year Mr I. Heymann was also elected Treasurer.

1920 – IMPORTANT YEAR OF CHANGE

The year 1920 brought about great changes in the Orphanage. Not only did the critical position of the Home become acute owing to the increased lack of accommodation and the urgent necessity of providing more accommodation, but there was also a growing feeling of dissatisfaction in regard to its management. Many felt that the Institution was important enough and the work entailed sufficient to warrant its existence as an independent organisation, and not simply as a branch of a Society which also dealt with other matters. A movement was set afoot, headed by Messrs M I Isaacson, David Getz and W Jacobson, to separate the Orphanage from the League, and to have male members included on the Governing Committee.

At a meeting held on 1 October 1920, with Mr H Newhouse, husband of the President and a well-known figure then in financial circles, in the Chair, Dr A J Orenstein – an authority on children, who was present by invitation – advocated the cottage system of housing the children, especially as vast alterations were necessary to the present building in Kensington in order to provide adequate and suitable accommodation for the children, who were being overcrowded. This proposal, he urged was in accordance with contemporary ideas of the scientific housing of children. He would recommend a number of smaller houses, with open-air sleeping accommodation.

It was suggested that the Kensington property be sold and a plot of ground purchased in the neighbourhood of Parkview, and Mr Newhouse said, the Corner House would sell the Orphanage a plot of ground about seven acres in extent for about £1,000, in the neighbourhood of the Zoo, whereon buildings for housing 100 children could be erected and fitted, at a cost of about £30,000.

These proposals were referred to a Special General Meeting held on 12 October 1920, at which Mr Newhouse also presided. It was there resolved to approve of the principle of selling the existing property, building a new Orphanage and to instruct the Committee to bring a report within three months showing the outlines of a scheme for carrying this out, and for the collection of funds for this purpose.

At a special meeting of the Committee held on 24 October 1920, it was resolved that the League and the Orphanage be separated, and that the Orphanage take over all the assets, with the exception of the cash in the bank in the name of the League. This resolution was carried with one vote against.

A Sub-Committee was then appointed to draft a Constitution and Rules and Regulations for the South African Jewish Orphanage, the name of the Institution to be "The South African Jewish Orphanage (Founded by the Jewish Ladies' Communal League)", and also to draft a Constitution for the Jewish Ladies' Communal League.

The same meeting also resolved that the personnel of the Committee of the Orphanage shall consist of 17, of whom not less than eight should be women and not less than five shall be men.

The above Sub-Committee submitted drafts of two Constitutions and Bye-Laws, one for the League and the other for the Orphanage, to a Special General Meeting of the League on 14 December 1920, at which they were adopted.

FIRST MEETING OF THE SOUTH AFRICAN JEWISH ORPHANAGE

An historic date in the annals of the Orphanage is Wednesday, 19 January 1921, for on that day the first meeting of the South African Jewish Orphanage as an independent Institution was held, at which the first Committee was elected and the first Constitution was adopted.

The following constituted the first Committee of the South African Jewish Orphanage: President, Mr D Starfield; Vice-Presidents, Mr B I Bloom and Mrs S B Asher; Honorary Treasurer, Mr S Schneier; Honorary Secretary, Mr David Getz; Trustees, Sir George Albu, Mr I W Schlesinger and Mr A Atkins; Committee, Mrs D A Bradlow, Mr M I Isaacson, Mrs M Israel, Miss R Jacobs, Mrs H Lipschitz, Mrs I Marks, Mr M Reuvid, Mrs P Sand, Mr A Sive, Mrs A Shapiro, Dr C Shapiro, Mrs S Nathanson.

Appropriate votes of thanks were passed to the League Committee, who had managed the Orphanage for the previous 17 years, and especially to the Honorary Secretary, Mrs E M Davis-Marks, who had occupied that office throughout that period.

THE GREAT PROBLEM – LACK OF ACCOMMODATION

In the year 1921 there were 64 children in the Orphanage – 40 girls and 24 boys.

The Kensington home was originally built to accommodate 32 children, so that now, with double that number to provide for, it can be well understood that the first and most urgent task of the Committee was to increase the accommodation, either by enlarging the present building or to build a new home elsewhere. It is not surprising that under these conditions the Committee were compelled to refuse some applications for admission.

The members gave the Committee a definite mandate to devise ways and means to provide, at the earliest possible opportunity, the increased accommodation essential for the needs of the Institution.

The Committee, soon after taking office, discussed the question of finding additional accommodation, and came to the conclusion that the present site was not sufficiently large nor suitable for additional building operations. Efforts were directed in the first place towards finding possible sites for a new building. In this connection it is worth noting that the Committee was somewhat limited in its choice by the following important considerations: the necessity that the Home should be situated in a district where the difficulty of obtaining school accommodation should not be insurmountable, that the centre in which the Home is located should be one to which easy access is obtainable and which was not too far distant from the Jewish neighbourhood. After consideration of various sites, the choice was made of a site of 13 acres, which was considered most suitable for the needs of the Institution.

An offer for this ground was made and accepted, and the site known as Langerman's Gardens, in Kensington, was purchased, at the price of £4,198. It was then described as one of the finest sites in Johannesburg, and magnificently laid out.

THE CONSTITUTION AND BYE-LAWS

The Constitution, Bye-Laws and Regulations adopted at this first meeting in January, 1921, have been considerably amended from time to time, as the necessity and circumstances required, and at present the objects of the Institution are stated to be as follows:-

1) To provide a Jewish Home for destitute orphans and other destitute children of the Jewish Faith, and to provide for their upbringing, maintenance and education.

2) To establish, manage, conduct and support, or aid in the establishment, management, conduct and support of a Home or Homes for indigent or partially indigent young persons of the Jewish Faith.

THE WAR ORPHANS FROM EASTERN EUROPE

It was in 1921 that the late Mr Isaac Ochberg, the President of the Cape Jewish Orphanage, working in conjunction with the Jewish Relief, Reconstruction and Orphans Fund,

brought out to this country 167 Jewish war orphans from Eastern Europe, 89 of whom were taken over by the Cape Orphanage and 78 by the Fund in Johannesburg.

A number of these orphans were privately adopted, and the Fund remained with 67 orphan children on its hands. The Fund Committee had several consultations with the Orphanage Committee with regard to the Orphanage taking over these overseas children, and as a result it was agreed that the needs of the Community would be best served by the erection of a building capable of housing both the children in the Orphanage and the orphans from Eastern Europe.

The Jewish Relief, Reconstruction and Orphans Fund, in consideration of these arrangements, agreed to contribute £12,500 towards the cost of a new building.

The Orphanage Committee agreed to undertake the care in the future of the 40 orphans then in the charge of the Fund, and that the Committee of the fund would have the right to appoint four members of the Fund to represent them on the Orphanage Committee.

Resolutions giving effect to this arrangement were passed at the 1922 Orphanage Annual Meeting, and the first four representatives of the Fund on the Orphanage Committee were Mr Bernard Alexander, Mr Richard Feldman, Mr M. Udwin and Mrs S. Epstein. In June 1932, this arrangement was cancelled by agreement.

Some of the Orphans and nurses on their way to South Africa

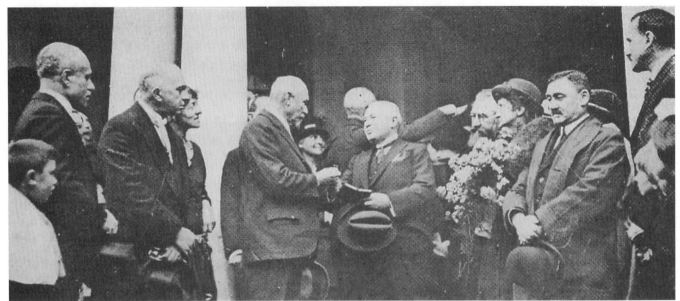

The Official Opening of Arcadia by Jan Smuts – 18 July 1923. Mr Schlesinger is presenting the key to General Smuts. On the right are Rabbi Dr J L Landau and Mr I Heymann. On the left is Mr M I Isaacson.

ARCADIA

During the year 1922 the Committee learned, mainly through the late Mr Bernard Alexander, that "Arcardia," the 26-acre home of Sir Lionel Phillips, in Parktown, could be purchased. This information started a series of negotiations, as the result of which, instead of proceeding with the plans for building in Langerman Gardens, it was decided at a special General Meeting to purchase Arcadia for the sum of £30,000, and to sell Langerman's Gardens, as well as the Home in Benbow Street.

At this time there were 81 children in the Kensington Home, but, in spite of this increase of 16 over the previous year, a number of applications had to be refused because of lack of accommodation.

With the purchase of Arcadia, this reason for refusing applications no longer applied, for Arcadia was large enough not only to provide a Home for the 81 children, but also for the 67 orphans from Eastern Europe, as well as for new applicants. Even after the sale of the two properties mentioned and the Relief Fund's payment of the £12,500 agreed upon, there was still a shortage of £10,000. This was obtained as a loan, and a campaign was launched to collect contributions from the Jewish Community, which met with a fair amount of success.

Considerable work had to be done at Arcadia to make it suitable for an Orphanage, and it was on 18 July, 1923, that Arcadia was officially opened, in the presence of a large and representative gathering, by the late General Smuts, who was then Prime Minister.

The official report of the opening said: "The occasion will long be remembered in the annals of the Jewish Community of the Witwatersrand as one of the most notable days in its history."

Villa Arcadia

Chapter 88 – THE SAJO AND THE SAMUELS FAMILY (1903)

The South African Jewish Orphanage in Johannesburg initially came into being when the Jewish Community had to take care for the Samuels children following the death of their mother.

THE HISTORY OF THE SAMUELS CHILDREN
Written by Arlene Beare Beare the daughter of Louis Samuels, born in 1899 and was the eighth of the nine Samuels children.

I have done extensive research into the history of the Orphanage with assistance by Prof Reuben Musiker.

I read through the minutes of the Jewish Ladies Communal League which make fascinating reading and I would recommend that anyone interested in the early years of the Orphanage read them in the Archives of the Jewish Board of Deputies in Johannesburg.

Benjamin (born in Krakow Poland) and Annie (Cohen) Samuels arrived in Johannesburg at the turn of the century with eight children. Three were born in London, four in Cardiff and the eighth Louis may have been born on the ship they arrived on. Their names were Abraham, Sophia, Rose, Ada, Esther, Eva, Dora and Louis (my father).

The ninth child Elma, was born in Johannesburg on the 10 September 1902. Annie, her mother died on the 12 September 1902. Benjamin abandoned the children and they were taken into care.

Elma was adopted, although not formally, by Mrs Pauline Jacobs who cared for her from the age of six weeks, and she took the name Elma Jacobs

The Samuels family prior to leaving England

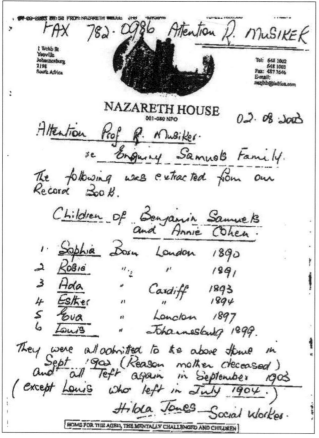

Nazareth House records

Abraham who was 17 probably found work and little is known of what became of him. There is mention in the minutes that he arrived to see his sisters, but was not allowed into the Orphanage. No reason is given in the minutes for his denial of entry.

Sophia, Rose, Ada, Esther, Eve and Louis were taken into the Nazareth House, a home for Christian children. Dora and possibly Abraham were in the Undenominational Children's Home, also a Christian Institution.

A meeting was held on 26 November 1902 in the Old Synagogue, President Street at which the plight of the Samuels orphans was discussed. They stated that every effort should be made to start a Jewish home for orphans or to try to get them accepted by the Jewish Orphanage at Norwood in England.

The minutes of 13 January 1903 record that Mr Goldreich explained that the object of the meeting was to send Jewish orphans now in the Nazareth Home and Undenominational Children's Home to the Jewish Orphanage in London.

However Dr Hertz stated that the amount required would be 100 guineas per child and that the Jewish Ladies Communal

League could only give £150 towards this objective. Rabbi Dr Hertz protested that the Chevra Kadisha should not stand by and see these children converted without raising a finger to help.

They also discussed the possibility of getting a house and approaching Mr Samuels who was living in Pretoria, to take back the responsibility of raising his children. The minutes of 12 May 1903 record that the father Benjamin refused to care for them.

Sophia Samuels was sent back to the Jewish Society for the Protection of Women and Girls in England as there was insufficient money to send all of the children. Mr Goldreich had written to his brother to arrange that Sophia would be met at Southampton with a Matron from the Home.

The minutes of the 20 July 1903 resolved that the Institution to care for the children would be called the South African Jewish Orphanage and would be connected with the Jewish Women's Communal League. The first premises were Alexander House at a rental of £35 per month.

A letter was sent to Mr Samuels for him to give permission to take the children from the Nazareth House and they were taken from there on the 2 of September 1903.

My father Louis was not admitted into the Orphanage as they had resolved on an age limit and he was too young. He remained in Nazareth House and was subsequently adopted by a Mr Goldman from Krugersdorp. Eva was adopted from the Orphanage by a Mr Hartfield.

Ada and Rose were very active in the daily running of the Orphanage standing in as cook or maid when they were short staffed. The minutes are full of references to them. Esther who was also in the home was offered a job and thus left the Orphanage.

Ada and Rose were both married from the Orphanage and the weddings were written up in the Jewish Chronicle. See below

In June 1904 the Minutes record the place of the meeting as at the Orphanage 51 Pretoria Street.

A special meeting was held on 21 July 1904 to discuss the offer of a house in Doornfontein but it was decided that they should rent a property rather than buying one and at the time. 23 Esselen Street was decided upon provided certain alterations could be done.

March the 23 1905 the foundation stone of the first Jewish Orphanage to be owned and not rented was laid by Mrs Max Langerman. This date is recorded as the date of the birth of the South African Jewish Orphanage but as I have shown from the minutes, the Orphanage came into being in 1903. "Arcadia" was the further development of the Orphanage.

Chapter 89 – MORRIS ISAAC AND MAVIS ISAACSON AND THE JEWISH RELIEF RECONSTRUCTION AND ORPHANS FUND

Morris Isaac Isaacson was one of three members of an advisory board that drafted a new constitution for the South African Jewish Orphanage (SAJO) so that it became an institution on its own and was no longer just a part of the Jewish Ladies' Communal League where it had been for 17 years.

Mr M I Isaacson was a member of the SAJO committee (1921-1923) and in 1924 he was appointed Chairman. In that year he married Mavis Myer who was the daughter of the then matron of the SAJO then housed in Kensington.

Mr Isaacson was also the Treasurer of the United South Africa Jewish Relief, Reconstruction and Orphan Fund that negotiated to bring to South Africa 200 Orphans from Poland and the Ukraine. Mavis took charge of 88 of the Orphans and they were temporarily housed at the Old Aged Home.

At the same time while plans were afoot to build a new Orphanage in Kensington the palatial residence "Arcadia" became available and it was acquired as the new home of the South African Jewish Orphanage and Mavis was then appointed Matron.

RAND PIONEER WHO ESTABLISHED "ARCADIA"
Extracts from an article by Richard Feldman

Jewish War Relief Fund

Simultaneously with his activities in the Labour Party, we find Morris Isaac Isaacson at the beginning of World War I, together with the respected representative of the orthodox Jews, Reb. Chaim Yankel Kark, as chief protagonists for the formation of a Jewish War Relief fund, which was at first strongly opposed by Mr Harry Graumann, at that time the leading spokesman of Johannesburg Jewry.

At the end of the First World War, Mr Isaacson was amongst the most prominent and active leaders of Johannesburg Jewry. He was President of the Jewish Guild, Treasurer of the Jewish War Memorial fund, Treasurer of the Jewish Relief and Reconstruction Fund, and chairman of the S A Jewish Orphanage.

Orphanage "Revolution"

His connection with the Orphanage needs to be written up at greater length, as it is the story of a bloodless "revolution" to establish democratic rule in one of the community's institutions. Briefly the facts are these. The Orphanage was not an independent body, and had no separate constitution, but was an activity of the Jewish Ladies' Communal League. Males could not have a say in the way the Orphanage was run. The League leadership was unsympathetic to the recent immigrants from Eastern Europe. Orphanage contributions had no legal rights, Member- ship fees were regarded as donations. Attendance at an annual meeting was a courtesy, not a right.

Morris Isaac Isaacson

Mr Isaacson, in collaboration with Mr David Getz (now of Cape Town), the late Mr W Jacobson, and other supporters, attended an annual meeting - by courtesy of the Committee – and demanded the independence and democratisation of the Orphanage. Seeing that the rebels had strong support, the Chairman adjourned the meeting for ten minutes, and on its resumption announced that the League was prepared to "abdicate", and an Interim Committee to draft a constitution was adopted. The old leadership refused to participate in the new Committee. "M I I" found himself with an Orphanage on his hands. Here he met Mavis Myers, the daughter of the Matron, and he married her in 1924.

The Relief fund was negotiating to bring to South Africa 200 orphans from Poland and Ukraine, and Mr Isaacson played a prominent part as Treasurer of the Fund in bringing together the local and overseas orphans.

Mavis Myers took charge of the 88 overseas orphans, who were temporarily housed at the Jewish Aged Home, and soon became "Mummy Myers" to them, as indeed "M I I" became "Pappa Isaacson". Their devotion to the young strangers was without bounds.

How "Arcadia" was acquired

Plans were ready for the building of a new Orphanage at Kensington at the cost of 35,000 pounds but the late Bernard Alexander, leader of South African Jewry at the time, and Chairman of the Relief fund, sent for Mr Isaacson and the late Peter Kaplan, and told them that Sir Lionel Phillips' palatial residence, "Arcadia", was for sale and it was bought for 30 000 pounds.

There was considerable opposition to this purchase on the ground that poor orphans should not be housed in a palace amidst beautiful surroundings. This opposition persisted until the official opening by General Smuts, who pointed out that the beauty of the surroundings was some compensation for these children who had no parents and no home of their own.

Mavis Myers was appointed matron and until her marriage she and Mr Isaacson devoted their spare time, their energy and love, to making "Arcadia" a home for its young residents.

In passing, it may be mentioned that Mr Isaacson wanted the Orphanage to be known as "Arcadia", and not the "Orphanage". He had witnessed some of the overseas children, when brought to the Cape Orphanage, reading the word "BET YESOIMIM" (House of Orphans) and crying: "So we have come from one Orphanage to another". This impressed him so much that his main endeavour was to free "Arcadia" from any institutional atmosphere.

Mavis Myer

Memorial to his wife

In 1926 the Isaacsons left for Warmbaths, and their active association with communal institutions stopped for some years, but many there are who have cause to remember them with affection and gratitude for the paternal care and assistance they rendered.

During the last war, Mrs Isaacson gave voluntary but full-time service to the Johannesburg Hospital, and at her death in 1949, sincere tributes were paid to her by the Hospital authorities for her devoted services.

As a memorial to his wife, Mr Isaacson, under the auspices of the City Council, built a Nursery School at Moroka Township – truly a fitting reminder of a partnership of service to different sections of the community.

ILLUMINATED ADDRESS from the UNITED SOUTH AFRICAN JEWISH RELIEF RECONSTRUCTION AND ORPHANS FUND to M I ISAACSON ESQ

Dear Mr Isaacson

On the occasion of your marriage we wish to place on record our deep appreciation of your great services to the cause of our people in Eastern Europe in your capacity as Hon Treasurer and Vice President of the Fund, particularly in the cause of our destitute orphans.

After the pogrom period in the Ukraine when the news of the terrible plight of hundreds of thousands of pogrom orphans reached us and South African Jewry deeply felt the great national tragedy, you placed yourself at the head of the Save the Orphans Campaign and since then you have worked wholeheartedly on behalf of these destitute orphans of ours. When the eighty eight orphans brought out by our Fund arrived in Johannesburg you entirely devoted yourself to caring for their well-being and happiness. Indeed you have been like a father to them.

It is not for us to thank you for your great and noble work, but we feel sure that on this your wedding day as well as all your life time you will feel happy and compensated in the knowledge of having to such an extent been instrumental in saving so many young lives, ensuring them of a happier future than that which faced them.

We also feel happy in the thought that your life's partner has also been associated with us in the caring of our orphans. Indeed Miss Mavis Meyers has as Matron been a true friend to them, giving them a mother's care and love.

We wish you both a very happy life – a life full of joy and sunshine.

With kindest regards – On behalf of the Central Executive Committee.

The document is signed by the President, Bernard Allexander, the Vice President, Natie Kirschner, the treasurer, S M Gordon, the Secretary, Percy Cowen, and Richard Feldman, the chairman of the Propaganda committee.

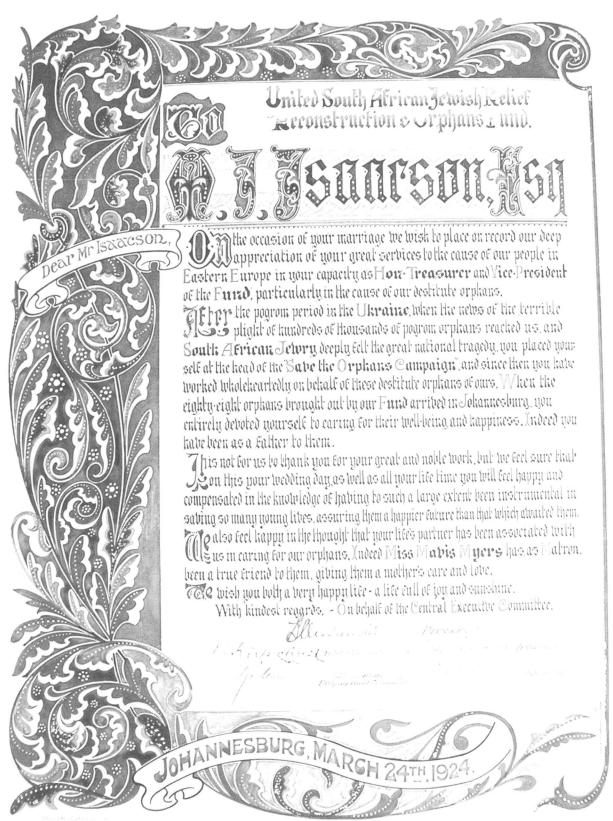

United South African Jewish Relief Reconstruction & Orphans Fund.

To M. J. Isaacson, Esq

Dear Mr Isaacson,

On the occasion of your marriage we wish to place on record our deep appreciation of your great services to the cause of our people in Eastern Europe in your capacity as Hon. Treasurer and Vice-President of the Fund, particularly in the cause of our destitute orphans.

After the pogrom period in the Ukraine, when the news of the terrible plight of hundreds of thousands of pogrom orphans reached us, and South African Jewry deeply felt the great national tragedy, you placed yourself at the head of the "Save the Orphans Campaign", and since then you have worked wholeheartedly on behalf of these destitute orphans of ours. When the eighty-eight orphans brought out by our Fund arrived in Johannesburg, you entirely devoted yourself to caring for their well-being and happiness. Indeed you have been as a father to them.

It is not for us to thank you for your great and noble work, but we feel sure that on this your wedding day, as well as all your life time you will feel happy and compensated in the knowledge of having to such a large extent been instrumental in saving so many young lives, assuring them a happier future than that which awaited them.

We also feel happy in the thought that your life's partner has been associated with us in caring for our orphans. Indeed Miss Mavis Myers has, as Matron, been a true friend to them, giving them a mother's care and love.

We wish you both a very happy life - a life full of joy and sunshine.

With kindest regards. - On behalf of the Central Executive Committee.

JOHANNESBURG, MARCH 24TH, 1924.

ILLUMINATED ADDRESS given to Morris Isaacs and Mavis Myers on the occasion of their wedding in thanks for their service given to the Ukraine Orphans.

Chapter 90 – THE PERSIAN FETE, A FUNDRAISER FOR THE "SAVE THE ORPHANS FUND"

THE PERSIAN FETE

A successful function held in Johannesburg in September 1921 to raise funds for the 'Save the Orphans Fund'

Reporter and newspaper unknown
Article sent in by Lionel Slier

Prior to leaving England, a friend mentioned that a Persian Fete was to be held in Johannesburg and concluded with the words 'you will be surprised'. Indeed, one cannot help being surprised at the success of the Persian Fete. For several months an energetic committee has been at work and in the face of many obstacles have achieved the impossible. It seems a great pity that Johannesburg, which prides itself on being such an up-to-date city, has no really large hall in the centre of the town. The Town Hall was far too small to stage the Persian Fete as it deserved, furthermore it was only with difficulty that only some of the thousands of people that wished to see the Fete were able to. Thousands were unable to get anywhere near the doors let alone inside, on the opening night. The hall itself was crowded to excess from the moment the doors were opened to closing time, so that the purveyors of all manner of articles, from a pin to tickets for the raffle of a motor car could only with difficulty carry out their duties.

His Worship the Mayor (Mr J Christie, MLA) and Mrs Christie opened the Fete on Tuesday, Mr Isaac Ochberg, Chairman of the Cape Jewish Orphanage who despite his recent arduous experiences in rescuing and bringing the orphans to South Africa, travelled specially from Cape Town to open the fete on the second day, whilst on the third day Mr Bernard Alexander, JP performed the opening ceremony.

On Wednesday and Thursday afternoons a "Fairy Flower Fantasy" was produced by Miss Madge Mann and Mrs E Solomon. The majority of those taking part in this production were young children, and large audiences showed in no unmistakable terms their appreciation of the youngsters' efforts. The singing, dancing and acting all call for special praise. The two ladies and their assistants deserve hearty congratulations for their excellent work, and it is to be hoped that it will perform in aid of other deserving objects in the near future.

Coming back to the Fete once more there were numerous stalls all of them tastefully decorated, space permit the mention of only a few. As usual the Jewish Guild worked hard, and in addition to being responsible for two stalls, lent valuable assistance to several others. The toiletries requisites' stall did a roaring trade and Mrs S L Sive and her helpers were kept busy in attending to the needs of their customers. Mr and Mrs I Belcher, who had charge of two stalls from the Doornfontein Branch, had all manner of articles which they quickly disposed of, they ranged from a Pomeranian puppy to juvenile clothing.

The furniture and jewellery stall had many hundreds of pounds worth of valuable articles for sale at reasonable prices, all of them the gifts of generous donors.

In addition there were stalls for the sale of flowers, refreshments of all descriptions, books, clothing, fancy goods, tobacco, fruit, provisions etc.

The music was provided by Mr Max Weinbrenn and his orchestra, Messrs Clarke and Adeler's orchestra and the Railway and Harbours band all of whom gave their services.

The object of the fete was to raise the substantial amount of £10,000 for the 'Save the Orphans Fund' and it is more than likely that this sum will not only be obtained but will be exceeded. The Honorary Organisers Mrs Joe Cohen and Mr Ernest Solomon and their numerous workers have the great satisfaction of knowing, that their labours have not been in vain and that their work for the needy has been appreciated.

TO-NIGHT'S
THE
NIGHT

PERSIAN
FETE
OPENS
TO-NIGHT
AT 8 p.m.

TOWN HALL
SEPTEMBER 27, 28, 29

OFFICIAL OPENING TO-NIGHT,
8 P.M. BY HIS WORSHIP THE
MAYOR AND MAYORESS
(Mr AND Mrs J Christie)

OFFICIAL OPENING WEDNESDAY
28th, 3 p.m. by Mr I Ochberg

OFFICIAL OPENING THURSDAY
29th 8 p.m. by Mr Bernard Alexander

FETE OPENS EACH DAY AT 11 AM
Morning and Afternoon Teas, Lunches
And High Teas served
ADMISSION 1 s

Chapter 91 – EXTRACT OF MINUTES OF ARCADIA (THE SOUTH AFRICAN JEWISH ORPHANAGE)

These extracts of minutes, which mention many of the Ochberg Orphan girls, were sent in by Lionel Slier

11 NOVEMBER 1923

House master
The Chairman reported that the Sub-Committee met in connection with a house master. He stated that Mr Israel's application was not being considered, and that we were expecting Rev Mr Ley. He also stated that Miss Barrkman had introduced another applicant for the post - Mr Kossik.

It was decided that the Committee meet at Mr Getz's office tomorrow afternoon to discuss the matter.

Drainage
Mr Udwin gave a full report on the necessary drainage alterations to be made in the building, as well as certain concrete steps required. The former to cost £60 and the latter £25. Mr Udwin suggested that Mr F A Sharman be engaged for this work, and the tenders placed by Mr Sharman for this work was produced at the meeting.

A discussion arose on Jewish workmen being employed for work to be done at the Orphanage.

The Secretary moved that in case of any work required for the Orphanage, that in the absence of any good reason to the contrary, the lowest tender should obtain the work. Preference to be given to Jewish contractors.

Seconded by Mrs Bradlow.   Carried

It was agreed that the expenditure £60 and £25 necessary for the alterations be sanctioned.

The alterations were left in the hands of Mr Edwin.

Kensington Property
The Secretary reported on this and stated that it would be necessary to call a meeting of the Jewish Ladies Communal League before the matter can be completed.

Miss Altuska's Holiday
The Chairman reported that Miss Altuska had left on a holiday to Cape Town and would be staying at the Cape Orphanage. He stated that he had paid £5.19.6 for her fare to Cape town.

21 SEPTEMBER 1924

Re Ratzer
With regard to this girl, who was being kept at Mr Judelowitz's house, Mr M Gordon proposed that she be taken into the Orphanage. The Chairman reported on this case and stated that it was not desirable that the girl should be in the Orphanage. After discussion, it was agreed that the girl be taken into the Orphanage.

Applications
The application of Mrs Glicksman of Benoni for the admission of her daughter aged seven was considered and granted.

Resignation of Mr Getz
A letter was read from Mr D Getz resigning his position as Honorary Secretary owing to his not being able to give sufficient time to it. The matter was discussed, and it was decided to write to Mr Getz asking him to reconsider his resignation in view of the present critical position of the Orphanage being such that no worker could be spared.

Correspondence
A letter was read from Mr Ravid, a collector for the Pretoria Branch, mentioning certain rumours that were being spread to the effect that the children were being insufficiently fed. It was decided to reply emphatically denying this statement and that, on the contrary, the children were being very well looked after.

A letter was read from the gardener complaining of the treatment he was subjected to and certain statements made to him. This was noted and the matter was left to the Chairman to deal with.

16 OCTOBER 1923

Sarah Gajer - To look for situation as milliner.

Elsie Ellman - To enquire of Mrs Levinson if she will take her as an assistant. Mrs Abelheim undertook to see Mrs Levinson.

- - - - - -

With regard to the following girls it was decided that they are to continue attending school, but so as to enable them to make more rapid progress, it was decided to engage a teacher to help them with their lessons and generally to enable them to skip a Standard.

Anna Bordweik	Frede Joffe	Tilly Walchuk
Rachel Bordweik	Polly Steinger	Sarah Altushka
Lily Faifer	Anna Garber	Zlate Knubowitz

- - - - - -

It was also decided that this teacher should give lessons in English to Gitel Gunifus, and Mindel Pensick, who are very backward in their studies.

- - - - - -

A Harris - to write to father if he can take the boy away, failing this to suggest sending him to be apprenticed at the Vereeniging Steel Works.

Harry Lissik - To suggest apprenticing to the Vereeniging Steel Works.

Mer Maltz - Application to be made for High School (if application has not already been made).

David Pensick - Mr M Gordon reported having obtained a good situation for this boy at L K Hurwitz.

The necessary application to School Board was being made and David commences work immediately. This was confirmed. Application to be made to the Twist Street School for High School tuition for this boy. He will in the meantime stay at the Orphanage.

Sarah Magrabi, Julius Victor and Betty Broudie - Matron Berliner reported that Dr Moll's assistant examined these children and they will soon be seen by Dr Moll. It was decided to be guided by Dr Moll's advice.

19 OCTOBER 1924

A meeting of the House Committee was held on 12 October 1924.

It was decided to get a certificated Nurse, preferably one who was at present at the Hospital, who should also be able to act as housekeeper, the engagement to be subject to one week's notice. The matter was left to Mrs Bradlow.

With regard to the staff, the following was decided:

Mrs Valensky	To remain in charge of the babies, at a salary of £10 per month.
Mrs Ulm	To remain in charge of the boys as far as the domestic arrangements are concerned, at £10. per month.
Miss Altushka	To remain in charge of the girls, at £8. per month.
Miss G Gunefas	To assist in kitchen and housekeeping, at a salary of £2.10.0 per month.
Miss A Datnovsky	To assist with the babies, salary £2. per month.
Miss M Penzik	To assist generally, salary £2. per month.
Mrs Amery (Sewing)	To remain at £10. per month.
Mr Lazarow	To look after the motor car, do handyman's work, and not to interfere with the housework.
Mr Goodman	As Handyman at a salary of £2.10.0 a month.

It was decided that the staff should have their meals with the children at breakfast and dinner, also that no electric irons were to be used by the children or assistants.

It was recommended to the Matron that she should establish sewing classes for the children.

It was decided to recommend that no individual member of the Committee should give instructions to the Matron but that this be done by the House Committee, two members of whom be appointed every month for the purpose of giving such instructions.

For this month Mrs Bradlow and Mrs Isaacson have been appointed.

OCHBERG ORPHAN SENT TO USA

The man in this picture was an Ochberg Orphan who was sent to the USA as he had an uncle there.

There are many lists of the children in Yiddish and English and handwritten and typed.
Following are two lists

Children sent to Johannesburg showing age, where born and where taken
Pages one and two

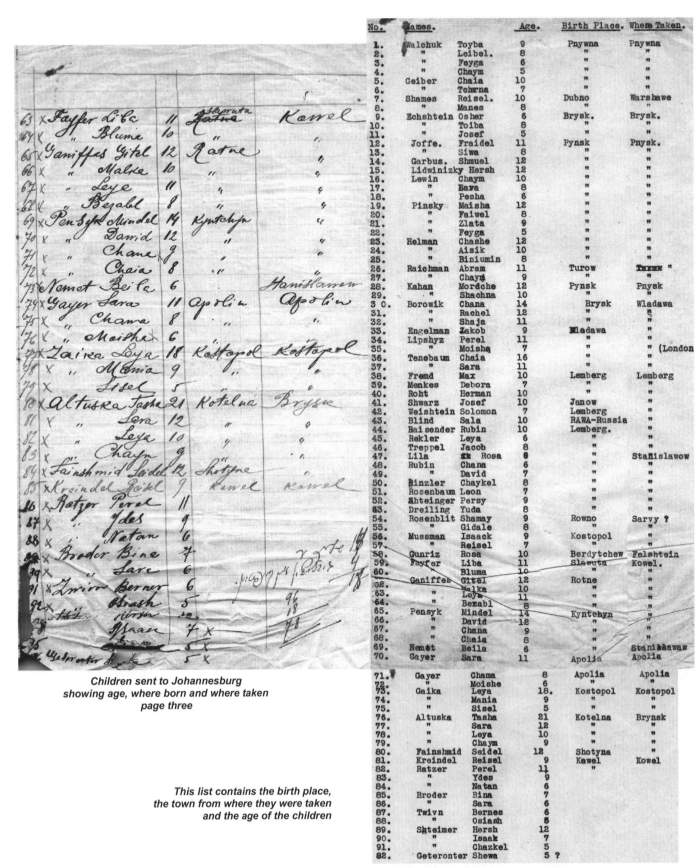

Children sent to Johannesburg
showing age, where born and where taken
page three

This list contains the birth place,
the town from where they were taken
and the age of the children

No.	Names.		Age.	Birth Place.	Where Taken.
1.	Walchuk	Toyba	9	Pnywna	Pnywna
2.	"	Leibel.	8	"	"
3.	"	Feyga	6	"	"
4.	"	Chaym	5	"	"
5.	Geiber	Chaia	10	"	"
6.	"	Tcherna	7	"	"
7.	Shames	Reisel.	10	Dubno	Warshawe
8.	"	Manes	8	"	"
9.	Echshtein	Osher	6	Brysk.	Brysk.
10.	"	Toiba	8	"	"
11.	"	Josef	5	"	"
12.	Joffe.	Fraidel	11	Pynsk	Pnysk.
13.	"	Siwa	8	"	"
14.	Garbus.	Shmuel	12	"	"
15.	Lidwinizky	Hersh	12	"	"
16.	Lewin	Chaym	10	"	"
17.	"	Bawa	8	"	"
18.	"	Pesha	6	"	"
19.	Pinsky	Maisha	12	"	"
20.	"	Faiwel	8	"	"
21.	"	Zlata	9	"	"
22.	"	Feyga	5	"	"
23.	Helman	Chashe	12	"	"
24.	"	Aisik	10	"	"
25.	"	Biniumin	8	"	"
26.	Raichman	Abram	11	Turow	Turow "
27.	"	Chaym	9	"	"
28.	Kahan	Mordche	12	Pynsk	Pnysk
29.	"	Shachna	10	"	"
30.	Borowik	Chana	14	Brysk	Wladawa
31.	"	Rachel	12	"	"
32.	"	Shaja	11	"	"
33.	Engelman	Zakob	9	Wladawa	"
34.	Lipshyz	Perel	11	"	"
35.	"	Moisha	7	"	(London
36.	Tenebaum	Chaia	16	"	"
37.	"	Sara	11	"	"
38.	Fremd	Max	10	Lemberg	Lemberg
39.	Menkes	Debora	7	"	"
40.	Roht	Herman	10	"	"
41.	Shwarz	Josef	10	Janow	"
42.	Weishtein	Solomon	7	Lemberg	"
43.	Blind	Sala	10	RAWA-Russia	"
44.	Baisender	Rubin	10	Lemberg.	"
45.	Rekler	Leya	6	"	"
46.	Treppel	Jacob	8	"	"
47.	Lila	th Rosa	8	"	Stanislawow
48.	Rubin	Chana	6	"	"
49.	"	David	7	"	"
50.	Rinzler	Chaykel	8	"	"
51.	Rosenbaum	Leon	7	"	"
52.	Shteinger	Persy	9	"	"
53.	Dreiling	Yuda	8	"	"
54.	Rosenblit	Shamay	9	Rowno	Sarvy ?
55.	"	Gidale	8	"	"
56.	Mussman	Isaack	9	Kostopol	"
57.	"	Reisel	7	"	"
58.	Gunriz	Rosa	10	Berdytchew	Felshtein
59.	Fayfer	Liba	11	Slawuta	Kowel.
60.	"	Bluma	10	"	"
61.	Ganiffes	Gitel	12	Rotne	"
62.	"	Malka	10	"	"
63.	"	Leya	11	"	"
64.	"	Bezabl	8	"	"
65.	Pensyk	Mindel	14	Kyntchyn	"
66.	"	David	12	"	"
67.	"	Chana	9	"	"
68.	"	Chaia	8	"	"
69.	Nemet	Beila	6	"	Stanislawaw
70.	Gayer	Sara	11	Apolia	Apolia
71.	Gayer	Chama	8	Apolia	Apolia
72.	"	Moishe	6	"	"
73.	Gaika	Leya	18.	Kostopol	Kostopol
74.	"	Mania	9	"	"
75.	"	Sisel	5	"	"
76.	Altuska	Tasha	21	Kotelna	Brynsk
77.	"	Sara	12	"	"
78.	"	Leya	10	"	"
79.	"	Chaym	9	"	"
80.	Fainshmid	Seidel	12	Shotyna	"
81.	Kreindel	Reisel	9	Kawel	Kowel
82.	Ratzer	Perel	11	"	"
83.	"	Ydes	9	"	"
84.	"	Natan	6	"	"
85.	Broder	Bina	7	"	"
86.	"	Sara	6	"	"
87.	Twivn	Bernes	6	"	"
88.	"	Osiash	5	"	"
89.	Shteimer	Hersh	12	"	"
90.	"	Isaak	7	"	"
91.	"	Chazkel	5	"	"
82.	Geteronter	Shewa	5 ?		

List kindly compiled by Anne Lapedus Brest from the original alphabetical list in the address book

NAME OF CHILD	CHILD PLACED IN THE CARE OF
No.83. ALTUSKA Chaim boy 9	gone to E. Joseph, 67, Terrace Road, Fordsburg. Returned.
No ALTUSKA Leah girl 10	
No ALTUSKA Tasha (Natasha) girl 21	
No ALTUSKA Sarah (girl 12)	
No. 47 BLIND Sala 10	B. Golomb Benoni
No. 35. BOROWIK SHAYA boy 11	gone to Mr. Kuper 68.
No. 34. BOROWIK Rochela Girl 12.	
No. 33. BOROWIK Chana 14.	
No. 91 BRODER Sara girl 6	Rubinstein
No. 90 BRODER Bina 7	Rubinstein
No. 36. ENGELMAN Jacob boy 9	to M. King, 56, Upper Ross Street
No. 13. ECHSTEIN Asher boy 8	still in cape Town
No. 12, ECHSTEIN Toiba girl 6	to A. Abrhamas.
No. 14, ECHSTEIN Joseph 5.	gone to L. Cohen.
No. 84. FAINSMID Leibel boy 12	
No. 63. FEIFER Liba girl 11 (2/2/1910)	to M.Lipman – returned
No. 64. FAIFER Bluma Girl 10	to Rosenkovitz 15, Upper Ross Street
No. 41. FREMD Max boy 10	
No. 76 GAYER Maisha boy 6	Fredman , fordsburg *(Friedman)*
No. 75 GAYER Chava girl 8	Fredman, Fordsburg. *(Friedman)*
No. 74 GAYER Sara girl 11	Rembach.
No. 62 GURWITZ Rosa left in CT . 10	Instructed to give away
No. 86. GELEREUTER Shewa 5	left in Cape Town
No. 17. GERBUS Shmuel boy 12	Gone to M. Golstein
No. 06. GUBER Tcharmag	
No. 05. GUBER Chaia girl 10	
No. 68 GANIFAS Becalel boy 8	Chasen
No. 67 GANIFAS Malka girl 10	to Ellenbogen, returned
No. 66 GANIFAS Leya girl 11 ``	Simon Selkin
No. 65 GANIFAS Gitel girl 12	~~Simon Selkin~~
No. 28. HELMAN Aisik boy 8	det. CT
No. 27 HELMAN Benjamin boy 10	det. CT
No. 26. HELMAN Chashe 12	~~left CT~~ Shamban.
No. 16. JOFFE Sirva girl 8	
No. 15 JOFFE Freidel girl 11	P Berman 74, Sherwell Street.
No. 51 LILA Rosa girl 9	Standerton Young Israel Society
No. 19. LEVIN Chaim boy 10	detained CT
No. 20 LEVIN Sara girl 8	~~det CT~~ toBen Falkow, *(Illegible, Reitz or Britz)*
No.21. LEVIN Peshe *(Geshe)* 6	~~Det. Ct.~~) Benj Falkov
No.37. LIPSHITZ Perel girl 11	~~Det CT~~
No.18 LIDWINSKY Hersh boy 12	~~Det CT~~
No.38 LIPSHITZ Moisha 7	CT

No.61.	MUSSMAN Reisel 7	B. GALANSKY, Benoni
No.60	MUSSMAN Yasaia 9	B GALANSKY, Benoni
No.42,	MENKES Debara girl 7	Mr and Mrs. B Stuppel.
No.73	NEMET Bila girl 6	gone to Bendet Friedland, Braamftonein.
No.46	NEISHTEIN Solomon 7	Joselowitz AE Doornfontein
No.25	PINKSY Feiga girl 5	S. Glass, Winburg OFS
No.24	PINSKY Zlata girl 9	Karensky
No.23	PINKSY Faivel boy 8	
No.22	PINSKY Maisha boy 12	
No.72	PENSIK Chaia girl 8	Mrs. And Mrs. A Meyerowitz
No.71	PENSIK Chana girl 9	A. Reichlin - Benoni
	PENSIK David boy 12	
	PENSIK Mindel girl 14	
No.54	RENSLER Chazkel boy 8	to Katzenellenbogen
No.55	ROSENBAUM Leon boy 7	
No.43	ROTH Herman boy 10	*illigible looks like* Borechovitz as preference.
No.48	RAISENDER Rubin boy 10	given to Isaac Judes, Box 84
No.89	RATZER Nathan boy 6	to JM Cohen, Berea
No.88	RATZER Yudes girl 9	Harry Barnard 95, Hopkins Street *(Yeoville, Johannesburg)*
No.87	RATZER Perel girl 11	To R. Woolf
No.30	RAICHMAN Chaim 9	To Max Israelsohn, Pietersburg
No.29	RAICHMAN Abram	To Kruger, Pietersburg.
No.53	RUBIN David boy 7	~~S. Levin~~
No.52	RUBIN Chana girl 6	~~Kessel Amoils~~ Selkin, Aliwal North,
No.59	ROSENBLATT Gidele boy 8	A. Nadelman Jeppe
No.58	ROSENBLATT Shamaya 9	CT
No.49	REXLER Leya	A. Baruch, Brits.
No.56	STAINGER Pese girl 9	~~Rose Goldstein~~
No.96	SHTEINER Hersh boy 12	
No.95	SHTEINER Isaac 7	detained CT
No.94	SHTEINER Chazkel boy 5	detained CT
No.11	SHAMES Manes boy 8	M. Favish, Benoni
No.10	SHAMES Reisel 10	
No 44	SHWARZ Joseph boy 10	detained CT
No 30	TREPPEL Jacob boy 8	taken by Sam Kruger 12, Goldreich St. Berea, *Johannesburg*.
No.40	TANNENBAUM Sara girl 11	Taken by *?* Bloch 52, Jules Street, Jeppe *JHB*
No.39	TANNENBAUM Chaia 16	
No.04	WALTCHUK Chayim boy 5	detained in CT keep for Mr. Klein
No.03	WALTCHUK Feiga 6	Mr. L. Braude 37, Observatory Ave *Jhb*
No.02	WALTCHUK Leibel 8	M. Cohen, Rouxville, OFS
No 01	WALTCHUK Toyba 9	detained in CT
No.93	ZWIRN Osiash boy 5	gone to Berachowitz.
No.92	ZWIRN Ber??? Boy 6	Gone to S. Lewin Brakpan
No.79	ZAIKA Lisel girl 5	can be separated R Kopelowitz Royal Arcade
No.78	ZAIKA Maura *??* girl 9	can be separated
No.77	ZAIKA Leya 18	will allow sister to *(be)* separated

LIST OF CHILDREN GOING TO JOHANNESBURG

CHILD PLACED IN THE CARE OF	NAME OF CHILD
1. ISAAC NEUSTAD 117	JUDEL DREILING 57
2. B. STUPPEL 18	DEVARA MENKES 42
3. M KUPER ?? 68	SHAYA BOROWICK 35
4. B FRIEDLAND 82	BILA NEMET 43
5. SAM KRUGER 119	JANKEL TREPPER 50
6. ~~B SHERLEY ?? 120~~	~~HERMAN Peter~~ 43
7. L COHEN 19	JOSEPH ECHSTEIN 14
8. AUG BARUCH 33	LEYA REXLER 49
9. I JUDES16	RUBIN REISENDER 48
10 L SHAMBAN 108	CHASA HELMAN 26
11 A. JOSELOWITZ 84	SOLOMON NEWSTAD 46
12 A SMITH 37??	MORDECHAI KAHN 31
13 B BEIRACHOWITZ 100	O.ZWIRN
14 A. ABRAHAMS 11	TOIBA ECHSTEIN 11
15/16 FREDMAN (Friedman) 85	MAISHA GAIER (Gayer) 76
15/16 FREDMAN (Friedman) 85	CHAVA GAYER 75
17 KRUGER 121	RAIFEL ~~TREPPLER~~ KREINDEL 85
18 HURWITZ 89	*32?? Kalman Shachne???*
19 KRUGER 23	ABRAM REICHMAN 29
20 NADELMAN 102	GIDELE ROSENBLATT
21. x ~~JOSEPHSON~~ 51	CHAIM ALTUSKA 83
22. M FAVISH	M. SHAMES 11
23. B. FALKOV 103	SARAH LEVIN 20
24. M.A. MEYEROWITZ 15	CHAIA PENSIK 72
25. S. LEVIN 59 (or 57?)	BERNER (Bener) ZWIRN 92
26. B. GOLOMB	SALA BLIND 47
27. x GALANSKY 94	MUSMAN REIZEL 61
28. x GALANSKY 94	MUSMAN YASAIA 60
29. x RUBENSTEIN 107	BRODER SARA 91
30. x RUBENSTEIN 107	BRODER BINA 90
31. L. BRAUDE 64	WALTZUK FEIGE 3
32. KOSELOWITZ 4	ZAIKA LESEL 79
33. GOLDSTEIN 81	GERBUS SMUEL 19
34. ~~COHEN J.M 101~~	~~RATZNER NATHAN 89~~
35 WOOLF R 44	RATZER PEREL 87
36. REICHLIN A 98	PENZIK CHANE 71
37. ~~PELINSKY 130~~	~~ENGLEMAN J (Jacob) 36~~
38. ISRAELSOHN 134	REICHMAN CHAIM 30
39. GLASS S. 133	PINSKY FEIGA *25*
40. M. COHEN	LEIBEL WALTCHUK *2*
41. ~~ROSENKOWITZ E 132~~	~~FAIFER BLUME 64~~

Comments of Anne Lapedus Brest.

The information supplied here was taken from the Little Black address book of Isaac Ochberg which I obtained with the kind permission of Naomi Musiker at the Library at Beyachad.
I apologise in advance for any mistakes but it was not easy to read, and the spelling in the address book itself was not always consistent.
The *italics* indicate I couldn't read the names and I also included the question marks which do not appear in the original data.
Where there is a "strikethough" a name, this is how it appears in the address book. This would indicate that the child was returned.

Chapter 94 – GROUP PHOTOS OF THE JOHANNESBURG CHILDREN

When the Ochberg Orphans arrived in Cape Town half of the children went to live in the care of the Cape Jewish Orphanage later to be called Oranjia. The other half were taken by train to Johannesburg and initially placed in the care of the The Jewish Relief, Reconstruction and Orphans Fund and then later in the care of the South African Jewish Orphanage, later to be called Arcadia.

Ochberg Orphans placed in the care of the South African Jewish Orphanage (Arcadia) in 1921

COMMENTS: I think my uncle David Rubin is the boy with his hands on his hips in the top left hand corner of this photograph and my mother Chana Rubin is the little girl third from the left in the front row. **Rhoda Fowler**

My mother Helen Penzik /Meyerovitz /Green is standing behind the bottom row of seated children and is 5th from the right wearing a hat. In the photo is also her brother David Penzik - top row standing on the right with a striped belt without a hat. Her sister Mindel Penzik/Davidow is also in the photo standing in front of David in the white dress. I unfortunately can't find her other sister Hannah Penzik/Sandler/Kahn in this picture, but am pretty sure she's somewhere there. **Yvonne Chenik**

In the 3rd row, there is a tall woman wearing a dark dress. To the right her is a little boy. Behind him is my Aunt Clare Tannenbaum. My Mom, Sally Tannenbaum, is on the little boy's right. Sally has her arms around the child in front of her.**Helen Kuttner**

I think but I'm not 100% sure that Zeidel Feinschmidt (Jack Fine) is in the back row, 5ᵗʰ from right. **Brian Fine**

2nd row extreme left is Cywje Joffe and 3rd row on left side of lady in dark dress is Freidel Joffe **Peter Larson**

Third row from top, second from right could be Gittel Gonifas and third from right could be Leah Gonifas **Dorothy Pantanowitz**

My dad Osher (Oscar) Echstein is third from the right in the bottom row standing, behind the row seated. There is a very strong Echstein family resemblance. **Harold Echstein**

The girl with her arm around the woman in the patterned dress could be my mom or aunt, blume or Liba Faifer. **Louise Bird**

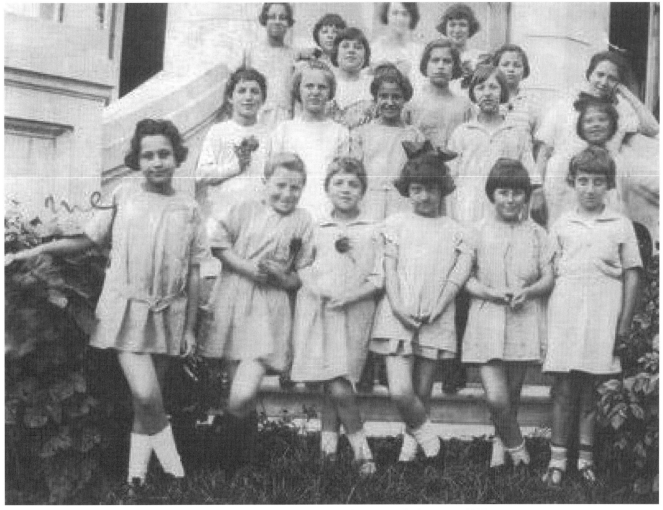

"Girls at the South African Jewish Orphanage", January ~ 1922

COMMENTS: **Ursula Rembach**, who sent in this photo identifies her mom, Leah Altuska, the first girl on left in front row)
I am convinced that the two girls on the top right hand side, one behind the other are Gittel Gonifas the top one, and Molly Gonifas the beauty beneath her. I think front row, 2nd from right is Leah Gonifas **Dorothy Pantanowitz** Front row extreme right is my aunt, Cywje Joffe **Peter Larson**
In the second row my mother, Blume Faifer is 2nd from left and her sister Lily is 2nd from right. Neither are smiling. **Louise Bird**

Girls in gyms - Sarah Altuska standing next to teacher
Annie Borowik is third from right

Group picture (Sarah Altuska 2nd from right)

Girls at the South African Jewish Orphanage ~1922
Tasha Altuska may be the grown up in white standing at the back (left of centre) with the very curly hair and glasses.

Sarah and Leah Altuska sitting in front of two unknown girls

Unknown girl and Sarah

Sarah at the back, Chaim in the middle and Leah Leah Altuska on the right. Jack Feinchmidt is the other boy. Girl on left unknown.

Some of the Ukrainian Pogrom and War Orphans(Ochberg Orphans) in Johannesburg, brought to South Afriica by Isaac Ochberg~ 1922 Isaac Ochberg is in the middle, Clara Tannenbaum is left of him (in the striped dress) and Sally Tannenbaum is standing behind him on the right. On his right is Leah Zaika. The two little children held by Isaac Ochberg are Hymie and Phyllis Wolchuk.

COMMENTS

Top row second from right is my aunt, Cywje Joffe. **Peter Larson**

The first boy on the left in the middle row (third) is definitely my uncle Isaac Helman and I think the first little chap in the front row on the left is his younger brother Benjamin Helman. **Julie Ross**

Chaim Altuska is the last boy on the right in the bottom row. **Ursula Rembach**

Fourth row, fifth from the left is Annie Borowik. **Barry Berelowitz**

In the middle of the back row is my mother, Blume Faifer and her sister Lily is to her right. **Louise Bird**

Second row on the extreme right hand side are Annie (Chaya) and Charlotte (Cherna) Guber, with hand on hip.

Third row third from left is Tasha Altuska, one of the 'Nurses" without her glasses.

Mavis, the Matron and Morris Isaacson, the Chairman, with the Ochberg Orphans ~ 1924

COMMENTS

Ursula Rembach, daughter of Leah Altuska, who sent in this photo identifies the three Altuska sisters. "Leah is on the right end of the first row of seated girls, Tasha is behind her with glasses and dark dress and Sarah is top row third from the right."

Jeff Isaacson living in Israel writes about the two adults in the second row
"Those are my parents, Mavis and Morris Isaacson, all right, but that's not the picture I had at home. There were many more children in my picture. In the picture my parents looked so young. What an extraordinary find! They must have been 24 and 46 respectively at the time."

Front row extreme left sitting on grass is Cywje Joffe and back row 2nd from right may be my mother, Freidel Joffe. **Peter Larson**

The little boy, in the front on the grass is probably Hymie Wolchuk. **Francine Blum**

The first girl on the left in the second row from the back is my mother Chassa Helman (Essie Zagey) **Julie Ross**

Second row, third from right Leah or Molly Gonifas, and third row, second from right is Gittel Gonifas **Dorothy Pantanowitz**

I am sure my mother, Salsa Blind or Sadie is in the middle row third from left, just behind Morris Isaacson. Her arm is around another girl. **Edna Rudnick**

Back row fifth from the left is Annie Borowik. I think that her sister Rachel is to her right. **Barry Berelowitz**

Chapter 95 – ARCADIA TODAY

ARCADIA 2002 AND ONWARDS → A NEW ERA
Tzivia Grauman, Group Communication Manager Chevah Kadisha

In the interests of the Jewish community, and at its request, the Chevrah Kadisha assumed financial, legal and management responsibility for Arcadia Jewish Children's Home in March 2002.

Arcadia had reached maximum capacity in 1939 when, due primarily to the influx of refugee children from Europe fleeing the nazi persecution, there were 400 children in its care.

As time went by the practice of placing children in the orphanage for financial reasons became increasingly undesirable. Progress in Social Services dictated the advantages of, as far as possible, keeping children at home with their parents by providing them with the financial means to do so.

With the war behind them and a new, enlightened approach to the importance of family, the 1950's - with its general improvement in the socio-economic situation and increased life expectancy - brought fewer orphans into Arcadia and numbers in the Jewish orphanage dwindled. By Arcadia's 75th Jubilee year in 1981 only 40 children resided there.

Long before the Chevrah Kadisha officially assumed responsibility for Arcadia, the organisation played a pivotal role in providing the funds that enabled parents to house, feed and educate their children themselves. Now, in 2011, the only children housed there are those whose parents are not able to take care of them.

> TODAY ALMOST EVERY CHILD AT ARCADIA IS PLACED THERE FOR THEIR OWN PROTECTION EITHER BY ORDER OF THE CHILDREN'S COURT OR THROUGH PRIVATE PLACEMENTS

By 2002 only a small section of Arcadia's sprawling 17 acre property in Parktown was occupied by the children who lived there and it was time for change.

One of the first efforts undertaken by the Chevrah Kadisha on behalf of the children was to relocate them to two renovated residential houses in Sandringham. Here the children enjoy a domestic, suburban environment that bears no semblance of institutionalisation. An intimate and homely atmosphere has been carefully created and nurtured.

The *After School Care Centre* provides supervised care not only for children resident at Arcadia, but also for some children of working parents in the community.

In *Residence* and at the *After School Care Programme*, full time and well-trained child-care workers supervise and tend the children by day and night. Healthcare, education, therapy, play and homework supervision are all part of the deal. Enormous energy is invested in offering Arcadia's children every opportunity for their futures.

Being located in a Jewish neighbourhood, in close proximity to youth movements and synagogues, the children are encouraged to take full advantage of their exposure to communal life.

The *After-Care Program* is designed to care for the financial, educational and emotional needs of post-matric youths who no longer live on campus. Arcadia provides them with tertiary education, accommodation and the kind of support and guidance normally provided by parents.

TODAY'S NUMBERS

- Forty two children and their families currently receive services from Arcadia
- Arcadia currently operates with a full staff complement
- There are currently 15 children designated to the care of Arcadia
- There are 16 children in the *After School Care Program* which is currently full
- The *After-Care Program* caters to seven adolescents who have completed their schooling
- A large number of volunteers are being screened for the Shabbos program
- Four volunteers currently assist with the afternoon program during the week
- All the children currently have Big Buddies

Arcadia's children receive excellent care. They also receive love, support and a warm, comfortable home. Schooling is selected to meet the needs of each individual child and counseling, religious studies, medical and dental care, and even exciting holiday programs, are all made available.

While no effort is spared to provide these children with every advantage of growing up in a normal family home, in truth we know that nothing can ever really replace that. These children have nowhere else to go and no-one else to depend upon.

YOU CAN HELP

Arcadia is not able to generate income in the form of fees and therefore the children are totally dependent on the facility for all the requirements - physical, emotional, intellectual and spiritual.

The support of the community is essential to their ongoing care. Your donation would be deeply appreciated.

For direct deposits, our banking details:

Arcadia:
Bank: First National Bank
Branch: Parktown
Branch Code: 250-455
Account No: 54860054731
Swift Code :   FIRNZAJJ

PLEASE HELP US TO IDENTIFY YOUR CONTRIBUTION
Please advise us of your contribution by email or fax
Fax: 011 640 2919
Email: pearl@jhbchev.co.za
Or mail your contribution to:
Private Bag X7, Sandringham 2131

בס״ד

Arcadia

February 2011
David Sandler
41 Bebich Drive
Wanneroo
WA6065
Australia

Dear David and all Friends who assisted you

On behalf of the Board of Governors and Management of the Chevrah Kadisha Group I thank you, and all those who assisted you with the production and distribution of the Arcadia Memory Books, for your sterling efforts on behalf of Arcadia Children's Home.

We deeply appreciate all the effort and financial outlay that you all selflessly committed to this project, which is clearly a labour of love for you.

We are also very grateful to you for directing all the proceeds from the books to Arcadia and can confirm that, as at the end of January 2011, Arcadia had received R479,543.54 from sales.

Thank you all for this truly wonderful generosity.

In the merit of your many great acts of kindness may you and your families be blessed with good health, peace and prosperity.

With best wishes

**MICHAEL SIEFF
GROUP CEO**

PART 3
JOHANNESBURG, SOUTH AFRICA

SECTION 10
LIFE STORIES OF OCHBERG ORPHANS PLACED IN THE CARE OF THE SOUTH AFRICAN JEWISH ORPHANAGE - ARCADIA

In this section you can read the individual life stories of the Ochberg Orphans who where placed in the care of the South African Jewish Orphanage – Arcadia written by their descendants

Chapter 96 – TASHA AND FEIGA ALTUSKA

Yetta, the daughter Sheina and Shepsel Pavin and her husband Labe Altuska lived in a village (Shtetl) on the outskirts of the city of Brest Liktov.

Leib died in 1920 and Yetta shortly afterwards leaving six children. Tasha the oldest, Sarah, Leah and Chaim were brought out to South Africa with the Ochberg Orphans, Faiga, the second oldest was left behind and the youngest Rochele sadly died in her infancy.

Yvonne daughter of Sarah and Yulanda daughter of Leah were named after Yetta while Lionel, Tasha's son, Lionel, Sarah's son and Leonard, Leah's son were named after Labe.

You can read about Chaim in the next chapter and Sarah and Leah Altuska in MORE ARC MEMORIES chapters 14 and 15. See www.arcadia.ca.com.au

TASHA ALTUSKA

Tasha Altuska was one of the five "nurses" Isaac Ochberg brought from Eastern Europe to help look after the children. After they landed in Cape Town in September 1921, Tasha accompanied the children sent to Johannesburg and there continued to look after the children who were then in the care of the South African Jewish Orphanage that was later to be called Arcadia.

One can see Tasha in many group photos of the Ochberg Children as she looked after them.

A TRIBUTE TO TASHA
Written by Yvonne Phillips (nee Slier), the daughter of Tasha's sister, Sarah Slier.

I always marvelled at how Tasha managed to look after her three little sisters and a baby brother during the First World War, with no or little food, no clothing, little warmth and no fixed accommodation.

Chaya Tannenbaum, Isaac Ochberg, Leah Zaicka and Tasha Altuska - the three nurses

The three nurses; Tasha Altuska, Leah Zaika and Chaya Tannenbaum with their younger siblings.
Chaim is standing to the left of Tasha and Sarah is behind her while Leah is on the far right with a white ribbon.
Manya is standing behind Leah Zaika while Sally is standing behind Clara Tannenbaum

Sometime during the war, the parents died and Tasha carried on caring for this family; how hard must that have been for a girl of 14 when the war began in 1914. Eventually they all ended up in an orphanage in Brest Litovsk and that is where Isaac Ochberg found them. He decided to take two sisters and the brother with him. One sister was in hospital and was promised that she would be on the next group but that was never to be.

My mother, Sarah, refused to go without Tasha so Isaac Ochberg made a plan and took Tasha along as a nurse to assist with the 200 children on their voyage to Africa.

The two younger sisters and the boy were placed in Arcadia and Tasha worked as a helper. After a while she went out to work and established a home in a rented house. When her family left the orphanage, they lived with her and she taught the girls to cook, knit and sew. She made all their clothing.

Tasha married and had three sons but things did not go well for the Rachmans because the recession of 1929 hit them very badly and they were very short of money. Life was a battle for Tasha and she also worked as an alteration hand in a dress shop.

My earliest memory of her was Tasha in her kitchen serving her visitors black tea and homemade grape jam. Many of her visitors were girls from the Arc. The family was very close to Tasha in fact, my brother Lionel Slier was more like a brother than a cousin to the Rachman boys

Tasha died in the old age home in Johannesburg and if I may quote from the song "She was just an angel in disguise sent to earth for us to love".

MY MOTHER, TASHA ALTUSKA
Written by Stanley (Jack) Rachman

My Mother, **Tasha Altuska**, and her three younger siblings, Sarah, Leah and Chaim, were among the orphans rescued by Mr Ochberg; another daughter, Feiga, who was in hospital at the time, was left behind. The five Altuska children were born and lived in Brest Litovsk but, to my deep regret, I never asked or learned about her life there, how they came to be orphaned, their rescue and early days in S A.

For a number of years they were sheltered in the Arcadia orphanage in Johannesburg, and on those rare occasions when she mentioned Arcadia it was with some warmth and nostalgia. There are two differing accounts of how and when her parents died. She told us, in short, that they had been killed by Cossacks in one of the recurrent pogroms. On the other hand one of my Mother's sisters said that their parents had died during the influenza epidemic. It remains unclear what happened.

At the time of their rescue my Mother was over the age limit for inclusion as an orphan, and was therefore given a role as an aide/nurse assistant. She took this responsibility seriously, and always spoke of it with pride.

She never told us about their time in the orphanage in Russia or of their rescue and journey to England and finally to South Africa. Instead we heard occasional anecdotes about London and especially the journey on the Edinburgh Castle to Cape Town. She cherished a card and a menu from the ship. In addition to helping care for the orphans she had a special responsibility for looking after her own three siblings. Throughout her life and theirs she was an anchor and informal maternal guide for the remnants of the family. The four Ochberg orphans remained very close throughout their lives. Their children, "the cousins", saw each other regularly and some established strong lifelong bonds.

Tasha had a strong character and remarkable stamina. She was a dedicated mother who was proud and was

The three Altuska sisters; Sarah, Leah and Tasha

protective of her children. Her love and affection embraced her own children and also those of her siblings. Similarly, Tasha's sisters and brother were fond of Tasha's boys. She had a fine sense of humour and used it to encourage or discourage us. Tasha was gregarious and her most enjoyable leisure activity was playing rummy with her pals.

In 1929 Tasha married Harry Rachman, the brother of Benny and David, whose family had emigrated from Plunge in Lithuania. They had three sons, Lionel, Bernard and Stanley.

My Father, Harry, was an insatiable reader who greeted visitors with the query, "Did you bring any reading matter?" He was a *luftmensch* totally unsuited for business (he called himself a 'jobber' whatever that meant) and was so hapless that he struggled unsuccessfully to make a living. The family was always short of money, and had some very hard times. In addition to carrying out her many domestic tasks my Mother did some dress-making at home in order to help pay the bills. She also sewed most of our clothing, including our white school shirts and grey shorts.

Her eldest son, Lionel, was a cheery non-conformist who disdained conventions, and carried on in the certainty that the Traffic Code did not apply to him. For example, he notoriously drove without a licence throughout his life, and collected a formidable collection of unpaid parking fines. He was an exceptional scofflaw but an unexceptionally hopeless businessman.

The second son, Bernard, was an adventurer and left home at the age of 17. He and a friend spent nine months working their way up Africa, and ended up in London. There he joined Hashomer Hatzair, (The Young Watchmen) a Zionist youth group, and after a period of training went to Israel where he lived on Gal-on kibbutz for a few years. After his return to S A he married and had two daughters, Aviva and Sandra. Aviva has four boys and lives on kibbutz Chamadia, Israel. Sandra is a G P in London and has two children.

Nurse Tasha Altuska, (2nd from right) at the SAJO (Arcadia)

Stanley (Jack), Bernard and the eldest, Lionel
Yeoville Boys' School ~1940

The youngest of Tasha's three sons, Stanley (always called "Jack" for unknown reasons), studied and then taught psychology at Wits University before emigrating to London in 1959. He worked in London University for 23 years, latterly as a Professor, and then emigrated to Canada in 1982. He has two daughters, Carla and Emily Tasha, and two sons, Gideon and Tom, and six grandchildren, one of whom is called Tasha.

True to the family pattern, Tasha's family as well as Harry's family, none of their offspring took to the life of business. Their children and grandchildren have accumulated 10 university degrees, including five post-graduate degrees, and published nine books, with three more on the way. There are two university teachers, two journalists, one novelist, one US Government analyst, and one doctor.

Remarkably, prior to and during World War II my Mother and all of the adults in our extended family protected all of us children from the horrors and terror of world events. They never discussed in front of us the horrific news from Europe, and never mentioned their fears and grief about the fate of their relations in Europe; the letters that were never answered or were returned as undeliverable. Until we were old enough to read the newspapers we were protected. We were of course aware that there was a war going on and admired the uniformed soldiers we encountered, but were shielded from the horrors that were under way, and also from the anguish that our parents were experiencing. Mr Ochberg rescued our orphaned parents, and they protected their children.

All of Tasha's children knew the bare outlines of Mr Ochberg's saintly rescue, but it is only in the past few years that we have learned, and are learning, the amazing details of the rescue and the full magnificence of Isaac Ochberg.

Ursula Rembach, daughter of Leah Altuska,

Tasha then aged 17 who was too old to be termed an orphan left to work as a seamstress in a clothing factory and took up lodgings in a boarding house in Doornfontein. At her place of work she met a young woman called Bella Krauthamer, newly emigrated from Palestine. The two became firm friends and shared their lodgings.

Together the two friends would visit the children at Arcadia on the weekends, taking them for day trips and treats. Tasha met a man called Harry Rachman and began dating him. Harry Rachman was a chemist and worked in a pharmacy in Judith's Paarl. At the pharmacy, an optician David Rembach had recently been employed. Since David was an immigrant from Palestine, Harry thought it was a good idea to introduce him to Tasha's friend Bella, also recently arrived.

The two couples later married and were "Unterfurers" at each other's weddings, their friendship enduring all their lives and also involving in the coming years the families of Sarah and Leah. In fact I, the youngest child of Leah was to marry the youngest child of Bella and David Rembach. We have known each other since we were infants. I am a strong believer of Besheit. Fate

Rose Rachman, Tasha's daughter-in-law writes

As far as I know Tasha continued to look after the children at the orphanage. Later I think she worked in a shop where she met her husband Harry Rachman.

I was married to Tasha's middle son Bernard Rachman who died in 1987. Tasha herself died I think in 1971. Bernard and I married in 1956 and emigrated to the UK in 1960. His contact with his mother was very limited so I have no documentation with which to begin to compile a family history. I have some memories of my contact with her for the first three years of my married life and on my visit to South Africa in 1966; and then of course there are the family stories I recall her sister Sarah telling me, but very little concrete information.

Wedding of Rose and Bernard - 1956
"Cheryl, daughter of Chaim Altuska is the flower girl
Front: Tasha, Bernard, myself, my mother and sister
Back: Hymie Schles, Harry Cohen (friends of Bernard) Jack his brother , Basil Fine, Harry Rachman, Shim Lakofski my Uncle and Lionel Rachman on the side of his father

Aviva Dan, Tasha's granddaughter, writes

My name is Aviva Dan and I live in Israel on a kibbutz. My grandmother was one of the orphans to be taken out of Russia by Isaac Ochberg and to go to Arcadia orphanage with her two sisters and brother. Her name was Tasha Altuska.

My grandmother was taken as a nurse because she was 15 at the time. She met my grandfather in South Africa, married and had three boys, Bernard, my father, Lionel and Stanley. My father and mother met in South Africa, where I was born then moved to England, were my sister was born. I have been living in Israel since 1977.

I am married and have four boys. My sister is married and has two children and lives in London. I recently met with my cousin who is the grand daughter of my grandmother's sister, Sarah, who was bought to South Africa together with my grandmother. She also now lives in Israel. She has a sister and a brother. Her sister lives in England and her brother in China.

I have no pictures of Tasha. My memory of her is from the year 1966. I visited South Africa with my mother and sister. My memory of her is of a white haired old lady who was very demanding in a house full of "treasures", lots of packets and bags full of all sorts of things. What I do remember though is in the hallway a large bar with glass counter. Under the glass were lots of pictures.

I have no idea what happened to the pictures. Recently her oldest son died and I know that the family are wanting to sell his flat and that the flat was full of books and papers and maybe also pictures. As her grand children all lived in England I don't know that there are any photos with her. There is one surviving son living in Canada who is not in touch with most of the family but is in touch with my sister.

I have been in touch with Sarah's granddaughter who now lives in Israel and she has been to visit me at my house.

Sandra Rachman, Tasha's granddaughter, writes

We visited South Africa in 1966. I was six years old and the trip was hugely exciting and left many memories.

I remember going to visit Tasha in hospital. She was gravely ill and very deaf so we weren't really able to communicate. For the rest I remember the family stories; how hard she had worked all her life to keep the family together, both her siblings and the story of the orphanage and then subsequently her own family in severe poverty.

It is great that you are compiling this book. I have shared all this with my own children (aged 19 and 14) and they are fascinated by the story. My son has commented how incredibly lucky we/they were to be among the chosen children out of so many, particularly in light of the fact that Tasha was in fact too old and the rules were bent to accommodate her. It is a story of survival and determination, and luck of course.

I have a wallet of Tasha's old photos which my Dad Bernard brought back to London after her death in 1971. My mother gave them to me for safekeeping when she moved from London. I have looked through these with Carla a year or two ago (Jacks oldest daughter) and we have put names to faces.

Harry and Tasha Rachman

TASHA ALTUSKA'S PHOTOS
Sent in by Sandra Rachman, her grand daughter

Tasha was a nurse on the journey to Cape Town who looked after the Ochberg children and later accompanied them up to Johannesburg and continued to look after them at Arcadia (SAJO).

Tasha, I believe, was more than just a carer to the other Ochberg Orphans (in the eyes of the children who had no family) but more like a relative, a mother figure to the little ones and an aunt or older sister to the older ones.

I believe in Tasha's album we have photos sent to her by other Ochberg Children who would share their simchas and adventures with her with cards and photos as we would all share with family. Here are some of the photos.

Message on reverse of last photo with translation

2/VII 22
To my dear sister
I send you my
picture in
remembrance

From me your
precious sister.

Is this Feiga, the sister left behind?

While the photos of the people above have not been identified, the three photos alongside and other photos have been identified

-Hymie Wolchuk and (Anna Chaya) Tannenbaum – chapter 128
-Freidl and Livia Joffe – chapter 111 and 112
-Manya and Lisa Zaika – chapter 129

-Also see chapter 13 for the photos of the children in the youth villages; Meir Shfeya and Kfar

Eli Nayman   *Hymie and Anna*   *Freidl and Livia Joffe*   *Manya and Lisa Zaika*

FEIGA ALTUSKA THE SISTER LEFT BEHIND
Written by Lionel Slier (Son of Sarah Altuska)

The lost sister Feigel with her husband and three of their eight children in front of their home - mid 1950s.

Years later we heard that Feigel, the sister left behind, had met and married a man by the name of Millztein and in 1925 or 1926 they had gone from Brest-Litovsk to Argentine.

They lived in Tucuman in Argentine and had eight children. Somehow my mother and Feigel established contact. In 1973 Feigel's eldest daughter, Anna (Yentle), came to visit us in South Africa and with her limited English we managed to communicate somehow. She told us that her mother would never ever talk about her life in Russia. However Anna did tell us that when her mother came out of hospital and found that her siblings had all been taken to 'Africa' by a strange man, she became severely traumatized and was unable to comprehend fully what had happened.

Even 50 years later she had not really recovered from the shock she had received as a girl of 12 years – her family gone and she left alone. No explanations, no goodbyes, nothing.

My mother and her sister, Leah, went to Argentine in the mid-seventies to see Feigel but my mother told me that because of the language difficulties they could not really communicate and the meeting was not a great success.

Anna did keep in touch and we learnt that Feigel had passed away but the connection is flimsy, to say the least. We know that one grandchild, a girl, made aliyah and married a religious man whose parents were from Morocco.

So this is a story of a family and a divided fate. If Ochberg had stuck to the letter of General Smut's conditions and left my mother in Brest Litovsk in 1921 then?

"That's my mother Sara's wedding (she's not in the picture) with my father Leon (who's hugging his mother Faigel).
It was 1st October 1966. The others are brothers, from left to right: Enrique, Bernardo and Miguel, Sara, Clara and Elisa, my grandmother and my father Leon. The only absent sister is my aunt Yenta and my grandfather. As my mother told me, she remembers she took that photograph to the hotel when visiting Buenos Aires." Gustavo Milsztein

Fany Twizer, Feiga's grand daughter writes

In the photo (above) are my uncles Enrique, Bernardo and Miguel (deceased), my mother Sara, my aunts Clara and Elisa, my grandmother Feiga and my uncle Leon (deceased). The other photo (below) is my aunt Yenta or Anna as you call her.

Yenta, Feiga's oldest daughter

The reason that my grand mother Feiga did not travel with her family is because she had some bites on her ankle and she was in the hospital when everybody left. She was under the care of her aunt and uncle but I do not know their names. She met my grandfather at the water well and after three months they got married.

His intention was to go to Canada, but, my family do not remember very well why, he missed the boat and he took another one to Argentina. After a while my grandma and her first daughter Yenta came too.

GRANDCHILDREN MEETING UP IN ISRAEL
Written by Ursula Rembach

I have just recently returned from a magnificent trip to Israel. Much of our time was visiting my husband's extensive extended family. But more amazing than anything else is that while in Israel I found Fany the granddaughter of Feigel, my mother's sister, who was left behind in Brest Liktov in 1921.

I visited with her in Jerusalem and also took along Paula Slier, the granddaughter of Sarah (and of course Lionel Slier's daughter) who also lives in Israel. The two young women are of a similar age and seemed to get on well together. I hope they will keep up this friendship. While I was with Fany we called the family in Argentina and were able to chat. While Fany did not know too much about the history of her grandmother she was able to fill us in about the eight children of Feigel.

I am hoping that through Fany we will be able to get more information as to how Feigel ended up in Argentine and also about where she spent the years after she was separated from her siblings when they left for SA with Isaac Ochberg.

I took pictures of Paula and Fany together in Jerusalem so maybe that is something that could be included. I think it is simply stunning that after what can only be alled an amazing life journey two grandchildren meet up almost 90 years later! Extraordinary – don't you think?

Paula Slier and Fany Milsztein met for the first time in Jerusalem in July 2009

I hope that both Paula and Fany, and also Tasha's granddaughter Aviva, who also lives in Israel, can represent the Altuska's at the Ochberg reunion later this year in Israel.

So, for me this was the result of very many years of searching – goes to show that if one does not give up finally something or rather someone turns up.

Fany Milsztein and her husband and daughter Abigail, the only great grandchild of Feigle

SARAH (ALTUSKA) SLIER

Yvonne Phillips writes
"Here are two photos of my mother Sarah (Altuska) Slier. Can anybody identify the young man? I think that the picture might have been taken at Arcadia as she looks about 16 years old. My mother married when 18 and I was born when she was 20"

Lionel Slier Remembers

A few years after my mother, Sarah Altuska, had married Jack Slier, they moved into a house in Orange Grove, Johannesburg and my uncle Harry (Chaim Altuska) came to live with her. Jack Kruger and another (Ochberg Orphan) man from Arcadia, Jack (Itzik) Mussman who was a glazier also came. I was born in that house and grew up with my uncle and the two Jacks sharing a sleeping porch. Later my younger sister arrived.

My sister, Yvonne Phillips, myself (sic,) my second sister, Deborah Shine who now lives in New York and our cousin, Stanley Jack Rachman, third son of Tasha (Altuska) Rachman who lives in Vancouver. It was at a child's birthday party.~1940

I do remember that Kruger had a motorbike, which he kept in the back yard, and later he traded it in for a two-door car (Chevrolet?) with a dickey-seat, which caused great joy among us three children whenever we were given a ride.

Jack Kruger was South African born but placed in Arcadia where he became friendly with my uncle Chaim Altuska (later became Harry Gordon). Kruger became a glazier as it was the custom at Arcadia in the Thirties to place boys in trades as soon as they turned 16 unless they showed academic potential. My uncle became a pharmaceutical apprentice but for reasons I do not know, he did not pursue this career.

Jack Kruger married Janie Goldstein, sister-in-law of Natie Ratzer, (both from Arcadia) and gradually drifted out of our lives.

About Mushie (as everybody called him) I know very little except that he served in the South African forces and was Up North as Egypt, Libya and Italy were then referred to).

I once asked my sainted father how did he manage with three young children and three adult single men living in one house and he answered, "Your mother wanted them to stay."

Polly Stanger married Natie Joffe and had two daughters. The older daughter Sybil married and went to live in Australia many years ago. I remember meeting her at a theatre in Johannesburg in the late 1960s and I believe that she emigrated soon after that.

Polly Stanger, unknown, and my mother Sarah Altuska Slier.   *Jack Kruger on his motor bike*

She was stunningly beautiful; that I remember. Myra is the name of the younger sister.

Polly, who was for years a great friend of my mother, passed away some time ago, as indeed so did my mother.

THE ALTUSKA FAMILY TALLY
Written by Lionel Slier (Son of Sarah Altuska)

Isaac Ochberg rescued four of the five Altuska children from the orphanage at Brest-Litovsk and as you know he ignored General Smut's condition about not breaking up families and left sister Feigel (who was in hospital) behind.

In fairness to him, he was not being callous and planned to return the following year and bring, possibly, 200 more children to South Africa. He actually got to England where he was informed that the new Communist government said that they would not allow their children to be taken to a Capitalist country.

However I have asked some questions and done the arithmetic and from the four Altuska children, three girls and a boy, that did come to Arcadia there have been 86 offspring to date (August 2009).

They live in the following cities: Durban, Cape Town, Johannesburg, Givat-tayim, Shanghai, Datchett (Berkshire), Boston, Washington, New York, San Francisco, Toronto, Atlanta, France, Rome, Melbourne, Sydney. Vancouver. London

Leah's line accounts for 32; her four children and grandchildren and Ursula Rembach can let you know where they all live.

Aviva, daughter of late Bernard (Tasha's second son) lives on a moshav in Israel with four sons, but I do not know its name). I know that one served in Gaza.

So if you take 86 descendents from just four rescued orphans and know that 187 orphans eventually came to South Africa it would be amazing to eventually know how many descendents there are at this time. Actually Lauren Snitcher in Cape Town is building a database and in time she may be able to answer the question.

Chapter 97 – CHAIM ALTUSKA

CHAIM ALTUSKA
Ursula Rembach, daughter of Leah Altuska, writes

While Leah and Sarah settled down to their new life at Arcadia, the brother Chaim, was adopted and his name was changed to Harry Gordon.

Chaim was not happy and after running away several times he was returned to Arcadia.

Entry in the register kept at Arcadia showing Chaim going to the Josephson family but then being returned

Group Passport 4 – Chaim is the boy third from the right in the top row aged either six or seven years.

Chaim and Tasha with Sarah behind

Chaim in the middle with Sarah behind and Jack Feinschmidt on the right – others unknown

My Uncle Chaim or Harry Gordon as he liked to be called was in reality known to us as Uncle Jumbuck. And, I simply don't know why. Everyone called him Jumbuck. He was exceptionally clever and handsome. I adored him all my life. He was very eccentric. I remember visiting him once and remarked that he

Harry Gordon (Chaim Altuska)

had about three or four Cadillacs parked in the driveway of his house in Malvern. He just brushed it aside as though everyone had that many Caddys outside. He had taught himself to read Russian and always had open books nearby. His home was filled with tabletop cigarette lighters that were absolutely beautiful and always filled and in working condition. There were clocks everywhere that were wound each day and they all kept perfect time. I was always impressed that there were cut glass crystal glasses in the kitchen and even as a young child I was allowed to drink from them. For all this he was not a rich man!

To me he was this man of mystery who I adored and held in the highest esteem. Like Tasha he had the most beautiful blue eyes (that his three children inherited) and with his steel grey hair and immaculate dress he was dapper and smart and in my eyes simply wonderful!

Rose Rachman, Tasha's daughter-in-law writes

The story of Tasha's brother was really interesting. I never knew he had been adopted nor that his name was Chaim. I knew him in his later life and he was always Gordon. He married an Afrikaans woman called Corrie and had three children with her. The eldest, Cheryl, was a flower girl at my wedding. She had two brothers called Ian and Keith. I am not sure what happened to all these children.

We left South Africa in 1960 and my next visit was 1966 after that I don't think I saw very much of Gordon and Corrie on my brief visits to South Africa. I do remember visiting them in their home and seeing the three children.

My memory of Harry Gordon was that he was a most generous man. When I visited SA in 1966, Lionel Rachman and I made a trip to Basutoland which was celebrating its independence. Lionel had a friend staying there and Harry Gordon lent us a car in which to make the trip.

MY FATHER HARRY GORDON
Written by Cheryl Gordon

These memories I sent you, although prompted by your request for memories of my father, were actually written for my niece, Chivaugn, who did not really know her grandfather or the circumstances of his life. Perhaps I was trying to let others know how lives through the generations have been affected by the ravages of war and the repulsive treatment of the Jews at that time and in that place.

I know it is a bit long and sometimes brutally honest, but I had more than one motive for writing it. The lives of the Ochberg Orphans were greatly affected by their early childhood experiences and I feel that this should be known. It would be dishonest to paint a rosy picture.

His friends and acquaintances knew Harry as a cultured, literary young man, immaculately dressed in a three-piece suit, turn-ups on the trousers, a shirt with collar and cuffs ironed precisely in the way he preferred and with cufflinks, braces and a beautiful tie, sometimes with a gold tiepin. It would have to be gold as nothing less would do. His hair started greying when he was a young man and he never wore a hat. There was a nautical star tattooed on his arm. A proud man but not vain, simply a man with fine tastes. He did not like his photo taken and he would lift his arm to cover his face. His family called him Jumbock because, with his broad chest, he had the strength of a Jumbo, the elephant. For Corrie, his wife, her family and their friends, he was HG, his initials. Somehow he was too reserved a man to be called by his real name as it was too personal. He was never able to call his wife or children by their names either for the same reason, I think. So my mother was Carrots, because her hair had been blonde with a reddish tone when he first met her. Ian, his older son, he called Tiger also because of that inherited physical strength. Keith, his younger son had a curious name. He had been nicknamed Ducktail by my father because his hair had a huge curl when he was a baby. My aunt Tasha was not able to say this word correctly. She pronounced it Dokkel so Dokkel it was. And I was Sugar Puff or Little girl. When we were children, he was Daddy, but now he is "the old man". Daddy seems to be too familiar for the father we remember with such mixed feelings. He was left-handed, but as a child he had been forced to write with his right hand with his left hand was tied behind his back and the resultant handwriting was very distinctive. Ian is also left-handed and so is his son, Jay.

My father smoked English cigarettes Mills and Players, always in a tin; and a Dunhill pipe, with the characteristic white spot, occasionally a genuine meerschaum, Dunhill tobacco, also in a tin and he used a Dunhill lighter. He also smoked cigars (never cheroots) Romeo y Julieta Cuban cigars. As children we kept the wooden boxes for storing crayons and so on. Smoking was to be the cause of his death many years later.

Although he kept a liquor cabinet, he never drank a drop of liquor. He did not know what alcohol tasted like. There is a tale told of him that when he was a young man some friends held him upside down over a bath, trying to force him to drink wine. Even in that precarious position he refused. But then Harry Gordon was renowned for his stubbornness.

Harry Gordon

He was also known for his generosity and gave gifts for all his friends and acquaintances; chocolates and whisky. He did not seem to be able to say no.

I remember one couple he befriended and he got my mother to make their curtains for them. Some time later, we heard that the woman had murdered her husband. I learnt very early not to admire anything in his presence or he would buy it for me. He would give us gifts anyway; jewellery, porcelain, watches. He had a strong predilection for clocks and watches and could not resist a good timepiece. The clocks were always wound and we all had several watches in our possession. We still have some in the family, and my mother also has splendid clocks. She has a collection of porcelain, most of it English, which my father accumulated over the years. In particular, he loved Royal Dalton.

My mother recalls the first time she visited Harry, accompanied by her parents, and they were served tea in a Royal Blue tea set with a gold border. That tea set is still in my mother's cupboard. Tea was always very strong and he never drank coffee. I made countless cups of tea for my father. Meat was forbidden in his diet and he refused to eat it, having seen a dreadful railway accident which killed some cows. He could never eat meat again after that. In later years, his diet was curtailed even more because he had ulcers. One night, an ulcer burst and he got peritonitis and an ambulance came to fetch him and his life was saved. Years later, when the ulceration became really bad again, he suffered indescribable pain. His pride did not allow him to admit it. We would find him, late at night, doubled-up, on his knees beside his armchair, unable to bear the pain. Not a murmur or a moan. Eventually, most of his stomach was removed, and he lived on vegetable soups, bread and tea, of course. He loved sweets, too. He always had boiled sweets and chocolates nearby. We would visit Dick's Sweets in the city and he would buy whatever we wanted. His particular favourites were pear drops and aniseed. We were taught excellent British table manners; forks with the tines facing down, rest knife and fork between mouthfuls, break your bread, never cut it and so on. But not once ever did my father sit at the dinner table with us to share in the family meal. I do not recall even one instance when he did that.

But more than anything, he loved books and classical music. Our home was filled with Mozart, Beethoven, Puccini and Verdi but not Wagner for a twofold reason; his music was a cacophony, my father said, and he was German. The music was our lullaby at night and the accompaniment to our daily activities. I barely knew any other kind of music existed until I was about twelve and today, that music is as much part of me as my own flesh. He loved going to concerts, but that was before I was born. The shelves were full of the finest literature can offer; the classics, the ancient Greeks, plays, poetry and philosophy, beautiful leather bound quarto volumes of Shakespeare, leather bound Milton, Wordsworth, Tennyson, Byron, complete sets of Dickens, Thackerey, Meredith, some of the moderns, usually pre-second-world war, Steinbeck, Upton Sinclair, Dreiser and Wodehouse. In amongst those books was Das Kapital, also several volumes of Lenin's writings. In the apartheid era, these books were an ominous presence, with the government's threat of the Red Danger, communism. Harry had been a card-carrying member of the communist party in his youth, and he supported communistic ideals throughout his life, refusing to acknowledge the breakdown of the philosophy in implementation.

We were allowed free access to those shelves and so was born my ever-abiding love of books. My father seemed to know everything. His vocabulary was superb. He loved to give information so I asked and he told. I could ask him the meaning of any word at all. He always knew. He taught me to look up anything I did not know and I still do. That was the only communication he was comfortable with when speaking to his children. I cannot recall conversations about everyday matters or anything about personal concerns. He could not break those barriers.

He never spoke about his childhood. The only memory he mentioned was a recollection about the large central stoves in Russian homes. He said he could remember the benches which surrounded the stove where the family slept for warmth. Other memories of his childhood came indirectly from my mother, and that wasn't very much either. We knew he had been orphaned and we were told that his mother had died whilst holding him in her arms (but I do not know whether that was true) and that he had spent six months in London before coming to South Africa by ship. We knew he had been adopted by the Gordon family and that he had run away. When he was about twelve, he renounced Judaism and all religious beliefs and tradition and

chose a secular path, not because he felt that the faith had not sustained him through troubled times but because it was simply that religion was a foolish mumbo-jumbo. He never wavered from that choice. My favourite memory of his childhood is the one where he found a shilling in the playground and he stood with his foot over it for an hour so that no one else could take it. When the area cleared he took the money to buy of course a book; Sexton Blake, a detective story. Another memory that is special is that at the age of nine, after learning English for only about three years, he won the English essay prize for the entire Transvaal province. He always loved the English language deeply, something I share. He wrote poetry, limericks, and humorous aphorisms. We had more of a British upbringing than a South African one, I think.

We know that he lived with Sara and her husband Jack and that he started a career as a pharmacist, but did not complete the training, opting to work in Jack's jewellery shop instead. That's where he met my mother. She had come with a friend who wanted to buy a pearl necklace. When he saw my mother he told a friend that she was the girl he was going to marry, this after many years of being the debonair young-man-about-town with many girlfriends. He was twelve

Harry Gordon (Chaim Altuska)

Harry and Corrie's children, Cheryl and Keith

years older than she was and she was from a Christian Afrikaans family but that was no deterrent to my father. My mother recalls that, upon meeting Tasha for the first time, my aunt, without saying anything, simply took my mother into her arms and gave her a loving, warm hug of welcome into the family. They married in a registry office. This was in 1948, post Second World War. Harry had tried to enlist, but had been turned down because he had flat feet. This had been a great disappointment to him, and he developed a fervent interest in the war which was to remain with him for the remainder of his life. In fact, all I seem to remember my father reading was books on the Second World War.

He was very knowledgeable about all aspects of the war but along with that came a penetrating, intense hatred of the Germans and everything German, except, of course the composers of an earlier era. We were not allowed to own anything German. He said that the Germans had a cold spot in their brains which caused them to desire to kill. I think that the news of the concentration camps affected him a great deal and his hatred of the Third Reich deepened with each revolting revelation. He was not a proponent of Churchill, either and in later years he was to spend much of his time writing a scathing biography of the statesman. He wrote page after page, but he did not number them and he did not complete the book. When, after his death, the manuscript fell out of a dropped suitcase, the pages became scattered and jumbled. At one time, I thought I might try to assemble the pages in order, but the memories of my father would be too overwhelming and the task become one of sadness.

Why the sadness? The relationship with my father was not an easy one for any of us. He had a violent temper and we spent much of our childhood in a state of anxiety, waiting for the next onslaught. It could be anything that set him off; the tap was dripping, the soap was soggy, the screwdriver wasn't in the toolbox, the breadknife wasn't in the drawer. I recall picking up cutlery many times after he had thrown a drawer onto the floor. Eventually, we acquired kitchen cabinets which had drawers that could not be pulled completely out. I remember taking a tray of tea to him on the veranda one day. Something angered

him and he threw the entire tray down the length of the veranda. When the Gordon children began asserting their own personalities as adolescents, he could not accept our choice of music or clothing. He attempted to throw away our records, but we were able to retrieve them. He did succeed in discarding our collection of Mad magazines, though. My brother Keith had to leave home because he wore jeans. He did not return for a year. My father was not always at ease when he interacted with others and it was as though there was an impenetrable casing about him. He was not entirely aloof, but was reserved and inclined to retreat to his own world of books. His common form of conversation with friends and relatives was one of badinage, clever puns and humorous comments and anything more personal would have invaded his comfort zone but people liked him. They enjoyed his company and his largesse. He did not relish going on family outings. The only occasions he would accompany the family was on an outing to his sister Sara or to my mother's sister, Elsie, however, he seemed reluctant to go, always procrastinating while we waited patiently in the car for him to emerge from the house. When he finally got into the car, he would fiddle with the radio or the mirror. Usually, my mother drove, and in later years, his children did while he sat as a passenger and threw insults at passers by that he did not like. I cannot recall my father taking us to the park, or to the cinema. He did not play games with us, nor did he tell us stories. Only once did he tell us a bedtime tale and that was the story of Sinbad the Sailor and the Roc on the beach. There was one exception, chess was a favoured pastime, and he would play games with my brothers and with Jack, Sara's husband. He never participated in sports, but he enjoyed watching boxing and English soccer. And he loved the challenge of a really difficult crossword. Each year he would anticipate the full-page crossword issued annually by the Star newspaper.

We did go on family holidays to Durban when we were young children. He did not venture onto the beach but would sit at a table in a restaurant on the promenade, cup of tea and book to hand. I have been told of a trip we took to Durban when I was about three. When we got there, no accommodation was available so we drove all the way back to Johannesburg. According to the tale, I stood all the way there and back. When we arrived at home, I asked my father for sugar sweets. He did not know what these were, but he set out to hunt them down anyway, until he found what I wanted. When those holidays ceased, he kept a packed suitcase in the boot of one of his cars for about nine years just in case he decided to go to Durban but he never did. He had many cars and at one time, there were thirteen cars parked about the house. He had a penchant for English cars; Jaguar, Rover, Wolseley, and he also owned Cadillacs and Buicks. All these cars were bought from auctioneers and they were the bane of our lives as they had so many mechanical faults and to this day, I cannot drive a car, without expecting it to break down at any moment: because those cars did. My brothers installed batteries, changed tires and there was always something they had to do to those cars and an endless stream of mechanics passed by our doors. He was generous with the cars and we all were given cars and a couple of other people as well. It is possible that these elegant cars were a link to the life he wished he had lived but by that time, circumstances had changed.

Harry and Corrie

He owned a small scrap-metal business for many years. It was filthy work and I think he loathed it. At times the income was excellent and he would buy generously and give generously. He began to hoard and we had cartons of everything we needed in pantry, 50 pound bags of sugar and 20 crates of cold drink stacked in the garage. Other people bought a slab of chocolate, we had boxes of twenty four slabs, tinned fruit, tissues and rice and the pantry shelves were piled high with groceries. He would bring boxes of goods received in the business that he deemed worth keeping. Occasionally, there was something curious or useful, but most of it was junk. My brothers had to carry the boxes in every evening and they did not relish the task. Then there were the periods of bleakness at an earlier period when we were young children (I was seven then) and we moved from the house the family owned because he could no longer keep up the payments. We lived in a series of dreary flats on rice and milk (I don't eat rice these days) and there were times when we would not have eaten at all had not my maternal grandparents brought us food. Eventually, we moved into their home. My father had stood surety for a friend who had reneged on the deal. Our furniture was taken and the lounge was empty. We children would take our friends around the back way and we didn't want them to see. At that time my father had to walk seven miles to and from his little business and my mother went out to work.

When we finally became stable again we moved to a house owned by friends. There was an unfortunate corollary to this as the friends would arrive, night after night to visit, and my parents had to endure hours of trivial conversation. I know my father ached to get to his books. He would sit to two o'clock in the morning reading, making up lost time. The business did fairly well during those years. Often, he would phone home in the mid-afternoon, asking us to bring him money for change. So off one of us would go, into the heavy traffic on the highways, hoping the car would not fail us. It was then that he was attacked one day in his shop and a gun held to his head. He was made to lie on the grimy cement floor and then the assailant spat on his face. That was probably one of the worst moments in that proud man's life.

His health started deteriorating as the years of smoking were taking their toll. We moved again and he became increasingly unsettled. He was too proud to admit that his sight and his hearing were failing. He started reading with a magnifying glass as he did not think he needed spectacles. When we spoke to him he became angry with us, saying we were speaking too softly. I think he was afraid of what was happening. The music was no solace anymore as he could not hear. He got lost a couple of times on the way home and I had to fetch him. His health deteriorated so much that he had to stop working and he seemed to tunnel into a place of disquiet. He became more and more irritated with family members, suspicious and moody. There were a few bright spots for him then and his grandchildren brought some joy in his life. His little grand daughter, Chivaugn, Keith's daughter, came to live with us when she was six, after the loss of her mother in a car accident. She brought some delight into his life. His grandson, Ian's son, was a baby and I think that the knowledge that he was leaving a legacy pleased him. His companion was his beloved dog, a fox-terrier. Formerly, my father had been extremely fond of bulldogs, but this dog was special for him. The dog was treated daily to a piece of chocolate, and when she became diabetic, he insisted on buying diabetic chocolate for her. He and I had many quarrels, and there were periods when we would not speak to each other. Then I would start communicating again because he was too proud to apologise. He hated the music I listened to and would come into the kitchen where I had a radio playing and switch it off. The relationship between my brother Keith and my father broke down completely and they never spoke again. In retrospect, I know that he was lonely, afraid and sad and I wish so much now that I could have been able to rise above my own emotional fragility and give him the succour he so desperately needed and yet so furiously spurned.

He had developed emphysema and it became worse to the point of desperation. He could not even walk to the bathroom and all his strength was seeping out of him and he could not breathe. He had an oxygen tank but it did not help much. By now my father had withdrawn so much we were unable to break through that wall of suffering and we weren't speaking again and that's how it was when he died. One of his most loved pieces of music, Beethoven' s Piano Concerto No 5, The Emperor, was played at his funeral.

If his children were to be asked what the strongest immediate memory of their father is, they would each of them say, without hesitation and without consultation, "He is sitting on the veranda, book in hand, tea-tray on the chessboard table, pipe in mouth and the music would be playing, of course and he would be content."

My father stopped working in 1984 and died in 1989.

Family dates and details

Ian (born 16/11/53) has a partner Helen Lovkis, who is an estate agent. Their son, Jay, recently turned 21.

Keith (born 16/06/55) married Jenny Kieser in 1978. She did fashion modelling and co-owned a small boutique making exclusive clothing and died 10/01/86 in a car accident. Chivaugn was six at the time and lived with my parents, and after my father died, she lived with my mother, until she was 22.

I (Cheryl born 23/07/52) have chosen to not marry while my Mom is now almost 83, and maintains her own home and still enjoys baking.

Ian, Keith and Cheryl

Corrie

Corrie and Chivaugn

Jay and Chivaugn

Chivaugn Gordon, Harry's grand daughter writes

I am ashamed to say that I knew only vaguely about grandpa's history. He never spoke about it, having been deeply traumatised, I'm sure. He also turned his back on his faith; probably as this was what caused these terrible things to happen to him. He also held an understandably bitter hatred toward all things German. I distinctly recall Grandpa (who was a devout lover of books) having torn out of a compendium about classical musicians the entire chapter about Wagner. Because he didn't eschew any of the Jewish teachings or faith, and because my gran was from a Christian background, his children and grandchildren were not raised to be Jewish.

As time moved on, we gradually lost touch with his side of the family; many of them moved to other parts of South Africa and some to Australia. We moved away ourselves, when I went to university in 1998.

A few months back, I happened upon a documentary on our version of cable/ satellite TV. It was about the Ochberg Orphans. I had never heard of this man! All I knew was that grandpa and his sisters, amongst others, were shipped here in the 1920's. As the story progressed, I couldn't believe what I was hearing as they were telling the exact same story as grandpa's and I cried and cried.

I told my gran Corrie, Harry's wife, who is still alive and well, and is the best baker in the southern hemisphere, and she confirmed that Grandpa was indeed an Ochberg Orphan!

His daughter Cheryl has done research on Grandpa's history and I chatted to her too. She and gran are the best people to liaise with about grandpa. They will give excellent accounts of his life story. He had three children: Cheryl, Ian and Keith, who are all in the jewellery business. Keith is my dad. Ian has a son, Jay and we are Harry's only grandkids. Jay is an artist and graphic designer, and I am a doctor.

Part of my mission has also been to find and frame black and white photos of the family. There are a few lovely ones of Harry. He hated the camera and so the photos are like hen's teeth. I have also found as many of his relatives (all my cousins) on the social blight Facebook (which I admit I love!) as I could. Thankfully, they remembered me as it has been well over 20 year since I have seen them. I did see Lionel, Gerald and Yvonne in 2004 when I was working near Durban. Lionel drew the family tree for me, which I still have.

Corrie, my gran is 83, and starting to reminisce about life and though she is well, I feel a sense of urgency in getting the information from her as one never knows what tomorrow holds. She would love to be involved and is so glad I am getting all this info as it is she who put me in touch with Lionel via Auntie Yvonne. It would be a zenith of sorts for gran and Cheryl will definitely be keen to contribute.

I recall that grandpa was writing a book of his own, but he never completed it, and didn't number the pages or keep them in any kind of order, so we have a stack of jumbled paper that is in a suitcase in the cupboard! I also have some of his poems and puns.

This has been a fantastic journey of discovery for me, as I contemplate the true meaning of "family" on the eve of my wedding!

Chapter 98 – SALA BLIND (1910-1991)

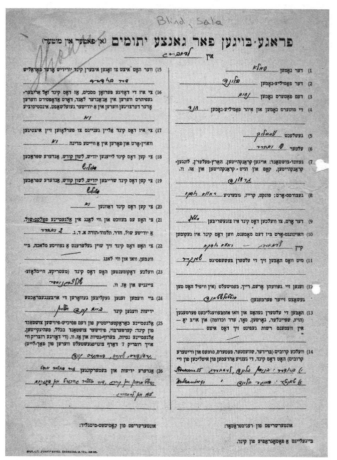

Questionaire on Sala Blind completed in Yiddish in Lemberg with translation by Veronica Belling following.

Name: Sala Blind **Age:** 10 years **Physical condition:** Healthy
Fathers name: Nachum   **Mother's name:** Chana
Place of birth: Rova Ruska (this is what it seems to be)
Place where she was living: Rova Ruska, Lemberg
Father's occupation: Inn keeper
Financial condition of family: average
Relatives: Brother: Binyomin Blind, Lemberg; Aunt: Feige Blind, Lemberg
Authority over the child: Brother
Is this person agreeable that the child be taken out of the country: Yes
Is the child herself prepared to leave her present place of residence: Yes
Can the child read Hebrew, Yiddish: Yiddish
Can the child write Hebrew, Yiddish: Yiddish
Can the child daven (say the blessings): Yes
Has the child attended school: For two years
Does the child have any personal documents: Shul certificate
Source of this information: Child herself
General physical and mental characteristics: Healthy
Other remarks: The father was killed in the war, the mother was killed in the 1918 pogrom in Lemberg.

My mother in school uniform – 8 September 1925
The photo from my mother to "Dear Ray"
Notice that my mother is wearing a tie.

SADIE SAUS (SALA BLIND)
Written by Edna Rudnick (Saus)

My name is Edna and I live with my husband Dennis, in Sydney. I am now 76 years old and I'm trying to get information about my late mother, Sadie Saus, nee Blind or Blinde. While my mother was alive, she would never ever discuss her family or past life.

My Mother said nothing about her life in Eastern Europe other than that the last she saw of her mother was her being dragged behind a horse ridden by a Polish soldier. We don't know what happened to her father.

She once mentioned she had an older brother of about 17 who was conscripted into the Polish Army. She never mentioned anything else.

We remember her saying she was at Arcadia, but she did not seem to have any friends except for one very good friend Sarah Altuska, whose married name was Slier.

Extracts from the register kept by the orphanage
Sala, aged 10, went to live with the Golomb family in Benoni.

She went to live with the Golomb family in Benoni and I recall that my Mom mentioned that she went to Hebrew High. In later years when we were children and doing sewing and knitting at school she said she did that at the Benoni Convent but I am told that the only convent in the early days was in Boksburg not Benoni. I spoke to one of my sisters, and she cannot ever remember my mom saying that she went to Benoni Convent. The only photo I have of my Mother as a child was in her school uniform.

I don't know how my parents met and have no wedding photos but I know they were married in the Arc Shul on 11 September 1932 and she mentioned the name of a millionaire, Schlesinger, who paid for some of the Arc girls' weddings and later went to live in America.

When my Mom got married, she started to work as a Saleslady at the OK Bazaars in Eloff Street. After several months of working, she gave notice, telling my father that the OK Bazaars did not employ pregnant women. It was an excuse to stop working as my father was giving his earnings to his mother at the end of each month. My grand-mother would then give my mom a small allowance.

My mother always looked very smart and elegant and I always picture her baking and cooking. She read a lot and was very quiet and never spoke. She never kept a maid and never really took an interest in what we did. My Mother was a good cook and baker and learned this from her Mother-in-law.

Our father Joe Saus came out from Lithuania with his older sister Fannie and a brother Sidney. They worked and saved and brought out the rest of the family one by one including their parents Yetta and Isaac.

They came from a very large family of seven brothers and three sisters with their Mom ruling the roost. After Fannie, Sidney and Joe there was Edi, Bennie, Lipka, Louis, Dorris and Victor. I'm sure my Mom found them a bit overpowering.

We lived in Doornfontein at the corner of Bertams Road and Chalton Terrace. I was born in 1933 and was a sickly child. Next came Gertie, then Fay (Phyllis) and Renee born in 1940. We all went to Doornfontein school. I went to Commercial High while my sisters went to Athlone. Dad used to come and watch us at school galas and netball but our Mom was never involved in our activities. I remember Dad and Mom were friendly with Leslie Wolchuk.

My Mother, a friend Mrs Hurwitz and my sisters, Phyllis, late Renee, born 1940, me and Gertie.
I am the eldest, then Gertie, Fay (Phyllis) and Renee and she is eight years younger than me
and must have been almost a year old. I am not sure of the ages.

Saus Brothers - Lipka, Louis (father of Kenny and Jeanette Saus), Joe (my Dad), Victor and Sydney

Sadie and Joe

I married Dennis Rudnick, born 1927, the son of Abraham and Bella (Nee Lazar). Their family lived in Three Anchor Bay but after the death of the father they went to live in Johannesburg. Dennis matriculated, became a fitter and turner and was an active member of Betar. He was part of a group of eight volunteers selected and sent via Italy to Israel and fought in the Israeli War of Independence. In 1950 Dennis was one of 40 mechanics who volunteed to spent two years training in the USA and they eventually returned to Israel with four upgraded aircraft which became the fleet of the newly founded Israeli Airlines El Al.

Aliens registration certificate of my mother issued in 1940. She arrived in South Africa on 19 September 1921. She came with a several hundred orphans from Poland. Her address was listed as Lemberg and then crossed out. The certificate states that she was born 10 July 1910. Country of birth is Poland. Nationality by marriage is Lithuanian. She passed away 26 September 1991.

My mother always spoke about Sarah Slier, a friend from Arcadia, however, we never ever met her or saw her with my mother. My mother never had friends, or entertained or invited friends over. She was such a loner and only after she died did we realize she suffered from severe depression.

Our dad died in August 1983 and our mother lived on her own for a number of years then went into the Jewish Old Aged home in Sandringham where she died in 1991.

Dennis meeting David Ben Gurion

Wedding of Edna and Dennis.
Bridesmaid is Fay. Sadie and Joe on the right

Grandchildren Candice Lee, 25, Justin 22 with Brandan 6, and my husband Dennis 82 holding Jared 10 and Asher 3

I have copy of *100 Years of Arc Memories* from my sister-in-law in Johannesburg. My husband and I knew and know a number of the people you have written about in the book. My three sisters were all friends with a number of the girls and boys in Arcadia. I also had two cousins, Jeanette and Kenny Saus, who grew up in Arcadia in the 1950s and they were the children of Louis Saus who had married Rosalyn.

I was a Saus prior to marriage. My sister has a son Alan Norman who married Wendy Rabinowitz who also grew up in the Arc.

Wedding of Edna and Dennis - 12 September 1954

Gary and Susan, Charlene Green and Saul and Tami

Dennis and I have four children who all live in Sydney:
Aubrey is not married.
Charlene Green is separated and had a daughter Candice and a son Justin.
Gary married Susan Gubbay. She lost her first son and has a second one Jared now 10. They had Brandon 6 and Asher 3.
Saul married Tami Grungrass and she had one daughter Ella

Dennis with our Grandchildren - Asher, Jared, Brandan and in front three year old Ella

OUR FAMILY HISTORY
Written by Barry Berelowitz and Helen Birin (nee Berelowitz)

Our mother Mary (Alta) came from Brest Litovsk in what is now Belarus, near the Polish border. Brest Litovsk was about two-thirds Jewish, according to an 1897 census. During World War I, the Jews were driven out on 1 August 1915 by order of the Russian high command. Shortly afterwards the Austro-German army occupied the city and many of the exiles returned, only to be expelled again by the Germans.

Our grandmother had died from typhus carried by the soldiers. Our grandfather, a prosperous merchant, fled to Poland with his five children to wait out the war. One day, while going out to find food for the family, he was killed by a stray bullet, and the children were orphaned.

The Borowiks had been in Brest Litovsk since 1804, when Moishka Borowik arrived from Bialystock with his wife and five children. The city, situated in the Pale of Settlement, was part of Lithuania until 1921 (which is what "Litovsk" denotes); today it's known as Brest.

Alta and Chana at the back and Rachel and Shia in front. Photo taken at the end of World War I.

Our great-grandfather was a highly respected rabbi, and when he died, his body was carried into every shul in Brest Litovsk as a mark of honor. Avraham Mordechai, our maternal grandfather, was able to provide his family with a high standard of living. The girls wore expensive dresses, which Avraham bought on business trips to Warsaw.

During the war the oldest of the Borowik children, Yankel, got a job with the German railways. After the war he married a Polish Jewess and settled in Metz, near Strasbourg in Alsace Lorraine.

Our mother, Mary, was the second oldest and took on the role of mother to her younger siblings, Chana (Annie), Rachel and Shiah, who were placed in an orphanage in Poland at the end of the war. (When our mother was hit by the great flu epidemic of 1918/19 and was in danger of dying, she was given a new name, Alta, in accordance with Jewish tradition; it means "the old one," because she was the oldest daughter.)

Annie told us that one day, the orphans were summoned to assemble and then divided into three groups, with siblings staying together. They were told that one group was going to America, one to Palestine and one to South Africa. Annie, Rachel and Shiah were in the latter group. They were very nervous about going to Africa, because they thought it was a dangerous place with lots of wild animals.

Our Zayda - Avraham Mordechai Borowik

Shia and Chana (Annie) immediately before coming to SA

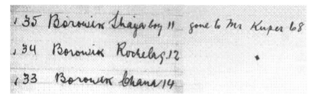

Extracts from the register kept by the orphanage in Johannesburg that cared for the three siblings. The age of the children is listed; Shiah, age 11, went to live with the Kuper family.

When the Borowik children arrived at Arcadia, Shiah was quickly adopted by the Kuper family. Mrs Kuper had come to Arcadia with a bag full of sweets and asked who wanted some. The children jumped up and down, noisily shouting "me, me." But one child quietly and politely raised his hand—that was Shiah. Mrs Kuper was so impressed by the boy's good manners that she arranged to adopt him.

The Kupers had two other sons, Simon and Leo. Simon eventually became a Supreme Court judge and president of the South African Jewish Board of Deputies, and Leo became an anthropology professor who taught at the University of California Los Angeles. Simon was murdered by an unknown assailant in his home in 1963.

Shia, Annie and Rachel attended the Jewish Government Primary School and the Hebrew High School in Johannesburg.

SallyTannenbaum is top right and the other children are the three Borowik siblings; Rachel and Shiah in the front and Annie on the left at the back

Rachel and Shia at Jewish Government School

The photograph is of the Arcadia girls that my aunt, Chana kept under the glass top of her sideboard for all the years that I lived with her. A message at the back translates "In memory for my dearest sister from all the great children in the African Orphanage, which are 'engaged' in gymnastics with our instructor Mr 'Lily' who is one of the best in Johannesburg, from your dear Chana." (Photo in full above and then part only enlarged below)

Kanter and Shia at the back and Rachel (Ray), Mrs Steiman and Chana (Annie) in the front and unknown young girl.

Unknown Arcadia Girls. Woman on the right side of the second row may be Rachel.

After leaving Arcadia, Annie and Rachel boarded with a Mrs. Isaacman in Doornfontein. At first Annie worked in a shoe store and Rachel as a secretary. Our mother's sisters married before our mother, but they always sought our mother's advice!

YANKEL

Our uncle Yankel died in 1950 in France, having survived World War II. He had divorced his Polish wife in the early 1930s after having a daughter with her, Helena. A few years ago we obtained a report from the International Red Cross confirming our assumption that Helena was murdered in Auschwitz; her mother presumably suffered the same fate.

Yankel remarried and had four children with a Catholic woman. He hid out with her family in rural France during the war years.

Yankel's children were brought up as Catholics. Barry first met the family in 1962. They managed to communicate by Barry speaking Yiddish and the French family speaking Alsacian German. The children had picked up Alsacian German from their mother who had once lived in Alsace Lorraine, which at various times was part of Germany.

Barry again met two of the cousins in Paris in 1967 on his honeymoon. They asked if the couple had been married in church. Barry was uncomfortable; he had no idea if his cousins were aware of their Jewish ancestry and how their husbands might react on finding out that Barry had been married in a synagogue. After all, France is a very anti-Semitic country.

Barry equivocated suggesting that it wasn't a church exactly but offering no details. But when one of the cousins visited us in South Africa in 1978, it became clear she was aware that her father was Jewish and we discussed our Jewishness openly. She told us that her name, Borowik, had elicited anti-Semitic inquiries at her job as to whether she was Jewish.

As with most of the Ochberg orphans, the irony of our family story is that had our grandparents not died tragically during World War I, they would most likely have eventually returned to their home in Brest Litovsk. When the Germans came to Brest during World War II, there were not yet concentration camps and so they took the entire Jewish community—some 30,000 people—to a nearby forest, where machine gunners were waiting for them. Our whole family would have been wiped out.

Barry and his wife Marlene recently returned from a Jewish heritage tour of Lithuania. (Most South African Jews came from Lithuania and Latvia). There are more than 200 killing fields where Lithuania's 200,000 Jews were murdered during the Holocaust; the bodies were dumped into mass graves.

When we look at photos of the Ochberg children, we are thankful for Isaac Ochberg bringing them to South Africa, for General Smuts providing government support of the venture, and for the wonderful South African Jewish community, which provided funds for bringing the children over and supporting them.

ALTA (BOROWIK) AND SAM BERELOWITZ

At 19, our mother was too old to go with her younger siblings but yearned to be with them. She remained in Poland and worked as a milliner while boarding with a family. In 1929, when she had saved enough money to go to South Africa, the family begged her to stay and marry their son. They promised she would never be short of anything. But her heart was with her siblings, and so she departed for South Africa shortly before the Immigration Quota Act of 1930 came into force, ending what had been full freedom of entry into the country.

My father, Sam Berelowitz, came from Yurburg in Lithuania and arrived in South Africa in 1929 to join two sisters who had come earlier.

Sam and Mary (Alta) on their wedding day

Our mother met and married Sam Berelowitz in 1933. It was a happy marriage, but sadly it did not last long as our father died of a heart attack in 1942, when we were four and seven years old, respectively. In 1950 we suffered another tragedy when our mother died at the age of 48 of a heart problem that stemmed from the flu she had suffered during the epidemic at the end of World War I. We were then 11 and 14 years old.

At some point before his death, my father bought a horse and cart and made a very good living by going to the produce market early in the morning and buying kosher poultry which he sold to kosher butcheries and boarding houses.

Neither my mother nor his sisters ever told me anything about my dad presumably because they did not want to bring up a painful subject.

Since my father died when I was only four, I remember very little of him.

Sam and Mary with Helen and Berry

After my father died in 1942, my mother struggled. At first she opened a dress shop but was unable to make a living out of it. She sold the family home which was near Athlone High School in Johannesburg and for a time we lived in a rented room in Bertrams.

She then bought a complex of four flats in Judith's Paarl and got a job as a clerk at a nearby laundry. It was at this time that her health became a problem since she suffered from a leaking heart valve, a condition which she developed during the great flu epidemic of 1918/19. Financially things were very tough. My mother was in and out of hospital with her heart condition until she died in 1950.

I remember my mother as a very gentle and refined woman. I remember her telling my aunt her experience at the theater or bioscope and she said that during the interval she went to the toilet. She put her hand in front of her mouth and lowered her voice before saying "toilet" as if to do otherwise would pollute the room.

Helen Mom and Berry in Johannesburg)

Berry Mom and Helen

Shiah recommended that we be placed in Arcadia, but Annie, who never had children of her own, insisted on taking us in.

ANNIE (BOROWIK) AND BENNY CENTNER

Annie at Jewish Government School and in her twenties

Annie had two short and very unhappy marriages before marrying Benny Centner in the mid-1930s.

Annie on her wedding day in about 1936 when she married Benny Centner

Benny, a plumber, volunteered for the army during the Second World War even though he was over 40. His father, who was over 70 when the war broke out and who had fought for the Boers in the Anglo Boer War, also volunteered and was accepted for duty in South Africa. Benny fought with the Allied forces in North Africa and Italy.

After the war Benny had difficulty finding a steady job. One day, coming out of the famous Jewish bakery, Crystals in Doornfontein, Annie came across a city councilman, Mr Weiner, who had been on Arcadia's board when she was growing up there. On the spur of the moment she told him about Benny's situation and asked if he could help. Weiner found Benny a position with the Johannesburg City Council, a job he held until his death in 1968. (Benny was not a registered plumber, and after a council review of workmen's qualifications in 1961, he was in danger of losing his job. Annie once again called on Weiner, who resolved the problem.)

Annie and Benny lived in Bez Valley, in Johannesburg and they took us in when my mom died. Since their home had only two bedrooms, they increased their mortgage so they could build on an extra room, allowing each of us to have separate bedrooms. Annie worked as a clerk for various big companies. Benny was a supervisor building homes in what is now Soweto. Annie was a very loving and devoted caregiver and did her utmost for us. Annie and Benny earned a modest living and our mother's estate brought in a meager income that was barely sufficient to support us.

In all the years we lived with Annie, a gentleman on a motorbike would come to our home every month to collect a regular donation that Annie made to Arcadia.

Helen lived with Annie until 1955, when she married Harry Birin, a pharmacist from Port Elizabeth. Barry matriculated from Athlone High in 1955 with a first class pass and a couple of distinctions. He went on to study accountancy while working as an articled clerk. Barry lived with Annie until 1967, when he married Joan Merkel.

Until shortly after Benny died, Annie worked as a bookkeeping assistant at various large companies. Annie was what would be described in Yiddish, as a *beria* (a highly competent homemaker). Her weekdays would start at 5.00 am when she would get up to make lunch for everyone to take to work or school and would arrange the food to be prepared by the maid for dinner. However, on one day a week she would be up at 4.00 am to go the butcher to buy meat and fish for the forthcoming week. At 6.00 am she would bathe and then do the exercise program broadcast by the SABC. She would leave the house shortly after 7.00 am to catch two buses to work. Benny would leave the house at 6.00 am to go to work. She and Benny enjoyed playing bowls on the weekend at the municipal bowling club in Emmarentia.

In 1968, while driving to Margate for their annual holiday, Benny was killed in a car accident. Annie was devastated by the loss and by the shock of witnessing the accident. About a year later, she decided to emigrate to Israel. Her hope was to work as a volunteer in an orphanage. But within a short time she met a distinguished Yiddish-speaking Israeli man and they got married, though this meant Annie had to forego payouts from Benny's pension fund. Her husband died after about three years. Annie died in Israel in 1977 at age 69.

Helen's wedding with Annie and Benny

Annie (Chana) and Benny with Helen's children ~ 1964

461

Annie had no children and thus there are no grandchildren. However, to Annie my sister Helen and Barry were like her own children.

Barry continues

From my standpoint Annie was as loving and caring a caregiver as I could ever have hoped for. She was extremely devoted to me and she did her utmost for me.

My mother's estate brought in a modest income which was barely sufficient to support Helen and me. I remember a lot of economic privation during my teenage years. I remember taking my shoes to the shoemaker to have the soles replaced for the umpteenth time and the shoemaker sorrowfully telling me that the shoes had been repaired so many times that there was no place on the welt where he could put in any more stitches. I managed to finish my matric by virtue of getting a fifty pound book bursary from the United Building Society.

I was a good scholar and matriculated from Athlone High in 1955 with a first class pass and a couple of distinctions. I wanted to study nuclear physics but the only affordable way to get an education was to study accountancy where I could work during the day and go to university at night. I was the second top student at Witwatersrand University where I graduated in 1959. In 1960 I passed the uniform national exam to become a chartered accountant.

Helen lived with Annie until 1955 when she married Harry Birin of Port Elizabeth. I lived with Annie until 1967 when I married Joan Merkel of Johannesburg. We have two daughters, Marian and Karen.

Shortly after Annie died, I was appointed managing partner of a 90-person accountancy firm, one of the largest in Johannesburg. However, at the end of 1978, in the wake of the police shooting schoolchildren in Soweto, I emigrated with my family and parents-in-law to Los Angeles.

Over the following 15 years, Helen, her husband and both their children and their families also emigrated to America.

Helen remembers

We lived with our mom in Natlea Court, Judith Paarl, until she died in 1950.

I remember Tania Jacobson (Bornstein) and her sister Rita. My mother and my aunts never ever went to Muizenberg without visiting Yetta Bornstein at home or popping in to their fish business.

One year my cousin Clara (Rachel's daughter) and I went to camp at Lakeside. Yetta invited us to come and take a bath there on Sundays and wash our hair too. I had long very curly hair and I clearly remember how she tried to help me get the knots out at the back of my head! The memory of the hospitality will always remain.

I remember her daughters Tania and Rita very well and I remember especially seeing granny Sheihdle always sitting on the verandah.

RACHEL (RAE) BOROVIK
Written by her daughter Claire Rushovich (Klein).

Rachel as a young lady

My name is Claire Rushovich (nee Klein). My Mother, Rachel (Rae) Borowik, may she rest in peace, was an Ochberg Orphan who died at the very young age of 40. She was from Brest Litofsk. She came to South Africa with her sister Annie (Chana) and her brother Shia. Her older sister Mary (Alta) was too old to go with them and she worked making hats in Warsaw until she could come to South Africa.

Their mother had died from contracting typhus from a neighbour she was taking care of. Their father was killed by a stray bullet while going out to buy food. My Mom told me they hid away, from soldiers, in toilets. Mary took care of them.

She was in the Jewish orphanage in Johannesburg, later called Arcadia. I remember she mentioned they were only allowed to shower a couple of times a week. So she and Anne got up very early, 4.00 am, to shower, until the matron caught them and put a stop to that.

When she left Arcadia she worked as a typist for African Studios. She married my Father, may he rest in peace, Hymen (Hymie) Louis Klein. I remember going with her to listen to a rabbi (I think rabbi Landau) at Arcadia.

She was a wonderful, good mother who could cook and bake and knit beautifully. She kept in touch with Polly Joffee (Sybil and Myra) and Chasha Zagey, Julie Ross her daughter. As children we played together.

My Mom and her sisters lived near each other and were close sisters. My Mom encouraged me to play tennis and said maybe I would meet my future husband playing tennis. And I did. I met David, may he rest in peace, my darling husband, who had also grown up in Arcadia.

We had two daughters. My older daughter, Heather, lives in Johannesburg and has a seven year old daughter Daniella. My younger daughter Robyn, lives in Israel, Raanana, with three children Daniel nine, Yoni six, and Liora two. She is married to Marcello Del Monte who is from Italy.

I live in Johannesburg and visit Israel each year for two months at a time.

SHIAH
Written by Sonia Rheiner, the daughter of Shiah

From some research, I understand that my father was about six years old when he arrived in South Africa. In any event, I always thought that he was born in 1910. After being rescued from Russia, he was taken into the Arcadia Orphanage. There he was adopted by the Kuper family, who were well known and highly respected in SA. He changed his name to Borwick and added on this the Cooper name (he changed the name from Kuper to Cooper). Apparently he was not terribly happy with his adopted family, but as a child, I remember him taking us to see his adopted mother, whom we called Granny Kuper. I believe she and her daughter, Anne were the only two Kupers with whom he stayed in touch, more or less.

He was married in 1937 to Gladys Gerber of Cape Town. Her parents also came originally from Russia. My grandfather came to South Africa before my grandmother who remained in Russia. My grandmother had a brother already in South Africa whose name was Abraham Faber and he apparently had connections and managed to get boat tickets for his sister who already had two small children. At that time, there were pogroms in Russia and my grandmother fled with the two children. Their names were Lettie aged six and Nat aged four. They went through terrible hardships, walked through deep snow but my grandmother urged the children on even though they complained of how cold it was and eventually they reached the boat which took them to South Africa.

In South Africa they tried many things and tried farming, but they were burgled when living in Wynberg. Eventually they opened a furniture store in Claremont. My grandmother was a very strong woman and if someone wanted something which she did not have in her store, she would go upstairs to their living quarters and take that item out of her own home and supply it to the customer.

Eventually they had another two daughters, I believe, both of whom died.

When Lettie was 18 and Nat 16, my mother Gladys was born. My grandmother was busy in the shop so my aunt Lettie practically brought up my mom. There is a story of when Lettie had to practice the piano she tied a piece of string onto the leg

of the piano and the other end onto the leg of my mom so she would not crawl down the stairs of their apartment.

My dad Shaih married my mother, Gladys in 1937. They moved to Johannesburg where my dad was a building contractor and built a magnificent house in Westcliffe. My bother Arnold was born in September of the same year.

I was born five years later and by that time, we had moved to Lower Houghton. My sister, Sharon Ester was born in 1950.

Arnold, my brother is a CPA. His wife Lola, is a lawyer. They have three children, Steven living in America, Janine living in JHB and Lynne, now moved to Australia.
Steven has two children; Shai (after my dad) who is 19, and Liron who is nine.
Janine has a boy and a girl.
Lynne has two girls

I live in Israel and have three children, all married; a daughter Ainat living in the States, Barak also living in the States and my youngest daughter, Miri living in Israel near me
Barak is married to Julia but does not have children.
Miri has two boys; Stav 16 and Aviv 11.

My sister Ester, has one child, Yael who is in her 20's.

My father was a wonderful father, a loving father who cared very much for his children. He was a very good looking man and was even once mistaken for my older brother.

Shia in his Freemason regalia

463

Chapter 100 – BINA AND SARAH BRODER

Bina Broder was born, 30 September 1913 in Kowel Stanislawow (now Ivano Frankovsk) in the Ukraine. Not much is known of her early history other than that she and her sister Sarah were both part of the group of 167 orphans brought out to Cape Town in September 1921 by Isaac Ochberg.

Group Passport One Bina Broder is in the front row, 7th from the right, and, her sister Sarah is in the back row, 5th from the right.

They were part of the group of the 78 children who were taken by train to Johannesburg on arrival in Cape Town and were placed in the care of the then South African Jewish Orphanage SAJO that in 1923 acquired the Arcadia estate as a home and also adopted the name Arcadia.

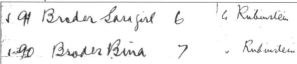

Extracts from the register kept by the SAJO that cared for the two siblings. The age of the children is listed after the name and they both went to live with the Rubenstein family.

They were adopted by Max and Yettie Rubenstein, of Lichtenberg in the Western Transvaal and the family moved to Durban in 1934

Max and Yettie Rubenstein who adopted Bina and Sarah Broder

On 25 July 1937 Bina married David Stange (born Heilbron 8 March 1908) in Durban and they had two sons, Max Stange born 18 November 1940 and Peter Stange born 15 March 1945.

The bride Bina Rubenstein (Broder) with her sister Sally (Sarah) (Broder) outside the Durban Jewish Club Durban where she had her wedding reception on 25 July 1937

OUR MOTHER BINA STANGE (RUBENSTEIN BRODER)
Written by Max Stange

My late Mother, of Blessed Memory, was an Ochberg Orphan, something that my brother, Peter, and, I only found out in 2006! Her original name was Bina Broder, and, she, and, her younger sister, Sarah, who also was an Ochberg Orphan, were fortunate enough to be adopted by Max and Yettie Rubenstein, owners of the International Hotel, Lichtenberg, soon after they arrived at Arcadia.

Max Rubenstein had arrived in South Africa from Neustadt in Germany at around 1900. Both her adoptive parents must have been remarkable people to have adopted two little girls. I never knew her father, Max but Yettie lived with us to a ripe old age in Durban.

Their surnames were changed to Rubenstein, and, the Family moved to Durban in 1934 as it was thought that the climate would be better for Max's failing health (asthma). Unfortunately, this advice was totally incorrect, and, Max passed away on 30 December 1937.

My Mom was engaged to David Stange, who was born in Heilbron, OFS., and, who had gone to Lichtenberg with his Father and Brother, in search of fame and fortune in the Diamond Diggings, neither of which was to be found.

My Dad then went to work for his Uncle, Benny Datt, selling Ford cars, and, when Max Rubenstein suddenly passed away in Durban, Dad was asked to come and run the Family business, which was the Umbilo Road Bottle Store.

Bina and Max in the centre with two friends

Our Mother, and, her sister, Sarah (aka Sally), were very close, and, used to see each other almost on a daily basis. They never mentioned a single word of their background as Ochberg Orphans.

Our Mother was a very devoted and dedicated Member of the Durban Jewish Social Services (previously known as Durban Jewish Welfare), and, was involved for many years with Sick Visiting and Fund Raising. She was recognized when she received Honourary Life Membership of the organisation. She always brought us up with the credo that we should never use the word "hate"!

Mom played a reasonably good game of tennis, and, was a member of the Circle Club for many years. She was well-known for being ambidextrous and would change the racquet to either hand. In later years she was a keen bowler, as was our Father, Dave, who was the first member of the Circle Bowling Club to win the All-Natal Pairs Championships in 1965. Dad skipped and the late Barney Gamsy (father of Springbok wicket-keeper, Dennis), played lead.

Our Father had a great love for Horseracing, and, would attend every meeting throughout the year. Mom shlepped along, but, only to keep him company, and, to take care of his "winnings", which he always gave to her. He never discussed the "losses". They were a fixture at the Greyville and Clairwood Courses, where they always had their own reserved tables in the Member's enclosure.

I recall, at their Golden Wedding anniversary, held at the Durban Jewish Club, when addressing the guests, I made the following comment. "Dad, as far as racing is concerned, I have never known anybody to back so many winners, and, come out losing!" This brought the house down, since all their friends, knew of his love for the Sport of Kings.

We always celebrated Shabbat at our home on Friday nights, and, Peter and I dutifully recited the *brachot* for the *kitkah* and wine, together. Mom used to really love going to Shul on a Friday night, and, her belief in the All mighty was sacrosanct.

Reminiscing about Mom, what seems to be a recurring theme is the fact that she was always such a serene, calm, soft-spoken lady. I cannot recall her ever losing her temper.

In fact, when our good friend, Dr Jonathan Beare, learned that our Mom was an Ochberg Orphan he sent me the following message.

"Your Mom did not keep the story to protect you from the trauma. I think she did not discuss it because it was so painful for her. I know many of the Jews who left Lite never talked to their children about *der heim*.

The trauma of losing one's family and never seeing them again was for a young person so traumatic that these people could not deal with telling it to their kids. My mom who was very close to her mom knew less than zero about her mother's family. Where did the mother come from? Did she have siblings? Who were her parents? All information that went to the grave with her in 1932.

You should now follow up in the records of the shtetl from where your mom came and tell me if you find out anything about the family. How was your Mom able to remain sweet and warm after such a terrible traumatic youth?"

Peter, Bina and Alec Levy, Sally's late son

*Bina Stange, Max Stange, Sally Levy in the top row,
and, Peter Stange, Yettie (Ouma) Rubenstein and
Alec Levy in front*

PETER STANGE WRITES

My Dad's parents were Anne (nee Shochat) and Samuel. He was one of four children: Gerald, Harry, David and Sophie. Dad was born in Heilbron in the Free State. He later lived in Lichtenburg in the Transvaal, where he worked at his uncle Ben Datt's garage and Ford agency. The only date he mentioned was that of his late grandfather's (Meyer Shochat) arrival in South Africa around 1896. Meyer was married in Riga. About his family on his father's side we know very little. Dad later followed my mother to Durban when she moved there with her adoptive parents – Yettie and Max Rubenstein and of course they married in Durban. He had presumably met my mother when her parents were running the International Hotel in Lichtenburg (grand name for a dorp!). They owned the Umbilo Road Bottle Store in Durban which my Dad inherited from my late grandparents and ran for 40 years. My mother's 'parents' also owned the Butterworth Hotel in Durban for a while.

My Mom passed away on 13 July 1997 (just a week or two short of their 60th wedding anniversary which they had planned to hold again at the Durban Jewish Club where they'd held their wedding reception in 1937, and for which invitations had already been sent out). She was also very active on the Durban Jewish Welfare and was a regular hospital visitor for many years.

I'd been back from the funeral for a short while when I was informed that my Dad had passed away, on 18 August 1997 and so off I went again to Durban.

I've thought long and hard about how I discovered my Mom was an Ochberg orphan and I really don't know the answer. Strange as that may sound? Beschert?

I can tell you a little bit though. A couple of years ago I was sitting at a table at a wedding reception (in Israel) for a friend's daughter (Ivan Kessel in Sydney) and overheard Bennie Penzick at our table discussing Ochberg and his story. I don't know what prompted me to ask him about it – I guess I had heard rumours that my Mom was an orphan and was keen to know more.

And that's how it started. He put me in touch with Brian Fine in Sydney and the rest, as they say, is history. Brian was able to locate the actual documents attesting to my mother's background.

*Dave and Bina Stange in their bowling togs
(both were keen bowlers)*

DISCOVERING MOM WAS AN OCHBERG ORPHAN

It was in 2006 that Peter, happened to attend a wedding in Israel, where he overheard a conversation between two guys who were discussing the Ochberg Orphans. Peter, amazingly and intuitively, asked them how he could find out more about the Ochberg Orphans and, he was given the e-mail address of Brian Fine of Sydney, Australia, whose Father was also an Ochberg Orphan, and, who had apparently saved the original Ship's Manifest with all the names handwritten in script. Peter wrote to Brian who responded immediately, and, asked Peter for our Mom's and Aunt's first names. Peter e-mailed this to Brian who responded by sending a photocopy of the Manifest which clearly indicated Bina Broder and Sarah Broder.

What an overwhelming revelation this was for us to find this out at this stage of our lives! To be honest, I still have difficulty coming to terms with it.

Shortly after we discovered this news, I happened to be in Durban with my Family on our annual holiday, when a certain lady, who was at our home for dinner, and, who knew nothing of our Mom's background, etc, happened to mention that she'd just read a fascinating book *The Night of the Burning* by Linda Press-Wulff, and, she told us that is was a fascinating story of two sisters who were among the Ochberg Orphans.

I could not get to the bookstore early enough the next day, where I purchased two copies (one for my brother, Peter), and, I read the book in one sitting. It was very sad and I realised, as I was reading, how this story might just as well have been written about our Mom and Aunt, except for the important fact that they were both adopted by the same Parents, and, grew up so very close together.

SALLY (SARAH) LEVY (RUBENSTEIN BRODER)

Sally (Sara) Levy

Sadly, there is nobody left on my Aunt Sally (Sarah) side of the family, as her only Son, Alec Levy, passed away several years ago. He left a wife and two daughters, but, they have no knowledge whatsoever of the family history, etc.

Alec would not have known that his Mother was an Ochberg Orphan. Alec was the President of the Chevra Kaddisha in Durban at the time of his passing. Alec went to Kearsney College and would have been 63 this year.

DURBAN JEWISH CENTRE FUNCTION
August 2008

Here are my closing remarks at a function that was held at the Durban Jewish Center in August, when we invited Lauren Snitcher-Tyfield to show us her Film.
"Rabbi Zekry,

Ladies and gentlemen, in concluding today's presentation by our guest, Lauren, I would like to begin by reading a poem.

It is titled *The poem of the orphan on his way to South Africa* and was written by an anonymous Jewish child from the Ukraine:

Poem of the orphan on his way to South Africa
written by an anonymous Jewish child

Merciful father in heaven
Who in his mercy toward children left orphans
Forced to leave their homes
Has sent Father Ochberg to make us citizens of South Africa
God blessed us that we found ourselves among good people
Our worries ended when we received the letter
Our group, hundreds of children, would not be separated
We would live as brothers!
A miracle will happen and when we grow up and stand on our feet
We will never forget the poor and needy
We left behind us ruins when we started on our way
We took leave of our friends
And hoped that fate would allow
That we would live as Jews
Father Ochberg came to rescue us ....
We will love as Jews
And to Zion come ....

As you all know, my late mother, Bina Stange, of blessed memory was an Ochberg Orphan.

It was not until 18 months ago, thanks entirely to the intuitive alertness of my brother, Peter, that we made this amazing discovery!

Subsequently, we managed to establish that she and her younger sister, Sally, were born in what is today known as Ukraine, and, that their original maiden name was Broder.

They were aged seven and five respectively when they landed in South Africa in 1921, the same age as our daughter, Bina, who we are blessed to have with us today.

As you can well imagine, this discovery was a hugely emotional experience for Peter and me, since our mother never told us the story of her very sad childhood.

Researching the amazing story of Isaac Ochberg, led me to connect with our guest of honour, Lauren Snitcher Tyfield, herself the granddaughter of an Ochberg Orphan. Lauren has dedicated herself to creating a very comprehensive database covering each and every Ochberg Orphan, together with their descendents. This is an ongoing project which Lauren works on constantly.

Lauren, may I take this opportunity, on behalf of all of us present today, to thank you most sincerely for your excellent film presentation and discussion, and, most importantly, for giving up your precious time, to fly from Cape Town to be with us.

Thank you"
Max Stange

Chapter 101 – YUDA DREILING

MY DAD, JULES FISHER (YUDA DREILING)
HIS LIFE AND LEGACY
Written by Michael Fisher

WAS MY FATHER REALLY ONE OF THE OCHBERG ORPHANS?

Extract from an affidavit dated 1974:
I, Jules Fisher, hereby make oath and say that:
(1) I am not in possession of my birth certificate. I was born at Stanislawov, Poland, on 10 June 1916.
(2) My parents died when I was a very young child and after their death I was brought to South Africa in 1921 and taken into an orphanage."

How this bare statement belies the trauma and events that befell a young child, his parents and siblings, and countless thousands of others in that era! And how it simply alludes to the legacy of Isaac Ochberg, who saved him and 166 other boys and girls and gave them the chance of a new life.

That he had been born in Poland and had somehow been sent to South Africa as a child, and that he grew up at Arcadia Children's Home in Parktown, Johannesburg was really all I ever knew about his early life. My Dad, like most who had experienced great trauma early on in life, kept that part of his life as his personal closed-book. It was only in 1997, when I was living in Sydney, that I learned the story of Isaac Ochberg and his mission to save the fate of Jewish children in Eastern Europe from the ravages of the pogroms, disease and hunger that they faced, and that my Dad had been one of those fortunate children.

The late Hanna Fine, mother of my very close friend, Brian Fine, had often mentioned that her late husband and my Dad had both come out on the *Edinburgh Castle* in 1921 and had been at Arcadia together. This was validated by my mother. It was only after Lauren Snitcher, from Cape Town, had contacted Brian and told her of the research she had been doing into the "Ochberg Orphans" that we became aware of the true story. The revelation was stunning. We hungered for as many facts as possible. It answered so many questions and at the same time posed more questions which, for me, still remain unanswered. I flew to Cape Town and met with Lauren, who took me to the University of Cape Town's archives and to the Jewish Museum and shared the copious research she had so passionately compiled.

While I knew Dad had been on the *Edinburgh Castle*, I could find no reference to him on any of the manifests or passport lists. I searched for a "Yudel", or "Fisch", which I knew was his name before he had it changed to "Fisher". Then a name caught my eye: on one handwritten list there I noted :
    "57. Dreyling Yuda, 8, Stanislawow",

On the schedule attached to a group passport photo of the children taken at the time of their transfer out of Poland: "8. Dreyling Juda, 8". Yes!- he had been born in Stanislawow

This photo is from Group passport No. 4.
Although Yuda Dreyling is listed on Group passport No.1, the uncanny family resemblance makes me sure this is in fact my father.

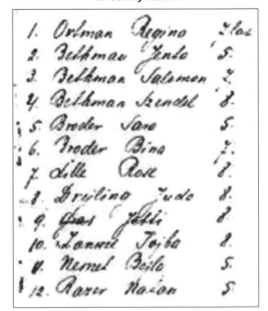

List of children from Group passport No 1.
No 8 on list is "Dreyling Juda, 8"

(which at various times had been part of Poland and at other times part of Ukraine). Vaguely I recalled that the name "Dreyling" had appeared on a document lodged by my father with the South African Government to verify his citizenship. But was this boy and my father one and the same?

Next I went to Arcadia and met with Selwyn Chalmers, who obligingly trawled through their records. I was amazed to see how basic they were- just an entry in a hard cover book and a 3x 5 card. The card noted on one side " *No 57 Dreiling Yuda, Male age 8. Remarks: Went to Isaac Neustad, 371 Proes St, Pretoria N117".*

Selwyn wrote to me saying *"The only document in the file was the card showing Yudel had been adopted by Isaac Neustad in Pretoria. It seems that Jules Fisch/Fisher is the same person as Yudel Dreiling".* And in a photocopy of a handwritten page, headed "From notebook marked Isaac Ochberg" was similarly recorded *"1. Isaac Neustad 117 – Yudel Dreiling 57".* Then followed on this page a list numbered up to 41 similarly coded: Adopter – Adoptee. That comprised the record of adoption of these children.

But had my Dad been adopted? I recalled that he had once regaled us at dinner with some rare glimpses into his life at Arcadia and a few youthful escapades. He told us that he had been taken for adoption by a man in Pretoria – after a few days he discovered this man was working with "dead bodies" – and in fear and panic he had run away and made it back to Arcadia. And he never again consented to be adopted. (Did this Isaac Neustadt work for the Chevra Kadischa, I wonder.)

I have the photograph of the children who are listed on the schedule to the aforementioned group photograph, yet I am unable to make out which was my father. Then in another photo from the archives, there is a boy marked "57" – and that boy bears an uncanny resemblance to me at a similar age".

I record this quest, as unlike most other Ochberg children, my father's identity as one of them, was not self-evident.

As explained above, my dad never mentioned his early childhood – no mention of his parents or siblings, no mention of Isaac Ochberg – we only knew that for some inexplicable reason he had arrived as an orphan in South Africa at the age of eight. At one time we were under the impression that his parents, only too aware of the risks of likely fate of their son if he remained in the Ukraine, selflessly and with courageous foresight, put their son on a boat to a place they hoped would be a haven and provide a life that could not otherwise be assured.

Now we believe that both parents were deceased, that dad indeed had an older brother, Jacob, and an older sister Klara, from whom he was separated. They apparently were being cared for by an uncle in Dresden. How was Dad then in a pitiful orphanage in Stanislawow – in the epicentre of a region notorious for repeated pogroms and atrocities?

When Dad was in his twenties, having somehow kept contact with his sister, he received several letters from her, telling him of the imminent danger which awaited the Jews of Europe, as Hitler took control of Germany. She begged Jules to get her, then pregnant, her husband and two little girls to South Africa and for money to escape. Struggling to make a living for himself, he sacrificed his savings and sent what money he could to the Bank of England. Needless to say, the money was never claimed and they perished, together with their brother Jacob.

In the article "The Ochberg Orphans – An Episode in the History of the Cape Jewish Orphanage" by Jonathan Boiskin (Jewish Affairs 1994), there is a quote from Poly Joffe (born Stanger) who was five when her father was conscripted by the Russians and sent off to Odessa. *"Although only five years old I can remember my elder sister and I living with a German woman...but later my sister died of illness. It was then that I was taken to the orphanage in Stanislawow. Here I remained for three arduous years before Mr Ochberg arrived to choose the younger children to go with him. The years I spent in the orphanage were most horrible. Very often we had nothing to eat and when fighting broke out in the town, we were chased into the countryside for safety. I remember sleeping in a filthy stable on one such occasion, while in another we hid in the forest for hours watching the Russians tear the town apart..."*

My dad, Yuda, who was the same age as Polly, must have endured the same horrors and deprivation.

EARLY LIFE IN SOUTH AFRICA

One cannot possibly comprehend the rollercoaster ride of emotions that these children must have experienced. From the time Isaac Ochberg took them under his wing; then during the arduous journey to London, where they would have relished hitherto unknown food, shelter and pampering as they were prepared for the ocean trip; the long trip itself and the wonderment and bewilderment of arriving to an embracing welcome in a strange land. For half of them, it meant further dislocation and separation from others they had befriended along the way, as not all the children could be absorbed into the Cape Town facilities. They were put on a train to Johannesburg and their final destination - Arcadia.

What kind of a scholar he was, what sport he might have played, who his friends were, his fears, torments, memories, hopes, what he enjoyed and what he yearned for – all that we as parents so intently concern ourselves with in our children – of that, no one would have had any inkling

At around the age of 15 he left school and the orphanage to make his way in the world. He tried his hand at various jobs. He once related to us that he had taken a job at the Johannesburg Hospital as an ambulance attendant. It was not long before he was required to remove a corpse from the ambulance – and as he told it, he grabbed his jacket and bolted!

FAMILY LEFT BEHIND

He had two siblings who did not come over with Ochberg; a sister Klara and brother Jacob. They managed to trace him to Arcadia in the early 1930s and I have copies of correspondence from them. As the 1930s progressed they implored him to help them get out of Germany.

As a young man he did not have the resources to help, although he sent money, but the money order was never redeemed.

The last correspondence in 1938 was just prior to their (brother and wife, and sister and husband) deportation from Dresden where they had been residing - and his sister was pregnant at that time.

Jules and Mussie at their Wedding - 28 February 1943

EARLY CAREER

He then became trained as a technician, repairing various amusement machines – jukeboxes, pinball and arcade machines, He spent some time living in Kimberley during this period. After he moved back to Johannesburg, he saved and bought some of these machines for himself over time, and gradually built up his own "round". This involved placing these machines in cafes, restaurants and amusement arcades.

As his business expounded, he began to prosper. He became quite the dapper, debonair young man. He had a penchant for cars and at one time drove a flashy black Buick. Home to Dad was the Radium Hotel in Jeppe.

He met my mother, a rather shy, attractive brunette – Mercia Mandel (known by all as Mussie), the second youngest of five sisters, when he visited her family home with a friend. Mom was born in 1920 in Vryheid. Her parents, Michel Leib and Sora Riva Mandel had emigrated from the town of Pokroy in Lithuania in 1909. Her father died when she was five and her mother battled to support her five daughters from her income from the general store she ran in Germiston.

In Mussie's words, "From the time he met me he never left me alone! We met when I was 18 and a year later I remember sitting in the lounge with him when we heard over the radio that war had been declared." Almost four years after they had met, Jules and Mussie got married on 21 February 1943 at the Great Synagogue in Wolmarans Street, Johannesburg. They lived in a semi-detatched house in Derby Road in the Johannesburg suburb of Judith's Paarl, close to where Dad had his amusement machine business. In April 1946 I, Michael, was born into the world. With a second child on the way, dad built a modern, then state of the art home in the newly opened suburb of Greenside Extension. I vividly remember the day my mom came home from the hospital with my new-born sister Sharon in 1949.

INNOVATOR AND ENTREPRENEUR

In 1952 my Dad decided to travel to Europe and America to explore what new ideas he could possibly bring back to South Africa. In those days a flight to London was not an overnight trip – it entailed hopping up Africa, across to the European continent and then on to London – over nearly four days. He spent three months travelling through Europe and then on to the US. We received regular letters, frequent "trunk calls", and to my and Sharon's delight, regular surprise packages of amazing toys. Oh how he spoiled us! In hindsight, I guess he wished to indulge us in a way he never was.

On his return he was laden with ideas and various novelties, such as the first transistor radio. He believed he had come across a brilliant business concept – parking meters!

He excitedly took the idea to the Johannesburg City Council – "Parking meters – whatever for – what a ridiculous idea" they scoffed and laughed him out of City Hall. That is an insight into his foresight and commercial instinct.

During his travels in the US, he forged ties with the leading manufacturers of jukeboxes and pinball machines (names like Gottlieb and Seiburg), and paved the way for importing the latest machines into S A. He also saw an innovation that so impressed him – tin cans which had a nozzle top, that when pressed, could spray any manner of products. Yes, the aerosol can! Not yet seen in South Africa, Dad negotiated the rights from one of the pioneering companies in the US to manufacture under license in SA.   Further travels followed in 1954 as the ground work was laid. In around that year Aeropak was formed.

The business had to import all the components – the cans, the valves – and a local gas supplier had to be found and educated as to what was required. Even though formulations were provided by the US licensor, much work was required to get the products just right. And so were launched a range of new products – "Body Guard" and personal spray deodorant, "Supertan" and Coppertan" suntan sprays, "Gloire" hairspray, "Bug Bomb" and "Roach and Ant Killer" insecticides, and "Aerolak" spray paints. Over the next ten or so years these products were marketed throughout the country. But as the multinationals which were producing such personal-care products, insecticides and the like, had far greater muscle, marketing budgets and distribution, Dad decided to limit his business to the one area in which he had built a distinctive and strong brand "Aerolak" spray paint.   The brand became the generic for spray paint – as Kleenex was for tissues. All these years, it was not easy as the business was undercapitalised and in fact its growth was funded by the amusement machine business. But over time – into the seventies particularly – new generations of amusement machines evolved with video games emerging. Dad did not invest in this trend, rather allowing his business to taper off, with the exception of the "kiddie rides" which he placed in shopping centres around the Witwatersrand.

Dad worked with steady, unremitting intensity six days a week. He never entirely switched off – in the evenings and on weekends, sitting in his favourite chair, a pencil and notebook were close at hand, and he was forever jotting down his thoughts. He was almost secretive, taking few into his confidence – but I was pleased that I was always one of the few.

As a young boy I would stand and wait each night by the window for his return from the office, and then run down to greet him. He was the most gentle of souls, seldom given to anger, never one to raise his voice or his hand, only to issue the mildest of curses – say to a traffic offender ("You silly son of a sea cow" – was the strongest epithet he could muster!) Again – no doubt with the lingering memory of his own.

Michael's Barmitzvah 1959

*Jules and Mussie on their 25th Wedding Anniversary
(28 February 1968) with Michael, Sharon and Melanie*

childhood – he would admonish –"don't knock the stuffing out of kids – let kids be kids".

I spent many happy Saturday mornings playing the pinball machines at his workshop – my friends vied for the chance to join me on these days. I could also boast an extensive record collection, thanks to the jukebox business. I always had the current "Top 10" in my bedroom!

In 1958 my youngest sister Melanie, a "laat lammetjie", was born, just eight months before my Barmitzvah. I went to the bimah at the old Emmarentia Shul, one of the last to be held there before the new shul was opened. I can vividly recall the lavish Barmitzvah reception held at the Ciros Nightclub in the city, where we were entertained by Dan Hill and his band and singer Peter Lotis. I had the first dance with my gorgeous young sister Sharon.

I went on to finish high school (Roosevelt and then Greenside High), to the army and then to Wits University. I married Beverley Suskin, the love of my life, in 1969 and after a year at Cape Town Business School we settled in Glenhazel and our first child, Ryan was born in 1971.

In January 1972 my sister Sharon married one Michael Witt. Ten days later she died in a car accident on their honeymoon in Swaziland. The news devastated our family – my Dad was cut to the core, and like my mom we never got over the loss of their shy and gentle daughter and our sister.

Dad doted on my children, Ryan, Stacey (born 1974) and Jared (1979) and I would like to think to some degree this helped to assuage the ache he and mom suffered from their loss.

Then to our deep dismay, Dad was diagnosed with lung cancer in 1979. Through the compassionate care of his physicians who knew it was terminal, through moderate treatment, they ensured that he had reasonable quality of life. We would have a standing date to meet for lunch every Wednesday at Waggenheimer's in Doornfontein for lunch, when we would discuss various matters related to the business. While his stamina gradually diminished, he survived for a further three years, and even attended work the day he died. He came home early, complaining of chest pains. Sitting in my office that morning, I felt an urgent need to contact him and I called him at home - he passed away on his bed while talking to me on the phone.

We laid him to rest, the epitaph on his stone recording that he was *"a man of courage, humility and integrity"*. These three words capture the essence of our Dad. He had stoically come through a childhood of unimaginable trauma and deprivation, having been rescued and placed in a haven, albeit without the warmth of parents and family, had gone forth into the world, with courage, vision, ingenuity and tenacity, nurtured his own nuclear family, gave them every comfort and security he himself had not known, and instilled in his children the values by which he had lived and built his legacy.

My mom, Mussie, approaching her 90th birthday in October 2010, lives in Melrose, Johannesburg.

She says, "He often bought me and the children expensive presents and he was devoted to his family and his grandchildren. He enjoyed entertaining friends at home, showing home movies, years before anyone else did that. He was very involved in his business, working seven days a week at times. Even as his disease progressed and he weakened, he wouldn't complain, despite his pain and discomfort."

My sister Melanie Hall, a vibrant and passionate schoolteacher with multiple talents and interests lives in Berario, Johannesburg with her husband Geoff and three children.

My Dad taught me so many values which I still hold dear. He was my best friend, companion and teacher of life. When I was a little boy, he would take me on an outing every Sunday, whether it was to the swimming baths, the zoo, Zoo Lake or to visit friends, He would often come home with a surprise gift, for no special occasion. I loved getting up early on a Saturday morning so that I could go with Dad to work, where I had fun playing on the machines, learning to type labels for the jukeboxes and then be sent to the Café with one of the staff members to buy a treat. Saturday evening was theatre or movie night in town, followed by a sumptuous meal. Dad appreciated the good life and he loved to share it with his family, who meant the world to him. He so deserved to enjoy what he had created all on his own through his hard work and entrepreneurial spirit. I can recall Dad driving us down to Durban every December, where he booked us into a beachfront hotel for many wonderful holidays.

We could talk about many things, but I regret not learning about his past from him. It was a closed door; all I knew was that Dad came from Poland and that he grew up in the orphanage.

He loved to laugh, and he enjoyed listening to popular music. He was very innovative and made silent home movies with his 16mm camera way back in the 50's.

I still keep a photo of my Dad next to my bed, which always reminds me of his unconditional love, his gentleness and zest for life. Taken away far too soon, it saddens me deeply that my children never got to know their "Zaida Jules", my hero and best friend."

My wife Bev and I migrated to Sydney in 1988 with our three children, all now happily married, and we count our blessings for the joys that life has brought, with special emphasis on our four wondrous grand-children. Surely this is the ultimate legacy of Isaac Ochberg.

Yes, thanks to Isaac Ochberg for providing salvation to the boy then known as Yuda Dreyling -aka Judel Fisch – my beloved father Jules Fisher – whose memory we will always cherish.

Jules

Chapter 102 – JOSEPH, TOIBA AND ASHER ECHSTEIN

THE ECHSTEIN SIBLINGS
Written by Harold Echstein

There were seven Echstein siblings, Tzirka, Shmuel, Berel, Joseph, Toiba, Asher and Mordechai. Their mother Bessie and eighth child died during childbirth and later the father, Isaac (Yitzchak) who was a horse dealer was killed by robbers. The older children and their grandmother looked after the family. While Joseph, Toiba and Asher were selected to be taken to South Africa by Isaac Ochberg the other four remained behind in Poland.

Our families after the war managed to locate Mordechai in Israel, but we do not know what happened to the eldest three siblings Berel, Tzirka and Shmuel. There were stories that Berel went to Russia, but I only wish that there was some way that I could trace him. Tzirka and Shmuel we assume perished in the Holocaust. I submitted forms, together with pictures of each sibling to the data base at Yad Vashem some 10 years ago and never got confirmation of their names appearing in any list of holocaust deaths.

Tilly arm around Jack, their grandmother and Oscar Taken in Poland before departure

The Echstein siblings who remained behind – Poland 1930
Mordechai (settled in Israel), Berel (the eldest brother), Tzirka (the eldest sister) and Shmuel.
On the back is written "For eternal remembrance we send you a photo from your brothers and sister Tzirka Echstein"

JOSEPH, TOIBA AND ASHER ECHSTEIN
Written by Arnold Rabinowitz

My Mother's birthday was on 1 September and she would have been 98 this year. The word didn't exist when she was young but an accurate description of Tilly (Toiba) would have been feisty. You only have to look at the picture of her in the Ochberg group prior to embarkation to see what I mean. Her memories of home were clear and precise: she was sure she lived in a comfortable, well provided for home. Her father, my Grandfather, was a butcher or meat dealer who disappeared one night. My Uncle Jack (Jacob) used to infuriate her by insisting that he had gone out to rustle cattle and was killed in the process. The truth is that he was probably killed by marauding Anti-Jewish groups in a sort of mobile pogrom.

How my Great Grandmother was persuaded to give up four of her children for adoption no one knows and no one knows what happened to her and the remaining children. They certainly lived on for a while after the first four left, but for exactly how long it has been impossible to ascertain. They were certainly alive, and there was some contact with my Mother, into the mid-30's and, after that, nothing. It is not difficult to guess their fate.

"In Group Passport 9, I am certain that Asher (Oscar) Echstein is fourth from the left in the bottom row wearing suspenders."

"In Group Passport 8, I am also certain that my mother Toiva (Tilly) Echstein (adopted by the Abrahams family) is middle row, third from the left."

TILLY RABINOWITZ (TOIBA ECHSTEIN)

My Mother, Tilly from then on, felt responsible for her two younger siblings and was devastated when, on arrival in Johannesburg, they were split and then adopted, except for Asher (Oscar), by different families. She was always furiously resentful that there never appeared to have been any effort made to keep the family together or to encourage contact between the siblings once they had been sorted, settled and disposed of. It was only through her doggedness and driving sense of duty that they maintained contact and were able, always, to act and relate as brothers and sister in a relatively normal way.

Extract in the register kept at Arcadia (SAJO)
Toiba went to stay with A Abrahams and Joseph went to stay with L Cohen and was later known as Jack Cohen.

Tilly, ah yes Tilly, well she was different from her brothers. She was adopted by the Abrahams family, a patrician and prosperous family with deep roots in South Africa and also in Palestine which they visited frequently. Tilly's adoption was arranged because the family, like so many others in Johannesburg, thought they ought to do something to help these newly arrived poor, sad children, the famous orphans saved by Isaac Ochberg.

Tilly

Two members of the Abrahams family, Doddie and Becky, were what today would be called intellectually challenged and neither worked or was capable of working. They lived in a large, dilapidated house on the edge of Yeoville and were supported by the family. When it became part of local obligation to adopt an orphan Doddie was sent off to the Orphanage to choose one. Out of all the newly arrived, cropped children Tilly stood out. She was the only redhead and it was because of this that she caught Doddie's attention. Back home he told the family that the one he fancied was the red haired one and they made all the appropriate approaches and arrangements for the adoption. Like Jack, she was given no say in the matter and was eventually moved out of Arcadia to live with Doddie and Becky. I don't know the circumstance of her later childhood and adolescence. I know that she lived largely with Doddie and Becky but spent a great deal of time with the Abrahams family and regarded the children of that family as surrogate or supplementary siblings.

Tilly had the same combative spirit and intellectual independence as her brothers but none of their cynicism or ability to accept what life offered with equanimity. She desperately wanted to be accepted into the society that had adopted her but, for much of her life, had to contend with the inbuilt snobbery and class consciousness of the established Johannesburg Jewish community. The general attitude of the community was that it was a mitzvah to have adopted one of those poor orphans made available by the saintly Isaac

Tilly Echstein / Abrahams on her wedding day

Ochberg, a good deed in a dark world, but you really wouldn't want one of them to marry into your family, would you? After all, you knew nothing of their parents and extended family, their health history and their genetic background. This is a generalisation that isn't true of all the adopters but it was certainly true of a fair number, nervous, insecure, only one generation from the Stetl themselves and determined to do nothing that would jeopardise their increasing prosperity and emergent social solidity.

Again, I know little of Tilly's school years, but I do know that she left school and went to work at about the age of 16. She desperately wanted to go to University but that wasn't thought a reasonable ambition by her family and so she went to work as a typist, ending up in Saul Pincus, Jewellers, which was owned by the husband of one of Tilly's surrogate aunts, Esther. I don't know how she met my father but I think it was somehow through the Pincus/Abrahams connection.

My father's family was a relatively well established Johannesburg/Rand family. My Grandfather, Joseph, was a successful businessman who had emigrated to South Africa in the very early 1900's and who had later established a very successful Hides and Skins business, tanning and making industrial leather. I think he was a fairly ruthless businessman and was know as someone you crossed or controverted at your peril. Through his marriage he became connected to the extensive Saffer clan, another successful and ambitious group of immigrants. Danny, my father, was injured at birth and was never able to walk properly. Because of this he was very much protected by the family and never really allowed to become totally independent. A cheerful and sociable and basically kind man, genuinely gay in the old fashioned sense of that word, he became a competent pianist and a passionate supporter of Germiston Caledonian football team. He was also something of a man about town and one of my first memories was of a car we had, a convertible with a dickey seat at the back. It was thrilling. His work was, I am sure, all arranged by his father.

There was a great deal of opposition to their proposed marriage. My Father's family was against the match because Tilly was an orphan from an unknown background. Tilly's family were against the match because, in the words of Aunt Esther, related to me by her daughter Zelda. "You don't want to marry that cripple. You can do better than that." But they married and made everyone unhappy for a while. Joseph suspected that Danny had been inveigled into marriage and was never really prepared to accept Tilly into his family.

Danny continued to work for Joseph but I think they clashed and it became necessary for Danny to leave Johannesburg. In about 1940 he and Tilly took over a hotel in Muizenburg and that is where I spent much of my primary school life. The hotel did reasonably well but eventually they decided to move back to Johannesburg and the rest of the family and settled in Hendon Street, Yeoville.

As I mentioned earlier, Tilly had the same restless intellectuality as her brothers and was always curious about the world. She read constantly, comprehensively and unselectively and was always prepared to share her knowledge with friends and family. Occasionally she was flooded by resentment at the fate that history had bequeathed her and often felt that she had

been adopted by the wrong family. Her own sense of family was incredibly strong and she made sure that family connections and standards were rigorously maintained. She certainly was able to transmit her frustrated academic ambitions to her children, all four of whom went to university, graduated well and followed independent professional careers and subsequently brought up ambitious, intellectual and interesting children of their own. After the death of my father she moved to Canada to be near Lila, who was in Toronto, and David, in Boston a little further south.

Cyril, Arnold, Lila, Tilly, and David
Tilly Rabinowitz (Toiba Echstein) with her four children
just after the death of her husband Danny in 1982.

Tilly aged about 70

JACK COHEN (JOSEPH (JACOB) ECHSTEIN)
Written by Arnold Rabinowitz

Jack Cohen (Joseph Echstein)

Jacob (Jack), who had lost a leg during the journey to South Africa, was adopted by the Cohen family, a family of well-to-do lawyers who lived in an affluent part of Johannesburg. Despite his disability he lived a full life, learning to drive and to play golf with a remarkable, flexible stroke that always gained him a point or two from incredulous new opponents. Much the same applied to his Poker playing where he was a relentless risk taker who usually prospered simply because of the incredulity he engendered in others. No one would believe the risks he was prepared to take. He did well at school and eventually qualified as a lawyer. One of his earliest friends in the community of Lawyers was Nelson Mandela and they did a number of cases together. At about the same time he veered away from the fledgling ANC and joined the Communist Party where he eventually became a local organiser and legal radical. His unrepentant and irrepressible radicalism led to him being "Banned" by the Nationalist Government of the time and he was forbidden to carry on working as a Lawyer. He carried on writing and supporting those who were working to bring an end to Apartheid and earned his living running a progressive bookshop, Pilgrim Books, in downtown Johannesburg.

His personal life was as racy as his political life and he flirted with danger by having relationships across what was then called the colour barrier. Many of his personal friends were Black and many of his girlfriends, much more dangerously, were Asian. He was, like his younger brother, a committed cynic with a dry sense of humour and great appreciation of honesty and directness and great impatience with dishonesty and dissimulation.

He never dissembled or deceived and was open and encouraging to his younger relatives. I loved him dearly. Jack introduced me to a wide range of esoteric literature and to the Gollancz Left Book Club, my bible and inspiration for many years. He was my true role model and it was he who steered me away from a conventional Johannesburg Jewish career path, Accountancy, Marriage, Three Children, membership of the Synagogue, Chevrolet, Holidays in Durban, political anaemia and intellectual paralysis. Through him I was able to work a couple of times, for experience, as Court Clerk in the law firm of Tambo and Mandela, meeting both at one stage while still at University, to make contact with the Communist Party. Eventually, when all this threatened to cause me problems at University and socially (I was President of the Students' Liberal Association - about as dangerous, really, as a toothless poodle- which caused me more problems with the Police and the authorities).

Because of Apartheid laws, Jack had to leave South Africa and work in Southern Rhodesia, now Zimbabwe. I know exactly when that was because I went to work with him during two University holidays. That was 1952 and 1953 and he was managing a concession store for African Stores in the N'daweri reserve.

He got me a job driving because some of the deliveries were beyond even his skill as a one legged driver in the days before automatic gear changes. To get from one store to another was always an epic journey along unmade roads and dongas. Fifteen miles usually took between three and four hours depending on the weather.

Phone contact was difficult and in order to keep in touch with his political friends and colleagues he had to have mail smuggled to him. Openly addressed mail was usually intercepted on the South African side. One of the reasons he wanted me to come and work there was so that I could carry large bundles of post, books and other material. The nearest town was Fort Victoria and the Zimbabwe Ruins which didn't offer all that much in terms of recreation: a few bars, one small bookshop, a general store and a wholesale warehouse specialising in suspicion.

These metropolitan delights ensured that most evenings were spent in our rooms at African Stores in pursuit of excellence: whiskey, card games and bad jokes with occasional sorties to the local horse races.

Jack supported me in my aim to leave South Africa as soon as I could. He was a wonderful man, literate, intelligent, knowledgeable and kind. He married late in life, Eineke and eventually moved to Natal. He died, too young, about 20 years ago.

Jack as remembered by Harold Echstein

My Uncle Jack (Joseph) never had children of his own, marrying late in life. He lost a leg in 1929 as a result of an injury in Poland that never healed, but even with his handicap, he was a very good sportsman, playing golf, swimming and also driving a car. He became a lawyer and befriended Nelson Mandela and Oliver Tambo who together with Walter Sisulu were founding members of the ANC Youth League. In 1942 they were outlawed by the South African apartheid government (under the Suppression of Communism Act). At the time of Mandela's imprisonment, an order was issued by the said government for my Uncle's arrest, but he managed to skip the country and spent a few years in then, Southern Rhodesia. He was later pardoned, returned to South Africa on condition that he did not practice law.

I remember that Jack was very attached to Eineke's two children from her previous marriage. They lived in a home in Germiston, not far from where we lived at the time. Eineke was Dutch, her children spending time between Holland and South Africa. The boy was called up to the South African Defence Forces where he was killed in a freak army accident. This devastated Jack, who never got over the incident. I think that they moved to Petermaritzburg in Natal after that where Jack spent the last years of his life in a wheelchair. He was a broken man and eventually died of a broken heart.

Jack Tilly and Oscar

OSCAR (ASHER) ECHSTEIN
Information from an interview of Oscar ~1998

The family lived in Brest Litovsk, about a half hour by train from the shul, and his Dad took Oscar to shul but not the other brothers.

His Dad was a horse dealer who used to go into the forest for six months at a time and collect 200 to 300 horses and then sell them to the Polish Army. The family had a big comfortable house and at the back they kept the horses and on one occasion the oldest brother Berel was was bitten by a horse.

There were seven siblings and their mother died giving birth to the eighth child while the Dad was caught by robbers and killed.

Oscar did not remember leaving the family house, catching a train or the voyage but when the ship arrived in Cape Town he and five other children were put into quarantine by a health

Oscar

inspector. The six children stayed in Cape Town in the Orphanage that was just being built and had a wonderful time, however, by the time he went up to the Orphanage in Johannesburg his siblings had been adopted.

Although he could not read or write when he went to Johannesburg he picked up English in no time. Initially he went to a foster home but as the woman there did not feed them he went on a strike and was returned to Arcadia.

Stompie Shaer, the superintendent of Arcadia from 1924, and Oscar were friends but he often used to wack Oscar.

Oscar who was born in 1913 said he went to Rhodesia when he was 16 and worked in a store in the bush. He bought cattle for his boss and took them to Fort Victoria 50 miles away and was in charge of about 20 black workers.

Although it was compulsory to register for the army at the drill hall Oscar did not.

Oscar remembered by Arnold Echstein

The youngest brother Asher (Oscar) was never adopted and lived all his adolescence at Arcadia. He had the same irritable independence of spirit as his two siblings but, for him, this was a disadvantage. The few attempts that were made to arrange his adoption failed because of his intransigence and unwillingness to pretend to be something that he was not; a nice, obedient, conventional boy. Unsurprisingly he didn't do that well at school, despite his intelligence, left as soon as he could and started work as a skilled Trouser Cutter at Alba Spads as soon as he had finished his apprenticeship. At that time, the late 30's and early 40's, all trousers were cut by hand and well trained and steady cutters were in great demand. He stayed in this line of work until mechanisation became more sophisticated and, eventually, left to sell furniture and to retire to Durban.

He died only a few years ago, sharp, perceptive, iconoclastic, irreligious and irreverent as his brother to the end. Both brothers were reluctant to talk about their childhoods and the process which brought them to South Africa. They had, I think, only very vague and disturbed memories of their early years and, in typical Jack and Oscar fashion, were more concerned with the present and the future than the past. Brian and Harold, his sons, and his two daughters will tell you about his lovely wife Nettie, an American, and their family life. Both he and Jack lived moderate lives. They drank a little, smoked a little, told jokes incessantly, loved playing Klaberjas and relaxing with friends and family.

Harold Echstein his son writes

My favorite story told by my Dad was that my grandfather was a horse thief murdered by other horse thieves. I only learnt this was not true in later years when I met my Uncle Mordechai who was the youngest sibling and did not sail with the Ochberg children as his grandmother would not let him go. He only arrived in Palestine at the age of 19. He told us that my Grandfather was a horse dealer selling horses to the Polish army and was murdered by bandits. I really never knew if my Dad believed the story he told us or whether it was part of his sense of humour.

My Dad Osher, aged six and two siblings, Toibe nine and Joseph four were amongst these fortunate 167. On arriving in Cape Town, my Dad was suspected of having some sort of virus, leaving him there in quarantine for two months, while his sister and brother were sent to Johannesburg where they were finally adopted. My Aunty Tilly (Toibe) went on to marry Danny Rabinowitz, with whom she had four children. One now lives in London, one in Canada, one in Boston USA and the other remaining in South Africa.

My Dad was never adopted, not for want of trying. He was very rebellious, very angry, and was rejected by most adopted families. He spent many years in the Arcadia Orphanage, where at the age of 16, went out to work.

The people in the wedding photo are mainly Mom's family, except in the far right middle row is Tilly and behind her is Danny, Tilly's husband, and behind Dad stands Jack.

Oscar and Nettie on their wedding day - 1938.

He remembered that one of his jobs was as a boss boy in Southern Rhodesia. He says that although he was so young the African labourers accepted him because he was white. Oscar later went to work for Alba Spads as a trouser cutter, working there for more than 20 years.

On 20 December 1938 Oscar married Nettie Fisher, who was born in Manhattan, New York City, on 21 January 1917. Her family emigrated to South Africa when she was nine years old, my late grandfather believing that the streets of Johannesburg were paved in gold. She passed away on 7 September 1999 at the age of 82.

Brian, Roslyn and Harold – 1951

478

Oscar and Nettie had four children, Harold, Brian, Roslyn and Erica. There is 13 years difference between Harold and Erica and she was born two months before his Barmitzvah.

Harold and Brian - Barmitzvah 1954

It was a strong character and an ability to forgive that left my Dad as a calm, loving and understanding person. I never heard him raise his voice, not even when we had, as children, done something wrong.

I remember him waking early every morning, eating a slice of toast and fishpaste and sharing the other slice between myself, my brother and my cousin Richard.

Oscar with grandson Gary 1965

Richard's father had passed away when Richard was four years old and Dad took in Richard, his sister Sandra and my aunty Mamie (Mom's sister). Where we all slept in the tiny house in 25 Raleigh Street Yeoville, I cannot remember. Dad at one time also took in his Brother Jack, who had been banned by the Apartheid government for his political views and activities. I remember very clearly waking one morning and standing next to our beds were three bicycles, one for each of us. I know at one time that Dad owned a bicycle store in Kempton Park, and also a pet shop in Germiston and one in Hillbrow. None of these projects lasted long, and finally, in 1961, he gave up Johannesburg, to work in Durban. Dad moved first, on his own, to find accommodation and establish himself in his new job. He was getting a good salary, affording us the privilege of living in a big block of new apartments on the beach front. On going to work one morning he found that the doors to the firm were locked and the police waiting outside. Apparently his boss had skipped the country with all the assets. Dad was a proud man and never took charity from anyone, but this time he had no choice. The Jewish community

Brian, Harold, Nettie and Oscar 1988

of Durban came together, found a job for Dad at the OK Bazaars as a furniture salesman. Dad worked hard at his job and eventually became the top furniture salesman in Natal and won many prizes for his achievements. He remained at the OK Bazaars until his retirement some 20 years later.

We also moved into a flat off Musgrave Road, where Mom and Dad stayed until they moved back to Johannesburg in the early 1980's. When we wanted to immigrate to Israel in 1982, we received Dad's blessings, saying that we must follow our dreams, something that he wanted to do when he was younger. He wanted to go to then Palestine, but did not want to leave his father-in-law, who had just lost his wife. We were taking away his two baby grand daughters, justifying it with the promise that he and Mom would come to visit every year. It never worked that way, they only managed to visit twice, once in '83 and again in '87. After mom passed away, Dad paid his last visit to us here on the kibbutz in 2000 at the age of 87.

I do not remember Dad intimately after we immigrated to Israel, although I did try my best to visit every two years or so. On my visits I found him very quiet, reserved, living his life for his wife and companion of 61 years, and I felt that the fire that had kept him going all his life had burnt out. He moved into the Sandringham Old Age home shortly after Mom passed away in 1999. Although he maintained his magic sense of humour, he just wanted to be left alone to spend his last days in quiet and seclusion. He still had an active mind, played bridge and solitaire until the day he died.

Tillie (Toiba), Eineke (Joseph's wife), Nettie and Oscar 1988

His grandson, Gary, had come from the States to visit, bringing with him his daughter Leah, Dad's first great-grandchild. On the Friday before he died, he called Gary aside, shook his hand and said "when you come to visit on Monday I won't be here." Monday morning he turned around in his bed and went "to sleep". He always said to me that it was enough, he wanted to "go". I always replied that please G-d we can choose our own time to go. Well, he did just that! He always wanted to be cremated, not wanting to be a burden to anyone. We took it as a joke, and also not believing in cremation, we never pursued the subject. It just goes to show what type of character he was. On the day of his funeral, the biggest and nastiest storm blew up, the wind and rain coming in at 90 degrees, that my sister Ros commented that it was like out of a horror movie just watching the mourners struggle up the hill with his coffin to his gravesite. I actually thought that I would die of the cold and be buried there and then with him. When we finally arrived at the open grave, Dad was laid to rest, but with the wind and rain so powerful that his grave wasn't covered in and was left to be done later. I am sure that Dad was lying at the bottom, saying, "There, I told you so, when I asked you to cremate me you never took any notice. Now that you all have suffered this storm, leave me alone and get back inside where it is warm and dry" His indomitable sense of humour prevailed until the end.

My brother and sister live in Johannesburg and my baby sister now lives in Ballarat Australia.

Oscar and Erica at Sandringham Gardens

The surviving "Ochberg orphans" and their children are fully aware that "Isaac Ochberg snatched us from the jaws of death. If we hadn't died from famine and disease we would have perished 20 years later in the gas chambers."

We honor and thank Isaac Ochberg who saved not only the 167 children he brought out of the jaws of death of Eastern Europe, but also their growing Jewish seed who now number 2,400 and are scattered around the world.

Until some 20 odd years ago, a stone monument, erected in memory of Isaac Ochberg, stood at the Elyakim Junction between Zichron Yaakov and Yochnam in North Central Israel. The monument was removed when plans were made for the widening of the road and was rediscovered in early 2009 in a JNF warehouse. It has been planned to re-erect it in an area overlooking the Isaac Ochberg tract, a piece of land on which the Kibbutzim Dalya and Gad-Ed are situated today and which was redeemed by the JNF, with the magnanimous bequest by Isaac Ochberg in the 30's, the largest single private donation ever made.

Oscar who passed away 30th July 2006, at the age of 93

Chapter 103 – MORDECHAI AND ASHER ECHSTEIN

Mordechai Echstein went to live in Palestine and was not an Ochberg Orphan while his brother Asher (Oscar) was.

MORDECHAI ECHSTEIN
Written by Harold Echstein

We always knew that we had an uncle in Israel as I remember the parcels Mom and Dad made up of our old clothes and second hand stuff to send to Mordechai and family in Israel, as they were very poor. My one dream in life was to meet Mordechai and the family, which eventually came true in 1967. The Six Day war broke out and the country was calling for Jewish volunteers from all over the world to come to Israel and relieve the dire situation in the towns and mainly kibbutzim, as the workforce was serving in the army defending the country. I was on my way to work in Durban one morning when I heard the call on the radio. I turned my car around and drove to the SA Zionist Federation and signed up there and then as a volunteer.

It was heart warming to see most of my friends had done the same. A week later, having disappointed my sister Roslyn by reneging on a promise to be pole holder at her upcoming wedding which was to take place two weeks later, and giving up my job, as a second hand car salesman, and leaving behind family, I boarded a plane for Israel and a new and exciting adventure in my life. To my pleasant surprise I saw my cousin, David Rabinowitz had also volunteered and was on the same plane.

That aircraft was the first to fly directly over the Sinai into Israel in 15 years, and to make it all the more exciting and surreal there was a fighter escourt for us on the last leg of our journey. On landing in Israel the first thing David and I did was to set out to find our uncle Mordechai. We left our luggage at the staging center at the Tadmor Hotel in Hertzlia and by bus, "tramp" and whatever means we could, we landed up in Nordau Street, Hertzlia, but could not find no 10, which was Mordechai's address.

We saw a tiny *markolit* (supply store) so decided to go in and ask directions. As we stepped inside, there was my father standing, or an older looking version of him, and straight away we realised that was Mordechai. Just thinking and writing about it still brings tears to my eyes and gives me goose bumps. We intoduced ourselves and in his broken English Mordechai accepted us into his family. We returned to the staging point at the hotel and were assigned to Kibbutz Erez on the Israeli Gaza border.

On our first leave we went back to Mordechai's house and met the rest of our family. Lotte, his wife; his children Danny, who was a soldier in the tank force and on leave from the fighting; Yigal, who was still at school; and Channah, a 12 year old sabre, cheeky and at the same time shy and very much in "charge".

Mordechai, Harold, Danny, Yigal, Lotte, Channah 1967

That night we slept in Mordechai and Lotte's bed, not knowing that they had given up their sleeping arrangements for us. Mordechai slept on the couch in the lounge and Lotte shared a bed with Channah in her room.

Lotte was a seamstress, sewing dresses for individual customers and also a *metapelet (*baby sitter) for a child of a young family nearby. Mordechai had a Jeep truck from which he drove around selling fruit and vegetables. He used to wake up at four o'clock every morning to go to the market to purchase the fresh produce to sell.

Mordechai arrived in then Palestine at the age of 19 from Poland and joined the army. At one stage the young boys of marriagable age were asked by the Jewish agency to go to Holland and pick a "wife" and return with her to Israel. At that time there were many refugees from war-torn Europe in Holland, many of them orphans who had lost their parents in the Holocaust. Lotte was one of them, her parents having perished in the gas chambers in Auschwitz. The idea was to "marry" the girls of their choice, bring them to Israel and then have the choice, once they were safe on Israeli soil, to either to stay with them as husband and wife or to part and go on their own way. Mordechai and Lotte chose to stay together as they were very much in love. They bore three children, as I mentioned before, Danny, Yigal and Channah.

David stayed on in Israel for a while longer and eventually went to live in the USA. I returned to SA three months after volunteering, thinking that I could go back and slot into my old job and way of life.

Little did I know the effect that Israel had on me and the change that I had gone through that three months later I was back in Israel as a permanent citizen. I remained in Israel for three years, living in Tel Aviv and working at the Kol Bo Shalom as a window dresser.

I returned to SA in 1970 after a hike through Europe. I met my wife Jeanette, who gave birth to two lovely girls, Nicole and Michelle. 12 years after my return to SA, Jeanette woke up one morning and asked "Do you still want to return to Israel?" I was always talking about the holy land, taking Jeanette to many talks on Israel and numerous films on the subject, never losing my love for my adopted country.

Six months later, on 18 June 1982, Jeanette, Nicole (Niki), aged six, and Michelle two, and a dog from SA, and I landed up back "home" on the absorption centre at Kibbutz Tzora. That same day we travelled by bus to introduce my family to Mordechai and his family. Jeanette was immediately accepted into their lives. I am not sure if it was because of Jeanette's warmth and easy way in which she handled people or because of the fact that on seeing Lotte's sink full of dishes she immediately set out to washing them! Lotte never forgot that and always said that that was the daughter that she wanted. Lotte and Mordechai became our mother and father away from home and always treated us as their children.

David and I were the first of our SA family to meet Mordechai, Dad being reunited with him in the 1970s, some 50 years after being parted in 1921. Unfortunately they met again as strangers and parted as strangers, not really making that important connection as brothers.

Lotte has her own story. She was orphaned at the age of 15 when her Mother and Father were transported to Auschwitz and were murdered in the gas chambers. Lotte escaped to France and later to Holland where she became a runner for the underground. I am not sure if that was in France or Holland. She related a story where she was given a message to be passed from one underground agent to another. The message was hidden in her underwear, which she had to remove when she had an urgent call of nature. She placed the message on the toilet cistern. When she was finished, she left and forgot the message in the toilet where she had placed it. On remembering that she had forgotten the message, she ran back to the toilet to discover that it was untouched exactly where she had left it.

Lotte could speak, read and write in four languages; German, Dutch, English and Hebrew. She in fact read most of the books in English that I had already read which I passed on to her. I always remember Lotte sitting in front of the TV on Independence Day Holidays and Holocaust and Rememberance Day watching films of the concentration camps and tears running down her face. On asking her why she tortured herself so, she replied, "I am looking for my parents!" She never did see them but in later years there was a manuscript published with the official names of the people murdered in Auschwitz and her parents names were there. Little comfort for her was that confirmation.

I am in constant contact with two of Mordechai's siblings. They all live here in Israel, are Sabras and speak Hebrew. Danny, Yigal and Channah are all married and have children of their own. Unfortunately I do not have any contact at the moment with Yigal and his family, but I speak to and visit with Danny and Channah. Mordechai passed away some 15 years ago. He married Lotte from Holland who is still alive but sadly in a home in Bat Yam as she has Alzheimer's.

Oscar, Nettie, Mordechai, Jossie, Channah, Nicole, Lotte Kibbutz Tzora 1983

ASHER (OSCAR) ECHSTEIN
Written by Brian Echstein, Harold's brother

I have a story about my Dad, Oscar, from just before he died.

It was 2006 and he was living at Sandringham Gardens at the time and had been there for about five years. He had Parkinson disease and was handling it extremely well. His body was starting to suffer, but his mind was as sharp as a bell. He could still remember the days cricket scores and knew what was going on around him.

In February I told Dad that I would be bringing to South Africa from the USA, his grandson Gary, whom he had not seen in 17 years, and Gary's Daughter Leah, Dad's great granddaughter, whom he had never seen. She was then going on 11 years old and Gary was turning 42.

Dad, who had just turned 93, had started almost every conversation with how tired he was and that it was high time that he went to "the Hotel in the sky" and be with his late wife Nettie. He was very excited about the news of his grandchildren coming to SA and said that he would wait for them to arrive. They were due to arrive the last week of July.

At the beginning of July, he told me that it was time to go and asked where Gary and Leah were? .I asked him to have patience as they were arriving in a few weeks time. I also said that he must hang on, see the kids, and then, jokingly, said that he can do what he likes after they arrived. They duly arrived and saw Dad every day for a week. He was thrilled to see them.

On the Saturday afternoon a week after they had arrived, we went to the home to see Dad. He was a bit dehydrated and on a drip in the hospital. We were about to leave when he looked at Leah and told her that she would not see him again. Gary and I poopoed this, told him to not be silly and that we would see him the next day.

The next morning, Sunday, I got a call from Sandringham to say that Dad had just passed away.

It's amazing the power of the mind. He had made up his mind to go and did just that. It was not so hard losing him like that as we knew that that is what he wanted.

Chapter 104 – BLUME (1911-1982) AND LIBA (1910-1984) FAIFER

Details extracted from Registration Forms filled out in Yiddish at the Orphanage in Kovel

Faifer, Libe, Blume (Full orphans: Kovel)
Libe aged 11; Blume aged 10
With whom are they living: *In the orphanage.*
Father's name: *Avraham*; Mother's name: *Shaindel*
Nearest relatives: *Eliah Faifer and Moshe Faifer, a tailor.*
Remarks: *Born in Slavuta, Ukraine. The father died of typhus, the mother of lung disease. Left without parents in Slavuta, they were brought to the Orphanage in Kovel.*

The register at Arcadia, the South African Jewish Orphanage shows

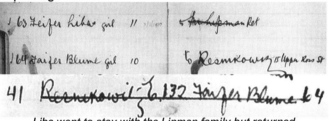

Liba went to stay with the Lipman family but returned
Blume went to the Resnikowitz family at 15 Upper Ross Street and also returned to Arcadia

Group Passport Photos and Lists
Louise Bird writes

"I have to say that I think an error may have occured with the passport photos somewhere along the line as I don't recognise my mom, Blume, at all on Group Passport 6 where she is number 8 on the list.

"I was always led to believe by her that she was on Group Passport 8.

GROUP PASSPORT 8 – Liba Fayfer is no 17 on list
She is the little girl in the white dress and blonde hair, top row second from the left while Lily is the girl in the top row, third from the right. If you look at the two girls, you can see the similarity.

BLUME AND LILY (LIBA) FAIFER (FAYFER)
Written by Louise Bird

My Mom, Blume, was very blonde with a very fair skin. She had a photo of herself, her parents and Lily, taken in Russia when younger. I remember as a child, looking at the photo, but it has since disappeared. From that photo one could instantly recognise my mom in the group photo, as well as Lily. She was the one who pointed herself out in that photo, to my sister and I.

There was two years between the sisters, but my mom was always a tall girl. They came from Kowel, an orphanage there.

My aunt, the older of the two, really never wanted to talk about that part of their lives as I think it was too painful, but my mother told me that they took on the name of their gran, Faifer, but she believed their surname was Schweitzer.

Their mother died at, or shortly after, childbirth. I do not know what happened to their father or their other siblings, but they were alone and walked what seemed to be forever until they reached their gran. Somehow they landed up at the orphanage and were fortunate enough to be picked by Daddy Ochberg to go to a faraway land where they would be happy.

After leaving London and arriving at Cape Town, they were soon 'sorted out' in groups, with some going to Johannesburg, Lily and Blume were two of those children.

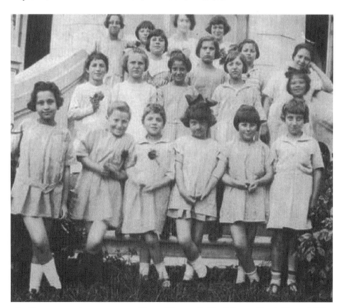

In the second row my mother, Blume is 2nd from the left and Lily is 2nd from the right, neither are smiling!

Blume was given the opportunity of possibly being adopted by a wealthy family in Johannesburg and to be company for their invalid daughter, but she missed her sister very much and was returned to the orphanage. I am not sure how long they lived there, but I do know that they were inseparable.

Just behind the woman with a patterned dress is a girl with her arm around this woman. This child could be either my aunt (Liba Faifer) or my mother (Blume Faifer)

I believe that is my mother, Blume Faifer, in the middle of the back row standing behind Sally Tannenbaum and to the right of the girl embracing another girl!
The girl to Blume's right definitely does look like Lily!

I do remember my mother telling me the children having their hair shaved off due to a lice problem and she did tell me that she and Lily were fortunate to keep their hair.

My mom said she was 11 years old when she went to work at The French Hairdressing Salon in Johannesburg, washing towels. It was owned by a Mr Cohen. I do not know if this was only in the afternoons or part-time, as I do know that she attended the Hebrew High School in Wolmarans Street, Johannesburg for a time. I am not too sure how long she worked for Mr Cohen, but she also mentioned that, because she had such a beautiful skin, she also worked behind the counter with cosmetics.

Around that time, Lily and my mom moved into a boarding house in Doornfontein. On weekends a whole crowd of friends used to meet and go out for picnics and this, I understand, is where my mom and dad met. I believe that it was love at first sight! She used to sing at these picnics as she apparently had a lovely voice and that's where he saw her for the first time.

She was, as I said before, very fair with green eyes and very attractive. He was smitten but shy so it took him a while to make contact. I remember my mother telling me how, one evening she was in her room at the boarding house, on the first floor, when she heard someone singing "My Yiddishe Mama" from outside. It was my father serenading her! and that was that. My father took her to Vereeniging to meet his family and she instantly was made to feel at home.

Blume as a young lady

Blume on her wedding day

Lionel Abrahams and Blume on their wedding day

She loved them very much. She at last had a family that she had yearned for, since she and Lily left their home in Russia.

My father opened up a practice in Vereeniging and they got married and stayed with the Abrahams family for a while until they 'got on their feet' and bought their own home in Stanley Avenue.

They had been married for a few years when my sister Sheena was born in 1946. Sheena was named after my mom's mother Shayna. I, Louise was born in 1950.

Blume and her daughter Sheena

She was so happy. My father was her 'other half", her life partner, her soul mate. On the 12 May 1956 he had a stroke and was taken to hospital. It was quite severe and she was told that if he lived he would be like a vegetable. She was prepared for anything, just as long as he was alive. He was 43 when he passed away. My mom was devastated. She felt like a half a person. She mourned the death of my father until she passed away on 24 November 1982.

My father was David Lionel Abrahams, born in Vereeniging on 23 October 1912 to the first Jewish family to settle in that town, I understand. His grandfather was the Shachet. He used to slaughter the animals and bless them for the Synagogue. My father came from a family made up of mother, Bessie Abrahams (nee Gluckman) and Louis Abrahams (yes, I was named after him) and three siblings. He was the eldest. He had two sisters, Adele and Yvonne, and a brother Peter Godfrey who later became a well known Ellerie Queen Author and had a book made into a film, "The Girl in the Black Silk Stockings".

Blume Sheena and Lionel with little Louise in front

My father, even though I say so myself, was a brilliant Lawyer. He went to school at Jeppe Boys in Johannesburg and then went through University entirely on bursaries. Although he died when I was just five years old, I remember him well. He loved my mother very much.

When my father passed away so suddenly, my mother was left with very little else except her memories. We sold our house and moved from flat to flat. My father's sister Adele was married to Issie Cartoon and he opened up a shop called The Leather Centre for my mom to manage for him. Later on, after a couple of years, she bought the shop from him, but things didn't work out and she closed the shop and we moved to Berea, Johannesburg, in the same block of flats where Lily was living.

Blume in the1960s

Lily had found her a job at Stuttafords but after a while, mom found herself a nice job at a chemist. She seemed fairly happy. My sister was married by then and lived close by. I, on the other hand, did not like Johannesburg and moved to Cape Town, where I stayed for 15 years and got married there. I visited mom as often as I could, sometimes two to three times a year.

It was very unfortunate that my children did not know their grandparents. I was pregnant with my first child, Samantha, when my mother passed away. Samantha, although dark-haired and takes after my husband's side of the family, has my mother's smile, while my younger daughter Stephanie strongly resembles my mother with her fair skin, greenish eyes and dark-blonde hair.

My mother was a wonderful and very special woman and she loved very deeply: my dad, his parents, my aunt Lily, my sister and I. She is always in my thoughts and I thank G-d regularly for the time I had with her.

LILY BEHRMAN (LIBA (FAIFER) FAYFER)

Lily married Teddy Behrman from Witbank. Teddy and Lily had no children.

Lily on her wedding day

Teddy Behrman and Lily (Liba) Faifer on their wedding day

Lily was a very kind, loving person and adored my mother. As you can imagine, they were extremely close. She moved with Teddie Behrman to Witbank after they married, where they had a small shop. They use to visit us quite regularly in Vereeniging.When her husband passed away she moved to Johannesburg, where she worked for a while and then retired.

My mother passed away in November 1982; Lily passed away in September 1984.

Chapter 105 – ZEIDEL FEINSCHMIDT (SYDNEY JACK FINE)

FINDING OUT ABOUT MY FATHER
Written by Brian Fine

My father Zeidel Feinschmidt, known as Jack Fine, was an Ochberg Orphan, but he never shared that with me. He did not speak one word about it and I found out everything by accident and weird coincidences. My Dad, however, occasionally took me to visit Arcadia.

I only discovered the Ochberg Orphan connection after he died when I was researching my genealogy and I received a report from a researcher. I found out my Dad's real name, from the name plate in the Chumash that he had received for his bar mitzvah in 1922, and when I went to the Shul to change the name I use on Yortzeit for my Dad. Someone overheard me talking and told me that one of her parents was also an Ochberg Orphan.

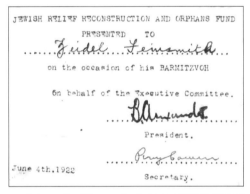

The name plate on the Chumash given to Zeidel Feinschmidt by the Jewish Relief Reconstruction and Orphans fund, the South African Charity that raised funds to bring the Ochberg Orphans to South Africa. In 1922 Zeidel was in the care of Arcadia (The South African Jewish Orphanage)

One night I was out and by coincidence someone who we were with, told me that one of her parents was also an Ochberg Orphan.

Only after my Dad had passed away did I start to question my mother about my Dad and she filled me in with many details and things from the past started to make sense.

The children on the day they had their passport picture taken. Third from right is Zeidel Feinschmidt (Jack Fine)

Group Passport No 3
Jack is sixth from the left in the middle row

There was a photo of a young girl in our photo album and when I asked my mother about it she told me that a man had come to our house one day. He told my parents he was from Russia and that my Dad had a brother. He gave them the photo of the young girl who was my uncle's daughter. My parents tried unsuccessfully to help the girl immigrate to South Africa.

Generally while the younger children could not remember, the older children had traumatic memories and did not share them and did not interact the same as other people. Other Ochberg Orphan descendants I have met, described their parents with the same characteristics as my father.

The details I have written about below come from what my mother told me and from bits and pieces gleaned from other sources.

THE STORY OF ZEIDEL FEINSCHMIDT
Written by Brian Fine

Zeidel was born in the town of Shershov in northern Ukraine. His parents Louis and Esther were killed in a pogrom in 1918, leaving Zeidel alone in a very hostile world. He had heard stories about a brother that he had who lived about 100 miles away in the town of Brest. With nobody to turn to this seven year old set out with one mission in mind, to find his brother. In the freezing cold of winter he set out on foot on a journey that was to take him six months to complete.

Zeidel was a survivor and in the aftermath of the Great War with food shortages, diseases and rampant defectors all around, he slowly made his way.

Fleeing from the Russian soldiers who were now engaged in the Russian Revolution and their sport of killing the Jew constantly on his mind, scavenging food from dustbins around army camps and sleeping in drainpipes was part of his daily routine. He did recall times that he was so hungry that his entire body was racked with pain. He teamed up with a few youngsters in similar situation and this gang would survive through the skills they had acquired in these tough times. They had recollections of removing whatever could be found on corpses, and there were many along the way.

This journey turned out to be in vain and he was never able to find his long lost brother. He was eventually found by relief workers scavenging amongst the ruins in the city of Brest which was to become famous for the signing of the armistice which marked the end of the war.

His vibrant personality made him stand out amongst the children and although he was not large in stature his presence would always be felt.

He hated the life that had been thrust upon him and when Isaac Ochberg arrived at the orphanage, Zeidel saw this as his way of getting out and starting a new life. He recalled how he begged Isaac to take him and how he refused to leave the room until a promise was made to include him.

The saving of the children and the subsequent journey to South Africa is well documented. As a born leader Zeidel persuaded the children from Brest to stick together and many of them landed up at the Arcadia Orphanage in Johannesburg. Their friendship solid they remained as family to each other in the difficulty that lay ahead.

Zeidel hated the life in the orphanage and at the age of 13 he wrote a letter begging them to allow him to leave and go out and find a job. He even changed his name to Sydney and was given the nickname of Jack by his friends.

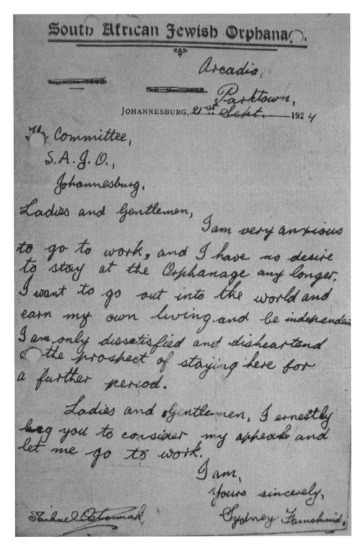

The committee at the orphanage would hear nothing of his request to leave and every effort was made to have him adopted. He was sent to a family in Mayfair and after only three days he ran away refusing to have anything to do with another family. The story goes that the man of the house where he was sent had said something about his parents and this enraged him so much that he struck the man resulting in a swift return to the orphanage.

The great traumas of his past had now become the demons that he had to live with on a daily basis. The memories of seeing his parents slaughtered followed by the food shortages and pain would haunt him the rest of his life.

By the age of 14 he had run away from the orphanage and changed his name to Sydney

I knew my father as a gentle man who was always kind and fair. He was a pacifist and believed strongly in the rights of all men. His past had made its mark on his personality and there were certain peculiarities that I would come to understand later on in my life. For instance, we would never be able to leave the table until our plates were clean and every morsel of food had been eaten. He could never walk past a begger without trying to

Sarah Altuska at the back, Chaim Altuska in the middle and Jack Feinschmidt on the right. The others are not known

assist. He hated any form of violence and encouraged us to walk away from any fight. He never had much, but was willing to share with everyone what he had.

After leaving the orphanage Jack became an apprentice plumber and eventually he had his own plumbing business. He met and married Hannah Kay and eventually had a family that lived in Highlands North in Johannesburg. Three sons Leonard, Brian and Martin made up what was to be the Fine Family.

The most outstanding characteristic that Jack had was the ability to make friends with everybody. He was very well-known in Johannesburg and had hundreds of friends.

Jack as a young man

Life in the Fine family was tough but it was always a happy open house. In all those years Jack shielded his past life from his family as it was too traumatic and sad to him to revisit. And so it was to be that only long after Jack had passed away did we begin to hear the story of the Ochberg Orphans. Many of the details of his early life were relayed to us through his friends from the orphanage.

Jack passed away at the young age of 56.

IN MEMORY OF 500,000 FORGOTTEN SOULS.
This story is about my father Zeidel Feinschmidt later known as Sydney Jack Fine

"Go now my child and G-d be with you."

Jews have always been expert at saying goodbye and this was no exception. To the six year old it was just another of those crazy moments that he had learned to accept in his father's now erratic behaviour. To the father these words meant the difference of life and death and although disguised these words were said with love and much pain. "No I won't go " said the boy in defiance.

"Go before I lather your hide."

"No" cried the petrified boy "I don't want to, I am scared, I hate it out there."

With that the old man struck the boy in desperation sending him flying into the thorny bushes. By now both were crying. The boy outwardly cried from pain while the father cried from his very depths of his soul.

How could he strike his son whom he loved so dearly? Is this what his G-d had made him do? His heart cried out in pain and he longed to pick up the boy and hold him close and show his love. But he dare not in fear that the boy would misinterpret this as another opportunity to deny his wishes and that he knew could be a fatal error.

"Get out" he screamed "Follow the bigger kids before I hit you again".

In fear of further onslaught the boy tearfully took off. How he hated this man he called father. The father watched in despair as the boy disappeared into the distance. How could this act of love ever be justified? How could one send one's own son away into the freezing snow possibly to face a terrible death?

"I curse the day I was born a Jew." he cried.
"Why do you do this to us?" he asked as he finally broke down.

He would never know the answer to that question. Two hours later he together with his wife and fifty seven other Jews lay dead; beaten, raped and hacked to death. They had become the main attraction in a day's sport for the drunken barbarians who were bent on destroying our people. The tenth of Av had indeed been another good day for killing Jews.

The children meanwhile had experienced this before. Cold, hunger and the frightening dangers of the wild would be their companions as they lay in hiding deep in the forest waiting for the moment when it was safe to return. Day turned into night and brought with it the horrors that no child should endure. The snow lay thick on the ground and the icy wind and cold soon claimed two of the weaker children. Frozen souls returned to their maker. Days passed and still no word from the town. Eternity for a young boy is more than forever. The days were bearable in spite of the hunger pains and biting cold. It was the nights that introduced hell to this miserable band of survivors. The wolves, ghostly shadows of the night, constantly howling, as they surrounded and tormented the children. Hours turned to eternity as the children, as they had been instructed, fought them off with sticks and the odd stone. Then came the screams of horror as the wolf pack broke the wall of resistance and someone near you was taken and dragged away screaming. At least this brought some peace as the pack disappeared for a while to enjoy their harvest.

Five days latter the boy, together with the surviving 30 children returned. Six had perished.

Now was the "Safe" time to return. Yes the Jew Haters had left.

The barbarians had arrived and left regularly to Brest-Letovsky the border town that nobody held for too long. If it were not the Germans it was the Poles, if not the Poles the Red army or the White or as on this fateful day a band of rough criminals made up of deserters from any of the various armies. Rape and plunder were their speciality, an art they had mastered to perfection. On that fateful day they had tested their various skills on the boy's parents and left them lying in the gutter for all to see. Nobody should dare and defy any of Groulco's men. Nobody did. The boy returned to find his father's bloody remains still lying beside his beloved mother.

This picture would haunt the boy for the rest of his life. On that freezing day in 1918 the boy, my father had become just another of the 500,000 Ukrainian orphans.

The greater majority of these orphans were destined to die over the next few years from plague, hunger and if lucky, a quick death like my grandfather's at the hands of murderers or in the hell of war. The next three years were to become the second act of the nightmare that no person should be cursed to live through. Survival at all cost is what the children learned. There were no teachers, no one to guide them as their own instincts took over. They quickly learned to scavenge for food in bins on rubbish dumps, anywhere that a scrap was left. But there were days, I learned about later, when there was no food to be found and the pain of hunger became a regular part of life.

A certain experience that lived permanently in my father's mind was of a time when he had nothing to eat for days and how he and a few others came across some unripe turnip still in the ground. Without washing off the dirt he devoured this treasure. This explained his absolute obsession that nothing, nothing, remain on a food plate. Who could know where the next meal may come from? No home, no hope the band of children slept in doorways or in the forest when the snow permitted it. Each day was the same battle to survive.

Thousands of people were dying all around. Initially they died in the war which devastated this part of the Ukraine. The Germans won battles as did the Poles as did the Russians. Every victory brought with it its own new form of misery. The locals were always punished for helping the other side during their brief possession of Brest. And who better to punish than the Jews. Always the Jews felt the brunt of the inevitable lesson that was taught with such commitment and enjoyment. But the boy was now streetwise, at seven years of age he had learned when to hide and when to reappear, when there may be food in the bins of the victors and when their time to be replaced came round again. Also he learned how to beg without getting beaten up and how to keep that which was yours when the older children ran short of food. War was everywhere about and he soon learned how best to take advantage of this, how to and what to remove from a rotting corpse and how to stay invisible at all times.

The nightmare was to continue for long after peace came to Europe. The Russians had now decided to have their own revolution and soon the area was again at the forefront of the action. New murderers arrived or should I say old murderers in new clothing. They were as determined as ever to demonstrate their barbaric ways and they had little trouble in finding the most vulnerable and the easiest targets so that they could justify their evil presence.

Death and misery were the boy's inheritance, one which he shared with all around him.

By this time it was 1921 and the plight of the Ukrainian orphans was brought to the attention of the Jewish agencies. Half a million Jewish starving orphans whose fate it was to perish in the holocaust that had enveloped the region for over eight long years. The failure of the crops and the resulting famine and plague brought welcome death to many of these forgotten children. Orphanages were full to capacity and could take no more. Anyway nobody cared enough to give relief to the misery. Not the Russians, nor the Poles nor the Germans. Everyone had their own problems and anyway who cared about starving Jewish children.

The battles were becoming more ferocious as the importance of the strategic value of the town was recognised by all sides. One day a group of about 50 children had taken refuge in the nearby forest that had saved them so many times before. The word was out that the Russians were around. Little did these poor children know that forest was to become the centre of a fierce and bloody battle. Trapped in heavy bombardment for four long days only twelve children were to survive. My father was one of them. Wounded, traumatised, hungry and mentally scarred for life, my father was picked up wondering about the battlefield and taken first to a field hospital and handed over to a Jewish orphanage which had little choice but to accept him.

Isaac Ochberg was such a very special person. As a 30 year old he went back to Eastern Europe to bring the children out to South Africa. I have set up a website on the Ochberg Orphans

Chapter 106 – SHMUEL GARBUS

SIDNEY GARBUS (BORN SHMUEL GARBUZ and also known as SHMUEL CHAIM BEN SHIMON YEHUDA HALEVI)
Written by Lawrence I Garbuz

My grandfather, Shmuel Garbuz, was born in Pinsk, Poland in 1909. He was later known as Sidney Garbus, and also known as Shmuel Chaim ben Shimon Yehuda HaLevi. My grandfather was one of the orphans rescued by Isaac Ochberg and was brought to South Africa.

My grandfather was the youngest child of his parents, Shimon Yehuda and Shifra Garbuz. He had seven older siblings, of which only two others, who also had left Europe, ultimately survived the Holocaust. His mother died while he was very young and his father passed away by the time he reached the age of about 10. His older siblings were unable to care for him so he was put into an orphanage. He hated Pinsk and so, even as a young boy, he dreamed of leaving Poland.

My grandfather's recollections of Pinsk were of harsh conditions and oppressive anti-Semitism. He would often recall the cold and hunger that he endured as a child, and often commented that hunger is a personal experience that can never be described. The persistent acts of violence against the Jews of Pinsk were ingrained in my grandfather's memory - whether it be of a religious Jew's beard being hacked off with a bayonet,

Shmuel Garbuz – as a young man

or the local constable's son (who died when he fell through some ice) who used his late father's position to terrorize the local Jewish population. This convinced my grandfather early in his life that there was little future for Jews in Poland.

He went to listen to Isaac Ochberg when he came to his orphanage and tell the children about this wonderful country called South Africa. He told his siblings about the opportunity to go with the other children. At first, his siblings refused to let him go, saying they would never see him again but eventually they relented knowing how difficult life was for him and how very unhappy he was. My grandfather knew very little about South Africa, nevertheless, he decided to leave Pinsk with Isaac Ochberg, leaving his siblings behind in Europe.

To his credit, my grandfather did not intend to change his name or seek to sever any relations that he had with his family. He remained in contact with his siblings in Europe until World War II, and spent a considerable amount of time after the war to try and learn if any of his siblings had survived. His eldest brother, Joseph Garbuz (Yossel or Jose) had left Pinsk in 1923 for Havana, Cuba. Another sister, Dora, left for the United States. Another brother, Lazer, remained in Pinsk, and he and his wife and two young children were murdered in the Holocaust along with the rest of the family.

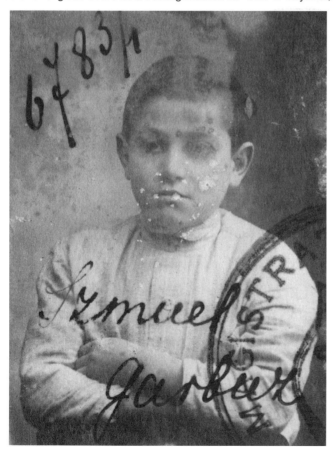

Shmuel Garbuz – photo from Pinsk Travel Document

Upon Sidney's arrival in South Africa, he was sent to Johannesburg and to the orphanage at Arcadia. From the moment he arrived in South Arica he fell in love with the country. One day a group of young women came to Arcadia to see the newly arrived orphans. One of the young ladies was Lilly Goldstein, one of four sisters, and was very taken with my grandfather. She went home to her parents and told them of this little orphan. He was adopted by the wonderful Goldstein family who had three other daughters: Rose, Ann and Cissie. They were all wonderful to him and he loved his new family; but he insisted that he keep his family name.

| 17 Gerbus Shmuel boy 12 | Gone to M Goldstein |

Entry in register kept at Arcadia shows he was aged 12 and placed in the care of the Goldstein Family

My grandfather learned English quickly and adapted to his new country. A story that he often liked to tell was when he was in class that he was asked to spell Canada. Having recently learned English he thought that Canada with the hard 'C' should be spelled with a 'K'. After his classmates laughed at him for misspelling Canada, he resolved to master English and worked so hard that he ultimately was able to skip a year in school. Following high school, he did not have any formal college education and went to work for a wholesale bicycle company.

My grandfather married my grandmother, Sophie Garbus (nee Lunsky) (1912 - 1986) in 1933, and they had two children: Lionel Garbus born in 1934 and Sheila Garbus born in 1938.

The Garbus Family – Lionel, Sidney, Sophie and Sheila

My grandfather moved to the Orange Grove suburb of Johannesburg. He opened his own motorcycle business and after he built that business, he opened a wholesale auto parts company and eventually employed his son, Lionel, in the business.

During World War II, he was asked to go to North Africa to head the army motor pool for South Africa. He declined so that he could stay with his family and accepted an offer to train an all female unit to be dispatch riders.

My grandfather and grandmother enjoyed playing bowls on the weekend. They took family vacations, particularly to Durban, Cape Town, Kruger Park and Mozambique.

Politically, my grandfather joined the Revisionist Party in South Africa. He raised money for the Irgun and supported the young State of Israel.

My grandfather and grandmother came to the United States in 1962. They lived happily near both of their children Lionel and Sheila in Costa Mesa, California for the balance of their lives. Lionel Garbus married Arlene Feldman and Sheila Garbuz married Leon Garbuz Shmulewitz. Lionel presently resides in Marina Del Rey, California. Sheila lives in Boca Raton, Florida.

Sidney Garbus was the proud father of two children and three grandchildren; Cheryl Shmulewitz who married Aaron Shmulewitz, Estelle Bloch and Lawrence I Garbuz who married Adina Lewis. He was fortunate enough to see his first great-grandchildren and there are now eight, who range in age from five to 27; Joseph Shmulewitz married Shira Saltzman, Isaac L Shmulewitz, Ariella Bloch, Serena Shmulewitz, Ella Sophia Lewis Garbuz, Liav Garbuz, Jonah Henry Lewis Garbuz (also known as Shmuel Yonah) and Eva Lindsey Lewis Garbuz.

As of this date, 13 lives have sprung from the rescue of my grandfather, Sidney Garbus, by Isaac Ochberg in Pinsk.

Sidney

THE FIVE GONIFAS SIBLINGS;
ENYA, GITTEL, LEAH, MALCA AND BEZALEL
Written by Dorothy Pantanowitz the daughter of Enya Gonifas

There were five Gonifas children, my Mother, Enya, then Gittel, Leah, Moly (Malca) and Charles (Bezalel).

The Gonifas parents' names were Moshe, who was some type of builder, and Shayne Mirel. Shayne Mirel died when my mother was around 12, and my mother did the cooking and babysitting till their father died when my mother was around 15. At that time my mother was already working as a domestic at 16 years old while the other four were in orphanages.

My mother was sixteen when Isaac Ochberg collected the orphans from the various orphanages and so she remained in Poland.

The four younger siblings would have accompanied Isaac Ochberg to London and then later set out by ship to Cape Town and they would have been included in the group of children that were sent up to Johannesburg

Extracts from the register kept by the South African Jewish Orphanage that cared for the four younger siblings. The age of the children is listed after the name and it seems that the children went to live with families.

MY MOTHER, ENYA

Once the orphans (Gittel, Leah, Malca and Bezalel) were working they collected money for my father's fare to South Africa. He worked for three years to support his wife and three children in Poland, and to save for their passage. He also sent money to support his mother and sister which also helped the family of my late uncle Hershel, (my father's brother) who was a communist and in jail a lot of the time.

My mother came out of Poland with three children, my two brothers and sister. She, the eldest, was the last of the Gonifas children, to arrive in South Africa, independently, but of course with the vital help of her Ochberg siblings.

These photos of my mother and of her and her family are probably ones sent by my mother from Poland-Ukraine in the 1920s to the Gonifas family in South Africa.

My mother, Enya Gonifas ~1923

Group passport No 4 used by the Ochberg Orphans in 1921 when they came out to South Africa. Is Charlie that boy in the middle of the bottom row with a 29 on him?

My parents and two brothers ~1926. The boy on the horse is my late brother Morris Leslie Segal. The baby is Simmie Segal.

This photo from 1930 was probably sent to my father in South Africa. The boy in the centre is Morris, the second boy is Simmie and the girl is Mickey (Muriel) Segal Robinson.

MY AUNT GITTEL

My aunt Gittel died in the 1940s when I was little.

MY AUNT LEAH

Leah Gonifas married Sol Berkman on 12 June 1932

The wedding of Leah Gonifas and Sol Berkman in 1932.

My aunt Leah Gonifas had three children who have all passed away now; my cousin Neville many years ago, Shirley about seven or eight years ago, and Ghita just three or four years ago in Cape Town.

Shirely has two children, Sharyn Behr and Sean. Last time I saw them in Johannesburg about six years ago. I don't know the names of Neville's children (I have been living in Israel since 1960) and Ghita had a son and a daughter Lauren who lived in Cape Town.

The wedding of Molly (Malca) Gonifas with Dave Blumberg from Benoni
From right to left, Sholoma Segal, Enya (Gonifas) Segal, Sol Berkman, Leah (Gonifas)Berkman, unknown, Dave Blumberg,
Molly Gonifas, Gittel Gonifas and on the left, the couple is Dave's parents, whose first names I think I never knew.

MY AUNT MOLLY

Molly married David Blumberg. Of their children only Stanley remains and he is living in Johannesburg as far as I know. I have no contact with him.

CHARLES (BEZALEL) GONIFAS

Charles (Bezalel) Gonifas has one daughter from his first marriage, Paddy Tayar, who lives in Johannesburg and grew up with her mother. He also had a son Maurice from that marriage but he died some years ago. He married a second time to Ivy and had three children, Cherry (I think Du Plessis) who lives in England, Nick who lives in South Africa and Geoffry with whom I am in contact, who is in the USA.

Geoffry Gonifas writes from the USA
Before my Dad died I got him to record the story of the earlier part of his life. It has always been my intention to write my own book about his life. Time has also been a problem in accomplishing this. I have family that would like copies. However before I distribute them I will have them legally copyrighted. I know this seems mean of me to some, but my Dad's story is so incredible it is worth a book in itself.

Although I am very proud of my Jewish heritage I am a pastor of a Pentecostal church and I considered myself a Messianic Believer. I believe that Yeshua is the Messiah of Israel.

Charles (Bezalel) Gonifas

I WATCHED IN HORROR AS THEY SHOT MY UNCLE
THE CAPE ARGUS 16 OCTOBER 1971 Staff Reporter

'When the reprieved prisoners attacked my uncle's farm in the Ukrainian countryside the children fled into the forest and hid there for a month,' Mrs Leah Berkman, one of the 200 orphans, recalled as she vividly described her early life in Russia.

'For a month we ate berries, leaves and whatever natural food we could find. It was a terrible time in my life which I will never forget.

'My uncle was a wealthy man and I remember watching in horror as they shot him in the head. My two sisters, Molly, Gitle and I went to the orphanage in Kowel after that.'

Mrs Berkman's elder brother, Charles, was taken away by the communists and it was only years later that they were united again.

'I was nine when we buried my father. It was after the funeral that we left for my uncle's farm - but even there the pogroms hounded us.' Mrs Berkman said.

'Life in the orphanage was difficult although the committee did all they could to provide us with food and clothing. If it were not for Mr Ochberg we would all have been dead a long time ago in Russia.' she added.

In South Africa she was educated at the Hebrew Girls High School and the Jewish Government School. My first job was that of a dressmaker. I later married (her maiden name was Gonifas) and have three children, all of them married.'

After her husband's death, Mrs Berkman managed their business in Germiston on her own for a while, but later sold it.

'I later managed to get my brother to South Africa from the Ukraine and we have rebuilt our lives here.'

Although not sure of the exact dates, Mrs Berkman remembers minute details of the event which changed her life completely.

'I can still clearly see the fatal wound on my uncle's head when the prisoners shot him. They looted the farm and also killed other families and relations in the area. Although I will never forget the past I do not like recalling it very often.' she added.

Mrs Berkman is in Cape town especially to attend the golden jubilee celebration of their arrival here in 1921.

THIS EARLY PHOTOGRAPH shows the Berkman family re-united again in South Africa after the terror of Russia.

496

Chapter 108 – CHAYA AND TCHARNA GUBER

CHAYA AND CHERNA (TCHARNA) GUBER (GOUBER)
Written by Chaya's sons Frank, Monty, Ralph and Leon.

Ochberg was a man of the "old" world whose vision and determination enabled Jews to escape to "the new world".

What customs, values and obligations did they bring with them that influenced, guided and coloured their way of life as they adapted to the peoples of South Africa? What helped them be successful?

Where did their strength, resilience and persistence come from, as shown in the way they became a Jewish community and contributed in a very significant way to the local South African community and country?

These qualities came from life's experience and traditions and the quality and character of the people's response to adversity.

EARLY LIFE

Chaya, later called Annie, and her sister Cherna, later called Charlotte, were born in 1912 and 1914 in Lvov (Lemberg). Their parents were Rifka and Efraim Guber.

Efraim's siblings were Moshe Bear, Bentja, Shimon, Ruchel Devora, and Abram. They spelled their family name "Gruber".

Annie was nine and Cherna seven when they were collected by Isaac Ochberg from an orphanage and taken via Warsaw and London to South Africa.

Group Passport Eight - Annie is in the middle row fifth from the left her sister Cherna is in the front row third right

Cherna and Annie were housed and accommodated in "Arcadia" orphanage but we could not obtain any information regarding the two sisters in the orphanage from when they arrived until the day they left. We only received two pages from 17/4/1924 that were their report cards when Cherna was in standard 3 and Annie standard 5, both had good results.

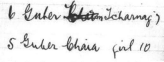

Entry in the register kept at Arcadia

Annie and Charlotte

At the age of 16 or 17 years of age, four females left the orphanage and rented a house in Doornfontein. We assume that it was the two sisters along with two of their friends.

CHARLOTTE ODES (CHERNA GUBER)

Cherna, later called Charlotte, was a very attractive, glamorous and outgoing person. She was very popular with the lawyers and doctors.

She was generous and kind and could not do enough for others. Charlotte and her big sister Annie were always close and supportive. Regardless of their tough beginnings, they were always happy and never dwelled on their trying past.

Charlotte married Maurice Odes. They had one son, Gerald, who was born in July 1946. Together, Charlotte and Maurice ran their general dealer shop in Malvern. Neither of them had a driver's licence so they took the bus to work 5:30 every morning. They worked tirelessly, never complaining, and return home late in the evening.

Annie and Charlotte

On Sunday the sisters and their families got together. In winter, they came over to Annie's house, but in summer, they'd all go together and spend time at the Rosedale swimming pool.

Initially, Charlotte and her family lived in Yeoville. Later they moved to a house directly opposite the Sydenham Highlands North Shul.

After moving to Sydenham, they used to walk over to Annie's home for the Friday night Shabbat meal and Yom-tov.

Family get together were a time of joy and laughter for the sisters and plenty of noise and activity from the five boys.

Maurice (groom) and Charlotte (bride) with Annie (on the far right)

Charlotte as a bride   *Gerald her son*

Charlotte passed away on 21January 1970.

Maurice and Gerald (her son) lived together in the house in Sydenham until Maurice unfortunately became blind. Maurice spent the next five years of his life in the care of the Sandringham Jewish Old Age Home, while Gerald lived in a residential hotel in Hillbrow.

Although Gerald was a very shy person, he had a group of very good friends. He worked as a manufacturer jeweller and spent his free time reading.

Sadly, Gerald never married. He spent most Yom-tovs with the cousins and attended all the family celebrations. He passed away on November 28, 2009 without leaving any descendents.

ANNIE (CHANA) GUBER

Annie was an extremely good looking lady who presented herself very well and had a very outgoing personality. She was bubbly and full of life and for these reasons she achieved many things in her life. She worked at a pharmaceutical firm "Sive and Karnofsky" which later became "S A Druggists".

Annie Guber married Morris Segal in Johannesburg. We think they met at the Lion Shul, Sivewright Avenue, Doornfontein. Their oldest son Frank was born on 15 May 1935 in Doornfontein. From Doornfontein they moved to Becker Street, Yeoville, where the second son Monty was born on 24 April, 1940. The family finally settled in 1 Armadale Street, Sydenham, where the famous twin palm trees of Sydenham still exist. Ralph was born on 8 May 1944 and Leon on 16 April 1946.

Annie was a peacemaker and was extremely ethical. She always was there for everybody and worried about herself last.

Annie never drove and what a walker she was. She played tennis twice a week in white dress and tackies.

She looked after two apartment blocks owned by the family and handled all the complaints on the phone. She was always there for Morris who had asthma and put up with a lot of nonsense from us four sons.

The Segal Famil - Leon Ann and Ralph in front and Monty Morris and Frank behind

Morris and Annie Segal

Morris Segal was a manufacturing jeweller. He worked for Laserson brothers and was unfortunately retrenched.

Annie's strength, resilience and work ethics were what sustained Morris's situation in his time of need. This motivated Morris to start his own business in their home in Becker Street. Morris was appointed by the prestige firm "Katz and Lurie" to be their manufacturer.

This was the beginnings of the firm "Morris Segal Jewellers", established in 1937 and still going strong. The firm was always a family business led by Frank and Leon and assisted by Monty and at various times Ralph. Today, Frank is partnered by his son Rael.

Morris was an extremely hard worker, working long hours. He was a heavy smoker with a quick explosive temper. He was very house proud and grew fruit trees. He wanted quiet at supper time and listened to the news on the radio. He was a very private man, not one for chatting or small talk.

In his youth he was an outstanding gymnast and represented Maccabi on the rings. He liked cars and was crazy about, and supported soccer. His sons did him proud, they all excelled at sports. Morris dealt with gold and jewellery every day, but his gems were his grandchildren. He was such a proud grandfather.

Holidays were often in Durban at the "Manora" hotel as well as in a town called "Parys" in the Orange Free State. In fact Leon met his wife Shula at the Manora hotel, when he came to fetch his mom Annie!

Annie's cooking and baking was appreciated by all. She always kept a strictly and completely kosher home. She appreciated life, had a joyous nature and oh, how she liked to laugh! Up would go her arms, and with her head thrown back her whole body shook with laughter.

Morris and Annie adopted a young orphan girl in Israel. After a few years, Annie received word that her adopted daughter had found her maternal mother. Annie approved the request to reunite mother and daughter. She was so happy for them.

Annie and Morris were very generous, always in the most discreet way. They frequently sent parcels to Russia to relatives, friends and people in need.

Annie and Morris contributed to the community to the "Dvinsk" society, a secret society. We only found out of late that the society's real function was to provide charity, employment, shelter, and scholarships. Most importantly, the society ensured that no family was without sustenance. The Dvinsk society always operated in the most discreet way.

The Dvinsk Society - Back: Morris, ?,?, ?Kwasnik, Lilly Kwasnik, Bessie Blacher Charlotte and Maurice Odes   Front: ?

Annie and Morris's success can be measured by the way they brought up and educated their four sons, as members of the community and members of the Sydenham Highlands North Hebrew congregation. They also had financial success and owned their home, their own business and properties.

Morris passed away on 4 December 1967, one week after Monty and Norma's wedding. Annie was a widow at 55 years old. After his death Annie would cry herself to sleep every night in her bedroom.

The following year Annie visited her relatives in Israel, Efraim Guber, a professor of Architecture and his sister Tziporah. During this visit Annie met Morris's childhood friend Ike Levin from Lithuania.

Ike was a widower and he lived in Israel. They spent time together and married in November 1969.They made a home together in central Tel-Aviv.

Annie, being the loving grandmother she was, couldn't stay away from her grandchildren in South Africa. She travelled to South Africa to be with the family. She visited at least once a year for Yom-tov and always flew in for a special events like a wedding, a briss or barmitzvah.

To Annie, family was very important. She tracked down her father's family in American and kept in touch with her cousins.

Annie passed away suddenly on 9 September 1982, leaving four sons and 11 grandchildren.

Annie's Hebrew name, Chaya, means "living", from the word "chai". She passed on her essence and her legacy to her children and grandchildren. They too live their lives with the same values and sense of what's important: family, community, helping others, and a wholesome dash of laughter.

Ike Levin and Annie   **Annie and granddaughter Shelley**

GROWING UP IN THE SEGAL HOUSE

All the Segal boys attended Sydenham Highlands North Nursery School, Orange Grove Primary School and Highlands North High School and Wits University- except for Leon who was drafted into the South African army, and on completion of his service furthered his studies at Damelin College while he worked in the family business Morris Segal Jewellers.

All four Segal brothers attended Bnei Zion Youth Movement. For them, this was a formative experience that played an important role in their lives. For example, Frank met his wife Hilda there. From a social point of view, it provided a framework of friends and a way of relating to other people. It taught them discipline and put them on the right path for the future.

All the Segal boys excelled at sport. Ralph was very successful in soccer, swimming and water-polo. In fact, his water-polo was so good; he was chosen to be the instructor. He always made first team at high school and first league Balfour Park Club, and this was in addition to rugby, which was compulsory at high school.

Ralph also played soccer for the professional reserve team Highlands Park and Junior Colts (no mean achievement).

Ralph remembers: "On Saturday nights Mom and Dad went to the movies and Mom always had chocolate for me when she returned. Every night she would bring me coffee and a sandwich in bed. She never spoke of her childhood to me. Dad was a very proud Zaida and I can see him standing under the huge palm tree with his eldest grandchild Steve cradled in his arms and his face was beaming."

Leon was a complete all-rounder sportsman. He played rugby, squash, water-polo, swimming, cricket, soccer. He was the fastest swimmer in primary school and in cricket won the Transvaal provincial cup. In Standard 5, he played at the Rand Stadium and his team won the McCulloch & Bothwell Cup. In water-polo he played in the same team as Ralph who is two years his senior. In rugby Leon played in all the first teams in high school. In soccer, he also played with Ralph in the Colts for Highlands Park and was chosen for the Southern Transvaal

team. Through the provincial ranking, he was chosen for South African Schools team, one of two Jews on these teams, along with Lennie Gerber.

Leon sang in the Shul choir, and earned the princely sum of 25 cents a week and a big bonus of R1 per wedding. With this 25c he bought material to make neckties, using Annie's famous sewing machine, with the assistance of their maid Petronella. That's how Leon started in business, and the rest is history

Leon remembers: "Our driveway was the centre of all the action in the neighbourhood after school. In cricket, it was a tradition that the batsman would hit the ball into Ralph's window, usually smashing it. In soccer, the guys would always wreck the flower-bed. This would usually lead to Mom coming out like a warrior, with her broomstick in hand, to chase the errant boys and disperse the crowd."

The boys also excelled at school. Leon clearly remembers his mother's gleaming face as she watched Ralph teach students maths, which was his forte.

Annie loved to dance and Leon has fond memories of grabbing his mom and waltzing with her all around the kitchen.

Thursday nights was fish night and as Petronella (the maid) took the fish out the pan to lay it on the brown paper on the plate, the boys would pass by and pinch a piece of fried fish. Annie and the maid would chase them with a broomstick.

Here is Annie's famous recipe for toasted cheese. Ingredients: cheese, bread and, wait for it, an iron. She would put greaseproof paper over the bread and simply iron it into a toasted cheese. The tastiest ever! Also, our taste-buds still have the memory of the great tomato soup, fruit salads, semolina pudding and her cold borscht soup with sour cream and potatoes.

The boys brought their friends over and to eat at their house. One of Monty's friends at Highlands was a "Kaaskop" Frank de Zeeuw, and his favourite food was schmaltz on rye bread!

As if the Segal home wasn't hectic enough with all the boys, their friends, and the rest of the neighbourhood, Monty had a menagerie at home.

Monty's affinity to feathered birds didn't taper off completely. In fact, to this day Monty raises birds in his home.

At Highlands, Monty was co-commander of the Signals Corp. He took part successfully in competitions sending Morse Code Messages and Heliograph communications as well as flag signals.

Monty remembers: "Mom used to prepare three to four different meals almost every evening because each of us all ate differently, and she never complained! She was always tolerant, patient, and joyful with her lot. Unfortunately, she was very secretive about her past experiences and never offered any anecdotes. She had her hands full raising four rambunctious sons with such different personalities and demands. She was a wonderful mother. If only I had shown more appreciation."

Since their father died young, Frank ran the family business while he studied at night school. Monty remembers how Frank helped him to become a Chartered Accountant. His first job as a cost-accountant was at a mattress and furniture company called Edblo.

The house was always full of noise, laughter and music. Morris bought Frank a 60 base Galanza accordion when Frank was only eight years old. Frank loved music. Annie always told him to go practice when he already had the accordion in his hands.

Frank was so thankful to his father for getting him his first accordion. He learned to read music and later Frank taught himself to play the organ. He plays both instruments to this day, and even has his original Galanza.

Frank sang in the first Sydenham Highlands North Shul choir at age 10. At age14, he began to earn money from choir. At age 16, he had saved enough to buy a second hand Vesper scooter. It was a great deal at R20, probably because it was pink. Annie was frantic, but managed to talk him out of it.

Photo of shul choir - Back Row: Louis Sacks (tenor), Mr Julius Katz (Bass), Shraga, Dennis Port, Barry Nathan, Issy Abel, ? and Bob Borowsky.   Middle: Arthur Lederman, Benny Kaplan, Selwyn Colombick, Barry Levin, Rabbi Altshuler, B Berman (Choirmaster), Levy, Philip Gershater, Bernie Bortz and Ruby Katz
Front: Neville Nathan, Henry Gaddin, Leon Druckmen, Frank Segal, Basil Weinberg and Leo Herdan

In standard five, Frank was chosen for the lead in the school musical production. A week before the actual performance, he got mumps and the late Joe Zimmerman took his place. The only good thing about the mumps was that he didn't have to write final exams.

At Sydenham Highland North high school, Frank captained the under 14 and under 15 rugby teams. He was a lieutenant in charge of the Signals team and in his Matric year, he was a prefect.

He was in charge of ringing the bell. This was great because he was the only boy who got to spend time on the girl's side of school. That's why he learned to play netball. Either he'd referee the game, or if the girls were short a player, he'd fill in. Later, he'd have to dash to the boy's side and ring the bell there.

Frank wanted to study dentistry with the late Elie Laserson and Sid Zetzer. It was the vacation before first year and Frank was

working with his father when he got accepted to dentistry. Annie told him "Frankie, you got to go study". Morris told him "Be aign en twantich ya must du machen a leben. (At 21, you got to make a living.)"

Frank decided to stay on and run Morris Segal Jewellers, but a year later he enrolled in night school to get his BComm.

He was 16 when he met Hilda at Beni Zion camp in Muizenberg. They married when Frank was 22 years old, and together with Morris, ran Morris Segal Jewellers, and went to night school at Witwatersrand University.

Frank remembers: "After Hilda and I'd been going out for about a few years, Hilda bought me a record with the song "You've got to have money in the bank Frank". My mom nearly "platsed"! The concern was written all over her face. But Mom and Hilda got on like a house on fire. I've been happily married ever since, I'm not sure about my wife.

As the house was strictly kosher, any wrong use of a utensil was immediately buried in the ground-and the kids were grounded too!

Yom-tov was a very special time. The house was thoroughly cleaned, new clothes bought and a real sense of difference and specialness pervaded the house. Annie would always dress up for Shul and Ralph would watch her powder her face at her dressing table, while looking at him in the mirror. "Mom, you look good", he would say, and that used to make her really happy.

Leon emigrated to Israel in 1977 with his young family. Being the entrepreneur that he is, he started another jewellery business and later a plastic factory, Bendaplast Industries, which has grown to be the largest thermo-forming food packaging plant in the Middle-East, and being the largest employer in an area of northern Israel.

MEMORIES FROM ANNIE'S GRANDCHILDREN
Written by Leon's children

We, the son and daughters, of Leon Segal, Annie's youngest son, would like to write a few words in memory of our dear grandma, Bobba Annie.

Although you are gone, the memories remain of what used to be; your beautiful smile, the sound of your laugh, your heart of gold and those big brown eyes filled with love. But most of all, the love you gave. You always had faith. You never gave up. You always found a way to make us laugh,

You cuddled us tightly right from the start and as we grew older, pulled us close to your heart. Weekends with you, laughing and giggling and making small chat. You were a treasure of gold sent to us from above. Your strength and your faith in times of distress are like rose petals bound in a book, neatly pressed.

In our dreams we hug you again, we kiss you again, and we take you by the hand. We sing once again, we laugh and we smile. Dear Bobba, you will always remain in our hearts.

Although we were all quite young when our dear Bobba Annie passed away, our memories of her are strong and clear.

We all remember her amazing liveliness! When Bobba Annie came in to the room, all the attention was drawn to her.

Her dynamic personality, huge smile and big brown eyes are three things we all remember about her.

Her routine of staying with us during the weekends and never forgetting to buy us our favourite nuts in a brown bag.

We all regret the fact that we did not have many more years to be with her and learn from her.

We believe that her marvellous personality, wisdom and strength could have guided us through the paths of life.

We are truly sad that our dear Bobba did not see our children come in to this world, we are sure it would have given her great joy and happiness.

We all miss her very much and she will always remain close to our hearts.

With all our love, Daniela, Alon, Liora and Dina, your loving grandchildren.

The greatest honour that could be bestowed on Annie, was that Alon named his first child after her, Ann.

Faye Gruber (Annie's cousin from Denver) Norma, Annie Front: Melissa, Shelley, Craig (Monty's children)

MY BOBBA ANNIE GUBER
Written by Batyah Rubin

My Bobba Annie z"l was a bundle of energy. I remember her as particularly soft, lovable and cuddly. When she laughed, it was with a radiant smile, pink cheeks, and a twinkle in her eye. She was no slacker and even though she was short, she was a powerhouse of physical strength.

She had a great love for "Am Yisrael" and "Eretz Yisrael", as did my Zayda Morris, her husband. She told me how my Zayda waved the Israeli flag from the top of their home in South Africa when Israel gained independence in 1948. Unfortunately, Zayda Morris passed away before I was two years old.

Bobba Annie was certainly adventurous! I was very young when she made aliya to remarry and to settle in Tel-Aviv. She used to return to South Africa for the "Chagim", so I got to spend time with her then. But she never spoke about her escape, her life in the orphanage, or even how she met Zayda Morris. It may have been because I was her fourth grandchild and she'd told the stories so many times before, but more likely, it was simply the Segal way: Speak little, do much, and keep marching forward.

In 1981 I spent three months in Israel on a school program called Ulpan. I spent quality time with Bobba Annie, she was about 63 at the time. I was astounded by her "get-up-and-go" attitude. I remember us trekking down the flights of stairs (there was no elevator in her building) and all the way to Shuk HaCarmel, to buy strawberries and cream, just because it was my favourite dessert.

My Bobba Annie passed away tragically from a heart attack at 65 years young, but my sister Elana z"l constantly did things which reminded us of Bobba Annie. The way she embraced life, laughed with no bounds and handled anything that came her way.

Today, I live in Israel with my husband and children. My third child Adina Chaya, is named after Bobba Annie, whose Hebrew name was Chaya. Adina too displays the same wonderful traits that my Bobba did.

In 1989, I used my inheritance from Bobba Annie, to bring our lift from South Africa to Israel. I hope my Bobba is pleased that I used it in that way and that I followed in her footsteps.

Isaac Ochberg saved my Bobba Annie and many more orphans like her. By doing so, he saved so many branches of "Am Yisrael". It's no wonder he shared the name of a vital link in our heritage, our forefather Yitzchak.

Hilda and Frank Segal getting married with Bobba Annie and Zayda Morris on the right

DESCENDANTS OF ANN AND MORRIS

Ann and Morris had four sons: Frank, Monty, Ralph and Leon, and there are now 11 grandchildren and 28 great grandchildren, (14 boys and 14 girls) in the family.

Leon Segal and his family have lived in Israel since 1977 and also the younger daughter of Frank, Batyah Rubin and family.

Leon, Ralph, Monty and Frank sons of Ann and Morris Segal

Frank married Hilda Gordon in 1958 and they had:
Steven (20.9.1959), Elana (11.8.1960-18.12.2008), Raell (9.11.1963) and Batyah (15.10.1965).
 -Steven married Arlene Novis in 1958 and they had:
 Ariel (25.4.1988), Daniel (21.5.1990) and Cayley (11.8.1994).
 -Elana married Peter Whittaker in 1984 and they had:
 David (9.5.1985), Laura (13.3.1987) and Kevin (24.9.1990).
 -Raell married Hilary Gerschlowitz in 1989 and they had:
 Joshua (1.3.1994), Shira (23.9.1996) and Aharon (6.1.2000).
 -Batyah married Paul Rubin in 1987 and they had: Yonatan (23.4.1988), Talya (3.9.1989), Adina (1.8.1992), Dana (22.10.1994), Gabriella (8.6.1997) and Benyamin (14.5.1999).

Hilda and Frank and their children
Hilda Rael Batyah Elana (Deceased 2008) Steven Frank

Hilda and Frank's eldest son Steven and Arlene and their three children - Steven, Ari, Cayley, Arlene and Daniel

Peter and Elana Whittaker (Segal) (Deceased 2009) and their children: Kevin, Laura, and David with Shira a cousin in front

Rael and Hilary and children Joshua, Aharon and Shira

Paul and Batyah Rubin (nee Segal) and their family
Yonatan, Binyamin, Talya, Gavriella, Adina, Dana, Paul, Batyah

Monty: married Norma Green in 1967 and they had:
Melissa (23.1.1970), Shelley (22.5.1972) and Craig (6.2.1974).
-Melissa married Darryl Luboff in 1993 (Darryl deceased 7.3.2010) and they had: Aaron (24.9.1995) and Jared (24.6.1998).
-Craig married Kerri Brickman in 2007 and they had:
Tanna Jade (9.12.2009).

Michael, Shay Shapiro, Lior, Daniella (Segal) and Liad

Craig and Kerri's wedding - Norma, Craig, Kerri, Monty, Shelley, Shulamit, Leon, Melissa and Darryl Luboff. In front are: Aaron and Jared Luboff children of Melissa and Darryl

Ralp had no children

Leon: married Shulamit Davidowitz in 1969 and they had:
Daniela (12.12.1971), Alon (3.12.1972), Leora (24.2.1974) and Dina (6.9.1975).
-Daniela married Shay Shapira in 1991 and they had:
Liad (6.5.1993), Lior (22.5.1996) and Michael (5.3.2000)
-Alon married Orit Schnal in 1995 and had Ann (11.9.1996) and got divorced. Alon remarried to Orit Rasohl in 2003 and they had: Lia (8.10.2004) and Nellie (11.10.2006)
-Leora married Shay Sidi in 2002 and they had:
Romi (8.10.2004) and Sean (2.5.2005)
-Dina married Tamir Pritsch in 2002 and they had:
Schahaf (06.12.2004) and Eli (23.03.2008)

Leora (Segal), Shay, Romi and Sean

*Front: Romi Sidi, Loir Shapira...Middle: Sean Sidi, Michael and Liad Shapira, Alon Segal, Lia Segal
Back: Daniella (Segal) Shapira and Ann Segal*

*Leon and Shulamit's wedding
Ann Segal and Shulamits parents Michael and Lili Davidowitz.*

Monty Leon Ralph and Frank

504

CHASHE, ISAAC AND BENJAMIN HELMAN
Written by Julie Ross

As far as I am aware my mother's father was murdered in a pogrom as well as her older sister. My grandmother remarried and her second husband was not a "tzadik" and insisted that the two younger brothers, Isaac and Ben be sent to the orphanage and my mother was sent to live with an aunt, also not a mensch. The aunt treated my then 12 year old mom, Chashe, as a domestic servant. Naturally, Chashe was not enamoured with the aunt and the chores she had to perform. When she heard about Pappa Ochberg and where her brothers were to be taken to, she somehow prevailed upon the powers that were in charge, to take her with and threatening to drown herself if they didn't. Thank G-d her threats didn't fall on deaf ears and she came to South Africa with her brothers and was sent to Arcadia. Her and her brothers were at the orphanage in Pinsk andI believe they came from a shtetl very near Pinsk. Any rate all three of them loved Arcadia and went to Jewish Government School.

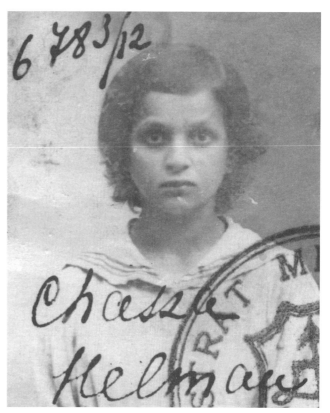

Chashe Helman
Photos from Pinsk travel documents

Chashe Helman

No.	\ames.		Age.	Birth Place.
12.	Joffe.	Fraidel	11	Pynsk
13.	"	Siwa	8	"
23.	Helman	Chashe	12	"
24.	"	Aisik	10	"
25.	"	Biniumin	8	"

Extract of the list of children sent to Johannesburg

Group Passport no 8 Chashe Helman no 27 on list and in the top right-hand corner

28 Helman Aisir boy 8	det. CJ.
27 Helman Benyomin boy 10	det CJ.
26 Helman Chashe 12	

Extract of the register held at the South African Jewish Orphanage (later Arcadia) and it shows; Aisik (later Isaac) aged eight, Benjamin aged 10 and Chashe (later Essie) aged 12

My mom was very pretty and had a slight squint and in fact very bad eyesight which gave her a huge complex. She was eternally grateful that my brother and I had good eyesight and was delighted that her four grandchildren didn't have her eyes.

I assume this photo was at the home of the family who adopted mom. Chashe (Essie) Ben and Isaac are in the bottom left hand corner behind the two men on the left.   Photo enlarged below

Young Chashe and Chashe with Mr Shamban

My mom was adopted by an elderly couple whose name I never knew as she never ever told me the name of her adoptive parents. Unfortunately, the wife wasn't happy about the attention the old man gave to my mother and she was returned to Arcadia very traumatized. My mom never ever used the name Shamban - her K'tuba and other documents state Helman.

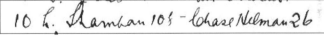

Chashe Helman was sent to stay with the Shamban Family (L Shamban) and there is nothing to indicate she was returned to Arcadia

Chasshe in front on right next to Rachel Klein (Borowik) in a swimming costume

Mom with friends, Mary and Rachel, also Ochberg orphans.

When she was old enough to work, the committee organised her with a job at the OK Bazaars at the haberdashery counter. Mom was introduced to my father Rubin Zagey, a very good looking immigrant from Rakishok, Lithuania. They married in March 1932 in the grounds of Arcadia.

Mom and Dad's wedding

Mom and friends

Mom inside a car - a momentous occasion.

The group wedding photos at Arcadia

We had a very happy home living firstly in Bez Valley then graduating to Kensington. I have only one brother Hymie.

Family photo taken 1945
I was 12 and my brother Harry was seven.

Mom was a very resilient person who had many friends - most of them being Ochberg children - I remember meeting them and their families during my childhood. Among my mother's friends were Polly Joffe (nee Stanger) and other Stangers, Anna Segal, whose daughter is Dot Pantanowitz who lives in Israel, Leah Berkman, Leah Greenblatt and Sarah Slier (Altuska sisters) Mary Berelowitz, Annie Centner and Rachel Klein (three sisters) Harry, Issy and Charlie Steiner, Morris Pinsky. I'm sure you have stories from most of these people's families.

To tell you more about my mother- she was a very down to earth person who never complained about anything except my brother losing his school bag, books and soccer boots - her philosophy was "Never look up - always look down and you'll be happy with what you have" That too is my mantra.

My father was a blacksmith and farrier, as was his father, from Rakishok, Lithuania. He left Rakishok in 1928 in order to avoid conscription to the Russian (Cossack) army - the only one of his family to come to SA. Without knowing anyone he somehow made his way to Standerton where he worked on a farm owned by the Orelowitz family - I dont know for how long

but he decided to come to Johannesburg to open his own business - and boarded with the Subel family in Mayfair who introduced him to my mother.

He was an extremely good-looking man with black hair and deep blue eyes - my friends all thought he looked like King George V - the closest we got to royalty. He was kind and generous and a man of his word to the nth degree. Although we weren't wealthy, I distinctly remember Sunday mornings when his less fortunate friends would arrive to ask for a loan - repayable whenever without any IOUs and nobody went away empty handed. My mother who was the financial controller would be at her wits end. There was actually an article in an Afrikaans newspaper in about 1959 about my father being the last blacksmith left in Newtown. He had a man working for him for many, many years, both working from 6.00 am to 6.00 pm. Weekends were for enjoyment, like picnics and playing klaberjas, visiting, weddings and barmitzvahs and kleibing nachas from his children.

Although my father was a Kohan he was not religious and lost all interest in religion when his whole family were annhilated in 1941 except for a niece who survived and now lives in Israel.

Hymie is marrried and has two sons and one grandchild from each son. I too have a daughter and son and am blessed with six grandchildren. My father passed away in March 1975 and my mother in January 1983.

Questionaire on the Helman children completed in
Yiddish in Pinsk with translation following.

QUESTIONNAIRE FOR FULL ORPHANS: (WITHOUT FATHER OR MOTHER)...
Hellman Yochanan Binyamin and Chasha

1. **Name** 1)Chanan   2) Aysik (crossed)
3)Binyamin and Chasha

2. **Surname** Helman

3. **Father's name** Yoel 45

4. **Mother's name and maiden name**
Chaya Valavelsky 43 years

5. **Sex**

6. **Age** 10 years and 8 years

7. **State of health. Eye disease, heart complaints, lung-complaints, head and skin diseases, etc.**
Healthy

8. **Place of birth, place, circuit, district.**
Lubashov (Circuit Pinsk)

9. **Place where the child was assigned** Lubashov

10. **Address before the child was admitted to**
Lubashov

11. **What was the parents occupation. ...**
Business of grocery wares

12. **Were they poor, rich, average (estimate of their worth)**
Middle

13. **Did the parents own immovable property (house, granary/barn, garden, orchard, land, etc.) If yes, who is looking after it now.**
Own house

14. **Relatives (brothers, sisters, uncles, aunts, and further relatives) Does the child have the exact address of any of them.**
Mother, brother sister. The mother is sick and poor and cannot take care of the children. The brother is 12 years the sister is 12 years. The family lived rich and respectable. The children have a doctor, an uncle in Russia by the Bolshevist.

15. **Who has legal authority over the child:**
The mother

16. **Is this person agreeable that the child be taken away to another country, to be adopted or to be brought up in a Jewish environment, institution there**.   Yes

17. **Is the child itself inclined to leave his present home and to travel to a faraway country**.   Yes

18. **Can the child read Yiddish, Hebrew, other languages?** .
Yes

19. **Can the child write Yiddish, Hebrew, other languages?** .
Yes

20. **Can the child** *daven*? .   Yes

21. **Has the child attended a general folkshul, a Jewish school, *kheyder*, Talmud Torah, etc. and for how long**: .
Yes

22. **Has the child learnt a specific trade, with whom, where, and how long** . No

23. **What certificates does the child have (matric, school leaving certificate etc.)**
Registry of birth, School Testimonies, Certificates, Certificates from the Orphanage

24. **From whom is the information about the child obtained**
The mother

25. **General psychological-physical condition of the child: build, general physical condition, abilities, general inclinations, vocational leanings etc. (this section as well as section 7 should be filled in by trades people.**
None written

26. **Other information and comments.**
The father murdered in a pogrom by the Bolshevist bands. When they demanded money, and not having to give, they took him out of the house and 30 paces from the house they shot him and took out of the house everything.
When 21 year old Rachel followed to retrieve the father and the things, they brutally hit her, raped her, cut off her fingers and murdered her.
The family all escaped into the forest.

Translated by C T Olswane   25 June 2010
(Nee Gelman(Helman) Chana (Chone's) daughter)

Julie writes
"I find the translation of the Application which was originally in Yiddish absolutely heart-rending and it is important and should be included in the book.

Tamar's comments on the document are that it doesn't mention my mother's age (which doesn't worry me) and the family seem to have been quite wealthy before the First World War.

Be that as it may, fortunes change. I researched on Shtetlinks and could find no mention of the town of Lubashov but did find my grandmother's maiden- name "Volovelsky" as being the owners of a grocery business in Pinsk. I dont know if it's related but it could be.

While Isaac and Ben, mom's two younger brothers and mom came to South Africa with Isaac Ochberg, there was also

another brother Chone, younger than my mother, who could not come to South Africa because he was ill at the time. I'm told this by my cousin Tamar who is Chone's daughter who lives in Johannesburg.

Yudel, their older brother, came to South Africa first but did not stay here. He apparently went on to Argentina an subsequently sent for Chone who settled in Argentina. Yudel came back to South Africa and settled here. He went into business with Isaac in Rietfontein and later Comet Supply Stores in Boksburg. He married a lovely lady Rachel Alpert in 1933. They had three children Rhita, Joel and Morris. Morris died of a heart attack at age 42 and Joel died in his sixties. Rhita is widowed and lives in Cape Town and I'm constantly in touch with her.

Now Ben, my uncle, lived with us as did my other two uncles before they were married, and joined the army when WW2 broke out. I remember being happy to polish the buttons on his uniform whenever he came home on leave. He would take me to town and to the "bioscope" and generally spoil me. and I loved him to bits. He married Hetty Hack in about 1942/3 and had three daughters, Renee (Hetty's daughter from her first marriage) Sheila and Marlene. Renee died some years ago and Sheila and Marlene now live in Toronto. On leaving the army Ben and a friend bought a brickyard and did pretty well businesswise. I think he was in his early 60s when he passed away. Sadly Sheila's husband Reuben Psek passed away about two weeks ago.

All my uncles and my mother had a pretty wry sense of humour and found just the right nicknames for everyone.

My mother and her two brothers Isaac and Ben, who are standing behind her. The older brother Julius (Yudel) who is seated actually went to Argentina and then came to South Africa. ~1931

ISAAC HELMAN
Written by Rhona Goldberg

Isaac Helman
Photos from Pinsk travel documents

Isaac left Arcadia at the age of 14 and was trained as a watchmaker, a trade he hated. On completion of the course he went to work in a concession store. I am not quite sure how long or for whom he worked, but I do know that from the time he started work as a young boy to the time of his retirement in his late seventies he worked hard from morning to night.

He and his brother Julius bought a bicycle shop from which they managed to make a living and a few years later opened a general dealer store in Boksburg which they called Comet Supply Stores. Isaac was an incredibly shrewd business man with a natural flair for figures. Had he been given the opportunity and had his life turned out differently I believe he could have been a top class accountant. He could add a column of figures in his head and come up with the correct answer long before the man on the adding machine.

As a result of Isaac's deprived childhood and the fact that he often went to bed hungry he was always very careful with money, always saving for a rainy day. He invested in property and shares, the latter becoming his hobby. He knew every share in his portfolio, how much he bought it for and the present trading rate. He made a few mistakes but I assure you not too many.

He was also an excellent klaberjas player and from his winnings on a Sunday morning, my sister Vivien and myself were given our weekly pocket money. The amount varied according to the winnings. On the odd occassion that he lost, we had to forgo the week's handout. An an early age I learnt that in order to keep my kitty full I had to make sure that I saved a little every week.

Isaac was introduced to Cecily Gordon by landsleit and they were married in March 1939. They had three children, Vivien, Rhona and Leonie. Unfortunately Leonie was born with complications and only lived for three weeks. They started their married life in Doornfontein and eventually moved to Kensington, where I was brought up. Their first house, 40 Nile Street, was a two bedroom home with an outside toilet. I lived there for about 12 years until we moved to a much larger house but also in Kensington. Vivien and I went to Leicester Road School, Vivien then went to Queens High and I went to Jeppe High.

Throughout these years of growing up dad was always working. He would leave for work at 6.30am and return between 7.00 pm and 7.30 pm Monday to Friday. Saturday he came home a little earlier, around 5.00 pm and on Sunday he played klaberjas in the morning and usually took us out in the afternoon. He never took time off, never went on a holiday and never complained about his hard life. He gave his family what he could and we learnt that we often had to go without. Most important of all there was always enough food on the table.

My mother Cecily came from Bialystok where she was a school teacher. She too lost her family apart from her father, Leon Gordon. Leon was the only grandparent we knew and he stayed with us until he died at the age of 65 from a heart attack. He was the kindest man I knew and always helped us with our homework and would tell us stories and read to us. Our parents were married for 45 years. Cecily died from kidney complications at the age of 74. When dad lost mom he was devastated, a lost soul living on his own in a big house, until he met Gita, a very lovely lady and at the age of 79 he and Gita were married. They bought a flat in Berea and lived there until dad had a stroke and passed away on 1st November 1993. He was 82.

Isaac was not a religious man, but he could tell you anything you needed to know about Abraham, Isaac or Moses. He always attended Shul on the High Holy days. I have always felt that had cirumstances been different he would have liked to be more observant. He was a member of Kensington Shul for many years, and today Roy Levy his son in law is a respected member of the same Shul. He was a man of integrity, was honest as the day is long and on closing a deal a handshake was all you needed from Isaac, he never went back on his word.

Vivien married Roy Levy. They live in Rembrandt Park, Johannesburg. They do not have children. Rhona married Richard Goldberg and had three children. Wendy, Jody and Gavin. they were married for 27 years and have been divorced for 17. Wendy is married to Tyrone Zinman and they have six children. Alon, Carli, Talia, Gilad, Tiferet and Gavrielle. Jody has three children, Danielle, Shira and David and Gavin married Lisa Levy. They have three children, Ethan, Jaymie and Mackenzie.

Unfortunately I do not know much about his life before he came to South Africa. He and his siblings, being Chonie, Julius, Benjamin and Essie, never spoke about it. I guess it was just too painful and they dealt with it the only way they knew how and that is to put it away. When I saw the video on the Ochberg Orphans I was saddened beyond words. My admiration for my father knows no bounds with him coming from such a disadvantaged childhood and having made a success of his life. I wish I could turn the clock back and learn more about his childhood, but that of course is not possible. I hope my grandchildren and great grandchildren will one day be as proud of Isaac as I am.

Isaac and Cecilia on their wedding day
With flowergirls Julie and Rhita

Isaac on right next to grandson Gavin, the Barmitzvah boy

Rhona, Isaac, Gita and Vivien

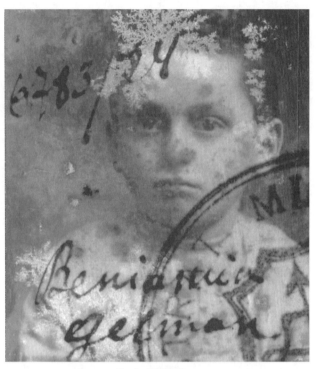

Benjamin Helman
Photos from Pinsk travel documents

BENJAMIN HELMAN,
Written by Sheila Psek

My Dad was one of the Ochberg Orphans. We knew that he had been in the orphanage *(Arcadia - The South African Jewish Orphanage)* for a number of years, but he never told us any details of his journey from Europe to Cape Town. My Dad's name was Benjamin (Ben) Helman and he was born on 23 March 1912.

He was the younger brother of Isaac and Essie, both of whom were in the orphanage with him. Their eldest brother Yudel was also in South Africa, but not in the orphanage. Sadly all have since passed away. My Dad passed away on 16 June 1976.

He was such a kind, gentle and loving man and taking care of his family was his main aim in life. This he did so well and with so much love. I know that after he left the orphanage, he worked in a trading store on one of the mines. I'm not sure how long he worked there and if he worked anywhere else before he enlisted in the army. He fought up north and was awarded two medals.

HELLMAN B is on this plaque which lists all the children of Arcadia on active service in WWII

Benjamin (Ben) Helman in his army uniform

I have a wedding photo of my Dad in his army uniform and his naturalisation papers. He married my momHetty Glass (nee Hack) in 1943 and adopted Renee, my adored older sister who passed away in 1995.

After the war ended, he and his partner started a brick making firm in Elandsfontein, which they ran together for about 20 years.

I have a younger sister Marlene Merwitz, who also lives in Toronto with her daughter Terry Kotton and her family. Her son Brad lives in South Africa.

My husband Reuben and I first lived in Pretoria, where Reuben worked with Bennie Penzik whose Dad was together with my Dad in the orphanage and was also one of the Ochberg orphans.

We then moved to Johannesburg where we lived until we emigrated to Toronto nearly three years ago to be with our three children who all live in North America; Jady Kallan, born 26 August 1967, Kevin born 12 June 1969 and Wayne born 11 June 1972 and two wonderful grandchildren, Kevin and Talya's son Justin born 5 May 2003 and Rachel Kallan born 24 April 2004.

Hetty, Ben, Marlene and Sheila

Terry Kotton, Benjamin's granddaughter writes

My name is Terry Kotton Granddaughter of Benjamin Helman. I could not believe this whole story when my Aunt Sheila found out and told me. It is incredible that none of us knew that my Grandfather was an Ochberg Orphan.

I wish I knew my Grandfather, but unfortunately I was only two years old when he passed away, so all I have to go on is what my mother has told me over the years. She has always spoken so highly of him, of what a gentle kind soul he was. My mother was the baby so he really fussed over her. She remembers that he would be the one to take her to school on the first day and be waiting for her when she came out. He would take them into Town on a Saturday which was such a treat and was always there for her over the years. He never spoke of his childhood. All he would say was that he had a cow and ate lots of potatoes and then came on a boat to South Africa and that was it.

This has been such an incredible learning experience for us! And we thank you for putting so much time and effort in putting all this information together. It is greatly appreciated!

I am the daughter of Marlene and Neville Merwitz (whom you may know as well, because he was an Arc resident too) I am married to Lance Kotton, and have two children; Sean who is ten years old and Alyssa who is seven years old. We have been living in Ontario, Canada for almost 14 years now.

Ben with his daughters Sheila (Psek) and Marlene (Merwitz)

Chapter 111 – FREIDL JOFFE (1910-1995)

The Joffe Family originally lived in Latvia and made their way to Pinsk after the father, Moshe deserted the Russian Army to avoid being sent off to the Russia-Japanese war. Later at the time of WW1 he was rounded up by the Germans (or Russians) for forced labour and died from typhus leaving the mother Mariasha and her three daughters, Sarah, Freda (Freidl) and Sylvia (Livia) to fend for themselves.

While Freda and Sylvia went to South Africa with Isaac Ochberg, Mariasha their Mother and Sarah their older sister remained behind and it is believed, perished in the Holocaust. (see end of chapter)

Freda left a detailed first hand account of her experiences as an Ochberg Orphan (see Part 1 Section 5) and now her son Peter Larsen continues her story.

FREDA LARSEN'S STORY (FREIDL JOFFE)
Written by Peter Larsen I

This is the story of my mother, Freidel Joffe (Freda Larsen), of her life-challenging journey after she left Arcadia.

Some of it is about me, my sister and my father. Freda's story, after she left Arcadia, and ours are intertwined and while not all that eventful, reflects more on her life circumstances, her tenacity - the way she coped with the situations that life presented - her indomitable spirit! Not really a cheerful story - it is not one of any notable achievements or success in the usual sense, but rather one of ongoing struggle, endurance and sacrifice for much of the time with some measure of well-deserved reward in the end - the reward of having seen her family through trying times and taking pride in what they eventually accomplished.

Freda was born in Pinsk, White Russia (later Poland, now Belarus) around 1910; she chose randomly September 13, never being sure of her exact date of birth.

Her early childhood is recounted in the interview recorded on tape, which has been transcribed by David Sandler and will be found in his book.

On reading further, it will immediately become apparent that her indomitable spirit, manifested in childhood, prevailed throughout subsequent years, enabling her to carry on against much adversity and eventually win through.

Freidel (Freda) and Cywje (Sylvia) Joffe
Photos from Travel Permits from Pinsk Magistrate

ARCADIA

Freda (Freidl) and her younger sister, Sylvia (Ciwje) were Ochberg Orphans cared for at Arcadia from 1923 having been initially accommodated in the Jewish Old Age Home in 1921 while the newly acquired Arcadia was being suitably fitted out as an orphanage. I know almost nothing of her days at Arcadia except that my Auntie Sylvia once told me that at one point after arriving in South Africa, Freda was taken in by a family for foster care or possible adoption but, apparently, she was treated more like a servant, and she didn't choose to stay. I have an idea that she didn't get further than about standard four in primary school and that she might have left Arcadia when she was quite young. It would seem that her tuition at Arcadia must have included piano lessons because in later life it was apparent that she had had quite a good grounding in piano playing and theory.

16 Joffe Livia girl 8
15 Joffe Freidel girl 11   *P Berman 74 Sherwell St*

The entry for the children in the register kept at the South African Jewish Orphanage (Arcadia)

The Borowic sisters with Freda   *Unknown friend with Freda*

EARLY ADULTHOOD

After leaving Arcadia, Freda might have sought work in a chemist shop where she possibly met my father, Arthur. He was training to be a pharmacist but never qualified as he became very ill with sugar diabetes and landed up in hospital not long after they married. For the rest of his life he had to be on insulin injections. It is interesting that insulin treatment had only become generally available a few years prior to this.

It was probably in the early 1930s that they met and married. Born in 1896, he was 14 years older than Freda. She was a young, innocent woman and she says that for a long time she continued to call my father Mr Larsen!

He had a sporting background and golf was his passion throughout his life (although he excelled in most sports in his youth). My mom at one stage even tried her hand at swinging a golf club. He was a very fine golfer, winning the tournament at the Houghton Golf Course, the Joel Cup, in four successive years in the late 1920s. His name still appears on the Champions Board which also bears the names of Gary Player, Ernie Els and the like.

A cartoon of my dad as a serious golfer with a pharmacy background

Arthur and Freda

I know at one stage, early on, my parents lived in Irene, near Pretoria, and it is likely that Arthur was either a golf-pro or worked in a chemist shop there. General, later Field Marshall, Smuts had his farm in Irene and my mother couldn't resist telling how he once walked into the Post Office where she happened to be and remarked on her "pragtige krule hare"(beautiful curly hair) which was also jet-black with natural waves. It was certainly no exaggeration on his part!

Throughout these difficult pre-war times, both Freda and her sister, Sylvia, always tried to send money, no matter how little,

My Mom as a young woman

to their mother and elder sister in Pinsk to help alleviate their poverty.

Being the second eldest in a family of 15 (originally 16) children, my father found himself in the position of being the main contributor in supporting his family who ran an old boarding house in Port Alfred where all the children had been reared. This was a financial burden which carried over into his early married life. This was at a time just after the 1929 Great Depression.

The early years were marked by illness and financial hardship which dogged them for the rest of their lives. Compared to today (2009), in the early days diabetic care was very rudimentary and difficult, so landing in a coma, infections, and hospitalization just became part of living with the ailment. But Freda stood by him and coped admirably with his illness which was punctuated by life-threatening episodes. It wasn't easy!

My sister, Ida, was born in Pretoria in 1935. I'm not sure what intervened, but they then landed up in the small town of Vereeniging, where I was born in 1938.

FREDA'S DAUGHTER IDA

Early on in the course of my father's illness, Ida at the age of three had to be looked after in Port Alfred by several of my dad's sisters at the old boarding house which was run by them. They were childless and naturally she was much fussed over.

After many months she was welcomed back into her home where, by contrast, her parents were in no position to give her what she had been experiencing with the relatives. And now there was a home with a new baby brother with whom she would have to share the attention.

Ida grew up to be exceptionally gifted, beautiful and vivacious, with a flair for writing, poetry and painting, playing the piano and most of all she had a remarkable coloratura soprano voice which she might have inherited from her parents who both had nice singing voices. She loved opera and learned to speak Italian. She was self-taught in all her accomplishments and she has made a meaningful contribution to society. It has always saddened me that circumstances got in the way of her pursuing a singing career.

PRETORIA

Soon after I was born, the family moved to Pretoria where we lived in a small two-bedroomed rented house. It stood out rather conspicuously from all the other average middle-class homes in the street, although around the corner, there were also other small dwellings similar to ours, all built by a speculator offering cheap housing.

Freda and son Peter

Interestingly, my mom was friendly with a Mrs Wells, a widow, who lived with her daughter in one of these houses. Mrs Wells' husband, Frederick, was the man, a mineworker at the Premier Diamond Mine near Pretoria, who in 1905 found the famous Cullinan diamond sticking out of the ground. He was given a reward but he later apparently turned to drink and became somewhat delusional. It seems on one occasion, he stopped a train by standing on the tracks in order to ask for a cigarette light!

Anecdotally, that's not the only connection I had with the Cullinan diamond. In 1964 I met an elderly lady who was the granddaughter of General Louis Botha, the first Prime Minister of the Union of South Africa. She was wearing a ring with a beautiful big diamond and two earrings, each with a large, beautiful diamond. They had been handed down from her grandfather who had been given these jewels made from fragments of the original huge Cullinan diamond!

Although our house was small, we were nevertheless grateful to have a roof over our heads. A coal-stove had to be prepared daily if the family was to have some hot water. Every day someone had to clean it out, chop wood, fetch a bucket of coal and make the fire. This slow-combustion stove was in the small kitchen and heated the water in the hot-water tank which was in the cupboard of my sister's small bedroom which tended to be warm in winter but hot in summer. But she was lucky to have her own room as I had to share the other small bedroom with my parents. Ours was one of the few remaining houses in the vicinity which still had an outside toilet, out of sight, somewhere at the very back of the house and not very convenient!

One cheerful aspect of our home was the small garden where my dad, who was a good gardener, would always have a bed or two of lovely, colourful, flowers and sometimes a few vegetables. At one stage we kept some chickens.

MORE ON ARTHUR

Arthur was a Gentile but was very protective of my mother when it came to her being Jewish. He would never tolerate anti-Semitic sentiments or remarks from anybody.

He was a good, kind, highly principled man, a real gentleman, charming, well-liked and well thought of by people from all walks of life. His family background was Anglican but I never knew him to go to any church. There were no luxuries like books in the house and only occasionally did the children get toys. We did have a few 78 rpm records, bought by my dad, which gave a lot of pleasure and fostered in us a deep and enduring love of music. He loved, especially, the singers of old and he, himself, had a good baritone voice.

My father, like many others in those days liked his smokes and his tipple which helped to ease the stresses in his life. Who could really blame him? This was, however, not without its drawbacks when it came to family harmony and the fact that there was less money for food. Also, it certainly didn't combine well with being a diabetic on insulin, sometimes landing up with him in a coma and the ambulance at the gate. His life was anything but easy but I cannot stress enough what a good man he was 'more sinned against than sinning' as my mother was wont to say! In spite of these shortcomings and stress that they caused, there was a great deal of love and devotion between them. My mother was a very giving, forgiving, demonstrative person. When things improved in later years his intemperance no longer manifested itself.

There was very little income and no steady job. He was, nevertheless, generous and many a time he would give his last penny to a down-and-out person, irrespective of colour or class, even a tramp.

There were phases throughout his life where he managed to eke out a small living as a golf professional, or on a few occasions working in a sports shop. He was good at stringing tennis racquets which he did on the sitting room table and this brought in a few pounds, until the automatic machines eventually replaced him and put an end to that little source of income. He also made a little out of giving occasional golf lessons and in this respect he was an excellent teacher. These sporadic ups and downs were part of our somewhat precarious existence.

For many years my father rode a motor bike – until one day he had an accident and we realized that it would be safer for him to drive a car. So he bought an old Opel Kadet which struggled up any slight incline and broke down every five minutes. We were never in a position to fix it properly.

At one stage he found a job as golf-pro at the Witbank Golf Course which was over 100 km away but we usually saw him on weekends. We used to worry about whether, being on his own away from home, he would go into a hypoglycemic or a diabetic coma, and whether he'd be safe as there had been a break-in at the clubhouse where he slept on his own. A further concern was that his old car was forever breaking down on the open road! This was a very unsettling time in our lives but it brought in a little much-needed income. This job, however, did not last very long.

HOME LIFE

Unlike almost all of the middle-class and affluent people in the country, we never employed a servant, so Freda had to cope with a lot of arduous housework; floor-polish for the wooden floors and stoep-polish for the tiny entrance and then for hours on hands and knees to get a shine to brighten up our lives. In later years we acquired an electric floor polisher and even a washing machine, the old kind with a spindle and a mangle.

My mom did all of the chores when we were small and continued with laborious housework even when we were older. She was a good cook. Tasty fried meat-balls which she called rissoles were served up now and then and she sometimes came up with nice Jewish dishes which we always enjoyed. Potato latkes were one of our favourites and sometimes gribinis or chicken-skin crackling. She occasionally made nice pickled herring with bay-leaves and peppercorns and we used to enjoy her beetroot set in raspberry jelly.

Our lives would have been more precarious were it not for my mother's resilience, resourcefulness and sacrifice! She did much to keep the ship afloat.

FREDA'S WORKING YEARS

Freda, with her very elementary school education, became a sales-lady behind the Kosher counter at the OK Bazaar in Pretoria, where she worked for 15 years. There were no supermarkets in those days so she was running up and down on her feet all day long serving customers some of whom made her life difficult, as did some of the supervisors. She would usually come home tired and complaining about the job and then still have to cope with house-work! She didn't bottle things up and venting her emotions helped to keep her going. There were occasional arguments which could be ascribed to general stress and financial worries. She was always aware of the contrast between her life and circumstances and those of many of the well-off people she had to serve and who sometimes flaunted their riches. Some, of course, were very nice, and not difficult as customers.

One of the well-disposed people who crossed our paths was Mrs. Grossfeld, who was my old primary school teacher and later principal of the Carmel Jewish School. Knowing a little of our background she encouraged my parents to give me some religious upbringing irrespective of which one, but obviously Jewish would be logical. So that led to my Barmitzvah at the Old Pretoria Synagogue. In 1962 this building, no longer used as a synagogue, served as the court for the Treason Trial of Nelson Mandela and others. The trial itself proved to be a milestone in the forging of South Africa's history. In 1977 the inquest into the death of Steve Biko, leader of the Black Consciousness Movement, was also held in the Old Synagogue.

When Freda worked at the OK she was burdened with quite a few troublesome ailments which made her job even more arduous. But she had no choice and her small income helped to keep our heads above water.

My father, after not having had any steady job for many years, was eventually given a job at Pretoria Wholesale Druggists owned by the Goldstein brothers. This was a kindly gesture on their part considering that my father had not worked in the pharmacy line for over 40 years and this job necessitated some knowledge of pharmacy and making up various pharmaceutical concoctions. But he obviously had had a good grounding, as apothecaries in bygone days regularly made up medicines in the dispensary themselves using the good-old apothecary-ware such as a weighing balance, pestle and mortar and measuring flask.

Their combined salaries helped send me to Medical School. I specialized as a pathologist. So there was something to show for both my parents' hard toil and sacrifice. I will forever be grateful to them.

ISSY COHEN

My father died in 1964. About eight years later Freda met Issy Cohen. He had attended my bris but it was many years thereafter that she was to meet up with him again. As a lonely elderly widow she was relaxing on a bench on the Durban beachfront, no doubt gazing out and praying for better things, when fortuitously and unexpectedly he walked into her life again.

They traveled around the country a bit; he had a little caravan at one stage. They even tried their hand at bowls. Issy, who had originally come with nothing in his pocket to South Africa, probably from Eastern Europe, with practically no formal education, had worked very hard all his life. He was very bitter from all he had gone through over the years, especially as all 13 of his close family had perished in the Holocaust. My mom quoted him as saying that he would wash his hands in the blood of Germans whom he called 'Amalek'! It is understandable that he did indeed feel very strongly about the matter. He had lovely photos of his sister, who was a very nice person. They killed the lot. He found that out when he was eventually able to communicate with some other people who had survived the Holocaust.

My mom did a lot to soften aspects of his character and make him more tolerant although it was difficult for him to ever overcome the strong feelings he expressed towards all those associated with taking the lives of his entire family.

Issy and Freda

Issy died in about 1985. Freda's latter years were spent living in a flat in Pietermaritzburg where we tried our best to see to all her needs and make her life pleasant. Nevertheless, she experienced the loneliness of old age and eventually became frail and senile and had to be looked after in an old age home. She passed away peacefully on 19 December 1995 at the age of 85. The first of her four great grandchildren, John, was seven days old but she was too uncomprehending and frail to have partaken in the joy.

FREDA AS A PERSON

My mother inculcated in us good principles and our circumstances were such that some well-meaning people would from time to time try to impart their Christian beliefs. Over the years she found herself befriended by a number of Christian people and was to some extent influenced by them to believe in many of the Christian tenets. She would often stress the principle of forgiveness and the comfort and hope offered to the downtrodden with whom she obviously identified. But she was very Jewish all the same. In other words, she drew on whatever gave her sustenance to carry on in her often lonely and difficult situation. She relied heavily on faith and the power of prayer to get her through difficult times.

People from all walks of life felt drawn to her. She was quite captivating, with a certain charm, bonhomie and affability, together with language proficiency stemming from her love of reading, and well-liked for her colourful conversation and wonderful sense of humour. She could quote many expressions and aphorisms from English and Yiddish. In particular, we loved her Jewish expressions which seemed to have no English equivalents in their aptness, succinctness and wit. For instance, if a person is down she would say "oyfn kop shpringen alle tzign!" (all the goats jump on your head!). Many people found her strong Jewish accent most appealing.

She had the gift of innately empathizing with people. They always asked her to read their cards and she was more often than not accurate with her fortune-telling. The cards were merely a guide but she had the gift of elaborating on what the cards showed and making riveting and convincing projections as she went along. People hung onto her every word. She had to be frank but tactful when a dark card, presaging a bad event, came up. She handled it all very convincingly and professionally, but she never charged for her fortune-telling except once when she did it at a fete for charity and she dressed up like a gypsy!

Freda's makeup was characterized by strength of character, fortitude under very trying circumstances, resilience, resourcefulness, sacrifice, good moral values - all these qualities - and above all, generosity. She was blessed with a degree of innate optimism. Following any disappointment, she would typically say: "When one door closes another door opens". While not being observant in any religion; she had unwavering faith, which might have stemmed from her mother's influence in childhood where faith and prayer probably played a huge role in sustaining her family through the most harrowing trials and tribulations. Freda believed strongly in the principle of forgiveness.

Like many or most mothers, she doted on her son. When she called me tati, tatele, or tatele meine, I accepted it as a well-meant term of endearment. It, however, caused me slight embarrassment when she occasionally did this in the presence of others but I knew there was nothing I could or should do about it. I never asked what those words actually meant! It has only now, after all these years, dawned on me that in Yiddish tati refers to daddy and that tatele would be the diminutive, little daddy. When I think back I feel a bit sorry for my embarrassment because I now realize that it is not unusual for a mother to look upon her son as a substitute for her father and she had, after all, lost her father when she was a very small child.

Like most of us she wasn't perfect. A small flaw was perhaps a chip she sometimes carried on her shoulder which could express itself unexpectedly. But it was usually well-grounded, based on past hurts that she had suffered from some person. This imperfection can easily be forgiven.

A selfless person, she cared little for material possessions, denying herself things in favour of her family's needs. She was the quintessential *Wonderful Yiddishe Momme.*

MY AUNT SYLVIA CHASTEAU: (Cywje Joffe)

I loved my mom's 'swester', my Auntie Sylvia. She and my mom were very close. Sylvia had a good command of English and a flair for writing and storytelling. She aspired to being a writer, penning many articles for newspapers and magazines but, sadly, she never recorded her life story.

Like my mom, she could sum up a situation and find just the right comment, always perspicuous and often tinged with a little witty cynicism, so that her comments would be amusing and often memorable. Once, on the phone, I was expressing concern about my son who at that time was in a dead-end job in Cape Town from which he was unable to extricate himself. I ended by suggesting to Sylvia that maybe we should pray for him. Her reply was unexpected but typical: "Peter, I am not the

Freda and Sylvia

praying type but I will pray in an emergency!" She would say of someone who always wanted to be the focus of attention: "Wants to be the bride at the wedding, and the corpse at the funeral!" She described a very thin person as "a match stick with the wood scraped off!"

On an overseas trip with her grown-up daughter, Yvonne, the Louvre in Paris was a port of call where they were to see the Mona Lisa. Not having been able to get close to the relatively small but famous masterpiece which was protected by a special thick glass plate, Sylvia didn't mince matters when she later told my mom: "Swester, I have seen it better on the back of a cigarette box!"

Sylvia was popular, with many good friends. Many of her friends and various hangers-on were attracted to her uncanny skill in reading tea-cups. It got to a point where, sometimes, in desperation, she had to disappoint uninvited guests who would have begged the favour after finishing their tea, by without warning, using a tea-strainer!

She lived in Johannesburg and we were in Pretoria. Her life also was not all that easy but overall her family was better off than ours, with a more stable income, particularly from the time when she was able to use her skills in full-time employment as a secretary.

They lived in Yeoville in a small semi-detached house slightly bigger, and in my eyes, much more inviting than ours; as a child I used to love visiting them. Their garden was not much bigger than a postage-stamp and my cousin Victor and I would often choose to play on the tin roof!

She was always very supportive during our hard times. Many a phone-call to her swester would include a mention of her sending some money – invariably for a new pair of "broeks" (knickers) for my mom.

Yes, I was very fond of my Auntie Sylvia and her husband Uncle George. He was a well-read, talented, philosophical man of deep insight and intellect, who complemented Sylvia's character and intellect very well.

FREDA'S DESCENDANTS

Freda had two children, me and my sister Ida. Ida married but had no children.

Peter, Rosa, Freda, Sylvia and George

Rosa and I have two children, Mara and Peter; and lived in Pietermaritzburg for close on 30 years and then moved to Perth, Western Australia in 2009.

Mara and her husband Greg have two sons and now live in Perth, Australia. Peter and his wife Caren have a son and a daughter and live in Toronto, Canada.

Mara, Greg, and sons   *Caren and Peter Jnr,*
Nicholas (L) and John (R)   *Solar and Adam*

I will always be extremely grateful for what my parents did for us and the sacrifices they made, and we all owe a deep debt of gratitude to Isaac Ochberg and all those other good people involved in my mother's life and who ultimately made it possible for me to relate this story.

CORRESPONDENCE WITH FAMILY LEFT BEHIND IN PINSK MARIASHA AND SARAH

While Freda and Sylvia went to South Africa with Isaac Ochberg, Mariasha their Mother and Sarah their older sister remained behind and here are postcards received from them.

Mariasha and Sarah

Card 1 - Sarah's photo, with message and translation following

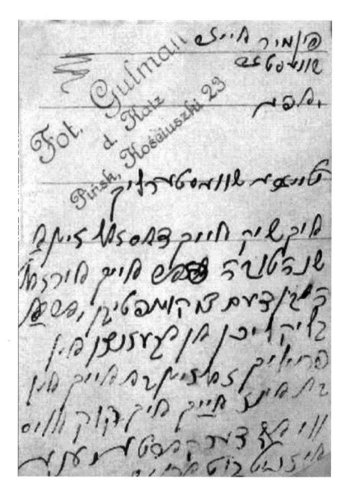

It clearly seems to be a New Year greeting.
Here is what I can make out, I am afraid that it is not that much.
On top, it looks like an address, but actually reads:

"From me your sister"
Dear little sister I am sending you this hearty?
a happy and... Shana tova that I.... in the coming year. a happy and....of joy to be....."

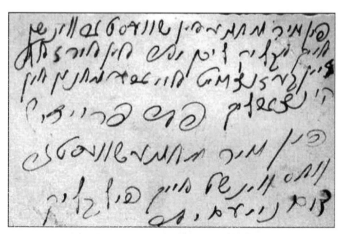

Card 2 Message with translation following

520

From your sisters who wish you a happy...... in ... [signed] Freidl.
From your sister who wishes you much happiness in the new year.
[no name] "

Translations by Veronica Belling

Card 3 Photo above with message in English below

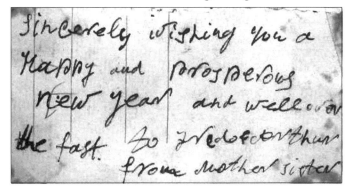

FAMILY LEFT BEHIND IN PINSK
MARIASHA AND SARAH JOFFE

While Freda and Sylvia Joffe were rescued by Isaac Ochberg in 1921, their mother, Mariasha and elder sister Sarah (aka Goda), remained behind in Pinsk.

Over the years Freda and Sylvia sent whatever money they could from South Africa to help the two in Pinsk who continued to suffer hardship and deprivation.

Soon after WWII started a letter was received asking the girls to please stop sending anything as post was being intercepted. One letter had said that they were ordered to report at certain barracks and that there were frightening rumours about what was happening to people. Sylvia wrote back trying to allay their fears by saying that the authorities were not likely to harm civilians. There was no reply.

Communication ceased except for one postcard, received in 1942, which was sent from the post office in the main street of the Pinsk Ghetto (22 Polnocna Strasse), coming to South Africa via the Red Cross and via Turkey as could be determined from

the postmarks. It is only after recently learning the full story of WWII Pinsk that we can surmise that the postcard must have been heavily censored by the Germans and was probably only allowed as a smokescreen to conceal the truth about what was really happening in Pinsk at the time. This postcard was in the possession of Sylvia but might have been misplaced when she was clearing her papers before moving to a frailcare home. Unfortunately the family hasn't been able to find a copy so we don't know the contents.

Freda and Sylvia both lived to about 86 years old without really knowing what had happened to their loved-ones in Pinsk. We had always assumed that they perished in the gas-chambers.

Now, with the advent of the Internet and the release of the German records held in the Soviet Union, we are able to piece together the circumstances of their deaths by massacre in Pinsk at the hands of the Germans.

The Germans kept meticulous records and we entered the name Joffe in the database held by Yad Vashem and found our grandmother and aunt listed there. Connected with my aunt Goda (aka Sarah) was the surname Glouberson.

A list of some of the people living at 87 Sumpfstrasse (Swamp Street) in the Pinsk Ghetto.

	Age/gender	Occupation
Bluma Glouberson	70 F	Housewife
Mariasha Joffe (mother)	65 F	Housewife
Salman Glouberson	41 M	Artisan
Goda Joffe (Sister Sarah)	36 F	Tailor/Seamstress
Feiga Joffe/Glouberson	16 F	
Frejda Joffe	13 F	
Mejer Glouberson Wolpus	13 M	
Isaak Joffe	12 M	
Judyta Joffe	5 F	
Wigdor Joffe	5 M	
Mojsiej Joffe	<1 M	

What can we deduce from examining this list?

-These 11 people could have occupied a single room in the dwelling as each person was allotted about a square metre so that 10 people occupied one room.

-It can be assumed that there were several families and many more people living in the same dwelling.

-Freda and Sylvia assumed that Sarah never married but there is no reason to doubt that she might have had children unbeknown to her sisters in South Africa.

-Some of the childrens' names are intriguing. Freda was Sarah's sister's name, Victor was the name of her then two year old nephew, Sylvia's son in South Africa, while Moshe was her father's name. Could we have had cousins in the ghetto?

-One wonders whether Salman Glouberson and Goda (Sarah) were the parents of the children in question.

Conditions in the ghetto have been described as atrocious. Many were given forced employment in factories and workshops outside the ghetto, working for the Germans' war effort and the city's residents; Sarah was probably usefully employed as a seamstress. But the people were kept on the brink of starvation. They were not allowed to bring food into the ghetto when they returned from work. They were tortured or even murdered for this "crime". Cooking facilities and access to water were extremely limited; the living conditions were inhuman.One can do no more than speculate on what they really went through.

A model of the Pinsk Ghetto found in the Ghetto Fighter's Museum at kibbuts Lohamey Hagetaot near Nahariya.

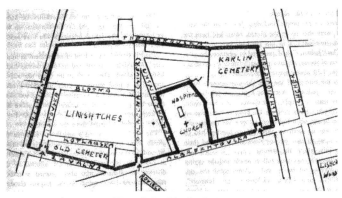

Map of the Pinsk ghetto

A brief history of the Pinsk Jews in WWII.

-The German army invaded Pinsk on 4 July 1941 and the liquidation of the Pinsk Jews began the following month with the murder of 11,000 men and boys.

-About 20,000 persons were left in the town, mostly women and children and some men who had managed to escape the first slaughter.

-During August of '41 almost all the Jews from the little towns around Pinsk (more than seven surrounding towns) were murdered. The remaining Jews were forced into the Pinsk Ghetto in early May 1942.

-Earlier on, Himmler had actually ordered that all the Jews were to be killed and the Jewish women and children were to be pushed into the Pripet marshes and drowned. But it would appear that this could not be carried out because the swamps were not deep enough at that time of the year. So the process was to be delayed and the majority of the inhabitants' lives were lengthened for at least a year.

-The Pinsk Ghetto's final liquidation was in October 1942, after six months of starvation and extreme suffering of its inhabitants.

-It finally culminated in the slaughter of groups of 200-300 people who were taken to pits outside Pinsk where they were shot. They were first ordered to strip and sort their clothing in piles according to type.

-The ghetto existed for six months – from May 1942 until its elimination at the end of October 1942. Almost 20,000 people were killed.

-About 140 people with useful skills were confined in a "small" ghetto and killed on 23 December 1942

-Only a small handful managed to escape to the forests and join the partisans and to eventually relate what happened. There were one or two people among the general population who were also able to give eye-witness accounts.

Chapter 112 – CIWJE JOFFE

The Joffe Family originally lived in Latvia and made their way to Pinsk after the father, Moshe deserted the Russian Army to avoid being sent off to the Russia-Japanese war. Later at the time of WW1 he was rounded up by the Germans (or Russians) for forced labour and died from typhus leaving the mother Mariasha and her three daughters, Sarah, Freda (Freidl) and Sylvia (Livia) to fend for themselves.

While Freda and Sylvia went to South Africa with Isaac Ochberg, Mariasha their Mother and Sarah their older sister remained behind and it is believed perished, in the Holocaust.

Freda left a detailed first hand account of her experiences as an Ochberg Orphan (see Part 1 Section 5) and her son Peter Larsen continued her story in chapter 111.

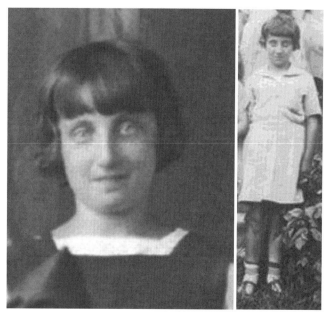

Ciwje (Sylvia) Joffe at Arcadia ~ 1922

SYLVIA, MY MOTHER
Written by Victor Chasteau - New Zealand March 2011

My mother Sylvia was an Ochberg orphan. Her original name was Ciwje, which became Sylvia as the closest name in English. She was about ten years old when she and her older sister Freda (Fredja) were taken from Pinsk, to South Africa in 1921 and sent to Arcadia orphanage in Johannesburg by Isaac Ochberg. On my South African birth certificate of November 1935 she is recorded as 25 years old. Because she was so young when she left Pinsk and with language difficulties at the time, her exact birth date is not known; we always celebrated her birthday on 26 September.

Strictly, she and Freda were not orphans as their mother (and an older sister) cared for them in Pinsk. Their father Moshe Joffe had died earlier during WW1 in either a German or Russian prisoner of war camp and their mother Mariasha was struggling to care for her children, Their early life has been covered to some extent in the record based on a tape recording made by Freda's son, Peter Larsen. This has already been ably documented and their connection with Arcadia, the beautiful home in Parktown, Johannesburg, built by Sir Lionel and Lady Phillips

At Arcadia, Sylvia was, of course, brought up in the Jewish faith; she was schooled to a level where she could become a shorthand typist, a not uncommon training for more "intellectually" oriented young women in those days, where other professions were generally out of their reach. She had a fascination with literature and used to read widely from the library at Arcadia. She told us that at night she would often sit on the main hallway steps to read as this was the best illuminated area, and many a time she heard the lions roaring in the zoo, which was close by. She dreamed of one day becoming an author herself.

Ciwje (Sylvia) Joffe
Photo from Pinsk Travel Permit

Ciwje (Sylvia) Joffe and little Hymie Wolchuk 1922

At the age of 14 Sylvia met Ray Newman at a school camp near Gordon's Bay in the Cape. A lifelong friendship with the Newmans, a well established Jewish family in Johannesburg was the outcome. This brought exposure to music, symphony concerts, opera, ballet and literature. Ray had always wanted a friend called "Viv" and this became Sylvia's name in this circle of friends. Sylvia adopted Viv as her nom de plume later when writing stories and articles. The many Jewish friends she made at Arcadia and through Ray were a valued part of the texture of the lives of her children.

Sometime around about 1930, I presume, Sylvia went to Vereeniging where she was employed as a typist and bookkeeper, by the Indian-owned general trading firm of Dadabhay, one of the first few Indian families given permission to settle in the Transvaal. At that time she met my father, George Chasteau, who was a technician employed by the Victoria Falls and Transvaal Power Company (VFP) at the power station next to the Vaal river.

VFP was an electricity generating company, set up to generate electricity for the Witwatersrand mining industry. The Victoria Falls part never materialised but the VFP in Vereeniging was eventually absorbed into Escom, the state-run power company for the whole of South Africa. It is interesting to note that Sammy Marks and Isaac Lewis, Jews originally from Lithuania, were largely responsible for the creation of the VFP.

George was a very serious, artistic and musically accomplished handsome young man. He was inspired by writers such as H G Wells, and was at the time writing a novel he titled Zia Zambia, about a new mysterious source of great energy for power generation (atomic?) and set in an African country. Zambia was actually only so named in 1964. Sylvia's connection with George was as a typist of his manuscript. Their mutual interest in writing and literature became a bond that linked them. Their relationship blossomed and they were married in 1933

George's father, Louis Chasteau, had come to South Africa from France around the turn of the century and married his best friend's widow who was of Dutch descent. They were caught up as non-combatants in the turmoil of the Anglo-Boer war, and were living in the Cape Province at the time of my father's birth in 1904. My father was initially brought up to some extent in the

Catholic faith by his father, but between this and the more general protestant connection of his mother he ended up rather a free-thinker and a philosopher. George's father returned to France around 1918, as far as I can determine, to sort out some family finances but succumbed there, possibly in the Spanish flu epidemic. My grandmother was left somewhat impoverished with my father and several half-siblings from her earlier marriage. My father grew up in the Orange Free State and was largely influenced by his mother's Afrikaner connections there.

My father finished high school but did not pursue any tertiary education till somewhat later. During the tough times of the depression he was fortunate to be working in an essential industry, electrical power generation. When they were first married my father and mother lived with his family in the village of Evaton, near Vereeniging. Living with the in-laws meant great adjustments for Sylvia; she, an English-speaking "penniless Jewish orphan", had to fit into a conservative Afrikaans community. These were difficult times for my mother

Sylvia and George Chasteau at Johannesburg Zoo 1931
with the message on the reverse side below

as she was a young woman with a new baby, my sister Yvonne, and with no family other than her sister Freda. She was inexperienced in housekeeping and had to win over a very domineering mother-in-law who was very attached to her youngest son, my father. She made every effort to learn the housewifely skills valued in the community: baking, cooking, fruit-bottling, jam-making sewing and so on. Sylvia's warmth and personality won over the family and "Sylf" became loved by all. None of my father's family held any very strong religious sentiments, and I don't believe there was any anti-Semitism, as such. Sylvia always kept up some degree of observance of the Jewish faith, but I was not brought up as a Jew, no bris! In later years, when we lived in Yeoville, Johannesburg, with many Jewish neighbours, Sylvia always informally acknowledged the various Jewish holy days and celebrations. We, her children, can, remember her, for instance, fasting on Yom Kippur.

By the time I was born, Sylvia and George were living more independently in Vereeniging and soon after George became employed by the Rand Water Board (RWB) and they moved to the residential property complex surrounding the RWB pumping station on the outskirts of Vereeniging. The Rand Water Board was the main supplier of water to the Witwatersrand. The water was drawn from the Vaal River and purified before being pumped to Johannesburg, about 40 miles away and 2000 feet higher up. During WW2 this plant was obviously of high security and was electrically fenced and patrolled. This led to a rather tight-knit community of the residents on the property and my sister and I as young children formed many close friendships. My parents also formed friendships, some of which lasted life-long. Sylvia was probably the only Jew amongst these people. While there, George studied extramurally with the University of South Africa and attained a Bachelor of Arts degree.

Some time around 1941 we moved to Johannesburg where George took up employment as a production engineer with the Coca Cola company, which had only recently entered the market in South Africa. Although George's degree was a B A his leanings were always more of a technical and engineering nature. He also had a spell working for Pepsi Cola and the small privately owned Victoria Mineral Water Company in Jeppestown.

Johannesburg opened up a whole new world of Jewish connections for Sylvia. There were Arcadians she had kept contact with and other friends she had made through her friendship with Ray Newman. We lived in Yeoville, surrounded by mainly Jewish neighbours. My younger sister, Madeleine, was born there in 1942.

When Madeleine started school, Sylvia returned to full-time employment as a secretary. Over the years she worked for many prominent corporations such as BOAC (which later became British Airways), and Chloride Electrical, the manufacturers of Exide batteries. Later, around 1960, after my parents moved to Vanderbijlpark, she was secretary to senior staff at Vecor and Iscor Engineering. Sylvia's generous and sympathetic spirit and her wisdom brought her many friends in her personal life.

Sylvia had always kept up correspondence with her mother and sister in Pinsk and when possible sent them monetary help. This came to an end with WW2. The last correspondence from them was via the Red Cross through Turkey, around the end of 1941 when the Jews of Pinsk were confined to the ghetto there.

Sylvia never knew the fate of her mother and sister but realised they had perished when the full horrors of the holocaust were revealed at the end of the war. In 1995 my mother gave me the details of her mother and sister's last known address in Pinsk. Some years after my mother's death, with the ever expanding capabilities of the internet, I searched for Pinsk and came upon the records of the Pinsk ghetto. My grandmother and my aunt were listed exactly as named by my mother and the last address she had given me was the main street of the Pinsk ghetto. On around 28 October 1942 the remaining inhabitants of the ghetto were taken to a nearby village and massacred. Amongst these was certainly Sylvia's mother. Her sister may have been spared for a short time as she was a skilled seamstress and their services were still required up to the time, a few months later, when they too were massacred in Pinsk. As can well be appreciated, these were extremely sad events in Sylvia's life. Throughout the years Sylvia did write and had articles, letters and stories accepted, but we have always felt great regret that she never wrote the story of her own life. It was too painful for her. The welfare and happiness of her family came first. She gave them unstinting love and care.

George and Sylvia lived at Loch Vaal near Vanderbijlpark for about 28 years. These were happy and settled years with their children being married and six grandchildren forthcoming. Eventually they moved to stay near Yvonne in Linden, Johannesburg. George passed away in 1989. Sylvia spent her final years in a retirement village, Sonneglans, She passed away peacefully on 18 June 1998.

Sylvia and George Chasteau - 1988

SYLVIA AND GEORGE'S DESCENDANTS

George and Sylvia had three children, Yvonne, my eldest sister, myself, Victor and my youngest sister Madeleine. We were all encouraged by George and Sylvia to be studious and pursue careers.

Yvonne was a university trained secondary school teacher. She married Laurence Cortie and over the years they built up a very successful engineering workshop business. Yvonne was a co-

Sylvia and George with their daughter Madeleine, son Victor and his wife Marion and daughter Yvonne with her huband Laurie Cortie and their younger son Alan

director and after Laurie's death in 1994 she took over the management of their financial affairs. Yvonne has two sons; the eldest, Michael, has three sons and lives near Wollongong in Australia; Alan, childless, lives in Baltimore, USA. Both are graduate engineers; Michael is Professor of Nanotechnology at the University of Technology in Sydney and Alan is a specialist in railway engineering. At present Yvonne lives in Randburg but is considering relocating to Australia to be near her son.

Sylvia's daughter Yvonne with her son Michael and his wife Linda and their three sons Colin, Steven and David

I am a graduate engineer who did research at the CSIR in Pretoria and lectured at universities in South Africa and New Zealand. I am married to Marion de Maar who immigrated to South Africa in 1955 from the Netherlands with her family. We immigrated to New Zealand in 1974 and now, since my retirement, live on a small farm near the beautiful Pakiri beach, north of Auckland. Marion trained as graduate secondary school teacher in South Africa and pursued a career in New Zealand as an accomplished jeweller, with a Master of Philosophy degree in Fine Arts; she now has a very great involvement in practising and teaching Yoga. We have three daughters who all live in New Zealand. Monique, the eldest, living in Auckland, is a university trained secondary school teacher and counsellor; she has two daughters. Louise, also

living in Auckland, is a medical doctor, at present doing additional training in the field of Occupational Therapy; she has no children. Our youngest daughter, Colette, also a graduate secondary school teacher and now training as a careers advisor, has a son and a daughter. They live in a separate house on the farm close to us and we are privileged to see a great deal of these grandchildren. A fourth daughter, Jeanne, died tragically 18 years ago.

Marion Chasteau and three daughters Louise, Colette and Monique *Jeanne-Claire Chasteau (deceased)*

Madeleine studied music to the level of a performing licentiate in piano and has been a music teacher for many years. She is married to Silvio Buffler, an architect, and they live on a small farm, part of a subdivision of General Smuts's farm near Irene. She is childless. She and Silvio have been very involved in Indian-based philosophy and were among only a handful of like-minded followers permitted to visit India at the time when South Africans were persona non grata there.

Silvio and Madeleine Buffler and Sylvia *George Sylvia and Vic Chasteau - 1988*

We (and our spouses and children) are to various degrees all spiritually-aware free-thinkers, proud of our Jewish origins.

To those happenings, beyond our rational thinking, which, all those years ago, saw Sylvia accepted as an orphan by Isaac Ochberg and gave her the chance to be nurtured at Arcadia we, her descendants, give our sincerest thanks.

Sylvia's great grand children: Eva, Sara, Finian and Sylvia

Chapter 113 – SARA, CHAIM AND PESHE LEVIN

MEMORIES OF MY MOTHER, SARAH LEVIN,
now known as CYNTHIA CHAIT
Written by Annette Grauman

My mother was born on 5 September 1913, and she together with her siblings Hymie and Polly, were lucky enough to be three of the 167 orphans rescued by Isaac Ochberg from Europe and brought to South Africa in 1921. At the time she was eight, her older brother was ten and her younger sister, six. They were known by their Yiddishe/Polish names of Chaim, Sore and Pesze, which were later anglicised to Hymie, Sarah and Polly. Their birthplace was Pinsk, Poland.

Unfortunately, I know very little of her early life as I never really questioned her when I was very young, and as I grew older and began to wonder about her past history she never told me very much. She either said she couldn't remember as she was very young when she was orphaned, or else the memories were so traumatic that she blocked them out of her mind. What I do know for certain is that her mother's name was Chana and her father was Shmariyu. I am named after my grandmother (I have her Hebrew name, Chana) and my brother Sidney after my grandfather (his Hebrew name is Shmuel). I also have a pair of shabbes candlesticks which my mother gave me and she told me that they were her mother's, which I treasure today and use them every Friday night.

RESEARCHING FAMILY DETAILS

My brother, Sidney Chait, went to Cape Town some years back and went to find out whatever details he could from both the Orphanage and the Jewish Museum and so he got copies of the group passport photos which he sent me.

Group Passport 2

I can't really recognise my family as the picture is too grainy, but think I worked out that my mother (Sarah) is the first one on the right sitting in the front and my uncle is in the back row, the 4th from the left wearing a cap, but I can't really be sure. According to details I have, my mother and her siblings were born in Pinsk, Poland but the ages are different from the ages listed on the passport. I have my mother's date of birth listed as 5 September 1913, which would make her eight years old (not five as shown on the list), and my uncle Hymie's date of birth is 15 September 1909 (which would make him twelve and not nine).

I also have these copies of three individual certificates signed and stamped by the magistrate from Pinsk.

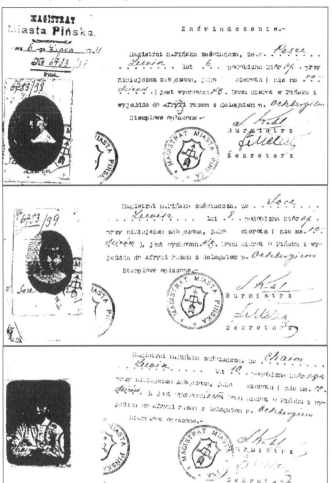

Kindly translated by Jack Goldfarb
The three similar affidavits grant permission for the three Levin siblings to be placed in the care of Mr Ochberg for the journey to South Africa. The Affidavits were written in Polish. Pinsk was actually located in White Russia, an area ceded to Poland in 1918, but then returned to Russia later.

6783/38 **Affidavit Issued by the Magistrate of the Town of Pinsk on 6 July 1921.**
The Magistrate of Pinsk states that PESCE LEVIN, of six years, whose photograph is attached, and is an orphan without parents, who resides in the Orphanage, is to depart for Africa with Caretaker OCHBERG.
Stamped and Sealed by two secretaries of the Magistrate of the Town of Pinsk.

The other two Affidavits were issued with the same wordings:
6783/39 **SORE LEVIN** (Pronounced in Yiddish: So-rah) eight years old Orphan Caretaker: Mr. Ochberg

(No Number) **CHAIM LEVIN** 10 years old Orphan Caretaker: Mr. Ochberg

AFTER ARRIVING IN SOUTH AFRICA

On arrival in South Africa there were too many orphans to all be accommodated in Cape Town, so half of them were sent to Johannesburg, and the three Levin siblings were brought up in Arcadia, until Polly was adopted and left the orphanage.

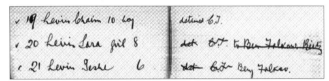

Extracts from the register kept by the South African Jewish Orphanage in Johannesburg that cared for the three siblings. The age of the children is listed after the name and Peshe (Polly) went to live with the Falkov family.

They went to the Hebrew High School on the corner of Claim and Wolmarans Streets in Johannesburg and a copy of my mother's Standard 3 school report shows that she was a very bright student.

Sarah (Cynthia) and Sam Chait getting engaged 1937

Unfortunately she never had the opportunity of furthering her studies, so when she left school she worked as a shop assistant until after her marriage, when my parents opened up a grocery store, and she seemed to be involved with food from then on.

I don't have any details of when my mother left the orphanage, how or when she met my father. I had always assumed that she met and married him in Cape Town, as I think that his family lived in Cape Town. However, on reflection recently, I am of the opinion that my father must have gone to Johannesburg where they met and married on 2 January 1938, as I know that the first seven years of my life we lived in Hillbrow, Johannesburg, and we only went back to Cape Town when I was seven and my brother Sidney was three, living in Muizenberg.

Sarah (Cynthia) Hymie and Polly as young adults

Sarah (Cynthia) 1937 and 1940

528

My mother had a very close friend, Dora (known as Dee) Abrahams from the time they worked together before getting married, and the close friendship lasted through the years and to this day Dee's daughter, Leonie, and I are still best friends. However, Dee decided that Sarah was too common a name and decided to call her Cynthia instead, and forever after my mother was always known by that name to everyone.

I also remember Fanny Lockitch from the orphanage as being very close friends with my mother, and in Muizenberg we were often in and out of each other's homes. Another very good friend of hers from the orphanage was Yetta Bornstein. My first bicycle was a second hand bike bought from Yetta when her daughter, Tania, outgrew it.

My mother was extremely hard working and always gave 100% effort to whatever she tackled. When they first went to Muizenberg they had a grocery store and later took on a fresh fish shop as well. Apart from working in the shop all day, she also took orders for home-made bagels, bulkes, taiglach, biscuits etc. Her cooking and baking were legendary and the house always smelled wonderful from all the baking.

During the summer season (the six weeks of school holidays at the end of the year) they also ran a hotel. Their first one was a small boarding house, called the Annsid Hotel and then in later years they had the Sandown on Sea Hotel, right on the beach. Every Sunday morning my mother got up at the crack of dawn to bake fresh bulkes for breakfast for every guest in the hotel.

My mother was always a very hospitable and sociable person, and their leisure time (what little they had) was spent playing cards on a Sunday. I well remember the days when they had several tables of cards, the women playing rummy and the men, either poker or solo. They always took off money from each table, which was donated to charity. They always had dinner, morning and afternoon tea and again there was always wonderful cooking and baking.

However, once they learned to play bridge that became their game of choice, and many years later, once I had learned bridge, my mother and I played every Saturday afternoon together with two friends of mine. I still remember those times very fondly.

Once I matriculated I went to Johannesburg on a holiday, met Abe and the rest, as they say, is history. We married on 4 September 1960 and although both Abe and I were living in Johannesburg, we had the engagement and later the wedding in Cape Town, as my parents couldn't get away from the shop for too long. The engagement party was held in December, which was the time the hotel was open and full of guests, so apart from our personal friends, every guest in the hotel was invited to the party as well, for which my mother oversaw the catering.

Every holiday, once we were married, was spent in Muizenberg, so that we could spend time with my parents. Sadly, the shop never closed so they were never able to get away on holiday together and I don't remember having "family holidays".

Uncle Hymie became a potato farmer once he left the orphanage and farmed in Delmas in the Transvaal. He never married, saying that he led such a lonely and isolated existence

Abe Grauman, Polly, Sarah, Annette and Hymie

that he felt it wouldn't be fair to expect any woman to share that sort of life with him.

But he regarded Sidney and me as his extended family and whenever he did come into town and we got together, he always was delighted to be with us and showered us with gifts.

Aunty Polly was adopted from the orphanage by a family called Falkov, so her name was legally changed from Levin to Falkov. Unfortunately her adopted parents were elderly and sickly so she often had to give up her friends and social life to stay home and care for them, and she too, never married.

In 1967 when my mother had been on her own for several years, and Sidney had graduated from University, she decided to move from Cape Town to Johannesburg, so that she could be nearer to us and get to know our children. She took a flat in Yeoville together with Aunty Polly (who had been living on her own in a boarding house in Hillbrow for many years until my mother arrived in Johannesburg), who had contracted osteoporosis at a very young age and was then unable to work. My mother was left to carry the bulk of the responsibility of working to support both of them, as well as caring for her sister in her illness. She took a job at the Zionist Federation running the kitchen for their frequent meetings etc. When she first started there they used to order in all the requirements, but my mom soon put a stop to that saying it was a huge waste of money, and instead they could make everything themselves. Her cooking became well known and everyone loved coming to the Federation offices at lunch or tea time as they were assured of a fabulous meal or tea.

At this time we had a house in Victory Park and it became the custom every Sunday for my mom and Aunty Polly, together with Abe's parents, Louis and Bella Grauman, to spend the day with us. My mother always arrived with tins full of home made cake or biscuits etc, as well as chocolates and treats for the children.

My mother was very easy to get along with and she and my in-laws became firm friends right from the beginning. In fact, soon after we emigrated to Australia, my mother and mother-in-law came out together on a three month visit to see us and both of them stayed with us at our home in Doncaster.

Family was the most important thing in my mother's life. She was lucky enough to know my husband (Abe Grauman) and children Elana, Bradley and Nadine, as well as Sidney's wife (Mary Bougin) and their sons, Gavin and David. Unfortunately she wasn't able to attend any of our children's weddings and she never got to know our grandchildren, Jarryd, Kaidyn and Shayn (Elana and Ian's sons), Simone and Adam (Brad and Dina's children), and Yazmin, Brooklyn and Harlan (Nadine and Daniel's children). She also never lived long enough to be at the weddings of Gavin to Rudilynn and David to Isobel, Sidney's sons.

However, she was a realist and when things started becoming difficult in South Africa, she was the first one to encourage us to take our children, leave the country and make a better and safer life for them elsewhere, knowing that we would be so far away and probably not see her very often once we moved. She selflessly put the needs of us and our children before her own.

As Aunty Polly's illness became worse she was unable to live at home as my mom couldn't care for her any longer, and sadly she had to put her into the hospital section of Our Parent's Home in Norwood, Johannesburg. A few years later, when my mother too, became too frail to take care of herself, she too moved into Our Parents Home, to be close to her sister and spent most of the day with her.

Later, after Uncle Hymie had stopped farming and when it became too difficult for him to remain in the hotel in Berea on his own, he too, went into Our Parents Home where he lived until the age of 90. My mother died at the age of 86 on 10 April 1999, and was buried in Port Elizabeth where Sidney and Mary live. Aunty Polly lived on in her frail state in the hospital section until she eventually died at the age of 85. Both Uncle Hymie and Aunty Polly are buried in the Johannesburg Cemetery. So the small family of the three Levins ended their lives together as they started it, all together in the Home, and each taking care of the other.

Hymie, Gavin, David, Polly and Sarah

My mother was a perfectionist in everything she undertook, she was very hard working and humble, very kind, warm and generous and had a very loving nature, and I am so proud to call her "My Mom".

NADINE'S MEMORIES OF BOBBA CHAIT

I remember Bobba Chait coming with Auntie Polly to our house in Victory Park, on Sundays, with Bobba and Zaida Grauman. I loved that they all came together on the weekends and had such a good time. I thought this was completely normal, for in-laws to have a genuine friendship like this. I liked how we referred to them by surname, so I knew where they came from! Thought this was normal too!

I remember Bobba Chait once giving me undies for my birthday...not very cool!! But I was probably only seven or eight years old!

I remember going to her flat, climbing the dark stairway, I think painted and cold concrete floors (was it the third floor?) and coming into the flat. I think the kitchen was on the right hand side as you came in. I remember there were always rows and rows of biscuits of various kinds. In fact, every time I see a glace cherry I think of her. She took such care in decorating and presenting her goodies. She was very matter-of-fact about it all. Just got it all out on the table without any fuss. It wasn't til I was an adult, entertaining guests myself, that I realized how much trouble she went to every weekend.

I remember Bobba Grauman for the savoury and Bobba Chait for the sweet! We never went hungry with either.

I remember that I always felt sorry for Uncle Hymie, because you used to talk of how hard it was for him, with there being drought. I remember as a child wondering what would happen to him. Would he have enough to eat? How was he making a living? With the current drought in Australia, I always think of him and wonder why he didn't do something else; why he chose such a solitary life. How did he end up potato farming??

I remember not knowing much about Auntie Polly. Not knowing even that she had been adopted out. I remember always feeling sorry for her too, always applying the word "invalid" to her. It seemed to me that Bobba took charge. Polly was totally dependent on her.

I remember when the two Bobbas came to visit us in Melbourne. I remember waiting for it so anxiously and living through the three months with equal measures of adolescent impatience and child-like fascination for her grandparents. I loved that they came together. When they left I remember wondering if I would ever see them again.

I remember taking Daniel to meet Bobba Chait in JHB in 1992. It was so difficult for her because she really couldn't see much anymore. She was adept at "feeling" her way around. I remember looking at her hands- which had become her eyes- and thinking they looked old, swollen. I wanted to tell her it was OK to touch my and Daniel's faces, as I sensed she couldn't really make them out so well anymore. But I didn't want to embarrass her. I remember her and Polly and Hymie's joy at our visit. I remember Polly was tiny in her chair. Like a small child. We went to Bobba's room, then had tea out on the patio. It was a lovely sunny day. When we left I knew that would be the last time we saw them. I was so glad they got to meet Daniel.

I remember that Uncle Hymie always smiled. He had small, crinkly eyes, surrounded by smile lines. I don't remember his face being stern, serious or even just neutral. Just smiling all the time. Always.

I don't have any other specific memories…just a general sense of Bobba. She was a giver; a feeder. She was not demonstrable with her love. I don't recall being covered in kisses or being hugged and held. I recall being fed. I recall her smile.

Brad, Elana and Nadine
18 Feb. 1996 Elana's wedding

Annette, Brad and Abe
12 June 1994 - Brad's wedding

Ian and Elana, Abe and Annette, Nadine and Daniel and Dina and Brad at Nadine and Daniel's wedding on 5 September 1995

Gavin, Mary, Sidney and David at David's wedding

BRAD'S MEMORIES OF BOBBA CHAIT

What I remember is going to visit Bobba and Aunty Polly in their flat on weekends. I remember the lavish tea parties with lots of cakes and biscuits. I remember the chocolate eclairs and the home made waffles. I know there was a park not too far away from their flat which had a water slide. I remember them coming to our house too, but I can't say I remember having much interaction with either of them. Aside from a sloppy kiss and a friendly smile, I can't honestly say that I recall things like having long conversations, playing games, or going to the movies with either of them. Perhaps because neither of them drove a car, I don't remember doing any activities that I see my kids now do with their grandparents.

I remember uncle Hymie coming over to visit on rare occasions. I think I remember him bringing a supermarket paper bag filled with chocolates for the kids. I remember that he would take me for drives in his ute - I would stand in the back and hold on to the bar. Other than this, again I don't recall any personal interaction with him. He may very well have spent one on one time with me but I can't honestly say I recall kicking a ball with him or having a chat about school. I certainly don't remember ever visiting him on his farm.

SARAH'S GREAT GRANDCHILDREN

Jarryd, Kaidyn and Shayn (Elana and Ian Chait's sons)

Jarryd   *Kaidyn*   *Shayn*

Simone and Adam, children of Brad and Dina Grauman.

Yazmin, Brooklyn and Harlan, children of Nadine and Daniel Judd.

Back Adam and Brooklyn
Front Simone and Yazmin

Harlan

QUESTIONAIRE FOR MOISHE LIPSHITZ

This questionnaire was filled in for Moishe and his siblings on admittance to the orphanage in Rovno which was supported by the Joint Distribution Committee.

Perel Lipschitz

Last address: Vishke in Vladeve

Name of mother: Sheindel; [Living with] family: Shneiderman
Which of the parents died: Father;

Cause of death: He was murdered by the Balachowitzes

When: September 1920

Does he have any property: Everything was destroyed

How many children: six; Boys three; Girls three.

Name and condition of the children over 14 years:
Freyde, 17 years old, was raped by the Balachowitzes; Perel 12 years old; Beile nine years old; Pesakh four years old was adopted.

Has the child attended school: Yes; Which one: a kheyder.

Receiving a subsidy: Yes

TRANSLATION OF QUESTIONAIRE
Courtesy Veronica Belling

Region: Vladeve; City: Vladeve   Province: Siedlicz; Date 5/II

Name and surname: Moishe Lipshitz

With whom is the child living: With the mother; Address 449 Vladeve Vishker

Date of birth: 1914

Name of father: Avraham Yitzhak; Occupation: Land worker;

PEREL AND MOISHE LIPSHITZ
Written by Harriette Zive

My mother Perel Lipshitz was born in Vlodawa Poland. Her father was in the forest industry. Perel once told me that he wanted to immigrate with the family to the USA, however, he was turned down as he had trachoma, which today is curable.

She saw her father shot and killed by a Polish soldier and ran with her younger brother, Moishe and other children into the forest.

The children were subsequently rescued and taken to South Africa. Perel and Moishe were taken into Arcadia orphanage.

She left the orphanage at age 14 and subsequently worked in a department store in Johannesburg. She never liked to talk about her experiences.

Perel married my father Abel and they had two children, Adele and me, Harriette. We grew up in Johannesburg.

Moishe unfortunately died as a young man and had no family.

Perel had four grandchildren, Sheryl, Janette, Kevin and Laurian. After my father Abel passed away Perel came to Canada to join Harriette's family. She never discussed her life in Poland or in the orphanage. She loved being with us in Cananda.

Her hobbies were knitting, crocheting and embroidering.

She was very happy when Adele and her family also immigrated to Canada.

She passed away in 2002.

My sister, Adele has one daughter, Laurian, who is married, lives in Canada and has two children, Taryn and Joshua. My husband, Max and I were married in South Africa. We have three children, Sheryl, Janette and Kevin. They are all married and live in Toronto Canada. Sheryl has three children, Ethan, Drew and Reid. Janette has two children, Sophia and Madeleine and Kevin have two children Lilly and Ella.

Perel in front, daughter and son-in-law behind

Perel and her grandchild

Perel and her husband Abel

Perel and her granddaughter

Chapter 115 – REISEL AND ITZIK MUSSMAN

A STORY OF TWO ORPHANS
Written by Lali Sher

Most South African parents travel all over the world visiting their children and grandchildren, and we are no exception. On a trip to Australia last year after seeing our son and daughter-in-law in Perth, we spent some time in Melbourne with my husband's niece, Joan and her husband Jack Queit.

One evening as we were sitting and chatting late into the night, I shared with them the mystery of my ancestry. For some time now I have been thinking about my mother's life and feeling a strange emptiness in my heart. It was a story untold. My mother had simply told me that she was an orphan and was adopted by the Golanskys who lived in Benoni.

She spoke very little about her childhood except to say that she had a sad and difficult time and she was a very unhappy little girl. She remembered that she was found with her older brother holding her hand and brought to South Africa on a ship. She had no memory of any details (or maybe did not want to talk about it).

As I was telling this story I noticed Jack looking at me very strangely. "But that is my mothers story" he said! And I have found out what happened to her" He then proceeded to tell me the Ochberg story!

He introduced me to David Sandler, who was a veritable mine of information, and then to Lauren Snitcher who introduced me to Solly Jossel. Seeing the wonderful documentary at his flat was a very moving and emotional experience!

My mother's name was Reisel (Ray) Mussman and my uncle, Itzik (Jack) Mussman. Lauren sent photographs and passport numbers 7 and 9. I think I recognise my mother but I am not yet sure. My uncle was immediately recognisable. I have established that he grew up at Arcadia, but the only mention of his name in the Arcadia Centenary book was in a list of those who served in World War 2.

I found out that my mother was in Arcadia for the first three years and then she and Itzik were both signed for and taken to Benoni by Bertha Golansky. (It seems that there was no such thing as formal adoption in those days.) Itzik was subsequently sent back to Arcadia. (I haven't found out why, maybe he was too naughty.)

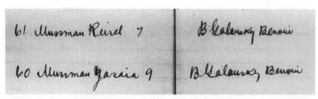

Extracts from the register kept by the South African Jewish Orphanage - The age of the children is listed after the name and they both went to live with B Golansky who lived in Benoni.

Morris and Bertha Golansky who adopted Ray

My uncle was known as Jack Mussman, and may be remembered by that name. He was married and had a beautiful daughter, Jacqueline and a grandchild, but I have been unable to trace them. The last time I saw them was at Jack's funeral in 1991 and I am very keen to contact them.

My mother's stories about her childhood sound like the story of Cinderella. She was a sad and lonely little girl, brought up as an only child. They called her Ray. She had two cousins. Rita was glamorous with long black hair, and Lucy was the perky, mischievous one. My mother felt that they were the favourites in the family, and was often left out.

I can't imagine how it must have been for this childless couple to adopt a child who couldn't speak English, and had suffered such trauma in her short life.

Ray left school at sixteen and went to a commercial college. When she qualified she went to work as a secretary in a hardware business called "Cohen and Levin". It wasn't long before she recognised her handsome prince and fell in love with her boss, Abe Levin.

By the time she was eighteen, they had a dream wedding. Within a year I was born, followed twenty two months later by my sister Ellinore. The youngest daughter, Glenda, was born twelve years after me. I always had the feeling my father would have loved to have a boy in the family

Ray at 19

The Jewish press cutting of the wedding of Ray Golansky (Reisel Mussman) to Abe Levin which took place on January 6th 1935, in Benoni

GOLANSKY - LEVIN

The marriage was solemnised at the New Synagogue, Benoni on Sunday evening, between Ray, only daugher of Mr and Mrs M Golansky of Benoni, and Abe, eldest son of Mrs S Levin and the late Mr Levin.

The bride, who was given away by her father, wore a beautiful gown of white satin which was cut on slim-fitting lines and terminated in a long train. It was trimmed with silver and appliqued with net, and her pretty Juliet cap of silver trellis work secured her graceful veil of white tulle. She carried a bouquet of white roses and maidenhair fern.

The Rev S Backon officiated at the ceremony and the Synagogue was packed with friends and well wishers of the bride and bridegroom.

The bridesmaids - Misses Sylvia Cohen, Phyllis Peltz, Freda Steinbaum and Rita Sack wore pretty frocks of green, pink and parma violet respectively, their headdress being Juliet caps of silver and tulle. They carried bouquets of pink carnations and maidenhair fern.

The two little flower girls, Mary Price and Sylvia Saffer, wore dainty frocks of pink. Messrs Jack Morrisman, Joe Golomb, Oscar Levin and Louis Chamey were the canopy bearers, and the groomsmen were Messrs Michael Kasin, Issy Kay, Mannie Pelts and Hyman Kasin.

Mr and Mrs R Golansky and Mr and Mrs H Flocks acted as unterfuhrers.

The Reception

Following the religious ceremony, a largely attended reception was held in the Hebrew Hall, where the Rev S Backon proposed the toast of the bride and bridegroom and Mr S Legator vice president of the BOD presented the Kiddish Cup.

The bride's mother, Mrs Golansky, wore a charming navy two-piece ensemble trimmed with lace and Mrs Levin, mother of the bridegroom was attired in a smart black two-piece gown.

When Mr and Mrs Levin left for their honeymoon, which is to be spent on a trip round the coast, the bride wore a becoming two-piece suit of Marina blue with hat and shoes to match.

Ray with Lali (Lorraine) aged two

Abe and Ray with Lali and Ellinore

Ray and Abe with Lali and Ellinore and little Glenda

I remember Morris Golansky as a genial smiling huggable grandfather who owned a bakery in Benoni called 'Rae's Bakery." My memories of him are filled with the smell of freshly baked bread. Friday night's challah was a delight to look forward to. Our birthday cakes were creative masterpieces, each year a new creation.

My father was something of a visionary. He was born in Lithuania and came out to seek his fortune on the diamond mine in Lichtenberg and was able to bring almost his entire family to South Africa.

With his new wife he started from a humble beginning in an old Terrace Road, Doornfontein home to a face brick house across the road from Darras Nurseries in Kensington. Then he followed his vision to a magnificent heritage home in Parktown with the lush garden that he had envisioned for so many years.

"This is an aerial photo of the 2.5 acre home that Abe and Ray lived in for many years, giving an idea of Ray's rags-to-riches Cinderella life."

Morris Golansky with Ray about 1946

536

JACK (ITZIK) MUSSMAN, MY HERO
A story I wrote about my uncle Jack (Itzik) Mussman.

"YOUR COUNTRY NEEDS YOU" screamed the poster.

Uncle Jack answered the call and went up North to fight the enemy. Eye-tye and Jerry he called them. Yanks and Brits were the Allies. The year was 1940.

My sister and I, too young to remember him, heard mom and dad tell about how brave he was. We were proud that we had an uncle who was a soldier, and carried a gun.

Our childhood loss in a war-torn world was the absence of chocolate and chewing gum. "Rationing" mom said. She knitted socks for Uncle Jack, packed into boxes with bully beef tins, soup and dried milk.

Every day we waited at the little red post box for a letter from Uncle Jack. When we heard the dogs barking up the road we knew the postman was on his way. One day he flung an official looking envelope into my hands and walked on. My mother opened it with trembling hands
.
"We regret to inform you that Private Jack Musman has been taken prisoner and is presently in an Italian Prisoner of War camp"

Mom gasped and ran inside. Had to lie down….a headache. She often had headaches after that day.

We played games imagining how it feels in a prisoner of war camp. When my sister was the prisoner. I tied her up with my favourite blue hair ribbon. Made her stand in a corner until she begged for mercy. We ate bread and water for lunch to see what it feels like. Afterwards we gobbled cottage pie.

Four years later the great day came, 8 May1945.

We listened to the radio A tinny voice crackled the news "the war is over and peace is declared Germany surrenders…Hitler is dead…Unconditional surrender." and no school today!
Whirling a desert sandstorm around the room…listening again and again to the news. What does all this mean? Uncle Jack is coming home.

For weeks we were in a flurry of cooking and cleaning and shining the house for Uncle Jack. He had not slept in a real bed for five years, or tasted home-made soup. Mom made a get-better soup for us when we were ill. A simmer of fresh vegetables, bay leaves and chicken. A healing balm to this day.

We wanted to make everything perfect for Uncle Jack to make him feel welcomed and loved because mom and her brother were war orphans. Mom at two and Uncle Jack a year older wandered the snowy fields in war torn Poland. Hand in hand, both with cornflower blue eyes. Rescuers found them and brought them to South Africa in a ship

A new bed, soft and comfy as a mother's love. Fresh brand-new linen, crisp as a biscuit. Cuddly blankets and the view of a Jacaranda garden.

My sister and I drew big posters in rainbow colours welcoming our hero home.

On an early wintry morning crowds surged into the Union Grounds from all over Johannesburg. Children waiting for fathers never known, wives whose lives had changed, families who did not know if their loved ones would return.

My sister and I wore our prettiest dresses - candy frills in pink and blue, with big bows in our newly washed hair. Aglow with excitement. Will he see me first?

Our family took our places high up on the grandstand looking down on rows of expectant faces and the still empty parade ground. We yo-yo'd up and down the steps waving our flags, stamping and chanting our little song---

"Uncle Jack
just got back
haven't seen you
For donkeys ears
But I still nose you!"

Mom and Dad were strangely quiet, Mom twisting her handkerchief in her hands. I thought I saw a tear in her eye, but I couldn't be sure, maybe dust? After all, who would want to cry on a day like this?
The band played my favourite song…

We'll meet again
don't know where
don't know when
we'll meet again
some sunny day.

Today was the day! All eyes on the gate.

A hush fell upon the crowd. In the distance we could hear the rhythm of the march, getting louder and louder. The crowd began to cheer as stamping feet swayed the grandstand. .

The phalanx of soldiers appeared, marching in perfect time, eyes straight ahead. A field of golden brown reeds spreading rhythmically over the parade ground.
"There he is!"
"I see him!"
"No that can't be him!"
"But it is …"

The crowd surges forward as the troops break ranks and golden brown is everywhere. People are running to their loved ones… Except us….
"Where is Uncle Jack?"
A sea of people … nobody looks familiar.

I see mom crying and hugging someone… a man brown as a nut, with eyes the same deep-sea blue as hers. Could that be Uncle Jack?

I feel shy and hide behind my sister. He walks over and lifts us both high in the air with strong arms. As the swift adrenaline hits my stomach the tears spurt. We are all crying and laughing and hugging.

At home we can't wait to show Uncle Jack what we have prepared for him. We run ahead pointing to his brand new bed, the room filled with flowers from the garden; a blue shirt to match his eyes, folded carefully on the plump eiderdown. He looks doubtful and calls it "civvies." We pull him into the dining room to see the table with the embroidered cloth only for visitors.

Mom brings out the meal she has lovingly prepared…. aromatic chicken soup, lamb chops grilled with fresh vegetables. .

Uncle Jack takes two spoonfuls of soup and puts his spoon down. We stare at him confused.
"Sorry I just can't eat this. I'm not used to eating rich food."

Mom looks at Dad and I see her lip trembling. Uncle Jack digs in his pocket and pulls out a silver tin with a picture of a camel on it.
"Think I'll have a smoke."

In seconds the room is filled with smoky spheres. We climb onto his knee, squealing with glee as we compete to break the most smoke circles.

After supper he opens his kitbag filled with loot. We cluster around and a handful of stars spill over the deep burgundy of the carpet. Jewels of every colour- gold, silver, butterfly wings. A treasure trove of Egyptian magic. Images of pyramids, palm trees, a shimmer of oasis in a mirage. Adorned and glowing we dance around him singing our special song.

"Uncle Jack
just got back
haven't see you
for donkeys ears
but I still nose you!"

We got to sleep late that night, warm in teddy bear pyjamas. I dreamed of flying over the pyramids on the sheen of a butterfly's wing.

Uncle Jack's midnight screams howl through the quiet suburban streets.

The next morning we found uncle Jack curled up in his khaki sleeping bag on the cement floor of the veranda.
"Sorry, not used to sleeping on a bed."

"Uncle Jack
just got back……….

WHEN THE ORPHANS CAME TO DINNER

This is a piece I wrote the first time I went to Arcadia. At that point I did not know anything about my Mom or Uncle being Ochberg Orphans nor did I know that my Uncle had been in the care of Arcadia. I did not even know that it used to be an orphanage! I simply went to a dinner and book launch.

May 2007- Launch of David Goldblatt's book of photographs

I dined last night in "Arcadia"
a silvery room, high ceilinged
redolent of haute cuisine
antique crystal and silk tablecloths

Once the mansion of a Randlord
A Herbert Baker home.

now a conference venue
elegant icon of urban crawl

I hear whisperings
under the table
wide-eyed children
spat out of the pogroms of Poland

I see shadowy figures
the ghosts of orphans
who lived here, rescued
after world wars.

small children
invisible among the guests
their empty bellies groan
skinny legs goosebumped

They wander pale
amongst the crowd
searching each face for signs
'Are you mine?'

One boy
with cornflowers in his eyes
my mother's eyes,
cornflowers too
his eyes beseech me

oblivious, guests laugh and guzzle
Wine flowing
intent on fine conversation,
the completion of a meal.

They go home,
kiss their children good night
tuck them into bed
leaving the cries
unheard.

All night,
the unwanted stalk my dreams

Two small children
brother and sister
walk hand in hand
amongst the dead.

together on the ship
nametags
around their necks
not knowing where or why
they yearn for mama.

 A wisp of memory
tickles my heart
a disconsolate man
an uncle tall and pale.
a man with cornflower eyes
He told me a tale of the 'Arc'

in my childish way
it seemed to be Noah's Ark
a sturdy houseboat
Carrying giraffes, tigers,
leopards, elephants

Now I know it was that night
at the place of silver and silk .
Arcadia, once an orphanage
In a room that resonated
with sacred liturgy
and the prayers of children
mourning the dead.

I dined on ancestral ground

this blue eyed boy
the link to my origins.
did he live those days
unloved?

Jack Mussman with daughter Jackie

JACARANDA SHADE
A fragment of childhood memory

After school afternoons
Tea on the lawn
Shaded with Jacaranda…
mulberry jam sandwiches
crunchy apples
juice dribbles
sticky, on the mohair rug

Mom tells stories of when she was a little girl
 adopted by a heartless woman
who gave bread without butter
 a home without love
One day a handsome prince on a white steed
 galloped to her rescue
 they lived happily ever after
.
We burst into delighted laughter
mom's stories always end in happily- ever- afters

As the Jacaranda purples my hair
I am wombed in its shade.

RAY'S LATER YEARS AND HER DAUGHTERS

By this time my parents had acquired a knowledge and love of antiques and their new home was filled with rare and special pieces. My mother loved beauty and colour. She filled our home with great jugs of cascading greenery, garnished with brilliant colours, the garden a never ending source of inspiration for her.

This beautiful garden was the scene of our wedding on 25 November 1956.

My husband, Raphael Sher and I have four sons... Steven was born in 1957, twins Graeme and Russel in 1959 and Brett in1963. They all had a loving relationship with their adoring grandparents.

Soon after Brett was born my father had a heart attack and was told by the doctors to take it easy, give up the business and take up a "hobby" And so it was that he became a numismatist, and opened a little coin shop in Jeppe Street. He was passionate about his hobby, which soon included small antique pieces, and became a thriving business.

About eight years later he was diagnosed with cancer A few months later he died, and my mother was once again abandoned and alone. Our family were living in Cape Town and my sisters were overseas.

My mother was desolate and inconsolable and began to have some strange symptoms which manifested in an inability to walk. She was soon confined to a wheel chair. Doctors diagnosed a mild stroke as the cause of the problem, but sadly without a solution. We came back to live in Johannesburg. Ellinore was still living in Israel and Glenda in America.

It was quite amazing how my mother coped with her disability. She took up bridge and played regularly. She still ran a beautiful home, always flower-filled, and the fridge full of home cooked and baked goodies. She started painting, and her walls were filled with paintings of biblical themes in luminous colours. Needing more help, she moved to a retirement village and employed a day and night nurse. It was only in the last two years that she had to give up her little flat and move to frail care where she became the beloved patient of her caregivers.

When I look at her life I am filled with admiration for her courage in the face of the childhood trauma which was repeated in later years when she was left vulnerable and alone and in a wheelchair for twenty four years. I will always remember her smiling with a twinkle in her cornflower blue eyes.

My sister Ellinore lived in Israel with her husband Cecil and two children Hayley and Andrew. Sadly Ellinore died of ovarian cancer at the age of sixty four, in 2002. Andrew now lives in Chicago with his wife Dana and three children Dean, Aaron and Maya. Hayley lives in Tel Aviv with her two children Eilon and Ohad

After a few years in the USA, my sister, Glenda came back to Johannesburg. Sadly she died at the age of fifty three on her birthday. She had no children.

When I think of my wonderful family, my husband Raphael, darling sons and daughters-in law and grandchildren, I am so grateful for the miracle of Isaac Ochberg.

I honour this man who had the courage to take this journey which changed the lives of so many.

Ray with Jack's daughter, Jacqueline

Ray's birthday, probably 1973, after Abe had died and she was already in a wheel chair. Ellinore is on the left, Lali behind her, Glenda next to her mother.

FOR ELLINORE

A poem I wrote for my sister on the day she died of ovarian cancer. April 2002

Eastern gold splashes into the city
the tree outside my window loses another leaf
already an icy sky
just another day.

I think of you this morning, my sister
separated by many countries
across the patchwork of Africa
yet we share our mother's womb
I, softening the way for you
we share the innocence of our childhood….
sitting on the worn mohair rug spread on the lawn
hair purpled by Jacaranda blossoms
a platter of thinly sliced fruit between us…
our mother tells us stories of heroines
with long golden hair
awakened by lovers, and carried off
on the back of a white steed.
open mouthed in deep listening
we jump for joy to hear the end…
they always lived happily ever after...
a lifetime of secrets and ceremonies
taffeta dresses…
tears and giggles

locked in the dark of the cupboard
I try not to cry
you cry for me, my sister…
I wait, alone and afraid…
your tears beg for my release…
 for my release..
I tumble out into the light

… and then our lovers came along
awakened us,
carried us off on their white steeds…
to vow our sacred pact
under the silken canopy…
and life became serious.
and then you went away
 left the golden city
for the spirit of Jerusalem.

our children changed our lives forever
they taught us love
we nurtured and grew them into heroes and princesses.
our grandchildren taught us how to laugh and play
and awed us with the miracle of their being.

an ordinary day….
but not for you.

long blonde hair gone
you ride the raging bull of cancer
bareback
alone you face the great mystery
I cry for you, my sister
my tears beg for your release
you gather fierce courage
to scream breathlessly through a seamless wall of fire
scorching your body…purifying your heart…
and then you see your soul in the face of God.

MY TRIBUTE TO ISAAC OCHBERG

Written by Raphael Sher

I first became aware of Isaac Ochberg when visiting the Jewish Museum in Cape Town in 2007. A lifesize photograph was displayed with details of the Ochberg Orphan story. At the time I noted the exhibit with no more than passing interest, but today he has become vivid in my experience.

I am only now beginning to realise how powerfully his initiative in 1921 influenced my life.

The curious thing is that every time I think or speak of him, the image of an apple comes to mind. Why an apple, what's the connection?

It's this quotation:
"You can count the seeds in an apple, but you will never be able to count the apples in just one seed."

Isaac Ochberg in what appeared to be an act of kindness and generosity, (although in fact, it was an intentional, purposeful, socially-conscious act) saved the lives of one hundred and sixty seven hopeless, pathetic war-torn orphans, and what followed has affected me in the outworking.

One orphaned girl, Reisel Mussman, rescued by Ochberg lived out her Cinderella charmed life. She provided the gift of my wife, our four wonderful sons, and our four beautiful grandchildren.

How many apples from the Ochberg tree? How about the other one hundred and sixty six apples? And who knows how many more that followed? *Overcountable,* we used to say in grade one.

I acknowledge with gratitude the enormous impact of Isaac Ochberg's legacy. His heroic intervention has enriched the lives of countless people continuing over generations.

The wedding of Jacqueline, daughter of Jack (Itzik) and Audrey Musman. Jack is on the left, next to his wife and daughter. That marriage produced one child and since Ray died in 1995, we haven't seen Jacqie and have been unable to trace her. We know that she divorced some fifteen years ago. That picture is a rare one showing Jack in happier moments of a tough life.

Chapter 116 – SOLLY JOSSEL (SALOMON NEUSTEIN)

Solly Jossel has a very detailed chapter in More Arc Memories where he relates his experience as a seven year old Ochberg Orphan. Also included in part one of this book is his Solly's first hand account.

Solly, Aaron and Nechama Josselowitz and their daughter Ethel – "Solly's wonderful adopted parents"

REMEMBERING SOLLY'S ADOPTIVE PARENTS, AARON AND NECHAMA JOSSELOWITZ.
Written by Solly's wife Sylvia

I express these stories from the bottom of my heart to show you how much both his adopted parents adored him and in turn, how much Solly adored them from the very day he set eyes on this woman Mrs Josselowitz who he attached himself to as a five year old. He was a true son to them both in every possible way.

Solly's adoptive parents Aaron and Nechama Josselowitz were extremely poor. They had a little grocery store and his Dad was a very soft hearted man. When people weren't able to pay their monthly bill he would always say to his wife, "Don't worry them for payment. They need what they have bought. Let them enjoy the food."

Being so poor themselves, when Solly turned 16 they told him they could no longer afford to spend more money for his education and he should therefore go and look for a job. Solly then found himself a job with a firm S Malk & Co, wholesalers. He was employed as a clerk with the salary of five pounds sterling, which in those days was a lot of money.

For this salary he had to pack goods into the shelves etc and it was at this stage when the boss wasn't looking he used to study in order to better himself.

However, when he received his very first salary (five pounds sterling) his adopted Mother immediately sent this money to his biological Mother, although she needed it herself as she knew how much this money would mean to Eva Neustein. That was the sort of Parents that adopted this little boy. Warm caring loving people.

It was this little story that made me look up old photos of Solly with his Mother (Mrs Nechama Josselowitz) which was taken a few years after Solly and I were married.

Nechama, Solly and Sylvia and their children

Solly with his Mother Nechama   *Nechama and Sylvia*

In September 1947 Solly had to travel to Beira on a business trip. His Father Mr Aron Josselowitz was at the time 79 years old. He took ill and in fact actually went into an unconscious state. I desperately tried to reach Solly by phone, but the lines between Beira and Johannesburg were down. About two days later Solly reached Lourenza Marques and in the normal way he had whilst away from home he phoned me. I told him to rush home immediately as his Father was so critically ill and he did so.

Just before his Father went into a state of unconsciousness he made a statement to us all on his dying bed in fact. He said in Yiddish to us who were at his bedside together with the Doctor in attendance "Children - don't worry about me. I will not die

until my son Shleime (he always used this name rather than Solly) is at my side." The Doctor told us that there was no hope any more - the man was in fact dying.

Solly arrived at the airport at 10 am on 10 September 1947 and I rushed him to his Father's side. His Father opened his eyes for the first time in two days, took Solly's hand in his and said "Shleime, my Son". The Doctor pronounced him dead at 2:15 pm on 10 September 1947.

This was the bond they shared and they were connected through love and not blood. His Father had actually waited for Solly to be at his side before he let go.

Five months later I delivered a bonnie little boy, Anthony whom we named after his beloved Father, Aaron which is our middle son's Hebrew name.

MY GRANDPA SOLLY
Written by Jodi Fittinghoff

Great Grandpa Solly with Tayne who is blessed to have four living Grandparents in his life.

My Grandpa Solly is the most humble, yet strong man. Full of wisdom on life and life events which have carved him to be the unique gentleman he is today. Because of his presence the world is simply a better place. Because of the care and love he shows to others, lives are touched and changed. Because of the generosity of his spirit, others feel hope.

There is a special bond and relationship I share with my grandparents. I am so blessed to have them both as such big parts of my life. They have made an impact on my life that I will never every forget.

Four generations – Jodi, Granny Sylvia holding
Tayne (Jodi's son) and Bernice (Jodi's Mom)

I never dreamt that I would have so much more than just a Grandpa and that I do and so my wish for my Grandpa is that he has and will always get more than he dreams of.

May my Grandpa Solly always know that I love him and am so very proud of him and who he is, and very proud to be his Granddaughter. This I do think he knows.
And to end, a quote which sums it all up,
"Grandpas are dads with lots of frosting."

Sylvia, champion More Arc Memories bookseller writes "Photo of our Great-grandchildren taken 13 August 2009, our 65th wedding anniversary. Solly turned 95 on 27 July.
Front: Sylvia, Tayne 4 months, Rafael 20 months and Solly
Back: Amy 19 months, Ryan 7 years and Saul 3 years."

MY HUSBAND SOLLY
Written by Solly's wife Sylvia

Usually it is either children or grandchildren who would write something about their parent but I feel that there is nobody better able than me, his wife, to tell you something about this amazing man. After all, who would know him better? It is indeed my privilege to be married for the past 65 years to 'an Ochberg Orphan', Solly Jossel, born Salomon Neustein who was adopted by the family Josselowitz at the age of six years old.

My first meeting with Solly was actually when I was only a child of ten years old. My late Father was doing business with him and he came to our house on a business meeting. I was in school uniform and he was a grown up man. Little did I know then that fate was to play its part in both our lives.

Eight years later I was introduced to Solly at a function of the Red Cross Organisation by the partner I was with and that evening set the path of this story. I was then 18 years old doing Army service in the South African Forces and Solly was a young man of 29 discharged from the Army through ill health.

After we were formally introduced it was only a matter of a week later that he phoned me requesting a date. I was not aware then that he was the young man whom I had seen meeting with my Father. I only discovered this some months after we were dating, as my Father had passed away when I was 15 years old.

We dated for a number of months and I was almost sure from the first date that he would be the man I would marry. I knew very little about him then, other than the fact that he was a charming young man who had been an Orphan and had been brought up by loving parents whom I only met after we had been dating for three months.

I was on embarkation leave at the time and his proposal to me was "Why go to Egypt and become a Mummy? If you get out of going I will make you a South African Mummy"

It was not easy for me to get out of the Army as I had taken "The Red Tape Oath" and my unit was due to leave in a matter of days, however, on his medical grounds discharge I was able to get out by informing my Commanding Officer that we were going to get married and Solly needed somebody to look after him. Pulling lots of strings at the time I managed to avoid going overseas.

My Mother was strongly against my marriage and tried her best to stop it. Both Solly and I understood her reasonings; firstly because she knew he was a sick man suffering from a bleeding ulcer which my Father had passed away from and secondly because she kept saying that we really didn't know anything about his biological family and who they were or what sort of people had he been born to.

Against all arguments I just knew that he could not have come from anything but good people as he himself was such a warm, loving and honourable man and his adoptive parents were highly respected people who had brought him up with love and care. No doubt his illness of the ulcer was caused from malnurtrition having been in an Orphanage from the age of barely two years old.

Our marriage took place on 13 August 1944. He was indeed a very sick man and had many days when his ulcer would bleed and he spent a lot of time in hospital. We still managed to produce a son and although he was so ill he was involved in many charitable affairs. As you will see from his CV he was involved in everything that was either charity or religous. He always said and still to this day says, he wanted to give back what he had received and in order to do this he has spent his entire life doing charitable work both in Jewish and Non Jewish communities.

Solly was born on 27 July, which makes him a Leo and believe me he is indeed "The Lion" in every respect. He has always been a leader, very determined but in a very gentle manner. He was very strict bringing up his three children and particularly with his daughter Bernice, but again only with love and gentleness. He demands obedience in everything he does.

When our son Manfred was nine months old, Solly was forced to have an operation for his ulcer. He was forced to give up his wholesale business which he managed to sell to his existing partner. The operation was one of the first of its kind in those days. Until then, the operation was a short circuit of the ulcer but in Solly's operation they did a new experimental operation and removed three quarters of his stomach. As you know TG he has survived and is now almost 96 years old. He is still capable of being "A Lion", still full of the joys of living, still always the centre of attention whereever he goes in spite of his poor eye-sight and hearing problem.

He still works from home doing what he does best, looking after his existing clients in the Insurace field. His advice to his clients is always taken as his clients adore him and they won't allow him to give up on them. He works now mornings only instead of full day which I believe gives him the will to carry on living. His brain is as sharp as it was when we got married and his memory is outstanding. He is an amazing gentleman loved by his three children, their respective spouses, his grandchildren and his great-grandchildren and by me, Sylvia his wife. I cannot even imagine a life without him.

Solly and Sylvia Jossel at the Arc Reunion 1 November 2009

A TRIBUTE TO SOLLY
Written by son Manfred

I consider it a very special honor to share memories of Solly Jossel, my dad.

One of the lucky "Ochberg Orphans" brought to South Africa in 1921 by the philanthropist, Isaac Ochberg, dad was placed in an orphanage in Johannesburg, together with the other Ochberg Orphans.

Word spread quickly and the intrigued and inquisitive came to look at these orphan children from Poland. One elderly couple, with no intention whatsoever of adopting a child, were part of the crowd visiting the orphanage. During their visit, a small six year old boy clung desperately to the woman's skirt and would not leave her side. She must have reminded him of his own loving mother he had sadly left behind in Poland. Being compassionate and caring, this wonderful couple adopted the clinging child into their family and so began the rest of my dad's journey...

Dad's new parents were extremely poor and as they could not afford to educate him, he was forced to leave school at an early age. Working odd jobs to help support his new parents and to educate himself, he eventually achieved his higher education by attending night school. Solly Jossel is the true essence of what it means to become a successful self-made man!

I always believed that dad would be the most unlikely person to live a long, healthy and prosperous life. During our annual vacations, we would be sitting on the beach and I would invite my dad to swim with me in the ocean. "No thanks, I don't like swimming." Or, I would beg him to play ball with me, and the answer was always a polite but firm, "No, I don't enjoy doing that." Whenever I asked him to help me fly my kite—that too was declined with a firm, "Sorry but it's not my thing." Whenever his friends invited him to play tennis, he would decline, albeit graciously, with, "I'll just sit and enjoy the sun."

Sadly, all of the friends he turned down have passed on, and here's my dad—enjoying life—and still watching everyone else play sport. He believes that we are given a certain amount of heart beats, and by participating in physically demanding activity one uses up the beats! By sitting around, and observing others has possibly saved the beats which have allowed him to keep going past what is considered a "normal" lifespan.

Thinking back, the only time I remember my dad doing anything resembling exercise was when he chased me around the house and into the garden after I had done something inappropriate. He finally caught up with me... I ducked—and instead of his hand connecting with my head—it hit the wall and began to bleed. That was the one time I ever recall him running. It was also the last time I ever attempted to escape his wrath!

The closest my dad ever got to swimming was when he would ease himself slowly into the water of our home swimming pool. Gripping the edge of the pool with one hand and with a bristle brush in the other, he would carefully maneuver his way around and scrub the walls. When he reached the deep end he would take a breath, let go and while underwater begin scrubbing returning to the surface when he ran out of breath. There was a day when instead of remaining close to the wall, he pushed back a little too far and could not find the edge he needed to cling to. After a while, I noticed both of his hands flaying desperately above his head and felt that he might need help. I dived and saved him from drowning. He never got into the pool again.

Dad has always kept a small pocket diary in his top pocket to record important family birthdays and anniversaries. One day concerned that the swimming pool was not being kept clean, he leaned over to look at the bottom of the pool and his diary fell into the water. For hours the entire family took turns blow drying the small diary one page at a time.

Contrary to medical advice and despite eating three full meals each day, dad constantly grazes on candy, cookies, dried fruits and nuts. Having had major abdominal surgery as a young man, he feels that he needs to eat all day to remain healthy. Although he takes in a huge amount of calories daily, he maintains the same weight as he had as a young man. During our telephone calls I often ask what he has eaten that week and he always responds with *herring*. Naturally, I eat herring, as I too strive to live to a healthy ninety-seven!

Dad is constantly looking for new doctors, as his [doctors] are no longer around. Perhaps they should have followed his advice about eating herring and not exerting oneself ?

Catnaps are an important part of my dad's life. He has the ability to fall-asleep standing in a store line while waiting to be served and immediately wakes up feeling as though he had just had a good eight hour sleep. He has been able to do this his entire life and I believe this too has enhanced the many years he now enjoys.

Even though my dad is not a particularly religious man, he set a wonderful example by taking me to shul every Saturday. My mom has always kept a strict kosher home out of respect for dad. He was president of our synagogue for as long as I can remember and active in city government for many years. An astute and successful businessman, we learned by watching and listening. Even to this day, whenever we discuss a business transaction over the phone, he always suggests trying for another ten percent, if possible. Even though he was never one for coming to school activities, sports days or listening to me play in my band, he always encouraged me in everything I did.

I have a charitable dad who has always taught the importance of giving to those less fortunate. Even the small gesture of offering a piece of candy when he has run out of pocket change is touching. He fills his pockets with loose change and candy before leaving home every day. He has an effective way of diffusing an argument or stopping a fight by reaching into his pocket and taking out a piece of candy as a peace offering. And, it always works. My dad enjoys complimenting the ladies, letting them know how beautiful they look. By offering them a piece of candy they reward him with smiles and hugs. … We all know he does it for the hugs!

He is a stubborn man and will continue to argue about being right even if he is not. Offering him candy does not quite work in the same way with him…

My dad always stressed the importance of good manners and my siblings and I learned how to sit properly at the table and how to pull back a chair or open a car door for mom. This has stood me in good stead, as my wife appreciates it too. However, there was a time that I forgot my manners and something my mom often reminds me about. During meals I sat on the right of my dad at the dining table. I had a bad habit of always smelling the food placed in front of me and dad constantly told me that it was bad manners, and not to do it. One shabbos dinner, and as was my custom, I put my nose close to a bowl of hot chicken noodle soup and began to sniff. Without a word, my dad pushed my face straight into the bowl of soup. I never smelt my food again, and neither did I sit next to him again. This is fondly remembered as the "Manfred wore his noodles," incident.

To this day, at least twice a week my mom and dad get into their car and drive many miles to the surrounding casinos to enjoy dancing, gambling and eating. When last visiting Johannesburg, my wife and I spent a few hours with them at a local casino, where we were introduced to some of their friends and all four of us danced to the music of a local band. The highlight of the day is sharing their free muffin! They are a tremendous inspiration to everyone who knows them.

This remarkable man nearing ninety-seven years old is still vibrant and healthy with a remarkable zest for life. My dad's memory and his mind are sharp. He can figure out an amount faster than those using a calculator. From time to time he apologises for living on my third of the inheritance, to which I always respond, "Keep using it, it's my pleasure, enjoy." When asked what keeps him going for so many years he responds, "When one reaches 100 years one gets a Birthday congratulations letter from the Queen of England." He always continues with, "I'm nearly there I only hope that she'll still be here!"

My dad's eyesight is fading, but my mom reads the news to him every morning to keep him up to date with local and world events. My beautiful mom, ten years his junior, has been at my dad's side for over sixty-six years. She has loved him, worked with him, played with him and has supported and inspired him throughout their time together.

We talk often by phone, as I live in Los Angeles with my own family. Conversations are lively and interesting. Dad always has a joke to share, offering tidbits of social and political gossip, lessons on gold as a commodity and how the Rand has devalued or how much mom won at the poker machines. Of course there is always an in-depth report on his brilliant youngest great-grandchild.

I always promised myself that I would never repeat some of what my dad used to say, to my own growing children. The most annoying being, "When I was young I never had shoes and had to walk uphill bare feet in the snow by myself in the dark and here you are *needing* a car, and you are only 16?" Well dad—I did exactly the same—thanks for the lesson! How privileged I am at the age of almost sixty-six to still have a dad to learn from, especially from such a kind, generous man. He continues to be the best teacher one could ever wish for.

Mom and dad,
Your American children, grandchildren and great-grandchildren love you and wish you many more happy, healthy and enjoyable years for us to enjoy. We may be far away in miles and time, but you are always in our hearts.

SOLLY JOSSEL TURNS 96
Speech made by Jodi and Adam, Solly's grandchildren.

Jodi – "This is really a very special occasion -- it's all about a very special, unique gentleman and we are all gathered here today to help celebrate our Grandpa Solly's 96th birthday and third Barmitzvah - and that's just incredible to us.
Incredible because what a milestone to reach for any human being, and incredible because our Grandpa still has all the remarkable energies and enthusiasm of someone a lot younger. We are truly blessed to be his Grandchildren and in his honor would like to say a few words to him."

Adam – "Starting his life witnessing tragedy after tragedy, Grandpa Solly arrived in South Africa as one of the Ochberg Orphans. From an orphan of 7 who could not speak a word of English, to an extremely successful businessman who stills handles clients' accounts at the age of 96! What more can we say! Grandpa Solly has been successful at everything he has ever done and has never failed at anything he has ever tried. Highlights of every Shabbat dinner are hearing the emotional stories of his upbringing and incredible path of life, we hang on to every word you say and can only learn from your strength and wisdom."

Jodi - "One does not have to do anything to become a grandfather. It simply happens when your child has a child. It is up to you to decide how involved you will be in your grandchild's life. There is an inherent biological relationship but the emotional bonding between grandfather and grandchild comes only with effort. It happens when the grandchild sees that you are open to forming a relationship. It happens when you get off your easy chair and make the effort to see what matters to your grandchild"

These words are true to the relationship between my Grandfather and my brother Adam and myself. Adam and I were always aware of the effort both my Granny Sylvia and Grandpa Solly made in being a big part of our lives right from the very beginning and this has never stopped. This has led to the special bond and relationship that we share with them to this day....we are so blessed to have them both as such big parts of our life.

Adam – We always thought, or Grandpa Solly made us believe, that with age came poor eyesight. For Example, serving him meals at dinner, reading the newspaper to him, which don't get me wrong we are blessed to be able to do, but the question we always wonder is when Wednesday and Friday come around, this 96 year old man can cruise through Monte, Carnival and Gold Reef casinos on his own hitting every slot machine and seeing everyone of his jackpots perfectly. Just the other night at about 11:30, Kerryn and I, having come out of the monte theatre, heading towards our car, bump straight into Granny Sylvia and Grandpa Solly eating ice cream and just beginning their night! …Gran and Gramps, may you both win many more jackpots!!

Jodi - What children need most are the essentials that grandparents provide in abundance, and this is true as my Grandpa has always given us unconditional love, kindness, patience, humor, comfort, lessons in life. And, most importantly, sweets and chocolates. There is never a time that my Grandpa does not have a sweet to offer in his pocket!!!! Anyone who has met or knows my Grandpa will know that whenever he says goodbye, he leaves you with a sweet out of his pocket - a way that he passes on his touch and sweetness to the world - and in turn - He also has passed on that sweet tooth of his onto me.

Adam – Grandpa Solly, The King of comedy! Whats so amazing about our grandpa is that you can be talking about ANYTHING and I mean anything and the first response from him is "that reminds me of a story when". and this leads into a fresh, unheard joke with perfectly timed punch line and all! I give you all permission to try this on him today, I can guarantee he won't let you or me down! I guess 96 years of life can give anyone a great database of fresh jokes!!! Seriously, Gramps may you always know that we love you and are so very proud to be your Grandchildren, may you keep telling great jokes for many more years!

Jodi - In the presence of your family and your friends we would like to express our gratitude and Love to you. We thank you for the years lit up with your presence and your loving and caring attitude.

Adam - For all that you have accomplished in your life…your loving family, for your energies and strength, and for the ways in which you continue to inspire us, may this birthday be your happiest. And may you Please G-d have many more, all of them in the best of health.
We wish you years filled with the same joy you bring to others

SPEECH AT SOLLY'S THIRD BARMITZVAH
Made by son Anthony

Mom, Dad, Family and Friends,

We welcome you all here today to this very unique occasion in our lives, as how many sons have the opportunity to be at a Fathers 3rd Barmitzvah.

A very special welcome to those who have travelled from all corners of the earth to be here today, and thank you for making the effort to be here to help us celebrate this very special occasion. Thanks Manf and Lorraine for coming all the way from America. I think that having all three children and their respective spouses together is indeed a unique event, let alone so many of the Grandchildren and Great Grandchildren.

A very big thank you to Bernice and Barry, for having made this wonderful party possible, and for all the hard work and effort that went into making it the most memorable and successful occasion.

Dad, on hehalf of us all, we all wish you a very happy birthday for this coming Tuesday 27th, and Mazel Tov on your Barmitzvah anniversary.

It was 73 years ago that you celebrated your Barmitzvah and recited your Haftorah portion Nachamo, as a young boy of 13, and it was a great privilege to be present in Shul with you yesterday to hear your recite the Brachot, so fluently from memory.

What can a son say to a Father at a time like this, other than we wish you many more healthy, and happy years, and may you continue to be an inspiration to us all.

You have always been a most wonderful Husband, Father, Grandfather, Great Grandfather and friend to us all, and you have set a wonderful example for us to follow.

You have always said "that a man is as old the woman he feels, and that you never stop feeling," so carry on, it seems to be working for you.

They say that behind every successful man is a successful woman, and this certainly applies to you, having had Mom by your side all your married life.

I would like to take this opportunity to wish you and Mom a very happy 66th anniversary for the 13th of next month, and may you both be blessed with many more healthy and happy years together.

The two of you always remind me of the characters "Darby and Joan'

The term 'Darby and Joan' is defined by the Random House Dictionary as "a happily married couple who lead a placid, uneventful life.

I would like to quote an extract from a poem by :Bernard Shaw

"There they sit, day by day,
They do not talk, there is nothing to say.
Darby and Joan the eighties for bye.
Enjoying the Sun and the light blue sky.
They smile to each other a tender smile.
Theirs has been truly a life worth while.
Children give them a great delight.
They feed the birds, a wonderful sight."

This certainly depicts the Mom and Dad, that we all love so much, but instead of "They feed the birds, a wonderful sight" I must substitute "They feed the machines at Monty all day and night"

Will you please rise and join me in drinking a toast to our very special Mom and Dad

LETTER FOR DAD
Written by daughter Bernice Thal

Sometimes the poorest man leaves his children the richest inheritance. ~ Ruth E Renkel. This quote is so true when it comes to describing my Father - Solly Jossel – not that he struggled financially all his life, but more so that he experienced a childhood of poverty and sadness.

My father being one of the Ochberg Orphans and who experienced a childhood that no parent wishes for their child, has truly been the biggest inspiration to me all my life – and someone to whom I look up to and respect.

I was never made to be aware of my Father's hardships or the fact that his life had been one rather different from most. He had always just been my Dad, quite normal, just like the rest of the Dads around.

I do not remember my father ever dwelling on his past or making his children aware of the experiences he had growing up. Instead he loved us and showered us with everything and anything a child desires. We were blessed with a very privileged life.

My Dad never raised his voice at me and I never ever, not even once, received a hiding. He had a quiet manner of authority, which I highly respected and never challenged. I was brought up to be a lady with good morals and values and I was encouraged never to swear, and to this day to my children's astonishment, I still do not. Any man can be a father, but it takes a special person to be a dad.

My Dad is most definitely the figurehead of our family. He has always been the decision maker, the disciplinarian, the strict but fair parent, always there for us in a loving, gentle, kind and generous manner. He has an extremely sharp sense of humour and a very sarcastic mind. His ability to calculate figure work in his mind is quite incredible. Even his Grandchildren using a calculator are not as quick as him.

They say that the most important thing a father can do for his children is to love their mother and this is so true of the relationship between my parents. I am so grateful to have parents who have set such a wonderful example of what a marriage should be. I can honestly say that they are true role models for a very successful, long marriage even 66 years down the line!!!

A touching gesture, which my parents still live by, is wishing each other a "Happy Anniversary" on the 13th of every month. This special tradition is something, which my husband and I have now followed since we got married.

My father is and has always been an extremely charitable man and spent a huge amount of his valuable time working for many different charities. He was also very active on the Bulawayo Hebrew Congregation and held the position of President of the Shul for many consecutive years.

I remember being a very young child and going with him every Saturday morning to Shul. My greatest excitement was being able to sit in the Gubbas box on his knee and looking up with such pride and joy at my friends sitting upstairs in the girl's section.

I was once asked what my father did for a living and with all the innocence of youth I said everything because of all the different positions he held. I genuinely believed he did everything.

Being the youngest of three children, and the only girl, I have always been very lovingly protected and sheltered and I feel so honoured to have been brought up in such a warm loving happy home.

Friday night dinners at our home always had many strangers joining us, people from out of town whom my father met at Shul and would bring home with him for dinner. How my mother coped is amazing, as she never really knew who would be sitting at our Shabbat table.

This applied to all the Yom Tovs and Jewish festivals. So many people to this day remember the warmth and hospitality given to them, by both my parents in our home in Bulawayo.

My Dad never told us how to live; he lived, and let us watch him do it and in doing so we learnt beautiful ways from him, which I please G-d hope to continue to live by and pass on to my children.

I have many beautiful and happy memories of my youth. My father loves sweets and he always kept a big tin filled with assorted sweets in a cupboard. After lunch each day one of us children would shout "Can we have sweets and can I share them out". Whoever said it first got to hand out a handful of sweets to the others.

He was a strict Father but extremely fair. He was very protective of me and an incident, which always brings a smile to my face, is when I first started dating, and if my curfew was 10pm and I happened to get home at 10.10pm there he was waiting at the front door in his pajamas!!!

My parents have always worked together, and it was something I found very special, so when I got married it was only natural that I should follow in their footsteps and work with my husband. I am proud to say that for the past 37 years my Husband and I have worked side by side too, very successfully.

Meal times in our home were very important. It was quality time when we each got to talk about the day's happenings and even if the phone rang or there was a special show on T V nothing was allowed to interrupt meal times. This was something my Father found very important and took seriously, and something we all respected.

A favorite game my brother Anthony and I shared was to hide on the back floor of my parent's car just before they left to go to work. They would go half way up the block when we would jump up and "surprise" them. They in turn acted shocked at seeing us and then they would have to go back home to drop us off. What patience they had, because this used to happen almost every day.

I would like to make mention of my Bobba, the angel who adopted my father, and the memories, which I hold of her, are still so very clear. She was truly an angel and so typical of what a person imagines a Bobba to be. She was such a gentle and kind lady and spoke with a true Yiddish accent. Her hair was grey and she always wore it neatly tied up in a bun. At night she would let her hair down, and it would fall beautifully long and straight.

She always called me "My Shayna Maidel" and to this day I can still feel her presence. I strongly believe she is my guardian angel looking down at us and protecting us.

I am honoured to have been given her wedding band, which I treasure with all my heart.

One of the many lessons she taught me was about patience. An example was if I got a ball of wool tangled up, she taught me to sit down quietly and gently tackle the task of undoing the knots. She would always say "My Shayna one day your future mother in law will judge you for your patience, so learn now to have it while you are still young"

To this day when faced with a difficult task I remember her words and feel her presence.

How could my father not possibly have turned out to be the secure, successful and loving human being he is. He was blessed to have been given a second chance in his young life by this incredible lady. Thank you Bobba.

How lucky I am, a woman in her sixties to be able to say a personal thank you to my father for my very blessed life. Thank you for sharing all our simchas, for filling all our lives with so much wisdom, love, warmth, laughter and happiness. Thank you for teaching us respect, understanding, gratitude and loyalty and for making us such secure happy human beings.

It could have been so different, and only now as adults and parents do we really realize and understand what you must have gone through at such a tender age, and we are so terribly grateful for the incredible life you have given us. Thank you Dad.

We love you dearly and ask Hashem to continue blessing you and Mom and our whole family to see many more years together filled with love, laughter, health and happiness.

It doesn't matter who my father was and what kind of childhood he experienced. What does matter is that we remember who he is and the life he continues to live, which is a life we should all be as blessed to live!

LETTER TO MY DAD, SOLLY JOSSEL
Written by Anthony Jossel

The name of the Late Isaac Ochberg may not be known to many people, but to our family, it is with gratitude, love and respect that we thank this most wonderful human beings, who brought my Dad, Solly Jossel, at the tender age of six, to South Africa as one of the "Ochberg Orphans"

Dad, as child I remember hearing your stories of how your life began, and how as a little boy aged 2 you were placed in an orphanage by your Mother who couldn't look after you, and your siblings after the loss of your Father. I have always considered your survival as a heavenly sent miracle, as Mr. Ochberg was mandated to take 200 healthy true orphans from Poland to South Africa, and that you, with a living Mother, were chosen from among some 400 orphans in the orphanage and some

500,000 orphans in general, and how you were adopted by the Josselowitz family. It pained me so much, and I spent so many sleepless, tearful nights imagining the trauma and emotions that you must have gone through. They say that hardships are what make a man, and in your case this certainly is true.

Fortunately, Hashem has been good to you, and you have been blessed with a long, healthy and happy life, with a wonderful, loving and caring wife, who has always been at your side, and supported you through thick and thin.

It has often been debated whether a persons character is influenced by "nature or nurture" whether it is hereditary factors or environmental influences that shapes ones character.

Well Dad, in your case, from what I have learned about your biological Neustein parents, from the family that you and Mom have so diligently traced, all over the world, combined with the wonderful upbringing you had from your adoptive parents, it is no wonder you blossomed into the great man that you are.

As a child, when we lived in Bulawayo, I remember you and Mom were always travelling overseas, leaving me and my siblings with a trained nurse, and Miriam, our devoted nanny. At that stage, all that concerned me was, when would you be home, and what presents would you be bringing back with you. However, as I grew up, I realized what your trips actually meant. You and Mom were searching for any living relatives who may have survived World War 2, and who could tell you anything about your biological family, about whom you knew so little. Your quest for knowledge of your heritage was not in vain, and you did in fact trace family in Europe, North and South America, as well as your only surviving sibling in Poland. Coupled with Moms exceptional communication skills, you were able to find further family members in many other parts of the world.

I was 9 years old, when you managed to bring your Brother, your only surviving immediate family member, "Uncle Filip" whom you hadn't seen for 35 years, from behind the iron curtain. As he only spoke Polish and Yiddish, I never really learned first hand about your background, but as I grew up, I began to understand and appreciate what a wonderful family you had come from, and how your Father gave his own life, trying to save a fellow Jew.

I, now as an adult, understand where you learned to be so charitable, and how acts of true Chesed (kindness) have always been so natural in you daily life, not only in Jewish circles, but in all spheres, including being the Gabba of the Shul, a City Councilor, an executive member of the SPCA, Chaplin to the Jewish prisoners, just to name a few. In between all of this you even managed to run a successful business, and raise a family, thanks to Mom who was always at you side. I was once asked- "which committee does your Dad sit on?" to which I replied- "which committee does he not sit on?"

Dad – you have always been an inspiration to me, and I have always know that I could rely upon you, not only for advise, but for unconditional love and support. Your kindness and generosity through out my life, to me and my family, has been exceptional and unlimited. I have always looked up to you with admiration and respect.

Despite the fact that you have always had so much energy and enthusiasm to do so much for others, your adult life has not been without its adversities. As a young newly married man, you had major stomach surgery that nearly cost you your life. I recall you once telling me how you applied for life assurance, as you were concerned about your young wife and infant child, but every Company you applied to, declined your application. It just goes to show that despite actuarial calculations, you have outlived the Agents, the Doctors, the Actuaries, and even the Life Assurance Companies.

So, to what do you attribute your longevity? I believe it is your wonderful sense of humour, together with your zest for live. You are always full of fun, and everything reminds you of some story or a joke, that you remember and tell so well. You have often said that having changed your name from Salomon Neustein to Shleima Josselowitz and then to Solly Jossel has confused the The Angel of Death to such an extent, that he doesn't know who he was sent to fetch and has missed you out. This is why you have lived so long you have confused this Angel.

You have always been full of the joys of life, and always ready for fun. Despite your inability to hear or see too well, in your latter years, no one would ever know how handy capped you are, as you are still great fun to have round, and always ready for some fun. Although you may be old in age, believe me, you are young in spirit.

Dad, thank you for giving me the opportunity of being brought up in a Jewish home, by loving parents who taught me truly Jewish morals and values, and not only spoke about them, but lived them day by day. I never remember being smacked or punished, as it was instilled in me that reward for good behavior, was far more effective than punishment for bad. I recall as a young boy, being caught smoking. Without any suggestion of punishment, you took me into the lounge, and offered me a large cigar. You insisted, "why smoke a nasty cheap cigarette when there are such beautiful large cigars?" I puffed and puffed on the cigar until I was green, and have never smoked again.

Dad, I must confess that I do recall one rather sneaky move that you and Mom pulled on me and my siblings. You used to travel from Bulawayo to Johannesburg on business, and whilst you were away, we would phone you in the morning before going to school. Whilst you were away Mom would ask us what we hoped you would bring from Johannesburg. Strangely, you would arrive with what we had hoped for, and we had heard the telephone conversation and there was no mention of our desires. It was many years later that it was revealed that you never did in fact shlep presents for us, but Mom had bought them and left them in the car, for you to distribute on your arrival back from your trip.

Dad, what a privilege it is for me, as man over 60, to go Shul on the Yom Tovim when Yizkor is recited, and to be able to walk out of Shul, so proudly, prior to the Yizkor service, as I have living parents, and have never been required to say Kaddish.
May Hashem bless you with many more healthy and happy years, filled with much "nachas' from your children, grand children and great grand children. May you continue to bring happiness and joy to all who are fortunate enough to cross your path, and remain the most wonderful Patriarch and example for us all to follow.

I love you lots.
Your devoted son, Anthony

Chapter 117 – MINDEL PENZIK (1905-1956)

Minnie Davidow (Mindel Penzik) has a detailed chapter in More Arc Memories written by her daughter Rita Chimes.

MY MOTHER MINNIE DAVIDOW
Written by Bessie Izikowitz

I am the youngest daughter of the late Mina Davidow Nee Penzik. My name is Bessie Izikowitz and I was the youngest child of six, four boys and two girls.

My mother was an Ochberg and Arc Orphan, who arrived in South Africa in 1921 with Uncle Isaac Ochberg and she always told us what a good man Uncle Isaac was. She arrived here with her brother and two younger sisters. She told us that her two sisters were adopted soon after they had arrived. They were my Aunties Hannah and Helen. I don't remember who adopted Hannah

Helen was adopted by the Meyerowitz family who were wonderful people. They promised my Mom and uncle Dave, that they would always be in contact with them, and they saw them every weekend, as promised. When it was time for Uncle Dave to leave the Arc, they found him a job and my Mom said she was very sad that Dave left, but they were still in contact. We did not see much of Auntie Hannah until we were young children.

When it was time for my Mom to leave the Arc, they asked her if she would stay and work in the laundry. She was so happy growing up in the orphanage and we loved hearing all the lovely stories my mom told us. My mom was a very popular girl, liked by everyone and she also liked going to visit the children who were in the hospital,

One Sunday David Davidow came with some friends to play tennis at the Arc, and that is when she met my Dad. The Arc gave them a wonderful wedding, on 26 March 1926, which is written about in the second edition of the Arc Memories. My mom always told us about her happy days in the Arc as we were growing up and that the little we have we must appreciate. My mom had such good qualities and she always thanked the Arc for giving her a chance in life, and she in turn instilled this in all of us. So coming from humble beginnings, we always knew that my Mom never let us go to an orphanage. She had hard times during her marriage, but kept us all together.

When we were growing up every Yomtov my Mom would make Tagel, for the Arc children and she never forgot. We would go two at a time to walk from Yeoville to Oxford Road to take the Tagels to the Arc. I liked going to the Arc because there was a picture hanging in the hall, of my Mom and Dad's wedding.

The eldest Sydney and the youngest, me, Bessie, looked like the Penzik's and the rest of our siblings like the Davidow family. My Mom often spoke about her friends at the Arc; to name a few; Sarah, Leslie, Pearl, and Hymie.

I want to mention a very important day in my life. I was seventeen, and had started a career in nursing, in 1951/2 at the Lady Dudley Nursing Home. There was a man in a private ward. I can't remember his name and it could have been Goss and

Helen is the little one with the cropped hair, Hannah has the plaits, Dovid is the younger boy and Mindel is standing behind. Isaac seated, the older brother was 21 years and left behind and we presume he perished in the Holocaust

every time I went into the ward, he always stared at me. I told the head sister that I felt uncomfortable and she said that I should ask him why does he stare at me and ask if there was a problem. This I did and the man told me that he grew up in the Arc and there was a girl who I reminded him of. When I said it must be my Mom Mina Penzik, he just started to cry. I told him I couldn't wait to get home to tell her and he cried even more. My Mom cried too. His name was Hymie and he promised me that when he got home from the hospital, that as soon as he was well enough, he would phone me and he and his driver would take me to see my Mom. He asked me if my Mom still liked fruit and chocolates, which she always did.

Needless to say the day came for them to meet and they both laughed and cried. I will never forget that day when he brought her a large basket of chocolates and fruit. The driver's name was Abel. Thanks to the Arc man Hymie for making our Mom so happy and for being so good to her. My father had already passed away when I was 12 years old.

This old photo showing Minnie, Anna, Ida and David Penzick as children is all Mr. Abraham Yankel Katz has to remind him of his cousins who he believes now to be living in South Africa.

DO YOU KNOW THE KUPITCHEVER PENZICKS?

Mr. Abraham Yankel Katz, of Michigan, U.S.A., is anxious to trace four cousins, who he believes to be living in South Africa. His cousins are Minnie, Anna, Ida and David Penzick — the children of Mr. and Mrs. Zalman Penzick, of Kupitchev. The last news Mr. Katz heard of his cousins was many years ago, when they were reported to be living in the Transvaal. Mr. Katz's parents were Michoel and Mnucah-Rivkah Katz.

Anyone who can give Mr. Katz any information regarding his cousins is asked to write to him at 22041 Beverly Street, Oak Park 37, Michigan, U.S.A.

Mr. I. Elias, of Box 4545, Cape Town, has a letter written by Mr. Katz, which he would like to hand over to any member of the Penzick family.

Bennie Penzik, son of David Penzik, writes

These are my recollections of the Yom Kippur when we got home from Shul to read the accompanying article in the Jewish Times of 5 October 1965.

There was great excitement and furious thumbing through my Dad's little black diary where he kept addresses and snippets of information including notes made when he was obliged to take leave of his beloved brother, Isaac, in Kowel, 1921. We were told that Isaac was unable to join his siblings because he had passed his 21st birthday.

Abraham Yankel Katz was an uncle to the five Penzik siblings and had emigrated to the USA in the early 1900's. Along with numerous others who made their way from Eastern Europe, he had decided that Detroit was the place to be, especially as the motor industry was paying five dollars a day!

It transpired that my Dad had written to Mr Katz in the early thirties asking him to help bring Isaac out of the Ukraine. At that time Isaac had married and was the father of two daughters. No response was forthcoming and no further word was heard and my Dad was sorely depressed. He believed that the insertion in the 1965 newspaper was an act of remorse and an effort to verify the safety of the remaining four siblings. After sending an affirmative response, efforts at further contact yielded nothing.

It was in 1995 that I met with close family of mine, still living in the Detroit area, and we verified that Mr Katz was indeed very disturbed at his inability to answer the plea that my Dad had made all those years back. I have retained contact with the Detroit branch of the family over the past fourteen years and a strong bond has developed.

Minnie's Family – Back row: Morris, Reuben, Joe and Rita
Front: Bessie, David, Mina and Sidney.

Chapter 118 – DAVID PENZIK

David Penzik and his wife Chaya Gabbe have a detailed chapter in More Arc Memories written by his son Bennie Penzik.

Here is further information on David Penzik and you can also read more on Chaya Gabbe in chapter 61 of this book.

NEWSPAPER CUTTINGS FROM THE CAPE ARGUS DATED 16 OCTOBER 1971 *By a Staff Reporter*

DAVID PENZIK

Mr David Penzik was one of the original 200 destitute orphans who arrived penniless in Cape Town in 1921.

Today, 50 year later, he is the director of a large wholesale firm and lives happily in Pretoria. His story is not unlike others of the 200 children.

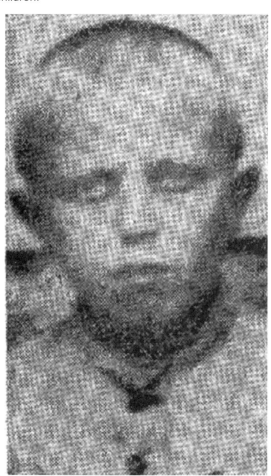

Then: David Penzik the orphan

'I lost my mother at the age of four. We - there were five of us, my youngest sister being nine months old at the time - were living in a town called Kupichev in the Ukraine. Life was difficult and I can remember the famine which stalked the country.

'My father died in 1919. I was nine then and we were taken to an orphanage in Sadowa Street, Kowel, where I stayed until Mr Ochberg arrived.'

Although then only 11, Mr Penzik, now 63, said he was already working as a compositor on a local newspaper. 'Because of this job I did not qualify to go to South Africa,' he said.

Eventually, after explaining his predicament personally to Mr Ochberg, he was allowed to leave with his three sisters for Cape Town.

'We travelled from Warsaw to Danzig by cattle truck and from there onwards by boat to England. Finally, after a very tiring and difficult journey, we arrived here on the *Edinburgh Castle* in 1921.'

After receiving his school-leavers' certificate through night school, Mr Penzik started work at a bicycle business in 1923. Sixteen years later, he branched out on his own, and, in his own words 'Things have since looked up and up.'

Now: David Penzik, successful businessman

Of the original 31,000 Jewish citizens in Kowel during the Russian Revolution only three were left in 1964.

From minutes of meeting at Arcadia SA Jewish Orphanage - October 1923

"David Penzik – Mr M Gordon reported having obtained a good situation for this boy at L K Hurwitz. (the giant of the cycle business)

The necessary application to School Board was being made and David commences work immediately. This was confirmed. Application to be made to the Twist Street School for High School tuition for this boy. He will in the meantime stay at the Orphanage."

This heralded the Penzik family's entry into the bicycle industry marked, in 1973, by the presentation of a plaque to Dad recognising his 50 years of service to the South African Cycle Industry and culminating in the sale of the family concern shortly thereafter.

The Who's Who of South African Jewry in the fifties made mention of Dad's service in the NVB (National Volunteer Brigade) during WW2.

David Penzik in uniform

The photo *David Penzik in uniform* was taken a very few years after his arrival in South Africa and bears testimony to his pioneering and volunteering spirit, characteristics which remained with him all his life. We suspect that the uniform he wore in this photo may have been the Active Citizen's Force.

That was Dad, no bells, no whistles, just the traditional 'back room boy' who simply did his job without the fanfare. I grieve the fact that I did not press him to talk about these issues which so typified his life.

PENZIK, David. Merchant. Born Kowel, Poland, 15th April, 1908; son of Zalman and Rifke Penzik. Came to South Africa 1921. Wholesale cycle merchant. Member, Pretoria United Hebrew Congregation. Member, Wingate Park Country Club. Was member of National Volunteer Brigade during World War II. Married Clara Gaby, 15th February, 1931; one son, one daughter. Add.: 1061 Duncan Street, Brooklyn; P.O. Box 570, Pretoria.

Extract from South African Jewry 1967-68

The Harpaz family Ramon, Jonathan, Rita, Dani and Tal

Bennie's children, Dov and Dalia Penzik, as university students in the UK during the early 1990's

Chapter 119 – CHANA PENZIK

HANNAH KAHN (SANDLER) (CHANA PENZIK)
Written by her daughter Rhoda Gien

Hannah Penzik arrived in Cape Town with the Ochberg group and was sent to Johannesburg and placed in the care of the South African Jewish Orphanage later to be called Arcadia.

Hannah was adopted by Aaron Reichlin and his wife from Benoni. They already had two sons. She had a little bit of schooling in Benoni and at age about 16. worked as a shop assistant. She never spoke much about her life with her adopted family, but we did visit them in Benoni occasionally at their home at 111 Atthill Avenue. Her stepmother died and then her stepfather married his late wife's sister who had a family of her own in Witbank. Hannah was very fond of this family and they kept in touch for a long time.

Hannah and her two adopted brothers lost touch with each other when they married and moved to Cape Town.

Hannah married Joseph Sandler 19 October in 1930 at age 19. She went to live in Charles Celliers with the Sandler family consisting of Joe's parents and some cousins and Joe's two sisters. Her son Stanley was born in Benoni and daughter Rhoda was born in Charles Celliers.

They moved to Gingindhlova (Natal) and then to Nongoma (Zululand) and then Vryheid (Natal). Berenice was born on 16 June 1940. They then moved to Amersfoort (Transvaal) and lived there from 1945 - 1953. Joseph died on 27 December 1951 and she continued to live in Amersfoort where she ran a family garage and filling station.

Hannah was only 40 when Joe died suddenly and she was left alone in Amersfoort to deal with business affairs of which she had no knowledge, but she managed and eventually after settling the estate and selling her house and business, she moved to Johannesburg as Stanley and Rhoda were living there by that time. Her brother David Penzik lived in Pretoria at that time.

In Johannesburg she went to work as a shop assistant at John Orr & Co. for a number of years. She then worked for a photo and camera importer when she met Max Kahn, a widower. They were married for about ten years when he became ill and died a few months later.

Hannah Penzik with her husband Joseph Sandler and children Stanley Sandler, Rhoda (Gien) and Berenice (Lasarow)

The Four Penziks at Hannah Penzik's wedding to Joseph Sandler - 19 October 1930
Helen seated left, David, Joseph with Hannah seated and Clara standing

She continued to run his business for a while and then sold the scrap metal business and moved to a residential hotel in Hillbrow. She lived there for about 20 years until it was no longer safe for elderly people then she moved to Sandringham Gardens where she still resides at the age of 98.

Hannah and daughter 1960

Hannah and sister Helen

Hannah was very plucky despite the fact that she had had a hard life and very little education. She spoke English with no foreign accent and was really beautiful. She was able to run the businesses in which her husbands were involved.

The grandchildren remember Hannah as a feisty lady who spoke her mind. She now has Alzheimer's and does not remember her grandchildren, however, she does remember her children

Rhoda Gien and her husband Aubrey

Berenice Lasarow (husband Leon Lasarow) and their daugher Merryl and grandchildren

Chapter 120– CHAIA PENZIK (1916-1990)

Helen Green/Meyerovitz (Chaia Penzik) has a detailed chapter in More Arc Memories written by her daughters Rene Aron and Yvonne Chenik.

Helen was one of five Penzik siblings; Isaac, Mina (Minnie Davidow) born 1905, David born 1908, Chana (Hannah Kahn (Sandler)) and Chaia (Helen Green (Mayerovitz)) born 1916.

Isaac, the oldest was over 16 and remained behind while the four younger siblings accompanied Isaac Ochberg to South Africa. You can read more about David, Minnie and Helen in chapters 7, 8 and 9 of "More Arc Memories".

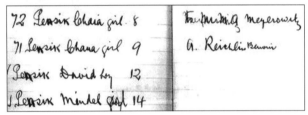

Extracts from the register kept by the orphanage in Johannesburg. The age of the children is listed after their names; Chana, aged 11, went to live with the Reichman family in Benoni and Chaia aged 8, went to stay with the Meyerovitz family.

MY GRAN HELEN (CHAIA PENZIK)
Written by Jacqui Bayala

When I remember my Gran, one of the very first things that spring to mind is her making ringlets in our hair with her old bobby pins. We would all take turns to sit at her dressing table, which was filled with an assortment of perform bottle and decorative bottles filled with coloured sand and which we were not allowed to touch, while she slowly wound small strands of our hair around her fingers. Then we would go out and play in her garden for a few hours until our hair was completely dry. After this, she would brush our ringlets, piece by piece.

My Gran was quite a no nonsense sort when it came to some of our childish antics and very pragmatic and her pet focus with me was my extreme fussiness with food. She always maintained that I would just try something. One particular evening she made sweet potatoes, which of course I refused to eat. I was told that if I ate them and liked them, I would get five rand to spend at the shops. I dutifully ate my sweet potatoes gushing about how great they tasted, earned my five rand which I spent on pick up sticks the very next day. Poor Gran decided to make sweet potatoes again the following evening as I had enjoyed them so much and true to form I refused to eat them as no payment was offered.

Possibly my sharpest and most painful memory of my Gran was the day following my grandfather's death. I was sixteen at the time and had once asked him if I could "inherit" a caricature of him drawn for his seventieth birthday by a family friend. At their house, with all the pictures either covered or down my Gran, as always together and strong, came up to me and passed me this piece of art. It's in the lounge room of my home today.

Helen Penzik's wedding to Harry Green - 21 July 1940
Jacqui was born 21 July 1971

My Granny never actually shared any of her past with us grandkids nor did she mention being an Ochberg Orphan. I'm not even sure whether she remembered very much as she was so young, but if she did no details were ever shared with her grandchildren. The only story I can recall was "When Granny was very little her parents died, so a very kind man took her and Aunty Hannah and Uncle Dovid on a ship and brought them to South Africa.

Granny's hair was cut very short like a boy's. One day at the orphanage, she was playing and ran into a man and a lady who were looking for a baby to take home with them. They liked

Helen, Harry, Errol, Yvonne and Renée – January 1949

Jacqui and Belinda with grandparents Helen and Harry

Granny and asked her if she wanted to come home with them and she said yes, but first they had to ask Uncle Dovid and Mindel if this was okay. Granny went home with Ouma and Oupa but they made sure she always got to see Aunty Hannah and Uncle Dovid." Whenever I heard this story told Isaac Ochberg was always referred to as "the very kind man".

As we grew up we always were aware that Granny had a "real" brother, Uncle Dovid, and a "real" sister, Aunty Hannah in contrast to her adopted siblings who we were never as close to. I never met Mindel but my Uncle Dovid was such a sweet loving man who would always hug and kiss us and had lots of time to speak and play with us even when the grown-ups were around. He also always managed to slip us kids a few coins each time he saw us. In particular I remember how incredibly supportive he was of my Gran once my Pops died. She went to

live with him at the Old Aged Home (Jaffa) in Pretoria where they had rooms next door to each other.

My Great Aunty Hannah has always been just that, a great aunt; always upbeat and happy and smiling and capable. As with Uncle Dovid she was a tremendous support to my Gran once my Pops died. From my perspective she always seemed the "most modern" of our group of grandparents and great aunts and uncles. When I was young I thought she was just so cool as she lived in a hotel! She also wore such interesting glasses. She related to us on a more adult level in comparison to other aunts and uncles which made us feel important. I can hardly ever remember her complaining of aches and pains or problems and she was just always so together and positive. I'm so lucky that I got to introduce my husband and children to her.

David, Hannah, Clara Gabbe, married to David, and Helen

"Descendants of Helen Green (Penzik) - Left to right: Jared (holding daughter Leora) and Debbi Levy (holding son Asher)-(our daughter Debbi), then Alan and Yvonne (myself) Chenik, Peter and Jacqui Byala (Jacqui is my sister Renee's oldest daughter), their children Megan and Zack, then Albert and Renee Aron (my sister) their younger daughter Belinda and Raffy Levy and their two children Shane and Cindy (in front), on the right in the blue shirt is my son Gary Chenik with Jacqui's older daughter Emma"Yvonne Chenik.

Chapter 121 - THE PINSKY FAMILY
MEISH, DWORA, ZLATA, FAYWEL AND FEYGA PINSKY

THE PINSKY FAMILY – Dwora (Dora), Meish (Morris), Zlata, Faywel (Phillip) and Feyga.

We have an unsolved mystery with the Pinsky Family.

Dwora Pinska – Photo from Pinsk Magistrate Travel document

Dwora (Dora), the oldest sister, is clearly listed and pictured in Group Passport Eight and we have a Pinsk Magistrate Travel document photo for her, however, she is not shown on any list as having arrived in South Africa or on the Oranjia or Arcadia lists or registers.

On the other hand Maisha (Morris), the oldest boy, while on the Arcadia lists and register, is not on any group passport and neither do we have a Pinsk Magistrate Travel document photo for him.

Following is information from the questionnaire filled in on admittance of the children into the orphanage in Pinsk.

QUESTIONAIRE FOR THE PINSKA FAMILY
Names:Moshe 12, Zlata 9, Faivel 8, Feigel 5 (full orphans)
Surname: Pinsky
Father Aharon; Mother Yenta
Place of birth: Pinsk
Father's occupation: carpenter.
Other comments:
Father died of hunger and the struggle to survive.
The mother died from the Balachovitches, she contracted syphilis from being raped by them.
The children had nowhere to go.

Gitta Stanger writes

"Eunice Green (the daughter of Zlata Dembo - nee Pinsky) remembers her mother telling her that at the last minute, just before the orphans were due to leave for South Africa, Dwora (Dora) did not join the group.

That would explain why Dwora's name did not appear on the list. She obviously came to South Africa at a later stage but we don't have any further details.

Zlata Pinska – Photo from Pinsk Magistrate Travel document

Group Passport Eight
No 8 Zlata Pinska aged 6 is front left on end
No 21 Dwora Pinska aged 10 is back row 4th from left

Fegel Pinska – Photo from Pinsk Magistrate Travel document

Faywel Pinska – Photo from Pinsk Magistrate Travel document

Group Passport Six
No 3 Feiga Pinska aged 3 – front left on end

Ochberg Orphan		Placed in the Care of:
No.22	PINSKY Maisha boy 12	
No.23	PINKSY Faivel boy 8	
No.24	PINSKY Zlata girl 9	Karensky
No 25	PINKSY Feiga girl 5	S. Glass, Winburg OFS

Extract from the register kept at the South African Jewish
Orphanage (Arcadia) –
Zlata was placed in the care of the Karensky Family
Feiga was placed in the care of the Glass Family

MAISHA PINSKY
Written by Gitta Stanger (Pinsky)

My father, Morris (Meish) Pinsky, was one of the Ochberg Orphans brought to Arcadia, Johannesburg in 1921. He never ever discussed his youth so, regrettably, his early years are shrouded in mystery. We know that he came from Pinsk and that the family had been caught up in the turmoil of the years post World War 1.

His siblings were Dora Jarzin, Slata Dembo, Birdie Glaser and Philip Pinsky. I know that my Aunt Slata was one of the Ochberg Orphans but am uncertain as to how or when the other Pinsky siblings arrived in South Africa.

My father and mother, Leah Godin, were married in Johannesburg in 1931. My sister Ada Shiller was born in 1932, I, Gitta Stanger in 1937, and my brother, Charles Pinsky in 1944. Another son was born between 1932 and 1937 but unfortunately he died at six months of age.

Meish was born in February 1909 and was 12 years of age when he arrived in South Africa. The only tangible piece of evidence we have of my father's time at Arcadia is the Tanach which was presented to him on the occasion of his Barmitzvah by the President of the Orphanage. This book is of great sentimental value to our family and is currently in the possession of my son, Aaron Stanger, who lives in Johannesburg with his wife Gwen and sons Noah and Ben.

If memory serves me correctly, my father was apprenticed to a furniture manufacturer at the age of 15 and he worked as a cabinet maker until the age of 69. He made bedroom suites and kists, and he always took great pride in his work. Ada, Charles and I grew up with the wonderful smell of wood, and some of my earliest memories are of my father working at the back of our house in Judith Paarl where he had a covered yard that enabled him to work in all weathers.

In the entrance to my flat in Melbourne where I live with my husband Monty Stanger, stands Meish's kist for all to see and admire. No fancy machines for my father - I can still see him carefully cutting out the dovetailing for the joints by hand.

It was only in 1971 when a reunion of the Ochberg Orphans had been planned, that I first heard about my father's connection to the amazing philanthropist, Isaac Ochberg. One weekend with various members of the family sitting around the dining table, I heard my husband's aunt, Polly Joffe (nee Stanger), ask my father whether he was going to Cape Town for the reunion. Aunty Polly, also one of the Ochberg Orphans, tried to convince my father to attend but in the end he decided not to go.

So it was only 50 years after the event that we finally heard about this group of children who had been plucked from the ruins of Europe. (Aunty Polly's daughter Sybil Keats also lives in Melbourne). On occasion my father mentioned the name David Penzik and I now know that he too was an Ochberg Orphan.

My mother passed away in 1973 and my father came to stay with us until his death in 1979. Our children, Aaron and Gabi, were very fond of their Zaida Meish and Monty and I were grateful for the years we were able to share with him. My late sister Ada, was married to Aubrey Shiller and they had one son, Saul. Saul lives in Johannesburg with his wife Lynn, and they are the proud owners of many pieces of furniture made by their Zaida Meish many years ago.

My brother Charles left South Africa in 1977 and lives in New Orleans with his wife Teresa. It is left to their two sons Ivan, married to Angela and now the father of three daughters, and Stefan to perpetuate the Pinsky name.

Gabi, our daughter, came to Melbourne 21 years ago and is married to Rob Selzer. They have two children, Tahlia and Amiel. Monty and I came to Australia in March 1997.

Birdie and Percy Glaser
"A photograph of my dad's sister (Morris Pinsky's sister), Feiga. She was adopted and became Birdie Glass, then married Percy Glaser. Wonderful people. I loved them very much." Jeff

Chapter 122 – CHANA AND DAWID RUBIN

FAMILY HISTORY AND LIFE IN POLAND
Written by Rhoda (Stock) Fowler

My mother Chana was born to Hersch (Hirsch/Herz) Rubin, a metal dealer from Dolina born in 1875 and the son or grandson of Solomon Rubin, and Jides Muhlstock (Milstock) Teichberg, born in 1877, and the daughter of Berl/Beril Teichberg and Sura/Sara Muhlstock of Boszowce. On her Ochberg passport my mother's date of birth is listed as 1915 and her place of birth as Stanislawow. My mother celebrated her birthday on July 11. So according to these records, she was actually six years old when she arrived in South Africa and Dawid was seven.

Solomon Rubin
Paternal grandfather

Berl Teichberg,
Maternal grandfather

I have managed to find birth records for a number of Chana Rubin's siblings:
1899 - Abraham in Bolzowce – no record of what happened
1901 -Zelman in Bolzowce (Salmon/Sigmund/Sigmond) Rubin survived and went to Israel and had a family)

1903 - Chaim - no record of what happened
1905 - Meilech - no record of what happened
There are also records of other siblings who died shortly after birth.

Recalled in 1998 by Uri Millstock, son of my mother's uncle Abraham, who was living in Israel with his wife Grania.

"Grandfather Berel had a barn. They had horses and they also grew vegetables. He loved agriculture! He made his living from selling crops and lived at Polshovse (Bolschowce Poland now Bolshovtsy).

Uri and his family lived at Podhayze (Podhajce/ Podgaytse) and Nahum lived at Tishminze"

The family was religious. His father (Abraham) had a beard and "peot". They donated money to the temple and were honoured. "The family was respected and rich. Learned and known for their generosity.

"Till 1933 life was very good. We had a cloth store. In the year 1933 a new law was published: Polish people were free of their debt to Jews. Then began Anti-Semitism. The Russians entered our city in 1939 and they confiscated Jewish goods. They took the store from us! We hid some goods and later we sold it secretly. So we made our living. I began working as a clerk and helped the family. In 1941 I was called to the Russian Army for three months. I left the house and since then never came back. The Germans entered Poland, my family were killed and I as a Russian soldier withdrew with all the others into Russia. As the Nazis advanced we moved…

"In 1943 I was transferred into a labour camp in a place called Shamlook, working in a coal mine, 160m underground. I stayed there for three years till the end of the war. On the way back from Russia to Poland I found that <u>all</u> my family were killed. I stayed in a camp in a place called Shevionitz, there I met my wife Granya. We got married in 1946"

Group Passport One - Dawid is the second from the right in the top row and Chana (we think) is the third from the right bottom row of the passport photo.

Copies of correspondence between the Selkon family and the Cape Jewish Orphanage

Letter dated: 11 March, 1921

From: S. Selkon, Somerset St, Aliwal North
To: The Cape Jewish Orphanage,
        PO Box 2730, Cape Town

Dear Sirs,
Some time ago I saw an appeal in the Zionist Record for a number of Pogrom Orphans who are being brought to this country. I accordingly made an application to the Johannesburg Orphanage I received a letter from them advising me to apply to you and they also advised me that they have transferred my application to you. I wish to adopt a little girl about three or four years. The home of mine to which she will come is a good one and I am prepared to come to Cape Town on the 18th instant
I will therefore esteem it a great favour if you will let me know if my application will be accepted and when Mr Ochberg is due to arrive back in South Africa.
If you would like to have further details you can refer to my son J N Selkon, at present studying medicine at the University of Cape Town. You can drop him a few lines on the above address and he will come to see you.
Trusting to be favoured with a favourable reply within the course of a few days, I more over promised a donation of five pounds five shillings to defray part of your expenses in bringing them out.
With Zionist Greetings
Yours faithfully
S. Selkon

Letter dated: 27 August, 1921

S. SELKON,
MERCHANT TAILOR.

SOMERSET STREET,
Aliwal North

No 153

PERFECT FIT · LATEST STYLES.
WORKMANSHIP GUARANTEED.

ALL WORK DONE BY EXPERIENCED EUROPEAN TAILORS.

SUITS TO MEASURE AT LOWEST PRICES, ALSO LADIES' COSTUMES.

LATEST SEASON'S PATTERNS STOCKED.

27th August 1921. 192

The Cape Jewish Orphanage,
P.O.Box 2730,
CAPE TOWN.

Dear Sir,
    1 have noticed in the Cape Times, that Mr Ochberg has, been successful in getting the first 100 orphans from the Ukraine;
    I am therefore under the impression that he will arrive in South Africa about the time of the New Year holidays. Please advise me by return of post when Mr Ochberg will definitely arrive and wether 1 am to come down to Cape Town to pick the child.
In your of the 15th April you wrote me that you would advise me in this matter, but thus far 1 have received no communication from you.
Please advise me further in this matter by return.

Yours faithfully,
Selkon

Letter Dated: 12 September, 1921

From; Secretary The Cape Jewish Orphanage
To: Mr S Selkon, P.O. Box 20 Aliwal North
Dear Sir
 Am in receipt of yours of the 27th August and in reply, beg to say that Mr Ochberg has not yet arrived with the pogrom Children, and the Committee have still the matter of their adoption under consideration. As soon as we have their final decision we will let you know when to come down to choose a child.
Yours truly Secretary

Letter Dated: 21 October, 1921

From: Secretary The Cape Jewish Orphanage
To: Secretary, Hebrew Congregation Aliwal North
Dear Sir:-
At a meeting of the Adoption Committee held recently it was decided to ask the Aliwal North Hebrew Congregation to be good enough to investigate the case of Mr S Selkon, Somerset St Aliwal North who made application for the adoption of a child, and to report soon, to the above committee as to whether they are fit and proper persons for such,
Thanking you in anticipation
I am yours faithfully   (Miss) SEC Secretary

Letter dated: 14 November, 1921

14th November, 1921

The President,
Hebrew Congregation,
Aliwal North.

Dear Sir:-

    We received an application from S. Selkon of Somerset Street, Aliwal North in which he applies for the adoption of a little girl from the Orphans whom we recently brought over from Eastern Europe, and we should be greatly obliged if you could report to us fully on this gentleman. We particularly desire to know whether he is keeping a thorough Jewish House so that the child could be brought up in a proper Jewish atmosphere, whether they are people without a stain on their character, are able to give the child an English education and take care of her otherwise.

    We will appreciate your frank report, and we need hardly assure you that all your remarks will be treated with stric confidence.

Yours truly,

PRESIDENT.

Letter dated: 14 November, 1921

From: President The Cape Jewish Orphanage
To: J W Selkon Esq.,
        c/o University, Cape Town
Dear Sir:-
I shall esteem it a favour if you will come in to see me re application made by your father to adopt a child from the Pogrom Orphans recently brought out to this country
Yours truly
PRESIDENT

Letter dated: 17 November, 1921

> A. N. Hebrew Congregation
> P.O. Box 9.
> 17.11.21.
>
> Mr J. Ochberg:
> President
> Cape Jewish Orphanage.
> Cape Town.
>
> Dear Sir,
> In reply to your letter of 14th inst.
> ... Mr Selkow of this town, I beg to inform
> you that he has already been granted
> a little girl from Johannesburg which
> child is now in his possession.
> Should you still require the information
> I may add that he is a fit & proper Jewish
> man, quite in a sound position to give the
> child an average education and a
> comparatively comfortable home.
> Trusting that this will meet with
> your requirements
> I remain
> Yours faithfully
> A. Bendelstein
> Hon Sec.

Dawid and Chana Rubin

Chana as a young girl

DAWID AND CHANA (DAVID AND ANN)

I cannot be sure why Dawid and Chana were placed in an orphanage. Hersch Rubin their father was still alive in 1932, as I have a document signed by him (a Heimats Schein) on that date. My cousins in Israel tell me that their father (my uncle Sigmond) told them that he was 14 at the time, - eight years older than Chana. Their mother was killed in a pogrom (there is some confusion about the date of her death) and their father placed the smaller children in an orphanage because he had to go away. When he came back he found that Chana and Dawid had been sent to South Africa.

My mother Chana Rubin and her brother Dawid were among the orphans brought to South Africa from the Ukraine by Isaac Ochberg. Their names appear on a list entitled "First Contingent of Pogrom Orphans" and they arrived in South Africa on the Edinburgh Castle on 19 September 1921.

We only found out about the Ochberg connection after her death in 1993, so piecing together what had happened to her and her brother was not an easy task.

> 53 Rubin David boy 7
> 52 Rubin Chana girl 6 ...S. Selkin
> Box 20 Aliwal North

Extract from register kept by Arcadia (SAJO)
This shows that Chana and her brother went to Johannesburg and record the fact that Chana was subsequently adopted by the Selkons. We also now know that Dawid stayed on at Arcadia. The age of the children is listed after the name.

We knew that our mother had been adopted by a family named Selkon. She mentioned that they were an older couple with several grown up sons and had always longed for a daughter.

She spoke of her upbringing in Aliwal North in the Cape, where she lived happily with her adopted parents and the convent where she was educated by very strict nuns. She told us how she had lived in Aliwal North until she left school and went to work in Johannesburg at OK Bazaars, joining her brother David she boarded with a family named Steinberg in Doornfontein.

It was here that she met my father Josef Stock who had fled from Nazi Germany.

Josef and Ann on their wedding day – 1938

David at the wedding of Josef and Ann   *Josef Ann and James-1941*   *Dawid and Rhoda Fowler ~1950*

Josef and Ann were married in 1938 and in 1940 their son James was born, followed by a daughter Rhoda in 1943 and a son Leonard in 1948.

However, when we asked my mother how she had arrived in South Africa as an orphan, she simply replied that she was very young (we gained the impression that she was two or three years old) and could only remember being on a big ship and nothing else. She said she thought that she had come from Austria.

Leukaemia while still a comparatively young man when I was about 10 or 11 and I remember him as a rather sad and lonely person and as a gentle man. I was very fond of him and recall that he came to visit us in Durban.

I also knew that my mother corresponded with an older sibling, Sigmond Rubin, who lived in Israel and a cousin Ruth in the USA. In 1965 with these scant facts, I began to try to find out what had happened to my mother's original family.

Ann and Josef with James Rhoda and Leonard ~ 1953

Sigmund Rubin
Chana's older sibling who went to Israel

She told us that her brother David had not wanted to be adopted so he had stayed in an orphanage. He had never married and had worked as a projectionist in Johannesburg where he lived until his death in approx 1953. He died of

Today, 16 years later after my mother's death, with the help of cousins in Israel, the internet and my US relatives, I have quite a bit more information, however many areas are still a mystery.

Chapter 123 – MANES SHAMES (1912-1994)

Feiga Mirel Shamis, Manny's mother, tells her life story in Part 1 Section 5 of this book.

MANNIE FAVISH (MANES SHAMIS)
Written by Mannie's wife, Nora (Austoker) Favish, and extracted from the preface of "Shalom Shalom My Dear Children" and the booklet "From Poland to Paardeberg"

Mannie Favish, my late husband, was born in Verba (which was formerly in Poland and is now in the Ukraine) in 1912. In 1920, when he was eight years old, he and his sister Rose, who was ten, were brought to South Africa by the philanthropist Isaac Ochbherg who rescued two hundred orphans from the Ukraine.

The orphans had been living in extreme poverty, many were sick and starving. He brought them to South Africa and this transfer of orphans was referred to as the Ukrainian Adventure. Some were taken to the Cape Town Orphanage and the rest went to Arcadia Orphanage in Johannesburg. There Rose refused adoption. She received her education in Johannesburg, worked there, and married Lulu Miller on 10 December 1931. They had a very happy marriage.

Mannie was adopted by Israel and Shaina Favish of Benoni where he received his schooling and studied law through the University of South Africa. He qualified with a BA LLB and practised as an attorney in Benoni until his death in 1994. In 1946 he married me, Nora Austoker, and we had 48 wonderful years together. It has ever been my regret that I did not meet his adoptive parents, especially his mother who gave him so much love.

Mannie (Shames) Favish

MEETING MANNIE

At the end of my first year working at *Die Vaderland* Newspaper in December 1939, I was 20 and my parents encouraged me to develop a sense of independence and I was made to take Bella, my younger sister, who is four years younger than me, away on holiday. We booked to go to a boarding house in Margate.

On the train in the compartment next door to ours, was a young man whom I met. It was inevitable. On the train people would stand in the corridors for hours on end staring at the passing scenery and talking to each other. The young man next to us was magnificent looking: tall, blond hair and blue eyes. He was going on holiday to Durban and tried to persuade me to cancel my booking in Margate and come with him to Durban and book in at the same hotel as him. This was certainly an appealing offer and it was definitely something that I wanted to do. However, I was responsible for the booking in Margate and I couldn't make such a decision until Bella and I had been to Margate and had discussed the option of cancelling our booking with the proprietor of our boarding house, and had found out what our responsibilities were in terms of payments.

On the first night at the boarding house in Margate I met a couple whom I knew from Johannesburg. They were Ros and Syd Barnett. I discussed my predicament with them. Ros suggested I speak to an attorney whom she had met there the previous evening, and he would advise me on the legalities of my dilemma.

After breakfast the next morning, Ros called me and introduced me to the attorney who hailed from Benoni. His name, Mannie Favish. Of course I did not know that then, but I know it now – that moment was the most momentous one in my whole life.

I told Mannie of my situation and how I wanted to transfer to Durban. I asked for his advice. Well, years later I challenged him and told him he had not given me the correct legal advice, but had rather done what his heart had dictated. Of course, his advice was that I should stay in Margate with Bella and spend the holiday there.

It was only afterwards that Mannie told me, that after our first meeting, he had decided that he was going to marry me one day.

MEETING UP WITH HIS MOTHER AGAIN

In 1941, when Mannie was serving with the South African Forces in Egypt during the Second World War, he took leave and visited his biological mother on the *kibbutz*. He spent a day and a night with her – mother and son had not seen each other for twenty years. One can only imagine the emotions they each experienced during this touching meeting. When he awoke from his sleep on the *kibbutz* he found his mother sitting in a chair and looking at him. She had apparently spent the night in that chair – probably remembering the tragic separation from her two young children twenty years before.

Feiga Mirel and Mannie, Givat Chaim, Palestine 1941

MARRIAGE

December 1939 was a momentous occasion in my life – when I met Mannie. Thereafter followed seven years of our romance.

I entered medical school in 1942 and only qualified in 1947. From the time when Mannie returned from Egypt in 1943, he pursued me, he loved me and tried to persuade me to marry him. The first present he gave me on 5 March 1945 was a watch on my birthday with the following engraving. *Leonora – my times are in your hands, Mannie.* Of course, I did love him but I found it very difficult to make such a major decision in my life when I had just embarked on a demanding career. So I just kept putting it off. However, in February 1946 I made the decision.

Mannie and I had one of our many 'breaks', and he said that seeing as though we were not going to see each other ever again, he wanted a photograph of me. At that point, I made the best decision I have ever made in my whole life, I would marry him!

I phoned Mannie and said that I did not have a photograph of myself, but would he accept the original? He left his game of bridge and rushed from Benoni to my house in Highlands North. We decided that night that we would get married on 5 February 1946.

A touching moment in our courtship which I would like to mention is that I received a telegram from Mannie on 8 March 1945.

It was addressed to: Miss L Austoker
Women's Common Room, Medical School, Jhb

This is what it said: *Sonnet 27 – Shakespeare, Love Mannie*

The Sonnet, I discovered, went as follows:

Weary with toil, I haste me to my bed,
The dear repose for limbs with travel tired;
But then begins a journey in my head,
To work my mind, when body's work's expired:
For then my thoughts, from far where I abide,
Intend a zealous pilgrimage to thee,
And keep my drooping eyelids open wide,
Looking on darkness which the blind do see;
Save that my soul's imaginary sight
Presents thy shadow to my sightless view,
Which, like a jewel hung in ghastly night,
Makes black night beautous, and her old face new.
Lo, thus, by day my limbs, by night my mind,
For thee and for myself no quiet find.

I told Phyllis Knocker, who was involved with Zolly Frank, that Mannie and I were going to get married. They decided that they too would come to the Magistrates Court in Benoni to get married. In those days it was necessary to have a marriage certificate from the Magistrate prior to marriage, unless one had put up wedding banns at Shul four weeks before the wedding.

We had an arrangement, Mannie would phone the secretary at Medical School after having spoken to the Magistrate in Benoni to find out when he would have a spare five minutes to marry us. One Friday afternoon, 1 February 1946, we were at an Eye clinic with Doctor Franks at the Johannesburg Hospital. The secretary from Medical School phoned to say that Mannie had called and he wanted us to come through as soon as possible and to meet him at the Magistrates Court in Benoni. His typist, in the meantime, had gone out and bought two gold rings – our wedding bands.

I went to Dr Franks to ask if I could please be excused. In front of 20 other medical students, he asked me if I was not feeling well. I replied, 'No – I am well, but I am going to get married.' The group burst out laughing. At this, Phyllis went up to him and asked if she could also be excused. To which Dr Franks replied. 'Oh, are you also going to get married?' and Phyllis said, 'Yes, as a matter of fact, I am!' With that, the two of us left the class, met Zolly and went through to Benoni, to meet Mannie at the Magistrates Court where we were duly married.

Before I tell you about our wedding. I would like to share a touching story about the engagement ring.

Mannie said to me a day before our Shul marriage that he would very much like to get me an engagement ring. I duly went to the manicurist and had my nails beautifully done. I then met him in front of the jeweller's shop. When we got there, I said to him that we had so many other expenses and a ring was really too expensive for us and that I did not need an engagement ring, but that I would like a memento. So we went to the jewellery counter at the OK Bazaars and I chose a ring which the saleslady said would cost two shillings, which is approximately 20 cents. Mannie said with tongue in cheek that that was too expensive, to which the saleslady replied, 'Ag foeitog!'. I thereupon chose something cheaper, probably costing about 10 cents. It was a green bead on a gold band. This ring was very special to me. It was my engagement ring!

On our tenth anniversary, Mannie said that he would like to get me a real diamond ring. So again, I went off to the manicurist and had my nails done, and met Mannie outside the jewellery shop and again, I said to him, that we needed a fridge and that was of more importance than a diamond ring, but that again, I wanted a memento. So yet again, we went next door to the OK Bazaars to the jewellery counter. Mannie bought me a ring with a beautiful glass stone – my first really official engagement ring!

On our 25th anniversary, Mannie decided that this time he would buy me a real diamond. And so yet again, I went through the procedure of getting my nails done, meeting Mannie outside the jewellers and then saying to him that it was unnecessary to spend that amount of money on a ring when we wanted to save money for Janet and Judy to go overseas and for other things we had planned. I really am very romantic, but I am also very practical. So again, we went to the OK Bazaars and chose a beautiful ring with three stones that resembled diamonds. We had a very lavish 25th anniversary celebration. It was in our garden and we had a marquee. During the evening, I glanced down at my ring and saw that there was a gaping, large cavity from which one of the glass stones had fallen out. I made an announcement that the guests should please look carefully on the grass for this missing 'diamond'. Everyone thought it was a genuine diamond and therefore, a genuine loss. But of course, it was not and the 'diamond' could not be found. I told them the real story. So again, I did not have a diamond ring.

On our 40th anniversary, I accepted Mannie's offer to buy me a real diamond. We went to Desmond Miller, our nephew, who had a diamond works and we chose a beautiful stone. That was my first engagement ring. I wore that ring for three years until one day I came home and felt something clawing at my cardigan. I looked down and saw that the diamond had gone and it was the ring itself that was catching on my jersey. I was heartbroken, of course.

The moral of this tale is that it is not the ring that is important in the marriage, but it is the love that a couple enjoy.

Our wedding was very austere. I did not wear a wedding dress. Many years later, when Janet was four years old she came back from visiting a friend. She said that she had seen her friend's mommy's photograph in a bridal dress. It was a beautiful picture, and where was mine? I said that I did not have a picture of myself in a bridal dress because I did not wear a wedding dress and we did not have any pictures. (I shall tell you the story of the pictures later.) She was absolutely heartbroken. She cried and said, 'You're not married!' She thought we weren't married. So Mannie said he knew what to show her to convince her we were married. The next day he arrived home from the office with our marriage certificate and our ante-nuptial contract. He proceeded to explain to this little four year old that we were really married. I do not know if it was of much comfort to her because she still did not have a photograph of her mommy in her wedding dress.

The reason we do not have photographs of our wedding is because, Boris Wilson, who was a very dear friend of ours and a good photographer suggested that I do not book a photographer because he would like to take photos of the wedding. We were very glad to have him do this. After the wedding, he said that he would come to see us when he returned from England where he was going to the next morning. He would bring the photographs with him then. He duly returned from England and came to visit us. He walked into our flat and looked very, very sheepish. I asked him where our photographs were. He replied that he was sorry and that he had a confession to make. There was no spool in the camera! Again the moral of the tale is clear. It is not the photographs that are important. Of course, I would have dearly loved to have had photos of that day, but Mannie and I could remember every detail of our wedding, in spite of the fact that there were no pictures to remind us.

The story of Boris Wilson has a sequel. Boris was a member of the Progressive Party when it was formed in South Africa. He was very politically involved. He subsequently wrote his autobiography entitled *A Time of Innocence.* He gave us a copy of his book with the inscription:

To Nora Austoker and Mannie
I wrote this specially to make up for lost
Wedding photographs!
Love Boris

RETIREMENT AND TRAGEDY

In March 1993 Mannie and I made a momentous decision. We left Benoni and moved to a retirement village, Elphin Lodge, in Johannesburg. At that time Mannie was consulting at his previous legal firm on one day a week and I was lecturing part-time at Rietfontein Hospital on Tuberculosis control. In March I had a serious fall and injured my eye. This sadly ended my working career. My eye recovered well after plastic surgery.

Mannie and I spent a wonderful year together. In 1994 on the evening of 19 April, Mannie suffered an annihilating stroke and passed away at midnight, in my arms, without regaining consciousness. This was a tragic loss for me.

I was totally devastated. It was the greatest tragedy of my life. I felt totally bereft. I do not know how I got through the days and months that followed. If breathing were not automatic, I would have stopped breathing.

A TRIBUTE TO MANNIE

Mannie and I had 48 glorious years together. Your grandfather was a remarkable man. The history of his childhood is described in a book written by his biological mother. It is entitled *Shalom, Shalom My Dear Children.*

Above all else, your grandfather had integrity and humility. He had a brilliant mind and a wonderful sense of humour. In spite of a very traumatic childhood, he grew up to be a strong and stable adult. He was a devoted and loving husband and father. He was an avid reader and had a particular love of Shakespeare. He studied the bard and Latin all his life. On one Father's Day he received a telegram from Judy who was living in Cape Town. He was touched when he read it:

Spero felicem patriam day habiturum esse, Love, Judy
Translated from Latin, it reads: *I hope you have a Happy Father's day.*

Mannie qualified as an attorney and then received his (BA) LLB degree from UNISA. He had a very successful career and was the town attorney in Benoni for many years. He was an authority on municipal law.

Mannie was truly in every sense, my husband, my friend, my lover and my mentor. He was also an inspiration to me all my life. The album I have put together for you contains all the letters and cards that Mannie gave me during our marriage. They speak for themselves.

Sydney Poitier in his autobiography said, *What is the measure of a man? His relationship with his family and his children.* Mannie's and my relationship was the best it could ever be. We did not need Feng Shui – there was always harmony and balance in our home. Manfred may not have been tall, but he was indeed larger than life in character. Mannie was so secure as a person, he encouraged and supported me always, and took pride in my achievements.

After reading the story of his childhood, one would realise how painful it must have been, and how traumatic, to have been separated from his mother and siblings at such a young age. This painful past was buried in Mannie's subconscious mind, never to surface. He never once spoke of the first eight years of his life, and when questioned about it he always replied that he did not remember anything.

He left me a treasured legacy – everlasting love. A quotation he often repeated to me was, *Grow old along with me, the best is yet to be* by Robert Browning. I would like to conclude this tribute to Mannie with these words from Shakespeare:

> *His life was gentle,*
> *And the elements so mixed in him,*
> *That nature might stand up,*
> *And say to all the world:*
> *This was a man*

Mannie (Shames) Favish

Nora (Austoker) Favish

570

Chapter 124 – REISEL SHAMES

Rose(Rosie) (Reisel) was born on 4 April 1910 in Verba Poland (Ukraine), and was admitted to Arcadia aged 10 after she arrived in South Africa as an Ochberg orphan in 1921.

Feiga Mirel Shamis, Reisel's mother, tells her life story in Part 1 Section 5 of this book.

ROSE (REISEL SHAMES) MILLER
Written by Sheila Landau

My mother never spoke about her childhood. She always said what she remembered of it was very sad. She would say her nanny would hide them in the forest from the bad men. There were 12 children in the family and their father died at a young age so my late grandmother, Feiga Mirel Shames reared them on her own, with great hardship. She came from a little shtetl called Verba near Dubno in the Ukraine.

Two of the siblings moved to Poland, two came to America, four died during the Holocaust, one went to Israel, Rose and Mannie to South Africa and one died in infancy.

I think my mother always expected her own mother to come and find her and therefore, although she had an opportunity to be adopted by a wonderful family, she said she would remain at Arcadia. Uncle Mannie (Manes Shames) was adopted by the Favish family from Benoni. Uncle Mannie was fortunate enough to meet his mother again, she had made her way to Israel to be with her youngest daughter. When uncle Mannie went up north to fight in the South African army, he was able to see her again, after many years.

Rosie Shames

While the siblings are entered in the Register of the children at Arcadia (South African Jewish Orphanage) one cannot find them listed on any group passport

Rosie Shames

A concert put on by the children of Arcadia
Rose is in the back row 2nd from the right

My mother was a wonderful person. She grew up in the orphanage and left from there to her wedding ceremony.

Polly Stanger, Sarah Altuska and Rosie Shames

Rosie Shames

Rose and Lulu (Loius Miller) were married on 10 December 1933. I never knew who gave my mother away or who walked down the aisle with her. I have only found out recently, through the newspaper clipping. I wish I had met all these wonderful people who took such good care of her, just to say thank you.

Following are news clippings of the engagement, the wedding announcement and the wedding and photos.

Shames-Miller – The engagement is announced of Rose Shames and Louis (Lulu) Miller, second son of Mr and Mrs S Miller. Both of Johannesburg.

The marriage will take place at 11 am on Sunday, December 10 at the Berea Synagogue of Miss Rose Shames to Mr Louis Miller. The reception will be held at the bride's residence, in Yeoville.

SUNDAY WEDDING Miller Shames

A lovely gown of ivory satin cut on straight lines with a panelled skirt and a bead-embroidered bodice was worn by Miss Rose Shames for her marriage yesterday to Mr Louis (Lulu) Miller, second son of Mr and Mrs Sam Miller. Her veil of embroidered silk net was held in place with a cap of pearls and she carried a sheaf of lilies.

The Rev S Steinberg officiated in the Berea Synagogue, which was decorated with palm and pink flowers, the colour of the bridal retinue. Mrs A Nathan and Mr B Mendelsohn gave the bride away and the unterfuhrers were Mr and Mrs S Miller, Mr B

Mendelsohn and Mrs A Nathan. Mr Mannie Favish (brother of the bride). Mr Larry Miller, Mr Bennie Lang and Mr Harry Fleisher were the canopy bearers. The brother of the bridegroom, Mr Abe Miller was the best man and Messrs Phil Sacks, Sammy Esakov, Max Kay and Dave Shaffer were groomsmen.

Miss Dorothy Kabatznik, the maid of honour, wore a dress of salmon pink crepe trimmed with grey cire satin with a coatee of satin.

The bridesmaids, the Misses Hilda Kabatznik, Rae Davis, Sylvia Shapiro and Ann Sapire, looked charming in pink and grey plaid organdie frilled on the skirt and sleeves. They carried bouquets of roses and wore large hats. Rene Levy, as flowergirl looked pretty in pink organdie frilled from the waist to the hem. She carried a basket of rose petals.

Rose Shames and Louis (Lulu) Miller on their wedding day and on honeymoon in Muizenberg

Mrs A Nathan looked well in black georgette with a black hat, and she carried tea roses. Mrs S Miller wore a handsome gown of black and fawn lace, with a hat to match. Her bouquet was of roses.

The reception was held at Ginsberg Hall, and about 200 guests were present. Toasts were proposed by Mr B Mendelsohn, Mr I Heyman and Mr H J Marks.

The members of the family present included Mr and Mrs J Kabatznik, Mr and Mrs H J Marks, Mrs Lipschitz, Mrs Miller and her sons, Mr and Mrs Shapiro (of Meyerton), Mrs B Greenberg, and Mr and Mrs L Heyman.

A pink dress with a silver-grey coat and pink hat was chosen by the bride for the honeymoon which will be spent at Muizenberg.

ESTABLISHED 1908

ISAAC OCHBERG

P O BOX 1305
TELEGRAMS: OCHBERGCO
CABLES: OCHBERG
TELEPHONE: CENTRAL 72
CODES:
A B C 5TH EDITION,
BENTLEY'S PHRASE.
WATKINS. PRIVATE.

COMMISSIONER OF OATHS

OCHBERGS BUILDINGS
ADDERLEY STREET
CAPE TOWN

27th November, 1933.

Miss Rose Shanes,
45 Hunter Street,
YEOVILLE.
JOHANNESBURG.

My dear Rose,

I just returned from Europe and found your invitation to your Wedding, which is to take place on Sunday the 10th December.

I need hardly tell you that if I will be in Johannesburg I will be only too happy to be present at your wedding. I did not even know of your engagement, and was rather taken by surprise to hear that you are getting married shortly.

On the "Warwick Castle" I spoke about you to Mr. Heyman (of Heyman & Gordon) also to Mr. Cohen of the O.K.Bazaars.

I hope that the young man you are marrying is a very nice fellow, which you undoubtedly fully deserve, and that he will take great care of you.

Appreciating the fact that you have not forgotten me on this great occasion of your life,

Sincerely yours,

Letter from Isaac Ochberg addressed to Rose

My mother kept a wonderful Jewish home for all of us. I had two siblings, my sister the late Carmen Nathan and my brother Des Miller. My parents always taught us to share everything and to respect our elders and each other.

My mother had a lonely life as my late father was a commercial salesman and was gone from home from Monday to Friday. Weekends were always wonderful and social. There were always friends around and music and singing.

I remember mostly the wonderful dinners at Pesach and Roshashana Yom Kippur with family and friends. Shabbat was kept always.

I often wondered how she did all this and who had taught her all this, especially as she never had her mother near her.

She loved all her children. If one asked her who is her favourite child, she would say "I love you all the same." She always had a smile and nothing was too much for her.

When my late father passed away, Rose came to live with my husband and myself. She lived with us for 17 years. My children adored her and they have very wonderful memories of her. She moved with us to Los Angeles but missed Desmond and Carmen (my late sister) very much, and then she decided she would spend six months at a time with us and six months with Carmen and Desmond and their families. Mom is buried here in Los Angeles, where she passed away in 1992.

My parents also helped raise funds to build the Shul, in Orchards, where my brother Desmond Miller was the first Barmitzvah to be held there after the Shul first opened (Pine

Sheila, Granny Rose and Joe

Street Shul) and in the same month my husband Joe Landau and I had the first wedding ceremony to be performed there. That was in May 1961. Joe was born in Alexandria, Egypt and immigrated to South Africa around 1945.

Joe and I have four daughters;
Kim, married to Matt Bedrosian, have a son Noah.
Lauren, married to David Hines, have two sons, Hugo and Oscar.
Gina, married a Miller, and has a son and daughter Danny and Carly-Rose,
Gaby, married to Michael Laur, have two daughters, Eden-Rose and Elle.

REMEMBERING GRANNY ROSE

Lauren Hines writes

We were the lucky cousins, lucky because Granny lived with us. I find it hard to conjure a memory of early childhood without the loving presence of Granny Rose. She spoiled us silly in her simple ways. She always so generously shared her comic books and peppermints. What really always mattered and what Granny Rose tried to teach us was the true meaning of family.

As a child I did not know to what extent Granny had suffered, how fraught with incredible loss her childhood must have been. Her life story was always a mystery, a pain too great to share or feelings so grave she simply chose not to remember.

The only time I remember Rose becoming upset was when we kids would argue amongst ourselves. I have vivid memories of Granny lecturing us on how awful it is to fight and most importantly how we should never use the word 'hate'. She always admonished; 'you have no idea what it means to hate'.

Looking back with adult eyes I realise how little Rose took from life and how much she gave. How few worldly possessions she desired or needed. Her need was for family, her tireless and endless devotion to her children and grandchildren.

Toward the end of Rose's life, she bestowed upon me the biggest gift of all. She had come to visit us in America, on the occasion of my sister's wedding. During her visit she became ill and was diagnosed with a brain tumour. Thus began her journey toward death. What an honour and privilege it was to sit, to love and to care for Rose until she had made her peace with this world and was finally able to let go. It was during this time that I began to understand the circle of life, family, love and devotion.

Fairly recently, with the translation of Rose's mother's story from Yiddish into English finally published, I am beginning to learn more about Rose Miller's life.

Kim Bedrosian remembers

Not too many kids can say they were fortunate to grow up with their grandmother living in their home. Granny Rose came to live with us when my Grandfather passed away, and lived with us throughout my childhood when I lived in South Africa. We were her family and the family she never had while growing up in the orphanage.

She seldom talked about her life as a child. She said it was too sad to talk about. We knew that her mother had given her a diary when she sent her and her brother to South Africa, but she would not allow anyone to read it saying it was much too painful to relive that time of her life.

She was always a huge part of our lives. She was always very supportive and interested in everything we did. We loved having her around. It was like having two moms. She was a comic book fiend and one of my favourite memories was spending afternoons with her in her room, reading her comics.

Granny Rose came to visit us here in Los Angeles for my wedding in 1992. While here, she was diagnosed with a brain tumour and passed away during her visit. I feel she came home to us her family to spend her last days. I think of her often and miss her very much. I wish my son would have had the opportunity to meet her.

Gina Miller remembers

Granny Rose was always there when my mother and father weren't. I always had the comfort of knowing that when I woke up in the middle of the night, and I was scared of the dark, she was awake in her room, directly across the hallway. She was always available to comfort me. She always seemed to be awake in the middle of the night.

Granny Rose taught me to have compassion, she taught me how to empathize and she taught me how to forgive, the biggest gift, anyone has ever bestowed upon me.

Gaby Lauren Joe Kim Matt Sheila and Gina

Granny Rose had a devastating childhood. Granny Rose lost her parents as a child and escaped to a foreign country, only to grow up in an orphanage. She held no grudge, no hatred towards anyone. She was thankful for surviving and thankful to her mother for giving her up. I believe that Granny's childhood created a lifetime of inability for her to take care of herself. It was almost as though she remained a child. She never learned how to drive, and I don't believe she completed her education. She never learned how to pay the bills, or write a cheque. She was an exquisite young lady, and married quite young.

Lulu, my grandfather, took care of her. Lulu died at a very young age, in his late fifties, of lung cancer. Granny was not able to take care of herself. She moved in with my Mom and Dad, and so, from then on she was taken care of by family.

Granny Rose always loved with an open heart. She didn't have a negative thought toward anyone or anything. She was so accepting, and never held blame toward anyone for her childhood. She was always just thankful for her family, and thankful for being alive. I am forever grateful for having her raise me along with my Mom and Dad. She helped to make me who I am today; she gave me my heart.

was still alive living in the Ukraine and she later got to Israel where she lived out the rest of her life. Rose's father had died.

She often told us that she refused to be adopted and remained at Arcadia until she was 16. Her brother Mannie who was eight years old when they arrived was adopted by the Favish family. Rose and Mannie were two of 12 children, wrote their mother Feiga in her diary.

Of her days at Arcadia I wish I could recall more. She did not speak in depth about her experiences there to me, in those early years of my marriage to Des her son.

Rose married Loius (Lulu) Miller, had three children, Carmen (deceased) Sheila and Des.

When our three sons saw that "the *four* cousins *in LA*" had each written a paragraph on their feelings about Granny Rose they asked if they could do the same. These grandchildren all loved this lady more than one can imagine.

REMEMBERING GRANNY ROSE

Craig Miller remembers

I am 35 years old I am one of Granny Rose's grandchildren. I have four children Taye nine years, Demi six years and Jed and Cal three year old twins.

Granny lived with us for many years and although I was very young I can remember so many good times and good memories with Granny. Most important is our family grounding and foundations that Rose laid down for the generations to come. Morals, respect, love, kindness, compassion, the ability to enjoy sharing and giving are a few of the traits that I have learned from my parents. These are the ways of my family and the ways that my children and their children have and will learn. How someone could survive such a challenge and find one self in an orphanage in a strange country at such a young age and after all that to come out at the other side and be such a good person, parent and example makes my Granny a hero.

The whole world should see what has come from my Granny's life, if only she was alive to see my kids and what unbelievable children they are and how all their morals, values, ethics etc are as a result of her and what she taught my parents.

I can't imagine how difficult gran's youth was especially because she never spoke about it, but after all that she raised a unique family.

Something I can remember granny always saying was, "Never say never" and never say, "I hate". Can you imagine after all she went through telling your grandchildren to never say the word "Hate." Wow that says a lot and has to give us all an idea of how to rise from any situation.

In conclusion I wish I had been able to spend more time with granny. I do think of her a lot because my family has a special closeness and caring for each other that I just don't see very often when I look at other families and I truly believe that its mostly due to the way my parents were brought up and the ways I was taught by them.

Thanks Gran.

Lonn Miller writes

My Granny Rose was as much a part of my life as my right hand. My memories of Granny Rose extend as far back as I am able to remember. Writing this I get a tear in my eye and a lump in my throat. I remember the last time I saw Granny Rose and I miss her whenever I think of her which is often when wishing she could have met my kids.

Granny Rose was the personification of family and love of family and she was a Jewess.

My seventh birthday present from Granny Rose was my very first siddur and today 32 years later it sits on a book shelf in my home, one of my most prized and valued possessions, the inside front cover inscribed with her unique hand-writing and signed-off with her trademark "G-d Bless".

Granny Rose lived with us in our house until my brothers and I were well into our teens. She always had good advice for us and was always concerned we would leave the house and get a cold. I couldn't count the times she would say to us "Take a jersey. You'll get a cold".

Granny Rose would spoil us and treat us to gifts of pocket money and other presents regularly; especially before each Yom Tov. She was an integral part of our lives and if we all merit being half the grand parent she was, we will have done well.

G-d Bless Granny Rose.

Glenn Miller remembers

I am Glenn Miller and the youngest of the three Miller brothers, the sons of Des and Margot Miller.

I am here today because of Granny Rose and may her memory linger on to my children as I recall her. I am so grateful for this book so that my children can also read the memories shared by the rest of her loving children and grand children.

Granny rose passed away when I was very young. I am her youngest grandchild so I don't have a library full of many memories of Granny Rose but the ones I do have I cherish with meaning as much as life itself. I feel I was most disadvantaged because Granny Rose was a most special person in the world.

My memory holds pictures of a lonely woman though. She lived alone because my Grandpa Lulu passed away even before I was born.

Granny Rose never opened up, not to me anyway and I don't know if she did with anyone else for that matter either. I just wish she spoke more about her past because I always felt she reserved her emotions and filed them away in a box somewhere in her mind. She spent a lot of time with us on and off through the years. I recall daily when she was with us how she would just sit on a couch whilst my brothers and I played as boys do and made a noise and ran in and out the room she was in, either sleeping or awake. Looking back now, I think that that those emotions may have been all she was thinking of all those times.

Granny Rose was a giver but not in a material kind of way. She was a giver of only genuine love and adoration. I don't think she valued anything material, however, of the very little she seemed to have, she always found a way of giving my brothers and I such that I valued her giving far beyond anything material a young child could value or have or need. For instance she would collect all her coins in jars and bottles for months at a time, sometimes one bottle for each of my brother and I or sometimes one massive bottle to share. She'd surprise us and give them to us. My brother and I would spend hours counting the coins. Sometimes she'd help us count and sort the 'load' or join us on the outing to the bank to 'cash' it in. This added to our pocket money so the value of that gift lingered and the memory grew in whatever it was we consumed from that money so looking back we would think of her with every dollar spent. She was very smart like this but more importantly was her company we shared each time. She would always follow up and get involved with what we bought.

Pesach time was usually also *Easter* time and she always arrived with *Easter* eggs for us and now, not an *Easter* goes by I don't think of her because of that.

I always feel like I missed and still miss her since maturing into an adult. Children visit Disneyland only to find it a minute place when they grow up. I think my memory of Granny Rose was the complete opposite. I think that I only had time to get to know the tip of the iceberg and I know that I am the man I am today because of her and I am eternally grateful and indebted to her for this.

I love you Granny Rose.

ROSIE (SHAMES) MILLER
As remembered by Yvonne (Slier) Phillips

Rosie was an Ochberg orphan and was brought out to Arcadia at the same time as my mother Sarah (Altuska) Slier. She was very beautiful as you see in the photograph following sent in by Ursula Rembach.

When I first met Rosie, she was married to Louis (but always called) Lulu Miller and they lived in Orange Grove, Johannesburg not very far from where we were living. Lulu Miller was a commercial traveller and was often away from home, 'on the road', so Rosie was rather lonely and spent a lot of time with my mother. She would arrive at our home, often, in the mornings, with her daughter, Carmen and sit reading our American comics which she loved. She was so much part of our family that when Carmen started school at Orange Grove Primary, she told everyone that she was related to the Sliers

Rosie had a younger daughter, Sheila and a son Desmond. Carmen became a Professor of Law at the University of Bophutushwane but died at a very young age.

Her daughter, Sheila married Joe Landau, and emigrated to Los Angeles where he was in the diamond business. Desmond became a diamond cutter and emigrated to Australia.

My husband, Gerald Phillips and I moved to Durban in 1956 as did my parents at a later date. My mother's sister, Leah, also went to Durban after her husband, Maurice Rosenblatt passed

away and her four children had 'left the nest. (Incidentally they all live in Melbourne). It was a similar story with Rosie. Lulu died and she used to holiday in Durban, so there was a minor reunion of three Ochberg children.

We now saw a great deal of Rosie who had become a great part of our lives again. On Friday evenings when we went to my sister Phyllis's home for Shabbat, my husband would do what he called 'the milk run' picking up the three women from their different homes and afterwards bringing them back again.

Sheila Landua adds
My Mom lived with us for 17 years, but she used to go to Durban for three months from July to September every year as we had a holiday home there.

The Slier families were wonderful to my mother and Rose was heartbroken when they moved to Durban. I remember the Rummy games, Aunty Sarah's cheese cake, it was the best, Yvonne with her piano accordion, Debora a fashion designer who once made a whole wardrobe of clothes for my doll,

I think Phyllis was younger than me and of course Lionel was older.

ROSE'S FAMILY
Written by her grandson Steven Nathan

Rose was an Ochberg Orphan and spent her youth in the Arc prior to marrying Lulu (Louis Miller). Lulu and Rose had three children, Carmen was the eldest, then there is Sheila and last, there is Desmond.

Sheila married Joe Landau and now lives in Los Angeles with her four children Kim, Lauren, Gina and Gaby and their respective children; nine grandchildren in all.

Des lives in Sydney with his wife Margot, their three boys, Lonn, Craig and Glen and their grandchildren.

Carmen, the first child of Lula and Rose Miller, married Arthur Nathan, and had two children, my older sister Melanie and me.

My name is Steven Nathan and I currently reside in Vienna, Virginia (greater Washington DC metropolitan area) with my wife Romy and our two boys Jack (age nine) and Max (age seven). I have been asked to write a little and provide some background on my Granny Rose and also on my late Mom, Carmen, the first child of Lula and Rose Miller.

MY GRANNY ROSE
Written by Steven Nathan

It is a little difficult for me to write too much about my Granny Rose. She was always just "there" for a large part of my life. I didn't have a full concept of her background growing up. Although she was very reluctant to share anything of her childhood with any of us, I did know that she was from Russia, had been sent to South Africa at an early age and lived in the Arc prior to her marriage to my Grandpa Lulu. Lulu died at a relatively early age. He was a big smoker, developed lung cancer and succumbed to this when I was about five years old. Granny Rose must have been about 50 years old at the time. In retrospect this seems so young, since I am writing this at age 51. Granny Rose was very dependent, I guess she had depended on Lulu most of her adult life and became dependent on her kids and their respective spouses after Lulu's death.

She lived together with Desmond, her youngest, for a short period of time before Des got married to Margo. After this, she lived mostly with Sheila, her second daughter and my late Mom Carmen's sister, and Joe Landau, Sheila's husband.

Initially, I lived with my family in Port Elizabeth and as I recall she would come about once a year for a visit, as she did when Lulu was still alive. When we moved to Johannesburg, Rose continued to live with Sheila and Joe. The times that she did come and visit us, I sensed that she and my late Mom Carmen sometimes butted heads. Sheila and Joe moved with their four daughters to the US in about 1975. From that time onwards, Rose lived with Des and Margo and their three sons, but would visit Sheila and Joe in the US. I moved to the US myself in 1985 with my sister Melanie herself moving over a few months later.

We were all living in Los Angeles at the time and as I recall, Granny Rose would come and visit and stay with Sheila for a good few months at a time. It was around one of these visits in 1992 that Granny Rose got ill with severe headaches. She had a CT scan of the head which showed evidence of cancerous lesions that had likely spread from elsewhere. The most likely primary source were her lungs as she had been a heavy smoker most her life. She had only given up smoking about four years prior when her breathing became a little difficult. She never complained about her breathing but one could tell that she got a little winded with excess activity and she very likely had a "touch" of emphysema. Together with Sheila and her family, I had the privilege of taking care of Granny Rose in her final weeks. She was buried at a cemetery in Los Angeles and as I recall I delivered a eulogy at her graveside, but I cannot recall a word of what I said.

What Granny Rose was like as a person I find difficult for me to say. She was not one who readily engaged in conversation and was always kind of in the background of any social gatherings. I think she was content to live her life somewhat vicariously through her children (especially Sheila) and her grandchildren. She spent a lot of time reading her comic books and when TV became available transitioned to that very readily. "Sister Louis" and "Look" were soon replaced by "Days of our lives" and other daytime soaps. The reason I remember the names of these photo comic books is that I shared Granny Rose's comic book interests and would read them myself. She was loving in her own way to all of us, although she was not one to be demonstrably affectionate.

There was one incident that I still cannot explain, but was quite profound and difficult for all of us to comprehend. Many years ago when we were all back in South Africa, one of her sisters who she had been separated from in Russia and who went to live in Israel, came to visit us, specifically Rose, in South Africa. This was a big deal for all of us and I think we might have all been a little excited to know that Rose would be reunited with one of her siblings. Well, it didn't turn out as planned and as I recall Rose was less than warm and welcoming to her sister and cut her cold for the most part. When confronted about this, she blamed it on the language barrier that now existed between the two of them. However, it turned into a very uncomfortable scenario for all and one that left us all scratching our heads a little. After her sister left (quite upset herself as I recall), the two never communicated again to my knowledge.

It is interesting to try and put Rose's life with us in the perspective of her background and speculate how that likely affected her in terms of her subsequent familial interactions. However, I don't think that any of us can fully comprehend the events and circumstance of her early life and how that impacted and moulded her apparent introspective nature and rather passive life with which she appeared quite content.

MY MOTHER CARMEN (MILLER) NATHAN
Written by Steven Nathan

It has been almost 20 years since my mother died and this is how I remember her life.

Carmen accomplished a lot in her life. She married my Dad, Arthur Nathan, at the age of around 20. As I recall they met at the Yeoville Swimming Pool, were engaged three weeks later and married nine months after that. My one and only sibling Melanie was born two years after their marriage and two years later I came along. My Mom was unable to have any more kids after that.

Carmen worked as a paralegal in her early career and also did some modelling. Soon after Melanie was born, the family moved to Port Elizabeth where Arthur worked as a travelling salesman. Carmen was at first 'a stay at home mom', but when I was about five, she decided to go back to school and enrolled at the University of Port Elizabeth for a B.Juris degree. I recall there was a local joke going around amongst all her friends as to how long she would last at this. I think the longest anyone gave her was six months at it before rejoining the tea party crowd.

Carmen was a very hard worker, very smart and dedicated and surprised everyone by soon emerging at the top of her class and graduating cum laude. Around this time, it became evident that the family would be moving back to Johannesburg after being in Port Elizabeth for about 11 or so years. Carmen therefore enrolled for her LLB degree through the University of South Africa and once again through the move and everything else emerged at the top of her class and once again graduated cum laude.

She then took a position as a lecturer at the University of South Africa (Unisa) and used to commute on a daily basis between our home in Johannesburg and the University in Pretoria. This was the start of a great and very accomplished legal academic career. Carmen was very busy and exemplified the example of "if you want something done, then give it to a busy person". Her juggling act included supporting and schlepping me through a successful swimming career which culminated in me receiving my Springbok colors in 1978 and 1979.

Carmen and Arthur's Wedding
Front row: Unknown girl and Desmond Miller (Rose Miller's son and youngest of three)
Second Row: Louis (Lulu) Miller, Rose Miller, Carmen Nathan (bride and Rose's eldest), Arthur Nathan (groom), Millie Nathan and Clarence Nathan

While at Unisa, Carmen co-wrote a major legal textbook, that I believe is still in print and used today. She continued to excel in her writing and wrote, co-authored and translated a number of books through her career. This was aside from the many articles she wrote. After a period of time at Unisa, Carmen took a position at the University of the Witwatersrand where she lectured for a number of years.

It was around this time that her marriage to Arthur began to fall apart, ultimately leading to their divorce in about 1980. By this time, Melanie had completed her BA/LLB and was herself practicing law while I was completing my medical school at Wits. After I graduated at the end of 1981, Carmen took the position of Professor of Law and became Dean of the Law School at the University of Bophuthatswana. By this time, her career had evolved further so that she enjoyed an International reputation as a champion of human rights, specifically woman and children's rights. She also had her own radio show "Let's make it Legal", which allowed her a measure of fame outside the academic world. I believe that there was always some criticism of her going to Bop (Bophuthatswana) which was perceived by some as an endorsement of apartheid. However, her view on it was that it was an island(s) and perhaps an example, of what South Africa could become. Aside from her Law School duties, Carmen found a very interesting and full life for herself in Bop where she, amongst other things, became an adviser and close confidant to the President of Bophuthatswana, Lucas Mangope.

Carmen would come and visit us at least once a year. About 10 days after her last visit over the Rosh Hashanah/Yom Kippur Holidays in 1990, she suffered a collapse at her home in Bop and died before her time at the early age of 55. Lucas Mangope sought the family's permission and we agreed that she should be buried in the President's personal family cemetery. Melanie and myself were accompanied by Sheila and travelled from Los Angeles to South Africa for the funeral . We were joined at the funeral by the rest of our family including my late Granny Rose (Ochberg orphan), as well as Desmond and Margot.

The funeral was almost "State-like" and was attended by a few thousand people with Carmen's coffin flown in by helicopter. I delivered a eulogy at the graveside and I wish I could find it as it summarized her life and accomplishments a little more completely and with fresher memory than I currently enjoy.

Although the so-called homelands are gone and incorporated in the new South Africa, in retrospect perhaps history will judge them, not for their intent, but on the unintended consequence of demonstrating that a black government and co-existence could work. Maybe this was another brick in the foundation that provided a measure of comfort for white South Africans to vote for the dismantling of apartheid and enable a peaceful transition. Carmen would have been proud.

The political circumstance of the day was one of the primary reasons I left South Africa in 1985 after completing my mandatory two years in the South African army. Melanie also left SA in 1985 and settled in California. She now lives in Marin County in Northern California where she works as a mediator and gay rights activist. She is married to her partner, Dorit Israel and has two kids; Hannah (12) and Rafael (three).

After my residency in Internal Medicine at Long Island Jewish in New York, I completed my fellowships in Pulmonary, Critical Care and Transplantation at Cedars-Sinai Medical Center in Los Angeles. While working at Cedars around 1992, my granny Rose visited and was staying with Sheila and her family when she became ill. It was soon evident that she had widespread cancer. I had the privilege of functioning as her doctor and together with Sheila and her family helped to take care of her during her last weeks. In some circle of irony, I had been trained and was in a position to take care of my Gran as she came to the end of her life's journey.

My current position is as medical director of the advanced lung disease and lung transplant program at Inova Fairfax Hospital, which is a large Hospital in the Washington DC suburbs about 12 miles west of the White House. I was somewhat aware of my Gran's childhood, but did not know all the details since she wasn't one to speak much of her past. As I think about how my own life might have been affected by this, I do recall an incident in my formative high school years that in some subliminal way might have helped fashion the course of my career. Granny Rose's brother, Mannie Favish (Ochberg orphan), had married Nora, who was herself a doctor, Specifically, Nora was a Tuberculosis doctor, a specialty of the time that is commonly regarded as the Pulmonologist of yesteryear.

I do recall that she had asked us to hold onto a specimen of TB lung, which was in a formalin glass case, to be picked up by a pathologist we knew, D. Jack Abramowitz. Anyway, Dr A was a little slow in stopping by and the specimen sat in our dining room as a visual accompaniment to many family dinners over the next six months. I also do recall the daily drive from our

Granny Rose and her four grandsons – June 1985
Rose and Lonn Miller at back and Craig Miller,
Steven Nathan and Glen Miller in front

I am indebted to the goodwill and work of Mr Ochberg, whose deeds have had a profound and extraordinary effect on many. My mom, Carmen's life is an attestation to how his deeds have been magnified generationally.

The Nathans; Steve and Romy (Gunter) with sons Jack and Max

house in Saxonwold to Parktown Boys High from 1971 until my matriculation in 1975. We passed the Arc daily and if we didn't get up Oxford Road early enough, many was the day when traffic would back up behind Mr Klevansky's "jalopie". I was one of "Klev's" Latin pupils for three years and through his renowned cajoling was one of his many Latin distinction students; no doubt this played some part in my acceptance to medical school.

ROSE'S FAMILY - Front row: Max Nathan, Elle Lauer, Romy Nathan, Oscar Hines
Middle row: Carly Miller, Hugo Hines, Eden Lauer, Jack Nathan
Back row: Joe Landau, Daniel Miller, Sheila (Miller) Landau, David Hines, Michael Lauer, Steve Nathan, Lauren (Landau) Hines, Gaby (Landau) Lauer, Kim (Landau) Bedrosian, Gina (Landau) Mille

Chapter 125 – HERSH, ISAAC AND CHASKEL SHTEINER

CHASKEL, HERSH AND ISAAC SHTEINER later known as Charles, Harry and Isadore Steiner.

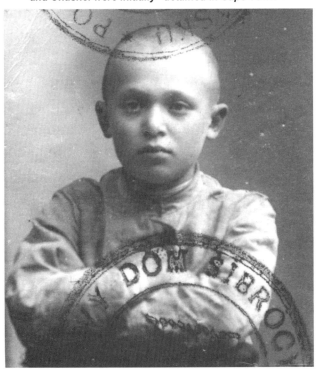

The entry in the register kept at The South African Jewish Orphanage (later called Arcadia) shows Hersh aged 12, Isaac seven and Chaskel five. While all boys went up to Arcadia, Isaac and Chaskel were initially "detained in Cape Town".

Hersh Shteiner
Photo from Travel Permits from Pinsk Magistrate

Group Passport Three
Hersh Shteiner, is no 28 on the list and shown as aged 8. I believe Hersh is in the first row, furthest on the right.

HARRY STEINER (HERSH SHTEINER)
Written by Audrey Rubin (nee Steiner)

My late father Harry (Hersh) and his late brothers Isadore (Issy) and Charles (Charlie) were Ochberg Orphans.

Harry was born in Libshei, Poland on 13 April 1909. His parents were Boruch and Brocha (nee Barenboim) Steiner. On his mother's side of the family, his grandparents were Naomi and Zvi Hersh Barenboim and the names of his father's parents are unknown.

After his father was shot one Saturday morning when he was going to Shul his mother took him and his brothers to her sister, Bashe's family. Chaya, the sister of the three boys, did not go with as she was waiting to tell her husband. Chaya's husband was in the army (presume in the resistance). The journey in the snow was too much for Brocha and she died from pneumonia. Before she died she made Harry promise to look after his brothers. Luckily he managed to keep that promise to her. He waited to see that his brothers were married before he decided it was time for him to get married. He was also the last to pass away.

While my dad was working at his uncle's farm, somebody came rushing to tell him that someone was going to take his brothers to South Africa. Needless to say Harry ran to see what this was all about. The rest is history.

My dad told us that when the ship wanted to dock in England there were shots fired some distance away from the ship. Eventually they were allowed to land. He also mentioned that two children remained in England. Maybe they had family there or else they were adopted.

Brocha (nee Barenboim) Steiner seated and her three Barenboim brothers; Samuel, the oldest, Hyman, the youngest and Joseph

581

Chaya (Shteiner) Friedman (Fleishman)   *Chaya, her child and husband and her two children - all perished in the Holocaust*

Unknown relative   *Yentel Fleishmam*   *Feigel and Reftel Barenboim*   *Joseph Barenboim's Family in USA*

Charlie, Harry and Issy   *Charlie, Harry and Issy*   *Charlie and Issy*   *Charlie, Harry and Issy*

Harry in rugby togs   *Harry and Charles*   *Harry in Rhodesia*   *Harry 1928*

Harry and Annie (Klevansky)   Harry, Bertha, Issy and Annie
Wedding March 8 1935

Harry, Bernard and Annie with Audrey behind
Bernard's Bar Mitzva 1951

Audrey, Harry and Bernard

My father did not tell me much about his life. A cousin, late Marsha Gross nee Barr, shortened in America from Barrenboim, told me what happened to the family as told her by her late granny Basha (Bessie.) She was my late father's mother's sister. I do have some photos with Yiddish writing on the back of the photos but do not know who they are from. Most of them write that things are not good and end the letters 'from your loving cousin.'

Stella Steiner, Issy's daughter, also found some letters, also in Yiddish, written to my late father Harry when my father was in the orphanage in Parktown.

How my late father made contact with his American family was through a Jewish newspaper brought to him one Sunday morning by a friend, Judel Hellman, who was also an Ochberg Orphan. His Uncle Jacob Stein, shortened from Steiner, was looking for information about my late father and his brothers. I was young at the time and just before my dad passed away I got the address of the Barr family but not the Stein family. I'm still in touch with Helen Barr.

He then got in touch with his mother's side of the family. After my mother passed away we lost touch with both families. When

Barney Steiner, Moira Wacks, Bernard, Annie and Harry and
Audrey (Steiner) and Lionel Rubin
Wedding Kensington Shul 1957

my father remarried his second wife Doris started writing to them again but got no reply from his Uncle Jacob Stein. Some years later I decided to try to write direct to Helen Barr and Marsha Gross. Some years ago Marsha came to South Africa to meet me. She stayed with us and I made a party for her and her husband Shia so that she could meet the rest of the South African family. Most of the information I have was given to me by her.

As far back as I can remember once a month on a Sunday morning Mr Stanger (also an Ochberg orphan) arrived at our house on his motor bike to collect a donation for the Orphanage.

When I asked my father why he did not go back to see where he had lived he told me it's too cold. He told me that his sister had married a Friedman, Friedland or something like that but did not know their daughter or son's first names. He told me that although he was the oldest he was the last to get married as the last thing his mother made him promise to do was that he would look after his two brothers and so he had waited until they were both married before he got married.

We used to go to Durban by train for our holidays. Bernard and I thought it was great fun, except that we had to get to the station hours before the train left. My dad's motto was that we could wait for the train but the train would never wait for us. We stayed at the only kosher hotel in Durban I think it was called the Sharon. It was owned by Solly Kursner's parents.

Eventually my father bought a Morris (Minor). When we went on outings or to visit family or friends and if the weather looked like it was going to rain, we all had to quickly get into the car and head for home. My father would park the car in the garage and take out his towels and clothes and give the car a good rubbing down. We all laughed and said that the car would not get a cold.

When the Second World War started they were calling for volunteers, Harry applied. The doctor who examined him would not pass him as he had an ulcer. Harry pleaded, he even cried with him to pass him. The doctor eventually passed him. My dad left by train and when lunch time came around they gave him a tin of Bully Beef; just what a good kosher Jewish man did not need. His ulcer flared up and he was very sick. The army doctor told personnel that they would have to send him home. No begging on my dad's part would change their minds. When the train stopped at the next station he had to get off and return home.

Harry was a very private, independent and extremely tidy person. He had wonderful 'green fingers'. He could plant anything, anywhere, anytime and it would grow. We always had some fresh fruit and vegetables He enjoyed nothing more than spending a Sunday morning pottering around in his garden.

We used to tease him and say that if we blindfolded him and asked him to go to his wardrobe and pick out his blue socks he would do just that. No ways would he bring us any other coloured socks. He loved watching rugby being an ex player.

On Saturday nights he enjoyed playing rummy with the Zageys or the Helmans. Other times he would go with my mother to bioscope to see a film and Bernard and I would sometimes go with. On most Sunday mornings he would come to visit us and his grandchildren. The grandchildren looked forward to seeing him. Hopefully it was not just to get some sweets or money from my father and Doris.

Lastly, I would like to record my deepest thanks to Isaac Ochberg and the South African Jewish Community and everybody else who was involved in bringing the orphans to South Africa. Without them we would not be here to relate our stories to the rest of the world.

Harry passed away in Johannesburg on 15 July 1999.

Harry's 90th birthday –
with Bernard's family and grandchildren

Gaby Laur remembers

I was 9 years old when we left South Africa. I realized all that Gran was to us when we moved.

Gran lived with us in South Africa. She was a part of our everyday lives. She was always around, always at home and always with a cigarette and box of peppermints. I remember her smile, her beautiful lips and her tanned skin. I remember Gran keeping to herself and meshing into the every day chaos a family of four children is sure to bring with it. I remember the simplicity Gran brought along with her, appreciative of everything around her in her life, never needy, never wanting and simply happy to enjoy the experience of everyday life alongside us. I never knew much of Granny's life back then. She never talked about it.

I remember feeling the void when we moved. Each year Gran would spend half with us here in the US and half with the rest of our family in SA. I always thought it so sad that her home as she knew it was split apart upon our move, however, when Gran would come and spend time here she would mesh right in, yet again riding alongside our everyday lives as if she never left. She was yet again appreciative, never asking for anything, keeping much to herself yet very much a part of our family home.

The blessing that Gran bestowed on all of us here in the US is that she came home to die, here with us, her home. My favourite thing of all is that when she was ill and practically on her death bed she had a conversation with my then boyfriend of four years, Michael, and made him promise her that he intended to marry me in the future. Gran wanted to know that he would take care of me. She loved Michael. This was so important to her. Michael and I were engaged six months after Gran died and have been happily married now going on 16 years. Thank you Granny Rose!

And thank you Granny Rose for teaching us to be simply happy, not needy or wanting just happy with the greatest gifts of life; family and love.

ROSE (MILLER) SHAMUS
Written by Joe Landau

Rose was my mother-in-law. I was so privileged to have a mother-in-law like her, Rose was wise, loving and understanding.

After reading what my wife Sheila and four daughters, Kim, Lauren, Gina and Gaby, had to say in their comments, I find myself with nothing more to add to what my family said except...

Rose was blessed to have great logic, wisdom and common sense. When Sheila and I had important decisions to make, including immigrating to America with four girls ages nine to 15 she gave us the courage we needed to face the move. We had her blessings.

She brought our two cultures together, Eastern European and Sephardic. Rose made it very easy for me. She always agreed with what I said, even if I was wrong, she always stood by me. What a gracious lady she was.

We nursed her through the most devastating illness and even then, she never complained. On her Death bed, she called us altogether and presented us with whatever she had brought with her from South Africa (only supposedly for a visit), her little pieces of jewelry and then gave us permission to read her mother's journal.

The fact that she is buried here, in Los Angeles has given us roots. It has made us feel like we belong here.

With Love.
Joe Landau

Rose and Family September 1987
Carmen Nathan - older daughter, Des Miller - son,
Lonn and Craig (front) Miller - grandsons, Margot Miller, Rose, Kim
Bedrosian - granddaughter and Sheila Landau - daughter.

ROSIE (SHAMES) MILLER
As remembered by Margot Miller

I am Desmond's wife and his Mom, Rosie (Shames) Miller, was an Ochberg orphan and sister of Manes Favish. I hope Sheila Landau, Des's sister who lives in Los Angeles, will write to you with Rosies story, but I hoped I might also add my little bit.

I first met Rosie in 1964 when I met Des who was six years later to become my husband, Rose never ever mentioned that she was an Ochberg Orphan but she did often tell us stories of how she lived in Poland (now the Ukraine) in a village where her father was the mayor. She spoke about a nanny who would take her into the woods, I assume to play. She had a diary given to her by her mother, as did her brother but he never read his copy which was written in a Polish/Yiddish dialect, which she also never ever read as she did not want to. We all assumed this was because whatever was written in it was too painful to read.

In 1998 after her and Mannie's death Nora Favish, Mannie's wife, went to great lengths to get the diary translated. She printed this out and gave each of us a copy. In this diary Rose and Mannie's mother documents as best she could the events (ie the pogroms) leading up to her placing them in an orphanage, where Ochberg found them.

During Nora's research she discovered that Rose (Reisel) who was born on 4 April 1910 in Verba Poland (Ukraine), was admitted to Arcadia when she arrived in South Africa as an Ochberg orphan when she was 10 years old. In fact her mother

Audrey, Harry and Bernard at Harry's 90th birthday

On the last Sunday in every month the Steiner cousins Barney, Stanley, Stella, Beryl, and I and our wives, husbands and partners and my daughter, Janice, go out for lunch together. It is a time when we can all get together. Afterwards who ever's turn it is to choose the restaurant has everybody over to their house for tea. This month it is my turn. to have everybody over for tea.

ISAAC SHTEINER later known as Isadore Steiner.
Written by Stella Steiner

My Dad was born in Pinsk on 18 September 1913 and was, therefore, seven years old when he arrived with his two brothers, Harry (Eldest brother) and Charlie (Younger than my Dad) in South Africa in 1921. They lived at the Jewish Orphanage in Parktown (Arcadia). I can't remember if he had to leave the orphanage at the age of 16 or 18. During his early years, he attended the Jewish Government School. When he left Arcadia, he went to live with a Jewish lady and her husband that took in boarders. I can't remember her name. He also boarded at a gentleman named Solly Bassman, whose mother took in boarders.

I don't know very much about my late Dad's early life as he seldom spoke about it.

After leaving school, my Dad did his apprenticeship as a motor mechanic. He met my Mom Bertha Steiner (nee Weitzman) and they married on 15 December 1935. They had three children, Barney, Stanley and myself. I arrived 15 years after Barney and 11 years after Stanley, so I'm known as the "Laat Lammetjie".

All I can remember about my Late Dad is that he worked hard at work and at home, working on cars. He was always working on cars. He built up a big private clientele. In fact, Barney and Stanley followed in my Dad's footsteps and are both motor mechanics themselves. My Dad suffered a massive stroke, after fixing my car in fact, and at the age of 74 became wheel-chair bound. He was paralysed on the right side of his body. He lived until 81 when he passed away at Hospice from cancer. I just wish I knew more now.

The mother and sister of the three Steiner siblings Brocha (nee Barenboim) Steiner and Chaya

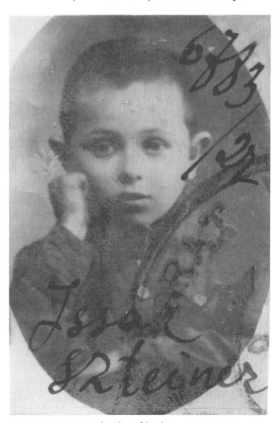

Isadore Shteiner
Photo from Travel Permits from Pinsk Magistrate

The three Steiner brothers; Charlie, Harry and Isadore

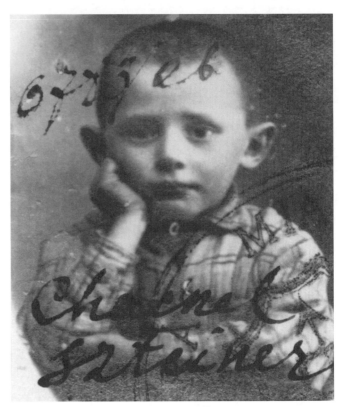

Chaskel Shteiner
Photo from Travel Permits from Pinsk Magistrate

CHARLES STEINER (CHASKEL SHTEINER)
16 October 1914 to 14 February 1959
Written by Gila Waichman (Heather Steiner)

My father, Charles, fondly called Charlie was born Chaskel in Libshei, Poland. His parents, Baruch and Brocha (nee Barenboim) had four children: Chaya, Hersh, Isaac and Chaskel. After Baruch was murdered during one of the many pogroms, Brocha fled with her children to her sister in Belarus. Soon after their arrival, Brocha died from pneumonia. Chaya remained with her aunt's family. She later married and her married name was Friedman. Tragically, she, her husband and two children, and the rest of the family died in the Holocaust. Sadly, this is all I know about that side of my dad's family.

Thanks to the humanitarian kindness and generosity of Isaac Ochberg, the three little boys, Chaskel aged five, Isaac six and Hersh nine were among the lucky ones who were selected and sent to South Africa. At age 14 my dad left the South African Jewish Orphanage in whose care the boys had been placed and he (and I think also his brothers) went to live with Solly Bassman and his family in Bertrams /Doornfontein. As far as I know Charles did not stay in touch with any of the other orphaned children.

He never ever spoke about his parents and sister, or his life as a child, adolescent or young adult. All I really knew was that he grew up in an orphanage, and his only immediate family were his two older brothers, Harry (Hersh) and Isadore (Isaac). I did not know much about Israel until the Six Day War and until I immigrated to Israel in 1969. I had no inkling of pogroms, the holocaust or anti-Semitism. We were just an average South African family and I was too young to even think about asking about our "roots".

My mother, Esther, daughter of Fanny Silver from Poland and Louis Weitzman from Latvia was the fifth of eight siblings and was born 22 March 1916 in Boksburg, South Africa. The family moved to Doornfontein when she was seven.

Charles and Esther met in the year 1932 in Doornfontein and were married on 23 December 1934 at the H O D Hall in Doornfontein. Charles was 20 and Esther only 18 years old. As you can see from the wedding invitation, Mr and Mrs. L Shemer were cited as the groom's family. The Shemers were cousins of my grandmother, Fanny Weitzman.

A year later Charles' elder brother Isadore (Issy), married my mother's elder sister, Bertha on 15 December 1935.

Charles was a wonderful, devoted, loving husband and father and a kind, gentle, soft-spoken and patient man. He was a good all round sportsman playing tennis, swimming, fishing and football and excelled at everything he did. Every Friday and Saturday would be spent in family activities, going for drives in the country, teaching and encouraging us to take part in sports, or visiting family and friends.

Ours was a loving, happy middle class family. We lived in Yeoville, opposite the Yeoville Convent, where all three daughters were educated. My father volunteered to do all building and maintenance work at the Convent and School, and in return our family was allowed to play on their tennis and netball courts when school was out. Our home was always full of pets; dogs, cats and birds, living in perfect harmony. I was the "spoilt, little girl". Our garden was on a deep slope. I remember at age five, that I used to ride my tricycle and when I was tired of riding for the day, I would ride full tilt down this deep slope and hit a brick wall at the bottom , thus buckling the front wheel. My dad, faithfully each night, would repair the buckled wheel so his little angel could carry on the next day with her wild antics.

Charles was a building contractor and among his many projects was the reconstruction of the Cyrildene Synagogue and numerous housing projects in Krugersdorp. My dad served in the Army during World War II and was stationed in Egypt.

Charlie passed away in 1959 at the age of 44. I was 12 years old. We were all devastated at his early demise. My whole world was turned upside down. My mom had to go to work, we had to leave our beautiful home and my precious animals and I had to change schools. If I found this upsetting and overwhelming at my age, I can only imagine the trauma my dad must have experienced, at his tender age, at the upheaval in his life: losing his beloved parents, being separated from his sister, and being shipped off to a foreign country.

After my dad passed away my mom wrote,
"Charles, My beloved darling, my love, my life
To the world you were my husband, to me you were the world.
Always a smile, never a frown
Always a hand when one was down
Always loving, thoughtful and kind
These are the memories you left behind
Your dear image is always in my heart, though G-d has taken you from my side"

Esther regrettably passed away at the age of 72 in 1988 in Israel, two days before she was due to return to South Africa and never lived to see all her great-grandchildren.

We, their descendants, will be eternally grateful to a wonderful, generous man, Isaac Ochberg, for granting us the privilege of "being here today".

Our most heartfelt gratitude and "Kol Hakavod" to all those numerous righteous kind souls associated with the rescue and nurturing of the Ochberg orphans.

CHARLES STEINER (CHASKEL SHTEINER)
Written by Shirley (Steiner) Shamos with photos from Gila

Group Passport Four
Chaskel Shteiner is no one on the list aged five
and Isaac is no three on the list aged six.
"My father, Charles Steiner, is in the first row, furthest
on the right in the group photo" Shirley Shamos

Seeing my father, Charles Steiner, in the group passport photo, at five years of age, shoeless and very gaunt, broke my heart. It brought home to me the realization of how he must have suffered in his early childhood. His father, a scribe in the Shul,

Harry and Charles Steiner
Photo taken at Arcadia

was shot by Bolsheviks, in front of his family on the way back from the Synagogue. His mother fled in the middle of winter with her daughter aged 11 and three sons aged four, six and eight to her sister in Belarus and died on arrival from pneumonia. The daughter remained with the sister's family and the boys were sent to South Africa with the Ochberg Orphans. How does a child of five survive the loss of his parents, one after the other? And then is sent to a strange country, and a strange new language? Luckily he had two older brothers with him. The sister who remained in Belarus died in the Holocaust with her husband and two children.

My father went to the Oranjia orphanage in Cape Town, and then to Arcadia in Johannesburg.

As an adult he worked in the building trade and eventually started a contracting builders company with a partner: Steiner and Schneid. He met my mother Esther Weitzman and they married in 1934. Two brothers married two sisters.

Charles Steiner
Photo taken at the tennis court at Arcadia

Esther and Charles Steiner 1930s

Charles, Esther (in black) and Esther's sisters

Esther, Charles and Rachel

Esther

Mr. & Mrs. L. Weitzman
and
Mr. & Mrs. L. Shemer
request the pleasure of your company on the occasion of the Marriage of

Esther Weitzman

to

Charles Steiner

On Sunday, December 23rd, 1934.
Ceremony and Reception 7 p.m.
At H.O.D. Hall, 14 De Villiers Street, Johannesburg.

R.S.V.P.:—"BELSTONE"
45 Bertrams Road,
New Doornfontein.   Johannesburg.

Wedding Invitation

My father volunteered in the army and was sent "up north" in 1939. I was six months old at the time. He was away for two years. He remained a soldier till the end of the war in 1945. I remember him in his uniform. I was so proud. He was an exceptional father.

Charles Steiner in Uniform - WWII

The Roll of Honour of all Arcadians who served in WWII
Steiner C is the 5th name in the names starting with "S"

Esther and Charles

Charles

Smith T
Smith B
Shain H
Sagoria E
Steiner C
Sullivan L
Starkowitz A
Slater M
Sacks M
Slavin C

Charles in uniform

Barney Silver (Esther's cousin) Charles Steiner, and Harry Weitzman (Esther's elder brother)

Esther and Charles in the 1950s

He spent a lot of time with us and he adored his three "princesses". We were always taken on new adventures to see the country.

Esther and baby Heather 1946

Charles holding Heather, Esther and Beryl and in front Shirley – Late 1940s

Beryl, Esther, Charles, Shirley and in front
Heather-Mid 1950s

I would come home on a Friday from school and find our suitcases packed and the car ready to set off for a surprise weekend trip to somewhere new.

He was an excellent sportsman; good at tennis and table tennis. He also loved playing cards.

When I met and then married Yitzie Shamos in 1958, he finally found his longed for son. They were very competitive. Both were excellent all rounders. Often in our courtship, I would go to bed while my dad and Yitzie would be playing klaberjas or table tennis till all hours. They loved and respected each other.

My parents were very happily married until my dad died of cancer in 1959 at age 44. We were all distraught at his early demise. I was 20 at the time. My mom was 42, but she never remarried. He was the love of her life.

My mom was wonderful with children and was asked to start a crèche of five children of doctors and nurses at the Childrens' Hospital in Johannesburg. She eventually became Administrator of the department which grew to 250 children.

After our marriage, we lived in Germiston until we came on aliya to Israel in 1969. Yoel, our eldest son was born in 1960, our second son, David, in 1962 and our daughter Dina, in 1965. My husband's family, the Dunsky family, were committed Zionists, the majority having emigrated to Israel in the 1950s, so it was inevitable that we would follow. It was a good move, although very hard for me to leave my mother and older sister, Beryl, her husband Ruby and their only child Carol who was and still is in the Selwyn Segal home in Johannesburg. My younger sister, Heather, now Gila, emigrated with us in 1969. She has her own wonderful family around her and all live in Israel.

My dad never spoke about his early childhood and we were too young to know to ask. We got all the information about him and his family from relations in America some years ago. Hearing about him being an Ochberg Orphan has made me so curious to know as much as I can about their ordeal. The fact that they were saved by this saint of a man is an incredible act of human kindness and compassion.

CHARLES STEINER (CHASKEL SHTEINER)
Written by Beryl Bark (nee Steiner)

Charles – 1950s

My Dad, Charles Steiner (Chaskel Shteiner) was only five years old, when he and his two older brothers were orphaned, and were saved by Isaac Ochberg. May his memory be blessed, what a great man!

My heart aches and the tears still flow when I think of my Dad having to live through those horrific first years. He told us about the time Solly Bassman wanted to adopt him, but his older brother Hersh (Harry) insisted that the three brothers had to stay together.

After my Dad left the orphanage he worked in the building trade and became a building contractor. He was such a kind, loving and caring family man. He married our Mom, Esther Weitzman, in December 1934. We were a very close and happy family, always together. His three daughters, Beryl, Shirley and

Beryl and Carol

Heather (Gila) were his pride and joy. Our parents had a wonderful marriage until my Dad became ill with a brain tumour in late 1958. He passed away in February 1959, at age 44, a devastating blow to our family. I was only 22, my sister Shirley was 20 and Heather was just 12.

In 1960 I married Ruben (Ruby) Bark, an accountant. He was 13 years older than I and in 1962 our beautiful Carol was born. When she was 15 months old, another tragedy struck us. Carol contracted T.B meningitis. She was in a coma for three months,

Carol and Ruby Bark - Selwyn Segal Hostel

which resulted in her becoming brain-damaged and physically handicapped (cerebral-palsied). Carol had to undergo very many orthopedic operations. Carol is now 48 years old, is in the Selwyn Segal home in Johannesburg, and is loved by all. She is so brave, always excited to see me, but has a lot of problems. My husband died in October 2008, after many years of suffering.

I live in a retirement home in Johannesburg. I had, for 28 years imported the "Eezy Fabric Comb" from Melbourne which I marketed in South Africa, until the last few years, but now they have become too expensive.

DESCENDANTS OF CHARLES STEINER

The three Steiner Girls, the daughters of Charles;
Beryl Bark, Shirley Shamos and Gila Waichman - 1990

GILA WAICHMAN (HEATHER STEINER)

My name is Heather, born 1946, and I changed it to Gila when I made aliya in 1969. I am the youngest of three daughters. My sisters are Shirley Shamos, born 1939, who lives with her entire family in Israel, and Beryl Bark, born 1936 and living in Sandringham, SA, whose only daughter Carol is a resident of Selwyn Segal. Beryl's husband, Ruby passed away a few years ago.

Soon after my arrival in Israel I met my husband, Arie Waichman who was born in Poland and made aliya with his parents and twin sisters to Israel in 1957. We were married in 1970. We have three children Yaron born 1971, Elad born 1974 and Yovav born 1984.

Our eldest son, Yaron, was born in 1971 and is happily married to Osnat (nee Goldstein) whose grandparents originated from Russia and Hungary. They were married in July 1996 and have three beautiful children; two boys and a girl. Or (born April 2000), Nitzan (born May 2003), the second son, and their daughter, Shai-Li was born in April 2008. Yaron practises 'Alternative and Chinese Medicine' and Osnat is a qualified engineer. They live in Herzliya.

Elad, our middle son (born in 1974) is happily married to Yael Omidi (her parents are from Iran, but she was born in Israel). They were married in December 2006, and have two daughters: Anat (born January 2008) and Adi (born March 2010) who is the newest addition to the family. Elad is a Computer Programmer and Yael is a lawyer. They live in Ramat Chen.

Gila and Arie Waichman

Gila and Arie's three sons
Yovav, Elad and Yaron and Yaron's son Nitzan

Our youngest son, Yovav (born 1984) is in the 2ⁿᵈ year of his Computer Science Course at Bar Ilan University, and still lives at home. We live in Kochav Yair. Yovav and his girlfriend, Meerav Or, have been going steady for three years already.

I am a medical secretary and my workday is divided between two of the largest hospitals in Israel (they are in the same complex). Arie is an electrician and electronic technician and is self-employed.

My only regret is that my dad never lived to see and enjoy his grandchildren and great-grandchildren and among them the "sons" he never had.

SHIRLEY (STEINER) SHAMOS

I started a medical publishing business with a partner in 1972. We publish a bi-monthly journal called Medic, which lists details of all medications available in Israel. My husband Yitzie, is a Chartered Accountant and is also in the business as a financial controller. We live in Raanana.

Yoel, our son, aged 49, has been twice divorced and is now very happily married to Yael, originally from Uruguay. They have a one year old son, Liam. Yoel has three sons from his first marriage; Adam, 25, a second year law student, Yoni, 23, a choreographer and dance instructor and Ben, 19, a soldier. He also has two daughters, Gali, 12, and Mai, 10 from his second wife. He is the CEO in his publishing and internet company in Netanya. Yael, his wife is marketing and sales director at Satlink, a worldwide satellite company. They live on Moshav Yanuv.

David, our second son, aged 47 is recently divorced, has two children; Daniel, seven and Jessica, six. He studied art in Florence for seven years and is a talented painter and works as a graphic designing artist. He lives on Moshav Mishmeret.

Dina, our daughter, now aged 45 has a doctorate in psychology and philosophy from the Hebrew University in Jerusalem. She is a university lecturer. Her husband Gil was a career soldier for 25 years. He recently became a partner in a security options

firm. They have two children: Andrea, 18, a soldier and Dani, 15. They live in Raanana.

Shirley Shamos (nee Steiner) and husband Yitzie

David, Daniel and Jessica   *Daniel, Dina Nir (Shamos),*
                                      Andrea and Gil

Left to right: Adam, Yael, baby Liam, Yoel, Gali, Mai, and Yoni.
Yoel (centre) with his wife Yael, son Adam on the left, then baby Liam and Gali and Mai and Yoni. Ben, a soldier is not in the picture

POLLY (PAULINE) JOFFE (PESE STANGER)
Written by Sybil Keats

BACKGROUND

My mother was one of seven children born to Sima and Mordchai Stanger and Beryl Rinzler. They were: Chone, Malka, Polly, a set of twins and two others. Four of the children died but we are not sure when.

Their father, Mordchai Beryl, was taken in a pogrom and, presumably, killed by the Russians. The mother, Sima, died shortly afterwards. After her death Malka was sent to an orphanage in Stanislov. Chone may also have been sent there but we are unsure because he was in the Polish army. My mother was left in Ottinya in the care of one of the neighbours.

Malka later heard rumours that their father had returned. She left the orphanage and set off to find him, hitching lifts on a horse and cart but, sadly, the reports about her father proved incorrect. When she got to Ottinya, she found my mother sleeping in the back of a shop and Malka returned to the orphanage, taking my mother with her.

When Mr Ochberg arrived to take Jewish orphans to South Africa, my mother was chosen as they took the younger children. Malka and Chone were left in Poland as they were above the required age group.

My mother started working in Johannesburg as soon as she was of age and joined CTC Bazaar. She used to walk to work from Arcadia to save money in order to bring Malka to join her in South Africa. When Malka finally arrived, she started working straight away and they both eventually had enough money to send for their brother, Chone.

Polly (Pepy Shtanger) from Group Passport One

Group Passport One-
Polly (Pepy Shtanger) is no 23 on the list and aged nine
Polly is fourth from the right in the back row.

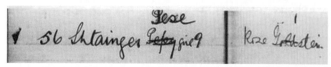

Entry in register at Arcadia – The South African Jewish Orphanage
Pese Shtainger, no 56 in the register and aged nine was initially
placed in the care of Rose Goldstein but the line through the
latters name indicates she returned to Arcadia.

I WATCHED THEM TEAR A TOWN APART
Extract from The Cape Argus – 16 December 1971

Mrs Polly Joffe was five years old when the Russians conscripted her father into a workforce and bundled him off to Odessa.

'There were seven of us in the family with only my mother left to care for us all. Although the Revolution had just ended there was a scarcity of everything in the country and to make matters even worse for us my mother died a little while later,' Mrs Joffe said.

'Although only five years old I can remember my elder sister and I living with a German woman for a while. She looked after us as best as she could, but later my sister died of illness too.

'It was then that I was taken to the orphanage in Stanislowow. Here I remained for three long, arduous years before Mr Ochberg arrived to choose the younger children to go with him. 'The years I spent in the orphanage were most terrible,' she said.

'Very often we had nothing to eat and when fighting broke out in the town we were chased out into the countryside for safety. 'I remember sleeping in a filthy stable on one such occasion, while on another we hid in the forest for hours watching the Russians tear the town apart for any possible Poles.'

Of her two brothers and five sisters only two sisters and a brother survived the Revolution. 'I must have been about eight years old when Mr Ochberg came to the orphanage.

'I was very difficult then and I did not want to go. Relations and other friends told me I should rather try to get to Israel, but not South Africa. Fortunately I did leave for Cape Town and have never regretted it.'

Mrs Joffe, who was born Stanger, said that as soon as she started to work she brought her sister out here too.

NOW: Mrs Polly Joffe photographed in Cape Town today.

'When I left Danzig they were too old to qualify to go as well - so I saved and borrowed money to get them here later. 'I was working as a sales assistant then and only earned the equivalent of R10 a month.'

She too had travelled to Cape Town for the celebration and to meet the rest of the 'Ochberg family.'

RECOLLECTIONS OF MY MOTHER

My mother spoke little about her past life except to praise Arcadia and her time there. She maintained that the past was behind her, although she was eternally grateful to Mr Ochberg and kept in close touch with fellow Arcadians for the rest of her life.

She took me to Arcadia a couple of times. I was overawed by the palatial house, the gardens but most of all, the sunken bath. It never dawned on me to question either of my parents on their life in Europe. The subject never came up in conversations at mealtimes, or elsewhere, as our lively conversations were always about current affairs and attitudes to life in South Africa.

My mother worked hard all her life, gradually rising in the stationery department of CTC Bazaar, later Greatermans and

the Belfast department stores, to the post of Stationery Buyer. She was held in high regard by everyone and my sister and I delighted in rooting through her bottom drawer where she kept presents and notes from grateful customers and suppliers. As the bottom drawer was forbidden territory, we took great pains to return everything as we had found it. Later, my own two daughters also took great pleasure in looking through 'the bottom drawer' but, as they did not have the same regard for the importance of the contents, they just shoved them back any old how. Their grandmother took great delight in their curiosity and they were never reprimanded.

When my mother eventually retired she was still called upon for advice from stationery salesmen and the managers at Belfast.

I often remark that my generation was "golden." As the offspring of immigrants, we were the first to be educated, to grow up in a free society (admittedly in a free white society) and our parents were slightly in awe of us. This made my mother very tolerant of my ideas and actions. Even when I brought home an African to dinner she was charming and welcoming and explained Kosher dietary laws so that he would not ask for butter to put on his bread. She herself took special interest in the African staff at the department stores and was very supportive of our maid running a shebeen in our back yard. Her attitude earned her protection from being the victim of any burglary, as some of Trafina's clients were policemen.

Her tolerance extended to me when I wanted to marry a non-Jew. After much soul-searching and conversations with an understanding rabbi, she finally consented and, as a tribute to how much she was loved, everyone in the family and all her Jewish friends turned up to celebrate my marriage.

Although she was the youngest of her surviving family, my mother was regarded as 'the head of the family.' She was very protective of her children, nieces and nephews.

One of my mother's great loves was the theatre. She never tired of telling us the impact on her when she saw Anna Pavlova dancing 'The Dying Swan' at the Standard Theatre. One of her great friends was the mother of Ivan Berold, then the leading musical star on the Johannesburg stage and we would go and see every musical in which he starred.

This interest extended to me taking ballet lessons and music lessons. My friends and I turned "professional" when she organised a concert in our backyard, charged the audience, paid us with sweets and the money raised went to charity.

I admired my mother greatly in what she had achieved and for being "her". When friends would discuss their mothers' failings (after all this was the time of the book "Her Mother's Daughter" by the feminist writer Marilyn French) I would truthfully say, "my mother was perfect".

My mother remained active and healthy till her final heart attack and I was fortunate to be visiting South Africa when she was rushed to hospital. I had to leave to return to my family and she died soon after in October 1981.

"My mother, Polly, kept in touch with fellow Arcadians for the rest of her life." Sybil Keats

Sybil, Polly, Lillie, Molly Blumberg and Ray - 1937
"Molly Blumberg, my aunt, was quite a beauty and my cousin Paddy, (uncle Charlie's daughter) looks exactly like Aunty Molly."
Dorothy Pantanowitz

"Standing at the left with the striped top is my late dad, David Penzik, with his hands on the shoulders of Ruthie, who passed away at the age of four, not long after this photo was taken. My late Mom, Clara Penzik, is seated in the foreground. Nathan and Polly are in the middle with daughter Sybil. The lady next to Polly is Becky Greenberg with her two children Basil and Marion!" Bennie Penzik

Polly (2nd from left), Gittel Gonifas in checked bathing suit and Sybil to her right - South Beach Durban
"Sitting 3rd from the left with her hands folded across her knees is my aunt, Peshe Levin, who became Polly Falkov." Annette Grauman
"Behind Gittel Gonifas is my late mother Judith Ratzer (aged 27) who later married Nathan Sherksne." Rachelle Meskin..

FAMILY

My mother married Nathan Joffe who had emigrated to South Africa from Lithuania with his parents, brother and sisters. As with my mother, he never spoke about his past and regrettably we never asked him. He had been a Yiddish typesetter and was associated with the Jewish Press in South Africa for some 30 years, even writing the occasional article. When he died in 1957 an obituary in *The Jewish Herald* observed that the Editorial Staff always found him an excellent friend as well as a first-class craftsman, devoted to his work, cheerful and obliging.

Myra's daughter Nadia   Sybil's daughter Alexia with son Joseph

Polly, Sybil and Nathan

Polly and Sybil with unknown (ex-Arcadian?) friends on right

Sybil's daughter Natasha Keats   Grandson Joseph

They had two daughters, one of whom - Myra - died suddenly in 2003. Myra had married and divorced Ugo Bacchini and had a daughter Nadia who lives and works in Johannesburg.

Judy Safro, Sybil and Mike – photo taken in Amsterdam

Polly and daughter Myra   *Myra*

I married Michael Keats, an Australian who was a foreign correspondent and later worked for various agencies of the United Nations. As a result, I have been fortunate to have lived in many countries and when, finally we reached "that certain age" we decided to retire to Melbourne. Our eldest daughter, Natasha, lives in London with three daughters and my other daughter, Alexia, lives in Melbourne with her son,

Pascale Lee sitting on her father Ben Lee's lap, Sybil's daughter Natasha Keats next to him with one of the twins, Saskia Lee on her lap. Sitting at the end is Sybil's daughter Alexia Keats and behind her is the other twin Imogen Lee.

Chapter 127 – CHAYA AND SARA TANNENBAUM

THE TANNENBAUM FAMILY HISTORY
Written by Helen Kuttner, daughter of Sally.

Israel and Shayndel Tannenbaum lived in Wlodawa, Poland, and had three children; Chaya (Clara), Sara (Sally), and a baby brother.

Israel was a shoemaker and was killed in one of the pogroms. Shayndel witnessed this and was also threatened by the Cossacks. A knife was held to her throat and she had to live with that experience all her life. It probably was this experience that led to her decision to send her daughters with Isaac Ochberg. According to family, Sara a very young child, also witnessed her father's death. Soon after the pogrom, there was a Typhus epidemic and the baby boy died.

Clara often spoke of how they were all ill and starving. They heard there were potatoes to be had in the next village and she, being the least ill, dragged herself there so that she could bring a small sack of potatoes back for the family and they would have something to eat.

Sally (Sara) Tannenbaum – Photo taken in Poland ~1921

Sally remembered salivating at the smell of fried liver and onions when she was starving. Sadly the leftovers were thrown in the garbage by someone close, an aunt, or perhaps a neighbour? Sally had scars on her body from sores suffered as a result of malnutrition.

Conditions were terrible and, when Shayndel heard of Ochberg, she went to tell him her story and begged him to take the two girls. Clara was 16 and Sally was 11.

Isaac Ochberg surrounded by "his" children Sally, an unhappy child, front row with her hand on her chin

Bobba Shayndel, Wlodawa, Poland, 1920

Sally Tannenbaum my aunt is in the back row, fifth from left in the dark dress - Group Passport photo eight

He must have taken pity on her and he accepted the girls, even though they were not orphans. What courage it took to let them go. Issa, the daughter of Clara, says, "I will never stop admiring Bobba. We can all be so proud to have Shayndel's genes as part of our makeup and, to this day, I honour her memory and her courage."

During the journey to Warsaw, they had to cross a river and Clara, who was holding Sally, dropped her in the water. Fortunately Sally was rescued by a man who fished her out. She always remained terrified of water that was deeper than a few feet.

Shayndel, Clara and Sally never ever spoke to us of the parting. It was probably too painful to recall. Ochberg decided that, as Clara was tall for her age, he would dress her as a nurse-aide for the trip and thus was able to take another small child in her place. In the Ochberg movie, the newsreel shows her on the left side of the screen ferrying the little ones onto the ship. Because Sally was too young to be accepted, her age was changed and so we really don't know her exact year of birth.

The journey to Africa was a wonderment for Clara. The boat docked in Las Palmas and it was the first time the children had ever seen bananas and pineapples. Clara was so taken with the pineapples that she consumed quite a bit of them and for days afterwards she suffered acid sores in her mouth. Soon after their arrival in Cape Town, Clara and Sally were part of the contingent sent to Arcadia. They found it hard to leave Daddy Ochberg. He gave Clara his cane which she, and later Issa, treasured for years. It is used in the movie and lies across the briefcase at the start of the movie. It will now be returned to the family who live in London.

Some time after they got to Arcadia, Sally was adopted by the wealthy Bloch family of Johannesburg, and became "sister" to Minnie, Becky, Rosie and Fanny Bloch and a "helper" to the family. Sally recalled running errands for the family and going to the grocery store with a list of items to purchase. Throughout her life, Sally remained in touch with these women and their families. She was especially close to Becky's daughters, Doffy and Pearly. Helen is still in touch with Pearly and her family who live in Charlotte, North Carolina.

Although Sally and Clara were separated, the Bloch's took care of Clara and she would holiday in their home. While Sally was brought up in the Bloch household, Clara, at the age of sixteen, went to work at Bloch's Wholesale. This belonged to a different Bloch family, not the foster family. From her earnings, Clara was able to start saving money with the objective of bringing their mother to join her and Sally in Johannesburg. Sally desperately wanted to study nursing. How different her life might have been had she had the opportunity. However, as soon as Sally was able to leave school, she went to work and lived with Clara. She saved every extra penny she earned, doing without any small luxury a young girl might want, to contribute to a savings account for her mother's journey from Poland.

When the girls left with Ochberg, Shayndel had gone to live in Warsaw with her brother, Moshe (Yossel Dreiman's father). This branch of the family survived the war and moved to Israel in the 1950's). Shayndel stayed with Moshe until the girls were able to bring her to South Africa. Shayndel and Moshe had another sister, Dvora, who, with her family, perished in the Holocaust.

The Bloch's might have helped financially for Shayndel to be reunited with her daughters, but this cannot be confirmed. It was Fanny Bloch who travelled to Cape Town to fetch Shayndel off the boat and escort her to Johannesburg. Can you

Sally

Sally, top right

imagine, Shayndel could only speak Polish and Yiddish, and Fanny only English! (For further reference, Dov Dori, son of Yossel Dreiman has just completed a book about the Dreiman family history. In Polish documents, Yossel's name appeared as Jozef Drejman. His Israeli passport had his name as Josef Dreiman. Dov writes about his father as Joseph Dreiman)

By the time Shayndel arrived in Johannesburg, both girls were working in the Wholesale. They had an apartment in Marlborough Court, Doornfontein, to which Shayndel was brought. She never managed to speak English and, as Issa never went to Cheder but went instead to the Yiddish Volkshule, Issa was able to communicate with her in Yiddish. Each day Shayndel and Issa spent time together conversing, and Issa says, "My abiding memory of Bobba is stoicism. She was often my anchor in a storm. I was lucky to have her in my life during my formative years. She did not have an easy life in South Africa but accepted what came her way. When I married and had to leave my family in Johannesburg and go to Cape Town to start a new life with my husband, I burst into tears on saying farewell. Bobba was the one who dried my tears and told me to go off and start my new life with courage and happiness."

As young adults, Clara and Sally led a full social life. Clara was very interested in drama and participated in Yiddish amateur theatre. She had a love of reading and always tried to better herself. Clara often spoke freely of her experiences as an Ochberg orphan and was quite happy to acknowledge this. She kept up her friendships with the Ochberg boys and girls and her daughters had many "Uncles and Aunts".

Sally, on the other hand, was quite traumatized by the whole Ochberg experience. Issa showed Sally a group picture of the Ochberg children and asked her to identify herself. Sally would not look at the picture, but said that she was the unhappiest child in the picture. Indeed, in the first row of the picture, there is Sally, a very sad little girl.

Helen says, "My mother would not speak about her childhood. I always knew not to press her. When she lived with our family in Canada, her grandchildren often asked questions to gather material for their school projects on family history. My mother would respond to these requests by saying, 'It is not a pretty story'. As a result, her three children, Ron, Neil and Helen, have only a handful of stories to share and these have been incorporated in this text."

Judy Levine, the daughter of Chaia, writes

My mother Chaia (Clara) and her sister Sorella (Sally) Tannenbaum were part of the Ochberg contingent. They came from a shtetl called Sieradski in Poland. That is the name that is mentioned on my mom's Naturalisation Papers.

Isaac Ochberg with a group of children– Johannesburg ~1922
Clara is sitting next to Ochberg on his right side (in the striped dress) and Sally is standing directly behind him on his left side.

*Chaia Tannenbaum, Isaac Ochberg, Leah Zaicka
and Tasha Altuska- the three nurses*

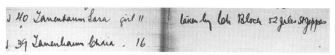

*Extracts from the register kept by the South African Jewish
Orphanage that cared for the two siblings. The age of the children
is listed and Sara went to live with the Bloch family.*

*The three nurses; Tasha Altuska, Leah Zaicka and and Chaia
Tannenbaum with their younger siblings.
Sally is standing behind Clara*

My mother Chaia came out on the ship as a nurse aide as she
was already 16 years old and apparently there was a cut-off
age for the orphans.

Sally and Clara (right)

Clara and Sally also feature in the photo on page 130 of "The Jews in South Africa" "The Jewish Workers' Club."

Clara is holding the left side of the banner and Sally is two away from her on her left side wearing a beret and a shirt and tie.

CLARA
Helen Kuttner, daughter of Sally continues

Sally (left) and Clara

Bobba Shayndel, Charles, Clara, Judy and Isaac, Issa and Henry,

Clara, Sally and friend

Clara married Isaac Steiman from Vilna, Lithuania. Both Clara and Sally were married on the same day in 1933. Isaac had been a Singer sewing machine salesman in Vilna. Their children are: Issa (married Werb) and Judy (married Levin).

In Johannesburg, Isaac became a demolisher of buildings and had a hardware store where he sold both new materials and salvage from his demolitions. His main trade was selling wood and iron to the Black population for building their homes in the Transkei. They would put down a deposit, choose their goods, and pay him off weekly. When the debt was completely paid up, the goods were railed to their given destination. Isaac and Clara had two daughters, Issa and Judy. They remember, "Our life in Johannesburg was interesting and simple. Though not affluent, there was always food on the table and a roof over our heads." Isaac passed away in 1971 and Clara passed away in 1988.

Dov Dori, Issa, Judy and, Neil, London 1996

SALLY

Sally was the softer and quieter of the two girls, so it was inevitable that, when she married, it was to a quiet, soft person. On 30 August 1933 she married Barney Egnal (Berel Ignal).

Barney and Sally's wedding – 30 August 1933

Barney and Ron   *Sally with Neil and Helen*

Neil, Bobba and Helen   *All the family*

Barney had come to South Africa in 1921 from Kelem, Lithuania. He was the sweetest, most gentle of men, always trying to please. He was a watchmaker by trade and, although the home was not an affluent one, they did their best for their children.

Sally became a widow at age 48. Helen says, "I can't imagine the terror my mother must have felt, but she continued to raise her children with determination and stoicism, like Bobba Shayndel before her.

Egnal Family Neil (tux), Ron, Barney, Helen, Sally, 1958

Wedding Neil and Denise Cape Town, 1970
Ron, Sally, Neil and Denise and Landau Family

Helen and Paul's Wedding Johannesburg 1970
Sally, Isaac, Helen, Paul and Clara

At the recent wedding of my younger son, Mark, I mentioned that I come from a long line of very strong women and, without daughters, I was passing the torch to my daughters-in-law, Mark's wife, Andrea, and Richard's wife, Katrin, with the expectation that they would not break this chain. I remember my mother as always being fearful of authority, never questioning people's actions. She taught me not to draw attention to myself. She and my father were very kind to people, especially to those in need. We had very little, but my father always managed to share what we had to help our relatives and friends who were in trouble, money, food and blankets. My mother placed great emphasis on education and books and her children are avid readers."

Sally's eldest son, Ronald, lives in Cape Town. He qualified as a jeweller and has been a dealer in jewellery and gems for many years. He is able to fix anything and everything, perhaps a skill inherited from his father. Neil became a psychologist and is now semi-retired and living in London, England. He and Denise have two children, Lee-Anne and Mark and two grandchildren, Aaron and Sam. Helen studied pharmacy and is living in Toronto, Canada. She and Paul have two children, Richard and Mark and a grandchild on the way (October 2009).

Sally was well into her seventies when she immigrated to Canada to be with Helen and family. In 1992, she proudly became a Canadian Citizen. Sally passed away on 15 June 1996 at Baycrest Centre. She is buried in Pardes Shalom cemetery, under a huge tree, surrounded by flowers and green grass in the summer and snow in the winter.

It is a very peaceful setting. As a result of her death at Baycrest, and because of the tremendous support offered to her family by the volunteers on the Palliative Care Unit, Helen trained as a volunteer on this unit. Since 1997, Helen has been actively involved with people who are dying. It is an enriching and fulfilling experience and Helen considers this opportunity a farewell gift to her from Sally.

SALLY'S GRANDCHILDREN

Children of Neil and Denise Egnal:
Lee-Anne Egnal, born in 1973, married to David Berns. They have twin boys, Sam and Aaron, born in 2004. Lee-Anne is a lawyer, currently living in Cairo with her family. David is with the U.S. State Department.
Mark Egnal, born in 1975, is a lawyer, currently living and working in New York City.

Children of Helen and Paul Kuttner:
Richard Kuttner, born in 1977, married to Katrin, currently living in Mountain View, California. Richard is a computer engineer.
Mark Kuttner, born in 1980, married to Andrea, currently living in Burlington, Ontario. Mark is a marketing executive. He and Andrea are expecting a baby in October.

Sally, Mark, Helen, Richard - Toronto

Ron and Neil at the back and , Helen, Bobba and Sally in front

Sally and Family - Greek Town, Toronto

EULOGY FOR SALLY EGNAL:
Surele (Sara) bat Shayndel V'Yisrael
21 May 1910 - 15 June 1996
Delivered by: Eli Rubenstein
Congregation Habonim, Toronto

Sally Egnal was born in Poland in 1910. Towards the conclusion of WWI, her father lost his life following a pogrom that took place during Pesach. At that time, there was great starvation in Poland and, the deprivation that Sally underwent during this period, left her with scars for the rest of her life. Because of the dire conditions in Poland, Sally and her older sister, Clara, were put on a refugee ship bound for South Africa - but they had to leave their mother behind. In South Africa, Sally was placed in a Jewish orphanage and then a Jewish foster home, but she was unhappy in both locations.

At about age 15, she moved into an apartment with her sister Clara. The two sisters worked and saved to bring their mother over from Poland. This was an enormous achievement.

On 30 August 1933, Sally married Barney Egnal, an immigrant from Lithuania, whose profession was watchmaker. Sally's mother lived with Sally and Barney for many years. Barney and Sally were observant for the sake of Sally's more traditional mother, but, Sally's mother moved to Clara's (according to family lore) after a maid mixed up the meat and milk dish cloths.

Sally gave birth to three children: Ronald first, followed by Neil, and Helen. Barney passed away in 1958, when Helen was 10, Neil was 17, and Ron was 22.

Sally remained close to Clara, who passed away in 1988. Sally loved Clara's two daughters, Issa and Judy. In 1994, Issa and Judy invited Sally for a three month visit to South Africa which she enjoyed immensely. Fortunately, she was also able to visit with Ron at this time.

After Barney's death, Sally raised the family on her own. Being Jewish was very important to her and she kept a strong Jewish home. Sally held the family home together by finding employment as a saleslady. She worked exceptionally hard, and denied herself to raise her children. Sally had always wanted to be a nurse, but there were no funds for this and she was always too busy working hard - first to bring her mother over and then to support her family - to find the time to dedicate to her own education. Remarkably, Sally worked in South Africa as a saleslady until the age of 78.

Towards the end of the 1970's, while Ron remained in South Africa, Sally's other children followed the route of many South African Jewish families and left South Africa for countries with a more stable political climate. Her daughter and son-in-law, Helen and Paul Kuttner, moved to Canada in 1978. Her son and daughter-in-law, Neil and Denise Egnal, moved to England in 1987. Sally was very fond and proud of Neil and Denise's children, Lee-Anne and Mark, whom she visited in England on several occasions.

In 1988, Sally moved to Toronto. It was a very difficult journey to take, but she wanted to be close to the people who mattered to her dearly: her daughter and her grandchildren. Sally was very fond of her grandchildren, Richard and Mark, and she was quite saddened by their move from South Africa which happened when Richard was one year old. She wanted to watch her grandchildren grow up.

Everybody loved Sally. She was a good listener. She was very kind to everyone. She was very positive and upbeat with people. She made friends extremely easily. She loved children. She worked very hard. She had a strong sense of right and wrong.

Above all Sally Egnal was a fighter. Her entire life was a battle for survival, and she waged this battle with courage and determination. Several times in the last 10 months, it looked as if she had lost the battle, but each time she rallied. When she had surgery in October of last year to have a tumour removed from her stomach, she said to her son Neil who was visiting her from London: "I was very ill, but I was called back."

Yet she was healthy for all but the last 10 months of her 86 years. Helen related to me that, the day before she was diagnosed with shingles - at 85 years of age - Sally walked 1.5 kilometres to the shopping mall and then walked the 1.5 kilometres back to the Kuttner home.

In Helen's words: "My mother was a very strong woman. She lived on sheer willpower and determination."

We remember Sally Egnal for her determination, her strength of character, her ability to overcome adversity. She will continue to be remembered through her children and grandchildren whose very existence are a testament to the life and spirit of Sally Egnal.

Pardes Shalom Cemetery, Toronto

CHAYA TANNENBAUM
As remembered by her daughters Issa Werb and Judy Levin

When Chaya's mother, Shayndel, learnt of Isaac Ochberg's search for Jewish orphans, she approached him and asked him to take both her daughters with him. According to our mother Clara, (as she became known) she had been born in 1905 and in 1921 that would have made her 16 years old and therefore too old for Ochberg to take, as an orphan as she was over the age limit allowed. We don't know what motivated him to take both Clara and Sara (Sally as she became known) but he was obviously moved by the plight of the family. Our mother was given the position as a nurse-aide to assist with the little ones and Sally was included as an orphan. There is no known passport photo of our mother at that time but Sally does appear in one of the group passport photos. In the Ochberg movie we saw Clara standing behind two little children framed in the window of a train and then in another shot ferrying the little ones onto the ship.

Clara never spoke about the experience of leaving her mother or of the journey that was undertaken. The story of her on-board experience of savouring the taste of fresh pineapple, eating too much at one go and burning her mouth from the acidity of the fruit was told to us not long before she passed away. When we read the stories of what life was like for the children in Poland we realize what remarkable strength of character our mother had and how her experiences made her the caring person that she was. She would go out of her way to help people and was very highly spoken of by those people who came in contact with her.

Our mother was not a tall person. In order for her to be accepted as an orphan when the ship docked in Cape Town her date of birth was given as 1st May 1910, the date that featured on all her legal, identification and passport documents until she passed away on the 8th November 1988. She and Sally were in the contingent of orphans who were sent up to Johannesburg and placed in the orphanage.

She spoke about attending school at the Jewish Paedagogic Centre in Wolmarans Street, across the road from the Wolmarans Street Shul but here again we don't know for how long she was a student there. She must have picked up the English language reasonably quickly as we were never aware of a Polish accent when she spoke. She went to work at M Bloch and Company, wholesalers in Market Street, and remained there until after she was married.

Sally was adopted by the Bloch family – no relationship to the owners of M Bloch & Company. My mother spoke about spending weekends in Benoni with one of their daughters, Becky, and her husband Harry and their two daughters Dorothy (affectionately
and only known as Doffy) and Pearl. Sally regarded them as sisters and by extension we thought of them as family and saw them often.

When Clara and Sally left their mother behind in Poland they made a vow that they would bring her to South Africa and to this end the girls saved whatever they could and in 1932 were able to be reunited as a family.

Clara was an avid reader and loved the theatre and encouraged us to appreciate the Arts. She joined the Yiddish Theatre group in Johannesburg and took part in theatrical productions that were staged by them. We never asked where and when she met our father, Isaac Steiman (from Lithuania). It's so sad that we were brought up as "children who should be seen but not heard" with the result that we never asked the pertinent questions that the youth of today ask and therefore know so little about what are really major events in our family history. They were married in September 1933 by Chief Rabbi Landau in his home. They didn't have the financial wherewithal to have a wedding with all the trimmings.

Bobba Shayndel stayed with Sally and her husband Barney for several years and then boarded with the Segal family (Abe Segal's parents) for a couple of years before coming to live with our family where she stayed until she passed away on the 20th August 1965.

One of our abiding memories of this wonderful and remarkable woman was her waiting for us to come home from school and, in the later years, from work. In warm weather she sat in her favourite chair on the verandah waiting and in winter she stood by the lounge window again waiting to see us safe and secure in our home. Another memory would be us coming home from school and finding her and our mother in the kitchen, making and baking together, in summer the stewed peaches that were bottled and lined the top shelf in the pantry and eaten right throughout the year and also the special Yomtov dishes prepared by them for Pesach, Shavuot and Rosh Hashanah. They were always there when we came home.

Another memory that comes to mind about our mother; Although her command of English was good, she used to keep a dictionary next to her when she had to write notes to our teachers excusing periodic absences from school. She said she never wanted to embarrass us in case she spelt any word incorrectly!

Clara and Sally were very close as sisters. They would speak to each other every day and we visited them regularly on the week ends. When Sally was widowed she moved to Pretoria with her younger two children, Neil and Helen. Ronnie opted to remain in Johannesburg as he was already working at that stage. We would go out to Pretoria at least once a month, and when Sally decided to come back to Johannesburg after several years absence, we were all delighted. Neil went to Cape Town to work and Helen went to Grahamstown to study so Sally would often spend week ends with us and a treat for us was to wake up to the smell of freshly baked scones for breakfast. She was a fantastic baker.

During the 2nd World War, when Germany invaded Russia, an organization was formed in Johannesburg, called Medical Aid for Russia, and both our parents were actively involved in hosting fund raising events to collect for the organization. After the war ended my mother learnt that the only surviving members of her family was a cousin, his wife and two children in Poland and his sister and her husband in Palestine (known in those years). My mother, regularly twice a year, made up parcels of clothes to send to the family in Poland. I remember her collecting the clothes and packing them into calico bags that she laboriously sewed together and addressed so that they would arrive intact at their destination. This went on until 1957 when these cousins made aliyah to Israel. In later years when we were able to meet with them they spoke so highly of my mother and my aunt Sally's efforts to send these parcels as they were able to sell the clothes and the money they made from the sales provided them with food to survive. My parents also sent suit lengths of cloth to my father's two sisters and their families in Vilna so that these could also be sold to obtain money to provide food for them.

Our mother loved to play bowls and she was also a very active member of the Jewish Womens' Benevolent Association and participated in all their activities. She also kept up friendships with ex Ochberg orphans Rosie Flink, Nellie Frankel (Jenny Segal's mother and aunt), Yetta Bornstein and Fanny Lockitch. The Flinks didn't live far from us in Johannesburg so we saw them on a regular basis and the siblings also formed friendships that survive to this day. Whenever we were down in Cape Town (a regular year-end occurence) we always visited with Nellie, Yetta and Fanny and their families. A wonderful friendship was also established by the siblings and in actual fact when Issa went down to Cape Town to be a bridesmaid at the wedding of Yetta's eldest daughter Rita, she met her husband Henry Werb. Rita unfortunately had a stroke several years ago and when her husband passed away last year her children felt that she should go into Highlands House. Issa regularly visits her once a week.

Our father was a building demolisher and eventually opened up a timber, paint and hardware store in Bree Street, Johannesburg. Clara would go in every day to help. In 1964 our parents went overseas for several weeks and visited with our father's family who were in London (a cousin), New York and Norfolk Virginia USA (two sisters) Moscow and Vilna (another two sisters) and Israel where Clara was able to meet up with her cousin Yossel Dreiman and his family who had made aliyah in 1957. After our father died in 1971 she ran the business for a year before selling it and 'retiring' from the commercial world. Every year she would go to Cape Town to spend a couple of months with Issa, Henry and their children. She made two more visits to Israel, the last one in 1976 and on her return she was diagnosed with Lupus which affected her kidneys. She lived on her own until 1983 when she came to live with Judy, her husband and three children. However at the beginning of 1988 she felt she needed to go into Our Parents Home and asked us to arrange this for her, which we reluctantly did. She passed away on 8 November 1988.

Abiding memories of a devoted daughter to Shayndel, sister to Sally, wonderful wife to Isaac, loving mother, mother-in-law and bobba to Issa and Judy, their spouses Henry and Boris and all her grandchildren. She was blessed to have had the pleasure of knowing two of her great-grandchildren, Craig and Bradley.

Isaac and Clara at their engagement party

CHAYA'S LEGACY
Written by her daughters Issa Werb and Judy Levin

Issa married Henry Werb and they had three sons;

Charles married Belinda and they live at the Gold Coast, Australia and had three children Craig (23), Bradley (21) and Gabriella (17)

Steven married Michelle and lives in London, and had three children Sasha (12), Gabriel (9), and Jonah (3).

David married Sarit and lives in Cape Town and had Ethan (3) and a baby due in December 2009

Judy married Boris Levin and had three children.

Johnathan married Robyn and lives in Sydney and they had Brandon (14) and twins Matthew and Darren (11)

Errol married Romy and lives in Johannesburg and they had Adam (11), Benjamin (9) and Kira (5).

Brenda married Bradley Rosenthal and lives in Johannesburg and they had Damian (6) and Natalya (22 months)

TOYBA, LEIBEL, FEIGA AND CHAYIM WOLCHUK
Written by Francine Blum

"I saw the movie about the Ochberg children and realised for the first time that my dad was one of them."

The Wolchuk family who were born in Pnywno, in what was then the Ukraine, were orphaned after both parents died of Typhus (according to the Ochberg records). They were later taken from there to an orphanage in Pinsk, after they had been found by Isaac Ochberg.

There were six siblings, two of whom were older and were able to take care of themselves, so they were not taken into the orphanage with the others. They were named Avrom and Getzel. We were never able to understand why they had left their younger brothers and sisters until we discovered that Ochberg was only permitted to bring children under the age of sixteen to South Africa and that they did not qualify to come.

They remained in Poland where they became partisans and later moved to Israel. They both married in Israel and had children and grandchildren, who all live in Israel, with the exception of one son Shmuel, who now lives in America. They have both passed on.

The names and ages on the passport documents of the remaining four children are very unreliable. My father Chayim, later called Hymie, was apparently born on 4 May 1918 and from what I can calculate about the time of the arrival in South Africa it seems that he must have been around three years old, not five as it states on the passport. I suspect that the ages of the other three are also not correct. He was one of the youngest children in the group, possible the youngest.

The South African names of the four siblings were Tilly, Leslie, Phyllis and Hymie.

Group Passport 9 - enlargement of right hand side

Extracts from the register kept by Arcadia (SAJO).
The approximate ages of the children are listed after the names..
Feiga (Phyllis) was adopted by the Braude family.
Leibel (Leslie) went to live with the Cohen family.

TILLY (TOYBA) WOLCHUK

Tilly was the oldest of the four Wolchuk children to come to South Africa. She was a sort of surrogate mother to Hymie, the youngest of the children, and was very protective of him.

Tilly was apprenticed to a milliner after leaving school and continued with this work until she married Barney (Baruch) Karlin from Zagar in Lithuania under a chupa in the garden at Arcadia on 13 April 1928 when she was 19. They had three children, Yettah, Salome and Sam.

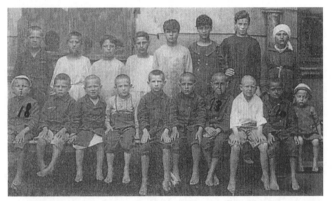

Group Passport 9 "I would say that Tilly might be the last girl in the back row right and that my dad (the tiny boy) is sitting directly in front of her in the front row right."

"Tilly Wolchuk's daughter Yettah gave me this photos that she found among her mom (Tilly's) things when she passed away. We couldn't identify Tilly in the picture, but little Hymie Wolchuk, her youngest brother, is the boy in the front row."

Yettah married Bernie Friedland and they had three children; Salome married Monty Orkin and they had two daughters who both live in the USA.

Sam died tragically at a young age leaving a wife and two sons. His wife died soon after and the boys were raised by a member of her family.

Tilly lived in Bulawayo for some time and died in Johannesburg aged 88.

PHYLLIS BRAUDE (FEIGA WOLCHUK)

"I suspect that in the picture of Ochberg surrounded by the children, where he is holding a small boy and girl in his arms, that they might well be my dad Hymie and his sister Phyllis."

Feiga, later called Phyllis Braude, is the younger of my dad's two sisters.

She was adopted by a family named Braude, who later immigrated to Israel, where she has lived ever since. She married a Major Frumkin, who fought in the Israeli army, and they had one daughter, who still lives in Israel.

HYMIE (CHAYIM) WOLCHUK

Photo from Tasha Altuska's Album
Message on back dated 17-1-1922 reads
"To dear Tilly,
From your loving friend Anne and Little Hymie."

Chayim, later known as Hymie, was probably the baby of the group. On the ship on the way to Cape Town Hymie contracted what was almost certainly small pox. We believe that one of the young women hired to take care of the children nursed him and kept him isolated until he recovered. He was left with pock marks on his nose and face which bears witness to the story.

The Wolchuk children were part of the group who could not be accommodated at Oranja and were moved to Arcadia.

Hymie was a sensitive child, very affectionate and kind. He attended Spes Bona School in Johannesburg. I obtained a copy of his file when Arcadia closed, which had some of his school reports in it. He did well in all his subjects, especially English but 'needed improvement in arithmetic'! He had to leave school early and stayed for a while with his sister Tilly and her husband.

He was trained to operate the large reel to reel bioscope projectors by African Consolidated Theatres, and worked for some time in the big cinemas of the day situated in the heart of Johannesburg city. This work was classified as an 'essential service' during the war, important for the morale of the people, and he was not drafted to fight as a result.

In 1942, he married Mary Kagan, who had come to Johannesburg at age 11 from Minsk in Latvia, after a dramatic journey across Europe to London and then to South Africa on one of the Union Castle liners. Hymie was 24 and Mary 20 and they married at the Wolmarans Street Shul. They had three children – Francine who married Robert Blum and now has three children and four grandchildren and lives in Johannesburg; Seymour, who married Glenda Schneider and has two daughters, all living in Dallas, Texas and Robert, who married Debbie Hepker and has a son and a daughter, also lives in Dallas.

Hymie working as a projectionist

Mary and Hymie getting married 1942

Mary, Hymie and Francine

Francine, Hymie and Seymour

My mom Mary is still in excellent health and plays a mean game of bridge!

Sadly Hymie passed away in 1996.

Mary, Dan Blum and Hymie at Dan's barmitzvah

WOLCHUK
HYMIE
Beloved husband of Mary, father of Francine, Seymour, Robert and Debbie, grandfather of Lisa, Melinda, Craig, Dan, Bodine, Kerry, Zachary and Samantha and great grandfather of Joshua passed away peacefully 28 November after a long illness bravely borne. We will all miss you always Zeida. Funeral West Park Jewish Cemetery. Sunday -01 Dec - 9:45 am.

LESLIE WOLCHUK
Written by Sandy Berkowitz

My Dad, Leslie Wolchuk, was born on the 10 October 1912, and came out to South Africa in 1921 with the Ochberg Children when he was nine years old. He and his siblings were sent up to Johannesburg and were placed in the care of Arcadia.

My late Dad, Leslie Wolchuk, his late brother Hymie and late sister Tilly were all at Arcadia. I also need to mention that there was another sibling, Phyllis. She was very young when they came over and was adopted an early age and the family later went to live in Israel.

Unfortunately I do not have any photos of them from when they were at Arcadia. I have seen the passport photos of the children, but unfortunately do not know which one of them is my dad, Hymie or Tilly as I do not know what they looked like when they were young.

Unfortunately I do not know much about the time my Dad spent at Arcadia, except that they were very happy times, and by the time I tried to get information from him, which was only in recent years, he already had Alzheimer's, and my Mom had passed away so I could not ask her.

I know at some stage he was either fostered or adopted, and went to live with the Cohen family in the Free State. I know that he had a step sister Bertha Lonstein, who was a school teacher and that she had two sons John and Jeffrey Lonstein.

My dad became an electrician and married my mom Daisy Pieterkosky (Simon) on 15 August 1937 and I attach a cutting from the newspaper describing the event.

In the 2nd World War my dad was in the Air Force and spent time away overseas. Later he had an electrical business called G W Electrical in Bertrams, Johannesburg and my Mom worked with him. The business had a little shop which sold school stationery as well. After many, many years, my dad gave up his business and went to work for the City Council before retiring.

They had two children, my brother Freddie (Frederick Edwin) born 20 July 1940 and myself Sandy (Sandra Yettah) Born 19 April 1947.

My dad loved the sport of boxing and went on to represent South Africa at the Maccabi games several times.

My dad was a caring and loving man, who's family and friends always came first. He was a wonderful grandfather to seven grandchildren and to date would have had 19 great grandchildren. He did a lot of charity work and belonged to an organisation called St Giles. He also played bowls which he really enjoyed.

My dad passed away on 22 February, 2006, and I love and miss him terribly. My one regret is that I did not listen more carefully when he used to tell us about his childhood and memories of Arcadia, but I was young at the time.

BOXER'S WEDDING Wolchuk - Simon

The marriage took place last Sunday, 15 August 1937, at the Womarans Street Synagogue of Daisy, second daughter of Mr and Mrs S Simon, of Johannesburg, to Mr Leslie Wolchuk, who represented South Africa as a boxer at the Maccabia Games. The ceremony was performed by Cantor Alter, assisted by the Rev AT Schrock.

The bride, who was given away by her father, wore a period frock of white chiffon velvet. Her veil was held in place by a halo of silver lamé and she carried a bouquet of lilies and carnations.

Miss Edith Simon, the maid of honour, wore a frock of gold embossed satin, with a halo and mittens of gold lamé. Miss Hannah Simon and Miss Tilly Wainer, the bridesmaids, wore similar frocks of silver embossed satin. They carried bouquets of gladioli.

Audrey Cohen and Yetta Karlin, as flower girls, wore frocks of silver embossed satin cut on the same lines as the bridesmaids and carried posies of pastel flowers. Dolores Cohen was a miniature bride in a replica of the bride's frock. Mr Ernest Levin was best man, assisted by Mr Louis Simon, Mr E Meyers and Mr J Desatnick.

The unterfuhrers were Mr and Mrs S Simon and Mr and Mrs B Karlin. Mr A Levin, Mr J Ratner, Mr L Karlin and Mr J Wainer were poleholders.

The bride's mother wore a handsome gown of black chiffon velvet trimmed with gold lamé. Her accessories were to match and she carried red gladioli. Mrs B Karlin, the bridegroom's sister, wore a frock of black embossed with gold. She too, carried red gladioli.

After the ceremony a guard of honour was formed outside the synagogue by Brethren of the Ancient Order of Foresters.

A reception was held in the Ginsberg Hall, after which the bridge and bridegroom left for their honeymoon. The bride travelled in a grey tailored suit with a silver fox fur and accessories to match.

Leslie Wolchuk

DIAMOND
ANNIVERSARY
WOLCHUK
LES AND DAISY
MARRIED
15/08/1937
Mazeltóv Móm and Dad on achieving 60 wonderful years together. May you be blessed to share many more. Love Fred, Flor, Sandy, David, all your grandchildren and great-grandchildren.

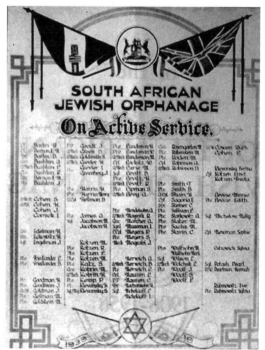

The Roll of Honour of all Arcadians who served in WWII
Wolchuk L is the 4th name in the names starting with "W"

Chapter 129 – MANYA ZEIKA

You can read more about Manya in section section five of this book. In chapter 38, Cissy Harris (Zeika) has written about the three sisters and chapter 39 are Manya's first hand recollections.

MANYA ZEIKA
Written by Frank and Viv Adler

Manya will be 100 years old on 2 May and we await the birth of her first great grandchild this week-100 years between them!!

Some of their story has been told in Jon Blair's wonderful film about the Ochberg Orphans in which Cissie travelled back to Kostopol in the Ukraine and Jon used some of the memories recorded by Manya.

Lisa was 18 or 19 and she travelled with the children as an assistant to Ochberg. She was an amazing woman. She looked after her family after her parents' death, probably from starvation, in ~1918.

There were two brothers Jack and Israel as well. Jack went off to Palestine very early but had to leave when he contracted malaria in the Hula swamps and joined his sisters in South Africa. Israel went to Vienna and worked as a dental mechanic for seven years before going to South Africa.

Lisa trained as a nurse and later worked as a matron in Bethel in the Transvaal. She later went to Palestine where she married a doctor, Saul Abend, and they worked together with Arabs and Jews in Sejera. She spoke many languages; Russian, Yiddish, Hebrew, English, Arabic, Polish, Afrikaans, Bulgarian and some more. She lived in Haifa in later life and was always a warm and involved aunt to her family and their children. She died aged 102.

Some of the stories that Manya told of her early life in Kostopol were:-
-of her family hiding political refugees in the attic;
-of her father having his beard pulled as he crossed the street;
-of how during a pogrom when Lisa was a child, walking outside the town and a Cossack on horseback stopped her and asked if there were any Jews around and then "Are you a Jew?" She answered "Me a Jew? Of course not!" and he left her safe;
-of picking wild strawberries, yagodi (bilberries) and mushrooms in the forest; and of how, after her parents died, it was arranged that Manya would be given to her aunt and uncle who had lost their daughter, but having waited for hours at the railway station for the train to Rovno, they were told it had been derailed and Liza said "das ist bechert" and they went home.

Manya lived in Arcadia, leaving when she was 16 years old. She loved ballet and trained as a ballet teacher. She married Nathan Adler who was articled to a firm of lawyers Alexander Brothers. At first they lived in various boarding houses in Johannesburg and when Nathan qualified he bought a small practice in Petrus Steyn in the Orange Free State. In their early

Manya and Lisa Zeika
Photo and message from Tasha Altuska's photo album

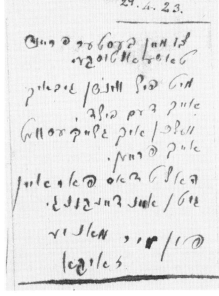

To my best friend Tashe Altuske

With many wishes I give you this picture that I believe will bring you joy.
Guard it well/ for remembrance

From me Manya Zeika   ***Translated by Veronica Belling***

The three nurses; Tasha Altuska, Leah Zaika and Chaya Tannenbaum with their younger siblings.
Chaim is standing to the left of Tasha and Sarah is behind her while Leah is on the far right with a white ribbon.
Manya is standing behind Leah Zaika while Sally is standing behind Clara Tannenbaum

schools for 13 years and then was the teacher-in- charge at the Simmons House Adolescent Unit for 20 years until he retired in 1997. Viv worked in comprehensive schools in London ending her teaching career as Deputy Head of Parliament Hill School. She retired in 1994 and retrained as a psychodynamic couple therapist. She now works for the Tavistock Centre for Couple Relationships.

Sarah qualified as a school teacher, as a maseuse and as a yoga teacher. She move to Manchester and spent 10 years in Australia before returning to England. Peter went to Dartington School before returning to London where he became a property developer. He now lives in Bournemouth with his partner Elisa Ponce-Villanueva. The birth of their daughter, Manya's great grand-daughter is joyfully awaited. Benjamin read English and Philosophy at Warwick University after which he worked his way up in television and now with his wife Patricia runs a very successful television company.

Viv and Frank Adler and family - 2010
Sara, Pat, Ben, Viv, Frank, Peter and Elisa

days there he introduced himself to a local farmer who said "I don't mind who you are as long as you are not a Jew". Later they moved back to Johannesberg and had three children; Erica, Frank and Henry.

Erica and Frank moved to London after taking degrees at Wits University. At Parktown Boys High School one of the teachers was Mr Klevansky, who continued to live at Arcadia as a member of staff and at university one of his lecturers was Jack Rachman the son of an Ochberg orphan who had been a good friend of Manya at Arcadia.

Frank led the Students Fellowship Society fighting for an end to racial discrimination at the university. After coming to London in 1960 he had the honour of being one of 35 South Africans abroad banned by the South African Government.

Erica left for London in 1959 and trained at the Rose Bruford Drama School. Frank followed in 1960, and Manya and Nathan and Henry came to London the following year. Erica went to Israel where she taught and had her poetry published. She has a daughter Shelley who studied International Relations at university in Jerusalem and married Oleg in 2010.

Henry left South Africa after his matric. He was always interested in film and Jazz and was a talented artist. He died tragically in his 40th year.

Frank did research at the Maudsley-Bethlem hospital from 1960 to 1964. He was very involved in the anti nuclear peace movement, as a member of the Committee of 100 he was arrested fifteen times and had three short spells in to prison as a consequence of civil disobedience demonstrations.

Frank married Tessa Holman in 1964. They had a daughter Sarah in 1965 and a son Peter in 1966. They divorced in 1969. Frank married Vivienne Mowatt in 1970 and had a son Benjamin in 1972. He worked as a teacher in comprehensive

Manya's 99th birthday May 2nd 2010

BERNER AND OSIACH ZWIRIN

Berner and Osiach, later called Barry and Issy, came from Stanislav and were in the group, of half of the Ochberg Orphans, who chose to go to Johannesburg, and there they were placed in the care of The South African Jewish Orphanage which later was called Arcadia.

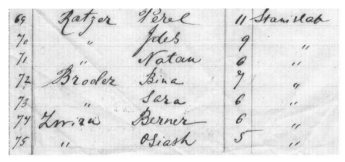

List of children send to Johannesburg

Group Passport 1 – Osiach and Berner Zwirin are the boys in the front row. They are 24 and 25 on the list and their ages are four and five.

Barry (Berner) went to live with the Lewin family in Brakpan. They must have adopted him as he took on their name and he is shown as aged six.

Issy (Osiach) went to live with the Berachovitz family in Brakpan. They adopted him and he took on their name which was later shortened to Beira. He is shown as aged five.

Extract from register of Ochberg Orphans who came up to Johannesburg

It seems that Barry was initially known as Barney Lewin and then in later years he changed his surname to Beira to be the same as his brother.

BARRY BEIRA (BERNER ZWIRIN/ TEIVN)
Written by Claire Steingo

I have little information to offer.

My parents were divorced when I was about five. I only saw my father once after that and have had no contact since. I have heard that he was charming but I have no memory of being with him. He must have left way before I was six.

My hope is that your efforts might help me find out more about him.

Sorry to tell you I really don't know anything about my dad.

I only knew he was an Ochberg orphan from your email. The little that I know was that his name was Barney Lewin. He changed his name before he married my mom. He then was married to a woman in Rhodesia.

I was the only daughter from this marriage. Marion Kimmel was a daughter from a previous marriage. I have only met her twice. I know nothing more about her. My cousin Shina Ospovat (nee Beira) knows Marion.

My mom's name was Jill, her Hebrew name Golda Leah and her nickname Jewel. My mom's maiden name was Rabinowitz.

Jill Rabinowitz and Barry Beira on their wedding day

Harry and Annie Rabinowitz the parents of Jill, Jill and Barry Beira and Mrs Beirachovitz and Issy Beira.

Sad to say I don't know when they were married or divorced. I would estimate it was between 1949 and 1954 Sorry I can't be of more help and I wish I knew more about him.

I was born 9 June 1950 and married Brian Steingo on 5 December 1971. I have two children Michael and Leanne and two grandchildren Ari and Joshua. I live in Ft Lauderdale Florida USA.

It is sad to say but that is it.

BARRY AND ISSY BEIRA (ZWIRIN)
Written by Dr Harold M Kimmel

Barry and Issy Zwirin were orphan brothers brought out by Isaac Ochberg and on arrival they were split up. Izzy, the youngest of all the orphans, was adopted by Beira family and Barry by the Lewin family.

They did not stay in contact with each other because of distance; Barry was in Springs and Issy in Cape Town. The Beiras were ultra orthodox but the Lewins were not. They did meet again as adults.

Barry as an adult joined the Royal Army and was a Physical Fitness Instructor in South Africa. He was not a commissioned officer. He then met and married Ethel Pack one of a family of five musical sisters, very well known in South African musical circles. In 1938 Barry was called to the UK and stationed at Aldershot, one of the main training centres in England. He took his wife Ethel with him and she lived nearby in Farnham next to Farnborough the Air-show airport. On 11 March 1940 they had a daughter Marian.

Ethel's family heard about the air attacks from Germany and pressured Ethel with her six month old infant to return to South Africa while Barry remained in UK until the war ended in 1945. He returned to South Africa but being a womaniser and gambler Ethel decided to divorce him. The terms of the divorce was that he would pay no alimony but would not have access to his daughter Marian.

In order to escape his gambling debts he regularly used the name Beira to avoid his creditors. We understand that he subsequently married a wealthy woman Claire Steingo's mother Jill who had daughters from another marriage Pam and Barbara, and gambled away her money leaving her poor. Being habitually short of money he then married another woman Ada Berman who Marian subsequently visited in the Old Aged Home many years later. Details are sketchy as in Ethel's family his name was never mentioned.

Marian married Harold Kimmel in 1965 and has had three sons Bryan in 1968, Warren in 1970 and Gary in 1974. Marian is a very well know Cellist.

Issy and Barry Beira.
Written by Shirna Ospovat

These two little brothers were not adopted after arriving in Cape Town, and were therefore sent in a group to Johannesburg for possible adoption there. When this group of children were brought to the local community hall, many Jewish people came to see them for adoption purposes, as well as just out of general interest, and curiosity.

My father (whom I think was the youngest child in his particular group), saw all these people gathered there, and noticed a middle aged woman in long black clothes amongst the bystanders. He ran towards her and shouted "mama mama", clutched her skirt, and would not let go. She comforted him, and felt she just had to take him home, as they were a childless couple anyway. However, when she heard there was an older brother, she was not willing to take both children, and a younger couple stepped forward willing to take the older brother. This was Mr and Mrs Lewin, from the East Rand, who took Berner, and raised him as Barry Lewin.

My father Issy, was therefore adopted by this middle age ultra orthodox Jewish couple, Mr and Mrs Beirachovitz, (later changed to Beira), from Doornfontein, Johannesburg.

Mrs and Mr Beira, my Bobba and Zeida, also adopted Freda, my Auntie, an older neice of my Bobba, who was brought out from Europe by them some years after they adopted Issy. Freda was always regarded as Issie's older sister. Freda married Joe Eliason, and they lived with my Bobba and kept up the house until they, Freda and Joe, were quite elderly, when they sold up and went to live at Sandringham gardens, where they remained for many years. Freda outlived all the males and died two years ago in 2008 at the age of 95. She and Joe did not have any children, and Issy's children were like her children.

Izzy grew up a very orthodox observant Jew, but went to a secular school during the day time as there were no Jewish schools in those days. Afternoons were spent at Cheder, and he became a soloist in the choir at the Lions Street Shul, Doorfontein.

Thelma Weinberg and Issy Beira on their wedding day

A younger Issy

Issy and Thelma

He grew up and went as a madrich to Habonim camp in Port Elizabeth where he met my mother, Thelma Weinberg, a secular Jewess from Port Elizabeth. They married and she came to live in Johannesburg. During the war years he was conscripted in North Africa, but returned safely home.

I, Shirna the eldest child was born in 1945, followed by a son, Bentley in 1946, and a third child Joel in 1949.

Issy was not a professional person but worked as a salesman and after the South African Govenment changed into Afrikaaner hands, they emigrated to Bulawayo, Rhodesia, to build a new life. We children all grew up there and we had a good life. He managed a fish and chips shop for years but when the company was taken over, we moved to Livingstone (close to Victoria Falls) for a few years where he managed a concession store. But things did not go well and we returned to Bulawayo for a few years, and finally returned to Johannesburg, South Africa in 1961 to seek better job opportunities. In 1962 we moved to Israel for a further year, and returned to

Johannesburg in mid 1963. There the family remained until Issy died in 1991.

Joel, the youngest child contracted cancer soon after their return to Johannesburg, and died at age 24 years, after many years of suffering, which was a huge hardship and blow to the family.

Shirna became a teacher, married and had a daughter and two sons, all of whom are very observant Jews. She now lives in Cape Town. The eldest son Clifford, lives in Johannesburg, and the youngest Hilton, lives in Cape Town, and is married with a sweet baby girl. The daughter Tanya and her family of three children, live in Ramat Bet Shemesh, a very religious area, in Israel.

Bentley is a successful businessman. He and his three sons are all married and live in Johannesburg and he has three grandchildren.

Berner (Barry) was adopted by a very secular Jewish couple from the East Rand which was far from Johannesburg. In those days transport and communication were not simple. The two families had very little connection, and so the brothers rarely saw or spoke to each other, and their connection and relationship degenerated completely.

Joel, Issy, Shirna, Thelma and Bentley

My father, however, was always fond of his older brother, and they finally did re-connect as adults, after they had both left home and started their adult lives. Both were in the South African army, but went in different directions. Issy was conscripted to North Africa, and Barry was sent to England.

Barry Lewin married Ethel Pack, a Jewish lady from Johannesburg, and their daughter was Marion Lewin, who today is a prominent and famous cellist. However, they were divorced when Marion was a tiny child of about two years old, and she barely remembers him, as he never saw her again. Some time after this divorce Barry changed his surname to Beira.

Barry in the meantime had married a lady Jill who had two older girls from a previous marriage, Pam and Barbara, whom he legally adopted. They had one child together a daughter Claire, now Steingo. The two brothers, even as adults only saw each other very occasionally. I do not know why.

Thelma Weinberg and Issy Beira

Issy was a good friend of Solly Jossel who was on the boat with him and also came to live in Bulawayo. Both the Jossel and Beira parents and all their children were very close friends sharing many Yom Tovim and good times together, until the Beira family left Bulawayo and returned to South Africa.

Once my parents, Issy and Thelma had emigrated to Rhodesia, the brothers lost touch, until one day suddenly, several years later Barry arrived in Bulawayo, to settle there, with his new wife, Ada, a widow, with a teenage daughter. They lived there for a short period (possibly 12-15 months), but this marriage also did not last, and one day when I was 14 years old, he suddenly disappeared never to be seen or heard of again.

No one knew or was able to find out what had happened to him. All enquiries came to nothing, and we all suspected that he quietly left the country to 'disappear' somewhere. My father Issy, tried several times to find him, but in vain, as he remained untraceable.

Issy, to his dying day, always hoped that some day, somehow, Barry would contact him and let him know of his whereabouts, but this never ever happened.

Issy and Thelma

MARIAN LEWIN - CELLIST

Marian Lewin is regarded as the doyenne of Cellists in South Africa and began playing the cello at the age of five studying with her aunt Betty Pack.

Marian won numerous awards in Eisteddfods and played regularly on the radio program "Young South Africa", and appeared three times with the J.S.O Youth Concerto Festival.

She obtained her University of South Africa Performers Licentiate in 1963 and was awarded an overseas scholarship.

In 1964 she joined the South African Broad Casting Orchestra and remained there until 1967, during which time she was appointed Acting Principal Cellist.

During the International Cello Week in Holland held in 1967 she was adjudged best cellist and appeared on Eurovision.

In 1971 she was appointed principal cellist in the PACT orchestra and held this post for 25 years.

She is a veteran broadcaster, and has appeared as soloist with the SABC, Natal Philharmonic and PACT Symphony Orchestras.

She was the Cellist of the Alma Musica Piano Trio for 34 years.

She is now a member of the Rosamunde String Quartet, the Hemanay Flute Trio, I Grande Violoncelliste, a six cello ensemble, the Festival Trio,
She is a past lecturer at the University of the Witwatersrand and taught at Pro-Arte art music and ballet school in Pretoria for 12 years.

She was nominated for 3 ARTES Awards for 1988, 1989 and 1995 and in 1998 was chosen as one of the top 10 musicians of the year by "Die BEELD"

Marian was a member of the jury for the International String Competition held at UNISA in 1992 and 2002.

She is regularly used as an external examiner for South African Universities as well as adjudicating various competitions and Eisteddfods.

Marian has recorded the complete collection of Glierre Cello duets on CD with Human Coetzee and recorded a Trio Hemany CD with Helen Vosloo and Malcolm Nay as well as Dances for Six, an internationally released CD of i Grande Cellisti and is currently making a CD with pianist Tertia Downie.

She is in great demand as a chamber musician.

Marian plays on a cello made in South Africa by Dawne Haddad who studied and had her own atelier in Cremona .

THE BEIRACHOVITZ FAMILY
Remembered by Freda (Koppel) Cheilyk

It so happens that my mother and my five brothers arrived in South Africa in November1936 and prior to our arrival my father used to board with a Mrs Beirachovitz.

She had to have been ultra-Orthodox for my father to have eaten there. Mrs. Beirachovitz lived in Sievewright Avenue in the house next door to the Alhambra Theatre.

On our arrival in Johannesburg we rented a house next door to the Lions Shul (so named because of the lions on each side of the entrance) in Siemert Road. Both these roads run parallel towards town.

On the first Saturday of our arrival Mrs Beirachovitz (shortened to Beira) arrived at our house with her daughter Freda (an adopted daughter of about 20 years of age) and told each of us what our names should be in English and we remained with those names given to us on that day.

Sometime in the 1980's I remember coming across Freda whom I got introduced to as Freda Beira. I thought that was her married name but now realise that she too must have shortened her name to Beira. One other time I saw Freda was at Sandringham Gardens but she had no idea who I was.

Strange how names come up and somewhere there is a connection in some hidden part of one's memory.

PART 3
THE OCHBERG ORPHANS

SECTION 11
ADDENDUM

This section of the book starts with
Isaac Ochberg's Bequests and Memorials,
the Golden Jubilee Reunion,
an article about the documentary "The Man from Africa"
and General Observations and Comments

It concludes with Acknowledgements
and an Index of the Ochberg Orphans

Chapter 131 – ISAAC OCHBERG – THE MAN, HIS FAMILY AND HIS BEQUESTS

ISAAC OCHBERG
Extract from article by Jonathan Boiskin "Jewish Affairs" 1994

Isaac Ochberg, the eldest son of Aaron and Sarah Ochberg, was born in 1878 in Uman, a small town in the Ukraine. His father Aaron had gone to South Africa in 1893 and Isaac followed him in 1895 at the early age of fifteen, making the trip alone. Several years later he established himself as one of Cape Town's leading entrepreneurs. Interestingly enough his success had in part been owing to his ventures in buying ships; on this account, the *Cape Argus* described him as the 'plucky shipowner'. Important purchases of property had also given Ochberg a high standing in the business community. Moreover, as the *Jewish Relief News* reported, his communal work had been of equal importance. He was a leading member of a number of charitable institutions in Cape Town and his special interest lay in making helpless children happy. His many business and family obligations did not by any means preclude him from participating fully in communal affairs, particularly Jewish ones.

Pauline (Polly) and Isaac

Isaac and Polly   *Isaac on board HMS Penelope*

He worked for the Helping Hand Society, the Jewish Orphanage, the Old Age Home, the *Dorshei Zion* Society, and was an active member of the New Hebrew Congregation of which he was subsequently elected vice- president. He was also an executive member of the South African Jewish Board of Deputies and an enthusiastic believer in Freemasonry. In her book *This Was a Man,* Bertha Epstein maintains that Ochberg was eventually recognised as one of the foremost social workers in South Africa, becoming associated in an important capacity with every Jewish organisation or institution in this country and with many overseas. He never refused to support a worthy cause; on the contrary, his creed was that since he had been enabled to achieve success in his own enterprises, he had a moral duty to help those less fortunate.

Isaac, Polly and family

Isaac Ochberg

One of Ochberg's most significant achievements was the evacuation of the pogrom orphans to South Africa. At his own expense, he travelled to that part of the Ukraine which had been overrun by bandits and brought back with him 200 orphans. His burning desire, however, was to see how his fellow Jews in the heart of the Ukraine were faring. After great difficulty he succeeded in getting permission to re-enter the country and was placed in charge of a special delegation appointed by the World Relief Conference, which sent through him shipments of foodstuffs, medical stores, clothing parcels and money. Becky Greenberg, herself an Ochberg Orphan, recalls that: *Isaac was a honey, he was like a father to us. There was no difference from one child to another, every child was a darling, everyone was lovely and everyone he patted. He was just wonderful.*

Isaac Ochberg was a man of heart and courage who always stood ready to proffer help whenever, wherever and to whomever it was needed.

Standing: Louis Melmed, Boris Crasnow, Polly Ochberg, and Leopold Davidowitz. Seated: Fay Ochberg, Joe Ochberg, Sara Ochberg, Isaac and Rose Ochberg. In Front: Bertha Ochberg,

EXTRACTS FROM THE PALESTINE POST
These Palestine Post extracts were sent in by Peter Stange.

CITATION FOR PROBATE
In the District Court of Haifa - No 42/38
First printed in the Palestine Post 1 August 1938

In the Matter of Isaac Ochberg, of Cape Town in the Union of South Africa, deceased.

In virtue of an order of the District Court of Haifa bearing date this day, I do hereby cite all and all manner of persons to appear in the said Court on or before Friday, the 23 September, 1938, at 9 am and show cause, if any they have, why the last Will and codicils thereto of Isaac Ochberg, deceased, should not be proved, approved and registered and probate thereof granted to Pauline Ochberg, Bertha Isabel Robinson born Ochberg (in the will described as Bertha Robinson) Julius Robinson, Boris Albert Crasnow, Leopold Dawidowitz, Jacob Gitlin, Cecil Louis Short in his capacity as nominee of Syfret's Trust Company Limited, and William Henry Low named therein, as, in default thereof the Court will proceed to grant the same accordingly.

REFLECTIONS
First printed in the Palestine Post 4 April 1941

The small Jewish community of South Africa has long been distinguished for its consistent generosity in supporting the upbuilding of Palestine. The forms which that support has sometimes taken may not be so familiar. Gifts have been forthcoming from all sections, but a few individuals have made specially outstanding contributions in the form of legacies.

Mr Isaac Ochberg of Cape Town, an active Zionist figure contributed lavishly and bequeathed £200,000 to Palestine, the larger part for the Jewish National Fund and the rest for the Hebrew University.

The money will be spent to acquire an area of land in the Hills of Ephraim. Mr Ochberg was in Palestine, and was more than once a delegate of South Africa at the World Zionist Congress. He directed that his estate was to be liquidated within seven years from his death.

Fifty thousand pounds is the sum left by the late Mr N Epstein of King Williamstown to the Jewish National Fund, on conditions however that postpone distribution for another decade. The testator was a bachelor and made the National Home his heir.

TRACT NAMED FOR ISAAC OCHBERG
First printed in the Palestine Post 25 June 1943

A tract of land in the Hills of Ephraim was formally named yesterday in honour of the testator of the funds which made its acquisition possible, the late Mr Isaac Ochberg of Cape Town, who was President of the local Zionist Organisation and a member of the Executive of the Board of Deputies.

He left the largest bequest known to Palestine from which the Jewish National Fund and the Hebrew University have each benefited by about £90,000 while further sums are expected from the estate.

In the centre of what will later become a civic square in Daliah, one of the settlements on the Tract, a 25 metre long pergola of stone pillars flanked by two 15 metre wings has been built on which a copper plaque bears the legend:

Erected in memory of the late Isaac Ochberg of Cape Town, through whose munificence the land of the Isaac Ochberg Tract was redeemed through the Jewish National Fund 1880-1937.

A pool has been constructed in front of the colonnade which will be surrounded with flower beds.

In unveiling this memorial, Dr A Granovsky, Managing Director of the JNF paid a warm tribute to the far sighted munificence of the donor who had taken a deep interest in the National Home and who loved Jewish youth. He had himself rescued pogrom orphans after the last war and bequeathed sums for Zionist youth education. On the Tract which at present comprises 9,000 dumans will arise several villages of which one will bear the name of the testator. He said that the testator was typical of the finest Zionist community - South Africa.

Prof Volcany spoke on behalf of the Hebrew University of their high appreciation of Mr Ochberg's bequest. The mukhtar of Daliah describing its progress said that they had proved that even from hard rugged terrain without irrigation they could get successful results.

The luncheon fare represented their first fruits. He added that a research laboratory for hill farming be established in the Ephraim Hills. The proceedings concluded with the singing of 'Hatikvah'.

Among the South Africans present were Mr D Dainow, Mrs Genusow, Messrs Friedman, A Levy, Manager of Dinyan Turtledove and H Zuckerman

Isaac Ochberg on the left, a delegate of South Africa at the World Zionist Congress Basle ~1932
Ochberg, Phili, Poliansky, Abrahams, and J Zukerman

A JEWISH NUFFIELD *by David Dainow*
First printed in the Palestine Post 25 June 1943

As reported above a tract of land in the Hills of Ephraim was named yesterday in honour of the late Isaac Ochberg, of Cape Town.

I knew Isaac Ochberg for over 25 years before he passed away in 1937. I had been on a relief mission to Poland just after the end of the last war when I came across a man engaged on a mission of mercy. His project was to collect a few hundred orphaned children from the pogrom areas in the Ukraine and bring them to South Africa. The difficulties of the task were enormous. I had the privilege of helping him. Finally the group of children was safely transported to the welcome shores of South Africa, where the children were placed in two orphanages. Within the first year, nearly 50 per cent of the orphans had been adopted by Jewish families and were brought up as their own children.

Isaac Ochberg came to South Africa as a poor immigrant and by dint of hard work, determination and a keen business sense, was able to attain great wealth. He was always, however, a very simple person and genuinely concerned in the poor and afflicted among his people. He gave generously during his lifetime. When his young daughter of 17 died suddenly some years ago in Cape Town, he gave an amount of £10,000 in her memory to the Hebrew University - an institution in which he was particularly interested.

It might well be said that Isaac Ochberg never knew the full total of his wealth. He had many interests, and bookkeeping and accounting were not his main concern. I believe he thought he was worth about a quarter-million pounds and that always seemed to be a burden to him. In the realisation of his properties and holdings since his death, the executors found that they had to deal with a fortune approximately three-quarters of a million pounds. After certain personal and public benefactions in South Africa and England, the bulk of his estate will finally go to Palestine - some hundred thousand pounds to the Jewish National Fund, and a similar amount to the Hebrew University, being among the fixed endowments. It will be the largest individual benefaction for the Holy Land in modern history.

Isaac Ochberg was buried in Cape Town on 13 December 1937

THE INVITATION TO THE GOLDEN JUBILEE 1921-1971
Invitation sent in by Freda (Koppel) Cheilyk

You are most cordially invited to a
Golden Jubilee Reunion
to be held at Oranjia,
Montrose Avenue, Oranjezicht, Cape Town
on Saturday, 16th October, 1971
to celebrate the
50th Anniversary
of the arrival in South Africa
of the
Ukrainian Pogrom Orphans
brought by the late Isaac Ochberg

Guests of honour:
His worship the Mayor
Councillor R. M. Friedlander and Mrs. Friedlander,
Mrs. Bertha Epstein (daughter of Mr. Ochberg)

Refreshments   8.00 p.m. for 8.15 p.m.

EVENTS IN THE LIFE OF ORANJIA

1911	Formation of Cape Jewish Orphanage.
1912	C.J.O. Land purchased in Montrose Ave.
1914	Outbreak of World War I.
1915	C.J.O. foundation stone laid by the Governor-General, Lord Buxton.
1916	New premises formally opened by Rev. A. P. Bender.
1918	End of World War I.
1920	Pogrom Orphan Fund started.
1921	Isaac Ochberg leaves for Eastern Europe.
	SEPTEMBER 19th 1921 Pogrom Orphans arrive in Cape Town with Isaac Ochberg.
1921	Ochberg Wing opened at C.J.O.
1922	Ochberg returns to Eastern Europe. Opens soup kitchens under auspices of C.J.O.
1930	Ochberg resigns after many years as president due to ill-health.
1937	Isaac Ochberg dies at sea December 11th—Leaves many charitable endowments including Higher Education Fund for C.J.O. and Dowry Fund for girls.
1939	World War II.
1945	World War II ends.
1961	Oranjia celebrates Golden Jubilee.
1971	Golden Jubilee Pogrom Orphan Re-union at Oranjia.

PROGRAMME OF EVENING

SATURDAY, OCTOBER 16th, 1971

———————

8.15	Guests Seated.
8.20	Chairman's introduction.
8.30	His Worship the Mayor, Councillor R. D. Friedlander welcomes guests.
8.45	Film of arrival of Isaac Ochberg and the children in Cape Town, in 1921.
9.00	Mrs. Fanny Lockitch talks about the Pogrom Orphans with whom she came.
9.15	Ian Webber, Mr. Ochberg's great-grandson says "Thank You".
9.25	Yehuram Ben-Dror of the Keren Kayemeth, Israel.
9.40	Tea Break.
10.40	Hatikvak and "get together".

THE POEM OF THE ORPHAN ON HIS WAY TO SOUTH AFRICA

Merciful Father in Heaven
Who in His mercy toward children left orphans
Forced to leave their homes
Has sent father Ochberg to make us citizens of South Africa
God blessed us that we found ourselves among good people
Our worries ended when we received the letter.
Our group, hundreds of children, would not be separated we would live as brothers!
A miracle will happen and when we grow up and stand on our feet
We will never forget the poor and needy.
Sins we have known
We will pray and ask blessings from heaven
We left behind us ruins when we started on our way
We took leave of our friends
And hoped that fate would allow
That we would live as Jews
To reach Zion is our dream.
Father Ochberg came to rescue us ...
And we will live as Jews
And to Zion come ...
So wrote an anonymous Jewish child from the Ukraine.

By a Staff Reporter

LIFE IN RUSSIA during the 1920s was a terrifying experience of tyrannical power and constant pogroms which plagued the existence of the Jewish population.

Amid famine and horror, pogroms daily created orphans until their number rose to 400 000.

Destitute, with little chance of survival, the children were shuttled between towns and orphanages as persecution spread. Jews around the world were alarmed at the appalling conditions and hardship under which the orphans existed.

Among the first to help the orphans were South African Jews in Cape Town in 1921.

A South African relief fund for Jewish war victims, came into operation on August 19, 1920.

The late Mr Isaac Ochberg of Cape Town proposed that the Cape Jewish Orphanage take responsibility for bringing orphan children out to South Africa.

In January 1921, Mr Bernard Alexander of Johannesburg persuaded the Union Government to give support on a pound for pound basis.

At his own expense Mr Ochberg went to Poland, the Ukraine and Galacta and established a temporary base — Sliska 28 — in Warsaw.

He chose younger children from various orphanages and with funds from South African Jews and the Union Government 200 set off from Danzig for South Africa.

The children landed in Cape Town on September 19 1921 and were first taken to Oranjia Orphanage. Soon, about half were sent to Arcadia, the sister institution of Oranjia, in Johannesburg.

Of those who survived many have become prominent and successful business and professional men and women.

And tonight survivors of those orphans are gathering at a reception at the Oranjia Orphanage to celebrate the golden jubilee of their arrival in Cape Town.

NOW HE LIVES HAPPILY

MR DAWID PENZIG was one of the original 200 destitute orphans who arrived penniless in Cape Town in 1921.

Today, 50 years later, he is the director of a large wholesale firm and lives happily in Pretoria. His story is not unlike others of the 200 children.

'I lost my mother at the age of four. We — there were five of us, my youngest sister being nine months old at the time — were living in a town called Kowel in the Ukraine. Life was difficult and I can remember the famine which stalked the country.

'My father died in 1919 (I was nine then) and we were taken to an orphanage in Sadowa Street, Kowel, where I stayed until Mr Ochberg arrived.'

Although then only 11, Mr Penzig, now 63, said he was already working as a compositor on a local newspaper.

'Because of this job I did not qualify to go to South Africa,' he said.

Eventually, after explaining his predicament personally to Mr Ochberg, he was allowed to leave with his younger sister and two brothers for Cape Town.

'We travelled from Warsaw to Danzig by cattle truck and from there onwards by boat to England. Finally, after a very tiring and difficult journey, we arrived here on the Edinburgh Castle in 1921.'

After receiving his school-leavers' certificate through night school, Mr Penzig started work at a Nigola business in 1922. Sixteen years later he branched out on his own and, in his own words 'things have since looked up and up.'

● Of the original 31 000 Jewish families in Kowel during the Russian Revolution only three were left in 1961.

THEN Dawid Penzik the orphan.

NOW: Dawid Penzik, successful businessman.

THE MAN they all remember — Mr Isaac Ochberg, who is being honoured at tonight's gathering of the 'Ochberg Family' — Jewish orphans who found refuge in South Africa.

THIS EARLY PHOTOGRAPH shows the Berkman family re-united again in South Africa after the terror of Russia.

I WATCHED AS THEY SHOT MY UNCLE

'WHEN THE REPRIEVED prisoners attacked my uncle's farm in the Ukrainian country-side the children fled into the forest and hid there for a month,' Mrs Leah Berkman, one of the 200 orphans, recalled as she vividly described her early life in Russia.

'For a month we ate berries, leaves and whatever natural food we could find. It was a terrible time in my life which I will never forget.

'My uncle was a wealthy man and I remember watching in horror as they shot him in the head. My two sisters, Molly, Gitle and I went to the orphanage in Kowel after that.'

Mrs Berkman's elder brother, Charles, was taken away by the communists and it was only years later that they were united again.

'I was nine when we buried my father. It was after the funeral that we left for my uncle's farm — but even there the pogroms hounded us.' Mrs Berkman said.

'Life in the orphanage was difficult although the committee did all they could to provide us with food and clothing.

'If it were not for Mr Ochberg we would all have been dead a long time ago in Russia,' she added.

In South Africa she was educated at the Hebrew Girls High School and the Jewish Government School.

'My first job was that of a dressmaker. I later married (her maiden name was Gonifas) and have three children, all of them married.'

After her husband's death, Mrs Berkman managed their business in Germiston on her own for a while, but later sold it.

'I later managed to get my brother to South Africa from the Ukraine and we have rebuilt our lives here.'

Although not sure of the exact dates, Mrs Berkman remembers minute details of the events which changed her life completely.

'I can still clearly see the fatal wound on my uncle's head when the prisoners shot him. They looted the farm and also killed other families and relations in the area.

'Although I will never forget the past I do not like recalling it very often,' she added.

Mrs Berkman is in Cape Town especially to attend the golden jubilee celebration of their arrival here in 1921.

FEAR OF BEING SOLD INTO SLAVERY

Mrs Leah Marks

TODAY an honorary life president of three Cape institutions, including the Women's Mizrachi, Mrs Leah Marks was a 17-year-old orphaned schoolteacher when she met Mr Ochberg in Poland for the first time.

'I was terrified at the time as I thought he was coming to kidnap the young girls at the school and sell them into slavery — which was a common thing during the Revolution,' Mrs Marks said at her home in Presnaye today.

'I was very young when the Russians came to take my father away from our home in Lemberg. The only thing I can remember about it was my mother throwing a parcel to him — and then he was gone.

'A month after we heard my father was dead, my mother died. She was only 35 but I think the experience was too much for her.'

Mrs Marks said that she then fortunately managed to get a bursary to study.

'My three sisters and a brother were sent to various orphanages in Russia. After completing my studies I returned to Lemberg to teach — and it was there that I met Mr Ochberg.'

Between helping Mr Ochberg, Mrs Marks undertook a hazardous journey to Kalush Hospital where her sister, Chana, was suffering from a contagious disease.

'They would not let me take her with me so I stole through a window, found her and carried her piggy-back to the station two miles away.

'Fortunately the train was delayed for four hours and we eventually managed to join up with the rest of the group gathered in Warsaw.

'Life was very cruel then and we never knew if there would be a tomorrow,' she added.

Mrs Marks said the orphans were in a terrible state when Mr Ochberg found them.

From Warsaw, they travelled to Danzig in cattle-trucks. Food was scarce and to keep their spirits up the orphans sang innumerable songs.

The arrival in Cape Town was 'overwhelming,' according to Mrs Marks, and on Cape Town harbour she met her present husband, Phillip Marks.

'Since then I have continually devoted my life to charitable work because I feel the need to help those who cannot help themselves. Even today I also remain grateful to Mr Ochberg who saved us from the horror of the pogroms and the fire we would have faced later during the Nazi regime.'

Today Mrs Marks has only one regret — and that is that through illness — she has a broken leg — she might not be able to attend the golden jubilee celebration.

I WATCHED THEM TEAR A TOWN APART

MRS POLLY JOFFE was five years old when the Russian conscripted her father into a work force and bundled him off to Odessa.

'There were seven of us in the family with only my mother left to care for us all. Although the Revolution had just ended there was a scarcity of everything in the country and to make matters even worse for us my mother died a little while later,' Mrs Joffe said.

'Although only five years old I can remember my elder sister and I living with a German woman for a while. She looked after us as best as she could, but, later my sister died of illness too.

'It was then that I was taken to the orphanage in Stanislowow.

Here I remained for three long, arduous years before Mr Ochberg arrived to choose the younger children to go with him.

'The years I spent in the orphanage were most terrible,' she said.

'Very often we had nothing to eat and when fighting broke out in the town we were chased out into the countryside for safety.

'I remember sleeping in a filthy stable on one such occasion, while on another we hid in the forest for hours watching the Russians tear the town apart for any possible Poles.'

Of her two brothers and five sisters only two sisters and a brother survived the Revolution.

'I must have been about eight years old when Mr Ochberg came to the orphanage.

'It was very difficult then and I did not want to go. Relations and other friends told me I should rather try to get to Israel, but not South Africa. Fortunately I did leave for Cape Town and have never regretted it.'

Mrs Joffe, who was born Stanger, said that as soon as she started to work she brought her sister out here too.

'When I left Danzig they were too old to qualify to go as well — so I saved and borrowed money to get them here later.

'I was working as a sales assistant and then only earned the equivalent of R16 a month.'

She too had travelled to Cape Town for the celebration and to meet the rest of the 'Ochberg family.'

THEN: Mrs Polly Joffe as she was at eight years old.

NOW: Mrs Polly Joffe photographed in Cape Town today.

The four newscuttings above can be seen in chapters:

POGROM ORPHAN GOLDEN JUBILEE
Held at the Cape Jewish Orphanage in the Ochberg Hall 16 October 1971

Written by Bertha I Epstein, the daughter of Isaac Ochberg, in THIS WAS A MAN, Cape Town, 1974

I am about to give my impression of the above occasion, because although it was extensively covered by the press, no such report could possibly give you a true picture of what it was really like. There were many factors which were of immense importance to me which would mean absolutely nothing to a reporter.

To start at the beginning. Of the original 200 orphans with whom my Father, the late Isaac Ochberg left the Ukraine in 1921, nine of them did not come to South Africa due to health reasons, so he actually arrived in Cape Town on the Edinburgh Castle on 19 September 1921 with a depleted company, and of these 25 have since died; some from natural causes, some in World War II (1939-1945).

With the devoted and able assistance of Julius Schochet who was in charge of the sub-committee for the Jubilee, and the willing co-operation of David Penzik, himself one of the Ochberg orphans, who lives in Pretoria, we managed to establish contact with every single one of the original children still alive. Scattered as they are all over South Africa, Rhodesia and even England, this was no mean achievement. Of the 400 people present in the Ochberg Hall at 'Oranjia' on Saturday, October 16th, 1971, 185 were the original pogrom orphans and their descendents.

Although we had invited every orphan still alive and offered to defray their expenses should it be needed, there were quite a few who were unable to come due to health or other personal reasons. Those who did come were either accommodated at 'Oranjia' or with one of the other 'orphans' in their own homes.

But every person actually present at the Golden Jubilee had some connection, directly or indirectly, with the project undertaken by my Father when he planned in 1920/21 to go to the Ukraine and rescue destitute Jewish children and bring them to South Africa. The records at the Cape Jewish Orphanage had been carefully and thoroughly searched until the committee lists of those who worked with him had been found and they, or if they were no longer living, their children or grandchildren were invited. Amazingly enough we did find two of the original pogrom orphan committee still alive, both of them now very elderly ladies, and they were both delighted to be with us that night.

All the Jewish members of the Cape Town City Council were invited, as were the Rabbis of all the local synagogues, and the Presidents of the various congregations. Every charitable organisation in Cape Town was asked to send a representative, and some members of the Government. We invited the last-named to show that although 50 years had passed, it had not been forgotten that my Father had received support from them, notably General Smuts and Sir Patrick Duncan. Both these gentlemen, in their official capacities had been instrumental in obtaining financial aid and permission for permits of entry.

Those who were unable to attend sent congratulatory messages and some of these were read at the reunion by the Chairman of the Orphanage, Mr R Chaitman. We received many letters, telegrams and cables of good wishes from America, Israel, England, and of course, from all parts of South Africa and Rhodesia.

Automatically the present committee of 'Oranjia' were also invited, but due to the limited capacity of the Ochberg Hall where the party was to be held, we had apologetically to restrict them to only two persons each. As it was, the hall was so crowded that every seat was squashed as close as possible to the next and there was hardly an inch to spare between them!

The atmosphere in the hall was positively electric. I have never in my entire life experienced anything like it.

Waves of joy and happiness seemed to wash almost visibly back and forth over the whole room.

There were only eight people at the 'top' table, in the order of seating they were: Ian Webber (my grandson); Phyllis Friedlander, the Mayoress; (by a most happy chance my first cousin), the chairman Mr Chaitman; myself; Dick Friedlander, the mayor; (he, incidentally, is a grandson of Mrs Natalie Friedlander through whose prompting the Cape Jewish Orphanage came into being in 1911), Fanny Lockitch one of

the Isaac Ochberg pogrom orphans and a past chairlady of 'Oranjia'; Yeruham Ben-Dror, from Israel, representing the Jewish National Fund, and Mrs Chaitman the chairman's wife.

Apart from a few round tables at the sides of the room for special guests, there were long continuous tables down the centre of the room in four rows.

At one of the side tables were seated all six Rabbis of the various congregations, with their wives. Here history was made as I was told it was the first time ever that Orthodox and Reform Rabbis had been seated together at a public function in Cape town. And what is more, they all seemed to be thoroughly enjoying themselves.

The seating arrangements had not been easy and we had spent many hours trying to get everyone placed in correct and congenial company. The pogrom orphans and their families were all placed in the long centre rows, each table bearing on large banners the name of the place from whence they originated.

Also placed at one of the side tables were other members of my family, who had come to celebrate with us this joyous affair. Our cousins, the Comay family from George with some of their children; Ethel Marcus, another cousin with her daughter and son-in-law; and my own two daughters, Noreen Webber, Ian'smother from Durban, and my eldest daughter Angela Snelgar, all the way from England.

The Ochberg Hall looked most attractive with all decorations, flowers, tablecloths, napkins, etc in blue and gold. The Union of Jewish Women had done large floral arrangements and these were outstandingly beautiful.

At each seating place was a printed program in blue and gold which I had had printed as a memento of the occasion. On the front was a reproduction of the photo taken of the pogrom orphan children on Waterloo Station in London. This together with a poem written by one of the children and used for the back of the program, I had found amongst my Father's personal papers. The poem was translated into English from the Yiddish in which it was written.

As one entered 'Oranjia' there were several large very lovely floral arrangements. From here one ascended a short flight of steps to the main entrance where I had placed two very large boards, having pinned on them the original photos of the children taken both individually and in groups. These too, I had found amongst my father's possessions. Can you just imagine the shrieks of mirth when these middle-aged men and women saw themselves as they had been 50 years before? They pushed and shoved striving to look closer at the photos, calling out to each other, 'Oy, look at this', and, 'Oh, it must be Chaya or Yankele', or whatever the case may have been. It was absolutely delightful to watch, and I congratulated myself on having thought of it. All the photos were given to the persons concerned after the party.

This foyer led in turn into a room in which was hung a large photo of the 1921/22 committee surrounded by flowers, with the figure 50 in gold on each side. On a table under this was a portrait of Isaac Ochberg, also bedecked with gold flowers, and a handsome gold candelabra with five long gold-coloured candles to represent the 50 years. This room lead directly into the Ochberg Hall.

If you are trying to imagine how I myself looked amidst all the splendour, I can tell you that I was wearing a simple gold-coloured silk two-piece suit, with a string of pearls, and pinned to my dress a cameo brooch on which was carved my Father's head. This had been made years before in Palestine as a gift for my Mother, and bequeathed to me by her. It is one of my most precious possessions. My cousin, the Mayoress, wore her handsome chain of office, and we each had on a spray of orchids which had been presented to us by the committee on our arrival. Mine was, most aptly, a gold one which matched my outfit perfectly, and hers was tinged with crimson which blended beautifully with the decorations on her dress and the Mayoress' chain. The Mayor, too, wore his official chain of office, as did the Deputy Mayor and Mayoress, Mr and Mrs David Bloomberg, who were in the receiving line. It all added charm and colour to the gaiety of the scene.

Now let's get to the party itself. When we were all seated the Chairman read out some of the messages of congratulations, and then introduced the next speaker, the Mayor, who in his capacity of first citizen of Cape Town extended a cordial welcome to our guests. After the Mayor's speech came the showing of 'THE FILM'.

Here I must explain that since my Father's death I have had in my possession a film of the pogrom orphans, made by Pathé Gazette, the British newsreel of the time. It is fairly short, showing firstly my Father and the children on Waterloo station in London, and then all of them embarking on the Edinburgh Castle in Southampton Docks, ready to sail to their new home in South Africa. This was taken on 5 September 1921, and my Father, in the style of the time wore formal morning suit with striped trousers and a top hat. He really looked very impressive.

When the film commenced there was total silence in the hall, but when the audience saw how comical some of the children looked in their peculiar clothes and with their shaven heads, many of them started to giggle. Suddenly they saw and recognised my Father and the clapping and cheering nearly raised the roof. 'Daddy Ochberg, Daddy Ochberg', they were shouting. To their intense delight at that moment my Father, almost as if he could hear them, raised his top hat and waved it cheerfully at us. This really hit them and they loved it.

From where I sat I could see the absorbed faces, most of them glistening with tears; not, I am sure, tears of sadness, but tears of happiness and very deep emotion. As the film ended there was an immediate clamour for it to be shown again, and it was. As it ended for the second time the lights went on and we proceeded to the next speech, somewhat chastened and having a little difficulty in composing ourselves.

The next speaker was Fanny Lockitch who, as Faygele Schrier, had been one of the pogrom children together with her brother, who was also present at the party wearing the very arm-band which had been given to them as identification when they arrived in London from Danzig, and which he has always treasured. He, by the way, is now a successful business man in Rhodesia, and had come to join us to celebrate the Golden Jubilee.

Fanny, all through the years, has retained her interest in 'Oranjia', has always served on the Committee, and was for some time their very able Chairlady.

She now proceeded to relate in very moving terms their terrible experiences in Russia before 'Daddy Ochberg' rescued them. She told of the horror of the pogroms; the starvation and sickness; the children's terror at the vile happenings they saw around them, and then of their salvation by my Father. She spoke of the love they bore him, how hard they worked to vindicate his trust in them and finally how successful and happy some of their lives had turned out. There cannot have been a dry eye in that entire room, and I saw some of the younger guests surreptitiously wiping their eyes and blowing their noses. As a matter of fact I had been a little apprehensive about the young people, afraid they might find the proceedings a bore, but I need not have worried because one by one they came afterwards and thanked me for the wonderful evening, and said how deeply moved they had been.

After Fanny's speech came the throat-clearing and it took a little while to become receptive to the next speaker who was Mr Ben-Dror. Amongst other things he mentioned the kibbutzim on the Isaac Ochberg Settlement in Israel which have become a haven of refuge for so many destitute and homeless people. He drew an interesting analogy between the Russia of 1921 and similar conditions there now. He ended his speech by reading part of that poem of 'An Orphan on his way to South Africa', printed on the back of the souvenir program.

Then, let me say, came my own big moment. My grandson, Ian was to speak on my behalf to thank everyone who had helped to make the Jubilee such a terrific success. All I had done in preparing him beforehand was simply to give him a list of the names that should be mentioned and tell him the rest was up to him. I certainly had no intention of letting him try to make a speech.

Well - I nearly burst with pride at what came forth! In a very clear and confident voice he spoke on behalf of the Ochberg family and to my astonishment as well as everyone else's he actually quoted some saying in Hebrew appropriate to the occasion. I thought he was wonderful.

We had arranged that at the end of his speech he was to call up Mr Schochet and give him a silver medallion which I had had made to a special design as a mark of my appreciation of all his yeoman work, and also to present Mr Chaitman as president of the Orphanage my cheque for R5,000 of which R2,000 was to be used to defray all the expenses of the party and the other R3,000 for refurnishing or redecorating 'Oranjia'.

While Ian was doing this I put on his plate a companion medal to the one I had given Mr Schochet, with his own name on it, as I wanted him to have a souvenir of this wonderful occasion which I hope will always bring him proud and happy memories.

In the weeks preceding the Golden Jubilee I had heard the word 'presentation' being whispered around, and I made it clear to all concerned that on no account whatsoever was I to be the recipient of any presentation. However, when I took my seat at the table on our arrival I found a small package addressed to me, and when unwrapped it found inside a beautiful antique gold locket. It opens from both sides, having on one side a photo of the 1921 orphan children with the following inscription: *commemorating the arrival of Daddy Ochberg's pogrom children in South Africa in 1921* and on the other side a small photo of my Father and these words: *Presented to Mrs Bertha Epstein by them in gratitude, at the Golden Jubilee, Oranjia 1971.*

I was so overwhelmed that at first I was quite speechless. When the full impact of all that it implied struck me, I was very close to breaking down completely. What an extra-ordinarily kind and gracious gesture. To show me in this tangible and moving form what their loving thoughts had been towards their beloved 'Daddy Ochberg'. Fifty years is a lifetime, but they had not forgotten him. This gift I will wear with pride and pleasure, and I hope it will ever remain a precious thing in the Ochberg family for all the coming generations.

By now, all emotion spent, we were more than ready for some refreshment. During the time this was being served, two of the younger girls of Oranjia entertained us with delightful songs in Yiddish. There were delectable things to eat and drink, and everybody settled down to do justice to the catering.

The excitement was still intense. There were laughter and tears, people dashing from table to table, greeting long-lost friends, showing each other photographs, introducing children and grandchildren, exchanging reminiscences - all in a happy pandemonium of the unleashed spirit of reunion.

Eventually 'Hatikvah' was sung, and the guests began to move homewards. Not so the '1921s'. For them this was by no means the end of the party. I was besieged by happy men and women telling me over and over again what a memorable evening it had been for them, and that it was something they would always remember.

For me too it had been a most momentous occasion. Honour had been paid where honour was due, with love and affection, in the living presence of my Father's greatest humanitarian achievement.

This had indeed been a Golden Jubilee to remember; the reunion of Isaac Ochberg and his beloved pogrom orphan children. God bless them all.

Lionel Slier sent this photo taken at 50th Year Anniversary Ochberg Orphan Reunion and comments.
"In Isaac Ochberg's will, he left a sum of money with his daughter for a 50 year reunion of the children to be held in Cape Town. There was money to pay for all 'children' who could not afford the fare to get to Cape Town and for their accommodation to be met. My mother, Sarah and her sister, Leah, went to the reunion in 1971. He truly was a wonderful man and a remarkable human being."
"Sarah Altuska with the white top and Leah Altuska with the black top are sitting together at the far side of the table"
My wife and I on left side, sitting with my mom, Fanny Lockitch (Shrier), who is obscured by the lady in the front" Barry Lockitch.
"In front are CK Friedlander, my father, Eva Smulowtiz (Chawa Pianka) my grandmother, and Edith Friedlander, my mother." Rae Sank

Chapter 133 – THE MAN FROM AFRICA - THE DOCUMENTRY

THE MAN FROM AFRICA

Written by David E Kaplan and first published in The Jerusalem Post, Metro magazine 4 April 2008.

Our knowledge of history is often lazily shaped by Oscar-winning movies. How many people gained their understanding of Jewish life under the Romans from the 1960s blockbuster *Ben Hur*, or the rebirth of modern Israel from Otto Preminger's *Exodus*?

But what about the movies that don't quite cut it at the Oscars? Have significant chunks of the past been relegated to the abyss of the unknown?

Such may be the case of a recent documentary by director and producer John Blair, who won the Best Documentary Feature statuette for his 1995 *Anna Frank Remembered*.

Blair's recent entry, *The Ochberg Orphans*, which deals with the rescue of Jewish children in 1921 from the war-torn Pale of Settlement and their resettlement in South Africa, failed to make the final five nominees at this year's Academy Awards, and an inspiring chapter of Jewish history may now never reach a wider audience.

An aside to this little-known story is that the documentary also brought a 90-year-old former South African residing in Haifa out of obscurity. In 2005, before Blair had begun making his documentary, *The Jerusalem Post* ran an appeal from the London-based director for information about South African philanthropist Isaac Ochberg, who helped finance and personally participated in the rescue. *Metro* contacted Sam Levin, a former Director of the South African Zionist Federation in Israel (Telfed), who in the 1920s had been a youngster in Cape Town, to ascertain whether he had any personal insights to impart to the director. Levin recalled meeting some of the rescued children at the Cape Town Jewish Orphanage, where his parents had been active volunteers. "One particular boy I will never forget," said Levin. "His arm was cut off below the elbow. The Cossacks had murdered his parents in front of him and when they were about to finish him off, he raised his arm to protect himself from the thrust of the sword. They sliced off his arm and left him to die."

In an article that appeared at the time, Levin surmised that it was unlikely that there were any Ochberg orphans alive today, particularly in Israel. So you can imagine the surprise when this writer received a phone call from a Cecilia Harris in Haifa, who revealed in a wavering voice: "I was an Ochberg orphan."

A few months later, Harris was on a flight to London, where she joined the film crew en route to Eastern Europe, where she starred in the documentary. Today, a giant poster of the movie hangs on a wall in her small Haifa apartment.

In the early 1920s, reports filtered through to South Africa of dreadful pogroms taking place in the Ukraine. Cataclysmic forces were in play and, unsurprisingly, Jews were caught in the middle. Following the collapse of the old Czarist Empire in 1917, rival armies, the Reds and the Whites, were fighting for control. Poor at the best of times owing to centuries of oppression, the Jews' condition deteriorated. Famine was followed by epidemics of typhoid and other diseases, and into this amalgam the most toxic of ancient antagonisms exploded to the surface - anti-Semitism. Ukrainian and Polish peasants joined forces with reactionary officers and troops to massacre Jews wherever they found them. Pogroms were being reported daily - full details and exact numbers of Jews killed arc unknown to this day. The Pale of Settlement became an open hunting season for Jews.

In despairing letters smuggled through enemy lines, Jews pleaded to their kinsman in South Africa and elsewhere for help. These pleas galvanized South Africa's Jewish communities like nothing before. "Why not try and mount a rescue operation and bring at least some of the children out?" people asked at meetings across the country. Overnight, an idea took shape and spread like wildfire. Before any organization could step in, generous offers of financial and other kinds of assistance were made. With abounding energy and enthusiasm, Cape Town businessman Isaac Ochberg embraced the plan.

Two further questions arose: How could the orphans be rescued from a war-torn region, and would the South African government create any difficulties in admitting them? Ochberg quickly met with then-prime minister Jan Smuts, who granted permission.

As reports of the Jews' plight continued to leak out, the dimensions of the tragedy became clearer. No fewer than 400,000 Jewish orphans were known to be destitute, so that whatever was done would only amount to a drop in the ocean. That did not deter the community, who were determined to save whomever they could.

The next step was for someone to travel to Eastern Europe and make arrangements on the spot. Without hesitation, Ochberg offered to undertake the mission. Fanny Frier, who would later become chairwoman of the Cape Jewish Orphanage, recalled being an orphan in Brest-Litovsk, waiting for "the man from Africa" to arrive.

"He was going to take some of us away with him and give us a new home on the other side of the world," Frier said. Understandably, the youngsters had mixed feelings. While they were excited about "going to a beautiful new country, we also heard stories of robbers and wild animals and we feared we might be eaten by lions or cannibals or sold off as slaves.

However, when he appeared with his reddish hair and cheery smile, we all took a great liking to him and called him 'Daddy.' He would spend hours talking to us, making jokes and cheering us up."

Ochberg's most traumatic problem was how to select whom to take and whom to leave behind. In the end, he decided to choose eight children from each institution - a total of 200. Since the South African government had stipulated that the children had to be in good physical and mental health, this required very careful selection. Only those who had lost both parents were accepted. Harris, who was three years old at the time, was selected together with her two older sisters. As no photographs survived, she has no knowledge of what her parents looked like. She does remember being sick on the ship to South Africa - the *Edinburgh Castle* - and her sister Lisa having to look after her.

Another contributor to the documentary was Liebe Klug from Cambridge, who spends part of the year in Beersheba, where her husband Aaron - a 1982 Nobel Laureate for chemistry - is on the Board of Governors at Ben-Gurion University of the Negev. Her father, Alexander Bobrow, was a key player in the drama that unfolded. "He had been an analytical chemist in a sugar factory," Klug told *Metro*. During the Great War, he changed professions to social work, joining the "Curatorium, which had been formed to help Jewish refugees in Pinsk. At 26, he accompanied the 200 rescued orphans on the ship to Cape Town, where he settled and met my mother," she recounts.

In testimony recorded before he died, Bobrow relates that "so many children were found that we set up three orphanages. At first, Pinsk was so isolated by the fighting that we were dependent solely on our own resources. We had neither beds, bedding nor clothes, and I recall using flour bags to make clothes for the children."

Bobrow relates how typhus broke out in one of the orphanages and how in the course of his duties he had to walk through the streets as shells were exploding. Balachou, the notorious Ukrainian, had descended on the city with his gangs and the pogroms raged for nearly a week. Bobrow recalled how an old lady tried to pacify the terror-stricken children by calling out: "The Almighty will keep us and save us - now repeat after me."

As order was restored, supplies began to arrive, first from the Juedischer Hilfsverein in Berlin and then from the Joint Distribution Committee - cocoa, condensed milk, cooking oil and clothes. One of the American relief workers Bobrow recalled meeting was "Henry Morgenthau, who would later become Secretary of the Treasury under president Franklin Roosevelt."

Like the Pied Piper of Hamelin, Ochberg moved from town to town, visiting cities - Minsk, Pinsk, Stanislav, Lodz, Lemberg and Wlodowa - as well as villages, collecting orphans. Three months later, with the 200 children in London, he wrote to the leadership in South Africa who were eagerly waiting for news.

"I have been through almost every village in the Polish Ukraine and Galicia and am now well acquainted with the places where there is at present extreme suffering. I have succeeded in collecting the necessary number of children, and I can safely say that the generosity displayed by South African Jewry in making this mission possible means nothing less than saving their lives. They would surely have died of starvation, disease, or been lost to our nation for other reasons. I am now in London with the object of arranging transport and I hope to be able to

Ochberg Orphans disembarking from Eastern Europe

advise telegraphically soon of my departure for South Africa with the children."

"Never, to my dying day, shall I ever forget our first sight of the lights of Cape Town and then the tremendous reception when we came ashore with half the city apparently waiting on the quay for us," Frier recorded. So large was the group of children that the Cape Jewish Orphanage was unable to house them all. A considerable number went to Johannesburg, including Harris and her two sisters as well as many others whose children now live in Israel. One was Phyllis Ratzer, whose daughter, Rene Simpson, lives in Tel Aviv. "She often spoke of 'Papa Ochberg' and died in Johannesburg at the age of 94," Simpson said. Another descendent of an Ochberg orphan is Yvette Shiloh of Haifa, whose mother, Andja Avin, was rescued in Warsaw and made aliya in 1960, settling initially on kibbutz Kfar Blum before moving to Kiryat Gat.

When Ochberg died in Cape Town, he left "what was then the largest single bequest to the Jewish National Fund," Sam Levin told *Metro*. "[The JNF] used it to redeem a piece of land in Israel called Nahalat Yitzhak Ochberg - which included the kibbutzim of Dalia and Ein Hashofet. In the course of years, the name Ochberg dropped off the signs and it's now known as Nahalat Yitzhak. I am certain there is hardly anyone in Israel today who would know which Yitzhak it was."

THE ISAAC OCHBERG MEMORIALS
Written by Bennie Penzik – February 2011

It all began in earnest in December 2008. I had read Bertha Epstein's book, *This Was a Man,* the life story of her father, Isaac Ochberg, on a number of occasions, but this time I focused on two specific issues - her descriptions of a1950 JNF film and a 1970 JNF brochure.

I retrieved the film from the Steven Spielberg Archives - what a revelation! A well-made production - *The Immortal Road* - designed to raise funds for the Jewish National Fund (JNF) primarily in the USA with 18 minutes focusing on the close bond between Isaac Ochberg and Kibbutz Dalia. The message of the film inferred that for man to achieve immortality, he should strive to establish his bond with the Land ensuring that, accompanied by an appropriate donation, his name will last forever!

Isaac Ochberg had made the largest single donation to the JNF, a record that stands to this very day. However, I discovered that people in the area, even residents of the kibbutz, had only sparse, if any, knowledge of the existence of the man. I interpreted this as an injustice and began the quest to achieve the righting of a grievous historic wrong.

I established that the JNF had indeed erected an impressive memorial monument of stone in Ochberg's honour, of which Bertha had written when she visited in 1970, at the Elyakim junction near Yokneam but this had been removed into storage when the road required widening during the nineties.

The monument as discovered in a JNF warehouse December 2008
Previously erected at the Elyakim junction near Yokneam

Negotiations began in earnest with the JNF and, as our small ad-hoc committee was to learn, many meetings needed to be attended, many visits were required to potential sites for the re-erection of the monument and extensive efforts on our part to convince the organisation that a debt of honour was owed and past due.

The plaque on the pergola wall in the 1960s Kibbutz Dalia
Photo from JNF brochure

In parallel, we met with the management of Kibbutz Dalia on numerous occasions to present our vision to establish the Isaac Ochberg Heritage Centre on the grounds adjacent to the pergola erected in Ochberg's memory in 1943. The story of the strong bond with the kibbutz was further covered in the 1970 JNF brochure printed in Jerusalem and thus pressure was brought to bear on the JNF management to, once again, correct a grievous historic wrong.

The plaque commemorating Isaac Ochberg - 2010 Kibbutz Dalia
The plaque is needing attention

Fast Forward to December 2010

After constant campaigning, the JNF finally agrees to acknowledge the recognition due to Isaac Ochberg and to finance the creation of a dedicated hilltop site at Ramat Menashe, replete with the re-erection of the original stone monument, the construction of a Memorial Wall of Names in memory of Ochberg's Orphans, a watch-tower overlooking the original Isaac Ochberg Tract, explanatory ceramic plaques, benches, a mini-amphitheatre, access paths and cycle parking. Our committee agreed that this gesture indeed went a long way in complying with the terms of our quest and correcting the perceived injustice to our esteemed 'patron'.

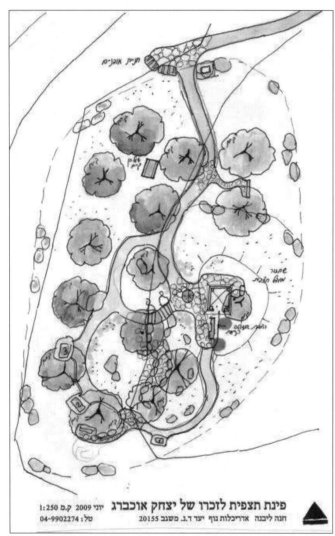

Sketch of the proposed JNF Ochberg Memorial Site at Ramat Menashe

At last!

19 July 2011 will witness the inauguration of the Isaac Ochberg Heritage Centre at Kibbutz Dalia.

The stone setting ceremony of the JNF Ochberg Memorial Site is set for 20 July 2011.

The year 2011 marks 90 years after a historic adventure which began in the orphanages of Eastern Europe via Warsaw and Danzig to Southampton and London, then southward bound on the epic voyage to Cape Town where the *Edinburgh Castle* arrived in September 1921 with its precious cargo of 181 orphans fortunate enough to have been selected to accompany Isaac Ochberg.

If I am to be permitted to end on a personal note....

My earliest recollections of my late Dad's commitment to the Arcadia orphanage in Parktown, Johannesburg, were how much he had enjoyed his sojourn, which period included both his Bar-Mitzvah and wedding. He was intimately involved in the support of Arcadia for 50 years. I recall the Sunday drives in the '34 Vauxhall with Dad and his little receipt book with its crumpled piece of carbon paper canvassing half-guinea donations from each Pretoria Jewish family.

To my everlasting chagrin, his requests of me as a teenager to accompany him on trips to the Parktown orphanage often fell on indifferent ears - after all, I had to play soccer or attend a Betar meeting so I was pressed for time.

I have ultimately joined the ranks of those who now want to ask questions and no-one is left to respond.

However, and this is the message I wish to convey to all descendants - it is never too late to pay homage. Now that I have been so intimately involved in the organisation of events in honour of his 'Daddy Ochberg', I pray that, *in absentia,* my Dad may be aware that I have endeavoured to live up to his expectations of me. It is exactly 40 years ago that he played an active role in organising the Golden Jubilee gathering of the original orphans and their families in Cape Town in 1971. I urge you all to step up to the plate and remember and honour Isaac Ochberg as befits his memory. Without him, we would not have been! February 2011

Bennie Penzik at the pergola 2010 – Kibbutz Dalia

Mountains of praise and thanks are due to Bennie Penzik by all Ochberg Orphan descendants for taking it upon himself to make it his business to rectify the errors of the past and to establish these Isaac Ochberg Memorials.

Bennie we all salute you!

GENERAL OBSERVATIONS AND COMMENTS ARISING FROM COMPILING THE OCHBERG ORPHAN BOOK
Written by David Solly Sandler

In compiling the individual life stories of the Ochberg Orphans, I encouraged descendants to write about the lives of the siblings, parents and other family left behind. Included in the index at the end of this section are the names of several siblings of Ochberg Orphans and their life stories are also told.

I encouraged descendants to include correspondence from family left behind and sadly there were many cases of correspondence ending when the Holocaust started and fruitless searches to find missing relatives after the war.

On the one end of the scale some descendants had comprehensive and well related life stories of their Ochberg Orphan forebears, while on the other end of the scale there were descendants who knew very little or did not want to share the stories they knew. While many Ochberg Orphans were successful with their lives and flourished and multiplied others did not.

For each of the Ochberg Orphans that survived there were many children that did not. I believe the stories of those who survived must be told to remember and honour the children who did not live to tell their stories.

VARIATIONS IN NAMES, DATES AND PLACES

Some children were found in terrible circumstances and there was not always an orderly handover of children in those desperate times. As a result, where the children came from and where and when they were born was not always known. Maybe a child told white lies to be accepted to go to South Africa and maybe those in charge could have told a little white lie about a child's age to help the child to be accepted.

The names of the children have been spelt in very many different ways. It is understandable, if we consider that the children were Russian, Polish or Ukraine and that their names were originally written down in Yiddish and then later different people would read the Yiddish written in the Hebrew script and then spell the name in English. Added to this are further complications and variations with the Anglicising of their names.

Ages vary between the group passports, the registers and the many lists made out for the children. One suggestion was that on the ship the children were listed as younger to pay a lower fee.

One descendant wrote, "My mother told me that although her birth date was shown as 1911, she was born a few years earlier. Apparently when she left for South Africa, she was listed as younger than she actually was, because it was felt that younger children were more acceptable for adoption."

Names of towns vary as well as the birth places of the children. In those desperate times of wars and revolution, with armies coming and going, borders moved and a town in one country could easily find itself in another country. Towns in the Pale of Settlement have various spellings in Russian, Polish, Ukrainian and maybe one or two more and then there is their present day name. To add to the confusion, Jews were at times forced to move by the changing authorities and sometimes they moved from one town to another on their own accord to avoid conflict. To further complicate matters some people wanted to hide from the authorities where they did in fact come from.

SILENCE, SHAME AND SADNESS

Some people today would not even know that they were descendants of Ochberg's Orphans. It was not something their parents readily spoke about and indeed many of them would have tried to hide the fact from their children so as to protect them.

There was, alas, also a shame attached to being an orphan.

Arnold Rabinowitz wrote, "The general attitude of the community was that it was a mitzvah to have adopted one of those poor orphans, a good deed in a dark world, but you really wouldn't want one of them to marry into your family, would you?

"After all, you knew nothing of their parents and extended family, their health history and their genetic background. This is a generalisation that isn't true of all the adopters but it was certainly true of a fair number, nervous, insecure, only to do nothing that would jeopardise their increasing prosperity and emergent social solidity."

What is very sad to see is that some descendants are embarrassed that their parents were Ochberg Orphans and were looked after by the Jewish Community. They are reluctant to write about their parents or send photos or let it be known their parents were Ochberg Orphans or to even make themselves known.

While we should all celebrate the lives of our ancestors who overcame hardship and tell their life stories for our grandchildren and their grandchildren, I can understand that sometimes descendants find the subject too sad or distressing to deal with.

BREAKING THE RULES

The *rules* prescribed by the South African Government for the admittance of the children were broken in more cases than they were adhered to. I understand that the children had to be healthy, double orphans (both parents deceased), could not be over 14 years old and could not be separated from siblings.

The life stories reveal that many of the Ochberg Orphans had family; siblings and sometimes parents left behind and some luckier ones were brought to South Africa by their Ochberg Orphan family. Others managed to emigrate from the 'Pale' and there were reunions of family members in other countries in later years. Sadly many of the family left behind perished in the Holocaust.

While some older siblings came as *nurses and carers* other siblings did not come as they were over the age limit, or not of good health or they chose not to come and ran away.

These were desperate times and at least one child denied her mother's existence to be accepted to go to South Africa. No doubt those in charge turned a blind eye to the *rules* to enable children to be accepted.

MARRIAGE

Once settled in South Africa I believe well meaning committee and care givers at Oranjia and Arcadia saw it as their responsibility to marry the girls off and that their duty ended when their charges were placed in the *bonds of holy matrimony.*

Celia Isaacman, the daughter of Regina Artman, wrote:
"*At the Ladies Section at Oranjia* there would be dances on Saturday nights and the girls could drop the names of young men they would like to invite into a box and those in charge of the hostel would invite the guys to come without mentioning who was actually the person asking them. In this way the hostel became a place where the young Jewish men could have a fun evening and meet the girls. Many girls met their husbands at the Saturday Night Dances (socials) in Cape Town."

Ursula (Rosenblatt) Rembach, the daughter of Leah Altuska, wrote in Leah's Story in More Arc Memories:
"In those days the main objective was for girls to be married off at an early age and when my mother and father married at Arcadia they were given a real "society" wedding, seemingly with no expense spared.

"My mother told me that for her to get married she would have to have finished school. I have the minutes from a board of trustees meeting at Arcadia where she seeks permission to do so. Before her 18th birthday on June 8 1930, Leah married Maurice.

"The Chupa took place on the lawns of Arcadia. The reception was a grand affair with 300 guests entertained at Arcadia, complete with a jazz band and children's choir from Arcadia. It was reported in *The Zionist Record* of June 13, 1930, a copy of which is one of my most treasured possessions.

"The Ladies Committee set up a trousseau fund for the Ochberg orphan girls so that they would go into marriage like any other girl, with new wedding dresses and a trousseau. This fund was continued for many years and when I married in 1969, I was considered a part orphan because my father had died when I was still a young girl, I too received a trousseau. I think that my mother considered Arcadia to be her home, the place where she grew up and was cared for. I don't think she ever thought of herself as an underprivileged orphan but rather someone special who had been given the gift of opportunity."

Several weddings took place at Arcadia and were reported in the press and I suspect that many *chance meetings* were engineered by these well meaning *match makers*.

MENTAL TRAUMA AND DISEASES

There is no doubt that many of the children arrived in South Africa traumatised from the horrors they had witnessed and also sometimes endured and some of the life stories clearly reveal this.

Social workers, clinical psychologists and child care workers were only introduced four or five decades later and there was no trauma counselling.

At least two children were violent as adults, two are known to have committed suicide and some had recurring nightmares as adults. Others no doubt bore their memories in silence or supressed them.

Several children were described as stoic and able to endure and cope with the ups and downs that life dished out.

As the life stories reveal a few Ochberg Orphans suffered from tuberculosis (consumption) and several succumbed to TB or other diseases at a young age, and of course some suffered from malnutrition as children which restricted their growth.

THE GENEROSITY OF THE JEWISH COMMUNITY

This book is about the suffering of the Jews in the 'Pale' and the help given to these desperate people in their time of need by their brethren, the Jewish Communities around the world.

Many life stories end with concluding paragraphs similar to Celia Isaacman's. "As I look at it, it is quite a sobering thought that had it not been for Isaac Ochhberg, my mother would have perished as we believe her sister and mother did in the Holocaust, and none of us would have been here."

I believe most readers of this book owe their very existence and the existence of their families to the generosity of the Jewish Community.

The Jewish Communities around the world saw it as their duty and responsibility to help fellow Jews (our ancestors) in their time of need and they did.

We too have a duty to help our fellow Jews who are presently in need of help in the Ukraine, South Africa and in Israel.

ACKNOWLEDGEMENTS

This book belongs to the Jewish Community and has been a grand collaboration with many people and organisations helping to shape it and nurture it along.

Our first and greatest thanks go to all the Ochberg Orphans and their descendants, who entrusted me with their memories, especially those who bravely opened up and shared their more sensitive and private stories.

Thank you to all others who have permitted us to include their work; Lionel Slier for *Europe, WW I and life in the 'Pale of Settlement' 1914-1920,* Dr Roman Serbyn for *Man-made Famine In Soviet Ukraine 1921-1923* and Veronica Belling for *The Cape Jewish Orphanage – Bes Yesoymim 1911-1939.*

Most of the firsthand accounts of the Ochberg Orphans at the end of part one of the book are extracted and adapted from the original transcript of interview courtesy Rainmaker Films. Thank you and also Janice Rosen, Archives Director, Canadian Jewish Congress Charities Committee National Archives and Solly Kaplinski, Misha Mitsel, Ninio Reeva and Lisa Margolin of the American Jewish Joint Distribution Committee for taking the time and trouble to help with information for the book.

Much thanks go to Bennie Penzik, son of two Ochberg Orphans, who like a benevolent older brother was always there to help and guide me and he contributed from the beginning; the title of the book, to the end; the chapter on Isaac Ochberg's Memorials.

Much thanks and praise is due to Veronica Belling (Jewish Studies Library UCT) for her invaluable and professional help. Not only did she send us archival information of the Cape Jewish Orphanage and contribute chapters to the book but also the book is peppered with her translations of letters and documents from Yiddish to English.

Thank you to Michael Perry Kotzen, an actor and octogenarian, initially from Israel and more recently from Sydney, the most prolific contributor of Arc Memories, who has always willingly helped with proof reading of both the initial and final drafts for this book.

I must thank my daughter Sarah, who helped design the cover and a very great thanks must go to Antoinette Weber, my partner of the past nine years, who gave very generously of her time and assisted with the typing and proofreading. I have once again tried to copy the very high standard of formatting she set in the first volume.

Then there are many people who took an interest in my work and helped and encouraged me along the way and gave me advice: Freda Cheilyk (Koppel), Monty Koppel, Alec Saul and Jules Gordon all Ex Arcadians and also Lionel Slier. Thank you all and also Rifka Gabbay, Eli Zagoria and Jack Goldfarb who helped translate documents.

Thanks must again go to two very close Arc 'brothers', David Kotzen and Dr Solly Farber who passed away in July 2002 a day apart. They both inspired and encouraged and helped me and set me on the path to compiling the volumes on Arcadia and this volume as a natural progression. As mentioned previously, I sometimes feel that it is not by chance that I share with them my names David and Solly. I hope that David and Solly, as well as Doc and Ma and all Old Arcs who have 'bunked over the hill' enjoy the book from above.

Also a very big thank you goes to all those that helped sell and store the Arc Memory Books:
Australia - Freda Cheilyk Gold Coast, Shelley Segal, Mannie Osrin and Lotte Herman in Melbourne and Hymie Sacks in Sydney.
Israel - Alec Saul in Hertzlia, Ronny and Dorothy Schreeuwer at Sdot Yam and Dave Samuel in Karmiel.
UK - Denise Sheer, and Monty Koppel in London.   **New Zealand** – Gary Blackman in Auckland
Canada - Mike and Felicia Saiet in Toronto and Pamela Chasen in Montreal.
USA - Sharmaine Palmer in Baltimore and Willie Isaacs and Gerald Sacks in Houston
South Africa - Jules Gordon, Max Goldman, Sylvia and Solly Jossel and Pearl Tennyson at the Arcadia Office selling and Graham Stoler and David Lasker storing the books in Johannesburg. Colin Rosenkowitz in Cape Town.

Lastly I thank all those who generously helped in sponsoring the printing and distribution of the *More Arc Memories*; Peter Hough from Sydney, Monty Koppel from the UK, Eric Herr, Aubrey Levy, Brian Hough, Eric Niedermeyer, Mark and Brett Levy, Effie Segal, Solly Jossel and Ekkie Litvin from South Africa, Jules Miller, Mark Jacobs, Hodda Lopis, Lotte Gaddin (Herman), Eli Zagoria and Hymie Sacks from Australia and Rita Chimes and Bennie Penzik and others who prefer to remain anonymous.

As mentioned in the foreword I hope to fund this third volume and distribute the books the same way as the first two volumes with all the costs being paid by contributions so that all sales proceeds go to Arcadia and Oranjia. As at the end of February 2011 approximately R500,000 had been raised for Arcadia and Oranjia. We still have many copies of the Arc Memory books on sale all around the world and I encourage you all to promote the book, and this sequel *The Ochberg Orphans,* with friends and to give them away as gifts. You can pay for them locally and have them delivered to friends overseas. Please see our website www.arcadia.ca.com.au and help us reach our target to raise R1,000,000 for Arcadia.

I plan next PG to compile a book on *Alter Bobrow and the Three Pinsk Orphanages* which will include over 100 letters written to Alter Bobrow by children and colleagues on his departure from Pinsk with the Ochberg Orphans in 1921.

Over many years I have also gathered my family history and PG *My Inheritance* may well be another book.

David Solly Sandler sedsand@iinet.net.au

INDEX OF OCHBERG ORPHANS

Birth Name			Later Name	Place Born		Born	Died	Chapters		
Altsefrum	Malka		Molly Suntup	Libov	~	1895		50		O
Altsefrum	Frieda		Freda Segal	Libov	~	1899		50		O
Altuska	Chaim		Harry Gordon	Brest-Litovsk		1914	1989	97		A
Altuska	Tasha		Tasha Rachman	Brest-Litovsk		1902	1971	96		A
Altuska	Leah		Leah Rosenblatt	Brest-Litovsk		1912	1993		V2 15	A
Altuska	Sara		Sarah Slier	Brest-Litovsk		1910	2001		V2 14	A
Altuska	Feiga	S		Brest-Litovsk				96	V2 15	
Artman	Regina		Regina Weintroub	Stanislav		1914	2001	51		O
Barmatch	Sara			Brest-Litovsk	~	1909				O
Berkowitch	Chava		Eva Berkowitz	Brest-Litovsk		1912	1964	52		O
Bernfeld	Chaya		Claire Klein	Warsaw		1911	2005	30	53	O
Bernfeld	Hersh		Harry Bernfeld	Warsaw	~	1909		53		O
Bettman	Chana		Chana Schneider	Stanislav	~	1908		54		O
Bettman	Leya		Leah Marks	Stanislav	~	1902		54		O
Bettman	Sheindel		Salka Sheiham	Stanislav	~	1912		54		O
Bettman	Solomon		Solly Bettman	Stanislav	~	1913		31	54	O
Bettman	Yenta		Pearly Trapida	Stanislav	~	1915		54		O
Blind	Salka		Sadie Saus	Rawa		1910	1991	98		A
Bornshtein	Isaac		Isaac Bornstein	Brest-Litovsk	~	1909		76		O
Borowik	Chana		Annie Centner	Brest-Litovsk	~	1907	1977	99		A
Borowik	Rochela		Rachel Klein	Brest-Litovsk		1905		99		A
Borowik	Shaya		Shia Borwick Cooper	Brest-Litovsk	~	1910		99		A
Borowik	Yankel	S	Yankel Borowik	Brest-Litovsk				99		
Borowik	Alta	S	Mary Berelowitz	Brest-Litovsk				99		
Broder	Bina		Bina Stange	Stanislav		1913	1997	100		A
Broder	Sara		Sarah Levy	Stanislav	~	1915		100		A
Cwengel	Saul			Wlodawa	~	1913				O
Derlowitz	Chana		Andja Avin	Lemberg	~	1911	1984	55		O
Dreiling	Juda		Jules Fisher	Lemberg		1916	1982	101		A
Echstein	Josef		Jack Cohen	Brest-Litovsk		1915		102		A
Echstein	Toiba		Tilly Rabinowitz	Brest-Litovsk		1910		32	102	A
Echstein	Asher		Oscar Echstein	Brest-Litovsk		1913	2006	102	103	A
Echstein	Mordechai	S		Brest-Litovsk				103		
Ellman	Yankel		Joe Ellman	Brest-Litovsk		1909	1968	56		O
Ellman	Bluma		Blume Kangisher	Domatchewo	~	1916	1973	56		O
Ellman	Feyga		Fanny	Domatchewo	~	1913	1940	56		O
Ellman	Jentel		Issy Elman	Domatchewo	~	1916		56		O
Elshtein	Abo		Alf Rubel	Pinsk	~	1909		57		O
Elshtein	Shlema		Solly Rubel	Pinsk		1914		57		O
Elshtein	Leibel		Louis Rubel	Pinsk	~	1916	1988	57		O
Engelman	Jakob			Wlodawa	~	1912				A
Faifer	Liba		Lily Behrman	Slavuta	~	1910	1984	104		A
Faifer	Blume		Blume Abrahams	Slavuta	~	1911	1982	104		A

Code: S - Sibling of Ochberg Orphan, ~ - approximate, V2 - More Arc Memories (Volume 2), A - Arcadia, O - Oranjia.

Birth Name			Later Name	Place Born		Born	Died	Chapters		
Feinschmidt	Zeidel		Sydney Jack Fine	Shershov	~	1909		105		A
Feldman	Mendel		Manuel Romanovsky	Shask	~	1912		58		O
Fremd	Max		Max Fremd	Lemberg	~	1911				A
Gabbe (Gaby)	Chaya		Clara Penzik	Trysk		1907	1987	61		O
Gabbe (Gaby)	Gittel		Gertie Shnaps	Trysk	~	1912		60		O
Gabbe (Gaby)	Peshe		Peggy Greenberg	Trysk	~	1910		59		O
Gayer	Moishe		Harry Friedman	Opalin		1913	1942		V2 12	A
Gayer	Chana		Eva Queit	Opalin		1914	1981		V2 12	A
Gayer	Sara		Sarah Gilinsky	Opalin		1909	1991		V2 12	A
Garbus	Shmuel		Sydney Garbus	Pinsk	~	1909		106		A
Gebengolz	Rochel			Shack	~	1911				O
Gelernter	Shewa		Hilda Modlin	Brest-Litovsk		1916	2003	33	49	O
Gershenabel	Moisha		Moshe Gershbone	Brest-Litovsk	~	1909				O
Gesunterman	Braindel		Bessie Morris	Pinsk	~	1911	1982	62		O
Gesunterman	Jochevet Sheina		Jessie Sher	Pinsk	~	1913		62		O
Gesunterman	Rochel		Janie Oddes	Pinsk	~	1909		62		O
Ginsburg	Mintcha			Wlodawa	~	1913				O
Gonifas	Betzalel		Charles Gonifas	Rotne		1912	1999	107		A
Gonifas	Malka		Molly Blumberg	Rotne		1909	1939	107		A
Gonifas	Gittel		Gittel Gonifas	Rotne	~	1909		107		A
Gonifas	Leya		Leah Berkman	Rotne		1906		107		A
Gonifas	Enya	S		Rotne	~	1905				
Gornshteyn	Abram		Abram Levitt	Pinsk		1910	1999	63		O
Gornshteyn	Chana		Connie Alhadeff	Pinsk	~	1913	2002	63		O
Greenshtein	Nachman		Nathan Greenstein	Berdichev	~	1913	1989	64		O
Guber	Chaya		Annie Segal	Pnywno		1912		108		A
Guber	Tcharna		Charlotte Odes	Pnywno	~	1914		108		A
Hans	Neta		Nellie Frankal	Rawaruska	~	1912		65		O
Hans	Ruza		Rosie Flink	Rawaruska		1912	1976	65		O
Heft	Rosha		Rosie Hoffman	Domatchewo	~	1912		66		O
Helman	Aisik		Isaac Helman	Pinsk		1910	1993	109		A
Helman	Benjamin		Benjamin Helman	Pinsk		1912		110		A
Helman	Chashe		Chassia Zagey	Pinsk		1907	1983	109		A
Hurwitz	Rosa			Berdytchew	~	1911				A
Joffe	Freidl		Freda Larsen	Pinsk		1910	1995	34	111	A
Joffe	Cywje		Sylvia Chasteau	Pinsk	~	1913	1998	112		A
Kahan	Golda			Pinsk	~	1904				O
Kahan	Mordehe			Pinsk	~	1909				A
Kahan	Shachna			Pinsk	~	1911				A
Kailer/Kohler	Rywka		Becky Greenberg	Kowel		1910		67		O
Kailer/Kohler	Zippe	S	Celia Jacobson	Kowel		1915		67		
Kailer/Kohler	Moshe	S	Morris Keller	Kowel		1913		67		
Karman	Benjamin		Benjamin Radomsky	Brest-Litovsk	~	1914	1974	68		O
Kaufman	Cypora			Wlodawa	~	1912				O

Code: S - Sibling of Ochberg Orphan, ~ - approximate, V2 - More Arc Memories (Volume 2), A - Arcadia, O - Oranjia

Birth Name		Later Name	Place Born		Born	Died	Chapters			
Kaufman	Solomon		Wlodawa	~	1914					O
Kawerberg	Mayer		Kowel	~	1908					O
Kawerberg	Moshe		Wlodawa	~	1908					
Kigielman	Jakob		Wlodawa		1912					
Knuboviz	Zlata		Pinsk	~	1909					O
Kolodner	Isaac	Isaac Aronowitz	Kowel		1918		69			O
Kolodner	Lieba	Lieba Singer	Kowel		1909	1974	69			O
Kolodner	Yenta	Hetty Nick	Kowel	~	1913	1990	69			O
Kreindel	Reisel		Kowel		1912					A
Lerman	Dwora	Deborah Wulf	Domatchewo	~	1913	1973	70			O
Lerman	Nechama	Naomi Miller	Domatchewo		1917	1970		V2 17		O
Levin	Chaim	Hymie Levin	Pinsk		1909	1999	113			A
Levin	Pasha	Polly Falkov	Pinsk	~	1915		113			A
Levin	Sara	Cynthia Chait	Pinsk		1913	1999	113			A
Lidvenitsky	Herschel	Harry Lidven	Pinsk		1908	1957		V2 10		A
Lila	Rosa	Rosa Braude	Lemberg		1913	1956				A
Lipshitz	Moishe		Wlodawa	~	1912		114			A
Lipshitz	Perel		Wlodawa		1910		114			A
Mandelblatt	Pesha	Polly Kapelus	Domatchewo	~	1911	1990	71			O
Margolin	Sara		Pinsk	~	1911					
Meikeffer	Franciszka		Lemberg	~	1912					
Menkes	Debora	Dorothy Weiner	Lemberg		1914	1999				A
Migdalowicz	Chonon	Charles Migdal	Pinsk		1908	2001	35	72		O
Migdalowicz	Nachman	Norman Migdale	Pinsk	~	1986	1986	72			O
Migdalowicz	Simon	Simon Migdale	Pinsk	~	1913	1977	72			O
Miler	Braindel		Kowel	~	1913					O
Mordochowitch	Gutro		Stanislav	~	1913					
Mordochowitch	Estel		Stanislav	~	1915					
Mussman	Isaac	Jack Musman	Kostopol	~	1912		115			A
Mussman	Reisel	Ray Levin	Kostopol		1916	1995	115			A
Neishtein	Sala	Celia Rakoff	Levov	~	1914		73			O
Nemet	Beila	Judith Smith	Kyntchyn		1915					A
Neustein	Solomon	Solly Jossel	Drohobycz		1914		36	116	V2 16	A
Ochshtein	Salomon		Pinsk	~	1912					
Orliansky	Abram		Brest-Litovsk	~	1909					O
Penzik	Mindel	Minnie Davidow	Kupichow		1905	1956	117	V2 8		A
Penzik	David	David Penzik	Kupichow		1908	1992	118	V2 7		A
Penzik	Chana	Hannah Sandler	Kupichow		1911		119			A
Penzik	Chaya	Helen Green	Kupichow		1916	1990	120	V2 9		A
Perechodnik	Szepsel	Samson Perch	Pinsk		1910	1974	74			O
Perechodnik	Yser	Oscar Perch	Pinsk	~	1907	~1970	74			O
Pianka	Chawa	Eva Smulowitz	Brest-Litovsk		1910	1983	75			O
Pinsky	Faywel	Philip Pinsky	Pinsk	~	1913		121			A
Pinsky	Feyga	Birdie Glaser	Pinsk	~	1916		121			A
Pinsky	Maisha	Morris Pinsky	Pinsk		1909	1979	121			A

Code: S - Sibling of Ochberg Orphan, ~ - approximate, V2 - More Arc Memories (Volume 2), A - Arcadia, O - Oranjia.

Birth Name			Later Name	Place Born		Born	Died	Chapters		
Pinsky	Zlata		Zlata Dembo	Pinsk	~	1912		121		A
Pinsky	Dvora	S	Dora Jarzin	Pinsk						
Ratzer	Ides		Judith Sherksne	Stanislav		1910	1965		V2 11	A
Ratzer	Natan		Natie Ratzer	Stanislav		1914			V2 11	A
Ratzer	Perel		Phyllis Ratzer	Stanislav		1908	2002		V2 11	A
Razu	Chaim		Chaim Rosier	Wlodawa	~	1912		78		O
Razu	Isaac		Itzik Rosier	Wlodawa	~	1913	1941	77		O
Razu	Yetta		Yetta Bornstein	Wlodawa	~	1911		76		O
Reichman	Abram		Abie Richman Kruger	Turow	~	1910				A
Reichman	Chaim		Hymie Richman Israelson	Turow	~	1912				A
Reisender	Rubin			Lemberg	~	1911				A
Rekler,	Leya			Lemberg	~	1915				A
Rinzler	Chaykel			Lemberg	~	1913				A
Roht	Herman		Harry Herman Roth	Lemberg		1910	1952		V2 13	A
Rosenbaum	Leon		Leon Rosenbaum	Lemberg	~	1914				A
Rosenblit	Gdalia			Rovno		1912				A
Rosenblit	Shamay			Rovno		1913				A
Rubin	Chana		Ann Stock	Lemberg		1915	~1994	122		A
Rubin	Dawid		David Rubin	Lemberg	~	1914	~1953	122		A
Ruchocki	Aron		Archie Ruch	Pinsk		1909	1976	79		O
Ruchocki	Faiwel		Philip Ruch	Pinsk		1911	2003	79		O
Ruchocki	Sholem		Solly Ruch	Pinsk		1913	1929	79		O
Samurina	Sima		Thelma Friedman	Pinsk		1912	1998	81		O
Samurina	Zlata		Charlotte Berman	Pinsk	~	1909		80		O
Sandak-Lewin	Simcha		Simon Sandak-Lewin	Wlodawa		1910		82		O
Schapira	Malka		Molly Cohen	Sarny		1913		37	48	O
Schrier	Jacob		Jack Schrier	Brest-Litovsk		1908	1984			O
Schrier	Feyga		Fanny Lockitch	Brest-Litovsk		1911	2005	38	83	O
Schwarz	Josef			Lvov	~	1911				A
Shamis	Manes		Manny Favish	Verba		1912	1994	123		A
Shamis	Reisel		Rose Miller	Verba		1910	1992	124		A
Shteiner	Chaskel		Charles Steiner	Libshei		1914	1959	125		A
Shteiner	Hersh		Harry Steiner	Libshei		1909	1999	125		A
Shteiner	Isaac		Isadore Steiner	Libshei		1913	~1994	125		A
Shtern	Solomon		Solomon Shtern	Wlodawa	~	1912				O
Shtrasner	Feyga			Stanislav	~	1915				O
Stanger	Pese		Polly Joffee	Lemberg	~	1912	1981	126		A
Stillerman	Hersh		Harry Stillerman	Lemberg	~	1909				O
Tannenbaum	Chaya		Clara Steiman	Wlodawa		1905	1988	127		A
Tannenbaum	Sara		Sally Egnal	Wlodawa		1910	1996	127		A
Treppel	Jacob		Jacob Trappel	Lemberg	~	1913				A
Wachtel	Sara		Sara Glaser	Stanislav	~	1912		84		O
Weidman	Sheindel			Stanislav	~	1914				O
Wolchuk	Chayim		Hymie Wolchuk	Pnywno		1916	1996	128		A
Wolchuk	Feiga		Phyllis Braude	Pnywno		1915		128		A

Code: S - Sibling of Ochberg Orphan, ~ - approximate, V2 - More Arc Memories (Volume 2), A - Arcadia, O - Oranjia

Birth Name		Later Name	Place Born		Born	Died	Chapters			
Wolchuk	Leibel	Les Wolchuk	Pnywno		1912	2006	128			A
Wolchuk	Toyba	Tilly Karlin	Pnywno		1912	~2000	128			A
Yagolkowsky	Yakov	Jack Yagalkovsky	Brest-Litovsk		1909	1956	84			O
Zaika	Manya	Manya Adler	Kostopol		1911		39	40	129	A
Zaika	Lysel	Cissy Harris	Kostopol	~	1915		39			A
Zaika	Leya	Lisa Abend	Kostopol	~	1903	~1905	39			A
Zwirin	Berner	Barry Beira	Stanislav	~	1915		130			A
Zwirin	Osiach	Issy Beira	Stanislav	~	1916	1991	130			A

Code: S - sibling of Ochberg Orphan, ~ -approximate, V2 - More Arc Memories (Volume 2), A - Arcadia, O - Oranjia.

ISAAC OCHBERG (1879-1937)

Isaac Ochberg was born in Uman, Russia on 31 May 1879 and died on the Pretoria Castle on 11 December 1937. He was buried in Cape Town on 13 December 1937. "He never refused to support a worthy cause; on the contrary, his creed was that since he had been enabled to achieve success in his own enterprises, he had a moral duty to help those less fortunate."

ARCADIA AND ORANJIA

"No one stands so erect than when they stoop to help a child"

Arcadia Jewish Children's Home (see chapter 95) and Oranjia Jewish Child and Youth Centre (see chapter 47) still exist in Johannesburg and Cape Town, South Africa taking care of Jewish Children in need.

Arcadia and Oranjia are fully dependant on the charity of the Jewish Community.

All the proceeds on sale of this third volume, **The Ochberg Orphans**, and the preceeding two volumes **100 Years of Arc Memories** and **More Arc Memories** go to Arcadia and Oranjia. You can order your books locally and have them delivered to friends and family around the world.
See our website www.arcadia.ca.com.au

Shalom

David Solly Sandler <sedand@iinet.net.au>

I was born in Johannesburg South Africa in 1952 and all my forebears originated in Lithuania. I spent most of my childhood, 1954-1969, in Arcadia from age three until 17, when I finished

school. I did my National Service in the SADF and did Articles and qualified as a Chartered Accountant in 1976.

In 1979 I married and have two daughters Sarah and Esther. At the age of 28 in 1981 I left Johannesburg and I have lived in Perth, Western Australia, ever since. In early 2007 I retired and compiling the three books has been the equivalent of about six years full time work.

PG there are still a few more compilations to come.